War Crimes and
War Crime Trials:
From Leipzig to the ICC
and Beyond

War Crimes and War Crime Trials: From Leipzig to the ICC and Beyond

Cases, Materials and Comments

John C. Watkins, Jr.
UNIVERSITY OF ALABAMA

and

John Paul Weber
JUDSON COLLEGE

CAROLINA ACADEMIC PRESS
Durham, North Carolina

Library of Congress Cataloging-in-Publication Data

Watkins, John C.
    War crimes and war crime trials : from Leipzig to the ICC and beyond : cases,
materials, and comments / by John C. Watkins, Jr. and John Paul Weber.
        p. cm.
    ISBN 0-89089-307-1
1. War (International law) 2. War crimes. 3. War crime trials. I. Weber, John Paul,
1942- II. Title.

KZ6385.W38 2004
341.6'9'0268--dc22

                                                            2005007636

Carolina Academic Press
700 Kent Street
Durham, North Carolina 27701
Telephone (919) 489-7486
Fax (919) 493-5668
www.cap-press.com

Printed in the United States of America

The laying a Country desolate, with Fire and Sword, declaring War against the natural rights of all mankind, and extirpating the Defenders thereof from the Face of the Earth, is the concern of every man....

Thomas Paine
(1737–1809)
Common Sense
February 14, 1776

Defeat cries out for explanation; whereas success, like charity, covers a multitude of sins.

Alfred Thayer Mahan
(1840–1914)
U.S. Naval Historian

International law should be realistic, creative, and axiologically oriented; it should take account of social psychology, sociology, economics, and politics, and it should furnish a functional critique in terms of social ends rather in terms of the norms themselves.

Hardy Cross Dillard
(1902–1982)
Judge, International
Court of Justice
(1970–1979)

*Dedicated to the men and women in international and national
tribunals who have labored over the years to bring justice
and peace to the community of nations and to make
the rule of law a living testament in
international relations*

Contents

Table of Cases   xvii
Foreword *by M. Cherif Bassiouni*   xix
Preface   xxiii
Acknowledgments and Permissions   xxvii
Editorial Note   xxix

Part One   Hague Peace Conferences; World War I; Treaty of Versailles;
League of Nations; Leipzig Trials (1899–1921)   3
Editorial Commentary   3
   1. Hague Conferences of 1899 and 1907   8
     (a) 1899 Hague Convention (No. II)
       Respecting the Laws and Customs of War on Land   8
     (b) 1907 Hague Convention (No. IV)
       Respecting the Laws and Customs of War on Land   13
   2. The Armenian Genocide (1915)   14
     (a) Vahakn N. Dadrian, "Genocide as a Problem of National and
       International Law: The World War I Armenian Case and Its
       Contemporary Legal Ramifications"   14
     (b) Peter Maguire, *Law and War: An American Story*   17
   3. Woodrow Wilson's "Fourteen Points"   17
   4. Conditions of an Armistice with Germany   19
   5. Covenant of the League of Nations Adopted by the Peace
     Conference at Plenary Session   22
   6. Excerpts from Address of President Wilson on Presenting the
     Draft Covenant of the League of Nations to the Third Plenary Session
     of the Peace Conference at Paris   25
   7. Excerpts from the Report of the Commission on the Responsibility
     of the Authors of the War and on Enforcement of Penalties to the
     Preliminary Peace Conference   28
       Memorandum of Reservations Presented by the Representatives of the
       United States to the Report of the Commission on Responsibilities   35
   8. Annex III
     Reservations by the Japanese Delegation   37
   9. The Status of William Hohenzollern, Kaiser of Germany,
     Under International Law   37
  10. Treaty of Peace with Germany   43
       Protocol Supplementary to the Treaty of Peace between the Allied
       and Associated Powers and Germany   47

11. Richard Overy, "The Versailles Settlement" in
    The Penguin Historical Atlas of the Third Reich   48
12. Treaty of St. Germain-en-Lave with Austria   50
13. The Leipzig War Crime Trials   51
    (a) Peter Maguire, *Law and War: An American Story*   51
    (b) *Current Notes:* German War Trials   52
    (c) U.S. Department of the Army Pamphlet No. 27-161-2
        II International Law 221–22 (1962)   52
    (d) Judgment in the *Case of Karl Heynen*   54
    (e) Judgment in the *Case of Emil Müller*   56
    (f) Judgment in the *Case of Commander Karl Neumann*   60
    (g) Judgment in the *Case of Lieutenants Dithmar and Boldt*   63
Suggestions for Further Reading   67

Part Two Weimar Republic:
          The Nazi Party and German Fascism; World War II and
          German War Crimes; IMT-Nuremberg; Nuremberg "Subsequent
          Proceedings"; Other Selected War Crime Cases—
          Great Britain and Norway (1921–1951)   71
Editorial Commentary   71
    1. Excerpts from the Weimar Constitution   85
    2. Richard Overy, "Weimar Germany" in
       The Penguin Historical Atlas of the Third Reich   89
    3. Richard Overy, "The German Slump" in
       The Penguin Historical Atlas of the Third Reich   90
    4. Kellogg-Briand Peace Pact (Pact of Paris)   91
    5. Paul Brooker, "Hitler's Regime in Germany" in
       Twentieth Century Dictatorships   96
    6. Charter of the International Military Tribunal   98
    7. Ann Tusa and John Tusa, *The Nuremberg Trial*   103
    8. Control Council Law No. 10
       Punishment of Persons Guilty of War Crimes,
       Crimes against Peace and against Humanity   109
    9. Gerry L. Simpson, "War Crimes Trials: Some Problems" in
       The Law of War Crimes: National and International Approaches 113
    10. Robert L. Birmingham, *Note*, "The War Crimes Trial: A Second Look" 117
    11. IMT-Nuremberg Defendants and Their Position(s) in the Third Reich 120
    12. *The United States of America, et al. against Herrmann
        Wilhelm Göering, et al.*   127
    13. The International Military Tribunal in Session at Nuremberg, Germany 143
        (a) Opening Statement   145
        (b) Closing Statement   151
        (c) Judgment of the Tribunal   159
    14. Summary of the Counts of the Indictment and Results of War
        Crimes Trial against Accused Individuals   161
    15. Organization Criminality   162
    16. Hans Ehard, "The Nuremberg Trial against the Major War
        Criminals and International Law"   162
    17. Georg Schwarzenberger, "The Judgment of Nuremberg"   174

18. Steven Fogelson, *Note*, "The Nuremberg Legacy:
    An Unfulfilled Promise"   181
19. Maximillian Koessler, "American War Crimes Trials in Europe"   186
20. German Occupation: "Subsequent Proceedings" under Allied
    Control Council Law No. 10   191
21. Selected "Subsequent Proceedings" Decisions   196
    (a) Tribunal II-A
        United States of America v. Otto Ohlendorf, et al.   196
    (b) Tribunal I
        United States of America v. Ulrich Greifelt, et al.   203
    (c) Tribunal V
        United States of America v. Wilhelm von Leeb, et al.   217
    (d) The Malmédy Trial   248
    (e) *United States of America v. Valentin Bersin et al.* (1946)
        The "Malmédy Massacre" Case   250
    (f) *Trial of Heinrich Gerike and Seven Others*
        (The Velpke Children's Home Case)   254
    (g) *Trial of Werner Rohde and Eight Others*
        (The SS Obergruppenführer Case)   259
    (h) *Trial of Gerhard Friedrich Ernst Flesch,*
        SS Ober-sturmbannführer, Oberregierungsrat   263
22. The Nuremberg Principles   272
Suggestions for Further Reading   274

Part Three   Japanese Imperialism in the 1930s; China and Manchuria;
             Nanking Massacre; Tripartite Pact; World War II and Japanese
             War Crimes; IMTFE Tokyo; Japanese Atomic Bomb Litigation
             (1927–1948; 1963)   277
Editorial Commentary   277
    1. Emperor Hirohito's Imperial Rescript   288
    2. *In re Yamashita*   289
    3. George F. Guy, "The Defense of Yamashita"   307
    4. Ann M. Prevost, "Race and War Crimes: The 1945 Trial of
       General Tomoyuki Yamashita"   311
    5. The Japanese Instrument of Surrender   315
    6. The Imperial Rescript of 2 September 1945   316
    7. Proclamation by the Supreme Commander for the Allied Powers 316
    8. Charter of the International Military Tribunal for the Far East 317
    9. IMTFE-Tokyo Defendants and Their Position(s) in Imperial Japan 323
   10. Judgment   325
       The United States of America, et al. against Sadeo Araki, et al. 325
   11. Dissent of Justice R. M. Pal   337
   12. *Hirota v. MacArthur, General of the Army, et al.*   343
   13. Elizabeth S. Kopelman, "Ideology and International Law:
       The Dissent of the Indian Justice at the Tokyo War Crimes Trial" 346
   14. The Imperial Rescript of 14 August 1945   352
   15. "Unit 731: The Hidden Atrocities"   353
   16. *Shimoda et al. v. State*   356

17. Richard A. Falk, "The Shimoda Case: A Legal Appraisal of the
    Atomic Attacks on Hiroshima and Nagasaki"   362
18. Yves Beigbeder, "The Legality of Atomic Bombing"   365
Suggestions for Further Reading   366

**Part Four   Israel and the Eichmann Case; Selected War Crime Cases
              Involving Former Nazis in Ghana (extradition); United States
              (civil damages); France (war crimes) and Canada (war crimes)
              (1960–62; 1966; 1980; 1985; 1994)**   369
Editorial Commentary   369
    1. The Indictment   374
       Peter Papadatos, *The Eichmann Trial*   374
       The Attorney-General v. Adolf, the son of Adolf Karl Eichmann
       aged 54, at present under arrest—the accused   374
    2. *The Attorney-General of the Government of Israel v. Eichmann* 383
    3. *Eichmann v. The Attorney-General of the Government of Israel* 396
    4. Nicholas N. Kittrie, "A Post Mortem of the Eichmann Case—
       The Lessons for International Law"   399
    5. *The State v. Schumann*   404
    6. *Rudolf Hess v. Federal Republic of Germany*   409
    7. *Handel v. Artukovic*   412
    8. *Federation Nationale des Deportes et Internes Resistants et Patriotes
       and Others v. Barbie*   420
    9. The Case of Paul Touvier   428
       Leila Sadat Wexler, "Reflections on the Trial of Vichy Collaborator
       Paul Touvier for Crimes against Humanity in France"   428
   10. *Regina v. Finta*   433
Suggestions for Further Reading   440

**Part Five   SEATO Treaty; Vietnam War; Gulf of Tonkin Resolution;
              Peers Commission Report; *Medina and Calley* Cases;
              Commentary on My Lai; U.S. District Court Cases on
              Legality of Vietnam Conflict (1964–1975)**   443
Editorial Commentary   443
    1. Michal R. Belknap, *The Vietnam War on Trial*   445
    2. Southeast Asia Collective Defense Treaty   448
    3. The Legality of United States Participation in the Defense of Viet-Nam 451
    4. The Gulf of Tonkin Resolution   460
    5. Headquarters: United States Military Assistance Command, Vietnam 461
    6. Jeffrey P. Addicott & William A. Hudson, Jr., "The Twenty-Fifth
       Anniversary of My Lai: A Time to Inculcate the Lessons"   463
    7. Michael Bilton & Kevin Sim, *Four Hours in My Lai*   465
    8. The Peers Commission Report   467
    9. *Medina v. Resor*   473
   10. Norman G. Cooper, "My Lai and Military Justice—To What Effect?" 475
   11. *United States v. Calley*   475
   12. *Calley v. Callaway*   483
   13. Kenneth A. Howard, "Command Responsibility for War Crimes"   487
   14. The Constitution, International Law and Vietnam   489

    (a) Jonathan M. Fredman, "American Courts, International Law
        and the War in Vietnam" 489
    (b) *United States v. Berrigan* 492
    (c) *Berk v. Laird* 495
Suggestions for Further Reading 498

Part Six   A Postscript on Twentieth Century Impunity; Selected ICTY and
        ICTR cases; International Criminal Court and the Rome Statute;
        Military Commission Controversy: History, Cases and Commentary;
        the *Hamdi* and *Padilla* Cases and the U.S. Supreme Court; Citizen
        Terrorists and the Constitution; Political Ethics and Terrorism
        (1990–2004) 501
Editorial Commentary 501
  1. Twentieth Century Impunity 503
    (a) Yves Beigbeder, *Judging War Criminals:*
        The Politics of International Justice 503
      (i) The Unpunished Soviet Massacres 503
    (b) M. Cherif Bassiouni, *Crimes against Humanity in*
        International Criminal Law 506
      (i) Selective Enforcement 506
    (c) Yves Beigbeder, *Judging War Criminals,*
        The Politics of International Justice 507
      (i) Indonesia: The 1965 Massacre 507
      (ii) China 508
      (iii) The Khmer Rouge Genocide 508
    (d) M. Cherif Bassiouni, *Crimes against Humanity in*
        International Criminal Law 509
  2. *Statute of the International Tribunal for the Former Yugoslavia* 511
  3. The *Tadic* Judgment of the ICTY 518
    (a) Karl A. Hockhammer, *Note,* "The Yugoslav War Crimes Tribunal:
        The Compatibility of Peace, Politics, and International Law" 519
    (b) *Prosecutor v. Tadic* 521
    (c) *Prosecutor v. Dusko Tadic* 525
  4. *Prosecutor v. Erdemovic* 527
  5. The Concept of Ethnic Cleansing 531
    (a) L.C. Green, *Notes and Comments:* "The Rule of Law and
        Human Rights in the Balkans" 532
    (b) John Quigley, "State Responsibility for Ethnic Cleansing" 533
  6. *Prosecutor v. Blaskic* 535
  7. The International Criminal Tribunal for Rwanda 541
    (a) Christina M. Carroll, "An Assessment of the Role and
        Effectiveness of the International Criminal Tribunal for Rwanda
        and the Rwandan National Justice System in Dealing with
        Mass Atrocities of 1994" 542
    (b) *Statute of the International Criminal Tribunal for Rwanda* 544
    (c) *Prosecutor v. Jean-Paul Akayesu* (Indictment) 549
    (d) *Prosecutor v. Jean-Paul Akayesu* 552
    (e) Diane Marie Amann, "Prosecutor v. Akayesu, Case ICTR-96-4T,
        'International Decisions' " 558

(f) *Prosecutor v. Georges Anderson Nderubumwe Rutaganda* (Indictment) 561

(g) *Prosecutor v. Rutaganda* 564

(h) Gabrielle Kirk McDonald, "The International Criminal Tribunals: Crime and Punishment in the International Arena" 570

(i) Michael P. Scharf, "The International Trial of Slobodan Milosevic: Real Justice or Realpolitik?" 572

8. The International Criminal Court, The Rome Statute and Commentary 576

(a) *The Statute of the International Criminal Court* as quoted in ch. 7, "International Prosecutorial Efforts and Tribunals," in I*nternational Criminal Law: Cases & Materials* 576

(b) The Rome Conference and the ICC Statute "The Rome Conference—15 June–7 July 1998," as quoted in Yves Beigbeder, *Judging War Criminals: The Politics of International Justice* 578

(c) Ceremony for the Opening for Signature of the Convention on the Establishment of an International Criminal Court, Rome, "Il Campidoglio" 581
Statement of Professor M. Cherif Bassiouni Chairman, Drafting Committee 581

(d) *Statute of the International Criminal Court* 582

(e) Michael P. Scharf, "The United States and the International Criminal Court: A Recommendation for the Bush Administration" 588

(f) "U.S. Policy and the International Criminal Court," Comments by Ambassador David J. Scheffer, U.S. Ambassador-at-Large for War Crimes Issues 591

(g) Alison M. McIntire, *Comment,* "Be Careful What You Wish for Because You Just Might Get It: The United States and the International Criminal Court" 595

(h) *American Servicemembers' Protection Act* 600

9. International Criminal Justice, Asymmetrical Warfare and the Military Commission Controversy 604

(a) *Public Law* 107-39, 107th Congress 604

(b) *Public Law* 107-40, 107th Congress 605

(c) W. Michael Reisman, *Editorial Comment,* "In Defense of World Public Order" 606

(d) Detlev F. Vagts, *Editorial Comments,* "Hegemonic International Law" 608

(e) United States Department of the Army, FM 27-10 (1956) 611

(f) (1) United States Code, 18 USC §2441 (2001) 611

(g) (2) United States Code, 10 USC §836 (2003) 612

(h) *Ex parte Milligan* 612

(i) *Ex parte Quirin* 618

(j) *Duncan v. Kahanamoku* 624

(k) *Johnson v. Eisentrager* 629

(l) *Reid v. Covert* 633

(m) Proclamation 7463 of September 14, 2001 638

(n) Military Order of November 13, 2001 640

(o) *Coalition of Clergy v. Bush* 643

(p) *Rasul v. Bush*   649
(q) *Al Odah v. United States*   650
(r) Kenneth Anderson, "What to Do With Bin Laden and Al Qaeda
    Terrorists? A Qualified Defense of Military Commissions and
    United States Policy on Detainees at Guantanamo Bay Naval Base"   653
(s) The *Hamdi* and *Padilla* Appeals: Citizen Terrorists and
    the Constitution   665
    (i) *Hamdi et al. v. Rumsfeld*   665
    (ii) *Rumsfeld v. Padilla*   677
(t) *Rasul v. Bush*   680
10. Epilogue: Michael Ignatieff, *The Lesser Evil:*
    Political Ethics in an Age of Terror   684
Suggestions for Further Reading   689

Appendices
Appendix A   General Orders No. 100   693
Appendix B   The Nuremberg Laws   697
Appendix C   Regulation on Military Government Courts, Issued by
              Letter of Headquarters, U.S. Forces, European Theater   700
Appendix D   Regulation on Military Commissions, Issued by Letter
              of Headquarters, U.S. Forces, European Theater   702
Appendix E   Regulations Governing the Trials of Accused War Criminals,
              GHQ, Supreme Commander for the Allied Powers [Tokyo]   704
Appendix F   Military Government—United States Zone Ordinance No. 7   708
Appendix G   Convention on the Prevention and Punishment of the
              Crime of Genocide   712
Appendix H   Convention for the Protection of Cultural Property in
              the Event of Armed Conflict   713
Appendix I   Convention on the Non-Applicability of Statutory
              Limitations to War Crimes and Crimes against Humanity   714
Appendix J   International Covenant on Civil and Political Rights   715
Appendix K   Protocol I Additional to the Geneva Conventions of
              12 August 1949, and Relating to the Protection of
              Victims of International Armed Conflicts   716
Appendix L   [United Nations] Security Council Resolution Condemning
              Hostage Taking   724
Appendix M   United States Code: 18 U.S.C. §2401,
              The War Crimes Act of 1996   724
Appendix N   Tables of International Legal Regimes and War
              Incident Values   725

Glossary   729
References   747
About the Editors   805
Name Index   807
Subject Index   815

Table of Cases

Ahrens v. Clark, 335 U.S. 188 (1948), 633

Al Odah v. United States, 321 F.3d 1134 (2003), 650

Alstoetter et al., United States v., 3CCL No. 10 Trials 954, 229

Araki et al., United States et al. v., MSS 78-3, Box Nos. 216–219, Spec. Coll., University of Virginia Law Library, 325

Attorney-General of Israel v. Eichmann, 56 Am. J. Int'l L. 805 (1962), 383

Augenblick, United States v., 393 U.S. 348 (1969), 486

Baker v. Carr, 369 U.S. 186 (1962), 494, 496–497

Baxley v. United States, 134 F.2d 937 (4th Cir. 1943), 492

Berk v. Laird, 317 F.Supp. 715 (E.D.N.Y. 1970), 495

Berrigan, United States v., 283 F.Supp. 336 (D. Md. 1968), 492

Bersin, Valentin et al., United States v., Rec. Gp. No. 153, Rolls 1–6, Nat'l Archives & Rec. Adm. (1946), 250

Bivens v. Six Unknown Federal Narcotics Agents, 403 U.S. 388 (1971), 415

Brady v. Maryland, 373 U.S. 83 (1963), 485

Brandenburg v. Ohio, 395 U.S. 444 (1969), 560

Brandt et al., United States v., I CCL No. 10 Trials 1, 192

Brown v. Allen, 344 U.S. 443 (1953), 682

Calley, United States v., 22 USCMA 534, 48 CMR 19 (1973), 475

Calley v. Callaway, 519 F.2d 184 (5th Cir. 1975), 483

Cantwell v. Connecticut, 310 U.S. 296 (1940), 493

Carbo v. United States, 364 U.S. 611 (1961), 679

Coalition of Clergy v. Bush, 189 F.Supp.2d 1036 (C.D. Cal. 2002), 652

Cox v. Louisiana, 379 U.S. 559 (1965), 493

Cuban-American Bar Assn. v. Christopher, 43 F.3d 1412 (11th Cir. 1995), *cert. denied,* 515 U.S. 1142 (1995), 648

DeBartolo Corp. v. Florida Gulf Coast Bldg & Const. Trades Council, 485 U.S. 568 (1988), 676

Dennis v. United States, 341 U.S. 497 (1951), 493

Dithmar & Boalt, In re, 16 Am. J. Int'l L. 708 (1922), 63

Dow v. Johnson, 100 U.S. 158 (1879), 628

Duncan v. Kahanamoku, 327 U.S. 304 (1946), 624, 676

Eichmann v. Attorney-General of Israel, 136 ILR 277 (1962), 396

Eisentrager v. Forrestal, 174 F.2d 96; (1949), 344

Endo, Ex parte, 323 U.S. 283 (1944), 344, 633, 676

Federation Nationale des Deportes et Internes Resistants et Patriots et al v. Barbie, 78 ILR 25 (1985), 420

Filartiga v. Pena-Irala, 630 F.2d 876 (2nd Cir. 1980), 413

Finta, Regina v., 104 ILR 285 (1994), 433

Flesch, Gerhard Friedrich Ernst, Trial of, 6 L.R.T.W.C. 111 (1948), 263

Flick et al., United States v., 6 CCL No. 10 Trials 1, 193

Gerike, Heinrich & Seven Others, Trial of, 7 L.R.T.W.C. 80 (1946), 254

Greifelt, Ulrich et al., United States v., 5 CCL No. 10 Trials 1, 196, 203

Hamdi et al. v. Rumsfeld, 542 U.S. ___ (2004), 665

Hamilton v. Regents of the University of California, 293 U.S. 245 (1934), 494

Handel v. Artukovic, 601 F.Supp. 1421 (C.D. Cal. 1985), 412

Hess, Rudolf, v. Federal Republic of Germany, 90 ILR 387 (1980), 409

Heynen, Karl, In re, 16 Am. J. Int'l L. 674 (1922), 54

Hirabayashi v. United States, 320 U.S. 81 (1943), 314

Hirota v, MacArthur, 338 U.S. 197 (1948), 343

INS v. St. Cyr, 533 U.S. 289 (2001), 682

Irvin v. Dowd, 366 U.S. 717 (1961), 476

Johnson v. Eisentrager, 339 U.S. 763 (1950), 629, 646, 650, 652, 681–682

Jones v. Cunningham, 371 U.S. 236 (1963), 645

Kalanianaole, In re, 10 Hawaii 29 (1895), 627

King v. Cowle, 2 Burr. 834, 97 Eng. Rep. 587 (K.B.), 683

Korematsu v. United States, 323 U.S. 214 (1944), 314

Kraunch et al., United States v., 8 CCL No. 10 Trials 1081, 194

Krupp, Alfried United States v., 9 CCL No. 10 Trials 1327, 194

Lambert v. California, 355 U.S. 225 (1957), 482

Lindh, United States v., 212 F.Supp.2d 541 (E.D. Va. 2002), 674

List et al., United States v., 11 CCL No. 10 Trials 757, 195, 281

Lotus Case, P.C.I.J., Ser. A; No. 10 (1927), 394

Luftig v. McNamara, 126 U.S. App. D.C. 4, 373 F.2d 664 (1967), *cert. denied*, 387 U.S. 945 (1967), 497

Marshall v. United States, 360 U.S. 310 (1959), 476

Mathews v. Eldridge, 424 U.S. 319 (1976), 672, 677

Medina v. Resor, 20 USCMA 403, 43 CMR 243 (1971), 473

Milch, United States v., 2 CCL No. 10 Trials 353, 192

Milligan, Ex parte, 71 U.S. (4 Wall.) 2 (1867), 612, 682

Mitchell v. Harmony, 54 U.S. (13 How.) 115 (1851), 183

Muller, In re, 16 Am. J. Int'l L. 684 (1922), 56

Murdock, United States v., 290 U.S. 389 (1933), 493

Neumann, In re, 16 Am. J. Int'l L. 704 (1922), 60

Ohlendorff, et al., United States v., 4 N.M.T. 411, 196

Ozawa v. United States, 260 U.S. 178 (1922), 312

Paguette Habana, The, 175 U.S. 677 (1900), 413, 490

Pohl et al., United States v., 5CCL No. 10 Trials 958, 196

Preiser v. Rodriguez, 411 U.S. 475 (1973), 682

Prosecutor v. Akayesu, ICTR-96-4-T (1998), 552

Prosecutor v. Blaskic, 122 ILR 2 (2000), 502–535

Prosecutor v. Erdemovic, IT-96-22-T (1996), 527

Prosecutor v. Rutaganda, ICTR-96-3-T (1999), 564

Prosecutor v. Tadic, IT-94-1-T (1997), 502

Quinn, Ex parte, 317 U.S. 1 (1942), 490, 618, 669, 682

Rasul v. Bush, 215 F.Supp.2d 55 (D.D.C. 2002), 649, 652

Rasul v. Bush, 542 U.S. ___ (2004), 680

Reid v. Covert, 354 U.S. 1 (1957), 633

Rohde, Werner & Eight Others, Trial of, 5 L.R.T.W.C. 54 (1948), 259

Rumsfeld v. Padilla, 542 U.S. ___ (2004), 677

Shaughnessy v. United States ex rel. Mezei, 345 U.S. 206 (1953), 682

Sheppard v. Maxwell, 384 U.S. 333 (1966), 476

Shimoda et al. v. State, 355 Hanrei Jiho 17 (1963), 356

Sisson, United States v., 294 F.Supp. 511 (D.Mass. 1968), 497

Spelar, United States v., 338 U.S. 217 (1949), 647

Swain v. Pressley, 430 U.S. 372 (1977), 682

Tel-Oren v. Libyan Arab Republic, 726 F.2d 774 (1984), 415

The State v. Schumann, 39 ILR 433 (1966), 404

United States ex rel. Toth v. Quarles, 350 U.S. 11 (1955), 636

United States of America et al. v. Hermann Wilhelm Göering, et al., 20 Temple L.Q. 168 (1946–47), 127

Vallandigham, Ex parte, 68 U.S. (1 Wall.) 243 (1863), 624

von Leeb, Wilhelm et al., United States of America v., 10 CCL No. 10 Trials 1, 217

Warth v. Seldin, 422 U.S. 490 (1975), 645

Watkins, Ex parte, 28 U.S. (3 Pet.) 193 (1830), 675

Weizsaeker, et al., United States v., 12 CCL No. 10 Trials 13, 193

West Virginia State Board of Education v. Barnette, 319 U.S. 624 (1943), 493

Whitmore v. Arkansas, 495 U.S 149 (1990), 645

Williams v. Kaiser, 323 U.S. 471 (1945), 681

Yamashita, In re, 327 U.S. 1 (1946), 289, 682

Yasui, United States v., 320 U.S. 115 (1943), 314

Yick Wo v. Hopkins, 118 U.S. 356 (1885), 630

Youngstown Sheet & Tube Co. v. Sawyer, 343 U.S. 579 (1952), 675

Zadvydas v. Davis, 533 U.S. 678 (2001), 647

Foreword

A disparity exists between human aspirations and their achievement. This is evident in the long history reflecting the evolution of fundamental human and humanitarian values applicable to the initiation and the conduct of war, and in later times, all types of armed conflicts. This historic evolution over the last 5,000 years witnesses the articulation of human and humanitarian values in the form of prohibitions in time of war against the killing of civilians and in general, the humane treatment of civilians, the non-destruction of religious establishments, and more recently, the protection of POWs and the sick, wounded, and injured in the field and at sea. A parallel track is evident in the evolution of doctrine and normative developments at the international and national levels, with doctrine being the driving engine for governments to adopt binding legal obligations.

All of this is evident in the writings of scholars from Sun Tzu in the Fifth Century BCE in China, Manu in the Fourth Century BCE in India, inscriptions on Mayan monuments in the Fourth Century BCE in South America, the practices of the Prophet Mohammed in the early Islamic battles in southern Arabia, followed by the specific prescriptions enunciated by the First Khalifa, Abu Bakr, to the Muslim troops going to the southern Mediterranean in the Seventh Century CE, the Christian European medieval code of chivalry in the Twelfth Century CE, and the writings of scholars, experts, and laypersons from the Seventeenth Century on.

This intellectual development, reflecting commonly-shared human values reflected in several civilizations, embodied in the values of the three Abrahamic faiths, led to specific international prescriptions and proscriptions applicable both to what was historically referred to as the *jus ad bellum* and the *jus in bello*. The result was a series of international instruments which developed along parallel tracks, namely, conventional and customary law applicable to conflicts of an international and non-international character. They are commonly referred to as the "Law of Geneva" and "Law of The Hague". The former in reference to the Conventions sponsored by the International Committee of the Red Cross in Geneva, starting with the First Geneva Convention of 1864, and ending, at this point in time, with the 1977 Additional Protocols to the Four Geneva Conventions of 1949. As to the "Law of The Hague," it originated with the First Hague Convention of 1899 soon amended in 1907, and which is still applicable as a restatement of customary international law, but which surprisingly has not been updated since then. The "Law of The Hague" also includes a number of conventions prohibiting the use of certain weapons which are deemed to be indiscriminate or to cause unnecessary pain and suffering.

As is evident in the history of what for lack of a better word we now call international humanitarian law, doctrine has always been far ahead of the willingness of governments to accept binding international obligations. Nevertheless, in recent times, particularly since the end of WWII, there has been a significant increase in international instruments with varying degrees of binding legal obligations evidencing prescriptive

norms for combatants, as well as proscriptive norms for the enforcement of these prohibitions. The adoption of these international norms has not, however, been paralleled
in the establishment of enforcement institutions. The post-WWI efforts of international
prosecution for violations of the *jus ad bellum* and *jus in bello* have been a step in the
right direction, but not one which has achieved its purposes, as no international prosecutions took place. Post-WWII efforts yielded a significant result in the Nuremberg and
Tokyo war crimes trials followed by national prosecutions brought by the Allies in their
respective zones of occupation in both theaters of the war. Other national prosecutions
in formerly occupied countries also occurred. The record of these proceedings is mixed.
For sure it evidences that international and national criminal justice for international
crimes is only for the defeated. However, substantial developments occurred in the
elimination of heads of state immunity for certain international crimes, and for the expansion of the law of command responsibility and the elimination of the automatic defense of obedience to superior orders.

The cold war brought this historic evolution to a temporary halt. However, during the
same period of time, another set of international legal norms developed, namely, international human rights law, which in many respects, overlaps with international humanitarian law. Thus, we have today two major sources of normative prescriptions and proscriptions which reflect certain commonly-shared values by the international community,
namely international humanitarian law and international human rights law. In the course
of their development, the former applied to the context of wars between states or what is
now called conflicts of an international character and to conflicts of a non-international
character, with some applications into what are also called conflicts of an internal character (which is particularly true with respect to genocide and crimes against humanity). As
to international human rights law, while it has originally been assumed to apply to times
of peace, it nevertheless evolved to apply to times of war as well. This was affirmed in the
2004 International Court of Justice Advisory Opinion on the Legal Consequences of the
Construction of a Wall in the Occupied Palestinian Territory, which recognized the joint
applicability of international human rights law and international humanitarian law in the
context of conflicts, as well non-conflict situations. In other words, international human
rights law is the general law applicable to all contexts and international humanitarian law
the more specific law applicable to conflict contexts. These two sources of applicable law
have, however, overlaps and gaps which have yet to be resolved, the two internal sources
of international humanitarian law, namely conventional and customary international
law, have overlaps and gaps which have not been resolved.

Notwithstanding the existence of multiple sources of law and their overlaps and
gaps, there has been a significant evolution in the enforcement of international criminal
law since 1992 with respect to what has now emerged as the three international core
crimes, namely, genocide, crimes against humanity and war crimes (with the politically
conspicuous disappearance from that list of "crimes against peace," which were prosecuted at Nuremberg and Tokyo, and which subsequently became aggression). As mentioned above, after a hiatus due to the cold war, a new political international resolve developed with the advent of the conflict in the former Yugoslavia, reflected in the security
council's decision in establishing a Commission of Experts to Investigate Violations of
International Humanitarian Law in that conflict, which then led the Security Council to
establish the International Criminal Tribunal for the former Yugoslavia (ICTY), followed by the International Criminal Tribunal for Rwanda (ICTR).

The Security Council's thrust in the arena of international criminal justice was soon
drained of its momentum, and the international community, particularly concerned

with the costs of the ICTY and ICTR, resolved to explore alternative mechanisms such as the mixed tribunals in Sierra Leone and East Timor. Both of these experiences, for lack of international commitment to them, as well as limited resources, cannot be held out as useful models without these missing ingredients. Lack of international political will has also prevented post-conflict justice in Cambodia. There are so many examples of situations where impunity has prevailed over accountability.

Since WWII, it is reported that over 250 conflicts have occurred throughout the world, resulting in 70 million casualties at the low range of estimates to 170 million casualties at the high range of estimates. Over the last half-century during which these atrocities have unfolded before the international community, with scant accountability befalling the leaders and senior perpetrators of these crimes, international civil society, as well as a number of governments have reaffirmed their beliefs in international criminal justice and worked towards the establishment of a permanent international criminal court—an idea that made its way to reality from the end of WWI to 1998 with the adoption of the Rome Treaty establishing the International Criminal Court.

The current thrust for the elimination of impunity and the establishment of accountability for international crimes is hopefully irreversible, though we have regrettably witnessed in recent times something else the international community thought to be irreversible, namely, the prohibition against torture, which some governments continue to practice, and which this Administration has institutionalized. How deep and how far the international community's commitment to international human rights law and international humanitarian law goes is something only time will tell. What is evident is the struggle between on the one hand human and humanitarian values and on the other *realpolitik*, or political realism. In a sense, this conflict may be simply viewed as a reflection of the struggle of good and evil in every individual which manifests itself in the behavior of societies from the beginning of time. With the advent of the nation-state, institutionalized rationalizations have been developed under the guise of "state interests," "strategic interests," and ultimately, under the overall umbrella of "political realism." What has changed, however, is the growing strength of international civil society which supports international criminal justice and opposes impunity.

The increase in the literature on these subjects evidences significant interest all over the world. This abundant literature includes contributions to the history and evolution of norms, what the author of this book refers to as "war crimes" and their enforcement, to which he refers as "war crimes trials." The material he offers in the six parts of this book is offered in a chronological order, covering a period of time ranging from 1899 to 2004. Most significantly, the material contained in these parts combine legal and political events, showing the interrelationship between norms, enforcement modalities, and the socio-political climate surrounding it.

While the first five parts offer the reader a thorough, conventional description of the course of events with appropriate excerpts from documents and other writings, it adds documents and comments seldom found in other similar writings. Among them for example, are those contained in part three, describing the rise of Japanese imperialism in the late '20s, and the Nanking massacre of 1937, which many similar writings have regrettably failed to adequately reflect. It also includes the 1963 Japanese civil litigation involving the atomic bombing by the United States in 1945 of Hiroshima and Nagasaki. Part 4 adds national prosecutions to the mix of international prosecutions, and includes the Vietnam war era and the Calley and Medina cases arising out of the My Lai massacre, which are somewhat forgotten in more contemporary writings on the enforcement of international criminal law. Part 6, which includes the ICTY and ICTR, as well as appropriate material on the ICC, also includes the U.S.'s position on the so-called "war against terrorism" and its aftermath. The book does not, however, cover mixed models and lesser known efforts such as in the case of Ethiopia. Probably because of timing, the book does not address Iraq's Higher Criminal Tribunal, established in December, 2003.

It would be appropriate to describe the contents of the book as a significant compilation of materials whose methodology and approach makes it readily usable in connection with teachings on international criminal law and on international humanitarian law. The author's didactic approach and the choice of materials, as well as the way they were excerpted, makes such a book not only appropriate in legal education, but also in the fields of political science and history.

It will not be difficult for anyone glancing at the table of contents to realize how comprehensive the material assembled by the author is, and how careful a surgeon he has been in cutting out the appropriate parts to make it all fit into a cohesive whole. Unlike similar works, this one is easy to read. The student and researcher will also find very useful the fourteen appendices containing significant documents directly applicable to the subject of the book.

Necessarily a book of this size will exclude cases and materials which are relevant to the subject. However, as a teaching tool, basically, everything needed is included in the book, and it may be that other scholars may be critical of a historic evolutionary approach, as opposed to a subject-matter oriented one. In my judgment, however, the historical and political contexts are indispensable to the understanding of how certain institutions developed, and how in turn these institutions developed jurisprudence, which in turn became foundational for further normative developments. Indeed, international criminal justice is not the product of an orderly intellectual or legislative development, instead, it is a haphazard product deriving from events, circumstances, and sometimes even the force of personality of certain individuals. The student of international criminal law must be mindful of how the history of war crimes and war crimes trials has developed, though admittedly I would have preferred a wider scope to show that the evolution of war crimes trials is part and parcel of the evolution of international criminal justice.

Professor John Watkins is to be congratulated on his effort, which I am sure will prove to be a significant contribution to the legal literature and that of other fields with respect to the subject of international criminal law.

Carolina Academic Press is also to be congratulated for publishing this book, and also for publishing other books on international criminal law.

M. Cherif Bassiouni
Distinguished Research Professor of Law, President
International Human Rights Law Institute, DePaul University College of Law
President, International Institute of Higher Studies in Criminal Sciences (Siracusa, Italy)
Honorary President, International Association of Penal Law (Paris, France)

Preface

This is a book about war crimes and war crime trials occurring for the most part in the twentieth century, with a concluding group of subsections in *Part Six* devoted to emerging twenty-first century geopolitical and military developments in response to transnational terrorism. All of us in the academic enterprise, in one degree or another, incorporate by reference the intellectual capital accrued by other scholars, both past and present. In this work we confess our collective debt to a number of gifted minds whose commentary make up a significant portion of the non-case law material included within these pages.

We have found that traditional casebooks that approach the subject of international criminal justice have often, in our view, neglected some of the historical dynamics that have driven war crimes jurisprudence. Our preference here is to provide the student of international criminal justice—primarily in the liberal arts field—with a short *précis* of certain events that have animated the trials of various individuals or groups who have flagrantly violated international legal norms. Nonetheless, because neither editor is a professional historian, we take full responsibility for any errors of historical omission or commission.

As lawyers, however, both of us appreciate the utility in placing these cases in a historical frame of reference, contingent as that may be. Traditional historical commentary, unlike the law, is almost always contingent and incomplete, awaiting yet again a new "slant," a new "analysis," a new prism as it were for the discovery of new evidence that may provide additional insight into a hodge-podge of conflicting narratives. On the other hand, law must generally eschew contingency and lack of finality. Its purpose, both in the international and domestic context, is to promote a reasonable degree of certitude, predictability and finality. Yet many jurists and lawyers who labor in the field of international criminal justice are also aware of the fact that this body of law is correspondingly affected by Jerome Frank's twin hobgoblins of jurisprudence—"fact skepticism" and "rule skepticism." Facts are subject to the human shortcomings of perception and narrative indeterminacy, while the rules are subject to a multitude of interpretations by judges from widely different cultural backgrounds and trained in diverse systems of law. The cases reported in the following pages reflect this duality at work on all levels of decision-making.

Despite the twenty-first century's new spectre of radical, religious-based, transnational terrorism, there is a positive side to the dilemma we face as a community of nations bound together ever closer by cutting-edge technology and economic interdependence. From the first Hague Peace Conference in 1899 to the present, there has been an ever-increasing recognition in international criminal justice of the primacy of human rights as a legitimate object of legal protection. Notwithstanding twentieth century impunity, the various international conventions, conferences and protocols, reinforced by both the Nuremberg and Tokyo judgments after World War II, have laid the groundwork for such developments as the Genocide Convention and the Universal Declaration of

Human Rights, among others. The principles, rules and regulations emerging from these various assemblies have added to the corpus of human rights recognized in international law that, in previous eras, had been left to the discretion of *ad hoc* tribunals or unilateral State action. The 1998 Rome Statute establishing the first permanent International Criminal Court is a positive step in the quest for global criminal accountability. At present, that Court's role in this quest is still a work in progress. The ICC does represent, however, the culmination of work first begun at the Hague Convention of 1899. Gross violations of human rights and war crimes may have at last been made amenable to a forum whose very existence may give pause to tyrants, great and small. It will be interesting to see whether or not the concerns raised by the United States to certain provisions of the ICC Statute will be a significant factor in determining that Court's future success. In the twentieth century, international criminal justice has moved from a State-centered to a more individual-oriented body of jurisprudence. Despite the asymmetrical, anomic and nihilistic nature of contemporary terrorism, the international accords and agreements put in place during the twentieth century provide a framework for dealing with a threat unenvisaged by those who drafted most of those instruments. Like the common law itself, international criminal law must adapt and change to meet this new accretion of atrocity, buttressed by the accumulated wisdom, experience and guidance afforded by a jurisprudence forged in the maelstrom of the world's bloodiest century.

In a seminal law review article published in 2001[1] Bradford remarked that "[I]n the past century, 203 million combatants and civilians have perished and vast fortunes have been squandered in war—a dysfunctional, yet ubiquitous, human social behavior that has threatened the very existence of mankind."[2] This book will illustrate in some small fashion the dysfunctionality of armed conflict and the attempts by international organizations and international and national tribunals to dampen violence in pursuit of political, economic, social and ideological objectives.

A work of this sort cannot cover an entire rogues gallery of all war criminals and other international outlaws of the past century, much less those of the nascent twenty-first. We have omitted, except for a few occasional references, coverage of the crimes perpetrated by Russian dictator Josef Stalin and Chinese Communist founder Mao Tse-Tung. Likewise, there is no coverage of crimes perpetrated in the name of Nicaraguan strongman Anastasia Garcia Somoza, Haiti's infamous Francois "Papa Doc" Duvalier, Cambodia's genocidal Pol Pot, Chili's Augusto Ugarte Pinochet, Kim II Sung of North Korea, Idi Amin of Uganda or Saddam Hussein of Iraq, to mention only the more notorious. Time and space constraints dictate such exclusion.

We've designed this work to be a teaching tool for a standard three-hour credit course that can be taught in departments of criminal justice, legal studies, political science, international relations and either as a stand-alone or supplementary casebook in schools of law. The book is divided into six *Parts* arranged in chronological order covering a time-span from the first Hague Peace Conference in 1899 up to the United States Supreme Court's decisions on terrorism and military tribunals in mid-2004. *Part One* covers the era from 1899 to 1921, including excerpts from the first and second Hague Conventions, World War I, the Treaty of Versailles of 1919, the Covenant of the League of Nations, Woodrow Wilson's "Fourteen Points" and four of the Leipzig Trials of 1921.

---

1. William C. Bradford, "International Legal Regimes and the Incidence of Interstate War in the Twentieth Century: A Cursory Quantitative Assessment of the Associative Relationship, 16 *Am. U. Int'l L. Rev.* 647 (2001).

2. *Id.* at 649–650.

Part Two includes the era from 1921 to 1951, including the inter-war years in Europe, the Weimar Constitution, the Kellogg-Briand Pact of 1928, the rise of Adolf Hitler and National Socialism in Germany, World War II and German war crimes, the London Charter of 1945, excerpts from the IMT-Nuremberg and selected "Subsequent Proceedings" cases in post-war Germany under Allied Control Council Law No. 10, two British war crime trial opinions as well as one post-World War II war crimes trial opinion by the Supreme Court of Norway and the United Nations' adoption of the so-called "Nuremberg Principles." *Part Three* is devoted to the years 1927–1948, and the year 1963, covering the rise of Japanese Imperialism in the Far East between the late 1920s and the beginning of World War II, the Nanking Massacre of 1937, the Tripartite Pact between Japan, Germany and Italy in 1940, World War II and Japanese war crimes, the IMTFE-Tokyo and the 1963 Japanese civil litigation involving the atomic bombing of Hiroshima and Nagasaki by the United States in August, 1945. *Part Four* covers selected events from 1960 to 1994, including the Israeli trial of Adolf Eichmann for his role in the Holocaust and selected war crime cases involving former Nazis in Ghana, the Federal Republic of Germany (West Germany), the United States, France and Canada. *Part Five* deals with the 1964–1975 time-period involving the SEATO Treaty, the Gulf of Tonkin Resolution, the Vietnam War, the Peers Commission Report on the My Lai atrocity, excerpts from both the *Medina* and *Calley* cases, commentary on My Lai and two United States district court opinions in the early 1970s addressing, among other things, the legality of the Vietnam conflict. *Part Six* covers the 1990–2004 period with an initial discussion of twentieth century impunity, selected decisions from the *ad hoc* United Nations' ICTY and ICTR rulings, selected provisions from the statute of the International Criminal Court and the United States' reservations and objections to the codification, selections regarding the military commission controversy from the post-Civil War United States Supreme Court decision of *Ex parte Milligan* of 1867 up to and including the June, 2004, Supreme Court opinions in the *Hamdi* and *Padilla* appeals involving American citizens in custody as suspected terrorists as well as *Rasul v. Bush*, dealing with Guantanamo Bay detainees. Trial by United States military commissions of suspected al Qaeda and other Islamic Jihadist from Afghanistan, Iraq and other Mid-East nations currently in custody at the United States Naval Base in Cuba, has aroused a robust public debate. How military commissions are organized and the procedures they employ to try accused persons is only dimly understood, if at all, by most of the American public. These forums, however, have a storied history going back in time as far as the American Revolution, but drawing more scrutiny after the Civil War. Military tribunals or commissions apply the laws and customs of war to their tasks, not the traditional and time-honored procedural protections taken for granted by Americans tried in regular state or federal criminal courts.

The Bush Administration characterizes the detainees it holds at Guantanamo Bay as *unlawful* "enemy combatants." Under such a rubric, these prisoners do not enjoy POW status, nor are they protected by all of the rules and regulations granted to *lawful* "enemy combatants" by international accords and conventions. The eleven cases selected for the final portion of *Part Six* illustrate the varied legal issues and tensions surrounding the question of trial by military commission and raise substantial public policy queries on how the United States treats captured asymmetrical warriors. This is followed by an *Epilogue* containing excerpts from the first chapter of Ignatieff's notable 2004 book, *The Lesser Evil: Political Ethics in an Age of Terror*, where that commentator lays out some final thoughts on how a liberal democracy should address issues of liberty, order and security when dealing with international terrorism. The book concludes with an eleven-entry *Appendices,* a *Glossary* containing over 200 entries, a *Reference* section of over 1,400 citations and a detailed *Name* and *Subject Index.*

A separate *Instructor's Manual* keyed to the Six *Parts* of the book supply background information for the instructor on selected topics and questions for classroom use. We believe this material can be usefully employed in either a classroom lecture format or in a small-group seminar format. We would suggest that no particular prerequisite be required, except, perhaps, upper-division undergraduate or graduate status.

John C. Watkins, Jr.
John Paul Weber
Tuscaloosa, Alabama
July 1, 2005

Acknowledgments
and Permissions

The editors wish to gratefully acknowledge the individuals and institutions whose names appear below for their assistance in the research and writing of this book.

Jacob A. Fuller, J.D. and Michael J. Musgrove, J.D., former third-year law students at The University of Alabama School of Law and Graduate Research Assistants to the lead editor, 2001–2002; Paul M. Pruitt, Jr., P.h.D., Special Collections Librarian and Penelope C. Gibson, M.L.S., Reference Librarian, Bounds Library of Law, The University of Alabama School of Law, Tuscaloosa, Alabama; Taylor Fitchett, M.L.S., Director, Arthur J. Morris Library of Law, University of Virginia School of Law, Charlottesville, Virginia and M. Alison White, M.L.S., Special Collections Librarian, Arthur J. Morris Library of Law, University of Virginia, Charlottesville, Virginia; Kevin M. Murphy, M.A., Editor-in-Chief, *American University International Law Review*, Washington, DC: Shelby J. Chandler, Program Assistant, College of Communication & Information Sciences, The University of Alabama, Tuscaloosa, Alabama; M. Cherif Bassiouni, S.J.D., Professor of Law, DePaul University College of Law, Chicago, Illinois; Kenneth C. Randall, J.S.D., Dean, The University of Alabama School of Law, Tuscaloosa, Alabama; the Hon. Frank J. Williams, J.D., Chief Justice, Supreme Court of Rhode Island, Providence, Rhode Island and military tribunal expert recently appointed a Review Panel Judge for the Quantanamo Bay, Cuba, military tribunals; Keith R. Sipe, Publisher, Carolina Academic Press, Durham, North Carolina, and Sallie A. Watkins, the lead editor's wife for her patience and computer research skills in tying up some final "loose ends" in the manuscript.

We also wish to thank the following institutions for their collective assistance in the overall research effort for this book: The Judge Advocate General's School, United States Army, Charlottesville, Virginia; the United States Military Academy, West Point, New York; the Virginia Military Institute, Lexington, Virginia; and the National Archives and Records Administration, Textual Archives Services Division, College Park, Maryland.

The following have kindly granted us permission to quote from their publications:

American Journal of International Law
American University International Law Review
Boston University International Law Journal
Brill Academic Publishers
Cambridge University Press
Canadian Year Book of International Law
Carolina Academic Press
Columbia Journal of Law & Social Problems

Columbia University Press
Continuum International Publishing Group
Harvard Journal of Law & Public Policy
William S. Hein & Co., Inc.
Human Rights Quarterly [John Hopkins University Press]
ILSA Journal of International & Comparative Law
Japanese Annual of International Law
Journal of Criminal Law, Criminology & Police Science
Journal of Public Law
Kluwer Law International
Alfred A. Knopf [a div. of Random House, Inc.]
Law & Social Inquiry [University of Chicago Press]
Maryland Journal of International Law & Trade
Military Law Review
N.Y.U. Journal of International Law & Politics
New York University Press
Oceana Publications, Inc.
Penguin Group (UK) Ltd.
Penguin Group (USA) Inc.
Frederick A. Praeger [a Div. of Greenwood Publishers Group, Inc.]
Princeton University Press
Random House, Inc.
Scholarly Resources, Inc.
Simon and Schuster Publisher, Inc.
Southern California Law Review
St. Martin's Press, Inc. [a division of Palgrave-Macmillian]
Suffolk Transnational Law Review
Temple Law Quarterly [*Temple Law Review*]
Tulane Law Review
University of California-Davis Law Review
University of North Carolina Press
University of Pittsburgh Law Review
University Press of Kansas
Vanderbilt Journal of Transnational Law
Viking Press [a div. of Penguin Group (USA) Inc.]
Wyoming Law Journal [*Wyoming Law Review*]
Yale Journal of International Law

The editors have made a concerted effort to obtain permissions to quote via personal letters, by telephone, by e-mail and by FAX to the periodicals and/or publishers of specific books. In some cases, periodicals or publishing companies have ceased to exist, or, for one reason or another, it has been impossible to locate them or individual authors. All permissions granted appear in the copyright format requested by the publisher concerned.

Editorial Note

Footnote citations in each of the six *Parts* conform to *A Uniform System of Citation,* Harvard Law Review Association (17th ed. 2000) The opinions of the German Supreme Court of the Empire in the Leipzig Trials are printed in the format appearing in the English translation of those decisions in volume 16 of the *American Journal of International Law.* Editorial comments, except those appearing at the beginning of each of the six *Parts,* are set off by brackets throughout the work. Citations in the *References* section are in a stylistic combination found in *A Uniform System of Citation* (17th ed. 2000) and in the *Publication Manual of the American Psychological Association* (5th ed. 2001). Footnotes in case law citations and in judicial opinions are selectively omitted, and, where used, are renumbered.

Minor omissions of words or parts of a sentence, paragraph subsection or section(s) in the text of judicial opinions, conventions, treaties, protocols and scholarly commentary are indicated by a series of ellipses. Major omissions of paragraphs, sections or pages are indicated by a series of asterisks. The majority of international agreements, judicial opinions and scholarly commentary have been edited due to space limitations. Foreign terms, words common to international law, phrases, acronyms and certain other terms of art are collected in the *Glossary.*

War Crimes and War Crime Trials: From Leipzig to the ICC and Beyond

Part One

Hague Peace Conferences; World War I; Treaty of Versailles; League of Nations; Leipzig Trials (1899–1921)

Editorial Commentary

Between 1899 and the end of World War I in 1918, two Hague Peace Conferences were convened while a third scheduled for the year 1915 was aborted by the First World War. In the summer of 1899, representatives from twenty-six nations met at The Hague in the Netherlands at the invitation of Czar Nicholas II of Russia and agreed upon a set of rules and regulations for the conduct of land warfare. These representatives, as well as those that again met at The Hague at the call of United States President Theodore Roosevelt in 1907, were motivated by a desire to codify basic international norms regarding the conduct of belligerents in hostilities primarily on land. Likewise, in both Hague Conventions, there was a healthy awareness of the multiform horrors attending nineteenth century warfare. The dawning of a new century, with both scientific and technological advances changing the face of war, demanded a fresh attempt at establishing at least some fundamental international norms. Thus, the 1899 and the 1907 Hague Peace Conferences set the stage for future twentieth century rule-making of the same genre.

Bradford[1] reminds us that:

> By the end of the nineteenth century, the rampart growth of international organizations had begun to draw aspects of international relations within the orbit of customary international law. Meanwhile, the horrors of the Napoleonic, Crimean, and United States Civil Wars provided the impetus for a universalized and codified international legal regime regulating war. The attention of scholars and statesmen soon turned to providing for the arbitration and

---

1. William C. Bradford, "International Legal Regimes and the Incidence of Interstate War in the Twentieth Century: A Cursory Quantitative Assessment of the Associative Relationship," 16 *Am. U. Int'l. L. Rev.* 647 (2001).

adjudication of disputes, the protection of the interests of neutral states, and the creation of bodies of formal rules and institutions to limit the scope and regulate the conduct of military operations.[2]

Bradford further notes that during the existence of the Hague Convention Rules from 1899 to the formation of the League of Nations in 1920, there occurred some 12,370,000 battle deaths in eleven international conflicts. World War I, of course, topped the list with approximately 12 million battle deaths and approximately 21 million wounded on all sides. The Allied naval blockade of Germany alone killed an estimated 750,000 Germans, most of whom were women and children who died of malnutrition, starvation, or both. From these figures, Bradford sadly concludes that the Hague Conferences were simply "a realist construction that offered little more than a modification of the jus in bello [law of war] and gave little if any consideration as to what law should govern the initial resort to force."[3] World War I and its inhumane engines of destruction had a profound impact on the International legal community in the short term, but its tragedies were soon either forgotten or ignored.

In the early years of the twentieth century, Europe was still ruled, in the main, by incumbents of the nobility. Empires were still intact and warfare was still conceived in the minds of many as a blood sport of princes. In order to protect themselves from enemies both perceived and real, European leaders and diplomats engaged in a set of entangling alliances that provided at least a façade of security to the affected parties. These alliances — many established for the safekeeping of empire — would eventually operate as a trip-wire for the initiation of hostilities in the summer of 1914, plunging the European continent, Japan and ultimately the United States and the Central Powers into a conflagration of immense proportion. Even now in the twenty-first century, what occurred in that 1914–1918 conflict and its aftermath, still haunts certain aspects of geopolitical accommodation as well as the conduct of international relations.

The twentieth century dawned peacefully enough until June, 1914. Then, on June 18th of that year, the heir-apparent of Austria, Archduke Francis Ferdinand, was assassinated in Sarajevo, Serbia, by a lone gunman by the name of Gavrilo Princip. Princip was a Bosnian Serb who, along with other conspirators, contemplated a Bosnia free from Austrian domination. This essentially political murder set in motion a chain of events which ignited the First World War later that summer.

The interlocking alliances and the nationalistic allegiances of 1914 pitted the Allies (the Triple Entente of Great Britain, France and Russia, along with Italy, Japan and later the United States) against the so-called Central Powers, consisting of Imperial Germany, Austria-Hungary, Turkey and Bulgaria. Because Archduke Ferdinand was the heir to the Austrian throne, Austria was justifiably eager to punish Serbia. The Russians, long an ally of Serbia because of its ethnic Slav population, threw their support behind the Serbian government. Imperial Germany, on the other hand, was committed to come to the aid of Austria in any dispute in the Balkans that might involve Czarist Russia. To complicate matters, France was also an ally of Russia and Germany had long considered the French to be her arch enemy dating back to the Franco-Prussian War of 1870–1871.

---

2. *Id.* At 685.
3. *Id.* At 689.

Imperial Germany, ruled by Kaiser Wilhelm II of Hohenzollern, was eager to bring down France and the Germans immediately began planning to implement the so-called *Schlieffen Plan* which envisaged a German attack on France through neutral Belgium. This war plan would allow German forces to drive southwest of Paris, then turn back and roll up the French Army from the rear-forcing it up against the Franco-German border. Alfred von Schlieffen was a student of the Prussian military genius Karl von Clauswitz, and the German military placed ultimate confidence in Schlieffen's strategic and tactical thinking. In order to subdue France, the Germans decided that the traditional neutrality of Belgium must be violated for the greater strategic and geopolitical good. Great Britain, on the other hand, had been guarantor of Belgium's neutrality as far back as 1839. When Germany marched on Belgium in order to put the Schlieffen Plan into operation against France, that act of unprovoked aggression brought Great Britain into the maelstrom. On July 28, 1914, Austria declared war on Serbia, confident that her ally, Imperial Germany, would lend its support. On July 29, 1914, the Imperial German Fleet was mobilized and placed on "war status." On that same day, the French mobilized and called to military duty nearly 3,000,000 Frenchmen. The following day, July 30, 1914, Czar Nicholas II of Russia ordered full mobilization to display Russia's solidarity with its fellow Slavs in Serbia. On August 3, 1914, Germany declared war on France as German troops were concurrently violating Belgium neutrality. On that same day—August 3, 1914—an obscure and somewhat pedestrian Austrian artist, drifter and rabid anti-Semite petitioned the King of Bavaria for permission to enlist in a Bavarian regiment. The following day, August 4, 1914, that request was granted to a young man named Adolf Hitler to fight for the Second Reich.

The British had repeatedly warned Germany not to violate Belgium neutrality. However, having word that German forces were already inside Belgian territory, Great Britain declared war on Imperial Germany one hour before midnight on August 4, 1914. By the end of that momentous day, five European empires were at war with each other: (a) Austria-Hungary vs. Serbia; (b) Imperial Germany vs. France; (c) Czarist Russia vs. Austria-Hungary and (d) Great Britain and France vs. Imperial Germany. Six nations—Holland, Switzerland, Spain, Denmark, Norway, and Sweden took no part in this European bloodletting.

The United States eventually joined the Allied war effort on April 6, 1917, when President Thomas Woodrow Wilson told the United States Congress that this conflict was being fought "to make the world safe for democracy." An irony of some moment occurred when the guns on the Western Front finally fell silent on November 11, 1918—the opposing armies faced one another at essentially the same geographic location where they first met in 1914! The carnage wrought by this conflict staggered the imagination; the nascent concept of "total war" had now emerged on the world scene. World War I saw the demise of the Romanov, Ottoman, Hapsburg and Hohenzollern Empires in the space of about four and a-half years. In defeated Germany, the seeds were planted in the soil of social, political and economic unrest in the 1920s and 1930s for the rise of yet another dictatorial regime far more sinister and bloodthirsty than its Second Reich predecessor.

On January 18, 1918, President Wilson addressed a joint session of Congress and laid out his vision for peace in Europe. Known as the "Fourteen Points," it collectively espoused a liberal, democratic and somewhat pacifist outlook for world cooperation and the peaceful settlement of international disputes. The "Fourteen Points" are reprinted in full (*infra*).

With the formal cessation of hostilities on November 11, 1918, the Allied Powers, in particular France and Great Britain, were anxious to bring certain Germans to trial for violation of the sanctity of treaties and for the commission of alleged war crimes. The Treaty of Peace with Germany, in Articles 230–277, accorded the right of the Allied governments not only to place Kaiser Wilhelm II on trial "for a supreme offense against international morality and the sanctity of treaties," but also to try and punish sundry other German nationals for "having committed acts in violation of the laws and customs of war." Kaiser Wilhelm escaped Allied retribution, and, in so doing, completely altered their plans for an international criminal assize featuring the former German Emperor as its centerpiece. On the morning of November 10, 1918, one day prior to the armistice, the Kaiser left his military headquarters in Spa, Belgium, and boarded a heavily-guarded train for exile in Holland. Thus, the grandson of England's Queen Victoria never returned to German soil. He took up residence in the small northern Dutch fishing village of Doorn and there he remained. Despite numerous entreaties, the Dutch Government (whose monarch at the time was Wilhelm's cousin), refused to surrender the Kaiser citing as a basis for refusal the fact that no international statute then in existence defined the specific offenses charged against the former German Emperor.

The Treaty of Versailles was signed on June 28, 1919. A portion of the language of that instrument provided that:

> A special tribunal be constituted to try Wilhelm II.... It will be guided by the highest motives of international policy with a view to vindicating the solemn obligations of international undertakings and the validity of international morality....

As Battle has noted:[4]

> In January, 1920, the Supreme Council of the Peace Conference made an official demand upon Holland for the surrender of Kaiser Wilhelm II. To this demand the Government of Holland made a flat refusal, stating, however, that precaution would be taken to guard this unwelcome guest. In March, 1920, this attitude of Holland was accepted by the Allies and no further efforts were made to extradite the former Emperor.[5]

The same month as the Allies had demanded the Kaiser's extradition, the German government suggested that German nationals accused of war crimes be placed on trial in a domestic forum in the southeastern German city of Leipzig. A lengthy list of some 895 names (the exact number varies in different accounts) were dispatched to the Supreme Court of the Empire sitting at Leipzig by the Allied Powers. Upon a review of this list, the German government drastically downsized it to only forty-six names. Of these forty-six, only twelve were charged and tried, and, of that twelve, six were convicted and six acquitted. Their sentences ranged from a minimum of six months to a maximum of four years in duration. At the end of *Part One*, we report excerpts from four opinions of the Supreme Court of the Empire in the cases of (a) *In re Heynen*; (b) *In re Muller;* (c) *In re Neumann;* and (d) *In re Dithmar & Boldt*. In historical hindsight, these decisions set a precedent of sorts, but not one most international lawyers would applaud. In fact, many characterized these proceedings as little more than a form of political theatre held by the Germans to appease the Anglo-French firebrands who sought

---

4. George C. Battle, "The Trials Before the Leipsic [sic] Supreme Court of Germans Accused of War Crimes," 8 *Va. L. Rev.1* (1921).

5. *Id.* at 4.

stern, draconian justice upon all responsible parties of the former German Empire im-plicated in the war. After 1922, however, no further attempt was made by the victors to force the Weimar Republic to continue the Leipzig litigation.

What, if anything, can we draw from this abortive attempt by a vanquished nation to deal with its own citizens charged with a violation of international law? Among some commentators there seems to be a view that perhaps at least two legal doctrines did emerge even in gossamer form from these less than adequate proceedings: (a) the so-called "act of State" doctrine and (b) the recognition of the defense of "superior author-ity." In reading the Leipzig opinions, you will note that the European style of decision-making and accompanying opinions of the jurists themselves differ from the Anglo-American traditional common law grand style. The *ratio decidendi* (rationale of the decision) of these cases must be gleaned from an extensive juridical narrative that omits any references to precedent. However, a close reading of these opinions reveal that the Leipzig court was following, what to it, were generally recognized international legal norms in place at the time. At the end of the Second World War, one of the chief factors motivating the Allies to opt for an International Military Tribunal prototype was the widespread distaste they harbored for the results reached in the Leipzig Trials a quarter of a century earlier.

Before proceeding to the Leipzig litigation, a brief background summary of the Hague Conventions of 1899 and 1907 may be helpful. Both of these international as-semblages laid the ideological and legal foundation for international criminal justice for the remainder of the twentieth century. In fact, the delegates accredited to both conven-tions were vitally interested in the concept of international *justice*. The 1899 conference lasted from May 18 to July 29, with twenty-six nations in attendance. The notion of state sovereignty, then as now, was held in high esteem by all State delegations. The first conference assembled in the Dutch summer palace, The House in the Wood. There, the various delegations tackled the nettlesome problems of warfare and how best to make armed conflict more humane and more rule-oriented. As Jones[6] has noted:

> The delegates were exactly what their names implied: representatives of a power not their own, deputed to defend and, if possible, secure the interests of that power in the meetings at The Hague. If that could be done through cooperation with the representatives of other states, well and good. If not—as in the case of the limitation of armaments—that was too bad. But in no case and in no wise must the state and the power of the state be diminished or undercut.... Only through the state could nationality be protected, independence be maintained, sovereignty be exercised, interests be pursued and freedom be kept free.[7]

Sovereignty as a concept was foremost on the minds of the delegates to the 1907 Hague Convention as well, convened at the behest of President Theodore Roosevelt of the United States. The 1907 conference assembled in the Hall of Knights at The Hague and was attended by forty-four state delegations, lasting from June 15 to October 18, 1907. It was here that the delegates once again tackled some of the major issues left unsettled at the 1899 conference. The 1899 Hague Conference (Hague I) did its work in three sep-arate conventions: (1) the Convention for the Peaceful Settlement of International Con-flicts; (2) the Convention for the Adaptation of the Red Cross to Maritime Warfare; and

---

6. Dorothy V. Jones, *Toward a Just World: The Critical Years in the Search for International Justice* (2000).

7. *Id.* at 6.

(3) the codification of laws and customs of land warfare. The work of the 1907 assembly (Hague II) was essentially two-fold: (1) it revised and enlarged the conventions of 1899 and published them in new and modified forms, and (2) to the three conventions of 1899, the 1907 conference added ten new conventions; yet the basic framework of the 1899 convention largely remained intact. In combination, delegates to both Hague Peace Conferences felt secure in the belief that warfare could be humanized and made manageable through law.

----

1. Hague Conferences of 1899 and 1907

(a) 1899 Hague Convention (No. II) Respecting the Laws and Customs of War on Land

1 *American Journal of International Law* (Supp.)
129; 132–139; 141; 147; 149; 151–152 (1907)
Reproduced with permission from 1 *American Journal of International Law* (Supp.) 129 (1907). © The American Society of International Law

Article I.

The High Contracting Parties shall issue instructions to their armed land forces, which shall be in conformity with the "Regulations respecting the Laws and Customs of War on Land" annexed to the present convention.

Article II.

The provisions contained in the Regulation mentioned in Article I are only binding on the Contracting Powers, in case of war between two or more of them. These provisions shall cease to be binding from the time when, in a war between Contracting Powers a non-Contracting Power joins one of the belligerents.

Article III.

The present Convention shall be ratified as speedily as possible. The ratification shall be deposited at the Hague. A proces-verbal shall be drawn up recording the receipt of each ratification, and a copy, duly certified, shall be delivered to the Contracting Powers through the diplomatic channel.

Annex to the Convention

Section I. On Belligerents

Chapter I. *On the Qualifications of Belligerents*

Article I

The laws, rights, and duties of war apply not only to armies, but also to militia and volunteer corps, fulfilling the following conditions:

1. To be commanded by a person responsible for his subordinates;
2. To have a fixed and distinctive emblem recognizable at a distance;

3.   To carry arms openly; and

4.   To conduct their operation in accordance with the laws and customs of war.

In countries where militia or volunteer corps constitute the army, or form part of it, they are included under the denomination "army."

Article II.

The population of a territory which has not been occupied who, on the enemy's approach, spontaneously takes up arms to resist the invading troops without having time to organize themselves in accordance with Article I, shall be regarded a belligerent if they respect the laws and customs of war.

Article III.

The armed forces of the belligerent parties may consist of combatants and non-combatants. In case of capture by the enemy both have a right to be treated as prisoners of war.

Chapter II. *On Prisoners of War*

Article IV.

Prisoners of war are in the power of the hostile Government, but not in that of the individual or corps who captured them.

They must be humanely treated.

All their personal belongings, except arms, horses, and military papers remain their property.

Article V.

Prisoners of war may be interned in a town, fortress, camp, or any other locality, and bound not to go beyond certain fixed limits; but they can also be confined as an indispensable measure of safety.

Article VI.

The State may utilize the labor of prisoners of war according to their rank and aptitude. Their tasks shall not be excessive, and shall have nothing to do with the military operations.

Prisoners may be authorized to work for the Public Service, for private persons, or on their own account.

Work done for the State shall be paid according to the tariffs in force for soldiers of the national army employed in similar tasks.

When the work is for other branches of the Public Service or for private persons, the conditions shall be settled in agreement with the military authorities.

The wages of prisoners shall go towards improving their position, and the balance shall be paid them at the time of their release, after deducting the cost of their maintenance.

Article VII.

The Government into whose hands prisoners of war have fallen is bound to maintain them.

Failing a special agreement between the belligerents, prisoners of war shall be treated as regards food, quarters, and clothing, on the same footing as the troops of the Government which has captured them.

Article VIII.

Prisoners of war shall be subject to the laws, regulations, and orders in force in the army of the State into whose hands they have fallen. Any act of insubordination warrants the adoption, as regards them, of such measures of severity as may be necessary.

Escaped prisoners, recaptured before they have succeeded in rejoining the army, or before quitting the territory occupied by the army that captured them, are liable to disciplinary punishment.

Prisoners who, after succeeding in escaping are again taken prisoners, are not liable to any punishment for the previous flight.

Article IX.

Every prisoner of war, if questioned, is bound to declare his true name and rank, and if he disregards this rule, he is liable to a curtailment of the advantages accorded to the prisoners of war of his class.

Article XII.

Any prisoner of war, who is liberated on parole and recaptured, bearing arms against the Government to whom he has pledged his honor, or against the allies of that Government, forfeits his right to be treated as a prisoner of war, and can be brought before the courts.

Article XVII.

Officers taken prisoner may receive, if necessary, the full pay allowed them in this position by their country's regulations, the amount to be repaid by their Government.

Article XVIII

Prisoners of war shall enjoy every latitude in the exercise of their religion, including attendance at their own church services, provided only they comply with the regulations for order and police issues by the military authorities.

Chapter III. *On the Sick and Wounded*

Article XXI.

The obligations of belligerents with regard to the sick and wounded are governed by the Geneva Convention of the 22nd August 1864, subject to any modifications which may be introduced into it.

Section II. On Hostilities

Chapter I. *On Means of Injuring the Enemy, Sieges and Bombardments*

Article XXII.

The right of belligerents to adopt means of injuring the enemy is not unlimited.

Article XXIII.

Besides the prohibitions provided by special Conventions, it is especially prohibited:

a. To employ poison or poisonous arms;

b. To kill or wound treacherously individuals belonging to the hostile nation or army.

c. To kill or wound an enemy who, having laid down arms, or having no longer means of defense, has surrendered at discretion;

d. To declare that no quarter will be given;

e. To employ arms, projectiles, or material of a nature to cause superfluous injury;

f. To make improper use of a flag of truce, the national flag, or military ensigns and the enemy's uniform, as well as the distinctive badges of the Geneva Convention;

g. To destroy or seize the enemy's property, unless such destruction or seizure be imperatively demanded by the necessities of war.

Article XXIV.

No rules of war and the employment of methods necessary to obtain information about the enemy and the country are considered allowable.

Article XXV.

The attack or bombardment of towns, villages, habitations, or buildings which are not defended, is prohibited.

Article XXVI.

The Commander of an attacking force, before commencing a bombardment, except in the case of an assault should do all he can to warn the authorities.

Article XXVII.

In sieges and bombardments all necessary steps should be taken to spare as far as possible edifices devoted to religious, art, science, and charity, hospitals, and places where the sick and wounded are collected, provided they are not used at the same time for military purposes. The besieged should indicate these buildings or places by some particular and visible signs, which should previously be notified to the assailants.

Article XXVIII.

The pillage of a town or place, even when taken by assault, is prohibited.

Chapter III. *On Flags of Truce*

Article XXXII.

An individual is considered as bearing a flag of truce who is authorized by one of the belligerents to enter into communication with the other, and who carries a white flag. He has a right of inviolability, as well as the trumpeter, bugler, or drummer, the flag-bearer, and the interpreter who may accompany him.

Article XXXIII.

The Chief to whom a flag of truce is sent is not obliged to receive it in all circumstances.

He can take all steps necessary to prevent the envoy taking advantage of his mission to obtain information.

In case of abuse, he has the right to detain the envoy temporarily.

Article XXXIV.

The envoy loses his right of inviolability if it is proved beyond doubt that he has taken advantage of his privileged position to provoke or commit an act of treachery.

Chapter IV. *On Capitulations*

Article XXXV.

Capitulations agreed on between the Contracting Parties must be in accordance with the rules of military honour. When once settled, they must be scrupulously observed by both the parties.

Chapter V. *On Armistices*

Article XXXVI.

An armistice suspends military operations by mutual agreement between the belligerent parties. If its duration is not fixed, the belligerent parties can resume operations at any time, provided always the enemy is warned within the time agreed upon, in accordance with the terms of the armistice.

Article XXXVII.

An armistice may be general or local. The first suspends all military operations of the belligerent States; the second, only those between certain fractions of the belligerent armies and in a fixed radius.

Article XXXVIII.

An armistice must be notified officially, and in good time, to the competent authorities and the troops. Hostilities are suspended immediately after the notification, or at the fixed date.

Article XL.

Any serious violation of the armistice by one of the parties gives the other party the right to denounce it, and even, in case of urgency, to recommence hostilities at once.

Article XLVII.

Pillage is formally prohibited.

Article LV.

The occupying State shall only be regarded as administrator and usufructuary of the public buildings, real property, forests, and agricultural works belonging to the hostile State, and situated in the occupied country. It must protect the capital of these properties, and administer it according to the rules of usufruct.

Article LVI.

The property of the communes, that of religious, charitable, and educational institutions, and those of arts and sciences, even when state property, shall be treated as private property.

All seizures of, and destruction, or intentional damage done to such institutions, to historical monuments, works of art or science, is prohibited, and should be made the subject of proceedings.

———————

(b) 1907 Hague Convention (No. IV) Respecting the Laws and Customs of War on Land

Article I.

The Contracting Parties recognize that hostilities between themselves must not commence without previous and explicit warning, in the form either of a reasoned declaration of war or of an ultimatum with conditional declaration of war.

Article 2.

The existence of a state of war must be notified to the neutral Powers without delay, and shall not take effect in regard to them until after the receipt of a notification, which may, however, be given by telegraph. Neutral Powers, nevertheless, cannot rely on the absence of a notification if it is clearly established that they were in fact aware of the existence of a state of war.

Article 5.

Non-signatory Powers may adhere to the present Convention. The Power which wishes to adhere notifies in writing its intention to the Netherland Government, forwarding to it the act of adhesion, which shall be deposited in the archives of said Government.

The said Government shall at once forward to all the other Powers a duly certified copy of the notification as well as the act of adhesion, stating the date on which it received the notification.

Convention Respecting the Laws and Customs of War on Land

[Many of the 1907 Hague Convention articles on the Laws and Customs of War are essentially duplicates of those same articles found in the 1899 Convention. The material below regarding the rights and obligations of neutral States also appeared in modified form in the 1899 Convention. We note them here for the first time as they appear in the 1907 Convention].

Chapter I. *The Rights and Duties of Neutral Powers*

Article 1.

The territory of neutral Powers is inviolable.

Article 2.

Belligerents are forbidden to move troops or convoys of either munitions of war or supplies across the territory of a neutral Power.

Article 3.

Belligerents are likewise forbidden to:

(a) Erect on the territory of a neutral Power a wireless telegraphy station or other apparatus for the purpose of communicating with belligerent forces on land or sea;

(b) Use of any installation of this kind established by them before the war on the territory of a neutral Power for purely military purposes, and which has not been opened for the service of public messages.

Article 4.

Corps of combatants cannot be formed nor recruiting agencies opened on the territory of a neutral Power to assist the belligerents.

Article 7.

A neutral Power is not called upon to prevent the export or transport, on behalf of one or other of the belligerents, of arms, munitions of war, or, in general, of anything which can be of use to an army or a fleet.

Article 10.

The fact of a neutral Power resisting, even by force, attempts to violate its neutrality cannot be regarded as a hostile act.

---

2. The Armenian Genocide (1915)

(a) Vahakn N. Dadrian, "Genocide as a Problem of National and International Law: The World War I Armenian Case and Its Contemporary Legal Ramifications"

14 *Yale Journal of International Law* 221; 315; 317–323 (1989)
Reproduced with permission from the
Yale Journal of International Law © 1989

[When World War I ended, Germany refused to hand over to the Allies Talat Pasa, the *de facto* head of the Turkish state. As with the Kaiser, the Allies were eager to try certain alleged Turkish war criminals for, among other things, deporting and killing countless Greeks and Armenians who were residing in the Ottoman state during the First World War. The Turks had previously massacred a number of ethnic minorities in Turkey, especially Armenians, during the so-called Hamidian massacres that took place during the period 1894 to 1897. The Triple Entente (Great Britain, France and Russia) issued a formal Declaration on May 15, 1915, to the Ottoman Turks that read: "In view of these new crimes of Turkey against humanity and civilization, the Allied governments announce publicly to the Sublime Porte that they will hold personally responsible [for] these crimes all members of the Ottoman Government and those by their agents who are implicated in such massacres." Turkey completely ignored this warning.

The Turkish response to the demand for the surrender of criminal suspects paralleled the German response. Not only did the Foreign Minister of the Istanbul government object to the surrendering of Turkish nationals to the Allies, but Mustafa Kemal, the head of the antagonistic Ankara government, rejected the very idea of "recognizing a kind of right of jurisdiction on the part of a foreign government over acts of a Turkish subject in the interior of Turkey herself"].

...On June 11, 1921, the Ankara government informed the British that..."those accused of crimes would be put on impartial trial at Ankara in the same way as German prisoners were being tried in Germany." This, as well as subsequent similar assurances, proved to be mere negotiating ploys.

* * *

...the Armenian genocide provides important insight into the roles of international actors in prevention or punishing genocide and the challenges that the international legal system faces in each case.... The Great Powers of Europe, through a misreading of the Turkish domestic situation and a hesitant fumbling policy of "humanitarian intervention," not only failed to prevent the genocide but exacerbated it by encouraging the Armenians to press for reforms and then failing to protect them from Turkish backlash.

* * *

The Armenian Genocide was a direct consequence of the socio-political system that existed in Ottoman Turkey during the years leading up to World War I. Because of certain intractable components, most notably religious beliefs which could not be reconciled with conceptions of Armeanian equality, the Ottoman system was subjected to unabating external and internal pressures. It is the basic thesis of this study that the genocidal nature of the Turkish response was in part conditioned by Ottoman traditions and theocracy. The norms and the associated corpus of the Ottoman customary and common law for subject nationalities and minorities not only allowed, but in many instances encouraged, such a drastic response as a form of crisis management. Thus, what was considered deviant by external, international standards was considered normal and functional by domestic Ottoman desiderata.

The concept of "status" provides the link between the social and legal criteria in the study of the Armenian genocide. The Armenians were not only an ethnic-religious minority with social disabilities, but also a politically disenfranchised group, denied legal equality. Their inferior status made them permanently vulnerable. The permeation of Islamic dogma and tradition into the Ottoman social system, reinforced by the martial traditions of the Empire, reinforced Armenian vulnerability. Most important, the Ottoman legal system became permeated with the elements of the Islamic canonic law, the Seriat, which required this unequal status as a fundamental and fixed truth under Islam.

The nineteenth-century "humanitarian interventions" of the Concert of Europe to protect the Armenians failed in large part because they did not give due consideration to the socio-political forces which forced the Armenians into an inferior position. By failing to address this central factor, the Europeans allowed the Ottoman state to pursue the more expedient but far less effective route of responding to the symptoms the socio-political system produced. A series of treaties and agreements signed between the European Powers and Turkey between 1856 and 1914 nominally obligated the Ottoman authorities to extend equality to their non-Muslim subjects. The Turkish authorities, while feigning concurrence with the need for reforms, ensured that these reforms never took actual effect. By pursuing a strategy of stalling and temporizing, while at the same time playing the Powers against each other, the Turks managed to defuse internationally explosive situations without taking any action contrary to their religious beliefs. At issue for the Turks was not the formal introduction of reforms, a series of which were in fact enacted and promulgated, but their effective implementation. The Armenians were not "entitled" to, and hence were not going to be accorded, equality in the Ottoman system.

When deception and deferral were ineffective, the Turks resorted to violent measures of repression, culminating first in the 1894–1897 Hamidian massacres. These massacres are important not only because they foreshadowed the subsequent genocide, but also because the perpetrators were not prosecuted. Given this precedent, the Turks had strong reason to believe that there would likewise be no punishment for subsequent killings.

These acts of annulment may technically be attributed to the effect of war; international law has no explicit or uniform rules for the preservation or annulment of treaties during war. The annulments acquire critical significance, however, when placed in the context of Ottoman Turkey's continuous flouting of treaty provisions in the decades preceding the war. The episodic pre-war massacres of Armenians occurred when these treaties were in force but not enforced. The European Powers elected to substitute expressions of outrage for any implementation of sanctions. While it must also be pointed out that the relevant treaties lacked self-executing provisions in case of violation, the fact remains that the Powers' inaction was not due to any sensitivity to legal niceties but rather to mutual suspicions and rivalries. The climax of this European ritual of alternately remonstrating with and threatening Turkey came in May 1915, with the initiation of the Armenian genocide. The genocide was consummated irrespective of Europe's threats, and perpetrators once more escaped punishment.

* * *

…The international efforts at retribution following World War I, both in the case of Turkey and its ally Germany, reveal the weakness of international punishment as an effective deterrent to future acts of genocide. The international efforts of the European Powers to bring the perpetrators of the Armenian genocide to justice fell victim to the overarching principle of national sovereignty and the machinations of international politics. By allowing the Ottoman government to remain in place following its defeat in the war, the European Powers gave up the authority that they needed to effectuate retribution for the massacre. The presence of a sovereign government in Turkey not only impeded the initiation of international trials through legal barriers, such as issues of jurisdiction, and the practical impediments, such as difficulties in securing the evidence needed for international prosecution, but led to the splintering of European resolve by fostering political maneuvering between the powers to curry favor with the Turkish government.

The efforts at domestic retribution for the Armenian genocide were similarly ineffective. Although Courts Martial were instituted in Turkey, and a great deal of damning evidence concerning the genocide was revealed, its perpetrators emerged relatively unscratched. The fact that these trials were held at all likely was due only to the efforts of a weak post-war government to secure more promising terms for peace. Thus, the courts were never given the power they needed to prosecute effectively the murderers of the Armenian people. Instead, the trials served only to stir a new ground swell of nationalist fervor among the Muslims which resulted in the emergence of the Kemalist regime. The Turks, like the Germans following World War I, were unwilling to accept the collective guilt that these domestic trials represented. Thus, after the Kemalist regime took power, the large number of Courts Martial that had not reached the verdict stage were dismantled, and the last opportunity of retribution disappeared. The European Powers, having lost the necessary cohesion and authority, were unable to prevent this result.

(b) Peter Maguire, *Law and War: An American Story*

75–76 (2000)
Reproduced with permission from Columbia University Press,
© 2000, Columbia University Press

…Rather than expel or resettle Turkey's minority Armenian population, Turkish leaders chose simply to kill them. When Turkey's Ittihad allied with Germany, its "Young Turk" leaders enslaved the Armenians and forced them to build public works projects. By 1915, according to David Kaiser,

> the Young Turks decided…to solve the problem of the Armenian minority by exterminating the Armenians…. The government disarmed the Armenians of Anatolia in 1915 and announced its decision to deport them to Mesopotamia. But the deportation was only a pretext: the Turks shot Armenian men and marched the Armenian women and children into the mountains and the desert, where they starved to death. Between 1 and 1.5 million Armenians perished.

The U.S. Government was divided over its official response. Although the U.S. Ambassador to Turkey, Henry Morgenthau, spoke out against the massacres, the State Department took a different view. In 1915, the governments of France, Great Britain, and Russia declared the Turkish atrocities "crimes against humanity and civilization" and threatened to hold the ringleaders "personally responsible." However, American leaders neither supported nor took actions against the perpetrators of the Armenian genocide.…

When President Woodrow Wilson unveiled his revolutionary peace plan in 1918, war crimes were a minor detail. His outline for an international political system was by far the most radical American attempt to dislodge the cornerstone of the old European state-sovereignty. Wilson's "Fourteen Points" set out to model international relations after a modern constitutional democracy, complete with "consent of the governed, equality of rights, and freedom from aggression."

* * *

Rather than fight, nations would enter into arbitration and settle differences diplomatically with nonmilitary sanctions. In the event of war, the League [of Nations] was to coerce the parties into arbitration. The terms "just" and "unjust" were changed to the more up-to-date "lawful" and "unlawful." The procedure for a lawful war was laid out in the League's Charter…. The traditional roles of the European state system were further challenged by the introduction of the concept of "war guilt."

---

3. Woodrow Wilson's "Fourteen Points"

(1918)

[In his message to the United States Congress delivered on January 8, 1918, and in his subsequent pronouncements, particularly in an address on September 27, 1918, Woodrow Wilson set out what he believed would contribute to international peace and world order after the conclusion of World War I. His "Fourteen Points" were both visionary and ground-breaking. He desired the society of nations to come together in a world ruled by law, not by force. The European Allies were less than enthusiastic about these global ukases and there was a standing joke making the rounds among them that, in effect, "God had only Ten Commandments; Wilson has Fourteen!" Wilson literally wanted to alter most of the old European rules of statecraft, but he was unsuccessful in a great many of his efforts. His own Secretary of State, Robert Lansing, along with James Brown Scott (the American representatives to the Versailles Peace Conference) saw to it that the long-venerated international law doctrine of sovereignty would remain a cornerstone of American foreign policy. The crowning blow to Wilson's vision for a New World Order after the chaos of the Great War was, of course, the failure of the United States to become a member of the League of Nations].

The "Fourteen Points"

1. Open covenants of peace, openly arrived at, after which there shall be no private international understandings of any kind, but diplomacy shall proceed always frankly and in the public view.

2. Absolute freedom of navigation upon the seas, outside territorial waters, alike in peace and war, except as the seas may be closed in whole or in part by international action for the enforcement of international covenants.

3. The removal, so far as possible, of all economic barriers and the establishment of an equality of trade conditions among all the nations consenting to the peace and associating themselves for its maintenance.

4. Adequate guarantees given and taken that national armaments will be reduced to the lowest point, consistent with domestic safety.

5. A free, open-minded, and absolutely impartial adjustment of all colonial claims, based upon a strict observance of the principle that in determining all such questions of sovereignty the interests of the populations concerned must have equal weight with the equitable claims of the government whose title is to be determined.

6. The evacuation of all Russian territory, and such a settlement of all questions affecting Russia as will secure the best and freest cooperation of the other nations in the world, in obtaining for her an unhampered and unembarrassed opportunity for the independent determination of her own political development and national policy and assure her of a sincere welcome into the society of free nations under institutions of her own choosing; and, more than a welcome, assistance also of every kind that she may need and may herself desire. The treatment accorded Russia by her sister nations in the months to come will be the acid test of their good-will, of their comprehension of her needs as distinguished from their own interests, and of the intelligent and unselfish sympathy.

7. Belgium, the whole world will agree, must be evacuated and restored, without any attempt to limit the sovereignty which she enjoys in common with all other free nations. No other single act will serve as this will serve to restore confidence among the nations in the laws which they have themselves set and determined for the government of their relations with one another. Without this healing act the whole structure and validity of international law is forever impaired.

8. All French territory should be freed and the invaded portions restored, and the wrong done to France by Prussia in 1871 in the matter of Alsace-Lorraine, which has unsettled the peace of the world for nearly fifty years, should be righted, in order that peace may once more be made secure in the interest of all.

9. A readjustment of the frontiers of Italy should be effected along clearly recognizable lines of nationality.

10. The people of Austria-Hungary, whose place among the nations we wish to see safeguarded and assured, should be accorded the freest opportunity of autonomous development.

11. Rumania, Serbia, and Montenegro should be evacuated; occupied territories restored; Serbia accorded free and secure access to the sea; and the relations of the several Balkan States to one another determined by friendly counsel along historically established line of allegiance and nationality; and international guarantees of the political and economic independence and territorial integrity of the several Balkan States should be entered into.

12. The Turkish portions of the present Ottoman Empire should be assured a secure sovereignty, but the other nationalities which are not under Turkish rule should be assured an undoubted security of life and an absolutely unmolested opportunity of autonomous development, and the Dardanelles should be permanently open as a free passage to the ships and commerce of all nations under international guarantees.

13. An independent Polish State should be erected which should be assured a free and secure access to the sea, and whose political and economic independence and territorial integrity be guaranteed by international covenant.

14. A general association of nations must be formed under specific covenants for the purpose of affording mutual guarantees of political independence and territorial integrity to great and small states alike.

---

4. Conditions of an Armistice with Germany
(1918)

13 *American Journal of International Law* (sect. 2) 97–100; 101–104 (1919)
Reproduced with permission from 13 *American Journal of International Law* (sect. 2) 97 (1919). © The American Society of International Law

(A) *On the Western Front.*

1. Cessation of hostilities on land and in the air six hours after the signature of the Armistice.

2. Immediate evacuation of the invaded countries: Belgium, France, Luxemburg, as well as Alsace-Lorraine, so ordered as to be completed within fifteen days from the signature of the Armistice. German troops which have not evacuated the above-mentioned territories within the period fixed will be made prisoners of war. Joint occupation by the Allied and United States forces shall keep pace with evacuation in these areas. All movements of evacuation or occupation shall be regulated in accordance with a Note (Annexe No 1), drawn up at the time of signature of the armistice.

3. Repatriation, beginning at once, to be completed within fifteen days, of all inhabitants of the countries above enumerated (including, hostages, persons under trial, or convicted).

4. Surrender in good condition by the German armies of the following war material: —

5,000 guns (2,500 heavy, 2,500 field).

25,000 machine guns.

3,000 trench mortars.

1,700 fighting and bombing aeroplanes—in the first place, all D7's and all night-bombing aeroplanes.

The above to be delivered *in situ* to the Allied and United States troops in accordance with the detailed conditions laid down in Annexe 1, drawn up at the time of the signature of the Armistice.

5. Evacuation by the German armies of the territories on the left bank of the Rhine. These territories on the left bank of the Rhine shall be administered by the local authorities under the control of the Allied and United States armies of occupation. The occupation of these territories shall be carried out by the Allied and United States garrisons holding the principal crossings of the Rhine (Mainz, Coblenz, Cologne), together with bridgeheads, at these points, of a 30 kilometer radius on the right bank, and by garrisons similarly holding the strategic points of each area. A neutral zone shall be reserved on the right bank of the Rhine between the river and a line drawn parallel to the bridgeheads and to the river, and at a distance of 10 kilometers from the Dutch to the Swiss frontier. Evacuation by the enemy of the Rhineland (left and right banks), shall be so ordered as to be completed within a further period of sixteen days—thirty-one days in all after the signature of the Armistice....

6. In all the territories evacuated by the enemy there shall be no evacuation of inhabitants; no damage or detriment shall be done to the persons or property of the inhabitants. No person shall be prosecuted for participation in military measures prior to the signatures of the Armistice. No destruction of any kind to be committed. Military establishments of all kinds shall be handed over intact, as well as military stores, food, munitions, and equipment not removed during the periods fixed for evacuation. Stores of food of all kinds for the civil population, cattle, &c., shall be left *in situ*. No measures of a general or official character shall be adopted which may result in a depreciation of industrial establishments or in a reduction of their personnel.

7. Roads and means of communication of every kind, railroads, waterways, main roads, bridges, telegraphs and telephones shall be in no way damaged. All civil and military personnel at present employed on them shall be maintained. 5,000 locomotives and 150,000 wagons in good running order, and provided with all necessary spare parts and fittings, shall be delivered to the Associated Powers within the period fixed by Annexe No. 2, which shall not exceed thirty-one days. 5,000 motor lorries in good running order shall also be handed over within thirty-six days.

The railways of Alsace-Lorraine shall be handed over within thirty-one days, together with all personnel and material belonging directly to these lines. Further, material necessary for the working of railways in the territories on the left bank of the Rhine shall be left *in situ*. All stores of coal and material for upkeep of permanent way, signals, and repair-shops, shall be left *in situ* and maintained by Germany as far as the working of these lines on the left bank of the Rhine is concerned. All barges taken from the Allies shall be restored to them....

8. The German Command shall be bound to disclose, within 48 hours after the signature of the Armistice, all mines or delay action apparatus disposed on the territory evacuated by the German troops, and shall assist in their discovery and destruction. The German Command shall also disclose all harmful measures that may have been taken (such as poisoning or pollution of springs, wells, &c.). All the foregoing under penalty of reprisals.

9. The right of requisition shall be exercised by the Allied and United States Armies in all occupied territories, settlement of accounts with the persons concerned being pro-

vided for. The maintenance of the troops of occupation in the Rhineland (excluding Alsace-Lorraine) shall be defrayed by the German Government.

10. Immediate repatriation, without reciprocity, of all Allied and United States prisoners of war (including those under trial or convicted), according to detailed conditions which shall be fixed. The Allied Powers and the United States shall dispose of these prisoners as they think fit. This condition cancels previous agreements on the subject of the exchange of prisoners of war, including the agreement of July, 1918, in course of ratification. The repatriation of German prisoners interned in Holland and in Switzerland shall, however, continue as before. The repatriation of German prisoners shall be settled upon the conclusion of the peace preliminaries.

11. Sick and wounded who cannot be removed from territory evacuated by the German armies shall be cared for by German personnel, to be left on the spot with the material required.

(B.) *Clauses Relating to the Eastern Frontiers of Germany*

12. All German troops at present in any territory which before the war belonged to Austria-Hungary, Roumania, or Turkey, must at once withdraw within the frontiers of Germany as they existed on August 1, 1914. All German troops at present in territories which before the war formed part of Russia shall likewise withdraw within the German frontiers as above defined, as soon as the Allies shall consider this desirable, having regard to the interior conditions of those territories.

13. Evacuation of German troops to begin at once, and all German instructors, prisoners, and civilian or military agents now within Russian territory (as defined on August 1, 1914), to be recalled.

14. German troops to cease at once all requisitions, seizures, or coercive measures for obtaining supplies intended for Germany in Roumania and Russia (according to frontiers existing on August 1, 1914).

15. Annulment of the Treaties of Bucharest and Brest-Litovsk and of supplementary treaties.

16. The Allies shall have free access to the territories evacuated by the Germans on their Eastern frontier, either via Danzig or by the Vistula, in order to revictual the populations of those territories or to maintain order.

* * *

(E.) Naval Conditions

20. Immediate cessation of all hostilities at sea, and definite information to be given as to the location and movements of all German ships. Notification is to be given to Neutrals that freedom of navigation in all territorial waters is given to the naval and mercantile marines of the Allied and Associated Powers, all questions of neutrality being waived.

21. Release, without reciprocity, of all prisoners of war in German hands belonging to the navies and mercantile marines of the Allied and Associated Powers.

22. Surrender to the Allies and the United States of all existing submarines (including all submarine cruisers and mine-layers) with armament and equipment complete, in ports specified by the Allies and the United States. Those which cannot be put to sea shall be paid off and disarmed, and shall remain under the supervision of the Allies and the

United States. Submarines which are ready to put to sea shall be prepared to leave German ports as soon as orders are received by wireless for them to proceed to the port of surrender, and the rest shall follow as soon as possible. The conditions of this clause shall be fulfilled within fourteen days after the signature of the Armistice.

* * *

26. The existing blockade conditions set up by the Allied and Associated Powers shall remain unchanged, and all German merchant ships met at sea shall remain liable to capture. The Allies and the United States contemplate the provisioning of Germany, during the Armistice, to such an extent as shall be found necessary.

* * *

This Armistice was signed on the 11th November 1918, at 5 a.m. (French time).

F. Foch	Erzberger
R.E. Wemyss	Oberndorff
Winterfeldt	
Vanselow	

Addendum

The Allied Representatives declare that, owing to recent events, it appears necessary to them that the following condition should be added to the clauses of the armistice:

"In the event of the German vessels not being handed over within the periods specified, the Allied and United States Governments shall have the right to occupy Heligoland so as to insure the surrender of the vessels."

---

5. Covenant of the League of Nations Adopted by the Peace Conference at Plenary Session

April 28, 1919, 13 *American Journal of International Law*
(sect. 2) 128; 129–134; 139 (1919)
Reproduced with permission from 13 *American Journal of International Law*
(Sect. 2) 128 (1919). © The American Society of International Law

In order to promote international co-operation and to achieve international peace and security by the acceptance of obligations not to resort to war, by the prescription of open, just and honorable relations between nations, by the firm establishment of the understandings of international law as the actual rules of conduct among governments, and by the maintenance of justice and a scrupulous respect for all treaty obligations in the dealings of organized peoples with one another, the High Contracting Parties agree to this Covenant of the League of Nations.

Article I

The original Members of the League of Nations shall be those of the Signatories which are named in the Annex to the Covenant and also such of those other States named in the Annex as shall accede without reservation to this Covenant. Such accession shall be effected by a Declaration deposited with the Secretariat within two months of the coming into force of the Covenant. Notice thereof shall be sent to all Members of the League.

Any fully self-governing State, Dominion or Colony not named in the Annex may become a member of the League of Nations if its admission is agreed to by two-thirds of the Assembly, provided that it shall give effective guarantees of its sincere intention to observe its international obligations, and shall accept such regulations as may be prescribed by the League in regard to its military and naval forces and armaments.

Any Member of the League may, after two years' notice of its intention to do so, withdraw from the League, provided that all its international obligations under this Covenant shall have been fulfilled at the time of its withdrawal.

Article II

The action of the League under this Covenant shall be effected through the instrumentality of an Assembly and of a Council, with a permanent Secretariat.

Article III

The Assembly shall consist of Representatives of Members of the League.

The Assembly shall meet at stated intervals and from time to time as occasion may require at the Seat of the League, or at such other place as may be decided upon.

The Assembly may deal at its meetings with any matter within the sphere of action of the League or affecting the peace of the world.

At meetings of the Assembly each Member of the League shall have one vote, and may have no more than three Representatives.

Article IV

The Council shall consist of Representatives of the United States of America, of the British Empire, of France, of Italy, and of Japan. These four members of the League shall be selected by the Assembly from time to time in its discretion. Until the appointment of the Representatives of the four Members of the League first selected by the Assembly, Representatives of Belgium, Brazil, Greece, Spain shall be members of the Council....

The Council shall meet from time to time as occasion may require, and at least once a year, at the Seat of the League, or at such other place as may be decided upon.

The Council may deal at its meetings with any matter within the sphere of action of the League or affecting the peace of the world....

At meetings of the Council each Member of the League represented on the Council shall have one vote, and may have not more than one Representative.

Article VII

The Seat of the League is established at Geneva.

The Council may at any time decide that the Seat of the League shall be established elsewhere....

Representatives of the Members of the League and officials of the League when engaged on the business of the League shall enjoy diplomatic privileges and immunities....

Article VIII

The Members of the League recognize that the maintenance of peace requires the reduction of national armaments to the lowest point consistent with national safety and the enforcement by common action of international obligations.

The Council, taking account of the geographical situation and circumstances of each State, shall formulate plans for such reduction for the consideration and action of several Governments.

Such plans shall be subject to reconsideration and revision at least every ten years....

Article X

The Members of the League undertake to respect and preserve as against external aggression the territorial integrity and existing political independence of all Members of the League. In case of any such aggression or in case of any threat or danger of such aggression the Council shall advise upon the means by which this obligation shall be fulfilled.

Article XI

Any war or threats of war, whether immediately affecting any of the Members of the League or not, is hereby declared a matter of concern to the whole League, and the League shall take any action that may be deemed wise and effectual to safeguard the peace of the nations. In case any such emergency should arise, the Secretary General shall, on the request of any Member of the League, forthwith summon a meeting of the Council.

Article XII

The Members of the League agree that if there should arise between them any dispute likely to lead to a rupture, they will summit the matter either to arbitration or to inquiry by the Council, and they agree in no case to resort to war until three months after the award by the arbitrators or the report to the Council....

Article XIII

The Members of the League agree that whenever any dispute shall arise between them which they recognize to be suitable for submission to arbitration and which cannot be satisfactorily settled by diplomacy, they will submit the whole subject matter to arbitration.

Disputes as to the interpretation of a treaty, as to any question of international law, as to the existence of any fact which if established would constitute a breach of any international obligation, or as to the extent and nature of the reparation to be made for any such breach, are declared to be among those which are generally suitable for submission to arbitration.

For the consideration of any such dispute the court of arbitration to which the case is referred shall be the court agreed on by the parties to the dispute or stipulated in any convention existing between them....

Article XIV

The Council shall formulate and submit to the Members of the League for adoption plans for the establishment of a Permanent Court of International Justice. The Court shall be competent to hear and determine any dispute of an international character which the parties thereto submit to it. The Court may also give an advisory opinion upon any dispute or question referred to it by the Council or by the Assembly.

Article XV

If there should arise between Members of the League any dispute likely to lead to a rupture, which is not submitted to arbitration as above, the Members of the League agree that they will submit the matter to the Council. Any party to the dispute may affect such submission by giving notice of the existence of the dispute of the Secretary General, who will make all necessary arrangements for a full investigation and consideration thereof.

Article XVI

Should any Member of the League resort to war in disregard of its covenants under Articles XII, XIII or XV, it shall ipso facto be deemed to have committed an act of war against all Members of the League, which hereby undertake immediately to subject it to the severance of all trade or financial relations, the prohibition of all intercourse between their nationals and the nationals of the covenant-breaking State and the nationals of any other State, whether a Member of the League or not.

It shall be the duty of the Council in such case to recommend to the several Governments concerned what effective military or naval force the Members of the League shall severally contribute to the armed forces to be used to protect the covenants of the League....

Any Member of the League which has violated any covenant of the League may be declared to be no longer a Member of the League by a vote of the Council concurred in by the Representatives of all the other Members of the League represented thereon.

Article XXVI

Amendments to this Covenant will take effect when ratified by the Members of the League whose Representatives compose the Council and by a majority of the Members of the League whose Representatives compose the Assembly.

No such amendment shall bind any Member of the League which signifies its dissent therefrom, but in that case it shall cease to be a Member of the League.

---

6. Excerpts from Address of President Wilson on Presenting the Draft Covenant of the League of Nations to the Third Plenary Session of the Peace Conference at Paris

February 14, 1918
13 *American Journal of International Law* 570; 572–573; 575–576 (1919)
Reproduced with permission from 13 *American Journal of International Law* 570 (1919). © The American Society of International Law

* * *

Now. as to the character of the document...it is, after all, very simple and in nothing so simple as in the structure which it suggests for the League of Nations—a body of delegates, an executive council, and a permanent secretariat. When it came to the question of determining the character of the representation in the body of Delegates, we were all aware of a feeling which is current throughout the world. Inasmuch as I am stating it in the presence of official representatives of the various Governments here present, including myself, I may say that there is a universal feeling that the world can not rest satisfied with merely official guidance. There reached us through many channels the feeling that if the deliberative body of the League was merely to be a body of officials representing the various Governments, the peoples of the world would not be sure that some of the mistakes which preoccupied officials had admittedly made might not be repeated.

* * *

And you will notice that this body has unlimited rights of discussion—I mean of discussion of anything that falls within the field of international relationships-and that it is specially agreed that war or international misunderstanding or anything that may lead to friction and trouble is everybody's business, because it may affect the peace of the world. And in order to safeguard the popular power as far as we could of this representative body, it is provided, you will notice, that when a subject is submitted, not to arbitration, but to discussion by the Executive Council, it can, upon the initiative of either one of the parties to the dispute, be drawn out of the Executive Council onto the larger forum of the general Body of Delegates, because throughout this instrument we are depending primarily and chiefly upon one great force, and that is the moral force of the public opinion of the world—the cleansing and clarifying and compelling influences of publicity—so that intrigues can no longer have their coverts, so that designs that are sinister can at any time be drawn into the open, so that those things that are destroyed by the light may be properly destroyed by the overwhelming light of the universal expression of the condemnation of the world.

Armed force is in the background of this program, but *is* in the background, and if the moral force of the world will not suffice, the physical force of the world shall. But that is the last resort, because this is intended as a constitution of peace, not as a league of war.

The simplicity of the document seems to me to be one of its chief virtues, because, speaking for myself, I was unable to foresee the variety of circumstances with which this League would have to deal. I was unable, therefore, to plan all the machinery that might be necessary to meet differing and unexpected contingencies. Therefore, I should say of this document that it is not a straitjacket, but a vehicle of life. A living thing is born, and we must see to it that the clothes we put upon it do not hamper it—a vehicle of power, but a vehicle in which power may be varied at the discretion of those who exercise it and in accordance with the changing circumstances of the time. And yet, while it is elastic, while it is general in its terms, it is definite in the one thing that we are called upon to make definite. It is a definite guarantee of peace. It is a definite guarantee by word against aggression. It is a definite guarantee against the things which have just come near bringing the whole structure of civilization into ruin. Its purposes do not for a moment lie vague. Its purposes are declared and its powers made unmistakable.

It is not in contemplation that this should be merely a league to secure the peace of the world. It is a league which can be used for cooperation in any international matter....

* * *

So I think I can say of this document that it is at one and the same time a practical document and a humane document. There is a pulse of sympathy in it. There is a compulsion of conscience throughout it. It is practical, and yet it is intended to purify, to rectify, to elevate. And I want to say that, so far as my observation instructs me, this is in one sense a belated document. I believe that the conscience of the world has long been prepared to express itself in some such way.

* * *

Many terrible things have come out of this war, gentlemen, but some very beautiful things have come out of it. Wrong has been defeated, but the rest of the world has been more conscious than it ever was before of the majesty of right. People that were suspicious of one another can now live as friends and comrades in a single family, and desire to do so. The miasma of distrust, of intrigue, is cleared away. Men are looking eye to eye and saying "We are brothers and have a common purpose. We did not realize it before, but now we do realize it, and this is our covenant of fraternity and friendship."

[The statesmen who assembled in Paris to debate not only the terms of the peace treaty with Germany, but also to debate the provisions of Woodrow Wilson's charter for world peace and prosperity, were similar to an international parliament of sorts. In historical hindsight, one can conclude today that the Covenant of the League of Nations was more a political than a legal instrument. Although the President of the United States sought a universal compact of nation-states, that simply did not happen. Two of the emerging twentieth century powers—the United States of America and the Union of Soviet Socialist Republics—failed to become members of the League. In a pragmatic sense, the League of Nations was really more of a multi-state debating society than it was an effective enforcement vehicle for violations of international law. Headquartered in Geneva, Switzerland, it was dependent, in large measure, on its more powerful Council members to implement its mandates—specifically Great Britain and France. Those two nations, however, were often diplomatically fickle, geopolitically timid and at the same time caught up in European post-war power politics which, in turn, made them unsure of what steps should be taken by the League to resolve the dilemmas of inter-war realpolitik machinations.

The Covenant's chief value lay in its paramount obligation for states to employ pacific means for settling international disputes. A resort to war was provided for, but only after all peaceful avenues to conflict were foreclosed. In context, the Covenant was clearly a document of its time and place in international relations, although its language by today's standards seems overly optimistic and somewhat naïve. Resort to armed conflict could not be eliminated from an instrument of this sort precisely because war had been an acceptable instrument of national policy by states willing to employ it throughout the nineteenth century and earlier ages. Nonetheless, the private nature of war between nations was replaced by a public international concern for peace. Article XI of the Covenant provided that war or its threat was a matter of utmost concern to the entire League. The League's abiding concern was that *justice* be upheld, even at the expense of international military conflict.

As noted previously, Woodrow Wilson's internationalist ideas were often mocked and derided by European statesmen who saw his efforts on behalf of the League of Nations to be both unrealistic and utopian. Another example of this mockery appeared in an expression published in the *Geneva Testament* in 1931 which declared:

> In the beginning, the hotels were empty, but the spirit of Wilson hovered over Lake Geneva.
>
> Darkness was everywhere, and the nations were separated by an abyss.
>
> The spirit of Wilson said: "Let there be light."
>
> Secret diplomacy disappeared at once! Three thousand journalists were accredited to the League of Nations, and Cook's Travel Agency began regular tours.
>
> Then the spirit created permanent delegates, visiting experts, lawyers, and international civil servants....
>
> And the Spirit blessed them and said: "Be fruitful and multiply."[8]

---

8. Alois Derso and Emery Kelen, *Le testament de Genieve* 8 (French trans.). (1931).

Mockery aside, in its attempt to restructure international statecraft in its own image, the League, in the words of Jones,[9] "could take notice of treaties that were out of date or that threatened world peace and could urge reformative action. The plan was for ongoing observation and assessment of the needs and stresses in the international system so that timely adjustments could be made and peace preserved"[10]].

---

7. Excerpts from the Report of the Commission on the Responsibility of the Authors of the War and on Enforcement of Penalties to the Preliminary Peace Conference

March 29, 1919
14 *American Journal of International Law*
95; 98–105; 107–118; 120; 127–128; 133–134; 144; 146–148 (1920)
Reproduced with permission from 14 *American Journal of International Law*
95 (1920). © The American Society of International Law

The Commission was charged to inquire into and report upon the following points:

1. The responsibility of the authors of the war.

2. The facts as to breaches of the laws and customs of war committed by the forces of the German Empire and their Allies, on land, on sea, and in the air during the present war.

3. The degree of responsibility for these offenses attaching to particular members of the enemy forces, including members of the General Staffs, and other individuals, however highly placed.

4. The constitution and procedures of a tribunal appropriate for the trial of these offenses.

5. Any other matters cognate or ancillary to the above which may arise in the course of the enquiry, and which the Commission finds it useful and relevant to take into consideration.

* * *

Chapter I

Responsibility of the Authors of the War

On the question of the responsibility of the authors of the war, the Commission, after having examined a number of official documents relating to the origin of the World War, and to the violations of neutrality and of frontiers which accompanied its inception, has determined that the responsibility for it lies wholly upon the Powers which declared war in pursuance of a policy of aggression, the concealment of which gives to the origin of this war the character of a dark conspiracy against the peace of Europe.

This responsibility rests first on Germany and Austria, secondly on Turkey and Bulgaria. The responsibility is made all the graver by reason of the violation by Germany and Austria of the neutrality of Belgium and Luxemburg, which they themselves had

---

9. *Supra*, note 6.
10. *Id.* at 28.

guaranteed. It is increased, with regard to both France and Serbia, by the violation of their frontiers before the declaration of war.

I. Premeditation of the War

A. Germany and Austria

Many months before the crisis of 1914 the German Emperor ceased to pose as the champion of peace. Naturally believing in the overwhelming superiority of his army, he openly showed his enmity towards France. General von Moltke said to the King of the Belgians: "This time the matter must be settled." In vain the King protested. The Emperor and his Chief of Staff remained no less fixed in their attitude.

On the 28th June, 1914, occurred the assassination at Sarejevo of the heir-apparent of Austria. "It is the act of a little group of madmen," said Francis Joseph. The act, committed as it was by a subject of Austria-Hungary on Austro-Hungarian territory, could in no wise compromise Serbia, which very correctly expressed its condolences and stopped public rejoicings in Belgrade. If the Government of Vienna thought that there was any Serbian complicity, Serbia was ready to seek out the guilty parties. But this attitude failed to satisfy Austria and still less Germany, who, after their first astonishment had passed, saw in this royal and national misfortune a pretext to initiate war.

* * *

Austria suddenly sent Serbia an ultimatum that she had carefully prepared in such a way as to make it impossible to accept.

* * *

Contrary to the expectation of Austria-Hungary and Germany, Serbia yielded. She agreed to all the requirements of the ultimatum, subject to the single reservation that, in the judicial inquiry which she would commence for the purpose of seeking out the guilty parties, the participation of Austrian officials would be kept within the limits assigned by international law. "If the Austro-Hungarian Government is not satisfied with this," Serbia declared she was ready "to submit to the decision of the Hague Tribunal."

* * *

The reiterated suggestions of the *Entente* Powers with a view to finding a peaceful solution of the dispute only produced evasive replies on the part of Berlin or promises of intervention with the Government of Vienna without any effectual steps being taken.

On the 24th of July Russia and England asked that the Powers should be granted a reasonable delay in which to work in concert for the maintenance of peace. Germany did not join in this request.

On the 25th July Sir Edward Grey proposed mediation by the Four Powers (England, France, Italy and Germany). France and Italy immediately gave their concurrence. Germany refused, alleging that it was not a question of mediation but of arbitration, as the conference of the four Powers was called to make proposals, not to decide.

* * *

As early as the 21st July German mobilization had commenced by the recall of a certain number of classes of the reserve, then of German officers in Switzerland, and finally of the Metz garrison on the 25th July. On the 26th July the German fleet was called back from Norway.

* * *

On the 1st August the German Emperor addressed a telegram to the King of England containing the following sentence: "The troops of my frontier are, at this moment, being kept back by telegraphic and telephone orders from crossing the French frontier."

Now, war was not declared till two days after the date, and as the German mobilization orders were issued on that same day, the 1st August, it follows that, as a matter of fact, the German army had been mobilized and concentrated in pursuance of previous orders.

The attitude of the *Entente* nevertheless remained still to the very end so conciliatory that, at the very time at which the German fleet was bombarding Libau, Nicholas II [of Russia] gave his word of honor to William II [of Germany] that Russia would not undertake any aggressive action during the pourparlers, [an informal preliminary conference] and that when the German troops commenced their march across the French frontier M. Viviani telegraphed to all the French Ambassadors "we must not stop working for accommodation."

On the 3rd August von Schoen went to the Quai d'Orsay [the Foreign Office of the French Government] with the declaration of war against France. Lacking a real cause of complaint, Germany alleged, in her declaration of war, that bombs had been dropped by French aeroplanes in various districts of Germany. This statement was entirely false. Moreover, it was later admitted to be so, or no particulars were ever furnished by the German Government.

Moreover, in order to be manifestly above reproach. France was careful to withdraw her troops 10 kilom. from the German frontier. Notwithstanding this precaution, numerous officially established violations of French territory preceded the declaration of war....

B. Turkey and Bulgaria

The conflict was, however, destined to become more widespread and Germany and Austria were joined by allies.

Since the Balkan War the Young Turk Government had been drawing nearer and nearer to Germany, whilst Germany on her part had constantly been extending her activities at Constantinople....

Finally, on the 4th August, the understanding between Turkey and Germany was definitely formulated in an alliance. The consequence was that when the *Goeben* and the *Breslau* took refuge in the Bosphorus, Turkey closed the Dardanneles against the *Entente* squadrons and war followed.

On the 14th October, 1915, Bulgaria declared war on Serbia, which country had been at war with Austria since the 28th July, 1914, and had been attacked on all fronts by a large Austro-German army since the 6th October, 1915. Serbia had, however, committed no act of provocation against Bulgaria.

* * *

Conclusions

1. *The war was premeditated by the Central Powers together with their Allies, Turkey and Bulgaria, and was the result of acts deliberately committed in order to make it unavoidable.*

2. *Germany, in agreement with Austria-Hungary, deliberately worked to defeat all the many conciliatory proposals made by the Entente Powers and their repeated efforts to avoid war.*

II. Violations of the Neutrality of Belgium and Luxemburg

A. *Belgium*

Germany is burdened by a specially heavy responsibility in respect of the violation of the neutrality of Belgium and Luxemburg. Article 1 of the Treaty of London of the 19th April, 1839, after declaring that Belgium should form a "perpetually neutral State," had placed this neutrality under the protection of Austria, France, Great Britain, Russia and Prussia....

It may be of interest to recall that the attributes of neutrality were specifically defined by the fifth Hague Convention, of the 18th October, 1907. That convention was declaratory of the law of nations, and contained these provisions—"The territory of neutral Powers is inviolable." (Article 1). "Belligerents are forbidden to move troops or convoys, whether of munitions of war or of supplies, across the territory of a neutral Power." (Article 2). "The fact of a neutral Power resisting even by force, attempts against its neutrality cannot be regarded as a hostile act." (Article 10).

There can be no doubt of the binding force of the treaties which guaranteed the neutrality of Belgium. There is equally no doubt of Belgium's sincerity or of the sincerity of France in their recognition and respect of this neutrality.

* * *

Meanwhile the attitude of the German Government remained enigmatic. At Brussels the German Minister, Herr von Below, made efforts in his discussions to maintain confidence, but at Berlin, in reply to the question which had been officially asked by the British Government, the Secretary of State informed the British Ambassador that "he must consult the Emperor and the Chancellor before he could possibly answer."...

* * *

It was only on the 4th August, after German troops had entered Belgian territory, that the Belgian Government sent his passports to Herr von Below, and it then appealed to Great Britain, France and Russia to co-operate as guaranteeing Powers in the defense of her territory.... Further, in his speech on the 4th August, the German Chancellor made his well-known avowal: "Necessity knows no law. Our troops have occupied Luxemburg, and perhaps have already entered Belgian territory. Gentlemen, that is a breach of international law.... We have been obliged to refuse to pay attention to the justifiable protests of Belgium and Luxemburg. The wrong—I speak openly—the wrong we are thereby committing we will try to make good as soon as our military aims have been attained. He who is menaced, as we are, and is fighting for his all can only consider how he is to hack his way through." To this avowal of the German Chancellor there is added the overwhelming testimony of Count von Lerchenfeld, who stated in a report on the 4th August, 1914, that the German General Staff considered it "necessary to cross Belgium: France can only be successfully attacked from that side. At the risk of bringing about the intervention of England, Germany cannot respect Belgium neutrality."

B. *Luxemburg*

The neutrality of Luxemburg was guaranteed by Article 2 of the Treaty of London, 11th May, 1867. Prussia and Austria-Hungary being two of the guarantor Powers. On the 2nd August, 1914, German troops penetrated the territory of the Grand Duchy. Mr. Eyschen, Minister of State of Luxemburg, immediately made an energetic protest.

The German Government alleged "that military measures had become inevitable, because trustworthy news had been received that French forces were marching on Luxemburg." This allegation was at once refuted by Mr. Eyschen.

Conclusion

The neutrality of Belgium, guaranteed by the treaties of the 19th April, 1839, and that of Luxemburg, guaranteed by the treaty of the 11th May, 1867, were deliberately violated by Germany and Austria-Hungary.

Chapter II

Violations of the Laws and Customs of War

* * *

In spite of the explicit regulations, of established customs, and of the clear dictates of humanity, Germany and her allies have piled outrage upon outrage. Additions are daily and continually being made.... Violations of the rights of combatants, of the rights of civilians, and of the rights of both, are multiplied in this list of the most cruel practices which primitive barbarism, aided by all the resources of modern science, could devise for the execution of a system of terrorism carefully planned and carried out to the end. Not even prisoners, or wounded, or women, or children have been respected by belligerents who deliberately sought to strike terror into every heart for the purpose of repressing all resistance. Murders and massacres, tortures, shields formed by living human beings, collective penalties, the arrest and execution of hostages, the requisitioning of services for military purposes, the arbitrary destruction of public and private property, the aerial bombardment of open towns without their being any regular siege, the destruction of merchant ships without previous visits and without any precautions for the safety of passengers and crew, the massacre of prisoners, attacks on hospital ships, the poisoning of springs and of wells, outrages and profanations without regard for religion or the honor of individuals, the issue of counterfeit money reported by the Polish Government, the methodical and deliberate destruction of industries with no other object than to promote German economic supremacy after the war, constitute the most striking list of crimes that has ever been drawn up to the eternal shame of those who committed them. The facts are established. They are numerous and so vouched for that they admit of no doubt and cry for justice. The Commission, impressed by their number and gravity, thinks there are good grounds for the constitution of a special commission, to collect and classify all outstanding information for the purpose of preparing a complete list of the charges under the following heads:

The following is the list arrived at:

   (1) Murders and massacres; systematic terrorism,

   (2) Putting hostages to death,

   (3) Torture of civilians,

   (4) Deliberate starvation of civilians.

   (5) Rape,

   (6) Abduction of girls and women for the purpose of enforced prostitution,

   (7) Deportation of civilians,

   (8) Internment of civilians under inhuman conditions,

(9) Forced labor of civilians in connection with military operations of the enemy,

(10) Usurpation of sovereignty during military occupation,

(11) Compulsory enlistment of soldiers among the inhabitants of occupied territory,

(12) Attempts to denationalize the inhabitants of occupied territory,

(13) Pillage,

(14) Confiscation of property,

(15) Exaction of illegitimate or exorbitant contributions and requisitions,

(16) Debasement of the currency, and issue of spurious currency,

(17) Imposition of collective penalties,

(18) Wanton devastation and destruction of property,

(19) Deliberate bombardment of undefended places,

(20) Wanton destruction of religious, charitable, educational, and historic buildings and monuments,

(21) Destruction of merchant ships and passenger vessels without warning and without provision for the safety of passengers and crew,

(22) Destruction of fishing boats and of relief ships,

(23) Deliberate bombardment of hospitals,

(24) Attack on and destruction of hospital ships,

(25) Breach of other rules relating to the Red Cross,

(26) Use of deleterious and asphyxiating gases,

(27) Use of explosives or expanding bullets, and other inhuman appliances,

(28) Directions to give no quarter,

(29) Ill-treatment of wounded and prisoners of war,

(30) Employment of prisoners of war on unauthorized works,

(31) Misuse of flags of truce,

(32) Poisoning of wells.

The Commission desires to draw attention to the fact that the offences enumerated and the particulars given in Annex I are not regarded as complete and exhaustive; to these such additions can from time to time be made as may be necessary.

Conclusions

1. The war was carried on by the Central Empires together with their Allies, Turkey and Bulgaria, by barbarous or illegitimate methods in violation of the established laws and customs of war and the elementary laws of humanity.

2. A commission should be created for the purpose of collecting and classifying systematically all the information already had or to be obtained, in order to prepare as complete a list of facts as possible concerning the violations of the laws and customs of war committed by the forces of the German Empire and its Allies, on land, on sea and in the air, in the course of the present war.

Chapter III

Personal Responsibility

The third point submitted by the Conference is thus stated:

The degree of responsibility for these offences attaching to particular members of the enemy forces, including members of the General staffs and other individuals, however highly placed.

...[T]he Commission desire to state expressly that in the hierarchy of persons in authority, there is no reason why rank, however exalted, should in any circumstances protect the holder of it from responsibility when that responsibility has been established before a properly constituted tribunal. This extends even to the case of heads of states. An argument has been raised to the contrary based upon the alleged immunity, and in particular the alleged inviolability, of a sovereign of a state. But this privilege, where it is reorganized, is one of practical expedience in municipal law, and is not fundamental. However, even if, in some countries, a sovereign is exempt from being prosecuted in a national court of his own country the position from an international point of view is quite different.

* * *

Conclusion

All persons belonging to enemy countries, however high their position may have been, without distinction of rank, including Chiefs of State, who have been guilty of offences against the laws and customs of war or the laws of humanity, are liable to criminal prosecution.

Chapter IV

Constitution and Procedure of an Appropriate Tribunal

* * *

Two classes of culpable acts present themselves:

   (a) Acts which provoked the world war and accompanied its inception.

   (b) Violations of the laws and customs of war and the laws of humanity.

In this class the Commission has considered acts not strictly war crimes, but acts which provoked the war or accompanied its inception, such, to take outstanding examples, as the invasion of Luxemburg and Belgium.

The premeditation of a war of aggression, dissimulated under a peaceful pretext, then suddenly declared under false pretexts, is conduct which the public conscience reproves and which history will condemn, but by reason of the purely optional character of the institutions at The Hague for the maintenance of peace (International Commission of Inquiry, Mediation and Arbitration) a war of aggression may not be considered as an act directly contrary to positive law, or one which can be successfully brought before a tribunal such as the Commission is authorized to consider under its terms of reference.

* * *

Conclusions

1. The acts which brought about the war should not be charged against their authors or made the subject of proceedings before a tribunal.

2. On the special head of the breaches of neutrality of Luxemburg and Belgium, the gravity of these outrages upon the principles of the law of nations and upon international good faith is such that they should be made the subject of a formal condemnation by the Conference.

3. On the whole case, including both the acts which brought about the war and those which accompanied its inception, particularly the violation of the neutrality of Belgium and Luxemburg, it would be right for the Peace Conference, in a matter so unprecedented, to adopt special measures, and even to create a special organ in order to deal as they deserve with the authors of such acts.

4. It is desirable that for the future penal sanctions should be provided for such grave outrages against the elementary principles of international law.

* * *

Annex II.

Memorandum of Reservations Presented by the Representatives of the United States to the Report of the Commission on Responsibilities

14 *American Journal of International Law* 127; 128; 132–134; 144; 146; 148 (1920) Reproduced with permission from 14 *American Journal of International Law* 127 (1920). © The American Society of International Law

April 4, 1919

The American members of the Commission on Responsibilities, in presenting their reservations to the report of the Commission, declare that they are as earnestly desirous as the other members of the Commission that those persons responsible for causing the Great War and those responsible for violations of the laws and customs of war should be punished for their crimes, moral and legal. The differences which have arisen between them and their colleagues lie in the means of accomplishing this common desire.

* * *

In the early meetings of the Commission and the three Sub–Commissions appointed to consider various phases of the subject submitted to the Commission, the American members declared that there were two classes of responsibilities, those of a legal nature and those of a moral nature, that legal offences were justiciable and liable to trial and punishment by appropriate tribunals, but that moral offences, however iniquitous and infamous and however terrible in their results, were beyond the reach of judicial procedure, and subject only to moral sanctions.

* * *

II

...The duty of the Commission was, therefore, to determine whether the facts found were violations of the laws and customs of war. It was not asked whether these facts were violations of the laws or of the principles of humanity. Nevertheless, the report of the Commission does not, as in the opinion of the American representatives it should, confine itself to the ascertainment of the facts and to their violation of the laws and customs of war, but, going beyond the terms of the mandate, declares that the facts found and the act committed were in violation of the laws and of the elementary principles of humanity. The laws and customs of war are a standard certain, to be found in books of authority and in the practice of nations. The laws and principles of humanity vary with the individual, which, if for no other reason, should exclude them from consideration in a court of justice, especially one charged with the administration of the criminal law. The American representatives, therefore, objected to the references to the laws and principles of humanity, to be found in the report, in what they believed was meant to be a judicial proceeding, as, in their opinion, the facts found were to be violations or breaches of the laws and customs of war, and the persons singled out for trial and punishment for acts committed during the war were only to be those persons guilty of acts which should have been committed in violation of the laws and customs of war....

* * *

There remain...two reasons, which...would prevent the American representatives from consenting to a tribunal recommended by the Commission. The first of these is the uncertainty of the law to be administered, in that liability is made to depend not only upon violations of the laws and customs of war, but also upon violations "of the laws of humanity." The second of these reasons is that heads of states are included within the civil and military authorities of the enemy countries to be tried and punished for violations of the laws and customs of war and of the laws of humanity. The American representatives believe that the Commission has exceeded its mandate in extending liability to violations of the laws of humanity, inasmuch, as the facts to be examined are solely violations of the laws and customs of war. They also believe that the Commission erred in seeking to subject heads of state to trial and punishment by a tribunal to whose jurisdiction they were not subject when the alleged offences were committed.

* * *

...The American representatives know of no international statute or convention making a violation of the laws and customs of war—not to speak of the laws or principles of humanity—an international crime, affixing a punishment to it, and declaring the court which has jurisdiction over the offence.

* * *

The American representatives therefore proposed that acts affecting the persons or property of one of the Allied or Associated Governments should be tried by a military tribunal of that country; that acts involving more than one country, such as treatment by Germany of prisoners contrary to the usages and customs of war, could be tried by a tribunal either made up of the competent tribunals of the countries affected or of a commission thereof possessing their authority. In this way existing national tribunals or national commissions which could legally be called into being would be utilized, and not only the law and the penalty would be already declared, but the procedure would be settled.

* * *

The majority of the Commission...was not influenced by the [American] argument. They appeared to be fixed in their determination to try and punish by judicial process the "ex-Kaiser" of Germany. That there might be no doubt about their meaning, they insisted that the jurisdiction of the high tribunal whose constitution they recommended should include the heads of states, and they therefore inserted a provision to this effect in express words in the clause dealing with the jurisdiction of the tribunal.

———————

8. Annex III
Reservations by the Japanese Delegation

14 *American Journal of International Law* 151–152 (1920)
Reproduced with permission from 14 *American Journal of International Law*
151 (1920). © The American Society of International Law

The Japanese Delegates on the Commission on Responsibilities are convinced that many crimes have been committed by the enemy in the course of the present war in violation of the fundamental principles of international law, and recognize that the principle responsibility rests upon individual enemies in high places. They are consequently of opinion that, in order to re-establish for the future the force of the principles thus infringed, it is important to discover practical means for the punishment of the persons responsible for such violations.

A question may be raised whether it can be admitted as a principle of the law of nations that a high tribunal constituted by belligerents can, after a war is over, try an individual belonging to the opposite side, who may be presumed to be guilty of a crime against the laws and customs of war. It may further be asked whether international law recognizes a penal law as applicable to those who are guilty.

In any event, it seems to us important to consider the consequences which would be created in the history of international law by the prosecution for breaches of the laws and customs of war of enemy heads of state before a tribunal constituted by the opposite party.

Our scruples become still greater when it is a question of indicting before a tribunal thus constituted highly placed enemies on the sole ground that they abstained from preventing, putting an end to, or repressing acts of violation of the laws and customs of war, as is provided in clause (c) of section (b) of Chapter IV.

---

9. The Status of William Hohenzollern,
Kaiser of Germany, Under International Law

53 *American Law Review* 401; 402–409; 412–416; 418; 422–426 (1919)

From time to time as the war progressed, suggestions have been made that, when it had been fought out to a successful issue, a fitting personal punishment should be visited on those in high places who have been guilty of ordering the unspeakable barbarities that have given to this war so hateful a distinction.

* * *

Suggestion has been made that the Kaiser, having fled into the Netherlands, should be extradited to Great Britain or to France. Already and during the pendency of the war the Kaiser has been indicted in some County of Great Britain for the deaths occurring in the Lusitania disaster. [The *Lusitania*, a British passenger liner, was sunk without warning by a German submarine off the Head of Kinsale on the Irish coast, May 7, 1915. This was a signal event that ultimately led to the entrance of the United States into World War I]. In the public prints a few days back it was stated that Mr. Clemenceau, Premier of France, has asked the head of the French bar for a ruling as to whether, in his opinion, extradition could be had between France and the Netherlands.

That in spite of his many atrocious crimes for which if not committed in war, under the doctrine of *qui facit per alium facit per se* [he who acts for another acts himself], the Kaiser could, under the common law, be tried and convicted, he must now go free because there is no law according to the principles of our municipal or international law under which jurisdiction can be obtained of his person, or under which he may be convicted, is a conclusion absolutely shocking to the moral sense. That he should escape punishment for these barbarities because our municipal law prescribes various rules and regulations as to jurisdiction, and as to trial and condemnation, which cannot by any extension of their principles be applied to this case, would be monstrous. On the other hand, that we should make a law to fit his case without reference to the reasons at the base of all law, or that we should strain existing procedure to meet his case, and thereby falsify the principles of the law we were using for the purpose, would be to commit judicial murder and place him in the position of a martyr.

It is deemed that under the general principles of the law and of the growth of institutions, there is warrant for our visiting upon the Kaiser the just penalty of his offenses without contradicting any principles applicable, and so as to make his punishment conformable, in the absence of precedent, to the just reasoning of the law.

It is important that we should accomplish this result without straining laws intended to meet different conditions as to make them apply to this extraordinary instance.

Under our municipal and international law there are two difficulties in the way of the prosecuting of the Kaiser.

1st. We must obtain jurisdiction of his person.

2nd. We must try to convict him of the perpetration of a crime (held to be such by common consent).

The crimes which the Kaiser has perpetrated have been as to situs committed in Belgium, the occupied portion of Northern France, the high seas (submarine operations), England and France (Zeppelin operations). The Kaiser has fled to Holland.

Under the circumstances different considerations of law, municipal and international, would apply under the extradition treaties, should France apply for extradition under its treaty with Holland for an offense committed in Northern France, or should England apply under its extradition treaty with the Netherlands, basing her application on the Lusitania murders or Zeppelin atrocities. In the event of the application of France, the question of the place of the crime would not be a bar to the application, because the crime has been committed in her territory. . . .

. . . But in the event of an application by Great Britain for extradition from the Netherlands, the application would be met by the suggestion that the crime had not been committed in Great Britain, and hence there is no jurisdiction to demand extradition.

* * *

Murder, which is the gravest crime under municipal law, is not a crime under international law when perpetrated *de jure belli* [by lawful war].

There stands the lion in the path.

Because of this objection we are compelled in the last analysis to rely for the conviction of the Kaiser after extradition upon the international law declared by the Hague Conference. . . and since we are compelled to do this, to make out the crime itself, we might as well refer our right to extradition not to the treaties, which were never made to cover this instance, but to the same warrant, the international law of murder as declared by the Hague Conference, and the process of an international court.

* * *

What, then, is the sound policy? What the honest course to be adopted by the Allied Nations?

The answer is that we must take international law as it is, and proceed to develop it along the course of the development of all law, and so developing it on principles of justice and equity, we will be enabled to enforce against William the penalty for his crimes.

All law, municipal and international, has grown from usage and custom by a steady slow growth. The rules of municipal law, at one time moral, have become law when to the consent of the majority that it was expedient that a certain moral rule should be observed, has been added the sanction of a penalty for its violation under the government prescribing the law.

* * *

A society of nations practically constituting a *quasi* sovereignty and equivalent in international law to the society of individuals constituting a sovereignty in municipal law has been in existence since the year 1648, made memorable by the Treaty of Westphalia. Great Britain, Russia and Poland were not represented at the Westphalia Peace but came into this Society of Nations by common consent and their joinder in the later treaties. So from time to time other nations have become members of this body and by various treaties between the nations of the world of a law-making character, among them the Vienna Congress of 1815, the Treaty of London of 1831, the Declaration of Paris of 1856, the Geneva Convention of 1864, and various others, a Society of Nations has been constituted. This Society of Nations met in the years 1899 and 1907 and laid down pure law-making treaties comprising various conventions and declarations which became and were a prescription of the international law as applied to the conduct of states in peace and war by which the various signatories were bound.

* * *

In follows, therefore, that the civilized nations of the world, prior to 1914, had, by common consent at The Hague Conference, declared certain moral rules to exist in respect to the conduct of nations in war. These customs and usages were thus made by common consent to apply to civilized nations, even in that province of their operation where, on account of the exigency of the occasion, it might be said that there is no law; or, that necessity knows no law (according to the German conception); yet, nevertheless, it is true that the civilized states of the world met and concluded upon a common ground to declare the rules they would be bound by, even in the abnormal conditions of the repudiation of all law known as the state of war....

These rules, therefore, although limited in their operation as an obligation founded on contract...remain as moral truths and moral rules recognized as such by all the nations of the world. That they should become laws binding on all nations waits only on the consent of the majority of nations recognizing them to prescribe a sanction for their violation.

Now, what have been the offenses against International Law which William has, under the guise of the German sovereignty, perpetrated upon the peoples of the nations which constitute the Society of Nations, and under which this Society of Nations is entitled, on principle and equity, to try and condemn him.

The answer is that the two Peace Conferences which were held at the Hague in 1899 and 1907, and which proceeded with the consent and approval of Germany to lay down certain principles to which Germany consented with reservations, sufficiently express the views of the Society of Nations as to the existence of certain ethical principles constituting customs and usages which did exist and should exist between them, and those usages have been violated by the Kaiser, representing Germany, and for those violations the Kaiser can be equitably and fairly punished without violating any moral rule.

Under the law—municipal and international—as it existed prior to the Hague Conference, murder occurring in the operations of war was not a crime. Under these conventions certain classes of murder occurring in the operations of war constitute a crime. [Here are discussed selected rules of the laws and customs of land warfare enunciated in both the 1899 and the 1907 Hague Convention].

* * *

These rules of war so laid down at The Hague Conference forbade the deportation of population of occupied territory, forced labor of civilians and prisoners, pillage, levies of excessive and improper fines, not to mention rape and cruelty, including treatment of prisoners,…the naval and military bombardment of undefended towns, the use of asphyxiating gases, and the activities involved in the submarine and Zeppelin operations as carried out by the Germans.

As to the expediency of some of these rules different views might be entertained. But so far as concerns the rules applying to murder through the operations of Zeppelins, submarines and asphyxiating gases, the concensus of opinion of the civilized world is clear and unanimous. A conviction on these grounds alone would fully satisfy the requirements of the situation, and therefore these are the irreducible minimum now required to be prescribed and enforced by the Nations.

* * *

Of these rules of law, Germany and the Kaiser have throughout this war been the violators. She has not only been the criminal violator thereof in each and every instance, but has, in addition publicly and intentionally and willfully done so, glorying in her denial of their existence or validity, and claiming that "might makes right."

Had Germany won this war, the Body of Customary usages and rules which for over two centuries we have known as "International Law" including these "Rules of the Hague" would have been cast into the scrap heap. The only law would have been Germany's will. Her Kultur [culture] would have illuminated and enslaved the world.

* * *

The Germans, by their ferocious and bestial methods, have acted in a manner without precedent in the conduct of this Society of Nations for over three centuries. We are consequently entitled, in maintaining our rule of law, to act without precedent under the law, but within the reason and necessity of the case. For them as for the Pirates an exception must be made.

* * *

Murder of the kind perpetrated by the Kaiser in the use of asphyxiating gases, the submarine and Zeppelin operations, [and] the Belgian atrocities…is a crime both under the municipal law and the international law of war as declared by The Hague and otherwise. It, then, should be punished as such.

Germany, by her high crimes and misdemeanors since 1914, is an outlaw. Whether she gave her consent to the principles of The Hague Conference of 1899 or 1907...is immaterial. She has placed herself beyond the pale. Her consent or dissent is of no importance.

We, the Allies, by virtue of our conquest of her, are the only ones to be considered on the question. We constitute the tribunal and the judge, and we should award and carry out the verdict.

Germany can only re-enter the Society of Nations by subscribing to this Code of The Hague Conference which we have elected to declare law. That Code declares that murder, perpetrated in war under the conditions stated, is murder, and not innocent. That law must be vindicated. The penalty incurred must be paid, and the law and sanction thus created made operative so as to deter from such crimes in the future.

Therefore, the Kaiser must die.

Only in this way and at this time shall we perform for the good of the world, the just verdict of civilization—an example and a warning for the future.

* * *

Let any madcap individual of the future know that when as King, Emperor or Prime Minister, he thus shall attempt to overturn the customs of war established by the concurrence of the Society of Nations, and glory in his crime, that the penalty of personal retribution hangs on the heels of his acts, and that he must make such a decision at his own personal risk and peril.

* * *

It is recommended, therefore, that the Allies proceed as follows:

Let them create a special international tribunal with jurisdiction and machinery to try the Kaiser and all other individuals responsible for the ordering or execution of these unspeakable crimes—preferable a kind of International Court, whose proceedings would not be hampered by the technical rules of evidence and procedure of municipal courts, but capable of deciding on moral evidence such as is now held sufficient for international tribunals and arbitrations.

* * *

The Kaiser, when hailed before an international tribunal such as is herein suggested, has outside of the denial of the actual doing of the acts claimed, which must be proved against him in the ordinary way, only one defense; that is, that his trial and punishment would be under an *ex post facto* law—a law making a crime of acts which had not hitherto been considered to be a crime.

In making this claim he will be claiming that certain principles of municipal law have been projected into international law so as to make that province of the law subject to the same moral principles as in municipal law. In so doing he would be acting in an utterly inconsistent manner, and yet appealing to the moral nature of the Allies to make out his plea, and claiming in the province of international law the existence of a limited law and order instead of chaos.

The answer of the Allies should be that they, as a majority of the individual sovereignties constituting the Society of Nations, have the right to make laws for the Society. The law making power is in the majority of the nations constituting the Society of Nations. That body has a right to sit and now, after the event, make laws, applying to these matters; and when they pass a rule and place a sanction upon it, such law becomes international law binding as such on the Society of Nations. Consequently, the majority of the nations constituting the Society of Nations may now enact the Rules of the Hague Conference and attach a penalty, and may make those rules retroactive....

For the interest of the Society of Nations as a whole, and the value of the rule of law prescribed, namely, that murder, under certain conditions occurring in war, shall constitute murder and be punishable as such, and that war, when waged, shall be waged under Civilized Rules, is of far more importance to the community of nations than the interests of the criminal who has committed the acts—the rule forbidding an *ex post facto* law being one founded on a policy of mercy to the criminal, and therefore being one which must yield to the greater law of the "safety of the public."

The rule forbidding murder is of primary ethical importance; the rule forbidding the passage of an *ex post facto* law is of secondary ethical importance. The latter must yield to the former when their clash imperils the greater interests of the community involved.

* * *

In view of the foregoing considerations, it is therefore advised as follows:

That a new meeting of the Society of Nations, or even preferably composed only of the Allies, similar to the former conferences at the Hague be called. At such meeting pass the necessary legislation to conform the previous rules of war of the Hague Conference, attach penalties to the prohibitions enacted, make the provisions of the rules retroactive so as to clearly apply to the deeds of the Kaiser and the other perpetrators of these wanton acts, and thereupon create a new international court with full jurisdiction to pass upon the offenses heretofore or hereafter occurring under the new Code.

By taking proceedings against the Kaiser in this way through an international tribunal, charging him with the breaches of international law of which he has been guilty and trying and condemning him accordingly, the Allies will proceed in strict compliance with the principles of Municipal Law and according to the justice and equity of the case. Thus they will, with frankness and truth, use their power in the premises without evasion or subtlety to declare on true principles involved in the laws and customs for which they stand, his liability to the penalties he has incurred, and thus exemplify the spirit of justice and equity for which they have fought.

And yet having thus proved that the Kaiser can be hanged according to due observance of certain preliminaries in municipal law, both according to the law and prophets, why, since no one will gainsay that the Allied Nations have the power so to accomplish his death strictly in accordance with the law, should we pause to go through the necessary formalities; why, having absolute power in the premises, being controlled only by our own sentiments, should we not expedite the result and cut the Gordian knot? For if he can be legally hanged,...; then, it will make no real difference, provided he be hanged, whether he be well hanged or not.

This suggestion that the Gordian knot should be cut without too much attention to formalities is worthy of due consideration. Under the extraordinary conditions of the problem, and the imperative necessity that the crimes of William Hohenzollern shall meet their well-merited punishment to so remain for all future time a lighted beacon before the eyes of all men, an example, greater even, if made in defiance of precedent, than if slavishly following the precedents,—these considerations and the weighing of expediencies involved, render it proper that the first plan above set forth to encompass his punishment should be carried out as suggested. For strong measures, when supported by strong reason are for strong men to use on strong occasions.

[These comments, filled as they are with of the rhetoric of the era, were written by R. Floyd Clarke, a member of the New York Bar. Mr. Clarke's position on Kaiser Wilhelm II and the recommended international trial that never took place, was shared by a number of American lawyers, international law commentators and a large segment of the general public both in the United States and in Europe. Nonetheless, there were also those who most assuredly did not share the views expressed by Clarke relative to the fate wished upon the Kaiser. Chief among some of the more prominent Americans who demurred to such views was Woodrow Wilson's Secretary of State, Robert Lansing. As Maguire notes,[11] "the American representative [Lansing] used his legal skills—he was America's most successful international lawyer, after all—to frustrate the European efforts to try the Kaiser and in the process to broaden the laws of war."[12] Further on, Maguire states that

> The American "Reservations" endorsed the principles of sovereign immunity with no reservations or qualifications: "the Commission erred in seeking to subject Heads of State to trial and punishment by a tribunal to whose jurisdiction they were not subject when the alleged offenses were committed." According to the American reading, "war was and is by its very nature inhumane, but acts consistent with the laws and customs of war, although these acts are inhuman, are nevertheless not the object of punishment by a court of justice." Most important, Secretary of State Lansing concluded that "[t]he essence of sovereignty was the abuse of responsibility. When the people confided it to a monarch or other head of State, it was legally speaking to them only that he was responsible, although there might be a moral obligation to mankind. Legally, however, there was no super-sovereignty."[13]

Lansing, along with a number of other international lawyers of the time, bristled at the suggestion that Kaiser Wilhelm II be put on trial to uphold the idea that he was, in his capacity as the former Emperor of Imperial Germany, *personally responsible* for war crimes and other wrongs. To their way of thinking, the well-recognized concept of *sovereignty* bestowed a mantle of protection about Wilhelm's misdeeds. In addition, Lansing and others of like mind also believed that such a procedure applied by victorious powers to a former enemy Head of State would be a blatant violation of the *ex post facto* doctrine].

----

10. Treaty of Peace with Germany
(Concluded at Versailles, June 28, 1919)
13 *American Journal of International Law* (sect. 2)
151; 179; 191–192; 194–195; 206–209; 215; 250–252 (1919)
Reproduced with permission from 13 *American Journal of International Law*
(sect. 2) 151 (1919). © The American Society of International Law

Bearing in mind that on the request of the Imperial German Government an Armistice was granted on November 11, 1918, to Germany by the Principal Allied and Associated Powers in order that a Treaty of Peace be concluded with her, and

----

11. Peter Maguire, *Law and War: An American Story* (2000).
12. *Id.* at 76.
13. *Id.* At 77.

The Allied and Associated Powers being equally desirous that the war in which they were successively involved directly or indirectly and which originated in the declaration of war by Austria-Hungary on July 28, 1914, against Serbia, the declaration of war by Germany against Russia on August 1, 1914, and against France on August 3, 1914, and in the invasion of Belgium, should be replaced by a firm, just and durable Peace,

For this purpose, the HIGH CONTRACTING PARTIES...[here follow the names of the representatives of the nations involved and then a series of Articles dealing with the establishment of the League of Nations. We take up selected provisions of the Versailles Treaty, beginning with Section V.].

* * *

Section V.

Alsace-Lorraine

The High Contracting Parties, recognizing the moral obligation to redress the wrong done by Germany in 1871 both to the rights of France and to the wishes of the population of Alsace and Lorraine, which were separated from their country in spite of the solemn protest of their representatives at the Assembly of Bordeaux,

Agree upon the Following Articles:

* * *

Article 51.

The territories which were ceded to Germany in accordance with the Preliminaries of Peace signed at Versailles on February 26, 1871, and the Treaty of Frankfort of May 10, 1871, are restored to French sovereignty as from the date of the Armistice of November 11, 1918.

* * *

Section VI.

Austria

Article 80.

Germany acknowledges and will respect strictly the independence of Austria, within the frontiers which may be fixed in a Treaty between that State and the Principal Allied and Associated Powers; she agrees that this independence shall be inalienable, except with the consent of the Council of the League of Nations.

Section VII.

Czecho-Slovak State

Article 81.

Germany, in conformity with the action already taken by the Allied and Associated Powers, recognizes the complete independence of the Czecho-Slovak State which will include the autonomous territory of the Ruthenians to the South of the Carpathians.

Germany hereby recognizes the frontiers of this State as determined by the Principal Allied and Associated Powers and other interested States.

Article 82.

The old frontier as it existed on August 3, 1914, between Austria-Hungary and the German Empire will constitute the frontier between Germany and the Czecho-Slovak State.

* * *

Section VIII.

Poland

Article 87.

Germany, in conformity with the action already taken by the Allied and Associated Powers, recognizes the complete independence of Poland, and renounces in her favor all rights and title over the territory bounded by the Baltic Sea, the eastern frontier of Germany as laid down in Article 27 of Part II...of the present Treaty...

The provisions of this Article do not, however, apply to the territories of East Prussia and the Free City of Danzig,...

The boundaries of Poland not laid down in the present Treaty will be subsequently determined by the Principal Allied and Associated Powers.

* * *

Section XI.

Free City of Danzig

* * *

Article 102.

The Principal Allied and Associated Powers undertake to establish the town of Danzig, together with the rest of the territory described in Article 100, as a Free City. It will be placed under the protection of the League of Nations.

Article 104.

The Principal Allied and Associated Powers undertake to negotiate a Treaty between the Polish Government and the Free City of Danzig, which shall come into force at the same time as the establishment of the said Free City...[Here is laid out six provisions giving Poland free access to the Baltic Sea as well as establishing diplomatic relations between Poland and the Free City of Danzig and empowering Poland to conduct diplomatic and foreign relations on behalf of the Free City of Danzig, among others].

Article 105.

On the coming into force of the present Treaty German nationals ordinarily resident in the territory described in Article 100 will *ipso facto* lose their German nationality in order to become nationals of the Free City of Danzig.

[Article 106 gave German nationals over age 18 domiciled in the Free City of Danzig a choice to opt for German nationality within two years of the Treaty of Versailles coming into force. If they so opted, they then had twelve months to relocate their domicile within the re-drawn boundaries of the German Weimar Republic].

Article 107.

All property situated within the territory of the Free City of Danzig belonging to the German Empire or to any German State shall pass to the Principal Allied and Associated Powers for transfer to the Free City of Danzig or to the Polish State as they may consider.

Part IV

German Rights and Interests Outside Germany

Article 118.

In territory outside her European frontiers as fixed by the present Treaty, Germany renounces all rights, titles and privileges whatever in or over territory which belonged to her or to her allies, and all rights, titles and privileges whatever their origin in which she held as against the Allied and Associated Powers.

[Articles 119 through 127 were specifically directed to Imperial Germany's overseas colonies. Articles 128 through 135 dealt with Germany's possessions and leaseholds in China acquired prior to World War I. Japan, being one of the Associated Powers allied with France, Great Britain and the United States, recognized a geopolitical opportunity in Germany's loss of her Chinese possessions. The Japanese moved to fill the vacuum left by Imperial Germany's departure from the Far East, and, by so doing, laid the groundwork for further Japanese imperialistic ambitions in that region of the world in the late 1920s and in the decade of the 1930s].

Part VII

Penalties

Article 227.

The Allied and Associated Powers publicly arraign William II of Hohenzollern, former German Emperor, for a supreme offense against international morality and the sanctity of treaties.

A special tribunal will be constituted to try the accused, thereby assuring him the guarantees essential to the right of defence. It will be composed of five judges, one appointed by each of the following Powers: namely, the United States of America, Great Britain, France, Italy and Japan.

In its decision the tribunal will be guided by the highest motives of international policy, with a view to vindicating the solemn obligations of international undertakings and the validity of international morality. It will be its duty to fix the punishment which it considers should be imposed.

The Allied and Associated Powers will address a request to the Government of the Netherlands for the surrender to them of the ex-Emperor in order that he may be put on trial.

Article 228.

The German Government recognizes the right of the Allied and Associated Powers to bring before military tribunals persons accused of having committed acts in violation of the laws and customs of war. Such persons shall, if found guilty, be sentenced to punishments laid down by law. This provision will apply notwithstanding any proceedings or prosecution before a tribunal in Germany or in any territory of her allies.

Article 229.

Persons found guilty of criminal acts against the nationals of one of the Allied and Associated Powers will be brought before the military tribunals of that Power.

Persons guilty of criminal acts against the nationals of more than one of the Allied and Associated Powers will be brought before military tribunals composed of members of the military tribunals of the Powers concerned.

In every case the accused will be entitled to name his own counsel.

Article 230.

The German Government undertakes to furnish all documents and information of every kind, the production of which may be considered necessary to ensure the full knowledge of the incriminating acts, the discovery of offenders, and the just appreciation of responsibility.

Part VIII

Reparation

Article 231.

The Allied and Associated Powers affirm and Germany accepts the responsibility of Germany and her allies for causing all the loss and damage to which the Allies and Associated Governments and their nationals have been subjected as a consequence of the war imposed upon them by the aggression of Germany and her allies.

Article 232.

The amount of the above damage for which compensation is to be made by Germany shall be determined by an Inter-Allied Commission, to be called the Reparation Commission...

* * *

Protocol Supplementary to the Treaty of Peace between the Allied and Associated Powers and Germany

Signed at Versailles, June 28, 1919
13 *American Journal of International Law* (sect. 2) 385–386 (1919)
Reproduced with permission from 13 *American Journal of International Law*
(sect. 2) 385 (1919). © The American Society of International Law

With a view to indicating precisely the conditions in which certain provisions of the Treaty of even date are to be carried out, it is agreed by the HIGH CONTRACTING PARTIES that:

(3) The list of persons to be handed over to the Allied and Associated Governments by Germany under the second paragraph of Article 228 shall be communicated

to the German Government within a month from the coming into force of the Treaty....

[Signed by the same Plenipotentiaries who signed the Treaty of Peace].

---

11. Richard Overy, "The Versailles Settlement" in *The Penguin Historical Atlas of the Third Reich*
14–15 (1996)
From *The Penguin Historical Atlas of the Third Reich* by Richard Overy, Copyright © 1996, by Richard Overy. Used by permission of Penguin Group (UK) Ltd.

On 7 May 1919 the German delegation to the Paris Peace Conference led by German Foreign Minister, Count Brockdorff-Rantzau, was presented with the terms of the settlement. There followed a long and bitter argument between German political leaders about whether to accept what they regarded as an unjust and vindictive peace. Only the view of army leaders that further military resistance was futile turned the tide and forced the government to accept. On 28 June German representatives signed the Treaty of Versailles in the Hall of Mirrors in the Palace of the French kings.

The terms of the Treaty went beyond anything even the most realistic German politicians had expected. Germany lost 13% of its territory; Alsace-Lorraine (taken from France in 1870), Danzig, a strip of territory through East Prussia to form a Polish "Corridor" to the [Baltic] sea, and areas in Schleswig, Silesia and on the Belgian frontier, where plebiscites were held to determine which state the populations should join. The Saar industrial region was placed under international control, but effectively under French influence. The plebiscites were conducted in 1920 and 1921. In Upper Silesia were extensive coal, iron and steel industries which the new Polish state wanted to control. The plebiscite held in March 1921 gave 707,000 votes in favour of Germany, 479,000 in favour of Poland. The Allied powers suspected that undue pressure had been put on Polish workers to vote for Germany, and divided the region on the basis of majority German or Polish voting. The result was that most of Silesian heavy industry went to Poland. In 1926 the German government presented Poland with a bill for 521 million marks in compensation.

The Treaty also contained punitive economic terms. Germany was forced to pay reparations for war damage, fixed in 1921 at 132 billion gold marks (to prevent Germany paying them with inflation marks). Nine-tenths of the German merchant fleet was confiscated. German overseas assets, totaling 16 billion marks, were seized. German colonies were taken over by the League of Nations and distributed as mandated territories to Britain, France and Japan.

Finally the Treaty provided for Germany's disarmament to prevent any resurgence of German power in Europe. The army was confined to 100,000 men on long-service contracts to prevent the regular training of conscripts. The General Staff was scrapped, most military installations and training schools closed down, and the Rhineland area demilitarized and occupied by Allied troops. The German air force was abolished, and the German navy was reduced to a maximum of 6 small battleships of only 10,000 tons each, 6 cruisers, 12 destroyers and no submarines. Any overtly "offensive" armament was forbidden. An Allied Control Commission oversaw the physical demolition of Germany's military structure and remained in Germany until 1926 verifying German compliance with the disarmament clauses.

The basis of the Allied punishment of Germany was contained in Clause 231 of the Treaty in which Germany was forced to confess her guilt for causing the war in the first place. This clause alienated opinion in Germany across the political spectrum. Versailles turned Germany into a revisionist state *ispo facto*. Only German powerlessness prevented efforts to overturn the Treaty in the 1920s. The Foreign Minister from 1924 to 1929, Gustav Stresemann, argued that Germany would gain more by working within the framework imposed by the Allies than by fighting against it. In 1925 Germany signed the Locarno Treaties with Britain, France, Belgium and Italy recognizing the territorial settlement in the west. In 1926 Germany joined the League of Nations, set up in 1920. German nationalists rejected all compromise with the Versailles system, but the general mood by the late 1920s was of reconciliation from necessity.

[The treaty regime ending World War I included, of course, (a) the Treaty of Versailles with Germany, June 28, 1919; (b) the Treaty of Saint-Germain-en-Lave with Austria, September 10, 1919; (c) the Treaty of Neuilly-sur-Seine with Bulgaria, November 27, 1919; (d) the Treaty of Trianon with Hungary, June 4, 1920; and (e) the Treaty of Sevres with Turkey, August 10, 1920. The Treaty of Sevres, however, was never ratified. Subsequently, on July 24, 1923, Turkey and the Allies signed the Treaty of Lausanne, which was ratified. All of these treaties forced upon the Central Powers rather unforgiving terms of peace. As noted by Overy [*supra*], the Treaty of Versailles was particularly galling to the Germans. The particular section of the Versailles Treaty dealing with war crimes was termed the *Schmachparagraphen* or ("shame paragraphs"). The myopia of the Allies regarding the overall political impact of the Versailles provisions was truly astonishing. Article 231, the infamous "war guilt clause" caused the German government to view the Treaty of Versailles with utter contempt and disdain. German political and public opinion from 1919 until the commencement of World War II in 1939, held fast to the premise that the Treaty of Versailles in general and Article 231 in particular imposed a retributive peace upon the German nation. By placing sole responsibility for the Great War on Imperial Germany, it has been argued that the Allied and Associated Powers created political conditions in Weimar Germany that spawned ultra-nationalist sentiment, right-wing militants, and a secret but determined effort by the German military, to rebuild German arms. However, before all this occurred, the Allies drafted plans for the trial of almost 1,000 alleged German war criminals in accordance with Article 229 of the Versailles settlement. France, Great Britain, Poland, Romania, Italy and Yugoslavia planned to prosecute various alleged German war criminals before military tribunals in their respective countries. Remarkably, for a host of reasons, none of these trials ever took place. An argument has been made that this collective abstention was due in large measure to the recognized fact that the United States itself was less than enthusiastic to compel the German government to hand over to the Allies these alleged offenders. This, because the United States government was unwilling to go on record in support of a post-war international criminal trial itself, despite the language contained in the Versailles Treaty. Because of America's unwillingness to be a party to the establishment of an international forum for the assessment of German war guilt, the political will of the remaining Allies to indict and try German war criminals in significant numbers, evaporated. This unwillingness on the part of the United States was also at least partially fueled by the State Department's antipathy toward an international trial of the Kaiser, as well as Woodrow Wilson's general disinterest in war crime trials altogether. Ultimately, this state of affairs led to trials of only a handful of alleged German war criminals in the German domestic legal system at Leipzig].

12. Treaty of St. Germain-en-Lave with Austria

September 10, 1919

14 *American Journal of International Law* (supp.) 1; 55–56 (1920)

Reproduced with permission from 14 *American Journal of International Law* (supp.) 1 (1920). © The American Society of International Law

Penalties

Article 173

The Austrian Government recognizes the right of the Allied and Associated Powers to bring before military tribunals persons accused of having committed acts in violation of the laws and customs of war. Such persons shall, if found guilty, be sentenced to punishment laid down by law. This provision will apply notwithstanding any proceedings or prosecutions before a tribunal in Austria or in the territory of her allies.

The Austrian Government shall hand over to the Allied and Associated Powers, or to such one of them as shall so request, all persons accused of having committed an act in violation of the laws and customs of war, who are specified either by name or by rank, office or employment which they held under the Austrian authorities.

Article 174.

Persons guilty of criminal acts against the nationals of more than one of the Allied and Associated Powers will be brought before military tribunals composed of members of the military tribunals of the Powers concerned.

In every case the accused will be entitled to name his own counsel.

Article 175.

The Austrian Government undertakes to furnish all documents and information of every kind, the production of which may be considered necessary to ensure the full knowledge of the incriminating acts, the discovery of offenders and the just appreciation of responsibility.

Article 176.

The provisions of Articles 173 to 175 apply similarly to the Governments of the States to which territory belonging to the former Austro-Hungarian Monarchy has been assigned, in so far as concerns persons accused of having committed acts contrary to the laws and customs of war who are in the territory or at the disposal of the States.

If the persons in question have acquired the nationality of one of the said States, the Government of such state undertakes to take, at the request of the Power concerned and in agreement with it, all the measures necessary to ensure the prosecution and punishment of such persons.

13. The Leipzig War Crime Trials

(a) Peter Maguire, *Law and War: An American Story*

80–82 (2000)
Reproduced with permission from Columbia University Press,
© 2000, Columbia University Press

On February 3, [1920] the victors called on the German government to live up to Article 228 of the Treaty of Versailles and hand over 854 men accused of war crimes. [Note that the number here vary, according to the particular source quoted]. Among them were some of Germany's most venerated military leaders; Ludendorff, von Moltke, von Tirpitz, and von Hindenburg. The German government refused and stated firmly, "the extradition of those blacklisted for a trial by an Entente court is a physical and moral impossibility." However, Germany did agree to try a limited number of men before the German Supreme Court (Reichsgericht) in Leipzig. The Associated Powers presented a revised list of 45 defendants. The British had been careful to choose cases where the violations of the laws of war were flagrant; in most, the infractions had been documented by both sides. The British submitted three submarine cases and three prison camp cases. Immediately following World War I, First Lieutenant Helmutt Patzig of U-86 returned home to Danzig and vanished, leaving his subordinates to take the fall. The political justice rendered by the Germans at the Leipzig Trials was... [in form] a sympathetic show trial as an appeasement measure to provide symbolic justice and little more.

The Leipzig trials opened on May 23, 1921, in the Reichsgericht with Dr. Schmidt, the presiding judge, and his six colleagues, cloaked in crimson robes and berets, sitting around a horseshoe-shaped table. Ludwig Dithmar and John Boldt, [case reported *infra*] the submarine defendants in one of the cases chosen by the British, were the subordinate officers of the U-boat that sank the hospital ship *Llandovery Castle*. Both refused to testify on the ground that they had taken an oath of silence concerning the events of the night of June 27, 1918.... The testimony of the other submarine crew members made it clear that First Lieutenant Patzig had attempted to cover up his action—not only did he alter the submarine's logs, he also changed the ship's course on the charts.

Based on the testimony of [the English witness] Chapman and the other survivors, the court determined that "the lifeboats of the *Llandovery Castle* were fired on in order to sink them."... The defendants were sentenced to four years imprisonment.

The decision in the British [prison camp] cases against Karl Heynen and Emil Muller [reported *infra*] were equally schizophrenic. Karl Heynen was in charge of British POWs in a Westphalian coal mine. When the prisoners refused to work, he beat some of them. Emil Muller, a German prison camp commandant, was similarly charged with nine instances of personal cruelty. They were sentenced to ten and six months respectively. While the court sternly condemned the defendant's beatings of the prisoners as "unworthy of a human being," nonetheless they concluded, "It must be emphasized that the accused has not acted dishonorably, that is to say, his honour as a citizen and as an officer remains untarnished."

The most uncomfortable moment of the Leipzig trials came when the court heard France's charge against Franz Stenger, a decorated German officer who had lost a leg to a French artillery shell. The officer was accused of issuing a no quarter order and ordering his men to shoot prisoners in August 1914....

In his final statement before the court, Stenger declared: "I did nothing in the war except my duty and obligation to the leaders of the German fatherland, to my Kaiser, the Supreme War Lord, and in the interest of the lives of my fighting German soldiers."

The speech was met with wild applause and an acquittal. His [Stenger's] German accuser [Major Benno Cruscius] was not so fortunate—Major Cruscius was sentenced to two years for "killing through negligence." The French prosecutors were heckled and spat upon by the unruly German spectators. After the defendants in three more of their cases were acquitted, the French withdrew from the trials. In the six British cases, five of the defendants were convicted; the French obtained only one conviction in their five cases. In their one case, the Belgians charged Max Ramdahr, the head of the German secret police in Belgium, with torturing young boys. The court acquitted him and maintained that the stories were merely the products of overactive adolescent imaginations. When Ramdohr was acquitted, the Belgians also withdrew from the trials.

(b) *Current Notes:* German War Trials

16 *American Journal of International Law* 628; 632 (1922)
Reproduced with permission from 16 *American Journal of International Law* 628 (1922). © The American Society of International Law

In accordance with the arrangement made between the Allies...whereby they agreed not to intervene in the trials but to leave the full responsibility to the Germans, the [British] mission took no part in the proceedings, and declined the offer of the German authorities to be joined as parties to the proceedings. The [British] mission obtained, however, and asserted on many occasions, the right to communicate in court with the *Oberreichsanwalt*, [public prosecutor] through the representative of the German Ministry of Justice, for the purpose of calling his attention to any point, which appeared to have been overlooked or imperfectly brought to the attention of the court by the necessary translation of the evidence of the witnesses.

In accordance with the practice prevailing in Germany and other Continental countries, the witnesses were examined and the proceedings were for the most part conducted by the president. The *Oberreichsanwalt* (Dr. Ebermeyer), appeared on behalf of the German State. The accused persons were present and were represented by legal advisors, who, although entitled to question the witnesses, took a relatively small part in the proceedings, and confined themselves to addressing the court after the examination of the witnesses had been concluded.

The *Oberreichsanwalt* summed up the evidence in his address to the court and indicated what charges in his opinion had, and which had not, been proved and where he had come to the conclusion that the accused was guilty demanded the sentence which he considered proper. The court then considered its decision and in due course delivered orally its judgment and sentence. The judgment was subsequently reduced to writing in a more extended form and a translation of the full judgment in each case...

(c) U.S. Department of the Army Pamphlet No. 27-161-2
II International Law 221–22 (1962)

The Leipzig Trials (1921)

Pursuant to articles 228–230 of the Versailles Treaty, Germany agreed to turn over suspected war criminals to the Allies for trial by Allied tribunals. At the Paris Peace Conference on February 6, 1920, the Allies formally demanded of Germany the extradition of 896 Germans accused of violating the laws of war. England demanded 97 for trial, France and Belgium 344 each, Italy 29, Poland 47, Rumania 31, and Serbia 4. Kurt von Lersner, head of the German peace delegation, refused to accept the extradition list. The German government was not very stable and compliance with the demand might have led to its overthrow. Von Lersner resigned from the Peace Conference and returned to Berlin.

As a compromise, the Allies, at the suggestion of Great Britain, agreed to accept an offer by Germany to try a selected number of individuals before the Criminal Senate of the Imperial Court of Justice of Germany. Forty-five names were selected. Of these forty-five only twelve were actually brought to trial, six at the insistence of the British, five accused by France, and one by Belgium.

The trial resulted in six convictions and six acquittals. Most of the acquittals resulted from a failure of the court to accept certain evidence as creditable. Disappointment was expressed not only over the comparatively light sentences meted out but also over the fact the trials dealt almost exclusively with the treatment of shipwrecked survivors of submarine activity and with the treatment of prisoners of war. No trials were held on the actual conduct of hostilities, such as the use of weapons and the destruction of life and property in combat. Another objection was the fact that the court itself was under pressure from the German press and German public opinion. Both were very hostile to the trials. For example, after the sentence was announced in the Llandovery Castle case the British observers had to leave by the side door under police escort.

The name of each accused, the charge, and the finding and sentence are as follows:

Sgt. Karl Heynen	Mistreatment of PW's	Guilty	10 months
Capt. Emil Muller	Mistreatment of PW's	Guilty	6 months
Pvt. Robert Neumann	Mistreatment of PW's	Guilty	6 months
Lt. Capt. Karl Neumann	Torpedoing hospital ship Dover Castle	N/G	
1st Lt. Ludwig Dithmar	Firing on survivors in lifeboats of hospital ship Llandovery Castle	Guilty	4 years
1st Lt. John Boldt	Firing on survivors in lifeboats of hospital ship Llandovery Castle	Guilty	4 years
Max Ramdohr	Mistreatment of Belgian Children	N/G	
Major Benno Cruscius	Passing on alleged order of Gen. Stenger	Guilty	2 years
1st Lt. Adolph Laule	Killing a PW	N/G	
Lt. Gen Hans Von Schock	Mistreatment of PW's	N/G	
Maj. Gen Benno Kruska	Mistreatment of PW's	N/G	
Lt. Gen. Karl Stenger	Ordering the killing of prisoners of war	N/G	

(d) Judgment in the *Case of Karl Heynen*

Supreme Court at Leipzig, Rendered May 26, 1921
16 *American Journal of International Law* 674–684 (1922)
Reproduced with permission from 16 *American Journal of International
Law* 674 (1922). © The American Society of International Law

IN THE NAME OF THE EMPIRE

In the criminal case against Karl Heynen, master cooper, of and born in Barmen on 22 June, 1875, for crimes and offences contrary to §§122, 55, 1, 121 Military Penal Code, and §74 Imperial Penal Code the Second Penal Senate of the Imperial Court of Justice at a sitting in public on 26 May, 1921, at which there took part judges [here is listed the President of the Senate, Dr. Schmidt and the six other judges as well as two officials from the Public Prosecutor's Department].

The accused is condemned to ten (10) months imprisonment on fifteen charges of ill-treating subordinates, and on three charges of insulting subordinates, and on charges of having treated subordinates contrary to the regulations; in other respects he is acquitted.

Reasons for the Decision

I. The accused...was called up in the autumn of 1914 as non-commissioned officer with the second Munster Landsturm Battalion. He took part in the campaign in Russia, was wounded on 29th December, 1914, on the Pelizza, then returned to Munster and was posted for a period of 7 months to the prisoners of war camp at Rheine. Deputy Officer Radenburg has testified to his great zeal, absolute trustworthiness and faultless conduct. There has been no complaint of any kind of excess towards the Russian prisoners of war, who were placed under him and were occupied with agricultural work.

At the beginning of October, 1915, he was recalled to the First Munster prisoners' camp, in order to take over the command of the new prisoners' camp to be organized at shaft V of the "Friedrich der Grosse" [Frederick the Great] mine near Herne. He received as his sentries a draft of 1 Lance Corporal and 12 Landsturm men, most of whom had only received their necessary training during the war.

There were placed under him 240 prisoners of war, of whom about 200 were English and 40 were Russian. They were to work in a colliery. This was kept secret from them, probably because it was foreseen that they might be unwilling to undertake such work. In fact they believed, from what they had been told, that they were to work at a sugar factory.

On 13 October 1915, accused with his detachment of sentries and the prisoners left Munster for Herne. He had received no further orders than that he had to see to it that the prisoners undertook the work intended for them; he was to make his own arrangements; until his arrival in camp in Herne he was to keep silent about their place of destination and the work intended for them.

On the way already discontent became apparent among the prisoners, because they saw that they were going to be made to work in a mine. They vented their discontent by such utterances as "Nix Minen" [no mine] and thus let it be understood that they would not work in a mine. It was impossible for the accused to make himself understood to the prisoners as he had not been allotted an interpreter.

II. After arrival at the railway station at Herne, the accused first endeavored to find amongst the English prisoners a man, who understood German sufficiently to be able to act to some extent as interpreter for his fellow prisoners. Such a man he found in the English prisoner Perry, who, however, at that time, had but little knowledge of German. Perry understood him only partially. In consequence the accused, according to Perry's statement which he considered to be credible, himself got angry and so irritable that he called him "Englisher Schweinhund" (Dog of an Englishman). He thus insulted this prisoner of war who, by being placed under his command, had become his subordinate. At this time the accused was endeavoring to carry out his duties. Therefore he is guilty of a breach of §121 para. 1, of the Military Penal Code and deserves increased punishment under §55, No. 2, of the Military Penal Code.

III. In consequence of the discontent generally prevailing among the prisoners, their march from Herne railway station to the camp at shaft V (a distance of about half-an-hour's walk) was very slow. On their arrival in camp the prisoners were very dilatory in obeying orders, which were repeatedly and emphatically given them; and this although most of them had already been prisoners for almost a year and must have known their obligations as regards obedience.

On this occasion the Englishman Gothard, in particular, disregarded the order to fall in, because he wished first to mix his cocoa at a hot-water pipe. Excited over this disobedience, the accused, as has been credibly stated by Gothard and other witnesses, hit Gothard on the head with the fist and as he ducked under the blows, gave him a blow on the nose and eye with his sheathed side-arm, thus drawing blood. In this the accused offended against §122, para. 1, 55, No. 2, of the Military Penal Code....

* * *

IX. On the other hand the accused has, in the following instances, assaulted prisoners who maintained that they were sick or while they were being treated temporarily by him:

(a) On 8th November [1915] he ill-used the English prisoner Jones by means of blows with the fist and kicks on the ground, alleging that he had reported sick but had been found fit by the doctor.

(b) He struck the same man Jones in the face with his fists on 10th or 11th November because Jones, who had a swollen cheek, declared he had a tooth-ache....

(c) At the beginning of November the English prisoner McLaren was in the sleeping room and the accused struck him with a broom, because he remained in bed on account of alleged sickness.

[The Court then continues its narrative of assaults and petty indignities committed by Heynen upon five other English prisoners who had allegedly violated either camp rules or one of more rules applicable to their work in the Frederick the Great mine].

* * *

XV. In deciding the measure of punishment the Senate has taken the following considerations into account:

Apart from the offenses of which he is now found guilty the accused bears an excellent and blameless character, both as a citizen and as a soldier. This holds good especially in regard to his later term of military service. He was removed from his command as soon as his offenses against prisoners became known in higher quarters, namely, on 26th November, 1915. On 5th April, 1916, he was sentenced by a court-martial, partly on account of the cases of ill-treating prisoners of which he now stands convicted. But afterwards he won back by a loyal performance of his duties the trust and appreciation of his superiors. He again reported himself at the front and during the years 1916–1918 he took part in the battles on the Western front. He earned the distinction of the Iron Cross of the II class, and on 17th April, 1918, he was promoted to Sergeant. When he was commandant of the prisoners' camp at Herne, there was also no lack of zeal. He was especially indefatigable as regards the arrangements for boarding and lodging the prisoners entrusted to him. Above all it has to be realized that he had had no adequate instruction in his duties and that his staff of sentries was inadequate both as regards quality and number. He was thus placed in an extremely difficult position, a position which was beyond his strength and abilities. The evidence has conclusively shown that his duties were rendered much more difficult, especially at the beginning, by the conduct of the English prisoners. Little as his failings can be excused, yet they can be explained to a large extent by the unstinting way in which he devoted his energetic personality to his appointed task. In carrying out his duties he spared himself least of all. He developed a state of irritability and excitement, which almost amounted to an illness, and this more and more undermined his self-control. This is shown clearly by the increasing number of offences towards the end of his period of command.

For all that, there can be no question of detention in a fortress in view of the nature of his offenses, especially those committed against prisoners who were undoubtedly sick. On the contrary a sentence of imprisonment must be passed so far as crimes against §122, 55, No. 2 of the Military Penal Code are concerned.

The ill-treatment of the prisoner Cross is considered to be the gravest case. For that there must be a punishment of 3 months' imprisonment. For each of the other cases of ill-treatment there must be 2 months' imprisonment. For the offences of throwing stones at prisoners there must be a sentence of three days medium arrest and for each case of insulting prisoners a sentence of a week's light arrest. In accordance with the terms of §54 of the Military Penal Code and of §74 o f the Imperial Code a comprehensive sentence has to be passed to include these separate sentences. The period of detention during the enquiry will be counted as part of the term of imprisonment now ordered; this is in accordance with §60 of the Imperial Penal Code.

[Here follow the signatures of the seven judges, the Clerk of the Court and the Seal of the Court].

––––––––––

(e) Judgment in the *Case of Emil Müller*

Supreme Court at Leipzig, Rendered May 30, 1921
16 *American Journal of International Law* 684–696 (1922)
Reproduced with permission from 16 *American Journal of International Law* 684 (1922). © The American Society of International Law

IN THE NAME OF THE EMPIRE

In the criminal case against Emil Müller, barrister, and Captain in the Reserve (retired), of Karslruhe, born on 24 July, 1877, in Mannheim, for crimes and offences against sections 122, 143, 55, 59, 1, 121, 7, of the Military Penal Code and section 74 of the Imperial Penal Code.

the second Criminal Senate of the Imperial Court of Justice at a Sitting held in public on 30 May, 1921, at which there took part as judges....

[Here the opinion lists the seven judges, the officials of the Public Prosecutor's Department, and the Clerk of the Court].

The accused is sentenced to six months' imprisonment for having ill-treated subordinates in nine instances: for having tolerated such ill-treatment in one instance; for having dealt with subordinates in four instances contrary to the regulations; and for having insulted subordinates in two instances. Of the remaining charges he is acquitted....

By Right

Reasons for the Decision

In March, 1918, the accused, who was a captain in the Reserve, commanded the II Company of the Gelsenkirchen Landsturm Battalion. In this capacity he was, in the beginning of April, placed in command of a camp for English prisoners of war at Flavy-le-Martel, which was being put in order by the battalion. He shared these duties with the commander of No. 1 Company, but each company took over a separate portion of the camp, and took up its quarters with the prisoners of war assigned to it. No commandant of the camp as a whole was appointed. The duties of the company commanders consisted solely in housing, feeding and supervising their prisoners, and in arranging, day by day, to provide the troops requisitioned for outside work. They had nothing to do with the regulation of this work itself or setting the hours of labor. This was the business of the commander of the battalion and of his subordinates. The company commanders took over a camp which was found empty. In the camp there were barracks and other buildings. These were the only buildings in the neighborhood. The company commanders had no choice of other buildings.

The accused held this position from the beginning of April until 5th May, 1918, that is to say, for a period of about five weeks. On the 4th May he was given leave, as he needed treatment for neurosis of the heart. He left the camp on 5th May and never returned.

The camp had shortly before been taken from the English during the so-called March offensive, and had previously been used by them as a camp for the temporary reception of German prisoners of war. It was in a wretched condition. It lay in a marshy and completely devastated district immediately behind the fighting line, where everything was still in constant movement. During the time the English had been in possession of it, it was unfit for human occupation....

[The Court then goes into a description of the camp's accommodations, its deteriorated condition as well as the effort expended by the defendant to afford his prisoners at least a modicum of comfort and minimum rations. However, despite Muller's efforts, the men under his supervision continued to suffer and grow weak from exhausting outside labor. The opinion continues]:

...Food remained insufficient.... The strength of the prisoners had not grown equal to the strenuous outside work. This work was necessitated by the fighting and, in determining it, the accused had in general no influence. Most of the prisoners grew weaker and weaker and they often collapsed at their work or on the march to their place of work as well as at the roll-calls in camp. Furthermore, infectious diseases broke out in the shelters, which were already overrun with lice and infected with germs of disease. The prisoners did not keep themselves clean and were unable to change either uniform or underclothing....

* * *

So far, therefore, as the general conditions in the prisoners' camp at Flavy-le-Martel are concerned, the accused must not only be acquitted of any blame, but it should be placed on record that the zeal with which he carried out his duties deserves high praise.

On the other hand, the same cannot be said about the way in which he treated the prisoners individually or his methods of maintaining order. It was precisely owing to his zeal and natural tendency for an impetuous and rigorous action (combined with a serious condition of nervous overstrain) that prompted him to commit a series of excesses, which constituted a breach not only of his official duties but also of the criminal law. These excesses cannot be justified by the circumstances. His attitude towards the prisoners was hard and over-severe, sometimes even brutal, and in other cases it was at least contrary to regulations. He treated them not as subordinates, and it was as such that he ought to have regarded his prisoners, but he treated them more like convicts or inmates of penitentiaries. His methods were those of the convict prison or such like institutions, although even on this standard his conduct could not be tolerated. The court has heard of his ill-treating prisoners by hitting and kicking them. He allowed his staff to treat them in the same manner. Insults were hurled at the prisoners and there was other ill-treatment which was contrary to the regulations. He habitually struck them when he was on horseback, using a riding cane or a walking stick; several prisoners have stated that they were struck with a riding whip, but this must be a mistake as the accused did not possess one.

I. Ill-treatment

[Here the Court narrated a series of nine separate incidents in which Muller committed assault and battery on various English POWs under his care, striking prisoners with a riding crop, ordering prisoners to be bound to posts for some infraction and striking those who requested improved working conditions. The opinion continues]:

In general the accused has admitted that it was his practice to enforce discipline, in cases of irregular behavior by means of light blows. He will not as a rule tax his memory about the details. He explains, however, it would have been impossible to attain rigid discipline if he had tolerated any lengthy explanations, especially as he and the prisoners could not understand each other's language. There may be some truth in this and there were no doubt serious difficulties in commanding such a camp. But nevertheless the accused never had any right to get over these difficulties by means of endless acts of violence.

* * *

...the accused, likewise acting continuously, often forced work on sick prisoners. When he could not muster the full complement of workers demanded or when supplementary demands arrived, he forcibly sent everyone out, even those entered as sick or who were obviously incapable of work; he tolerated no opposition.... The accused cannot answer this by pleading that he considered many of these alleged sick to be malingerers or that his strict orders obliged him to send out the number of workers that were demanded. For the first excuse contradicts the evidence of the witnesses, who declare that there could have been no doubt about the sickness of many of the men in question.

* * *

Thus it has been definitely established:...

I. In nine instances he deliberately kicked or struck English prisoners of war, his subordinates, or otherwise physically ill-treated them or caused injury to their health.

II. In one instance, as commanding officer of a military detachment, he allowed one of his subordinates, a non-commissioned officer, deliberately to strike an English prisoner of war with his fist. The accused thereby with knowledge permitted the committing of a criminal act, which he could have prevented, and which he was officially bound to prevent.

III. In two instances he insulted English prisoners of war, his subordinates, by using words of abuse.

IV. In four instances he is guilty of treating English prisoners of war, his subordinates, contrary to the regulations and as in the cases I and IV, he did this whilst carrying out his duties.

He is thus liable to punishment for crimes and offences according to Section 122, paras. 1, 143, 121; paras. 1, 55(2), 53, 7, of the Military Penal Code; Section 76 of the Imperial Penal Code...

In deciding the extent of punishment the following factors have had to be taken into consideration.

The accused is in no wise guilty to the extent which might appear from the results of the preliminary proceedings. The trial before this court has vindicated him on many points; in others it has proved that his offences were not so serious as had been expected.

* * *

But his personal treatment of the prisoners (and for this his temperament was less suited), he erred seriously. Instead of earning the prisoners' confidence, he got a reputation among them for being a tyrant.... But here, too, his excesses were only due to that military enthusiasm which worked him up to an exaggerated conception of military necessity and discipline. He made insufficient allowance for the special conditions in which prisoners in war-time find themselves. He showed himself and lacking in consideration but not deliberately cruel. His acts originated, not in any pleasure in persecution, or even in any want of feeling for the sufferings of the prisoners; but in a conscious disregard of the general laws of humanity. Had this not been so, he would not have generally troubled so much about the well-being of the prisoners, and his acts of ill-treatment would have caused more serious injury to those concerned than has been proved to have occurred. Not a single case has really serious consequences.

It must be emphasized that the accused has not acted dishonorably, that is to say, his honor both as a citizen and as an officer remains untarnished.... There has been an accumulation of offences, which show an almost habitually harsh and contemptuous and even a frankly brutal treatment of prisoners entrusted to his care. His conduct has some times been unworthy of a human being; these factors the court considers decisive. When he mixed with the prisoners there was seldom anything but angry words; attempts to ride them down; blows and efforts to push them out of his way: he never listened patiently to their grievances and complaints: he had not eyes for their obvious sufferings: he cared little for the individual, if only he could secure order among the prisoners collectively. It is impossible to consider his conduct as a number of separate instances of rash actions which he regretted: it appears rather as a deliberate practice of domineering disregard for the other men's feelings. It is no justification that his methods were intended to secure discipline. It is also no excuse that the conditions had been brutalized by war. The only possible excuse for him was he was over-excited: that he feared disorder, and that he did not know how to handle men. But even so, it must be recalled that he had under him prisoners who were peculiarly unfortunate, sick and suffering men who deserved protection. When these prisoners offended against the regulations, the cause for the most part lay in their miserable condition. Such men in such conditions were not likely to really be refractory. The accused should have avoided being unduly severe; and above all he ought not to have indulged in such reprehensible means of punishment as blows, kicks, tying-up and such like. Such conduct dishonors our army, and is singularly unfitting in a man of his education and military as well as civilian positions.

Therefore it seems to the court that detention in a fortress is too light a sentence to follow such an accumulation of offences.

The most grievous mistake of the accused having regard to the lamentable health conditions of the camp, is considered to be his compelling sick men to work.... For this there must be a sentence of 2 months' imprisonment.

* * *

[Here follows separate individual sentences for each charge].

Out of these separate sentences there will be a total sentence of 6 months' imprisonment in accordance with Section 74 of the Penal Code and Section 54 of the Military Penal Code. In respect of the other charges the accused is acquitted.

[Here follow the signatures of the seven judges, the Clerk of the Court of the Seal of the Court].

(f) Judgment in the *Case of Commander Karl Neumann*

Supreme Court at Leipzig, Rendered June 4, 1921
16 *American Journal of International Law* 704–708 (1922)
Reproduced with permission from 16 *American Journal of International Law* 704 (1922). © The American Society of International Law

IN THE NAME OF THE EMPIRE

In the criminal charge against Karl Neumann, Merchant, Commander (retired) of Breslau, born on 22nd December, 1887, in Kallowitz.

The Second Criminal Senate of the Imperial Court of Justice at a Sitting held in public on 4th June, 1921, at which there took place as Judges,...

[Here the opinion listed the seven Judges, the officials from the Public Prosecutor's Department, and the Clerk of the Court].

By Right

During the war the accused, as First Lieutenant in the Navy, was Commander of the Submarine U.C. 67. In the list communicated by the Allied Powers to the Government by virtue of Art. 228, par. 2, of the Treaty of Peace he was charged with having, on 26th May, 1917, torpedoed the English hospital ship *Dover Castle* without warning and with having sunk her with exceptional brutality...

The Attorney General has entered no indictment on this charge, but, in accordance with the law of 12th May, 1921, he has asked for an enquiry to decide the point whether the accused in the Tyrrhenian Sea [a portion of the Mediterranean bounded by Western

Italy, Corsica, Sardinia and Sicily], on 26th May, 1917, intentionally killed six men and whether these men were killed after full consideration.... The result of these proceedings is as follows:

On 26th May, 1917, the accused was in the Tyrrhenian Sea in command of the submarine U.C. 67.

During the day he sighted two steamers, escorted by two destroyers. The weather was clear and sunny. The accused was therefore soon able to see that the two steamers carried the distinctive outward signs laid down for military hospital ships by the 10th Hague Convention, in accordance with the principles of the Geneva Convention on naval warfare of 18th October, 1907. He approached nearer to the convoy, which was pursuing a zig-zag course and about 6.0 p.m. he fired a torpedo at the steamer nearest him. The steamer was hit; it remained stationary, but did not sink. One of the destroyers, which were accompanying it, came alongside its starboard side and took off its crew, as well as all the sick and wounded on board. Only after this had taken place, about 1 and one-half hours after the first torpedo, did the accused sink the vessel by firing a second torpedo. He then rose to the surface and found out from the markings on the unmanned life-boats which were drifting about that the sunken steamer was the *Dover Castle*.

According to the statement of the English Government, the *Dover Castle* had been serving for several years as a hospital ship and as such had regularly traveled from England to Malta and Salonica and from there back home. When torpedoed she had sick and wounded on board and was on her way to take them from Malta to Gilbralta. When the vessel was sunk not one of them perished. The first torpedo that was fired, however, caused the death of six members of the crew.

The accused frankly admits sinking the *Dover Castle*. He pleads that in doing so he merely carried out an order of the German Admiralty, his superior authority. With respect to this order the circumstances are as follows:

During the first years of the war the German Admiralty respected the military ships of their opponents in accordance with the regulations of the 10th Hague Convention referred to above. Later, however, they came to believe that enemy governments were utilizing their hospital ships not only to aid wounded, sick and shipwrecked people, but also for military purposes and that they were thereby violating this convention. In two memoranda, dated 29th January and 29th March, 1917, respectively, the German Government explained its attitude more clearly and gave proof in support of its assertions. It stated that it would not entirely repudiate the convention, but was compelled to restrict the navigation of enemy hospital ships. Accordingly it was announced in the second memorandum that henceforth, as regards the Mediterranean, only such hospital ships would be protected, which fulfilled certain conditions. The hospital ships had to be reported at least six weeks previously and were to keep to a given course on leaving Greece. After a reasonable period of grace, it was announced, all enemy hospital ships in the Mediterranean would be regarded as vessels of war and forthwith attacked.

The second memorandum reached the enemy governments in the early part of April, 1917.

It corresponds with the order of the Admiralty issued on 29th March, 1917, to the German Flotilla in the Mediterranean.

* * *

This order was communicated to the accused before his departure from Cattaro. Previously the two memoranda had been also brought to his knowledge. Exceptions in the case of hospital ships had not been arranged, as the enemy governments made no use of the opportunities to notify their hospital ships given in the memorandum of 29th March, 1917.

In the circumstances the acquittal of the accused has been requested.

It is a military principle that the subordinate is bound to obey the orders of his superiors. This duty of obedience is of considerable importance from the point of view of the criminal law. Its consequence is that, when the execution of a service order involves an offence against the criminal law, the superior giving the order is alone responsible. This is in accord with the terms of the German law, §47, para.1 of the Military Penal Code. It also accords with the legal principles of all civilized states… [citing examples].

The Admiralty Staff was the highest service authority over the accused. He was in duty bound to obey their orders in service matters. So far as he did that, he was free from criminal responsibility. Therefore he cannot be held responsible for sinking the hospital ship *Dover Castle* according to orders.

Under §47 of the Military Penal Code quoted above, there are two exceptional cases in which the question of the punishment of a subordinate who has acted in conformity with his orders can arise. He can in the first place be held responsible, if he has gone beyond the orders given him. In the present case the accused has not gone beyond his orders. It was impossible to give a warning to the *Dover Castle* before the torpedo was fired, because she was escorted by two warships. The accused is not charged with any peculiar brutality in sinking the ship. On the contrary he made it possible to save all the sick and wounded on board the *Dover Castle* by allowing about 1 and a half-hours to elapse between the firing of the first and the second torpedoes.

According to §47 of the Military Penal Code No. 2. a subordinate who acts in conformity with orders is also liable to punishment as an accomplice, when he knows that his superiors have ordered him to do acts which involve a civil or military crime or misdemeanor. There has been no case of this here. The memoranda of the German Government about the misuse of enemy hospital ships were known to the accused. The facts set out in them he held to be conclusive, especially as he had received, as he had explained, similar reports from his comrades. He was therefore of the opinion that the measure taken by the German Admiralty against enemy hospital ships were not contrary to international law, but were legitimate reprisals. His conduct clearly shows that this was his conviction. He never made any secret of the sinking of the *Dover Castle*. Not only did he report it to his superiors, but he has also frankly admitted it in the present proceedings. He has never disputed that he knew that the *Dover Castle* was a hospital ship. It is specially noteworthy that he allowed the English captain, whom he had on board his submarine as prisoner, to observe his approach to the *Dover Castle*. Although this enemy subject thus knew about the sinking of the hospital ship, the accused on going ashore gave him a certificate when he asked for one and signed it with his full name, giving his rank in the service. He would not have done this if he had considered that his orders or his execution of them were illegal.

The accused accordingly sank the *Dover Castle* in obedience to a service order of his highest superiors, an order which he considered to be binding. He cannot, therefore, be punished for his conduct. [Here follow the signatures of the seven judges, the Clerk of the Court and the Seal of the Court].

————————

(g) Judgment in the *Case of Lieutenants Dithmar and Boldt*

Supreme Court at Leipzig, Rendered July 16, 1921
16 *American Journal of International Law* 708–724 (1922)
Reproduced with permission from 16 *American Journal of International
Law* 708 (1922). © The American Society of International Law

IN THE NAME OF THE EMPIRE

In the criminal case against:

(1) Ludwig Dithmar of Cuxhaven, First Lieutenant and Adjutant of the Cuxhaven Command, at present detained during trial, born in Aix-la-Chapelle on the 13th May, 1892, and

(2) John Boldt of Altona, retired First Lieutenant, merchant, at present detained during trail, born in Dantzig on the 26th January, 1895.

The Second Criminal Senate of the Imperial Court of Justice, at its public Sitting on the 16th July, 1921, at which there took part as judges:...[Here the opinion listed the seven judges, the officials from the Public Prosecutors Department, and the Clerk of the Court].

...has pronounced judgment as follows, after hearing the evidence, namely

I. Each of the accused is sentenced to four years' imprisonment for having taken part in homicide:

II. Further,

(i) The accused Dithmar is ordered to be dismissed from the service,

(ii). The accused Boldt is deprived of the right to wear officer's uniform.

By Right

Reasons for the Decision

Up to the year 1916 the steamer *Llandovery Castle*, had, according to the statements of the witnesses Chapman and Heather, been used for the transport of troops. In that year she was commissioned by the British Government to carry wounded and sick Canadian soldiers home to Canada from the European theatre of war. The vessel was suitably fitted out for the purpose and was provided with the distinguishing marks, which the Tenth Hague Convention of the 18th October, 1907, (relating to the application to naval warfare of the principles of the Geneva Convention) requires in case of naval hospital ships. The name of the vessel was communicated to the enemy powers. From that time onwards she was exclusively employed in the transport of the sick and wounded. She never again carried troops in the light of the statements of the witness Thring, as well as of those witnesses who have been on board the steamer.

The witness Meyer, who saw the *Llandovery Castle* at the Port of Toulon, did not notice anything about her that could have led to the conclusion that she was being improperly used for war purposes. The court is convinced that the 120 men in Khaki, whom the witness Crompton saw go on board the *Llandovery Castle* in Tilbury Docks at the beginning of December, 1916, belonged to the Medical Corps.

At the end of the month of June, 1918, the *Llandovery Castle* was on her way back to England from Halifax [Nova Scotia], after having carried sick and wounded there. She had on board the crew consisting of 104 men, 30 officers and men of the Canadian Medical Corps, and 14 nurses, a total of 258 persons. There were no combatants on board, and, in particular, no American airmen. The vessel had not taken on board any munitions or other war material. This has been clearly established by the statement of the second officer, the witness Chapman. If a few witnesses draw the inference from the violence of the explosion, which they heard when the vessel went down, that not only the vessel's boilers but also munitions exploded, this is not conclusive in the light of the statement of the expert, Corvette Captain Saalwatcher. From the sound it is not possible to distinguish with certainty between an explosion of a boiler and one of munitions.

In the evening of 27th June, 1918, at about 9:30 (local time) the *Llandovery Castle* was sunk in the Atlantic Ocean, about 116 miles south-west of Fastnet (Ireland), by a torpedo from the German U-boat 86. Of those on board only 24 persons were saved, 234 having been drowned. The commander of U-boat was First Lieutenant Patzig, who was subsequently promoted to captain. His present whereabouts are unknown. The accused Dithmar was the first officer of the watch, and the accused Boldt the second. Patzig recognized the character of the ship, which he had been pursuing for a long time, at the latest when she exhibited at dusk the lights prescribed for hospital ships by the Tenth Hague Convention. In accordance with international law, the German U-boats were forbidden to torpedo hospital ships. According both to the German and British Governments' interpretation of the said Hague Convention, ships, which were used for the transport of military persons wounded and fallen ill in war on land, belonged to this category. The German Naval Command had given orders that hospital ships were only to be sunk within the limits of a certain barred area. However, this area was a long way from the point we have now under consideration. Patzig knew this and was aware that by torpedoing the *Llandovery Castle* he was acting against orders. But he was of the opinion, founded on various information (including some from official sources, the accuracy of which cannot be verified, and does not require to be verified in these proceedings), that on the enemy side, hospital ships were being used for transporting troops and combatants, as well as munitions. He, therefore, presumed that, contrary to international law, a similar use was being made of the *Llandovery Castle*. In particular, he seems to have expected (what grounds he had for this has not been made clear) that she had American airmen on board. Acting on this suspicion, he decided to torpedo the ship, in spite of his having been advised not to do so by the accused Dithmar and the witness Popitz. Both were with him in the conning tower, the accused Boldt being at the depth rudder.

The torpedo struck the *Llandovery Castle* amidship on the port side and damaged the ship to such an extent that she sank in about 10 minutes. There were 19 lifeboats on board. Each could take a maximum of 52 persons. Only two of them (described as cutters) were smaller, and these could not take more than 23 persons. Some of the boats on the port side were destroyed by the explosion of the torpedo. A good number of undamaged boats were, however, successfully lowered. The favorable weather assisted life-saving operations. There was a slight breeze and a slight swell.

* * *

Some time after the torpedoing, the U-boat came to the surface and approached the lifeboats, in order to ascertain by examination whether the *Llandovery Castle*, had airmen and munitions on board. The witness Popitz, who was steerman on board the U-boat, took part in the stopping of several lifeboats for that purpose. The occupants of the captain's boat gave a fuller description of this. It was called by the U-boat, while it was busy rescuing shipwrecked men, who were swimming about in the water. As it did not at once comply with the request to come alongside, a pistol shot was fired as a warning. The order was repeated and the occupants were told that, if the boat did not come alongside at once, it would be fired on with the big gun. The lifeboat then came alongside the U-boat. Capt. Sylvester had to go on board the U-boat. There he was reproached by the commander with having had eight American airmen on board. Sylvester denied this and declared that, in addition to the crew, only Canadian medical corpsmen were in the ship.

* * *

The U-boat then left the captain's boat, but, after moving about for a little time, returned and again hailed it. Although its occupants pointed out that they had already been examined, the captain's boat was again obliged to come alongside the U-boat. The witnesses, Chapman and Barton, the second and fourth officers of the *Llandovery Castle*, were taken on board the U-boat and were subjected to a thorough and close examination. The special charge brought against them was that there must have been munitions on board the ship, as the explosion when the ship went down had been a particularly violent one. They disputed this and pointed out that the violent noise was caused by the explosion of the boilers. They were again released. The U-boat went away and disappeared from sight for a time.

The U-boat soon returned, and made straight for the captain's boat. Its occupants feared lest they might be run down. The U-boat, however, passed by, made a big circle and again made straight for the lifeboat, but when quite close to it, it was steered slightly sideways, so that it passed by without touching the lifeboat. The occupants of the boat nevertheless thought that the U-boat wanted to ram it and thus destroy it. There is, however, no conclusive evidence of this, although suspicion cannot be refuted entirely....

After passing by the second time, the U-boat once more went away. The lifeboat, which had hoisted a sail in the meantime, endeavored to get away. But after a brief period, the occupants of the boat noticed firing from the U-boat. The first two shells passed over the lifeboat. Then firing took place in another direction; about 12 to 14 shots fell all told. The flash at the mouth of the gun and the flash of the exploding shells were noticed almost at the same time, so that, as the expert also assumes, the firing was at a very near target. After firing had ceased, the occupants of the lifeboat saw nothing more of the U-boat.

The captain's boat cruised about for some 36 hours altogether. On the 29th June, in the morning, it was found by the English destroyer *Lysander*. The crew were taken on board and the boat left to its fate. During the 29th June, the commander of the English Fleet caused a search to be made for the other lifeboats of the *Llandovery Castle*. The English sloop *Snowdrop* and four American destroyers systematically searched the area, where the boats from the sunken ship might be drifting about. The *Snowdrop* found an undamaged boat of the *Llandovery Castle* 9 miles from the spot on which the *Lysander* had found the captain's boat. The boat was empty, but had been occupied, as was shown by the position of the sail. According to observations made while passing by, the boat bore the number 6. Otherwise the search which was continued until the evening of the 1st July, in uniformly good weather, remained fruitless. No other boat from the *Llandovery Castle* and no more survivors were found.

The firing from the U-boat was not only noticed by the occupants of the captain's boat. It was also heard by the witnesses Popitz, Knoche, Ney, Tegtmeier and Kass, who were members of the crew of the U-boat.... Witnesses Popitz and Knoche took part in the interrogation, and confirm that no proof was obtained of the misuse of the *Llandovery Castle*.

* * *

The prosecution assumes that the firing of the U-boat was directed against the lifeboats of the *Llandovery Castle*. The court has arrived at the same conclusion as the result of the evidence given at this time.

* * *

...[T]he conduct of Patzig can only be explained on the supposition, that he does not regard himself as guilty only of the inexcusable torpedoing of the *Llandovery Castle*. It is clear that by every means he has endeavored to conceal this event. He made no entry of it in the vessel's log-book. He has even entered on the chart an incorrect statement of the route taken by the ship, showing a track a long way distant from the spot where the torpedoing occurred, so that, in the event of the sinking of the *Llandovery Castle* becoming known, no official enquiries into the matter could connect him with it. But his precautions extended further. The promise to maintain silence, which he extracted from the accused, has already been put in its true light.

* * *

On these various grounds the court has decided that the lifeboats of the *Llandovery Castle* were fired on in order to sink them. This is the only conclusion possible, in view of what has been stated by the witnesses. It is only on this basis that the behavior of Patzig and of the accused men can be explained.

The court finds that it is beyond all doubt that, even though no witness had direct observation of the effect of the fire, Patzig attained his object so far as two of the boats were concerned. The universally known efficiency of our U-boat crews renders is very improbable that the firing on the boats, which by their very proximity would form an excellent target, was without effect. This must be considered in conjunction with the special circumstances in this case.

* * *

The act of Patzig is homicide, according to para. 212 of the Penal Code. By sinking the lifeboats he purposely killed the people who were in them.... He has said that he would torpedo a hospital ship, with all its characteristic markings, in the expectation of being able to prove that it was being used for improper purposes. His hope was in vain. In spite of the most minute investigation, it was not possible for him to obtain any confirmation of his assumption. Then arose the question, how he could avert the evil consequences of his error of judgment. He had to decide quickly: he had to act quickly. Under this pressure of circumstances, he proceeded in a manner which the naval expert rightly described as imprudent.

* * *

The firing on the boats was an offence against the law of nations. In war on land the killing of unarmed enemies is not allowed... similarly in war at sea, the killing of shipwrecked people,, who have taken refuge in lifeboats, is forbidden. It is certainly possible to imagine exceptions to this rule, as, for example, if the inmates of the lifeboats take part in a fight. But there was no such state of affairs in the present case, as Patzig and the accused persons were well aware, when they cruised around and examined the boats.

* * *

The two accused knowingly assisted Patzig in this killing, by the very fact of their having accorded him their support in this manner, which has already been set out. It is not proved that they were in agreement with his intentions. The decision rested with Patzig as the commander. The others who took part in this deed carried out his orders. It must be accepted that the deed was carried out on his responsibility, the accused only wishing to support him therein. A direct act of killing, following a deliberate intention to kill, is not proved against the accused. They are, therefore, only liable to punishment as accessories. (Para 49 of the Penal Code).

* * *

In estimating the punishment, it has, in the first place, to be borne in mind that the principal guilt rests with Commander Patzig, under whose orders the accused acted. They should certainly have refused to obey the order. This would have required a specially high degree of resolution. A refusal to obey the commander on a submarine would have been something so unusual, that it is humanly possible to understand that the accused could not bring themselves to disobey. That certainly does not make them innocent.... They had acquired the habit of obedience to military authority and could not rid themselves of it. This justifies the recognition of mitigating circumstances. In determining the punishment under para. 213, 49, para. 2, 44 of the State Penal Code, a severe sentence must, however, be passed. The killing of defenseless shipwrecked people is an act in the highest degree contrary to ethical principles. It must also not be left out of consideration that the deeds throws a dark shadow on the German fleet, and especially on the submarine weapon which did so much in the fight for the Fatherland. For this reason a sentence of four years' imprisonment on both the accused persons has been considered appropriate.

In accordance with Section 34, para. 1, No. 2, Section 40, para. 1, and Section 36 of the Military Penal Code, the accused Dithmar is dismissed from the service, and the accused Boldt, is condemned to lose the right to wear officer's uniform. [Here follow the signatures of five judges and the Clerk of the Court and the Seal of the Court. Two members of the Court were absent when signatures were affixed].

Suggestions for Further Reading

(1) Adams, Williams, "The American Peace Commission and the Punishment of Crimes Committed During War," 39 *Law Quarterly Review* 245 (1923).

(2) Aufricht, Hans, *Guide to League of Nations Publications: A Biographical Survey of the Works of the League, 1920–1947.* New York: Columbia University Press (1951).

(3) Battle, George C., "The Trials Before the Leipsig Supreme Court of Germans Accused of War Crimes," 8 *Virginia Law Review* 1 (1921).

(4) Beals, Walter, *The First German War Crimes Trial.* Chapel Hill, NC: Documentary Publications (1985).

(5) Bellot, Hugh H. L., "War Crimes and War Criminals," 36 *Canadian Law Times* 754 (1916).

(6) Boyajian, Dickran H., *Armenia: The Case for a Forgotten Genocide.* Westwood, NJ: Educational Book Crafters (1972).

(7)   Boyd, Francis A., *Foundations of World Order: The Legalist Approach to Interna-
      tional Relations (1918–1922)*. Durham, NC: Duke University Press (1999).

(8)   Cadoux, C. J., "The Punishing of Germany After the War of 1914–1918," 43 *Hib-
      bert Journal* 107 (January, 1945).

(9)   Clark, J. B., "Shall There be War After War,?" 11 *American Journal of International
      Law* 790 (1917).

(10) Clarke, R. Floyd, "Germany Under International Law." 53 *American Law Review*
      401 (1919).

(11) Colby, Elbridge, "War Crimes and Their Punishment." 8 *Minnesota Law Review*
      40 (1923).

(12) Commission on the Responsibility of the Authors of the War and on Enforcement
      of Penalties, *Report Presented to the Preliminary Peace Conference*, 14 *American
      Journal of International Law* 95 (1920).

(13) Creel, George, *War Criminals and Punishment*. (ch. 8.). New York: McBride
      (1944).

(14) Dadrian, Vahakn, *The History of the Armenian Genocide*. Providence, RI:
      Berghahn Books (1995).

(15) *Das Diktat von Versailles*. (3 vols.). Essen: Essener Verlagasanstalt (1939).

(16) Davis, George B., "Doctor Francis Leiber's Instruction for the Government of
      Armies in the Field." 1 *American Journal of International Law* 13 (1907).

(17) Dunbabin, J. P., "The League of Nations' Place in the International System," 78
      History 421 (1993).

(18) Dunbar, N. C. H., "Act of State and the Law of War," 75 *Judicial Review* 246
      (1963).

(19) Dyer, Gwynn, "Turkish 'Falsifiers' and Armenian Deceivers: Historiography and
      the Armenian Massacres," 12 *Middle Eastern Studies* 99 (1976).

(20) Erickson, Otto, "A Judicial Reckoning for William Hohenzollern." 22 *Law Notes*
      184 (January, 1919).

(21) Fenwick, Charles C., "Germany and the Crime of the World War," 23 *American
      Journal of International Law* 812 (1929).

(22) Finch, George A., "Jurisdiction of Local Courts to Try Enemy Persons for War
      Crimes," 14 *American Journal of International Law* 218 (1920).

(23) _____, "Superior Orders and War Crimes," 15 *American Journal of Interna-
      tional Law* 440 (1921).

(24) Garner, James W., "Punishment of Offenders Against the Laws and Customs of
      War," 14 *American Journal of International Law* 70 (1920).

(25) Gregory, S. S., "Criminal Responsibility of Sovereigns for Wilfull Violations of the
      Laws of War," 6 *Virginia Law Review* 400 (1920).

(26) Hartigan, Richard S., *Leiber's Code and the Law of War*. Chicago: Precedent (1983).

(27) Jones, Dorothy, *Toward a Just World: The Critical Years in the Search for Interna-
      tional Justice*. Chicago: University of Chicago Press (2002).

(28) Matas, David, "Prosecuting Crimes Against Humanity: The Lessons of World War
      I," 13 *Fordham International Law Journal* 86 (1990).

(29) Mullins, Claude, *The Leipzig Trials: An Account of the War Criminals Trials and a Study of German Mentality*. London: H. F. G. Witherby (1921).

(30) _____, "War Criminals Trials," 116 *Fortnightly Review* 417 (September, 1921).

(31) "Punishing War Criminals: Holland Refuses Extradition of ex-Kaiser—Allies Agree to Trial of 890 Others at Leipsic." 11 *Current History* 375 (1920).

(32) Read, James M., *Atrocity Propaganda, 1914–1918*. New Haven, CT: Yale University Press (1941).

(33) Renault, Louis, "War and the Law of Nations in the 20th Century," 9 *American Journal of International Law* 1 (1915).

(34) *The Armenian Genocide in Perspective* (Richard Hovannisan ed.). New Brunswick, NJ: Rutgers University Press (1986).

(35) *The Kaiser and His Court: Note Books and Letters of Admiral Georg Alexander von Muller, Chief of Naval Cabinet 1914–1918*. London: MacDonald (1961).

(36) "The Leipzig Trials," 310 *Living Age* 241 (1921).

(37) Toynbee, Arnold J., *Armenian Atrocities: The Murder of a Nation*. London: Hadden & Stroughton (1915).

(38) _____, *The German Terror in Belgium: An Historical Record*. New York: Doran (1917).

(39) "Trial of Sovereigns for State and War Offenses," 43 *Judicial Review* 175 (1931).

(40) von Clausewitz, Karl, *War, Politics, and Power: Selections from On War and I Believe and Profess* (Edward M. Collins trans.). Washington, DC: Regnery Gateway (1962).

(41) Willis, William N., *The Kaiser and the Barbarians, An Authoritative Record of the Crimes Committed by the Germans in France and Belgium in the name of War: Together with the Official Reports of the Commission of Enquiry Appointed by King Albert of Belgium*. London: Anglo-Eastern (1914).

(42) Wright, Quincy, "The Legal Liability of the Kaiser," 3 *American Political Science Review* 120 (1919).

Part Two

Weimar Republic: The Nazi Party and German Fascism; World War II and German War Crimes; IMT-Nuremberg; Nuremberg "Subsequent Proceedings"; Other Selected War Crime Cases — Great Britain and Norway (1921–1951)

Editorial Commentary

The German empire came to an end in 1918 with the abdication of Kaiser Wilhelm II and his exile to Holland. This was followed with the passage of the Weimar Constitution on July 31, 1919, that brought into being the Weimar Republic—twentieth century Germany's first taste with popular democratic government. On its face, the Weimar Constitution was a well-drafted and to many an almost perfect instrument for popular sovereignty. In the fourteen years of its existence (1919–1933), the German nation and her politicians were animated by both this organic charter of government and by the provisions of the Treaty of Versailles. These two documents—the Weimar Constitution and the Versailles Treaty—had a profound influence on German politics during the 1920s and the early 1930s. History reveals that neither document was looked upon with any significant degree of public adulation. Both were subjected to mordant criticism by Germans of high and low rank, especially by those who were members of various political fringe groups that seemed to emerge almost overnight from the detritus of World War I.

Fischer, in his recent history of Nazi Germany,[1] notes that

> On January 19, 1919, the German people went to the polls to elect 421
> deputies to the National Constituent Assembly. The task of the assembly was to
> appoint a new government, write a constitution, and conclude peace with the
> Allied Powers.

> On Thursday, February 6, 1919, the National Constituent Assembly began its
> work in the New National Theater in Weimar. Located on the river Ilm about
> 150 miles southwest of Berlin, the city of Weimar had been picked by the
> government as a meeting place of the assembly because it offered a safer en-
> vironment than the volatile capital. Weimar also occupied a special place in
> the hearts of Germans because it was the city of Goethe, Schiller, and
> Herder, the Cynosure of the 'good' Germany of humane poets and philoso-
> phers. Psychologically, therefore, Weimar was not a bad choice for a new de-
> mocratic beginning.[2]

German politics remained volatile throughout the 1920s. The same year the Weimar
Republic came into being found an Austrian national, Adolf Hitler, joining an obscure
Bavarian political party in Munich, founded by Anton Drexler. Drexler called his orga-
nization the German Workers' Party. Adolf Hitler joined this party as member #7 in
September, 1919, and was placed in charge of party propaganda and member recruit-
ment. Schirer[3] informs us that Drexler was

> ...a locksmith by trade, who may be said to have been the actual founder of
> National Socialism. A sickly, bedspeckled man, lacking a formal education,
> with an independent but narrow and confused mind, a poor writer and a
> worse speaker...[4]

It was Drexler's ideas, however, that ignited Adolf Hitler's messianic mission to free
Germany from the perceived shackles of Western-style democracy and the onerous
burdens of the Versailles *diktat* [dictate]. After a brief period of self-doubt about
joining a ready-made political party, Hitler plunged into his new role with both
vigor and imagination. His association with the German Workers' Party also brought
him in contact with two other personalities who had a profound influence on the
subsequent rise of National Socialism — Ernst Röehm and Dietrich Eckart. Röehm
was later to command the *Sturmabteilung* (SA) or "Storm Troopers" as they were
known. The SA became the vanguard of National Socialism and subsequently performed a major portion of the party's "dirty work" for Hitler by guarding Nazi Party
rallies, and, when the occasion demanded, roughing up political opponents and
other obstructionists. Eckart, in Shirer's words, "was often called the spiritual
founder of National Socialism."[5] He was both a journalist and a thespian, and he employed these dual talents to great advantage in the early history of the Nazi Party.
Unlike Röehm, who became for a time a close confidant of Hitler until his assassination in 1934, Eckart died in 1923, apparently of alcoholism. Once Hitler had gained
control of Drexler's nascent political party, he changed the name of the party to the
National Socialist German Workers Party (NSDAP); the date was April 1, 1920.

---

1. Klaus P. Fischer, *Nazi Germany: A New History.* (1995).
2. *Id.* at 55–56.
3. William L. Shirer, *The Rise and Fall of the Third Reich* (1959).
4. *Id.* at 36.
5. *Id.* at 38.

Rather than refer to it by such a lengthy title, the acronym "Nazi" was established as a suitable abbreviation.

Hitler immediately set to work drafting a 25-Point Program with the assistance of Gottfried Feder, a German economist. In essence, this economic blueprint for German resurgence had definite anti-capitalist and anti-semetic overtones. In 1923, Hitler and the Nazis attempted a brazen coup [or *putsch*] to overthrow the Reich government. The scene of the so-called Munich Beerhall Putsch was the Burgerbräukeller some half-mile from the city center. On the evening of November 8–9, 1923, Hitler and a small band of Nazis and fellow sympathizers attempted to march on the Bavarian seat of government, overthrow it and then march on Berlin itself. They were singularly unsuccessful. Sixteen Nazis were killed that evening and scores were wounded when they were confronted by the Bavarian authorities. Two days later, Adolf Hitler was arrested and charged with high treason. He was tried by the People's Court in Munich, found guilty, and sentenced to a five-year prison term in Landsberg Prison with the possibility of parole after six months! His incarceration lasted only nine months, but, during that interval, he dictated to Rudolf Hess his political testament titled *Mein Kampf* [*My Struggle*]. This work, written in a poor and often rambling style, laid out the future dictator's goals for German reconstruction and expansion in a post-World War I world.

Hitler became convinced that electoral politics was the way to power in Germany and, with the able assistance of Gregor and Otto Strasser and the party's propaganda tactition, Dr. Paul Josef Goebbels, the Nazi Party moved out of its south German birthplace to encompass the nation as a whole. The Nazis had only small successes during the 1920s. The first real break came in the local elections held in Thuringia and Saxony in 1930. In those two regions in that year, the NSDAP polled more than ten per cent of all votes cast.

The Nazis were masters at mobilizing support from German workers and conservative elements of the middle class. All of these constituencies shared an intense dislike of Marxism and most were politically alienated from the programs of the Weimar Republic. By the fall of 1930, the NSDAP had become a political party to be reckoned with in a Germany just beginning to feel the real pains of an emerging global economic depression.

Fritzsche[6] notes "that German politics remained so volatile during the 1930s was due to the different emphases both voters and candidates put on the idea of *Volksgemeinschaft*."[7] [Community of the people]. He then goes on to say that

> Adolf Hitler…had grown up politically during the world war…. His vision of a racially pure, economically productive, and militarily powerful Germany led him to seek larger and larger audiences, to engage socialist workers, and to slowly build the machinery of a mass political movement…. A skilled activist and a superb orator, Hitler emerged as a charismatic leader…[8]

* * *

> Nazis did not take over innocent townspeople in some sort of audacious invasion; they gave sharp political definition to imprecisely held affinities and frustrated expectations.[9]

* * *

---

6. Peter Fritzsche, *Germans Into Nazis* (1998).
7. *Id.* at 183–184.
8. *Id.* at 185.
9. *Id.* at 190

Versed in the customs of tavern sociability, open to sympathizers without respect to status, the Nazis appeared to millions of Protestants and Catholics as representative of a genuine people's party.[10]

On the final page of his engaging book, Fritzsche remarks that

National socialism was rooted in the imagination because it appealed to populist aspirations that had been frustrated since German unification and to solidaristic virtues newly kindled by World War I.... Thus even as the Nazis upheld an integral, almost redemptive nationalism, they created new categories of outsiders, enemies, and victims.

Nazism was neither accidental nor unanimous.[11]

Added to the social and political unrest in Weimar Germany, there occurred another series of events that propelled National Socialism into the forefront of national life. Between 1920 and Hitler's assumption of power in 1933, several economic downturns took place. The most devastating of these, at least for the continued viability of the Weimar Republic, was the world-wide depression aggravated by the American stock market crash of October, 1929. Germany had already been under the yoke of the Versailles reparation provisions since the early 1920s. At that time, the Allies had established a committee to determine reparation payments. Until a final figure was determined, Germany was obliged to pay Allied governments an interim sum of 5 billion dollars by May 21, 1921. This figure, by itself, was an astronomical amount for a state to pay for war damages in that era. After the Reparations Committee met, it determined that besides the 5 billion demanded in 1921, Germany was obliged to pay an additional 25 billion dollars, plus other costs. In sum, Germany was to pay the Allies by the year 1963, a total sum of 32 billion, 500 million dollars in reparations! Such a demand was, of course, both outrageous and impossible to meet. As a result of other provisions of the Versailles Treaty, Germany was stripped of her overseas possessions and significant portions of her former continental territory that would have provided at least some basis for wealth generation. Noted international economist, John Maynard Keynes said that "[t]he policy of reducing Germany to servitude for a generation...should be abhorrent and detestable.... Nations are not authorized, by religion or by natural morals, to visit on the children of their enemies the misdoing of parents or rulers."[12] France, especially, and Great Britain to a somewhat lesser degree, demanded the lion's share of German wealth while correspondingly stripping the nation of economically productive regions. Under Versailles, France gained Alsace-Lorraine while the northern portion of Schleswig was awarded to Denmark. Belgium gained the German provinces of Eupen and Malmedy and the Rhineland was occupied by Allied forces. The rich industrial area of the Saarland was placed under international control and France was given the coal fields of the Ruhr. The nation had been split in half by the Treaty of Versailles with East Prussia being separated from the remainder of Germany by the so-called Polish Corridor; this was the Carthaginian Peace Germany was fated to endure before Hitler's ascendency.

By the time the "Great Depression" in the United States had reached international proportions in the early 1930s, Germany's ability to sustain itself as a viable state was in serious question. Under the Versailles Treaty, if Germany failed in making its reparation payments, even more German territory would be seized and occupied in order

---

10. *Id.* at 193.

11. *Id.* at 235.

12. John M. Keynes, *Economic Consequences of the Peace* 225 (1920).

to satiate the onerous conditions of that document. The Germans were thus both economically and politically vulnerable to a leader and a political party that offered them both a return to former geopolitical prominence and one that would free them from a ruinous economic malaise. National Socialism's hour had arrived by 1933. David Lloyd George, Great Britain's able Prime Minister during the Peace Conference of 1919, made a prescient observation about the future of the German State. As quoted by Lentin in his book on Lloyd George,[13] the British Prime Minister remarked that

> You may strip Germany of her colonies, reduce her armaments to a mere police force and her navy to that of a fifth-rate power; all the same, in the end, if she feels that she has been unjustly treated in the peace of 1919, she will find means of exacting retribution from her conquerors.[14]

German retribution would begin apace after Adolf Hitler took the reins of government on January 30, 1933. From 1933 until World War II broke out on September 1, 1939, the Third Reich began to mold both an economic resurrection and a police state that would be the envy of any tyrant.

During the inter-war years, international law had been struggling to define and eventually codify the concept of aggression. The only explicit reference to aggression in the Covenant of the League of Nations was found in Article 10. But that particular provision lost much of its impact because the overriding ambition of the League of Nations was really not to define aggression, but to abolish outright *war* as an instrument of national policy. In other words, war abolition trumped a precise definition of aggression. During the 1920s, the Geneva Protocol Draft of 1924 and the Locarno Treaties of 1925 attempted to establish forms of presumptive aggression, but these met with only limited success. The treaties that emerged from the Locarno Conferences between Germany, Belgium, France, Great Britain and Italy provided, in part, that these nations "will in no case invade each other or resort to war against each other" unless such is mandated in the "exercise of the right of legitimate defense" or "action taken by the Assembly or by the Council of the League of Nations."

All of this, in turn, led ultimately to the signing of the General Treaty for Renunciation of War of August 27, 1928. Known by its more familiar name as the Kellogg-Briand Pact [or Pact of Paris], two key articles in that treaty provided the following:

> Article I. The High Contracting Parties solemnly declare in the names of their respective peoples that they condemn recourse to war for the solution of international controversies, and renounce it as an instrument of national policy in their relations with one another.

> Article II. The High Contracting Parties agree that the settlement or solution of all disputes or conflicts of whatever nature or of whatever origin they may be, which may arise among them, shall never be sought except by pacific means.

A total of sixty-three nations either conformed to or ratified the Kellogg-Briand Pact. It was one of the chief international law precedents invoked by the Allied governments against the major Nazi war criminals at Nuremberg during the course of the IMT and in the various Subsequent Proceedings cases as well as against the Japanese war criminals tried by the IMTFE-Tokyo.

---

13. Anthony Lentin, *Lloyd George and the Lost Peace: From Versailles to Hitler, 1919–1940.* (2001).
    14. *Id.* at 10.

The inter-war years saw the League of Nations having only marginal success in its attempt to dampen international lawlessness. The League, of course, was President Thomas Woodrow Wilson's answer to ending once and for all the destructiveness, both human and material, wrought by the First World War. A native Virginian and the twenty-eighth President of the United States (1913–1921), Wilson was the first Southern post-Civil War Chief Executive. He was also a former governor of New Jersey, an academic holding a Ph.D. degree in American history, President of Princeton University and the recipient of the 1919 Nobel Peace Prize. Woodrow Wilson was also a devout and somewhat doctrinaire Presbyterian. This particular theological trait carried over into his political life. It often prevented him from seeking crucial political compromises with the United States Senate forces arrayed against America's membership in the League of Nations. In order to preserve world peace, the League would have to rely on the doctrine of *multilateralism* set forth in Article 10 of the Covenant and Wilson absolutely refused to either amend or delete it.

In the United States Senate, opposition to the entire concept of a League of Nations and especially to Article 10, was spearheaded by Senator Henry Cabot Lodge the elder, Republican of Massachusetts. Lodge was the Chairman of the powerful Senate Foreign Relations Committee and he, along with a host of his colleagues, believed very strongly that Article 10 imperiled United States sovereignty. To Wilson, however, Article 10 was at the very core of his global multilateral imperative; the United States Senate, on the other hand, demurred.

In order to defend his position before the nation, Wilson embarked on a nation-wide rail tour to swing public opinion in his favor regarding this grand design for world peace through law. It was on this tour on September 25, 1919, after a speech in Pueblo, Colorado, that the President suffered a stroke and had to curtail his national crusade for the League of Nations. Less than two months later, on November 19, 1919, the United States Senate voted 55–39 against League of Nations' membership.

In historical hindsight, it must be said that Woodrow Wilson was probably his own worst enemy when debate on membership in the League of Nations took place. Oftentimes he appeared unbending in his advocacy for a multilateral approach to international relations. David Lloyd George, Great Britain's Prime Minister and the chief British delegate to the Paris Peace Conference of 1919, remarked in his memoirs that "I really think that at first the idealistic president regarded himself as a missionary whose function it was to rescue the poor European heathen from their age-long worship of false and fiery gods." Republican Senator Frank Brandegee of Connecticut commented after meeting with Wilson regarding the Peace Treaty with Germany that it was though "I had been wandering with Alice in Wonderland and had tea with the Mad Hatter."

Despite America's rejection of the League of Nations, the organization initially began to flourish and resolutely adapted its mission to the provisions of the Covenant. Bradford[15] notes that "[r]elative peace and prosperity in the first decade of the League's existence nurtured the establishment of cooperative efforts in economic, social, and, to a lesser extent, security issue areas."[16] It soon became painfully apparent, however, that Wilson's ideal of a treaty-based form of multilateral cooperation would face daunting challenges. With the United States' rejection of the League, France and Great Britain be-

---

15. William C. Bradford, "International Legal Regimes and the Incidence of Interstate War in the Twentieth Century: A Cursory Quantitative Assessment of the Associative Relationship," 16 *Am. U. Int'l L. Rev.* 647 (2001).

16. *Id. at 696.*

came the dominant geopolitical partners in the confederation. Both still colonial powers, they now had to contend with the emerging twentieth century hydra-headed genie
of totalitarianism-strident nationalism, ideological fanaticism and a revitalized form of
imperialism. These together formed the cauldron which gave birth to such phenomena
as National Socialism in Germany, fascism in Mussolini's Italy and Japan's all-consum-
ing imperialistic ambitions in the Far East. "By the mid-1930s," according to Bradford,[17]
"…as expansionist and revionist powers forcibly reshuffled the international system and
insecure states reverted to the dubious shelter of bilateral non-aggression treaties and
regional security arrangements, the League imploded as an institution designed to prevent and punish aggression."[18] In a footnote, Bradford lists the following failures of the
League of Nations during the 1920s and 1930s that preceded World War II:

> (1) the Polish seizure of Vilna (1920); (2) the Lithuanian seizure of Memel
> (1923); (3) the Japanese invasion of Manchuria (1931); and Japan's withdrawal
> from the League to avoid sanctions for the same (1933); (4) the Italian invasion
> of Ethiopia/Abyssinia (1935); (5) the German remilitarization of the
> Rhineland (1936); annexation of the Studentenland (1937); and the annexa-
> tion of Austria (1938); (6) the Russian invasion of Finland (1939) and its ex-
> pulsion from the League for the same (1939); and the German invasion of
> Poland, which sparked World War II…. Although the Japanese refusal to ac-
> cept the recommendations of the League Council to quit Manchuria in Octo-
> ber 1931 inflicted damage on League credibility, the League might have sur-
> vived the Manchurian crisis had it been successful in reversing the Italian
> invasion of Ethiopia. Enforcement failures in China and Africa, however, bred
> enforcement failures in Europe, which utterly destroyed the League as an inter-
> national legal regime. League silence in responding to Nazi expansionism…
> drained the League of all practical and normative force and made global war an
> inevitability.[19]

Could the United States, had it joined the League of Nations, perhaps have prevented
World War II? That is a question no one is really able to answer. Even if the United
States had joined what many consider an impotent organization, America's emerging
power and world influence may have been able to provide a leveling influence on the
geopolitics of the times. Ferrell[20] reminds us that "[I]n 1919 the United States was
strong enough to have made the world safe for democracy. It possessed one of the rich-
est portions of the globe, the world's largest economy, had created the largest army, and
was building the largest navy."[21] Why did Woodrow Wilson fail to compromise with the
United States Senate? Again, Ferrell provides us with a plausible explanation when he
writes that

> Perhaps something in Wilson's Presbyterian soul, or his Princeton experience,
> or the times in which he lived, made compromise difficult if not impossible.
> His life from its beginnings in the manse at Staunton [Virginia] to his acade-
> mic duties at Princeton had taught him to stand for what he believed, and in
> deciding what to believe he did not always choose well…. Princeton may have
> dominated—twenty years on that campus…. The times, too, the high Victo-

17. *Id.* at 696–697.
18. *Id.*
19. *Id.* n. 174 at 697–698.
20. Robert H. Ferrell, *Woodrow Wilson and World War I 1917–1921* (1985).
21. *Id.* at 157.

rian age in which he came to manhood, may have reinforced his impulse to take a stand.... He addressed Congress after little or no consultation, failing to talk with Democrats and Republicans alike.[22]

Ambrosius[23] notes that

> ...Wilson had failed to make the world safe for democracy. Neither the Weimar Republic nor Soviet Russia, which were both excluded from membership in the League, embraced his vision of a new international order. Nor did the Allies entrust their future to this form of collective security.... The president, as he privately acknowledged, was painfully aware that his crusade for democracy had not transformed the Old World.[24]

Because of the wide-ranging and egregious behavior of the Third Reich insofar as specific war crimes are concerned, we will here give only a cursory review of the more gruesome details of German malevolence. More specific accounts will be set forth in the materials surrounding both the IMT-Nuremberg and the subsequent trials conducted under Allied Control Council Law No. 10. Perhaps one of the better brief synopses of Nazi brutality is found in Beigbeder's work[25] on war criminals published in 1999. He comments that

> The killings, devastation, losses and suffering caused by World War II, in the European Theatre, were not only larger than in World War I—ten million deaths in World War I, over 50 million in World War II—but they took another dimension as a result of the racist ideology of the Nazis, which caused the persecution of the Jews followed by their systematic extermination. The harassment and mass murder of Soviet prisoners of war, another class of 'subhumans', was in part due to the racist theories of Aryan superiority over the Slavs, and in part to the political and military struggle between Nazism and Communism. The Nazis had already tested extermination methods on their own citizens, mentally ill, handicapped persons, the infirm and other 'worthless' lives, on the biological altar of 'racial hygiene'; the so-called T4 programme killed 70,000 German victims from 1939 to 1941. Another 30,000 of these 'semi-humans' were eliminated in concentration camps in Mauthausen, in Dachau from 1941 to 1945.
>
> Robert Daniell,...was the British tank commander who in 1945 smashed open the gates of the Nazi concentration camp at Bergen-Belsen, where inmates, most of them Jews, had died for years of starvation, disease and torture. On Daniell's arrival, the camp still held more than 60 000 prisoners. In the first days of their liberation, 14 000 died and as many died in the following weeks.... Rudolf Höess was Commandant of the Auschwitz concentration camp from May 1940 until December 1943. In his testimony at the Nuremberg Tribunal on 15 April 1946...he estimated that 'at least 2,500,000 victims were executed and exterminated by gassing and burning, and at least another half-million succumbed to starvation and disease, making about 3,000,000'. Among them were 'approximately 20,000 Russian prisoners of war'. 'We executed approximately 400,000 Hungarian Jews in the single Auschwitz camp in the Sum-

---

22. *Id.* at 158–159.
23. Lloyd E. Ambrosius, *Wilsonian Statecraft: Theory and Practice of Liberal Internationalism during World War I* (1990).
24. *Id.* at 134–135.
25. Yves Beigbeder, *Judging War Criminals: The Politics of International Justice* (1999).

mer of 1944.' It is now estimated that 5 100 000 persons were murdered between 1941 and 1945 at the instigation of the Nazi power for the only reason
that they were Jews. The victims represented about two-thirds of the Jewish
population of Europe. As from the end of 1942, the Gypsies joined the Jews as
victims of the Nazi racist theories and cruelty: the number of deaths caused by
this other genocide range from 200 000 to 500 000, a genocide which was ignored by the Nuremberg Tribunal. According to a letter from Rosenberg to
Keitel of February 1942, of 3 600 000 Soviet prisoners of war, 'only several
hundred thousand are still able to work fully'. The others have 'starved or died
because of the hazards of the weather'. To these atrocities, one should add the
mass killings of Polish and Russian civilian populations, the deportation of political opponents from occupied countries and forced labour of civilians and
prisoners of war to German factories, as only samples of a global picture of organized terror.[26]

Add to this account the genocide and other atrocities committed by the Japanese in the
Far East and one must conclude that the Second World War was nothing less that barbarity writ large!

It was not until the end of the Second World War in Europe that the full enormity of
Nazi crimes became apparent. Word occasionally leaked out via immigrant groups and
escaped exiles and some of these crimes did come to the attention of the International
Red Cross, some of the Allied leaders and the Vatican. Before a complete military victory could be secured on the Continent, specific details of a large majority of these offenses were missing. Nonetheless, the Allied Powers who prosecuted the war in the European Theatre knew enough about German War crime activity prior to May, 1945, to
begin seriously considering how to proceed with Nazi perpetrators—to either simply
put them before a firing squad without any other legal formality, or, on the other hand,
to bring them to trial before a court established for that purpose. As far back as January
13, 1942, in the St. James Declaration issued at the behest of some nine exile governments, the wording of that document urged the Allied governments to "place among
their principal war aims the punishment, *through the channel of organized justice*" those
who have committed violations of international and military law. [Italics added]. Tusa
and Tusa[27] noted that

> [E]very Allied nation between 1939 and 1945 demanded punishment for those
> who committed war crimes. Criminals of all nations were denounced. During
> the War both German and Allied military authorities held courts martial of
> their own nationals. From 1942 an Extraordinary State Commission in the
> USSR was investigating German war crimes in Russia; in 1943, three German
> officers were tried in Kharkov and shot. Inevitably once the War finished there
> would be many more trials and executions of individuals who had committed
> atrocities. Yet, even more strongly than in the First World War, there was the
> conviction that the enemy's leaders constituted a criminal regime, that the inci-
> dents of atrocity were part of a deliberate policy of crime and that those who
> were most responsible and deserving of severest punishment were the Nazi
> leaders themselves.... In the First World War, the German General Staff and
> government may or may not have condoned war crimes; in the Second it was
> believed that the wholesale nature of such crimes could only be explained by

---

26. *Id.* at 29–31.
27. Ann Tusa, and John Tusa, *The Nuremberg Trial* (1990).

deliberate intention and use of resources—they were way beyond the nature and number to be expected simply from the vicious behavior of criminal individuals and groups.[28]

In 1943 the United Nations War Crime Commission was established in London to collect, review, collate and evaluate information coming to it about German war crime culpability. Seventeen nations composed this commission, although the USSR was not a member. Apparently, Stalin demanded that all Soviet Republics be included on the Commission. His request was not granted, hence Russia refused to join. Also in 1943, at the Moscow Foreign Ministers Conference, the Allies established what amounted to two groups of war criminals:

> ...national action for localized offences, and international action for those whose criminal orders had applied in several countries. But there was one important omission in the Moscow Declaration—there was no mention of trial before punishment for the major criminals. Indeed talk of punishment by 'joint declaration' seems to preclude trial. Why was there no mention of judicial proceedings? Was it the memory of the practical difficulties and the final farce of the Versailles discussions and the Leipzig trials? Or was it that the foreign ministers reckoned that justice was too good for such men?... There is... evidence that those present did not think the fate of leading Nazi criminals merited much time or trouble. At Moscow the U.S. Secretary of State, Cordell Hull, actually said: 'If I had my way I would take Hitler and Mussolini and Tojo and their accomplices and bring them before a drumhead court martial, and at sunrise the following morning there would occur an historic incident.'[29]

President Roosevelt and various other members of his administration had made general comments about the shocking nature of alleged Nazi crimes almost since the beginning of the war. But the Allies did not really get down to seriously considering what procedure to employ in dealing with Nazi criminals until after Allied forces had broken out of the Normandy beaches and headed inland into France. Another outspoken member of President Roosevelt's cabinet, Secretary of the Treasury Henry Morgenthau, Jr., supported a plan that called for "pasturalization" of Germany. It was Morgenthau's view that the German nation essentially be "plowed under" and converted into one giant pasture in central Europe! Morgenthau, like Cordell Hull, was of the opinion that the major German war criminals be summarily shot. On the opposite side of this issue stood Secretary of War Henry Stimson who opted, not for summary execution, but for a trial of those charged with major war crimes. Stimson was also adamantly opposed to Morgenthau's "pasturalization" plan.

The British, likewise, were initially in favor of summary execution and were leary that a trial of the major Nazi defendants might create more problems that it would solve. The early British view, in a nutshell, was that it would be far too impractical to hold a joint trial between the European Allies and the United States. Eventually, the Americans and the British decided at the Quebec Conference that Morgenthau's harsh solution be adopted. Things stood at that juncture until a member of the United States War Department's Personnel Branch stepped in and argued convincingly for a trial of

---

28. *Id.* at 20.
29. *Id.* at 24.

the Nazis that reinforced Secretary of War Stimson's point of view. Lt. Colonel Murray C. Bernays outlined a very comprehensive strategy that suggested a trial of both leading Nazi war criminals as well as Nazi *organizations*. Bernays opposed summary executions of German war criminals precisely because he felt very strongly that a trial would have a positive educative effect on both the German people and on the entire international community as well. He was also of the opinion that summary executions would run the risk of making martyrs of the offenders so judged. Subsequently, as the Allied advance continued on both fronts and inevitably squeezed Nazi Germany further and further into a giant vise, an incident occurred during the Battle of the Bulge in December, 1944, that assured the eventual implementation of a modified form of the Bernays Plan. On December 17, 1944, near the Belgian village of Malmédy, the 1st SS Panzer Regiment under the command of Lt. Colonel Joachim Peiper, captured and then murdered seventy-two American prisoners of war and left their bodies in a frozen, snow-covered field. This was apparently the first time during the European war that there had been a wholesale butchery of American servicemen by the Waffen SS. Public opinion was outraged and the Roosevelt Administration, taking note of this state of affairs, began clearly to see the utility of providing a trial for Nazi war crimes, not only to establish individual culpability, but also to establish *organizational* guilt.

Finally, the British changed their position when both France and the USSR agreed to a trial instead of other means of punishment. Some also suggest that Britain's change of mind might have been influenced by the fact that Adolf Hitler, Heinrich Himmler, Josef Goebbels and Benito Mussolini were all deceased by the late Spring of 1945. Whatever the reasons, the Allied Powers were now at least all on the same page insofar as the *form* to employ in the adjudication of guilt or innocence. The details that form would take would be worked out in London from June to August, 1945.

Thus, in the summer of 1945, Great Britain, the Free French, the Union of Soviet Socialist Republics and the United States of America negotiated, then drafted, then signed the Treaty of London, better known as the London Charter. This instrument served as the legal basis for charging, trying and punishing the leading surviving Nazi war criminals of World War II. Thus the IMT-Nuremberg became a multinational and not a unilateral effort by the Allied Powers to bring to justice those persons and organizations that unleashed upon the world a horror almost incomprehensible.

After extensive discussion, the Four Powers agreed in London to try the major Nazi war criminals within a modified Anglo-American form of trial procedure which included some characteristics of the continental European system. Several of the nettlesome problems confronting the delegates to the London conference were whether or not to charge the future defendants with the crime of conspiracy. Conspiracy is a criminal offense recognized only in Anglo-American law, not in the law of continental Europe, nor in the Soviet system of criminal law. The Americans, however, were adamant in their demand to insert a conspiracy count in the formal charges. The three remaining Allies finally agreed to have a charge of conspiracy included. The Soviet Union, in turn, desired to limit the charged crimes to those acts committed by the European Axis. The Russians feared that if the secret protocol of their non-aggression pact with Nazi Germany in 1939 became known, they too could be charged with the crime of aggression against Poland. This very real and explosive issue was solved by having language in the Charter state that the purpose of the International Military Tribunal was simply to prosecute crimes of the Axis. By so doing, the Russians were freed from having to sit in judgment of the self-same state behavior they committed in flagrant violation of international law.

The London Charter was signed on August 8, 1945. Among some of the Charter's more noteworthy provisions were (1) the establishment of an International Military Tribunal (IMT) for the trial of the major Nazi war criminals; (2) the setting forth of four charges against those to be tried, namely: (i) the Common Plan or Conspiracy; (ii) Crimes Against Peace; (iii) War Crimes; and (iv) Crimes Against Humanity; (3) disallowing the defense of "act of State" and "Superior orders," (4) defendants had no right to appeal an adverse judgment; and (5) the jurisdiction of the IMT could not be challenged by any of its members, nor by either the prosecution or defense. Six Nazi organizations were also declared to be criminal: (i) the Reich Cabinet (*die Reichsregierung*); (ii) the Leadership Corps of the Nazi Party (*das Korps der Politischen Leiter der National Sozialiltischen Deutschen Arbeiterpartei*); (iii) the SS (*die Schutzstaffeln*); (iv) the Gestapo (*die Geheime Staatspolizei*); (v) the SA (*die Sturmabteilungen der N. S. D. A. P.*): and (vi) the German General Staff and the High Command of the Armed Forces.

The tribunal consisted of eight jurists, a senior judge and an alternate from each of the four victorious powers. Before its work was concluded, the IMT had held a total of 403 public sessions with thirty-three witnesses for the prosecution and sixty-one for the defense. At first blush, these figures seem rather miniscule for a trial of this scope and length, but it must be remembered that the vast amount of evidence introduced at Nuremberg, especially for the prosecution, was *documentary* in nature. The Germans had the habit of keeping detailed written records of most of their nefarious activities, and the Allied prosecutors employed these written documents to good advantage. Thus, in a manner of speaking, the Nazis hoisted themselves on their own petard. Nineteen of the twenty-four defendants took the witness stand in their own behalf. In all, 38,000 affidavits were submitted on behalf of the political leaders, 136,000 on behalf of the SS, 7,000 on behalf of the General Staff and 2,000 on behalf of the Gestapo.

The trial commenced on the afternoon of November 20, 1945, in the Palace of Justice located in Fürth, a Nuremberg suburb. Sir Geoffrey Lawrence of Great Britain opened the initial session. The prosecution's case-in-chief took slightly over five months. The trial generated twenty-four written volumes of evidence, plus countless other pieces of documentation.

The four permanent judges of the tribunal and their alternates were: (1) Lord Justice Sir Geoffrey Lawrence, president of the Tribunal and his alternate, Justice Norman Birkett (Great Britain); (2) Mr. Francis Biddle and his alternate, Judge John J. Parker (United States); (3) Professeur Donnediue de Vabres and his alternate, Le Conseiller Robert Falco (France); and (4) Major General I. T. Nikitchenko and his alternate, Lieutenant Colonel A. F. Volchkov (U. S. S. R.).

The chief prosecutors were Sir Hartley Shawcross (Great Britain); United States Supreme Court Associate Justice, Robert H. Jackson (United States); M. Francois de Menthon and M. Auguste Champetier De Ribes (France); and General R. A. Rudenko (U. S. S. R.). The defendants were allowed counsel of their own choosing or appointed counsel, as desired. The trial itself was conducted under Anglo-American accusatorial practice with opening and closing statements, examination and cross-examination of witnesses, authentication and introduction of documentary evidence and with the panel of judges sitting as impartial referees rather than as active participants in the proceedings as under continental European practice.

Each prosecuting team was assigned the task of presenting evidence relative to each of the four charges leveled at the defendants. The conspiracy or "common plan" to commit the substantive charges was assigned to the United States. The British prosecution team handled the charges alleging that the defendants promoted aggressive warfare in violation of existing international treaties and agreements. The French and the Soviet prosecution teams were assigned the task of proof of war crimes and crimes against humanity by the Third Reich in both Western and Eastern Europe, respectively.

The twenty-four leading Nazis charged were: (1) Hermann Wilhelm Göering, Commander-in-Chief of the Luftwaffe (*OberKommando der Luftwaffe*) and successor, until near war's end, to Adolf Hitler; (2) Richard Rudolf Hess, Deputy Füehrer and successor-designate to Adolf Hitler after Göering, until his bizarre flight to England on May 10, 1941; (3) Joachim von Ribbentrop, Reich Minister for Foreign Affairs; (4) Robert Ley, Leader of the German Labor Front; (5) Wilhelm Keitel, Chief of the High Command of the German Armed Forces (*OberKommando der Wehrmacht*-OKW); (6) Ernst Kaltenbrunner, Chief of the Security Police and Security Service; (7) Alfred Rosenberg, Reich Minister for Occupied Eastern Territories and Nazi Party "philosopher': (8) Hans Frank, Governor-General of Occupied Poland; (9) Wilhelm Frick, Reich Minister of the Interior; (10) Julius Streicher, Editor-in-Chief of the anti-Semitic Nuremberg newspaper, *Der Stuermer*; (11) Walter Funk, President of the Reichsbank; (12) Hjalmar Schact, Reich Minister of Economics; (13) Gustav Krupp von Bohlen und Halbach, German armaments manufacturer; (14) Karl Döenitz, Commander-in-Chief of U-boats and the final testamentary successor to Adolf Hitler; (15) Erich Raeder, Commander-in-Chief of the Navy (*OberKommando der Kreigsmarine*); (16) Baldur von Schirach, Leader of the Hitler Youth (*Hitler Jügend*); (17) Fritz Saukel, Plenipotentiary for the Employment of Labor and the Gauleiter of Vienna; (18) Alfred Jodl, Chief of the Operations Staff of the Army High Command (*OberKommando des Heeres*-OKH); Franz von Papen, Vice-Chancellor to Adolf Hitler; (20) Arthur Seyss-Inquart, Reich Commisar for the Occupied Netherlands and the Austrian quisling;[30] (21) Albert Speer, Plenipotentiary for Armaments; (22) Constantin von Neurath, Reich Commisar for Occupied Czechoslovakia and Adolf Hitler's first Foreign Minister; (23) Hans Fritsche, Head of the Radio Division of the Department of Propaganda of the Nazi Party; and (24) Martin Bormann, Head of the Nazi Party Chancellory in Berlin and Keeper of "Hitler's Purse." A more complete background of these defendants appear in *Table I. (infra)*.

Of the twenty-one defendants physically present in the dock at time of sentencing, eleven received the penalty of death by hanging (Göering; von Ribbentrop; Keitel; Kaltenbrunner; Rosenberg; Frank; Frick; Streicher; Saukel; Jodl and Seyss-Inquart); seven received varying terms of imprisonment (Hess-life; Funk-life; Döenitz-ten years; Raeder-life; von Schirach-twenty years; Speer-twenty years; and von Neurath-fifteen years). Three were acquitted (Schacht; von Papen and Fritzsche). Robert Ley and Hermann Wilhelm Göering committed suicide while in custody. Gustav Krupp was judged to be too ill to stand trial and Martin Bormann was charged, tried, convicted and sentenced to death *in absentia*.

The prosecutors presented their case against each of the twenty-one defendants and charged organizations largely from written and photographic documents confiscated from the Germans by the advancing Allied forces. For example, under the conspiracy or common plan count of the indictment, the American prosecution team argued that a conspiracy to wage aggressive war, commit war crimes and crimes against humanity

---

30. The term "quisling" means "a person who betrays his own country by aiding an invading enemy, often serving later in a puppet government; fifth columnist. [after Vidkun *Quisling* (1887–1940), pro-Nazi Norwegian leader]," according to the *Random House Dictionary of the English Language* (unabridged ed.). 1181 (1967).

had been in place in Germany for a number of years, stretching supposedly as far back as the founding of the Nazi Party in 1919 up to the end of Hitler's Third Reich in May, 1945. Employing commentary from Hitler's *Mein Kampf*, published in 1925, and other various documents recording the history of the rise of National Socialism during the 1920s and the 1930s, the prosecution established what to it was a *prima facie* case of an organized criminal conspiracy to not only take over the German state, but to also launch a war of aggression in direct violation of treaties and protocols Germany had signed between Versailles in 1919 and her invasion of Poland on September 1, 1939. In particular, the conspiracy allegation was evidenced by: (1) the Nazi's disregard and repudiation of the Treaty of Versailles; (2) the Nazi acquisition of territories lost by Imperial Germany at the conclusion of World War I; (3) the systematic persecution and genocide of both German and other European Jews, gypsies, refugees and other *Untermenschen* (subhumans); (4) the Nazi regimentation of German Youth; (5) the destruction of German trade unions by Nazi Party directives; (6) the Third Reich's withdrawal from the League of Nations; (7) the Third Reich's initiation of aggressive war against a total of thirteen nations, beginning with Poland in 1939; and (8) by the introduction of compulsory military service throughout the Third Reich. Additionally, the common plan or conspiracy to wage aggressive war was buttressed by Hitler's so-called "Twenty-Five Points" of the National Socialist German Workers' Party which were included in his blueprint for world conquest in *Mein Kampf*.

Additionally, the prosecution alleged the commission of war crimes and crimes against humanity by the Third Reich in: (1) the torture and ill-treatment of prisoners-of-war; (2) the torture and ill-treatment of civilian populations for use as slave labor in German defense and public works projects; (3) the capturing and execution of hostages in civilian populations in nations and territories occupied by the Third Reich; (4) the systematic plundering of both public and private property in occupied territories in order to provide for the German war machine; and (5) the needless and wanton destruction of cities and towns by German armed forces which were without any military significance.

The major defenses raised by the Germans at Nuremberg were: (1) the *ex post facto* nature of the crimes charged against the accused; (2) the fact that international law, in the eyes of the accused, is concerned with acts of sovereign states only and provides no rationale for the punishment of individuals as such; (3) that individuals are not personally responsible for "acts of State"; and (4) that the obedience to superior orders (political or military) is a defense to criminal charges. None of these defenses were accepted by the Tribunal. The IMT officially concluded on October 1, 1946. All of the defendants sentenced to death by hanging were executed during the early morning hours of October 16, 1946, on gallows erected inside the prison gymnasium. Their bodies were cremated and their ashes disposed of at an unknown location in order to avoid the possibility that gravesites might serve as shrines for neo-Nazis, both in Germany and elsewhere.

The conclusion of the IMT-Nuremberg represented only what may be described as Phase One of war crime trials in Germany in the immediate post-war era. In addition to those tried, convicted and sentenced by the IMT, numerous other German nationals and those who assisted the Nazis in their reign of terror, were brought to trial in proceedings in the Allied Four Power Zones of Germany. When the Third Reich collapsed in May, 1945, Germany was left without a national government. The United States, Great Britain, France and the U.S.S.R. then became, for the time, the successor government of Germany until the political situation stabilized and the government of the newly-created state of West Germany could assume its role in world affairs. The Soviets, of course, created their own puppet state of East Germany, and this division existed until the fall of the Soviet Union in 1991.

Phase Two of the war crime trials in Germany were held under the auspices of Allied Control Council Law No. 10. Each of the Allied nations established tribunals in their own sectors to charge, try and convict individuals of war crimes in their respective jurisdictions, or elsewhere. Many of these trials lasted through the late 1940s and some into the early 1950s. Eventually, emerging Cold War politics between the West and the U.S.S.R. terminated the trials of lesser German war criminals, along with the creation of the new West German state whose view of continued war crime trials was looked upon with disfavor.

The IMT-Nuremberg set a benchmark in international criminal justice in several distinct ways. Among the more important general "principles' emerging from that proceeding were: (1) that international law must take into account individual rights, not those affecting state interests *per se*; (2) that concepts of "justice' and "morality" are not exclusive to one another in international law; (3) that the law of nations may take primacy over the concept of "sovereignty" in particular contexts; and (4) that private citizens, not just politicians and military personnel, have certain responsibilities under international law. These principles will emerge from the materials that follow. We will commence *Part Two* with the end of World War I and establishment of the Weimar Republic that replaced the Hohenzollern Empire.

---

1. Excerpts from the Weimar Constitution

(1919)

(*Die Anfange der Weimarer Republik,* August 11, 1919)

The German people, united in its tribes and inspired with the will to renew and strengthen its Reich in liberty and justice, to serve peace inward and outward and to promote social progress, has adopted this constitution.

First Part

Composition of the Reich and Its Responsibility

First Chapter: The Reich and the States

Article 1

The German Reich is a republic.

State authority derives from the People.

Article 4

The generally recognized rules of international law are valid as binding elements of German Reich law.

Article 17

Every state must have the constitution of a free state. State parliaments must be elected in a general, equal, immediate and secret ballot, in which all Reich German men and women participate, according to the principles of representative election. The state government requires the confidence of the state parliament....

Second Chapter: The Reichstag

Article 20

The Reichstag is composed by the representatives elected by the German people.

Article 21

Members of parliament represent the entire nation. They have to follow nothing but their conscience and they are not bound to instructions.

Article 22

Members of parliament are elected in a general, equal, immediate and secret election; voters are men and women older than 20 years; the election is held according to the principles of representation election....

Article 26

Reichstag elects its president, its vice-president and its secretaries. Reichstag establishes its rules of procedure.

Third Chapter: The Reich President and Reich Government

Article 41

The Reich President is elected by the entire German nation. Every German who has finished the 35th year of his life is eligible. Further details are provided by a Reich law.

Article 45

When it comes to international law, the Reich is represented by the Reich President. He concludes alliances and other treaties with foreign powers in the name of the Reich. He accredits and receives ambassadors.

War can only be declared and peace only be signed by Reich law. Alliances and treaties which relate to matters of Reich legislation require the approval of the Reichstag.

Article 47

The Reich President has the supreme command over the armed forces, in their entirety.

Article 48

If a state does not fulfill the obligations laid upon it by the Reich constitution or the Reich laws, the Reich President may use armed force to cause it to oblige.

In case public safety is seriously threatened or disturbed, the Reich President may take the measures necessary to reestablish law and order, if necessary using armed force. In the pursuit of this aim he may suspend the civil rights described in articles 114, 115, 117, 118, 123, 124, and 154, partially or entirely....

Article 50

All orders and edicts by the Reich President, including such pertaining to the armed force, in order to gain validity, require the countersignature of the Reich Chancellor or the responsible Reich ministers. The countersignatory assumes responsibility.

Article 52

The Reich government consists of the chancellor and the Reich ministers.

Fourth Chapter: The Reichsrat

Article 60

To represent the German states in Reich legislation and administration, a Reichstag is formed.

Sixth Chapter: Reich Administration

Article 78

Foreign relations are a matter of the Reich exclusively. In matters which underlie state legislation, the states may sign treaties with foreign countries; these treaties have to be approved by the Reich.

Article 79

Reich defense is a Reich matter. Military service will be regulated and uniform, with consideration to regional traditions.

Seventh Chapter: Jurisdiction

Article 102

Judges are independent and subject only to the law.

Article 104

Judges serving ordinary jurisdiction are appointed for a lifetime....

Article 105

Extraordinary courts are inadmissible. Nobody may be deprived of his ordinary judge. Legal regulations concerning military jurisdiction and court martial are not affected hereby....

Article 108

In accordance with a law, a supreme court will be established for the German Reich.

Second Part

Basic Rights and Obligations of the Germans

First Chapter: The Individual

Article 109

All Germans are equal in front of the law.

In principle, men and women have the same rights and obligations. Legal privileges or disadvantages based on birth or social standing are to be abolished....

No German may accept titles or orders from a foreign government.

Article 110

Nationality in the Reich and in the states is acquired and lost according to the specifications of a Reich law. Every state national simultaneously is a Reich national.

Every German, in every state, enjoys the same rights and obligations as the respective state nationals.

Article 118

Every German is entitled, within the bounds set by general law, to express his opinion freely in word, writing, print, image or otherwise.... There is no censorship; in case of the cinema, other regulations may be established by law. Also in order to combat trashy and obscene literature, as well as for the protection of the youth in public exhibitions and performances legal measures are permissible.

Second Chapter: Life Within a Community

Article 123

All Germans have the right to assemble peacefully and unarmed; such assemblies do not require any prior notification or special permit. A Reich law can require prior notification for assemblies taking place in the open, and it can, in case of imminent danger for public security, stipulate that such assemblies in the open may be prohibited.

Article 124

All Germans are entitled, for means which do not conflict with penal laws, to form clubs or societies. This right may not be limited by preventive measures. These regulations also apply for religious societies.

Every club is free to acquire legal capacity. No club may be denied of it because of it pursuing political, socio-political or religious goals.

Third Chapter: Religion and Religious Communities

Article 135

All Reich inhabitants enjoy full freedom of liberty and conscience. Undisturbed practice of religion is guaranteed by the constitution and is placed under the protection of the state. General state laws are not affected thereby.

Article 137

There is no state church.

Freedom to form religious communities is guaranteed. Regarding the unification of religious communities within the Reich territory there are no limitations....

Article 140

Soldiers have to be given appropriate free time to fulfill their religious obligations.

[As expected, the Weimar Constitution came in for its share of both fulsome praise and robust criticism. Two noted historians of Nazi Germany give contrasting views. Shirer[31] remarks that

> The constitution which emerged from the Assembly after six months of debate...was, on paper, the most liberal and democratic document of its kind the twentieth century had seen, mechanically well-nigh perfect, full of ingenious and admirable devices which seemed to guarantee the working of an almost flawless democracy. The idea of cabinet government was borrowed from England and France, of a strong popular President from the United States, of the referendum from Switzerland. An elaborate and complicated system of proportional representation and voting by lists was established in order to prevent the wasting of votes and give small minorities a right to be represented in Parliament. The wording of the Weimar Constitution was sweet and eloquent to the ear of any democratically minded person.[32]

Fischer,[33] on the other hand, notes that

---

31. William L. Shirer, *The Rise and Fall of the Third Reich* (1959).
32. *Id.* at 56–57.
33. *Supra.* note 1.

[t]he Weimar Constitution was a hodge-podge of principles drawn from Socialist and liberal agendas; it represented so much confusion in regard to economic objectives and unresolved class conflicts that German democracy was stymied from the beginning.

Although an impressive democratic document, the Weimar Constitution contained a number of provisions that could be construed autocratically as well as democratically.... The central government gained sole control over the armed forces; directed all matters pertaining to foreign policy; raised and levied taxes as required; and made all civil servants, formerly subject to the states, directly responsible to Berlin.... Even the name of the new nation did not differ from the old one, for the framers of the constitution, in their eagerness to preserve a sense of historical continuity, retained the word *Reich* in referring to the new republic. It was not clear just how the idea of empire, with all the imperial symbols it evoked, and the idea of a democratic republic could be harmonized. The truth was that the contradictions inherent in such efforts caused psychic dissonances that were made all the more acute by the pressures of economic hardship and national humiliation.[34]

Fischer's reference to "economic hardship" perhaps was an understatement. Germany's post-war economy was extremely fragile and sensitive to economic turbulence throughout the 1920s].

---

2. Richard Overy, "Weimar Germany" in *The Penguin Historical Atlas of the Third Reich*
12–13 (1996)

From *The Penguin Historical Atlas of the Third Reich* by Richard Overy,
Copyright © 1996 by Richard Overy. Used by permission
of Penguin Group (UK) Ltd.

...In January, 1919, a Constitutional Assembly was elected and was dominated by the moderate parties of the center and left. Meeting at Weimar... the delegates approved a democratic constitution.

The new regime faced enormous difficulties. Domestic order was restored with the help of the army and volunteer forces (*Freikorps*) many of whom were violently hostile to democracy. A crippling peace treaty was signed with the Allies in June 1919. The economy was in deep crisis. A 150 billion marks debt was inherited from the war which weakened the German currency. The low output of food and industrial goods and high state spending to cope with demobilization all fuelled inflation. After a brief period of stabilization in 1921, helped by large loans from abroad, the murder of Foreign Minister Walther Rathenau in June 1922 precipitated a speculative crisis. The mark plunged on world currency markets. When France and Belgium occupied the Ruhr industrial area in January 1923 it was only one-trillionth of its value in 1914 and the state's massive war debt was reduced to only 15 pfennings. In December 1923 a package was agreed by Germany and the Allied powers to refund the German currency and in 1924 a measure of financial and economic stability was at last introduced, at the cost of impoverishing millions of German savers.

---

34. *Id.* at 56–57.

During the following four years a fragile peace returned to German politics. Between 1919 and 1923 the state had been faced with coup attempts from right and left, of which the most serious, the army-backed Kapp Putsch of 1920, was only overturned by a General Strike called in Berlin. German society was bitterly divided. The nationalist right was completely unreconciled to the parliamentary state. They blamed Jews and Marxists for Germany's defeat and the problems of democracy. Anti-semitism became the hallmark of the radical right and led to regular attacks on synagogues and the desecration of Jewish graveyards. Despite the disarmament of Germany enforced through the peace settlement, the army kept alive the skeleton of military organization, and secretly developed weapons. Popular militarism continued to flourish, and manifested itself in the growth of para-military organizations tied to the parties of both right and left.

---

3. Richard Overy, "The German Slump" in *The Penguin Historical Atlas of the Third Reich*
16–17 (1996)
From The Penguin Historical Atlas of the Third Reich by Richard Overy, Copyright © 1996 by Richard Overy. Used by permission of Penguin Group (UK) Ltd.

The effort to restore economic and political stability in Germany between 1924 and 1928 was destroyed by the economic recession between 1928 and 1932. For many Germans the slump was the final straw after defeat, revolution and inflation. Parliamentary politics was undermined and the moderate centre-ground collapsed.... When the first signs of recession appeared in 1928 confidence soon evaporated. Well before the Wall Street Crash marked the end of American, and world, prosperity in October 1929, the Germany economy was in decline. There were 3 million registered unemployed in February 1929. The German downturn became an economic disaster when it coincided with the wider world crisis. Loans were called in which could not easily be repaid. World trade slumped, cutting German exports in half. Prices, output and employment fell sharply precipitating the worst business slump in German history.... In 1930 the centre-left coalition in the Reichstag collapsed and the new Chancellor, the Catholic politician, Heinrich Bruning, ruled largely by Presidential emergency decree. Parliamentary government became almost superfluous and public confidence in democracy evaporated. In the 1930 Reichstag election the Nazi Party made its first real electoral breakthrough, but the Communist Party, formed in 1919 during the revolutionary crisis, began to attract the votes of urban workers disillusioned with social-democracy and the failure of German capitalism. In the major cities the radical left and right fought running street battles which left hundreds dead. By early 1932 Communist membership rose to 287,000. It was particularly strong in Saxony, Berlin and the northern port cities. In June 1932 the party set up an Anti-Fascist Action Front to organize a concerted fight against Nazism, but its continued hostility to the SPD, [Social Democratic Party] which was regarded as a reactionary 'social fascist' party, weakened its appeal. The revival of the revolutionary threat from the left did more than anything during the slump to push centre and right-wing voters towards the nationalist extremes. The centre-right parties collapsed electorally. With more than 8 million people out of work in 1932 moderate solutions no longer appealed.

---

4. Kellogg-Briand Peace Pact (Pact of Paris)

August 27, 1928, 46 Stat. 2343, 94 L. N. T. S. 57

THE PRESIDENT OF THE GERMAN REICH, THE PRESIDENT OF THE UNITED STATES OF AMERICA, HIS MAJESTY THE KING OF THE BELGIANS, THE PRESIDENT OF THE FRENCH REPUBLIC, HIS MAJESTY THE KING OF GREAT BRITAIN, IRELAND AND THE BRITISH DOMINIONS BEYOND THE SEAS, EMPEROR OF INDIA, HIS MAJESTY THE KING OF ITALY, HIS MAJESTY THE EMPEROR OF JAPAN, THE PRESIDENT OF THE REPUBLIC OF POLAND, THE PRESIDENT OF THE CZECHOSLOVAK REPUBLIC.

Deeply sensible of their solemn duty to promote the welfare of mankind;

persuaded that the time has come when a frank renunciation of war as an instrument of national policy should be made to the end that the peaceful and friendly relations now existing between their peoples may be perpetuated;

Convinced that all changes in their relations with one another should be sought only by pacific means and be the result of a peaceful and orderly process, and that any signatory Power which shall hereafter seek to promote its national interests by resort to war should be denied the benefits furnished by this Treaty;

Hopeful that, encouraged by their example, all the nations of the world will join in this humane endeavor and by adhering to the present Treaty as soon as it comes into force bring their peoples within the scope of its beneficent provisions, thus uniting the civilized nations of the world in a common renunciation of war as an instrument of their national policy;

Have decided to conclude a Treaty and for that purpose have appointed as their respective Plenipotentiaries...[here is then listed seventeen Plenipotentiaries (or delegates) that put their signatures to the Treaty] who, having communicated to one another their full powers found in good and due form have agreed upon the following articles:

Article I

The High Contracting Parties solemnly declare in the names of their respective peoples that they condemn recourse to war for the solution of international controversies, and renounce it, as an instrument of national policy in their relations with one another.

Article II

The High Contracting Parties agree that the settlement or solution of all disputes or conflicts of whatever nature or of whatever origin they may be, which may arise among them, shall never be sought except by pacific means.

Article III

The present Treaty shall be ratified by the High Contracting Parties named in the Preamble in accordance with their respective constitutional requirements, and shall take effect as between them as soon as all their several instruments of ratification shall have been deposited at Washington.

This Treaty shall, when it comes into effect as prescribed in the preceding paragraph, remain open as long as may be necessary for adherence by all the other Powers of the

World. Every instrument evidencing the adherence of a Power shall be deposited at Washington and the Treaty shall immediately upon such deposit become effective as between the Power thus adhering and the other Powers party hereto.

It shall be the duty of the Government of the United States to furnish each Government named in the Preamble and every Government subsequently adhering to this Treaty with a certified copy of the Treaty and of every instrument of ratification or adherence. It shall also be the duty of the Government of the United States telegraphically to notify such Governments immediately upon the deposit with it of each instrument of ratification or adherence.

IN FAITH WHEREOF the respective Plenipotentiaries have signed this Treaty in the French and English languages both texts having equal force, and hereunto affix their seals.

DONE at Paris, the twenty-seventh day of August in the year one thousand nine hundred and twenty-eight. [here follows the names of the major signatories, including Frank B. Kellogg, Secretary of State of the United States].

AND WHEREAS it is stipulated in the said Treaty that it shall take effect as between the High Contracting Parties as soon as all the several instruments of ratification shall have been deposited at Washington;

AND WHEREAS the said Treaty has been duly ratified on the parts of all the High Contracting Parties and their several instruments of ratification have been deposited with the Government of the United States of America, the last on July 24, 1929;

NOW THEREFORE, be it known that I, Herbert Hoover, President of the United States of America, have caused the said Treaty to be made public, to the end that the same and every article and clause thereof may be observed and fulfilled with good faith by the United States and the Citizens thereof....

[The Kellogg-Briand Pact became effective less than three months before the Wall Street Crash of October, 29, and less than six months before the beginning of the turbulent destabilizing decade of the 1930s. Dr. Gustav Stresemann, Minister of Foreign Affairs for the German Reich signed this instrument on behalf of the Weimar Republic, while Count Uchida, Privy Councilor, signed for the Emperor of Japan. Besides these and other signatories to the Treaty, the following states, possessions, territories and kingdoms deposited at Washington, DC, instruments of definitive adhesion: Afghanistan; Albania; Australia; Austria; Bulgaria; Canada; China; Cuba; Denmark; Dominican Republic; Egypt; Estonia; Ethiopia; Finland; Guatemala; Hungary; Iceland; India; Irish Free State; Latvia; Liberia; Lithuania; Netherlands; New Zealand; Nicaragua; Norway; Panama; Peru; Portugal; Rumania; Russia (U.S.S.R.); Kingdom of the Serbs and Slovenes; Siam; Spain; Sweden; Turkey; and the Union of South Africa. Through the remainder of the year 1929, Chile; Costa Rica; Danzig; Greece; Honduras; Luxemburg; Persia; and Venezuela agreed to adhere to the Kellogg-Briand language.

Thus, a significant number of nations of the globe had indicated their assent to the Kellogg-Briand Pact. In terms of length, this treaty was noteworthy for its brevity. The hope was that the treaty would not often call for interpretation by either jurists or publicists due to its adumbrated length and clearness of expression. The view taken by many in the international community of that era was that the multipartite nature of Kellogg-Briand would command general obedience. Nonetheless, the signatories reserved to themselves the question whether war may become necessary in case of self-defense.

In particular preliminary discussions leading up to the actual signing of the document, nations such as the United States, Great Britain, France, Germany, Japan, Poland,

Czechoslovakia and South Africa, for example, expressed concern over the issue of self-defense. The comments of the United States consultants were illustrative:

> There is nothing in the American draft of an anti-war treaty to restrict or impair in any way the right of self-defense. That right is inherent in every sovereign state and is implicit in every treaty. Every nation is free at all times and regardless of treaty provisions to defend its territory from attack or invasion, and it, alone, is competent to decide whether circumstances require recourse to war in self-defense. If it has a good case, the world will applaud and not condemn its action. Express recognition by treaty of this inalienable right, however, gives rise to the same difficulty in any effort to define aggression. It is the identical question approached from the other side. Inasmuch as no treaty provisions can add to the natural right of self-defense, it is not in the interest of peace that a treaty should stipulate a juristic conception of self-defense since it is far too easy for the unscrupulous to mold events to accord with an agreed definition.[35]

Likewise, the British opined that

> Its terms (do not) exclude action which a state may be forced to take in self-defense.... Mr. Kellogg regards the right of self-defense as inalienable.... There are certain regions of the world the welfare and integrity of which constitute a special and vital interest for our peace and safety. His Majesty's Government have been at pains to make it clear in the past that interference in these regions cannot be suffered. Their protection against attack is to the British Empire a measure of self-defense. It must be clearly understood that His Majesty's Government in Great Britain accept the New treaty upon the distinct understanding that it does not prejudice their freedom of action in this respect.[36]

Comments such as these were not meant to be *reservations* to the treaty provisions, rather only to suggest that many of the signatories were cognizant of the fact that national self-defense was implicitly recognized by the law of nations without specific mention in international agreements.

Wright[37] asks

> Assuming that the Pact creates legal obligations, what are these obligations? Under Article 1, parties have "condemned recourse to war for the solution of international controversies, and renounced it as an instrument of national policy in their relations with one another." This article appears to add nothing to Article 2 of the Pact but makes it probable that a state of war can never exist among parties to the Pact without violation of the Pact. It has been suggested that a state of war may be legally begun because of defensive necessity or in pursuit of the League of Nations Covenant or other guaranty agreements, but it seems doubtful whether the initiation of a state of war is ever a proper defense measure...

> It seems very doubtful, therefore, whether a state could under the Pact declare war as an act of self-defense, unless another state was already in a state of war against it, in which case the other state would already have violated the Pact.[38]

---

35. Quincy Wright, "The Meaning of the Pact of Paris," 27 *Am. J. Int'l L.* 39 (1933).
36. *Id.* at 42–43.
37. *Id.*
38. *Id.* at 50–51.

When Adolf Hitler assumed the mantle of Chancellor of Germany at 12:00 noon on January 30, 1933, most observers on the international scene would have concluded, at least at that time, that the German head of state would abide by international agreements entered into by the Weimar Republic. Hitler, however, had no real intention of abiding by agreements entered into by a despised socialist democracy. In fact, as the history of the 1930s reveal, he went about dismantling the few achievements of the Weimar experiment, first somewhat cautiously, then with caution thrown to the wind. Hitler, of course, was a devotee of the so called "stabbed in the back" legend of 1918 which suggested that Imperial Germany's defeat in World War I was not the result of a military defeat, but rather a geopolitical situation brought on by spineless German politicians, accompanied, of course, by the Versailles Treaty provisions. A year later, in 1919, was born the *Dolchstosslegend*—that the Imperial German Army was never defeated in the field, but defeated, instead by forces outside the ambit of military control, literally by a "stab in the back" by politicians. In particular, the army resented that provision of Versailles that reduced its manpower to 100,000 officers and enlisted personnel. In the early 1920s, then Army Chief of Staff, General Hans von Seeckt, began a covert rebuilding program of German arms through such organizations as the *Freikorps* and the so-called *Black Reichswehr*. In addition, the outlawed German General Staff was resurrected and renamed the *Truppenamt* and continued its work to reorganize and rebuild the Germany Army. Outside states were enlisted by Germany to assist it in armament procurement and the famous Krupp Works of Essen, Germany, began rebuilding armaments once again in foreign territories. For example, Spain secretly constructed submarines for the German *Kreigsmarine*, while Sweden, Holland, Denmark and the U.S.S.R. were all involved, in one form or fashion, in supplying post-World War I Germany with military hardware of varying types. Even the Swiss, on occasion, cooperated by providing armaments to the *Reichswehr* (Reich defense force).

As a result, when Adolf Hitler took over the German state in 1933, there was in place at lease a significant nascent infrastructure that would lend its support to dictatorial goals and imperial regeneration. Shirer[39] observes that

> The Hohenzollern Empire had been built on the armed triumphs of Prussia, the German Republic on the defeat by the Allies after a great war. But the Third Reich owed nothing to the fortunes of war or to foreign influence. It was inaugurated in peacetime, and peacefully, by the Germans themselves, out of both their weaknesses and their strengths. The Germans imposed the Nazi tyranny on themselves....[40]

Shirer's observations that "the Third Reich owed nothing to the fortunes of war or to foreign influence" is off the mark. Clearly, much of the national impetus that fed National Socialism was, at least in part, a consequence of German fortunes in World War I, and the "foreign influence" exerted by the victorious Allies, especially France and Great Britain upon both the post-war German economy and territorial acquisitions incident to the Versailles settlement. It would be sheer nonsense to believe that the vagaries of war and the intrusiveness of the intervention into German continental and overseas sovereignty by the World War I victors had little influence on the rise of the Third Reich.

In the early morning hours of September 1, 1939, Adolf Hitler's Third Reich unleashed a military onslaught on the state of Poland, second to none. World War II had

---

39. Shirer, *supra* note 3.
40. *Id.* at 187.

begun. Fifty-two well-equipped German divisions, employing the latest military technology on both land and air, encircled Poland from three sides. On September 17, 1939, forces of the Soviet Union crossed the eastern Polish frontier under the pre-arranged German-Soviet Non-Aggression Pact signed only weeks earlier by von Ribbentrop for the Nazis and Molotov for the Soviet Union. On September 28, 1939, Poland capitulated. According to the accounts of most historians, Adolf Hitler had expected his Polish incursion to be looked upon by the international community as strictly a local affair. Instead, he became immediately embroiled in a European war, first against Great Britain and France, and later in 1941, against both the Soviet Union and the United States. Germany now faced a two-front war far more disastrous in terms of men, material and civilian lives and property, than anything that had occurred in the 1914–1918 conflict.

Nazi Germany declared war on the United States four days after the Japanese attack on Pearl Harbor, December 11, 1941. Hitler's declaration of war against the United States is far more mysterious than Japan's open aggression against the Hawaiian Islands. German historian Fischer[41] remarks that

> [m]ost historians have described Hitler's declaration of war [against the United States] as an act of lunacy and a monumental blunder, arguing that attacking the most powerful economic country in the world, while at the same time being bogged down with his army in the second most powerful country in the world, [the U.S.S.R.] he virtually guaranteed Germany's defeat.[42]

To this day, no one is absolutely sure why Adolf Hitler joined battle against the United States shortly after the Japanese struck Pearl Harbor. Fischer, however, had a theory. He writes that

> First and foremost, it seems that Hitler's declaration of war on the United States was an act of willful defiance on the part of the vainglorious führer who was delighted after a year of provocations by the United States to smack the 'lout' Roosevelt publicly in the face…his declaration of war on the United States was the logical culmination of his racial policies. The führer now saw himself confronted by two interrelated foes; the United States and the Soviet Union, and the link between them was the Jew.[43]

The core emphasis in *Part Two* embraces selected excerpts from the wetherbell war crimes trial of the twentieth century—the International Military Tribunal-Nuremberg. We also look at other selected trials that took place in occupied Germany involving some of the lesser-known Nazi defendants as well as one trial conducted in Norway. In Germany, these "Subsequent Proceedings" under Allied Control Council Law No. 10, were conducted in the various Four-Power Zones of Occupation. A Brief summary of all American cases are noted [*infra*] while three decisions are reported in greater detail. These three are (i) the *Einsatzgruppen Case:* (ii) the *RuSHA Case;* and (iii) the *High Command Case*. In addition to these three, we include the case of *United States v. Bersin et al.,* better known as the *Malmédy Massacre Case*, against, among others, SS Lt. Colonel Joachem Peiper and some of his grenadiers assigned to *Kampfgruppe* (battlegroup) Peiper for the murder of seventy-two American POWs who had surrendered to the Germans in Belgium in December, 1944, during the Battle of the Bulge; (v) the *Case of Heinrich Gerike,* better known by some as the *Velpke Children's Home Case*, tried by a

---

41. Fischer, Supra note 1.
42. *Id*. at 475.
43. *Id*.

British military tribunal in Brunswick in 1946; (vi) the trial of *Werner Rohde et al.* by a British military tribunal in Wuppertal in 1946 and (vii) the trial of *Gerhard Flesch* by a trial court in Norway in 1946 and the eventual appeal to the Supreme Court of Norway in 1948].

---

5. Paul Brooker, "Hitler's Regime in Germany" in *Twentieth Century Dictatorships*
36–40 (1995)

Reproduced with permission of NYU Press from *Twentieth Centuy Dictorships* by Paul Brooker. Copyright © 1995 by Paul Brooker

The coming to power of Hitler and his Nazi Party…is one of the most written about topics in modern history. Even if the Nazis had not gone on to become a byword for evil, their spectacular rise to power through the ballot box rather than revolution or coup would have attracted much academic attention. A party which had won less than 3 per cent of the vote in the elections of 1928 saw its leader become the head of government in 1933 in accordance with the constitutional proprieties and, unlike the Fascist Party in Italy, because it held the largest number of seats in parliament.

It is often pointed out that Hitler and the Nazi Party did not come to power in truly democratic fashion. The Nazis and their Nationalist allies could not command a majority in the German parliament (the Reichstag) when Hitler became head of government (Reich Chancellor) on 30 January 1933. For the Nazi Party had won less than 33 per cent of the vote in the November 1932 elections to the Reichstag. As this had marked a significant decline from the more than 37 percent of the vote that the Nazis had won a few months earlier in the July elections, there was also reason to believe that the Nazi phenomenon had lost its momentum. (In particular the Nazis had been unable to break into the unionized working class constituencies of the Social Democratic and Communist parties or into the Catholic constituency of the Centre Party.) Furthermore, the actual decline in voting support between July and November seems to confirm that the earlier, 1930–2 massive rise in the Nazi vote was largely a protest vote produced by the cataclysmic economic crisis, known as the Great Depression, that had begun in 1929 and by late 1932 was beginning to ease.

Nevertheless, when President Hindenburg appointed Hitler to the office of Chancellor and head of a new government, the President was acting in a comparatively democratic manner.…

* * *

The Nazis' radically rightest, fascist ideology of National Socialism differed in several ways from its Fascist counterpart in Italy. For example, National Socialism did not espouse a corporativist ideal like the Corporative State and instead was committed to a form of 'socialism' and to the fraternal/populist ideal of a '*Volk* community.' However, the most significant difference between the two fascist ideologies was that National Socialism was based not on nationalism and statism but on racism.

The most famous or notorious elements of National Socialism was its racial *Weltanschauung* (world view) of a perpetual conflict between the 'culture-creating' Aryan race and the parasitical but cunning Jewish race. The cunning of the Jews was supposedly to be seen in their being behind such outwardly opposed forces as Bolshevism in Russia and in international financial capitalism in New York. Nazi racial doctrines also included a Social Darwinist belief in the 'survival of the fittest,' both in the deadly struggle between the races and in the social forms of struggle that existed within a race. An accompanying eugenic belief in the need to maintain the purity of health of the race would be used to legitimate not only the Nazis' eugenic policies, including the sterilization of 'defectives', but also the anti-Semitic 'Nuremburg' Laws for the Protection of German Blood. [*see*: Appendix B, infra]. Yet although the racial doctrines of Nazi ideology were used to legitimate many aspects of the regime's persecution of German Jews, these anti-Semitic doctrines were not used to legitimate publicly the ultimate, genocidal 'Final Solution', which was kept secret from the German people and even from the ordinary membership of the Party.[44]

National Socialism's conception of a racial clash of good and evil between Aryans and Jews was complicated by the existence of 'sub-human' races, such as Negroes and Slavs, and by the existence of national or ethnic subdivisions within the Aryan race. But as the German subdivision of the Aryan race was supposedly the purest and the most valuable, German nationalism could be accommodated within the racial ideological framework. The Nazis could exploit the already long-established doctrines of German nationalism by presenting their National Socialist ideology and propaganda in nationalist as well as racist guise.

However, neither nationalism nor racism was publicly used to support National Socialism's imperialist doctrine, for this *Lebensraum* doctrine was not propagated among the German people as part of the regime's official ideology. The Nazis were reticent about presenting the doctrine, let alone the actual policy implications, of the German Aryans' supposed need for more *Lebensraum* (living space) in the east, in the territories inhabited by the Slavs. Not surprisingly, the policy implications of this concept—a war of conquest against Eastern Europe and the Soviet Union—were not spelled out in public. Instead, Hitler portrayed himself as seeking to use peaceful means to attain Germany's limited and nationalist, not imperialist, foreign policy goals. Even the rearmament policy that would culminate in the autarkic Four Year Plan of 1936 was portrayed as helping to attain Germany's international goals peacefully, by allowing Germany to negotiate from a position of strength. Outwardly National Socialism had little in common with the open, almost bombastic imperialism and bellicoseness of Fascist ideology.

In contrast to the reticence shown in espousing the imperialist *Lebensraum* doctrine, great publicity was given to the Nazis' social ideal of the *Volksgemeinschaft* (Folk community), of establishing a fraternal and populist community of Aryan Germans free of class divisions and selfishness. The *Volksgemeinschaft* ideal was one of the key elements of National Socialist ideology and was used to legitimate much of the regime's social policy—not to mention providing support for the Nazis' opposition to liberal individualism and Marxist class antagonism. It was also linked to the socialist component of National Socialism, which was a social-welfarist 'German' socialism or 'socialism of the deed' that was expressed in such measures as the Winter Relief fundraising campaign to help the poor through the winter months.

The leader principle *Führerprinzip* was National Socialism's highly publicized and pervasive authority principle. It sought an end to collective (committees and parlia-

---

44. Some might take issue with an assertion of this sort, especially those who have read and agree with the conclusions reached in Daniel J. Goldhagen's *Hitler's Willing Executioners* (1996). For a highly critical evaluation of the Goldhagen work, *see* Norman G. Finkelstein & Ruth B. Birn, *A Nation on Trial: The Goldhagen Thesis and Historical Truth* (1998).

ments) and rule-governed (bureaucratic) forms of authority and to have them replaced by a personal form of authority exercised by individual leaders. As Hitler himself put it, such leaders were 'to receive unconditional authority and freedom of action downward, but to be charged with unlimited responsibility upward'. Throughout German society and even in the civil service there was an attempt to conform to the Nazi regime's leader principle. It was also used to legitimate the regime's production-oriented policy of increasing employers' power to direct their workforce—the 1934 Law for the Ordering of National Labour transformed employers into authoritarian 'leaders' of their employees. Furthermore, the leader principle legitimated the regime itself (or at least the form the regime took) by legitimating Hitler's absolutist leader position over the regime and the German people.

---

6. Charter of the International Military Tribunal

[London, August 8, 1945]
19 *Temple Law Quarterly* 162–168 (1945–46)
Reproduced with permission of Temple Law Review,
© *Temple Law Quarterly* (1945–1946)

I. Constitution of the International Military Tribunal

Article 1. In pursuance of the agreement signed on the 8th day of August 1945 by the Government of the United States of America, the Provisional Government of the French Republic, the Government of the United Kingdom of Great Britain and Northern Ireland and the Government of the Union of Soviet Socialist Republics, there shall be established an International Military Tribunal (hereinafter called "the Tribunal") for the just and prompt trial and punishment of the major war criminals of the European Axis.

Article 2. The Tribunal shall consist of four members, each with an alternate. One member and one alternate shall be appointed by each of the signatories. The alternates shall, so far as they are able, be present at all sessions of the Tribunal. In case of illness of any member of the Tribunal or his incapacity for some other reason to fulfill his functions, his Alternate shall take his place.

Article 3. Neither the Tribunal, its members nor their alternates can be challenged by the prosecution or by the Defendants or their Counsel. Each signatory may replace its member of the Tribunal or his alternate for reasons of health or for other good reasons, except that no replacement may take place during a Trial, other than by an alternate.

Article 4.

(a) The presence of all four members of the Tribunal or the alternate for any absent member shall be necessary to constitute a quorum.

(b) The members of the Tribunal shall, before any trial begins, agree among themselves upon the selection from among their number of a President, and the President shall hold office during that trial, or as may otherwise be agreed by a vote of not less than three members. If, however, a session of the Tribunal takes place on the territory of one of the Signatories, the representative of that signatory on the Tribunal shall preside.

(c) Save as aforesaid the Tribunal shall take decisions by a majority vote and in case the votes are evenly divided, the vote of the President shall be decisive: provided always that convictions and sentences shall only be imposed by affirmative votes of at least three members of the Tribunal.

Article 5. In case of need and depending on the number of matters to be tried, other Tribunals may be set up; and the establishment, functions, and procedure of each Tribunal shall be identical, and shall be governed by this Charter.

II. Jurisdiction and General Principles

Article 6. The Tribunal established by the Agreement referred to in Article I hereof for the trial and punishment of the major war criminals of the European Axis countries shall have the power to try and punish persons who, acting in the interests of the European Axis countries, whether as individuals or as members of organizations, committed any of the following crimes.

The following acts, or any of them, are crimes coming within the jurisdiction of the Tribunal for which there shall be individual responsibility.

(a) Crimes Against Peace: namely, planning, preparation, initiation or waging of a war of aggression, or a war in violation of international treaties, agreements or assurances, or participation in a common plan or conspiracy for the accomplishment of any of the foregoing;

(b) War Crimes: namely, violations of the laws and customs of war. Such violations shall include, but not be limited to, murder, ill-treatment or deportation to slave labor or for any other purpose of civilian population of or in occupied territory, murder or ill-treatment of prisoners of war or persons on the seas, killing of hostages, plunder of public or private property, wanton destruction of cities, towns or villages, or devastation not justified by military necessity;

(c) Crimes Against Humanity: namely, murder, extermination, enslavement, deportation, and other inhumane acts committed against any civilian population, before or during the war, or persecutions on political, racial, or religious grounds in execution of or in connection with any crime within the jurisdiction of the Tribunal, whether or not in violation of the domestic law of the country where perpetrated.

Leaders, organizers, instigators and accomplices participating in the formulation or execution of a common plan or conspiracy to commit any of the foregoing crimes are responsible for all acts performed by any person in execution of such plan.

Article 7. The official position of defendants, whether as Heads of State or responsible officials in Government Departments, shall not be considered as freeing them from responsibility or mitigating punishment.

Article 8. The fact that the Defendant acted pursuant to order of his Government or of a superior shall not free him from responsibility, but may be considered in mitigation of punishment if the Tribunal determines that justice so requires.

Article 9. At the trial of any individual member of any group or organization the Tribunal may declare (in connection with any act of which the individual may be convicted) that the group or organization of which the Individual was a member was a criminal organization.

After receipt of the Indictment the Tribunal shall give notice as it thinks fit that the prosecution intends to ask the Tribunal to make such declaration and any member of the organization will be entitled to apply to the Tribunal for leave to be heard by the Tribunal upon the question of the criminal character of the organization. The Tribunal shall have the power to allow or reject the application. If the application is allowed, the Tribunal may direct in what manner the applicants shall be represented and heard.

Article 10. In cases where a group or organization is declared criminal by the Tribunal, the competent national authority of any Signatory shall have the right to bring individuals to trial for membership therein before national, military, or occupation courts. In such case the criminal nature of the group or organization is considered proved and shall not be questioned.

Article 11. Any person convicted by the Tribunal may be charged before a national, military, or occupation court, referred to in Article 10 of this Charter, with a crime other than of membership in a criminal group or organization and such court may, after convicting him, impose upon him punishment independent of and additional to the punishment imposed by the Tribunal for participation in the criminal activities of such group or organization.

Article 12. The Tribunal shall have the right to take proceedings against a person charged with crimes set out in Article 6 of this Charter in his absence, if he has not been found or if the Tribunal, for any reason, finds it necessary, in the interest of justice, to conduct the hearing in his absence.

Article 13. The Tribunal shall draw up rules for its procedure. These rules shall not be inconsistent with the provisions of this Charter.

III. Committee for the Investigation and Prosecution of Major War Criminals.

Article 14. Each Signatory shall appoint a Chief Prosecutor for the investigation of the charges against and prosecution of major war criminals.

The Chief Prosecutor shall act as a committee for the following purposes:

(a) to agree upon a plan of the individual work of each of the Chief Prosecutors and his staff,

(b) to settle the final designation of major war criminals to be tried by the Tribunal,

(c) to approve the Indictment and the documents to be submitted therewith,

(d) to lodge the Indictment and the accompanying documents with the Tribunal,

(e) to draw up and recommend to the Tribunal for its approval draft rules of procedure, contemplated by Article 13 of this Charter. The Tribunal shall have the power to accept, with or without amendments, or to reject, the rules so recommended.

The Committee shall act in all the above matters by a majority vote and shall appoint a Chairman as may be convenient and in accordance with the principle of rotation: provided that there is an equal division of vote concerning the designation of a Defendant to be tried by the Tribunal, or the crimes with which he shall be charged, that proposal will be adopted which was made by the party which proposed that the particular Defendant be tried, or the particular charge be preferred against him.

Article 15. The Chief Prosecutors shall individually, or acting in collaboration with one another, also undertake the following duties:

(a) investigation, collection and production before or at the Trial of all necessary evidence,

(b) the preparation of the Indictment for approval by the Committee in accordance with paragraph (c) of Article 14 hereof,

(c) the preliminary examination of all necessary witnesses and of the Defendants.

(d) to act as prosecutor at the Trial

(e) to appoint representatives to carry out such duties as may be assigned to them,

(f) to undertake such other matters as may appear necessary to them for the purpose of the preparation for and conduct of the Trial.

It is understood that no witness or Defendant detained by any Signatory shall be taken out of the possession of that Signatory without its consent.

IV. Fair Trial for Defendants

Article 16. In order to ensure fair trail for the defendants, the following procedure shall be followed:

(a) The Indictment shall include full particulars specifying in detail the charges against the Defendants. A copy of the Indictment and of all the documents lodged with the indictment, translated into a language which he understands, shall be furnished to the Defendant at a reasonable time before trial.

(b) During any preliminary examination or trial of a Defendant he shall have the right to give any explanation relevant to the charges made against him.

(c) A preliminary examination of a Defendant and his trial shall be conducted in, or translated into, a language which the Defendant understands.

(d) A Defendant shall have the right to conduct his own defense before the Tribunal or to have the assistance of Counsel.

(e) A Defendant shall have the right through himself or through his Counsel to present evidence at the Trial in support of his defense, and to cross-examine any witness called by the Prosecution.

V. Powers of the Tribunal and Conduct of the Trial

Article 17. The Tribunal shall have the power

(a) to summon witnesses to the Trial and to require their attendance and testimony and to put questions to them,

(b) to interrogate any Defendant,

(c) to require the production of documents and other evidentiary material,

(d) to administer oaths to witnesses,

(e) to appoint officers for the carrying out of any task designated by the Tribunal including the power to have evidence taken on commission.

Article 18. The Tribunal shall

(a) confine the Trial strictly to an expeditious hearing of the issues raised by the charges,

(b) take strict measures to prevent any action which will cause unreasonable delay, and rule out irrelevant issues and statements of any kind whatsoever,

(c) deal summarily with any contumacy, imposing appropriate punishment, including exclusion of any Defendant or his Counsel from some or all further proceedings, but without prejudice to the determination of the charges.

Article 19. The Tribunal shall not be bound by technical rules of evidence. It shall adopt and apply to the greatest possible extent expeditious and non-technical procedure, and shall admit any evidence which it deems to have probative value.

Article 20. The Tribunal may require to be informed of the nature of any evidence before it is offered so that it may rule upon the relevance thereof.

Article 21. The Tribunal shall not require proof of facts of common knowledge but shall take judicial notice thereof. It shall also take judicial notice of official governmental documents and reports of the United Nations, including the acts and documents of committees set up in the various allied countries for investigation of war crimes, and the records and findings of military or other Tribunals of any of the United Nations.

Article 22. The permanent seat of the Tribunal shall be in Berlin. The first meetings of the members of the Tribunal and the Chief Prosecutors shall be held at Berlin in a place to be designated by the Control Council of Germany. The first trial shall be held at Nuremberg, and any subsequent trials shall be held at such places as the Tribunal may decide.

Article 23. One or more of the Chief Prosecutors may take part in the prosecution at each trial. The function of any Chief Prosecutor may be discharged by him personally, or by any person or persons authorized by him.

The function of Counsel for a Defendant may be discharged at the Defendant's request by any Counsel professionally qualified to conduct cases before the Courts of his own country, or by any other person who may be specially authorized thereto by the Tribunal.

Article 24. The proceedings of the Tribunal shall take the following course:

(a) The Indictment shall be read in court.

(b) The Tribunal shall ask each Defendant whether he pleads "guilty" or "not guilty."

(c) The prosecution shall make an opening statement.

(d) The Tribunal shall ask the prosecution and the defense what evidence (if any) they wish to submit to the Tribunal, and the Tribunal shall rule upon the admissibility of any such evidence.

(e) The witnesses for the Prosecution shall be examined and after that the witnesses for the Defense. Thereafter such rebutting evidence as may be held by the Tribunal to be admissible shall be called by either the Prosecution or the Defense.

(f) The Tribunal may put any question to any witness and to any Defendant, at any time.

(g) The Prosecution and the Defense shall interrogate and may cross-examine any witnesses and any Defendant who gives testimony.

(h) The Defense shall address the court.

(i) The Prosecution shall address the court.

(j) Each Defendant may make a statement to the Tribunal.

(k) The Tribunal shall deliver judgment and pronounce sentence.

Article 25. All official documents shall be produced and all court proceedings conducted in English, French and Russian, and in the language of the Defendant. So much of the record and of the proceedings may also be translated into the language of any country in which the Tribunal is sitting, as the Tribunal considers desirable in the interests of justice and public opinion.

VI. Judgment and Sentence

Article 26. The judgment of the Tribunal as to the guilt or the innocence of any Defendant shall give the reasons on which it is based, and shall be final and not subject to review.

Article 27. The Tribunal shall have the right to impose upon a Defendant, on conviction, death or such other punishment as shall be determined by it to be just.

Article 28. In addition to any punishment imposed by it, the Tribunal shall have the right to deprive the convicted person of any stolen property and order its delivery to the Control Council of Germany.

Article 29. In case of guilt, sentences shall be carried out in accordance with the orders of the Control Council of Germany, which may at any time reduce or otherwise alter the sentences, but may not increase the severity thereof. If the Control Council for Germany, after any Defendant has been convicted and sentenced, discovers fresh evidence which, in its opinion, would found a fresh charge against him, the Council shall report accordingly to the Committee established under Article 14 hereof, for such action as they may consider proper, having regard to the interests of justice.

[The following excerpts, taken from the Tusa and Tusa book on the Nuremberg trial mirror some of the intense negotiations that took place largely behind the scenes in the summer of 1945 by representatives of the four Allied governments assembled in London to craft a treaty (known as the "Charter") agreeable to all participants. Especially difficult was the task of reaching agreement on the forms and procedure of the trial itself, inasmuch as such an effort involved the melding together of essentially three totally different legal systems: the Anglo-American common law, the French civil law and the Soviet Union's system of Socialist jurisprudence].

---

7. Ann Tusa and John Tusa, *The Nuremberg Trial*
75–79; 81; 83; 85; 86–88 (1990)
Reprinted with permission of Scribner, an imprint of Simon & Schuster Adult Publishing Group, from *The Nuremberg Trial* by Ann Tusa and John Tusa, Copyright © 1983 by Ann Tusa and John Tusa

The London Conference opened on 26 June [1945] in Church House.... The meetings were held in private and they were informal-grueling though the full day sessions often became, at least they spared the delegates endless prepared official speeches. Perhaps, in fact, the meetings were too informal to be efficient. There seems to have been no agenda; if there was, it was ignored and the delegates rambled, interrupted and wandered off the point. The discussions were repetitious and frequently at cross-purposes.... At the main sessions the delegations submitted draft proposals and argued over them and the principles they raised. As time went on a drafting sub-committee was established to draw up final proposals on which agreement had been reached. There were fourteen full sessions in all, but plenty of informal meetings behind the scenes (alas, unrecorded)....

A high proportion of the time at the Conference was spent on procedural matters—working out how the trial should be run, what should happen when, who should have what powers. All were agreed that a military rather than a civil tribunal would free them to pool the best elements from all their national systems. Since they were embarking on a totally new enterprise they need not be hidebound by previously established procedures. For instance, they could ignore the rules of evidence which normally applied in trials with juries and allow the Tribunal to admit any evidence which seemed to have probative value-provided it was clearly relevant to the point it was substantiating and was not repetitious. All were agreed they could create a new court procedure for the occasion which must be efficient and fair. The trouble was they could not agree on how to do it. All tended to cling to the conviction that there own national way of doing things was best. This was illustrated most clearly in the recurring argument over the nature of the indictment.

In Anglo-American trials, the indictment is a brief statement by the prosecution of who is accused and on what charges. The prosecution presents it to a court which fixes the time of trial. Once the trial opens, the full prosecution evidence for the charges is produced in open session. The court hears it, weighs it against that of the Defense and then determines guilt. In Continental Law, however, preliminary work on a case is not carried out by the prosecution; it is the responsibility in France of a *juge d'instruction*, in Russia of a commission of enquiry. They prepare an indictment which not only states the charges but is accompanied by the full evidence on which they are based and the law which applies. The prosecution only takes over once the case comes to trial. Though a judge may later call for more evidence or witnesses to clarify points and allow the prosecution and defence to apply for more, the bulk of the prosecution evidence has been presented with the indictment and is available for the defence to study from the moment the accused have been served with the indictment.

And this, said the French and Russian delegates to the London Conference, is the best system: it is more efficient, because the case has been thoroughly examined to check its soundness before a court is asked to spend time on it; it is quicker, because only effective evidence and witnesses are called in court; and it is infinitely fairer to the defendants who will be spared a hearing if the case against them is poor, and who will have had ample opportunity to prepare a defence against the prosecution evidence should they be brought to trial. The French and Russians were deeply shocked that in the Anglo-American system, as Professor Gros put it: 'the prosecutor could come in out of the blue with evidences which were completely unknown until the moment of the trial.' Falco [of the French delegation] was so shocked he was actually stung to speech and complained that if the indictment did not present the full prosecution evidence, the defence would be faced during the trial with the 'opening of a Pandora's box of unhappy surprises.' Maxwell-Fyfe [of the British delegation] continued to assure them that he had worked with the short indictment for twenty years and had not found the system unfair in practice—the court could always give the defence time to prepare answers to unexpected evidence. He was willing to compromise and suggest a fuller indictment on Continental lines plus greater latitude to introduce new evidence in court than Europeans were used to, Jackson [the chief American prosecutor] was not. Day after day he argued for 'a longer trial but a shorter indictment.' In spite of constant reassurance, he continued to believe that the Continental system prevented the calling of new evidence and witnesses.... Jackson was never reconciled to the unfamiliar Continental system and remained blind to its virtues.... He spoke with the emotion of the Common Law courtroom lawyer when he finally complained that if all the evidence went into the indictment there 'wouldn't be anything left for a trial.'

There were arguments too over the role of the judges. The French and the Russians wanted their familiar system where judges intervene frequently to direct the course of the trial and examine defendants and witnesses. The British and Americans were more accustomed to the adversary process of challenge and cross-examination by opposing counsel. The Continental delegates also wanted to insist on the right of defendants to speak when not under oath and to make a final speech in their own defence....

On all procedural matters the French and Russians were the more prepared to compromise. Jackson was less willing to meet halfway. He was the first to confess that he was stubborn. He admitted that these procedural matters were 'so deeply ingrained in the thought of the American people' that alternatives were unacceptable. But it was not just that he was so stuck on the 'American Way' as to have tunnel vision. At the second session of the conference, Nikitchenko [of the Soviet delegation] had thrown a bombshell by suddenly announcing: 'We are dealing here with the chief war criminals who have already been condemned and whose conviction has already been announced by both the Moscow and Crimea Declarations by the heads of government.' So presumably Nikitchenko did not want a trial, merely formal confirmation of [a] political decision; saw no need for a careful examination of the evidence; thought the rights of defendants to be nothing more than an impediment to speedy punishment.

* * *

Whatever the reason, Nikitchenko's words caused a lot of damage to the negotiations in London. Jackson was constantly prepared to place the worst construction on any Russian suggestion. When they proposed a scheme for replacing judges during the trial, he instantly assumed they were suggesting replacing them for 'unsatisfactory decisions,' though the Russian draft had made it clear they were worried about judges becoming ill or being recalled for other work....

Suspicion and differences in legal thinking widened the rifts between the delegations when they began to discuss the American wish to indict the Nazi organizations. Nikitchenko's very first comment at the opening session was: 'I am not quite clear on the point of including the organization.' Jackson had hoped it was self-evident. From the days of the Bernays plan the declaration of criminality against the main organizations had been a fundamental part of trying the whole regime through its leaders. As the Americans saw it, these Nazi institutions had been the instrument through which the conspirators had carried out their evil plans. A legal pronouncement would confirm the criminality and speed up subsequent proceedings against members who would not be able to argue the matter all over again.

Nikitchenko tried to argue that no declaration was needed—the Moscow and Crimea Declarations had said that the Nazi Party and its organizations and institutions would be wiped out and they had been. All had been disbanded by the occupying forces; criminal proceedings and de-Nazification courts would deal with their members. But [professor] Gros quickly pointed out that the statements had made declarations of intention, not legal pronouncements. The French and Russians were in total agreement with Jackson that the Nazi organizations were criminal groups. They were, however, very dubious about the legality of a court pronouncement on their criminality.

* * *

...Jackson saw the charge of aggressive war as the cornerstone of the case against the Nazi regime.... The French too believed that the charge was 'morally and politically desirable.' The trouble was they did not think it was legal. They believed the Americans were trying to invent a crime which, however, unfortunately, did not exist in international law. And [professor] Gros quoted with approval Professor Trainin's opinion: 'The effort to make war of aggression a crime is still tentative.' To leap ahead of international decision and claim aggressive war as criminal was 'shocking' to the French. They thought it would be better simply to declare the intention to punish those who had launched wars. This might be arbitrary but it was less of an outrage against justice because it made no claim to be legal.

Nikitchenko agreed—he thought the United Nations must reach a decision on the criminality of aggression and that until they had defined it others must not pre-empt them. He and the French were only prepared to charge the defendants with specific acts of breaking treaties and invasions, 'deemed criminal,' and leave it to the judges to decide the law which covered them. Jackson, on the other hand,...was certain that the crime existed in law and wanted it clearly defined—he feared a trial becoming a platform for Nazi propaganda about 'self-defence' and 'fears of encirclement.' He could not stomach Russian draft proposals covering the question of aggression. They limited the definition to aggression committed 'by the Axis Powers.' This was because of their belief that all aggression was not yet criminal in international law.

* * *

The only American plan which was not discussed exhaustively day after day at the Conference was the intention to charge the Nazi leaders with conspiracy, the essential bond of the Bernays plan. The conspiracy charge, as Jackson argued at London, was to deal only with 'those who deliberately entered a plan aimed at forbidden acts' not with the millions of soldiers, or the farmers who occasionally employed slave labour at harvest time. He wanted to reach 'the planners, the zealots who put this thing across.' These were the people the British, French and Russians wanted to reach too. They just did not think that the American concept of conspiracy was the way to do it. The charge was little discussed at their main sessions—while it endured death by a thousand cuts in the drafting sub-committee. In draft and re-draft, conspiracy was either omitted altogether, or it was whittled away to an accusation of 'planning' or 'organizing' specific crimes.

The British might take the American concept for granted, but their pragmatism suggested its use was too vague, too grandiose to be effective in court. The Russians and the French were accustomed to the idea that conspiring to commit crimes is illegal, but in their law the concentration must be on the criminal act itself. Given their experience of invasion and occupation in recent years, it seemed only too obvious that the Nazis had committed crimes and that these crimes had been planned and supervised by their leaders. Why, then, bother to make planning, for which conspiracy only seemed a fancy word, a separate charge? There was evidence in plenty to prove the top Nazis committed actual crimes.

* * *

...[F]inally, on 8 August [1945] the heads of delegation in London signed two documents which they had been working on at the suggestion of the Russians from the earliest stages of the Conference. The first was a statement of the general intention to fulfill the wishes of the United Nations and the signatories of the Moscow Declaration. This London Agreement announced the intention to establish an International Military Tribunal 'for the trial of war criminals whose offences have no particular geographical location, whether they be accused individually or in their capacity as members of organizations or groups or in both capacities.' Nineteen other nations [Australia, Belgium, Czechoslovakia, Denmark, Ethiopia, Greece, Haiti, Honduras,

India, Luxemburg, New Zealand, Norway, Panama, Paraguay, Poland, The Netherlands, Uruguay, Venezuela and Yugoslavia] later expressed their adherence to this London Agreement.

Attached to it was a fuller document setting out the composition, jurisdiction, powers and procedures of the Tribunal. [*supra*]. The name for this document had caused a certain amount of bother to the drafting sub-committee.... Sir Thomas Barnes, the Treasury Solicitor, finally suggested the name which stuck—the Charter.

The Charter expressed the eventual happy union between the Common Law and Continental systems of procedure. As everyone had wished, the accused were given the right to counsel, and to an indictment and trial in their own language. As a compromise between the two systems the defendants would be served in advance of the trial with an indictment which gave a full summary of the evidence against them and which was accompanied with as many of the relevant documents as possible; others could then be produced in court and time given to the defence to study them.... Defendants would have the right to take the stand and testify under oath, subject to cross-examination (which is not usual on the Continent); and to make a final statement without prosecution challenge and not under oath (a right unfamiliar in Anglo-American courts). The results of the blend of the two systems was, in Jackson's view, to give rather more rights to the defendants than might have been available in either system separately.

When it came to a definition of the charges, however, the London Conference had found compromise more difficult. Some of the contentious issues had not been settled by the Charter. Nor had the French and Russian delegates been prepared to set out the law on which the charges were based—given the unprecedented nature of the trial and the uncertain state of international law, they insisted on leaving it to the judges. The conspiracy charge had virtually disappeared—into a phrase attached to the first count and a hazy sentence added to the other three. And the Charter was no clearer about asking the Tribunal to declare indicted organizations criminal. Thanks to delegates' doubts about the legality and practicality of the matter, Article 9 did not say the Tribunal 'must' decide the guilt or innocence of the groups; it merely said 'the Tribunal may.' Some sort of compromise between the warring viewpoints had been reached in the provision that the criminality of organizations must be connected with the criminal acts of individual defendants, together with the entitlement of members to be heard in their organization's defence.

Individual defendants and organizations were to be heard on three counts. The first was the crime of planning and waging aggressive war. It had been given a new name—previously coined by Professor Trainin—Crimes Against Peace. In view of the doubts of the French and the Russians as to the status of aggressive war in international law, it was not given a general definition, and the introduction to the charge made it clear that the Tribunal was empowered only to try and punish those who acted in the interests of 'the European Axis Powers.' This was an undoubted defeat for Jackson who had so longed for the chance to show that any war was criminal.... In defining a crime against peace as the waging of war, it had probably ruled out reference by the prosecution to the takeover of Austria in the Anschluss or the invasion of Czechoslovakia, since in those cases no actual fighting had occurred. Law Ten of the Allied Control Council cleared this up for subsequent proceedings by talking of wars *and* invasions....

Count Two dealt with War Crimes. At first glance this charge was less novel than Crimes Against Peace. The Charter's definition of War Crimes followed that of firmly established international agreements; war criminals had frequently been prosecuted and punished for these crimes. It was however an innovation to suggest that responsibility for these criminal activities ultimately rested with those who governed or commanded those who engaged them. Jackson may not have convinced the London Conference that war crimes were an intended result of the War rather than an unhappy by-product, nor had the wording of the Charter made clear his belief that the Nazi leaders had conspired from the beginning to commit them. But he had found ready ears for his argument that those at the top must bear the brunt of responsibility for the acts of their underlings. Article Seven of the Charter emphasized their view that those at the top could not shelter behind their official positions—holding high office was to be an implication of greater guilt, not a mitigating factor.

The final Count in the Charter—that of Crimes Against Humanity—was a totally new charge. The name first coined at Versailles was recommended to the Conference by Professor Hersch Lauterpacht to cover the persecution of racial and religious groups and the wholesale exploitation of European people and resources. Perhaps many of the acts covered by this charge could have been included in the list of war crimes. But existing laws did not always envisage the nature and scale of the atrocities which had been committed. Nor could the charge of war crimes be stretched to deal with, for example, the attempted extermination of German Jews. The charge of Crimes against Humanity expressed the revulsion against Nazi attitudes and methods which had been so strongly felt by those who drew up the Charter. As lawyers, however, some of them had felt scruples about the right of an international court to interfere in the domestic policy of a sovereign state. Strong though the temptation had been to prosecute German leaders for persecuting the Jews, the Christian churches, and political opponents in the 1930s, the Charter resisted it. Persecutions had to be examined 'in connection with any crimes within the jurisdiction of the Tribunal.' This strongly suggested that they must be directly connected with the War and probably had to be committed after 1939. Jackson would have a hard job to convince the Tribunal of his belief that they were all deliberately part of the entire Nazi design right from the beginning of the regime.

No such problems of limitations hedged Article Eight of the Charter which made clear that no defendant could claim the protection of having obeyed orders from a superior, though superior orders might be considered by the Tribunal as a mitigating factor in sentencing. The denial of the defence of superior orders has often been called the 'Nuremberg Principle.' It was not, however, new at the trial. It was perfectly familiar in national legal systems—and, indeed, it was probably even more familiar to the German military than to anyone. Every German soldier's paybook contained 'Ten Commandments' one of which stated that no soldier should obey an illegal order.... As Maxwell-Fyfe had pointed out at the London Conference, the defence of superior orders had not been allowed by German judges in at least one of the Leipzig trials after the First World War, and in recent editions of Oppenheimer—the Bible of international lawyers—superior orders were likewise inadmissible in international law.

Clear though the Charter might be on questions such as this, it was in fact riddled with unanswered questions; not least, what was the law on aggressive war? Had the Nazis planned to commit crimes other than launching war; if so, from what date? What makes a man a conspirator? Can declarations of criminality against organizations be made and then binding on subsequent courts? Nor had the framers of the Charter chosen to impose many rules on the Tribunal for handling the case in court.

It might have been expected that the signatories of the London Agreement would have invented the game, evolved rules for playing it which gave the advantage to one side only, then gone out to play certain of victory. Instead, thanks to lawyers' rectitude and national differences, the rule book was vague, the options available to the players ill-defined but not limited to one side, and even the size of the pitch was not specified. In this situation the referee can start to create much of the game. The Charter had established an outline for the trial of the Nazi leaders, but it left many of the important details to be settled by their judges. Through their analysis of the law and the interpretation of the sketch they had been given for the trial, by the way they chose to use the powers given to them and by the rules they evolved for controlling the process, they could shape it and largely determine its outcome. This was going to be very much a trial held by the judges, not one staged by the prosecution. The negotiators at the London Conference had all been agreed on one thing—that the case against the Nazi leaders was open and shut; they would all be found guilty and punished. Whether they now realized it or not, though, the Charter had taken the initiative from the prosecution and given it to the judges. A walkover victory for the prosecution was no longer guaranteed.

It might well be argued that this very failure to build in a guarantee of prosecution success was one of the great strengths of the Charter—even if it was not one of its intended virtues. It had other virtues too. Given the extent of the doubts and the intensity of the differences between the delegations it is perhaps surprising they could have agreed to so much. It is easy to accuse them of slack drafting in places—but this was necessary to avoid snapping national tolerance and in some cases an honest admission of uncertainty which they wished to leave to others to consider. The Charter certainly demonstrated the intention to hold a fair hearing according to commonly accepted principles of justice. Basic issues as well as prosecution and defence cases remained to be heard fully in court. The delegates in London had had to engage in negotiations and co-operation of a kind that seasoned diplomats would have found testing. As lawyers they were faced with the added nightmare of legal innovation. Under the circumstances the London Agreement and Charter were remarkable achievements.

---

8. Control Council Law No. 10
Punishment of Persons Guilty of War Crimes, Crimes against Peace and against Humanity
20 December 1945
1 TWC xvi; Taylor, Report, 250

In order to give effect to the terms of the Moscow Declaration of 30 October thereto and in order to establish a uniform legal basis in Germany for the prosecution of war criminals and other similar offenders, other than those dealt with by the International Military Tribunal, the Control Council enacts as follows:

Article I. The Moscow Declaration of 30 October 1943 "Concerning Responsibility of Hitlerites for Committed Atrocities" and the London Agreement of 8 August 1945 "Concerning Prosecution and Punishment of the Major War Criminals of the European Axis" are made integral parts of this Law. Adherence to the provisions of the London Agreement by any of the United Nations, as provided for in Article 5 of that Agreement, shall not entitle such nation to participate or interfere in the operation of this Law within the Control Council area of authority in Germany.

Article II. 1. Each of the following acts is recognized as a crime:

(a) *Crimes against Peace*. Initiation of invasion of other countries and wars of aggression in violation of international laws and treaties, including but not limited to planning, preparation, initiation or waging a war aggression, or a war in violation of international treaties, agreements or assurances, or participating in a common plan or conspiracy for the accomplishments of any of the foregoing.

(b) *War Crimes*. Atrocities or offenses against persons or property constituting violations of the laws or customs of war, including, but not limited to, murder, ill treatment or deportations to slave labour or for any other purpose, of civilian population from occupied territory, murder or ill treatment of prisoners of war or persons on the seas, killing of hostages, plunder of public or private property, wanton destruction of cities, towns or village, or devastation not justified by military necessity.

(c) *Crimes Against Humanity*. Atrocities and offenses, including but not limited to murder, extermination, enslavement, deportation, imprisonment, torture, rape, or other inhumane acts committed against any civilian population, or persecutions on political, racial, or religious grounds whether or not in violation of the domestic laws of the country where perpetrated.

(d) Membership in categories of a criminal group or organization declared criminal by the International Military Tribunal.

2. Any person without regard to nationality or the capacity in which he acted, is deemed to have committed a crime as defined in paragraph 1 of this Article, if he was (a) a principal or (b) was an accessory to the commission of any such crime or ordered or abetted the same or (c) took a consenting part therein or (d) was connected with plans or enterprises involving its commission or (e) was a member of any organization or group connected with the commission of any such crime or (f) with reference to paragraph 1(a), if he held a high political, civil or military (including General Staff) position in Germany or in one of its Allies, co-belligerents or satellites or held high position in the financial, industrial or economic life of any such country.

3. Any person found guilty of any of the Crimes above mentioned may upon conviction be punished as shall be determined by the tribunal to be just. Such punishment may consist of one or more of the following:

(a) Death

(b) Imprisonment for life or a term of years, with or without hard labor.

(c) Fine, and imprisonment with or without hard labor, in lieu thereof.

(d) Forfeiture of property.

(e) Restitution of property wrongfully acquired.

(f) Deprivation of some or all civil rights.

Any property declared to be forfeited or the restitution of which is ordered by the Tribunal shall be delivered to the Control Council for Germany, which shall decide on its disposal.

4. (a) The official position of any person, whether as Head of State or as a responsible official in a Government Department, does not free him from responsibility for a crime or entitle him to mitigation of punishment.

(b) The fact that any person acted pursuant to the order of his Government or of a superior does not free him from responsibility for a crime, but may be considered in mitigation.

5. In any trial or prosecution for a crime herein referred to, the accused shall not be entitled to the benefits of any statute of limitations in respect of the period from 30 January 1933 to 1 July 1945, nor shall any immunity, pardon or amnesty granted under the Nazi regime be admitted as a bar to trial or punishment.

Article III. Each occupying authority, within its Zone of occupation,

(a) shall have the right to cause persons within such zone suspected of having committed a crime, including those charged with crime by one of the United Nations, to be arrested and shall take under control the property, real and personal, owned or controlled by the said persons, pending decisions as to its eventual disposition.

(b) shall report to the Legal Directorate the names of all suspected criminals, the reasons for and the places of their detention, if they are detained, and the names and location of witnesses.

(c) shall take appropriate measures to see that witnesses and evidence will be available when required.

(d) shall have the right to cause all persons so arrested and charged, and not delivered to another authority as herein provided, or released, to be brought to trial before an appropriate tribunal. Such tribunal may, in the case of crimes committed by persons of German citizenship or nationality against other persons of German citizenship or nationality, or stateless persons, be a German court, if authorized by the occupying authorities.

2. The tribunal by which persons charged with offenses hereunder shall be tried and the rules and procedure thereof shall be determined or designated by each Zone Commander for his respective Zone. Nothing herein is intended to, or shall impair or limit the jurisdiction or power of any court or tribunal now or hereafter established in any Zone by the Commander thereof, or of the International Military Tribunal established by the London Agreement of 8 August 1945.

3. Persons wanted for trial by an International Military Tribunal will not be tried without the consent of the Committee of Chief Prosecutors. Each Zone Commander will deliver such persons who are within his Zone to that committee upon request and will make witnesses and evidence available to it.

4. Persons known to be wanted for trial in another Zone or outside Germany will not be tried prior to decision under Article IV unless the fact of their apprehension has been reported in accordance with Section 1(b) of this Article, three months have elapsed thereafter, and no request for delivery of the type contemplated by Article IV has been received by the Zone Commander concerned.

5. The execution of death sentences may be deferred by not to exceed one month after sentence has become final when the Zone Commander has reason to believe that the testimony of those under sentence would be of value in the investigation and trial of crimes within or without his Zone.

6. Each Zone Commander will cause such effect to be given to the judgments of courts of competent jurisdiction, with respect to property taken under his control pursuant thereto, as he may deem proper in the interest of justice.

Article IV. 1. When any person in a Zone in Germany is alleged to have committed a crime, as defined in Article II, in a country other than Germany or in another Zone, the government of that nation or the Commander of the latter Zone, as the case may be, may request the Commander of the Zone in which the person is located for his arrest and delivery for trial to the country or Zone in which the crime was committed. Such request for delivery shall be granted by the Commander receiving it unless he believes such person is wanted for trial or as a witness by an International Military Tribunal, or in Germany, or in a nation other than the one making the request, or the Commander is not satisfied that delivery should be made, in any of which cases he shall have the right to forward the said request to the Legal Directorate of the Allied Control Authority. A similar procedure shall apply to witnesses, material exhibits and other forms of evidence.

2. The Legal Directorate shall consider all requests referred to it, and shall determine the same in accordance with the following principles, its determination to be communicated to the Zone Commander.

(a) A person wanted for trial or as a witness in an International Military Tribunal shall not be delivered for trial or required to give evidence outside Germany, as the case may be, except upon approval of the Committee of Chief Counsel acting under the London Agreement of 8 August 1945.

(b) A person wanted for trial by several authorities (other than an International Military Tribunal) shall be disposed of in accordance with the following priorities:

(1) If wanted for trial in the Zone [in] which he is, he should not be delivered unless arrangements are made for his return after trial elsewhere;

(2) If wanted for trial in a Zone other than that in which he is, he should be delivered to that Zone in preference to delivery outside Germany unless arrangements are made for his return to that Zone after trial elsewhere;

(3) If wanted for trial outside Germany by two or more of the United Nations, or one of which he is a citizen, that one should have priority;

(4) If wanted for trial outside Germany by several countries, not all of which are United Nations, United Nations should have priority;

(5) If wanted for trial outside Germany by two or more of the United Nations, then, subject to Article IV 2(b) (3) above, that which has the most serious charges against him, which are moreover supported by evidence, should have priority.

Article V. The delivery, under Article IV of this law, of persons for trial shall be made on demands of the Governments or Zone Commanders in such a manner that the delivery of criminals to one jurisdiction will not become the means of defeating or unnecessarily delaying the carrying out of justice in another place. If within six months the delivered person has not been convicted by the Court of the Zone or country to which he has been delivered, then such person shall be returned upon demand of the Commander of the Zone where the person was located prior to delivery.

[The IMT-Nuremberg and Allied Control Council Law No. 10 were both *ad hoc* measures taken by the victors of World War II in Europe to deal with German war criminals on a broad scale. Because there had been a complete disintegration of the German government which was followed by the unconditional surrender of German armed forces, the Allies thereby exercised supreme governmental power over the boundaries of a defeated nation. Explaining this state of affairs in greater detail, Kelsen[45] writes:

---

45. Hans Kelsen, "Legal Status of Germany According to the Declaration of Berlin," 39 *Am. J. Int'l L.* 518–519 (1945).

…German territory, together with the population residing on it, has been placed under the sovereignty of the four powers. It means further that the legal status of Germany is not that of 'belligerent occupation' in accordance with Articles 42 to 56 of the Regulations annexed to the Hague Convention respecting the Laws and Customs of War on Land of 1907. After Germany's unconditional surrender and especially after the abolition of the last German Government, the Government of Grand Admiral Döenitz, the status of belligerent occupation has become impossible. This status presupposes that a state of war still exists in the relationship between occupant and state and the state whose territory is under belligerent occupation. This condition implies the continued existence of the state whose territory is occupied and, consequently, the continued existence of its government recognized as the legitimate bearer of the sovereignty of the occupied state. This is the reason why it is generally assumed that belligerent occupation does not confer upon the occupant power sovereignty over the occupied territory. By belligerent occupation the legitimate government is made incapable of exercising its authority and is only substituted for the period of occupation by the authority of the occupant power.…

It can hardly be doubted that Germany, after the unconditional surrender of her armed forces, did not fulfill the conditions essential to belligerent occupation. For the legitimate Government of Germany had ceased to exist. The unconditional surrender signed by the representatives of the last legitimate Government of Germany may be interpreted as a transfer of Germany's sovereignty to the victorious powers signatories to the surrender treaty.… By abolishing the last Government of Germany the victorious powers have destroyed the existence of Germany as a sovereign state. Since her unconditional surrender, at least since the abolishment of the Döenitz Government, Germany has ceased to exist as a state in the sense of international law.[46]

Subsequent to the International Military Tribunal, war crime trials at both Nuremberg and other locations throughout Germany were held under the aegis of Control Council Law No. 10. Selected cases tried under CCL 10 by the United States are reported *infra*. after the IMT-Nuremberg trial of the major Nazi war criminals and accompanying selected commentary].

---

9. Gerry L. Simpson, "War Crimes Trials: Some Problems" in *The Law of War Crimes: National and International Approaches*

4–9; 11–13; 16–17 (1997)
Reprinted with permission of Brill Academic Publishers NV.
© 1997 Kluwer Law International

A. The Problem of Partiality

On August 8, 1945, the Allies signed the London Charter establishing an international tribunal to try the major German war criminals. This was to presage a new era in

---

46. *Id.* at 518–519.

which the requirements of justice and the concerns of universal human rights were to guide the conduct of international relations. Acts of criminality during war were declared and the wholesale destruction of civilian populations was condemned as a crime against humanity. On the same day in 1945, the United States dropped its second atomic bomb on Japan devastating the city of Nagasaki and immediately killing at least 70,000 of its largely civilian inhabitants. The history of war crimes is a history suffused with irony but the conjunction of these two acts—one, a manifesto declaring the subordination of force to law, the other, an unprecedented act of violence contrary to a basic requirement of the laws of war—is perhaps the most tragically ironic of all. For some observers, Nagasaki is viewed as the symbol of the death of an idea at its birth, the idea of universal application of international criminal law to all offenders regardless of affiliation, status or nationality. Systematic and consistent regulation of international crime remains chimerical despite the efforts of the International Law Commission and various publicists.

In the absence of a uniform and global approach, there is a widespread assumption that the trials of war criminals have generally occurred only where defeat and criminality coincide.... The victorious allied powers tried their German and Japanese adversaries without ever considering the possibility of applying these same laws to their own war-time behavior. There is little doubt that some allied actions would have proved amenable to the laws of Nuremberg even if the jurisdictional and political barriers to prosecution were inevitably insurmountable. Indeed, the defence attorneys at Nuremberg invoked the *tu quoque* [thou also] principle several times pointing to the bombing of Dresden, for example, as evidence that the Allies had not come to Nuremberg with clean hands. The most successful use of this argument occurred in the case of Admiral Döenitz who argued, with some justification, that the "crime" of failing to pick up enemy survivors of submarine attacks was in fact the policy of U.S. forces in the Pacific under the command of [Admiral] Nimitz.

Regardless of how well-founded these *tu quoque* objections are, it is important to recognize that the Nuremberg and Tokyo proceedings are not typical of war crimes initiatives before or since. If they are models of victor's justice they are not models of war crimes trials generally. There are several respects in which this is true. First, the classical war crimes trials both prior to and since 1945 have generally occurred in domestic settings under national rather than international law. This was the case in Leipzig where German nationals were tried under German law for crimes committed during the First World War....

* * *

There is another sense in which the Nuremberg model is misleading. The vast majority of cases in which sanctions are imposed on violators of the laws of war take place under military jurisdiction. This is yet another irony of the area—that, for all their supposedly educative function, most war crimes trials are confidential and usually remain so. Here, again winners and losers alike try their own military personnel for breaches of the laws of war or war crimes.... The use of martial law is both unsurprising and perfectly appropriate in many circumstances. The Geneva Conventions and Protocols envisage sanctions along these lines in cases of war crimes or grave breaches of their provisions.

* * *

...In the sphere of international criminal law there is a regularized tension between the retributive urge and the realist demand, between the necessary and the possible, the visceral and the pragmatic. Each new atrocity brings in its train a fresh call for war crimes prosecutions. This, in turn, is routinely met with reluctance and caution from those with the power to set in motion the mechanics of such a trial. Justice and diplomacy are engaged in a perpetual *pas de deux* over whether to prosecute or rehabilitate. It is only an unexpected confluence of events that leads to the establishment of such tribunals.... So each war crimes trial is an exercise in partial justice to the extent that it reminds us that the majority of war crimes remain unpunished....

This area of law is partial and selective in other less obvious ways. War crimes jurisprudence generally — that is, the practice of courts and tribunals since 1945 — reveals an obsession with the trial and punishment of Nazi war criminals. This bias may have a number of explanations but it is particularly curious given the absence of any prosecutions involving Japanese war criminals after 1947 (it is significant, in this regard, that the Tokyo trials themselves have almost disappeared from history).

The metaphorical equation of war crimes with Nazis is inscribed on the culture. Most of the war crimes trials held since 1945 has been a restatement of this relationship. The Nazi regime remains the epitome of absolute evil in Western culture and each successive war crimes trial owes as much to this doctrine as to the tenacious efforts of Nazi hunters like Beate Klarsfeld and Simon Weisenthal. Why has there been a tendency to equate war crimes and the Nazi regime in Western jurisprudence and culture? Any answer to this question is likely to be complex and inconclusive. One way to approach the problem is to remember that war crimes trials (especially successful ones) have exculpatory effects as well as retributive consequences. As well as trying alleged war criminals, these trials serve as vindication of Western progress, they maintain the idea that National Socialism was an aberration in Western culture, they function as moral demarcations between the accused and the accusers, they even avert attention from war crimes closer to home and, finally, they contain the message that the untried crimes are not of this magnitude or order. The eternal pariah is Nazi Germany serving as a lesson not only that it must not happen again but perhaps it is *not* happening again.

The singular focus on Nazi war criminals has a curious legal consequence. The Nazis are taken as an exemplification of evil in the world and also an exception to universal humanism. This is why war crimes trials hover endlessly between upholding a universal morality and particularizing the crime in question as an historical exception. Ultimately, the performance of a war crimes trial is both situated in a history and yet seeks to transcend it. The trial confines a historical moment in its abnormality but wishes to make its lesson universal and timeless....

B. The Problem of Legality

War crimes trials have been impugned on many grounds over the last half-century. Perhaps the most serious group of objections concern the legality or procedural fairness of these trials... Judith Shklar, for example, has argued that war crimes trials bear an uneasy resemblance to the political or show trials regarded as the antithesis of the Western tradition of legalism. There is no question that war crimes trials raise delicate matters of procedure and jurisdiction.

Generality

A fundamental requirement of the rule of law is generality — that is, the principle that laws should be applied generally and uniformly to all activities regardless of the status of the actor. War crimes prosecutions have tended to suffer from defects in this regard also.

Prosecutions are often limited to a certain group (the Nazis), a certain time period or a particular locus.... The problems related to partiality are obviously linked closely to this concern for the legality of the individual trial. The selective application of international criminal law is a serious flaw in the international legal system itself (partiality) and, also, an impediment to the just application of these laws to individual defendants (legality).

Nullem Crimen Sine Lege

War crimes also suffer from vagueness deficiencies. The lack of any systematic definition of international criminal law (only now being remedied by the International Law Commission but still at the reform stage) means that categories such as crimes against humanity or crimes against peace remain underdeveloped. Meanwhile, the notion of war crime itself has given rise to a proliferation of meanings....

The absence of clear standards or precedents is another ground for suggesting that war crimes prosecutions have the potential to offend the principles *nullen crimen sine lege* [no crime without a law] and *nullen poena sine lege* [no punishment without a law]. This is particularly the case in international criminal law where the laws are rarely self-applying.... Crimes against humanity were defined in the International Military Tribunal Charter as war-time acts; genocide requires an intent that may be difficult to show; war crimes are hedged by military necessity defences; and international humanitarian law has not been fully extended to cover civil wars.... Each of these factors makes enforcement more difficult.

War crimes trials are also often criticized as an *ex post facto* application of alien law to acts whose criminality was not at all obvious at the time these acts were carried out. Indeed, this problem was fully exploited by the defence in the Nuremberg trial who argued that the absence of an international criminal law regime prior to 1945 meant that the Nazi defendants could not possibly know that they had offended any universal principles of criminality. These defences were rejected but only after a rather unconvincing trawl through pre-War international law for evidence of an incipient criminal law system....

* * *

C. Conceptual Difficulties Associated with International Criminality

The problem of definition creates due process difficulties related to vagueness but is also endemic to international criminal law at a deeper conceptual level. The attempt to develop a more general notion of criminality in international law has proved troublesome given the structure of the system itself. The international legal order was traditionally conceived as the private law between equal legal persons—the equivalent of tort and contract law in municipal systems. According to this once dominant positivistic reading of international law, the system lacks a public dimension because there is no public enforcement instrument and no substantive public law. International law is seen simply as the contractual relations between states. When States commit wrongs they become delictually liable to other States and not to some transcendent public administrative organ. This idea of horizontal responsibility exhausts the possibilities of punishment in the eyes of the classical scholars. According to them, crime is a concept alien or unknown to such a system.

However, there are many definitions of "crime" and the distinction between civil and criminal liability is not one that can be made with much confidence even in municipal systems where the distinction has been operative for centuries. Generally, it is thought that criminal law is an expression of a community's moral sense. As such, it is public, punitive, retributive and moral in ways that civil law is not. Consequently, violations of criminal law are said to have graver social consequences for the whole of society which demands, in turn, that the community acts through its public enforcement agencies to suppress these breaches.

Given this, the international legal order seems unsuited for a criminal role. There are at least three reasons why the notion of crime may not be readily transposed from municipal to international settings. First, there is no public system of sanction which might enforce such law. Criminal law seems to require the presence of an Austinian sovereign to carry out its dictates. Such a public centre of power is lacking in the statist order.... Second, international law *pace* Austin may be more positivistic than domestic legal orders. The moral or naturalistic orientation of much criminal law depends on a system of shared social ethics or an underlying natural law. Conversely, the international law regime is morally pluralistic and normatively consensual. Third, and very much associated with this point, the commission of crime often requires an element of intention or moral turpitude that States as corporate bodies may not possess. Certainly, States are less easily viewed as moral persons than human beings.

Whatever one thinks of these doubts, they have not proved fatal to the development of embryonic forms of criminal law within the international system. The nomenclature, and probably the substance, of criminality has now been introduced, most notably by the Nuremberg Tribunal and, more recently, by the International Law Commission, even if these two bodies have defined crime in two radically divergent ways. However, the questions as to whom it should apply and who should enforce it remain unresolved.

---

10. Robert L. Birmingham, *Note*, "The War Crimes Trial: A Second Look"

24 *University of Pittsburgh Law Review* 132; 133–139; (1962–63)
Reproduced with permission of the *University of Pittsburgh Law Review* ©
1962–63, Robert L. Birmingham, *The War Crimes Trial; A Second Look*,
24 *U. Pitt. L. Rev.* 132 (1962–63)

Introduction

The determination of the victorious Allies to assess individual responsibility for the nightmare of the Second World War through the innovation of the trial of the leaders of the vanquished powers has excited a seemingly endless flow of inconclusive legal analysis.... Questions concerning the legality of war crimes trials today seem moot; the prior proceedings are a *fait accompli* which will stand as precedent sufficient to support their reintroduction if the occasion arises.

* * *

A. War Crimes Trials: Efficacy and Fairness

1. War, Technology, and Nationalism

War has always brought sufferings to common combatants and to civilians caught in the path of fighting. Members of the aristocracy frequently, and at times apparently even traditionally, met death in battle. Nevertheless, the presumed manliness of physical aggression, the glory of victory, the grandeur of military display, and the appeals of patriotism combined to make most suffering tolerable.

* * *

Even though until the twentieth century weapons had only had limited powers of destruction, war has throughout history proved terrifyingly devastating. Kurt Reinhardt, describing the results of the Thirty Years' War of the seventeenth century, states:

> Some figures may illustrate the extent to which vitality of the German people was taxed and depleted by the successive waves of destruction. The city of Augsburg lost 62,000 of its 80,000 inhabitants. The population of the duchy of Würtemberg was reduced from 400,000 to 48,000. It is reliably estimated that the density of the population as a whole decreased by nearly two thirds....

The prevalence of militant nationalism makes the use of modern instruments of destruction possible if not probable. A relatively new force, its reception into the post-classical theory of politics appears to date from Bodin's isolation of the concept of sovereignty in the latter half of the sixteenth century. Machiavelli, who coined the term "state" (*lo stato*) over a century earlier, was interested in the power of the individual ruler rather than the institutional framework within which he operated.

In the past, patriotism has frequently consisted of little more than an attitude of comfortable superiority engendered by ethnocentrism. The British gentlemen of the nineteenth century, for instance, could enjoy the gratification of harmless hatred of everything French without stirring from his club chair. Since aggressiveness is not a prerequisite of patriotism, willingness to die for one's country does not necessarily imply approval of the sacrifice of lives to increase its power.

Nevertheless the ideology of nationalism may be adopted by the fanatic as the means of mobilizing consent to revolutionary change. Resulting encouragement of concern for country without regard for the welfare of mankind in general creates dangerous international instability in a world shrunken by air transportation and electronic communication.

* * *

2. The War Crimes Trial as a Preventive Measure

Having granted that thermonuclear war is a grave danger to mankind and that some reformulation of the structure of the international community is necessary to assure peace, we are confronted with the problem of determining whether war trials...are a step toward essential safeguards....

One may well doubt that the fear of punishment will go far to prevent future national leaders from initiating hostilities or acting inhumanely during war. Hitler, after all, hardly expected to be banished to Elba if his efforts at world conquest proved unsuccessful. Elimination of hope for mercy, on the other hand, may upon evident military failure lead to orgies or national self-destruction rather than life-saving compromise. Although some lessening of government efficiency may be expected if lower-level leaders are aware that obedience to orders may subject them to personal liability upon defeat, even here we must assume that the individual would prefer to be shot at as late a date as possible.

The war crimes trial may have some small value as a propaganda device through information dissemination and public condemnation of actions which the judges find morally reprehensible. This influence upon the ethical standards of mankind would, however, seem limited. A cursory comparison of behavior recommended by Christ to assure eternal glory and the history of Europe over the past twenty centuries will demonstrate a compartmentalization of the individual's spiritual nature which permits ostensible adherence to ideals even while compromising with reality.

3. The War Crimes Trial as a Mechanism for Revenge

The war crimes trial would seem most effective as a ritual of revenge. Hitler's madness devastated an entire continent and brought misery into countless American homes half a world away. The attempt to unify a people through the merciless destruction of a several-million-member cultural minority among them ranks with the most barbaric practices in history. Photographs of life in German prison camps such as Buchenwald simultaneously nauseate and enrage the viewer. Psychologically healthy expression of grief and anger may be obtained through a judicial proceeding such as the Nuremberg trials, which permits extensive public exhibition of the criminals and continued reiteration of their deeds.

Retribution as a theory of punishment has its basis in the Code of Hammurabi and the Mosaic laws of *Exodus*, where it was employed as a limitation on revenge. Seneca wrote that "it is but a just retaliation for anyone to suffer in his own person the evil that he intended to inflict upon another." Kant stated that "the right of Retaliation (*jus talionis*)…is the only Principle which in regulating a Public Court…can definitely assign both the quality and quantity of a just penalty. All other standards are wavering and uncertain…they contain no principle conformable to the sentence of pure and strict Justice." Nevertheless, the modern reader cannot help but feel revulsion upon reading Blackstone's argument that the corpse of a murderer hanging in chains on the gibbet was "a comfortable sign to the relations and friends of the deceased." There is a growing realization, receiving only limited recognition in the law, that asocial actions indicate character maladjustments which should be corrected rather than condemned.

4. Justice and the War Crimes Trials

The practical effectiveness of war crimes trials may be seriously questioned. Against whatever small degree of utility such proceedings may possess must be balanced their probably intrinsically unjust nature.

The defendants in the Nuremberg trials were not permitted to relieve themselves of individual responsibility by demonstrating that punishment of nationals of the prosecuting states guilty of equally heinous acts was not to be considered. This ruling would seem correct: "As far as the *tu quoque* argument is concerned, it need only be mentioned that it is no defence for an individual to claim that a crime for which he is being tried has also been committed by others." One should nevertheless remember that the atrocities perpetrated by the Russians during the decade preceding the Second World War rivaled in barbarity those of the Third Reich. Moreover, in the last moments of conflict America, albeit with probable justification, unleashed the terror of the atomic bomb on Japanese populations primarily composed of innocent women and children.

That reprehensible acts were committed in pursuance of superior orders did not absolve the defendants, since the courts maintained that those on trial were aware that their deeds violated the unwritten laws of humanity.… Most of the acts committed on German soil which the Tribunal found objectionable were legal under the degenerate form of national law then prevailing. In addition, the Nazi government had ostensibly made German law applicable to its citizens throughout the conquered territory.

[The preceding selections, published thirty-five years apart, discuss war crimes trials from a slightly different perspective. Because of the enormous diversity of opinion on this subject, even today, it is difficult to draw definite conclusions about either the utility or the disutility of such proceedings. Some commentators have elevated the so-called "Nuremberg Principles" to almost canonical status in international law, while others with distinctive national memories have been less effusive. Some praise particular portions of the Nuremberg ruling while damning portions they find disagreeable. Each of them in their own way have contributed to the massive literature surrounding this case alone. When juxtaposed beside its Asian counterpart, the Tokyo IMTFE, the Nuremberg trial stands alone as an international symbol of both due process and retribution combined. It has emerged as the twentieth century's pole star edict on state-sponsored atrocity and obscene violence. In addition, the IMT-Nuremberg opinion has been employed to justify other more recent *ad hoc* tribunal rulings in both the Balkans and in East Africa. Thus we turn now to the most discussed international criminal justice decision of the twentieth century. *Table I* that follows lists all twenty-four defendants charged with one or more violations of international criminal law at Nuremberg. Twenty-two of these defendants are listed in alphabetical order. Two, Robert Ley and Gustav Krupp von Bohlen und Halbach, were not tried. Ley committed suicide before trial and the elder Krupp was determined to be too ill to stand trial. His son, Alfried, was substituted in his place and tried in a separate proceeding under Control Council Law No. 10 in 1947–48].

Table I

11. IMT-Nuremberg Defendants and Their Position(s) in the Third Reich

(1)   Martin Bormann
(1900–1945)
Born: Halberstadt, Germany,
    June 17, 1900
Died: Berlin, Germany,
    May, 1945

*One-time Saxony farmer
*Head, Nazi Party Chancellery
*Manager of "Hitler's Purse"
*Executed "Master Race" Programs
*Final arbiter/decision-maker on most NSDAP Appointments
*Day-to-day NSDAP administrator
*In Berlin bunker and witnessed Hitler's marriage and suicide
*Tried *in absentia* and sentenced to death by the IMT
* Skeletal remains unearthed in a Berlin excavation in early 1970s
* Declared officially dead by a West German court in 1973

(2)   Karl Döenitz
(1891–1980)
Born: Grunau bei Berlin, Germany,
    September 16, 1891
Died: Hamburg Germany,
    December 24, 1980

*Commander of U-boats (*Befehlshaber der U-Boote* (Sept. 12, 1939)
*Supreme Naval Commander (*Oberbefehlshaber der Kreigsmarine* (1943)
*Broke off Battle of Atlantic (1943)
*Condemned the "dishonorable" officers who plotted Hitler's assasination on July 20, 1944

*Named final successor to Adolf Hitler
(May, 1945)
*Sentenced to 10 years imprisonment by
the IMT

(3) Hans Frank
     (1900–1946)
     Born: Karlsruhe, Germany,
          May 23, 1900
     Died: Nuremberg, Germany,
          October 16, 1946

*Member of Nazi Party's "Old Guard"
*Governor-General of Occupied Poland
*Established the Reich Legal Office
(*Reichsrechtamt*) in 1930
*Established Academy of German Law in
1933
*Nazi Party's leading lawyer
*Converted to Christianity and joined
Roman Catholic faith near war's end
*His ledger, kept from 1939 to 1945,
condemned him
*Responsible for sending thousands of
Poles and Jews to their death
*Wrote book, *Im Angesicht des Galgens*
(Facing the Gallows) before he was
executed

(4) Wilhelm Frick
     (1877–1946)
     Born: Alsenz, Germany,
          March 12, 1877
     Died: Nuremberg, Germany,
          October 16, 1946

*German politician and one of Hitler's
favorite bureaucrats
*Reich Minister of the Interior
*Instrumental in passage of infamous,
anti-Semitic "Nuremberg Laws"
*Considered to be architect of the Nazi
police state and co-developer of the terror
system of concentration camps
*Appointed Reich Protector of Bohemia
and Moravia in 1943

(5) Hans Fritzsche
     (1900–1953)
     Born: Bochum, Germany,
          April 21, 1900
     Died: Cologne, Germany,
          September 27, 1953

*German journalist and Director of the
news service in the Nazi Propaganda
Ministry (May 1933)
*Director, Radio Division on the Nazi
Propaganda Ministry (1942)
*Identified bodies of Josef Goebbels and
family in Berlin bunker to Soviets (1945)
*Taken to Moscow and placed in prison
*Returned to Nuremberg (1945)
*Acquitted by the IMT
*Sentenced to a work camp by a German
de-Nazification court in 1947
*Released, Sept. 29, 1950

(6) Walther Funk
     (1890–1960)
     Born: Trakehnen, Germany,
          August 18, 1890
     Died: Düsseldorf, Germany,

*German politician and economics expert
*Became Hitler's personal economics advisor
*Reich Economics Minister and General
Plenipotentiary for the War Economy
(1938)

May 31, 1960

*President of the Reichsbank (1939)
*Shared responsibility for looting of occupied territories
*Entered secret accord with *Reichsführer SS*, Heinrich Himmler, that enabled Reichsbank to store for the SS cash, gold, jewelry and other valuables taken from deported and/or murdered Jews
*Sentenced to life imprisonment by the IMT
*Released from Spandau Prison in Berlin in 1957 due to ill-health

(7) Herrmann Wilhelm Göering
(1893–1946)
Born: Rosenheim, Germany,
       January 12, 1893
Died: Nuremberg, Germany,
       October 15, 1946

*Highest ranking Nazi tried by the IMT
*Member of famed WW I Richthofen Flying Squadron
*Member of the Nazi "Old Guard"
*Prussian Minister of the Interior
*Organizer of state secret police (*Geheime Staatspolizei*) or the Gestapo
*Commander-in-Chief of the German Air Force (*Oberkommando der Luftwaffe*)
Reichsmarshal by appointment (July 10, 1940)
*Sentenced to death by IMT
*Committed suicide in custody one day before appointed execution

(8) Richard Rudolf Hess
(1894–1987)
Born: Alexandria, Egypt,
       April 26, 1894
Died: Berlin, Germany,
       August 17, 1987

*Early Head of Nazi Party Chancellery
*Deputy *Führer* to Adolf Hitler
*Involved in 1923 Beer Hall Putsch with Hitler
*Detained 18 months in Landsberg Prison and there took dictation from Hitler for *Mein Kampf*
*Flew to Scotland in ME-109, on May 10, 1941, in a futile attempt to negotiate a settlement between Nazi Germany and Great Britain
*Sentenced to life imprisonment by the IMT
*Committed suicide in Spandau Prison as the sole remaining inmate from the Nazi era

(9) Alfred Jodl
(1890–1946)
Born: Würzburg, Germany,
       May 10, 1890
Died: Nuremberg, Germany,
       October 16, 1946

*Front-line soldier in WWI
*Attained rank of Colonel General (Jan. 30, 1944)
*One of Hitler's closest military advisors
*Chief of the *Wehrmacht* Operations Staff
*Worked closely with both Hitler and Keitel

*Signed Germany's unconditional
surrender at Rheims, France on May 7,
1945
*Sentenced to death by the IMT
*On Feb. 28, 1953, a West German court
rehabilitated Jodl *posthumously*, finding
him not guilty of breaching international
law, but excluding the disputed charge of
committing Crimes Against Peace

(10) Ernst Kaltenbrunner
      (1903–1946)
      Born: Ried, Austria,
            October 4, 1903
      Died:: Nuremberg, Germany,
            October 16, 1946

*Austrian lawyer
*Austrian Minister of State Security
*SS-*Obergruppenführer*
*Member of the *Reichstag*
*Played key role in organizing police
activities in the Austrian *Anschluss* (1938)
*Prime mover in operationalizing the
"Final Solution" to the Jewish problem
*Adolf Eichmann's superior
*Head of the RSHA (Reich Main Security
Office) (1943)
*Sentenced to death by the IMT

(11) Wilhelm Keitel
      (1882–1946)
      Born: Helmscherode, Germany,
            September 22, 1882
      Died: Nuremberg, Germany,
            October 16, 1946

*Professional soldier and member of a
Freikorps in 1919
*Chief of Staff of the High Command of
German Armed Forces (*Oberkommando
der Wehrmacht*) (OKW)
*His signatures appeared on such infamous
documents as the *Commisar Order*, the
Bullet Decree and the *Night and Fog Order*
(*Nacht-und-Nebel Erlass*)
*Field-Marshal by appointment (1940)
*Part of all military plans under Hitler
*Member: Secret Cabinet Council and
Council for the Defence of the Reich
*Sentenced to death by the IMT; Request as
a soldier to be shot by firing squad was
denied

(12) Constantin Freiherr von Neurath
      (1873–1956)
      Born: Klein-Glattbach, Germany,
            February 2, 1873
      Died: Enzweihingen, Germany,
            August 14, 1956

*German politician and
SS-*Obergruppenfüherer*
*Diplomat in Papen government before
Nazi takeover
*German Foreign Minister (1933–1938)
*Replaced by von Ribbentrop (1938)
*President, Secret Cabinet Council
*Reich Protector of Bohemia and Moravia
(1939)
*Went on permanent "sick leave" in 1941
*Sentenced to 15 years imprisonment by
the IMT

*Granted early release in 1954 due to an eye ailment

(13) Franz von Papen
(1879–1969)
Born: Werl, Germany,
October 28, 1879
Died: Obersasbach, Germany,
May 2, 1969

*General Staff and cavalry officer during WW I
*German politician and diplomat
*Joined intrigue that brought Hitler to power
*Mediated Hitler's "Concordat" with Roman Catholic Church
*Appointed Ambassador to Austria (July, 1934)
*Helped ease the way for the German *Anschluss* with Austria
*Ambassador to Turkey (1939–1944)
*Acquitted by the IMT
*Sentenced to 8 years in a work camp by a West German court (1949)
*Wrote autobiography, *Der Wahrheit eine Gasse* (A Way to Truth), published in 1952
*Autobiography gave no insight into his fateful role in the liquidation of the Weimar Republic and the establishment of Nazi tyranny

(14) Erich Raeder
(1876–1960)
Born: Hamburg-Wandsbeck,
Germany, April 24, 1876
Died: Kiel, Germany,
November 6, 1960

*German Grand Admiral (*Grossadmiral*) (Apr. 1, 1939)
*Replaced as Grand Admiral by Hitler in 1943 by Karl Döenitz because of a disagreement involving U-boat warfare
*Sentenced to life imprisonment by the IMT
*Released from imprisonment at Spandau on Sept. 26, 1955, because of ill-health

(15) Joachim von Ribbentrop
(1893–1946)
Born: Wesel, Germany,
April 30, 1893
Died: Nuremberg, Germany,
October 16, 1946

*German politician and diplomat
*Hitler's Chief Foreign Policy advisor
*Reich Minister of Foreign Affairs (1938)
*Played key role in the Munich Pact of Sept., 1938, wherein Britain and France deserted their Czechoslovak ally and appeased Nazi Germany
*Signed the German-Soviet Non-Aggression Pact in Moscow containing secret clause to partition Poland and open the way for the German attack on Poland, Sept. 1, 1939
*Sentenced to death by the IMT

(16) Alfred Rosenberg
(1893–1946)
Born: Tallinn, Estonia,

*Baltic German who joined Nazi Party in 1919
*In 1923, became editor of the Nazi

January 12, 1893
Died: Nuremberg, Germany,
October 16, 1946

newspaper *Volkische Beobachter*
(Ethical/Racial Observer)
*Self-proclaimed ideologue of National
Socialism
*Founder, Fighting League for German
Culture
*Established *Einstab Rosenberg* to loot art
treasurers from occupied territories
*Minister for the Occupied Eastern
Territories (1941)
*Plenipotentiary for Labour Mobilization
(1942–1945)
*Sentenced to death by the IMT

(17) Fritz Sauckel
      (1894–1946)
      Born: Hassfurt, Germany,
            October 27, 1894
      Died: Nuremberg, Germany,
            October 16, 1946

*German politician and merchant seaman
during WWI
*Joined Nazi Party in 1923
*Appointed General Plenipotentiary for
Labor Deployment (Mar. 21, 1939)
*Member of the Reichstag
*Organized millions of alien workers to
work in German industry against their
wills under miserable working conditions
*Plenipotentiary for Labour Mobilization
(1942–1945)
*Sentenced to death by the IMT

(18) Hjalmar Schacht
      (1877–1970)
      Born: Tinglev, Germany,
            January 22, 1877
      Died: Munich, Germany,
            June 4, 1970

*German politician and financial expert
*Reared in United States by immigrant
parents
*President of the Reichsbank (1924–1929)
*Reich Finance Minister (1935–1937)
*Connected to the July 20, 1944 plot
against Hitler's life
*Arrested and imprisoned in German
concentration camp until war's end
*Was incredulous for being tried by the
IMT
*Acquitted by the IMT

(19) Baldur von Schirach
      (1907–1974)
      Born: Berlin, Germany,
            May 9, 1907
      Died: Krov/Mosel, Germany,
            August 8, 1974

*Joined Nazi Party in 1924
*Appointed Reich Youth Führer
(Reichsjügend Führer) (1928)
*Appointed Leader of Hitler Youth (*Die
Hitler Jügend*) (1934)
*By 1938, had built Hitler Youth
membership to 7.75 million
*Entered German Army in 1940 and
awarded Iron Cross, 2d Class
*Left army and assumed post of Governor
and *Gauleiter* of Vienna

*Sentenced to 20 years imprisonment by the IMT
*Released from Spandau Prison in 1966
*His memoirs, *Ich glaubte an Hitler* shed little light on Nazi era

(20) Arthur Seyss-Inquart
      (1892–1946)
      Born: Stannern bei Iglau,
          Moravia
      Died: Nuremberg, Germany,
          October 16, 1946

*Austrian politician and Vienna lawyer
*Champion of Austrian *Anschluss* with Nazi Germany
*Chancellor of Austria (Mar. 11, 1938)
*Reich Governor for Austria (Mar. 16, 1938)
*SS-*Obergruppenführer*
Reich Commissioner in the Netherlands (1940–1945)
*Sentenced to death by the IMT

(21) Albert Speer
      (1905–1981)
      Born: Mannheim, Germany,
          March 19, 1905
      Died: London, England,
          September 1, 1981

*Joined Nazi Party in 1931
*Hitler's favorite architect and Reich Minister for Armaments, succeeding Fritz Todt
*Prussian State Councillor
*Member of the Reichstag
*German arms production under Speer reached its peak in 1944
*Sabotaged Hitler's Nero Command and confessed his share of guilt at the IMT
*Sentenced to 20 years of imprisonment by the IMT
*Released from Spandau Prison in 1966, but, while there wrote his *Spandauer Tagebucher* (Spandau Diaries)

(22) Julius Streicher
      (1885–1946)
      Born: Fleinhausen bei Augsburg,
          Germany, February 12, 1885
      Died: Nuremberg, Germany,
          October 16, 1946

*German politician and publisher
*Founded an anti-Semitic political party in Bavaria in 1919 which eventually merged with the Nazi Party in 1921
*Published the anti-Semitic newspaper, *Der Sturmer* (The Stormer)
*Member of the Reichstag
**Gauleiter* of Franconia (1925)
*Member of the Bavarian legislature (1929)
*A rabid Jew-baiter; he was instrumental in various Nazi campaigns to ban Jews from all forms of public life in Germany
*Dismissed from all Nazi Party posts in 1940 because of his boorish behavior
*Sentenced to death by the IMT

The following two individual were charged with war crimes but were not tried:

(23) Robert Ley
      (1890–1945)

*German politician
*Member of the *Reichstag*

Born: Niederbreidenback, Germany,
      February 15, 1890
Died: Nuremberg, Germany,
      October 25, 1945

*Director, Working Committee for the
Protection of German Labor
(*Aktionskomitee zum Schutz der Deutscher
Arbeit*)
*Broke the German trade unions in 1933
and replaced them with the DAF (German
Labor Front)
*Established two major Nazi educational
institutions: the Adolf Hitler Schools and
the *Ordensburgen*
*Committed suicide before he could be
tried by the IMT

(24) Gustav Krupp von Bohlen
      und Halbach
      (1870–1950)
Born: The Hague, Netherlands,
      August 7, 1870
Died: Blühbach, Austria,
      January 16, 1950

*German industrialist, married Bertha
Krupp, sole heiress of the Friedrich Krupp,
AG, armaments works
*Trustee of the *Adolf Hitler Donation* of
German businessmen and put the Krupp
Works at the service of Nazi re-armament
as a "weapon smith"
*Named *Military Economic Führer* in 1937
*Awarded Gold Nazi Party Badge in 1940
*Not tried by IMT due to Ill-health
*Son, Alfried, stood trial in his father's
stead in a "Subsequent Proceedings" case
1947–48

INTERNATIONAL MILITARY TRIBUNAL

I

12. *The United States of America, et al. against Herrmann Wilhelm Göering, et al.*

19 *Temple Law Quarterly* 172; 173–188; 208–210; 223–226 (1945–46)
Reproduced with permission of Temple Law Review
© *Temple Law Quaterly* (1945–46)

II

INDICTMENT

I. The United States of America, the French Republic, the United Kingdom of Great Britain and Northern Ireland and the Union of Soviet Socialist Republics by the undersigned, Robert H. Jackson, Francois de Menthon, Sir Hartley Shawcross and R. A. Rudenko, duly appointed to represent their respective governments in the investigation of the charges against and the prosecution of the major war criminals, pursuant to the agreement of London dated 8 August 1945, and the Charter of this Tribunal annexed thereto, hereby accuse as guilty in the respects hereinafter set forth, of crimes against peace, war crimes, crimes against humanity and of a common plan or conspiracy to commit these crimes all as defined in the Charter of the Tribunal and accordingly name as defendants in this cause and as indicted on the counts hereinafter set out, [here follow the names of the twenty-four defendants as contained in Table. I, [*supra*].

II. The following are named as groups or organizations since dissolved, which should be declared criminal by reason of their aims and the means used for the accomplishment thereof and in connection with the conviction of such of the named defendants as were members thereof: [here follow the list of the six major Nazi organizations and their sub-components charged with "organizational criminality" [*infra*].

Count One:

The Common Plan or Conspiracy

Charter, Article 6, Especially (A)

III. *Statement of the offense:* All the defendants, with divers other persons, during a period of years preceding 8 May, 1945, participated as leaders, organizers, instigators or accomplices in the formulation or execution of a common plan or conspiracy to commit, or which involved the commission of, crimes against peace, war crimes and crimes against humanity, as defined in the Charter of this Tribunal, and, in accordance with the provisions of the charter, are individually responsible for their own acts and for all acts committed by any persons in the execution of such plan or conspiracy. The common plan or conspiracy embraced the commission of crimes against peace, in that the defendants planned, prepared, initiated and waged wars of aggression, which were also wars in violation of international treaties, agreements or assurances, in the development and course of the common plan or conspiracy it came to embrace the commission of war crimes, in that it contemplated and the defendants determined upon and carried out ruthless wars against countries and populations in violation of the rules and customs of war, including as typical and systematic means by which the wars were prosecuted, murder, ill treatment of prisoners for slave labor and for other purposes of civilian populations of occupied territories, murder and ill treatment of prisoners of war and of persons on the high seas, the taking and killing of hostages, the plunder of public and private property, the wanton destruction of cities, towns, and villages, and devastation not justified by military necessity.

The common plan or conspiracy contemplated and came to embrace as typical and systematic means, and the defendants determined upon and committed, crimes against humanity both within Germany and within occupied territories, including murder, extermination, enslavement, deportation and other inhumane acts committed against civilian populations before and during the war, persecutions on political, racial or religious grounds in execution of the plan for preparing and prosecuting aggressive and illegal wars, many of such acts and persecutions being violations of the domestic laws of the countries where perpetrated.

IV. Particulars of the nature and development of the common plan or conspiracy.

(A) Nazi party as the central core of the common plan or conspiracy.

In 1921 Adolf Hitler became the supreme leader or Fuehrer of the Nationalsozialistische Deutsche Arbeiterpartei (National Socialist German Workers' party, also known as the Nazi party), which had been founded in Germany in 1920. He continued as such through the period covered by this indictment.

The Nazi party, together with certain of its subsidiary organizations, became the instrument of cohesion among the defendants and their co-conspirators and an instrument for the carrying out of the aims and purposes of their conspiracy. Each defendant became a member of the Nazi party and of the conspiracy with knowledge of their aims and purposes, or, with such knowledge, became an accessory to their aims and purposes at some state of the development of the conspiracy.

(B) Common objectives and methods of conspiracy

The aims and purposes of the Nazi party and of the defendants and divers other persons from time to time associated as leaders, members, supporters or adherents of the Nazi party (hereinafter called collectively the "Nazi conspirators,") were, deemed or came to be, to accomplish the following by any means deemed opportune, including unlawful means, and contemplating ultimate resort to threat of force, force and aggressive war:

(1) To abrogate and overthrow the Treaty of Versailles and its restrictions upon the military armament and activity of Germany;

(2) To acquire the territories lost by Germany as the result of the World War of 1914–1918 and other territories in Europe asserted by the Nazi conspirators to be occupied principally by so-called "racial Germans";

(3) To acquire still further territories in Continental Europe and elsewhere claimed by the Nazi conspirators to be required by the "racial Germans" as "Lebensraum," or living space, all at the expense of neighboring and other countries. The aims and purposes of the Nazi conspirators were not fixed or static but evolved and expanded as they acquired progressively greater power and became able to make more effective application of threats of force and threats of aggressive war.

When their expanding aims and purposes became finally so great as to provoke such strength of resistance as could be overthrown only by armed force and aggressive war, and not simply by opportunistic methods theretofore used, such as fraud, deceit, threats, intimidation, fifth-column activities and propaganda, the Nazi conspirators deliberately planned, determined upon and launched their aggressive wars and wars in violation of international treaties, agreements and assurances by the phases and steps hereinafter more particularly described.

(c) Doctrinal techniques of the common plan or conspiracy.

To incite others to join in the common plan or conspiracy, and as a means of securing for the Nazi conspirators the highest degree of control over the German community, they put forth, disseminated and exploited certain doctrines, among others, as follows:

(1) That persons of so-called "German blood" (as specified by the Nazi conspirators) were a "master race" and were accordingly entitled to subjugate, dominate or exterminate other "races" and peoples.

(2) That the German people should be ruled under the Fuehrerprinzip (leadership principle according to which power was to reside in a Fuehrer from whom sub-leaders were to derive authority in a hierarchical order, each sub-leader to owe unconditional obedience to his immediate superior but to be absolute in his own sphere of jurisdiction; and the power of the leadership was to be unlimited, extending to all phases of public and private life).

(3) That war was a noble and necessary activity of Germans.

(4) That the leadership of the Nazi party, as the sole bearer of the foregoing and other doctrines of the Nazi party, was entitled to shape the structure, policies and practices of the German State and all related institutions, to direct and supervise the activities of all individuals within the State and to destroy all opponents.

(D) The acquiring of totalitarian control of Germany (Political):

(1) *First steps in acquisition of control of State machinery.*

In order to accomplish their aims and purposes, the Nazi conspirators prepared to seize totalitarian control over Germany to assure that no effective resistance against them could arise in Germany itself. After the failure of the Munich Putsch of 1923 aimed at the overthrow of the Weimar Republic by direct action, the Nazi conspirators set out through the Nazi party to undermine and capture the German government by "legal" forms supported by terrorism. They created and utilized, as a party formation, die Sturmabteilungen (SA, a semi-military, voluntary organization of young men trained for and committed to the use of violence, whose mission was to make the party the master of the streets).

(2) *Control acquired.*

On 30 January 1933, Hitler became Chancellor of the German Republic. After the Reichstag fire of 28 February 1933 clauses of the Weimar Constitution guaranteeing personal liberty, freedom of speech, of the press, of association and assembly were suspended. The Nazi conspirators secured the passage by the Reichstag of a "law for the protection of the people and the Reich" giving Hitler and the members of his then cabinet plenary powers of legislation. The Nazi conspirators retained such powers after having changed the members of the cabinet. The conspirators caused all political parties except the Nazi party to be prohibited. They caused the Nazi party to be established as a para-governmental organization with extensive and extraordinary privileges.

Resistance Exterminated

(3) *Consolidation of control.*

Thus possessed of the machinery of the German State, the Nazi conspirators set about the consolidation of their position of power within Germany, the extermination of potential internal resistance and the placing of the German nation on a military footing.

(a) The Nazi conspirators reduced the Reichstag to a body of their own nominees and curtailed the freedom of popular elections throughout the country. They transformed the several states, provinces and municipalities, which had exercised semi-autonomous powers, into hardly more than administrative organs of the central government. They united the offices of the President and the Chancellor in the person of Hitler, instituted a widespread purge of civil servants and severely restricted the independence of the judiciary and rendered it subservient to Nazi ends. The conspirators greatly enlarged existing state and party organizations and "coordinate" state agencies with the result that German life was dominated by Nazi doctrine and practice and progressively mobilized for the accomplishment of their aims.

(b) In order to make their rule secure from attack and to instill fear in the hearts of the German people, the Nazi conspirators established and extended a system of terror against opponents and supposed suspected opponents of the regime. They imprisoned such persons without judicial process and subjected them to persecution, degradation, despoilment, enslavement, torture and murder. These concentration camps were established early in 1933 under the direction of the defendant Goering and expanded as a fixed part of the terroristic policy and method of the conspirators and used by them for the commission of the crimes against humanity hereinafter alleged. Among the principal agencies utilized in the perpetration of these crimes were the SS and the Gestapo, which together with other favored branches or agencies of the state and party were permitted to operate without restraint of law.

Extermination of Opposition

(c) The Nazi conspirators conceived that, in addition to the suppression of distinctively political opposition, it was necessary to suppress or exterminate certain other movements or groups which they regarded as obstacles to their retention of total control in Germany and to the aggressive aims of the conspiracy abroad. Accordingly:

(i) The Nazi conspirators destroyed the free trade unions in Germany by confiscating their funds and properties, persecuting their leaders, prohibiting their activities and supplanting them by an affiliated party organization. The leadership principle was introduced into industrial relations, the entrepreneur becoming the leader and the workers becoming the followers. Thus any potential resistance of the workers was frustrated and the productive labor capacity of the German nation was brought under the effective control of the conspirators.

(ii) The Nazi conspirators, by promoting beliefs and practices incompatible with Christian teaching, sought to subvert the influence of the churches over the people and in particular over the youth in Germany. They avowed their aim to eliminate the Christian churches in Germany and sought to substitute therefor Nazi institutions and Nazi beliefs and pursued a program of persecution of priests, clergy and members of monastic orders whom they deemed opposed to their purposes and confiscated church property.

(iii) The persecution by the Nazi conspirators of pacifism groups, including religious movements dedicated to pacifism, was particularly relentless and cruel.

(d) Implementing their "master race" policy, the conspirators joined in a program of relentless persecution of the Jews, designed to exterminate them. Annihilation of the Jews became an official state policy, carried out both by official action and by incitements to mob and individual violence. The conspirators openly avowed their purpose.

* * *

These avowals and incitements were typical of the declarations of the Nazi conspirators through the course of their conspiracy. The program of action against the Jews included disfranchisement, stigmatization, denial of civil rights, subjecting their persons and property to violence, deportation, enslavement, enforced labor, starvation, murder and mass extermination.

The extent to which the conspirators succeeded in their purpose can only be estimated, but the annihilation was substantially complete in many localities in Europe. Of the 9,600,000 Jews who lived in the parts of Europe under Nazi domination, it is conservatively estimated that 5,700,000 have disappeared, most of them deliberately put to death by Nazi conspirators. Only remnants of the Jewish population of Europe remain.

Education Reshaped

(e) In order to make the German people amenable to their will and to prepare them psychologically for war, the Nazi conspirators reshaped the educational system and particularly the education training of the German youth, The leadership principle was introduced into the schools and the party and affiliated organizations were given wide supervisory powers over education. The Nazi conspirators imposed a supervision of all cultural activities, controlled the dissemination of information and the expression of opinion within Germany as well as the movement of intelligence of all kinds from and into Germany and created vast propaganda machines.

(f) The Nazi conspirators placed a considerable number of their dominated organization on a progressively militarized footing with a view to the rapid transformation and use of such organizations whenever necessary as instruments of war.

(E) The acquiring of totalitarian control in Germany (Economic)

The economic planning and mobilization for aggressive war.

Having gained political power, the conspirators organized Germany's economy to give effect to their political aims.

(1) In order to eliminate the possibility of resistance in the economic sphere, they deprived labor of its rights of free industrial and political association as particularized in Paragraph (D) (3) (i) herein.

(2) They used organizations of Germany's business as instruments of economic mobilization for war.

(3) They directed Germany's economy toward preparation and equipment of the military machine. To this end they directed finance, capital investment and foreign trade.

(4) The Nazi conspirators, and in particular the industrialists among them, embarked upon a huge rearmament program and set out to produce and develop huge quantities of materials of war and to create a powerful military potential.

(5) With the object of carrying through the preparation of war, the Nazi conspirators set up a series of administrative agencies and authorities. For example, in 1936 they established for this purpose the office of the four-year plan with the defendant Goering as plenipotentiary, vesting it with overriding control over Germany's economy. Furthermore, on 28 August, 1939, immediately before launching their aggression against Poland, they appointed the defendant Funk plenipotentiary for economics, and on 30 August, 1939, they set up the Ministerial Council for the Defence of the Reich to act as a war cabinet.

(1) Status of the conspiracy by the middle of 1933 and projected plans.

By the middle of the year 1933 the Nazi conspirators, having acquired governmental control over Germany, were in a position to enter upon further and more detailed planning with particular relationship to foreign policy. Their plan was to rearm and to reoccupy and fortify the Rhineland, in violation of the Treaty of Versailles and other treaties, in order to acquire military strength and political bargaining power to be used against other nations.

Versailles Treaty Attacked

(2) The Nazi conspirators decided that for their purpose the Treaty of Versailles must definitely be abrogated and specific plans were made by them and put into operation by 7 March, 1936, all of which opened the way for the major aggressive step to follow, as hereinafter set forth. In the execution of this phase of the conspiracy the Nazi conspirators did the following acts:

(a) They led Germany to enter upon a course of secret rearmament from 1933 to March, 1935, including the training of military personnel and the production of munitions of war and the building of an air force.

(b) On 14 October, 1933, they led Germany to leave the International Disarmament Conference and the League of Nations.

(c) On 10 March, 1935, the defendant Goering announced that Germany was building a military air force.

(d) On 16 March, 1935, the Nazi conspirators promulgated a law for universal military service, in which they stated the peacetime strength of the German Army would be fixed at 500,000 men.

(e) On 21 May, 1935, they falsely announced to the world, with intent to deceive and allay fears of aggressive intentions, that they would respect the territorial limitations of the Versailles Treaty and comply with the Locarno Pact.

(f) On 7 March, 1936, they reoccupied and fortified the Rhineland in violation of the Treaty of Versailles and the Rhine Pact of Locarno of 16 October, 1925, and falsely announced to the world that "We have no territorial demands to make in Europe."

(3) *Aggressive action against Austria and Czechoslovakia*

(a) The 1936–1938 phase of the plan:

Planning for the assault on Austria and Czechoslovakia. The Nazi conspirators next entered upon the specific planning for the acquisition of Austria and Czechoslovakia, realizing it would be necessary, for military reasons, first to seize Austria before assaulting Czechoslovakia. On 21 May, 1935, in a speech to the Reichstag, Hitler stated that:

> "Germany neither intends nor wishes to interfere in the internal affairs of Austria, to annex Austria or to conclude an Anschluss."

On 1 May, 1936, within two months after the reoccupation of the Rhineland, Hitler stated:

> "The lie goes forth again that Germany tomorrow or the day after will fall upon Austria and Czechoslovakia."

Thereafter the Nazi conspirators caused a treaty to be entered into between Austria and Germany on 11 July, 1936, Article I of which states that "The German Government recognizes the full sovereignty of the federated State of Austria in the spirit of the pronouncements of the German Fuehrer and Chancellor of 21 May, 1935." Meanwhile plans for aggression in violation of that treaty were being made. By the autumn of 1937 all noteworthy opposition within the Reich had been crushed. Military preparation for the Austrian action was virtually concluded.

* * *

(b) the execution of the plan to invade Austria:

November, 1937, to March, 1938

Hitler on 8 February, 1938, called [Austrian] Chancellor Schuschnigg to a conference at Berchtesgaden. At the meeting of 12 February, 1938, under threat of invasion, Schuschnigg yielded a promise of amnesty to imprisoned Nazis and appointment of Nazis to ministerial posts. He agreed to remain silent until Hitler's 20 February speech, in which Austria's independence was to be reaffirmed, but Hitler in his speech, instead of affirming Austrian independence, declared himself protector of all Germans. Meanwhile subversive activities of Nazis in Austria increased. Schuschnigg on 9 March, 1938, announced a plebiscite for the following Sunday on the question of Austrian independence. On 11 March Hitler sent an ultimatum demanding that the plebiscite be called off or that Germany would invade Austria. Later the same day a second ultimatum threatened invasion unless Schuschnigg should resign in three hours. Schuschnigg resigned. The defendant Seyss-Inquart, who was appointed Chancellor, immediately invited Hitler to send German troops into Austria to "preserve order." The invasion began on 12 March, 1938. On 13 March Hitler by proclamation assumed office as Chief of State of Austria and took command of its armed forces. By a law of the same date Austria was annexed to Germany.

Plan on Czechoslovakia

(c) The execution of the plan to invade Czechoslovakia: April, 1938 to March, 1939

(i) Simultaneously with their annexation of Austria, the Nazi conspirators gave false assurances to the Czechoslovak Government that they would not attack that country. But within a month they met to plan specific ways and means of attacking Czechoslovakia, and to revise, in the light of the acquisition of Austria, the previous plans for aggression against Czechoslovakia.

(ii) On 21 April, 1938, the Nazi conspirators met and prepared to launch an attack on Czechoslovakia not later than 1 October, 1938. They planned specifically to create an "incident" to "justify" the attack. They decided to launch a military attack only after a period of diplomatic squabbling, which, growing more serious, would lead to the excuse for war, or, in the alternative, to unleash a lightning attack as a result of an "incident" of their own creation. Consideration was given to assassinating the German Ambassador at Prague to create the requisite incident. From and after 21 April, 1938, the Nazi conspirators caused to be prepared detailed and precise military plans designed to carry out such an attack at any opportune moment and calculated to overcome all Czechoslovak resistance within four days, thus presenting the world with a fait accompli and so forestalling outside resistance. Throughout the months of May, June, July, August and September these plans were made more specific and detailed, and by 3 September, 1938, it was decided that all troops were to be ready for action on 28 September, 1938.

(iii) Throughout this same period the Nazi conspirators were agitating the minorities question in Czechoslovakia, and particularly in the Sudetenland, leading to a diplomatic crisis in August and September, 1938. After the Nazi conspirators threatened war, the United Kingdom and France concluded a pact with Germany and Italy at Munich on 29 September, 1938, involving the cession of the Sudetenland by Czechoslovakia to Germany. Czechoslovakia was required to acquiesce. On 1 October, 1938, German troops occupied the Sudetenland.

(iv) On 15 March, 1939, contrary to the provisions of the Munich pact itself, the Nazi conspirators caused the completion of their plan by seizing and occupying the major part of Czechoslovakia not ceded to Germany by the Munich pact.

(4) Formation of the plan to attack Poland: Preparation and initiation of aggressive war.

March, 1939 to September, 1939.

(a) With these aggressions successfully consummated, the conspirators had obtained much desired resources and bases and were ready to undertake further aggressions by means of war.

Attack on Poland Decided On

Following assurances to the world of peaceful intentions, an influential group of the conspirators met on 23 May, 1939, to consider the further implementation of their plan, the situation was reviewed and it was observed that "the past six years have been put to good use and all measures have been taken in correct sequence and in accordance with our aims," that the national-political unity of the Germans had been substantially achieved and that further successes could not be achieved without war and bloodshed. It was decided nevertheless next to attack Poland at the first suitable opportunity. It was admitted that the question concerning Danzig which they had agitated with Poland were not true questions but rather that the question was one of aggressive expansion for food and "Lebensraum." It was recognized that Poland would fight if attacked and that a repetition of the Nazi success against Czechoslovakia without war could not be expected. Accordingly, it was determined that the problem was to isolate Poland and, if possible, prevent a simultaneous conflict with the Western Powers. Nevertheless, it was agreed that England was an enemy to their aspirations and that war with England and her ally France must eventually result and therefore that in that war every attempt must be made to overwhelm England with a "Blitzkrieg." It was thereupon determined immediately to prepare detailed plans for an attack on Poland at the first suitable opportunity and thereafter for an attack on England and France, together with plans for the simultaneous occupation by armed forces of air bases in the Netherlands and Belgium.

The Danzig Issue

(b) Accordingly, after having denounced the German-Polish Pact of 1934 on false grounds, the Nazi conspirators proceeded to stir up the Danzig issue, to prepare frontier "incidents" to "justify" the attack, and to make demands for cession of Polish territory. Upon refusal by Poland to yield, they caused German armed forces to invade Poland on 1 September, 1939, thus precipitating war also with the United Kingdom and France.

(5) *Expansion of the war into a general war of aggression: Planning and execution of attacks on Denmark, Norway, Belgium, the Netherlands, Luxembourg, Yugoslavia and Greece.*

1939 to April, 1941

Thus the aggressive war was prepared for by the Nazi conspirators through their attacks on Austria and Czechoslovakia and was actively launched by their attack on Poland in violation of the terms of the Briand-Kellogg pact, 1928. After the total defeat of Poland, in order to facilitate the carrying out of their military operations against France and the United Kingdom, the Nazi conspirators made active preparations for an extension of the war in Europe.

In accordance with those plans, they caused the German armed forces to invade Denmark and Norway on 9 April, 1940; Belgium, the Netherlands and Luxembourg on 10 May, 1940; Yugoslavia and Greece on 6 April, 1941. All these invasions had been specifically planned in advance.

(6) The German invasion on June 22, 1941, of the U.S.S.R. territory in violation of the Non-Aggression Pact of August 23, 1939.

On June 22, 1941, the Nazi conspirators deceitfully denounced the non-aggression pact between Germany and the U.S.S.R. without any declaration of war, and invaded the Soviet territory, thereby beginning a war of aggression against the U.S.S.R.

From the very first day of launching their attack into Soviet territory the Nazi conspirators began to carry out the destruction of cities, towns and villages, the demolition of factories and plants, collective farms, electric stations and railroads, the robbery and barbaric devastation of the national cultural institutions of the peoples of the U. S. S R., the devastation of museums, schools, hospitals, churches, historical monuments, and the mass deportation of the Soviet's citizens for slave labor to Germany, as well as the annilation of adults, old people, women and children, especially Russians, Belo-Russians, Ukrainians, the extermination of Jews, committed throughout the invaded territory of the Soviet Union.

The above-mentioned criminal offenses were perpetrated by the German troops in accordance with the orders of the Nazi Government and the German General Staff and the High Command of the German Armed Forces.

(7) Collaboration with Italy and Japan and aggressive war against the United States.

November, 1936, to December, 1941

After the initiation of the Nazi wars of aggression the Nazi conspirators brought about a German-Italian-Japanese ten-year Military-Economic Alliance signed at Berlin on 27 September, 1940. This agreement, representing a strengthening of the bonds among those three nations established by the earlier but more limited pact of 25 November, 1936, stated:

> "The governments of Germany, Italy and Japan, considering it as a condition precedent of any lasting peace that all nations of the world would be given each its own proper place, have decided to stand by and cooperate with one another in regard of their efforts in Greater East Asia and regions of Europe respectfully wherein it is their prime purpose to establish and maintain a new order of things calculated to promote the mutual prosperity and welfare of the peoples concerned."

Japan Exhorted to Help

The Nazi conspirators conceived that Japanese aggression could weaken and handicap those nations with whom they were at war and those with whom they contemplated war. Accordingly, the Nazi conspirators exhorted Japan to seek "a new order of things." Taking advantage of the wars of aggression then being waged by the Nazi conspirators, Japan commenced an attack on 7 December, 1941, against the United States of America at Pearl Harbor and the Philippines and against the British Commonwealth of Nations, French Indo-China and the Netherlands in the Southwest Pacific. Germany declared war against the United States on 11 December, 1941.

(G) War crimes against humanity committed in the course of executing the conspiracy for which the conspirators are responsible:

(1) Beginning with the initiation of aggressive war on 1 September, 1939, and throughout its extension into wars involving almost the entire world, the Nazi conspirators carried out their common plan or conspiracy to wage war in ruthless and complete disregard and violation of the laws and customs of war. In the course of executing the common plan or conspiracy there were committed the war crimes detailed hereinafter in Count Three of this indictment.

(2) Beginning with the initiation of their plan to seize and retain total control of the German State and thereafter throughout their utilization of that control for foreign aggression, the Nazi conspirators carried out their common plan or conspiracy in ruthless and complete disregard and violation of the laws of humanity. In the course of executing the common plan or conspiracy there were committed the crimes against humanity detailed hereinafter in Count Four of this indictment.

(3) By reason of all the foregoing the defendants, with divers other persons, are guilty of a common plan or conspiracy for the accomplishment of crimes against peace, of a conspiracy to commit crimes against humanity in the course of preparation for war and in the course of prosecution of war and of a conspiracy to commit war crimes not only against the armed forces of their enemies but also against nonbelligerent civilian populations.

(H) Individual, group and organization responsibility for the offense stated in Count One:

* * *

Count Two

Crimes Against Peace

Charter, Article 6 (A)

V. Statement of the Offense

All the defendants with divers other persons during a period of years preceding 8 May, 1945, participating in the planning, preparation, initiation and waging of wars of aggression, which were also wars in violation of international treaties, agreements and assurances.

VI Particulars of the wars planned, prepared, initiated and waged.

(A) The wars referred to in the statement of offense in this Count Two of the indictment and the dates of their initiation were the following: Against Poland, 1 September, 1939; against the United Kingdom and France, 3 September, 1939; against Denmark and Norway, 9 April, 1940; against Belgium, the Netherlands and Luxembourg, 10 May, 1940; against Yugoslavia and Greece, 6 April, 1941; against the U.S.S.R., 22 June, 1941; and against the United States of America, 11 December, 1941.

* * *

Count Three:

War Crimes

Charter, Article 6, Especially (B)

VIII. Statement of the offense.

All the defendants committed war crimes between 1 September, 1939, and 8 May, 1945, in Germany and in all those countries and territories occupied by the German armed forces since 1 September, 1939, and in Austria, Czechoslovakia and Italy and on the high seas.

All the defendants, acting in concert with others, formulated and executed a common plan or conspiracy to commit war crimes as defined in Article 6 (B) of the Charter. This plan involved among other things, the practice of "total war," including methods of combat and of military occupation in direct conflict with the laws and customs of war and the commission of crimes perpetrated on the field of battle during encounters with enemy armies and against prisoners of war and in occupied territories against the civilian population of such territories.

The said war crimes were committed by the defendants and by other persons for whose acts the defendants are responsible (under Article 6 of the Charter) as such other persons when committing the said war crimes performed their acts in execution of a common plan and conspiracy to commit the said war crimes, in the formulation and execution of which plan and conspiracy all the defendants participated as leaders, organizers, instigators and accomplices.

Types of Laws Broken

These methods and crimes constituted violations of international conventions, of international penal laws and of the general principles of criminal law as derived from the criminal law of all civilized nations and were involved in and part of a systematic course of conduct.

(A)   Murder and ill treatment of civilian populations of or in occupied territory and on the high seas throughout the period of their occupation of territories overrun by their armed forces.

The defendants, for the purpose of systematically terrorizing the inhabitants, murdered and tortured civilians, and ill treated them and imprisoned them without legal process.

The murders and ill treatment were carried out by divers means, including shooting, hanging, gassing, starvation, gross overcrowding, systematic under-nutrition, systematic imposition of labor tasks beyond the strength of those ordered to carry them out, inadequate provision of surgical and medical services, kicking, beatings, brutality and torture of all kinds, including the use of hot irons and pulling out finger nails and the performance of experiments by means of operations otherwise on living human subjects.

In some occupied territories the defendants interfered with religious services, persecuted members of the clergy and monastic orders and expropriated church property. They conducted deliberate and systematic genocide, viz., the extermination of racial and national groups, against the civilian populations of certain occupied territories in order to destroy particular races in classes of people and national, racial, or religious groups, particularly Jews, Poles and Gypsies and others. Civilians were systematically subjected to torture of all kinds, with the object of obtaining information. Civilians of occupied countries were subjected systematically to "protective arrests" whereby they were arrested and imprisoned without any trial and any of the ordinary protections of the law, and were imprisoned under most unhealthy and inhumane conditions.

In the concentration camps were many prisoners who were classified "nacht und nebel." [night and fog]. These were entirely cut off from the world and were allowed neither to receive nor to send letters. They disappeared without trace and no announcement of their fate was ever made by the German authorities. Such murders and ill treatment were contrary to international conventions, in particular to Article 46 of the Hague Regulations, 1907, the Laws and Customs of War, the general principles of criminal law as derived from the criminal laws of all civilized nations, the internal penal laws of the countries in which such crimes were committed, and to Article 6 (B) of the Charter.

[Here the indictment then listed, by way of example, numerous war crime violations by German armed forces in France, Belgium, Holland, Estonia, the U.S.S.R. and in Yugoslavia. Included in this listing were violations regarding POWs, looting of public and private property, the plunder of cultural artifacts, destruction of schools, churches, museums, the illegal removal of raw materials and other natural resources and the deliberate and unnecessary destruction of villages, towns and cities in the various occupied territories].

* * *

Count Four:

Crimes Against Humanity

Charter, Article 6, Especially (C)

X. Statement of offense.

All the defendants committed crimes against humanity during a period of years preceding 8 May, 1945, in Germany and in all those countries and territories occupied by the German armed forces since 1 September, 1939, and in Austria and Czechoslovakia and in Italy and on the high seas.

All the defendants, acting in concert with others, formulated and executed a common plan or conspiracy to commit crimes against humanity as defined in Article 6 (c) of the Charter. This plan involved, among other things, the murder and persecution of all who were or who were suspected of being hostile to the Nazi party and all who were or were suspected of being opposed to the common plan alleged in Count One. The said crimes against humanity were committed by the defendants and by other persons for whose acts the defendants are responsible (under Article 6 of the Charter) as such other persons, when committing the said war crimes, performed their acts in execution of a common plan and conspiracy to commit the said war crimes, in the formulation and execution of which plan and conspiracy all the defendants participated as leaders, organizers, instigators and accomplices. These methods and crimes constituted violations of international conventions, of internal penal laws, of the general principles of criminal law as derived from the criminal law of all civilized nations and were involved in a part of a systematic course of conduct. The said acts were contrary to Article 6 of the Charter. The prosecution will rely upon the facts pleaded under Count Three as also constituting crimes against humanity.

* * *

The Nazis murdered amongst others Chancellor Dollfuss, the Social Democrat Breitscheid and the Communist Thaelmann. They imprisoned in concentration camps numerous political and religious personages, for example, Chancellor Schuschnigg and Pastor Niemoeller. In November, 1938, by orders of the Chief of the Gestapo, anti-Jewish demonstrations all over Germany took place. Jewish property was destroyed, 30,000 Jews were arrested and sent to concentration camps and their property confiscated. Under Paragraph VIII (A) above millions of the persons there mentioned as having been murdered and ill-treated were Jews....

* * *

As the Germans retreated before the Soviet Army they exterminated Jews rather than allow them to be liberated. Many concentration camps and ghettos were kept up in which Jews were incarcerated and tortured, starved, subjected to merciless atrocities and finally exterminated. About 70,000 Jews were exterminated in Yugoslavia.

* * *

Wherefore, this indictment is lodged with the tribunal in English, French and Russian, each text having equal authenticity, and the charges herein made against the above-named defendants are hereby presented to the tribunal.

[The indictment was followed by two Appendices. *Appendix A* listed all twenty-four defendants charged and gave a brief background précis of each. *Appendix B* dealt with the criminality of groups and organizations. Since we have previously listed the indicted defendants and given a brief background summary of each in Table I., we here include only *Appendix B*]

* * *

Appendix B

Statement of criminality of groups and organizations.

The statements hereinafter set forth, following the name of each group or organization named in the indictment as one which should be declared criminal, constitute matters upon which the prosecution will rely *inter alia* as establishing the criminality of the group or organization:

> "*Die Reichsregierung* (Reich Cabinet)" referred to in the indictment consists of persons who were: [i. Members of the ordinary cabinet after 30 January, 1933, the date on which Hitler became Chancellor of the German Republic; the term "Ordinary Cabinet" as used herein means the Reich Ministers, i. e., heads of departments of the Central Government; Reich Ministers Without Portfolio; State Ministers acting as Reich Ministers and other officials entitled to take part in meetings of this Cabinet. ii. Members of the *Ministerrat für die Reichvertiedigung* (Council of Ministers for the Defense of the Reich. iii. Members of the *Geheimer Kabinettsrat* (Secret Cabinet Council)].

Under the Fuehrer these persons functioning in the foregoing capacities and in association as a group, possessed and exercised legislative, executive, administrative and political powers and functions of a very high order in the system of the German Government. Accordingly, they are charged with responsibility for the policies adopted and put into effect by the Government, including those which comprehended and involved the commission of the crimes referred to in Counts One, Two, Three and Four of the indictment.

> "*Das Korps der Politischen Leiter der Nationalsozialistischen Deutschen Arbeiterpartei* (Leadership corps of the Nazi party)" referred to in the indictment consists of persons who were at any time, according to common Nazi terminology, "politishce Leiter" (political leaders) of any grade or rank.

The Politischen Leiter comprised the Leaders of the various functional offices of the party (for example, the Reichsleitung, or party Reich directorate, and the Gauleitung, or party Gau directorate), as well as the territorial leaders of the party (for example, the Gauleiter).

The Politschen Leiter were a distinctive and elite group within the Nazi party proper and as such were vested with special prerogatives. They were organized according to the leadership principle and were charged with planning, developing and imposing upon their followers the policies of the Nazi party. Thus the territorial leaders among them were called Hoheitstraeger, or bearers of sovereignty, and were entitled to call upon and utilize the various party formations when necessary for the execution of party policies.

Reference is hereby made to the allegations in Count One of the indictment showing that the Nazi party was the central core of the common plan or conspiracy therein set forth. The Politischen Leiter, a major power within the Nazi party proper and functioning in the capacities above described and in association as a group joined in the common plan or conspiracy, and accordingly share responsibilities for the crimes set forth in Counts One, Two, Three and Four of the indictment.

The prosecution expressly reserved the right to request at any time before sentence is pronounced that Politsche Leiter of subordinate grades or ranks or of other types or classes to be specified by the prosecution, be excepted from further proceedings in this case, but without prejudice to other proceedings or actions against them.

"*Die Schutzstaffeln der Nationalsozialistschen Deutschen Arbeiterpartei* (commonly known as the SS), including die Sicherheitsdienst (commonly known as the SD) referred to in the indictment consists of the entire corps of the SS and all offices, departments, services, agencies, branches, formations, organizations and groups of which it was at any time comprised or which were at any time intergrated in it, including, but not limited to, the Allgemeine SS, the Waffen SS, the SS Totenkopfverbande, Sicherheitsdienst des Reichsfüehrers SS (commonly known as the SD).

The SS, originally established by Hitler in 1924 as an elite section of the SA to furnish a protective guard for the Fuehrer and Nazi party leaders, became an independent formation of the Nazi party in 1934 under the leadership of the Reichsfuehrer-SS, Heinrich Himmler. It was composed of voluntary members selected in accordance with Nazi biological, racial and political theories, completely indoctrinated in Nazi ideology and pledged to uncompromising obedience to the Fuehrer. After the accession of the Nazi conspirators to power, it developed many departments, agencies, formations and branches and extended its influence and control over numerous fields of governmental and party activity. Through Heinrich Himmler as Reichsfuehrer-SS and Chief of the German police agencies and units of the SS and of the Reich were joined in operation to form a unified repressive police force. The Sicherheitsdienst des Reichsfuehrers-SS (commonly known as the SD), a department of the SS, was developed into a vast espionage and counter-interlligence system which operated in conjunction with the Gestapo and criminal police in detecting, suppressing and eliminating tendencies, groups and individuals deemed hostile or potentially hostile to the Nazi party, its leaders, principles and objectives, and eventually was combined with the Gestapo and criminal police in a single security police department, the Reich Main Security Office.

Other branches of the SS developed into an armed force and served in the wars of aggression referred to in Counts One and Two of the Indictment. Through other departments and branches the SS controlled the administration of concentration camps and the execution of Nazi racial, biological and resettlement policies. Through its numerous functions and activities it served as the instrument for insuring the domination of Nazi ideology and protecting and extending the Nazi regime over Germany and occupied territories. It thus participated in and is responsible for the crimes referred to in Counts One, Two and Four of the indictment.

"*Die Geheime Staatspolizei* (Secret State Police, commonly known as the Gestapo)," referred to in the indictment, consists of the headquarters, department, offices, branches, and all the forces and personnel of the Geheime Staatspolizei organized or existing at any time after January 20, 1933, including the Geheime Staatspolizei of Prussia and equivalent secret or political police forces of the Reich and components thereof.

The Gestapo was created by the Nazi conspirators immediately after their accession to power, first in Prussia by the defendant Goering, and shortly thereafter in all other states in the Reich these separate secret and political police forces were developed into a centralized uniformed organization operating through a central headquarters and through a network of regional offices in Germany and in occupied territories. Its officials and operatives were selected on the basis of unconditional acceptance of Nazi ideology, were largely drawn from members of the SS and were trained in SS and SD school. It acted to suppress and eliminate tendencies, groups, and individuals deemed hostile or potentially hostile to the Nazi party, its leaders, principles and objectives and to repress resistance and potential resistance to German control in occupied territories. In performing these functions it operated free from legal control, taking any measures it deemed necessary for the accomplishment of its missions.

Through its purposes, activities and the means it used, it participated in and is responsible for the commission of the crimes set forth in Counts One, Two, Three and Four of the indictment.

"*Die Sturmabteilungen der Nationalsozialistishchen Deutschen Arbeiterpartei* (commonly known as the SA), referred to in the indictment was a formation of the Nazi party under the immediate jurisdiction of the Fuehrer, organized on militant lines, whose membership was composed of volunteers serving as political soldiers of the party. It was one of the earliest formations of the Nazi party and the original guardian of the National Socialist movement. Founded in 1921 as a voluntary military formation, it was developed by the Nazi conspirators before their accession to power into a vast private army and utilized for the purpose of creating disorder and terrorizing and eliminating political opponents. It continued to serve as an instrument for the physical ideological and military training of party members and as a reserve for the German armed forces. After the launching of the wars of aggression referred to in Counts One and Two of the indictment, the SA not only operated as an organization for military training, but provided auxiliary police and security forces in occupied territories, guarded prisoner-of-war camps and concentration camps and supervised and controlled persons forced to labor in Germany and occupied territories. Through its purposes and activities and the means it used, it participated in and is responsible for the commission of the crimes set forth in Counts One, Two, Three and Four of the indictment.

The "General Staff and High Command of the German Armed Forces" referred to in the indictment consist of those individuals who between February, 1938, and May, 1945, were the highest commanders of the Wehrmacht, the Army, the Navy and the Air Forces. The individuals comprising this group are the persons who held the following appointments:

Oberbefelshaber der Kreigsmarine (commander in Chief of the Navy) *Chef* (and formerly *Chef des Stabes) der Seekriegsleitung* (Chief of Naval War Staff);

Oberbefelshaber des Heeres (commander in Chief of the Army), *Chef des Generalstabes des Heeres* (Chief of the General Staff of the Army);

Oberbefelshaber der Luftwaffe (commander in Chief of the Air Force), *Chef des Generalstabes der Luftwaffe* (Chief of the General Staff of the Air Force);

Chef des Oberkommando der Wehrmacht (Chief of the High Command of the Armed Forces):

Chef des Fuehrungstabes des Oberkommando der Wehrmacht (Chief of the Operations Staff of the High Command of the Armed Forces):

Stellvertretender Chef des Feuhrungstabes des Oberkommando der Wehrmacht (Deputy Chief of the Operations Staff of the High Command of the Armed Forces):

Commander in Chief in the field, with the status of *Oberbefelshaber*, of the Wehrmacht, Navy, Army, Air Force.

Functioning in such capacities and in association as a group at the highest levels in the German armed forces organization, these persons had a major responsibility for the planning, preparation, initiation and waging of illegal wars as set forth in Counts One and Two of the indictment and for the war crimes and crimes against humanity involved in the execution of the common plan or conspiracy set forth in Counts Three and Four of the indictment.

---

13. The International Military Tribunal in Session at Nuremberg, Germany
6 F.R.D. 69; 73–75 (1947)

THE RT. HON. LORD JUSTICE LAWRENCE (member of the United Kingdom of Great Britain and Northern Ireland) President

THE HON. MR. JUSTICE BIRKETT (alternate member for the United Kingdom of Great Britain and Northern Ireland)

THE HON. FRANCIS BIDDLE (member for the United States of America)

THE HON. JOHN J. PARKER (member for the United States of America)

M. LE PROFESSEUR DONNEDIEU DE VABRES (member for the French Republic)

M. LE CONSEILLER FALCO (alternate member for the French Republic)

MAJOR-GENERAL JURISPRUDENCE I. T. NIKITCHENKO member for the Union of Soviet Socialist Republics)

LT.—COLONEL A. F. VOLCHKOV (alternate member for the Union of Soviet Socialist Republics)

Prosecutors

Mr. Justice Robert H. Jackson:

Chief Prosecutor for the United States of America

M. Champetier de Ribes:

Chief Prosecutor for the French Republic

Rt. Hon Sir Hartley Shawcross, KC, MP.:

Chief Prosecutor for the United Kingdom of Great Britain and Northern Ireland

State Counsellor of the 2nd Class, R. A. Rudenko:

Chief Prosecutor for the Union of Soviet Socialist Republics

Counsels for the Defendants

Defendants	*Counsel*
Goering	Dr. Otto Stahmer
Hess	Dr. Alfred Seidl
Ribbentrop	Dr. Martin Horn
Keitel	Dr. Otto Nelte
Kaltenbrunner	Dr. Kurt Kaffmann
Rosenberg	Dr. Alfred Thoma
Frank	Dr. Alfred Seidl
Frick	Dr. Otto Pannenbecker
Streicher	Dr. Hans Marx
Funk	Dr. Fritz Sauter
Schacht	Dr. Rudolf Dix
Doenitz	Capt. Otto Kranzbuehle
Raeder	Dr. Walter Siemers
von Schirach	Dr. Robert Servatius
Jodl	Prof. Franz Exner
von Papen	Dr. Egon Kubuschok
Seyss-Inquart	Dr. Gustav Steinbauer
Speer	Dr. Hans Flaechsner
von Neurath	Dr. Otto Von Luedinghausen
Fritzsche	Dr. Heinz Fritz
Bormann	Dr. Friedrich Bergold

[The trial began on the morning of November 20, 1945 as scheduled. Proceedings were opened by the court President, Sir Geoffrey Lawrence, with a brief statement, noting that these proceedings were "unique in the history of jurisprudence…and of supreme importance to millions of people all over the globe." The actual courtroom in the Palace of Justice was located on the second floor. It was a space enclosed by wood-paneled walls with dark green curtains on the windows and green marble door facings. The judges sat on a raised dias and all of them, except the Russians, wore black robes. The Russians were in military uniform. Behind the judges were their national flags and a series of interpreters. German defense counsel were adorned primarily in academic robes of varying color. Captain Otto Kranzbuehle, counsel for defendant Döenitz, wore his naval uniform. The defendants themselves wore rather drab clothing and their appearance belied their former status. Most were dressed in civilian clothing, except for the former members of the German armed forces who wore their uniforms shorn of any insignia of rank or other decorations.

The first day was taken up with the reading of the indictment. Day two, among other things, was set aside for allocution, that is, requiring defendants to plead one way or another to the charges against them in the indictment. Tusa and Tusa's[47] account of that procedure notes that:

---

47. Tusa and Tusa, *supra* note 27.

Goering was the first to stand at the microphone in the dock. He held a type-written speech in his hand, 'Before I answer the question of the Tribunal whether or not I am guilty...."Before I answer the question of the Tribunal whether or not I am guilty...' Lawrence cut him off; defendants could only plead guilty or not guilty, speeches were forbidden. Baulked of his hopes of challenging the court and assuming the heroic role, Goering had to rest content with a brief statement, 'I declare myself in the sense of the indictment not guilty.' Ribbentrop, Rosenberg, Schirach and Fritzsche adopted the same formula. Sauckel, red-faced and with clenched fists, declared himself not guilty 'in the sense of the indictment, before God and the world and particularly before my people.' Jodl added to his plea of not guilty: 'for what I have done or had to do I have a pure conscience before God, before history and my people.'

The others gave the formal reply, Schacht emphasizing he was not guilty 'in any respect,' Papen 'in no way.' Hess shouted 'Nein' which Lawrence said would be entered as a plea of not guilty.[48]

It is beyond the scope of this book to include even a small portion of the contents of the forty-two volume record of the IMT. However, we do include portions from both the opening and closing statements of Mr. Justice Robert H. Jackson, the chief American prosecutor and note briefly the dissenting comments filed by the Soviet jurist, I. T. Nikitchenko].

(a) Opening Statement

By Robert H. Jackson
U.S. Chief of Counsel, International Military Tribunal
2 IMT 98 (1947)

The President: I will now call upon the Chief Prosecutor for the United States of America.

Mr. Justice Jackson: May it please your Honors:

The privilege of opening the first trial in history for crimes against the peace of the world imposes a grave responsibility. The wrongs which we seek to condemn and punish have been so calculated, so malignant and so devastating, that civilization cannot tolerate their being ignored, because it cannot survive their being repeated. That four great nations, flushed with victory and stung with injury, stay the hands of vengeance and voluntarily submit their captive enemies to the judgment of the law, is one of the most significant tributes that Power ever has paid to Reason.

This Tribunal, while it is novel and experimental, is not the product of abstract speculations nor is it created to vindicate legalistic theories. This inquest represents the practical effort of four of the most mighty of nations, with the support of seventeen more, to utilize International Law to meet the greatest menace of our times—aggressive war. The common sense of mankind demands that law shall not stop with the punishment of petty crimes by little people. It must also reach men who possess themselves of great power and make deliberate and concerted use of it to set in motion evils which leave no home in the world untouched. It is a cause of that magnitude that the United Nations will lay before Your Honors.

---

48. *Id.* at 150.

In the prisoners' dock sit twenty-odd broken men. Reproached by the humiliation of those they have led, almost as bitterly as by the desolation of those they have attacked, their personal capacity for evil is forever past. It is hard now to perceive in these miserable men as captives the power by which as Nazi leaders they once dominated much of the world and terrified most of it. Merely as individuals their fate is of little consequence to the world.

What makes this inquest significant is that these prisoners represent sinister influences that will lurk in the world long after their bodies have returned to dust. We will show them to be living symbols of racial hatreds, of terrorism and violence, and of the arrogance and cruelty of power. They are symbols of fierce nationalism and of militarism, of intrigue and war-making which have embroiled Europe generation after generation, crushing its manhood, destroying its homes, and impoverishing its life. They have so identified themselves with the philosophies they conceived, and with the forces they have directed, that any tenderness to them is a victory and an encouragement to all the evils which are attached to their names. Civilisation can afford no compromise with the social forces which would gain renewed strength if we deal ambiguously or indecisively with the men in whom those forces now precariously survive.

What these men stand for we will patiently and temperately disclose. We will give you undeniable proof of incredible events. The catalogue of crimes will omit nothing that could be conceived by a pathological pride, cruelty and lust for power. These men created in Germany, under the "Führerprinzip," a National Socialist despotism equaled only by the dynasties of the ancient East. They took from the German people all those dignities and freedoms that we hold natural and inalienable rights in every human being. The people were compensated by inflaming and gratifying hatreds towards those who were marked as "scapegoats." Against their opponents, including Jews, Catholics, and free labour, the Nazis directed such a campaign of arrogance, brutality, and annihilation as the world has not witnessed since the pre-Christian ages. They excited the German ambition to be a "master race," which of course implies serfdom for others. They led their people on a mad gamble for domination. They diverted social energies and resources to the creation of what they thought to be an invincible war machine. They overran their neighbors. To sustain the "master race" in its war-making, they enslaved millions of human beings and brought them into Germany, where these hapless creatures now wander as "displaced persons." At length, bestiality and bad faith reached such excess that they aroused the sleeping strength of imperiled Civilisation. Its united efforts have ground the German war machine to fragments. But the struggle has left Europe a liberated yet prostrate land where a demoralized society struggles to survive. These are the fruits of the sinister forces that sit with these defendants in the prisoner's dock.

In justice to the nations and the men associated with this prosecution, I must remind you of certain difficulties which may leave their mark on this case. Never before in legal history has an effort been made to bring within the scope of a single litigation the developments of a decade, covering a whole continent, and involving a score of nations, countless individuals, and innumerable events. Despite the magnitude of the task, the world has demanded immediate action. This demand has had to be met, though perhaps at the cost of finished craftsmanship. In my country, established courts, following familiar procedures, applying well-thumbed precedents, and dealing with the legal consequences of local and limited events, seldom commence a trial within a year of the event in litigation. Yet less than eight months ago to-day the courtroom in which you sit was an enemy fortress in the hands of the German SS troops. Less than eight months ago nearly all our witnesses and documents were in enemy hands. The law had not been codified, no procedures had been established, no tribunal was in existence, no useable courthouse stood here, none of the hundreds of tons of official German documents had been examined, no prosecuting staff had been assembled, nearly all of the present defendants were at large, and the four prosecuting powers had not yet jointed in common cause to try them. I should be the last to deny that the case may well suffer from incomplete researches, and quite likely will not be the example of professional work which any of the prosecuting nations would normally wish to sponsor. It is, however, a completely adequate case to the judgment we shall ask you to render, and its full development we shall be obliged to leave to historians.

Before I discuss particulars of evidence, some general considerations which may affect the credit of this trial in the eyes of the world should be candidly faced. There is a dramatic disparity between the circumstances of the accusers and of the accused that might discredit our work if we should falter, in even minor matters, in being fair and temperate.

Unfortunately, the nature of these crimes is such that both prosecution and judgment must be by victor nations over vanquished foes. The world-wide scope of the aggressions carried out by these men has left but few real neutrals. Either the victors must judge the vanquished or we must leave the defeated to judge themselves. After the First World War we learned the futility of the latter course. The former high station of these defendants, the notoriety of their acts, and the adaptability of their conduct to provoke retaliation make it harder to distinguish between the demand for a just and measured retribution, and the unthinking cry for vengeance which arises from the anguish of war. It is our task, so far as is humanly possible, to draw the line between the two.

We must never forget that the record on which we judge these defendants to-day is the record or which history will judge us tomorrow. To pass these defendants a poisoned chalice is to put it to our lips as well. We must summon such detachment and intellectual integrity to our task that this trial will commend itself to posterity as fulfilling humanity's aspirations to do justice.

* * *

If these men are the first war leaders of a defeated nation to be prosecuted in the name of the law, they are also the first to be given a chance to plead for their lives in the name of the law. Realistically, the Charter of this Tribunal, which gives them a hearing, is also the source of their only hope. It may be that these men of troubled conscience, whose only wish is that the world forget them, do not regard a trial as a favor. But they do have a fair opportunity to defend themselves—a favour which, when in power, they rarely extended even to their fellow countrymen. Despite the fact that public opinion already condemns their acts, we agree that here they must be given a presumption of innocence, and we accept the burden of proving criminal acts and the responsibility of these defendants for their commission.

When I say that we do not ask for convictions unless we prove crime, I do not mean mere technical or incidental transgressions of international conventions. We charge guilt on planned and intended conduct that is a natural and human, even if illegal, cutting of corners, such as many of us might well have committed had we been in the defendants' positions. It is not because they yielded to the normal frailties of human beings that we accuse them. It is their abnormal and inhuman conduct which brings them to this bar.

We will not ask you to convict these men on the testimony of their foes. There is no count in the Indictment that cannot be proved by books and records. The Germans were always meticulous record keepers, and these defendants had their share of the Teutonic passion for thoroughness in putting things on paper. Nor were they without vanity. They arranged frequently to be photographed in action. We will show you their own films. You will see their own conduct and hear their own voices as these defendants re-enact for you, from the screen, some of the events in the course of the conspiracy.

We would also make clear that we have no purpose to incriminate the whole German people. We know that the Nazi Party was not put in power by a majority of the German vote. We know it came to power by an evil alliance between the most extreme of the Nazi revolutionists, the most unrestrained of the German reactionaries, and the most aggressive of the German militarists. If the German populace had willingly accepted the Nazi program, no storm-troopers would have been needed in the early days of the Party, and there would have been no need for concentration camps or the Gestapo, both of which institutions were inaugurated as soon as the Nazis gained control of the German state. Only after these lawless innovations proved successful at home were they taken abroad.

The German people should know by now that the people of the United States hold them in no fear, and in no hate. It is true that the Germans have taught us the horrors of modern warfare, but the ruin that lies from the Rhine to the Danube shows that we, like our Allies, have not been dull pupils. If we are not awed by German fortitude and proficiency in war, and if we are not persuaded of their political maturity, we do respect their skill in the arts of peace, their technical competence, and the sober, industrious and self-disciplined character of the masses of the German people.

* * *

This war did not just happen—it was planned and prepared for over a long period of time and with no small skill and cunning. The world has perhaps never seen such a concentration and stimulation of the energies of any people as that which enabled Germany, twenty years after it was defeated, disarmed, and dismembered, to come so near carrying out its plan to dominate Europe. Whatever else we may say of those who were authors of this war, they did achieve a stupendous work in organization, and our first task is to examine the means by which these defendants and their fellow conspirators prepared and incited Germany to go to war.

* * *

The case as presented by the United States will be concerned with the brains and authority behind all the crimes. These defendants were men of a station and rank which does not soil its own hands with blood. They were men who knew how to use lesser folk as tools. We want to reach the planners and designers, the inciters and leaders without whose evil architecture the world would not have been for so long scourged with the violence and lawlessness, and ranked with the agonies and convulsions, of this terrible war.

* * *

The Charter of this tribunal evidences a faith that the law is not only to govern the conduct of little men, but that even rulers are, as Lord Chief Justice Coke put it to King James, "under God and the law." The United States believed that the law has long afforded standards by which a juridical hearing could be conducted to make sure that we punish only the right men and for the right reasons. Following the instructions of the late President Roosevelt and the decision of the Yalta Conference, President Truman directed representatives of the United States to formulate a proposed International Agreement, which was submitted during the San Francisco Conference to the Foreign Ministers of the

United Kingdom, the Soviet Union, and the Provisional Government of France. With many modifications, that proposal has become the Charter of this Tribunal.

* * *

It is true, of course, that we have no judicial precedent for the Charter. But international law is more than a scholarly collection of abstract and immutable principles. It is an out-growth of treaties and agreements between nations and of accepted customs. Yet every custom has its origin in some single act, and every agreement has to be initiated by the action of some State. Unless we are prepared to abandon every principle of growth for international law, we cannot deny that our own day has the right to institute customs and to conclude agreements that will themselves become sources of a newer and strengthened international law. International law is not capable of development by the normal processes of legislation, for there is no continuing international legislative authority. Innovations and revisions in international law are brought about by the action of governments such as those I have cited, designed to meet a change in circumstances. It grows, as did the common law, through decisions reached from time to time in adapting settled principles to new situations. The fact is that when the law evolves by the case method, as did the common law and as international law must do if it is to advance at all, it advances at the expense of those who wrongly guessed the law and learned too late their error. The law, so far as international law can be decreed, he had clearly pronounced when these acts took place. Hence we are not disturbed by the lack of judicial precedent for the inquiry it is proposed to conduct.

* * *

Our position is that whatever grievances a nation may have, however objectionable it finds the *status quo*, aggressive warfare is not a legal means for settling those grievances or for altering those conditions. It may be that the Germany of the 1920s and 1930s faced desperate problems, problems that would have warranted the boldest measures short of war. All other methods—persuasion, propaganda, economic competition, diplomacy—were open to an aggrieved country, but aggressive warfare was outlawed. These defendants did make aggressive war, a war in violation of treaties. They did attack and invade their neighbors in order to effectuate a foreign policy which they knew could not be accomplished by measures short of war. And that is as far as we accuse or propose to inquire.

The Charter also recognizes individual responsibility on the part of those who commit acts defined as crimes, or who incite other to do so, or who join a common plan with other persons, groups or organizations to bring about their commission. The principle of individual responsibility for piracy and brigandage, which have long been recognized as crimes punishable under international law, is old and well established. That is what illegal warfare is. This principle of personal liability is a necessary as well as a logical one if international law is to render real help in the maintenance of peace. An international law which operates only on States can be enforced only by war because the most practicable method of coercing a State is warfare.... Only sanctions which reach individuals can peacefully and effectively be enforced. Hence, the principle of the criminality of aggressive war is implemented by the Charter with the principle of personal responsibility.

Of course, the idea that a state, any more than a corporation, commits crimes, is a fiction. Crimes always are committed only by persons. While it is quite proper to employ the fiction of responsibility of a state or corporation for the purpose of imposing a collective liability, it is quite intolerable to let such a legalism become the basis of personal immunity.

The Charter recognizes that one who has committed criminal acts may not take refuge in superior orders nor in the doctrine that his crimes were acts of states. These twin principles, working together, have heretofore resulted in immunity for practically everyone concerned in the really great crimes against peace and mankind. Those in lower ranks were protected by the orders of their superiors. The superiors were protected because their orders were called acts of state. Under the Charter, no defence based on either of these doctrines can be entertained. Modern civilisation puts unlimited weapons of destruction in the hands of men. It cannot tolerate so vast an area of legal irresponsibility.

* * *

I am too well aware of the weaknesses of juridical action alone to contend that in itself your decision under this Charter can prevent future wars. Judicial action always comes after the event. Wars are started only on the theory and in the confidence that they can be won. Personal punishment, to be suffered only in the event the war is lost, will probably not be a sufficient deterrent to prevent a war where the warmakers feel the chances of defeat to be negligible.

But the ultimate step in avoiding periodic wars, which are inevitable in a system of international lawlessness, is to make statesmen responsible to law. And let me make clear that while this law is first applied against German aggressors, the law includes, and if it is to serve a useful purpose it must condemn, aggression by any other nations, including those which sit here now in judgment.... The trial represents mankind's desperate effort to apply the discipline of the law to statesmen who have used their powers of state to attack the foundations of the world's peace, and to commit aggressions against the rights of their neighbours.

* * *

No charity can disguise the fact that the forces which these defendants represent, the forces that would advantage and delight in their acquittal, are the darkest and most sinister forces in society—dictatorship and oppression, malevolence and passion, militarism and lawlessness. By their fruits we best know them. Their acts have bathed the world in blood and set civilisation back a century. They have subjected their European neighbors to every outrage and torture, every spoilation and deprivation that insolence, cruelty, and greed could inflict. They have brought the German people to the lowest pitch of wretchedness, from which they can entertain no hope of early deliverance. They have stirred hatreds and incited domestic violence on every continent. These are the things that stand in the dock shoulder to shoulder with these prisoners.

The real complaining party at your bar is Civilisation. In all our countries it is still a struggling and imperfect thing. It does not plead that the United States, or any other country, has been blameless of the conditions which made the German people easy victims to the blandishments and intimidations of the Nazi conspirators.

But it points to the dreadful sequence of aggressions and crimes I have recited, it points to the weariness of flesh, the exhaustion of resources, and the destruction of all that was beautiful or useful in so much of the world, and to greater potentialities for destruction in the days to come. It is not necessary among the ruins of this ancient and beautiful city with untold members of its civilian inhabitants still buried in its rubble, to argue the proposition that to start or wage an aggressive war has the moral qualities of the worst of crimes. The refuge of the defendants can only be their hope that international law will lag so far behind the moral sense of mankind that conduct which is crime in the moral sense must be regarded as innocent in law.

Civilisation asks whether law is so laggard as to be utterly helpless to deal with crimes of this magnitude by criminals of this order of importance. It does not expect that you can make war impossible. It does expect that your judicial action will put the forces of International Law...on the side of peace,...

(b) Closing Statement

By Robert H. Jackson
U.S. Chief of Counsel, International Military Tribunal
20 *Temple Law Quarterly* 85; 86; 90; 95–98; 102–107 (1946–47)
Reproduced with permission of Temple Law Review
© *Temple Law Quarterly* (1946–47)

An advocate can be confronted with few more formidable tasks than to select his closing arguments where there is a great disparity between his appropriate time and his available material. In eight months—a short time as state trials go—we have introduced evidence which embraces as vast and varied a panorama of events as has ever been compressed within the framework of a litigation. It is impossible in summation to do more than outline with bold strokes the vitals of this trial's mad and melancholy record, which will live as the historical text of the Twentieth Century's shame and depravity.

It is common to think of our own time as standing at the apex of civilization, from which the deficiencies of preceding ages may patronizingly be viewed in the light of what is assumed to be "progress." The reality is that in the long perspective of history the present century will not hold an admirable position, unless its second half is to redeem its first. These two-score years in this Twentieth Century will be recorded in the books of years as one of the most bloody in all annals. Two World Wars have left a legacy of dead which number more than all the armies engaged in any war that made ancient or medieval history. No half-century ever witnessed slaughter on such a scale, such cruelties and inhumanities, such wholesale deportations of peoples into slavery, such annihilations of minorities. The Terror of Torquemada pales before the Nazi Inquisition. These deeds are the overshadowing historical facts by which generations to come will remember this decade. If we cannot eliminate the causes and prevent the repetition of these barbaric events, it is not an irresponsible prophecy to say that this Twentieth Century may yet succeed in bringing the doom of civilization.

Goaded by these facts, we have moved to redress the blight on the record of our era. The defendants complain that our pace is too fast. In drawing the Charter of this Tribunal, we thought we were recording an accomplished advance in international law. But they say that we have outrun our times, that we have anticipated an advance that should be, but has not yet been made. The Agreement of London, whether it originates or merely records, at all events marks a transition in international law which roughly corresponds to that in the evolution of local law when men ceased to punish local crime by "hue and cry" and began to let reason and inquiry govern punishment. The society of nations has emerged from the primitive "hue and cry," the law of "catch and kill." It seeks to apply sanctions to enforce international law, but to guide their application by evidence, law, and reason, instead of outcry. The defendants denounce the law under which their accounting is asked. Their dislike for the law which condemns them is not original. It has been remarked before that—

"No thief ere felt the halter draw
With good opinion of the law."

...Of one thing we may be sure. The future will never have to ask, with misgiving, what could the Nazis have said in their favor. History will know that whatever could be said, they were allowed to say. They have been given the kind of a trial which they, in the days of their pomp and power, never gave to any man.

But fairness is not weakness. The extraordinary fairness of these hearings is an attribute to our strength. The prosecution's case, at its close, seemed inherently unassailable because it rested so heavily on German documents of unquestioned authenticity. But it was the weeks upon weeks of pecking at this case by one after another of the defendants that has demonstrated its true strength. The fact is that the testimony of the defendants has removed any doubts of guilt which, because of the extraordinary nature and magnitude of these crimes, may have existed before they spoke. They have helped write their own judgment of condemnation.

...Let me emphasize one cardinal point. The United States has no interest which would be advanced by the conviction of any defendant if we have not proved him guilty on at least one of the counts charged against him in the Indictment. Any result that the calm and critical judgment of posterity would pronounce unjust, would not be a victory for any of the countries associated in this prosecution. But in summation we now have before us the tested evidences of criminality and have heard the flimsy excuses and paltry evasions of the defendants. The suspended judgment with which we opened this case is no longer appropriate. The time has come for final judgment and if the case I present seems hard and uncompromising, it is because the evidence makes it so.

The Crimes of the Nazi Regime

The strength of the case against these defendants under the conspiracy count, which is the duty of the United States to argue, is in its simplicity. It involves but three ultimate inquiries: *First*, have the acts defined by the Charter as crimes been committed; *second*, were they committed pursuant to a common plan or conspiracy; *third*, are these defendants among those who are criminally responsible?

The charge requires examination of a criminal policy, not of a multitude of isolated, unplanned, or disputed crimes. The substantive crimes upon which we rely, either as goals of a common plan or as means for its accomplishment, are admitted. The pillars which uphold the conspiracy charge may be found in five considerations in appraising the proof of conspiracy.

[Jackson then lists the five "pillars" which characterize, in his judgment, the overt acts necessary to establish a conspiracy. These are, in order of presentation: *(1) The Seizure of Power and Subjugation of Germany to a Police State; (2) The Preparation of Waging of Wars of Aggression; (3) Warfare in Disregard of International Law; (4) Enslavement and Plunder of Populations in Occupied Territories; and (5) Persecution and Extermination of Jews and Christians.* Under each of these five headings, a detailed narrative is presented to establish a *prima facie* violation of The London Charter. He then proceeds to summarize the legal bases for the so-called "common plan or conspiracy"].

* * *

I pass now to the inquiry whether these groups of criminal acts were integrated in a common plan or conspiracy.

The Common Plan or Conspiracy

The prosecution submits that these five categories of premeditated crimes were not separate and independent phenomena but that all were committed pursuant to a common plan or conspiracy. The defense admits that these classes of crimes were committed but denies that they are connected one with another as parts of a single program.

The central theme in this pattern of crime, the kingpin which holds them all together, is the ploy for aggressive war. The chief reason for international cognizance of these crimes lies in this fact. Have we established the plan or conspiracy to make aggressive war?

Certain admitted or clearly proven facts help answer that question. First, is the fact that such war of aggression *did* take place. Second, it is admitted that from the moment the Nazis came to power, everyone of them and everyone of the defendants worked like beavers to prepare for some war. The question therefore comes to this: Were they preparing for the war which did occur, or were they preparing for some war which never has happened? It is probably true that in the early days none of them had in mind what month of what year war would begin, the exact dispute which would precipitate it, or whether its first impact would be Austria, Czechoslovakia, or Poland. But I submit that the defendants either knew or are chargeable with knowledge that the war for which they were making ready would be a war of German aggression. This is partly because there was no real expectation that any power or combination of powers would attack Germany. But it is chiefly because the inherent nature of the German plans was such that they were certain sooner or later to meet resistance and that they could then be accomplished only by aggression.

* * *

...A glance over the dock will show that, despite quarrels among themselves, each defendant played a part which fitted in with every other, and that all advanced the common plan. It contradicts experience that men of such diverse backgrounds and talents should so forward each other's aims by coincidence.

The large and varied role of Goering was half militarist and half gangster. He stuck a pudgy finger in every pie. He used his SA muscle-men to help bring the gang into power. In order to entrench that power he contrived to have the Reichstag burned, established the Gestapo, and created the concentration camps. He was equally adept at massacring opponents and at framing scandals to get rid of stubborn generals. He built up the *Luftwaffe* and hurled it at his defenseless neighbors. He was among the foremost in harrying the Jews out of the land. By mobilizing the total economic resources of Germany he made possible the waging of the war which he had taken a large part in planning. He was, next to Hitler, the man who tied the activities of all the defendants together in a common effort.

The parts played by the other defendants, although less comprehensive and less spectacular than that of the Reichsmarshal, were nevertheless integral and necessary contributions to the joint undertaking, without any one of which the success of the common enterprise would have been in jeopardy. There are many specific deeds of which these men have been proven guilty. No purpose would be served...to review all the crimes which the evidence had charged up to their names. Nevertheless, in viewing the conspiracy as a whole and as an operating mechanism it may be well to recall briefly the outstanding services which each of the men in the dock rendered to the common cause.

The zealot Hess, before succumbing to wanderlust, was the engineer tending the Party machinery, passing orders and propaganda down to the Leadership Corps, supervising every aspect of Party activities, and maintaining the organization as a loyal and ready instrument of power.

When apprehension abroad threatened the success of the Nazi scheme for conquest, it was the duplicitous Ribbentrop, the salesman of deception, who was detailed to pour wine on the troubled waters of suspicion by preaching the gospel of limited and peaceful intentions.

Keitel, weak and willing tool, delivered the armed forces, the instrument of aggression, over to the Party and directed them executing its felonious designs.

Kaltenbrunner, the grand inquisitor, took up the bloody mantle of Heydrich to stifle opposition and terrorize compliance, and buttressed the power of National Socialism on a foundation of guiltless corpses.

It was Rosenberg, the intellectual high priest of the "master race," who provided the doctrine of hatred which gave the impetus for the annihilation of jewry, and put his infidel theories into practice against the eastern occupied territories. His wooly philosophy also added boredom to the long list of Nazi atrocities.

The fanatical Frank, who solidified Nazi control by establishing the new order of authority without law, so that the will of the Party was the only test of legality, proceeded to export his lawlessness to Poland, which he governed with the lash of Caesar and whose population he reduced to sorrowing remnants.

Frick, the ruthless organizer, helped the Party to seize power, supervised the police agencies to insure that it stayed in power, and chained the economy of Bohemia and Moravia to the German war machine.

Streicher, the venomous vulgarian, manufactured and distributed obscene racial libels which incited the populace to accept and assist the progressively savage operations of "race purification."

As Minister of Economics Funk accelerated the pace of rearmament, and as Reichsbank president banked for the SS the gold teeth fillings of concentration camp victims—probably the most ghoulish collateral in banking history.

It was Schacht, the façade of starched respectability, who in the early days provided the window dressing, the bait for the hesitant, and whose wizardry later made it possible for Hitler to finance the colossal rearmament program and do it secretly.

Doenitz, Hitler's legatee of defeat, promoted the success of the Nazi aggressions by instructing his pack of submarine killers to conduct warfare at sea with the illegal ferocity of the jungle.

Raeder, the political admiral, stealthily built up the German navy in defiance of the Versailles Treaty, and then put it to use in a series of aggressions which he had taken a large part in planning.

Von Schirach, poisoner of a generation, initiated the German youth in Nazi doctrine, trained them in legions for service in the SS and *Wehrmacht,* and delivered them up to the Party as fanatic, unquestioning executors of its will.

Sauckel, the greatest and cruelest slaver since the Pharaohs of Egypt, produced desperately needed manpower by driving foreign peoples into the land of bondage on a scale unknown even in the ancient days of tyranny in the Kingdom of the Nile.

Jodl, betrayer of the traditions of his profession, led the *Wehrmacht* in violating its own code of military honor in order to carry out the barbarous aims of Nazi policy.

Von Papen, pious agent of an infidel regime, held the stirrup while Hitler vaulted into the saddle, lubricated the Austrian annexation, and devoted his diplomatic cunning to the service of Nazi objectives abroad.

Seyss-Inquart, spearhead of the Austrian fifth-column, took over the government of his own country only to make a present of it to Hitler, and then moving north, brought terror and oppression to the Netherlands and pillaged its economy for the benefit of the German juggernaut.

Von Neurath, the old-school diplomat, who cast the pearls of his experience before Nazis, guided Nazi diplomacy in the early days, soothed the fear of prospective victims, and as Reich Protector of Bohemia and Moravia, strengthened the German position for the coming attack on Poland.

Speer, as Minister of Armaments and War Production, joined in planning and executing the program to dragoon prisoners of war and foreign workers into German war industries, which waxed in output while the laborers waned in starvation.

Fritzsche, radio propaganda chief, by manipulation of the truth goaded German public opinion into frenzied support of the regime and anesthetized the independent judgment of the population so that they did without question their master's bidding.

And Bormann, who had not accepted our invitation to this reunion, sat at the throttle of the vast and powerful engine of the Party, guiding it in the ruthless execution of Nazi policies, from the scourging of the Christian Church to the lynching of captive Allied Airmen.

The activities of all these defendants, despite their varied backgrounds and talents, were joined with the efforts of other conspirators not now in the dock, who played still other essential roles. It could not from among its own ranks make up a government capable of carrying out all the projects necessary to realize its aims. Therein lies the special crime of betrayal of men like Schacht and von Neurath, Speer and von Papen, Raeder and Doenitz, Keitel and Jodl. It is doubtful whether the Nazi master plan could have succeeded without their specialized intelligence which they so willingly put at its command. They did so with knowledge of its announced aims and methods, and continued their services after practice had confirmed the direction in which they were tending. Their superiority to the average run of Nazi mediocrity is not their excuse. It is their condemnation.

The War Was Deliberately Planned

The dominant fact which stands out from all the thousands of pages of the record of this trial is that the central crime of the whole group of Nazi crimes—the attack on the peace of the world—was *clearly and deliberately planned*. The beginning of these wars of aggression was *not* an unprepared and spontaneous springing to arms by a population excited by some current indignation. A week before the invasion of Poland Hitler told his military commanders:

> "I shall give a propaganda cause for starting war—never mind whether it is plausible or not. The victor shall not be asked later on whether we told the truth or not. In starting and making a war, not the right is what matters, but victory."

The propaganda incident was duly provided by dressing concentration camp inmates in Polish uniforms, in order to create the appearance of a Polish attack on a German frontier radio station. The plan to occupy Belgium, Holland and Luxembourg first appeared as early as August 1938 in connection with the plan to attack Czechoslovakia. The intention to attack became a program in May 1939, when Hitler told his commander that

> "The Dutch and Belgian air bases must be occupied by armed forces. Declarations of neutrality must be ignored."

Thus, the follow-up wars were planned before the first was launched. These were the most carefully plotted wars in all history. Scarcely a step in their terrifying succession and progress failed to move according to the master blueprint or the subsidiary schedules and timetables until long after the crimes of aggression were consummated.

Nor were the war crimes and the crimes against humanity unplanned, or spontaneous offenses. Aside from our undeniable evidence of their plotting, it is sufficient to ask whether six million people could be separated from the population of several nations on the basis of their blood and birth, could be destroyed and their bodies disposed of, except that the operation fitted into the general scheme of government.

Could the enslavement of five millions of laborers, their impressments into service, their transportation to Germany, their allocation to work where they would be most useful, their maintenance, if slow starvation can be called maintenance, and their guarding have been accomplished if it did not fit into the common plan?

Could hundreds of concentration camps located throughout Germany, built to accommodate hundreds and thousands of victims, and each requiring labor and materials for construction, manpower to operate and supervise, and close gearing into the economy—could such efforts have been expended under German autocracy if they had not suited the plan?

Has the Teutonic passion for organization become famous for its toleration of nonconforming activity?

Each part of the plan fitted into every other. The slave labor program meshed with the needs of industry and agriculture and these in turn synchronized with the military machine. The elaborate propaganda apparatus geared with the program to dominate the people and incite them to a war their sons would have to fight. The armament industries were fed by the concentration camps. The concentration camps were fed by the Gestapo. The Gestapo was fed by the spy systems of the Nazi Party. Nothing was permitted under the Nazi iron rule that was not in accordance with the program. Everything of consequence that took place in this regimented society was but a manifestation of a premeditated and unfolding purpose to secure the Nazi state a place in the sun by casting all others into darkness.

* * *

In conspiracy we do not punish one man for another man's crime. We seek to punish each for his own crime of joining a common criminal plan in which others also participated. The measure of the criminality of the plan and therefore the guilt of each participant is, of course, the sum total of crimes committed by all in executing the plan. But the gist of the offense is participation in the formulation or execution of the plan. These are rules which every society has found necessary in order to reach men, like these defendants, who never get blood on their own hands but who lay plans that result in the shedding of blood. All over Germany today, in every zone of occupation, little men who carried out these criminal policies under orders are being convicted and punished. It would present a vast and unforgivable caricature of justice if the men who planned these policies and directed those little men should escape all penalty.

These men in the dock, on the face of the record, were not strangers to this program of crime, nor was their connection with it remote and obscure. We find them in the very heart of it. The positions they held show that we have chosen defendants of self-evident responsibility. They are the very top surviving authorities in their respective fields and in the Nazi State. No one lives who, at least until the very last moments of the war, out ranked Goering in position, power, and influence. No soldier stood above Keitel and Jodl, and no sailor above Raeder and Doenitz. Who can be responsible for the duplicitous diplomacy if not the Foreign Ministers, von Neurath and Ribbentrop, and the diplomatic handyman, von Papen? Who should be answerable for the oppressive administration of occupied countries if Gauleiters, Protectors, Governors, and Commissars such as Frank, Seyss-Inquart, Frick, von Schirach, von Neurath and Rosenberg are not? Where shall we look for those who mobilized the economy for total war if we overlook Schacht, and Speer and Funk? Who was the master of the great slaving enterprise if it was not Sauckel? Where shall we find the hand that ran the concentration camps if it is not the hand of Kaltenbrunner? And who whipped up the hates and fears of the public, and manipulated the Party organizations to incite these crimes, if not Hess, von Schirach, Fritzsche, Bormann, and the unspeakable Julius Streicher? The list of defendants is made up of men who played indispensable and reciprocal parts in this tragedy. The photographs and films show them again and again together on important occasions. The documents show them agreed on policies and on methods, and all working aggressively for the expansion of Germany by force of arms.

Each of these men made a real contribution to the Nazi plan. Every man had a key part. Deprive the Nazi regime of the functions performed by a Schacht, a Sauckel, a von Papen, or a Goering, and you have a different regime. Look down the rows of fallen men and picture them as the photographic and documentary evidence shows them to have been in their days of power. Is there one whose work did not substantially advance the conspiracy along its bloody path towards its bloody goal? Can we assume that the great effort of these men's lives was directed towards ends they never suspected?

To escape the implications of their positions and the inference of guilt from their activities, the defendants are almost unanimous in one defense. The refrain is heard time and again: these men were without authority, without knowledge, without influence, indeed without importance.

* * *

They do protest too much. They deny knowing what was common knowledge. They deny knowing plans and programs that were as public as *"Mein Kampf"* and the Party program. They deny even knowing the contents of documents they received and acted upon.

* * *

The defendants have been unanimous, when pressed, in shifting the blame on other men, sometimes on one and sometimes on another. But the names they have repeatedly picked are Hitler, Himmler, Heydrich, Goebbels and Bormann. All of these are dead or missing. No matter how hard we have pressed the defendants on the stand, they have never pointed the finger at a living man as guilty. It is a temptation to ponder the wondrous workings of a fate which has left only the guilty dead and only the innocent alive. It is almost too remarkable.

The villain on whom blame is placed,—some of the defendants vie with each other in producing appropriate epithets—is Hitler. He is the man at whom nearly every defendant has pointed an accusing finger.

I shall not dissent from this consensus, nor do I deny that all these dead or missing men shared the guilt. In crimes so reprehensible that degrees of guilt have lost their significance they may have played the most evil parts. But their guilt cannot exculpate the defendants. Hitler did not carry all responsibility to the grave with him. All the guilt is not wrapped in Himmler's shroud. It was these dead whom these living chose to be their partners in this great conspiratorial brotherhood, and the crimes that they did together they must pay for one by one.

It may well be said that Hitler's final crime was against the land that he had ruled. He was a mad messiah who started the war without cause and prolonged it without reason. If he could not rule he cared not what happened to Germany. As Fritzsche has told us from the stand, Hitler tried to use the defeat of Germany for the self-destruction of the German people. He continued the fight when he knew it could not be won, and continuance meant only ruin. Speer, in this courtroom, has described it as follows:

> "...The sacrifices which were made on both sides after January 1945 were without sense. The dead of this period will be the accusers of the man responsible for the continuation of that fight, Adolf Hitler, just as much as he destroyed cities, destroyed in the last phase, who had lost tremendous cultural values and tremendous numbers of dwellings.... The German people remained faithful to Adolf Hitler until the end. He has betrayed them knowingly. He has tried to throw it into the abyss...."

...But let me for a moment turn devil's advocate. I admit that Hitler was the chief villain. But for the defendants to put all blame on him is neither manly nor true. We know that even the head of a state has the same limits to his senses and to the hours of his day as do lesser men. He must rely on others to be his eyes and ears as to most that goes on in a great empire. Other legs must run his errands; other hands must execute his plans. On whom did Hitler rely for such things more than upon these men in the dock?... These men had access to Hitler, and often controlled the information that reached him on which he must base his policy and his orders. They were the Praetorian Guard, and while they were under Ceasar's orders, Ceasar was always in their hands.

If these dead men could take the witness stand and answer what has been said against them, we might have a less distorted picture of the parts played by these defendants. Imagine the stir that would occur in the dock if it should behold Adolf Hitler advancing to the witness box, or Himmler with an armful of dossiers, or Goebbels, or Bormann with the reports of his Party spies, or the murdered Roehm or Canaris. The ghoulish defense that the world is entitled to retribution only from the cadavers, is an argument worthy of the crimes at which it is directed.

We have presented to this Tribunal an affirmative case based on incriminating documents which are sufficient, if unexplained, to require a finding of guilt on Court One against each defendant. In the final analysis, the only question is whether the defendants' own testimony is to be credited as against the documents and other evidence of their guilt. What, then, is their testimony worth?

The fact is that the Nazi habit of economizing in the use of the truth pulls the foundations out from under their own defense. Lying has always been a highly approved Nazi technique. Hitler, in *"Mein Kampt."* advocated mendacity as a policy. Ribbentrop admits the use of the "diplomatic lie." Keitel advised that the facts of rearmament be kept secret so that they could be denied at Geneva. Raeder deceived about rebuilding the German navy in violation of Versailles. Goering urged Ribbentrop to tell a "legal lie" to the British Foreign Office about the Anschluss, and in so doing only marshaled him the way he was going. Goering gave his word of honor to the Czechs and proceeded to break it. Even Speer promised to deceive the French into revealing the specially trained among their prisoners.

Nor is the lie direct the only means of falsehood. They all speak with a Nazi doubletalk with which to deceive the unwary. In the Nazi dictionary of sardonic euphemisms "Final Solution" of the Jewish problem was a phrase which meant extermination; "Special treatment" of prisoners of war meant killing; "Protective custody" meant concentration camp; "Duty labor" meant slave labor; and an order to "take a firm attitude" or "take positive measures" meant to act with unrestrained savagery. Before we accept their word at what seems to be its face, we must always look for hidden meanings....

Besides outright false statements and doubletalk, there are also other circumventions of truth in the nature of fantastic explanations and absurd professions. Streicher has solemnly maintained that his only thought with respect to the Jews was to resettle them on the Island of Madagascar. His reasons for destroying synagogues, he blandly said, was only because they were architecturally offensive. Rosenberg was stated by his counsel to have always had in mind a "chivalrous solution" to the Jewish problem. When it was necessary to remove Schushnigg after the Anschluss, Ribbentrop would have had us believe that the Austrian Chancellor was resting at a "villa." It was left to cross-examination to reveal that the "villa" was Buchenwald Concentration Camp. The record is full of other examples of dissimulations and evasions. Even Schacht showed that he, too, had adopted the Nazi attitude that truth is any story which succeeds. Confronted on cross-examination with a long record of broken vows and false words, he declared in justification—

"I think you can score many more successes when you want to lead someone if you don't tell them the truth than if you tell them the truth."

This was the philosophy of the National Socialists. When for years they had deceived the world, and masked falsehoods with plausibilities, can anyone be surprised that they continue the habits of a lifetime in this dock? Credibility is one of the main issues of this trial. Only those who have failed to learn the bitter lessons of the last decade can doubt that men who have always played on the unsuspecting credulity of generous opponents would not hesitate to do the same now.

It is against such a background that these defendants now ask this Tribunal to say that they are not guilty of planning, executing, or conspiring to commit this long list of crimes and wrongs. They stand before the record of this trial as blood-stained Gloucester stood by the body of his slain King. He begged of the widow, as they beg of you: "Say I slew them not." And the Queen replied, "Then say they were not slain. But dead they are, * * *"

If you were to say of these men that they are not guilty, it would be as true to say there has been *no war*, there are *no slain*, there has been *no crime*.

(c) Judgment of the Tribunal
6 F.R.D. 69; 76–77; 147 (1947)

The Court:

* * *

The Tribunal was invested with power to try and punish persons who had committed crimes against peace, war crimes and crimes against humanity as defined in the Charter.

The Charter also provided that at the trial of any individual member of any group or organization the Tribunal may declare (in connection with any act of which the individual may be convicted) that the group of organization of which the individual was a member was a criminal organization.

In Berlin, on the 18th October 1945, in accordance with Article 14 of the Charter, an indictment was lodged against the defendants named in the caption above, who had been designated by the Committee of the Chief Prosecutors of the signatory Powers as major war criminals.

A copy of the indictment in the German language was served upon each defendant in custody at least thirty days before the Trial opened.

* * *

The defendant Robert Ley committed suicide in prison on the 25th October 1945. On the 15th November 1945 the Tribunal decided that the defendant Gustav Krupp von Bohlen und Halbach could not then be tried because of his physical and mental condition, but that the charges against him in the indictment should be retained for trial thereafter, if the physical and mental condition of the defendant should permit. On the 17th November 1945 the Tribunal decided to try the defendant Bormann in his absence under the provisions of Article 12 of the Charter....

In accordance with Articles 16 and 23 of the Charter, Counsel were either chosen by the defendants in custody themselves, or at their request were appointed by the Tribunal. In his absence the Tribunal appointed Counsel for the defendant Bormann, and also assigned Counsel to represent the named groups or organizations.

The Trial which was conducted in four languages...began on the 20th November 1945, and pleas of "not Guilty" were made by all defendants except Bormann.

The hearing of evidence and the speeches of Counsel concluded on 31st August 1946.

* * *

Much of the evidence presented to the Tribunal on behalf of the Prosecution was documentary evidence, captured by the Allied armies in German army headquarters, Government buildings, and elsewhere. Some of the documents were found in salt mines, buried in the ground, hidden behind false walls and in other places thought to be secure from discovery. The case, therefore against the defendants rests in large measure on documents of their own making, the authenticity of which has not been challenged except in one or two cases.

* * *

PREFACE TO INDIVIDUALS' JUDGMENT

Article 26 of the Charter provides that the Judgment of the Tribunal as to the guilt or innocence of any defendant shall give the reasons on which it is based.

The Tribunal will now state those reasons in declaring its Judgment on such guilt or innocence.

[The Court then went into a lengthy discussion of the events leading up to the judgment of each of the twenty-two defendants (Bormann included) and the reasons for such judgment. Beginning with Göering, the Court took up *seriatum*, Hess, von Ribbentrop, Keitel, Kaltenbrunner, Rosenberg, Frank, Frick, Streicher, Funk, Schacht, Döenitz, Raeder, von Schirach, Sauckel, Jodl, Bormann, von Papen, Seyss-Inquart, Speer, von Neurath and Fritzsche. After each defendant, the Tribunal recited the findings of guilt or innocence relating to each of the four counts in the indictment. At the conclusion of this narrative, a dissenting opinion was filed by the Soviet Member of the Tribunal, I. T. Nikitchenko. Judge Nikitchenko disagreed with the sentences handed down by the Tribunal regarding defendants Schacht, von Papen, Fritzsche and Hess. The Soviet jurist also dissented from the Tribunal's majority finding three Nazi organizations "not criminal," namely, (1) the Reich Cabinet, (2) the SA and (3) the General Staff and OKW. In sum, Nikitchenko remarked, "I can not agree with the decision adopted by the Tribunal as it does not correspond to the facts of the case and is based on incorrect conclusion." Tables II. and III. (*infra*) reflect a composite of the IMT verdicts].

Table II

14. Summary of the Counts of the Indictment and Results of War Crimes Trial against Accused Individuals

Count 1 — Conspiracy to commit acts named in the three other counts.

Count 2 — Crimes against peace, namely, the planning, preparation, initiation and waging of wars of aggression.

Count 3 — War crimes, namely: violations of the laws or customs of war.

Count 4 — Crimes against humanity, namely, murder, extermination, enslavement, deportation or other inhumane acts against any civilian population, before or during the war; or persecutions, political, racial or religious.

(Where there is no symbol in the Table, the accused was not charged).

Accused	Count 1	Count 2	Count 3	Count 4	Sentence
Hermann Göering	G	G	G	G	Hanging
Richard Rudolf Hess	G	G	I	I	Life
Joachim v. Ribbentrop	G	G	G	G	Hanging
Wilhelm Keitel	G	G	G	G	Hanging
Ernst Kaltenbrunner	I	—	G	G	Hanging
Alfred Rosenberg	G	G	G	G	Hanging
Hans Frank	I	—	G	G	Hanging
Wilhelm Frick	I	G	G	G	Hanging
Julius Streicher	I	—	—	G	Hanging
Walther Funk	I	G	G	G	Life
Hajlmar Schacht	I	I	—	—	Acquitted
Karl Döenitz	I	G	G	—	10 years
Erich Raeder	G	G	G	—	Life
Baldur v. Schirach	I	—	—	G	20 years
Fritz Sauckel	I	I	G	G	Hanging
Alfred Jodl	G	G	G	G	Hanging
Franz v. Papen	I	I	—	—	Acquitted
Arthur Seyss-Inquart	I	G	G	G	Hanging
Albert Speer	I	I	G	G	20 years
Constantin v. Neurath	G	G	G	G	15 years
Hans Fritzsche	I	—	I	I	Acquitted
Martin Bormann	I	—	G	G	Hanging

—————

Table III

15. Organization Criminality

Leadership Corps of the NSDAP	Declared criminal
The Gestapo and the SD	Declared criminal
The SS	Declared criminal
The SA	Declared non-criminal
The Reich Cabinet	Declared non-criminal
General Staff and High Command	Declared non-criminal

—————

16. Hans Ehard, "The Nuremberg Trial against the Major War Criminals and International Law"

43 *American Journal of International Law* 223; 224–226; 229–244 (1949)
Reproduced with permission from 43 *American Journal of International Law*
223 (1949) © Copyright the American Society of International Law

[Hans Ehard, *Minister-President of Bavaria*, presented the following account of the Nuremberg proceedings to a meeting of lawyers held in Munich, Germany, June 2, 1948. The presentation was recommended for publication by Mr. Justice Robert H. Jackson, not because he necessarily agreed with all of it, but, because, in his words, "… it places the discussion on a more profitable basis than some of the popular criticisms that have appeared. And at all events, the German viewpoint is worth considering in any appraisal of the trial." Excerpts from this paper, originally published in Germany in the German legal publication, *Suddeutsche Juristen-Zeitung (South German Legal Newspaper)* (July, 1948), vol. 3, No. 7, cols. 353–368, appear below].

"The trial which is now about to begin is unique in the history of the jurisprudence of the world and it is of supreme importance to millions of people all over the globe."

Thus spoke the President of the International Military Tribunal in Nuremberg, Lord Justice Lawrence, upon the occasion of the institution of the so-called Trial against the Major War Criminals on November 20, 1945. If his statement is correct, then the German people undoubtedly rank in first place among these millions. This also was the opinion of the chief prosecutor which recurred several times in his statements. Thus the French representative, Mr. Francois de Menthon, exclaimed:

> This work of justice is equally indispensable for the future of the German people…. The initial condemnation of Nazi Germany by your high Tribunal will be a first lesson for these people and will constitute the best starting point…of re-education which must be its great concern during the coming years….
>
> Your judgment…can serve as a foundation for the moral uplift of the German people, first stage in its integration into the community of free countries….

During the proceedings the German people have become only insufficiently aware of the importance of the trial such as it has been described in the quoted phrases by outstanding men of other nations. It was still too stunned from the collapse, too deeply mired in its increasing distress, too much under the spell of the power of war propaganda, of distrust and of disappointments, too little familiar with the horrible crimes of the deposed leaders, too unfamiliar with the entire proceedings. Furthermore, type of coverage given in the press and on the radio was not suited to create understanding and interest.

The passage of time has had a clarifying and calming effect in this respect. We have gained sufficient mental and psychological distance from the trial and the judgment to view them quietly. We now also have at our disposal the essential material required for this objective examination, namely, in the form of the official publication of the records which contain the text of the indictment and of the judgment as well as the transcript of the proceedings and the most important documentary evidence, and which, as is stated in a prefatory remark, is "published in accordance with the direction of the International Military Tribunal, under the jurisdiction of the Allied Control Authority for Germany."

The German people may no longer remain passive before this tremendous amount of material. A judgment which an international military tribunal has rendered on German territory, against Germans, should not leave any German unconcerned. Proceedings in which the law of nations is invoked for the first time in such a magnificent form against the abuse of power should find the lively attention of the German people even if Germany had not been directly involved. In my opinion it is now the duty and the gratifying task of German legal science and politics to investigate the voluminous material of the trial and to make use of it.

* * *

The basis in international law of the trial is the agreement between England, the United States, France and the Soviet Union signed on August 8, 1945, which is entitled: "Agreement for the Prosecution and Punishment of the Major War Criminals of the European Axis."

* * *

In its formal aspect, the Agreement represents so-called particular international law, which originates from an agreement, and, at first hand, is only binding upon the entire community of nations.

The Charter, in its contents, is substantive criminal law and procedural criminal law at the same time, It defines the punishable acts and provides the limits of punishment as is usual in a criminal code. It also contains the provisions regarding the composition of the tribunal and the rules of procedure such as we find them in a judiciary act and in a code of criminal procedure. The Charter represents, particularly in regard to procedural law, a compromise between Anglo-Saxon and continental legal doctrine.

* * *

The indictment was based upon an abundance of exact facts on each count. The main trial was instituted on November 20, 1945. The judgment is dated October 1, 1946.

From a technical point of view the trial was an important accomplishment. German, English, French and Russian were admitted as languages in which the proceedings could take place. Each word that was spoken in one of these languages could be heard over the ear-phones, translated into one of the other three languages. A tremendous amount of documentary proof was submitted, explained and worked over.

Within the framework set by the Charter all participants were obviously endeavoring to be objective. Occasional deviations from this rule were stopped immediately by the President.

The German defense saw itself faced with a difficult task, since in all technical questions it was dependent upon the court or the prosecution because it did not become cognizant of the tremendous amount of incriminating material of the prosecution during the course of the trial, and had to find its way in a trial procedure which deviates substantially from the German criminal procedure. The performance of the defense should receive particularly high credit under the circumstances.

* * *

The crushing documentary evidence which the prosecution submitted during the oral hearings for the most part was taken from captured German archives. Its authenticity could not be contested. The Indictment, the protocols of the proceedings and the judgment described the fateful course of National Socialism in Germany and in the world as objectively and impressively as hardly any German description could have done. We experience once again the entire development: the road to power, the strengthening of power by deception, compulsion, cunning and terror, the battle against the working class, against the Church, the persecution of the Jews, and the war with its horrors. Much is uncovered before our eyes which was unknown to the German people. The blush of shame must rise in the face of every German if he hears the incontrovertible proof thereof and sees how cowardly cruelty, currish fealty, insane obsession debased honor and humanity [had] forfeited the German reputation. One would like to tell every German to read these documents, particularly those people who forget too soon and would like to avert their eyes from the horrors of the near past. Then they would understand more readily that the tragic today had to develop from the criminal yesterday.

... [P]ermit me to pass onto the legal problems which we are to discuss today.

1. The criminal law which was to be applied is the Charter. It dates from August 8, 1945. However, the indictment is directed against acts which were committed before May 8, 1945, *i. e.*, long before the promulgation of the Charter. Furthermore, the Charter declares that, among other things, certain acts which heretofore had merely been judged as political or military conduct, but never had been subjected to an appraisal from the viewpoint of international criminal law, were declared by the Charter to be crimes....

In addition, the Charter makes responsible a group of persons such as has heretofore never been subjected to criminal jurisdiction under international law. According to the weight of doctrine, international law has only to do with nations, not with individual persons. In cases of acts of a predominately political character, also of the so-called political crimes, only the state as such, and not the offender personally, is responsible according to this view.

Therefore, the question comes up whether the principle almost generally recognized in the criminal law of civilized nations is not violated by the Charter and the proceedings, namely, that an act shall only be punished if at the time of its commission it was under penal sanction. It is the principle which excludes the retroactive force of penal laws and which is usually expressed by the Latin formula: *nulla poena sine lege* or *nullem crimen sine lege.* Many representatives of international law doubt whether this principle is applicable to international law at all, namely, because it would presuppose a stage in the legal organization which has not yet been attained in international law. But I need hardly enter upon this objection, since neither the prosecution nor the judgment have in principle denied that this principle also applies in international law....

2. The Charter has been promulgated by the victors and is directed exclusively against the vanquished. The party on the one hand is, as has been stated in the joint defense, "all in one; creator of the statute of the Tribunal and of the rules of law, prosecutor and judge." The question arises whether these facts do not run counter to the generally recognized principles of modern penal jurisprudence and to the requirements of an international court.

The prosecutors and the court could simply have avoided any discussion of these questions by referring to the Charter as the sole authoritative source of law. It is to the credit of the court as well as of the prosecution that, in putting full emphasis upon the authoritative importance of the Charter, they did not avoid these fundamental legal questions, but tried to meet the above-mentioned objections in their statements, which in part are masterpieces of forensic oratory, full of great perspicacity and considerable adroitness, although they did not all agree with one another on every detail and every argument.

The prosecutors themselves stress the novelty of the procedure. They admit that for the first time in history such an international criminal court is in session and that for the first time the men responsible for the war of aggression and its consequences are being taken personally to account. However, they nevertheless represent the viewpoint that the principle "*nulla poena sine lege*" has not been violated; that the legal norms applied are not fundamentally new but correspond to the general conviction of what is right. International law originates — so they state — not only from agreements between nations, not only as enacted law, but also from gradual observance, from customary law; that this customary law, which already before was in force, was, so to speak, codified in the Charter; that not the penal law as such, but only its formulation is new. Thus, for example, the chief American prosecutor states:

> It is an outgrowth of treaties and agreements between nations and of accepted customs. Yet every custom had its origin in some single act.... Unless we are prepared to abandon every principle of growth for international law, we cannot deny that our own day has the right to institute customs and to conclude agreements that will themselves become sources of a newer and strengthened international law.

Now, the indictment for planning and waging aggressive war is the salient part of the trial, as has been stressed again and again. If, however, aggressive war were not punishable, there would not be any basis for the punishment of crimes against peace, in other words, of the so-called political crimes which were so strongly emphasized. The chief prosecutors therefore have built up the thesis with a considerable array of oratory and historical material, that the war of aggression, defined as a crime in the Charter, was considered a crime under international law not later than after the Paris Pact of 1928 to Outlaw War, the so-called Briand-Kellogg Pact.

Now, if war of aggression is a crime — they argue, perhaps in a theoretically somewhat top-heavy argument — the aggressor automatically loses all rights which a party waging war has in a justified war. War of aggression therefore is nothing other than a murderous and predatory enterprise. The English chief prosecutor says:

> What statesman...could doubt, from 1928 onwards, that aggressive war...was unlawful and outlawed?

. . . .

It is, indeed, not necessary to doubt that some aspects of the Charter bear upon them the imprint of significant and salutary novelty. But it is our submission and our conviction, which we affirm before the Tribunal and the world, that fundamentally the provision of the Charter which constitutes wars...a crime, is not in any way an innovation. This provision of the Charter does no more than constitute a competent jurisdiction....

. . . .

It fills a gap in international criminal procedure.

According to the statements of the prosecutors, the personal liability on the part of the men responsible for the war also for the political acts committed in the name of the state is a logical conclusion and a requirement of justice. The state is only an idea. Acts, crimes are always committed by human beings only. Justice Jackson says:

The very minimum legal consequences of the treaties making aggressive war illegal is to strip those who incite or wage them of every defense the law ever gave, and to leave war-makers subject to judgment by the usually accepted principles of the law of crimes....

. . . .

The principle of personal liability is a necessary as well as logical one if international law is to render real help to the maintenance of peace....

. . . .

Those in lower ranks were protected against liability by the orders of their superiors. The superiors were protected because their orders were called acts of state.... Modern civilization puts unlimited weapons of destruction in the hands of men. It cannot tolerate so vast an area of legal irresponsibility....

Thus far Justice Jackson. The English chief prosecutor exclaims:

...the great powers responsible for this Charter...draw the inescapable conclusion from the renunciation, the prohibition, the condemnation of war...and they refuse to reduce justice to impotence by subscribing to the outworn doctrines that a sovereign state can commit no crime and that no crime can be committed on behalf of the sovereign state by individuals acting in its behalf.

* * *

The French chief prosecutor, in a well-founded legal construction, justifies the law of the Charter differently from Anglo-Saxon representatives. He states that the jurisdiction of the court rests upon the recognition in international law of the territorial principle in force in the sovereign states. According to this principle every nation may punish the crimes which are committed on its territory. Since the crimes of defendants apply to several national territories, the creation of a joint court seemed advisable. If responsibility under international law is recognized, it usually does not concern the individual but the national community as such. In such case, it is the duty of the state to deal with, either politically or as a crime, the conduct of the men who were the perpetrators of a violation of international law. At the present time, however, there is no German state. The highest authority in Germany is exercised by the four occupying Powers. Therefore, they have the right to have the guilt of German nationals tried before the court. According to this French thesis, therefore, the court would act as curator of German sovereignty.

The chief prosecutor of the Soviet Union, General Rudenko, does not recognize, in contradistinction to the other chief prosecutors, the customary law as part of the law of nations, but rather considers the agreements between states as the only source of establishing law and as the sole legal binding act. He says:

> The Charter…of the International Military Tribunal is to be considered an unquestionable and sufficient legislative act, defining and determining the basis of the procedure for the trial and punishment of major war criminals.

The references to the principle *nullum crimen sine lege*, he states further, "are not applicable because of the following fundamental, decisive fact: The Charter of the Tribunal is in force and in operation and all its provisions possess absolute and binding force."

These statements perhaps simplify the problem too much.

The judgment substantially follows the fundamental statements of the chief prosecutors. It emphasizes that the law of the Charter is binding for the court. According to the statement of the judgment, the Charter has been enacted on the basis of the indubitable right of the occupying Powers to enact laws for the occupied territories. The Charter does not represent an arbitrary exercise of power on the part of the victorious nations, but the expression of international law as it existed at the time of its creation.

With regard to the retroactive force of the Charter the judgment states the following:

> In the first place, it is to be observed that the maxim *nullem crimen sine lege* is not a limitation of sovereignty, but is in general a principle of justice. To assert that it is unjust to punish those who in defiance of treaties and assurances have attacked neighboring states without warning is obviously untrue, for in such circumstances the attacker must know that he is doing wrong, and so far from it being unjust to punish him, it would be unjust if his wrong were allowed to go unpunished.

If I understand these statements correctly, they state that the sovereign state may enact binding law for its courts without regard to the principle "*nullum crimen sine lege*," provided the higher justice requires it.

The judgment then states that war of aggression has been outlawed by the Briand-Kellogg Pact of 1928 as a crime.

* * *

The judgment argues that the Pact does not expressly state that such wars are crimes and does not appoint any courts for the trial of the aggressor. In interpreting the Pact, however,

> it must be remembered that international law is not the product of an international legislature, and that such international agreements as the Pact of Paris have to deal with general principles of law, and not with administrative matters of procedure. The law of war is to be found not only in treaties, but in the customs and practices of states which gradually obtained universal recognition, and from the general principles of justice applied by jurists and practiced by military courts. This law is not static, but by continual adaptation follows the needs of a changing world.

The responsibility of individuals under international law is affirmed by the court. In its opinion international law imposes duties and liabilities upon individuals as well as upon states. In this connection it is stated in the judgment: "only by punishing individuals who commit such crimes can the provisions of international law be enforced."

* * *

I shall now direct my attention to the more important question whether and to what extent new law has been applied in this trial and the principle *"nulla poena sine lege"* has been violated.

Let us again establish the meaning of the sentence first. We know that it is the purpose of all law to regulate the relations of men among themselves. The law tells everyone what he may do and what he may not do. Whoever commits an act must know what legal consequences it will entail. That is only possible if the rules of conduct are already fixed in advance. The more serious the legal consequences are, the more it is necessary that they be capable of being anticipated clearly and unequivocally. That is particularly true if the community claims the right to punish, which by its very nature is a painful interference with the legal sphere of the individual. The legal norm upon which a right to punish is based must declare certain conduct not only as unlawful, but must make it appear as punishable conduct, as a crime, and it must finally make provision for the execution of the right to punish. The legal norm which prohibits or outlaws the act must be accompanied by the penal sanction which is capable of execution in practice. It therefore does not suffice if the act is condemned from the moral point of view and is felt to be worthy of punishment; rather, it must also be branded as punishable. If, in the course of development, a legal norm evolves which makes punishable an act heretofore not punishable, then this norm, if it really is to be considered law, may only apply to the future. For, up to that time, the act was not contrary to law—and the legislator cannot change the past. This is the idea upon which the maxim *nulla poena sine lege* is based. In that connection the word *lex* should not only be taken to mean the law in the narrower technical sense, i. e., a rule issued in a definite form by authorities specially empowered, but it must be understood to include every legal norm, whether it be founded upon formal law or upon customary law, i. e., upon legal principles generally believed to be binding. The word *lex* in this connection corresponds to the concept of the English expression, "law," which in German also means "Gesetz" as well as "Recht" or "Rechtsnorm."

If we apply these criteria to the Nuremberg trial, the first question arises: Does the provision of the Charter, which designates the planning or waging of a war of aggression as a punishable crime, correspond to a legal norm laid down by international law or to general legal principles already in existence in 1939?

First, it must be stated that the concept of war aggression is not defined in the Charter and that no generally binding agreement has been reached in regard to this term in international law. This fact is not unimportant. Whoever starts a war will always be prepared with a more or less credible justification. We need only remember the speeches of Hitler. However, as the American chief prosecutor rightly emphasizes, "no political, military, economic, or other considerations shall serve as an excuse or justification for such actions…" Jackson quotes as an example the "Agreement concerning the Definition of the Concept of Aggression" which was signed in London in 1933 by the Soviet Union, the Baltic States, Poland, Rumania, Turkey, Persia and Afghanistan, and he designates it as "one of the most decisive sources of the law of nations." What now is termed a decisive source of international law at that time was considered merely a diplomatic maneuver on the part of the Soviet Union. Among the states represented in the court neither the United States nor England nor France has joined this or any agreement of similar contents, namely, for the reason that they did not want to have the definition apply to themselves. Incidentally, the agreement did not prevent the Soviet Union from moving into the territory of the contracting parties, of the Baltic States and of Poland, and from occupying Rumanian Bessarabia without worrying about its own definition of aggression and without regard to diplomatic protests.

Let us leave theory aside and assume without further discussion that the wars upon which the court had to decide were in fact wars of aggression in the meaning of article 6(a) of the Charter. What about the question whether these wars were punishable? One would think that, on such an important question, international law would provide a clear and unequivocal provision. Alas that is not the case. It is true that after a detailed description of the movements to prevent war since the time of the first World War, the indictment and judgment, as I have already stated, arrived at the conclusion that, at the latest, the General Treaty for Renunciation of War of August 27, 1928, which is better known under the name Paris Treaty to Outlaw War, or Kellogg Treaty, establishes punishment for wars of aggression....

This contractual renunciation of war as a tool of national politics implies, of course, that such a war is contrary to international law and that any nation which in spite thereof wages such a war commits a breach of contract. To this extent one must agree with the judgment. On the other hand, I do not find in the statements of the indictment and of the judgment any convincing proof for the further conclusion that after the treaty such a war was not only unlawful, but that those who plan such a war and wage it thereby commit a *crime*. In the treaty itself war is not designated as a crime and the renunciation is not reinforced by a sanction. It must be regretted that the treaty is a *lex imperfecta* to this extent, but in my opinion this cannot be disputed. It certainly is not satisfactory from a moral point of view if, subsequent to the treaty, monstrous deeds such as the waging of a war of aggression may be considered unlawful but not as a punishable offense. But such imperfections are not infrequent in the development of law and they are not always avoidable.

It is stated in detail in the trial and in the judgment that international law not only consists of treaties but also develops from usages and customs which gradually have found general recognition, and from legal principles which were worked out by jurists and which then slowly became general legal conviction. Furthermore, legal norms which originally were only contractual law may gradually become universal international law which applies to all nations. We fully agree with this view, which is also represented in German science of international law. Therefore, it remains to be examined in the present case whether war of aggression, even though no contractual norm has declared it punishable, perhaps was a punishable crime according to general legal conviction.

In this connection the judgment refers to resolutions which term war of aggression an international crime, namely, to a Resolution of the League of Nations dated September 24, 1927, and to a Resolution of the Sixth Pan American Conference in Havana dated February 18, 1928, as well as to the so-called Geneva Protocol of 1924. These demonstrations without a doubt show that in the community of nations the desire increased to see wars of aggression declared an international crime. But they in no way prove that this wish has already been realized in international law. On the contrary, it must be stated that none of the participating governments has gone beyond a declaratory or declamatory demonstration and that no government has committed itself to the international law viewpoint that war of aggression is punishable. The Geneva Protocol at that time was recommended for adoption by unanimous resolution of the Members of the League of Nations. But nevertheless it was never ratified and has never achieved validity as international law. This circumstance, in my opinion, speaks not for, but against, the existence of a general legal conviction.

Finally, let us consider the practice of nations, which is also an important source of international law.

If, since 1928, a general legal conviction had existed which regarded war of aggression as a punishable act under international law, it would in all probability have expressed itself in practical politics. There was no lack of suitable or even compelling occasions therefor. Japan started war against China and occupied Manchuria by armed force. Italy engulfed Abyssinia in a war, the Soviet Union conducted war against Finland. However, no official statement has become known in which the United States or the English, French or Soviet government would have designated these wars of aggression as international crimes under reference to the international law in effect, threatened with an international punishment and made the statesmen responsible for it personally liable. It is true that at the end of 1939 the Soviet Union was expelled from the League of Nations because of the war with Finland, but the prosecution and the judgment have not made reference to this resolution, nor to the "sanctions" decided upon in individual cases, as proof of the punishable character of a war of aggression under international law.

I believe that these facts and considerations must lead to the conclusion that the punishable character of the war of aggression stipulated in the Charter does not correspond to a general legal conviction in force in 1939, but that it is a *new* law and that to this extent the principle of *nullem crimen sine lege* has been violated.

We must ask ourselves why the punishable character of the war of aggression has been made the salient feature of the first Nuremberg trial, for the defendants would not have escaped their justified punishment because of their acts, which violate the penal laws of all civilized countries, even if the punishment of war of aggression as an international crime had been dispensed with. The explanation for this procedure probably lies more upon the political than upon the legal plane. A prosecution "in court" of the criminally induced world catastrophe just could not be avoided unless recourse was to be had to considerably more far-reaching methods, methods of punishment more questionable for the development of law which necessarily would have entailed a higher degree of arbitrariness. The emphasis upon war of aggression in the indictment has made it possible for the defendants to introduce primarily political viewpoints for their defense. This in part has had the regrettable consequence that their acts which would clearly have been punishable according to existing law, have to a certain extent been overshadowed by the controversial question whether war of aggression is an international crime which should be tried, if an individual is involved, before a tribunal of the victorious Powers.

But it would be much more regrettable if, in the future, because of the condemnation of war of aggression, the rules of warfare which are of primary importance for the protection of the individual, such as the Hague Rules of Land Warfare, the Geneva Convention on the Treatment of Prisoners of War and others should be neglected or ignored and lose their value. It is doubtful whether humanity will even succeed in making war impossible, but it is established beyond any doubt that, in view of the present state of technical progress, a barbaric method of total war would ensue, endangering the entire human race, if all warring parties, aggressors as well as defenders, did not feel themselves bound by these rule of warfare which have become established in the community of nations.

...The court rejected the view that persons who perform an official act assume no responsibility of their own under international law but are protected by the doctrine of the sovereignty of the state. In this connection it may be stated that the view at one time generally in vogue, that international law is only the law between nations that does not concern the individual, has not at all been generally relinquished. The allegations advanced several times, that crimes are always committed by individuals, is undoubtedly correct, but it is a truism. It applies to every human act and of itself proves nothing with regard to criminal responsibility in the individual case. I recall the English maxim: "The King can do not wrong." International military tribunals also are made up of human beings, conventions, also are entered into by human beings, a charter also is created by human beings, the indictment brought by individual human beings—and nevertheless the indictment in the trial begins with the words" "The United States of America, the French Republic, the United Kingdom of Great Britain and Northern Ireland, and the Union of Soviet Socialist Republics hereby indict...."

Finally the apodictic statement of the judgment that the principle of international law which, under certain circumstances, grants the representatives of the state protection, may not apply to acts which were branded as criminal by the law of nations, would require a more profound justification. In any event, no single case is known in which a statesman would have been subjected to criminal responsibility for any act committed in the name of the state. All representatives of the prosecution emphasize with fervor that the trial of those responsible for official acts is something completely new. Thus we come to the conclusion that, with regard to this question also, new law was applied with retroactive force.

Finally, a word on the procedural aspects of the trial. It is disposed of by the representatives of the prosecution in the otherwise extensive and thorough pleadings in a relatively short manner. It is true that all concede that this court is a novel institution and that no such international criminal proceedings have taken place, not even after the Treaty of Versailles which originally had provided for a trial of the war criminals. The prosecutors say: The Charter "only" fills a gap. The Charter "only" provides a competent jurisdiction. But these are in reality tremendous innovations. A law which fills a gap is new law; a law which creates jurisdiction not hitherto existing is also new law. It makes a great difference to the offender whether the judiciary act and the trial procedure were already determined at the time of the commission of the offense, or whether it was merely created subsequently, with confinement of its application to his case. It is not without reason that many constitutions and also Article 86 of the Bavarian Constitution declare special courts unlawful.

The observations which we have made, in my opinion, lead to the conclusion that the Charter and the trial have proceeded beyond international law as in force and have applied new law retroactively. I believe it would befit the reputation of the judge and international administration of justice better if we concede this fact than if we stretch the law upon the bed of Procrustes until it seems to serve the requirement of the hour.

The defenders of the Charter apparently have also felt that one cannot subsume satisfactorily the tremendous complex of political, military, and legal problems which faced the court under existing international law by means of legal constructions which depend entirely upon the substantive law in force. After exhausting all legal arguments they finally have made a subsidiary appeal against the restrictive substantive law to higher justice, to which all substantive law is to be subordinated. That is understandable. A number of horrible deeds have been committed. Was humanity to be deprived of the privilege of punishing these deeds and of exacting expiation from the guilty ones? Every feeling of law and order revolts against it. This desire for higher justice must be fulfilled even if one should have to proceed beyond the law as in force at the time of the commission of the deeds.

It probably is not coincidence that the prosecutors developed the noblest eloquence particularly on this point where substantive law no longer offers any conclusive arguments. Indeed, the ultimate and deepest justification of the Charter and the trial would be and would have to be the fulfillment of this ethical requirement. Whoever wishes to free the way to this higher justice would like to exclaim in the words of the British chief prosecutor:

> If this be an innovation, it is innovation long overdue—a desirable and benef-icent innovation fully consistent with justice, fully consistent with common sense and with the abiding purposes of the law of nations.

These are memorable words. If we follow them they will lead very far. Justice, sound human reasoning and the eternal aims of the law of nations demand that these norms, old or new, must apply to the strong as well as to the weak if they are to be felt to be law. For all actions are equal before the law of nations. It is contrary to law if one nation in-vokes legal norms against another nation which it does not consider binding also for it-self. It is regrettable that this general recognition [of the binding force] by the nations sitting in judgment has not been made expressly. The Powers could have solemnly de-clared in the London Agreement that they consider the norms established in the Charter as generally binding for the community of nations. They have not done so. The United Nations in whose interest the four Powers acted, as is stated in the preface to the Lon-don Agreement, have stated their "conviction" in a resolution of the General Assembly of December, 1946, with reference to the Nuremberg judgment, that the principles ap-plicable to the criminals of a war of aggression are to be generally valid. However, this resolution, just as the resolutions already mentioned, did not of itself create interna-tional law, but it is only a recommendation *de lege ferenda* [from law to be passed]. A competent court was not constituted.

It is true that the representatives of the prosecution have stated repeatedly that the signatory Powers have subjected themselves to this international law by virtue of the Charter. Thus the American representatives states:

> We must never forget that the record on which we judge these defendants today is the record on which history will judge us tomorrow. To pass these de-fendants a poisoned chalice is to put it to our own lips as well.

And in another place:

> And let me make clear that while this law is first applied against German ag-gressors, the law includes, and if it is to serve a useful purpose it must con-demn aggression by any other nations, including those which sit here now in judgment.

I am afraid that the light which this brilliant rhetoric sheds on sober reality is too rosy. At any rate the signatory Powers have not bound themselves in any way by contract to have the law of the Charter apply against themselves also.

Now we may perhaps be inclined to assume that the judgment must have binding force as a precedent particularly for the Anglo-Saxon mind. However, this hope might also be deceptive. The British chief prosecutor, it is true, stated once:

> Insofar as the Charter of this Tribunal introduces new law, it authors have es-tablished a precedent for the future—a precedent operative against all, includ-ing themselves....

However, the American chief prosecutor expressly stated during the oral argument:

> One of the reasons this was a military tribunal, instead of an ordinary court of law, was in order to avoid precedent-creating effect of what is done here on our

own law and the precedent control which would exist if this were an ordinary judicial body.

Since Jackson probably is the chief author of the Charter, his words have particular weight. It must be regretted that a judgment whose fundamental importance has been stressed on all sides so loudly was restricted so considerably in its legal effect.

Justice, sound human reasoning and the eternal aims of the law of nations also demand, finally, that the international jurisdiction, to which the lofty norms, may they be old or new, are entrusted for interpretation and application, offer in its constitution and in its composition every attainable guarantee of impartiality. The principles of modern criminal procedure are hardly disputed in this respect. It is the undisputed general sense of justice that the legislator should not also be prosecutor and judge. It is the general sense of justice that the accessory to the crime should not be legislator and judge over the perpetrator. Whoever himself enters into pacts with the aggressor, encourages him in his aggression and has shared the spoils with him is not justified in sitting in judgment upon him. It is the general sense of justice, and it is a practice of hitherto existing international jurisprudence, that the judicial decision should be made by neutrals and that the opposing parties should be represented.

It is regrettable that in Nuremberg that law was applied only by the victors. The assurance that, in spite thereof, not the law of the victors but only the law of nations was to be applied, would have been more convincing if the sword of law had been put into the hands of neutral Powers. It is true that there were few neutrals in this World War, but nevertheless there were Switzerland, Sweden, Portugal, countries in which persons conversant with international law and wise judges are not scarce.

Finally, the confidence in the jurisprudence of this court and the moral effect of the judgment would undoubtedly have been greater among the German people if German judges also would have been seated and had a voice in this court sitting over Germans.

However, all these statements should not in any way minimize the importance of the trial. It was, after all, our purpose in today's meeting to clarify in our minds the importance of the trial, not by regarding it from the narrow German viewpoint, but by setting it within the appropriate frame of the law of nations which embraces all civilized peoples. Only within this frame are we able to recognize to what extent the Charter and the trial represent and introduce a step forward.

Let us consider the following! During the trial nearly the entire law of nations, particularly the law in regard to the prevention of war and the rules of warfare, was restated by shrewd representatives of the four great victorious Powers. The conventions of the Hague, the law of occupation, the Geneva Convention Relating to Prisoners of War, everything which science has worked out, practice has observed and the governments have expressly and impliedly recognized, including the Charter, were submitted in the court as the law in force, as the expression of the general sense of justice, as the realization of justice, and the court was entreated to apply this law even if there were no precedent in the past for such application because otherwise the community of nations must perish! And the court, established by the four great Powers, manned by outstanding men from four nations, has confirmed that these norms contain or represent the general sense of justice and are generally binding!

Thus the trial and the judgment solemnly declared priority of law over force. This commitment to a law applying to all cannot be restricted to the individual case, but must morally bind all nations even if they have undertaken no express legal obligation. Nineteen nations have joined the London Agreement and the prosecutors have themselves declared that the law stated by them represents "the wisdom, the sense of justice, and the will of 21 governments, representing an overwhelming majority of all civilized people." This law applied for all times, in all places and for everyone, victor and vanquished. For victory and defeat may never establish a moratorium for law and justice.

Nor let us forget that the future is more important than the past! With this understanding we may salute the Nuremberg trial as a guidepost for the further development of the law of nations. A democratic Germany will further this development with all its strength. We also are of the opinion that it represents a tremendous advance of the law of nations if, in the future, war of aggression is prosecuted as an international crime without regard to the nation or the person, and if the responsible statesmen are personally taken to account. We consider it correct if, in the future, murder, ill-treatment of members of the civilian population of the occupied territories or their deportation for slave labor, or their banishment from their homes, the taking away of their property, plunder of public and private property, persecution for political, racial or religious reasons are punished by international law regardless of the person. We agree with the statement that it must be considered a punishable crime if the population of an occupied territory wastes away because of malnutrition and lack of fuel, if prisoners of war are mistreated and deported for slave labor, contrary to international agreements and the customary rule of international law. Subject to this law and on the basis of this law, we shall serve peace and reconciliation, when it will again be granted to us to cooperate, with our modest contribution, in the development of relations among nations.

---

17. Georg Schwarzenberger, "The Judgment of Nuremberg"

21 *Tulane Law Review* 329; 338–341; 343–353; 356–361 (1947)
George Schwarzenberger, *The Judgement of Nuremberg*, originally published in
21 Tul. L. Rev. 330–361 (1947). Reprinted with permission of the
Tulane Law Review Association which holds the copyright

[Georg Schwarzenberger is Reader in International Law in the University of London and Sub-Dean, Faculty of Laws, University College, London].

The International Military Tribunal for the Trial of German Major War Criminals has been described as a tribunal of a totally unprecedented character. It has been held that there *is* no precedent for this Tribunal, and that there is *no need* for any precedent. The first proposition seems hardly tenable, while the second is based on rather questionable assumptions.

* * *

Firstly, the Nuremberg Tribunal is international more in form than in substance. It is more akin to a joint tribunal under municipal law than to an international tribunal in the normal sense of the word.

Secondly, the status of the Tribunal within the judicial hierarchy of municipal courts and tribunals of the States which share it is that of a military *ad hoc* tribunal.

Thirdly, the status of the Tribunal as an agency which applies international law is similar to that of other courts which are composed of eminent exponents of municipal law, and the freedom of the Tribunal to apply international customary law is limited by its overriding duty to apply the law of its Charter whether or not such law is declaratory of existing international law.

The international basis of the Nuremberg Tribunal is provided by the Agreement of August 8th, 1945, as modified by the Protocol of October 6th 1945. The adhesion to the Agreement of nineteen members of the United Nations before delivery of the judgment further strengthened this source of the Tribunal's jurisdiction.

There is, however, another source of the Tribunal's jurisdiction: The exercise by the occupying Powers of *condominium* over Germany.... In the case of Germany,...there did not remain any "central Government or authority...capable of accepting responsibility for the maintenance of order, the administration of the country and compliance with the requirements of the victorious Powers." In view of Germany's complete breakdown owing to *debellatio*, [subjugation] the four Powers very logically declared that they assumed "supreme authority" over Germany.... [T]he joint sovereigns administer Germany as a separate international entity. In the words of a certificate, recently issued by the British Foreign Secretary, "the Allied Control Commission are the agency through which the Government of Germany is carried on."

In its Judgment, the Tribunal leaned heavily on this second source of its jurisdiction: "The jurisdiction of the Tribunal is defined in the Agreement and Charter.... The making of the Charter was the exercise of the sovereign legislative power by the countries to which the German Reich unconditionally surrendered."

The duality of the sources of the Tribunal's jurisdiction is legally significant from the point of view of the Judgment as *res adjudicata*. [A thing or matter finally decided on its merits by a court of competent jurisdiction]. The treaty basis of the judgment is valuable in that it gives the character of *res adjudicata* to the Judgment not only with regard to the original signatories of the Agreement of 1945, but also with regard to each of the nineteen States which adhered to the Treaty. Conversely, the character of the Judgment as a decision under German (Allied-decreed) municipal law makes the Judgment *res adjudicata* with effect against any court in Germany which has to administer Law No. 10.

In so far as the effect of the Judgment as a precedent in international law is concerned, it matters little whether emphasis is put on the international or municipal character of the Judgment. In the former case, the Judgment is merely a precedent in a nontechnical sense; for international law has not accepted the principle of *stare decisis*. In the latter, the Powers have made sure to avoid any such consequences, with regard to their own systems of municipal law, by giving the Tribunal the character of a military tribunal. From the point of view of international law the Judgment then may claim at most the standing of twenty-three identical judgments of municipal courts. The significance, therefore of the Judgment for the development of international law depends entirely on its persuasive authority, that is to say, on the question whether, and to what extent, the Tribunal has done more than merely apply its Charter: whether it has convincingly declared international customary law.

* * *

(a) *War Crimes*. "Violations of the laws or customs of war" (as war crimes in the narrower sense are defined in the Charter) have been treated of old as criminal acts for which members of the armed forces or civilians engaged in illegitimate warfare are held individually responsible by the enemy. In this regard, and especially in so far as violations of Hague Convention IV of 1907 are concerned, there is not doubt that such crimes are war crimes under international customary law. It may be controversial whether all rules of warfare which had been generally recognized by civilized nations in the pre-1914 period, have survived the impact on warfare of modern technological developments. Yet even allowing for an unprecedented and unavoidable measure of ruthlessness which follows from the use of the most up-to-date forms of mechanized mass-killing, there remain too many deeds for which even the conception of total war does not provide any cover. On this point, the Judgment of Nuremberg is on strong ground and may justly claim to be a fair exposition of international customary law. Whatever misgivings remain are connected with the *ad hoc* character of the Tribunal and the impossibility of referring to a tribunal similar to that set up at Nuremberg those who allege war crimes on the part of the United Nations and who especially point to the use of the atomic bomb on the eve of Japan's surrender.

An omission in the Indictment must be mentioned in this connection. In accordance with the established principles of land warfare, it might have been held that there was never a more indiscriminate weapon that the flying bombs and the rockets which were used by Germany against Great Britain. Yet there was no attempt to stigmatize the use of such weapons as war crimes. On the contrary, the competition of the United Nations in securing the services of the German technicians who had been engaged in the production of these weapons appears to amount to a recognition by implication of the legality of such weapons or at least to practically undisguised admission of an intention to use such weapons in any war of the future.

(b) *Crimes Against Peace.* This category of crime is defined in the Charter as "planning, preparation, initiation or waging of a war of aggression, or a war in violation of international treaties, agreements or assurances, or participation in a common plan or conspiracy for the accomplishment of any of the foregoing." As such acts had been crimes by the Charter, the Tribunal did not think it "strictly necessary to consider whether, and to what extent, aggressive war was a crime before the execution of the London Agreement." Thus, in spite of the fact that the subject was fully argued before the Tribunal by the Prosecution and the Defence, the views expressed by the Tribunal on the criminal responsibility under international customary law of offences against peace are merely *obiter dicta* [A thing said in passing].

Rightly, the Tribunal drew attention to Hague Convention IV of 1907 in order to show that the violation of an international treaty may amount to a war crime in the technical sense. Less convincing is the Tribunal's argument *a minore ad majorem* from the Hague Convention to the Kellogg Pact, the violation of which was held to be "equally illegal, and of much greater moment than a breach of one of the rules of the Hague Convention." The Hague Conventions were based on the assumption of the legality of even aggressive war and on the absence of any test in international law regarding the legality or illegality of war between sovereign States. If, however, the anology is derived from the illegality of a breach of treaty in both cases, such argument begs the question when the breach of a treaty also involves the commission of an international tort or of a crime analogous to war crimes in the technical sense. If the evil character of war and its disastrous effects on international society as a whole are adduced to give further support to the thesis of the criminal character of aggressive war in international customary law, such judgment involves a well-deserved condemnation of power politics. However, it ignores the function of war in a system of power politics and the legality of all forms of war under international customary law since at least the nineteenth century.

The Judgment's references to the Draft Treaty of Mutual Assistance of 1923, to the ungratified Geneva Protocol of 1924 and to the League Resolution of 1927 on aggressive war rather tend to weaken the conclusion at which the Tribunal arrived. Draft treaties and unratified conventions are legally non-existent and resolutions of the Assembly of the League of Nations—even if unanimously adopted—were widely held not to be legally binding on the members of the League of Nations....

Thus, the view expressed by the Tribunal on the character of aggressive war as a crime under international customary law in the inter-war period stands and falls with the criminal character of any breach of the Kellogg Pact: "In the opinion of the Tribunal, the solemn renunciation of war as an instrument of national policy necessarily involves the proposition that such a war is illegal in international law; and that those who plan and wage such a war, with its inevitable and terrible consequences, are committing a crime in so doing." It will be observed that again the Tribunal describes justly any breach of the Kellogg Pact as illegal, but, without further ado jumps to the conclusion that such an illegal act must be a crime. It is true that the stigmatization of war as a crime corresponds to a change in public opinion which has its roots in the experiences of the First World War. The Tribunal, however, chose to ignore the discrepancies between the standards which the man-in-the-street applied to the conduct of international affairs and those standards which governments applied to themselves and each other. It might not be irrelevant to quote the restrained opinions which, during the inter-war-period, some distinguished international lawyers expressed on the legal significance of the Kellogg Pact. It may suffice, however, to let State practice since the conclusion of the Kellogg Pact speak for itself.

In 1929 the Soviet Union seized forcibly two places in Manchuria, which were garrisoned by Chinese troops, and agreement with China was achieved only on the basis of a Russian ultimatum. Then came the Japanese invasion of Manchuria, repeated large-scale battles between Soviet and Japanese forces on the Soviet-Manchurian frontier at a time when both countries were formally not at war with each other; the Italian aggression against Abyssinia and the express recognition of the King of Italy as Emperor of Italian East Africa by France and Great Britain; the practically undisguised intervention of first Italy and Germany, and then France and the U.S.S.R., in the Spanish War; the German invasion of Austria and Czechoslovakia—the latter with Hungarian and Polish participation; Italy's occupation of Albania; the secret German-Soviet Protocols of August 23rd and September 28th, 1939; the Soviet occupation of the Eastern parts of Poland; the incorporation into the U.S.S.R. of the Baltic States and the preventive Soviet War against Finland. Even if judgment is suspended on the wars in disguise which are taking place at present in Greece, Persia and China—on the surface between partisans of one or the other faction in these countries—can it really be said that the governments of the world in the period since 1928 regarded the parties who were guilty of flagrant aggressions in most of these cases as criminals?

In Mr. Justice Jackson's words, "the world's statesmen again went only as far as they were forced to go. Their efforts were timid and cautious and often less explicit that we might have hoped." Yet not even by implication did the governments of the nations, which during the inter-war period permitted the aggressors to receive from their own countries indispensable raw and war materials, indicate that they considered such policies more than a breach of treaties. The actions—as distinct from the words—of these governments failed to conform with the standards of international morality which were postulated by wide sections of public opinion in the Western democracies.

* * *

Thus we are brought up against the question whether crimes against peace are merely *ex post facto* crimes and are so treated in the Charter contrary to the principle of *nullum crimen, nulla poena sine lege*. The Tribunal admitted the relevance of this maxim as a "principle of justice," but held that it did not apply to the present case; for "the attacker must know that he is doing wrong," and at least some of the accused "must have known that they were acting in defiance of all international law when in complete deliberation they carried out their designs of invasion and aggression."

In order to answer the question whether an act which has been made criminal under the Charter is only retrospectively of a criminal character, as distinct from an immoral or possibly tortuous character, it is important to understand the meaning of the term "crime" in the Charter. An international crime presupposes the existence of an international criminal law. Such a branch of international law does not exist. If the evolution of criminal law within the State offers any guidance, the reason for the absence so far of international criminal law is not far to seek. Criminal law postulates the existence of a strong government which is capable of enforcing order against even the mightiest transgressors. On the plane of inter-State relations, such central government is sadly lacking. Optimists may hold that the United Nations represents the transition from international anarchy to world order. Yet all that has happened so far is that the number of actually sovereign States has dwindled to two or possibly five world powers. The veto is the visible expression of this new hierarchy in world affairs.

In the absence, therefore, of a world authority which, in case of need, could confidently apply justice to such world powers as the United States and the U.S.S.R., it appears premature to speak of international criminal law. It may, however, be objected that this argument proves too much. Are not piracy and war crimes in the technical sense evidence of the reality of international criminal law? Actually, this is far from being the truth. In time of peace, any State may exercise jurisdiction only over ships sailing the high seas under its own flag. A pirate vessel, however, is not under the protection of any subject of international law. Thus, international law merely authorizes any State to exercise in such cases its criminal jurisdiction right to the limit, that is to say, including the application of the death penalty.

* * *

...Even in a system of power politics, there is a difference between a State which slides into war and international gangsters which (like totalitarian States) deliberately plan wholesale aggression and indiscriminately flout every rule of international law as well as all standards of civilization or humanity. Such States forfeit their international personality and put themselves beyond the pale of international law. In short, they become outlaws, and subjects of international law may treat them as their own standards and conscience permit. It is submitted that, in the present state of international society, such treatment of international gangsterism is less artificial than the assertion that aggressive war is already a crime under international customary law.

(c) *Crimes Against Humanity*. In Article 6(c) of the Charter as modified by the Protocol of October 6th, 1945, crimes against humanity are defined as "murder, extermination, enslavement, deportation, and other inhumane acts committed against any civilian population, before or during the war, or persecutions on political, racial or religious grounds in execution of or in connection with any crime within the jurisdiction of the Tribunal, whether or not in violation of the domestic law of the country where perpetrated."

* * *

As interpreted by the Tribunal, crimes against humanity are of a merely subsidiary character and cover acts as enumerated in Article 6(c) if a connection can be shown between such acts and crimes within the Tribunal's jurisdiction, that is to say war crimes and crimes against peace. In accordance with the Charter, it is then irrelevant whether crimes against humanity have been committed before or during the war and whether they have been committed in violation of the domestic law of the country where perpetrated. The significance of this auxiliary crime consists in the fact that, within the limits laid down by the Tribunal, it includes acts by civilians against civilians which either would be covered by the conception of exclusively domestic jurisdiction if committed before the war or, if committed during the war, would not amount to war crimes in the technical sense of the word.

* * *

In any case, the rather artificial limitation in the Charter of crimes against humanity to those connected with crimes against peace and war crimes hardly recommends itself as declaratory of international customary law. Under international customary law there is no room for such subtle qualifications. Either criminal responsibility exists for all forms of the abuse of national sovereignty with regard to individuals, such as extermination, enslavement or deportation of civilian populations, or such behavior is covered in peacetime by the conception of exclusively domestic jurisdiction. Then such deeds involve international responsibility only if practiced against populations of occupied territories in time of war and then amounting to war crimes in the technical sense....

* * *

(e) *Declaration of Groups and Organizations to be of a Criminal Character.* The Charter authorizes the Tribunal to declare at the trial of any individual member of any group or organization "that the group or organization of which the individual was a member was a criminal organization." The Charter further contains a procedural rule which defines the legal effects of such a declaratory judgments of the Tribunal. In the words of the Judgment, the meaning of Article 10 of the Charter is that "the declaration of criminality against an accused organization is final, and cannot be challenged in any subsequent criminal proceedings against a member of that organization."

Thus, Article 10 of the Charter defines the scope of *res judicata* of the declaratory part of the Judgment for any subsequent trials of individuals for membership in such organizations. In the Tribunal's view, a declaration of criminality with regard to organizations and groups determines the criminality of the members, as membership in such organizations or groups is likened to participation in a criminal conspiracy. In the circumstances, the Tribunal attempted at least to circumscribe such declarations so as to insure as much as possible the exclusion of innocent persons from the circle of those comprehended in the definition of criminal organizations and groups;...In dealing with the individual organizations and groups, the Tribunal was anxious not to cast its net too widely. In contrast to the views expressed by the Soviet member of the Tribunal, the majority was very much alive to the danger that the application of this procedure, "unless properly safeguarded," was likely to "produce great injustice."

The Tribunal twice emphasized the novelty of the doctrine of group criminality, and made it clear that it was going to exercise the discretion granted to it by the Charter in keeping with its status as a judicial body and "in accordance with well settled legal principles." From this starting point, the Tribunal proceeded to lay down tests on which the criminal character of a group or organization depends. The group or organization must have an individuality of its own and have acted as such. It must be connected with the commission of crimes within the meaning of Article 6 of the Charter. Such connection must not be too remote. Finally, the whole procedure being justified only by the mass character of the crimes which had been committed by the totalitarian aggressors, the organization or group must be big enough to justify resort to a procedure of such an unorthodox character.

Conclusions

The Judgment of the Nuremberg Tribunal is not unprecedented. It focuses attention, however, on sanctions of the rules of warfare which, throughout the centuries, have been known and applied. Its treatment of crimes against peace and humanity makes the world conscious of issues which, if settled at all, are settled so far only on paper.

The organization of the Court as a joint *ad hoc* tribunal of the victorious Powers and its military character should serve as warnings against attributing undue significance to the Judgment. If, in the respect, cautioned may be counseled, this is certainly not due to any lack in judicial bearing on the part of the members of the Tribunal or to any shortcomings in the actual conduct of the trial. Such reserve follows from the incongruity between parts of the Tribunal's Charter and the present state of world organization. The Charter did not overstep these bounds in its definition of war crimes in the technical sense of the word. It appears, however, that the signatories took a too narrow view of the phenomenon of totalitarian aggression when they attempted to include it within the categories of war crimes and crimes against peace and humanity. The leaders of the aggressor nations did not merely violate this or that rule of international law: they challenged world civilization as such and, therefore, necessarily came in conflict with all the basic principles of religion, morality and law. To attempt to deal with international gangsterism of this sort as a criminal phenomenon amounts to making a very large assumption. It means asserting that international society has exchanged the state of hue and cry for that of world order.

It was said before by the victors in another world war that "the trial and punishment of those proved most responsible for the crimes and inhuman acts committed in connection with a war of aggression, is inseparable from the establishment of that reign of law among nations which it was the agreed object of the peace to set up." The idealism of a credulous world has been disappointed once and given way to an air of skeptical detachment. In such an atmosphere, the outlawry of the chief totalitarian gangsters and even judicial proceedings against them on such a basis would have offered tangible advantages as compared with the procedure that was actually adopted. It would have made it clear that the totalitarian aggressors were different in kind from the rest of the world. It is true that in a world in which tribalism, race antagonism, emotional nationalism, imperialist greed, half-baked ideologies and the blind mechanics of power politics are rampart, Nazism, Fascism and Japanese militarism may be seen merely as the extremes of forces which are at work everywhere. Yet there comes a point where, in Hegel's language, quantity changes into quality. When this point is reached, a subject of international law becomes an outlaw and can no longer claim the protection of international law. He can merely rely on the limitations which civilized nations set themselves.

The four Powers aimed at a more ambitious goal. They have not merely tried to safeguard existing international society against its wholesale assailants, but they gave it to be understood—and the Tribunal supported this claim—that the law of the Charter was substantially declaratory of existing international law and thus applicable to any future aggressor. In the words of Mr. Justice Jackson, these principles applied as much to the nations "which sit here now in judgment" as to any other nation, and the trial had to be understood as "part of the great effort to make peace more secure." Assuming that the Charter and the Tribunal's Judgment could be interpreted in such a way, future transgressors are warned that:

Firstly, aggressive war involves personal responsibility of the leaders of aggressor States akin to responsibility for war crimes in the technical sense of the word.

Secondly, the same responsibility applies in the case of crimes against civilian populations if such offences against humanity are committed in preparation of, or in connection with, crimes against peace and war crimes.

In the age of the atomic warfare a premium is put on preventive war, and the origin of atomic bombs which have been deposited in enemy capitals beforehand, or are contained in directed missiles, may be hard to determine. Therefore, the unreality of the first rule only indicates the self-contradictions which are involved in the attempt to maintain a system of power politics and to establish the rule of international law.

The odd limitations of the second rule are again an uncomfortable reminder of the real crux of the matter: the sacrosanctity of the sphere of exclusively domestic jurisdiction.

What is certain, however, is that even the Judgment of Nuremberg has not led to the creation of an international criminal law. Within the framework of its Charter, the Nuremberg Tribunal has extended the normal range of municipal jurisdiction in the field of criminal justice and, in the respect, assimilated jurisdiction in crimes under the Charter to jurisdiction in war crimes under international customary law.

The successful combination of the accusatory and inquisitorial systems, and of Anglo-Saxon with Continental rules of criminal procedure in the Charter and during trial are pointers to the more constructive aspects of the matter. The results achieved within the framework of this *ad hoc* international institution indicate that when there is a will amongst the world powers to co-operate, a common denominator for such joint effort can be found. If in the future the Powers should be able to make such an effort not only *against* a common foe, but also *for* the common and over-riding purpose of establishing world order under law, those who consider Nuremberg a landmark and not merely an episode, as the expression of the moral conscience of organized mankind and not as a symptom of the hypocrisy of their leaders, may still be justified. Whether the "idealists" or "realists" are right can only be determined in retrospect. Both camps, however, may find common ground in the proposition that the Judgment of Nuremberg should not primarily be thought of as a matter of the past. It presents a challenge which has to be accepted in its full Magnitude. The evil has been diagnosed so often that a repetition of the diagnosis and of available cures must appear equally redundant....

---

18. Steven Fogelson, *Note*, "The Nuremberg Legacy: An Unfulfilled Promise"

63 *Southern California Law Review* 833; 858–866; 868–870; 883–885 (1990)
Reprinted with permission of the *Southern California Law Review*
© 1990 Southern California Law Review Association

IV. THE LEGITIMACY OF THE NUREMBERG TRIALS

An analysis of the Nuremberg Trials seems incomplete without discussing its legitimacy. The fact that the crimes had to be punished was beyond dispute. Murray Bernays and Telford Taylor's rationale that a trial would have more educational and political effect than summary executions can be viewed as purely political. Thus, it may appear that Nuremberg was merely a political "show trial" meant to carry out the will of the victors. The policymakers behind the trials took steps to counter these charges. They applied law that was grounded in existing international law, highlighted historical antecedents and more recent international agreements, and argued that they applied law that was completely consistent with these precedents. In order to further bolster the legitimacy of the trials, they also integrated several safeguards into the Charter to ensure that the procedure was fair.

* * *

Providing the vanquished defendants a fair judicial proceeding is evidence of the legitimacy of the proceedings, but the more basic question regarding the trial's legitimacy includes the legal and moral justification for holding a trial in the first place. The controversy surrounding the legitimacy of the Nuremberg Trials involves overlapping issues. First, commentators argue that the Tribunal applied *ex post facto* law because the actions of the Germans were not crimes at the time they were committed, but were only defined as criminal by the victors after the war ended. Second, and logically following from the first, commentators argue that the victors had no moral or legal right to try the vanquished, and consequently the victors merely exerted arbitrary power over them.

1. Historical Justification for Count Two

The argument that the Allies applied ex post facto law has superficial appeal, but it fails on closer scrutiny. Count Two is perhaps the most difficult aspect of the trial to justify as existing within international law at the time the acts were committed. Crimes Against Peace, including planning and launching a war, were generally considered to be within a sovereign's legitimate powers by the international legal community at the time of the Nuremberg Trial. However, as Justice Jackson noted in his *Report to the President, June 6, 1945,* the nineteenth century doctrine itself was a departure from earlier international legal principles as taught by Hugo Grotius. [Grotius, a Dutch scholar and diplomat, is considered by many to be the founding father of international law]. Grotius distinguished between just and unjust wars; while the former is permissible, the latter is not. Subsequently, this doctrine evolved into the proposition that aggressive wars were unjust, and defensive wars were just. On either count, the Nazi aggressions were unjustified. The inclusion of moral principles in international law steadily eroded as doctrines that supported the rights of nation states to act freely in pursuing their self-interest gained popularity in the nineteenth century.

An undercurrent of opposition to this statist view of international law persisted throughout the nineteenth century. Beginning in 1899, several nations entered into binding international agreements that rejected the notion of the absolute sovereignty of a nation state. The *Judgment* of the Nuremberg Tribunal acknowledged its reliance on these agreements. Among these agreements were the Hague Conventions of 1899 and 1907 which limited a state's right to launch a war.... Germany executed treaties of mutual guarantee with Belgium, France, Great Britain, and Italy. The treaties were signed at Locarno, Switzerland in 1925 and renounced any and all plans for territorial expansion. Germany, Poland, France, Great Britain, the United States, and several other countries signed the Kellogg-Briand Pact of 1928, explicitly outlawing aggressive war and the seizure of territories. In addition, the Versailles Treaty expressly required the demilitarization of the Rhineland, respect for the independence of Czechoslovakia and Austria, and Germany's renunciation of any rights in the Free City of Danzig. All of these agreements were violated by the Germans. Although Germany could claim that it agreed to the Versailles Treaty under duress, the same excuse could not apply to the other agreements.

Thus, Nuremberg continued the twentieth-century trend of rejecting the nineteenth-century nationalist conception of international law in favor of the emerging doctrine of limited sovereignty, which had its antecedents in the classical doctrines of international law. After the Tribunal decided to adhere to this emerging doctrine, and in light of the extensive and duplicitous violations of international agreements committed by Germany, the Tribunal had no trouble deciding that Count Two was both justified and adequately proven.

However, this historical perspective does not inevitably lead one to conclude that the Tribunal at Nuremberg was acting within the legitimate authority of international law. During World War II, if a nation violated an international agreement, the other nations to the treaty could justifiably disregard it with respect to the breaching party. They were not, however, necessarily entitled to try the officials of the breaching nation as common criminals.

There is, however, historical precedent that does support these actions. English and American common law have historically prosecuted breaches of international law as common law crimes. In general, judges in a common law jurisdiction draw upon "settled law [and] ideas…of what is moral, right, just; of what will further sound public policy, in the light of the customs and traditions" of the community to determine if the facts of the case before them should be classified as a crime. Furthermore, sovereigns as well as individuals should be expected to answer to international law.

2. Justification for Counts Three and Four

Nineteenth-century American cases establish that military personnel have a duty to disobey illegal orders; if they do not, they may be held liable in a court of law for the damages they cause. Chief Justice Taney stated in *Mitchell v. Harmony*, 54 U.S. (13 How.) 115, 137 (1851): "[I]t can never be maintained that a military officer can justify himself for doing an unlawful act, by producing the order of his superior. The order may palliate, but it cannot justify." The prosecution of Henry Wirz, the Confederate Commander of the prisoner of war camp at Andersonville [Georgia] during the Civil War, was consistent with earlier cases…. A total of approximately fourteen thousand Union soldiers met their death at this camp. Although Wirz produced evidence at his trial that he followed the orders of his superior, General John H. Winder, he nonetheless was found guilty of both conspiracy and murder in violation of the laws and customs of war.

These cases do not suggest that a soldier should question the legality of every order. Such a policy would jeopardize the efficiency and discipline that are often essential in military situations. Therefore, United States courts allow a presumption in military trials in favor of the lawfulness of military orders. At the same time, however, a soldier is never obliged to obey an order that is palpably illegal on its face.

* * *

Another issue that needs to be addressed is whether it matters that the defendants at the Trial of the Major War Criminals at Nuremberg were not soldiers who had followed palpably illegal orders, but rather held positions of high authority. The question then becomes whether they are shielded by virtue of their office. The Act of State Doctrine provides that "the courts of one country will not sit in judgment on the acts of the government of another, done within its own territory." However, this is American judge-made law and, therefore, not necessarily accepted in international law. Notwithstanding this admonition, the Nuremberg Charter arguably did not violate this doctrine because it did not prosecute crimes that occurred within the internationally recognized borders of Germany, except as they were connected to a conspiracy that involved crimes taking place outside of Germany. Though the Nazis committed reprehensible acts of repression and murder within the pre-war borders of Germany, their most shocking crimes, such as the death camps, took place outside of Germany....

It is therefore difficult to understand how some familiar with the workings of the Tribunal, the provisions of the Charter, and the actual crimes committed by the defendants can seriously claim that their prosecution was ex post facto. As many American policymakers as well as the Tribunal itself declared, most of the Nazi crimes violated the criminal law of all civilized countries in the world.

* * *

A. The Nuremberg Principles

...Many major principles emerged from Nuremberg due to the complexity of the Nazi crimes and the novel institution the Allies developed to cope with them. First and foremost is the proposition that international law should be applied toward the goal of achieving justice in line with morality. This concept is not hopelessly relativistic, as a strict formalist might suppose, but has evolved into a workable standard that includes internationally recognized norms of conduct as preemptory to any treaty or agreement in contravention of it. This concept is identified as *jus cogens* and is now embedded in international law. As defined in the Vienna Convention,[49] the *jus cogens* doctrine holds that "[a] treaty is void if...it conflicts with...a norm accepted and recognized by the international community of States as a whole...from which no derogation is permitted." Several human rights norms are accepted as *jus cogens*.

A companion concept holds that international law should take into account the rights of individuals. These rights are not generally accepted as part of international law immediately prior to Nuremberg. At that time, international law dealt with the rights and duties of states and applied only to interactions and conflicts among states. There is, however, evidence that individual rights were a concern of international law in the eighteenth century, but this interest faded in the nineteenth and twentieth centuries as the statist concept of international law gained popularity. Nuremberg revived this commitment to protect individual rights. Once again, it was primarily normative concerns that reinfused this concept into international law. Individuals suffered horribly at the hands of an alien government, and the Allies were resolved to include these crimes in the Tribunal's jurisdiction.

In the same manner that the rights of individuals would henceforth be a concern of international law, the conduct of individuals under the color of official state action would no longer be immune from the reach of international law. The Charter and the Tribunal made it exceedingly clear that individuals could be held criminally responsible for committing specific crimes that deserve the abhorrence of all civilized peoples. Similar to other principles of Nuremberg, this one had its antecedents in the eighteenth

---

49. The Vienna Convention on the Law of Treaties, May 23, 1969, 1155 U. N. T. S. 332; *Restatement (Third) of the Foreign Relations Law of the United States* §§102 comment K, 332(2) (b), comment e (1987).

century, but was largely ignored until Nuremberg. However, the concept of holding individuals responsible for some transgressions of international law was actively and continuously employed throughout modern history.

Closely related to this principle is the explicit recognition that a nation's sovereignty is limited by the demands of international law.... [A] state no longer possesses the sovereign right to plan and launch an aggressive war, and the sovereign itself would be held accountable for transgressions against specified offenses. Because of the very nature of these acts, their identification as offenses added morality and humanity to the application of international law. It is also fair to say that anyone who commits one of these offenses will be subject to universal jurisdiction. That is, the offender will be regarded as "an enemy of all mankind," *hostis humani generis*, and subject to the jurisdiction of the capturing sovereign.

The private citizen's responsibilities to international law were another controversial "innovation" of Nuremberg. This doctrine developed in cases against leading German industrialists. The industrialists were guilty of willingly cooperating with the Nazis and exploiting the slave labor programs that were instituted by the Nazis. The Allies intended for these citizens to be represented by Gustav Krupp [the elder] at the Trial of the Major War Criminals, but due to poor health Krupp was unable to stand trial.[50] Therefore, the doctrine was not fully defined until the judgment of the *The Flick Case* prosecuted under Control Council Law 10 which held: "International law, as such, binds every citizen just as does ordinary municipal law. Acts adjudged criminal when done by an officer of the government are criminal also when done by a private individual." In *The Justice Case*, the tribunal promoted these same principles by holding that citizens, like soldiers, have a duty to disobey illegal domestic orders when the orders conflict with international law. This infusion of morals and concern for individual rights into international law launched the modern doctrine of International Human Rights Law.

* * *

If the courts in the nineteenth century generally denied that fundamental principles and individual rights were a part of international law, Nuremberg signaled a return of these principles. The Trial at Nuremberg restored the principles of individual rights and fundamental norms of conduct into international law. The horror of the Nazi Holocaust impressed upon the nations conducting the trial that universal moral principles must be a part of international law. It is especially incumbent upon the United States, given its leading role in establishing and participating in the Tribunal at Nuremberg, to incorporate this aspect of international law into its domestic law. Moreover, our Constitution and the history of its creation mandate such an incorporation.

Both the doctrine of *jus cogens* and the resurgence of universal jurisdiction are direct outgrowths of the Trial at Nuremberg and reflect the idea that fundamental rights exist in international law, which may never be transgressed.... The Vienna Convention does not specifically name what peremptory norms are recognized, but rather leaves these definitions open to interpretation. However, the Vienna Convention does make it clear that a treaty in conflict with a peremptory norm is void *ab initio*. Similarly, a valid

---

50. Gustav's son, Alfried, was charged, tried and convicted in his father's stead. Sentenced to twelve years imprisonment on July 31, 1948, he was granted amnesty on May 31, 1951. Alfried resumed direction of the Krupp Works after making a solemn public vow that his company would never again produce armaments.

treaty will become void if it subsequently conflicts with a *jus cogens* norm. The Restatement (Third) of the Foreign Relations Law of the Untied States adopts the Vienna Convention's interpretation of *jus cogens*.

* * *

Universal jurisdiction is a time-honored doctrine that was accepted when the U.S. Constitution was written. Although it was neglected as positivism and statism gained popularity, it was never completely abandoned. Universal jurisdiction, simply stated, is the proposition that some crimes are universally recognized as so opprobrious that any state that captures the perpetrator is entitled to try and punish the criminal on behalf of all nations of the world. Piracy has long been the archetypal crime giving rise to universal jurisdiction. However, universal jurisdiction was never confined to piracy alone. The Nuremberg Charter effectively made Crimes Against Peace, War Crimes, and Crimes Against Humanity subject to universal jurisdiction. Additionally, the Restatement explicitly acknowledges that war crimes, genocide, slave trade and aircraft hijacking are subject to universal jurisdiction....

Nuremberg was a watershed event that pointed international law towards a more humane and enlightened interpretation and application. It also helped to revive universal jurisdiction and spurred the advent of *jus cogens* doctrine. These doctrines have given momentum to the pendulum of international law, which now swings back to include individual rights as well as fundamental norms of conduct as proper subjects of international law....

---

19. Maximillian Koessler, "American War Crimes Trials in Europe"

39 *Georgetown Law Journal*
18; 19–21; 23–26; 28–32; 34–37; 44–48; 55–56 (1950)

[Maximilian Koessler was an Attorney, War Crimes Group, United States Army, and a Member of the Legal Division, Military Government for Bavaria (1946–1949)].

* * *

World War II, as conducted by Germany and Japan, has set a record in modern history of a series of most shocking atrocities. This does not refer to occasional excesses of individuals which are regrettable but unavoidable in a war. Rather it refers to those crimes which were perpetrated on a grand scale in cold blood, according to policy directives issued right from the top of the government involved.... [A] substantial number of World War II atrocities, especially those perpetrated by the Germans, had not even the apparent justification of a pursuit of military objectives. They added to the evil necessarily inherent in war, the abject feature of a ruthless and cruel policy of subjection, persecution and even extermination of "inferior races," as Nazi arrogance had branded them.

Tortures of a medieval kind, the performance of which would shake even the most callous visitor of a "Grand Guignol" theater, were applied by Hitler's henchmen both for purely "ideological" purposes and in apparent pursuit of war objectives. The infamous institution of concentration camps furnishes an illustration of the merger of non-military and military motives in some of the German war crimes and "crimes against humanity." Originally instruments of political terror, they became during the war also sources for the supply of slave labor. To exploit them was not repellent to German industrial concerns of world-wide reputation.

The conscience of humanity required that such nefarious deeds should not remain unpunished. The different view of a minority of men of good will was no less unrealistic than the extremely opposite approach of the collective guilty advocates. To avoid enemy reaction under the pretext of retaliation, only a few war crimes trials were held on the Allied side while the fighting was going on. However, preparations were made for the punitive proceedings which were to follow the armistices in Europe and the Far East respectively. Taken as a whole, and especially in view of their unprecedented number, they represent the largest judicial enterprise recorded in the history of mankind.

* * *

Special war crimes tribunals, exclusively composed of Allied nationals, partly under the authority of a single Allied nation, were established.

* * *

...The most numerous ones [by a single Allied nation] are probably the American trials, and the most important ones, those that were conducted by American military commissions or military government courts in Germany, [were] commonly referred to as "The Dachau Trials."

The Dachau Trials

Apart from the twelve Nuremberg trials, [tried subsequently to the IMT]...World War II war crimes trials in the American occupation zone of Germany were conducted either before military commissions or before specially appointed military government courts. Most, though not all, of these non-Nuremberg trials took place in Dachau (Bavaria), within an American military compound established on the site of the one-time German concentration camp. Therefore, the whole groups are conveniently referred to as the "Dachau Trials"....

The United States sponsored a total of approximately nine hundred war crimes trials involving over three thousand defendants. About half of these were tried in Germany. The second largest group is represented by the trials in Japan. There were relatively few American war crimes trials in Austria. Italy, the Philippines, China and the Pacific Islands respectively, with the trial in the Philippines ranging highest in number among these minor groups. From the above mentioned German defendants, 1,380 were convicted and 241 acquitted by the respective trial courts. The sentences adjudged in the same group of cases included 421 death sentences, not all of which were approved on review, and of which 255 have been executed so far. There were 194 sentences of imprisonment for life adjudged by the trial courts of which about 136 were approved.

Little was known about the Dachau trials outside the small circle of those officially concerned or directly affected by them, until they came within the searchlight of publicity in connection with Congressional investigations of the sentence finally meted out to Ilse Koch, one of the defendants in the *Buchenwald Concentration Camp Case*, and of certain methods of pre-trial investigation applied in the *Malmédy Case*.

* * *

Turning now to certain general aspects of the Dachau trials, it may be stated that their external appearance was clearly akin to normal proceedings under the courts martial system of the United States Army. The tribunals were exclusively composed of American officers, at least one of whom would normally have had legal training or experience like the "law member" of a court martial. While an outward difference thus existed between the Dachau tribunals composed of officers and the Nuremberg courts composed of civilians in spite of their designation as "military tribunals," the underlying philosophy of the two groups of trials was the same. In both of them, the judges approached their difficult and delicate task in a truly judicial spirit and with the best intention of avoiding any emotional prejudice against the defendants.

At variance with the Nuremberg trials, where the vote of an unqualified majority of the members of the tribunal was sufficient for any judgment, including convictions and any kind of sentence, a majority of at least two-thirds of the members of the tribunal was required for a conviction or sentence in a Dachau trial. This, however, was sufficient even for a death sentence, contrary to the regular courts-martial system which requires a unanimous vote for capital punishment.

In accordance with applicable provisions, the Nuremberg judgments included reasonings justifying the tribunal's findings. By the thoroughness with which the judges discharged this part of their functions, they rendered an invaluable service to the clarification of certain legal issues involved and to those who in the present or at future times may benefit from this rich well of information. A corresponding feature is absent from the Dachau judgments. They consisted of the laconic verdict of "guilty" or "not guilty" and, in the case of a conviction, also of the sentence, but were not accompanied by any kind of reasoning.

Announcing in each case, by way of a standing clause, that the judgment had been reached with concurrence of at least two-thirds of the members present, the Dachau tribunals did not disclose whether the decision had been actually arrived at by a unanimous vote or was only carried by a vote of the qualified majority, required as a minimum. This was considerably different from Nuremberg, where not only the judgment of the tribunal was made public but also any concurring and dissenting opinion. The Dachau practice was in this respect like the continental one that abides by the principle of secrecy in polling the judges. The Nuremberg practice, in accordance with Anglo-American tradition but not indispensable to the realization of the Anglo-American ideal of justice, might better have been avoided as a matter of occupation policy since it impaired the prestige of the Nuremberg judgments in the eyes of the German public.

Both in Nuremberg and in Dachau the defendant was given adequate opportunity for assistance by learned counsel. The routine was not, however, the same in the two systems. In Nuremberg the defense was mainly entrusted to German attorneys who were only in a few instances assisted by unofficial American counsel, retained by the defendant subject to special admission by the tribunal. The defense in the Dachau trials was chiefly in charge of officially assigned American counsel, but a great number of German attorneys, either retained by the respective defendant or officially assigned to him were also engaged in this task. German counsel in Dachau would either act alone for a particular defendant or with liaison assistance of officially assigned American counsel. Both in Nuremberg and in Dachau, former Nazi affiliation would not bar a German attorney from the function as defense counsel in a war crimes trial. No American defense counsel was officially assigned in any of the Nuremberg trails. Officially assigned American defense counsel in Dachau would be taken from a panel of legally trained officers and Department civilians, jointly available for prosecution and defense purposes....

* * *

According to a famous dictum of the Supreme Court of the United States "... charges of violation of the law of war triable before a military tribunal need not be stated with the precision of a common law indictment." [In the *Yamashita* case, 1946]. Neither in Nuremberg nor in Dachau was there any remarkable ambition to make the written act of accusation more specific than was required under that announcement. Nevertheless, the respective practice was not the same in the Nuremberg and the Dachau trials. The indictment in the Nuremberg trials, patterned after the form used in the case against Hermann Göering and others, did not fully conform with the "dossier" or "Anklageschrift" (brief of accusation), traditional in the criminal procedure of civil law countries. Nor did it have the highly technical and most uncommunicative contents of a common law indictment. It was however a workable compromise between the two and showed the result of skillful and rather sophisticated draftsmanship.

Turning from the form to the substance of the accusation, it should be mentioned that, again different from the Nuremberg practice, no charge in a Dachau trial was in terms based on the conception of a crime against humanity. Nor was there any charge or participation in a crime against peace. The accusations in Dachau were phrased in terms of the traditional war crimes. Finally, the charges in the Dachau trials did not include the accusation of membership in an organization declared as criminal by the International Military Tribunal in Nuremberg.

* * *

An appeal technically was not provided for either...the Nuremberg or the Dachau trials. There was nevertheless a substantive difference between the two systems insofar as the final effect of the judgment was involved. In both systems it needed an executive confirmation. However, the military governor, passing upon a Nuremberg judgment, could only change a sentence in favor of the affected defendant, but he could not reform it *in pejus* nor set aside or alter any finding of the court regarding guilt or innocence respectively. In the Dachau trials, the judgments were subject to review and approval through channels. The appropriate military commander could not only alter a sentence but had the power of setting aside a finding of guilt. However, he had no power of setting aside an acquittal no matter how unjustified he may have found it. In any of these actions he was guided, through not bound, by an opinion of his Judge Advocate, commonly referred to as the "review" or "post-trial review."...

The question may well be raised whether there was any need for two different systems of war crimes trials in the American occupation zone of Germany. Why have both the Dachau *and* Nuremberg trials? The reason for this duplication was indeed not one of logic but of history. The Dachau proceedings revived the tradition of military commissions trying captured enemy nationals for violations of the law of war. The subsequent specially appointed military government courts were not part of the normal system of occupation courts established under this name. They were only by their designation different from the military commissions which had been their predecessors in carrying out the American war crimes trial program in Germany. The numerous so-called "flier cases," that is, trials against Germans who had participated in the lynching of bailed out American or British fliers, were of course much closer to the traditional activities of military commissions trying war criminals than the trials involving mass atrocities against civilians of Allied, but not American, nationality. In the last mentioned group of cases, American jurisdiction was nevertheless asserted on the basis of the alleged principle of universality of war crimes jurisdiction.

Different was the historical background of the later Nuremberg trials. The idea was apparently to have a series of trials against major war criminals in continuation of the *International Military Tribunal Case* but without Soviet participation. It was in line with this consideration that cases of major importance should be tried in Nuremberg and in close approximation to the pattern established there in the case against Hermann Göering. This automatically ruled out the military commissions and the sober arrangement of trials before them with practically no publicity at all. Rather it seemed preferable to retain and adjust the spectacular Nuremberg scene with the forms, technical paraphernalia and procedures developed there during the International Military Tribunal trial. In other words, the grand judicial show in Nuremberg should be continued in all its external aspects but as an American rather than an international performance.

A rather flexible European Theater directive defined the internal relationship between the two systems of war crime trials. The theoretical line of demarcation thus drawn was rather vague. The actual practice after the establishment of the later Nuremberg tribunals was that the Chief of Counsel for War Crimes in Nuremberg selected for his organization cases of top exponents of certain professional lines of cooperation with criminal policies of the Third Reich. The remaining bulk of the cases were handled as before, by the Theater Judge Advocate, more specifically by his Deputy for War Crimes. His was the general jurisdiction as it were; the Chief of Counsel for War Crimes had a special one.

It would be a mistake, however, to believe that only small fry were taken to account in the Dachau trials and that all the "big shots" were tried in Nuremberg. For instance, three army generals, one of them an army and one a corps commander, were among the defendants in the *Malmédy* trial. A police general was the main accused in another important Dachau case. A "Gauleiter and Reichsstatthalter" figured among those indicted in the *Mauthausen Concentration Camp* trial.... Several members of the medical profession were among the defendants in the *Hadamar* trial and in various concentration camp cases. Commanders of concentration camps were also tried in Dachau....

* * *

...[T]he first war crimes trials sponsored by the United States in Germany were conducted before military commissions which were such tribunals not only in fact but also by official designation. From some time in the winter of 1945 onward, the trials were conducted before so-called specially appointed military government courts which, it is submitted, were nevertheless military commissions for all practical purposes. In between there was a period of transition where certain was crimes trials were held before military commissions so designated, and others before specially appointed military government courts.

* * *

...As a matter of fact there was no important difference between a war crimes trial before a "military commission" so designated and a specially appointed military government court. Also these military government courts were appointed *ad hoc*, that is, separately and specifically for each case. They had in common with the military commissions so designated that they were American military tribunals proceeding under rules different from those applicable before a court martial. In other words, they were, as suggested hereinbefore, nothing else than the same military commissions under a different name.

* * *

It is obvious that the position of a defendant in a war crimes trial before an American military commission or an American military government court in Germany was less favorable than the position of a defendant before a United States court martial. For instance, according to Article of War 43, a unanimous vote of the members of a general court martial is required for death sentences and a three-fourths vote for sentences to life imprisonment or to confinement for more than 10 years, whereas both military commissions and military government courts could reach a finding of guilty and impose any sentence, including death, with the concurrence of two-thirds of the commission or court. Moreover, and perhaps more important, in a court martial the defendant is given the great advantage of the so-called exclusionary rules of the Anglo-American law of evidence....

This striking difference between the position of a defendant in one of the war crimes trials in question and the one of a defendant in an American court martial, gave defense counsel of those accused who had been members of the German Army, the opportunity of raising a special jurisdictional issue, related to the Geneva (Prisoners of War) Convention of July 27, 1929. It provides in its Article 63 as follows:

> Sentence may be pronounced against a prisoner of war only by the same courts and according to the same procedure in the case of persons belonging to the armed forces of the detaining Power.

Defense counsel claimed that the accused former members of the German armed forces were to be considered as prisoners of war, therefore entitled to the privilege under the above quoted Article 63 and consequently triable only before a U.S. Court martial and under the rules applicable thereto. The same jurisdictional objective had been raised before the American commission trying the German General Anton Dostler at Rome in the period October 8–12, 1945. The commission held Article 63 inapplicable without announcing its reasons for this conclusion.... Dealing with a similar jurisdictional objection of the Japanese General, [Yamashita] the majority opinion of the Supreme Court of the United States reached the result that Article 63 of the Geneva Convention was applicable only to a proceeding for an offence committed by the defendant in question while he was a prisoner of war but not to a proceeding for an offence committed while he was still a combatant.

* * *

Starting with the constitution of the courts, it should be pointed out that in the military commissions era as well as in the military government courts period, the war crimes tribunals were individually established for each specific case. There was an order of the so-called appointing authority, separately issued for each case, organizing the tribunal by appointing the officers to sit as members of the court and also those to conduct prosecution and defense respectively.... No instructions or directives whatsoever were, officially or unofficially, given to those appointed as members of the tribunal as to how they should live up to their judicial responsibilities. They were bound only by general regulations on the form of the procedure and on the prevailing principles of evidence, but they were not given any kind of lead or hint with regard to the decision of the individual case entrusted to them. This was left completely to their own discretion, to be solely controlled by their own judicial conscience.

---

20. German Occupation: "Subsequent Proceedings" under Allied Control Council Law No. 10

U.S. Department of the Army, Pamphlet No. 27-161-2, II
International Law 224, 226–33 (1962)

The Subsequent Proceedings at Nuremberg (August 1946–April 1949). Allied Control Council Law No. 10, 20 December 1945, was promulgated in order to establish a uniform legal basis in Germany for the prosecution of war criminals and other similar offenders, other than those dealt with by the International Military Tribunal. The American courts established under this law tried twelve cases, known as "The Subsequent Proceedings." These twelve cases, plus the single case tried by the International Military Tribunal at Nuremberg and the International Military Tribunal for the Far East make up the war crimes cases tried by international courts to which the United States was a party. The United States, acting alone, tried many more cases before military commissions....

Acting under this Control Council Law, the United States promulgated Military Government Ordinance No. 7. This ordinance provided that each tribunal was to consist of three members and an alternate. All were to be civilian lawyers from the United States. Six tribunals were formed composed of 18 judges and six alternates. These six tribunals heard twelve cases....

The Twelve Subsequent Proceedings

a. *U.S. v. Karl Brandt, et al.* (The Medical Case). The indictment named twenty-three defendants. The chief defendant, Karl Brandt, had, for a time, been one of Hitler's personal physicians and had risen to become Reich Commissioner for Health and Sanitation, the highest medical position in the Reich. The other defendants were the Chief of the Medical Service of the Luftwaffe, Chief Surgeon of the SS, Dean of the Medical Faculty of the University of Berlin, a specialist in tropical medicine, and lesser doctors in the military and civilian hierarchy. The principal count in the indictment charged the defendants with criminal responsibility for cruel and frequently murderous "medical experiments" performed without the victim's consent, on concentration camp inmates, prisoners of war, and others. The trial lasted from 9 December 1946 to 19 July 1947. The tribunal's judgment of 19 August 1947 convicted 16 defendants and acquitted seven. Karl Brandt, Gebhardt, Rudolf Brandt, Mrugowsky, Seivers, Brack and Hoven were sentenced to hang. Imprisonment was given to Becker-Freyseng (20 years), Beiglboeck (10 years), Handloser (life), Schroeder (life), Genzken (life), Rose (life), Fishcer (life), Oberheuser (20 years), and Poppendick (10 years). Rostock, Blome, Ruff, Romberg, Weltz, Schaefer and Pokorney were acquitted.

b. *U.S. v. Joseph Alstoetter, et al.* (The Justice Case). The fourteen defendants were all officials, as judges, prosecutors, or ministerial officers, of the judicial system of Nazi Germany. The main point of the prosecution's charge was that the defendants were guilty of "judicial murder and other atrocities, which they committed by destroying law and justice in Germany, and then utilizing the emptied forms of legal process for persecution, enslavement and extermination on a vast scale." The court, in its judgment, concluded that "The dagger of the assassin was concealed beneath the robes of the jurists." The sentences imposed were as follows: Schlegelberger (life), Klemm (life), Rothenberger (7 years), Lautz (10 years), Mettgenberg (10 years), Von Ammon (10 years), Joel (10 years), Rothaug (life), Oeschey (life), Altstoetter (5 years). Four of the fourteen defendants were acquitted. They were Bannickel, Petersen, Nebelung and Cuhorst.

c. *U.S. v. Milch.* This is the first of two cases dealing with government ministers. It is also the only subsequent proceeding with only one defendant. Erhard Milch was indicted on the basis of his activity as member of the Central Planning Board, established by a Hitler decree of 29 October 1943. The chief of this Board, Albert Speer, was tried by the International Military Tribunal. This Board had authority to instruct Saukel, also tried by the IMT, to provide slave laborers for industries under its control. Milch was also accused of complicity in the medical experiments for the German Air Force.

The Court's judgment, rendered on 16 April 1947, found Milch not guilty of implication in the medical experiments but guilty of complicity in the slave labor program. He was sentenced to life in prison.

d. *U.S. v. Ernst Weizsaeker, et al.* (The Ministries Case). This is the second of the two cases dealing with ministers. It was the longest and last of the Subsequent Proceedings. Seventeen months elapsed from the filing of the indictment to the rendering of the judgment, 15 Nov. 1947–14 April 1949. There were twenty-one defendants, eighteen of whom were ministers or high functionaries in the civil administration of the Third Reich. The defendants were lower echelon of the higher dignitaries who sat in the dock before the IMT.

The indictment consisted of eight counts: crimes against peace (1 and 2), mistreatment of PW's, against only seven defendants (3), crimes against humanity before the war (4), crimes against humanity and war crimes after the war started (5), plunder of property in occupied areas (6), deportation of slave labor (7), membership in criminal organizations (8). Count Four was dismissed [re: crimes against humanity before 1939]. The trial continued on the remaining seven counts. The sentences were as follows:

Berger	25 years
Lammers	20 years
Veesenmayer	20 years
Koerner	15 years
Pleiger	15 years
Kehrl	15 years
Krosigk	10 years
Keppler	10 years
Darryl	7 years
Woermann	7 years
Dietrich	7 years
Weizsaecker	7 years
Rasche	7 years
Von Mayland	7 years
Schellenberg	6 years
Bohle	5 years
Puhl	5 years
Ritter	4 years
Meissner	NG
Stuckart	Time Served
Erdmannsdorff	NG

e. *U.S. v. Flick.* Three of the twelve cases concerned industrialists. They were the Flick, I. G. Farben and Krupp trials. Flick was a powerful steel magnate and industrial promoter. He was indicted along with his five personal associates. The indictment contained five counts: (1) deportation of slave labor, (2) plunder of property in occupied areas, (3) crimes against humanity in the pre-war years, (4) financial support of the SS (two defendants only), and (5) membership in the SS (one defendant only). The indictment was filed on 8 February 1947 and the judgment reached on 22 December 1947.

The results of this trial are as follows:

Defendants	Counts	1	2	3	4	5	Sentence
Flick		G	G		G		7 years
Weiss		G	NG				2 and one-half years

Steinbrinck	NG	NG	G	G	5 years
Burkart	NG	NG			Acquitted
Kaletsch	NG	NG			Acquitted
Terberger	NG	NG			Acquitted

[count three was dismissed]

f. *U.S. v. Krauch* (I. G. Farben Case). Twenty-four individuals were indicted, twenty of whom were members of I. G. Farben's governing body, the "Vorstand." The other four were important officers of the corporation. Twenty-three were actually tried. The indictment contained five counts: (1) crimes against peace (aggressive war), (2) plunder of property in occupied areas, (3) slave labor, (4) membership in the SS, and (5) conspiracy to wage aggressive war. The judgment of the tribunal was handed down in July 1948. All twenty-three of the defendants were acquitted on counts 1 and 5. All three who were indicted under Count 4 were acquitted. Only five were found guilty under Count 3; Krauch, Ambros, Buetifisch, Duemfeld and Ter Meer. Nine were convicted and fourteen acquitted on Count 2. Ter Meer was the only defendant found guilty under two counts. Ten defendants were acquitted and thirteen convicted.

Sentences were as follows:

Ambros	8 years
Duemfeld	8 years
Ter Meer	7 years
Krauch	6 years
Buetifisch	6 years
Von Schnitzler	5 years
Schmitz	4 years
Ilgner	3 years
Haefliger	2 years
Oster	2 years
Buergin	2 years
Kugler	1 and one-half years
Jaehne	1 and one-half years

g. *U.S. v. Krupp.* This is the third and last trial of the industrialists. Gustav Krupp was indicted before the IMT. However, he was too infirm to stand trial. Here his forty-year-old son was indicted along with eleven other officials. The Krupp organization was the largest manufacturer in Germany. The indictment indicated that the officials of this firm were engaged in the slave labor program (Count Three) and in the economic plunder of occupied areas (Count Two) similar to the defendants in the *Flick* case. Two additional counts were added, that of crimes against peace (Count One) and conspiracy to commit crimes against peace (Count Four), because it was alleged that the Krupp firm took the lead in secret rearmament, supported Hitler's seizure of power, and cooperated willingly in the rearmament of Germany for foreign conquest.

The trial lasted from early December 1947 to the end of June 1948. On April 5, 1948 the Tribunal granted a motion for a finding of not guilty on Count One and Count Four. The following are the findings and sentences:

Defendant	Counts	2	3	Sentence
Alfried Krupp		G	G	12 years
Loeser		G	G	7 years
Houdremont		G	G	10 years
Mueller		G	G	12 years

Janssen	G	G	10 years
Ihn	NG	G	9 years
Eberhardt	G	G	9 years
Korschan	NG	G	6 years
Buelow	NG	G	12 years
Lehmann		G	6 years
Kupke		G	Time Served
Pfirsch	NG	NG	Acquitted

h. *U.S. v. Von Leeb* (The High Command Case). The cases of generals Von Leeb and List comprise, from the military point of view, two of the most important of the twelve subsequent Proceedings. Here were the trial of high military figures for the manner in which they conducted the war and the manner in which they governed unruly occupied areas.

The first was the trial of the high command of the German Army. Fourteen general officers were indicted under four counts: (1) crimes against peace, (2) war crimes, (3) crimes against humanity, and (4) conspiracy to commit these three crimes. The court dismissed charges 1 and 4. This was in line with the pattern in the Subsequent Proceedings. Rarely was an individual convicted of crimes against peace. The principal war crimes charged concerned the Commissar Order for the killing of Communist political advisors in the Russian Army, the Barbarossa Jurisdiction Order for the suppression of guerrilla warfare, the Commando Order for no quarter against British raiding parties and the Night and Fog degree for the secret deportation of individuals. Crimes against humanity (Count Three) dealt with the activities of race execution teams operating in areas controlled by the defendants. The following findings and sentences were handed down on 28 October 1948:

Defendant	Counts	2	3	Sentence
von Leeb		NG	G	3 years
Schniewind		NG	NG	Acquitted
Sperrle		NG	NG	Acquitted
Keuechler		G	G	20 years
Hoth		G	G	15 years
Reinhardt		G	G	15 years
von Salmuth		G	G	20 years
Hollidt		G	G	5 years
Roques		G	G	20 years
Reinecke		G	G	Life
Warlimont		G	G	Life
Woehler		G	G	8 years
Lehmann		G	G	7 years

i. *U.S. v. List* (Hostages Case). This second military case dealt principally with the actions of the occupation authorities in Yugoslavia and Greece. A second element was the destruction of property during evacuation of Finland and Norway. The case receives its name from the widespread use of hostages and reprisal prisoners in order to discourage partisan warfare in Yugoslavia and Greece.

Twelve German Army generals were indicted on four counts: (1) excess shooting of hostages, (2) plunder and destruction of property, (3) ill treatment of prisoners of war, and (4) slave labor. On 19 February 1948 the court handed down the following findings and sentences:

Defendant	Counts	1	2	3	4	Sentence
List		G	NG	G	NG	Life
Weichs		Not tried because of illness				
Rendulic		G	NG	G	G	20 years
Kuntze		G	NG	G	G	Life
Foertsch		NG	NG	NG	NG	Acquitted
Boehme		Suicide				
Felmy		G	G	NG	NG	15 years
Lanz		G	NG	G	NG	12 years
Dehner		G	NG	NG	NG	7 years
Speidel		G	NG	NG	NG	20 years
Geitner		NG	NG	NG	NG	Acquitted

j. *The SS Cases.* The SS Cases comprise the three remaining Subsequent Proceedings. They were *U.S. v Ohlendorf* ("Einsatzgruppen Case'), *U.S. v. Pohl* (concentration Camps and *U.S. v. Greifelt* (The RuSHA Case).

The Einsatzgruppen were extermination units whose mission was to kill minority races in occupied areas, particularly Jews and Gypsies. Twenty-two men were indicted. Twenty-one were convicted of serious participation in this murder program. The remaining defendant was sentenced to time already served. The sentences were severe compared to those handed down by the other tribunals. However, the enormity of the crime called for such punishment. Fourteen were sentenced to hang, two to life in prison, three to twenty years and the remaining two to ten years each.

Oswald Pohl and seventeen others were indicted principally for their administration of the concentration camps. Three were sentenced to hang, three to life in prison, two to 20 years, one to 15 years and six to ten years each. Three were acquitted.

The third SS case, known as the RuSHA case is a peculiar mixture of race hatred and pseudo-science. RuSHA is the German abbreviation for the Race and Settlement Main Office, an SS agency. Its purpose was to strengthen biologically and territorially the German nation at the expense of conquered countries. Fourteen were indicted. One was acquitted. Of the remaining thirteen one was sentenced to life in prison, two to twenty-five years, one to twenty years, three to fifteen years, one to ten years and five to time served.

---

21. Selected "Subsequent Proceedings" Decisions
(a) Tribunal II-A
United States of America v. Otto Ohlendorf, et al.
4 N.M.T. 411 (1948)

"The Einsatzgruppen Case"

Members of Military Tribunal II-A

Michael A. Musmanno, Presiding, Court of Common Pleas, County of Allegheny, Pennsylvania

John J. Speight, Member, Prominent Member of Alabama Bar

Richard D. Dixon, Member, Judge of the Superior Court of the State of North Carolina

Chief Prosecutor: Mr. Benjamin B. Ferencz

III. Opening Statement by the Prosecution

Mr. Ferencz: May it please your Honors: It is with sorrow and with hope that we here disclose the deliberate slaughter of more than a million innocent and defenseless men, women and children. This was the tragic fulfillment of a program of intolerance and arrogance. Vengeance is not our goal, nor do we seek merely a just retribution. We ask this court to affirm by international penal action man's right to live in peace and dignity regardless of his race or creed. The case we present is a plea of humanity to law.

We shall establish beyond the realm of doubt facts which, before the dark decade of the Third Reich, would have seemed incredible. The defendants were commanders and officers of special SS groups known as Einsatzgruppen—established for the specific purpose of massacring human beings because they were Jews, or because they were for some other reason regarded as inferior peoples. Each of the defendants in the dock held a position of responsibility or command in an extermination unit. Each assumed the right to decide the fate of men, and death was the intended result of his power and contempt. Their own reports will show that the slaughter committed by these defendants was dictated, not by military necessity, but by that supreme perversion of thought, the Nazi theory of the master race. We shall show that these deeds of men in uniform were the methodical execution of long-range plans to destroy ethnic, national, political, and religious groups which stood condemned in the Nazi mind. Genocide, the extermination of whole categories of human beings, was a foremost instrument of the Nazi doctrine. Even before the war the concentration camps within the Third Reich had witnessed many killings inspired by these ideas. During the early months of the war the Nazi regime expanded its plans for genocide and enlarged the means to execute them. Following the German invasion of Poland there arose extermination camps such as Auschwitz and Maidanek. In spring 1941, in contemplation of the coming assault on the Soviet Union, the Einsatzgruppen were ordered to destroy life behind the lines of combat. Not all life to be sure. They were to destroy all those denominated Jew, political official, gypsy and those other thousands called "asocial" by the self-styled Nazi superman. This was the new German "Kultur."

Einsatz units entering a town or city ordered all Jews to be registered. They were forced to wear the Star of David under threat of death. All were then assembled with their families to be "re-settled" under Nazi supervision. At the outskirts of each town was a ditch, where a squad of Einsatz men waited for their victims. Whole families were arrayed, kneeling or standing near the pit to face a deadly hail of fire.

Into the prisoner-of-war camps went the Einsatz units, selecting men for extermination, denying them the right to live.

Helpless civilians were conviently labeled "Partisans" or "Partisan-sympathizers" and then executed.

In the hospitals and asylums the Einsatzgruppen destroyed the ill and insane, for "useless eaters" could never serve the Third Reich.

Then came the gas vans, vehicles which could receive living human beings and discharge corpses. Every Einsatzgruppe had its allotment of these carriages of death.

These in short were activities of the Einsatzgruppen.

The United States, in 1942, joined 11 nations in condemnation of these Nazi slaughters and vowed that justice would be done. Here we act to fulfill that pledge, but not alone because of it.

Germany is a land of ruins occupied by foreign troops, its economy crippled and its people hungry. Most Germans are still unaware of the detailed events we shall account. They must realize that these things did occur in order to understand somewhat the causes of their present plight. They put their faith in Hitler and their hope in his regime. The Nazi ideology, devoid of humanism and founded on a ruthless materialism, was proclaimed throughout Germany and was known to all Germans. Hitler and other Nazi leaders made no secret of their purpose to destroy the Jews. As we here record the massacre of thousands of helpless children, the German people may reflect on it to assess the merits of the system they so enthusiastically acclaimed. If they shame at the folly of their choice they may yet find a true ideal in place of a foul fetish.

Proof of a million murders will not be the most significant aspect of this case. We charge more than murder, for we cannot shut our eyes to a fact ominous and full of foreboding for all mankind. Not since men abandoned tribal loyalties has any state challenged the right of whole peoples to exist. And not since medieval times have governments marked men for death because of race or faith. Now comes this recrudescence—this Nazi doctrine of a master race—an arrogance blended from tribal conceit and a boundless contempt for man himself. It is an idea whose toleration endangers all men. It is, as we have charged, a crime against humanity.

The conscience of humanity is the foundation of all law. We seek here a judgment expressing that conscience and reaffirming under law the basic rights of man.

Nazi Doctrine of Superior and Inferior Races

As this trial deals with the crime of genocide, it is essential to investigate the basic tenets and the development of the Nazi doctrine which inspired the crimes we shall prove. It is conceded that the Nazis neither invented nor monopolized this idea of superior peoples, but the consequences they wrought gave it a new and terrible meaning.... The motivation of the crime of genocide, as it was carried out by Hitler and his legions in all of the occupied and dominated counties, stemmed from the Nazi ideology of "blood and race." In this theory of the predominance of the alleged Nordic race over all others and in the mystic belief that Nordic blood was the only creative power in the world, the Einsatzgruppen had their ideological basis. In this primitive theory, derived in part from Nietzsche's teaching of the Germanic superman, the Nazis found the justification for Germany's domination of the world.

* * *

Hans Frank, the Governor General of occupied Poland, addressed a cabinet session in the government building at Krakow on 16 December 1941 and advocated the following solution of the Jewish problem:

> "Gentlemen, I must ask you to rid yourself of all feelings of pity. We must annihilate the Jews, wherever we find them and wherever it is possible, in order to maintain there the structure of the Reich as a whole."

The same Hans Frank summarized in his dairy of 1944 the Nazi policy as follows: "The Jews are a race which has to be eliminated. Wherever we catch one it is his end." And earlier, speaking of his function as Governor General of Poland, he confided to his diary this sentiment: "Of course, I cannot eliminate all lice and Jews in only a year's time."

* * *

...The prophecy of Hitler, made in his speech to the German Reichstag on 30 January 1939, that the result of war would be the annihilation of the Jewish race in Europe, came very near fulfillment. It is estimated that, of the 9,600,000 Jews who lived in Nazi-dominated countries, 6,000,000 have perished in gas chambers of the concentration camps or were murdered by Einsatzgruppen.

[Here follows copius documentation, examination and cross-examination of twenty-two of the twenty-four defendants charged. One defendant, SS Major Emil Haussmann committed suicide on 31 July 1947, while the other defendant, SS Brigadier General Otto Rasch was severed from the case because of the onset of Parkinson's disease].

* * *

XI. Opinion and Judgment

The indictment filed in this case on 29 July 1947 charged the 24 defendants enumerated therein with crimes against humanity, war crimes, and membership in criminal organizations. The 24 defendants were made up of 6 SS generals, 5 SS colonels, 6 SS lieutenant colonels, 4 SS majors, and 3 SS junior officers....

* * *

Although the indictment accuses the defendants of the commission of atrocities, persecutions, exterminations, imprisonment and other inhumane acts, the principle charge in this case is murder....

At the outset it must be acknowledged that the facts with which the Tribunal must deal in this opinion are so beyond the experience of normal man and the range of man-made phenomena that only the most complete judicial inquiry, and the most exhaustive trial, could verify and confirm them. Although the principle accusation is murder and, unhappily, man has been killing man ever since the days of Cain, the charge of purposeful homicide in this case reaches such fantastic proportions and surpasses such credible limits that believability must be bolstered with assurance a hundred times repeated.

The books have shown through the ages why man has slaughtered his brother. He has always had an excuse, criminal and ungodly though it may have been. He has killed to take his brother's property, his wife, his throne, his position; he has slain out of jealousy, revenge, passion, lust and cannibalism. He has murdered as a monarch, a slave owner, a madman, a robber. But it was left to the twentieth century to produce so extraordinary a killing that even a new word [genocide] had to be created to define it.

One of counsel has characterized this trial as the biggest murder trial in history. Certainly never before have twenty-three men been brought into court to answer the charge of destroying over one million of their fellow human beings....

If what the prosecution maintains is true, we have here participation in a crime of such unprecedented brutality and of such inconceivable savagery that the mind rebels against its own thought image and the imagination staggers in the contemplation of a human degradation beyond the power of language to adequately portray. The crime did not exclude the immolation of women and children, heretofore regarded the special object of solicitude even on the part of an implacable and primitive foe.

The International Military Tribunal in its decision of 1 October 1946 declared that the Einsatzgruppen and the Security Police, to which the defendants belonged, were responsible for the murder of two million defenseless human beings, and the evidence presented in this case has in no way shaken this finding. No human mind can grasp the enormity of two million deaths because life, the supreme essence of consciousness and being, does not lend itself to material or even spiritual appraisement. It is so beyond finite comprehension that only its destruction offers an infinitesimal suggestion of its worth. The loss of any one person can only begin to be measured in the realization of his survivors that he is gone forever. The extermination, therefore, of two million human beings cannot be felt. Two million is but a figure. The number of deaths resulting from the activities with which these defendants have been connected and which the prosecution has set at one million is but an abstract number. One cannot grasp the full cumulative terror of murder one million times repeated.

It is only when this grotesque total is broken down into units capable of mental assimilation that one can understand the monstrousness of the things we are in this trial contemplating. One must visualize not one million people but only ten persons—men, women and children, perhaps all of one family—falling before the executioner's guns. If one million is divided by ten this scene must happen one hundred thousand times, and as one visualizes the repetitious horror, one begins to understand the meaning of the prosecutor words,...

Judicial opinions are often primarily prepared for the information and guidance of the legal profession, but the Nuremberg judgments are of interest to a much larger segment of the earth's population. It would not be too much to say that the entire world itself is concerned with the adjudications being handed down in Nuremberg. Thus it is not enough in these pronouncements to cite specific laws, sections, and paragraphs. The decisions must be understood in the light of the circumstances which brought them about. What is the exact nature of the facts on which the judgments are based? A tribunal may not avert its head from the ghastly deeds whose legal import it is called upon to adjudicate. What type of reasoning or lack of reasoning was it that brought about the events which are to be here related? What type of morality or lack of it was it that for years bathed the world in blood and tears? Why is it that Germany, whose rulers thought to make it the wealthiest and the most powerful nation of all time, an empire which would overshadow the Rome of Caesar—why is it that this Germany is now a shattered shell? Why is it that Europe, the cradle of modern civilization, is devastated and the whole world is out of joint?

These Nuremberg trials answer the question, and the Einsatzgruppen trial in particular makes no little contribution to that enlightenment.

When the German armies, without any declaration of war, crossed the Polish frontier and smashed into Russia, there moved with and behind them a unique organization known as the Einsatzgruppen. As an instrument of terror in the museum of horror, it would be difficult to find an entry to surpass the Einsatzgruppen in its blood-freezing potentialities. No writer of murder fiction, no dramatist steeped in macabre lore, can ever expect to conjure up from his imagination a plot which will shock sensibilities as much as will the stark drama of these sinister bands.

* * *

The Einsatzgruppen were...instructed to shoot gypsies. No explanation was offered as to why these unoffending people, who through the centuries have contributed their share of music and song, were to be hunted down like wild game. Colorful in garb and habit, they have amused, diverted, and baffled society with their wanderings, and occasionally annoyed with their indolence, but no one has condemned them as a mortal menace to organized society. That is, no one but National Socialism which, through Hitler, Himmler and Heydrich ordered their liquidation. Accordingly, these simple, innocuous people were taken in trucks, perhaps in their own wagons, to the antitank ditches and there slaughtered with the Jews and the Krimchaks.

The insane also were to be killed. Not because they were a threat to the Reich, nor because someone may have believed they were formidable rivals of the Nazi chieftains.... These victims were grouped together under the title of "useless eaters."... Insane asylums were often emptied and the inmates liquidated because the invaders desired to use the asylum buildings.

"Asiatic inferiors" was another category destined for liquidation. This kind of designation allowed for a wide discretion in homicide. Einsatzgruppen and Einsatzkommando leaders were authorized to take executive measures on their own responsibility. There was no one to dispute with them as to the people they branded "Asiatic inferiors." And even less was there a curb on homicidal operations when they were authorized to shoot "Asocial people, politically tainted persons, and racially and mentally inferior elements."

And then, all Communist functionaries were to be shot. Again it was never made quite clear how broad was this classification. Thus, in recapitulation, the Fuehrer Order, and throughout this opinion it will be so referred to, called for the summary killing of Jews, gypsies, insane people, Asiatic inferiors, Communist functionaries and asocials.

* * *

Prisoners of War

The extermination program on racial and political grounds also extended to prisoners of war. Even in the first weeks of Germany's war against Russia, large numbers of civilians from the invaded areas were indiscriminately thrown into prisoner-of-war camps, run by the PW department of the High Command of the Wehrmacht. On 17 July, 1941, Heydrick issues Operational Order No. 8, which contained "directives" for the Einsatz units "detailed to permanent PW camps (Stalags) and transit camps (Dulags)." These directives not only grossly violated the provisions of the Hague Regulations of prisoners of war and civilians in belligerently occupied territories and of century-old rules and customs of warfare, but outraged every principle of humanity. They provided for nothing less than the cold-blooded mass-murder of prisoners of war and of civilians held in PW camps. The directives state as their "purpose" —

> "The Wehrmacht must immediately free itself of all these elements among the prisoners of war who must be regarded as Bolshevist influence. The special situation of the campaign in the East, therefore, demands *special measures* [italics original] which have to be carried out in a spirit free from bureaucratic and administrative influences, and with an eagerness to assume responsibility."

The directives instruct the Einsatz units as to which categories of persons to seek out "above all." This list mentions in detail all categories and types of Russian government officials, all influential Communist Party officials, "the leading personalities of the economy," "the Soviet Russian intellectuals," and as a separate category which was again to yield the largest number of victims of this "action" — "all Jews."

* * *

The Füehrerprinzip

In every Nuremberg trial, an invisible figure appears in the defendant's dock. As each session in this Palace of Justice, he has entered the door and quietly moved to his place among the other defendants. For over two years he has been making his entrance and exits. He never takes the witness stand, he never speaks, but he dominates every piece of evidence, his shadow falls over every document.

Some of the accused are ready to charge this sinister shadow with responsibility for their every reverse and misfortune. But were he to cast off the cloak of invisibility and appear as he was, the animadversions of the other occupants of the defendants' box might not be so audible, because he knows them well. He was no sudden interloper in Germany's destiny. He did not appear in a flash and order his present companions into action. Had it happened that way, the story of physical and moral duress they recounted from the witness stand would not be so incongruous. But, of their own free will, they threw in their lot with that of the specter's, and in their own respective functions enthusiastically carried out the shadow's orders, who was then not a shadow but a fire-breathing reality.

In explanation of their willingness to follow him in those days, they explain they had no reason to doubt him. He had been so successful. But the very successes they cheered most were usually this man's greatest crimes. Each defendant has claimed that the propaganda of the day assured them that Germany was always fighting a defensive war, but these men were not outsiders, nor were they children. They were part of the government, they belonged to the regime. It is incredible that they should believe that Germany was being attacked by Denmark, Yugoslavia, Czechoslovakia, Greece, Belgium, and even little Luxembourg. Indubitably they reveled in these successes. One of the defense counsel declared that the defendants could well believe of Hitler that "here was a man whom no power could resist."

And indeed never did a man wield so much power and never was a living man so ignominiously and stupidly obeyed by other men. Never did living beings, made in the image of man so pusillanimously grovel at feet of clay. But it is not true that no one could resist him. There were people who could resist him, or at least refused to be a party to his monstrous criminality. Some voluntarily left Germany rather than acknowledge him as their spiritual leader. Others opposed him and ended up in concentration camps. It is mistake to say or assume that all the German people approved of nazism and the crimes it fostered and committed. Had that been true, there would have been no need of Stormtroopers in the early days of the Party, and there would have been no need for concentration camps or the Gestapo, both of which institutions were inaugurated as soon as the Nazis gained control of the German State.

* * *

These defendants were among those who made it possible for a megalomaniac to achieve his ambition of putting the world beneath his heel or to bring it crashing in ruins about his head. Some of these defendants, in following Hitler, may have believed that, in executing his will, they were serving their country. Their sense of justice staggering from the intoxication of command, their normal reactions drugged by the opiate of their blind fealty, their human impulses twisted by the passion of their ambitions, they made themselves believe that they were advancing the cause of Germany. But Germany would have fared better without such patriotism. When Samuel Johnson uttered his cynical line that patriotism is the last refuge of a scoundrel, he could well have had in mind a Hitlerian patriotism.

Hitler struck the match, but the fire would have died a quick death had it not been for his fellow arsonists, big and little, who continued to supply the fuel until they, themselves, were scorched by the flame they had been so enthusiastically tending. If history had taught anything, it has demonstrated with devastating finality that most of the evils of the world have been due to craven subservience by subchiefs upon a man who through boundless ambition unrestrained by conscience has formulated plans which, proposed by anyone else, would be rejected as mad.

Dictatorship in government can only lead to disaster because whatever benefits derive from centralized control are lost in the infinite damage which inevitably follows lack of responsibility. That unlimited authority and power are poisons which destroy judgment and reason is a demonstrable fact as conclusively established as any chemical formula tried and tested in a laboratory. The genius of true democratic government is that no one person is allowed to take the nation with its millions of people into the valley of decisive action without the advice, counsel and approval of those who are to be subjected to the hazards, hardships and potentially fatal consequences of that decision.

The defendants must have found themselves repeatedly at the crossroads where and when there was still the opportunity to turn in the direction of the ideals which they had once known, but the willful determination to follow the trail of blood prints of their voluntarily accepted leader could only take them to the goal they had never intended. It is possible that currently the defendants realize the mistakes which they made. Though most of them have sought to rationalize their deeds, though they attempted to explain that every executioner's rifle was aimed at a national peril, it is possible that they now grasp the disservice they have done not only to humanity but to their own Fatherland. It may even be that through this trial with its sobering revelations, they will have demonstrated what are the inevitable consequences of any plan which stems from hatred and intolerance; and here they may have proved what has never been disproved: There is only one Fuehrer, and that is truth.

* * *

That so much man-made misery should have happened in the twentieth century, which could well have been the fruition of all the aspirations and hopes of the countries which went before, makes the spectacle almost unsupportable in its unutterable tragedy and sadness. Amid the wreckage of six continents, amid the shattered hearts of the world, amid the sufferings of those who have borne the cross of disillusionment and despair, mankind pleads for an understanding which will prevent anything like this happening again. That understanding goes back to the words spoken 1900 years ago, words which had they been honored in the observance rather than in the breach would have made the events narrated in this trail impossible—

"Therefore, all things whatsoever ye would that men should do to you, do ye so to them."

[The Court then pronounced sentence individually upon twenty-two defendants, beginning with Otto Ohlendorf and ending with Mathias Graf].

(b) Tribunal I
United States of America v. Ulrich Greifelt, et al.
5 CCL No. 10 Trials 1 (1948)

"The RuSHA Case"

Members of Military Tribunal I.

Lee B. Wyatt, Presiding, Associate Justice, Supreme Court of Georgia

Daniel T. O'Connell, Member, Associate Justice, Superior Court of Massachusetts

Johnson T. Crawford, Member, Judge, District Court of Oklahoma

Chief Prosecutor: Mr. James M. McHaney

A. Opening Statement of the Prosecution

Mr. McHaney: May it please the Tribunal, the crimes of these defendants, thirteen men and one woman for which they stand here accused, are the result of a vast and premeditated plan to destroy national groups in countries occupied by Germany. This program of genocide was part of the Nazi doctrine of total warfare, war waged against populations rather than against states and armed forces. Hitler once said that—

> "The French complained after the war [World War I] that there were twenty million Germans too many. We accept the criticism. But our friends will have to excuse us if we subtract the twenty million elsewhere. After all these centuries of whining about the protection of the poor and lowly, it is about time we decided to protect the strong against the inferior. It will be one of the chief tasks of German statesmanship for all time to prevent, by every means in our power, the further increase of the Slav races. Natural instincts bid all living beings not merely to conquer their enemies, but also destroy them."

All of these defendants played an active and leading role in carrying out this broad program which had the two-fold objective of weakening and eventually destroying other nations while at the same time strengthening Germany at their expense, territorially and biologically, in order to secure German domination first of Europe and finally the world.

This program was primarily based upon the two Nazi concepts of Race and Lebensraum [living space]. Belief in German racial supremacy is not new in German thought. At the end of the 19th century it became crystallized in the theory of Aryan supremacy. The "Aryan" had long been used to denote that family of languages to which ancient Norse, Greek, and Sanskirt belonged. Now the term Aryan was applied to a mythical race which was creator of all the culture existing in the world.

As Hitler himself said in "Mein Kampf"—

> "All the human culture, all the results of art, science and technology that we see before us today, are almost exclusively the creative product of the Aryan."

This theory of race played a prominent role in the rise to power of the Nazis. It convinced the German masses of Aryan supremacy and taught them that the Germans were more entirely Aryan than any other race. They were the "Nordic Germanic race," the Master Race. Thus, the German people, by purifying themselves, casting out Jews, Slavs, and other non-Aryans, were to become the foremost race on earth. Himmler, in a speech to high-ranking army officers in 1935, said—

> "I am a convinced supporter of the idea that what matters in the world ultimately is only good blood. * * * I have approached my task from this angle. It means that actually the only good blood, according to our reading of history, is the leading creative element in every state, and in particular, the blood engaged in military activity, and, above, all, Nordic blood."

This reconstituted Aryan people was to be the strongest race in the world. Therefore, in accordance with nature's law of survival of the fittest, the Aryan race would conquer the world, enslave all other races and everywhere spread Aryan culture (for Aryans only, of course) in a new Pax Germanica.

Inside Germany this racial theory coordinated everything in public and private life according to the tenets of Nazism. In foreign affairs, it became the slogan for the unification of all Germans, holding out to them a glittering vision of world mastery as both a possibility and a right.

This theory of race matched with the theory behind Lebensraum. The Nazis made much of Germany's over-population with respect to its area. But they were not really concerned with over-population. In fact, the Nazis constantly proclaimed the duty of all good Germans to have as many children as possible. Lebensraum was not, as many think it, a cry of an underprivileged people for the possibility of existence. It was a demand for more and more land, in fact, for more land that the German people could use at that time. The Nazis felt that only by expansion into a great state, territorially, could Germany proceed to become mistress of the world. In short, Lebensraum was a slogan for an aggressive drive by the German people under the Nazi leadership to expand its borders regardless of economic need. This cumulated in wars of aggression to gain territory and populations at the expense of neighboring countries.

In the course of the war, as the Nazis overran Poland and most of the rest of Europe, they gained the opportunity to put these theories of Race and Lebensraum, this crime of genocide, into practice. The main drive for expansion was in the East. Himmler, in 1942 explained it as follows:

> "It is not our task to Germanize the East in the old sense, that is, to teach the people there the German language and German law, but to see to it that only people of purely German blood live in the east."

In November 1939, the Office for Racial Policy of the Nazi Party put forth a treatise with the weighty title of "The Problem of the Manner of Dealing with the Population of the Formerly Polish Territories on the Basis of Racial-Political Aspects." In this treatise, which formed in part the basis of actions taken by these defendants, it stated—

> "The aim of the German policy in the new Reich territory in the East must be the creation of a racial and therefore intellectual-psychical as well as national-political uniform German population. This results in the ruthless elimination of all elements not suitable for Germinazation.

> "This aim consists of *three interwoven tasks*.

> "*First*, the complete and final Germanization of the population which seems to be suitable for it.

> "*Second*, deportation of all foreign groups which are not suitable for Germanization, and

> *Third*, the resettlement by Germans."

It must be realized that under the Nazi theory of race, non-Aryans simply did not matter. Hitler stated this clearly in *Mein Kampf* when he said, "All who are not of good race in this world are chaff." This is again clearly brought out in the judgment of the International Military Tribunal, where it is stated— "When the witness Bach-Zelewski was asked how Ohlendorf could admit the murder of 90,000 people, he replied, 'I am of the opinion that when for years, for decades, the doctrine is preached that the Slav race is an inferior race, and Jews not even human, then such an outcome is inevitable.'"

It may seem somewhat inconsistent for the Nazis to prate of race and purity of blood on the one hand and on the other to take Poles, Czechs and nationals of many other countries and decide, upon the basis of physical characteristics such as blue eyes and blond hair, that these people can be Germanized. This was a measure to which the Germans were forced because they found that their own population was not sufficient to fulfill the Nazi scheme of expansion. This taking of non-Germans and calling them Germans was also justified on the ground that Germany was thereby taking the best blood from the other nations and thus weakening them as well as strengthening itself.

The seemingly insurmountable theoretical barrier of race was avoided very neatly. It was obvious, they said, that for a thousand years and more, Germanic peoples had gone forth over the map of Europe. Thus, when a Polish family showed no signs of any German ancestry for hundreds of years, if the physical characteristics were compatible with those of the mythical super race, it meant that sometime in the dim past Nordic blood had forgotten its heritage and become Polonized. Nevertheless, they said, this blood was still valuable blood and could be reclaimed and this Polish family could be Germanized. There was to be a gradual sifting of the peoples of the East until finally all the Aryan blood had been reclaimed.

* * *

In 1942 the defendant Meyer-Hetling drew up a broad plan for the ethnic reconstruction of Eastern Europe which was entitled the "General Plan East." According to this plan the regions around Leningrad, the Crimea and Kherson in Russia, and Memel in Lithuania, and Narew, were to become German colonies, and within 25 years to be resettled with a large German population. This plan was forwarded by the defendant Greifelt to Himmler who gave his wholehearted approval to it, and asked the defendant Meyer-Hetling to draft also a plan embracing the incorporated Polish territories, Bohemia and Moravia in Czechoslovakia, Alsace, and Lorraine in France, and Upper Carniola and South Styria in Yugoslavia. This was to be a 20-year plan, so Himmler said, and was to bring about a thorough Germanization of Esthonia and Latvia, as well as of the General Government in Poland.

This then was the program of genocide. It was a coordinated plan aimed at the destruction of the essential foundations of the life of national groups. This destruction can be and was accomplished with the help of these defendants by a number of different means, which may be broadly classified as physical, political, biological and cultural. They sought [as Lemkin noted] the "disintegration of the political and social institutions of culture, language, national feelings, religion, and the economic existence of national groups, and the destruction of the personal security, liberty, health, dignity, and even the lives of the individuals belonging to such groups."

In another courtroom of this same building, 23 leaders of the notorious Einsatzgruppen of the Security Police and SD are being tried [the *Ohlendorf Case*] for the mass annihilation of Jews and Russians. While a number of defendants in this dock also participated in those very same crimes and others of similar nature, their main efforts were devoted to the destruction of national groups by other methods. The technique of these defendants was the mass deportation of oppressed peoples, the deprivation of their means of livelihood by the wholesale confiscation of property, the forced Germanization of citizens of occupied countries, and the destruction of their national culture, folkways, and educational facilities, the creation of conditions which increased the mortality rate and prevented increase of the population, and the kidnapping of children.

These techniques of genocide, while neither so quick nor perhaps so simple as outright mass extermination, are by the very nature of things far more cruel and equally effective. If crimes such as these are allowed to go unpunished, the future of humanity is in far more danger than if an occasional murderer goes free. It is the enormity and far-reaching effects of these crimes that give this case its significance.

* * *

I turn now to a description of the Main Staff Office of the RKFDV, VoMi, RuSHA, and Lebensborn and the positions of these defendants in those organizations.

Perhaps the most important organization involved in this trial is the Staff Main Office of the Reich Commissioner for the Strengthening of Germanism. Heinrich Himmler, Reich Leader of the SS and Chief of the German Police, was appointed RKFDV by Hitler's decree of 7 October 1939. In this decree Hitler said—

> "The consequences which Versailles had on Europe have been removed. As a result, the Greater German Reich is able to accept and settle within its space German people who up to the present had to live in foreign lands and to arrange the settlement of national groups within its spheres of interest in such a way that better dividing lines between them are attained. I commission the Reich Leader SS with the execution of this task in accordance with the following instructions:

> I

> "Pursuant to my directions the Reich Leader SS is called upon—

> "1. To bring back those German citizens and racial Germans abroad who are eligible for permanent return into the Reich.

> "2. To eliminate the harmful influence of such alien parts of the population as constitutes a danger to the Reich and the German community.

> "3. To create new German colonies by resettlement, and especially by the resettlement of German citizens and racial Germans coming back from abroad.

> "The Reich Leader SS is authorized to give such general orders and to take such administrative measures as are necessary for the execution of these duties."

* * *

Himmler in his capacity as RKFDV had jurisdiction over all matters connected with the strengthening of Germanism, such as resettlements, racial screening, deportations, confiscations and the like. In addition to the members of the Staff Main Office, VoMi, and the other offices of the SS, numerous government and Party officials were subject to Himmler's authority insofar as their activities related to the strengthening of Germanism. Thus, Himmler as RKFDV, and in practice the defendant Greifelt as his deputy, could give orders to the Gauleiters and Reich Governors. The Staff Main Office also had its own branch offices in the occupied territories and the General Government.

* * *

The Repatriation Office for Ethnic Germans (VoMi) existed long before the outbreak of the war. The defendant Lorenz was appointed the head of VoMi on 1 January 1937 by Rudolf Hess and was subordinated to him and the Chief of the Foreign Office, Joachim von Ribbentrop. Shortly after the appointment of Himmler as RKFDV in 1939, Lorenz was commissioned by Himmler with the task of carrying out the registration and evacuation of ethnic Germans from their former homes, and their transportation to collecting camps for Germanization. On 11 June 1941, the section of VoMi which was engaged in this activity was established as a Main Office of the SS, the Repatriation Office for Ethnic Germans, with Lorenz as its chief. The defendant Brueckner was connected with numerous resettlement and deportation actions.

* * *

The Race and Settlement Main Office (RuSHA) was one of the oldest Main Offices of the Supreme Command of the SS.

* * *

RuSHA's concern with and experience in racial matters made it the logical agency to take over the racial problems inherent in Himmler's program of genocide and Germanism. It was apparent that someone had to screen the millions of people about to be uprooted from their homes and tossed about the map of Europe.

* * *

Lebensborn was a registered society which was founded in December 1935. It was at first a department of RuSHA, but in 1936 it became part of the Personal Staff of Himmler.

The early aim of Lebensborn was the perpetuation of the blood of the members of the SS. The minimum family expected of an SS man was four.

* * *

Those unable to have children of their own were expected to adopt suitable children and bring them up on National Socialist lines. Lebensborn was to assist in their process and insure the support of both legitimate and illegitimate children of SS men. Its tasks were to help large families "valuable from the racial and hereditary and biological point of view" and to take care of pregnant women and their children. The prerequisite of this care was an assurance through racial and health examinations of these women and their mates that the parents were of good health and race and that the future children would possess the same qualities.

* * *

The defendant Viermetz joined Lebensborn in September 1938. Soon after the outbreak of the war, she reorganized and was placed in charge of the employment office for Lebensraum mothers. Early in 1940 she reorganized the department dealing with Homes and Adoptions and was in charge of both this department and the Employment Department until the beginning of 1941.... From the middle of 1942 until the middle of 1943, the defendant Viermetz carried out special tasks for Lebensborn including negotiations with respect to the transfer of children to Germany from various countries and the establishment of Lebensborn homes.

* * *

Mr. Lamb [Associate Counsel for Prosecution]: In the course of their execution of genocide and Germanization, all of the defendants participated in the plunder of public and private property. As time will not permit a detailed discussion of all of these crimes, we will limit ourselves to the most important points.

The Staff Main Office under the defendant Greifelt was particularly active in the mass confiscation of property from Poles and other persons evicted from their farms. This served the dual purpose of depriving those people of their means of livelihood and providing land and houses for resettlers.

* * *

An idea of the extent of the plunder engineered by the Staff Main Office can be obtained from the following figures. On 3 August 1942, the defendant Greifelt reported to Himmler that by 1 July 1942 a total of 626,642 enterprises (85 percent rural, 5 percent urban) had been taken away from Jews and Poles in Danzig, Wartheland, Eastern Prussia and Silesia by the Central Land Office. In a pamphlet called "Folkdom and Soil" issued by the Staff Main Office it was noted that by 31 December 1942 a total of 193,427 enterprises covering a territory of 804,880 hectares had been registered for seizure and confiscation in lower Styria and South Carinthia, that a total of 2,998 enterprises covering an area of 99,175 hectares had been seized, and a total of 1,094 enterprises of 28,042 hectares had been confiscated. Also, it was pointed out that in Lorraine an area of 214,445 hectares had been registered for seizure and confiscation and in Alsace a total of 10,561 hectares. In October 1943 the defendant Greifelt estimated that the total value of the confiscated land amounted to from 7 to 8 hundred million marks.

[The prosecution then details the persecution of the European Jews by RuSHA and other Nazi organizations, the kidnapping of alien children, the removal of infants from Eastern workers in German industry, the methods employed to prevent reproduction among enemy nations, the punishment for sexual intercourse with Germans by foreign workers, and other indignities practiced by the Nazis on their captive populations. The prosecution then concludes its opening statements with the following comments].

Civilized usage and conventions to which Germany was party had prescribed certain immunities for peoples unfortunate enough to dwell in lands overrun by hostile armies. Today, we have briefly outlined before this Tribunal the crimes committed by these fourteen defendants in which man's dearest and most sacred rights were denied to hundred of thousands throughout Europe. These crimes represent but a partial fulfillment of their genocidal plans. One shudders to think how Europe would appear today if these defendants and their collaborators still remained in their positions of power.

From these defendants we shall soon hear variously formulated and developed apologies and excuses in justification or mitigation of their crimes. When they are heard, let this Tribunal not forget that these crimes were not of an occasional or casual character but were deliberate and integrated parts of the sinister program of genocide, a program to strengthen Germany at the expense of other peoples and nations. To the successful fulfillment of this program, all of the defendants in the dock devoted their untiring efforts and abilities. Each held a position of responsibility which was endowed with the power to decide the fate of men and to destroy all which interfered with their conception of a Germanic world. For their crimes we seek from this Tribunal a just restriction and a reaffirmation of man's right to live in peace and dignity under the law.

[After an Opening Statement for the defendant Greifelt by his defense counsel, there followed an Order of the Tribunal concerning time allotted for presentation of defense evidence and cross-examination by the prosecution. Evidence was then presented by the prosecution regarding the forced Germanization of enemy nationals and selected extracts of testimony by various defendants were presented in question and answer form. This aspect of the trial consumed a great deal of time and generated a voluminous record too lengthy to reproduce. Numerous documents were also introduced by both prosecution and defense in an attempt to either establish or rebut various accusations and charges].

* * *

Extracts from the Closing Statement of the Prosecution

Mr. Shiller: May it please the Tribunal:

Today we approach the end of this proceeding which began on 20 October 1947. Fifty-seven trial days have been consumed, nine hundred and four exhibits have been introduced by the prosecution and over one thousand by the defense. Thirty-two witnesses have been heard for the prosecution and eighty-four for the defendants, and the record comprises 4,780 pages.

This tribunal was established for the particular purpose of hearing and deciding this one case. It was constituted pursuant to international agreement, and the crimes with which these defendants are charged are crimes under international law. The result of this trial is the concern of all the people of the world, and the judgment in this case will become a part of the body of international law and will be a precedent for the guidance of all civilized nations of the world for years to come.

The crimes with which the defendants are charged include murders, brutalities, cruelties, tortures, atrocities, deportations, enslavement, plunder of property, persecution and other inhuman acts.

But the importance of the issues to be settled here cannot be measured in terms of trial days, exhibits, and witnesses, nor does the mere listing of the crimes, grave and shocking through they are, properly indicate the seriousness of the task which your Honors have here undertaken, or tell why it was considered proper to bring these charges before a specially established tribunal having the jurisdiction and dignity of an international court. The thing that makes this case so important and justifies its being brought before this international Court is the motive which prompted the commission of these criminal acts and the fact that the concerted effort with which they were carried out threatened, and very nearly accomplished, the destruction of entire nations.

The motive in this case was what the Nazis termed the "Strengthening of Germanism," which was their way of describing a program that has generally been known as "genocide."

These defendants are not charged with the generic crime of genocide as such, but are specially charged with many criminal acts which had a clear genocidal purpose—that of strengthening Germany through the destruction of her neighbors. To judge these defendants this motive must be considered....

Genocide, as practiced by the Nazis, was a two-edged sword, both aspects of which were equally criminal. The positive side, according to the German concept, was the Germanization program by which they sought to strengthen themselves by adding to their population large groups of people selected from among the populations of the conquered territories, and by forcing the German language, culture, citizenship, and ideals upon those so selected. The negative side of this program, through which the so-called positive side was in equal measure accomplished, was the deliberate extermination and enslavement of the remaining population of these conquered territories. Thus, Germany would be strengthened by adding to its population, and its neighbors would be weakened by subtracting from their population, and the strength of Germany would thereby be proportionately increased.

It is the first time in history that such elaborate plans were laid and such appalling crimes committed in an effort to carry out a program of genocide. Only by learning the truth about this criminal plan, by making a permanent record of what is learned, and by punishing the perpetrators of these enormous crimes, can it be hoped to forestall the development of similar schemes in the future.

There have been trials by other Military Tribunals here at Nuremberg in which defendants were charged with participation in certain phases of this genocidal program. But in those cases it was primarily the negative side of the program, that is, the actual extermination of populations that was involved. The case at bar is the first where the entire program of Germanization and genocide with all its ramifications has been completely brought to light. The Office of the Reich Commissioner for the Strengthening of Germanism, with which all the defendants in this case were directly or indirectly connected, was created for the particular purpose of planning and executing this program, and it is this office and its satellites with which the evidence in this case is primarily concerned. Nowhere else can the world gain so complete a picture of the extremes to which the Nazis went in their attempts to carry out this program as in the record of this proceeding.

The crimes charged here were not committed in a heat of passion brought on by overzealous wartime patriotism. These were premeditated acts. They had long been contemplated and their seeds are to be found in the avowed aims of the Nazi Party itself. On 5 January 1919, not two months after the conclusion of the armistice which ended the First World War, the Nazi Party had its beginning and adopted a platform. This program, which remained unaltered until the Party dissolved in 1945, consisted of twenty-five points. The first four points contain the Nazi doctrines of Lebensraum and the inferiority of other races, which were the immoral bases for the detailed program launched during the war.

* * *

Throughout the years that followed the first pronouncement, the members of the Nazi Party and the world in general were constantly reminded of the objectives of the Nazis. Hitler's "Mein Kampf," the Nazi bible, continued to preach the same doctrine. This book was published about 1925 and, as the International Military Tribunal judgment expressed it,

> "* * * was no mere private diary in which the secret thoughts of Hitler were set down. Its contents were rather proclaimed from the house tops. It was used in the schools and universities * * *. By the year 1945 over 6.5 million copies had been circulated. The general contents are well known * * *." "The second chapter of book one of *Mein Kampf* is dedicated to what may be called the 'Master Race' theory, the doctrine of Aryan superiority over all other races, and the right of the Germans in virtue of this superiority to dominate and use other peoples for their own ends. * * *

> "The greatest emphasis was laid on the supreme mission of the German people to lead and dominate by virtue of their Nordic blood and racial purity; and the ground was thus being prepared for the acceptance of the idea of German world supremacy."

Within the launching of the wars of aggression by the Third Reich, it became possible to put these noxious principles into practice. By the middle of 1940, a very definite plan was being effectuated. This is shown by the top secret document which Himmler wrote, entitled "Reflections on the Treatment of Peoples of Alien Races in the East." This treatise by Himmler was given to Hitler and was approved by him. On 28 May 1940, in a memorandum attached to this highly secret document, Himmler stated that he had shown it to Hitler a few days before, and that—

> "the Fuehrer read the six pages and considered them very good and correct. He directed, however, that only very few copies should be issued; that there should be no large edition, and that the report is to be treated with utmost secrecy."

Hitler agreed that the report would be considered as a directive; that one copy could be given to Lammers, who in turn was authorized to divulge its contents to four or five of the highest ranking Reich Ministers and Gauleiter [district leaders]; that another copy might be given to Bormann, who was Hitler's right-hand man; another to the defendant Greifelt; and still another to the chief of the Race and Settlement Main Office, who at that time was the defendant Hofmann.

* * *

An examination of these "Reflections on the Treatment of Peoples of Alien Races in the East," of which the defendants Greifelt, Creutz, Meyer-Hetling, and Hofmann had first-hand knowledge, will explain why even these evil men were ashamed of it. The treatise starts off by naming the various ethnic groups that make up the population of the so-called Government General of Poland and observes that these people must not be allowed to unite....

* * *

Himmler's plans with reference to the Jews and Poles were different. The directive goes on to say:

> "I hope that the concept of Jews will be completely extinguished through the possibility of a large emigration of all Jews to Africa or some other colony. Within a somewhat longer period it should also be possible to make the ethnic concepts of Ukrainians, Goralen and Lemken disappear in our area. What has been said for these fragments of peoples is also meant on a correspondingly larger scale for the Poles."

Himmler then orders that some of the children are to be kidnapped and others are to be brought up in ignorance and slavery.

* * *

Himmler then showed that he was conscious of his guilt and made excuses for his actions by saying that it was better to make slaves of these people than to exterminate them. The directive then goes on to say:

> "Cruel and tragic as every individual case may be, this method is still the mildest and best one if, out of inner conviction one rejects as un-German and impossible the Bolshevist method of physical extermination of a people."

The defendants may contend that this was Himmler's plan and they had nothing to do with the preparation of it. Our only answer to this is that whether they had anything to do with the preparation of the plan or not, the things which they actually did followed the directive to the letter. The things which Himmler here "prophesied" came to pass, and it was through the activities of these defendants and their collaborators in the Staff Main Office, VoMi, RuSHA and Lebensborn, that they did come to pass.

These defendants and the four organizations which they ran, the Staff Main Office, VoMi, RuSHA and Lebensborn, were the leaders in both the planning and the execution of this criminal common design.

* * *

The guilt of the defendants in this case has been proved by evidence of the highest known character. The prosecution has relied almost entirely upon documentary evidence, the authenticity of which has only in the rarest of occasions been questioned by the defendants. In most instances the defendants have taken up the prosecution exhibits, document by document, discussed them in detail and admitted their genuineness. They have given various and sundry unconvincing excuses as to why these documents did not incriminate them, but it was seldom, if ever, claimed that a document was not authentic.

* * *

Most of the prosecution's exhibits are orders, letters, decrees, reports, directives and the like. Many of them are signed by the defendants themselves. This is the type of evidence which we have mainly relied on and which we think proves the guilt of all the defendants beyond every reasonable doubt. The few affidavits which we have introduced, including those of the defendants, merely clarify and corroborate what is contained in the other documents.

* * *

The defendants always blamed someone else who had a higher position than they, such as Himmler, or some irresponsible subordinate. They would have us believe that Himmler personally attended to everything connected not only with SS offices involved here but all the twelve Main SS Offices over which he had control. They have all testified that they did not approve of Hitler or Himmler and that they did not approve of the objectives of the agencies here involved. But none resigned because of this.

Inasmuch as these defendants have denied absolutely all connection with the crimes here charged and have said that these documents which we have introduced do not mean what they say, we think a question of credibility is a principal issue before the Tribunal. We submit that it is incredible that all of the many incriminating documents which have been submitted by the prosecution are mistaken in what they say. This question of credibility is clear cut. Either the documents are all entirely wrong or these defendants are guilty. In their testimony the defendants took no half-way measures. They looked at incriminating document after incriminating document squarely in the face and simply said these documents didn't mean what they said. They called black white without the slightest hesitation. They read their lines without faltering. It was only on cross-examination that they would sometimes admit an "unfortunate term" had been used.

These defendants always blamed someone else, yet they were careful never to implicate any of their co-defendants. The obvious reason for this stems from the fact that all of these defendants were engaged in a common cause and each knows of all the work done by the other.... They always blamed someone who is dead or whose whereabouts is unknown, and remained loyal to their fellow brothers in the SS.

* * *

Most of the defendants' witnesses were former SS men and practically all of them were Nazis. A typical witness was General Karl Wolff...who was head of Himmler's Personal Staff. He testified that he knew most of the defendants personally, that they all were sterling characters, that none of them wanted to work for Himmler but were just victims of circumstances. He further testified that he did not know the SS was killing Jews....

* * *

A common defense in this case has been that what the defendants did was in accordance with German law at that time. Of course, the German laws after 1933 were nothing except the expression of "Hitler's will." When, therefore, a defendant says that what he did cannot be a crime because it was authorized by the German law, he is in effect saying that what he did cannot be considered a crime because Hitler wanted it done.... But this is obviously no defense; Tribunal III in Case No. 3, the Justice Case, gave a correct statement of the law when it said:

"In German legal theory Hitler's law was a shield to those who acted under it, but before a tribunal authorized to enforce international law, Hitler's decrees were a protection neither to the Fuehrer himself nor to his subordinates if in violation of the law of the community of nations."

Another defense of equal invalidity is that certain territories over-run by Germany, for example parts of Poland and Luxembourg and Alsace and Lorraine, were incorporated into the Reich and must be considered as a part of Germany. The burden of this argument is that since these territories were absorbed by the Reich, the laws and customs of war no longer applied and hence no war crimes could have been committed. This contention was disposed of by the International Military Tribunal in the following language:

"A further submission was made that Germany was no longer bound by the rules of land warfare in many of the territories occupied during the war, because Germany had completely subjugated those countries and incorporated them into the German Reich, a fact which gave Germany authority to deal with the occupied countries as though they were part of Germany. In the view of the Tribunal it is unnecessary in this case to decide whether this doctrine of subjugation, dependent as it is upon military conquest, has any application where the subjugation is the result of the crime of aggressive war. The doctrine was never considered to be applicable so long as there was an army in the field attempting to restore the occupied countries to their true owners, and in this case, therefore, the doctrine could not apply to any territories occupied after 1 September 1939...."

* * *

Another contention has been that certain of the incorporated territories were German territories prior to the Treaty of Versailles and that the Germans were therefore justified in treating this territory as German. This defense was rejected by the International Military Tribunal. Whatever one's view may be on the merits of the treaty, there can be no disagreement that it could not be validly abrogated by unilateral action of the German Government and least of all through aggressive war.

* * *

Opinion and Judgment

* * *

When it is considered that the oral and documentary evidence in this case consists of approximately 10,000 pages, it becomes readily apparent that any effort to even summarize the evidence would be impracticable. We shall, in the main, therefore record here our findings. Those interested in the details of evidence must be referred to the record....

Considerable evidence on the part of the defense was adduced to the effect that certain functions, actions and measures taken, were Party matters while others came under the competency of offices of the government. In our opinion this attempted differentiation of spheres of competency makes no difference. In practice the Nazi Party and the Government in Germany under Hitler were one and the same thing. In fact, the law in Germany under date of 1 December 1933 declared the unity the Nazi Party and the German State.

The indictment in this case is framed in three counts. The first and second counts charge the commission of crimes against humanity and war crimes, respectively.

* * *

Judged by any standard of proof, the record in this case clearly establishes crimes against humanity and war crimes, substantially as alleged in the indictment under counts one and two.

The acts and conduct, as set forth in this judgment, and as substantially charged in the indictment, constitute crimes against humanity as defined in Article II (c) of the Control Council Law No. 10, and are violative of international conventions, and particularly Articles 23, 45, 46, 47, 52, 55 and 56 of the Hague Regulations (1907), and are violative of the general principles of criminal law as derived from the criminal laws of all civilized nations and of the internal penal laws of the countries in which such crimes were committed.

The acts and conduct set forth in this judgment, and as substantially alleged in the indictment, also constitute war crimes, as defined in Article II(b) of Control Council Law No. 10, and are violative of international conventions, and particularly of Articles 23, 45, 46, 47, 52, 55 and 56 of the Hague Regulations (1907), and are violative of the general principles of criminal law as derived from the criminal laws of the civilized nations and of the internal penal laws of the countries in which such crimes were committed.

It has been insisted repeatedly by the defendants that numerous activities were not within their sphere of competency but on the contrary some other person or some other organization was charged with the performance of these various tasks. We have given careful consideration to these assertions, and in instances we have determined that certain assertions of this nature were creditable; and in such instances the defendant has not been held responsible for those activities....

* * *

Another defense urged is that, in performing certain functions, the defendants were acting under superior orders. By Control Council Law No. 10 it is expressly provided that superior orders shall not free a defendant from responsibility for crime but this fact may be considered in mitigation of punishment. We have, in passing judgment on all the defendants, given due consideration to this defense as it might affect the punishment of the individual defendants. It is our view in this respect that justice demands a fair consideration of the fact that each and all defendants occupied a subordinate position, being answerable to Himmler, and several of the defendants were even subordinate to other defendants at bar.

Still another defense often asserted is to the effect that if certain events happened, or certain orders or memoranda were issued, the defendants knew nothing of these transactions. Such a defense is of no avail when it appears, as it does in many instances, that the defendant urging such a defense actually issued an order or memorandum, or actually received it, or otherwise had full knowledge, at the time, of the commission of various acts.

It has been urged and argued at length that certain territories, such as the Incorporated Eastern Territories of Poland and parts of Luxembourg, Alsace and Lorraine, were incorporated into the Reich and thereby became a part of Germany during the war. Hence, it is urged, the laws and customs of war are inapplicable to these territories.

Any purported annexation of territories of a foreign nation, occurring during the time of war and while opposing armies were still in the field, we hold to be invalid and ineffective. Such territories never became part of the Reich but merely remained under German military control by virtue of belligerent occupation. Moreover, if it could be said that the attempted incorporation of territories into the Reich had a legal basis, it would avail the defendants nothing, for actions similar to those occurring in the areas attempted to be annexed also occurred in areas which Germany never professed to have incorporated into the Reich.

Count three of the indictment charges all defendants, except the defendant Viermetz, with membership in a criminal organization, namely, the SS. This charge will be dealt with in passing upon the guilt or innocence of the individual defendants.

[The Tribunal then passed judgment and sentence upon all fourteen defendants, respectively, beginning with defendant Ulrich Greifelt and ending with defendant Inge Viermetz. Defendant Viermetz, the only female charged, was acquitted. Of the remaining thirteen, Greifelt was sentenced to life imprisonment, while all others received sentences ranging in duration from twenty-five years to time served. Judge Daniel T. O'Connell concurred in part and dissented in part. Excerpts from his concurrence and dissent appear below].

Concurring and Dissenting Opinion
Judge Daniel T. O'Connell

With all findings of the Tribunal and disposition of indictments as applicable to all defendants, I concur, except in respect to sentences of imprisonment imposed upon the defendants Greifelt [life], Creutz [15 years], Lorenz [20 years], Brueckner [15 years], Hofmann [25 years] and Hildebrandt [25 years]. I dissent from the majority of the Tribunal in the extent of terms of imprisonment as applicable to the aforesaid defendants and for reasons hereafter stated.

It is my reasoned judgment, based upon nineteen years of judicial service, related in large measure to imposition of prison sentences, that in respect to each of the above-named defendants, the sentence imposed is too extreme in fixed duration of time when consideration is given to the character and scope of the duties each performed. Severity of sentence is erroneously believed by many to be a preventive of future crime by others. I do not subscribe to such a belief.

These six defendants, associated with other defendants, some of whom have been found not guilty of the crimes alleged in counts one and two, were essentially employed in civilian capacities. Their duties related almost exclusively to direction, or aiding in direction, of bureaus subordinate to governmental control, springing from the power Himmler exercised as delegated by Hitler, and accompanied with all its ruthlessness as disclosed by the evidence before us.

Their guilt is fixed by the findings heretofore set forth, is entwined with military mandates and superiority of direction. Grave difficulty exists in effecting separation of dominant governmental and military superiority of direction from civilian association and support.

All governments engaging in war, of necessity, must have the aid of civilian bureaus operating under governmental direction, and functioning closely with the armed forces. It is difficult to draw a line fixing to what extent punishment can be inflicted upon those associated with civilian bureaus, also how far down the line of authority in the direction of bureau activities, responsibility is to be fixed in decreeing punishment and the extent of punishment the civilian invites for himself or herself in participating in actual war activities. It is also most difficult to determine to what extent the civilian bureau official joins in spirit, or without definite objection or protest, against acts calculated to further the perpetration of criminal acts.

* * *

...It is, therefore, a warranted judicial conclusion that the sentences imposed upon these civilian officials, even though all enjoyed military titles, awarded as establishing greater and perhaps more effective prestige in executing their civilian duties should be less in severity than as fixed by the majority of the Tribunal.

In no instance as affecting these defendants do I believe a sentence of life imprisonment is warranted; neither is it warranted to fix upon sentences which in duration carry the person to an age which, based upon normal life expectancy, is the equivalent of a life sentence.

I believe, also, sound reasoning in respect to decreeing of imprisonment should include a stated direction that the sentence imposed is to be reduced by subtraction of the period of time covered by imprisonment while awaiting trail.

I concur with the majority of the Tribunal in respect to the sentences imposed upon the defendants [Herbert] Huebner and [Fritz] Schwalm.

(c) Tribunal V
United States of America v. Wilhelm von Leeb, et al.
10 CCL No. 10 Trials 1 (1948)

"The High Command Case"

Members of Military Tribunal V.

John C. Young, Presiding, Formerly Chief Justice of the Supreme Court of the State of Colorado

Winfield B. Hale, Member, Judge of the Court of Appeals of the State of Tennessee

Justin W. Hardin, Member, Formerly District Judge of the First Division, Territory of Alaska

Chief Prosecutor: Mr. Paul Niederman

II. Arraignment

Presiding Judge Young: Military Tribunal V will come to order. The Tribunal will now proceed with the arraignment of the defendants in Case No. 12 pending before this Tribunal.

Dr. [Hans] Laternser (counsel for the defendant von Leeb): If your honors please, I am Dr. Laternser, and I am defense counsel for the defendant von Leeb. I have also been chosen spokesman for the defense. Before this Tribunal proceeds with the arraignment of the defendants, I would like to put a motion for the whole of the defense.

I move that this Tribunal pronounce itself incompetent to try these defendants, and I would like to give my reasons for this motion. All generals who are defendants here were during the last war officers of the German Armed Forces. They were combatants in the meaning of Article I of the Annex to the Hague Convention for Land Warfare, and as such, they were captured by the enemy. According to the Geneva Convention they are consequently entitled to be recognized as prisoners of war. Already during peacetime it was recognized that a soldier is under a special law; soldiers have to be his judges. It is so everywhere, because even in peace the life of a soldier is governed by different conditions compared with the life of an ordinary citizen. Much more so does this apply in war. It is therefore all the more important that actions committed in war by a soldier should be judged by a court consisting of soldiers. The rights of the soldier prisoner of war are governed by the Rules of the Geneva Convention. In accordance with Article 63, sentence on a prisoner of war can only be pronounced by the same courts and according to the same procedure as applied to a member of the state holding the prisoner. It is however, not undisputed whether or not the state holding the prisoner is at all competent to try acts which were committed by the prisoner before he was captured. If one answers this question in the affirmative, irrespective of what reasons, then Article 63 of the Geneva Convention applies to this extent. The range of acts committed during captivity is not a very extensive one. They are mainly questions of disobedience, insubordination towards sentries and superiors, mutiny, etc., but that the Geneva Convention for these offenses provides for trial by a military court will not be disputed even by the prosecution. The legal basis for this provision applies all the more to acts committed in war, which were committed within the sphere of the high military leadership and within OKW. All these are acts, the judgment of which requires special expert knowledge based on personal experience.

Your Honor, this is not only recognized by British courts, which, for instance held the proceedings against Field Marshall Kesselring before a proper military court; the practice of the United States runs along similar lines. Thus recently, in the proceedings against Skorzeny [Otto Skorzeny, Austrian Waffen-SS officer in the *Liebstandarte Adolf Hitler*, German soldier-of-fortune and rescuer of Benito Mussolini from confinement in the Hotel Campo Imperatore in the Appennines, September 13, 1943] before a military tribunal in Dachau, the tribunal consisted of American officers. This conclusively proves that the defendants have the right to a trial before a military court, which according to Article 12 of the Articles of War of the United States, should be a general court martial. This general court martial according to Article 16 of the same rules, has to consist of officers of at least the same rank.

For these reasons, Your Honor, I have put the motion that this Tribunal should pronounce itself not competent to judge these defendants.

Presiding Judge Young: May I inquire if counsel has filed this motion with the Secretary General?

Dr. Laternser: If your Honor please, I have not filed this motion in writing because, on the basis of the Rules of Procedure, that is on the basis of Article II, I am of the opinion that the question of competence will become clear from the proceedings; and for such questions as arise from the proceedings, as I understand the Rules of Procedure, we have the oral pleadings.

If the Tribunal so desires, I shall certainly immediately put this motion in writing. I put this motion this moment, Your Honor, because in the opinion of the defense, the defendants are only obliged to plead before a competent tribunal. If this Tribunal should reach the opinion that it is not competent, this arraignment of the defendants here would then be obviated.

Presiding Judge Young [addressing U.S. Army Lt. General Telford Taylor, Chief Counsel]: General Taylor, have you any comments too make on this motion?

General Taylor: Your Honor, I would like to make three very brief comments. Firstly, as to procedure: This is the type of motion which has invariably been filed in writing under Rule No. 10 of the Uniform Rules. We, of course, have not seen it. I would respectfully suggest that Dr. Laternser should be asked to file a motion in writing; the prosecution will answer it in writing; and the Court can, if it so desires, set it for argument.

Secondly, the question raised in the motion is not novel, as the same point has been made in other proceedings here and has been rejected. I also believe it to be dealt with in the Wehrmacht decision of the Supreme Court, all of which matters we can cover in our answer to the motion.

Thirdly, different charges against officers of the German armed forces in this theater have been a matter of general policy. It is not a matter peculiar to this case in any way. Under general theater policy all officers of the German Armed Forces have been charged, and there is nothing peculiar about the situation of the defendants in that regard.

That is all I have to say.

Presiding Judge Young: Under the circumstances,... counsel representing the defendants will file this motion with the Secretary General,...

The Secretary General will call the roll of the defendants.

[Here, each defendant's name was called and the Court asked each of the defendants how he pleads to the indictment. All plead "not guilty."]

A. Opening Statement of the Prosecution

General Telford Taylor: If it please Your Honors. The prosecution will observe the injunctions of the Court laid down this morning, and as to the matter of expedition, it is our estimate that we can put in the prosecution's case in less than 20 trial days.

Your Honors. This year is the three hundredth since the end of the Thirty Years' War, which once was thought the most destructive in the history of man, and Nuremberg lies among its battlefields; a few miles from here Gustavus Adolphus and Wallenstein fought at the "Alte Feste." These 30 years left much of Germany devastated, and dislocated its economy for decades. But all that misery was the merest trifle compared to the havoc recently wrought in six short years, throughout Europe and the Orient.

The comparison between 1648 and 1948 is not original, and few will openly dispute its cogency. Men at war have ceased to toy with popguns and have taken to hurling thunderbolts, and civilization can no longer afford such mutilation. It was the acute awareness of these truths, forced upon us by the First World War, which has led to the general condemnation of those who willfully launch a war of conquest as criminals in the deepest and most serious sense.

These proceedings at Nuremberg, in which crimes against peace are charged, are vitally important because the principles to be applied here are man's best protection against his capacity for self-destruction. When we say that aggressive war is a crime, we mean it to exactly the extent to which we are prepared to treat it as criminal in a judicial proceeding. No principle deserves to be called such unless men are willing to stake their conscience on its enforcement.

In this proceeding, we ask the Tribunal to test the conduct of men who stood at the top of the German profession of arms. In most countries, arms is one among a number of callings. It is a necessary profession as long as organized force plays an important part in the affairs of men. But it is the true and high purpose of this profession to protect, not to subject. The military art is never to be practiced for its own sake; the death and destruction which the use of arms entails is redeemed and ennobled only when the sword is the guardian and restorer, not the destroyer, of peace.

But in Germany, the military profession was not merely one among many. The German officer was accorded a very unique and exalted role. A century and a half ago the

Frenchman Mirabeau wrote that "Prussia is not a state that possesses an army; it is an army that has conquered a nation." And it is because of the dominant part which military matters have played in the life and thought of Germany ever since the time those words were written, that this twelfth and last case before the Nuremberg Military Tribunals may well prove of greater importance to Germany than any other case heard in this courtroom. In saying this, we by no means, mean to depreciate the significance of the issues at stake in other cases which are being or have been held here. But the evidence here is closely related to one of the strongest currents in German thought, which may be aptly entitled "Arms and the German."

The defendants are charged not only with the unlawful use of war, but also with its abuse. The laws and customs of war, which mitigate its ravages, have never won more than lip loyalty from the German militarists. The German Military Manual openly scoffs at the Hague Convention as being derived from "humanitarian considerations which not infrequently degenerated into sentimentality and flabby emotion." The terrible consequences of this ruthless nihilism are not, even today, fully grasped. Millions of innocent civilians were slaughtered by troops under the command or control of the defendants and their colleagues, not in pursuit of any legitimate military objective, but in furtherance of the basest Nazi racial and social myths. The defendant von Kuechler, for example, as the documents prove, observed Christmas Day in Russia in 1941 by authorizing the killing of 230 incurable invalids in an asylum at Makarevskaya [Markarevskaya] on the basis of the subordinate report which stated that...:

"* * * according to German conception the inmates of the asylum no longer represent objects with lives worth living."

We have said that the military profession was esteemed above all others by many Germans, and the German Officers' Corps included men of great ability and high character. To these men we mean no dishonor in this proceeding. The issues here are far too grave to warrant any tricks of advocacy; the evidence is quite compelling enough and will provide its own eloquence. These members of the German Officers' Corps who have the capacity for clear vision and the courage to face the facts will welcome the opportunity for emergence of truth.

Counts One and Four—The Reichswehr and the Weimar Republic (1919–1933)

In presenting the evidence under count one of the indictment [Crimes Against Peace], the prosecution plans to deal summarily with the years prior to the advent of Hitler. But we must not overlook the fact that most of these defendants were not Nazis in the usual sense of the word, and that they are charged with the commission of crimes, not as Party members, but as military leaders. The moral outlook and purposes which resulted in these crimes were not invented by Hitler, but were developed by the defendants and their predecessors in the German Officers' Corps. Mr. Justice Oliver Wendell Holmes has observed that, in some circumstances, "a page of history is worth a volume of logic." And we believe that the story of the German Army since the First World War, very briefly treated, will do much to illuminate the issues in this case.

The Arms Limitations and the Versailles Treaty

The most fundamental circumstance in Germany's military structure during the Weimar Republic was, of course, the Treaty of Versailles. Under part V of the treaty, the military, naval and air clauses, precise limitations were prescribed for the size and nature of the German Armed Forces, and compliance with these provisions was to be ensured by Inter-Allied Commissions of Control. Such commissions—military, naval and aeronautical—arrived in Germany in September 1919.

The air clauses of the treaty need not detain us long. Military and naval aviation was completely prohibited by providing that "the Armed Forces of Germany must not include any military or naval air forces."

The naval clauses were, of necessity, more elaborate. Like military aircraft, submarines were completely prohibited. As for surface craft, the navy was restricted to six each of battleships and light cruisers, and twelve each of destroyers and torpedo boats. The tonnage of newly-built units was limited: battleships 10,000 tons, light cruisers 6,000 tons; and the rate at which naval units could be replaced was also specified. The personnel of the German Navy was not to exceed 15,000 officers and men.

Most important for our purposes are the military clauses. By Article 160 it was stipulated that, after 31 March 1920, the German Army should not exceed ten divisions—seven infantry and three cavalry divisions—comprising not over 100,000 officers and men, and grouped under not more than two corps headquarters. The so-called "Great German General Staff" was to be dissolved and not "reconstituted in any form" The army was not to be designed for any warlike purpose; it was expressly stated in the treaty that: "The army shall be devoted exclusively to the maintenance of order within the territory, and to the control of the frontiers."

Other provisions were intended to ensure that the "100,000-men Reichswehr" should not be used as a means of training a large reserve. Compulsory military service was abolished. Newly appointed officers had to agree to serve 25 years, and enlisted men for 12 years.

The armaments and munitions limitations were equally important. Tanks and poison gas were prohibited. Precise schedules fixed the maximum amounts of guns and small arms of specified calibers, and stocks of ammunition, which were permitted to be maintained. Within Germany, arms could be manufactured only at certain factories listed by the Allied powers; all other munition plants were to be "closed down."

And, finally, special safeguards were provided by the demilitarization of the Rhineland. In Germany, west of the Rhine and east of the Rhine, to a depth of fifty kilometers, no armed forces were to be maintained or assembled. Forts and field defense works were likewise forbidden within this area.

Organization of the Armed Forces

The organization of the German Armed Forces under the [Weimar] Republic reflected these arms limitation clauses. There was no German Air Force. The army and navy were brought together in a single cabinet ministry, which was pacifically named the Reich Defense Ministry (Reichswehrministerium).

Sovereign authority over the Reichswehr was divided between the President of Germany and the Cabinet, acting through the Chancellor and the Reich Defense Minister. The President was the Supreme Commander of the Armed Forces. But because of the parliamentary form of government, the development and execution of government policies was in the hands of the Cabinet. Therefore all presidential orders pertaining to the armed forces had to be counter-signed by the Reich Chancellor or the Reich Minister of Defense.

* * *

In the field, Germany was divided into seven military districts (Wehrkreise), corresponding to the seven infantry divisions allowed by the treaty.... Again following the treaty limitation of the army to two corps headquarters, the military districts of eastern Germany were grouped under an "Army Group Headquarters" (GruppenKommando) at Berlin, and those in western Germany under a similar headquarters at Kassel. There were also three cavalry divisional headquarters without territorial jurisdiction.

Clandestine Rearmament—Von Seeckt (1920–1926)

Restricted by the treaty provisions described above, the Reichswehr of the Weimar Republic bore little outward resemblance to the mighty army of the Kaiser. But the purpose, the intelligence, and the energy, and the determination to salvage as much as possible from the wreckage, and start to rebuild Germany's military might, were not lacking, either in the army or the navy. They found their most effective focus in the brain of the Chief of the Army Command, General Hans von Seeckt.

There is no occasion now to debate the merits or demerits of the Treaty of Versailles. The important fact here is that, whatever they might say publicly, von Seeckt and the other military leaders of Germany unqualifiedly rejected the treaty, and all their plans were directed to its overthrow. Their immediate purpose, therefore, was to bring about as soon as possible a state of affairs which would permit Germany to recreate her once formidable military engine.

Von Seeckt's plan of campaign to achieve these ends was flexible, but was based upon about half a dozen basic principles. The first of these principles, designed to preserve the army's prestige in the eyes of the German people, was intensive cultivation of the legend that the German Army was not defeated in the First World War....

* * *

Secondly, the traditions of the old imperial army were to be preserved. There was to be no "democratizing" of the new Reichswehr. Prussian concepts of discipline and "honor" persisted, and the prerogatives of the Officers' Corps were safeguarded...the spirit of the Officers' Corps continued to be autocratic; monarchism was tolerated and was not uncommon.

Von Seeckt's third basic principle was that the Reichswehr should hold itself aloof from and above internal party politics in Germany.... Rather than risk the army's prestige in [the] maelstrom of party politics, von Seeckt wisely held the army apart from any party, and discouraged political party activity within the Officers' Corps.

But this is not to say that the army was not a political fact, or that von Seeckt had no political attitude. Quite the contrary; the army was above politics because, in a sense, it dominated them. Sedulously and skillfully, von Seeckt brought about, among the leading politicians of all parties, a feeling that the government was dependent upon the Reichswehr for its protection and to insure its continued existence.... When the more serious threat of reactionary revolution culminated in actual attempts to overthrow the Republic—such as the Kapp Putsch of 1920, and the Hitler-Ludendorff Putsch of 1923—the army again emerged in the role of saviour, despite the fact that military leaders were among the participants.

Fourthly, von Seeckt brought about close relations between the Reichswehr and the Soviet Union's Red Army.... The Treaty of Rapallo, signed by Germany and the Soviet Union in 1922, set the official seal upon the military leaders of the two countries.

Fifthly, von Seeckt saw that the Reichswehr could best compensate for its small size by keeping in the forefront on questions of military technique. The greatest emphasis was put on the improvement of weapons and equipment, and on experience in handling the newer weapons, such as tanks. German officers were sent to Russia to train with the Red Army in the handling of heavy artillery, tanks, and other weapons forbidden to Germany under the Versailles Treaty.

The training of German officers with the Red Army was, indeed, only one of the many ways in which the arms provisions of the treaty were evaded and violated by the Reichswehr. And von Seeckt's sixth and last principle was that the treaty imposed no obligation on the Wehrmacht [the German Armed Forces] to comply with its provisions, and should be violated in every way which would further the rebuilding of Germany's armed might. Contempt for the binding character of treaties was not an invention of Adolf Hitler.

Clandestine Rearmament—von Schleicher (1927–1933)

By the time of von Seeckt's retirement in October 1926, Germany's military and political situation was greatly improved. Hindenburg, the nation's idol, had become President after Ebert's death in 1925. With Hindenburg's support, Gustav Stresemann achieved a measure of political stability within Germany, and abroad; he joined in the Locarno Pact, under which Allied evacuation of the Rhineland began in 1926, and Germany was admitted to the League of Nations.

Within Germany, the prestige of the army had been reestablished. The election to the presidency of Hindenburg—a retired field marshall and, in public estimation, Germany's greatest military hero—strengthened the Reichswehr enormously in a political sense. More practical military advantages accrued from the Locarno Pact; in the course of the Locarno settlement, Stresemann's arguments, that the Inter-Allied Control Commissions should be wound up and withdrawn, prevailed. In January 1927, the last staff members of the commission left Germany, and thereby Allied supervision of compliance with the arms limitation clauses of the treaty came to an end.

New faces appeared in the highest positions at about this time.

* * *

Behind many of these personnel changes, and taking a constantly larger share in guiding the destinies of the Reichswehr, was General Kurt von Schleicher.

* * *

Von Schleicher, as is well known, became the last Chancellor of the Weimar Republic, save only Hitler himself, who destroyed it.

* * *

But if the era of von Schleicher had been one of political vicissitudes, the Reichswehr itself had been further strengthened. Although von Schleicher himself became enmeshed in party politics, the army as a whole did not, but continued in the general lines laid down by Seeckt. In particular, clandestine rearmament in violation of the Versailles Treaty continued with quickened pace, and with the strong moral support of Hindenburg's secret approval.

It was, of course, well understood by all concerned that this secret rearmament was not only a violation of international law, but was also forbidden by Germany's internal law. The legal expert of the Reich Defense Ministry, in an opinion written in January 1927, declared that, "* * * the Peace Treaty of Versailles is also a law of the

Reich, and by reason of this, it is binding on all members of the Reich at home. This commitment ranks superior even to the provisions of the Constitution of the Reich * * *."

* * *

By the time the Weimar Republic was nearing its end, the Reichswehr had ample cause for satisfaction with the progress it had made in rearmament despite the Versailles Treaty. At Christmas time in 1932, Colonel Zengauer, a department chief in the Army Ordinance Office, accompanied the season's greetings to [Gustav] Krupp with the information that, "The department is convinced that, thanks to your active cooperation and valuable advice, our armament development in 1932 has made great progress, which is of great significance to our intent of rearming as a whole."

When this was written, Hitler's appointment as Chancellor was only 5 weeks in the future. Many terrible things were in store for Germany, but it is a mistake to overlook that the Weimar Republic and the Third Reich had numerous common denominators, and that the Reichswehr was the most important link between the two. What the German military leaders accomplished under the Republic was a vitally important part of the process of German rearmament for aggressive war....

[Here follows a lengthy overview of the Wehrmacht and the Third Reich from 1933 to 1938. The prosecution presents a detailed historical tapestry about the Nazi regime and the generally willing accommodation accorded it by the leaders of the German military. The Austrian, Czechoslovakian and Sudentenland crises are discussed as well as the infamous Munich conference between Hitler and British Prime Minister Neville Chamberlain. Chief Prosecutor McHaney then details the top secret plans of the Wehrmacht high command for the unprovoked assault on Poland which initiated the Second World War, thence on to the German invasion of Norway, Denmark, the Low Countries and France. Lastly, McHaney briefly reviews the German offensive in the East against Soviet Russia in the summer of 1941. Prosecutor Eugene H. Dobbs then proceeds to address the Tribunal with Opening Statements regarding Counts Two and Three, namely, war crimes and crimes against humanity].

Mr. Dobbs: We now turn to the war crimes and crimes against humanity in which all the defendants participated in the course of waging wars of aggression. Under count two of the indictment [war crimes], the defendants are charged with the commission of crimes against enemy belligerents and prisoners of war, while count three [crimes against humanity] charges them with crimes against civilians of countries overrun by the Wehrmacht.

Every war involves killing. Any war means death, and pain, and grief. For centuries the civilized nations of the world have attempted to reduce the death and suffering by observing the laws and usages of war. By international conventions and agreements, such as the Hague and Geneva Conventions, and by general custom, certain practices are internationally regarded as cruel, inhumane, and criminal. Such barbarities include the killing of surrendered belligerents, the refusal of quarter, and torture or other ill-treatment of belligerents or inhabitants of occupied countries. Such acts are crimes and, if they result in death, are murders.

It will be said that in time of war some such crimes must occur in every army. That, undoubtedly, is true. But as Justice Jackson has said, "It is not because they yielded to the normal frailties of human beings that we accuse them. It is their abnormal and inhuman conduct which brings them to this bar." The prosecution will not present isolated cases of spontaneous brutality by German soldiers. Instead, it will portray a deliberate policy—emanating from the highest levels of the Wehrmacht—of murder and ill-treatment of civilians and prisoners of war, applied in every theater of war and by all of these defendants. This policy is rooted in the contemptuous and scornful attitude toward the law of war which has characterized the German Officers' Corps for decades past. At the very outset we mentioned the scoffing attitude toward the Hague Conventions expressed in the German military manual; on this matter, a distinguished American commentator [J. W. Garner] has written:

> "One can scarcely determine from a reading of the German manual whether the rules of the Hague Convention were ever intended to bind belligerents in the conduct of war. In fact, they are rarely mentioned, and when they are referred to it is usually in derision. A good many of its rules are clearly in conflict with the Convention, and various regulations annexed to the Convention are cynically dismissed with the statement that they are excessively humane, or that they are good in theory but will never be observed by belligerents in practice, etc. The fact is, the General Staff does not look with favor upon the movement to reduce the law of war to written form, for the reason that the effect would be to limit the arbitrary powers of military commanders and thus to put an obstacle in the way of military success."

The First World War accomplished nothing in the way of changing the attitude of the German Officers' Corps toward the laws of war. A most revealing memorandum from the files of the Reich Defense Ministry, written in September 1924, by Lieutenant Colonel Otto von Stuelpnagel, embodies his suggestions as to what attitude the Wehrmacht should take toward a revision of the Hague rules, in the event of a new Hague Conference. After conceding grudgingly that it would be wise to participate in such a conference, inasmuch as "refusal to accept an invitation * * * would only be used to Germany's detriment for propaganda purposes by our ex-enemy nations, and would again be misrepresented as malicious intentions on the part of Germany," the author stated that "the first basic question to be answered is: What attitude should the German delegation take at a new Hague Conference?" In view of the small size of the German Forces at that time and the restrictions of the Versailles Treaty, the writer thought that the answer to this question depended upon whether "the possibility of a struggle for liberation exists in the not too distant future." His memorandum continued:

> "*Can we, in consideration of the present political situation, at all afford to advocate a ruthless use of force?* Is this not likely to result in another hate-campaign against Germany, in new and more intensive measures of control and a closer coordination of our enemy nations? The ex-enemy powers, quite aware of their present military superiority, will undoubtedly advocate a strictly regulated conduct of war and lay the greatest stress upon observance of all laws of humanity."

The evidence under counts two and three will abundantly demonstrate the poisonous effect of these views on German methods of warfare during the Second World War, and especially their shocking and disastrous impact upon the civilian populations of countries occupied by Germany. For the most part, those criminal policies were embodied in orders and directives framed at the very top level of the Wehrmacht, usually with direct participation by Warlimont and Lehmann, and, within his fields of work, of Reinecke also. These orders were distributed through regular military channels to the highest field commanders, including all of the other defendants in this case, and were by them passed down to the lower formations, where the orders were actually carried out.

In outlining the charges under counts two and three, it will be most convenient to deal first with the criminal orders and directives which were chiefly intended for the conduct of the war and the German military occupation in western and southern Europe, and secondly with those which were especially connected with the war against the Soviet Union. In all theaters of war, of course, these criminal orders and the crimes which resulted therefrom, sprang from the same disregard for the laws of war and the dictates of humanity. Likewise, numerous types of war crimes and crimes against humanity were common in all theaters. Nevertheless, there were certain significant distinctions, arising chiefly out of differences in the technique of warfare in the West as compared to the East, and out of the different occupational tactics which the Germans chose to apply among the various occupied countries.

Finally, after sketching the chief categories of crimes in the West and in the East, we will outline the Wehrmacht's participation in the German slave labor program, which was a malignant common denominator of German occupation policy in all countries.

War Crimes and Crimes Against Humanity Committed in Western and Southern Europe

Under count two of the indictment, the principal charge of war crimes committed in western and southern Europe relates to the so-called "Commando," and "Terror Flier" orders. Under count three of the indictment, we will be chiefly concerned with criminal measures taken by the German Army in the occupied countries, involving the execution of hundreds of thousands of hostages, and the secret deportation and execution of many others under the notorious "Night and Fog Degree" [Nacht und Nebel Erlass].

In the autumn of 1942, the Nazis were still at the climax of their power and the Allies in the initial stage of their preparations for the invasion which was to follow two years later. In August of that year British and Canadian "commandos" raided Dieppe [a seaport in northern France on the English Channel]. It was the first time since Dunkirk that Allied Forces had crossed the channel in strength to probe the German fortifications in the west, as a first rehearsal for the still distant invasion of "Fortress Europe."

In the following months, small groups of Allied soldiers dressed in uniform and carrying weapons openly—so-called "Commando" units—were landed on the continent, mainly in France and Norway, to accomplish special combat missions which consisted predominantly in the destruction of highly important military installations. The Wehrmacht's answer to these legitimate acts of warfare was the notorious "Commando Order," which directed the summary execution of captured commando troops, even if fully uniformed. When the defendant Warlimont came to his office at the OKW on 8 October 1942, he found on his desk Hitler's directive for the drafting of the "Commando Order," together with the text of the official German radio announcements of 7 October 1942, which read as follows…:

> "All terror and sabotage troops of the British and their accomplices who do not act like soldiers but like bandits have in future to be treated as such by the German troops, and they must be slaughtered ruthlessly in combat wherever they turn up."

Immediately after receipt of the text of the radio announcement, Warlimont gave the following instructions with respect to its enforcement:

> "1. Transposition into order-form.

> "2. * * * this order too, must—in accordance with the legal department and counterintelligence—be very carefully considered and correctly worded. Dis-

tribution only as far as the armies, from there only orally. To be destroyed after reading * * *."

By 9 October, the defendant Lehmann had completed a draft of the order, which was transmitted by Warlimont to the OKW Intelligence Department under Admiral Canaris for his comments. Canaris voiced strong objection; his words deserved to be quoted because they show not only that the utter illegality of the Commando Order was well known to those who prepared and executed it, but also that some of Hitler's military leaders dared to voice their opposition when they were so minded. In a memorandum received by Warlimont, Lehmann and Reinecke, Canaris stated:

"* * * Sabotage units in uniform are soldiers and have the right to be treated as prisoners of war * * *. Reprisals on prisoners of war, according to the agreement ratified in 1934, are absolutely not permitted."

This respect for international law was not unique to Canaris in the days when the Germans were themselves making widespread use of paratroops for sabotage purposes. As early as June 1938, the defendant Sperrle had stated in a plan for the employment of his Air Fleet 3 against France, in case of her intervention against the seizure of Czechoslovakia, that...:

"It is intended to use parachute sabotage troops * * * for the purpose of destroying suitable targets, against which bombing raids cannot guarantee decisive success."

And in June 1940, the OKH advised all army groups that...:

"German parachutists are elements *of the German Armed Forces* ('Regular Troops'). They are legal combatants and they carry out justified acts of warfare. Where they are committed (whether at the front, or behind the enemy lines, or in the rear) does not affect their quality as combatants. Their position as justified by martial law remains unchanged * * *."

But the accepted German view underwent a marked reversal when the shoe was on the other foot. Lehmann put forward the following pseudo-legal justification as an excuse for murdering commandos:

"Whoever performs acts of sabotage as a soldier, with the idea in mind to surrender without a fight after the act is successfully completed, does not conduct himself as an honorable warrior. He *misuses* the rights of article 23c, Hague Convention, since such methods of warfare had not been thought of at the time this article was formulated."

On 17 October 1942, Jodl submitted the final draft of the "Commando Order," prepared by Warlimont and Lehmann, to Hitler, and on the following day it was issued, starting in part...:

From now on all enemies on so-called commando missions in Europe or Africa challenged by German troops, even if they are to all appearances soldiers in uniform or demolition troops, whether armed, in battle, or in flight, are to be slaughtered to the last man. It does not make any difference whether they are landed from ships or airplanes for the actions, or whether they are dropped by parachute. Even if these individuals, when found, should apparently be prepared to give themselves up, no pardon is to be granted them on principle * * *.

"If individual members of such commandos, such as agents, saboteurs, etc., fall into the hands of the armed forces by some other means, through the police in occupied territories, for instance, they are to be handed over immediately to the Security Service * * *."

Because commando operations were most prevalent in the western and southern theaters of war, it was in those theaters that the order was of most importance. It was, however, distributed by the OKH to all three branches of the service—army, navy and air force—and to all theaters under the OKH, including Norway, Africa, the Balkans, the Mediterranean, France, and the Low Countries. It was passed to Himmler's SS and Police Force, and the OKH sent the order down to all army groups and armies in the East. Each and every defendant in the dock—except Leeb, who had retired some months earlier—was familiar with the Commando Order, and each of them, like every other German officer, knew perfectly well that it required the commission of murder. Pursuant to this order, British and Norwegian commandos were executed in Norway in 1942 and 1943, American commandos were shot in Italy in 1944, and other Allied soldiers were murdered in these countries and elsewhere.

The first executions of captured commandos occurred not more than a fortnight after the order was issued. On 21 November 1942, Warlimont received the following report from Air Fleet 5 in Norway:

"Following supplementary report is made about landing of a British freight glider at Hegers in the night of November 11:

'a. No firing on the part of German defense.

'b. The towing plane (Wellington) has crashed after touching the ground, 7-man crew dead. The attached freight glider also crashed, of the 17-man crew, 14 alive. Indisputably a sabotage force. Fuehrer order has been carried out,'"

And so the reports came in—British, American, French, Norwegian, Greek commandos, slaughtered in battle, slaughtered in captivity; the laconic reports tell a story of foul murder. A telegram signed by Warlimont to the Commander in Chief Southeast directed...:

"* * * The English radio operator Carpenter and the Greek sailor Lisgaris, captured at Alimnia, are no longer needed and are released for special treatment, according to Fuehrer order."

"Special treatment" is a German euphemism for murder; another is "dealt with."

* * *

On 22 June 1944, Warlimont gave an enlightening explanation of the "German concept of usage and customs of warfare" in a memorandum to the legal department under Lehmann...:

"The Fuehrer order is to be applied even if the enemy employs only *one* person for a task. Therefore, it does not make any difference if several persons or a single person take part in a commando operation. The reason for the special treatment of participants in a commando operation is that such operations do not correspond to the German concept of usage and customs of warfare."

Nor did the murder of Allied commandos cease with the invasion of France by Anglo-American forces on 22 June 1944. On 23 June, Rundstedt requested OKW to clarify the applicability of the order in view of the large-scale landing. In a reply the following day, Warlimont directed that the Commando Order should be enforced against all paratroopers found outside of the immediate combat zone. Daily reports of the number "liquidated" were also required. The order was sent through military channels on 29 June to the defendant Blaskowitz, then Commander in Chief of Army Group G in southern France. He in turn passed the order down to units subordinated to him, including the First Army, whence it reached the LXXX Corps under the First Army. The order passed down by Blaskowitz explicitly required all executions of commandos to be reported through army channels. A few days later, on 3 July 1944, thirty odd British and American commandos were captured by troops of the LXXX Corps and summarily executed.

When any Allied method of warfare started to prove effective against the Wehrmacht, the usual first reaction of its leaders was to declare such methods of warfare criminal and threatened with death the enemy troops engaged therein. A year after the successful commando raids aroused the German wrath, the growing strength of the Allied Air Forces began to be acutely felt. In view of the wondrous shortness of the German memory, we will do well to remind ourselves that in the field of aerial attacks against enemy cities, the Allies were imitators, not originators; Warsaw, Rotterdam, London and other cities were flattened or badly scarred long before any German city suffered severely. Nonetheless, by the fall of 1943 Allied attacks in Germany aroused indignant screeches from Goebbels and Himmler. The former used the press and other means to incite the German civilian population to lynch American and British fliers who had been forced to parachute from disabled planes over Germany, and Himmler directed the German police not to protect Allied fliers from these lynching bees.

As was often the case, the German soldier was more chivalrous when acting on his own initiative than when following the orders of his highest superiors. On several occasions Wehrmacht troops protected Allied fliers from civilian attacks, as indeed the laws of war required, for the airmen were unarmed, endeavored to surrender, and were entitled to the status of prisoners of war.

Such soldierly conduct could not be tolerated by OKW; on 9 July 1944, an order prepared by Warlimont's section was issued by OKW which directed that Wehrmacht troops should not protect so-called Anglo-American "terror flyers" against action by the civilian population....

* * *

This order, together with a similar order by Hitler and murderous incitement by Goebbels through the press, led to the slaughter of numerous Allied airmen in flagrant violation of the rules of war.

Civilians — "Night and Fog" Decree

Mr. Barbour: The Wehrmacht's policies and practices in governing the occupied countries were characterized by a blind and unimaginative faith in the use of ruthless force and methods of intimidation and terrorism. This policy was not only brutal and criminal; it was senseless and bound to end in failure. Catastrophe was the price that the leaders of the Third Reich had to pay for their arrogant disregard of law and for their failure to realize that in the end stupid violence is a weapon which recoils upon its user. The so-called "Night and Fog' (Nacht und Nebel) Decree was the foundation of a system which embodied these principles to perfection. It was the means through which the Wehrmacht sought to "pacify" the countries of western Europe. The IMT found in connection with this decree, that "The evidence is quite overwhelming of a systematic rule of violence, brutality, and terror." The circumstances surrounding the issuance and enforcement of the Night and Fog Decree were the subject of extensive testimony before Military Tribunal No. III in Case No. 3 [*United States v. Alstoetter et al. (The Justice Case)*].

That Tribunal stated, in its judgment:

"The Night and Fog Decree (Nacht und Nebel Erlass) arose as the plan or scheme of Hitler to combat so-called resistance movements in occupied territories. Its enforcement brought about a systematic rule of violence, brutality, outrage and terror against the civilian populations of territories overrun and occupied by the Nazi armed forces...."* * * civilians of occupied territories accused of alleged crimes in resistance activities against German occupying forces were spirited away for secret trial by special courts of the ministry of Justice within the Reich; that the victim's whereabouts, trial and subsequent disposition were kept completely secret, thus serving the dual purpose of terrorizing the victim's relatives and associates, and barring recourse to evidence, witnesses, or counsel for defense. If the accused were acquitted or if convicted, after serving his sentence, he was handed over to the Gestapo for 'protective custody' for the duration of the war. These proceedings resulted in the torture, ill-treatment and murder of thousands of persons."

On 12 December 1941, the OKW, through Keitel, issued the Night and Fog Decree, which had been prepared by the defendant Lehmann in the OKW Legal Department.... It provided in part as follows:

"I. In case of criminal acts committed by non-German civilians and which are directed against the Reich or the occupation power, endangering their safety or striking power, the death penalty is applicable in principle.

"II. Criminal acts described in paragraph I will, in principle, be tried in the occupied territories only when it appears probable that death sentences are going to be passed against the offenders, or at least the main offenders, and if the trial and the execution of the death sentence can be carried out without delay. In other cases the offenders, or at least the main offenders, are to be taken to Germany.

In a covering letter, also written by the OKW Legal Department, the purpose of the decree was given:

"Efficient and enduring intimidation can only be achieved, either by capital punishment or by measures by which the relatives of the criminal and the population do not know the fate of the criminal. The aim is achieved when the criminal is transferred to Germany."

A copy of this order, which was made effective in France, Holland, Norway, Bohemia and Moravia and the Ukraine was received by the defendants Warlimont and Reinecke.

* * *

Civilians — Hostages and Reprisals

We have seen in the previous section the criminal measures devised by the Wehrmacht for the imprisonment, deportation, or execution, without trial or with only the form of a trial, of persons suspected of hostile action against the German authorities. The other principal method adopted by the German occupational authorities was equally savage and senseless; it consisted in the indiscriminate murder of many thousands of innocent civilians — murder committed under the pretext of calling such persons "hostages" — in the absurd belief that the civilian population would be "pacified" by such measures. In fact, as could have been foreseen, such wholesale executions served rather to arouse and enrage the inhabitants, who thus saw thousands of their friends and relatives executed even though they had not lifted a finger against the occupying authorities.

While terroristic measures of this kind were not confined to any particular occupied country, they were applied with particular severity in western Europe and in the Balkans. Particularly in Greece and Yugoslavia, fantastically high execution ratios— ranging up to the execution of one hundred hostages for the killing of one German— were applied. During the fall of 1941, such ratios were adopted as standard German Army policy. On 16 September 1941, an OKW order, prepared in Warlimont's department and initiated by him, called attention to disturbances which had occurred in the occupied countries and stated...:

> "a. It should be inferred in every case of resistance to the German occupying forces, no matter what the individual circumstances, that it is of Communist origin.

> "b. In order to nip these machinations in the bud, the most drastic measures should be taken immediately on the first indication, so that the authority of the occupying forces may be maintained and further spreading prevented. In this connection it should be remembered that a human life in the countries concerned frequently counts for nothing, and a deterrent effect can be attained only by unusual severity. The death penalty for 50–100 Communists should generally be regarded in these cases as suitable atonement for one German soldier's death. The way in which sentence is carried out should still further increase the deterrent effect."

While this order laid great stress on Communist responsibility for these uprisings, it was by no means intended that the hostages executed should in all cases be Communists. Quite the contrary.

* * *

The execution of hostages in Greece and Yugoslavia is one of the major charges against the defendants in Case No. 7, (*United States v. Wilhelm List et al.*) [*The Hostages Case*] now pending before Military Tribunal V. In the present case we will present evidence of similar crimes in other occupied countries, including France. For example, during July and August 1944, numerous hostages were executed in the area of Army Group G, commanded by the defendant Blaskowitz. A month earlier, despite the fact that units of the French resistance forces fulfilled all the conditions for recognition as properly constituted armed forces, and had been proclaimed part of the Allied forces, Blaskowitz issued to his subordinate units an order that "members of the French resistance movement are to be treated as guerrillas." That of course, meant immediate execution upon capture.

War Crimes and Crimes Against Humanity Committed in Eastern Europe

In turning from the western to the eastern theater of war, we will find nothing to mitigate the black criminality of the Commando Order and the Night and Fog Decree. Quite on the contrary. In western and southern Europe, the Wehrmacht was at least anxious to keep up the appearance of compliance with the laws and customs of war. But during the warfare in the East, the leaders of the Wehrmacht were totally uninhibited by consideration of law and humanity. Hitler and the generals laid their plans for the war against Russia on the basic assumption that every Slav is subhuman, and every Jew is subhuman and criminal as well. The Russians, therefore, were to be treated like beasts, and the Jews were to be killed like dangerous beasts. Orders and directives in line with these malignant views and policies were prepared by the military leaders, and distributed throughout the Wehrmacht. In the formulation and enforcement of these orders the German warlords sank far below the imagined qualities of the peoples they affected to despise and brutalized the German soldiers who trusted their leadership. Germany's treatment of the Jews of Europe and the Slavs of eastern Europe is the blackest page in the history of European civilization.

The murderous measures laid down within the German Army, in advance of the attack on Russia, were directed both at the soldiers of the Soviet Army and at the Russian civilian population. Attached to the combat units of the Russian Army were special officers who can best be described as "political commissars"; they represented the Communist Party and were responsible for the political indoctrination and morale of the Russian troops. However, they were not just pep talk boys; they were part of the Russian Army, wore its uniform, carried arms openly, and fought with conspicuous courage as part of the army at the front. But by express order of the German military leaders, laid down at highest level, these soldiers were not to be taken prisoner under any circumstances, but, like the commando units on the western front, were to be slaughtered to the last man.

Within the Russian territory overrun by the Wehrmacht, all the safeguards required by the laws of war for the maintenance of order and the protection of the civilian population were done away with. German troops were encouraged and, indeed, ordered to practice the utmost brutality in dealing with the Russian population. Except under very limited circumstances, no German soldier was to be punished for excesses against the civilian population. As if this were not enough, very special measures were taken to make sure that all Jews and all political officials of any importance, would be hunted down and murdered as soon as possible. For this purpose, special SS and Police forces were organized, furnished and instructed by Himmler. These gangs were to move into Russia with the German Army, and, with the full administrative support of the army, were to carry out their murderous mission.

The horrible purposes which we have just described were discussed between Hitler and the leading generals more than 3 months before the attack in the East was launched. On 17 March 1941, at a conference in which Hitler and the Chief of the Army General Staff, General Halder, participated, Hitler stated…"

> "* * * The intelligentsia working for Stalin must be exterminated. The hierarchy of the Russian Empire must be crushed. Maximum brutality must be applied throughout the Russian area. The ideological ties of the Russian peoples are not strong enough. They will break with the elimination of the functionaries."

* * *

For these manifold crimes in western and Eastern Europe all the defendants bear responsibility except Sperrle and Blaskowitz, who were never involved in the Russian campaign. The defendant Schniewind was relieved as Chief of Staff of the Naval War Staff (6 June 1941) just before the attack was launched, but prior to his transfer participated actively in the planning of the campaign against the Soviet Union, was present at conferences at which these criminal policies were discussed, and received, and distributed to naval units certain of the criminal orders mentioned above. The defendants Warlimont, Lehmann, and Reinecke, as leading officers of the OKW, were heavily involved in the formulation and distribution of these orders.

The remaining eight defendants were all high-ranking field commanders during the Russian campaign; they received these orders from the OKW and the OKH, and passed them down to their subordinate units, and the orders were executed by troops under their command. The defendant Leeb was Commander in Chief of Army Group North until January 1942, when he retired from active service at the age of 65. The defendant Kuechler, Commander in Chief of the Eighteenth Army at the outset of the campaign, succeeded Leeb as commander in chief of the army group. The defendant Hoth, who led a Panzer group into Russia, was promoted to the command of the Seventeenth Army in Rundstedt's Army Group South in October 1941, and in May 1942 was transferred to the command of the Fourth Panzer Army. The defendant Reinhardt, at first a corps commander, succeeded to the command of Hoth's Armored Group, which was later designated as the Third Panzer Army. Reinhardt was made a full general in 1942, and became the Commander in Chief of Army Group Center in August 1944. The defendant Salmuth was also promoted from corps to army command, and became a full general in 1943. From June 1942 to August 1943, he commanded successively the Seventeenth, the Fourth, and the Second Armies on the Eastern Front; from August 1943 to August 1944, he commanded the Fifteenth Army in France. The defendant Hollidt, who led the 50th Infantry Division into southern Russia, rose rapidly to corps command in January 1942, and became Commander in Chief of the Sixth Army in March, 1943; in that same year he, too, became a full general. The defendant von Roques remained an army group rear area commander until December 1942, when he went back into retirement. The defendant Woehler served as Chief of Staff of the Eleventh Army—first under von Schobert and later under von Manstein—until February 1943. After a brief period of service as Chief of Staff of Army Group Center, and as a corps commander, he was promoted to the rank of lieutenant general and made Commander in Chief of the Eighth Army in southern Russia in August 1943, and in December 1944, became the Commander in Chief of Army Group South.

The "Commissar Order"

On 8 June 1941, two weeks before Russia was attacked, Field Marshall von Brauchitsch, Commander in Chief of the German Army, issued an order, entitled, "Directives for the Treatment of Political Commissars," to the commanders of the army groups and armies then deployed along the Russian border awaiting the word to attack. This order read in part as follows...

"When fighting bolshevism one cannot count on the enemy acting in accordance with principles of humanity or international law. In particular it must be expected that the treatment of our prisoners by the political commissars of all types, who are the true pillars of resistance, will be cruel, inhuman and dedicated to hate.

"The troops must realize— "(1) That in this fight it is wrong to treat such elements with clemency and consideration in accordance with international law. They are a menace to our own safety and to the rapid pacification of the conquered territories.

"(2) That the originators of the Asiatic barbaric methods of fighting are the political commissars. They must be dealt with promptly and with the utmost severity.

"Therefore, if taken while fighting, or offering resistance, they must, on principle, be shot immediately.

"For the rest, the following instructions will apply:... "2. Political commissars in their capacity of officials attached to the enemy troops are recognizable by their special insignia—red star with an inwoven golden hammer and sickle on the sleeves * * *. They are to be segregated at once, i. e., while still on the battlefield, from the prisoners of war. This is necessary in order to deprive them of any possibility of influencing the captured soldiers. These commissars will not be recognized as soldiers; the protection granted to prisoners of war in accordance with international law will not apply to them. After having been segregated they are to be dealt with."

If there were no other proof to be offered in this proceeding except that concerning the issuance and execution of this one order, it would still more than justify the presence in this dock of every defendant except Sperrle, Blaskowitz, and Schniewind. The Commissar Order was formulated by the defendants Lehmann and Warlimont; issued by Warlimont to 19 different offices of the Wehrmacht, including the OKH; distributed by the OKH to the defendants Leeb, Kuechler, Hoth, and Woehler; passed on to Reinhardt, Salmuth, Hollidt, and Roques; and executed by units subordinated to them. Reinecke saw to its enforcement in the prisoner of war camps under his jurisdiction.

The Commissar Order was not the exclusive achievement of any one man. On 6 May 1941, the OKH forwarded to Warlimont a proposed draft of an order for the treatment of commissars. Warlimont submitted this draft to the defendant Lehmann in the Legal Department of the OKW. Lehmann approved the draft with minor changes and returned it to Warlimont the next day. On 12 May, Warlimont submitted the draft, as approved by the Legal Department, to Jodl together with a memorandum in which he stated...:

"* * * Military functionaries (commissars) are to be dealt with according to proposal OKH. They are not recognized as prisoners of war and are to be liquidated at the latest in the transient prisoner of war camps, and under no circumstances to be removed to the rear area."

On 6 June, Warlimont issued the order to the supreme commanders of the army, navy and air force, with instructions that it was to be distributed in writing to army and air fleet commanders and orally to lower commands. Two days later Brauchitsch passed down the order with the amendment that, "Political commissars attached to the troops should be segregated and dealt with by order of an officer, inconspicuously and outside the battle zone proper." From army group to army, army to corps, corps to division, division to regiment—down went this order for murder until it was well known over the entire eastern front.

* * *

Whatever...defendants may conjure up in their defense they can never honestly say that they did not know that this criminal order was being executed by units subordinated to them.

* * *

Belligerents and Prisoners of War—Murder and Ill-Treatment Generally

As we have just seen, the murder of commissars, who were uniformed members of the Red Army, was the task of the German combat troops. The fate in store for commissars was soon noised about in the Red Army, and naturally some of the prospective victims went to some pains to conceal their identity from the Germans in the event of capture. General Halder noted in his useful diary on 1 August 1941, with respect to the "treatment of captured commissars," that they were, "for the most part identified only in prisoner of war camps." This possibility the Wehrmacht had anticipated. The defendant Reinecke, as chief of the OKW department with jurisdiction over prisoner of war matters, entered into an agreement with the notorious Reinhard Heydrich, chief of the Security Police and Himmler's right hand man. This agreement covered not only the apprehension of commissars, but also the weeding out from Russian prisoners of certain type categories regarded as "subversive," which was to be accomplished by the special SS gangs called, "Einsatzgruppen."

* * *

The agreement further provided that "suspects" and "intolerable elements" among the prisoners should be segregated by the Einsatzkommandos and surrendered to them by the camp officials. The fate of the prisoners selected is made all too clear by Heydrich's instructions that:

> "Executions must not be carried out in or near the camp. If the camps are in the Government General [of Poland] close to the frontier, prisoners are to be moved to former Soviet territory, if possible, for special treatment."

* * *

This order, like the "Commando Order," was reviewed by Admiral Canaris. In this case, too, Canaris' opinion that the order was a flagrant violation of international law was clearly given:

> "The Geneva Convention for the treatment of prisoners of war is not binding in the relationship between Germany and the U.S.S.R. Therefore only the principles of general international law on the treatment of prisoners of war apply. Since the 18th century these have gradually been established along the lines that war captivity is neither revenge nor punishment, but solely protective custody, the only purpose of which is to prevent the prisoners of war from further participation in the war. This principle was developed in accordance with the view held by all armies that it is contrary to military tradition to kill or injure helpless people * * *. The decrees for the treatment of Soviet prisoners of war enclosed are based on a fundamentally different viewpoint."

The order just quoted, played an important part in the IMT's conviction of General Keitel, who noted on Canaris' memorandum of protest, "These objections arise from the military concept of chivalrous warfare. This is the destruction of an ideology. Therefore, I approve and back the measure."

Such orders as these inevitably resulted in cruelty and inhumanity on a wide scale. As the IMT stated in its judgment: "The treatment of Soviet prisoners of war was characterized by particular inhumanity. * * * It was the result of systematic plans to murder." These "systematic plans" were embodied in orders from the OKW, prepared by Warlimont and Lehmann; orders for the transfer of prisoners to concentration camps, signed by Reiecke; OKH orders, distributed by field commanders, for the shooting of Russian soldiers in uniform on the pretext that they were "guerrillas"; orders for the killing of escaped prisoners upon recapture, a flagrant violation of the usages of war; and the other similar directives.

* * *

Civilian—Murder and Ill-Treatment Generally

Mr. McHaney: As we mentioned earlier, the Germans had very far-reaching economic and political designs with respect to the Russian territories overrun by the

Wehrmacht. In order to exploit these areas for the benefit of Germany, it was planned to "pacify" and crush all opposition, to obliterate the Soviet political system and set up new regional political administrations, and to convert the productive resources of the land to the uses of the Third Reich.

* * *

Within the limits of available time, we can only sketch the outlines of this criminal structure. The basic order was issued by the OKW some five weeks before the invasion, on 15 May 1941, to the commanders in chief of the army, navy and air force. This order, in unmistakable terms, legalized the murder of Russian civilians by German troops. It accomplished this in two ways. Firstly, for the punishment of Russian civilians suspected of unfriendly acts, the order substituted summary execution by the troops for action by military courts.

* * *

The second part of the order was even more vicious; it guaranteed German soldiers against any fear of punishment for crimes committed against the civilian population, unless such crimes were likely to undermine the discipline of the army.

* * *

Warlimont and Lehmann were in a unique position to know the purpose of this order—the so-called "Barbarossa Jurisdiction Order"—inasmuch as they formulated it. Drafts of the order were prepared by them and the OKW as early as April 1941. These drafts were discussed (as his diary shows) with the Chief of the Army General Staff, General Halder, on 6 May; it appears that Halder wished to preserve the jurisdiction of the military courts over minor offenses. [That request was granted by OKW. The prosecution then goes into a detailed discussion of the persecution of the Jews in Soviet territory and the slave labor apparatus, all under the umbrella of protection provided by the Wehrmacht].

* * *

General Taylor: If it please your Honors. The wide scope of the subject matter of this case has made it quite impossible to set forth the evidence in any detail within the compass of this presentation. We have sought only to outline the charges, and the same limitation of time and space rule out any full analysis of the legal matters which the defense will, no doubt suggest in due course.

* * *

It is perfectly legal for military men to prepare military plans to meet national contingencies, and such plans may legally be drawn whether they are offensive or defensive in a military sense. It is perfectly legal for military leaders to carry out such plans and engage in war, if in doing so they do not plan and launch and wage illegal aggressive wars. There may well be individual cases where drawing the line between legal and illegal behavior might involve some difficulties.... But we do not believe that there is any such doubt or difficulty here.

The military defendants will undoubtedly argue that they are pure technicians. This amounts to saying that military men are a race apart from and different from the ordinary run of human beings—men above and beyond the moral and legal requirements that apply to others, and incapable of exercising moral judgment on their own behalf.

In the nature of things, planning and executing aggressive war in accomplished by agreements and consultation among all types of a nation's leaders. And if the leaders in any notably important field of activity stand aside, or resist, or fail to cooperate, then the criminal program will at the very least be seriously obstructed. That is why the principal leaders in all fields of activity share responsibility for the crime, and military leaders no less than the others. As the IMT stated in its judgment:

> "Hitler could not make aggressive war by himself. He had to have co-operation of statesmen, military leaders, diplomats, and business men. When they, with knowledge of his aims, gave him their cooperation, they made themselves parties to the plan he had initiated."

* * *

The question here is not one of personal likes and dislikes, but of acts. If these defendants and their fellows did not give Hitler their trust, they certainly lent him their active and energetic collaboration and put their talents at his disposal. They swore an oath of loyalty to his person. They built him a gigantic war machine. Under his political leadership, they provided the military leadership which guided this machine on its course of conquest in Europe. They used the machine to perpetrate the most catastrophic crimes in modern history of the profession of arms.

* * *

And therefore, shocking and incredible as is the evidence in this case, there is nothing herein that should come as a complete surprise to any one who understands the history and ideology of the German Officers' Corps. Men who believe in war are not likely to take a strong stand in opposition to invading the neutrality of Belgium, Holland, or Norway. An Officers' Corps whose military manual scoffs openly at the laws of war is not likely to take a strong stand in opposition to even the most outrageous criminal measures called for by their leaders. A profession which for decades has rigorously excluded Jews, has already made progress towards understanding the reasons for their eradication. No matter how much they may throw up their hands in feigned horror, they will not be found ready to risk much in opposition; nor, even, will they be unwilling to lend it support, if what they conceive to be "larger objections" so require.

* * *

...And so it comes to pass that the only way in which the behavior of the German troops in the recent war can be made comprehensible as the behavior of human beings, is by a full exposure of the criminal doctrines and orders which were pressed upon them from above, by these defendants and others. In that exposure, the German people themselves have the greatest stake.

* * *

[Dr. Hans Laternser, defense counsel for defendant von Leeb, then proceeded to present the opening statements in defense of his client. In a lengthy historical, political and legal defense of both von Leeb in particular and the German Officers' Corps in general, Laternser outlined for the Tribunal his rebuttal of prosecution charges. We present only selected excerpts of some of his more cogent arguments].

Dr. Laternser: May it please the Tribunal.

In view of Germany's plight today, a plight brought about by proper to proceed on the assumption that only history will render the guilt of her National Socialist leadership, it might perhaps be an objective verdict on the measures taken against her military leaders. [*This paragraph is, apparently, a translation error in the official trial record*].

There must be special reasons, indeed, if, at the very beginning of such a trial, criticism is voiced in the countries of our former enemies, and by men whose judgment carries some weight in the world.

I have before me the evening edition of the *News Chronicle*, dated 20 February 1948. In this issue the noted British military critic, Liddell Hart, comments on this Nuremberg Trial, "I was rather amazed," he states, "to see the names of some of the people whom the Americans have decided to bring to trial." Referring to my client, Field Marshall von Leeb, he goes on to write: "The case of von Leeb, who also is charged with the planning of aggressive war, is equally curious. He was the principal proponent of the defensive theory in the German Wehrmacht. He was one of those who tried to dissuade Hitler from invading Russia, and he was regarded by Hitler as an 'incorrigible anti-Nazi.'"

I propose to set forth and prove that Field Marshall von Leeb is not guilty of the crimes he is charged with, but that, on the contrary, his is a personality of great integrity and honesty of conviction in the best military tradition.

* * *

If we examine in the light of historical facts the prosecution's contention that German military leaders throughout the last century instigated one war after the other, we shall at once note that it is incorrect.

On the promise that the prosecution disregards the wars of the Napoleonic era, I may start with the Russo-Turkish War in 1854, in which neither Russia nor Germany took part, as the event and date inaugurating the turbulent century which the prosecution has in mind. First of all, a glance at any history book is sufficient to verify the statement that quite a number of wars have since been waged in Europe and outside it without Germany's participation. Throughout the whole century, from 1815–1914, Prussia and/or Germany participated in warlike conflicts only for a short period of six years, from 1864–1870. These conflicts were the Wars of 1864, 1866 and 1870–71, immediately preceding the creation of German Reich.

* * *

It is well known that the Franco-Prussian War of 1870–71 was initiated and declared by France on the idle pretext of frustrating the candidacy of a German prince aspiring to the Spanish throne, and that, in keeping with the traditions of French policy, it aimed at preventing the formation of a unified German State.

The unified German Reich drew the logical conclusion after this war, built up a strong army in view of Germany's vulnerable position in the center of Europe, and thus maintained peace for a long time.

Only in 1914, did the neighboring states feel themselves strong enough and drove the *entente cordiale* to war. Every historian worthy of note knows this fact today.

* * *

The First World War was unleashed by shots fired in the Balkans. We know that the same danger is again threatening from that area, the only difference being that the team on the one side has changed. Russia's far-ranging objectives, which have for so long made this a focal point of politics, have remained unchanged.

* * *

Even the outbreak of the Second World War can only ostensibly support the prosecution thesis that the German officer's corps had brought about one war after another. The contribution made by the German officers' corps and its leaders merely consists in this:

By education and ethical convictions, they were unprepared for the means with which Hitler fought; they were not equal or able to cope with his demoniac personality; it was too late when they recognized the true nature of this man to whom they had—not quite voluntarily—sworn the oath of allegiance after the death of Reich President Hindenburg.

Only thus was it possible that Hitler secured for the execution of his plans the effective instrument of the German Armed Forces, destined by its military leaders solely for defense.

* * *

One cannot do justice to the part played by the armed forces and the Officers' Corps in German life without realizing that Germany in the heart of Europe for a long time acted as a shock absorber, cushioning the impact of the natural pressure of the Slav masses and the very strong expansionist power of the Russian State, while at the same time she was threatened in the back by France which, in a 1,000 years' struggle, was able steadily to advance her frontiers eastward. This mission has now devolved on other nations and even today we can perceive the influence which this fact exerts on their military struggle.

* * *

I do not know on what grounds the prosecution base their contention that the German officer was inspired by the belief that war constituted a natural and admirable part of life and that this belief has been frequently expressed in the writing of German military leaders through almost two centuries.

Professor de Martens, the author of the Russian draft agreement of the laws and customs of war for the Brussels Conference of 1874, who, next to Dr. Lieber, was the father of the modern laws of war, and who was Chairman of the Hague Peace Conference of 1899, has examined the literature of the various nations with respect to the reflections on war contained therein. The result he arrived at differs substantially from that attained by the prosecution. The advocates of war are not German generals, far from it, but above all the Piedmontese De Maistre and the celebrated French philosopher Proudhon for who war is actually something devine

The German contribution to the philosophy of war consists in the statement of the Prussian general and eminent student of the war, *Clausewitz*, which has universal validity, that war is only a means, a political instrument, which powers use to obtain their objective. According to him, war is the continuation of politics with other means and possesses no quality peculiar to itself; both politics and war partake of the same nature.

Clausewitz's perspicacious and objective mind has moulded generations of German officers. His book, "On War," has been included by the Army of the United States as Volume 1 in the series of their military dossiers.

II. The German Officers' Corps and the Laws of War

The prosecution's charge that the German Officers' Corps has always displayed a nihilistic attitude towards the laws of war, and only paid lip service to the laws and customs of war, is as incorrect as their assertion that the German Officers' Corps has brought about one war after another during the past century.

Professor de Martens also investigated the problem of the attitude displayed by various nations towards the laws of war. During the Franco-Prussian War of 1870–71, he followed events as a neutral observer in close proximity to the theater of war and carefully collected and examined such facts as were claimed by the one side or the other to constitute a violation of the laws of war. He did not find any attitude of German nihilism towards the law of war. Rather, he came to the conclusion that events on both sides were a consequence of the fact that the belligerent parties could not reach an understanding about customs of war for which they claimed obligatory powers.

* * *

Also the events in Belgium during the First World War which were not only objects for an anti-German propaganda, but also subjects of exacting investigations, were to a large extent attributable to the different concepts of the two parties with reference to the law applicable to belligerent participation by the civilian population. It is correct, however, that the Germans shot hostages in Belgium in several instances during the First World War and, in the case of Dinant, probably unjustly. But a conclusion that the laws of war were disregarded cannot be derived from this. American Military Tribunal V. has stated in its judgment, dated 19 February 1948, in the case against Field Marshall List and the other generals of the Southeast that according to the laws of war not only partisans and franc-tireurs [a term designating a sharp-shooter in the French Army] may be shot, but also the killings of hostages is permissible in connection with illegal resistance activities.

* * *

As counsel for the defense of the General Staff and the OKW before the International Military Tribunal in Nuremberg, I have already given a short survey of the fate of the highest military leaders: —

Of 17 Field Marshals, active in the army, 10 were relieved of their positions during the war; 3 lost their lives in connection with the plot against Hitler on 20 July 1944; 2 died in combat; 1 became a prisoner of war [von Paulus to the Russians]. Only one remained in his position until the end of the war. Of 36 Generalobersten, 26 were removed from their positions, among them three who were executed in connection with the events of 20 July 1944, and two who were dishonorably discharged; 7 fell in battle; and only 3 remained until the end of the war.

If you, Your Honors, take into consideration that these disciplined officers were highly qualified and battle-proved leaders, then you will see from this impressive survey, which will be further expanded, that they were not blindly subordinated to Hitler, as charged by the prosecution, but rather made use of the possibilities at their disposal, existing in a dictatorship.

Whether German men with an attitude, as we shall prove it to you, Your Honors, will stand up to the judgment of history, will have to be established in the future by an objective recording of history. Prosecutors who see only a distorted picture, and want only to see such a picture, will no longer play a part in this.

[Dr. Laternser then goes into a spirited defense of his client regarding the Commissar Order, participation in wars of aggression and the treatment of civilians in occupied territories. He continually argued that von Leeb was always a defensive-minded Field Marshall who opposed Hitler's plans in the West and that he was in total agreement with Field Marshall von Brauchitsch, Commander in Chief of the German Army, that an offense in the West was ill-advised and would be fatal to Germany's plans in the East against the U.S.S.R. These comments are then followed by opening statements from various defense counsel for defendants Hoth, Schniewind, Woehler, Warlimont and Reinecke. Following this is a detailed presentation of the organization of the German

Armed Forces from *German Army Manual 90*, June 1938. This was followed by examination and cross-examination of defense witnesses and defendants themselves as well as further selections from the argumentation on the charges of aggressive war plus extensive extracts from a variety of documentary evidence from OKW and OKH and Hitler's directives and speeches. The "Terror Flyer Order," the "Night and Fog Decree," the issue of the deportation and enslavement of civilian populations and the plunder of pubic and private property not justified by military necessity were all taken up in that order. The trial concluded with the closing statement of the prosecution, followed by the closing statements of defendants Reinhardt, Warlimont and Lehmann. Closing briefs were filed on behalf of defendants Kuechler, Hoth, Reinhardt, Hollidt, von Roques and Woehler. Field Marshall von Leeb made a final statement to the Tribunal on behalf of himself and all charged defendants. Finally came the judgment on each of the four counts charged, namely, (1) crimes against peace; (2) war crimes; (3) crimes against humanity; and (4) a common plan or conspiracy to commit the first three crimes.

We include excerpts from the Closing Statements of the prosecution and excerpts from the Final Statement of defendant Field Marshall Wilhelm von Leeb. The case report concludes with the judgment of the Tribunal handed down against each individual defendant. The "High Command Case" record consumes about one and two-thirds volumes, that, with the *Preface*, totals some 2,095 pages].

* * *

IX. Final Argumentation

Only a small fraction of the final argumentation at the close of the trial has been reproduced below.... The closing statements of the prosecution and the defense required 4 days to deliver, the prosecution's closing taking less than one full day and the defense closing taking more than 3 days. In addition voluminous briefs were filed by both the prosecution and defense which total hundreds of pages....

* * *

...Among the topics covered are a number of special arguments which include: the effect of superior orders, the justification of alleged military necessity, the principle of *tu quoque* ["thou also"], the responsibility of a chief of staff, the nature of command authority and executive power in the areas occupied by the German armed forces, and the international law applicable to prisoners of war, partisans and civilians....

B. Extracts from the Closing Statement of the Prosecution

Mr. Fulkerson: The evidence which the prosecution has submitted in support of the charges in count two and three of the indictment is very extensive. We shall not attempt today to describe again the terrible events which the documentary evidence so eloquently portrays. The criminal responsibility of each of the defendants under counts two and three will be established in detail in the individual briefs. At this time we shall content ourselves with calling to the Tribunal's attention only such portions of the evidence as are relevant to meet the conglomerations of vague, implausible, and mutually contradictory defenses which have been raised under these counts.

A. The "Commissar Order"

Under subdivision A. of count two of the indictment, dealing with the so-called Commissar Order, Sperrle and Schniewind are not charged. The responsibility of Warlimont and Lehmann in connection with the drafting and distribution of the order, as well as the responsibility of Reinecke for the execution of the order at prisoner of war camps has, we submit, been clearly established. The remaining eight defendants—von Leeb, von Kuechler, Hoth, Reinhardt, von Salmuth, Hollidt, von Roques and Woehler are all charged with the distribution and execution of the Commissar Order in their capacities as field commanders. All of them have resorted to substantially identical excuses and explanations. [The record then takes up the prosecution's argument against three of the eight defendants mentioned above, namely, von Leeb, Von Kuechler and Hoth, regarding their alleged distribution of the Commissar Order. Excerpts below are taken from prosecution comments regarding Field Marshall von Leeb].

* * *

... [T]he record proves incontrovertibly that the Commissar Order was distributed and carried out within von Leeb's Army Group, with von Leeb's knowledge, and resulted in the outright murder of numerous prisoners of war. We will dispose of these defenses *seriatim*.

a. The fact that von Leeb protested against the order to von Brauchitsch and Keitel is, of course, no defense if he in fact distributed and executed the order. Like his memorandum to von Brauchitsch advising against the invasion of Belgium and Holland, these protests merely established conclusively that he was fully aware of the wrongful character of his actions.

b. Whether or not von Leeb personally passed the Commissar Order to the commander of his rear area, it is perfectly clear that the order reached the rear area, because on 19 December 1941 the 281st Security Division, then subordinated to the rear area, reported that two commissars had been shot.... The headquarters of von Leeb's Army Group North was the only headquarters which could have reissued the Commissar Order to the rear area....

* * *

c. Generals Busch, Hoepner and the defendant von Kuechler, who commanded the three armies under von Leeb's Army Group, were directly subordinate to von Leeb in the chain of command. Von Leeb testified that all three of them shared his own view that the Commissar Order was unlawful.... Von Leeb could have instructed them not to pass it down, and there is absolutely no basis in the record for assuming that the three generals would not have followed his instructions...there is no evidence in the record that von Leeb made any attempt to prevent the army commanders from disseminating the order.

* * *

d. While there is no reason to doubt von Leeb's testimony that he disapproved of the Commissar Order, there is absolutely no evidence that he took any action which was effective, or could have been expected to be effective, to prevent its execution within his army group.

* * *

But the defendants are not accused here only of sins of omission, regardless of how grave an offense their failure to take preventive action, without more, may be. These men participated affirmatively in the commission of these murders by putting the order into the hands of their subordinates. These defendants or members of their staff, took further steps to insure the execution of the order, by passing down supplementary directives in connection therewith. Their guilt for these crimes has been established beyond any shadow of a doubt, and the crime for which they bear this guilt is the crime of murder.

B. The "Commando Order"

Mr. Higgins: If your Honors please.

We turn now to the Commando Order. The events which preceded its issuance were various raids carried out between 19 August and 6 October 1942 by English commando units on Dieppe, the island of Sark, and the various installations in Norway.

On 7 October a German radio broadcast announced "all terror and sabotage troops of the British and their accomplices who do not act like soldiers but like bandits have in the future to be treated as such by the German troops, and they must be slaughtered ruthlessly in combat wherever they turn up." The next day the defendant Warlimont directed the Legal Department of the OKW, headed by defendant Lehmann, to draft a formal order.... Warlimont then sent [a draft order] to the office of Foreign Counterintelligence under Admiral Carnaris and asked for his comments. Canaris immediately objected to the legal department draft, root and branch.

* * *

The illegality of the Commando Order is clear, and has been established by the decision of the IMT and by the opinion in United States vs. Wilhelm List, et al. Lehmann himself said on the stand that he considered the order to have been an "inadmissible reprisal" to the extent that it applied to uniformed military personnel.

* * *

...Warlimont and Lehmann, of course, as the draftsmen of the Commando Order, are criminally responsible for all the murders committed thereunder, whether in the East or in the West.

C. Other Crimes Against Prisoners of War

Paragraphs 50 to 57 of count two of the indictment charge all the defendants except Schniewind with other crimes against prisoners of war. An abundance of evidence has been introduced in support of these charges... we will limit ourselves here to a very few brief observations.

The defendants have relied heavily on the circumstances that the Soviet Union was not a party to the Geneva Convention with respect to the treatment of prisoners of war, but it is well settled—and was so held by the IMT—that the general principles of international law with respect to the treatment of prisoners of war were applicable as between Germany and the Soviet Union. The German High Command was fully aware of this, and Admiral Canaris of the OKW set forth this viewpoint in a memorandum of 15 September 1941, protesting against proposed regulations for the treatment of Soviet prisoners. Under these well-established principles, war captivity is not a "punishment," and prisoners of war are not fit objects for revenge or reprisals. They must not be subjected to dangerous employment, not required to work against the interests of their own country by being forced to engage in any type of labor directly related to war operations.

* * *

The treatment which Russian prisoners of war habitually received while in German custody is one of the most appalling parts of this appalling case. In connection with the Commissar Order, we have already mentioned that the inmates in the prisoner of war cages were screened for the purpose of removing those of them who fell within the meaning of that lethal ordinance. But the screening process went much further. All the prisoners of war were put into one of several classifications. Into the first of these three classifications fell ethnic Germans, Ukrainians and natives of the three Baltic countries [Estonia, Latvia and Lithuania]. Into the second fell Asiatics, Jews and German-speaking Russians. The third category consisted of persons classified as "politically intolerable and suspicious elements, commissars and agitators."

Theoretically, the treatment was to vary according to the classification. The first group was earmarked for service as auxiliaries of the German Army and, sometimes, even as combat troops; the third group was considered as temporary boarders who were to survive only until firing squads could be organized. The Jews were taken care of by the extermination squads of the Einsatzgruppen, and the remainder were scheduled to be shipped to Germany to work in the armament industry or to operate antiaircraft guns. [The prosecution proceeded to summarize various other alleged offenses committed by or under the direction of the defendants throughout their commands in all theaters of operation in which they were involved. Closing briefs and statements were then submitted by several defendants. Before the Tribunal retired to reach its final judgment, Field Marshal von Leeb was allowed to present a final statement to the court. Excerpts from that statement are set forth below].

* * *

B. Final Statement of the Defendant von Leeb

Presiding Judge Young: Dr. Laternser.

Dr. Laternser: If the Court please, I want to announce to the Court that Field Marshal von Leeb will speak the last word for all of the defendants. I ask that he be permitted to do so from the prosecutor's stand.

Presiding Judge Young: He will have that permission in just a moment. In view of the fact that one of the defendants, Field Marshal von Leeb, will speak for all, he, of course, will not be limited to ten minutes if he desires more time than was in the order assigned to each defendant. The Tribunal will now hear such statement as Field Marshal von Leeb desires to make and he may make it from the podium.

Defendant von Leeb: May it please the Tribunal, I have been allotted the task of making the final speech on behalf of all the defendants.

I believe that we will not be looked upon as presumptuous in upholding our opinion that the German officer was respected beyond the boundaries of his own country. He was respected not only on account of his technical qualifications, but mainly because of his soldierly qualities which form the essence of the soldier's profession. We deem these qualities to include loyalty, close ties between officers and men, obedience, a sense of duty, unselfishness and personal gallantry. The unusually high casualties among officers in both World Wars, including general officers, give proof of our readiness to lay down our lives.

We, the defendants, have belonged to this body of officers for many years. We have been trained and have grown up in this spirit of the soldier's profession. We have fulfilled our duty as soldiers with equal loyalty under the German Emperor, during the First World War, under the Weimar Republic, and in the Third Reich. However, in the Third Reich, under the dictatorship of Hitler, we found ourselves faced with a development which was in contrast to our principles and nature. It is not true to say that we as officers changed—the demands made of us became different.

We sought to oppose this evolution under the Third Reich, but we lacked the means which might have been effective under dictatorship.

Above all, the body of officers as a whole was the only section of the population in Germany which, according to the constitution and to tradition, possessed no civil rights. We held no right of franchise or election. We were not permitted any activity in any political sphere whatsoever, be it domestic or foreign politics.

Therefore no one among us was able to exert any influence on Hitler's conduct of the affairs of state at home or abroad. We were neither able nor permitted to enter politics. We were merely required to be soldiers.

Even as soldiers we did not incite to war. We, of all people, were familiar with war and all its attendant horrors from personal experience of front-line combat during the First World War. On the contrary, we did everything in our power to dissuade Hitler from his bellicose plans.

However, once the head of state, who alone was vested with unlimited powers of decision on war or peace had commanded the initiation of acts of war against the will and advice of his generals, we were bound to do our duty as soldiers like any other Germans.

We were not entitled to demand enlightenment on the political reasons underlying a war and to refuse our services if such reasons should appear inadequate to us. We are not prepared to believe that the leading generals of any other state would have refused their services in the same situation....

In the East the grim aspect of the war was determined by Russia. Stalin's appeal for the slaughter of all Germans induced the partisans to pervert the conduct of the war.

We, as German soldiers, had up to that moment refrained from such conduct, and we had not desired and sought such extremes; neither in Russia nor in other theaters. We were forced to seek effective protection against this degeneration in warfare. We acted in self-defense.

In regard to Hitler's instructions which went against our humane and soldierly feelings, we were never merely his tools without a will of our own. We did oppose his instructions as far as we deemed this to be possible or advisable and we toned their wording down and rendered them ineffective or mitigated them in practice....

No blame attaches to the Wehrmacht for anything that may have happened on Russian soil beyond the purely *belligerent* purpose of the war. Such actions occurred without our knowledge or participation. None of the defendants had any knowledge of the secret Fuehrer Decree and the organized mass murder carried out by the Einsatzgruppen which were *not* subordinated to us.

We are unable to grasp the charge contained in count four, according to which we are supposed to have participated in a common plan and conspiracy for the commission of crimes under Control Council Law No. 10.

In summarizing, I wish to state that we, the defendants, were required to do our duty as soldiers under dictatorship in its most severe form, with unlimited legislative power, with manifold abuses, and with violent distrust of our persons, which gradually turned into hatred and called forth the reaction shown in the events of 20 July 1944.

Outwardly we were fighting our enemies abroad, but at the same time we were fighting at home against the Party with its influences, it demands, and its almost unlimited-power especially on the subject of military jurisdiction—and we were even fighting against our own Supreme Commander. What a terrible tragedy is revealed by the fact that we as the appointed *guardians of the soldiers' duty to obey* were forced to act towards our own Supreme Commander in defiance of this chief axiom of soldierly conduct.

No soldier in all the world has ever yet had to fight under such a load and such a tragedy.

In the First World War we did not infringe any laws, and we remained what we were during in the Second World War. We were not guided by criminal instincts, as the prosecution seeks to convey, but we now *look back* upon a life of disinterested service and unselfish fulfillment of duty towards our country and men.

There is no need, nor is it in fact possible, to tear the mask from our face, as the prosecution has told the German public over the radio, because we never wore a mask.

We are soldiers who upheld their soldierly honor even in their Second World War amidst the turmoil of dictatorial violence. As *our* witnesses we call upon those hundreds of thousands of frontline soldiers who fought under our orders.

Presiding Judge Young: We appreciate the assistance of counsel for defense and prosecution in the presentation of this case and in bringing it, so far as the evidence is concerned and the arguments, to a conclusion. The Tribunal will now be recessed for preparation of its judgment, subject to call, of which, of course, you will have proper notice.

XI. Judgment

Presiding Judge Young: The Tribunal will now proceed to read the judgment.

* * *

The indictment named as defendants:

Generalfeldmarschall (General of the Army) Wilhelm von Leeb, General Feldmarschall (General of the Army) Hugo Sperrle, Generalfeldmarschall (General of the Army) Georg Karl Friedrich-Wilhelm von Kuechler, Generaloberst (General) Johannes Blaskowitz, Generaloberst (General) Hermann Hoth, Generaloberst (General) Hans Reinhardt, Generaloberst (General) Karl Hollidt, Generaladmiral (Admiral) Otto Schniewind, General der Infanterie (Lieutenant General Infantry) Karl von Roques, General de Infanterie (Lieutenant General Infantry) Hermann Reinecke, General der Artillerie (Lieutenant General, Infantry), Otto Woehler, and Generaloberstabsrichter (Lieutenant General, Judge Advocate) Rudolf Lehmann.

The defendant General Johannes Blaskowitz committed suicide in prison on 5 February 1948, and thereby the case against him was terminated.

* * *

Sentences

Presiding Judge Young:...

The reading of the opinion and judgment having been concluded, the Tribunal will now impose sentences upon those defendants who have been adjudged guilty in these proceedings....

As the name of each defendant is called, he will arise, proceed to the center of the dock and put on the earphones.

Otto Schniewind, the Tribunal having found you not guilty, you will arise and retire with the guards. You will be released as heretofore ordered when the Tribunal presently adjourns.

Hugo Sperrle, having been found not guilty, in accordance with the order heretofore made, will be released when the Tribunal presently adjourns.

The defendant Wilhelm von Leeb will arise.

Wilhelm von Leeb, on the count in the indictment on which you have been convicted [Count 3], the Tribunal sentences you to three years' imprisonment. You will retire with the guards.

[Field Marshall Wilhelm Ritter von Leeb received the lightest sentence of the remaining eleven defendants subsequent to the acquittals of Schniewind and Sperrle; Reinecke and Warlimont received life sentences, while the remaining nine were sentenced to prison terms varying in length from five to twenty years. The *von Leeb* case on the defensive side attempted to draw a distinction between Nazi crimes perpetrated by the rogue elements of the Hitler regime (such as the Gestapo, the SS and other groups) and the so-called "purity of arms" of the German *Wehrmacht* itself. Only in recent years has this "purity of arms" myth been exposed as just that—a myth. Evidence coming to light over the past half-century clearly implicates the German profession of arms in extermination operations of all kinds from the top echelons through the junior officer corps and down to the rank and file.

Some commentators legitimately questioned the terminology employed in describing the twelve "Subsequent Proceedings" cases at Nuremberg as proceedings "international" in character. The origin of these courts rested, of course, on the provisions of Allied Control Council Law No. 10, implemented by *Ordinance No. 7* of the American Military Government in Berlin, dated October 18, 1946. These cases commenced on October 26, 1946, and concluded on April 14, 1949.

In effect, cases heard in these twelve courts were tried by "Military Tribunals" in name only, not in fact. There were no military judges sitting on these courts. All were staffed by American civilian judges who were members of various state judiciaries, plus an alternate for each trial. All members of these tribunals had to be admitted to the practice of law in an American jurisdiction for at least five years prior to their appointment. Only the "United States" was designated as the prosecuting party of record and certain visible paraphernalia and invocations employed gave these courts the appearance of a purely American forum. No one can legitimately claim that the "Subsequent Proceedings" courts, the military commissions and the military government courts established by the United States in occupied Germany were international tribunals. They have always been understood to be purely American in both procedure and substance.

Of the 177 German defendants tried in the twelve Nuremberg "Subsequent Proceedings" cases, 35 were acquitted. A total of 888 witnesses testified for the various defendants, while 467 testified for the prosecution. There were 375 defense attorneys that represented various individuals and ninety-four prosecutors. Article 2 of *Ordinance No. 7* brought in an additional multitude of Germans for trial before United States Military Tribunals in the American Zone of Occupation. In at least one important respect, the "Subsequent Proceedings" trials differed from their IMT-Nuremberg counterpart. The major Nazi war criminals tried by the IMT were *not* tried for crimes committed by them prior to September 1, 1939, the date Germany invaded Poland to formally commence World War II. However, in the "Subsequent Proceedings" cases, German nationals accused of war crimes could be charged, tried and convicted for crimes they committed *before* the date recognized as the anniversary date for World War II. Worldwide, of the 3,306 individuals accused of war crimes and tried after World War II by various *United States* military courts, 471, or slightly over fourteen percent, were acquitted].

(d) The Malmédy Trial

[On an overcast and bitterly cold 12-degree Sunday, December 17, 1944, an event occurred in the Ardennes region of Belgium that subsequently had a significant impact on the Allied decision to place Germans on trial for war crimes. At the Baugnez cross-roads near the village of Malmédy there occurred an event perpetrated by the *Waffen-SS* that politically energized the United States government to persuade the British, French and Russians that war crime trials were the appropriate international response to Nazi brutality.

The United States Army's 7th Armoured Division was conducting a southward move from Holland to St. Vith, Belgium, in the heavily wooded Ardennes sector of Belgium. Battery B of the 285th Field Artillery Battalion was one of the force elements assigned to the 7th Armored Division. As this latter group advanced near the village of Malmédy, they were confronted by advance elements of *Kampfgruppe Peiper's 1st SS Liebstandarte Adolf Hitler Panzer Division*. After the Germans opened fire on the Americans, the members of Battery B, taken by surprise and overwhelming force, surrendered. It was later reported that a passing Panzer officer shouted out to the Americans in heavily-ac-cented English: "The 1st SS Panzer Division welcomes you to Belgium, gentlemen."

The American POWs were immediately rounded up and forced to assemble in a nearby field. Lt. Colonel Peiper, passing the Americans in his command vehicle, report-edly shouted to them in English: "It's a long way to Tipperary boys!" (Tipperary is the name of a town in Ireland and the song, *It's a Long Way to Tipperary*, became one of the most popular songs of World War I among British, German and Russian troops). After all the American stragglers had been rounded up, what happened next, like most situa-tions in combat, is subject to widely conflicting accounts.

In a nutshell, however, it is known from the sworn testimony of one of the survivors that one of Peiper's men shouted to his comrades, "Macht alle Kaputt"! ("Kill them all.") At that moment, machine guns and pistols from several panzers opened fire on the huddled Americans. Altogether, some seventy-two GIs were murdered in a fulisade of fire from the panzers and grenadiers situated close to the Baugnez road crossing. Re-markably, there were a number of survivors who would later bear witness against Peiper and members of the *Sixth Panzer Armee*.

In May, 1946, *SS-Obergruppenfuehrer* Sepp Dietrich, one of Nazi Germany's "veteran fighters" and the leader of the "Adolf Hitler Life-Guards" before 1933, in his position as commander of the *Sixth Panzer Armee*, along with Lt. Colonel Joachim Peiper and members of *Kampfgruppe Peiper*, which had been assigned to the *Sixth Panzer Armee*, Fritz Kramer, the *Sixth Panzer Armee* Chief of Staff, Hermann Priess, Commander of the *1st Panzer Korps*, and a number of other personnel, were all put on trial by an American General Military Government Court. This tribunal sat in the former Dachau Concentration Camp near Munich. Seventy-four Germans were charged and tried. Of that number, forty-three received the death penalty. Sentences of life imprisonment were meted out to twenty-two, while another eight were sentenced to varying degrees of lesser punishment. The trial lasted from May 16 to June 16, 1946.

The so-called "Malmédy Massacre" became a *cause celebe* in large measure because of the notoriety of defendants Sepp Dietrich and Joachim Peiper and also because that event judicially investigated the first American encounter in World War II with the savage *modus operandi* of the *Waffen-SS*. That organization had perfected its style of battle and warriorhood with a "take-no-prisoners/full reprisals" combat ideology perfected and practiced with lethal efficiency on the bloody Eastern Front while fighting the Red Army.

However, in the overall scheme of things during the last six-months or so of World War II in Europe, Parker[51] notes that "...[T]he Malmédy Massacre was a minor incident in the Ardennes Campaign. However, it did give the American GI a taste of the mentality that had produced the *SonderKommandos* of the Eastern Front, Oradour-sur-Glan in France and the diabolical concentration camps within Germany."[52]

Another unusual episode connected with the *Malmédy Case* was the allegation of improper and unconstitutional pre-trial interrogation methods employed by United States Army investigators against potential defendants awaiting trial in the American prison located at Schwäbisch Hall, Germany. The criticism became so intense, both by German nationalists and others in the United States, that Congress was moved to conduct several investigations into the entire American war crimes program in occupied Germany.[53] The United States Supreme Court became involved in 1948 when it denied an application for a writ of *habeas corpus*[54] filed by defense counsel on behalf of all the defendants tried in the Dachau proceeding. Even the Secretary of the Army became involved in the controversy and caused a board of review to be established (the Simpson Commission) to review all death sentences handed down in the Malmédy trial. Subsequently, that Commission recommended that all death sentences be commutted to life imprisonment. Other controversies swirled about the case, its investigation and outcome, as the international geopolitical spectre of the emerging Cold War began to influence the later decisions regarding the entire war crimes trial efforts in Germany. Ultimately, in January, 1950, the remaining six defendants who still had a death sentence pending, had their capital sanctions commuted to life imprisonment. Thus, no executions of *any* individuals involved in the *Malmédy Case* ever took place! Defendant Sepp Dietrich was released from confinement in August, 1951. Joachim Peiper walked out of Landsberg Prison a free man on December 22, 1956. Nearly twenty-years later, however, a strange twist of fate ended the life of this former *SS* officer.

Peiper, his wife and son had decided to live in France. On July 14, 1976 (Bastille Day), Joachim Peiper's home in Traves, France, was firebombed by unknown assailants and his body (never positively identified by the French) was found in the ruins of his home. His wife and child had previously left Traves. In his book on the military exploits and trial of Joachim Peiper, Reynolds[55] makes this interesting observation in the final chapter:

> The police files in the Peiper case are still held in Dijon [France] and have been seen by the author; there are four of them and they are each four inches thick. Follow-up investigations included ballistic tests, house searches of suspects and dozens of interrogations. They all proved fruitless.

> Amazing scenes had followed the events of 14th July 1976. Right-wing hooligans in France attacked various Communist Party Offices and in Germany a campaign started to have an 'Oberst Peiper Denkmal' (Memorial)

---

51. Danny S. Parker, *The Battle of the Bulge: Hitler's Ardennes Offensive, 1944–1945* (1991).

52. *Id.* at 124.

53. *See, Malmedy Massacre Investigation*, Hearings Before a Sub-committee of the Senate Comm. on Armed Services, 81st Cong., 1st Sess. (1949).

54. 334 U.S. 824 (1947).

55. Michael Reynolds, *The Devil's Adjutant: Jochen Peiper, Panzer Leader* (1995).

erected at, of all places, Dachau. Hinrich Peiper [his son] did not support the campaign but tried to persuade various German politicians to have his father's reputation cleared of all ignominy. He failed.[56]

On May 9, 1958, the last defendant convicted of a war crime by any of the courts sitting at Camp Dachau was released from confinement at Landsberg Prison. Altogether, there were 489 cases tried at Dachau implicating 1,672 defendants. Of that number, 256 were acquitted while 426 received a sentence of death. Life imprisonment was imposed upon 199 while 791 defendants received lesser prison sentences of varying length].

(e) *United States of America v. Valentin Bersin et al.* (1946) The "Malmédy Massacre" Case

Camp Dachau, May 16–July 16, 1946

[There was no reported "opinion" by the Court in this case. We include selected excerpts from archival microfilm, Record Group No. 153, rolls 1–6, from the National Achieves and Records Administration, College Park, Maryland. The Dachau court was one of many American General Military Government Courts sitting in Occupied Germany. This particular tribunal came into being by virtue of two Special Orders from Headquarters, 3d United States Army, the first dated April 9, 1946 and an amended by Special Order dated May 10, 1946. The first session of the court took place on May 16, 1946.

The prosecution was led by Lieutenant Colonel Burton F. Ellis, Trial Judge Advocate, assisted by four Assistant Trial Judge Advocates and a 1st Lieutenant William R. Perl, Special Assistant to the Prosecution. The defendants were represented by a team of both American and German defense counsel. The American defense team was led by Colonel Willis M. Everette, Jr. with four additional assistant defense counsels. The German defense team consisted of six lawyers authorized to practice law before Military Government Courts. These six were: Dr. Max Rau, Dr. Heinrich M. Wieland, Dr. Otto Leiling, Dr. Franz J. Pfister, Dr. Eugene Leer and Dr. Hans Hertkorn. Members of the court who sat in judgment in this case were: Brigadier General Josiah T. Dalbey, Colonel Paul H. Weiland, Colonel Lucien S. Berry, Colonel James C. Watkins, Colonel Wilfred H. Steward, Colonel Raymond C. Conder and Colonel A. H. Rosenfeld].

PRESIDENT: Take seats. Court will come to order.

PROSECUTION: Prosecution is ready to proceed in the case of Valentin Bersin et al. The accused are all present…together with the regularly appointed defense counsel.

PRESIDENT: Whom does the accused desire to introduce as counsel?

DEFENSE COUNSEL: May it please the Court, at this time the accused desire the United States officers and civilians heretofore appointed by the Third Army as their defense counsel. The accused further desire to introduce the following named German counsel, who are practicing attorneys are qualified to practice before this court: [here follows the list of German defense counsel and the list of the members of the Court].

PROSECUTION: The general nature of the charges in this case is the violation of the laws and usuages of war in that the above named accused, charged as being parties concerned, did willfully, deliberately, and wrongfully permit, encourage, aid, abet, and par-

---

56. *Id.* at 268.

ticipate in the killing, shooting, ill-treatment, abuse and torture of members of the Armed Forces of the United States of America, and of unarmed allied civilians.

The prosecution will not call any members of the Court as a witness, nor will the accused.

DEFENSE COUNSEL: May it please the Court, the Defense Counsel does not anticipate calling any members of the Court as a witness...

We respectfully request the President to determine if any member of this Court has any prior knowledge of the facts in this case by virtue of his participation in the Ardennes Offensive commonly referred to as the "Battle of the Bulge" which could prejudice him in his judgment. If so, we respectfully request that he be excused for cause.

* * *

DEFENSE COUNSEL: Let the record show that all members of the Court have answered in the negative. [Here follows other preliminary questions and answers by both sides. There then follows a listing of all defendants along with their name, rank and unit affiliation].

* * *

3. [Defense Counsel continuing]: On 1 November 1943, three great powers, the United States, Russia and Great Britain enumerated a policy concerning the trial of war criminals. The conference at which this policy was formulated is now commonly referred to as the "MOSCOW CONFERENCE." The declaration on atrocities which became a part of that conference is as follows:

'At the time of the granting of any Armistice to any Government which may be set up in Germany, those German officers and men, members of the Nazi Party, who have been responsible for or who have taken a part in the above atrocities, massacres, and executions, will be sent back to the country in which these abominable deeds were done, in order that they may be judged and punished according to the laws of these liberated countries and of the free Governments which will be erected therein.'

[Defense counsel then made a motion that argued that the Court was without jurisdiction to try the charged defendants and that, instead, they should be extradited to Belgium for trial. There then followed a lengthy colloquy between the President of the Court and defense counsel concerning specific defendants and the jurisdiction of the Court to try them on specific charges as well as the substantive content of some of the charges. The defense motion was then denied by the Law Member].

* * *

PRESIDENT: The Court has satisfied itself that it is properly constituted under the laws and rules governing General Military Government Courts and has jurisdiction over the person and offences of the accused....

PRESIDENT: There being no grounds for challenge, the Court is declared to be properly constituted and the trial will be conducted in open Court.

* * *

PROSECUTION: If the Court please, the prosecution does desire to make an opening statement.... We will briefly outline the evidence that we expect to show.

The offensive which is referred to in this trial was known to the Germans as the Eifel Offensive. To the Americans it is more commonly referred to as the Battle of the Bulge, the Rundstedt Offensive or the Ardennes Offensive. We expect to show that for this offensive there existed a general policy to spread terror and panic, to avenge the so-called terror bombings and to break all resistance by murdering prisoners of war and unarmed civilians....

We expect the evidence to show that the 6th Panzer Army, commanded by the accused Dietrich, passed on the tenor of Hitler's speech [of December 16, 1944, where he extorted his field commanders to show no humane inhibitions]...in words and substance to the effect that 'considering the desperate situation of the German people, a wave of terror and fright should precede the troops...that prisoners of war must be shot when the local conditions of combat should so require it.' This order was passed on down through Corps, Divisions and Regiment.

The 1st SS Panzer Regiment, commanded by the accused Peiper, passed on this order to subordinate commands in words and substance to the effect that "this fight will be conducted stubbornly, with no regard for Allied prisoners of war who will have to be shot, if the situation makes it necessary and compels it." This order was read to subordinate commanders who in turn passed it on down to Company Commanders who likewise passed it to lower echelons and to the troops.

* * *

We expect the evidence to show that throughout this offensive the troops of the 1st SS Panzer Regiment proceeded to execute their orders to kill unarmed and defenseless prisoners of war and unarmed Allied civilians with zeal and enthusiasm. We expect the evidence to show that they murdered them not only at the crossroads south of MALMEDY, where the bodies of 71 American prisoners of war were found, and where 43 other Americans whom they attempted to kill escaped...

* * *

...We expect the evidence to show that in the short space of time covered by the Charge, the 1st SS Panzer Regiment murdered in at least 94 known incidents 538 to 749 Americans who had surrendered and were prisoners of war, and over 90 Belgian civilians. It must be pointed out that figures do not represent the historical truth as to the total number of victims murdered by the SS Panzer Regiment during this offensive, but only the number the prosecution expects the evidence to show.

* * *

We now expect to be able to prove that the 74 defendants now on trial before this court being concerned as parties, did, in conjunction with other persons, willfully, deliberately, and wrongfully permit, encourage, aid, abet and participate in the killing, shooting, ill-treatment, abuse and torture of members of the Armed Forces of the United States who were prisoners of war of the German Reich and of unarmed Allied civilian nationals.

* * *

DEFENSE COUNSEL: The Defense desires to make a short opening statement:

It must be remembered that this case which we are now dispassionately judging a year after the cessation of the European War, transpired when the Allies were rapidly forging their way to Berlin. It was then Total War.

Here are seventy-four accused and it must be emphasized that before the Prosecution is entitled to a verdict of 'guilty' they must show a premeditated plan or malice aforethought for these men to be called murderers. We believe the evidence will show, that in the absense of any preconceived murderous plan, the maximum penalty that could be imposed by this justice tribunal would be that for manslaughter which does not carry any death penalty in our courts. Again and again, it must be emphasized that these accused are members of a Spearhead fighting desperately under the worst battle conditions. Each of you must bear in mind that this was an armoured unit advancing rapidly into enemy territory and being totally cut off from supplies and reinforcements. The practical difficulty of armoured units taking prisoners is well recognized, as they are tightly organized and have absolutely no men to spare for evacuating of prisoners of war.... We believe the evidence will show why no prisoners could be taken in this rapidly advancing column and we believe the Court has already recognized that "motioning prisoners of war to the rear" was necessary.

* * *

We believe the evidence has shown and will further show that the breaking of ranks and dispersing of prisoners of war was the primary factor of most of the deaths at Malmedy.

* * *

We believe the evidence will show that violations of land warfare are rare in this case and when the true combat situation has been shown to this Court, two words can accurately describe the over-all picture "intense combat."

* * *

This is strictly a heat of battle case, a desperate counter-offensive by our beaten enemy, a "lost battalion" without the benefit of supplies and communication.

[The prosecution maintained that Peiper, Dietrich, Kraemer and Priess, along with seventy other German combat personnel, were criminally responsible for the deaths of at least 460 Americans, including those killed at the Bangnez crossroads, as well as 106 Belgians. Unfortunately, the proceedings in this particular case do not reflect well on American military justice in the context of those times. Astonishingly, the tribunal heard each of the defendants' cases on an average of less than *three minutes each*! After all the evidence was in, the Court handed down forty-three death sentences, Joachim Peiper included. Twenty-two accused were sentenced to life imprisonment, while the remainder were given sentences varying in duration from ten to twenty years. One defendant, Marcel Boltz, because he was an Alsatian, was handed over to the French authorities. Boltz was subsequently set free due to insufficient direct evidence of his involvement in the Malmédy affair. All defendants sentenced to death by hanging were removed to Landsberg Prison. Ironically, this was the same prison where Adolf Hitler was held after the failed 1923 Beerhall Putsch and where he had dictated the manuscript of *Mein Kampf* to Rudolf Hess. Controversy followed the Malmedy trial long after it was concluded. It is generally conceded that the most problematic element in this case surrounds the subject-matter of the case-in-chief by the prosecution buttressed by the use of the accused's own confessions which were corroborated only by out-of-court-statements made by *other defendants* on trial!

Subsequently, after an investigation by a United States Senate Sub-Committee, all death sentences accorded the Malmedy defendants were committed. The last defendant to be paroled—Joachim Peiper—was released in December, 1956, after having spent nearly five years in solitary confinement].

(f) *Trial of Heinrich Gerike and Seven Others*
(The Velpke Children's Home Case)

British Military Court, Brunswick
20th March–3rd April, 1946
7 LRTWC 80 (1946)

A. CUTLINE OF THE PROCEEDINGS

The accused, Heinrich Gerike, Georg Eessling, Werner Noth, Hermann Muller, Gustav Claus, Doctor Richard Demmerich, Fritz Flint and Frau Valentina Bilien, were charged with committing a war crime "in that they at Velpke, Germany, between the months of May and December, 1944, in violation of the laws and usages of war, were concerned in the killing by willful neglect of a number of children, Polish Nationals."

It was established that a home for infant children of Polish female workers was established in Velpke in about May, 1944, that the children were to be compulsorily separated from their parents, and that the purpose of the separation was to advance the work on the nearby farms in order to maintain the supply of food in the year 1944. In view of the protests to the effect that the tending of their babies by Polish women was hindering the production of food on the farms where they worked, the accused Gerike, then Kreisleiter of Helmstedt, was ordered by his Gauleiter to erect a home where the children could be kept after being taken away from their mothers. Gerike chose, though according to his account only as a temporary expedient, a corrugated iron hut, without running water, light, telephone or facilities for dealing with sickness. As a matron for the home, the Labour Officer sent, against her will, the accused Valentina Bilien, who stated in Court that she had been married to a Russian, but that her father was German and that she came to Germany in February, 1944. She had formerly been a school teacher in Russia and had had no previous experience running a clinic for infant children. She was at first provided with no staff, no medical equipment and no records except for a register of incoming children. Gerike ordered her not to return the children to their mothers and not to send any to hospital. She was instructed to "call a doctor if necessary." She later had the assistance of four helpers, Polish and Russian girls, but conditions were largely the same when, six months later, possession of the premises was required by the Volkswagon makers.

Gerike, though he knew of the death-rate, never visited the home or interviewed Frau Bilien after the final selection of the barracks. Nor did he engage the services of a trained nurse who lived in the village of Velpke.

Frau Bilien claimed that she was ordered by the Labour Office, and then by Gerike, to take over her post at the home. The evidence showed that the premises were infested with flies and the sick children were not adequately separated from the rest. The infants' clothing was not kept clean, and there were no scales for weighing them. The matron went away for her meals and to do shopping, and was never in the home at night, though the helpers stayed there. During six months, more than 80 Polish infants died. The evidence of the village registrar showed that the three most frequent causes of death as certified by the doctors were general weakness, dysentery, and what they called catarrh of the intestines.

As administrator of the home, Gerike appointed the accused Hessling, who was also without previous experience of operating a children's clinic. Hessling called at the home at least once a month, and knew of the death-rate. Frau Bilien testified that she made many complaints to him, but that nothing was achieved except the raising of the entry age for children, which was previously eight to ten days after confinement, to four to six weeks thereafter. Hessling claimed that his only duty was to arrange the finances, but Gerike denied this. One witness testified that Frau Bilien, on finding that some of the children were dying because they needed mothers' milk, sent some back to their mothers, but that Hessling, on discovering her action, forbade such a course.

Two doctors paid rare visits to the home before September, 1944, when the accused Dr. Demmerick, though without official instructions, started to visit the home and to tend sick infants. Later in the period from September to December, 1944, however, Demmerick, falling in with the matron's suggestions, only tended such of the children as Frau Bilien brought to him, and only visited the home to sign death certificates. Demmerick claimed that, due to his large practice, he could find no time to write any letters of protest to persons in authority, or, in the later period, to visit the babies.

The accused Muller was an Ortsgruppenleiter, the leading Nazi in the village. He had seen the home and disapproved of it, but Gerike had told him that it was not his responsibility. Nevertheless, he once telephoned Gerike, told him of the frequent deaths and received an assurance that something would be done to improve matters. After that he appears not to have pursued the matter any further.

The accused Noth was Burgomeister in the village, and held no official position in the Nazi party, though he was a member thereof. He knew of the state of affairs at the home, advised against its establishment and wanted to see it removed.

The accused Claus, a farmer of Velpke, was found not guilty immediately after giving his evidence. He admitted that he sent at least two children to the home against the parents' will, but it was not proved that he knew of the neglect shown in the institution. The accused Flint died during the course of the trial.

Gerike, Hessling, Demmerick and Frau Bilien were found guilty. Muller and Noth were found not guilty.

Subject to confirmation by superior military authority, Valentina Bilien was sentenced to fifteen years' imprisonment, Dr. Richard Demmerick to ten years' imprisonment, and Georg Hessling and Heinrich Gerike to death by hanging. The findings and sentences were confirmed.

B. NOTES ON THE NATURE OF THE OFFENSE

The war crime of which the accused were found guilty was of a very unusual type and would repay a little examination. In the absence of a Judge Advocate's summing up, the arguments of Counsel can most profitably be examined in making an attempt to throw light on the legal nature of the offense.

The Prosecutor referred to Article 46 of the Regulations annexed to the Hague Convention No. IV of 1907, which forms part of Section III (*Military Authority over the Territory of the Hostile State*) and which provides that:

> "Art. 46. Family honour and rights, individual life, and private property, as well as religious convictions and worship, must be respected.
>
> Private property may not be confiscated."

Counsel pointed out that under international law it was forbidden in time of war to kill the innocent and defenceless population of any country overrun, "either in their own country or in the country of the occupying power." He added that it was unlawful for an occupying power to deport slave labour from the occupied country to its own territory, in the first place.

Elaborating his legal argument further, the Prosecutor quoted a number of passages from Archbold's *Pleading, Evidence and Practice in Criminal Cases* which expounded certain aspects of the English law of murder and criminal negligence. These were as follows:

"If a man, however, does any other act, of which the probable consequences may be and eventually is death, such killing may be murder, although no stroke were struck by himself; as was the case of the gaoler, who causes the death of a prisoner by imprisoning him in unwholesome air; of the unnatural son, who exposed his sick father to the air against his will, by reason whereof he died; of the harlot, who laid her child in an orchard, where a kite struck it and killed it; of the mother, who hid her child in a pig-sty, where it was devoured; and of the parish officers, who moved a child from parish to parish till it died from want of care and sustenance."

"Neglect of the helpless: Premeditated neglect or ill-treatment by persons having custody, charge, or control of helpless persons, whether children, imbeciles, or lunatics, or sick or aged, by deliberate omission to supply them with necessary food, etc., if attended with fatal results, may be murder; and if the same result flows from gross neglect in such a case, the offender is guilty of manslaughter."

"If a grown-up person chooses to undertake the charge of a human creature helpless either from infancy, simplicity, lunacy, or other infirmity, he is bound to execute that charge without wicked negligence; and if a person who has chosen to take charge of a helpless creature lets it die by gross negligence, that person is guilty of manslaughter. Mere negligence will not do; there must be negligence so great as to satisfy a jury that the prisoner was reckless and careless whether the creature died or not. 'Reckless' is a more accurate epithet to be applied to the negligence required than 'wicked.' If a person has the custody of another who is helpless, and leaves that other with insufficient food or medical attendance, and so causes his death, he is criminally responsible."

"Where death results in consequence of a negligent act, it would seem that to create criminal responsibility the degree of negligence must be so gross as to amount to recklessness. Mere inadvertence, while it might create civil liability, would not suffice to create criminal liability." The next paragraph reads: "In explaining to juries the test which they should apply to determine whether the negligence in the particular case amounted or did not amount to a crime, Judges have used many epithets such as 'culpable,' 'criminal,' 'gross,' 'wicked,' 'clear,' 'complete.' But whatever epithet is used and whether an epithet be used or not, in order to establish criminal liability, the facts must be such that, in the opinion of the jury, the negligence of the prisoner went beyond a mere matter of compensation between subjects and showed such disregard for the life and safety of others as to amount to a crime against the State and conduct deserving punishment."

In general it is recognized that the distinction made in English Law between murder and manslaughter is not relevant in trials of war criminals, and the Prosecutor did not in fact indicate on which of the above statements he chose to place most reliance in the present case.

The Prosecutor placed particular stress on the claim that once the child came from the farm where the female Polish worker had it and passed into the home, then all the obligations of motherhood, and the tests laid down by those passages, became applicable to Gerike, Hessling and Bilien. From the moment Gerike established the home for infant children of female Polish workers, whose children were to be taken away from their parents if necessary by force, "the Home became a Party affair, an NSDAP institution, entrusted by the Gauleiter to the control, administration and responsibility of the Kreisleitung of Helmstedt.... As long as the children of these workers remained in the custody of their mothers, albeit they were working on the farms, then if harm or hap should come to those children, then it may have been the fault of the Polish mother, but once you have removed those children by force and against the will of the mother into that Home which is run by the [Nazi] Party and from Kreis downwards, then and there the Party at the Kreisleitung takes over the parental responsibility of those infant children, and with that responsibility they take over naturally a whole burden of complicated duties relating to every branch of ordinary child welfare." Counsel claimed that the case of infant children had from time immemorial been "the act and attribute of a civilized community." In dealing with Frau Bilien he pointed out that: "Although she has said that what she did she did under order, she seems to have had very little idea of service and devotion and sacrifice to duty. If you undertake a task of skill then in law you are called upon to show the skill of the task that you have undertaken."

A case which turned mainly if not entirely on allegations, not of acts, but of omissions necessarily raised difficult questions as to what standard of care each accused could reasonably have been expected to observe. The Prosecution claimed that the accused, each "according to his function," had been guilty of such a gross and criminal disregard of their duties towards these defenceless Polish infants as to show a total disregard as to whether they lived or whether they died, and were therefore guilty under the charge. For various accused it was argued that they had done all that they could in the difficult position as regards accommodation, transport, suitable labour and medical services which resulted from the war. For Noth it was claimed that he had no power to alter a state of affairs which was actually under the control of the Nazi party.

The Court refused to support the allegation of the Prosecution in all cases. For instance, the Prosecution, while pointing out that Muller had, unlike Demmerick, Hessling and Gerike, never assumed the care of the children, submitted that Muller was neglectful in his functions as chief Nazi in the village, and that he thus "did contribute to the whole miserable affair and allowed it to go forward." Ortsgruppenleiter Muller was nevertheless acquitted. So also was the Burgomeister, Noth, who, according to the Prosecution's submission, turned a blind eye to the home, while he and the Ortsgruppenleiter together could have done much to relieve the conditions and death-rate therein. On the other hand, the Court inflicted a term of ten years' imprisonment on Dr. Demmerick, who had never received official instructions to tend the babies but who, according to the Prosecution, had by his acts "assumed the care of those children in place of their mothers."

It is to be noted that Article 46 of the Hague Convention No. IV of 1907, which was drafted at a time when deportations for forced labour on the scale carried out by Nazi Germany could not have been contemplated, strictly speaking applies only to behaviour of the occupying Power *within occupied territory*. Nevertheless, it is clear that the general rule laid down therein must be followed also in respect of inhabitants of occupied territory who have been sent into the country of the occupant for forced labour, as had the mothers of the children who were sent to the Velpke home, and to children born to them while in captivity. It was pointed out by the prosecutor that such deportation was itself contrary to international law, as was stated in Oppenheim-Lauterpacht, *International Law,* Vol. II, 6th Edition, on pp. 345–6, in the following passage:

> "…there is no right to deport inhabitants to the country of the occupant, for the purpose of compelling them to work there. When during the World War the Germans deported to Germany several thousands of Belgian and French men and women, and compelled them to work there, the whole civilized world stigmatized this cruel practice as an outrage."

It could have been argued by the Defence in the present case that the offence of deportation was committed by persons other than the accused; nevertheless, it seems reasonable to assume that the inhabitants of an occupied territory keep their rights under international law when forced to leave their own country, even though this is not expressly provided in the Hague Convention. Indeed, the Tribunal which conducted the *Justice Trial* [at Nuremberg] stated clearly that the transfer of "Night and Fog" prisoners from occupied territories to Germany did not cleanse the "Night and Fog" Plan of its iniquity "or render it legal in any respect."

Similarly, the Judge Advocate acting in the Trial of Georg Tyrolt and others by a British Military Court, Helmstedt, 20th May–24th June, 1946, said of the victims of the offences charged in that case: "Quite obviously if it is wrong to show lack of respect to their family life and individual life in their own country, you cannot get out of that obligation simply by taking them to your country and then ill-treating them there."

The last-mentioned trial is indeed a useful parallel to the *Velpke Children's Home Case.* The charge against the accused…[was] concerned in "killing by willful neglect a number of children of Polish and Russian nationals." The general facts of the case were also very similar to those in the trial of Gerike and others and again concerned the operation of a children's home. In his closing address the Prosecutor quoted the first three passages from Archbold which are cited above and added:

> "In a war crime we do not have to distinguish in charging a person between murder and manslaughter. To kill infant children who are admittedly helpless and in their care either by premeditated neglect or by wicked neglect is equally a war crime whether it be murder or manslaughter, but it is for you to decide in the case of each accused which degree is applicable to each accused."

The Judge Advocate referred to the Prosecutor's words as follows:

> "Again, I have no quarrel whatever with the authorities that Major Draper cited to you in support of his contention that these accused, if they did what is alleged against them, come within the doctrines of our English law regarding the standard of behavior that must be expected of persons who undertake the care of young children…. I agree with those submissions in law that he has made to you, and my advice to you is that they are sound and that they should govern your decisions when you come to consider the verdict. Either of those standards would include the wording of the charges in this case, namely 'concerned in killing by willful neglect' and the final question of which of those two standards any one of those accused neglected to observe, if any of them did, can only affect, in my opinion, your sentence at a later stage and not your verdict."

Death sentences were passed on the accused Dr. Korbel, [in the *Tyrolt Case*] who had been responsible for the medical care and health of the children, and on Ella Schmidt, a nurse in whose charge they were placed. A sentence of five years' imprisonment was passed on Liesel Sacher, a nurse who had also had charge of the infants for a period. Seven others accused were found not guilty. The findings and sentences were confirmed.

(g) *Trial of Werner Rohde and Eight Others* (The SS Obergruppenführer Case)

British Military Court, Wuppertal, Germany,
29th May–1st June, 1946
5 LRTWC 54 (1948)

A. OUTLINE OF THE PROCEEDINGS

Wolfgang Zeuss, Magnus Wochner, Emil Meier, Peter Straub, Fritz Hartjenstein, Franz Berg, Werner Rohde, Emil Bruttel, and Kurt Aus Dem Bruch, were charged with committing a war crime in that they at Stuthof/Natzweiler, France, in or about the months of July and August, 1944, in violation of the laws and usages of war, were concerned in the killing of four British women when prisoners in the hands of the Germans.

The accused were all officials attached to Stuthof/Natzweiler camp, except Berg, who was a prisoner there. It was shown that two members of the Womens Auxiliary Air Force (W. A. A. F.) and two of the First Aid Nursing Yeomanry (F. A. N. Y.), British Units, one of the four being of French nationality, had been sent to France in plain clothes to assist British liaison officers whose mission was to establish communications between London and the Resistance Movement in France. They were captured and eventually taken to Karlsruhe prison. After some weeks they were delivered to Natzweiler camp, where they were injected with a lethal drug and then cremated. It was alleged that the circumstances of their death constituted a war crime for which the accused were in different ways responsible. Counsel for Meier and Aus Dem Bruch were told by the Judge Advocate that they need not deal with these two accused in the final address, and the two were found not guilty.

Hartjenstein was Kommandant of the camp. There was no definite evidence that he was present at the killing, and he claimed that he was away from the camp at the time and that he did not know of the events alleged until after capture. It was established, however, that he was present at a party in the camp, the date of which was, according to some evidence, the same as that of the killings.

Wochner was the head of the political department at the camp, being independent of Hartjenstein and directly under the orders of the Security Police in Berlin. He claimed that someone from the criminal department at Karlsruhe brought the four women to his office, saying that they were to be executed and that he sent them away, saying that the matter did not concern him. He also denied having had any knowledge of the actual killings until after his capture. There was no evidence that he was present at the killings, but one witness said that Straub could not perform a cremation without Wochner's authority.

Rohde was a medical officer at the camp and admitted giving at least one injection, intending to kill. He claimed, however, that he only performed this distasteful task because he had orders to do so from one Otto; the latter, however, was shown to be merely an officer under a course of instruction with no official authority in the camp.

Rohde admitted that Otto showed him no evidence of a sentence of death having been passed on the victims.

Straub was in charge of the camp crematorium, but claimed that he was in Berlin at the time of the offence; on this point, however, there was a conflict of evidence, and one witness stated that Straub had actually told him that he was present at the execution.

Against Zeuss, a staff sergeant at Natzweiler, the evidence consisted of an affidavit statement, that he, along with Straub, had been seen "taking prisoners backwards and forwards," and the evidence of Wochner, that Zeuss was usually present at executions. Zeuss claimed that he was on leave at the time of the killings, and in this he was to some extent supported by other accused.

Berg was a prisoner whose task was to work the oven of the crematorium. He admitted that he lit the oven on the occasion but without knowing that there was anything unusual in the circumstances. No one claimed that he took part in the execution, and his own account was that he was locked in his room and that a fellow-prisoner watched and related the events to him as they happened.

Bruttel, a first aid N. C. O. at Natzweiler, admitted that he obeyed in order to bring the drug and that he heard, in conversations between the doctors and other officers in the camp, references to "the four women spies," "we cannot escape the order" and "execution." He claimed, however, that he had no clear idea that an execution was intended when he received his order. He was outside the room where the executions took place; he would have preferred to leave the crematorium altogether but could not do so without a lamp.

It was not shown that there existed any warrant for the execution of the victims. There was evidence that the papers relating to three of them during their stay in Karlsruhe prison provided no record of a trial or a sentence of death.

Zeuss, Meier and Aus Dem Bruch were found not guilty. The remaining accused were found guilty. Rohde was sentenced to death by hanging, Hartjenstein to imprisonment for life, and Straub, Wochner, Berg and Bruttel to imprisonment for thirteen, ten, five and four years respectively.

The findings and sentences were confirmed, and put into execution.

B. NOTES ON THE CASE

1. The Offence Alleged

The charge alleged a killing, contrary to the laws and usages of war, of British women prisoners in German hands. Neither the Prosecutor nor the Judge Advocate attempted to argue on the basis of the Geneva Prisoners of War Convention, however, and the only references to conventional International Law were made to Articles 29 and 30 of the Hague Convention. The lack of greater clarity in the allegation would seem to have arisen out of the prevailing doubts as to the legal status of the victims.... In discussing the plea of superior orders, the Judge Advocate stated: "You begin, of course...from the point of view that *the laws of humanity* demand that no one shall be put to death by a fellow human being..."

Regarding the meaning of the term "concerned the killing," contained in the charge, the Judge Advocate explained that to be concerned in a killing it was not necessary that any person should actually have been present. None of the accused was actually charged with killing any of the women concerned. If two or more men set out on a murder and one stood half a mile away from where the actual murder was committed, perhaps to keep guard, although he was not actually present when the murder was done, if he was taking part with the other man with the knowledge that that other man was going to put the killing into effect then he was just as guilty as the person who fired the shot or delivered the blow.

2. The Plea That The Killing Was Legal Under Articles 29 and 30 of the Hague Convention

Articles 29 and 30 of the Regulations annexed to the IVth Hague Convention of 1907 read as follows:

> "Art. 29. A person can only be considered a spy when, acting clandestinely or on false pretences, he obtains or endeavors to obtain information in the zone of operations of a belligerent, with the intention of communicating it to the hostile party.

> "Accordingly soldiers not wearing a disguise who have penetrated into the zone of operations of the hostile army for the purpose of obtaining information are not considered spies. Similarly, the following are not considered spies: Soldiers and civilians entrusted with the delivery of dispatches intended either for their own army or for the enemy's army, and carrying out their mission openly. To this class likewise belong persons sent in balloons for the purpose of carrying out dispatches and, generally, of maintaining communications between the different parts of an army or a territory."

> "Art. 30. A spy taken in the act shall not be punished without previous trial."

One of the Defence Counsel, acting on behalf of all the accused in this instance, argued that the evidence had shown that the four victims were spies and that Article 30 had been fulfilled. A spy was one who secretly or under false pretext received or attempted to receive messages in the country occupied by the enemy. The victims had landed in France without uniforms and had contacted the Resistance Movement. Article 30 simply stated that a sentence must have preceded the execution, but nowhere was it explained how such a sentence should have been arrived at. Counsel quoted the opinion of Professor Mosler, that: "Treatment according to usages of war does not require the lawful guarantee of a proper trial. It is sufficient to ascertain that a war criminal offence has been committed.... Usages of war do not know of any regulations on who could pass the sentence. Normally the commanding officer of the troops who brought about the arrest would be the one to ascertain the guilt, the punishment, and the execution, and would order the execution." It must be remembered that the Nazi regime used unusual methods in some of its activities. Counsel for the Prosecution had alleged that the documents of the prison showed that no legal proceedings had taken place because nothing was mentioned in those documents concerning a sentence. The sentence was only entered on such documents, however, when the institutions concerned also carries out the execution, so that they could know how many days the party concerned was confined. In the case of political crimes where usually the Gestapo dealt with the matter the prison was given no such instruction. Counsel stated: "For us Germans the government in the last years have given us an enormous number of special courts amongst which I myself have found S. S. courts S. D. Courts, courts who everywhere decided the fate of a human being and normally passed sentences of death.... Quite a number of the ac-

cused in as much as they are only small men cannot be expected to know that perhaps there was no sentence, and finally it is my point of view that the sentence by a
full court was not required in this case but a sentence by a single person may have
sufficed."

International Law, it was argued, did not lay down the manner in which spies should
be executed, and instantaneous painless death by injection could be considered a humane method. Counsel suggested that a soldier might have found difficulty in shooting
or hanging women.

In reply to these arguments, the Prosecutor admitted that, while the victims' mission
was not connected with espionage, they might nevertheless, on the least favorable interpretation, be possibly classified as spies. Had they had a trial by a competent court and
subsequently been lawfully executed by shooting this case would never have been
brought. The Defence, however, had not shown that there was any trial. No death sentence was ever communicated to these women nor did they ever, in the Prosecution's
submission, appear before any court. Someone in authority issued orders for all inmates to be indoors between eight and nine during the evening. The victims were injected with secrecy and at the same time they were told they were being injected against
typhus. They were then immediately cremated. Could the secrecy and the circumstances of their killing be reasonable [sic] inferred to be in the interests of humanity?

In his summing up, the Judge Advocate began by pointing out that a person who
takes part in a judicial execution bears, of course, no criminal responsibility. There was
no real definition of a spy, but Article 29 gave several examples of persons who could
not be regarded as such. The Court might choose to interpret the reference to "persons
sent in balloons for the purpose of carrying dispatches and generally, of maintaining
communications between the different parts of any army or a territory" as including
within its scope persons sent by aircraft for the purpose of maintaining communications. If the victims had been obviously spies, their being such might have been a mitigating circumstance which the accused could possibly plead, but the doubt which existed on the point made it all the more clear that they should have been given a trial....
The Judge Advocate, after reviewing the evidence on the point, concluded that he
could see no proof that a trial in any real sense was held. A separate issue was whether
or not the accused actually regarded the execution as being a judicial one; the Judge
Advocate thought it legally sound to plead that the accused did so, if it could be proved
in fact.

3. The Plea of Superior Orders

On behalf of the accused, it was pleaded that German Military Law demanded that
an order had to be carried out unless the accused knew positively that the deed was unlawful. The Judge Advocate pointed out that, even if an order had been given, no one
was obliged to obey an unlawful order. The Defence, he continued, had argued in effect that in Germany at the time an order to kill someone in the circumstances of this
case would not be regarded as unlawful. He felt bound, however, to advise the Court
that this did not provide a sufficient answer, if they were "satisfied that the order was
one which could not have been tolerated in any place where a system of justice was
used," and made the following comment: "If you were to go to a lunatic asylum to visit
a field-marshal who was an inmate there and he said: 'Go and kill the head warden.'
you would not, I imagine, go and do so and say: 'Well, I had to as the field-marshal
said "do it." That would not be an answer. That is what you are up against in this particular trial; a question of whether if anyone gives an order, emanating even from the

highest authority, which *obviously cannot be permitted*, you are going to obey it or not."
(Italics inserted).

4. Evidence By Accomplices

In summing up, the Judge Advocate pointed out that, in this case, a great deal of evidence was provided by accomplices "that is, persons who are also charged, or obviously could be charged, with having taken part in the same offence." He warned the Court "that the evidence of an accomplice must be regarded always with the greatest suspicion. Every accomplice is giving evidence which is of a tainted nature. He may have many reasons for not telling the truth himself. He may be trying to exculpate himself and throw the blame on somebody else, and there may be a hundred and one reasons why he should not be telling the truth.... This does not mean that you cannot believe him or you cannot accept the evidence of an accomplice, but it means that before you do so you must first caution yourself on those lines. If, having done so and in spite of having so warned yourselves, you believe that what he is saying is true, you are perfectly free to act upon his evidence." He added: "When you are looking for corroboration of an accomplice's evidence an accomplice cannot corroborate another."

In making these remarks the Judge Advocate was applying to the case the practice followed in English Criminal Law, according to which, "where a witness was himself an accomplice in the very crime to which an indictment relates, it is the duty of the judge to caution the jury strongly as to the invariable danger of convicting upon such evidence without corroboration. Moreover this corroboration must confirm not merely a material particular of the witness's story, but some particular which connects the prisoner himself with it.... Corroboration by another accomplice, or even by several accomplices, does not suffice.... But these common law rules as to the necessity of corroborating accomplices amount only to a caution and not to be a command."

(h) *Trial of Gerhard Friedrich Ernst Flesch,*
SS Ober-sturmbannführer, Oberregierungsrat

Frostating Lagmannsrett (Nov.–Dec., 1946)
Supreme Court of Norway (February, 1948)
6 LRTWC 111 (1948)

A. OUTLINE OF THE PROCEEDINGS

1. The Indictment

The defendant Flesch was charged by the Director of Public Prosecutions with having committed war crimes amounting to murder and torture...

* * *

The individual counts of the indictment made the following charges:

Count I

(a) In November, 1942, the defendant gave orders to the Commandant of Falstad Concentration Camp for the shooting of three Norwegian citizens of Jewish descent.

(b) In February, 1943, the defendant gave orders for the shooting of the Norwegian citizen Toralf Berg.

(c) In March, 1944, the defendant gave orders for the hanging of nine Russian prisoners of war. The defendant himself supervised the execution.

(d) In August–September, 1944, the defendant gave orders for the hanging of 15 Russian prisoners of war. The defendant himself supervised the execution.

(e) In October, 1944, the defendant gave orders for the shooting of the Norwegian citizens Kjell Barre, Kaare Storaas, Hans Fredrik Bye and three other persons, to take place while they were being arrested. As a result Kjell Barre and Hans Fredrik Bye were shot.

(f) In October, 1944, Johnny Pevik was hanged on the defendant's orders.

(g) In February, 1945, the Norwegian citizens Ingar Trooen and Ole Kvernrod were shot on the defendant's orders while being arrested.

Count II

(a) In March, 1942, the defendant took part in the "versharfte Vernehmung" of Hans Konrad Ekornes.

(b) In the autumn of 1942, the defendant gave orders to his subordinates to employ flogging as an ordinary means of punishment for Jewish prisoners in Falstad Concentration Camp.

(c) In February, 1944, the defendant gave orders for the "verscharfte Vernehmung" of Peter Helland Hansen.

(d) In May, 1944, the defendant gave orders for the "verscharfte Vernehmung" of Magne Flem.

(e) In November, 1944, the defendant gave orders for the "verscharfte Vernehmung" of Arne Tommeraas.

(f) In March, 1945, the defendant gave orders for the "Verscharfte Vernehmung" of Ingeborg Holm.

Count III

In September, 1943, the defendant, who was at that time Chief of Falstad Concentration Camp, refused permission for the taking to hospital of prisoner Erling Borg who was suffering from acute diphtheria. Borg died as a result of the illness on 22nd September, 1943....

2. The Position of the Accused

The evidence showed that Gerhard Friedrich Flesch was born on 8th October, 1909, in Poznan. In 1934, he took his degree in law and was appointed by Heydrich to the Gestapo where he was in control of the religious sects of Germany. In 1938, he took part in the German march into the Sudetenland, and in 1939, in the annexation of Bohemia and Moravia, and was later appointed political advisor to Gauleiter Sauckel in Thuringia. After the outbreak of the war in September, 1939, he became leader of an "Einsatzkommando" in Poznan. In 1940, he joined an SS Totenkopf-division in their march into France.

The defendant came to Norway on 23rd April, 1940, as Kommandeur of the SIPO and the SD in Bergen, and from October, 1941, held the same position in Trondhjem and district, covering most of Northern Norway. As Kommandeur of the district, he was also chief of Falstad Concentration Camp outside Trondhjem and prisons in Trondhjem. He was given the rank of Obersturmbannfuhrer and received the title of Oberregierungsrat. His immediate superior was Fehlis.

3. Judgment of the Frostating Lagmannsrett [trial court] of 2nd December, 1946

Flesch was found guilty on all counts, except points *a* and *c* of Count I, and was sentenced to death by shooting. The reasons of the Lagmannsret for reaching its decision are set out below.

Count I(a)

During the state of emergency in the Trondhjem area in the autumn of 1942, all male Jews were arrested and taken to Falsted Concentration Camp. Among them were Schidorsky, aged 55, Glick, aged 65 and Abrahemsen, aged 70. All three were sick men and were allowed to lie in a loft during the day. One day in November, the defendant came to inspect the camp. When he saw the three sick men, he said: "Sick Jews lying about! There is only one thing to do, dig a grave and everything will be right." (Aber Sie lassen doch keine kranken Juden liegen. Draussen ein Grab graben und alles ist in Ordnung).

The defendant denied having said anything to that effect but the Lagmannsrett felt bound to believe three witnesses, one of whom was Dr. Eitinger, the German M. O. in charge of the sick. Some days later Dr. Eitinger had gone to the Lagerkommandant and asked for permission to take one of the sick Jews to hospital. The Lagerkommandant had thereupon gone to Trondhjem to get a permit for the transfer of all three sick men to hospital. When he returned the same evening, the three men were taken from the camp.

Since then these three Jews had not been heard of, neither had it been possible to trace their names in any hospital register. The only evidence that has come to light is a letter from the SIPO to the Swedish Consualte General in Oslo, dated 31st May, 1943, which, in reply to some investigations started by Schidorsky's relatives in Sweden, stated that Schidorsky had died of pyaemia in Falstad Camp on 13th November, 1942.

The defendant insisted that he had not seen the Lagerkommandant as he had been in Germany at that time. It has not been possible to ascertain that it was the defendant who saw the Lagerkommandant or that it had been he who had given the actual orders for the extermination of the three Jews, and the court, therefore, felt bound to acquit him on *Count I(a)*.

Count I(b)

Toralf Berg, who had been one of the leaders of the local branch of the Military Organization—the Norwegian underground movement—had been arrested on15th August, 1942, and was sent to Falsted Camp where he had been badly ill-treated during several interrogations. He was shot on 16th February, 1943, on the defendant's orders.

The defendant had admitted to having given the orders but had maintained that Berg had been sentenced to death by a German military court in Dombaas, about 150 miles from Trondhjem. The Lagmannsrett could not accept that explanation. Berg had shared a cell with seven other prisoners to whom he had spoken freely but to whom he had never mentioned having been tried or court-martialled. Nor was there any proof that Berg had been taken from the camp to Dombaas where the court had ostensibly sentenced him to death. A letter received by Berg's father from the SIPO informing him of his son's suicide also contradicts defendant's statement.

The Lagmannsrett found that the defendant was guilty of having caused Berg's death without a trial, and that he had thus violated the laws and customs of war.

Count I(c) and (d)

The defendant had admitted having given the orders for the execution of two lots of Russian prisoners of war. He had stated that the prisoners had been sent to Falstad from various camps in the district and had all been guilty of criminal acts, such as attacks with explosives, murder and preparations for mass escapes. He maintained that every one of the prisoners had been sentenced to death by a Wehrmacht court martial. The reasons why they had not been executed by the Wehrmacht, but sent to him, were that he had been commissioned to investigate through interrogations how far Norwegians and Norwegian illegal organizations had been implicated in those subversive activities.

On the basis of the evidence submitted in the case, the Lagmannsrett assumed that before 1943 prisoners of war who had committed offences while in camp were dealt with by the Wehrmacht, and that the Wehrmacht courts martial only were considered competent to try such cases. In 1943, however, it had been decided that the SIPO should take over cases against prisoners of war who had escaped from the camps and had committed criminal acts while at liberty. After Himmler in July–August, 1944, had become in charge of matters concerning prisoners of war, it was decided that the SIPO should also take over cases against prisoners of war who had committed crimes while in camp without formal sentence being passed. Circumstances indicate that no sentences whatever had been passed on any Russian prisoners of war or at any rate not on those referred to in Court I(c) and (d).

As far as the prisoners of war referred to in point (c) are concerned, the evidence submitted to the court did not, however, prove sufficient to dismiss the defendant's statement that they had been sentenced by a court martial. Assuming that to be correct, the defendant's acts could not be characterized as being at variance with the laws and customs of war, in particular Article 8 of the Hague Convention concerning land warfare. The prosecution had not succeeded in proving that these prisoners of war had not been court-martialled and the Lagmannsrett, therefore, acquitted the defendant on that point.

As regards point (d), however, the Lagmannsrett could not accept the defendant's statement. Several German witnesses who had been in charge of the investigation into the cases against a number of these prisoners of war had stated that none of them had been sentenced for if they had been tried, they would in the course of their duties have been informed whether they had been sentenced or not. The Lagmannsrett, therefore, found it proved beyond doubt that the prisoners referred to in point (d) had been executed without a previous trial and that defendant had been cognizant of the fact. His actions, therefore, were at variance with the laws and customs of war, in particular Article 8 of the Hague Convention regarding land warfare. As the defendant had committed those acts knowingly and intentionally, he had also violated §233 of the Norwegian Civil Criminal Code.

The Lagmannsrett regarded as immaterial the defendant's plea that the German treatment of Russian prisoners of war must be adjudged in the light of the Russian treatment of German prisoners of war.

Count I(e)

The Lagmannsrett found it proved that in October, 1944, defendant had given orders for the arrest of a number of Norwegian citizens, and that in the course of the arrest six of them were to be shot from behind as if hit while escaping. Of the three Gestapo men who were in charge of the arrests, Roth arrested his seven men but did not shoot two of them as ordered. Koczy shot Barre but not Bye, who, he stated was wanted in connections with some investigations. Bye was shot later by Koczy ostensibly while trying to escape. The third Gestapo man, Dudeck, had made his arrests but had not carried out the order as to the shooting of two of the men.

The defendant had stated that he gave those orders in accordance with written directives received from Fehlis who had said that the men to be shot had already been sentenced by a Standgericht. The conclusion is inevitable, however, that the real reasons for the arrests and the shooting were reprisals against the Norwegian underground movement whose activities were allegedly in violation of international law.

According to defendant, he had sent a report to Fehlis mentioning the persons who, in his opinion, would be arrested, and Fehlis, relying upon the authority of an Erlass [decree] from Himmler concerning subversive activities in occupied territories, had decided which of them were to be shot.

The defendant's orders to his underlings had been to shoot the six men as soon as they were identified. The Lagmannsrett found that even though the six persons may have been guilty of subversive activities, the whole procedure was at variance with the laws and customs of war. According to Article 30 of the Hague Convention regarding land warfare, even spies caught *in flagrante delicto* [in the very act] could not be shot without trial, and persons who had committed such acts as the six men had been charged with could obviously not be placed in a less favourable position. As mentioned above, the defendant maintained that he had been told by Fehlis that all six persons had been sentenced to death by a Standgericht, but the Lagmannsrett found that even if defendant were to be believed on this point, he must have known that such "sentences" were actually only administrative decisions taken by Fehlis which could not be regarded as a sentence in the sense as understood by international law. The defendant himself had admitted that the shooting of the persons in question was an act of reprisal camouflaged by a Standgericht sentence. It must be remembered that of those doomed persons who had not been shot by the Gestapo men on the spot, not one was executed later.

The Lagmannsrett could not accept the defendant's plea that the procedure applied in these instances could be regarded as justifiable acts of reprisal. Experts on international law are divided in their opinion as to the legality of reprisals. Whatever the legal position, an act of reprisal can in no circumstances be pleaded in exculpation unless it was, at the time, announced publicly as such, or it appeared from the act itself that it was intended as a reprisal and showed clearly against what unlawful acts it was directed. None of the incidents in question fulfilled any of these minimum demands. Gestapo man Dudeck had stated that defendant had given explicit orders to shoot the persons in question from behind so as to make it seem as if they had been shot while escaping. It was not at all clear from these acts of alleged reprisals against what definite kinds of breaches of international law or German criminal provisions they were intended to serve as reprisals. The defendant had maintained that the acts of reprisal in question were directed against a number of subversive acts described in quite general terms, such as sabotage, guerrilla warfare, etc. The Lagmannsrett, however, could not regard guerrilla warfare in general as a breach of international law. It is a fact that soldiers had been sent to Norway from England to sabotage factories and military objectives, but in dealing with cases like that, the Germans had never distinguished between such acts having been executed by men in uniform or by soldiers in civilian disguise. When such acts of sabotage had been carried out by soldiers in uniform, they did not constitute a breach of international law.

The Lagmannsrett thus came to the conclusion that the acts in question could not be regarded as reprisals but must be considered as acts solely intended to terrorize the population in order to stem the underground movement. It was significant in the Lagmannsrett's opinion that the defendant's underlings had reacted against the inhumane orders by trying to avoid carrying them out.

The Lagmannsrett found that the shooting of Barre had been carried out in accordance with detailed instructions. Consequently this act was a violation of §233 Norwegian Civil Criminal Code. As regards the defendant's orders for the shooting of the others, the Lagmannsrett found that this constituted attempted murder, an act punishable according to §233, cf. §49 of the Civil Criminal Code.

Count I(f)

Pevik was arrested in the autumn of 1943, on suspicion of having smuggled arms and taken part in sabotage. During various interrogations he had been cruelly ill-treated until in October, 1944, the defendant had given orders for his hanging.

The defendant had made several contradictory statements on that count. In the first place he had maintained that the execution was based on a sentence by the SS und Polizeigericht Nord in November or December, 1943, but had been postponed pending investigations into other cases. Later he had stated that Pevik was kept alive because he was regarded as a hostage, later still that he was to be exchanged for a German prisoner. In October, 1944, the defendant had allegedly received orders from Fehlis to execute the sentence. The defendant denied the ill-treatment.

The Lagmannsrett found it proved that Pevik had not been sentenced by any court. Several German witnesses closely connected with the SS und Polizeigericht Nord, among them the secretary to the court, denied that Pevik had been tried, and one German witness had stated that the defendant had told him that Pevik was to be executed pursuant to the "Nacht und Nebel Erlass." [Night and Fog Decree]. In the light of all the available evidence, the Lagmannsrett found that Pevik had been executed at variance with the laws and customs of war. As the defendant committed those acts knowingly and intentionally, he had also violated §233 of the Norwegian Criminal Code.

Count I(g)

The Lagmannsrett found it proved that the defendant on 15th February, 1945, gave orders for the arrest of Ingar Trooen and Ole Kvernrod and for their shooting while being arrested. Trooen was shot while he was leaving his house, whereas Kvernrod was arrested to begin with, but shot later when allegedly trying to escape. Even though Trooen and Kvernrod as section leaders of the Military Organization were liable to be sentenced to death by a German court martial, the Lagmannsrett found that the procedure followed by defendant, as far as Trooen was concerned, was at variance with international law. As to Kvernrod, however, the Lagmannsrett could not but accept the possibility that it might have been true that he was shot while trying to escape as stated by the German witness who had shot him. As defendant had acted knowingly and intentionally, he had at the same time violated §233, cf. §42 of the Norwegian Civil Criminal Code.

Count II

In accordance with what defendant himself had explained, the Lagmannsrett found it proved that the so-called method of "verscharfte Vernehmung" [aggravated examination] of prisoners, in order to extract information, was brought into force in Norway in 1940–41. The Polizeikommandeurs [police commanders] were vested with the authority to issue written permits for the application of that method. Later the individual investigators (Sachbearbeiter) were delegated with authority to use this method if they found it necessary.

The Lagmannsrett then turned to the individual instances of torture covered by Count II and found it proved that all the victims had been tortured in the most appalling way by the application of the most vicious and sadistic methods of torture ever employed by the Germans, and that these acts of torture had been carried out either on special orders or with the connivance or approval of the defendant. As, however, these acts of torture did not give rise to any legal problems, it is considered beyond the scope or purpose of these present Reports to go into further detail as regards the evidence of the individual acts of torture. It will suffice to state that the Lagmannsrett, on the basis of the overwhelming evidence submitted to the court, found that these acts were committed in violation of §229 of the Civil Criminal Code as all the acts of torture referred to had been carried out according to the authority or general directives from defendant who must have been aware of the fact that these would result in grave bodily harm. The defendant thus violated §232 of the Civil Criminal Code in so far as the acts had been committed knowingly and intentionally and in a particularly painful way.

The defendant had pleaded that all his acts had been carried out on superior orders either according to general or special directives. The Lagmannsrett, however, found that as the defendant had been aware that his acts were in violation of international law, superior orders could not be invoked in exculpation.

Count III

Erling Borge was taken in Falstad Concentration Camp on 8th September, 1943, suffering from diptheria. The M. O. repeatedly asked the camp commandant for permission to have the patient taken to hospital but was refused. The Lagmannsrett found it established that the camp commandant had applied to defendant for permission to move Borge to hospital but that the defendant had said that the patient was going to die in any case and could thus as well remain in his cell. Borge died on 22nd September.

The Lagmannsrett found that the defendant, by refusing Borge's admission to hospital, had willfully and knowingly violated §242 of the Civil Criminal Code.

4. The Appeal to the Supreme Court of Norway

The defendant appealed to the Supreme Court against the sentence of the Lagmannsrett primarily on the grounds that:

(a) the Lagmannsrett had wrongly applied the provisions of the law on criminal procedure, and

(b) the Lagmannsrett had wrongly interpreted and applied the provisions of international and Norwegian substantive law.

He also appealed on the grounds that the punishment decided upon by the Lagmannsrett was too severe.

The details on the points of the appeal will appear from the account of the decision of the Supreme Court.

5. The Decision of the Supreme Court on 12th February, 1948

The defendant's appeal was unanimously rejected.

JUDGE SOELSETH in giving the reasons for the court's decision dealt with defendant's appeal point by point.

The defendant had maintained that whilst the preparations for the trial were going on, he had been taken to Bergen and other places for interrogation purposes. Because of that he had not been able to study the voluminous material submitted to the court and to prepare his defence as thoroughly as he would have like to. Furthermore, during the trial his opportunity to confer with his German counsel had been limited, and according to prison regulations, he had not been allowed to work on his defence after 10 p.m. This complaint was ruled out by Judge Soelseth who found that defendant had been given ample time to prepare his defence, confer with his counsel and explain himself in court.

The defendant had complained that the Lagmannsrett had refused to summon or order the interrogation of four German witnesses, one of whom could have testified that death sentences had been passed on the Russian prisoners of war mentioned in Count I(d) of the indictment whilst the other witnesses could have stated that death sentences had also been passed on Toralf Berg and Johnny Pevik, cf. Count I(b) and (f) respectively. Judge Solseth observed that according to the records of the Lagmannsrett trial, the court had requested the prosecution to try to trace these German witnesses. The prosecution had done its utmost but had not been able to trace them. The Lagmannsrett had found that there was not sufficient reason to adjourn the trial because of this as it was considered doubtful whether their evidence would have been of any decisive importance in view of the convincing evidence already submitted to the court. Before the case came up before the Supreme Court, two of the witnesses had been found and interrogated but their evidence, quite unexpectedly to the defendant, had supported the prosecution's contention.

Judge Soelseth then went on to discuss the defendant's allegation that the Lagmannsrett had wrongly applied the law. The defendant had contended that the Lagmannsrett had erroneously assumed that the executed persons mentioned in Court I(b), (e), (f) and (g) of the indictment could not be legally executed without a previous trial. According to the defendant, these persons were franc-tireus [war traitors or turncoats] whose actions were at variance with international law and consequently they were not entitled to be treated according to regulations laid down by international law. Judge Soelseth ruled out this objection. In his opinion it was quite clear that in the prevailing circumstances the fight of the underground movement against the Germans could not in itself be regarded as being at variance with international law. The question whether such resistance against the occupying Power was a breach of international law or not had no bearing on the question at issue, namely, what procedure the occupying Power was bound by international law to apply against people who had taken part in subversive activities. Judge Soelseth held that it was an unquestionable principle of international law that punishment could not be inflicted unless the guilt of the accused had been established through judicial procedure and he made reference to Konz's *Kriegsrecht und Neutraliatsrecht,. [The Law of War and the Law of Neutrality]* page 97. He also recalled that the Supreme Court had taken the same view in the cases against Oscar Hans and against Latza and two others. It might not be clear according to international law what requirements the tribunal or the authorities which take the decision must fulfill, but Judge Soelseth felt satisfied that the minimum demand for such procedure was that the accused could not be sentenced without having his guilt investigated in a proper and fair manner. To ensure this result, it was necessary that the accused be informed of the charge and the evidence brought against him, and that he be given opportunity to defend himself and to offer counter-evidence. The Lagmannsrett found that as regards the Norwegian citizens who had been executed, no such trial or proper investigation had been instituted. Judge Soelseth agreed with the Lagmannsrett that the procedure applied by the German authorities in these instances did not fulfil the minimum demands as laid down by international law. Thus it has been established as regards the persons mentioned in Court I(e) and (g) respectively, that they had been arrested subsequent to the decision for their execution, and that they had not been interrogated at all.

Judge Soelseth agreed with the view held by the Lagmannsrett to the effect that the execution of the Norwegian citizens without previous trial could not be regarded as constituting justifiable reprisals and made reference to what had been held by the Supreme Court in the case of Bruns and others.

As to the Russian prisoners of war referred to in Count I(d) of the indictment, the defendant had maintained that the Lagmannsrett had wrongly considered it immaterial that the Russians shot German prisoners of war. In this connection the counsel for the defence had pointed out that Russia had not become a signatory to the Geneva Convention and that she had decreed that she would not treat members of the German armed forces in accordance with the Geneva Convention. Counsel for defence claimed that German prisoners of war were shot by the Russians when taken prisoners, a fact which in his opinion justified the Germans to shoot Russian prisoners of war without trial, at any rate those who were guilty of criminal offences. Judge Soelseth did not find it necessary to deal with the question whether or not Russia had complied with the provisions of the Geneva Convention in her treatment of German prisoners of war. He found it sufficient to point out that it did not follow from the fact that Russia had not become a signatory to the Geneva Convention that the general provisions of international Law should not be complied with by the Germans when dealing with Russian prisoners of war.

Defendant had pleaded superior orders and maintained that he could not be held responsible unless it could be shown that he had known that the orders were illegal. Judge Soelseth observed, however, that superior orders could not be pleaded in exculpation, cf. §5 of Law No. 14 of 13th December, 1946, and it was clear from what had been stated by the Lagmannsrett that defendant had in all instances been aware that he had acted in violation of international law.

As to Bye and Bvernrod, cf. Count I(e) and (g) respectively, defendant had maintained that he could not be found guilty of the attempted murder of these persons. Although he had given the orders for their execution, they were not actually shot as a consequence of these orders. In their attempt to escape, a new situation had arisen which constituted the immediate cause for their shooting. Thus it had come to a break in the causative relation between his orders and the shootings. Judge Soelseth felt satisfied that the Lagmannsrett had interpreted the law correctly when finding defendant guilty of attempted murder in the case of Bye and Bvernrod.

A subsidiary appeal had been launched by defendant against the degree of punishment imposed by the Lagmannsrett. Judge Soelseth held that in view of the fact that the defendant had held the high position of a Kommandeur of the SIPO since October, 1941, he could justly be made personally responsible for the acts carried out by his underlings. According to Judge Soelseth it could not be pleaded in mitigation that it might have been possible that several of the executed persons would have been legally sentenced to death by a proper tribunal. On the other hand, however, it had to be remembered that the defendant had by his orders and actions deprived these persons, who were in his power, of the opportunity of having the charges against them tried in a proper way. Thus Judge Soelseth agreed with the Lagmannsrett that the supreme penalty had to be applied in the case at hand.

The remaining Judges, Berger, Schei, Stenersen, Krog, Gaarder, Holmboe, Bonnevie and Stang concurred in Judge Soelseth's opinion.

[Between 1945 and the early 1950s, the war crimes trial program by the Allies in Western Europe against the Nazis wound down due to a variety of factors, chief among which were the differing *realpolitik* developments between the West and the Soviet Union. Simpson[57] asks once again:

> …Why has there been a tendency to equate war crimes and the Nazi regime in Western jurisprudence and culture?… One way to approach the problem is to remember that war crimes trials (especially successful ones) have exculpatory effects as well as retributive consequences. As well as trying alleged war criminals, these trials serve as vindication of Western progress, they maintain the idea that National Socialism was an aberration in Western culture, they function as moral demarcations between the accused and the accusers, they avert attention from war crimes closer to home and, finally, they contain the message that the untried crimes are not of this magnitude or order. The eternal pariah is Nazi Germany serving as a lesson not only that it must not happen again but that perhaps it is *not* happening again.… The singular focus on Nazi war criminals had a curious legal consequence. The Nazis are taken as an exemplification of evil in the world and also an exception to universal humanism. This is why war crimes trials hover endlessly between upholding a universal morality and particularizing the crime in question as an historical exception. Ultimately, the performance of a war crimes trial is both situated in a history and yet seeks to transcend it. The trial confines a historical movement in its abnormality but wishes to make its lesson universal and timeless.[58]

In order to permanently imprint the judgment of the IMT in international law, the General Assembly of the United Nations asked the International Law Commission to draft a document that incorporated by reference the basic canons of the Nuremberg trial. The ILC prepared what has become known as the "Nuremberg Principles" which was adopted by the U. N. General Assembly on December 12, 1950. This document lays out in rather specific language what the international community deems the basic essentials of a fair trial and the offenses deemed to be universally condemned by the law of nations. We conclude *Part Two* with the "Nuremberg Principles"].

---

22. The Nuremberg Principles
1 U.N. GAOR (Part II) at 188, U.N. Doc. A/61/ADD.1 (1946)

Principle I. Any person who commits or is an accomplice in the commission of an act which constitutes a crime under international law is responsible therefore and liable for punishment.

---

57. Timothy L. H. McCormick, & Gerry J. Simpson, *The Law of War Crimes: National and International Approaches* (1997).
    58. *Id.* at 9.

Principle II. The fact that domestic law does not punish an act which is an international crime does not free the perpetrator of such crime from responsibility under international law.

Principle III. The fact that a person who committed an international crime acted as Head of State or public official does not free him from responsibility under international law or mitigate punishment.

Principle IV. The fact that a person acted pursuant to order of his government or of a superior does not free him from responsibility under international law. It may, however, be considered in mitigation of punishment, if justice so requires.

Principle V. Any person charged with a crime under international law has the right to a fair trial on the facts and law.

Principle VI. The crimes hereafter set out are punishable as crimes under international law.:

a. Crimes against Peace:

(1) Planning, preparation, initiation or waging of a war of aggression, or a war in violation of international treaties, agreements or assurances;

b. War Crimes: namely, violations of the laws or customs of war. Such violations shall include, but not be limited to, murder, ill-treatment or deportation to slave labour or for any other purpose of civilian population of or in occupied territory, murder ill-treatment of prisoners of war or persons on the seas, killings of hostages, plunder of public or private property, wanton destruction of cities, towns or villages, or devastation not justified by military necessity.

c. Crimes against Humanity: namely, murder, extermination, enslavement, deportation and other inhuman acts done against a civilian population, or persecution on political, racial or religious grounds, when such acts are done or such persecutions are carried out in execution of or in connection with any crime against peace or any war crime.

Principle VII. Complicity in the commission of a crime against peace, a war crime or a crime against humanity, as set forth in Principle VI, is a crime under international law.

[Between 1948 and 1960, courts in West Germany conducted so-called *Kameradenschinder* trials, that is, trials of Germans who had tormented their comrades while both were in Soviet captivity as POWs. These West German courts applied a more draconian yardstick to Germans who committed offenses against other Germans held by the Russians than they did to those offenses committed by Germans against other Germans during the Hitler regime. Most of these trials were commenced by former German POWs who had returned to Germany from Russia, and, once back in West Germany, had accused fellow Germans in Soviet captivity of various crimes such as beatings of fellow captives or other forms of collaboration with Soviet authorities. There was, however, an interesting prosecutorial omission in these *Kameradenschinder* tribunals; West German courts during this era abstained from the prosecution of German soldiers for alleged war crimes committed by them against *non-German* victims on the Eastern front. By and large, *Kameradenschinder* trials were conducted under the rule of law by members of an independent judiciary unlike their East German counterparts who conducted state purges of political enemies in the German Democratic Republic (GDR). The West German judges studiously refrained from sitting in judgment of what would be classified today as blatant political prosecutions. This abstention was a welcome counterpoint to the East German political trials held under Soviet auspices].

Suggestions for Further Reading

(1) Ball, Howard, *Prosecuting War Crimes and Genocide: The Twentieth Century Experience.* Lawrence, KS: University Press of Kansas (1999).

(2) Bankier, David, *The Germans and the Final Solution: Public Opinion Under Nazism.* Cambridge, MA: Harvard University Press (1992).

(3) Barry, John V., "The Trial and Punishment of Axis War Criminals," 17 *Australian Law Journal* 43 (1943).

(4) Bassiouni, M. Cherif, "Nuremberg Forty Years After: An Introduction," 18 *Case Western Reserve Journal of International Law* 261 (1986).

(5) Bernays, Murray, "Legal Basis of the Nuremberg Trials," 35 *Survey Graphics* 390 (January, 1946).

(6) Bial, L. C., "The Nuremberg Judgment and International Law," 13 *Brooklyn Law Review* 34 (1947).

(7) Black, Naomi, "Decision-making and the Munich Crisis," 6 *British Journal of Interantional Studies* 278 (1980).

(8) Boozer, Jack S., "Children of Hippocrates: Doctors in Nazi Germany," 45 *Annals of the American Academy of Political and Social Science* 83 (July, 1980).

(9) Bowett, Derek, "Reprisals Involving Recourse to Armed Force," 66 *American Journal of International Law* 1 (1972).

(10) Bracher, Karl D., *The German Dictatorship: The Origins, Structure, and Effects of National Socialism.* New York: Praeger (1970).

(11) Broszat, Martin, *The Hitler State.* New York: Longman (1981).

(12) Buchheim, H., *The Third Reich: Its Beginning, Its Development, Its End.* Munich: Kosel (1961).

(13) Buscher, Frank W., *The U.S. War Crimes Trial Program in Germany, 1946–1955.* Westport, CT: Greenwood Press (1988).

(14) Bush, Jonathan A., "Nuremberg: The Modern Law of War and Its Limitations," 93 *Columbia Law Review* 2022 (1992).

(15) Carroll, Berenice A., *Design for Total War: Arms and Economics in the Third Reich.* The Hague: Mouton (1968).

(16) Combs, William L., *The Voice of the SS: A History of the SS Journal DAS SCHWARZE KORPS.* New York: Peter Lang (1986).

(17) Davidson, Eugene, *The Trial of the Germans: An Account of the Twenty-One Defendants Before the IMT at Nuremberg.* New York: Macmillian (1966).

(18) Delarue, Jacques, *The Gestapo: A History of Horror.* New York: Morrow (1964).

(19) Eitner, Lorenz, "The Criminal State and Its Servants: Reminiscences of the Nuremberg War Crimes Trials," 3 *Minnesota Law Review* 162 (1963).

(20) Feig, Konnilyn G., *Hitler's Death Camps: The Sanity of Madness.* New York: Holmes & Meier (1981).

(21) Frei, Norbert, *National Socialist Rule in Germany: The Führer State, 1933–1945.* (Simon B. Steyne trans.). Oxford, UK: Blackwell (1993).

(22) Friedlander, Henry, *Origins of Nazi Genocide: From Euthanasia to the Final Solution*. Chapel Hill, NC: University of North Carolina Preess (1995).

(23) Graber, G. S., *The History of the SS*. New York: David McKay (1978).

(24) Hessler, Curt A., "Command Responsibility for War Crimes," 82 *Yale Law Journal* 1274 (1973).

(25) Kochavi, Arieh J., *Prelude to Nuremberg: Allied War Crimes Policy and the Question of Punishment*. Chapel Hill, NC: University of North Carolina Press (1998).

(26) Laffin, John, *Hitler Warned Us: The Nazi's Master Plan for a Master Race*. New York: Barnes & Noble (1995).

(27) Lambert, Thomas F., Jr., "Recalling the War Crimes Trials of World War II," 149 *Military Law Review* 15 (1995).

(28) Marrus, Michael R., *The Nuremberg War Crime Trial 1945–46, A Documentary History*. Boston: Bedford Books (1997).

(29) Massey, Stephen J., "Individual Responsibility for Assisting the Nazis in Persecuting Civilians," 71 *Minnesota Law Review* 97 (1986).

(30) Neumann, Franz, *Behemoth: The Structure and Practice of National Socialism 1933–1944*. New York: Harper & Row (1966).

(31) Reitlinger, Gerald, *The SS: Alibi of a Nation 1922–1945*. New York: Viking Press (1957).

(32) Russell, Edward F. L., *The Scourge of the Swastika: A Short History of Nazi War Crimes*. New York: Philosophical Library (1954).

(33) Viereck, Peter, *Metapolitics: The Roots of the Nazi Mind*. New York: Capricorn Books (1965).

(34) Weindling, Paul J., *Nazi Medicine and the Nuremberg Trials*. New York: Palgrave Macmillan (2004).

(35) Wright, Quincy, "Legal Positivism and the Nuremberg Judgment," 42 *American Journal of International Law* 409 (1948).

(36) _____, "War Criminals," 39 *American Journal of International Law* 257 (1945).

Part Three

Japanese Imperialism in the 1930s; China and Manchuria; Nanking Massacre; Tripartite Pact; World War II and Japanese War Crimes; IMTFE Tokyo; Japanese Atomic Bomb Litigation (1927–1948; 1963)

Editorial Commentary

At the end of World War I, the Japanese began to expand their interests on the Asian mainland and elsewhere. Japan, of course, was an ally of the United States and the *Triple Entente* during the Great War, and, after Imperial Germany surrendered in 1918, the Japanese under the authority of a League of Nation's mandate, moved to occupy Germany's former leaseholds in China. In addition, the Japanese also began to occupy Germany's island colonies in the Western Pacific north of the equator under similar mandates from the League.

As early as 1922, certain ultra-nationalist elements in Japanese political and military sectors began to assert themselves. In that year, as a result of negotiations spelled out by the *Washington Naval Conference*, the British and American negotiators persuaded the reluctant Japanese to limit the size of the Imperial Japanese Fleet to three-fifths the size of the Anglo-American navies. While Japan was not in total accord with such a proposal, she agreed nonetheless to abide by such strictures. Even making allowance for that concession, the three-fifths ratio gave Japan what amounted to naval superiority in the waters of the Western Pacific and along the length and breadth of the coast of China. For a maritime nation with imperialistic ambitions, the 1922 negotiations were the most Japan would concede.

Japan was also a signatory to another naval treaty signed in 1930. The *Treaty for Limitation and Reduction of Naval Armaments* of April 22, 1930, was entered into by Japan with Great Britain, India and other British dominions as well as with the United States. This treaty, signed at London, simply provided for continued limitations on naval armaments within the general framework of the 1922 *Washington Naval Conference*. Although subsequently ratified by Japan, the language of the 1930 treaty gave rise to considerable political and military opposition within the country.

Japanese land expansion and other imperial ambitions were outlined in a secret government document in 1927, called the *Tanaka Memorial*. The contents of this directive were top secret and geopolitically sensitive. Among other things, its provisions outlined Imperial Japan's blueprint for how Manchuria, Mongolia and China could be incorporated into what the Japanese propagandists would later term the "Greater East Asia Co-Prosperity Sphere."

The prelude to World War II in the Far East began in 1931. On the evening of September 18, 1931, the so-called "Mukden Incident" in Manchuria initiated a Japanese military presence on the mainland of Asia from that date through the end of World War II. A firefight broke out near the Mukden railway station on the South Manchurian Railway between Chinese troops and the Japanese. Sometime later, Japanese infantry attacked the city of Mukden itself. Lord Russell[1] notes that:

> There is overwhelming evidence that the Mukden Incident was carefully planned by officers of the Army General Staff, officers of the Kwantung Army, members of the Cherry Society [a secret Japanese military society] and others, with the object of affording a pretext for the occupation of Manchuria by that [Japanese] Army, and the setting up of a new State [in Manchuria] as a satellite of Japan.[2]

As a result of the Mukden encounter, the Japanese Kwantung Army moved into Manchuria and virtually occupied the country. Mayer[3] exclaims that:

> [t]he invasion of Manchuria was a bad omen for things to come.... The Manchurian incident inaugurated a series of episodes in which decisions which vitally affected the course of Japanese history and diplomacy were made by army officers in the field while the government in Tokyo stood by powerless to act except in response to *faits accomplis*.[4]

By January, 1932, for all intents and purposes, active hostilities in Manchuria were concluded. However, continuing hostilities with China did not abate. With Japanese forces continuing to pour into Northern China, the Chinese government invoked Article II of the Covenant of the League of Nations and requested the Council of the League to take whatever action was necessary to restore the territorial *status quo* in the region. Responding to China's request, the League appointed a Commission of Enquiry, headed by Lord Lytton of Great Britain, to investigate and report back to the Council its findings regarding Japanese occupation of Manchuria and continued Japanese incursions on the Chinese mainland, with special attention being given to the events that occurred in Mukden on September 18–19, 1931. The Lytton Commission spent a total of

---

1. Lord Russell of Liverpool, *The Knights of Bushido: A Short History of Japanese War Crimes (1958).*

2. *Id.* at 7.

3. *The Rise and Fall of Imperial Japan* (S. L. Mayer ed. 1976).

4. *Id.* at 96

six months in the Far East investigating and interrogating various officials in both the Japanese and Chinese governments. During this six-month interval, the Japanese further complicated the work of the Lytton Commission by installing Pu Yi, the last emperor of the Ching Dynasty, as the head of the new Japanese puppet state of Manchukuo (formerly Manchuria). The Lytton Commission could not, of course, give formal recognition to the government officials of this new Japanese creation. The final report by the Lytton Commission was made to the League of Nations in September, 1932. In it, the Commission was critical of Japanese intervention in Manchuria and Japan was called upon to make a voluntary withdrawal. However, a sharp controversy arose between the disputants as to whether the Japanese actions at Mukden in 1931 were legitimate acts of self-defense or acts of unwarranted aggression. The verbatim findings of the Lytton Commission on this point were ambivalent at best. They read:

> The military operations of the Japanese troops during this night [September 18–19, 1931], which have been described above, cannot be regarded as measures of legitimate self-defence. In saying this, The Commission does not exclude the hypothesis that the officers on the spot may have thought they were acting in self-defence.[5]

The Japanese government was incensed by the overall tone and findings of the Lytton Commission, seeing its recommendations as merely another example of occidental meddling in Japanese affairs of State. Instead of acceding to the finding of the Lytton Commission, the Japanese instead withdrew from the League of Nations on March 27, 1933. By now it was painfully obvious to most international observers that Japan was on the road to further martial conquests. Writing in 1934 in the *American Journal of International Law* Lauterpacht,[6] a noted scholar in that field, observed that:

> …The charter of the community of nations organized in and through the League proved, at all appearances, to be of illusory value in its fundamental aspect, namely, in the undertaking to protect the members of the League from external violence and aggression. The prediction of the skeptics that the authority of the League would be unable to assert itself if challenged by one of the Great Powers seemed to have been amply confirmed. It seemed to have been fulfilled by a successful defiance of the Covenant so unprecedented in its magnitude, obviousness and persistence as to constitute a fair test case of the value and of the potentialities of the League.[7]

On June 15, 1936, Japan formally withdrew from the accords reached at the London Naval Conference in 1930. By 1936, all indications were that the Japanese military had gained a virtual stranglehold on the civilian government in Tokyo. In July, 1937, Chinese and Japanese forces clashed in and around the cities of Peking and Nanking. On November 11, 1937, after occupying and seizing control of Shanghai, the Japanese army moved against Nanking. Strong opposition by the Chinese at Peking, Shanghai and Nanking apparently infuriated the Japanese; they had not expected the Chinese to resist with such vigor. On December 9, 1937, the Japanese launched a murderous attack on Nanking. At that time, Nanking was a city of over one million, many of its inhabitants having fled from the Kwantung Army from the north which had invaded China in 1931.

---

5. As quoted in Editorial Comment, "The Lytton Report on the Manchurian Crisis," 27 *Am. J. Int'l L.* 96, 98 (1933).

6. Hersh Lauterpacht, "'Resort to War' and the Interpretation of the Covenant During the Manchurian Dispute," 28 *Am. J. Intl' L.* 43 (1934).

7. *Id.*

On December 12, 1937, the Chinese troops defending Nanking decided to withdraw to the opposite side of the Yangtze River. The following day, December 13, 1937, the Japanese 6th and 116th divisions entered Nanking. The Imperial Navy then arrived to support the army and it took up positions on both sides of the Yangtze; Nanking fell to the Japanese that same day. It is what transpired in Nanking during the following six weeks or so that became known to the world as the "Rape of Nanking" or the "Nanking Massacre." Casualty figures will never be precisely known, but it is conservatively estimated that at least 300,000 Chinese soldiers and civilian non-combatants were killed and about 20,000 Chinese women of all ages were raped and tortured by the invaders. In addition to widespread rape, the Japanese army burned, looted and vandalized Nanking. In the horrendous aftermath, the city of Nanking was reduced to nothing more that a gigantic pile of smoldering rubble that ultimately became an international symbol of Japanese insensitivity to civilized norms of behavior regulating international hostilities between nation-states. To this day, the official Japanese government response to what it terms the "Nanking incident" has been one of bold denial. Nonetheless, what transpired at Nanking in those weeks of tumult set the tone for future Japanese war crimes committed throughout the Far East in the course of World War II.

As the 1930s came to an end, it was becoming quite clear that Japan was being more and more diplomatically isolated from the West. As an island nation, Japan's industrial development and her capacity for sustaining international mischief as well depended heavily on a sustained source of secure markets and a continuous flow of raw materials. Petroleum, of course, was a key natural resource. During the 1930s, the United States supplied Japan with sixty-five percent of her petroleum imports! If this huge oil import quota were cut off, Japan would be faced with a shortfall of staggering and disastrous proportion.

In his exhaustive and thoroughly-researched book on the American occupation of Japan after the war, Takemae[8] writes that:

> Washington...viewed Japanese aggression in China as an attempt to terminate American influence throughout Asia and responded with economic sanctions. In July, 1939, the United States signaled its intention to terminate Japan's Most Favored Nation status and subsequently outlawed the export of scrap metal.... In late July 1941, following the Imperial Army's march into southern French Indo-China...Britain, the Netherlands and the United States froze Japanese assets. For Tokyo, the final blow fell on 1 August 1941 when Washington embargoed oil exports.[9]

He then notes that:

> The crucial decision leading to war was taken at the Imperial Conference of 2 July 1941, when the government and military high command endorsed the establishment of a Greater East Asia Co-Prosperity Sphere in Asia and agreed to advance southwards, preparing for hostilities with the Anglo-American alliance should negotiations fail.[10]

About a year earlier on September 17, 1940, Japan became a signatory to the *Tripartite Pact* along with Nazi Germany and Fascist Italy. She then moved diplomatically to secure her northern flank by negotiating with the Soviet Union the *Russo-Japanese Neu-*

---

8. Takemae, Eiji, *Inside GHQ: The Allied Occupation of Japan and Its Legacy* (2002).
9. *Id.* at xxxii.
10. *Id.* at xxxv.

trality Agreement in April, 1941. When Nazi Germany invaded the Soviet Union on June 22, 1941, Premier Stalin felt secure enough on his eastern frontier with Japan to turn most of the Soviet war effort against the invading Hun from the West. Russia did not finally enter the war against the Japanese until August 8, 1945, less than one month before Japan's surrender.

While the Roosevelt Administration's time and talent were taken up with extricating America from the toils of the Great Depression, the events unfolding in the Far East, as noted, were not ignored. In 1941, the Japanese government posted Admiral Kichisaburo Nomura to Washington as its ambassador to the United States. The Japanese government was hopeful that Nomura would be able to persuade the Roosevelt Administration to reconsider some of its previous economic decisions affecting Japan and begin to restore normal Japanese-American commercial relations. Nomura was authorized to tell Washington that Tokyo was ready and willing to renounce the use of military force in Asia if proper economic ties could be reestablished with the United States. However, the overall American response to Nomura's overtures were ambivalent at best.

When the Japanese moved to occupy southern Indo-China in February, 1941, that action began a series of economic reprisals that lasted up to the attack on Pearl Harbor. Between February, 1941 and December, 1941, there were often intense efforts to restore some semblance of mutual trust between the two nations. However, diplomacy could not overcome the years of animosity and distrust that had accumulated between the United States and Japan over the preceding decade. American Secretary of State, Cordell Hull, with the President's approval, demanded that for Japanese-American relations to improve, Japan must withdraw her forces from Manchuria, China and Indo-China. Rightly or wrongly, the Japanese took this to be an ultimatum and refused to even consider such a suggestion, let alone put it in force. The ill winds of war increased for the two nations when President Roosevelt refused to heed a Japanese call for a bilateral conference to defuse the impasse. Japanese Prime Minister Prince Fumimaro Konoye (who was succeeded in office by Hideki Tojo), had urgently requested such a conference with American representatives as late as August, 1941, in Honolulu; the United States alternately suggested Juneau, Alaska. However, this meeting never took place largely because of State Department objections.

By 1941, Japanese strategic thinking both in Asia and in the Pacific generally was a combination of carrot and stick. The Japanese view seemed to be that if Japan invaded Burma, the Dutch East Indies, Malaya and the Philippine Islands, then neutralized the United States Pacific Fleet anchored at Pearl Harbor, the American government would then be willing to seek a permanent diplomatic accord with Japan over all outstanding issues. In turn, the Japanese were confident that America's colonial Allies in the Far East (the British, the French and the Dutch) would automatically follow America's lead in a diplomatic *entente cordiale*. While surely both utopian and geopolitically naïve, such a Japanese mind set was fully in place on the eve of the attack on Pearl Harbor on December 7, 1941. Reflecting on events over six decades ago, it is perhaps difficult to envision the world the Japanese saw in 1941. Nonetheless, their worldview was strikingly at odds with that of the Western Allies.

To the political and military elite in Japan, the West, and especially the United States was seen in a most unfavorable light. Coffey,[11] reflecting on this mindset in his notable book on the Japanese experience in the Second World War, writes:

---

11. Thomas M. Coffey, *Imperial Tragedy, Japan in World War II: The First Days and the Last* (1970).

The white nations of the West…had now become even bolder and more aggressive in their attempts to enslave Japan. America, Britain, China and the Dutch (The ABCD Powers) were engaged in a deliberate plan to encircle Japan and reduce it to insignificance. The white nations had always treated Japan with arrogance. Ever since Admiral Perry had arrived [in 1853] with his cannons and forced the country to accept him, Americans had been coming in and out of Japan as if they owned it. But at the same time they had passed a race-insulting immigration law to stop the Japanese and other Asians from going to America. The time had now come for the arrogant, bigoted, Americans to learn that there was a limit to Japanese patience.[12]

Views such as these in conjunction with the various economic sanctions and embargos visited by the United States and others on the Japanese in the late 1930s and up to December 7, 1941, fostered a culture of oppression and reprisal in the eyes of Imperial Japan. When Hideki Tojo became Japanese Prime Minister on October 18, 1941, also simultaneously holding the posts of a general officer in the army, Minister of Munitions and War Minister, the die had been cast. During the summer of 1941, secret plans were being formulated for the Pearl Harbor attack. By September, 1941, the Naval War College in Tokyo had conducted its final "War Games" for both an attack on the American Pacific Fleet in Hawaii, and also for attacks on the Chinese coast and military operations in Malaya, Singapore and the Dutch East Indies.

On November 26, 1941, Secretary of State Cordell Hull delivered to the Japanese Special Envoy to the United States, Saburo Kurusu, the "final conditions" for a diplomatic settlement. In brief, the full note contained three points: (1) a non-aggression pack should be negotiated by all nations who had an interest in the Far East; (2) the Japanese must withdraw all their military forces from China and French Indo-China; and (3) the Japanese government must renounce its support for and abolish the puppet government it had established in Manchuria. On that same date, the carrier attack force of the Japanese Imperial Navy, under the command of Admiral Chuchi Nagumo, weighed anchor at Hitokappu Bay on Etorofu Island in the southern Kurile Islands under radio silence and set sail for Hawaii across the vast and desolate expanse of the northern Pacific Ocean. This route was specifically chosen by Japanese naval planners because it avoided the heavily-traveled merchant shipping sea lanes and was far distant from American naval installations. On December 2, 1941, the Japanese carrier attack force received a coded message: "Climb Mount Niitaka." Those three words sealed the fate of both Pearl Harbor and the Japanese Empire and irrevocably ordered the attack to proceed as planned.

On Sunday morning, December 7, 1941, at 0600 hours, Pacific time, some 275 nautical miles north of the Hawaiian Islands, Coffey[13] paints this brief verbal picture of history in the making:

> The six large carriers [*Akagi, Kaga, Soryu, Hiryu, Zuikaku and Shokaku*], turning into the north wind to facilitate takeoff, proceeded in parallel columns of three, with two battleships protecting them at the corners astern and two heavy cruisers at the corners in front. A light cruiser led the formation. Nine destroyers hovered around it. A fleet of supply ships followed it, almost 200 miles ahead, three submarines acted as its forward eyes. There had been no attempt

---

12. *Id.* at 100–101.
13. *Id.*

to camouflage or conceal the identity of the ships. It would have been pointless.... The Rising Sun, therefore, flew openly from the masts of all the ships and was painted prominently on the wings and fuselages of all the planes.

* * *

...the first attack wave of 183 planes turned and flew at 125 nautical miles per hour toward the Hawaiian island of Oahu, slightly more than 200 miles away.[14]

World War II in the Pacific had begun on the heels of a Japanese surprise naval maneuver considered by many to be the greatest single tactical military success of the twentieth century. United States losses at Pearl Harbor were significant. Of the ninety-six vessels anchored at Pearl Harbor on that fateful morning, nineteen major warships were either sunk or seriously damaged. In addition, the United States Navy lost ninety-six aircraft while the United States Army Air Force lost a similar number. In terms of personnel, United States losses totaled 2,403 killed and 1,178 wounded. At approximately 1630 hours (4:30 p.m.), the Japanese carrier force, having recovered all the aircraft that had returned, set sail on a northwesterly compass bearing across the Pacific for the Japanese port of Kure. The entire surface fleet escaped unharmed.

The following day, Monday, December 8, 1941, President Franklin D. Roosevelt delivered his war message to a joint session of Congress. The following are excerpts from that message:

Yesterday, December 7, 1941—a date which will live in infamy—the United States of American was suddenly and deliberately attacked by naval and air forces of the Empire of Japan.

The United States was at peace with that Nation and, at the solicitation of Japan, was still in conversation with its Government and its Emperor looking toward the maintenance of peace in the Pacific. Indeed, one hour after Japanese squadrons had commenced bombing Oahu, the Japanese Ambassador to the United States and his colleague delivered to the Secretary of State a formal reply to a recent American message.

While this reply stated that it seemed useless to continue the existing diplomatic negotiations, it contained no threat or hint of war or armed attack.

It will be recorded that the distance of Hawaii from Japan makes it obvious that the attack was deliberately planned many days or even weeks ago. During the intervening time the Japanese Government has deliberately sought to deceive the United States by false statements and expressions of hope for continued peace.

The attack yesterday on the Hawaiian Islands has caused severe damage to American naval and military forces. Very many American lives have been lost. In addition, American ships have been reported torpedoed on the high seas between San Francisco and Honolulu.

* * *

Japan has, therefore, undertaken a surprise offensive extending throughout the Pacific area. The facts of yesterday speak for themselves. The people of the United States have already formed their opinions; and well understand the implications to the very life and safety of our Nation.

---

14. *Id.* at 11–12.

As Commander-in-Chief of the Army and Navy I have directed that all measures be taken for our defense.

Always we will remember the character of the onslaught against us.

No matter how long it may take us to overcome this premeditated invasion, the American people in their righteous might will win through to absolute victory.

I believe I interpret the will of the Congress and of the people when I assert that we will not only defend ourselves to the uttermost but will make very certain that this form of treachery shall never endanger us again....

I ask that the Congress declare that since the unprovoked and dastardly attack by Japan on Sunday, December seventh, a state of war has existed between the United States and the Japanese Empire.

Franklin Delano Roosevelt

President of the United States

The Japanese, unlike their European counterparts, acted on a strategic military and geopolitical blueprint that had been in the planning stages for quite some time. To advance the success of the "Greater East Asia Co-Prosperity Sphere," they immobilized (temporarily) United States Naval power in the Pacific in order to extend their empirial reach from the two Aleutian islands of Kiska and Attu in the far north to the Marshall, Mariana and Caroline islands in the south which directly threatened the north coast of Australia. In between, the Japanese Empire would encompass Manchuria, Northern China, Korea, Taiwan, the Philippines, French Indo-China (now Vietnam), Malaya, Singapore, the Dutch East Indies, portions of New Guinea and the Pacific islands as far west as the Gilbert islands, including Tarawa, and as far south as Guadalcanal.

The task facing principally both the United States and Great Britain was to roll back Japan from these Far East and Western Pacific enclaves. America, Britain and their European and Asian allies finally prevailed after some three years and nine months of brutal, non-forgiving warfare with an enemy that showed little regard for the niceties of the rule of law in international conflict. The Japanese came in for legitimate international criticism for their indiscriminate murder and ill-treatment of Allied prisoners of war, the rape and execution of countless civilian non-combatants, the pillaging of cities, towns and villages which had no military significance and their cruel exploitation of POWs and native populations in furtherance of Japanese war aims.

Under Japanese rule, anywhere between 80,000 and 100,000 Korean women were rounded up and forced into prostitution throughout Asia. In addition, countless civilians and POWs suffered treatment at the hands of the Japanese contrary to the laws and customs of war in such occupied areas as Borneo, China, Burma, the Dutch East Indies, Hong Kong, the Phillipines, Malaya, Indo-China and Thailand. While casualty figures will never be accurately determined, it is estimated that some 10 to 15 *million* Chinese alone perished during the Japanese invasion and occupation of China between 1931 and 1945. In what was then known as French Indo-China (now Vietnam), somewhere between one and two *million* starved to death between 1944 and 1945 as a direct result of Japanese economic policies and the employment of favorable rice requisitions for the Japanese military. It was reported that approximately 30,000 Dutch and other European nationals living in various Far Eastern colonial possessions perished during Japanese hegemony and nearly 100,000 Filopinos were killed in the Battle of Manila alone. An estimated four *million* were killed in Indonesia from a combination of Japanese hostilities and draconian occupation policies, while India reported some 180,000 of its nationals killed by the Japanese.

The Japanese saw themselves as a superior culture to occidental societies and this ethnocentricity early on grafted itself upon the Japanese military from the War Minister down through the lowest enlisted ranks. Contrariwise, in Western eyes, Japan was frequently viewed as a dynastic, backward and brutal warrior nation that disavowed all semblance of abiding by international legal norms. It was this dissensus that often played a prominent role in the racial attitudes adopted by both contending adversaries and exascerbated the inhumane atrocities that emerged in the Pacific War.

In Japan itself, nearly 3 *million* people perished. Most of the nation's major urban areas and infrastructure lay in ruins and it was estimated that at least 10 *million* Japanese throughout the home islands were on the brink of starvation at war's end. It was into this human, social and economic chaos that General Douglas MacArthur stepped when he officially accepted the surrender of Japan aboard the battleship *USS Missouri* anchored in Tokyo Bay on September 2, 1945.

The air raid sirens had barely ceased at Pearl Harbor in 1941 when word came to the Allied authorities of widespread Japanese atrocities being committed throughout the Far East. The Japanese government was immediately warned about the ultimate consequences of their criminal behavior. On December 18, 1941, eleven days after the Pearl Harbor attack, Secretary of State Hull pointedly warned the Japanese Foreign Ministry that the Allied governments fully expected the Japanese military to adhere to the provisions of the Geneva Convention of July 27, 1929. Likewise, on August 21, 1942, President Roosevelt noted in a public address that he had "been aware" of war crimes committed by all the Axis Powers, Japan included. After the infamous "Bataan Death March" in the Phillipines became known to the United States government in January, 1944, Secretary of State Hull issued yet another warning to Japan about her continued and open violations of treaty provisions and the laws and customs of war. Finally, the *Potsdam Declaration* of July 26, 1945, contained language setting forth the basic Allied policies that would be put in place for the eventual trial and punishment of Japanese war criminals. When Japan surrendered, the Japanese government informed the Allies that it accepted the terms and conditions set forth in the *Potsdam Declaration* applicable to alleged war criminals.

Thus, on a composite human scale alone, the Pacific theatre in World War II was on a par with, if not more cruel and deadly than, the war conducted in the European theatre against Nazi Germany and Fascist Italy. Oddly enough, however, the Pacific war against Imperial Japan and the subsequent Japanese war crime trials have always seemed to be of secondary significance to the European hostilities, both in terms of international notoriety and in terms of the jurisprudence developed by the IMTFE-Tokyo.

Unlike the Nuremberg War Crimes Trial of the major Nazi war criminals, the trial of the major Japanese war criminals in Tokyo began later, lasted longer and was staffed by more judges than its European prototype. Known officially as the International Military Tribunal for the Far East (IMTFE), this trial was discussed and early plans drafted at the Cairo Conference of December 1, 1943. The IMTFE was premised upon an entirely different organic legal document than the IMT-Nuremberg. The *Charter* of the IMTFE-Tokyo originated under the terms and conditions contained in the *Proclamation of the Supreme Commander for the Allied Powers*, January 19, 1946, signed by General Douglas MacArthur. That document, along with the provisions of the *Charter* of the IMTFE-Tokyo, is reported (*infra*). The Tokyo proceedings were both in form and substance "international" in character. However, the IMTFE was more than just a tribunal to try Japanese war criminals; it was, in fact, a forum that played a significant role in later United States post-war occupation policies in Japan as well.

Under the terms drafted by General MacArthur, he and he alone was vested with sole authority to select not less than six nor more than eleven judges whose names were submitted to him by the eleven belligerents who had fought against Imperial Japan. MacArthur was given further authority to appoint the President of the tribunal. The IMTFE was officially organized on April 29, 1946, and twenty-eight Japanese defendants then in custody were indicted.

The defendants presented themselves with their defense counsel in the auditorium of the War Ministry Building in Tokyo on May 3, 1946. After arraignment, the trial commenced on June 3, 1946, and concluded on November 4, 1948. During 818 sessions that lasted nearly two and one-half years, two defendants died and one was unable to stand trial due to mental incompetence. The IMTFE-Tokyo was presided over by judges from six nations and five of their territorial possessions. These included Australia, Canada, China, Great Britain, France, India, the Netherlands, New Zealand, the Philippines, the U.S.S.R. and the United States. The accused faced a three-count indictment: (1) "murder" alleged in sixteen charges; (2) "crimes against peace" alleged in thirty-six charges; and (3) "other conventional war crimes and crimes against humanity" alleged in three charges. No "organizational criminality" charges were preferred against the Japanese defendants as was the case in the IMT-Nuremberg proceedings.

In all, 419 witnesses testified before the Tribunal. Additionally, there were 779 witness statements represented by either deposition or by affidavit. Like the IMT-Nuremberg, the volume of paperwork generated by the IMTFE was staggering. The transcript of the trial alone consumed 49,858 pages! The majority opinions, supported by eight of the eleven judges, consisted of five separate opinions, some of which were highly critical of the proceedings in general. The prosecution presented its case-in-chief, rebuttal and summation in 192 days, while the defense consumed a total of 225 days in its case-in-chief, rebuttal and summation. The Tribunal consisted of eleven judges with no alternates. The jurists and the nations they represented were: (1) Sir William F. Webb, Presiding Judge (Australia); (2) John P. Higgins (later replaced by Major General Myron C. Cramer, (United States); (3) Lord Patrick (Great Britain and Northern Ireland); (4) Henri Bernard (France); (5) I. M. Zaryanov (U.S.S.R.); (6) E. Stuart McDougal (Canada); (7) Ju-Ao Mei (China); (8) Delfin Jaranilla (The Philippines); (9) Bernard Victor A. Röling (The Netherlands); (10) Erima Harvey Northcroft (New Zealand); and (11) Radhabinod M. Pal (India). The Chief Prosecutor was Joseph B. Keenan of the United States. Each of the other ten nations or possessions had their own prosecutor assigned to the case. An American lawyer headed the defense staff, assisted by four additional American attorneys plus one Japanese-counsel assigned to each defendant. Like Nuremberg, there was a simultaneous translation system in operation and the proceedings were heard in five languages: English, French, Chinese, Russian and Japanese. Despite this advantage, however, on cross-examination and other forms of colloquy between trial counsel and the bench, translations had first to be put into each language and then distributed to the appropriate parties. This procedure caused a tremendous amount of delay and accounted, in part, for the inordinate length of the entire trial.

Lord Russell,[15] in remarking on certain trial procedures, had this to say.

---

15. Russell, *supra* note 1.

The Japanese language was also a great practical difficulty, for literal translation from Japanese into English, or vice versa, is seldom possible. Much could merely be paraphrased, and so great were the discrepancies that the Tribunal was forced to set up a Language Arbitration Board to settle matters of disputed interpretation.[16]

In alphabetical order the defendants were: (1) Sadeo Araki: (2) Kenji Dohihara; (3) Shunoku Hata; (4) Kingoro Hashimoto; (5) Kiichiro Hiranuma; (6) Koki Hirota; (7) Naoki Hoshino; (8) Seishiro Itagaki; (9) Okinori Kaya; (10) Koichi Kido; (11) Heitaro Kimura; (12) Kuniaki Koiso; (13) Iwane Matsui; (14) Yosuke Matsuoka; (15) Jiro Minami; (16) Akira Muto; (17) Osami Nagano; (18) Takasumi Oka; (19) Shumei Okawa; (20) Hiroshi Oshima; (21) Kenryo Sato; (22) Mamoru Shigemitsu; (23) Shitetaro Shimada; (24) Toshio Shiratori; (25) Teiichi Suzuki; (26) Shigenori Togo; (27) Hideki Tojo; and (28) Toshijiro Umezo. Matsuoka and Nagano died during the proceedings while Okawa was found to be insane and was dismissed from prosecution. Of the twenty-eight accused, the only name even vaguely familiar to most Americans, and probably to most Allies as well (because of wartime propaganda) was Hideki Tojo. Unlike the Nuremberg trial *all* defendants who remained on trial to the end were found guilty. Seven were sentenced to death by hanging (Dohihara, Hirota, Itagaki, Matsui, Muto, Kimura and Tojo). This group was executed inside Tokyo's Sugamo Prison on December 23, 1948. Sixteen accused were sentenced to life imprisonment. The remaining two defendants, Togo and Shigemitsu were sentenced to prison terms of twenty and seven years, respectively. The lightest sentence was passed upon Mamoru Shigemitsu who had been a career Foreign Ministry official, serving as Foreign Minister for a brief period before war's end and one of two Japanese officials who signed the instrument of surrender on September 2, 1945. Excluding Shigemitsu, not a single remaining IMTFE defendant who received a prison sentence served more than ten years behind bars.

A significant criticism of the IMTFE surfaced shortly before the trial even began and continues to resonate negatively even today in some international law commentary. That was the decision apparently made at the highest levels of the United States government, in consultation with General Douglas MacArthur, to *exempt* Japanese Emperor Hirohito from indictment and trail as a war criminal. He was never called as a witness by either side during the entire trial. This was a rather bizarre turn of events, given the wording of the IMTFE's *Charter* which specifically denied immunity to any individual for war crimes committed during the Pacific conflict. O'Neill[17] writes that:

> ...it appears that...extralegal concerns drove the legal [outcome]. The decision not to indict Hirohito sprang from a multitude of factors; political need formed by internal Japanese pressures, General MacArthur's desire for a smooth transition in postwar Japan, a bitter anti-Japanese racism that existed during World War II, and the research of social scientists.[18]

There was also a feeling in some quarters that the Japanese Emperor was nothing more than an innocent pawn in the grip of a militaristic cabal that effectively ruled Japan from the late 1920s until 1945. Postwar Germany has continued to try surviving Nazi

16. *Id.* at 285.
17. Kerry C. O'Neill, "A New Customary Law of Head of State Immunity?: Hirohito and Pinochet," 38 *Stan. J. Int'l L.* 289 (2002).
18. *Id.* at 290.

war criminals since the late 1940s. On the other hand, no such complimentary war crime trials have ever taken place in a domestic Japanese court since early 1946.

In addition to selected excerpts from the IMTFE proceedings, we also include in *Part Three* excerpts from several United States Supreme Court decisions that were decided either during or shortly after the conclusion of the Second World War involving various Japanese military defendants whose trials and convictions were challenged on numerous constitutional grounds. Probably the most noteworthy of these was the case of Japanese General Tomoyuki Yamashita tried by a United States military commission in the Philippines before the establishment of the IMTFE. *In re Yamashita* (1946) details the events surrounding General Yamashita's trial in the Philippines, his appeal from an order of the Supreme Court of the Commonwealth of the Philippines and the application for a writ of *habeas corpus* to the United States Supreme Court.

Along with the *Yamashita* case, and subsequent to the IMTFE opinions, we include the 1948 United States Supreme Court decision of *Hirota v. MacArthur* and the concurring opinion of Mr. Justice Douglas in the same case written in June, 1949. The petitioners in the *Hirota* litigation were either high government officers or officers in the Japanese Army during World War II and were being held in custody pursuant to the judgment of the IMTFE-Tokyo. They were all found guilty of certain war crimes committed during World War II. Other respondents included General Walker, United States 8th Army Commander, the Army Chief of Staff, the Secretary of the Army and the Secretary of Defense.

We commence materials in *Part Three* with Japanese Emperor Hirohito's Imperial Rescript (or official announcement) to the Japanese people of the declaration of war on the United States and Great Britain by Japan at approximately 11:45 a.m. (Tokyo time), on December 8, 1941. We conclude *Part Three* with the *Hirota* case and excerpts from the 1963 *Shimoda* decision involving a Japanese civil action arising out of the August, 1945, bombings of Hiroshima and Nagasaki, with selected commentary.

----

1. Emperor Hirohito's Imperial Rescript
December 8, 1941

We, by the grace of Heaven, Emperor of Japan, seated on the throne of a line unbroken for ages eternal, enjoin upon ye our loyal and brave subjects:

We hereby declare war on the United States of America and the British Empire. The men and officers of our army and navy shall do their utmost in prosecuting the war. Our public servants of various departments shall perform faithfully and diligently their appointed tasks, and all other subjects of ours shall pursue their respective duties; the entire nation with a united determination will mobilize its total strength so that nothing will miscarry in the attainment of our war aims.

To ensure the stability of East Asia and to contribute to world peace is the far-sighted policy which was formulated by our great illustrious imperial grandsire and our great imperial sire succeeding him, and which we lay constantly to heart. To cultivate friendship among nations and to enjoy prosperity in common with all nations has always been the guiding principle of our empire's foreign policy. It has been truly unavoidable and far from our wishes that our empire has now been brought to cross swords with America and Britain. Moreover, these two powers, inducing other counties to follow suit, increased military preparations on all sides of our empire to challenge us. They have obstructed by every means our peaceful commerce, and finally resorted to a direct severance of economic relations, menacing gravely the existence of our empire. Patiently have we waited and long have we endured, in the hope that our government might retrieve the situation in peace. But our adversaries, showing not the least spirit of conciliation, have unduly delayed a settlement; and in the meantime, they have intensified the economic and political pressure to compel thereby our empire to submission.....[19]

---

2. *In re Yamashita*

Supreme Court of the United States
327 U.S. 1 (1946)

Mr. Chief Justice STONE delivered the opinion of the Court.

[This] is an application for leave to file a petition for writs of habeas corpus and prohibition in this Court [and] a petition for certiorari to review an order of the Supreme Court of the Commonwealth of the Philippines...denying petitioner's application to that court for writs of habeas corpus and prohibition. As both applications raise substantially like questions, and because of the importance and novelty of some of those presented, we set the two applications down for oral argument as one case.

From the petitions and supporting papers it appears that prior to September 3, 1945, petitioner was the Commanding General of the Fourteenth Army Group of the Imperial Japanese Army in the Philippine Islands. On September 25, by order of respondent, Lieutenant General Wilhelm D. Styer, Commanding General of the United States Army Forces, Western Pacific, which command embraces the Philippine Islands, petitioner was served with a charge prepared by the Judge Advocate General's Department of the Army, purporting to charge petitioner with a violation of the law of war. On October 8, 1945, petitioner, after pleading not guilty to the charge, was held for trial before a military commission of five Army officers appointed by order of General Styer. The order appointed six Army officers, all lawyers, as defense counsel. Throughout the proceedings which followed, including those before this Court, defense counsel has demonstrated their professional skill and resourcefulness and their proper zeal for the defense with which they are charged.

On the same day a bill of particulars was filed by the prosecution, and the commission heard a motion made in petitioner's behalf to dismiss the charge on the ground that it failed to state a violation of the law of war. On October 29th the commission was reconvened, a supplemental bill of particulars was filed, and the motion to dismiss was denied. The trial then proceeded until its conclusion on December 7, 1945, the commission hearing two hundred and sixty-eight witnesses, who gave over three thousand pages of testimony. On that date petitioner was found guilty of the offense as charged and sentenced to death by hanging.

The petitions for habeas corpus set up that the detention of petitioner for the purpose of the trial was unlawful for reasons which are now urged as showing that the mil-

---

19. Coffey, *supra* note 11, at 101–102.

itary commission was without lawful authority or jurisdiction to place petitioner on trial, as follows:

(a) That the military commission which tried and convicted petitioner was not lawfully created, and that no military commission to try petitioner for violations of the law of war could lawfully be convened after the cessation of hostilities between the armed forces of the United States and Japan.

(b) that the charge preferred against petitioner fails to charge him with a violation of the law of war;

(c) that the commission was without authority and jurisdiction to try and convict petitioner because the order governing the procedure of the commission permitted the admission in evidence of depositions, affidavits and hearsay and opinion evidence, and because the commission's admitting such evidence were in violation of the 25th and 38th Articles of War (10 U.S.C. ss 1946, 1509, 10 U.S.C.A. ss 1496, 1509) and the Geneva Convention (47 Stat. 2021), and deprived petitioner of a fair trial in violation of the due process clause of the Fifth Amendment.

(d) that the commission was without authority and jurisdiction in the premises because of the failure to give advance notice of petitioner's trial to the neutral power representing the interests of Japan as a belligerent as required by Article 60 of the Geneva Convention, 47 Stat. 2021, 2051.

On the same grounds the petitions for writs of prohibition set up that the commission is without authority to proceed with the trial.

The Supreme Court of the Philippine Islands, after hearing argument, denied the petition for habeas corpus presented to it, on the ground, among others, that its jurisdiction was limited to an inquiry as to the jurisdiction of the commission to place petitioner on trial for the offense charged, and that the commission, being validly constituted by the order of General Styer, had jurisdiction over the person of petitioner and over the trial for the offense charged.

In Ex parte Quirin *[infra]*, we had occasion to consider at length the sources and nature of the authority to create military commissions for the trial of enemy combatants for offenses against the law of war. We there pointed out that Congress, in the exercise of the power conferred upon it by Article I, s 8, Cl. 10 of the Constitution to 'define and punish * * * Offenses against the Law of Nations * * *,' of which the law of war is a part, had by the Articles of War...recognized the 'military commission' appointed by military command, as it had previously existed in United States Army practice, as an appropriate tribunal for the trial and punishment of offenses against the law of war. Article 15 declares that 'the provisions of these articles conferring jurisdiction upon courts-martial shall not be construed as depriving military commissions * * * or other military tribunals of concurrent jurisdiction in respect of offenders of offenses that by statute or by the law of war may be triable by such military commissions * * * or other military tribunals.'"

We further pointed out that Congress, by sanctioning trial of enemy combatants for violations of the law of war by military commission, had not attempted to codify the law of war or to mark its precise boundaries. Instead, by Article 15 it had incorporated, by reference, as within the preexisting jurisdiction of military commissions created by appropriate military command, all offenses which are defined as such by the law of war, and which may constitutionally be included within that jurisdiction. It thus adopted the system of military common law applied by military tribunals so far as it should be recognized and deemed applicable by the courts, and as further defined and supplemented by the Hague Convention, to which the United States and the Axis powers were parties.

We also emphasized in Ex parte Quirin, as we do here, that on application for habeas corpus we are not concerned with the guilt or innocence of the petitioners. We consider here only the lawful power of the commission to try the petitioner for the offense charged. In the present case it must be recognized throughout that the military tribunals which Congress has sanctioned by the Articles of War are not courts whose rulings and judgments are made subject to review by this court.... They are tribunals whose determinations are reviewable by the military authorities either as provided in the military orders constituting such tribunals or as provided by the Articles of War. Congress conferred on the courts no power to review their determinations save only as it has granted judicial power 'to grant writs of habeas corpus for the purpose of an inquiry into the cause of the restraint of liberty.'... The courts may inquire whether the detention complained of is within the authority of those detaining the petitioner. If the military tribunals have lawful authority to hear, decide and condemn, their action is not subject to judicial review merely because they have made a wrong decision on disputed facts. Correction of their errors of decision is not for the courts but for the military authorities which are alone authorized to review their decisions....

Finally, we held in Ex parte Quirin...as we hold now, that Congress by sanctioning trials of enemy aliens by military commission for offenses against the law of war had recognized the right of the accused to make a defense.... It has not foreclosed their right to contend that the Constitution or laws of the United States withhold authority to proceed with the trial. It has not withdrawn, and the Executive branch of the government could not, unless there was suspension of the writ, withdraw from the courts the duty and power to make such inquiry into the authority of the commission as may be made by habeas corpus.

With these governing principles in mind we turn to the consideration of the several contentions urged to establish want of authority in the commission. We are not here concerned with the power of military commissions to try civilians.... The Government's contention is that General Styer's order creating the commission conferred authority on it only to try the purported charge of violation of the law of war committed by petitioner, an enemy belligerent, while in command of a hostile army occupying United States territory during time of war. Our first inquiry must therefore be whether the present commission was created by lawful military command and, if so, whether authority could thus be conferred on the commission to place petitioner on trial after the cessation of hostilities between the armed forces of the United States and Japan.

The authority to create the commission. General Styer's order for the appointment of the commission was made by him as Commander of the United States Armed Forces, Western Pacific. His command includes, as part of a vastly greater area, the Philippine Islands, where the alleged offenses were committed, where petitioner surrender [sic.] as a prisoner of war, and where, at the time of the order convening the commission, he was detained as a prisoner in custody of the United States Army. The Congressional recognition of military commissions and its sanction of their use in trying offenses against the law of war to which we have referred, sanctioned their creation by military command in conformity to long established American precedents. Such a commission may be appointed by any field commander, or by any commander competent to appoint a general court martial, as was General Styer, who has been vested with that power by order of the President.

Here the commission was not only created by a commander competent to appoint it, but his order conformed to the established policy of the Government and to higher military commands authorizing his action. In a proclamation of July 2, 1942...the President proclaimed that enemy belligerents who, during time of war, enter the United States, or any territorial possession thereof, and who violate the law of war, should be subject to the law of war and to the jurisdiction of military tribunals. Paragraph 10 of the Declaration of Potsdam of July 6, 1945, declared that '* * * stern justice shall be meted out to all war criminals including those who have visited cruelties upon prisoners.'.... This Declaration was accepted by the Japanese government by its note of August 10, 1945....

By direction of the President, the Joint Chiefs of Staff of the American Military Forces, on September 12, 1945, instructed General MacArthur, Commander in Chief, United States Army Forces, Pacific, to proceed with the trial, before appropriate military tribunals, of such Japanese war criminals 'as have been or may be apprehended.' By order of General MacArthur of September 24, 1945, General Styer was specifically directed to proceed with the trial of petitioner upon the charge here involved. This order was accompanied by detailed rules and regulations which General MacArthur prescribed for the trial of war criminals. These regulations directed, among other things, that review of the sentence imposed by the commission should be by the officer convening it, with 'authority to approve, mitigate, remit, commute, suspend, reduce or otherwise alter the sentence imposed,' and directed that no sentence of death should be carried into effect until confirmed by the Commander in Chief, United States Army Forces, Pacific.

It thus appears that the order creating the commission for the trial of petitioner was authorized by military command, and was in complete conformity to the Act of Congress sanctioning the creation of such tribunals for the trial of offenses against the law of war committed by enemy combatants. And we turn to the question whether the authority to create the commission and direct the trial by military order continued after the cessation of hostilities.

An important incident to the conduct of war is the adoption of measures by the military commander, not only to repel and defeat the enemy, but to seize and subject to disciplinary measures those enemies who, in their attempt to thwart or impede our military effort, have violated the law of war.... The trial and punishment of enemy combatants who have committed violations of the law of war is thus not only a part of the conduct of war operating as a preventive measure against such violations, but is an exercise of the authority sanctioned by Congress to administer the system of military justice recognized by the law of war. That sanction is without qualification as to the exercise of this authority so long as a state of war exists—its declaration until peace is proclaimed.... The war power from which the commission derives its existence, is not limited to victories in the field, but carries with it the inherent power to guard against the immediate renewal of the conflict, and to remedy, at least in ways Congress has recognized, the evils which the military operations have produced....

We cannot say that there is no authority to convene a commission after hostilities have ended to try violations of the law of war committed before their cessation, at least until peace has been officially recognized by treaty or proclamation of the political branch of the Government. In fact, in most instances the practical administration of the system of military justice under the law of war would fail if such authority were thought to end with the cessation of hostilities. For only after their cessation could the greater number of offenders and the principal ones be apprehended and subjected to trial.

No writer on international law appears to have regarded the power of military tribunals, otherwise competent to try violations of the law of war, as terminating before the formal state of war has ended. In our own military history there have been numerous instances in which offenders were tried by military commission after hostilities and before the proclamation of peace, for offenses against the law of war committed before the cessation of hostilities.

* * *

The extent to which the power to prosecute violations of the law of war shall be exercised before peace is declared rests, not with the courts, but with the political branch of the Government, and may itself be governed by the terms of an armistice or the treaty of peace. Here, peace has not been agreed upon or proclaimed. Japan, by her acceptance of the Potsdam Declaration and her surrender, has acquiesced in the trials of those guilty of violations of the law of war. The conduct of the trial by the military commission has been authorized by the political branch of the Government, by military command, by international law and usage, and by the terms of the surrender of the Japanese government.

The Charge. Neither Congressional action nor the military orders constituting the commission authorized it to place petitioner on trial unless the charge preferred against him is of a violation of the law of war. The charge, so far as is now relevant, is that petitioner, between October 9, 1944 and September 2, 1945, in the Philippine Islands, 'while commander of armed forces of Japan at war with the United States of America and its allies, unlawfully disregarded and failed to discharge his duty as commander to control the operations of the members of his command, permitting them to commit brutal atrocities and other high crimes against people of the United States and of its allies and dependencies, particularly the Philippines; and he * * * thereby violated the laws of war.'

Bills of particulars, filed by the prosecution by order of the commission, allege a series of acts, one hundred and twenty-three in number, committed by members of the forces under petitioner's command, during the period mentioned. The first item specifies the execution of a 'deliberate plan and purpose to massacre and exterminate a large part of the civilian population of Batangas Province, and to devastate and destroy public, private and religious property therein, as a result of which more than 25,000 men, women and children, all unarmed noncombatant civilians, were brutally mistreated and killed, without cause or trial, and entire settlements were devastated and destroyed, wantonly and without military necessity.' Other items specify acts of violence, cruelty and homicide inflicted upon the civilian population and prisoners of war, acts of wholesale pillage and the wanton destruction of religious monuments.

It is not denied that such acts directed against the civilian population of an occupied country and against prisoners of war are recognized in international law as violations of the law of war Articles 4, 28, 46 and 47, Annex to Fourth Hague Convention, 1907, ... But it is urged that the charge does not allege that petitioner has either committed or directed the commission of such acts, and consequently that no violation is charged as against him. But this overlooks the fact that the gist of the charge is an unlawful breach of duty by petitioner as an army commander to control the operations of the members of his command by 'permitting them to commit' the extensive and widespread atrocities specified. The question then is whether the law of war imposes on an army commander a duty to take such appropriate measures as are within his power to control the troops under his command for the prevention of the specified acts which are likely to attend the occupation of hostile territory by an uncontrolled soldiery, and whether he may be charged with personal responsibility for his failure to take such measures when violations result. That this was the precise issue to be tried was made clear by the statement of the prosecution at the opening of the trial.

It is evident that the conduct of military operations by troops whose excesses are unrestrained by the orders or efforts of their commander would almost certainly result in violations which it is the purpose of the law of war to prevent. Its purpose to protect civilian populations and prisoners of war from brutality would largely be defeated if the commander of an invading army could with impunity neglect to take reasonable measures for their protection. Hence the law of war presupposes that its violation is to be avoided through the control of the operations of war by commanders who are to some extent responsible for their subordinates.

This is recognized by the Annex to Fourth Hague Convention of 1907, respecting the laws and customs of war on land. Article I lays down as a condition which an armed force must fulfill in order to be accorded the rights of lawful belligerents, that it must be 'commanded by a person responsible for his subordinates.' Similarly Article 19 of the Tenth Hague Convention, relating to bombardment by naval vessels, provides that commanders in chief of the belligerent vessels 'must see that the above Articles are properly carried out.' ... Article 43 of the Annex of the Fourth Hague Convention,... requires that the commander of a force occupying enemy territory, as was petitioner, 'shall take all the measures in his power to restore, and ensure, as far as possible, public order and safety, while respecting, unless absolutely prevented, the laws in force in the country.'

These provisions plainly imposed on petitioner, who at the time specified was military governor of the Philippines, as well as commander of the Japanese forces, an affirmative duty to take such measures as were within his power and appropriate in the circumstances to protect prisoners of war and the civilian population. The duty of a commanding officer has heretofore been recognized, and its breach penalized by our own military tribunals. A like principle has been applied so as to impose liability on the United States in international arbitrations....

Congress, in the exercise of its constitutional power to define and punish offenses against the law of nations, of which the law of war is a part, has recognized the 'military commission' appointed by military command, as it had previously existed in United States army practice, as an appropriate tribunal for the trial and punishment of offenses against the law of war....

We do not make the laws of war but we respect them so far as they do not conflict with the commands of Congress or the Constitution. There is no contention that the present charge, thus read, is without the support of evidence, or that the commission held petitioner responsible for failing to take measures which were beyond his control or inappropriate for a commanding officer to take in the circumstances. We do not here appraise the evidence on which petitioner was convicted. We do not consider what measures, if any, petitioner took to prevent the commission, by the troops under his command, of the plain violations of the law of war detailed in the bill of particulars, or whether such measures as he may have taken were appropriate and sufficient to discharge the duty imposed upon him. These are questions within the peculiar competence of the military officers composing the commission and were for it to decide.... It is plain that the charge on which petitioner was tried charged him with a breach of his duty to control the operations of the members of his command, by permitting them to commit the specified atrocities. This was enough to require the commission to hear evidence tending to establish the culpable failure of petitioner to perform the duty imposed upon him by the law of war and to pass upon its sufficiency to establish guilt.

Obviously charges of violations of the law of war triable before a military tribunal need not be stated with the precision of a common law indictment.... But we conclude that the allegations of the charge, tested by any reasonable standard, adequately allege a violation of the law of war and that the commission had authority to try and decide the issue which it raised....

The Proceedings before the Commission. The regulations prescribed by General MacArthur governing the procedure for the trial of petitioner by the commission directed that the commission should admit such evidence 'as in its opinion would be of assistance in proving or disproving the charge, or such as in the commission's opinion would have probative value in the mind of a reasonable man,' and that in particular it might admit affidavits, depositions or other statements taken by officers detailed for that purpose by military authority. The petition in this case charged that in the course of the trial the commission received, over objection by petitioner's counsel, the deposition of a witness taken pursuant to military authority by a United States Army captain. It also, over like objection admitted hearsay and opinion evidence tendered by the prosecution. Petitioner argues as ground for the writ of habeas corpus, that Article 25 of the Articles of War prohibited the reception in evidence by the commission of depositions on behalf of the prosecution in a capital case, and that Article 38 prohibited the reception of hearsay and opinion evidence.

We think that neither Article 25 nor Article 38 is applicable to the trial of an enemy combatant by a military commission for violations of the law of war. Article 2 of the Articles of War enumerates 'the persons * * * subject to the articles,' who are denominated, for purposes of the Articles, as 'persons subject to military law.' In general, the persons so enumerated are members of our own Army and of the personnel accompanying the Army. Enemy combatants are not included among them....

* * *

By thus recognizing military commissions in order to preserve their traditional jurisdiction over enemy combatants unimpaired by the Articles, Congress gave sanction, as we held in Ex parte Quirin, to any use of the military commission contemplated by the common law of war. But it did not thereby make subject to the Articles of War persons other than those defined by Article 2 as being subject to the Articles, nor did it confer the benefits of the Articles upon such persons. The Articles recognized but one kind of military commission, not two. But they sanctioned the use of that one for the trial of two classes of persons, to one of which the Articles do, and to the other of which they do not apply in such trials. Being of this latter class, petitioner cannot claim the benefits of the Articles, which are applicable only to the members of the other class. Petitioner, an enemy combatant, is therefore not a person made subject to the Articles of War by Article 2, and the military commission before which he was tried, though sanctioned, and its jurisdiction saved, by Article 15, was not convened by virtue of the Articles of War, but pursuant to the common law of war. It follows that the Articles of War, including Articles 25 and 38, were not applicable to petitioner's trial and imposed no restrictions upon the procedure to be followed. The Articles left the control over the procedure in such a case where it had previously been, with the military command.

Petitioner further argues that by virtue of Article 63 of the Geneva Convention of 1929,...he is entitled to the benefits afforded by the 25th and 38th Articles of War to members of our own forces. Article 63 provides: 'Sentence may be pronounced against a prisoner of war only by the same courts and according to the same procedure as in the case of persons belonging to the armed forces of the detaining Power.' Since petitioner is a prisoner of war, and as the 25th and 38th Articles of War apply to the trial of any person in our armed forces, it is said that Article 63 requires them to be applied in the trial of petitioner. But we think examination of Article 63 in its setting in the Convention plainly shows that it refers to sentences 'pronounced against a prisoner of war' for an offense committed while a prisoner of war, and not for a violation of the law of war committed while a combatant.

* * *

We cannot say that the commission, in admitting evidence to which objection is not made, violated any act of Congress, treaty or military command defining the commission's authority. For reasons already stated we hold that the commission's rulings on evidence and on the mode of conducting these proceedings against petitioner are not reviewable by the courts, but only by reviewing military authorities. From this viewpoint it is unnecessary to consider what, in other situations, the Fifth Amendment might require, and as to that no intimation one way or the other is to be implied. Nothing we have said is to be taken as indicating any opinion on the question of the wisdom of considering such evidence or whether the action of a military tribunal in admitting evidence which Congress or controlling military command has directed to be excluded may be drawn in question by petition for habeas corpus or prohibition.

Effect of failure to give notice of the trial to protection power.... Petitioner relies on the failure to give the prescribed notice to the protecting power to establish want of authority in the commission to proceed with the trial.

For reasons already stated we conclude that Article 60 of the Geneva Convention... applies only to persons who are subjected to judicial proceedings for offenses committed while prisoners of war.

It thus appears that the order convening the commission was a lawful order, that the commission was lawfully constituted, that petitioner was charged with violation of the law of war, and that the commission had authority to proceed with the trial, and in doing so did not violate any military, statutory or constitutional command. We have considered, but find it unnecessary to discuss other contentions which we find to be without merit. We therefore conclude that the detention of petitioner for trial and his detention upon his conviction, subject to prescribed review by the military authorities were lawful, and that the petition for certiorari, and leave to file in this Court petitions for writs of habeas corpus and prohibition should be, and they are

Denied.

Writs denied.

Mr. Justice MURPHY, dissenting.

The significance of the issue facing the Court today cannot be overemphasized. An American military commission has been established to try a fallen military commander of a conquered nation for an alleged war crime. The authority for such action grows out of the exercise of the power conferred upon Congress by Article I, s 8, Cl. 10 of the Constitution to 'define and punish * * * Offenses against the Law of Nations * * *.' The grave issue raised by this case is whether a military commission so established and so authorized may disregard the procedural rights of an accused person as guaranteed by the Constitution, especially by the due process clause of the Fifth Amendment.

The answer is plain. The Fifth Amendment guarantee of due process of law applies to 'any person' who is accused of a crime by the Federal Government or any of its agencies.

No exception is made as to those who are accused of war crimes or as to those who possess the status of an enemy belligerent.

Indeed, such an exception would be contrary to the whole philosophy of human rights which makes the Constitution the great living document that it is. The immutable rights of the individual, including those secured by the due process clause of the Fifth Amendment, belong not alone to the members of those nations that excel on the battlefield or that subscribe to the democratic ideology. They belong to every person in the world, victor or vanquished, whatever may be his race, color or beliefs. They rise above any status of belligerency or outlawry. They survive any popular passion or frenzy of the moment. No court or legislature or executive, not even the mightiest army in the world, can ever destroy them. Such is the universal and indestructible nature of the rights which the due process clause of the Fifth Amendment recognizes and protects when life or liberty is threatened by virtue of the authority of the United States.

The existence of these rights, unfortunately, is not always respected. They are often trampled under by those who are motivated by hatred, aggression or fear. But in this nation individual rights are recognized and protected, at least in regard to governmental action. They cannot be ignored by any branch of the Government, even the military, except under the most extreme and urgent circumstances.

The failure of the military commission to obey the dictates of the due process requirements of the Fifth Amendment is apparent in this case. The petitioner was the commander of an army totally destroyed by the superior power of this nation. While under heavy and destructive attack by our forces, his troops committed many brutal atrocities and other high crimes. Hostilities ceased and he voluntarily surrendered. At that point he was entitled, as an individual protected by the due process clause of the Fifth Amendment, to be treated fairly and justly according to the accepted rules of law and procedure. He was also entitled to a fair trail as to any alleged crimes and to be free from charges of legally unrecognized crimes that would serve only to permit his accusers to satisfy their desire for revenge.

A military commission was appointed to try the petitioner for an alleged war crime. The trial was ordered to be held in territory over which the United States has complete sovereignty. No military necessity or other emergency demanded the suspension of the safeguards of due process. Yet petitioner was rushed to trial under an improper charge, given insufficient time to prepare an adequate defense, deprived of the benefits of some of the most elementary rules of evidence and summarily sentenced to be hanged. In all this needless and unseemly haste there was no serious attempt to charge or to prove that he committed a recognized violation of the laws of war. He was not charged with personally participating in the acts of atrocity or with ordering or condoning their commission. Not even knowledge of these crimes was attributed to him. It was simply alleged that he unlawfully disregarded and failed to discharge his duty as commander to control the operations of the members of his command, permitting them to commit the acts of atrocity. The recorded annals of warfare and the established principles of international law afford not the slightest precedent for such a charge. This indictment in effect permitted the military commission to make the crime whatever it willed, dependent upon its biased view as to petitioner's duties and his disregard thereof, a practice reminiscent of that pursued in certain less respected nations in recent years.

In my opinion, such a procedure is unworthy of the traditions of our people or of the immense sacrifices that they have made to advance the common ideals of mankind. The high feelings of the moment doubtless will be satisfied. But in the sober afterglow will come the realization of the boundless and dangerous implications of the procedure sanctioned today. No one in a position of command in any army, from sergeant to general, can escape.... Indeed, the fate of some future President of the United States and his chiefs of staff and military advisors may well have been sealed by this decision. But even more significant will be the hatred and ill-will growing out of the application of this unprecedented procedure. That has been the inevitable effect of every method of punishment disregarding the element of personal culpability. The effect in this instance, unfortunately, will be magnified infinitely for here we are dealing with the rights of man on an international level. To subject an enemy belligerent to an unfair trial, to charge him with an unrecognized crime, or to vent on him our retributive emotions only antagonizes the enemy nation and hinders the reconciliation necessary to a peaceful world.

That there were brutal atrocities inflicted upon the helpless Filipino people, to whom tyranny is no stranger, by Japanese armed forces under the petitioner's command is undeniable. Starvation, execution or massacre without trial, torture, rape, murder and wanton destruction of property were foremost among the outright violations of the laws of war and of the conscience of a civilized world. That just punishment should be meted out to all those responsible for criminal acts of this nature is also beyond dispute. But these factors do not answer the problem in this case. They do not justify the abandonment of our devotion to justice in dealing with a fallen enemy commander. To conclude otherwise is to admit that the enemy has lost the battle but has destroyed our ideals.

War breeds atrocities. From the earliest conflicts of recorded history to the global struggle of modern times inhumanities lust and pillage have been the inevitable byproducts of man's resort to force and arms. Unfortunately, such despicable acts have a dangerous tendency to call forth primitive impulses of vengeance and retaliation among the victimized peoples. The satisfaction of such impulses in turn breeds resentment and fresh tension. Thus does the spiral of cruelty and hatred grow.

If we are to ever develop an orderly international community based upon a recognition of human dignity it is of the utmost importance that the necessary punishment of those guilty of atrocities be as free as possible from the ugly stigma of revenge and vindictiveness. Justice must be tempered by compassion rather than by vengeance. In this, the first case involving this momentous problem ever to reach this Court, our responsibility is both lofty and difficult. We must insist, within the confines of our proper jurisdiction, that the highest standards of justice be applied in this trial of an enemy commander conducted under the authority of the United States. Otherwise stark retribution will be free to masquerade in a cloak of false legalism. And the hatred and cynicism engendered by that retribution will supplant the great ideals to which this nation is dedicated.

This Court fortunately has taken the first and most important step toward insuring the supremacy of law and justice in the treatment of an enemy belligerent accused of violating the laws of war. Jurisdiction properly has been asserted to inquire 'into the cause of restraint of liberty' of such a person.... Thus the obnoxious doctrine asserted by the Government in this case, to the effect that restraints of liberty resulting from military trials of war criminals are political matters completely outside the arena of judicial review, has been rejected fully and unquestionably. This does not mean, of course, that the foreign affairs and policies of the nation are proper subjects of judicial inquiry. But when the liberty of any person is restrained by reason of the authority of the United States the writ of habeas corpus is available to test the legality of that restraint, even though direct court review of the restraint is prohibited. The conclusive presumption must be made, in this country at least, that illegal restraints are unauthorized and unjustified by any foreign policy of the Government and that commonly accepted judicial standards are to be recognized and enforced. On that basis judicial inquiry into these matters may proceed within its proper sphere.

The determination of the extent of review of war trials calls for statesmanship of the highest order. The ultimate nature and scope of the writ of habeas corpus are within the discretion of the judiciary unless validly circumscribed by Congress. Here we are confronted with a use of the writ under circumstances novel in the history of the Court. For my own part, I do not feel that we should be confined by the traditional lines of review drawn in connection with the use of the writ by ordinary criminals who have direct access to the judiciary in the first instance. Those held by the military lack any such access; consequently the judicial review available by habeas corpus must be wider than usual in order that proper standards of justice may be enforceable.

But for the purposes of this case I accept the scope of review recognized by the Court at this time....

* * *

The Court, in my judgment, demonstrates conclusively that the military commission was lawfully created in this instance that petitioner could not object to its power to try him for a recognized war crime...however, I find it impossible to agree that the charge against the petitioner stated a recognized violation of the laws of war.

It is important, in the first place, to appreciate the background of events preceding this trial. From October 9, 1944, to September 2, 1945, the petitioner was the Commanding General of the 14th Army Group of the Imperial Japanese Army, with headquarters in the Philippines. The reconquest of the Philippines by the armed forces of the United States began approximately at the time when the petitioner assumed this command. Combined with a great and decisive sea battle [Battle of Leyte Gulf], an invasion was made on the island of Leyte on October 20, 1944. 'In the six days of the great naval action the Japanese position in the Philippines had become extremely critical. Most of the serviceable elements of the Japanese Navy had become committed to the battle with disastrous results. The strike had miscarried, and General MacArthur's land wedge was firmly implanted in the vulnerable flank of the enemy * * * There were 260,000 Japanese troops scattered over the Philippines but most of them might as well have been on the other side of the world so far as the enemy's ability to shift them to meet the American thrusts was concerned. If General MacArthur succeeded in establishing himself in the Visayas where he could stage, exploit and spread under cover of overwhelming naval and air superiority, nothing could prevent him from overrunning the Philippines.' Biennial Report of the Chief Staff of the United States Army, July 1, 1943, to June 30, 1945, to the Secretary of War, p. 74.

By the end of 1944 the island of Leyte was largely in American hands. And on January 9, 1945, the island of Luzon was invaded. 'Yamashita's inability to cope with General MacArthur's swift moves, his desired reaction to the deception measures, the guerrillas, and General Kenney's aircraft combined to place the Japanese in an impossible situation. The enemy was forced into a piecemeal commitment of his troops.' Ibid. p. 78. It was at this time and place that most of the alleged atrocities took place. Organized resistance around Manila ceased on February 23. Repeated land and air assaults pulverized the enemy and within a few months there was little left of petitioner's command except a few remnants which had gathered for a last stand among the precipitous mountains.

As the military commission here noted, 'The Defense established the difficulties faced by the Accused with respect not only to the swift and overpowering advance of American forces, but also to the errors of his predecessors, weaknesses in organization, equipment, supply with special reference to food and gasoline, training, communications, discipline and morale of his troops. It was alleged that the sudden assignment of Naval and Air Forces to his tactical command presented almost insurmountable difficulties. This situation was followed, the Defense contended, by failure to obey his orders to withdraw troops from Manila, and the subsequent massacre of unarmed civilians, particularly by naval forces. Prior to the Luzon Campaign, Naval forces had reported to a separate ministry in the Japanese Government and Naval Commanders may not have been receptive or experienced in this instance with respect to a joint land operation under a single commander who was designated from the Army service.'

The final day of reckoning for the enemy arrived in August, 1945. On September 3, the petitioner surrendered to the United States Army at Baguio, Luzon. He immediately became a prisoner of war and was interned in prison in conformity with the rules of international law. On September 25, approximately three weeks after surrendering, he was served with the charge in issue in this case. Upon service of the charge he was removed from the status of a prisoner of war and placed in confinement as an accused war criminal. Arraignment followed on October 8 before a military commission specially appointed for the case. Petitioner pleaded not guilty. He was also served on that day with a bill of particulars alleging 64 crimes by troops under his command. A supplemental bill alleging 59 more crimes by his troops was filed on October 29, the same day that the trial began. No continuance was allowed for the preparation of a defense as to the supplemental bill. The trial continued uninterrupted until December 5, 1945. On December 7 petitioner was found guilty as charged and was sentenced to be hanged.

The petitioner was accused of having 'unlawfully disregarded and failed to discharge his duty as commander to control the operations of the members of his command, permitting them to commit brutal atrocities and other high crimes.' The bills of particular further alleged that specific acts of atrocity were committed by 'members of the armed forces of Japan under the command of the accused.' Nowhere was it alleged that the petitioner personally committed any of the atrocities, or that he ordered their commission, or that he had any knowledge of the commission thereof by members of his command.

The findings of the military commission bear out this absence of any direct personal charge against the petitioner. The commission merely found that atrocities and other high crimes 'have been committed by members of the Japanese armed forces under your command * * * that they were not sporadic in nature but in many cases were methodically supervised by Japanese officers and non-commissioned officers * * * that during the period in question you failed to provide effective control of your troops as was required by the circumstances.'

In other words, read against the background of military events in the Philippines subsequent to October 9, 1944, these charges amount to this: 'We, the victorious American forces, have done everything possible to destroy and disorganize your lines of communication, your effective control of your personnel, your ability to wage war. In those respects we have succeeded. We have defeated and crushed your forces. And now we charge and condemn you for having been inefficient in maintaining control of your troops during the period when we were so effectively besieging and eliminating your forces and blocking your ability to maintain effective control. Many terrible atrocities were committed by your disorganized troops. Because these atrocities were so widespread we will not bother to charge or prove that you committed, ordered or condoned any of them. We will assume that they must have resulted from your inefficiency and negligence as a commander. In short, we charge you with the crime of inefficiency in controlling your troops. We will judge the discharge of your duties by the disorganization which we ourselves created in large part. Our standards of judgment are whatever we wish to make them.

Nothing in all history or in international law, at least as far as I am aware, justifies such a charge against a fallen commander of a defeated force. To use the very inefficiency and disorganization created by the victorious forces as the primary basis for condemning officers of the defeated armies bears no resemblance to justice or to military reality.

International law makes no attempt to define the duties of a commander of an army under constant and overwhelming assault; nor does it impose liability under such circumstances for failure to meet the ordinary responsibilities of command. The omission is understandable. Duties, as well as ability to control troops, vary according to the nature and intensity of the particular battle. To find an unlawful deviation from duty under battle conditions requires difficult and speculative calculations. Such calculations become highly untrustworthy when they are made by the victor in relation to the actions of a vanquished commander. Objective and realistic norms of conduct are then extremely unlikely to be used in forming a judgment as to deviations from duty. The probability that vengeance will form the major part of the victor's judgment is an unfortunate but inescapable fact. So great is that probability that international law refuses to recognize such a judgment as a basis for a war crime, however fair the judgment may be in a particular instance. It is this consideration that undermines the charge against the petitioner in this case. The indictment permits, indeed compels, the military commission of a victorious nation to sit in judgment upon the military strategy and actions of the defeated enemy and to use its conclusions to determine the criminal liability of an enemy commander. Life and liberty are made to depend upon the biased will of the victor rather than upon objective standards of conduct.

The Court's reliance upon vague and indefinite references in certain of the Hague Conventions and the Geneva Red Cross Convention is misplaced....

* * *

The provisions of the other conventions referred to by the Court are on their face equally devoid of relevance of significance to the situation here in issue....

* * *

Even the laws of war heretofore recognized by this nation fail to impute responsibility to a fallen commander for excesses committed by his disorganized troops while under attack....

* * *

The Government claims that the principle that commanders in the field are bound to control their troops has been applied so as to impose liability on the United States in international arbitrations.... The difference between arbitrating property rights and charging an individual with a crime against the laws of war is too obvious to require elaboration. But even more significant is the fact that even these arbitration cases fail to establish any principle of liability where troops are under constant assault and demoralizing influences by attacking forces. The same observation applies to the common law and statutory doctrine, referred to by the Government, that one who is under a legal duty to take protective or preventive action is guilty of criminal homicide if he willfully or negligently omits to act and death is proximately caused.... No one denies that inaction or negligence may give rise to liability, civil or criminal. But it is quite another thing to say that the inability to control troops under highly competitive and disastrous battle conditions renders one guilty of a war crime in the absence of personal culpability. Had there been some element of knowledge or direct connection with the atrocities, the problem would be entirely different. Moreover, it must be remembered that we are not dealing here with an ordinary tort or criminal action; precedents in those fields are of little if any value. Rather we are concerned with a proceeding involving an international crime, the treatment of which may have untold effects upon the future peace of the world. That fact must be kept uppermost in our search for precedent.

The only conclusion that I can draw is that the charge made against the petitioner is clearly without precedent in international law or in the annals of recorded military history. This is not to say that enemy commanders may escape punishment for clear and unlawful failures to prevent atrocities. But that punishment should be based upon charges fairly drawn in light of established rules of international law and recognized concepts of justice.

But the charge in this case…was speedily drawn and filed but three weeks after the petitioner surrendered. The trial proceeded with great dispatch without allowing the defense time to prepare an adequate case. Petitioner's rights under the due process clause of the Fifth Amendment were grossly and openly violated without any justification. All this was done without any thorough investigation and prosecution of those immediately responsible for the atrocities, out of which might have come some proof or indication of personal culpability on petitioner's part.... We live under the Constitution, which is the embodiment of all the high hopes and aspirations of the new world. And it is applicable in both war and peace. We must act accordingly.

* * *

…These are the reasons that lead me to dissent in these terms.

Mr. Justice RUTLEDGE, dissenting.

Not with ease does one find his views at odds with the Court's in a matter of this character and gravity. Only the most deeply felt convictions could force one to differ. That reason alone leads me to do so now, against strong considerations for withholding dissent.

More is at stake than General Yamashita's fate. There could be no possible sympathy for him if he is guilty of the atrocities for which his death is sought. But there can be and should be justice administered according to law. In this stage of war's aftermath it is too early for Lincoln's great spirit, best lighted in the Second Inaugural, to have wide hold for the treatment of foes. It is not too early, it is never too early, for the nation steadfastly to follow its great constitutional traditions, none older or more universally protective against unbridled power than due process of law in the trial and punishment of men, that is, of all men, whether citizens, aliens, alien enemies or enemy belligerents....

This long-held attachment marks the great divide between our enemies and ourselves. Theirs was a philosophy of universal force. Ours is one of universal law, albeit imperfectly made flesh of our system and so dwelling among us. Every departure weakens the tradition, whether it touches the high or the low, the powerful or the weak, the triumphant or the conquered. If we need not or cannot be magnanimous, we can keep our own law on the plane from which it has not descended hitherto and to which the defeated foes' never rose.

With all deference to the opposing views of my brethren, whose attachment to that tradition needless to say is no less than my own, I cannot believe in the face of this record that the petitioner has had the fair trail our Constitution and laws command.

Because I cannot reconcile what has occurred with their measure, I am forced to speak. At bottom my concern is that we shall not forsake in any case, whether Yamashita's or another's, the basic standards of trial which, among other guaranties, the nation fought to keep; that our system of military justice shall not alone among all forms of judging be above or beyond the fundamental law or the control of Congress within its orbit of authority; and that this Court shall not fail in its part under the Constitution to see that these things do not happen.

This trial is unprecedented in our history. Never before have we tried and convicted an enemy general for action taken during hostilities or otherwise in the course of military operations or duty. Much less have we condemned one for failing to take action. The novelty is not lessened by the trial's having taken place after hostilities ended and the enemy, including the accused, had surrendered. Moreover, so far as the time permitted for our consideration has given opportunity, I have not been able to find precedent for the proceeding in the system of any nation founded in the basic principles of our constitutional democracy, in the laws of war or in other internationally binding authority or usage.

The novelty is legal as well as historical. We are on strange ground. Precedent is not all-controlling in law. There must be room for growth, since every precedent has an origin. But it is the essence of our tradition for judges, when they stand at the end of the marked way, to go forward with caution keeping sight, so far as they are able, upon the great landmarks left behind and the direction they point ahead. If, as may be hoped, we are now to enter upon a new era of law in the world, it becomes more important than ever before the nations creating that system to observe their greatest traditions of administering justice, including this one, both in their own judging and in their new creation. The proceedings in this case veer so far from some of our time-tested road signs that I cannot take the large strides validating them would demand.

It is not in our tradition for anyone to be charged with crime which is defined after his conduct, alleged to be criminal, has taken place; or in language not sufficient to inform him of the nature of the offense or to enable him to make defense. Mass guilt we do not impute to individuals, perhaps in any case, but certainly in none where the person is not charged or shown actively to have participated in or knowingly to have failed in taking action to prevent the wrongs done by others, having both the duty and the power to do so.

It is outside our basic scheme to condemn men without giving reasonable opportunity for preparing defense; in capital or other serious crimes to convict on 'official documents * * *; affidavits; * * * documents or translations thereof; diaries * * *, photographs, motion picture films, * * * and newspapers' or on hearsay, once, twice or thrice removed, more particularly when the documentary evidence or some of it is prepared ex parte by the prosecuting authority and includes not only opinion but conclusions of guilt. Nor in such cases do we deny the rights of confrontation of witnesses and cross-examination.

Our tradition does not allow conviction by tribunals both authorized and bound by the instrument of their creation to receive and consider evidence which is expressly excluded by Act of Congress or by treaty obligation; nor is it in accord with our basic concepts to the tribunal, specially constituted for the particular trial, regardless of those prohibitions, the sole and exclusive judge of the credibility, probative value and admissibility of whatever may be tendered as evidence.

The matter is not one merely of the character and admissibility of evidence. It goes to the very competency of the tribunal to try and punish consistently with the Constitution, the laws of the United States made in pursuance thereof, and treaties made under the nation's authority.

All these deviations from the fundamental law, and others, occurred in the course of constituting the commission, the preparation for trial and defense, the trial itself, and therefore, in effect, in the sentence imposed. Whether taken singly in some instances as departures from specific constitutional mandates or in totality as in violation of the Fifth Amendment's command that no person shall be deprived of life, liberty or property without due process of law, a trial so vitiated cannot withstand constitutional scrutiny.

One basic protection of our system and one only, petitioner has had. He has been represented by able counsel, officers of the army he fought. Their difficult assignment has been done with extraordinary fidelity, not only to the accused, but to their high conception of military justice, always to be administered in subordination to the Constitution and consistent Acts of Congress and treaties.... I rest my judgment that the commission was without jurisdiction from the beginning to try or punish the petitioner and that, if it had acquired jurisdiction then, its power to proceed was lost in the course of what was done before and during trial.

Only on one view, in my opinion, could either of these conclusions be avoided. This would be that an enemy belligerent in petitioner's position is altogether beyond the pale of constitutional protection, regardless of the fact that hostilities had ended and he had surrendered with his country. The Government has so argued, urging that we are still at war with Japan and all the power of the military effective during active hostilities in theatres of combat continues in full force unaffected by the events of August 14, 1945, and after.

In this view the action taken here is one of military necessity, exclusively within the authority of the President as Commander-in-Chief and his military subordinates to take in warding off military danger and subject to no judicial restraint on any account, although somewhat inconsistently it is said this Court may 'examine' the proceedings generally.

As I understand the Court, this is in substance the effect of what has been done. For I cannot conceive any instance of departure from our basic concepts of fair trial, if the failure here are not sufficient to produce that effect.

We are technically still at war, because peace has not been negotiated finally or declared. But there is no longer the danger which always exists before surrender and armistice. Military necessity does not demand the same measures. The nation may be more secure now than at any time after peace is officially concluded. In these facts is one great difference from Ex parte Quirin... Punitive action now can be effective only for the next war, for purposes of military security. And enemy aliens, including belligerents, need the attenuated protections our system extends to them more now than before hostilities ceased or than they may after a treaty of peace is signed. Ample power there is to punish them or others for crimes, whether under the laws of war during its course or later during occupation. There can be no question of that. The only question is how it shall be done, consistently with universal constitutional commands or outside their restricting effects. In this sense I think the Constitution follows the flag.

* * *

...My primary concern will be with the constitution of the commission and other matters taking place in the course of the proceedings, relating chiefly to the denial of reasonable opportunity to prepare petitioner's defense and the sufficiency of the evidence, together with serious questions of admissibility, to prove an offense, all going as I think to the commission's jurisdiction. [Here, Justice Rutledge reviews the commission's authority according to General MacArthur's directive to General Styer, especially with reference to the rules of evidence. The Justice then continues]:

II.

* * *

A more complete abrogation of customary safeguards relating to proof, whether in the usual rules of evidence or any reasonable substitute and whether for use in the trial of crime in the civil courts or military tribunals, hardly could have been made. So far as the admissibility and probative value of evidence was concerned, the directive made the commission a law unto itself.

It acted accordingly. As against insistent and persistent objection to the reception of all kinds of 'evidence,' oral, documentary and photographic, for nearly every kind of defect under any of the usual prevailing standards for admissibility and probative value, the commission not only consistently ruled against the defense, but repeatedly stated it was bound by the directive to receive the kinds of evidence it specified, reprimanded counsel for continuing to make objection, declined to hear further objections, and in more than one instance during the course of proceedings reversed its ruling favorable to the defense, where initially it had declined to receive what the prosecution offered. Every conceivable kind of statement, rumor, report, at first, second, third or further hand, written, printed, or oral, and one 'propaganda' film were allowed to come in, most of this relating to atrocities committed by troops under petitioner's command throughout the several thousand islands of the Philippine Archipelago during the period of active hostilities covered by the American forces' return to and recapture of the Philippines.

* * *

But there is not a suggestion in the findings that petitioner personally participated in, was present at the occurrence of, or ordered any of these incidents, with the exception of the wholly inferential suggestion noted below. [Here the inference was made by the prosecution that because of the widespread and extensive crimes perpetrated by soldiers under petitioner's command, he must have had knowledge of their occurrence and failed to put an end to such activities].

* * *

[The] vagueness, if not vacuity, in the findings runs throughout the proceedings, from the charge itself through the proof and the findings, to the conclusion. It affects the very gist of the offense, whether that was willful, informed and intentional omission to restrain and control troops known by petitioner to be committing crimes or was only a negligent failure on his part to discover this and take whatever measures he then could to stop the conduct.

Although it is impossible to determine from what is before us whether petitioner in fact has been convicted of one or the other or of both these things, the case has been presented on the former basis and, unless as is noted below there is a fatal duplicity, it must be taken that the crime charged and sought to be proved was only the failure, with knowledge, to perform the commander's function of control, although the Court's [majority] opinion nowhere expressly declares that knowledge was essential to guilt or necessary to be set forth in the charge.

* * *

Petitioner asserts, and there can be no reason to doubt, that by the use of all this forbidden evidence he was deprived of the right of cross-examination and other means to establish the credibility of the deponents or affiants, not to speak of the authors of reports, letters, documents and newspaper articles; of opportunity to determine whether the multitudinous crimes specified in the bills were committed in fact by troops under his command or by naval or air force troops not under his command at the time alleged; to ascertain whether the crimes attested were isolated acts of individual soldiers or were military acts committed by troop units acting under supervision of officers; and, finally, whether 'in short, there was such a 'pattern' of conduct as the prosecution alleged and its whole theory of the crime and the evidence required to be made out.'

* * *

So far as I know, it has not yet been held that any tribunal in our system, of whatever character, is free to receive 'such evidence' as in its opinion would be 'of assistance in proving or disproving the charge' or, again as in its opinion, 'would have probative value in the mind of a reasonable man'; and, having received what in its unlimited discretion it regards as sufficient, is also free to determine what weight may be given to the evidence received without restraint.

When to this fatal defect in the directive, however innocently made, are added the broad departures from the fundamentals of fair play in the proof and in the right to defend which occurred throughout the proceeding, there can be no accommodation with the due process of law which the Fifth Amendment demands.

* * *

VI.

I cannot accept the view that anywhere in our system resides or lurks a power so unrestrained to deal with any human being through any process of trial. What military agencies or authorities may do with our enemies in battle or invasion, apart from proceedings in the nature of trial and some semblance of judicial action, is beside the point. Nor has any human being heretofore been held to be wholly beyond the elementary procedural protection by the Fifth Amendment. I cannot consent to even implied departure from that great absolute.

It was a great patriot [Thomas Paine] who said:

'He that would make his own liberty secure must guard even his enemy from oppression; for if he violates this duty he establishes a precedent that will reach himself.'

Mr. Justice MURPHY joins in this opinion.

[The military Board of Review which received the trial record of the *Yamashita* proceedings in December, 1945, came to the conclusion that, indeed, there was sufficient credible evidence establishing that General Yamashita had failed to exercise appropriate command responsibility during his tenure as commander of Japanese forces in the Philippines. This failure exascerbated the widespread criminal behavior of the troops under his command. The Board's evaluation of the record read, in part:

Upon this issue a careful reading of all the evidence impels the conclusion that it demonstrates this responsibility. In the first place the atrocities were so numerous, involved so many people, and were so widespread that accused's professional ignorance is incredible. Then, too, their manner of commission reveals a striking similarity of pattern throughout.... In many instances there was evidence of prearranged planning of the sites of the execution.... [There was] direct proof of statements by the Japanese participants that they were acting pursuant to orders of higher authorities.... There was some evidence in the record tending to connect accused more directly with the commission of some of the atrocities. His own Staff Judge Advocate, Colonel Hishiharu, told him that there was a large number of guerrillas in custody and not sufficient time to try them.... It is also noteworthy that the mistreatment of prisoners of war at Ft. McKinley occurred while accused was present in his headquarters only a few hundred yards distant.... [20]

The following selected excerpts are taken from two articles written some forty-three years apart. Both comment on the *Yamashita* case from different perspectives. The first selection by Guy narrates a close-up view of the trial by one of the appointed American defense lawyers. In reading this material, bear in mind that these are expressions of a defense trial advocate, not an individual who approaches the case with a sense of detached reflection. Major Guy, along with five other United States Army defense lawyers, provided the accused with a sustained and robust defense in the best traditions of American trial advocacy, from submission of the initial charges, up to and including a final plea of clemency addressed to President Harry S. Truman.

The selection by Prevost also reviews the trial procedures in *Yamashita* as well as the often unremarked racial encumbrances that may have played a role in the ultimate fate of General Yamashita. Prevost also comments on the make-up of the United States Supreme Court bench at the time and how Chief Justice Harlan Fiske Stone attempted to craft a unanimous decision in *In re Yamashita*. We include only excerpts involving the racial overtones in the case and selected comments concerning the personnel of the Supreme Court sitting in the immediate postwar era].

---

3. George F. Guy, "The Defense of Yamashita"

4 *Wyoming Law Journal* 153, 154; 156; 158–59;
161–62; 166; 171–75; 176; 178–79 (1949–50)
George F. Guy, *The Defense of Yamashita*, originally published in
4 *Wyo. L. J.* 153–180 (1949–50). Reprinted with
permission of the Wyoming Law Review

* * *

I am aware that the officers assigned to the defense approached their task with uncertainty, concern and curiosity. We had all seen the ravages and destruction in Manila itself and many of us had seen similar sights out in the provinces and in other cities in the Philippines. We all knew that Yamashita was entitled to a defense, but we all wondered, "Why does it have to be us"?

The war was so recently over that it was difficult to regard any Japanese other than as an enemy and it was particularly difficult to regard the Commanding General of the

---

20. *Review of the Record of Trial by a Military Commission of Tomoyuki Yamashita, General, Imperial Japanese Army,* Gen. H. Q., U.S. Army Forces, Pacific, Office of the Theatre Judge Advocate Dec. 26, 1945, as quoted in Paust, Jordan J., et al., *International Criminal Law: Cases and Materials,* 2d ed. 52 (2000).

Japanese Forces in the Philippines as anything but the representative of all that was re-
pugnant and brutal and cruel and treacherous in the Japanese system—as the prime
standard bearer of that inhuman power that had looted, burned, murdered and raped
Manila, the "Pearl of the Orient" and her sister cities of the Philippines. Therefore, it
was indeed with mixed emotions, including no small amount of curiosity, that we six,
who had been appointed as defense counsel, approached our task and our first interview with our client at New Bilibid Prison, Muntinglupa Province, Luzon, on October
4, 1945.

* * *

We shortly and quickly got down to the serious business at hand and, working
through Mr. Hamamoto [the interpreter], were soon in the midst of the allegations of
the charge against Yamashita. That charge is as follows:

> "Tomoyuki Yamashita, General, Imperial Japanese Army, between 9 Octo-
> ber, 1944 and 2 September, 1945, at Manila and at other places in the Philip-
> pine Islands, while commander of armed forces of Japan at war with the
> United States of America and its allies, unlawfully disregarded and failed to
> discharge his duty as commander to control the operations of the members of
> his command, permitting them to commit brutal atrocities and other high
> crimes against people of the United States and its allies and dependencies, par-
> ticularly the Philippines; and he, General TOMOYUKI YAMASHITA, thereby
> violated the laws of war.

Dated 25 September, 1945   /s/ALVA C. CARPENTER

                                                Colonel, JAGD

                                                United States Army."

That charge had been served on Yamashita a few days before by…one of the prosecution staff, but it was not until this afternoon [October 4, 1945] that Yamashita, after
conference with his counsel, had any real concept of understanding of the nature of the
charge against him. After that very first moment of comprehension of the full import of
the charge, Tomoyuki Yamashita firmly and solemnly maintained his innocence of such
charge.

* * *

…By mid-October, it seemed that all of America, yes, all of the occidental world, not to
mention all the Philippines, believed firmly that all Japanese army officers were "Samurai
fanatics," "Greater East Asia exponents," "Empire Imperialists," etc., whose hands dripped
with blood of helpless and innocent women and children. All Japanese officers were regarded alike, regardless of what individual records might be. In the case of Yamashita, the
popular concept was even darker and bloodier, because he was commonly referred to in
the press of the world as the "Tiger of Malaya." This appellation gave rise to the popular
picture of Yamashita as the Japanese conqueror who raged down the Malayan Peninsula
like a roaring Tiger, devouring and destroying as he went…. By virtue of this press
buildup, Yamashita was already convicted in the eyes of the world, and certainly in the
eyes of the Filipinos, even before a shred of evidence had been introduced against him. I
fear that a great majority of American military personnel in the Philippines was satisfied,
from this mass of publicity, that Yamashita was guilty of anything that might be said.

Under such conditions, and with the trial held in Manila, the very center and vortex
of these swirling animosities and predetermined public concepts of guilt, the task confronting the defense seemed enormous indeed.

* * *

The lay public must understand that the trial before the Military Commission was no trial in the ordinary sense of the term, and the lay public must disassociate from its mind the usual conception of a criminal trial with a judge, learned in the law, sitting as the trier of questions of law and with a jury sitting as the trier of questions of fact of the evidence presented to it within the usual rules of admissibility as determined by the judge. The Military Commission which tried General Yamashita had no "judge learned in the law" sitting with it. True, one of the officers was designated as "law member," but he is not a lawyer and is not "learned in the law" and not a member of the legal profession. The Commission as a whole—that is, the five members, all Generals—sat also as a jury in determining the facts as presented. The Rules of Evidence were especially prepared for this trial. They provided numerous exceptions to the usual safeguards thrown about accused persons in the criminal or military proceedings. A clear exception, for example, was made in the case of hearsay evidence. One of the basic rules of our law of evidence for hundreds of years has been the hearsay rule; i. e., a witness cannot testify as to what someone else told him. This was entirely eliminated in the Yamashita case. Under this elimination, hearsay was freely accepted as were statements of absent and even unidentified persons. This rule also permitted the introduction of diaries of Japanese troops and enemy orders found on the battlefield without identification of the authors or the units to which they belonged. All of these were unquestionably inadmissible under the usual rules of evidence. The defense vigorously contested these rules and carried that part of the fight into the Supreme Court of the Philippines and finally into the Supreme Court of the United States itself....

The proof of murder, torture, rape and maltreatment of thousands of Filipinos and of hundreds of Americans and of some scores of other nationalities was clear and overwhelming. These outrages occurred at points in the Philippines from Bataan Island north of Luzon itself to Davao in southern Mindanao. There is no denying that Japanese personnel indulged in the most revolting outrages and in some instances, seemed to conduct their activities on almost an organized basis with officers and non-coms directing the activities. The Japanese personnel involved were variously identified as Navy, Army and Merchant Marine, but there is no doubt that the atrocities complained of did occur. Witness after witness testified to these crimes until tales of horror, death, mutilation, starvation, maltreatment and abuse became almost commonplace.

* * *

The most significant point made by the defense was that throughout the great mass of prosecution testimony and evidence there was not one word or one shred of credible evidence to show that General Yamashita ever ordered the commission of even one of the acts with which he was charged or that he ever had any knowledge of the commission of any of these acts, either before they took place, or after their commission.

* * *

At the conclusion of the prosecution's case, the defense made a motion for a finding of "Not Guilty" on the ground generally that there was no proof of any kind to connect Yamashita with what did happen. This motion was over-ruled and the defense was directed to proceed with its evidence. A defense motion for a continuance, based upon an indication given at the time the trial opened that such continuance would be granted at the close of the prosecution's case, was denied. Thereupon the defense evidence was presented.

* * *

Numerous witnesses testified for the defense.... General Muto, Yamashita's Chief of Staff, was perhaps the most important defense witness, aside from the accused himself. Muto had been Chief of Staff in Sumatra and did not arrive in the Philippines until about October 20, 1944, or at the time of the initial American assault on Leyte.... He was subsequently tried along with several others including General Tojo before the International Military Tribunal Far East in Tokyo and was finally executed.... He positively testified that never at any time had Yamashita ordered the commission of any atrocities against the Filipinos or anyone else. There never had been any prosecution evidence that such orders *had* been given, but any inference of their having been given or having been condoned, was certainly effectively refuted by General Muto's testimony.

* * *

[Regarding Yamashita's testimony, Guy notes]: He took the stand in his own behalf, after explanation by General Reynolds that he did not need to, and that he could make an unsworn statement or remain silent as he liked, but that if he did take the stand as a witness, he would be subject to cross-examination. He elected to take the stand as a witness and did so, and was on the stand all told for about 18 hours. His testimony was frank, forthright, full and complete.

* * *

The whole essence of the Charge against Yamashita was that he "failed to control" his troops, thereby "*permitting*" them to commit crimes, etc. He was subjected to a long and searching cross-examination by Major Kerr, the Chief Prosecutor, the dramatic climax of which was reached in the following cross-examination, appearing at page 3660 of the record of the trial:

> "Q. You admit, do you, that you failed to control your troops in the Philippines?
>
> A. I have put forth my maximum efforts in order to control the troops, and if this was not sufficient, then somehow I should have done more, but I feel that I have done my very best.
>
> Q. Did you fail to control your troops? Please answer 'yes' or 'no.'
>
> A. I believe I did control my troops.

[After the accused was found guilty by the court, defense counsel filed papers with the Supreme Court of the Philippines for both a writ of prohibition and a writ of habeas corpus. Service of these writs was made upon Lieutenant General Wilhelm. D. Styer on November 13, 1945].

* * *

The reader must realize that our system of law does not permit any direct appeal from the decision of a court-martial or Military Commission; in other words, there is no procedure provided whereby an appeal can be taken from conviction by the military tribunal to civilian courts for the purpose of reviewing those decisions. The only means of judicial escape for Yamashita, or for that matter, for an American so convicted by a military court, is by habeas corpus and prohibition. In order to make these remedies available, it is essential that petitioner show that the military court which tried him was without jurisdiction.... The Philippine Supreme Court announced its decision denying the petition on December 4th, the day before the conclusion of the final argument before the Military Commission.

* * *

...General Yamashita was brought into the jam-packed court room...[and] was directed to take a stand in front of General Reynolds accompanied by Colonel Clarke, senior defense counsel. Almost immediately General Reynolds commenced reading the prepared statement which constituted the Commission's findings, judgment and sentence.... [H]istory was being made in the field of International Law, for this was the first time in American history that a Commander of a defeated enemy army was convicted as a war criminal upon the theory of command responsibility alone.

* * *

The case was set down for oral argument before the United States Supreme Court on January 7, 1946, and it was there presented by my three colleagues, who had flown to Washington from Manila. The Government's case was presented by the newly appointed Solicitor General Mr. Howard McGrath, his assistant, Mr. Judson, and the Attorney General, Mr. Tom Clark.

* * *

The matter was taken under advisement, and on February 4th, the Supreme Court announced its momentous denial of the writs sought and this meant death for Yamashita. The majority opinion was read by...Mr. Justice Stone. It considered each of the points made by the defense and concluded that the Articles of War did not apply to Yamashita and that he, therefore, could not complain if the procedure did not conform to the standards set by our military code....

* * *

Following the action of the United States Supreme Court, Colonel Clark made [a] supreme final effort on behalf of Yamashita by taking an appeal for clemency to President Truman. The President, however, declined to act and thereby left the matter entirely in the hands of the military.

* * *

In due time, General MacArthur announced that he had confirmed the sentence of the Commission and on February 23, 1946, at Los Banos Prison Camp, 30 miles south of Manila, Tomoyuki Yamashita paid with his life for the crimes of his troops.

---

4. Ann M. Prevost, "Race and War Crimes: The 1945 Trial of General Tomoyuki Yamashita"

14 *Human Rights Quarterly* 303; 304–309; 321, 328; 329 (1992)
Ann M. Prevost, *Race and War Crimes: The 1945 Trial of General Tomoyuki Yamashita*. 14 *Human Rights Quarterly* 303 (1992), 303–309, 321, 328–329.
© The Johns Hopkins University Press. Reprinted with
permission from the Johns Hopkins University Press

* * *

The case of General Tomoyuki Yamashita is one of the most renowned of the war crimes trials of World War II. The trial of the Japanese commander of the Philippines was and continues to be a case surrounded in controversy. It is noted particularly for the precedential charge applied to the general, known today as command responsibility.

Under this charge, the American military tribunal was able to convict Yamashita without any showing of culpability on his part.

* * *

...During the Pacific War, the Philippines and the U.S. soldiers fighting there had suffered tremendously at the hands of the Japanese. The atrocities committed by naval forces in Manila, for which Yamashita was charged with command responsibility, were some of the most brutal of the war. Not surprisingly, the mood at the opening of the trial—so soon after the war—was one of revenge. General Douglas MacArthur, the Supreme Commander for the Allied powers, Far East, and his military tribunal were blindly determined to convict Yamashita. Indeed the procedures put in place by the tribunal to try Yamashita were so onerous that even the press reported them to be outside the norms of "Anglo-Saxon justice."

* * *

...Yamashita was not convicted merely because he was a commander; he was convicted because he was a *Japanese* commander. The influence of racial prejudice in Yamashita's trial and the controversial Supreme Court decision which followed has never been adequately addressed. Yet it is a fact that the *Yamashita* version of command responsibility theory was not used against German war criminals at Nuremberg, nor was it applied to U.S. officers during the Vietnam War. The courts have applied it only to alleged Japanese war criminals. Yamashita was convicted of this charge, and it was used at the international tribunal in Tokyo. Indeed, racism and the Pacific War is a subject which only recently has been examined....

When the government secures such a conviction as a result of racial prejudice, it is not unlikely that the conviction will later be found to be a terrible yet irretrievable mistake. In this respect, the *Yamashita* case ends with just such an unsettling twist. This author discovered, as a result of an interview with *Yamashita* defense counsel A. Frank Reel, that just two years after Yamashita's conviction Admiral Soemu Toyoda, Japan's highest ranking naval officer, was charged with the *identical* war crimes. Toyoda's own testimony at trial reveals that Yamashita was not in command of the forces that committed the atrocities for which he was hanged. It was Toyoda who put the perpetrators of those crimes in a position to commit them. Interestingly, the trial of Admiral Toyoda has virtually disappeared from recorded history. To date the United States has never acknowledged its mistake.

A. The Yellow Peril and the Second World War

American prejudice against the Japanese and Asians in general—evidenced by the once-common fear of the "Yellow Peril"—has had a long and shameful history. Such racism first appeared in the United States during the nineteenth century when Chinese immigrants came to the west coast to work on the transcontinental railroad [principally over the Sierra Nevada mountain range via Donner Pass in north-central California]. By 1882 Congress had passed the Chinese Exclusion Act in order to restrict Chinese Immigration.

At the turn of the century Japanese immigrants met with this same race hatred. Initially the racial tension was relegated to the west coast where the majority of Japanese had immigrated. However, as a result of the Russo-Japanese War of 1905 the Yellow Peril fear and anti-Japanese hysteria spread throughout the country; for the first time in modern history, an Asian nation had defeated a European nation.

In 1922 the Supreme Court decision *Ozawa v. United States* [260 U.S. 178] held that Japanese were not eligible for naturalization as U.S. citizens because they were not of the Caucasian race. In 1924 Congress prohibited all persons ineligible for citizenship from immigrating; the Immigration Act of 1924 thus entirely eliminated Japanese immigration to the United States.

The Yellow Peril fear was dormant for several years until it was reactivated by the bombing of Pearl Harbor on 7 December 1941. During the war, race-based propaganda against the Japanese became overwhelming. Professor John W. Dower, who has written extensively on the subject of racism in the Pacific War, has noted that Americans persisted in the notion that the Japanese were "subhuman, inhuman, lesser-than-human" or, conversely, "superhuman." [see: Dower in *Reference* section]. As a practice, the U.S. and the Allies used images of apes to describe the Japanese.

In addition, Professor Dower has pointed out that this component of racial prejudice was not present in the European sphere of the war. Throughout the war the Allies maintained a skewed vision toward their European and Asian foes. Despite the brutality of the Germans, a generally "enlightened attitude" was assumed by the Allies, who took care to distinguish "good" and "bad" Germans. Further, Professor Dower has written that the Allies tended to describe German atrocities as "Nazi" crimes rather than as behavior "rooted in German culture or personality." In contrast, Asian brutality was presented simply as "Japanese." There was no Japanese counterpart to the "good" German, hence the war-time saying, "The only good Jap is a dead Jap."

Throughout the war, Yamashita was a victim of this racist vision. As early as 1942 the Allied notion of Japanese as subhuman and ape-like was applied to the General. As an illustration, in February of that year Yamashita captured the British fortification at Singapore. The British had considered Singapore invulnerable to attack, yet General Yamashita rapidly negotiated his troops through the dense jungle and offered surrender terms as he reached the gates of the city. Not knowing that Yamashita's forces were numerically inferior, Sir Arthur Percival accepted Yamashita's terms.

Instead of acknowledging that they had been outdone by the brilliant strategy of Japan's great field general, the British portrayed their defeat as having been accomplished by savage beasts. In cartoon form, the British magazine *Punch* depicted Yamashita's forces as apes making their way to Singapore swinging from tree to tree.

At the very same time Yamashita was securing victory in Singapore, his German counterpart, Field Marshall Erwin Rommel, was destroying the British in North Africa. Far from being hated, however, Rommel was becoming a legendary figure to the Allies. Indeed, it was precisely because of his successes against the British that Rommel was considered by them to be "one of the greatest military leaders in history." He was hailed as a "pure genius who made the Afrika Corps unbeatable." This analysis of the two great Axis field generals underscores Professor Dower's theory that the Allied vision of their enemies was racially skewed. Rommel, who became known as the "Desert Fox" for his accomplishments on the battlefield, was considered a romantic figure. Yamashita, who became known as the "Tiger of Malaya" for his battlefield successes, was considered a savage.

Yamashita, however, was quite different than he was depicted by the Allies. After considerable investigation into his character and background, *Yamashita* defense counsel George Guy found that, in fact, "Yamashita had never been a 'political' General and that he had earned his high rank by sheer efficiency." Guy found also that Yamashita had a "reputation for fairness and for being a firm and strong disciplinarian and that he had never been part of extremist groups."

On the contrary, Yamashita had actually been opposed to the war with the Allies. Defense counsel Feldhaus recounted that in 1940, after an inspection tour in Europe, Yamashita reported to Tojo that, compared to the European armies, the Japanese army "left much to be desired." Yamashita also recommended that the "Chinese War be brought to an immediate close" and suggested that peaceful relations with Great Britain and America be "maintained at all costs." Yamashita's analysis put him in great disfavor with Tojo and the military clique in power in Japan. By September 1941 Yamashita found himself in command of an "unimportant post" in the Japanese puppet state of Manchukuo.

It was not until later that year, when war with the United States was imminent, that he was given command of the 25th Japanese Army in the Malayan peninsula. It was at this point that Yamashita captured Singapore. Defense counsel Reel recounted that overnight Yamashita became a "national hero." Prime Minister Tojo, however, feared Yamashita's new political influence and refused to allow him to come to Tokyo to make his report to the Emperor. Instead, Tojo ordered Yamashita once again to an obscure command in Manchukuo. It was not until some two years later, when Tojo's government fell on 18 July 1944, that Yamashita was given command in the Philippines.

* * *

... [T]he Supreme Court was overwhelmed early on by pressures stemming from the Pacific War. *In re Yamashita* was just one of several war-related cases decided by the Supreme Court under the guidance of Chief Justice Harlan Fiske Stone (1941–1946). A number of these earlier wartime cases involved Japanese-American citizens. In these cases the Supreme Court had been unwilling to challenge the decisions of the military. The treatment of Japanese-Americans in the United States is a forceful example of the racial prejudice of the Pacific War and the "official endorsement" it received.

The Court sanctioned military restrictions on Japanese-Americans and resident aliens in such infamous cases as *Hirabayashi v. United States* [320 U.S. 81 (1943)]; *Yasui v. United States* [320 U.S. 115 (1943)]; and *Korematsu v. United States* [323 U.S. 214 (1944)]. The Court relied on an unconditional doctrine of judicial restraint in arriving at these decisions. Chief Justice Stone had formulated this theory soon after President Roosevelt's court-packing plan of 1937 as a way to protect the Court. In adhering to this principle Stone hoped to gain the confidence of the President. One observer [Mason] has noted that by applying this strict interpretation as a rationalization for the Japanese-American cases the Court carried its idea of judicial restraint to the point of "judicial abdication."

* * *

To date, the version of the command responsibility doctrine invoked in the *Yamashita* trial has been applied only to Japanese officers whose troops have committed atrocities. In the Nuremberg trials the U.S. judges abandoned the "must have known" reasoning of the *Yamashita* decision. Instead, they required "proof of a causative, overt act or omission from which a guilty intent can be inferred before a verdict of guilty will be pronounced." [Reel]. The Vietnam War also revealed problems inherent in the charge. The case of Captain Ernest Medina [*infra, Part Five*], in 1971, was the only command responsibility prosecution to be brought against a US officer during the war.

* * *

Indeed, General Telford Taylor, former American Chief Prosecutor at Nuremberg, states that "if you were to apply to [General William Westmoreland] and other US generals [in Vietnam] the same standards that were applied to General Yamashita, there would be a strong possibility that they would come to the same end as he did."

* * *

It is not surprising, then, that the international community rejected the *Yamashita* version of the command responsibility doctrine in the 1977 Geneva Protocol regarding the punishment of war crimes. The proposed US amendment suggested that the definition include a "should have known" clause, under the reasoning set forth in the *Yamashita* decision. The Geneva delegations, however, found this proposal to be "unacceptable as a basis for future war-crimes prosecutions."

---

5. *The Japanese Instrument of Surrender*

Hans Dollinger, *The Decline and Fall of Nazi Germany and Imperial Japan*
(Arnold Pomerans trans.) 403 (1967)

We, acting by command of and on behalf of the Emperor of Japan, the Japanese Government and the Japanese Imperial General Headquarters, hereby accept the provisions set forth in the declaration issued by the heads of the Governments of the United States, China and Great Britain on 26 July 1945, at Potsdam, and subsequently adhered to by the Union of Soviet Socialist Republics, which four powers are hereafter referred to as the Allied Powers.

We hereby proclaim the unconditional surrender to the Allied Powers of the Japanese Imperial General Headquarters and of all Japanese armed forces and all armed forces under Japanese control wherever situated.

We hereby command all Japanese forces wherever situated and the Japanese people to cease hostilities forthwith, to preserve and save from damage all ships, aircraft and military and civil property and to comply with all requirements which may be imposed by the supreme Commander for the Allied Powers or by agencies of the Japanese Government at his direction.

We hereby command the Japanese Imperial General Headquarters to issue at once an order to the Commanders of all Japanese forces and all forces under Japanese control wherever situated to surrender unconditionally themselves and all forces under their control.

We hereby command all civil, military and naval officials to obey and enforce all proclamations, orders and directives deemed by the Supreme Commander for the Allied Powers to be proper to effectuate this surrender and issued by him or under his authority and we direct all such officials to remain at their posts and to continue to perform their non-combatant duties unless specifically relieved by him or under his authority.

We hereby undertake for the Emperor, the Japanese Government and their successors to carry out the provisions of the Potsdam Declaration in good faith, and to issue whatever orders and take whatever action may be required by the Supreme Commander for the Allied Powers or by any other designated representative of the Allied Powers for the purpose of giving effect to that Declaration.

We hereby command the Japanese Imperial Government and the Japanese Imperial General Headquarters at once to liberate all allied prisoners of war and civilian internees now under Japanese control and to provide for their protection, care, maintenance and immediate transportation to places as directed.

The authority of the Emperor and the Japanese Government to rule the state shall be subject to the Supreme Commander for the Allied Powers who will take such steps as he deems proper to effectuate those terms of surrender.

Signed at *Tokyo Bay, Japan at 0908 on the second day of September 1945.*

/s/ MAMORU SHIGEMITSU

by Command and on behalf of the

Emperor of Japan and the Japanese Government

/s/ YOSHIJIRO UMEZU

by Command and on behalf of the

Japanese Imperial General Headquarters

---

6. The Imperial Rescript of 2 September 1945

Hans Dollinger, *The Decline and Fall of Nazi Germany and Imperial Japan* (Arnold Pomerans trans.) 403 (1967)

Accepting the terms set forth in Declaration issued by the heads of the Governments of the United States, Great Britain and China on 26 July 1945 at Potsdam and subsequently adhered to by the Union of Soviet Socialist Republics. We have commanded the Japanese Imperial Government and the Japanese Imperial General Headquarters to sign on Our behalf the Instrument of Surrender presented by the Supreme Commander for the Allied Powers and to issue General Orders to the Military and Naval forces in accordance with the direction of the Supreme Commander for the Allied Powers. We command all Our people forthwith to cease hostilities, to lay down their arms and faithfully to carry out all the provisions of Instrument of Surrender and the General Orders issued by the Japanese Imperial Government and the Japanese Imperial General Headquarters hereunder.

This second day of the ninth month of the twentieth year of Syowa.

Seal of the Emperor   HIROHITO

[Here follow the names of fifteen various Japanese government ministers].

---

7. Proclamation by the Supreme Commander for the Allied Powers

January 19, 1946

Whereas, the United States and the Nations allied therewith in opposing the illegal wars of aggression of the Axis Nations, have from time to time made declarations of their intentions that war criminals should be brought to justice.

Whereas, the Governments of the Allied Powers at war with Japan on the 26th July 1945 at Potsdam, declared as one of the terms of surrender that stern justice shall be meted out to all war criminals including those who have visited cruelties upon our prisoners;

Whereas, by the Instrument of Surrender of Japan executed at Tokyo Bay, Japan, on the 2nd September 1945, the signatories for Japan, by command of and in behalf of the

Emperor and the Japanese government, accepted the terms set forth in such Declaration at Potsdam;

Whereas, by such Instrument of Surrender, the authority of the Emperor and the Japanese Government to rule the state of Japan is made subject to the Supreme Commander for the Allied Powers, who is authorized to take such steps as he deems proper to effectuate the terms of surrender;

Whereas, the undersigned has been designated by the Allied Powers as Supreme Commander for the Allied Powers to carry into effect the general surrender of the Japanese armed forces;

Whereas, the Governments of the United States, Great Britain and Russia at the Moscow Conference, 26th December 1945, having considered the effectuation by Japan of the Terms of Surrender, with the concurrence of China have agreed that the Supreme Commander shall issue all Orders for the implementation of the Terms of Surrender.

Now, therefore, I, Douglas MacArthur as Supreme Commander for the Allied Powers, by virtue of the authority so conferred upon me, in order to implement the Term of Surrender which requires the meting out of stern justice to war criminals, do order and provide as follows:

Article 1. There shall be established an International Military Tribunal for the Far East for the trial of those persons charged individually, or as members of organizations, or in both capacities, with offenses which include crimes against peace.

Article 2. The Constitution, jurisdiction and functions of this Tribunal are those set forth in the Charter of the International Military Tribunal for the Far East, approved by me this day.

Article 3. Nothing in this Order shall prejudice the jurisdiction of any other international, national or occupational court, commission or in any territory of a United Nation with which Japan has been at war, for the trial of war criminals.

/s/ Douglas MacArthur

General of the Army, United States Army

Supreme Commander for the Allied Powers

---

8. Charter of the International Military Tribunal for the Far East
(19 January, 1946, amended 26 April 1946)
TIAS 1589; D/S Pub. 2613 & 2765

I. CONSTITUTION OF TRIBUNAL

Article 1

Tribunal Established. The International Military Tribunal for the Far East is hereby established for the just and prompt trial and punishment of the major war criminals in the Far East. The permanent seat of the Tribunal is in Tokyo.

Article 2

Members. The Tribunal shall consist of not less than six members nor more than eleven members, appointed by the Supreme Commander for the Allied Powers from the names submitted by the Signatories to the Instrument of Surrender, India and the Commonwealth of the Philippines.

Article 3

Officers and Secretariat

(a) *President.* The Supreme Commander for the Allied Powers shall appoint a Member to be President of the Tribunal.

(b) *Secretariat.*

(1) The Secretariat of the Tribunal shall be composed of a General Secretary to be appointed by the Supreme Commander for the Allied Powers and such assistant secretaries, clerks, interpreters and other personnel as may be necessary.

(2) The General Secretary shall organize and direct the work of the Secretariat.

(3) The Secretariat shall receive all documents addressed to the Tribunal, maintain the records of the Tribunal, provide necessary clerical services to the Tribunal and its Members, and perform such other duties as may be designated by the Tribunal.

Article 4

Convening and Quorum, Voting and Absence

(a) *Convening and Quorum.* When as many as six members of the Tribunal are present, they may convene the Tribunal in formal session. The presence of a majority of all members shall be necessary to constitute a quorum.

(b) *Voting.* All decisions and judgments of this Tribunal, including convictions and sentences, shall be by a majority vote of those Members of the Tribunal present. In case the votes are evenly divided, the vote of the President shall be decisive.

(c) *Absence.* If a member at any time is absent and afterwards is able to be present, he shall take part in all subsequent proceedings; unless he declares in open court that he is disqualified by reason of insufficient familiarity with the proceedings which took place in his absence.

II. JURISDICTION AND GENERAL PROVISIONS

Article 5

Jurisdiction Over Persons and Offenses. The Tribunal shall have the power to try and punish Far Eastern war criminals who as individuals or as members of organizations are charged with offenses which include Crimes against Peace.

The following acts, or any of them, are crimes coming within the jurisdiction of the Tribunal for which there shall be individual responsibility:

(a) *Crimes against Peace:* Namely, the planning, preparation, initiation or waging of a declared or undeclared war of aggression, or a war in violation of international law, treaties, agreements or assurances, or participation in a common plan or conspiracy for the accomplishment of any of the foregoing;

(b) *Conventional War Crimes:* Namely, violations of the laws or customs of war;

(c) *Crimes against Humanity:* Namely, murder, extermination, enslavement, deportation and other inhumane acts committed against any civilian population, before or during the war, or persecutions on political or racial grounds, in execution of or in connection with any crime within the jurisdiction of the Tribunal, whether or not in violation of the domestic law of the country where perpetrated. Leaders, organizers, instigators and accomplices participating in the formulation or execution of a common plan or conspiracy to commit any of the foregoing crimes are responsible for all acts performed by any person in execution of such plan.

Article 6

Responsibility of Accused. Neither the official position, at any time, of an accused, nor the fact that an accused acted pursuant to order of his government or of a superior shall, of itself, be sufficient to free such accused from responsibility for any crime with which he is charged, but such circumstances may be considered in mitigation of punishment if the Tribunal determines that justice so requires.

Article 7

Rules of Procedure. The Tribunal may draft and amend rules of procedure consistent with the fundamental provisions of this Charter

Article 8

Counsel

(a) *Chief of Counsel.* The Chief of Counsel designated by the Supreme Commander for the Allied Powers is responsible for the investigation and prosecution of all charges against war criminals within the jurisdiction of this Tribunal, and will render such legal assistance to the Supreme Commander as is appropriate.

(b) *Associate Counsel.* Any United Nation with which Japan has been at war may appoint an Associate Counsel to assist the Chief of Counsel.

III. FAIR TRIAL FOR ACCUSED

Article 9

Procedure for Fair Trial. In order to insure fair trial for the accused the following procedure shall be followed.

(a) *Indictment.* The indictment shall consist of a plain, concise, and adequate statement of each offense charged. Each accused shall be furnished, in adequate time for defense, a copy of the indictment, including any amendment, of this Charter, in a language understood by the accused.

(b) *Language.* The trial and related proceedings shall be conducted in English and in the language of the accused. Translations of documents and other papers shall be provided as needed and understood by the accused.

(c) *Counsel for Accused.* Each accused shall have the right to be represented by counsel of his own selection, subject to the disapproval of such counsel at any time by the Tribunal. The accused shall file with the General Secretary of the Tribunal the name of his counsel. If an accused is not represented by counsel, the Tribunal may appoint counsel for an accused if in its judgment such appointment is necessary to provide for a fair trial.

(d) *Evidence for Defense.* An accused shall have the right, through himself or through his counsel (but not through both), to conduct his defense, including the right to examine any witness, subject to such reasonable restrictions as the Tribunal may determine.

(e) *Production of Evidence for the Defense.* An accused may apply in writing to the Tribunal for the production of witnesses or of documents. The application shall state where the witness or document is thought to be located. It shall also state the facts proposed to be proved by the witness of the document and the relevancy of such facts to the defense. If the Tribunal grants the application the Tribunal shall be given such aid in obtaining production of the evidence as the circumstances require.

Article 10

Applications and Motions before Trial. All motions, applications, or other requests addressed to the Tribunal prior to the commencement of trial shall be made in writing and filed with the General Secretary of the Tribunal for action by the Tribunal.

IV. POWERS OF TRIBUNAL AND CONDUCT OF TRIAL

Article 11

Powers. The Tribunal shall have the power

(a) To summon witnesses to the trial, to require them to attend and testify, and to question them,

(b) To interrogate each accused and to permit comment on his refusal to answer any question,

(c) To require the production of documents and other evidentiary material,

(d) To require of each witness an oath, affirmation, or such declaration as is customary in the country of the witness, and, to administer oaths,

(e) To appoint officers for the carrying out of any task designated by the Tribunal, including the power to have evidence taken on commission.

Article 12

Conduct of Trial. The Tribunal shall

(a) Confine the trial strictly to an expeditious hearing of the issues raised by the charges,

(b) Take strict measures to prevent any action which would cause any unreasonable delay and rule out irrelevant issues and statements of any kind whatsoever,

(c) Provide for the maintenance of order at the trial and deal summarily with any contumacy, imposing appropriate punishment including exclusion of any accused or his counsel from some or all further proceedings, but without prejudice to the determination of the charges,

(d) Determine the mental and physical capacity of any accused to proceed to trial.

Article 13

Evidence.

(a) *Admissibility:* The Tribunal shall not be bound by technical rules of evidence. It shall adopt and apply to the greatest possible extent expeditious and non-technical procedure, and shall admit any evidence which it deems to have probative value. All purported admissions or statements of the accused are admissible.

(b) *Relevance.* The Tribunal may require to be informed of the nature of any evidence before it is offered in order to rule upon the relevance.

(c) *Specific evidence admissible.* In particular, and without limiting in any way the scope of the foregoing general rules, the following evidence may be admitted:

   (1) A document, regardless of its security classification and without proof of its issuance or signature, which appears to the Tribunal to have been signed or issued by any officer, department, agency or member of the armed forces of any government.

   (2) A report which appears to the Tribunal to have been signed or issued by the International Red Cross or a member thereof, or by a doctor of medicine or any medical service personnel, or by an investigator or intelligence officer, or by any other person who appears to the Tribunal to have personal knowledge of the matters contained in the report.

   (3) An Affidavit, deposition or other signed statement.

   (4) A dairy, letter or other document, including sworn or unsworn statements which appear to the Tribunal to contain information relating to the charge.

   (5) A copy of a document or other secondary evidence of its contents, if the original is not immediately available.

(d) *Judicial Notice.* The Tribunal shall neither require proof of facts of common knowledge, nor of the authenticity of official government documents and reports of any nation nor of the proceedings, records, and findings of military or other agencies of any of the United Nations.

   (3) *Records, Exhibits and Documents.* The transcript of the proceedings, and exhibits and documents submitted to the Tribunal, will be filed with the General Secretary of the Tribunal and will constitute part of the Record.

Article 14

Place of Trial. The first trial will be held in Tokyo and any subsequent trials will be held at such places as the Tribunal decides.

Article 15

Course of Trial Proceedings. The proceedings at the Trial will take the following course:

(a) The indictment will be read in court unless the reading is waived by all accused.

(b) The Tribunal will ask each accused whether he pleads "guilty" or "not guilty."

(c) The prosecution and each accused (by counsel only, if represented) may make a concise opening statement.

(d) The prosecution and defense may offer evidence and the admissibility of the same shall be determined by the Tribunal.

(e) The prosecution and each accused (by counsel only, if represented) may examine each witness and each accused who gives testimony.

(f) Accused (by counsel only, if represented) may address the Tribunal.

(g) The prosecution may address the Tribunal.

(h) The Tribunal will deliver judgment and pronounce sentence.

V. JUDGMENT AND SENTENCE

Article 16

Penalty. The Tribunal shall have the power to impose upon an accused, on conviction, death or such other punishment as shall be determined by it to be just.

Article 17

Judgment and Review. The judgment will be announced in open court and will give the reasons on which it is based. The record of the trial will be transmitted directly to the Supreme Commander for the Allied Powers for his action thereon. A sentence will be carried out in accordance with the order of the Supreme Commander for the Allied Powers, who may at any time reduce or otherwise alter the sentence, except to increase its severity.

By command of General MacArthur:

RICHARD J. MARSHALL

Major General, General

Staff Corps, Chief of Staff

OFFICIAL:

B. M. FITCH

Brigadier General, AGD

Adjutant General

[Thus, unlike the London Charter, drafted by representatives of the four victorious European allies for the trial of the major Nazi war criminals at the IMT-Nuremberg, the Tokyo Charter was the product of a General Order issued by the Supreme Commander of the Allied Powers, General of the Army, Douglas MacArthur. Both the Emperor of Japan and the entire Japanese government was made subject to the directives of General MacArthur. On September 21, 1945, the United States Joint Chiefs of Staff approved a directive that ordered the investigation, apprehension and detention of all Japanese personnel who were suspected of war crimes. On January 19, 1946, that Joint Chiefs of Staff directive was followed by a Proclamation by General MacArthur [*supra*] which formally established the International Military Tribunal for the Far East (IMTFE). Beigbeder[21] notes that:

> As for Nuremberg, the intention was to assign criminality to individuals, and to reject the charge of collective responsibility of a whole nation and

---

21. Yves Beigbeder, *Judging War Criminals: The Politics of International Justice* (1999).

people. However, unlike Nuremberg, the drafting of the Charter for the Tokyo Tribunal was not submitted to an international conference: it was essentially an American project.... The Allies were only consulted after its issuance, a subordinate position justified politically by the primary military role played by the USA in fighting the Japanese and in achieving victory.

* * *

Unlike Nuremberg, where there were four prosecutors, equal in rank if not in actual performance and influence, in Tokyo there was one Chief of Counsel (Prosecutor), an American, and ten associate counsels, each having the nationality of the ten countries other than the USA.... Finally, no provision was made at Tokyo for the trial of allegedly criminal groups or organizations.[22]

What follows in *Table I.* is a listing, similar to *Table I.* in *Part Two.* It identifies the major IMTFE defendants, along with a short explanation of their respective roles in governmental, diplomatic and/or military affairs both before and during the Allied hostilities with Imperial Japan in World War II].

Table I

9. IMTFE-Tokyo Defendants and Their Position(s) in Imperial Japan

(1) Hideki Tojo	Chief-of-Staff, Kwantung Army, 1937; Vice-Minister of War, 1938; Minister of War, 1940; Minister of Munitions and Prime Minister, 1941–1944
(2) Marquis Koichi Kido	Lord Keeper of the Privy Seal; chief personal confidant to Emperor Hirohito on political matters; largely responsible for Hirohito's appointment of Hideki Tojo as Prime Minister
(3) Shigenori Togo	Japanese diplomat; Foreign Minister, 1941–1942; 1945; Signed postwar agreement between Japan and Soviet Union regarding boundary between Manchuria and Outer Mongolia
(4) Koki Hirota	Japanese Diplomat; Foreign Minister, 1933–1936; 1937–1938; Prime Minister, 1936–1937; Member: Council of Senior Statesmen
(5) Baron Kiichuro Hiranuma	President of the Privy Council, 1936–1939; Prime Minister, January–August 1939; Vice-Premier, July, 1940–October, 1941; Council of Senior Statesmen, 1941–1945
(6) Mamoru Shigemitsu	Japanese diplomat; Ambassador to Soviet Union, 1936–1938; Ambassador to Great Britain, 1938–1941; Ambassador to China, 1942–1943; Foreign Minister,

---

22. *Id.* at 55–56.

	1943–1945; one of two signatories of Instrument of Surrender abroad USS *Missouri* September 2, 1945
(7) Sadeo Araki	Japanese Army General, Minister of War, 1931–1934; Education Minister, 1938–1939
(8) Kenji Doihara	Japanese Army General, Commander, Japanese 5th Army, Manchuria in 1938; Inspector-General of Military Aviation, 1941; Commander, Japanese 7th Army in Malaya, Sumatra, Java and Borneo, 1944–1945
(9) Kingoro Hashimoto	Arch propagandist of Japanese aggression and plotter to remove "moderates" from Japanese government; commanded an artillery regiment during the "Rape of Nanking" in 1937
(10) Shunroku Hata	Japanese Army General and Minister of War, 1939–1940; Commander of Japanese Expeditionary Forces in China 1938; 1941–1944; Inspector-General of Military Education
(11) Naoki Hoshino	President of the Planning Board; Vice-Chief of the Finance Ministry of Manchukuo, 1936; Chief of the General Affairs Board of Manchukuo, 1936; Minister w/o Portfolio, 1940; Chief Secretary in the Tojo Cabinet and Councilor of the Planning Board, 1941
(12) Hiroshi Oshima	Japanese Diplomat; Ambassador to Nazi Germany, 1939–1945
(13) Kenryo Sato	Japanese Army General, Chief of the Military Affairs Section of the Military Affairs Bureau; Chief, Military Affairs Bureau, 1942–1944
(14) Shigetaro Shimada	Admiral, Imperial Japanese Navy; Naval Minister in Tojo Cabinet, 1941–1944; Chief of the Naval General Staff, February–August, 1944
(15) Toshido Shiratori	Japanese Diplomat; Chief, Information Bureau of the Foreign Office, 1930–1933; Minister to Sweden, 1933–1937; Ambassador to Italy, 1938; Advisor to the Foreign Office, 1940–1941
(16) Teiichi Suzuki	Japanese Army General, 1937; President, Cabinet Planning Board, April, 1941–July, 1944
(17) Yoshiiro Umezu	Japanese Army General, Chief of the Army General Staff, Vice War Minister, 1936–1938; Commander of Kwantung Army in China, 1939–1944; one of two signatories of Instrument of Surrender abroad USS *Missouri*, September 2, 1945
(18) Seishiro Itagaki	Japanese Army General, Vice Chief of Staff, Kwantung Army, Minister of War, June, 1938–August, 1939; Commander of Japanese forces in Java, Sumatra, Malay and Borneo, April–August, 1945
(19) Okinoro Kaya	Japanese bureaucrat; Minister of Finance in the Tojo Cabinet

(20) Heitaro Kimura	Japanese Army General, Vice-Minister of War, 1941–1944; Commander of Japanese forces in Burma, August, 1944–1945
(21) Kuniaki Koiso	Japanese Army General, Overseas Minister in Cabinet, 1939–1940; Prime Minister, 1944–1945
(22) Iwane Matsui	Japanese Army General; Commander, Shanghai Expeditionary Force which captured Nanking, December 13, 1937; Cabinet Member, July, 1938–January, 1940
(23) Jiro Minami	Elder Japanese Army General; Governor-General of Korea, 1936–1942
(24) Akira Muto	Japanese Army General; Chief Military Affairs Bureau, October, 1939–April, 1942; Commander of Second Imperial Guards Division in northern Sumatra, 1942–1944; Chief of Staff-Philippines, 1945
(25) Takasumi Oka	Admiral, Imperial Japanese Navy; Chief, Naval Affairs Bureau of the Imperial Japanese Navy, 1940

10. Judgment

INTERNATIONAL MILITARY TRIBUNAL FOR THE FAR EAST

The United States of America, et al. against Sadeo Araki, et al.

Reprinted by Permission from Special Collections, University of Virginia Law Library: The Personal Papers and Official Records from the International Military Tribunal for the Far East, 1945–1948, MSS 78–3

(a) JURISDICTION OF THE TRIBUNAL

SIR WILLIAM F. WEBB, PRESIDNG JUDGE: In our opinion the law of the Charter is decisive and binding on the Tribunal. This is a special tribunal set up by the Supreme Commander under authority conferred on him by the Allied Powers. It derives its jurisdiction from the Charter. The Order of the Supreme Commander, which appointed the members of the Tribunal, states: "The responsibilities, powers, and duties of the Members of the Tribunal are set forth in the Charter thereof…" In the result, the members of the Tribunal, being otherwise wholly without power in respect to the trial of the accused, have been empowered by the documents, which constituted the Tribunal and appointed them as members, to try the accused but subject always to the duty and responsibility of applying to the trial the law set forth in the Charter. The foregoing expression of opinion is not to be taken as supporting the view, if such view be held, that the Allied Powers or any victor nations have the right under international law in providing for the trial and punishment of war criminals to enact or promulgate laws or vest in their tribunals powers in conflict with recognized international law or rules or principles thereof. In the exercise of their right to create tribunals for such a purpose and in conferring powers upon such tribunal belligerent powers may act only within the limits of international law.

The substantial grounds of the defense challenge to the jurisdiction of the Tribunal to hear and adjudicate upon the charges contained in the indictment are the following:

(1) The Allied Powers acting through the Supreme Commander have no authority to include in the Charter of the Tribunal and to designate as justifiable "Crimes against Peace" (Article 5(a));

(2) Aggressive war is not per se illegal and the Pact of Paris of 1928 renouncing war as an instrument of national policy does not enlarge the meaning of war crimes nor constitute war a crime;

(3) War is the act of a nation for which there is no individual responsibility under international law;

(4) The provisions of the Charter are "ex post facto" legislation and therefore illegal;

(5) The Instrument of Surrender which provides that the Declaration of Potsdam will be given effect imposes the condition that Conventional War Crimes as recognized by international law at the date of the Declaration (26 July, 1945) would be the only crimes prosecuted;

(6) Killings in the course of belligerent operations except in so far as they constitute violations of the rules of warfare or the laws and customs of war are the normal incidents of war and are not murder;

(7) Several of the accused being prisoners of war are triable by court martial as provided by the Geneva Convention 1929 and not by this Tribunal.

Since the law of the Charter is decisive and binding upon it this Tribunal is formally bound to reject the first four of the above seven contentions advanced for the Defence but in view of the great importance of the questions of law involved the Tribunal will record its opinion on these questions.

[A close reading of the trial record also reveals that defense counsel filed serious objections to several members of the Tribunal's bench. For example, Sir William Webb, Chief Justice of the Supreme Court of Queensland, Australia, and President of the Tribunal, had previously been involved in investigations of Japanese atrocities in New Guinea; neither the French nor the Soviet judges spoke either official languages of the Tribunal; Judge Cramer of the United States, at that time a Major General in the U.S. Army, was appointed to succeed Judge John P. Higgins of the Superior Court of Massachusetts after some 2,300 pages of trial testimony had been heard and transcribed; the Chinese Member of the Tribunal, Mei Ju-Ao, was a politician, not a lawyer; Judge Jaranilla, Associate Justice of the Supreme Court of the Philippines, was a survivor of the Bataan "Death March" and Judge Pal missed a total of eighty-one out of 417 court days due to the illness of his wife in India. Any one, or a combination of these events, would, in a domestic Anglo-American trial for felony, be grounds for an immediate mistrial].

After this Tribunal had in May 1946 dismissed the defence motions and upheld the validity of its Charter and its jurisdiction there-under, stating that the reasons for this decision would be given later, the International Military Tribunal sitting at Nuremberg delivered its verdict on the first of October 1946. That Tribunal expressed inter alia the following opinions: [here the Tribunal quoted from the Nuremberg judgment wherein that Tribunal rejected, for all practical purposes, the self-same arguments previously put forth by Japanese defense counsel. The IMTFE's opinion then continues]:

With the foregoing opinions of the Nuremberg Tribunal and the reasoning by which they are reached this Tribunal is in complete accord. They embody complete answers to the first four grounds urged by the defense as set forth above. In view of the fact that in all material respects the Charters of this Tribunal and the Nuremberg Tribunal are identical, this Tribunal prefers to express its unqualified adherence to the relevant opinions of the Nuremberg Tribunal rather than by reasoning the matters anew in somewhat different language to open the door to controversy by way of conflicting interpretations of the two statements of opinions.

The Fifth ground of the defence challenge to the Tribunal's jurisdiction is that under the instrument of Surrender and the Declaration of Potsdam the only crimes for which it was contemplated that proceedings would be taken, being the only war crimes recognized by international law at the date of the Declaration of Potsdam, are Conventional War Crimes as mentioned in Article 5(b) of the Charter. Aggressive war was a crime at international law long prior to the date of the Declaration of Potsdam, and there is no ground for the limited interpretation of the Charter which the defence seek to give it.

A special argument was advanced that in any event the Japanese Government, when they agreed to accept the terms of the Instrument of Surrender, did not in fact understand that those Japanese who were alleged to be responsible for the war would be prosecuted. There is no basis in fact for this argument. It has been established to the satisfaction of the Tribunal that before the signature of the Instrument of Surrender the point in question had been considered by the Japanese Government and the then members of the Government, who advised the acceptance of the terms of the Instrument of Surrender, anticipated that those alleged to be responsible for the war would be put on trial. As early as the 10th of August, 1945, three weeks before the signing of the Instrument of Surrender, the Emperor said to the accused KIDO, "I could not bear the sight…of those responsible for the war being punished…but I think now is the time to bear the unbearable."

The sixth contention for the Defence, namely, that relating to the charges which allege the commission of murder will be discussed at a later point.

The seventh of these contentions is made on behalf of the four accused who surrendered as prisoners of war—ITAGAKI, KIMURA, MUTO and SATO. The submission made on their behalf is that they, being former members of the armed forces of Japan and prisoners of war, are triable as such by court martial under the articles of the Geneva Convention of 1929 relating to prisoners of war, particularly Articles 60 and 63, and not by a tribunal constituted otherwise than under that Convention. This very point was decided by the Supreme Court of the United States of America in the Yamashita case. The late Chief Justice Stone, delivering the judgment for the majority of the Court said:

> "We think it clear from the context of these recited provisions that Part 3 and Article 63, which it contains, apply only to judicial proceedings directed against a prisoner of war for offenses committed while a prisoner of war. Section V gives no indication that this part was designated to deal with offenses other than those referred to in Parts 1 and 2 of Chapter 3."

With that conclusion and the reasoning by which it is reached the Tribunal respectfully agrees.

(b)

Prisoners taken in war and civilian internees are in the power of the Government which captures them. This was not always the case. For the last two centuries, however, this position has been recognized and the customary law to this effect was formally embodied in the Hague Convention No. IV in 1907 and repeated in the Geneva Prisoner of War Convention of 1929. Responsibility for the care of prisoners of war and of civilian internees (all of whom we will refer to as "prisoners") rests therefore with the Government having them in possession. This responsibility is not limited to duty of mere maintenance but extends to the prevention of mistreatment. In particular, acts of inhumanity to prisoners which are forbidden by the customary law of nations as well as by conventions are to be prevented by the Government having responsibility for the prisoners.

In the discharge of these duties to prisoners Governments must have resort to persons. Indeed the Governments responsible, in this sense, are those persons who direct and control the functions of Government. In this case and in the above regard we are concerned with the members of the Japanese Cabinet. The duty to prisoners is not a meaningless obligation cast upon a political abstraction. It is a specific duty to be performed in the first case by those persons who constitute the Government. In the multitude of duties and tasks involved in modern government there is of necessity an elaborate system of sub-division and delegation of duties. In the case of the duty of Governments to prisoners held by them in time of war those persons who constitute the Government have the principal and continuing responsibility for their prisoners, even though they delegate the duties of maintenance and protection to others.

In general the responsibility for prisoners held by Japan may be stated to have rested upon:

(1) Members of the Government;

(2) Military or Naval Officers in command of formations having prisoners in their possession.

(3) Officials in those departments which were concerned with the well-being of prisoners;

(4) Officials, whether civilian, military, or naval, having direct and immediate control of prisoners.

It is the duty of all those on whom responsibility rests to secure proper treatment of prisoners and to prevent their ill-treatment by establishing and securing the continuous and efficient working of a system appropriate for these purposes. Such persons fail in this duty and become responsible for ill-treatment of prisoners if:

(1) They fail to establish such a system

(2) If having established such a system, they fail to secure its continued and efficient working.

Each of such persons has a duty to ascertain that the system is working and if he neglects to do so he is responsible. He does not discharge his duty by merely instituting an application. An Army Commander or a Minister of War, for example, must be at the same pains to ensure obedience to his orders in this regard as he would in respect of other orders he has issued on matter of the first importance.

Nevertheless, such persons are not responsible if a proper system and its continuous efficient functioning be provided for and conventional war crimes be committed unless:

(1) They had knowledge that such crimes were being committed, and having such knowledge they failed to take such steps as were within their power to prevent the commission of such crimes in the future, or

(2) They are at fault in having failed to acquire such knowledge.

If, such a person had, or should, but for negligence or supineness, have had such knowledge he is not excused for inaction if his Office required or permitted him to take any action to prevent such crimes. On the other hand it is not enough for the exculpation of a person, otherwise responsible, for him to show that he accepted assurances from others more directly associated with the control of the prisoners if having regard to the position of those others, to the frequency of reports of such crimes, or to any other circumstances he should have been put upon further enquiry as to whether those assurances were true or untrue. That crimes are notorious, numerous and widespread as to time and place are matters to be considered in imputing knowledge.

* * *

(c) THE INDICTMENT

Under the heading of "Crimes Against Peace" the Charter names five separate crimes. These are planning, preparation, initiation and waging aggressive war or a war in violation of international law, treaties, agreements or assurances; to these four is added the further crime of participation in a common plan or conspiracy for the accomplishment of any of the foregoing. The indictment was based upon the Charter and all of the above crimes were charged in addition to further charges founded upon other provisions of the Charter.

A conspiracy to wage aggressive or unlawful war arises when two or more persons enter into an agreement to commit that crime. Thereafter, in furtherance of the conspiracy, follows planning and preparing for such war. Those who participate at this stage may be either original conspirators or later adherents. If the latter adopt the purpose of the conspiracy and plan and prepare for its fulfillment they become conspirators. For this reason, all the accused are charged with the conspiracies, we do not consider it necessary in respect of those we may find guilty of conspiracy to enter convictions also for planning and preparing. In other words, although we do not question the validity of the charges we do not think it necessary in respect of any defendants who may be found guilty of conspiracy to take into consideration nor to enter convictions upon counts 6 to 17 inclusive. [The Tribunal then proceeds to abstain from considering additional counts in the indictment for varying reasons which will not here be detailed. In all, there were a total of fifty-five counts charged against twenty-five accused, but a significant number of the original counts were dropped before the actual proceedings commenced. The Tribunal then goes into a lengthy discussion of Japanese military incursions into both China and the Soviet Union by the Japanese Kwantung Army in the 1930s. Following this, there is an equally lengthy discussion relating to Japanese aggression in the Pacific War with the United States, Great Britain and their Allies. The following excerpts conclude that section of the Tribunal's opinion regarding the Pacific War].

CONCLUSIONS

It remains to consider the contention advanced on behalf of the defendants that Japan's acts of aggression against France, her attack against the Netherlands, and her attacks on Great Britain and the United States of America were justifiable measures of self-defence. It is argued that these Powers took such measures to restrict the economy of Japan that she had no way of preserving the welfare and prosperity of her nationals but to go to war. The measures which were taken by these Powers to restrict Japanese trade were taken in an entirely justifiable attempt to induce Japan to depart from a course of aggression on which she had long been embarked and upon which she had determined to continue. Thus the United States of America gave notice to terminate the Treaty of Commerce and Navigation with Japan on 26th July 1939 after Japan had seized Manchuria and a large part of the rest of China and when the existence of the treaty had long ceased to induce Japan to respect the rights and interests of the nationals of the

United States in China. It was given in order that some other means might be tried to induce Japan to respect these rights. Thereafter the successive embargoes which were imposed on the export of materials to Japan were imposed as it became clearer and clearer that Japan had determined to attack the territories and interests of the Powers. They were imposed in an attempt to induce Japan to depart from the aggressive policy on which she had determined and in order that the Powers might no longer supply Japan with the materials to wage war upon them. In some cases, as for example in the case of the embargo on the export of oil from the United States of America to Japan, these measure were also taken in order to build up the supplies which were needed by the nations who were resisting the aggressors. The argument is indeed merely a repetition of Japanese propaganda issued at the time she was preparing for her wars of aggression. It is not easy to have patience with its lengthy repetition at this date when documents are at length available which demonstrate that Japan's decision to expand to the North, to the West and to the South at the expense of her neighbors was taken long before any economic measures were directed against her and was never departed from. The evidence clearly establishes contrary to the contention of the defence that the acts of aggression against France, and the attacks on Britain, the United States of America and the Netherlands were prompted by the desire to deprive China of any aid in the struggle she was waging against Japan's aggression and to secure for Japan the possessions of her neighbors in the South. The Tribunal is of the opinion that the leaders of Japan in the years 1940 and 1941 planned to wage wars of aggression against France in French Indo-China. They had determined to demand that France cede to Japan the right to station troops and the right to air bases and naval bases in French Indo-China. They did make such demands upon France under threat that they would use force to obtain them, if that should prove necessary. In her then situation [due to the German invasion and occupation] France was compelled to yield to the threat of force and granted the demands.

* * *

The Tribunal is further of opinion that the attacks which Japan launched on 7th December 1941 against Britain, the United States of America and the Netherlands were wars of aggression. They were unprovoked attacks, prompted by the desire to seize the possessions of these nations. Whatever may be the difficulty of stating a comprehensive definition of "a war of aggression," attacks made with the above motive cannot but be characterized as wars of aggression.

It was argued on behalf of the defendants that, is as much as the Netherlands took the initiative in declaring war on Japan, the war which followed cannot be described as a war of aggression by Japan. The facts are that Japan had long planned to secure for herself a dominant position in the economy of the Netherlands East Indies by negotiation or by force of arms if negotiations failed. By the middle of 1941 it was apparent that the Netherlands would not yield to the Japanese demands. The leaders of Japan then planned and completed all the preparations for invading and seizing the Netherlands East Indies. The orders issued to the Japanese army for this invasion have not been recovered, but the orders issued to the Japanese Navy on 5th November 1941 have been adduced in evidence. This is the Combined Fleet Operations Order No. 1 already referred to. The expected enemies are stated to be the United States, Great Britain and the Netherlands. The order states that the day for the outbreak of war will be given in an Imperial General Headquarters order, and that after 0000 hours on that day a state of war will exist and the Japanese forces will commence operations according to the plan. The order of Imperial General Headquarters was issued on 10th November and it fixed

8th December (Tokyo time) (7th December, Washington time) as the date on which a state of war would exist and operations would commence according to the plan. In the very first stage of the operations so to be commenced it is stated that the Southern Area Force will annihilate enemy fleets in the Philippines, British Malays and the Netherlands East Indies area. There is no evidence that the above order was ever recalled or altered in respect to the above particulars. In these circumstances we find in fact that orders declaring the existence of a state of war and for the execution of a war of aggression by Japan against the Netherlands were in effect from the early morning of 7th December 1941. The fact that the Netherlands, being fully apprised of and thus officially recognized the existence of a state of war which had been begun by Japan cannot change that war from a war of aggression on the part of Japan into something other than that.

* * *

Count 31 charges that a war of aggression was waged against the British Commonwealth of Nations. The Imperial Rescript which was issued about 12 noon on 8th December 1941 (Tokyo time) states: "We hereby declare war on the United States of America and the British Empire." There is a great deal of lack of precision in the use of terms throughout the many plans which were formulated for an attack on British possessions.... That by the use of the term "the British Empire" they intended the entity which is more correctly called "the British Commonwealth of Nations" is clear when we consider the terms of the Combined Fleet Operations Order No. 1 already referred to.

* * *

It is charged in Count 30 of the Indictment that a war of aggression was waged against the Commonweath of the Philippines. The Philippines during the period of the war were not a completely sovereign state. So far as international relations were concerned they were part of the United States of America. It is beyond doubt that a war of aggression was waged against the people of the Philippines. For the sake of technical accuracy, we shall consider the aggression against the people of the Philippines as being a part of the war of aggression waged against the United States of America.

CONVENTIONAL WAR CRIMES
(ATROCITIES)

After carefully examining and considering all the evidence we find that it is not practicable in a judgment such as this to state fully the mass of oral and documentary evidence presented; for a complete statement of the scale and character of the atrocities reference must be had to the record of the trial. The evidence relating to atrocities and other Conventional War Crimes presented before the tribunal establishes that from the opening of the war in China until the surrender of Japan in August [sic.] 1945 torture, murder, rape and other cruelties of the most inhumane and barbarous character were freely practiced by the Japanese Army and Navy. During a period of several months the Tribunal heard evidence, orally or by affidavit, from witnesses who testified in detail to atrocities committed in all theatres of war on a scale so vast, yet following so common a pattern in all theatres, that only one conclusion is possible—the atrocities were either secretly ordered or willfully permitted by the Japanese Government or individual member thereof and by the leaders of the armed forces.

* * *

...from beginning to end the customary and conventional rules of war designed to prevent inhumanity were flagrantly disregarded. Ruthless killings of prisoner by shooting, decapitation, drowning, and other methods; death marches in which prisoners including the sick were forced to march long distances under conditions which not even well-conditioned troops could stand, many of those dropping out being shot or bayoneted by the guards; forced labor in tropical heat without protection from the sun; complete lack of housing and medical supplies in many cases resulting in thousands of deaths from disease; beatings and torture of all kinds to extract information or confessions or for minor offences; killing without trial of captured aviators; and even cannibalism: these are some of the atrocities of which proof was made before the Tribunal. The extent of the atrocities and the result of the lack of food and medical supplies is exemplified by a comparison of the number of deaths of prisoners of war in the European Theatre with the number of deaths in the Pacific Threatre. Of United States and United Kingdom forces 235,473 were taken prisoner by the German and Italian Armies; of these 9,348 or 4 percent died in captivity. In the Pacific Theatre 132,134 prisoners were taken by the Japanese from the United States and United Kingdom forces alone of whom 35,756 or 27 per cent died in captivity.

* * *

DEATH MARCHES

The Japanese Army did not observe the laws of war in the movement of prisoners of war from one place to another. Prisoners were forced to march long distances without sufficient food and water and without rest. Sick and wounded were forced to march in the same manner as the able. Prisoners, who fell behind on such marches were beaten, tortured and murdered. We have furnished evidence of many such marches. The Bataan March is a conspicuous example. When General King surrendered his forces on Bataan on 9 April 1942, he was assured by Japanese General Homma's Chief of Staff that his soldiers would be treated humanely. General King had saved sufficient trucks from demolition to move his men from Bataan to the prisoner of war camp. The American and Filipino soldiers on Bataan had been on short rations and the sick and wounded were numerous. However, when General King suggested the use of the trucks, he was forbidden to do so. The prisoners were marched in intense heat along the highway to San Fernando, Pampanga, which is a distance of 120 kilometers or 75 miles. The sick and wounded were forced to march. Those who fell by the roadside and were unable to continue were shot or bayoneted. Others were taken from the ranks, beaten, tortured and killed. The march continued for nine days, with the Japanese guards being relieved at five kilometer intervals by fresh guards who had been transported in the American trucks. During the first five days the prisoners received little or no food or water. Thereafter, the only water available was that from an occasional artesian well or caribou wallow. When the prisoners grouped around a well in an attempt to get water the Japanese fired upon them. Shooting and bayoneting of prisoners were commonplace. Dead bodies littered the side of the road. Murata, who had been sent to the Philippines in February 1942 by War Minister TOJO as a civilian advisor to General Homma, drove along this highway and saw the dead bodies along the highway in such great numbers that he was prompted to ask General Homma about the situation. Murata testified that "I merely saw it, I did not complain about it, I just asked questions." At San Fernando, the prisoners were crowded into railway freight cars to be transported to Camp O'Donnell. They were forced to stand through lack of space and many died in the cars from exhaustion and lack of ventilation. It is not clear how many died in this movement from Bataan to Camp O'Donnell. The evidence indicates that there were approximately 8,000 deaths of American and Filipino prisoners. At Camp O'Donnell, the evidence shows that from April to December 1942 no less than 27,500 Americans and Filipinos died.

TOJO admitted that he heard of this March in 1942 from many different sources.... TOJO also admitted that the United States Government's protest against unlawful treatment of these prisoners had been received and discussed at the bi-weekly meetings of the Bureau Chiefs of the War Ministry soon after the death march occurred, but that he left the matter to the discretion of the Bureau Chiefs. TOJO said that the Japanese forces in the Philippines were not called upon for a report on the incident and that he did not even discuss the matter with General Homma when that General visited Japan in early 1943. TOJO said that he first inquired into this subject when he visited the Philippines in May 1943, and at that time he discussed it with General Homma's Chief-of-Staff, who informed him of the details. TOJO explained his failure to take action to prevent a repetition of similar atrocities as follows:

> "It is Japanese custom for a commander of an expeditionary army in the field
> to be given a mission in the performance of which he is not subject to specific
> orders from Tokyo, but has considerable autonomy."

This can mean only that under the Japanese method of warfare such atrocities were expected to occur, or were at least permitted, and that the Government was not concerned to prevent them. Such atrocities were repeated during the Pacific War which it is reasonable to assume resulted from the condonation of General Homma's conduct at Bataan.

[The Tribunal then discusses in great detail other Japanese war crimes such as additional force marches in British New Guinea, Borneo and other southeast Asia locations. The infamous Burma-Siam Railway constructed by Japanese prisoners of war was reviewed, along with the illegal movement of prisoners by sea in prison hulks that were dangerously overcrowded and often became unwitting targets for Allied submarines and aircraft. The Allied governments made numerous formal and informal protests to the Japanese Foreign Office and other governmental agencies throughout the duration of the war, apparently with little effect. The following excerpts by the Tribunal take note of Japanese behavior regarding Allied charges of atrocities.]

Formal and informal protests and warnings against violations of the laws of war lodged by the Allied Powers and the Protecting Power during the Pacific War were ignored; or when they were answered, the commission of the offenses was denied, or untruthful explanations were given.

* * *

In addition to formal protests, radio broadcasts were regularly made over Allied stations detailing the atrocities and other violations of the laws of war being committed by the Japanese armed forces and warning the Japanese Government that it would be held responsible for these offenses. These broadcasts were monitored by the Japanese Foreign Ministry and distributed to all ministries, bureaus and officials concerned.... The formal protests delivered were too numerous for detailed mention here. In general it may be said that these protest related to the violations of the laws of war which we have mentioned as well as to many others. In each case, specific and detailed facts were stated which permitted complete investigation. The same thing may be said of the protests and warnings over the radio.

* * *

FINDINGS ON COUNTS OF INDICTMENT

In Count 1 of the Indictment it is charged that all the defendants together with other persons participated in the formulation or execution of a common plan or conspiracy.

The object of that common plan is alleged to have been that Japan should secure the military, naval, political and economic domination of East Asia and of the Pacific and Indian Oceans, and of all countries and islands therein or bordering thereon, and for that purpose should, alone or in combination with other countries having similar objects, wage a war or wars of aggression against any country or countries which might oppose their purpose. There are undoubtedly declarations by some of those who are alleged to have participated in the conspiracy which coincide with the above grandiose statement, but in our opinion it has not been proved that these were ever more than declarations of the aspirations of individuals. Thus, for example, we do not think the conspirators ever seriously resolved to attempt to secure the domination of North and South America. So far as the wishes of the conspirators crystallized into a concrete common plan we are of opinion that the territory that they had resolved Japan to dominate was confined to East Asia, the Western and Southwestern Pacific Ocean and the Indian Ocean, and certain of the islands in the oceans. We shall accordingly treat Count 1 as if the charge had been limited to the above object.

* * *

...[W]hen Tanaka was premier, from 1927 to 1929, a party of military men, with Okawa and other civilian supporters, was advocating this policy of Okawa that Japan should expand by the use of force. The conspiracy was now in being. It remained in being until Japan's defeat in 1945. The immediate question when Tanaka was premier was whether Japan should attempt to expand her influence on the continent—beginning with Manchuria—by peaceful penetration, as Tanaka and the members of his Cabinet wished, or whether that expansion should be accomplished by the use of force if necessary, as the conspirators advocated. It was essential that the conspirators should have the support and control of the nation. This was the beginning of the long struggle between the conspirators, who advocated the attainment of their object by force, and those politicians and latterly those bureaucrats, who advocated Japan's expansion by peaceful measures or at least by a more discreet choice of the occasions on which force should be employed. The struggle culminated in the conspirators obtaining control of the organs of government of Japan and preparing and regimenting the nation's mind and material resources for wars of aggression designed to achieve the object of the conspiracy. In overcoming the opposition the conspirators employed methods which were entirely unconstitutional and at times wholly ruthless. Propaganda and persuasion won many to their side, but military action abroad without Cabinet sanction or in defiance of Cabinet veto, assassination of opposing leaders, plots to overthrow by force of arms Cabinets which refused to cooperate with them, and even a military revolt which seized the capital and attempted to overthrow the government were part of the tactics whereby the conspirators came ultimately to dominate the Japanese polity.

As and when they felt strong enough to overcome opposition at home and latterly when they had finally overcome all such opposition the conspirators carried out in succession the attacks necessary to effect their ultimate object that Japan should dominate the Far East. In 1931 they launched a war of aggression against China and conquered Manchuria and Jehol. By1934 they had commenced to infiltrate into North China, garrisoning the land and setting up puppet governments designed to serve their purposes. From 1937 onwards they continued their aggressive war against China on a vast scale, overrunning and occupying much of the country, setting up puppet governments on the above model, and exploiting China's economy and natural resources to feed the Japanese military and civilian needs.

In the meantime they had long been planning and preparing a war of aggression which they proposed to launch against the U.S.S.R. The intention was to seize that country's eastern territories when a favorable opportunity occurred. They had also long recognized that their exploitation of East Asia and their design on the islands in the Western and Southwestern Pacific would bring them into conflict with the United States of America, Britain, France and the Netherlands who would defend their threatened interests and territories. They planned and prepared for war against these countries also. The conspirators brought about Japan's alliance with Germany and Italy, whose policies were as aggressive as their own, and whose support they desired both in the diplomatic and military fields, for their aggressive actions in China had drawn on Japan the condemnation of the League of Nations and left her friendless in the councils of the world. Their proposed attack on the U.S.S.R. was postponed from time to time for various reasons, among which were (1) Japan's preoccupation with the war in China, which was absorbing unexpectedly large military resources and (2) Germany's pact of non-aggression with the U.S.S.R. in 1939, which for the time freed the U.S.S.R. from threat of attack on her western frontier, and might have allowed her to devote the bulk of her strength to the defence of her eastern territories if Japan had attacked her.

Then in the year 1940 came Germany's great military successes on the continent of Europe. For the time being Great Britain, France and the Netherlands were powerless to afford adequate protection of their interests and territories in the Far East. The military preparations of the United States were in the initial stages. It seemed to the conspirators that no such favorable opportunity could readily recur of realizing that part of their objective which sought Japan's domination of Southwest Asia and the islands in the Western and Southwestern Pacific and Indian Oceans. After prolonged negotiations with the United States of America, in which they refused to disgorge any substantial part of the fruits they had seized as a result of their war of aggression against China, on 7 December 1941 the conspirators launched a war of aggression against the United States and the British Commonwealth. They had already issued orders declaring that a state of war existed between Japan and the Netherlands as from 00.00 hours on 7 December 1941. They had previously secured a jumping-off place for their attacks on the Philippines, Malaya and the Netherlands East Indies by forcing their troops into French Indo-China under threat of military action if this facility was refused to them. Recognizing the existence of a state of war and faced by the imminent threat of invasion of her Far Eastern territories, which the conspirators had long planned and were now about to execute, the Netherlands in self-defence declared war on Japan.

These far-reaching plans for waging wars of aggression and the prolonged and intricate preparation for and waging of these wars of aggression were not the work of one man. They were the work of many leaders acting in pursuance of a common plan for the achievement of a common object. That common object, that they should secure Japan's domination by preparing and waging wars of aggression, was a criminal object. Indeed no more grave crimes can be conceived of than a conspiracy to wage a war of aggression or the waging of a war of aggression, for the conspiracy threatens the security of the peoples of the world, and the waging disrupts it. The probable result of such a conspiracy and the inevitable result of its execution is that death and suffering will be inflicted on countless human beings.

The Tribunal does not find it necessary to consider whether there was a conspiracy to wage wars in violation of the treaties, agreements and assurances specified in the particulars annexed to Count 1. The conspiracy to wage wars of aggression was already criminal in the highest degree.

The Tribunal finds that the existence of the criminal conspiracy to wage wars of aggression as alleged in Count 1, with the limitation as to object already mentioned, has been proved. The question whether the defendants or any of them participated in that conspiracy will be considered when we deal with the individual cases.

The conspiracy existed for and its execution occupied a period of many years. Not all of the conspirators were parties to it at the beginning, and some of those who were parties to it had ceased to be active in its execution before the end. All of those who at any time were parties to the criminal conspiracy or who at any time with guilty knowledge played a part in its execution are guilty of the charge contained in Count 1.

In view of our finding on Count 1 it is unnecessary to deal with Counts 2 and 3, which charge the formulation or execution of conspiracies with objects more limited than that which we have found proved under Count 1, or with Count 4, which charges the same conspiracy as Count 1 but with more specification.

Count 5 charges a conspiracy wider in extent and with even more grandiose objects than that charged in Count 1. We are of the opinion that although some of the conspirators clearly desired the achievement of these grandiose objects, nevertheless there is not sufficient evidence to justify a finding that the conspiracy charged in Count 5 has been proved.

For the reasons given in an earlier part of this judgment we consider it unnecessary to make any pronouncement on Counts 6 to 26 and 37 to 53. There remain therefore only Counts 27 to 36 and 54 and 55, in respect of which we now give our findings. Counts 27 to 36 charge the crime of waging wars of aggression and wars in violation of international law, treaties, agreements and assurances against the countries named in those counts. In that statement of facts just concluded we have found that wars of aggression were waged against all those countries with the exception of Commonwealth of the Philippines (Count 30) and the Kingdom of Thailand (Count 34). With reference to the Philippines, as we have heretofore stated, that Commonwealth during the period of the war was not a completely sovereign state and so far as international relations were concerned it was a part of the United States of America. We further stated that it is beyond doubt that a war of aggression was waged in the Philippines, but for the sake of technical accuracy we consider the aggressive war in the Philippines as being a part of the war of aggression waged against the United States of America.

Count 28 charges the waging of a war of aggression against the Republic of China over a lesser period of time than that charged in Count 27. Since we hold that the fuller charge contained in Count 27 has been proved we shall make no pronouncement on Count 28. Wars of aggression having been proved, it is unnecessary to consider whether they were also wars otherwise in violation of international law or in violation of treaties, agreements and assurances. The Tribunal finds therefore that it has been proved that wars of aggression were waged as alleged in Counts 27, 29, 31, 32, 33, 35 and 36. Count 54 charges ordering, authorizing and permitting the commission of Conventional War Crimes. Count 55 charged failure to take adequate steps to secure the observance and prevent breaches of conventions and laws of war in respect of prisoners of war and civilian internees. We find that there have been cases in which crimes under both these Counts have been proved....

* * *

VERDICTS

The Tribunal will now proceed to render its verdict in the case of each of the accused. Article 17 of the Charter requires that the judgment shall give the reasons on which it is based. Those reasons are stated in the recital and the statement of findings, the reading of which has just been completed. Therein the Tribunal has examined minutely the activities of each of the accused concerned in relation to the matters in issue. Consequently, the Tribunal does not propose in the verdicts now to be read to repeat the many particular findings on which the verdict is based. It will give its reasons in general terms for its findings in respect of each accused...

* * *

[The Tribunal then, in alphabetical order, rendered separate verdicts on each of the twenty five defendants who had been present in court during the twenty-nine month trial. In each instance, the Tribunal briefly recounted the particular defendant's role in Japan's involvement in World War II. Although some defendants were exonerated of certain charges, all were found guilty on at least one of several Counts in the fifty-five count indictment by a vote of eight to three. The three dissenting votes were cast by Justice Bernard of France, Justice Röling of the Netherlands and Justice Pal of India. With the exception of defendants Matsui and Shigemitsu, all remaining defendants were found guilty of a conspiracy to wage aggressive war. Of the Twenty-five in the dock, seven were hanged; five generals and two politicians (Koki Hirota and Hideki Tojo) both of whom were former Prime Ministers of Japan. All remaining defendants were sentenced to a term of years ranging from life to seven years. On November 24, 1948, the Supreme Allied Commander, General MacArthur, put his confirmation upon the convictions and ordered that the sentences be executed. What follows are selected excerpts from the vociferous dissent filed by Justice Pal, the only international law scholar among the eleven judges. Pal rested his disagreement with The Tribunal's majority judgment on three major theses: (1) that all Japanese defendants were being tried for *ex post facto* crimes (i.e., "crimes against peace") that were non-existent in international law before both the IMT and the IMTFE; (2) that the charge that a "conspiracy" existing as far back as 1928 was absurd because numerous Japanese cabinets had come and gone during that period; and (3) the hypocritical attitudes of both the United States and Great Britain regarding their "just war" crusade to rid the Japanese archipelago of imperial hubris that had evolved in Japan from the late 1920s until the end of World War II. Beyond Pal's dissent, the IMTFE "precedent" was further sullied by four additional events that still haunt the international law legitimacy of that trial: (1) the failure to bring Emperor Hirohito to trial for war crimes; (2) the failure to prosecute any Japanese involved in the infamous "Unit 731" medical experiments on Allied POWs in Manchuria; (3) the failure to prosecute any Japanese officials for the enslavement of many thousand so-called "comfort women" to provide sexual favors to the armed forces of Imperial Japan; and (4) the failure by the tribunal to investigate the alleged deployment by the Japanese of chemical warfare in China. These oversights, coupled with Pal's dissent have led many to conclude that the IMTFE was and still remains a weak and questionable precedent in war crimes jurisprudence].

---

11. Dissent of Justice R. M. Pal

I sincerely regret my inability to concur in the judgment and decision of my learned brothers. Having regard to the gravity of the case and of the questions of law and of fact involved in it, I feel it my duty to indicate my view of the questions that arise for the decision of this Tribunal.

The charges against those accused persons are laid in fifty-five counts grouped in three categories:

1. Crimes against Peace (Count 1 to Count 36).

2. Murder (Count 37 to Count 52).

3. Conventional War Crimes and Crimes against Humanity (Count 53 to Count 55).

* * *

In presenting its case at the hearing the prosecution offered what it characterized to be "the well-recognized conspiracy method of proof." It undertook to prove:

1. (a) that there was an over-all conspiracy;

   (b) that the said conspiracy was of a comprehensive character and of a continuing nature;

   (c) that this conspiracy was formed, existed and operated during the period from 1 January 1928 to 2 September 1945;

2. that the object and purpose of the said conspiracy consisted in the complete domination by Japan of all the territories generally known as Greater East Asia described in the indictment;

3. that the design of the conspiracy was to secure such domination by

   (a) war or wars of aggression

   (b) war or wars in violation of

      (i) international law

      (ii) treaties

      (iii) agreements and assurances

4. that each accused was a member of this over-all conspiracy at the time any specific crime set forth in any count against him was committed.

The prosecution claimed that as soon as it would succeed in proving the above matters, the guilt of the accused would be established without anything more and that it would not matter whether any particular accused had actually participated in the commission of any specified act or not.

* * *

The prosecution case is that these accused persons did the acts alleged in course of working the machinery of the Government of Japan taking advantage of their position in that Government.

* * *

The acts alleged are, in my opinion, all acts of state and whatever these accused are alleged to have done, they did that in working the machinery of the government, the duty and responsibility of working the same having fallen on them in due course of events. Several serious questions of international law would thus arise for our consideration in this case. We cannot take up the questions of fact without coming to a decision on these questions

The material questions of law that arise for our decisions are the following:

1. Whether military, naval, political and economic domination of one nation by another is crime in international life.

2.   (a) Whether wars of the alleged character became criminal in international law during the period in question in the indictment.

If not,

(b) Whether any ex post facto law could be and was enacted making such wars criminal so as to affect the legal character of the acts alleged in the indictment.

3.   Whether individuals comprising the government of an alleged aggressor state can be held criminally liable in international law in respect of such acts.

* * *

The accused at the earliest possible opportunity expressed their apprehension of injustice in the hands of the Tribunal as at present constituted. The apprehension is that the Members of the Tribunal being representatives of the nations which defeated Japan and which are the accusers in this action, the accused cannot expect a fair and impartial trial at their hands and consequently the Tribunal as constituted should not proceed with the trial.

* * *

The fear of miscarriage of Justice is constantly in the mind of all who are practically or theoretically concerned with the law and especially with the dispensation of criminal law. The special difficulty as to the rule of law governing this case, taken with the ordinary uncertainty as to how far our means are sufficient to detect a crime and coupled further with the awkward possibilities of bias created by racial or political factors, makes our position one of very grave responsibility. The accused cannot be found fault with, if, in these circumstances, they entertain any such apprehension, and I, for myself, fully appreciate the basis of their fear. We cannot condemn the accused if they apprehend, in their trial by a body as we are, any possible interference of emotional factors with objectivity.... We, on our part, should always keep in view the words of the Supreme Commander for the Allied Powers with which Mr. Keenan [the prosecutor] closed his opening statement and avoid the eagerness to accept as real anything that lies in the direction of the unconscious wishes, that comes dangerously near to the aim of the impulses. With these observations I persuade myself to hold that this objection of the accused need not be upheld.

* * *

A war, whether legal or illegal, whether aggressive or defensive, is still a war to be regulated by the accepted rules of warfare. No pact, no convention has in any way abrogated jus-in-bello. So long as States, or any substantial number of them, still contemplate recourse to war, the principles which are deemed to regulate their conduct as belligerents must still be regarded as constituting a vital part of international law. There is a persistent tendency on the part of belligerents to shape their conduct according to what they consider to be their own needs rather than the requirements of international justice. Strong measures are required to curb this tendency in the belligerent conduct. War crimes stricto sensu [in a strict sense], as alleged here, refer to acts ascribable to individuals concerned in their individual capacity. These are not acts of State and consequently the principle that no State has jurisdiction over the acts of another State does not apply to this case.

* * *

The first substantial objection to the jurisdiction of the Tribunal is that the crimes triable by this Tribunal must be limited to those committed in or in connection with the war which ended in the surrender on 2 September 1945. In my judgment this objection must be sustained. It is preposterous to think that defeat in a war should subject the defeated nation and its nationals to trial for all the delinquencies of their entire existence. There is nothing in the Potsdam Declaration and in the Instrument of Surrender which would entitle the Supreme Commander or the Allied Powers to proceed against the persons who might have committed crimes in or in connection with any other war.

The prosecution places strong reliance on the Cairo Declaration read with paragraph 8 of the Potsdam Declaration and urges that the Cairo Declaration by expressly referring to all the acts of aggression by Japan since the First World War in 1914 vested the Allied Powers with all possible authority in respect to those incidents. The relevant passage in the Cairo Declaration runs thus: "It is their purpose that Japan shall be stripped of all the islands in the Pacific which she has seized or occupied since the beginning of the First World War in 1914 and that all the territories Japan has stolen from the Chinese, such as Manchuria, Formosa, and the Pescadores, shall be restored to the Republic of China. Japan will also be expelled from all other territories which she has taken by violence and greed. The aforesaid three great powers, mindful of the enslavement of the people of Korea, are determined that in due course Korea shall become free and independent." The Potsdam Declaration in paragraph 8 says: "The terms of the Cairo Declaration shall be carried out and Japanese sovereignty shall be limited to the islands as we determine." [In effect, to the Japanese home islands].

These Declarations are announcements of the intention of the Allied Powers. They have no legal value. They do not by themselves give rise to any legal right in the United Nations. The Allied Powers themselves disown any contractual relation with the vanquished on the footing of these Declarations;...

As I read these Declarations I do not find anything in them which will amount even to an announcement of intention on the part of the declarants to try and punish war criminals in relation to these incidents. I am prepared to go further. In my judgment, even if we assume that these Declarations can be read so as to cover such cases, that would not carry us far. The Allied Powers by mere Declaration of such an intention would not acquire in law any such authority. In my view, if there is an international law which is to be respected by the nations, that law does not confer any right on the conqueror in a war to try and punish any other unconnected war or incident. The Cairo Declaration referred to in the Potsdam Declaration rather goes against the contention of the prosecution. That Declaration expressly refers to certain specified past matters and proclaims what steps should be taken in respect to them. I do not find anything in that Declaration which would suggest any trial or punishment of any individual war criminal in connection with those past events. Nor do I find anything in the Charter which would entitle us to extend our jurisdiction to such matters. In my opinion, therefore, crimes alleged to have been committed in or connection with any conflict, hostility, incident or war not forming part of the war which ended in the surrender of the 2d September 1945 are outside the jurisdiction of the Tribunal. The defense claims the following incidents to be thus outside our jurisdiction, namely,

1. The Manchurian Incident of 1931.

2. The activities of the Japanese Government in the Provinces of Liaoning, Kirin, Heilungkiang and Jehol.

3. The armed conflicts between Japan and the U.S.S.R. relating to Lake Khassan affairs and Khalkin-Gol River affairs.

...Apart from their being parts of the overall conspiracy charged in count 1, the hostilities relating to these matters ceased long before the Potsdam Declaration of 26 July 1945 and the Japanese Surrender of 2 September 1945.

* * *

In my judgment no category of war became a crime in international life up to the date of commencement of the world war under our consideration. Any distinction between just and unjust wars remained only in the theory of the international legal philosophers. The Pact of Paris did not affect the character of war and failed to introduce any criminal responsibility in respect of any category of war in international life. No war became an illegal thing in the eye of international law as a result of this Pact. War itself, as before remained outside the province of law, its conduct only having been brought under legal regulations. No customary law developed so as to make any war a crime. International community itself was not based on a footing which would justify the introduction of the conception of criminality in international life.

In prescribing the rules of evidence for this trial the Charter practically discarded all the procedural rules devised by the various national systems of law, based on litigation experience and tradition, to guard a tribunal against erroneous persuasion, and thus left us, in a matter of proof, to guide ourselves independently of any artificial rules of procedure.

* * *

Following these provisions of the Charter we admitted much material which normally would have been discarded as hearsay evidence.

[Justice Pal then proceeds to a lengthy analysis of each of the four alleged stages of conspiracy that involved the various accused, in one form or fashion, between 1928 and 1945. Stage One involved obtaining control of Manchuria; Stage Two, from domination of Manchuria to the remainder of China; Stage Three concerned the alliance with the European Axis (Nazi Germany and Fascist Italy) and Stage Four consisted of the further expansion of Japanese hegemony into the central and southeastern Asia mainland, the western Pacific islands and the Indian Ocean. He then addresses his dissent to what he considers to be the cumulative effect of the prosecution's case-in-chief].

OVERALL CONSPIRACY — CONCLUSION

It remains only to consider the cumulative effect of the entire evidence led before us so far as this question of over-all conspiracy is concerned.... As I have already pointed out, there is no direct evidence of this conspiracy or design. The factum of this alleged conspiracy, design or plan has not been attested to directly by any witness, thing, or document. By evidence the prosecution has sought to establish certain intermediate facts which, according to it, are sufficiently proximate to the principal fact to be proved, so as to be receivable as evidentiary of it. The evidentiary facts thus brought in are only of presumptive value; the connection between them and the principal fact to be proved is not of any necessary consequence of the laws of nature; their connection is only such as to make the inference of the principal fact a probable one from these evidentiary facts. Absolute certainty amounting to demonstration is seldom to be had in the affairs of life. We are, therefore, obliged to act on degrees of probability which may fall short of certainty. But the degree of probability must be so high as to justify one in regarding it as certainty. Conjecture or suspicion must not be confused with this probability.

* * *

Keeping everything in view, and on a careful consideration of the entire evidence of the case, I have arrived at the conclusion:

1. That no conspiracy either "of a comprehensive character and of a continuing nature," or of any other character and nature was even formed, existed or operated during the period from January 1, 1928 to September 2, 1945 or during any other period;

2. That neither the object and purpose of any such conspiracy or design for domination of the territories, as described in the indictment, nor any design to secure such domination by war has been established by evidence in this case;

3. That none of the defendants has been proved to have been members of any such conspiracy at any time.

* * *

RECOMMENDATIONS

For the reasons given in the foregoing pages, I would hold that each and everyone of the accused must be found not guilty of each and every one of the charges in the indictment and should be acquitted of all those charges.

I have not considered whether or not any of the wars against any of the nations covered by the indictment was aggressive. The view of law that I take as to the criminality or otherwise of any war makes it unnecessary for me to enter into this question. Further, I have indicated the difficulty that I feel in defining "aggressive war," keeping in view the general prevalent behaviour of the powers in international life.

* * *

It has been said that a victor can dispense to the vanquished everything from mercy to vindictiveness; but the one thing the victor cannot give to the vanquished is justice. At least, if a tribunal be rooted in politics as opposed to law, no matter what its form and pretenses, the apprehension thus expressed would be real, unless 'justice is really nothing else than the interest of the stronger."

Had we been openly called upon to decide such political issues, the entire proceeding would have assumed a difference appearance altogether, and the scope of our enquiry would have been much wider than what we allowed it to assume. The past conduct of the persons under trial in such a case would have simply furnished some evidentiary facts; the real ultimate probandum would have been the future threat to the "public order and safety" of the world. There is absolutely no material before us to judge of any such future menace. The parties were never called upon to adduce any evidence in this respect. The matter would certainly involve extensive investigation of facts perhaps hitherto undisclosed to the world. When the Nazi aggressors are all eliminated and the Japanese conspirators are well secure in prison, we are still authoritatively told that "never before in history has the world situation been more threatening to our ideals and interest." So, it may be that the world's attention has not yet been directed in the right direction....

It is indeed a common experience that, in times of trial and stress like those the international world is now passing through, it is easy enough to mislead the people's mind by pointing to false causes as the fountains of all ills and thus persuading it to attribute all the ills to such causes. For those who want thus to control the popular mind, these are the opportune times; no other moment is more propitious for whispering into the popular ear the means of revenge while giving it the outward shape of the only solution demanded by the nature of the evils. A judicial tribunal, at any rate, should not contribute to such a delusion. The name of justice should not be allowed to be invoked only for the prolongation of the pursuit of vindictive retaliation. The world is really in need of generous magnanimity and understanding charity....

---

12. *Hirota v. MacArthur, General of the Army, et al.*
Supreme Court of the United States
338 U.S. 197 (1948)

PER CURIAM.

The petitioners, all residents and citizens of Japan, are being held in custody pursuant to the judgment of a military tribunal in Japan. Two of the petitioners have been sentenced to death, the others to terms of imprisonment. They filed motions in this Court for leave to file petitions for *habeas corpus*. We set all the motions for hearing on the question of our power to grant the relief prayed and that issue has now been fully presented and argued.

We are satisfied that the tribunal sentencing these petitioners is not a tribunal of the United States. The United States and other allied countries conquered and now occupy and control Japan. General Douglas MacArthur has been selected and is acting as the Supreme Commander for the Allied Powers. The military tribunal sentencing these petitioners has been set up by General MacArthur as the agent of the Allied Powers.

Under the foregoing circumstances the courts of the United States have no power or authority to review, to affirm, set aside or annul the judgments and sentences imposed on these petitioners and for this reason the motions for leave to file petitions for writs of *habeas corpus* are denied.

MR. JUSTICE MURPHY dissents.

MR. JUSTICE RUTLEDGE reserves decision and the announcement of his vote until a later time. [Justice Rutledge died September 10, 1949, and never announced his vote].

MR. JUSTICE JACKSON took no part in the final decision on these motions.

MR. JUSTICE DOUGLAS, concurring.

These cases present new, important and difficult problems.

Petitioners are citizens of Japan. They were all high officials of the Japanese Government or officers of the Japanese Army during World War II. They are held in custody pursuant to a judgment of the International Military Tribunal for the Far East. They were found guilty by that tribunal of various so-called war crimes against humanity.

Petitioners at the time of argument of these cases were confined in Tokyo, Japan, under the custody of respondent Walker, Commanding General of the United States Eighth Army, who held them pursuant to the orders of respondent MacArthur, Supreme Commander for the Allied Powers....

First. There is an important question of jurisdiction that lies at the threshold of these cases. Respondents contend that the Court is without power to issue a writ of *habeas corpus* in these cases. It is argued that the Court has no original jurisdiction as defined in Art. III, §2, Cl. 2 of the Constitution, since these are not cases affecting an ambassador, public minister, or consul; nor is a State a party. And it is urged that appellate jurisdiction is absent (1) because military commissions do not exercise judicial power within the meaning of Art. III, §2 of the Constitution and hence are not agencies whose judgments are subject to review by the Court; and (2) no court of the United States to which the potential appellate jurisdiction of this Court extends has jurisdiction over this cause.

It is to the latter contention alone that consideration need be given. I think it is plain that a District Court of the United States does have jurisdiction to entertain petitions for *habeas corpus* to examine into the cause of the restraint of liberty of the petitioners.

* * *

Habeas corpus is an historic writ and one of the basic safeguards of personal liberty.... There is no room for niggardly restrictions when questions relating to its availability are raised. The statutes governing its use must be generously construed if the great office of the writ is not to be impaired. In *Ahrens v. Clark* [335 U.S. 188],...denial of a remedy in one District Court was not a denial of a remedy in all of them. There was a District Court to which those petitioners [in *Ahrens*] could resort. But in these cases there is none if the jurisdiction of the District Court is in all respects restricted to cases of prisoners who are confined within their geographical boundaries.

Such a holding would have grave and alarming consequences. Today Japanese war lords appeal to the Court for application of American standards of justice. Tomorrow or next year an American citizen may stand condemned in Germany or Japan by a military court or commission. If no United States court can inquire into the lawfulness of his detention, the military have acquired, contrary to our traditions...a new and alarming hold on us.

I cannot agree to such a grave and startling result. It has never been deemed essential that the prisoner in every case be within the territorial limits of the district where he seeks relief by the way of *habeas corpus*. In *Ex parte Endo*, 323 U.S. 283,...a prisoner had been removed, pending an appeal, from the district where the petition had been filed. We held that the District Court might act if there was a respondent within reach of its process who had custody of the prisoner. The aim of the statute is the practical administration of justice. The allocation of jurisdiction among District Courts, recognized in *Ahrens v. Clark*, is a problem of judicial administration, not a method of contracting the authority of the courts so as to delimit their power to issue the historic writ.

The place to try the issues of this case is in the district where there is a respondent who is responsible for the custody of petitioners. That district is obviously the District of Columbia. That result was reached by the Court of Appeals for the District of Columbia in *Eisentrager v. Forrestal*, 84 U.S. App. D. C. 396, 174 F. 2d 961....

* * *

It is therefore clear to me that the District Court of the District of Columbia is the court to hear these motions. The appropriate course would be to remit the parties to it, reserving any further questions until the cases come here by certiorari. But the Court is unwilling to take that course, apparently because it deems the cases so pressing and the issues so unsubstantial that the motions should be summarily disposed of.

Second. The Court in denying leave to file states:

> "We are satisfied that the tribunal sentencing these petitioners is not a tribunal of the United States.... The military tribunal sentencing these petitioners has been set up by General MacArthur as the agent of the Allied Powers...."

But that statement does not in my opinion adequately analyze the problem. The formula which it evolves to dispose of the cases is indeed potentially dangerous. It leaves practically no room for judicial scrutiny of this new type of military tribunal which is evolving. It leaves the power of those individuals absolute. Prisoners held under its mandate may have appeal to the conscience or mercy of an executive; but they apparently have no appeal to law.

The fact that the tribunal has been set up by the Allied Powers should not of itself preclude our inquiry. Our inquiry is directed not to the conduct of the Allied Powers but to the conduct of our own officials. Our writ would run not to an official of an Allied Power but to our own official. We would want to know not what authority our Allies had to do what they did but what authority our officials had.

If an American General holds a prisoner, our process can reach him wherever he is. To that extent at least, the Constitution follows the flag. It is no defense for him to say that he acts for the Allied Powers. He is an American citizen who is performing functions for our government. It is our Constitution which he supports and defends. If there is evasion or violation of its obligations, it is no defense that he acts for another nation. There is at present no group or confederation to which an official of this Nation owes a higher obligation than he owes to us.

I assume that we have no authority to review the judgment of an international tribunal. But if as a result of unlawful action, one of our Generals holds a prisoner in his custody, the writ of *habeas corpus* can effect a release from that custody. It is the historic function of the writ to examine into the cause of restraint of liberty. We should not allow that inquiry to be thwarted merely because the jailer acts not only for the United States but for other nations as well.

* * *

The war crimes policy of the Allied Powers as respects Japan seems to have been first suggested in the Cairo Declaration (December 1, 1943). The Potsdam Declaration promised that "stern justice" would be meted out "to all war criminals."

The Far Eastern Commission on April 3, 1946, adopted a policy decision which defined "war crimes" as including "Planning, preparation, initiation or waging of a war of aggression or a war in violation of international treaties, agreements and assurances, or participation in a common plan or conspiracy for the accomplishment of any of the foregoing." It provided that the Supreme Commander for the Allied Powers should have power to appoint special international military courts to try war criminals. Prior to this time the Supreme Commander had constituted a court for that purpose [the IMTFE] and had appointed judges from various nations to it. . . .

So I think there can be no serious doubt that, though the arrangement is in many respects amorphous and though the tribunal is dominated by American influence, it is nonetheless international in character. But it should be noted that the chain of command from the United States to the Supreme Commander is unbroken. It is he who has custody of petitioners. It is through that chain of command that the writ of *habeas corpus* can reach the Supreme Commander.

* * *

The political nature of the decision which brought these petitioners before the International Military Tribunal is emphasized by the rulings which that tribunal made. The Charter of the Tribunal was constituted by an order of the Supreme Commander. It established the tribunal, determined its procedure, and described its jurisdiction. It described the "crimes" that came within the jurisdiction of the tribunal and the standard of responsibility of the accused.

* * *

The conclusion is therefore plain that the Tokyo Tribunal acted as an instrument of military power of the Executive Branch of government. It responded to the will of the Supreme Commander as expressed in the military order by which he constituted it. It took its law from its creator and did not act as a free and independent tribunal to adjudge the rights of petitioners under international law. As Justice Pal said, [in dissent] it did not therefore sit as a judicial tribunal. It was solely an instrument of political power. Insofar as American participation is concerned, there is no constitutional objection to that action. For the capture and control of those who were responsible for the Pearl Harbor incident was a political question on which the President as Commander-in-Chief, and as spokesman for the nation in foreign affairs, had the final say.

[William O. Douglas was a dedicated civil libertarian. Although he ultimately concurred in the decision to deny granting *habeas corpus* to these IMTFE defendants because they were beyond the reach of United States Supreme Court power, he was troubled by the entire process. To Douglas, basic due process rights that should have been accorded to the Japanese defendants were trampled by the manner and form in which the Tokyo tribunal was conducted. It should come as no surprise, then, that Justice Douglas agreed with Judge Pal in some of the latter's reasoning in his lengthy 701-page dissent. Taken as a whole, the Pal dissent from the IMTFE judgment was, at one and the same time, both truly bizarre and, in places, exceptionally well-reasoned. Interestingly, it has evoked only scant attention since 1948. Kopelman,[23] in her exhaustive analysis of Pal's dissent, sheds new light on the controversial legal opinion written by the Justice from the High Court of Calcutta].

---

13. Elizabeth S. Kopelman,
"Ideology and International Law: The Dissent of the Indian Justice at the Tokyo War Crimes Trial"

23 *New York University Journal of International Law and Politics*
373; 374–375; 377–378; 380; 406–411;
414–417; 423; 428; 430–431; 440 (1991)
Elizabeth S. Kopelman, *Ideology and International Law:
The Dissent of The Indian Justice at The Tokyo War Crimes Trial*, 23 N.Y.U.J.
Int'l L. & Pol. 373 (1991), © New York University Journal
of International Law and Politics (1991)

The ideology of the *pox americana* that emerged from the Second World War was based on premises about the illegality of aggressive war and the nature of individual responsibility for acts of state, along with corollaries relating to the nature of aggression, self-defense, and conspiracy in the international legal context. These assumptions were first systematized and codified in an operational way in the Charters of the Nuremberg and Tokyo Trials of the major Axis leaders. Two generations later, many of these assumptions seem naïve, ethnocentric and hypocritical and precisely because of these flaws, are full of lessons for a multipolar and multicultural world once again on the threshold of reinventing the international legal order.

---

23. *See* sec. 13, above.

* * *

The Dissent by the Indian Justice, Dr. Rahadbinod Pal, protesting the majority judgment of the International Military Tribunal for the Far East…argued for the acquittal on all counts of the accused Japanese wartime leaders. This astonishing conclusion, and the premises underlying it, are two of the most understudied aspects of a trial already suffering from a pronounced dearth of historical and legal scrutiny.

Pal objected strenuously to what he perceived as the "politicalization" of the Tokyo Trial—its infusion with crusading ideology of its American sponsors, who were striving to create an international legal community in their own image. Yet Pal's ideology remains somewhat puzzling. Was he a strict legal positivist objecting to what he saw as reckless innovations in international jurisprudence? Was he a lone voice for a differing pan Asian perspective on a Eurocentric international legal order? Or was he perhaps simply a finicky professor from a country spared dramatic wartime devastation and with no stake in the Nuremberg principles on which the Tokyo Trial was based?

How we choose to frame Pal's objections shapes our analysis not only of the Tokyo Trial itself, but also of several central assumptions about contemporary international law relating to aggression and self-defense, individual responsibility under international law, and the doctrine of military necessity. Examining these assumptions can also tell us something about past efforts at constructing "new world orders."

* * *

…From November 4, to 12, 1948, Presiding Judge Webb of Australia delivered the 1,211 page Judgment which made no finding on or found "not proved" the charges in forty-five counts, but nevertheless sentenced seven defendants to death by hanging, sixteen to life imprisonment, one to twenty years imprisonment, and one to seven years, based on the findings on the remaining ten counts.…

Justice Pal exploded in a 701-page Dissent. He was not alone among the judges in finding fault with the conclusions of the majority; five separate opinions were filed, none of which was made part of the record or referenced in the Judgment. Pal, however, stood alone in that he dissented entirely from the majority on questions of jurisdiction, law, evidence, and procedure, and concluded that all of the accused should have been found not guilty of every count in the Indictment and acquitted on all charges.

* * *

The Allies had three options for disposing of the enemy leaders after World War II: they could deal with them by executive fiat (which would have involved either shooting them or confining them in political imprisonment), they could let them go free, or they could put them on trial. All three choices were problematic. Wholesale executions without trial would have been ideologically awkward for the democracies in light of their contemporaneous pronouncements on the new United Nations and the rule of law. Simple confinement in a remote area by executive fiat, along the lines of the "Elba solution" for Napoleon, probably would have outraged public opinion enough to be politically unfeasible. The second option of actually freeing such dastardly enemies of humankind as Goering and Tojo might have appeared to imply that the sacrifices of millions of Allied soldiers and civilians had been in vain, and was therefore never seriously considered.

Given the available options, putting the defeated wartime leaders on trial was the only politically viable solution that could accommodate the multiplicity of Allied goals. These purposes were essentially fourfold: (1) to eliminate proven malefactors; (2) to set an example that would act as a deterrent in the future; (3) to establish international law by setting a respected precedent; and (4) to vindicate the Allied cause in the eyes of the general public and justify the sacrifices made in its name. Justice Pal's view was that this last goal, concerned with wider issues of Allied policy and perceptions of that policy, overwhelmed and subsumed the first three. Pal felt that the Trial's role as a public morality play would ultimately determine the legacy of what Presiding Judge Webb called "the greatest trial in history" and defendant Hideki Tojo labeled "merely a victor's trial."

* * *

...Pal contrasted Kaiser Wilhelm II's rationale for the 1914 version of total war with the American justification for the use of atomic weapons and found them morally and logically identical.

* * *

...For Pal, the rationale behind [U.S.] Secretary [of War] Stimson's "necessity" justification for the use of atomic weapons merely accentuated the hypocrisy of America's high moral tone at Tokyo. Pal was outraged by the concept of trying leaders for crimes of which the prosecutors were themselves guilty. The decision of the American government to drop atom bombs on Hiroshima and Nagasaki was, in his assessment, a prime example of a crime against humanity.

* * *

Not only would the victor be the judge of war crimes, but it would be allowed to act without restraint in order to become the victor.

In the name of its just cause—which Pal seemed to perceive as little more than a continuation of imperialism in the guise of "progress"—the American government felt itself justified in sweeping aside the conventional laws of war, the entire *jus in bello* tradition which limited the means of injuring the enemy.

This disgusted Pal:

> The feeling that "we are a unity of humanity, linked to all our fellow human beings, irrespective of race, creed or color, by bonds which have been fused unbreakably in the diabolical heat of those explosions" might have been a result of these [atomic] blasts. But certainly these feelings were non-existent AT THE TIME WHEN the bombs were dropped. I, for myself, do not perceive any such feelings of broad humanity in the justifying words of those who were responsible for their use.

However, Stimson argued that his government had little real scope for moral choice. He stated that "[i]n the light of the alternatives which, on a fair estimate, were open to us I believe that no man, in our position and subject to our responsibilities, holding in his hand a weapon of such possibilities for...saving those lives [of Allied servicemen] could have failed to use it and afterwards looked his countrymen in the face." Pal's view, however, was closer to that of the ethicist Michael Walzer, who felt that the saving of American (and Japanese) lives was not sufficient to justify the bombing, and that preserving the quality of life, civilization and morality ought to have been additional concerns.

* * *

Justice Pal began his Dissent by examining the Tribunal's jurisdiction and the Charter's basis in international law, concluding that the Charter did not invest the Tribunal with any legal authority in addition to the international law existing among nations at the time the alleged crimes were committed. His general position was that prior to World War II no authoritative and binding body of international law had succeeded in actually outlawing war, and he discussed in detail numerous authorities supporting his contention that aggressive war was not illegal.

* * *

On the subject of individual responsibility for acts of aggression and criminal conspiracy, he argued that individuals were not liable for acts of state, especially when there had been no meeting of the minds of the defendants. He was also unconvinced that the atrocities with which the defendants were charged had been ordered, authorized, or permitted by them.

* * *

Pal felt that the only real barrier between the defendants at both Nuremberg and Tokyo and something truly barbaric was the integrity and objectivity of the individual justices themselves. He wrote that the law as prescribed by the Charter would be "a sham employment of legal process for the satisfaction of a thirst for revenge.... Such a trial may justly create the feeling that the setting up of a tribunal like the present is much more a political than a legal affair, an essentially political objective having been thus cloaked by a judicial appearance."

* * *

According to Pal, the question was not how badly the individuals on trial had behaved in bringing their own nation to grief, but whether they had made themselves answerable to international society. In his opinion they had not because,...he thought that holding policy-makers accountable under international law would abrogate the sovereignty of the states they led.

* * *

...Pal took issue with the Tribunal's application of the notion of "negative criminality" to civilian leaders, asserting that no evidence existed whatsoever "which would in any way led to the inference that the Government in any way permitted the commission of such offenses."...

* * *

In Pal's view, the use of the notion of a broad web of conspiracy as an explanation for a wide variety of events over an extended period of time [1928–1945] was simplistic and completely illegitimate. To Pal, the Judgment amounted to sitting in judgment over a nation's historical evolution.

* * *

...Because Pal was further distanced from the wartime fray than many of his colleagues, the judge from Canada excepted, he was able to speak dismissively of the Bataan Death March as "an isolated instance of cruelty" in a way that Justice Jaranilla [of the Philippines] never could. Thus one could also see Pal's Dissent as a puritanical reaction to the perceived hypocrisy of the Allies, with whom he did not particularly identify.

* * *

Pal saw the "international community" in whose name this litigation had been conducted as a Eurocentric club, not as a true community. His perspective was that of an outsider, and he was hostile to insiders who attempted to change the rules of the game just as new members with different interests began to join.

* * *

Pal attacked the crusading ideology of America's just war against the Japanese Empire, the logic of which manifested itself in two ways: in the bombing of Hiroshima and Nagasaki, and in Tokyo at the International Military Tribunal for the Far East. The Tokyo Trial was a child of the Potsdam Declaration, that instrument to eradicate irresponsible militarism, and the heart of Pal's Dissent was his objection to the implications of this just war ideology.

* * *

In arguing throughout his Dissent for the evenhanded enforcement of the conventional rules of war, Pal insisted that until nations came to adopt the same standards of morality, world law could not regulate their behavior. Nor could international institutions, or international military tribunals, "produce by sleight of hand a moral consensus where none exists. World law must express world community; it cannot create it." Pal did not explore the underlying circularity of his positivistic arguments which rested ultimately on sovereign consent. Although the logic implicit in his criticism was circular, at least it was not disingenuous. Pal's Dissent illustrates that the fundamental problem with the Tokyo Trial was America's attempt to make a moral and legal virtue out of a political necessity. In retrospect, the hubris of such an attempt now seems breathtaking.

[Part of Justice Pal's disenchantment with the Allied "moral crusade" to make the Japanese pay for their former delicts was his absolute disagreement with the United States' decision to employ atomic weapons on the Japanese mainland. However, the United States had been pursuing the development of an atomic bomb as far back as 1939 when Albert Einstein sent a letter to President Roosevelt that portrayed the enormous potential for such a weapon. On February 12, 1942, physicist Enrico Fermi succeeded in producing the first nuclear chain reaction in his laboratory under the football stadium at The University of Chicago. By the spring of 1943, the entire atomic bomb project was under the control of the United States Army. In early June, 1945, the first trial bomb was developed. On July 16, 1945, the United States conducted its first successful test explosion of this new weapon at Alamogordo, New Mexico. Theory had now merged with operational fact to produce a weapon unlike any other known in the history of warfare. The debate now shifted to whether or not the United States should deploy this new technology in the service of both military and political ends. The scientific community was not at all in one accord on this issue. For example, Enrico Fermi, J. Robert Oppenheimer and some of their other colleagues in nuclear physics suggested that the United States first demonstrate the bomb's devastating potential in a non-military setting to impress upon the Japanese the mortal threat hanging over their head. However, this idea was apparently scuttled on the premise that the Japanese would not be deterred by such an exhibition in their suicidal and fanatical struggle to save their homeland from an Allied invasion. Thus, the military option then became all the more attractive.

On July 26, 1945, the United States, Great Britain and China convened in Potsdam, Germany, a suburb of Berlin, to discuss various issues surrounding the eventual capitulation of Imperial Japan. Out of that meeting emerged the *Potsdam Declaration*, calling for Japan's unconditional surrender. During the Potsdam negotiations, President Harry S. Truman received a secret message in three words: "Babies satisfactorily born," indicating a successful test of the atomic bomb in the New Mexico desert. With this weapon in hand, the United States was emboldened to increase the pressure on Japan to surrender under the terms of the *Potsdam Declaration*. The Japanese Government, however, continued to vacillate, paralyzed by the stand-off between hard-line militarists who wanted to fight the Allies to the bitter end and other more moderate officials who urged an accommodation with those seeking an immediate surrender. On July 30, 1945, scientists and technical support staff from the Los Alamos Laboratory in New Mexico, arrived on the island of Tinian in the Marianas to assemble the components of the bomb dubbed "little boy." One week later, on August 6, 1945, the United States dropped "little boy" (the first of two atomic bombs) on Hiroshima. Walker,[24] a historian with the United States Nuclear Regulatory Commission, narrates that world-changing episode in these words:

> At 2:45 a.m. on August 6, 1945, a B-29 under the command of Colonel Paul W. Tibbets, a 29-year-old veteran pilot, began to roll down the runway on Tinian Island to take off on its historic mission to Hiroshima. The plane, which Tibbets had named *Enola Gay* after his mother, carried a crew of twelve men and an atomic bomb fueled with uranium 235. As it flew over Iwo Jima, it was joined by two other B-29s; their crews would seek scientific information on and take photographs of the blast. Tibbets informed his crew that the cargo they would deliver was an atomic bomb, but otherwise the flight was uneventful. The weather was clear and the *Enola Gay* did not encounter resistance from antiaircraft fire or enemy fighters. The fleet of just three planes caused little alarm when it appeared over Hiroshima, no warning sirens sounded and citizens saw no reason to seek shelter.
>
> At about 8:15 a.m. (Hiroshima time) the Enola Gay's bombardier released the bomb.... Forty-three seconds after leaving the plane, the bomb exploded, proving that the uranium 235, gun-type design worked as Manhattan Project scientists had promised.

* * *

> On the ground the bomb produced a ghastly scene of ruin, desolation, and human suffering. After the bomb exploded in the air about 1,900 feet above Hiroshima, witnesses reported seeing a searing flash of light, feeling a sweeping rush of air, and hearing a deafening roar, which was intensified by the sound of collapsing buildings.

* * *

> The permanent population of Hiroshima at the time of the attack was roughly 245,000.... [T]he number of people in the city on August 6, including transients, conscripted workers, and Japanese troops, was probably about 350,000. It is impossible to measure precisely how many people were killed by the atomic bomb.[25]

Official casualty figures at Hiroshima gave 78,150 killed, 13,983 missing and 37,425 wounded. Three days later, another B-29 named *Bock's Car* took off from Tinian with the objective of dropping a second bomb dubbed "Fat Man" on the city of Kokura. Due to inclement weather, the secondary target city of Nagasaki was chosen instead. Using the city stadium as a landmark, *Bock's Car* released its plutonium bomb over the industrial city of approximately 270,000 population. Again, actual casualty figures are in dispute, but the United States Strategic Bombing Survey gave a casualty estimate of about 35,000 killed.

---

24. Samuel J. Walker, *Prompt and Utter Destruction: Truman and the Use of Atomic Bombs Against Japan* (1997).

25. *Id.* at 76–77.

Walker informs us that "more recent studies have raised the figure to between 60,000 and 70,000 by the beginning of November 1945."[26] Still, the Japanese Government remained eerily silent and generally inscrutable regarding both the Allied surrender proposal and the shocking devastation wrought by the atomic attacks on Hiroshima and Nagasaki. Coffey[27] addressed that immediate state of affairs by noting that:

> [c]ontrary to widespread supposition, those who decided Japan's fate in the closing days of the war were not just frightened men trying to escape doom. They were men who had been trained in an extraordinary tradition, and who sought to solve a cataclysmic dilemma without betraying that tradition, without being unfaithful in their beliefs or to themselves.[28]

Five days after the Nagasaki bombing, however, Emperor Hirohito was moved to issue an Imperial Rescript that acknowledged the seeming futility of the military struggle on Japan's part, expressed thanks to the nation for its sacrifice, noted the atomic assault on his homeland and, most importantly, accepted the provisos of the *Potsdam Declaration*. The text of that Rescript appears below].

---

14. The Imperial Rescript of 14 August 1945

Haruka T. Cook & Theodore F. Cook, *Japan at War: An Oral* History
401 (1992) as quoted in Yves Beigbeder, *Judging War Criminals:*
The Politics of International Justice 51 (1999)
Copyright © Yves Beigbeder, From: *Judging War Criminals:*
The Politics of International Justice by Yves Beigbeder.
Reprinted with permission of Palgrave Macmillan

To Our good and loyal subjects:

After pondering deeply the general conditions of the world and the actual conditions obtaining in our Empire today, We have decided to effect a settlement of the present situation by resorting to an extraordinary measure.

…We declared war on America and Britain out of Our sincere desire to assure Japan's self-preservation and the ability of East Asia, it being far from Our thought either to infringe upon the sovereignty of other nations or to embark upon territorial aggrandizement. But now, the war has lasted for nearly four years. Despite the best that has been done by everyone—the gallant fighting of military and naval forces, the diligence and assiduity of Our servants of the State and the devoted service of our one hundred million people, the war situation has developed not necessarily to Japan's advantage, while the general trends of the world have all turned against her interest. Moreover the enemy has begun to employ a new and most cruel bomb, the power of which to do damage is indeed incalculable, taking the toll of many innocent lives. Should We continue to fight it would not only result in the ultimate collapse and obliteration of the Japanese nation, but also it would lead to the total extinction of human civilization. Such being the case how are We to save the millions of Our subjects or to atone Ourselves before the hallowed spirits of Our Imperial Ancestors? This is the reason Why we have ordered the acceptance of the Joint Declaration of the Powers…[issued at Pots-

---

26. *Id.* at 80.
27. *Supra* note 11.
28. *Id.* at v.

dam]. We are keenly aware of the innermost feelings of all ye, Our subjects. However, it is according to the dictate of time and fate that We have resolved to pave the way for a grand peace for all the generations to come by enduring the endurable and suffering what is insufferable...

The 14th day of the 8th month of the 20th year of Shōwa (August 14, 1945).

[One matter of note in the Imperial Rescript were the words that commended "the diligence and assiduity of Our servants of the State..." The major war crimes committed in the name of Imperial Japan were, for the most part, determined and tried by the IMTFE-Tokyo. However, there was one particularly egregious atrocity by Japanese "servants of the State" that was *never* introduced in evidence at the Tokyo Tribunal and only came to public attention decades later. Beigbeder explains in the following excerpts]:

---

15. "Unit 731: The Hidden Atrocities"

Yves Beigbeder, *Judging War Criminals:*
The Politics of International Justice 72–75 (1999)
Copyright © Yves Beigbeder, from: *Judging War Criminals:*
The Politics of International Justice by Yves Beigbeder.
Reprinted with permission of Palgrave Macmillan

A particular atrocious Japanese war crime, similar to the medical experiments carried out in Nazi concentration camps under the direction of Josef Mengele, was deliberately withheld from the [IMTFE] Tribunal by the American authorities, for political-military reasons.

Unit 731 was the Japanese army's principal bacteriological warfare research and experimentation organization, led by Army Medical Lieutenant General Ishii Shiro, officially designated as a 'Water Purification Unit.' Established near the Manchurian city of Harbin in 1932, the facility and its work were classified top secret by the military. Between 1932 and 1945, it is estimated that 5000 Japanese military, medical and civilian personnel were employed in the base. Unit 731 was the site of experiments aimed at developing and testing bacteriological agents and means of delivering them as weapons of war. This entailed the use of live beings as experimental animals by exposing them to diseases such as bubonic and pneumonic plague, anthrax, epidemic hemorrhagic fever, typhoid and syphilis, to mustard gas, to scorching heat and subzero cold, and to a pressure chamber. Their endurance was tested until death. At open-air testing grounds, prisoners were chained and bombarded with bacterial weapons. Victims were subject to vivisection. At least 3000 prisoners of war, mostly Chinese and Russian, but also Korean, and a few British and Dutch, were slowly tortured and murdered in unbearable suffering, and then incinerated. According to recent research, this estimate may be increased to at least 12000 murdered in the Unit itself, and more in clandestine field tests, such as poisoned water wells. The interview of Tamura Yoshio, a 'chemical-weapon handler,' directed like those of his colleagues by bacteriological scholars—most of them former senior professors at prestigious universities—is revealing and frightening. He recognized that he was a war criminal because of the things he did. However, at the time, he had no feelings of pity, 'We disparaged all other races. That kind of racism. If we didn't have a feeling of racial superiority, we couldn't have done it...hatred was there, but I simply had to ignore it. In other words, they [the victims] were valuable experimental animals.' As in Nazi Germany, total secrecy was imposed.

Following the entry into the war of the USSR (8 August), all installations were destroyed between 10 and 13 August 1945 and 400 prisoners executed. In 1947, in a secret 'pact with the devil,' the US authorities gave immunity from prosecution to Ishii Shiro and all those who participated in the experiments with a guarantee of secrecy, in exchange for the results of their 'research work,' perhaps also fearing that the information would fall into Soviet hands. The case was not submitted to the Tokyo Tribunal. Neither the Japanese authorities nor the Japanese Medical Association have initiated any official investigation on the Unit. In 1982, the Japanese Ministry of Health recognized that Unit 731 had existed, but said that they had no proof of the experimentation, although public reports and other publications have revealed in detail the reality of the Unit's activities. In 1993–94, an exhibition on Unit 731 was traveling in Japan, and a number of its former members have given public testimonies on their work in the Unit as an act of repentance.

Breaking the official secret, in December 1996, the US Justice Department's Office of Special Investigations announced that it had added sixteen Japanese World War II veterans to its 'watch list' of war criminals who are banned from entering the USA. This list includes surviving members of Unit 731. [Beigbeder then continues with a critique of the IMTFE-Tokyo in these words]:

CONCLUSION

It is clear that the Tokyo Trial suffered from many flaws, some common with Nuremberg, some of its own. Among the common flaws was the creation and running of both Tribunals by the victors, while trial and punishment was strictly reserved for the vanquished. The open domination of the Tokyo Tribunal by the American government and occupation forces tainted even more than in Nuremberg its 'international' label. In substance, the same criticisms were addressed to both Tribunals on the application of *ex post facto* international law regarding crimes against peace and crimes against humanity. Procedural flaws were more apparent in Tokyo and the final division of the judges into a majority judgment and separate or dissenting opinions seriously weakened the value and impact of the Tribunal's findings and sentences. Under the *tu quoque* [thou also] argument, the US use of atomic bombs continues to weigh heavily, particularly in the minds of the Japanese people, as a blatant, unacknowledged and unpunished war crime. Finally, the later discovery that the USA had secretly bargained with and granted immunity to the leaders of Unit 731 could only be taken as an affront to any human rights concern, besides making the USA a belated accomplice to a particularly odious war crime and crime against humanity.

The judgment of the Tribunal as a whole, including the majority judgment, the separate, dissenting and concurring opinions and the Official Transcript of the Proceedings, were only published in 1977, at the initiative of former Justice Röling and C. F. Rüter, Professor of Criminal Law at the University of Amsterdam. Was the American decision not to publish the Tribunal's judgment due to the fear that publication might have attracted too many and too public legal challenges as well as potentially embarrassing political and moral questions? In contrast, the 42-volumes of the Nuremberg Tribunal's records were promptly published in 1947.

The decision to grant immunity to the Emperor, a political decision with valid reasons for the maintenance of the constitutional Japanese order and as a basis for a progressive democratization of the country, faulted the equity of the trial: there was evidence that the Emperor was not only a figurehead, but that he had approved the decision to declare war in the Pacific as well as the final decision to surrender. The Emperor's immunity could not but affect the assessment of criminal responsibility on to the defendants, in spite of their loyal and constant determination to protect him. One may also wonder whether the reluctance of the Japanese government and people to acknowledge their aggressive expansionism since the 1930s and the concurrent war crimes committed by their armed forces—their apparent amnesia—is not due at least in part to the Emperor's immunity, which may have appeared as a declaration of innocence for the country, while the few real villains, those who had lost the war, were being punished by the Allies. History books have not been revised, in contrast with the attitude adopted by the German governments after World War II: most of the Japanese believe that Japan's advance in other Asian countries was an understandable reaction to Western colonialism and expansionism, to the benefit of their populations. Furthermore, the use of atomic bombs has allowed the Japanese to transfer any possible feelings of war guilt to the Americans and to show themselves as victims.

In Asia, countries that were conquered and occupied by the Japanese during the Asia-Pacific War have long pressed for a formal apology for Japan's wartime aggression and atrocities. After a long public and political debate, the Japanese government adopted, on 6 June 1995, a formal declaration expressing what was translated as 'deep remorse' for its wartime aggression. A group of former 'comfort women' also want formal apologies and government-paid compensation for the surviving victims. Finally, in August 1996, Prime Minister Ryutaro Hasimoto expressed his 'sincere apologies and remorse' and stated that Japan was 'painfully aware of its moral responsibility in the affair.'

In spite of its faults, the Tokyo Trial confirmed and reinforced the Nuremberg precedent in recognizing the individual criminal responsibility of high-level officials for launching an aggressive war, for conventional war crimes and for crimes against humanity. Tokyo made an additional, albeit controversial, contribution to international criminal law in establishing criminal liability for omission. The Tokyo Judgment concluded 'the atrocities were either secretly ordered or willfully permitted by the Japanese Government or individual members thereof and by the leaders of the armed forces.' Count 55 of the...[indictment] alleges that the accused...'deliberately and recklessly disregarded their legal duty to take adequate steps to secure the observance and prevent breaches' of the laws of the war. Seven accused were sentenced under this count. When he published the Judgment of the Tokyo Tribunal, in 1977, Röling expected that recognized liability for omission could have an important function in the prevention and termination of what is called 'systemic war criminality.'

One of the purposes of both the Nuremberg and the Tokyo trials was to individualize punishment in order to avoid German or Japanese collective criminal responsibility. Has this aim succeeded too well in the case of the Japanese?

[By 1958, all convicted Axis war criminals were set free. In Europe, the French granted extensive pardons and amnesties to all but the most serious malefactors. In Austria, some half-million Austrians were purged from government service who had been former Nazis or Nazi sympathizers, but no legal proceedings against them were invoked. Likewise, in Italy, Poland and the Netherlands, no significant war crime trials were held for those who had committed atrocities in the name of the Third Reich. West Germany, on the other hand, did conduct a number of domestic proceedings against former Nazis well after the conclusion of the IMT-Nuremberg. In Japan, the Commanding General of the Eighth U.S. Army, under the authority of SCAP (Supreme Commander Allied Powers), in a letter dated December 5, 1945, convened military commissions at Yokohama to try former members of the Japanese military and selected civilians who were alleged to have committed sundry violations of the laws and customs of war].

16. *Shimoda et al. v. State*

Tokyo District Court, December 7, 1963
355 Hanrei Jiho [Decisions Bulletin] 17
8 *Japanese Annual of International Law* 212; 218; 219–220; 249–250 (1964)
Reproduced with permission from 8 *Japanese Annual of International Law*
212 (1964); Kazuhiro Nakatani, Secretary, ILA Japan Branch (2004)

PLAINTIFFS:

Ryuichi Shimoda, No. 945 Nakahiro-Machi, Hiroshima, and four others, represented by Takahisa Kato, Yasuhiro Matsui, Kinju Morikawa, Kenichi Mizuta, Shuzo Furuno, Toru Suzuki, Hiroshi Ashida, Masao Ono, and Sumio Shinagawa, attorneys-at-law.

DEFENDANT:

The State (Japanese Government), represented by Okinori Kaya, Minister of Justice, and Hatsuo Usami and Noboru Minami, attorneys-at-law.

JUDGMENT:

1. The claims of the plaintiffs are dismissed on the merits.

2. The cost of litigation shall be borne by the plaintiffs.

FACTS:

I. Claims of the plaintiffs.

The plaintiffs seek the following judgment and declaration of provisional execution:

1. The defendant State shall pay R. Shimoda, plaintiff, 300,000 yen and interest thereon at the rate of 5% per annum from May 24, 1955, until paid in full. [The Court then lists the names of the other defendants with each claiming 200,000 yen apiece, or a total of 800,000 yen plus the 300,000 yen claimed as compensation by Ryuichi Shimoda, for a total of 1,100,000 yen altogether].

II. Claims of the defendant State.

The defendant State seeks the judgment to the same effect as in the text of Judgment above.

III. Cause of the plaintiff's claims.

1. Atomic bombing and its effect.

(1) Around 8:15 a.m. on August 6, 1945, a B-29 bomber piloted by Colonel Tibbets, U.S. Army Air Forces, dropped a bomb called a uranium bomb on the City of Hiroshima under the orders of U.S. President H. S. Truman. The uranium bomb exploded in the air. A furious bomb-shell blast with a streak of strong flash followed, and buildings in Hiroshima collapsed with a crash. The city was blacked out by a cloud of dust caused by the blast, and was everywhere enveloped in raging flames. All mortals including pregnant women and babies at the breast of their mothers who were within a radius of some four kilometers of the epicenter, were killed in an instant. Also, in other areas people were horribly wounded on their bodies, owing to the special power of injury of the explosion; or they were flooded with radial rays and suffered from atomic bomb injuries, although they were not scarred on their bodies. And there is still no end to consequential deaths even today, ten and several years after.

(2) Around 11:02 a.m. on August 9,1945, three days after the aerial bombardment of Hiroshima, another B-29 bomber piloted by Major Sweeney, U.S. Army Air Forces, dropped a bomb called a plutonium bomb on the City of Nagasaki. The plutonium bomb exploded in the air into a fire-ball of some 70 meters in diameter. The next instant, the fire-ball expanded quickly, struck the earth, and turned into white smoke while changing all things on the earth into radioactive things. Consequently, also in Nagasaki, the same destruction and extremely cruel casualty to innocent people occurred as in Hiroshima.

(3) Neither the existence nor the name of the uranium bomb which was dropped on Hiroshima, or of the plutonium bomb dropped on Nagasaki, were known to mankind that day; but they were later called atomic bombs, and were to put the people of the world into deep fear. The atomic bomb discharges energy generated from the nuclear fission of the uranium atom and the plutonium atom, and energy generated from the chain reaction of the nuclear fission in the shape of light, heat, radial rays, pressure from bomb explosion, etc. The bomb not only has a destructive power beyond the imagination of mankind, both in quantity and quality, but also by thermo-radiant rays sets fires to things not directly destroyed, and gives people burns by flash (different from burns by flame). The bomb inevitably results in indiscriminate casualties over some four kilometers in radius from the epicenter, destroys buildings by bomb-shell blast, and further gives rise to atomic bomb injuries by radial rays and causes people to die gradually.

(4) Among the casualties of the atomic bombs dropped on Hiroshima and Nagasaki, the number of killed and wounded is shown in Exhibit I.... Numbers, however, fail to describe the disastrous scene after the atomic bombing. People in rags of hanging skin wandered about and lamented aloud among dead bodies. It was an extremely sad sight beyond the description of a burning hell, and beyond all imagination of anything heretofore known in human history. Thus, the effect of injury of the atomic bomb is remarkably great in comparison with the highly efficient bombs of the past, and besides the atomic bomb gives excessively unnecessary pain. Moreover, it is inevitable that atomic bombing results in indiscriminate bombardment. Therefore, use of the atomic bomb is an extremely cruel means of injuring the enemy.

2. International law aspects.

The dropping of the atomic bomb was a hostile act taken by the United States, which was then in a state of war with Japan, and was an illegal act of hostility contrary to the positive international law of that day (treaties and customary laws).

(2) (a) By the St. Petersburg Declaration (December 11, 1868), the parties agreed upon the following matters: The crisis of war must be limited as much as possible with the advance of civilization. The one just objective of war is to weaken the enemy's military force, and in order to accomplish this objective, as many people as possible must be placed out of battle. The use of a weapon designed to increase the pain of people placed out of battle, or to bring about their death, is beyond the limits of the above objective of war and contrary to humanity. Therefore, in case of war, the contracting parties promise to renounce the freedom of use by land forces or sea forces of explosives and combustive projectiles under 400 grammes.

(b) The Hague Regulations respecting the Laws and Customs of War on Land, 1899, which are a code pertaining to the general law of war on land, mention in article 22 the use of poison or poisonous weapons, and the use of such weapons, projectiles, and other materials causing unnecessary pain as matters especially prohibited. The same

Regulations prohibit in article 25 attack and bombardment on undefended cities, and provide for the necessity of previous notice in case of bombardment (article 26) and the limitation of the objective of attack to military objectives (article 27).

(c) The same conclusion is drawn from the interpretation of the Declaration (1907) prohibiting the use of special projectiles (dum-dum bullets by popular name), which was adopted at the Second Hague Conference, and the Protocol (1925) respecting the prohibition of poison gas, etc., which was adopted in Geneva.

(d) Article 22 of the Draft Rules of Air Warfare, 1923, prohibits aerial bombardment for the purpose of terrorizing the civilian population, destroying private property not of military character, or injuring non-combatants. The same Draft Rules provide in article 24 that aerial bombardment is legitimate only when directed at a military objective (paragraphs 1 and 2); that the bombardment of cities, towns, villages, dwellings, or buildings not in the immediate neighborhood of the operations of land forces is prohibited (paragraph 3); that in cases where bombardment cannot be made without the indiscriminate bombardment of civilian population, bombardment must be abstained (paragraph 3); that in the immediate neighborhood of the operations of land forces, bombardment is legitimate only where the military concentration is sufficiently important to justify such bombardment, having regard to the danger caused to the civilian population (paragraph 4); and that a belligerent State is liable to pay compensation for injuries to persons and property caused by violation of the provisions of this article (paragraph 5). The Draft Rules of Air Warfare are not positive law, but we can recognize the effect of their contents as a logical international law or a customary international law.

(2) (a)...The effect of the atomic bomb was a well-known fact among persons who had hands in the research and production of the atomic bomb in the United States, including President Truman. Further, the Hiroshima and Nagasaki of that day were not centers of war potential of Japan; and they were neither important military bases nor so-called defended places against occupation. Therefore, the acts of atomic bombing Hiroshima and Nagasaki were so-called indiscriminate bombardments. The acts were clearly contrary to the express provisions of articles 24, 26 and 27 of the Hague Regulations respecting the Laws and Customs of War on Land, and to articles 22 and 24 of the Draft Rules of Air Warfare.

(b) The severity and cruelty of the pain caused to the human body by the power of injury of the atomic bomb, is more tremendous than that of poison or poisonous weapons which are prohibited by article 26 of the Hague Regulations respecting the Laws and Customs of War on Land; and the act of use of the atomic bomb is necessarily illegal from the interpretation of the Declaration prohibiting dum-dum bullets and the Protocol respecting the prohibition of poison gas, etc.

(c) Japan of that day had no atomic bomb, of course. It is a matter of general anticipation that the defeat of Japan was inevitable, and the defeat was regarded as a matter of time. Therefore, the atomic bombs were not dropped for the purpose of crushing the war potential of Japan, but as a terrorizing measure intended to make officials and people of Japan lose their fighting spirit. Nor were they dropped as a measure of defense of the United States, or for retaliation. Such is clear from the fact that a committee on the social and political meaning of atomic power, which was composed of seven scientists including Professor James Frank as chairman, recommended against the atomic bombing of Japan and so informed the Secretary of the Army. At the same time, 64 scientists who participated in the research and production of the atomic bomb presented a petition to the President to the same effect as the report of the above committee. The report and the petition, however, were disregarded; and the atomic bomb was dropped without notice on Hiroshima and Nagasaki.

(3) The defendant State alleges that it is difficult to form an immediate conclusion on the question whether the atomic bombing was contrary to international law, and as a reason alleges that no positive international law existed on the use of the atomic bomb, and that the illegality of the atomic bomb cannot be deduced from the interpretation of treaties like the Hague Regulations respecting the Laws and Customs of War on Land. However, since logical interpretation is admitted as a general principle of interpretation of international law, the allegation of the defendant State is without reason. The Japanese Government presented a letter of protest…to the Government of the United States through the Government of Switzerland on August 10, 1945. The defendant State says that its present view results from objective considerations apart form the standpoint of a belligerent, but does it follow that the Japanese Government of that day did not make a proper interpretation of international law?… Further, the defendant State seems to have the view that any measure except those definitely prohibited can be used in war until the enemy surrenders. This view is, however, that of a Merchant of Death, or a Politician of Death, and is highly regrettable.

(3) Municipal law aspects.

An act of atomic bombing is contrary to international law, as stated above, and is contrary to municipal law at the same time.

(1) That all homicides are illegal acts, is a universal principal of mankind, which is adopted in the law of every country. However, where homicide is committed as an act of hostility, only where it is regarded as a legal act of hostility, in international law may it be justified and excused in municipal law…. Since the act of atomic bombing is contrary to international law, and is not justified, it therefore constitutes an illegal act in municipal law.

(2) In the present case, those who assume responsibility for the illegal act are the United States and President Truman, who ordered the dropping of the atomic bomb, but in order to claim damages against them a suit must be filed in the district court of the United States. The *lex causae* applied in this case is decided by the conflict of laws of the United States, but there is no doubt that in the case of an illegal act, the *lex causae* is the law of the place of the illegal act and where that place lies over two countries, the law of the place of the result of the illegal act applies. Therefore, the *lex causae* in the present case is the law of Japan, the place of the result of the illegal act. According to the Japanese law of that day, it is clear that the State assumed responsibility for illegal acts performed by a member of the state organ, and that the member himself was not excused from liability.

(3) The defendant State tries to exclude the act of atomic bombing from the object of judicial review, by broaching the theory of Act of State (acte de gouvernement). Indeed, such an act as proclamation of war may be an Act of State, but there is no reason why an individual act of hostility is an Act of State. The so-called theory of Act of State is that, in case of conflict between the Act of State and fundamental human rights, judicial review does not intervene in the conflict; and this is clear from the historical development of the theory.

(4) Further, the defendant State broaches the old-fashioned theory of Immunity of the Crown in English law, but is sufficiently clear in the Declaration of Independence of the United States that the United States did not adopt the theory. Even if there is room for applying the theory, the application must be subject to reasonable restriction; and it

goes without saying that such exemption theory cannot apply to the use of atomic bombs, which people agree can evaporate the earth and ruin mankind. This suit must start off with calm, exact, and serious recognition of the horrible power of destruction of the atomic bomb.

4. Claims for damages to sufferers.

(1) As stated above, the acts of atomic bombing by the United States were contrary to international law; and with regard to such acts, not only the defendant State but also the injured individuals may claim damages in international law, both as the subject of rights in international law. Article 19(a) of the Treaty of Peace with Japan (hereinafter referred to as the Japanese Peace Treaty), which provides that: "Japan waives all claims of Japan and its nationals against the Allied Powers and their nationals arising out of the war or out of actions taken because of the existence of a state of war," clearly assumes the existence of Japanese individuals' claims against the Allied Powers (against the United States in the present case).

(2) The defendant State alleges that the plaintiff's claims are abstract and theoretical, and are not rights since they have no means of realization. If the view of the defendant State is recognized, international law in time of war will be denied generally. The logical extension of the defendant State's view is that, even if a country uses a weapon which is strictly prohibited, the country is excused from a charge of illegality in case of victory; that, even if it observes international law, a defeated country cannot charge the other country's illegality; and that therefore, a country may use a prohibited weapon in order to win a war. The defendant State's theory that a right which cannot be exercised is not a right, is nothing but dogmatism. The rights of the plaintiffs are exercised by the Government of Japan; and it is enough if the government of their own country can exercise their rights, since a democratic country exists for its people. We must say that the theory that the rights of people in international law must depend on whether or not the government of their own country exercises their rights for them, is a poor theory.

(3) Further, the defendant State alleges that the plaintiffs' claims do not exist; that their claims in international law did not exist even before the conclusion of the peace treaty; and that there is no example in history where a claim for damages by the sufferers of the defeated country was realized. Rights, however, are always abstract in substance; their existence is confirmed by the application of a country's norm of law or norm of international law. The realization of a right is influenced by various relations of power such as military power or economic power, but the existence of a right itself is not influenced by them.

* * *

5. ... Japan has waived the claims in municipal law as well as the claims in international law against the United States and President Truman. Consequently, the plaintiffs legally have completely lost the claims for damages against the United States and President Truman.

[In the Treaty of Peace between the Allied Powers and Japan, concluded at San Francisco on September 8, 1958, retroactive to April 28, 1952, Article 19(a) provides that: "Japan waives all claims of Japan and its nationals against the Allied Powers and their nationals arising out of the war or out of actions taken because of the existence of a state of war, and waives all claims arising from the presence, operations or actions of forces or authorities of any of the Allied Powers in Japanese territory prior to the coming into force of the present Treaty."]

* * *

6. Defendant's responsibility for waiver of claims.

(1) The plaintiffs allege that the defendant State lost the plaintiffs' claims for damages in international law and municipal law against the United States and President Truman by waiving them. *It is, however, ... that claims in international law were not the object of waiver in the above-mentioned provisions; and it is as already explained that there is no admitting the existence of even the claims in municipal law which were made the object of waiver. Such being the case, it follows that the plaintiffs had no right to lose, and accordingly there is no reason for asserting the defendant's legal responsibility therefore.* (Italics in original).

(2) Everyone has a whole-hearted compassion for those who suffered damages by the dropping of the atomic bombs, which possess the largest-scale and strongest destructive power in human history. It is a common desire of mankind to totally abolish war, or at least to limit it to the minimum and confine damage to the minimum; and for that purpose we, mankind, are persevering in our efforts day and night.

However, if a war unfortunately occurs, it goes without saying that every country is required to minimize damage and to protect its nationals. In this light, the question of State redress on the basis of absolute liability will arise necessarily for war calamity.... The defendant State caused many nationals to die, injured them, and drove them to a precarious life by the war which it opened on its own authority and responsibility. Also, the seriousness of the damage cannot compare a moment with that of the general calamity. Needless to say the defendant State should take sufficient relief measures in this light.

That is, however, no longer the duty of the Court, but a duty which the Diet or legislature of the Cabinet or the executive must perform. Moreover, it is by such a procedure that relief measures can be taken not only by the parties to this suit, but also by general sufferers of the atomic bombs; and there lies the *raison d'etre* of the legislature and the administration. It cannot possibly be understood that the above is financially impossible for Japan, which has achieved a high degree of economic growth after the war. We cannot see this suit without regretting the political poverty.

7. Conclusion.

For the above reasons, the plaintiffs' claim in this suit are ruled improper, without considering the other issues; and we can only dismiss the plaintiffs' claims on the merits. Accordingly, applying articles 89 and 93 of the Code of Civil Procedure to the costs of litigation, we decide as in the text of the judgment above,

Civil Affairs Division No. 24, Tokyo District Court.

Presiding Judge Toshimasa Koseki, Judge Yoshiko Mibuchi, Judge Arira Takakuwa.

[The Associated Press reported on May 11, 2005, that a Hiroshima district court ruled against the city of Hiroshima which had twice previously rejected claims for monetary relief from survivors of the atomic attack on that city in 1945. Under Japan's *Atomic Survivor's Support Law,* survivors of the 1945 bombings of both Hiroshima and Nagasaki are eligible for government-sponsored health care, funeral expenses, and are allowed up to $1,260.00 per month in reparation].

17. Richard A. Falk, "The Shimoda Case: A Legal Appraisal of the Atomic Attacks on Hiroshima and Nagasaki"

59 *American Journal of International Law* 759; 760–769; 774–777; 780 (1965)
Reproduced with permission from 59 *American Journal of International Law*
759 (1965). © The American Society of International Law

In May of 1955 five individuals instituted a legal action against the Japanese Government to recover damages for injuries allegedly sustained as a consequence of the atomic bombings of Hiroshima and Nagasaki in the closing days of World War II. On December 7, 1963, the twenty-second anniversary of the surprise attack by Japan upon Pearl Harbor, the District Court of Tokyo delivered its lengthy decision in the case....

The Japanese court reached the principal conclusion that the United States had violated international law by dropping atom bombs on Hiroshima and Nagasaki. It also concluded, however, that these claimants had no legal basis for recovering damages from the Japanese Government. Both sides in the litigation refrained from exercising their right of appeal to a higher Japanese court. Apparently, the five plaintiffs, although disappointed by the rejection of their claim for compensation, were satisfied enough by the finding of the court that the attacks themselves were illegal to let the litigation lapse, and the defendant Japanese Government, although unpersuaded by the finding that the attacks were illegal, was willing to forego an appeal in view of the rejection by the court of the damage claim.

The *Shimoda* case seems eminently worthy of attention.... First, it is the one and only attempt by a court to assess the legality of atomic, and, by extension, nuclear weapons. The decision thus offers a focus for a more general inquiry into the continuing relevance of the laws of war to the conduct of warfare in the nuclear age. Second, the case is an illustration of an attempt by a court in a country defeated in war to appraise the legality of a major belligerent policy pursued by the victor. Third, the Japanese locus of the litigation gives us an unusual example of an Asian court taking for granted the validity and applicability of a body of international law developed by Western countries, although Japan, it should be noted, is not a newly independent Asian country, nor one that has joined in the attack upon traditional international law. Fourth, the decision grapples with the problem of determining the extent to which individuals may assert legal rights on their own behalf for causes of action arising out of violations of international law. Fifth, the decision discusses the extent to which principles of sovereign immunity continue to bar claims by individuals against governments. Sixth, the decision considers the legal effect of a waiver in a peace treaty of the claims of nationals against a foreign country. Seventh, the court confronts a rather difficult question of choice of laws because of the need to decide whether the existence of the right of recovery is to be determined by Japanese or by United States law, And eighth, the whole nature of the undertaking by this Japanese court raises the problem of identifying the appropriate role for a domestic court in this kind of an international law case.

* * *

The plaintiffs begin by describing the atomic attacks and their effects upon the cities of Hiroshima and Nagasaki.

* * *

In fact, the plaintiffs contend that the use of atomic bombs against these Japanese cities violated both conventional and customary international law.... In main, the claims were based upon the series of formal international acts prohibiting recourse to poisonous gas, restricting rights of aerial bombardment, buttressed by the more general condemnation of terror tactics that inflict indiscriminate injury and unnecessary sufferings upon civilians. The principal argument is that the atomic attacks are covered by these pre-atomic legal instruments either directly or *mutates mutandis*, and furthermore, that even if it is found that positive international law does not directly condemn these atomic bombings, these rules indirectly or rather "their spirit must be said to have the effect of natural law or logical international law"…and by this process support a finding of illegality.

* * *

The complaint…tries to demonstrate why a Japanese domestic court is the only appropriate forum for the litigation. The plaintiffs argue that the waiver in Article 19(a), because treaties are the supreme law of the land, would be effective to bar the presentation of the claim in a United States court, so that their only remedy is to proceed in Japan. The statement goes on, somewhat gratuitously, to say that, if the plaintiffs did institute the action in the United States, they could not "easily obtain the cooperation of lawyers or the support of public opinion," adding that even in Japan, "it is extremely difficult to find cooperators."

The final step of the argument in the complaint is to show that the Government of Japan wrongfully waived the claims of its nationals, and as a consequence, is responsible for the losses thereby inflicted.

* * *

…On the main issue of legality, the Japanese Government contends that the atomic bombs were new inventions and hence not covered by either customary or the conventional rules of the international law of war. Since the use of atomic bombs was not expressly forbidden by international law, there is no legal basis upon which to object to their use by a belligerent.

* * *

…It is significant that the Japanese Government is willing to associate itself, even for purposes of defense in this action for compensation, with the official justification of the use of atomic weapons that has been offered by the United Sates. The defense goes so far as to say: "with the atomic bombing of Hiroshima and Nagasaki, *as a direct result*, Japan ceased further resistance and accepted the Potsdam Declaration."

* * *

Even if international law covers the atomic bombing, there is no cause of action, the defense contends, created in municipal law. The law of war is a matter of state-to-state relations and there is no expectation that individuals injured by a violation of the laws of war can recover directly or indirectly from the guilty government. The defense then considers the outcome of this litigation if it is treated as though it is brought against the United Sates in an American domestic court. And as courts in the United States refrain from questioning the legality of belligerent acts undertaken by the Executive to carry on a war, they would refuse to examine the legality of the use of atomic bombs against Japan.… At the time of the attacks, furthermore sovereign immunity would bar, under the municipal law of the United States, claims of this sort being brought against either the United States Government or the public official responsible for the alleged wrongdoing.

* * *

The Japanese Government also denies the standing of the claimants to institute action on their own behalf. The defense subscribes to the traditional theory that it is the government on behalf of national victims, and only the government, that has the capac-

ity, in the absence of a treaty conferring capacity on individuals, to assert claims against
a foreign state.

* * *

In concluding its presentation, the defense describes itself as "unstinting in its deep
sympathy" with the survivors of the atomic attacks, but points out that "the way of consolation for these people must be balanced with the consolation for other general war
victims, and by taking into due consideration the actual circumstances of finance of the
State, etc." These matters of social justice are asserted to be matters of politics, not law,
and must therefore, be left for settlement to the wisdom of the legislature; they are not
resolvable by exercise of the adjudicative powers of the courts. And until the legislature
sees fit to act, the Japanese Government, as such, cannot be said to have an obligation
to compensate.

* * *

...[I]n a strict legal sense it is important to govern one's perception of the case in accord with the restrictive conception set forth by the Japanese court. And in this regard,
it is well to emphasize that the opinion does not attempt to deal with the legality of
atomic weapons as such, but only with their legality of their use against Hiroshima and
Nagasaki. This accords with the best tradition of judicial craftsmanship; namely, the
narrowing of the dispositive issue to the greatest extent possible. But even here there is
an inevitable ambiguity arising from the fact that most of the legal authority found relevant by the court was developed to proscribe or restrict the use of weapons with certain characteristics (*e. g.*, poisons, dum-dum bullets, bacteria) rather than to regulate
their use against certain kinds of targets.

* * *

The principal holding of the court is, of course, that the attacks with atomic bombs
upon Hiroshima and Nagasaki on August 6 and 9 of 1945 were in violation of international law.

* * *

...The language used in the opinion is not entirely clear, but the court seems to affirm the potential capacity of the individuals to enforce international law. At the same
time, the court denies that this capacity always, or even generally, exists in present-day
international law. On the contrary, the individual only possesses a legal capacity to proceed on his own when the capacity has been specifically conferred in an international
agreement.

* * *

The opinion ends with a statement expressing compassion for the victims of atomic
attack and looking forward to the abolition of war. The court even ventures to comment upon the non-legal obligations of the Government of Japan to those who suffer
war damage.

───────────

18. Yves Beigbeder, "The Legality of Atomic Bombing"

Yves Beigbeder, *Judging War Criminals:*
The Politics of International Justice 69–71 (1999)
Copyright © Yves Beigbeder, from: Judging *War Criminals:*
The Politics of International Justice by Yves Beigbeder.
Reprinted with permission of Palgrave-Macmillan

On 7 December 1963, the Tokyo District Court rejected the claims of R. Shimoda and four others for financial compensation for damages suffered by them as a result of the atomic bombing of Hiroshima and Nagasaki, alleged to be an illegal act of hostility contrary to positive international law of that period.

* * *

On 15 December 1994, the UN General Assembly requested the International Court of Justice for an urgent advisory opinion on the question: 'Is the threat or use of nuclear weapons in any circumstance permitted under international law'?... The controversial resolution, which followed intense lobbying by pacifist and human rights non-governmental organizations, was adopted by less than two-thirds majority and opposed in particular by France, Russia, the UK and the USA. The Court's divided and inconclusive advisory opinion of 8 July 1996 reflected the division of the international community on this issue. The main opposition was between those states who condemn the use or threat of nuclear weapons as illegal in any circumstances whatsoever and those, led by the USA, who consider that events have demonstrated the legality of the threat or use of nuclear weapons in extraordinary circumstances, and that nuclear deterrence is 'not only eminently lawful but intensely desirable.' In its advisory opinion the Court held:

(A) unanimously, that neither customary nor conventional international law specifically authorizes the threat or use or nuclear weapons;

(B) by eleven votes to three, that neither customary nor conventional international law comprehensively and universally prohibits the threat or use of nuclear weapons;

(C) unanimously, that a threat or use of force by means of nuclear weapons that is contrary to Article 2, paragraph 4 of the UN Charter and that fails to meet all the requirements of Article 51 is unlawful;

(D) unanimously, that a threat or use of nuclear weapons should be compatible with the requirements of the international law applicable in armed conflict (including international humanitarian law) and specific obligations under treaties and other undertakings expressly dealing with nuclear weapons;

(E) by seven votes to seven, by the President's casting vote, that the threat or use of nuclear weapons would generally be contrary to the rules of international law applicable in armed conflict, and in particular the principles and rules of humanitarian law, but that in view of the current state of international law and the facts before the Court, it could not conclude definitively whether the threat or use of nuclear weapons would be lawful or unlawful in an extreme circumstance of self-defense, in which the very survival of the state would be at stake; and

(F) unanimously, that there exists an obligation to pursue in good faith and bring to a conclusion negotiations leading to nuclear disarmament in all its aspects under international control.

While refraining from a determination that the threat or use of nuclear weapons was illegal, the Court provided all the basic elements for such a determination.

In applying the relevant law, the Court 'considered it imperative to take into account certain unique characteristics of nuclear weapons, in particular their destructive capacity, which can cause untold human suffering for generations to come'... The Court noted that certain specific treaties dealing with the acquisition, manufacture, possession, deployment and testing of nuclear weapons, 'point to an increasing concern in the international community' with nuclear weapons and concluded they 'could therefore be seen as foreshadowing a future general prohibition of the use of such weapons, but they do not constitute such a prohibition by themselves'... By reference to its 1986 Judgment in *Nicaragua v. USA*, the Court made clear that, notwithstanding the absence of specific mention of proportionality in Article 51 of the UN Charter, 'there is a specific rule whereby self-defense would warrant only measures which are proportional to the armed attack and necessity to respond to it, a rule well established in customary international law'... The Court stated that the cardinal principles of international humanitarian law prescribing the conduct of military operations are (1) the protection of the civilian population and civilian objects and the prohibition of the use of weapons incapable of distinguishing between combatants and non-combatants, and (2) the prohibition on causing unnecessary suffering to combatants by using certain weapons.... While the Court affirmed that these constitute intransgressible principles of international customary law, to be observed by all states whether or not they have ratified the conventions that contain them..., it refrained from drawing the obvious conclusions from its previous findings on the ground that they were controversial.

Even though the Court made the unusual, non-legal recommendation that states had an obligation to pursue in good faith and bring to a conclusion negotiations leading to nuclear disarmament, a number of participants at the opening session of a UN Conference on Disarmament Issues held in Hiroshima expressed dismay at the Court decision. Yuzan Fujita, governor of the Hiroshima Prefecture, said that the Court's decision 'was a bitter disappointment for the people of Hiroshima, who have consistently insisted that the use and the threat of use of nuclear weapons violate international law.'

Suggestions for Further Reading

(1) Allen, Thomas B. & Norman Polmar, *Code-Name Downfall: The Secret Plan to Invade Japan — and Why Truman Dropped the Bomb*. New York: Simon & Schuster (1995).

(2) Bergamini, David, *Japan's Imperial Conspiracy*. New York: Morrow (1971).

(3) Bix, Herbert P., "Japan's Delayed Surrender: A Reinterpretation," 19 *Diplomatic History* 197 (Spring, 1995).

(4) Blewett, George F., "Victor's Injustice: The Tokyo War Crimes Trial," 4 *American Perspective* 282 (1950).

(5) Boling, David, "Mass Rape, Enforced Prostitution, and the Japanese Imperial Army: Japan Eschews International Legal Responsibility," 32 *Columbia Journal of Transnational Law* 533 (1995).

(6) Coffey, Thomas M., *Imperial Tragedy: Japan in World War II: The First Days and the Last*. New York: World (1970).

(7) Craig, William, *The Fall of Japan*. New York: Dial Press (1967).

(8) Daws, Gavan, *Prisoners of the Japanese: POWs of World War II in the Pacific*. New York: Morrow (1994).

(9) *Documents on the Rape of Nanking* (Timothy Brook ed.). Ann Arbor, MI: University of Michigan Press (1999).

(10) Dower, John W., *War Without Mercy: Race and Power in the Pacific War*. New York: Pantheon Books (1986).

(11) Edgerton, Robert, *Warriors of the Rising Sun*. New York: Norton (1957).

(12) Falk, Stanley L., *Bataan: The March of Death*. New York: Jove (1983).

(13) Fliess, Peter J., "Review of the Yamashita Precedent," 78 *American Journal of International Law* 256 (1984).

(14) Harris, Sheldon H., *Factories of Death: Japanese Biological Warfare 1932–1945 and the American Cover-Up*. London: Routledge, Kegan Paul (1994).

(15) Honda, Michael M., "Japan's War Crimes: Has Justice Been Served,?" 21 *Whittier Law Review* 621 (2000).

(16) Horwitz, Solis, *The Tokyo Trial*. New York: Carnegie Endowment for International Peace (1950).

(17) Maddox, Robert J., *Weapons for Victory: The Hiroshima Decision Fifty Years Later*. Columbia, MO: University of Missouri Press (1995).

(18) Minear, Richard H., *Victor's Justice: The Tokyo War Crimes Trial*. Princeotn, NJ: Princeton Unviersity Press (1971).

(19) Reed, Frank, *The Case of General Yamashita*. Chicago: The University of Chicago Press (1949).

(20) Russell, Edward F. L., *The Knights of Bushido: A Short History of Japanese War Crimes*. London: Greenhill Books (1958).

(21) Skates, John R., *The Invasion of Japan: Alternative to the Bomb*. Columbia, SC: University of South Carolina Press (1994).

(22) Tanaka, Uki, *Hidden Horrors: Japanese War Crimes in World War II*. Boulder, CO: Westview Press (1996).

(23) *The Rise and Fall of Imperial Japan* (S. L. Mayer ed.). Greenwich, CT: Bison Books (1984).

(24) *The Tokyo War Crimes Trial: Proceedings of the Tribunal* (22 vols.). (R. John Pritchard & Sonia Zaide eds.). New York: Garland (1981).

(25) Trefousse, Hans, *What Happened at Pearl Harbor?* New Haven, CT: College and University Press (1958).

Part Four

Israel and the Eichmann Case; Selected War Crime Cases Involving Former Nazis in Ghana (extradition); United States (civil damages); France (war crimes) and Canada (war crimes) (1960–62; 1966; 1980; 1985; 1994)

Editorial Commentary

The Israeli trial of Adolf Eichmann before a three-judge District Court in Jerusalem, presided over by Mr. Justice Landau, was a milestone in international criminal justice. It commanded wide international interest because of the idiosyncratic nature of some of the legal issues it raised and the response to those issues by the Jewish court. The proceedings began on April 11, 1961, and lasted until August 14, 1961. During that time, the court held 114 sessions, heard 120 witnesses and admitted some 1,500 pieces of documentary evidence. The judgment ran to a total of 197 pages, the first fifty-six of which concentrated on contentious jurisdictional issues and other legal matters. The remainder of the judgment, for the most part, dealt with the gruesome evidence adduced by witnesses and the sundry documents introduced by both sides. Eichmann's specific connection with the facts were also detailed in the court's opinion.

Adolf Eichmann was born on March 19, 1906, in Solingen, Germany, a town located in the Rhineland known worldwide for its fine cutlery. In 1910, he and his family moved to Linz, Austria. Eichmann joined the Austrian Nazi Party and the SS in 1932 at the invitation of Ernst Kaltenbrunner, the Austrian lawyer who was instrumental in helping to subvert Austria for the 1938 *Anschluss* (or annexation) with the Third Reich. As successor to Reinhard Heydrich, Kaltenbrunner would later be tried, convicted and sentenced to death by the IMT-Nuremberg for his role in the Holocaust.

Once gainfully employed in a position he thoroughly enjoyed, Eichmann immediately came to the attention of significant others in wider Nazi circles as a devoted and extremely efficient bureaucrat. In 1938, he was assigned the task of establishing a central office for Jewish emigration in Vienna. After being posted to Berlin in 1939, the defendant was placed in charge of Jewish deportation in the RSHA (Reich Main Security Office) as head of Section IV B-4. By 1941, Eichmann had risen to the rank of *Obersturmbannführer* (Lt. Colonel) in the SS. It was his devoted and tireless work in the so-called "*Dienststelle Eichmann*" (or the "Eichmann Authority") in that particular RSHA branch that placed in Eichmann's hands the power and official license to issue directives for the deportation and annihilation of at least three million European Jews—all under the very "legal" authority of the German Reich and its *Reichsführer-SS,* Heinrich Himmler. In fact, Rudolf Höss, the notorious former commandant of Auschwitz, testified at Nuremberg that all orders involving "mass executions through gassing" came "directly from Himmler through Eichmann."

In the chaotic months following the collapse of Nazi Germany and the end of World War II in Europe, Eichmann's pivotal role in the Nazi "Final Solution" directives was essentially overlooked. In footnote twenty-six in his article on the Eichmann case, Lippman[1] remarks that:

> Aided by two organizations of ex-Nazis—ODESSA (Organization der SS Angehoerigen) and Die Spinne (The Spider)—Eichmann was transported from Lower Saxony to a monastery in Genoa where a sympathetic Franciscan monk provided him with a refugee passport [used to escape to Argentina] bearing the name of Richardo Klement, a German national born in Bolzano, Italy. He was initially employed as a labor organizer...in the province of Tucuman,.... From 1952 on, Eichmann held various jobs; at the Mercedes-Benz firm he was known as "SS Lieutenant Colonel Adolf Eichmann, in retirement."[2]

In 1957, the Israeli government received information from various sources that Eichmann was, in fact, residing in Argentina and plans were set in motion to physically abduct him from that country and bring him back to Israel to stand trial for his part in Nazi war crimes. On May 11, 1960, Eichmann was kidnapped on a street in Buenos Aires by what Israel would later characterize as a group of "volunteers." It can reasonably be assumed, however, that this abduction was carried out by members of the Israeli Security Services with the approval of those at the highest levels in the government of Israel. On May 23, 1960, the Israeli Prime Minister, David Ben Gurion, announced to Israel's Parliament (the Knesset) that Eichmann had been located in Argentina, had been abducted and then flown to Israel on an El Al airliner without the consent of the Argentine government. At the time of Eichmann's abduction, there was no extradition treaty in force between Argentina and Israel. In his announcement to the Knesset, Mr. Ben Gurion said, in part:

> I have to inform the Knesset that a short time ago one of the greatest Nazi war criminals, Adolf Eichmann, who was responsible together with the Nazi leaders for what they called "The Final Solution of the Jewish Question," that is, the extermination of six million of the Jews of Europe, was discovered by the Israel Security Services. Adolf Eichmann is already under arrest in Israel and

---

1. Matthew Lippman, "The Trial of Adolf Eichmann and the Protection of Universal Human Rights Under International Law, 5 *Hou. J. Int'l L.* 1, 5–6 (1982).

2. *Id.*

will shortly be placed on trial in Israel under the terms of the law for the trial of Nazis and their helpers 5710-1950.[3]

With Adolf Eichmann thus physically present in the State of Israel and under the control of the Israeli authorities, a diplomatic furor immediately erupted between Argentina and Israel. The Argentine government charged Israel with violating its national sovereignty. In due course, Argentina filed a formal complaint with the United Nations Security Council under the provisions of article 33 of the U. N. Charter. A debate ensued in the Security Council followed by a resolution of that body censuring Israel for its actions and requesting the Israeli government make appropriate reparations to Argentina for Eichmann's abduction. Eventually, after some intense discussion, lengthy diplomatic dialog and an official apology by Israel, the two nations issued a joint communiqué on August 3, 1960, agreeing that the Eichmann "incident" was settled and no further action would be taken by Argentina. Interestingly, no other nation at the time in question, other than Israel, sought to bring Eichmann to justice. Argentina, the Federal Republic of Germany, Austria and Poland, to name but four, would certainly have had a legitimate jurisdictional and moral stake in seeing Adolf Eichmann tried and convicted. Apparently, the fear of possibly reviving latent memories of the Holocaust acted as a political impediment in those states for a trial of one of the key Nazi facilitators of genocide. Thus, for all intents and purposes, Israel was free, according to her own domestic law, to place Eichmann in the dock.

In a sense the trial of Adolf Eichmann was much more that a trial involving a murderous member of the Nazi darkness that had enveloped Europe from 1933 to 1945. It was also a trial that gave rise to disputed principles of international criminal law and jurisdiction and the duty devolving upon the surviving victims of the Holocaust to personally experience justice in some small but significant way. Additionally, the Eichmann trial was also a true "show trial" in the media sense of that word. The Israeli government went to great lengths to make sure that the physical venue of the tribunal allowed for maximum public exposure. The Beit Ha'am Municipal Theatre in Jerusalem was remodeled into a courtroom with the audience and the press seated in theatre seats below a three-tier, well-lit rostrum. The defendant was seated inside a glass enclosed booth on the first tier, guarded by Israeli security personnel. At an oblique angle in front of Eichmann sat the members of the prosecution and defense teams. The translators' desk and the witness box were located on the second tier at opposite ends of the bench which occupied the third tier. Facing the bench from left to right sat the three judges of the District Court of Jerusalem: Benjamin Halevi; Presiding Judge Moshe Landau; and Yitzchak Raveh. Arendt, in her acclaimed book on the Eichmann Trial,[4] gives the following account of the trial's opening:

> *"Beth Hamishpath"* — the House of Justice: these words shouted by the court usher at the top of his voice make us jump to our feet as they announce the arrival of three judges, who, bare-headed, in black robes, walk into the courtroom from a side entrance to take their seats on the highest tier of the raised platform.... Directly below the judges are the translators, whose services are needed for direct exchanges between the defendant or his counsel and the court; otherwise, the German-speaking accused party, like almost everyone else in the audience, follows the Hebrew proceedings through the simultaneous

---

3. As quoted in Jacob Robinson, *And the Crooked Shall Be Made Straight: The Eichmann Trial, the Jewish Catastrophe, and Hannah Arendt's Narrative* at 105 (1965).

4. Hannah Arendt, *Eichmann in Jerusalem: A Report on the Banality of Evil* (1963).

radio transmission,.... One tier below the translators, facing each other and hence their profiles turned to the audience, we see the glass booth of the accused and the witness box.

* * *

Eichmann, son of Karl Adolf Eichmann, the man in the glass booth built for his protection; medium sized, slender, middle-aged, with receding hair, ill-fitting teeth, and nearsighted eyes, who throughout the trial keeps craning his scraggy neck toward the bench (not once does he face the audience), and who desperately and for the most part successfully maintains his self-control despite the nervous tic to which his mouth must have become subject long before this trial started. On trial are his deeds, not the sufferings of the Jews, not the German people or mankind, not even anti-Semitism and racism.[5]

Attorney-General Gideon Hausner arose, addressed the court with the usual formalities and began the trial by remarking that:

> When I stand before you here, Judges of Israel, to lead the prosecution of Adolf Eichmann, I am not standing alone. With me are six million accusers. But they cannot rise to their feet and point an accusing finger towards him who sits in the dock and cry: 'I accuse.' For their ashes are piled up on the hills of Auschwitz and the fields of Treblinka, and are strewn in the forests of Poland. The graves are scattered throughout the length and breadth of Europe. Their blood cries out, but their voice is not heard.

Adolf Eichmann was charged by Israel with crimes that constituted official policy of the N. S. D. A. P. The murder of approximately six million Jews and other Nazi "undesirables" was a key element in the Third Reich's plan for world domination. The early German plan for harassment and deportation of the Jews failed to convince the Nazi leadership that these dual policies would solve the "Jewish problem." Hence, the National Socialists then decided to turn to the concentration camp device to effectuate their sinister aims. Reinhard Heydrich, *SS-Obergruppenführer* and alter ego of *Reichsführer-SS*, Heinrich Himmler, became Himmler's chief of Security Service (SD) in 1932. A tall, cold and brutal man with blond hair and a horse-like face, Heydrich chaired the notorious Wannsee Conference held on the outskirts of Berlin on January 20, 1942. Adolf Eichmann was in attendance at this meeting where a discussion ensued regarding how a more efficient and technologically-swift means could be usefully employed to annihilate the Jews. The Wannsee conferees agreed that all of European Jewry must be done away with as expeditiously as possible and that the most efficient way to accomplish such a diabolical plan was to transport the Jews for extermination to one of at least five major concentration camps located at Treblinka, Belzec, Sobibor, Majdanek and Auschwitz. The significance of the Wannsee Conference, and, by implication, Eichmann's criminal complicity in the "Final Solution," was that it initiated an across the— board *state effort* by all designated Nazi organs to implement the plan for the complete destruction of the Jews of Europe.

At Wannsee, Heydrich informed the assembled attendees:

> "Under suitable control...the Jews should be brought to the East, in the course of the 'final solution,' for use as labour. In big labour gangs, the sexes separated, the Jews capable of work will be transported to those areas and set to

---

5. *Id.* at 3–5.

road-building, in the course of which many, without doubt, will succumb through natural losses. The surviving remnant, surely those with the greatest powers of resistance, will be given special treatment (Sonderbehandlung), since they will constitute the natural reserve for the recreation of Jewry, as history has proved.

In execution of the final solution, Europe will be combed from East to West. The Jews will first be driven into Ghettoes, and from there to the East.... In the Occupied Territories and in those under our influence in Europe, the officer designated by the Security Police will operate in coordination with the appropriate representative of the Ministry for Foreign Affairs,"[6]

The Majdanek concentration camp near Lublin, Poland, was established in 1941. Nazi efficiency at Majdanek reached its zenith in November, 1943, when German records reveal that at least 18,000 Jews were slaughtered in one single day! The Treblinka camp near Warsaw, Poland, accounted for at least 750,000 Jewish deaths between the years 1942 and 1943. Treblinka was then destroyed by the Germans in 1943 in their attempt to erase clear evidence of genocide. The Chelmno concentration camp near Lodz, Poland, accounted for some 340,000 Jewish deaths. At Balzec, it is estimated that at least 600,000 Jews were murdered. And finally, at Auschwitz, located near Cracow, Poland, some 2.5 million internees, mostly Jewish, met an ignominious fate while at least an additional 500,000 died as a result of the combined effects of ill-treatment, lack of proper nutrition and disease. All of this, and more, was part and parcel of Adolf Eichmann's legacy of international savagery and destruction. While the majority of the program of genocide was conducted in concentration camps, the *Einzatzgruppen* units, along with other German police organizations who followed in the wake of the army's conquest, also conducted a number of mass murders throughout the conquered territories. Of course, there were other less visible killing fields in existence under the heel of Nazi tyranny, but those just mentioned will live in infamy as concrete and hideous examples of man's inhumanity to man in the twentieth century.

Besides acts of genocide that occurred in Eastern Europe and the occupied regions of the U.S.S.R., the Nazi grim reaper appeared in other European countries including Holland, whose Jewish population suffered almost total extinction, France, Yugoslavia, Greece and the Czech protectorate. The IMT-Nuremberg had this to say about Nazi organizations found to be "criminal" whose diverse activities throughout Europe clearly implicated and incriminated Adolf Eichmann:

The creation of the R. S. H. A. [*Reichssicherheitshauptampt*, or Reich Security Office, created September 27, 1939, and headed by Reinhard Heydrich] represented the formalisation at the top level of the relationship under which the S. D. [*Sicherheitsdienst*, or Security Service] served as the intelligence agency for the Security Police. Within Germany...the local offices of the Gestapo, Criminal Police and S. D. were formally separated.... In the occupied territories the formal relationship between local units of the Gestapo, Criminal Police, and S. D. was slightly closer.... As the Nazi programme of anti-Semitic persecution increased in intensity, the role played by [these] groups became increasingly important....

The Gestapo and S. D. were used for purposes which were criminal under the Charter, involving persecution and extermination of the Jews, brutalities

---

6. As quoted in Peter Papadatos, *The Eichmann Trial*, at 8 (1964).

and killings in concentration camps, excesses in the administration of occupied territories, and administration of the slave labour programme and the ill-treatment and murder of prisoners of war.[7]

During his trial, Eichmann spoke quite openly regarding these hellish activities and his moral insensitivity was clearly demonstrated when he testified at one point that "Ich sass am Schreibtish und machte meine Sachen" (I sat at my desk and did my work).

Following a reprint of the *Indictment*, we report excerpts from the opinion and judgment of the District Court of Jerusalem, excerpts from the appellate opinion of the Supreme Court of Israel along with commentary regarding some of the major legal issues raised by the Eichmann trial and its place in international criminal justice. Other post-war trials of incarcerated or renegade Nazis will be reported as well.

---

1. The Indictment
Peter Papadatos, *The Eichmann Trial*
Appendix, 111–124 (1964)

The Eichman Trial © Peter Papadatos 1964. Reproduced with permission of Greenwood Publishing Group, Inc.

The Attorney-General v.
Adolf, the son of Adolf Karl Eichmann
aged 54, at present under arrest — the accused

ADOLF EICHMANN
is hereby charged as follows:

FIRST COUNT

Nature of Offence

Crime against the Jewish people, an offence under section 1(a)(1) of the Nazis and Nazi Collaborators (Punishment) Law, 5710-1950, and section 23 of the Criminal Code Ordinance, 1936.

Particulars of Offence

(a) The accused, together with others, during the period 1939 to 1945, caused the killing of millions of Jews, in his capacity as the person responsible for the execution of the Nazi plan for the physical extermination of the Jews, known as 'the final solution of the Jewish problem."

(b) Immediately after the outbreak of the Second World War the accused was appointed head of a department of the Gestapo in Berlin the duties of which were to lo-

---

7. *Trial of the Major War Criminals before the International Military Tribunal, Nuremberg*, Nov. 14, 1945–Oct. 1, 1946, vol. 1 at pp. 263, 267 (1947).

cate, deport and exterminate the Jews of Germany and the other Axis countries, and the Jews of occupied areas. That department bore in succession the following distinctive numbers:

IV D4; IV B4; IV A4,

(c) Instructions for the execution of the plan of extermination in Germany were given by the accused directly to local commanders of the Gestapo, while in Berlin, Vienna and Prague the instructions of the accused were issued to central authorities (*Zentralstelle für jüdische Auswanderung*) for the direction of which the accused was personally responsible until their liquidation towards the end of the Second World War.

(d) In areas occupied by Germany the accused acted through the offices of the commanders of the Security Police and the S. D. and through those persons specially nominated to deal with Jewish affairs, who were appointed from the department of the accused in the Gestapo, and were subject to his instruction.

(e) In Axis countries and areas conquered by them the accused made use of the offices of the diplomatic representatives of Germany in each place, in continual co-ordination with the special departments of the German Foreign Ministry in Berlin which dealt with the Jewish Problem. Advisors were appointed in the offices of such diplomatic representatives from among the members of the department of the accused, who were subject to his instructions.

(f) The accused, together with others, secured the extermination of the Jews, by— among other means— their being killed in concentration camps the purpose of which was mass murder, the more important of such camps being as follows: [here the Indictment lists six concentration camps, *Auschwitz, Chelmno, Belzec, Sobibor, Treblinka* and *Majdanek*, and the extermination methods employed by each].

(g) Immediately after the invasion of Poland by the German army in September 1939, the accused committed acts of expelling, uprooting and exterminating the population, in co-ordination with massacre-squads, recruited from the ranks of the German Security Police and the S. S., which were known by the name of *Einsatzgruppen* (Special Action Groups). Groups of this name also operated after the invasion of the U.S.S.R. in 1941, and advanced in the wake of the German army. These groups received their orders directly from the Reich Security Head Office (RSHA), and each such group co-operated with the accused in the extermination of the Jews in the area of its jurisdiction. These groups operated in the main on the Sabbath and Jewish Festivals, which days were selected for the slaughter of Jews. These groups exterminated hundreds of thousands of Jews in the area occupied by Germany in Poland.

(h) Before the invasion by the German army of areas of the U.S.S.R. and the Baltic countries Lithuania, Latvia and Estonia, which were annexed to the U.S.S.R., four *Einsatzgruppen* co-operated with the accused in the extermination of Jews in the areas referred to, and in that portion of Poland which was annexed to the U.S.S.R. after September 1939. [the *Indictment* then details the number of Jews killed by *Einsatzgrupp* A, B, and D operating behind the German lines after the invasions of Poland and the U.S.S.R.].

(i) At the end of 1941 the accused ordered the deportation of thousands of Jews from Germany, Austria and Czechoslovakia (Protectorate) to ghettoes in Riga, Kovno and Minsk. These Jews were exterminated and, *inter alia:*

(1) A number of such Jews deported from the Reich (Germany) were murdered on November 30, 1941, together with some 4,000 from Riga;

(2) Some 3,500 Jews from Germany who were sent to Minsk as aforesaid pursuant to instructions issued by the accused, were exterminated by an *Einsatzgruppe* in Bielorussia together with 55,000 more Jews who were residents of that district.

(j) During the years 1940–1945 the accused, together with others, caused the killing of hundreds of thousands of Jews in forced labour camps which were conducted on the lines of concentration camps, and in which such Jews were enslaved, tortured and starved to death in Germany, and in countries occupied by Germany.

(k) The accused, together with others, caused the killing of still more hundreds of thousands of Jews during the years 1939–1945 in Germany and the other Axis countries, and the areas occupied by them, by their mass deportation and concentration in ghettoes and other concentration points under cruel and inhumane conditions, that is to say, in the following countries: Germany; Austria; Italy, Bulgaria; Belgium; U.S.S.R. and the Baltic States, Lithuania, Latvia and Estonia which was annexed to the U. S. S. R. after September 1939; Denmark; Holland; Hungary; Yugoslavia; Greece; Luxembourg; Monaco; Norway; Poland; Czechoslovakia; France, Rumania.

(1) The accused caused the killing of some half a million Hungarian Jews by means of their mass deportation to the extermination camp at Auschwitz and other places during the period from March 19 to December 24, 1944, at a time when he acted as head of the "Eichmann Special Action Group" (*Sondereinsatz-Kommando Eichmann*) in Budapest.

(m) All the acts mentioned in this count were committed by the accused with the intention of destroying the Jewish people.

SECOND COUNT

Nature of Offence

Crime against the Jewish people, an offence under section 1(a)(1) of the Nazis and Nazi Collaborators (Punishment) Law, 5710-1950, and section 23 of the Criminal Code Ordinance, 1936.

Particulars of Offence

(a) During the period from 1939 to 1945 the accused, together with others, placed many millions of Jews in living conditions which were calculated to bring about their physical destruction, and took steps towards this end in Germany and the other Axis countries, in the areas occupied by them, and in the areas under their *de facto* control. During the period aforesaid, and pursuant to his duties as stated in the first count, and for the purpose of executing "the final solution of the Jewish problem," the accused committed the following acts in respect of such Jews:

(1) Putting them to work in force labor camps;

(2) Sending them to ghettoes and detaining them there;

(3) Driving them into transit camps and other concentration points;

(4) Deporting them, and conveying them in mass transportation under inhumane conditions.

All the said acts were committed by the accused for the same purpose, in the same manner, and in the same places mentioned in the first count.

(b) All the said acts were committed by the accused with the intention of destroying the Jewish people.

THIRD COUNT

Nature of Offence [same as in Counts One and Two].

Particulars of Offence

(a) During the period of the Nazi regime the accused fulfilled certain duties in the Security Service of the S. S. (S. D.) in dealing with Jews, in accordance with the programme of the Nazi Party (N. S. D. A. P.) After the outbreak of the Second World War these duties were combined with the duties of the department in the Gestapo which is described in the first count, at the head of which stood the accused.

(b) During the whole of the period aforesaid the accused, together with others, caused serious physical and mental harm to millions of Jews in Germany and other Axis countries, in areas occupied by them and in the areas under their *de facto* control, in the countries detailed in the first count.

(c) The accused, together with others caused the serious harm aforesaid by the enslavement, starvation, deportation, and persecution of the said Jews and by their detention in ghettoes, transit camps and concentration camps in conditions which were designed to cause their degradation, the deprivation of their rights as human beings and to suppress them and cause them inhumane suffering and torture.

(d) The accused, together with others, committed the acts aforesaid through measures the more important of which were as follows.

(1) The sudden, mass arrest of Jews without any guilt on their part or judicial decision, and merely by reason of their being Jews, and the torture of such Jews in concentration camps such as those at Dachau and Buchenwald;

(2) The organization on the night of November 9–10, 1938, of the mass persecution of some 20,000 Jews from Germany and Austria by arrest, cruel beatings, causing serious bodily harm, and torture in concentration camps, [*Kristallnacht*].

(3) The organization of the social and economic boycott of Jews and their designation as a sub-human racial group;

(4) The application of the laws known as the "Nuremberg Laws" in order to deprive millions of Jews in all the countries specified in the first count of their human rights.

(e) The acts aforesaid were committed by the accused with the intention of destroying the Jewish people.

FOURTH COUNT

Nature of Offence [same as in Counts One and Two]

Particulars of Offence

(a) As from 1942 the accused, together with others, devised measures the purpose of which was to prevent childbearing among the Jews of Germany and countries occupied by her.

(b) The devising of such methods by the accused, by virtue of his duty as head of the Department for Jewish Affairs in the Gestapo in Berlin, was also designed to advance the "final solution of the Jewish Problem."

(c) The measure referred to include:

(1) The instruction of the accused to Dr. Epstein who was head of the Council of Elders in the Concentration Camp of Theresienstadt during 1943/1944, concerning

the forbidding of births in the camp and the interruption of pregnancy by artificial abortion in all cases and at all stages of pregnancy:

(2) An order by the German police in the Baltic countries in 1942 against Jewish women in the ghetto of Kovno forbidding birth and compelling such women to undergo operations for abortion in all states of pregnancy;

(3) On October 27, 1942, in the offices of the accused IV B4 (RSHA) in Berlin, the accused, together with others, devised measures for the sterilization of the off-spring of mixed marriages of the first degree among Jews in Germany and in areas occupied by her in accordance with the following principles:

(aa) The Sterilization of the offspring of mixed marriages, Jews or Jewesses, will be performed with their consent, in return for the favour of their being given the right to remain within the area governed by the German Reich;

(bb) The offspring of the mixed marriages will be entitled to choose between sterilization and deportation to extermination areas in the East;

(cc) It will be suggested by the authorities to the offspring of the mixed marriages to choose deportation;

(dd) Those who choose deportation will be separated according to their sex in order to prevent any further births;

(ee) The sterilization will be carried out secretly and in camouflaged manner.

(d) In devising the measures aforesaid, the accused intended to destroy the Jewish people.

FIFTH COUNT

Nature of Offence [same as in Counts One and Two, except under section 1(a)(2) of the Nazis and Nazi Collaborators (Punishment) Law].

Particulars of Offence

The accused, during the period 1939 to 1945, committed, in Germany and other Axis countries, in areas occupied by them and in the areas under their *de facto* control, acts constituting a crime against humanity in that, together with others, he caused the murder, extermination, enslavement, starvation and deportation of the civilian Jewish population in those countries and areas.

The accused committed those acts whilst functioning in the capacities specified in the first count.

SIXTH COUNT

Nature of Offence [same as in Count Five].

Particulars of Offence

The accused, in carrying out the acts described in counts 1 to 5 above, persecuted Jews on national, racial, religious and political grounds.

SEVENTH COUNT

Nature of Offence [same as in Count Five].

Particulars of Offence

(a) During the period of the Nazi regime in Germany and the other Axis countries, in the countries occupied by them and in the areas under their *de facto* control, the accused, together with others, caused the spoliation of the property of millions of Jews resident in the countries aforesaid, by means of inhumane measures involving compulsion, theft, terrorism and torture.

(b) Such measures included:

(1) The establishment, organization and operation of "the Central Authority for the Emigration of Jews" (*Zentralstelle für Jüdische Auswanderung*) in Vienna, from immediately after the entry of the Nazis into Austria in March 1938 until the end of the Second World War, through which authority the accused transferred the property of the Jews of Austria and all the Jewish communities of that State into German control. Part of this property was stolen for the purpose of financing the expulsion of the Jews of Austria to places beyond the borders of that State, and part of such property was transferred to the authorities by means of compulsion and measures of terrorism against its owners.

(2) The establishment of the "Central Authority for the Emigration of Jews" in Prague after the Nazi invasion of Czechoslovakia in March 1939, until the end of the Second World War, and the organization and operation of that authority by the accused in the same manner as the Central Authority in Vienna. By means of this authority a "special account" was operated through which the property of the Jews who had been robbed by the accused, together with others, in Czechoslovakia itself and in other countries, was transferred to the control of Germany.

(3) The establishment of a Central Authority for the Emigration of Jews and the Affairs of German Jews (*Reichszentrale*) in Berlin in 1939, and its operation by the accused until the end of the Second World War. By means of this Central Authority, as was the case with the Central Authority in Vienna, the accused, together with others, despoiled the property of the German Jews, both the individual property as well as the property of the various Jewish communities in that country, by the same methods and under the same conditions as were prescribed by him in regard to the authorities in Vienna and Prague.

(4) The accused compelled hundreds of thousands of Jews to finance their deportation to extermination camps and other centres of mass slaughter by the levy of compulsory payments upon deportees from Germany and areas occupied by her. For the purpose the accused conducted a special account "W" which was placed at the sole disposal of his department.

(5) The property of Jews who were murdered in German occupied countries in Eastern Europe was also stolen by their murderers—members of the S. S.

In order to centralize the acts of plunder special actions were organized in 1942/1943 within the framework of the special operation for the murder of Jews in Poland known as "Aktion Reinhard." The person in charge of this special operation was the commander of the Security Police and the S. D. in the District of Lublin. During the two said years property, the nominal value of which was two hundred million Marks, but the actual value of which was several times in excess of that sum, was stolen.

(6) During the Second World War and up to a short time before its conclusion, freight trains containing the moveable property of persons murdered in extermination camps, concentration points and ghettoes were run month by month from the occupied districts in the East to Germany. This property also contained vast amounts of parts of the bodies of the murdered persons, such as hair, gold teeth,

false teeth and artificial limbs; all other personal effects were also robbed from the bodies of the Jews before their extermination and thereafter.

(7) The accused, together with others, planned all the acts of extensive robbery in order that the property of the millions who were sent to extermination should be taken from them and conveyed to Germany. The extent of the success of such robbery is reflected by the fact that when the Germans, at the time of their retreat in January 1945, burnt twenty-five such stores which had been erected in the extermination camp at Auschwitz, the six stores saved from the fire were found to contain *inter alia:* 34,820 men's suits, 836,255 women's dresses and 38, 000 men's shoes.

(c) The accused committed the said acts until the end of 1939 in the exercise of his special functions in the Security Service of the S. S. (S. D.); and from the end of that year the accused combined these functions with his functions in Bureau IV of the RSHA.

(d) The accused executed the spoliation of the property of the Jews of Germany and the other areas occupied by her, in addition to those already mentioned in this count, by giving instructions to local commanders of the Security Police and, in Axis countries and areas occupied by such countries, through the offices of the diplomatic representatives of Germany as described in the first count.

EIGHTH COUNT

Nature of Offence

War crime, an offence under section 1(a)(3) of the Nazis and Nazi Collaborators (Punishment) Law, 5710-1950, and section 23 of the Criminal Code Ordinance, 1936.

Particulars of Offence

The accused, during the period of the Second World War, in Germany and other Axis states and in areas occupied by them, committed acts constituting a war crime in that, together with others he caused the ill-treatment, deportation and murder of Jewish inhabitants of the States occupied by Germany and other Axis states. The accused committed these acts whilst functioning in the capacities specified in the first count.

NINTH COUNT

Nature of Offence

Crime against humanity, an offence under section 1(a)(2) of the Nazis and Nazi Collaborators (Punishment) Law, 5710-1950, and section 23 of the Criminal Code Ordinance, 1936.

Particulars of Offence

The accused, between 1940 and 1942, in Poland, then occupied by Germany, committed acts constituting a crime against humanity in that, together with others, he caused the deportation of over half a million Polish civilians from their places of residence with intent to settle German families in those places.

The Polish deportees were in part transferred to Germany and German-occupied areas for the purpose of their employment and detention under conditions of enslavement, coercion and terrorism; in part abandoned in other regions of Poland and German-occupied areas in the East; in part concentrated under inhumane conditions in labour camps organized by the S. S.; and in part transferred to Germany for the purpose of re-Germanisation (*Ruckverdeutschung*).

The accused committed these acts under a special appointment dated December 1939, by which he was empowered by the head of the Security Police in Berlin to act as officer in charge of the "evacuation" of civilians.

TENTH COUNT

Nature of Offence

Crime against humanity, an offence under section 1(a)(2) of the Nazis and Nazi Collaborators (Punishment) Law, 5710-1950, and section 23 of the Criminal Code Ordinance, 1936.

Particulars of Offence

(a) The accused, in 1941, in the then German-occupied parts of Yugoslavia, committed acts constituting a crime against humanity in that, together with others, he caused the deportation of over 14,000 Slovene civilians from their places of residence, with the intention of settling German families in their stead.

(b) The Slovene deportees were transferred to the Serbian part of Yugoslavia by coercive, terrorist measures and under inhumane conditions.

(c) The planning of the deportation aforesaid was devised by the accused at the meeting which took place at Marburg (Untersteirmark) on May 6, 1941, to which the accused summoned the representatives of the other authorities concerned in the matter. The deportation headquarters continued to be located in that city, and operated under the direction of the accused.

The accused committed these acts under his special appointment referred to in the ninth count.

ELEVENTH COUNT

Nature of Offence [same as in Count Ten].

Particulars of Offence

The accused, during the period of the Second World War, in Germany and German-occupied areas, committed acts constituting a crime against humanity in that, together with others, he caused the deportation from their places of residence tens of thousands of gypsies, their concentration at concentration points, and their transportation to extermination camps in German-occupied regions in the East for the purpose of being murdered.

The accused committed these acts under his special appointment referred to in the ninth count.

TWELFTH COUNT

Nature of Offense [same as in Count Eleven].

Particulars of Offense

The accused, in 1942, committed acts constituting a crime against humanity in that, together with others, he caused the deportation of approximately 100 children, civilians of the village of Lidice in Czechoslovakia, their transportation to Poland, and their murder there.

The accused committed these acts in the discharge of his functions in the Gestapo in Berlin.

THIRTEENTH COUNT

Nature of Offence

Membership in a hostile organization, an offence under section 3(a) of the Nazis and Nazi Collaborators (Punishment) Law, 5710-1950.

Particulars of Offence

The accused, during the period of the Nazi regime in Germany, was a member of the organization known as *Schutzstaffeln der N. S. D. A. P.* (S. S.), and attained during his service in that organization the rank of S. S.-Obersturmbannführer.

This organization was declared a criminal organization by the judgment of the International Military Tribunal dated October 1, 1946, in accordance with article 9 of the Charter of the Tribunal annexed to the Four-Power Agreement of August 8, 1945, concerning the trial of the major war criminals.

FOURTEENTH COUNT

Nature of Offence [same as in Count Thirteen].

Particulars of Offence

The accused, during the period of the Nazi regime in Germany, was a member of the organization known as *Sicherheitsdienst des Reichsführers* S. S. (S. D.).

This organization was declared a criminal organization by the Judgment of the International Military Tribunal dated October 1, 1946, in accordance with Article 9 of the Charter of the Tribunal annexed to the Four-Power Agreement of August 8, 1945, concerning the trial of the major war criminals.

FIFTEENTH COUNT

Nature of Offence [same as in Count Fourteen].

Particulars of Offence

The accused, during the period of the Nazi regime in Germany, was a member of the Secret Police (*Geheime Staatspolizei*) known as the Gestapo, and served in it as Director of the Department for Jewish Affairs.

This organization was declared a criminal organization by the judgment of the International Military Tribunal dated October 1, 1946, in accordance with article 9 of the Charter of the Tribunal annexed to the Four-Power Agreement of August 8, 1945, concerning the trial of the major war criminals.

The notice of charges was handed to counsel for the accused on February 1, 1961, and he intimated that he waives his right to the holding of a preliminary hearing.

Jerusalem, this fifth day of Adar, 5721 (February 21, 1961).

Guideon Hausner
Attorney-General

2. *The Attorney-General of the Government of Israel v. Eichmann*

District Court of Jerusalem, Judgment of December 11, 1961
56 *American Journal of International Law* 805; 805–808; 810–816;
818–819; 821; 823–835; 843–844 (1962)
Reproduced with permission from 56 *American Journal of International Law*
805 (1962). © The American Society of International Law

Adolf Eichmann was abducted from Argentina and brought to trial in Israel under the Nazi Collaborators (Punishment) Law, enacted after Israel became a state and after the events charged against Eichmann during the Nazi era in Germany. Section 1(a) of the law provides:

A person who has committed one of the following offences—

1) did, during the period of the Nazi regime, in a hostile country, an act constituting a crime against the Jewish people;

2) did, during the period of the Nazi regime, in a hostile country, an act constituting a crime against humanity;

3) did, during the period of the Second World War, in a hostile country, an act constituting a war crime;

is liable to the death penalty.

Counsel for Eichmann objected to the jurisdiction of the Court *inter alia*, on grounds based on international law. [What follows are selected excerpts from the opinion of Jerusalem District Court prepared by Covey Oliver, a member of the Board of Editors of the *American Journal of International Law*].

* * *

8. Learned Counsel does not ignore the fact that the Israel law applicable to the acts attributed to the accused vests in us the jurisdiction to try this case. His contention against the jurisdiction of the Court is not based on this law, but on international law. He contends—

(a) that the Israel law, by inflicting punishment for acts done outside the boundaries of the State and before its establishment, against persons who were not Israel citizens, and by a person who acted in the course of duty on behalf of a foreign country ("Act of State") conflicts with international law and exceeds the jurisdiction of the Court.

9. Before entering into an analysis of these two contentions and the legal questions therein involved we will clarify the relation between them. These two contentions are independent of each other. The first contention which negates the jurisdiction of the Court to try the accused for offences against the law in question is not bound up with or conditional upon the circumstances under which he was brought to Israel. Even had the accused come to the country of his own free will, say as a tourist under an assumed name, and had he been here arrested upon the verification of his true identity, the first contention of Counsel that the Israel Court has no jurisdiction to try him for any offences against the law in question would still stand. The second, additional, contention is that no matter what the jurisdiction of the Israel Court is to try offences attributed to the accused in usual circumstances, that jurisdiction is in any case negated by reason of the special circumstances connected with the abduction of the accused in a foreign country and his prosecution in Israel. We will therefore deal with the two questions seriatim.

10. The first contention of Counsel that Israel law is in conflict with international law and that therefore it cannot vest jurisdiction in this Court, raises the preliminary question as to the validity of international law in Israel and as to whether in the event of a clash between it and the laws of the land, it is to be preferred to the laws of the land. The law in force in Israel resembles that which is in force in England. [The Court then quotes from several authorities from Great Britain and Australia, along with commentary from recognized publicist in international law and then continues].

* * *

Our jurisdiction to try this case is based on the Nazis and Nazi Collaborators (Punishment) Law, *a statutory law the provisions of which are unequivocal*. The Court has to give effect to the law of the Knesset, and we cannot entertain the contention that this law conflicts with the principles of international law. For this reason alone Counsel's first contention must be rejected.

11. But we have also perused the sources of international law, including the numerous authorities mentioned by learned Counsel in his comprehensive written brief upon which he based his oral pleadings, and by the learned *Attorney-General* in his comprehensive oral pleadings, and failed to find any foundation for the contention that Israel law is in conflict with the principles of international law. On the contrary, we have reached the conclusion that the law in question conforms to the best traditions of the law of nations.

The power of the State of Israel to enact the law in question or Israel's "right to punish" is based, with respect to the offences in question, from the point of view of international law on a dual foundation: The universal character as being designed to exterminate the Jewish people. In what follows we shall deal with each of these two aspects separately.

12. The abhorrent crimes defined in this law are crimes not under Israel law alone. These crimes which afflicted the whole of mankind and shocked the conscience of nations are grave offences against the law of nations itself ("delicta juris gentium"). Therefore, so far from international law negating or limiting the jurisdiction of countries with respect to such crimes, in the absence of an International Court the international law is in need of the judicial and legislative authorities of every country, to give effect to its penal injunctions and to bring criminals to trial. The authority and jurisdiction to try crimes under international law are *universal.*

13. This universal authority, namely the authority of the "forum deprehensionis" (the Court of the country in which the accused is actually held in custody) was already mentioned in the Corpus Juris Civilis...and the towns of northern Italy had already in the Middle Ages taken to trying specific types of dangerous criminals ("banniti, vagabundi, assassini") who happened to be within their area of jurisdiction without regard to the place in which the crimes in question were committed.... Maritime nations have also since time immemorial enforced the principle of universal jurisdiction in dealing with pirates, whose crime is known in English law "*piracy jure gentium.*"

* * *

It is therefore the moral duty of every sovereign state...to enforce the natural right to punish, possessed by the victims of the crime whoever they may be, against criminals whose acts have "violated in extreme form the law of nature and the law of nations." By these pronouncements the father of international law [Hugo Grotius] laid the foundations for the future definition of the "crime against humanity" as a "crime under the law of nations" and to universal jurisdiction in such crimes.

* * *

Cowles, in "Universality of Jurisdiction over War Crimes," 33 California Law Review (1945), p. 177 *et seq.*, states in the following terms the reasons for the rule of law as to the "universality of jurisdiction over war crimes" which was adopted and determined by the United Nations War Crimes Commission...:

> "The general doctrine recently expounded and called 'universality of jurisdiction over war crimes,' which has support of the United Nations War Crimes Commission and according to which every independent State has, under International Law, jurisdiction to punish not only pirates but also war criminals in its custody, regardless of the nationality of the victim or of the place where the offence was committed, particularly where, for some reason, the criminal would otherwise go unpunished."

Instances of the extensive use made by the Allied Military Tribunals of the principle of universality of jurisdiction of war crimes of all classes (including "crimes against humanity") will be found in Vols. 1–15 of the Law Reports of Trials of War Criminals.

16. We have said that the crimes dealt with in this case are not crimes under Israel law alone, but are in essence offences against the law of nations. Indeed, the crimes in question are not a figment of the imagination of the legislator who enacted the law for the punishment of Nazis and Nazi collaborators, but have been stated and defined in that law according to a precise pattern of international laws and conventions which define crimes under the law of nations. The "crime against the Jewish people" is defined on the pattern of the genocide crime defined in the "Convention for the prevention and punishment of genocide" which was adopted by the United Nations Assembly on 9.12.48. The "crime against humanity" and the "war crime" are defined on the pattern of crimes of identical designations defined in the Charter of the International Military Tribunal (which is the Statute of the Nuremberg Court) annexed to the Four-Power Agreement of 8.8.45 on the subject of the trial of the principal war criminals (the London Agreement), and also in Law No. 10 of the Control Council of Germany of 20.12.45. The offence of "membership of a hostile organization" is defined by the pronouncement in the judgment of the Nuremberg Tribunal, according to its Charter, to declare the organisations in question as "criminal organizations," and is also patterned on the Council of Control Law No. 10. For purposes of comparison we shall set forth in what follows the parallel articles and clauses side by side. [Comparison omitted]....

17. The crime of "genocide" was first defined by Raphael Lemkin in his book "Axis Rule in Occupied Europe" (1944) in view of the methodical extermination of peoples and populations, and primarily the Jewish people by the Nazis and their satellites (after the learned author had already moved, at the Madrid 1933 International Congress for the Consolidation of International Law, that the extermination of racial, religious or social groups be declared "a crime against international law"). On 11.12.46 after the International Military Tribunal pronounced its judgment against the principal German criminals, the United Nations Assembly, by its Resolution No. 96(I), unanimously declared that "genocide" is a crime against the law of nations. That resolution said:

> "Genocide is a denial of the right of existence of entire human groups, as homicide is the denial of the right to live of individual human beings; such denial of the right of existence shocks the conscience of mankind, results in great losses to humanity in the form of cultural and other contributions represented by these groups, and is contrary to moral law and to the spirit and aims of the United Nations.

"Many instances of such crimes of genocide have occurred when racial, religious, political and other groups have been destroyed, entirely or in part.

"The punishment of the crime of genocide is a matter of international concern.

"THE GENERAL ASSEMBLY, THEREFORE,

"AFFIRMS that genocide is a crime under international law which the civilized world condemns, and for the commission of which principals and accomplices—whether private individuals, public officials or statesmen, and whether the crime is committed on religious, racial, political or any other grounds— are punishable:

"INVITES the Member States to enact the necessary legislation for the prevention and punishment of this crime;

"RECOMMENDS that international co-operation be organized between States with a view to facilitating the speedy prevention and punishment of the crime of genocide, and, to this end,

"REQUESTS the Economic and Social Council to undertake the necessary studies, with a view to drawing up a draft convention on the crime of genocide to be submitted to the next regular session of the General Assembly."

18. On 28.5.51, the International Court of Justice gave, at the request of the United Nations Assembly, an Advisory Opinion on the question of the reservations to that convention on the prevention and punishment of the crime of genocide. The Advisory Opinion said *inter alia* (p. 23):

"The origins of the Convention show that it was the intention of the United Nations to condemn and punish genocide as 'a crime under international law' involving a denial of the right of existence of entire human groups, a denial which shocks the conscience of mankind and results in great losses to humanity, and which is contrary to moral law and to the spirit and aims of the United Nations (Resolution 96 (I) of the General Assembly, December 11th, 1946). The first consequence arising from this conception is that the principles... which are recognized by civilized nations as binding on States, even without any conventional obligation. A second consequence is the universal character both of the condemnation [of genocide and of the co-operation required] 'in order to liberate mankind from such odious scourge' (Preamble to the Convention). The Genocide Convention was therefore intended by the General Assembly and by the contracting parties to be definitely universal in scope. It was in fact approved on December 9th, 1948, by a resolution which was unanimously adopted by fifty-six states."

19. In light of the recurrent affirmation by the United Nations in the 1946 Assembly resolution and in the 1948 convention, and in the light of the advisory opinion of the International Court of Justice, there is no doubt that genocide has been recognized as a crime under international law in the full legal meaning of this term, and at that ex tunc; that is to say: the crimes of genocide which were committed against the Jewish people and other peoples were crimes under international law. It follows therefore, in the light of the acknowledged principles of international law, that the jurisdiction to try such crimes is universal.

20. This conclusion encounters a serious objection in the new light of Article 6 of the convention which provides that:

"Persons charged with genocide or any of the other acts enumerated in Article III shall be tried by a competent tribunal of the State in the territory of which the act was committed, or by such international penal tribunal as may have jurisdiction with respect to those Contracting Parties which shall have accepted jurisdiction."

Prima facie this provision might appear to yield support for an argumentum e contrario, the very contention voiced by the learned Counsel against the applicability of the principle of universal jurisdiction and even against any extraterritorial jurisdiction with respect to the crime in question: if the United Nations failed to give their support to universal jurisdiction by each country to try a crime of genocide committed outside its boundaries, but has expressly provided that, in the absence of an international criminal tribunal, those accused of this crime shall be tried by a "competent court of the country in whose territory the act was done" how may Israel try the accused for a crime that constitutes "genocide"?

21. To reply to that reservation we must direct attention to the distinction between the rules of customary and the rules of conventional international law, a distinction which also found expression in the Advisory Opinion of the International Court of Justice with respect to the convention in question. That convention fulfills two roles simultaneously: in the sphere of customary international law it re-affirms the deep conviction of all peoples that "genocide, whether [committed] in time of peace or in time of war, is a crime under international law" (Article 1). That confirmation which, as stressed in the Advisory Opinion of the International Court of Justice, was given "unanimously by fifty-six countries" is "of universal character," the purport of which is that "the principles inherent in the convention are acknowledged by the civilized nations as binding on the country *even without a conventional obligation*" *(ibid.)*. "The principles inherent in the convention" are *inter alia*, the criminal character of the acts defined in Article 2 (that is, the article upon which the definition of "a crime against the Jewish people" in the Israel law has been patterned), the penal liability for any form of participation is this crime (Article 3), the want of immunity from penal liability for rulers and public officials (Article 4), and the fact that for purposes of extradition no political "character" may be assigned to any such crime (Article 7). These principles are "recognized by civilized nations" according to the conclusion of the International Court of Justice, and are "binding on the countries even without a conventional obligation:' that is to say, they constitute part of the customary international law. The words "approve" in Article 1 of the convention and "recognize" in the Advisory Opinion indicate approval and recognition ex tunc, namely the recognition and confirmation that the above-mentioned principles had already been part of the customary international law at the time of the perpetration of the shocking crime which led to the United Nations' resolution and the drafting of the convention—crimes of genocide which were perpetrated by the Nazis. Thus far as to the first aspect of the convention (and the important one with respect to this judgment): the confirmation of certain principles as established rules of law in customary international law.

22. The second aspect of the convention, which is the practical object for which it was concluded, is: the determination of the conventional obligations between the contracting parties to the convention for the prevention of such crimes *in future* and the punishment therefore in the event of their being committed. Already in the UN resolution 96(I) there came, after the "confirmation" that the crime of genocide constitutes a crime under international law, an "invitation," as it were, to all States-Members of the United Nations "to enact the necessary legislation for the prevention and punishment of this crime," together with a recommendation to organize "international cooperation" between the countries with a view to facilitating the "prevention and swift punishment

of the crime of genocide," and to this end the Social and Economic Council was charged with the preparation of the draft convention. Accordingly the "affirmation" that genocide, whether committed in time of peace or in time of war, constitutes a crime under international law is followed in Article 1 of the convention by the obligation assumed by the contracting parties who "undertake to prevent and punish it," and by Article 5 they "undertake to pass the necessary legislation to this end."

In the wake of these obligations of the contracting parties to prevent the perpetration of genocide by suitable legislation and enforce such legislation against future perpetrators of the crime, comes Article 6 which determines the Courts that will try those accused of this crime. It is clear that Article 6, like all other articles which determine the conventional obligations of the contracting parties, is intended for cases of genocide which will occur in the future after the ratification of the treaty or adherence thereto by the country or countries concerned. It cannot be assumed, in the absence of an express provision in the convention itself, that any of the conventional obligations, including Article 6, will apply to crimes which had been perpetrated in the past. It is of the essence of conventional obligations, as distinct from the confirmation of existing principles, that unless another intention is implicit, their application shall be *ex nunc* and not *ex tunc*. Article 6 of the convention is a purely pragmatic provision, and does not presume to confirm a subsisting principle. Therefore, we must draw a clear line of distinction between the provision in the first part of Article 1, which says that "the contracting parties confirm that genocide, whether [committed] in time of peace or in time of war, is a crime under international law," a general provision which confirms the principle of customary international law that "is binding on all countries even without conventional obligation," and the provision of Article 6 which is a special provision in which the contracting parties pledged themselves to the trial of crimes that may be committed in the future. Whatever may be the purport of this obligation within the meaning of the convention...it is certain that it constitutes no part of the principles of customary international law which are also binding outside the conventional (contractual) application of the convention.

23. Moreover, even the conventional application of the convention, it cannot be assumed that Article 6 is designed to limit to the principle of territoriality the jurisdiction of countries to try genocide crimes. Without entering into the general question of the limits of municipal criminal jurisdiction, it may be said that all agree that customary international law does not enjoin to try its citizens for offences they committed abroad.... Had Article 6 meant to provide that those accused of genocide shall be tried *only* by "a competent court of the country in whose territory the crime was committed" (or by an "international court" which has not been constituted), then that article would have foiled the very object of the convention "to prevent genocide and inflict punishment therefor."...

* * *

...It is clear that the specification in Article 6 of the territorial jurisdiction, apart from the jurisdiction of the non-existent international tribunal, is not exhaustive, and every sovereign State may exercise its existing powers within the limits of customary international law, and there is nothing in the adherence of a country to the convention to waive powers which are mentioned in Article 6. It is in conformity with this view that the law [of Israel] for the Prevention and Punishment of Genocide, 5710-1950, provided in Article 5 that "any person who did outside of Israel an act which is an offence under this law may be tried and punished in Israel as though he did the act in Israel." This law does not apply with retroactive effect and does not therefore pertain to the offences dealt with in this case. Our view as to the universality of jurisdiction is not based on this law or on this interpretation of Article 6 of the convention, but derives from the basic nature of the crime of genocide as a crime of utmost gravity under international law. The significance of the treaty to this cause is in the confirmation of the international nature of the crime, a confirmation which was unanimously given by the United Nations Assembly and to which also adhered, among other peoples, the German people (in 1954 the German Federal Republic adhered to the convention and enacted a law... which gave effect to the convention in Germany, and added to the German criminal law Article 220A against genocide...a crime defined according to Article 2 of the convention). The "crime against the Jewish people" under section 1 of the Israel law constitutes a crime of "genocide" within the meaning of Article 2 of the [Genocide] convention, and inasmuch as it is a crime under the law of nations, Israel's legislative authority and judicial jurisdiction in this matter is based upon the law of nations.

* * *

It is hardly necessary to add that the "crime against the Jewish people," which constitutes the crime of "genocide" is nothing but the gravest type of "crime against humanity" (and all the more so because both under Israel law and under the [Genocide] convention a special intention is requisite for its commission, an intention that is not required for the commission of a "crime against humanity.") Therefore, all that has been said in the Nuremberg principles on the "crime against humanity" applies *a fortiori* [with greater force] to the "crimes against the Jewish people."

* * *

It is not necessary to recapitulate in Jerusalem, 15 years after Nuremberg, the grounds for the legal rule on the "crime against humanity," for these terms are written in blood, in the torrents of blood of the Jewish people which was shed. "That law," said Aroneanu in 1948, "was born in the crematoria, and woe to him who will try to stifle it."... (Quoted by Boissarie in his introduction to *Eugene Aroneanu*, Le Crime contre 1 'Humanite, 1961).

The judgment against the Operation Groups of 10.4.48, (*Einsatzgruppen* Case)... says on the same subject:

> "Although the Nuernberg trials represent the first time that international tribunals have adjudicated crimes against humanity as an international offense, this does not, as already indicated, mean that a new offense has been added to the list of transgressions of man. Nuernberg has only demonstrated how humanity can be defended in court, and it is inconceivable that with this precedent extant, the law of humanity should ever lack for a tribunal.

> "Where law exists a court will rise. Thus, the court of humanity, if it may be so termed, will never adjourn."

* * *

The courts in Germany, too, have rejected the contention that the crimes of the Nazis were not prohibited at the time, and that their perpetrators did not have the requisite criminal intent. It is stated in the judgment of the Supreme Federal Tribunal... that the expulsions of the Jews the object of which was the death of the deportees were a continuous crime committed by the principal planners and executants, something of which all other executants should have been conscious, for it cannot be admitted that they were not aware of the basic principles on which human society is based, and which are the common legacy of all civilised nations.

* * *

The Hebrew rule "No one may be punished unless he was forewarned," which corresponds to the principle of legality according to the Roman rule, hints at the importance of warning that a certain action is prohibited. During the World War Allied governments gave the Nazi criminals recurrent warnings that they would be punished, but these were of no avail. Henry Stimson was right when he said, as cited in the Judgment on "The Jurists" (p. 976):

> "It was the Nazi confidence that we would never chase and catch them, and not a misunderstanding of our opinion of them, that led them to commit their crimes. Our offense was thus that of the man who passed by on the other side. That we have finally recognized our negligence and named the criminals for what they are is a piece of righteousness too long delayed by fear."

28. Learned Counsel seeks to negate the jurisdiction of the State [of Israel] by contending that the crimes attributed to the accused in counts 1–12 had been committed, according to the Charge Sheet itself, in the course of duty, and constitute "acts of State," acts for which, according to his contention, only the German State is responsible.

* * *

Learned Counsel bases himself on the rule "par in parem non habet imperium," that is to say—a sovereign State does not dominate, and does not sit in judgment against, another Sovereign State, and deduces therefrom that a State may not try a person for a criminal act that constitutes an "act of State" of another State, without the consent of such other State to that person's trial. In view of Kelsen [an international law scholar] only the State in whose behalf the "organ" (ruler or official) had acted is responsible for the violation, through such act, of international law, [for] which the perpetrator himself is not responsible (with the two exceptions of espionage and war treason).

The theory of "Act of State" was repudiated by the International Military Tribunal at Nuremberg, when it said (pp. 222–223):

> "It was submitted that international law is concerned with the actions of sovereign States, and provides no punishment for individuals; and further, that where the act in question is an act of State, those who carry it out are not personally responsible, but are protected by the doctrine of the sovereignty of the State. In the opinion of the Tribunal, both these submissions must be rejected. That international law imposes duties and liabilities upon individuals as well as States has long been recognized. In the recent case of *Ex Parte Quirin* (1942), 317 U.S. 1, before the Supreme Court of the United States, persons were charged during the war with landing in the United States for purposes of spying and sabotage. The late Chief Justice Stone, speaking for the Court said:
>
> 'From the very beginning of its history this Court has applied the law of war as including that part of the law of nations which prescribes for the conduct of war, the status, rights, and duties of enemy nations as well as enemy individuals.'
>
> He went on to give a list of cases tried by the Courts, where individual offenders were charged with offenses against the law of nations, and particularly the laws of war. Many other authorities could be cited, but enough has been said to show that individuals can be punished for violations of international law. Crimes against international law are committed by men, not by abstract entities, and only by punishing individuals who commit such crimes can the provisions of international law be enforced.... The principle of international law which, under certain circumstances, protects the representatives of a state,

cannot be applied to acts which are condemned as criminal by international law. The authors of these acts cannot shelter themselves behind their official position in order to be freed from punishment in appropriate proceedings. Article 7 of the [London] Charter expressly declares:

> 'The official position of defendants, whether as heads of States, or responsible officials in government departments, shall not be considered as freeing them from responsibility, or mitigating punishment.'

> On the other hand the very essence of the [London] Charter is that individuals have international duties which transcend the national obligations of obedience imposed by the individual state. He who violates the laws of war cannot obtain immunity while acting in pursuance of the authority of the state if the state in authorizing action moves outside its competence under international law.

It is clear from the context that the last sentence was not meant, as Counsel contends, to limit the rule of the "violation of the laws of war" alone. The Court expressly said, as quoted above, that "the principle of international law [which] under certain circumstances protects the representatives of a State cannot be applied to acts which are condemned as criminal by international law."

Indeed, the theory of Kelsen and his disciples...and also the 'limited' theories referred to by Learned Counsel...are inadmissible.... A State that plans and implements a "final solution" cannot be treated as "Par in parem," but only as a gang of criminals. In the judgment on "The Jurists" [at one of the twelve Nuremberg trials after the IMT] it is said (p. 984):

> "The very essence of the prosecution case is that the laws, the Hitlerian decrees and the Draconic, corrupt, and perverted Nazi judicial system themselves constituted the substance of war crimes and crimes against humanity and that participation in the enactment and enforcement of them amounts to complicity in crime. We have pointed out that governmental participation is a material element of the crime against humanity. Only when official organs of sovereignty participated in atrocities and persecutions did those crimes assume international proportions. It can scarce-be said that governmental participation, the proof of which is necessary for conviction, can also be a defense to the charge."

Drost says in his "The Crime of State (Humanicide)" pp. 310–311 (under the caption—"State Crime as Act of State"):

> "Any state officer irrespective of his rank or function, would necessarily go unpunished if his acts of state were considered internationally as the sovereign acts of a legal person. The person who really acted on behalf of the state, would be twice removed from penal justice since the entity whom he represented, by its very nature would be doubly immune from punishment, once physically and once legally. The natural person escapes scot-free between the legal loopholes of state personality and state sovereignty. But then, this reasoning in respect of these too much laboured juristic conceptions should not be carried into the provisions of penal law.

> "Immunity for acts of state constitute the negation of international criminal law which indeed derives the necessity of its existence exactly from the very fact that acts of state often have a criminal character for which the morally responsible officer of state should be made penally liable."

The contention of Learned Counsel that it is not the accused but the State in whose behalf he had acted, that is responsible for his criminal acts is only true in its second part. It is true that under international law Germany bears not only moral, but also legal, responsibility for all the crimes that were committed as its own "Acts of State," including the crimes attributed to the accused. But that responsibility does not detract one iota from the personal responsibility of the accused for his acts.

* * *

For these reasons we dismiss the contention as to "Act of State,"

* * *

30. We have discussed at length the international character of the crimes in question because this offers the broadest possible, though not the only, basis for Israel's jurisdiction according to the law of nations. No less important from the point of view of international law is the special connection the State of Israel has with such crimes, seeing that the people of Israel (Am Israel)—the Jewish people (Ha'am Ha'yehudi—to use the term in the Israel legislation)—constituted the target and the victim of most of the crimes in question. The State of Israel's "right to punish" the accused derives, in our view from two cumulative sources: a universal source (pertaining to the whole of mankind) which vests the right to prosecute and punish crimes of this order in every State within the family of nations; and a specific or national source which gives the victim nation the right to try any who assault their existence.

This second foundation of penal jurisdiction conforms, according to the acknowledged terminology, to the protective principle or the *competence reelle*.

* * *

31. *Dahm* says [that]:

> "Penal jurisdiction is not a matter for everyone to exercise. There must be a 'linking point,' a legal connection that links the punisher with the punished. The State may, insofar as international law does not contain rules contradicting this, punish only persons and acts *which concern it more than they concern other States*" (italics by author).

Learned Counsel has summed up his pleadings against the jurisdiction of the Israel legislator by stressing…that under international law there must be a connection between the State and the person who committed the crime, and that in the absence of an "acknowledge linking point" it was ultra vires the States to inflict punishment for foreign offences….

32. We have already stated…the view of Grotius on "the right to punish," a view which is also based on a "linking point" between the criminal and his victim. Grotius holds that the very commission of the crime creates a legal connection between the offender and the victim, and one that vests in the victim the right to punish the offender or demand his punishment. According to natural justice the victim may himself punish the offender, but the organsation of society has delegated that natural right to the sovereign State. One of the main objects of the punishment is—continues the author [Grotius] of the "The Law of Peace and War" (Book 2, chapter 20)—to ensure that "the victim shall not in future suffer a similar infliction at the hands of the same person or at the hands of others…

Grotius also quotes an ancient authority who said that the punishment is necessary to "defend the honour or the authority of him who was hurt by the offence so that the failure to punish may not cause his degradation;"…and he adds that all that has been said of the jurisdiction applies to the infringement of all of his rights.…

* * *

Notwithstanding the difference of opinion as to the closeness of the requisite link, the very term "connection" or "linking point" is useful for the elucidation of the problem before us. The question is: What is the special connection between the State of Israel and the offences attributed to the accused, and whether this connection is sufficiently close to form a foundation for Israel's right of punishment as against the accused. This is no merely technical question but a wide and universal one; for the principles of international law are wide and universal principles and not articles in an express code.

33. When the question is presented in its widest form, as stated above, it seems to us that there can be no doubt as to what the answer will be. The "linking point" between Israel and the accused (and for that matter between Israel and any person accused of a crime against the Jewish people under this law) is striking and glaring in a "crime manifest against the Jewish people," a crime that postulates an intention to exterminate the Jewish people in whole or in part. Indeed, even without such specific definition—and it must be noted that the draft law had only defined "crimes against humanity" and "war crimes"…—there was a subsisting "linking point," seeing that most of the Nazi crimes of this kind were perpetrated against the Jewish people; but viewed in the light of the definition of "crime against the Jewish people," the legal position is clearer. The "crime against the Jewish people," as defined in the law, constitutes in effect an attempt to exterminate the Jewish people, or a partial extermination of the Jewish people. If there is an effective link (and not necessarily an identity) between the State of Israel and the Jewish people, then a crime intended to exterminate the Jewish people has a very striking connection with the State of Israel.

34. The connection between the State of Israel and the Jewish people needs no explanation. The State of Israel was established and recognized as the State of the Jews. The proclamation of Iyar 5, 5705 (14.5.48)…opens with the words: "It was in the land of Israel that the Jewish people was born," dwells on the history of the Jewish people from ancient times until the Second World War, refers to the Resolution of the United Nations Assembly of 29.11.47 which demands the establishment of a Jewish State in Eretz Israel, determines the "natural right of the Jewish people to be, like every other people, self-governing, in its sovereign State." It would appear that there is hardly need for any further proof of the very obvious connection between the Jewish people and the State of Israel: this is the sovereign State of the Jewish people.

Moreover, the proclamation of the establishment of the State of Israel makes mention of the very special tragic link between the Nazi crimes, which form the theme of the law in question, and the establishment of the State:

> "The recent holocaust which consumed millions of Jews in Europe, provides fresh and unmistakable proof of the necessity of solving the problem of the homelessness and lack of independence of the Jewish people by re-establishing the Jewish State which would fling open the gates of the fatherland to every Jew and would endow the Jewish people with equality of status within the family of nations.

> The remnants of the disastrous slaughter of the Nazis in Europe together with Jews from other lands persisted in making their way to the Land of Israel in defiance of all difficulties, obstacles and dangers. They have not ceased to claim their right to a life of dignity, freedom and honest toil in their ancestral home.

"In the Second World War the Jewish people in Palestine made its full contribution to the struggle of the Freedom and peace-loving nations against the
Nazi forces of evil. Its war effort and the blood of its soldiers entitled it to rank
with the peoples that made the covenant of the United Nations."

These words are no mere rhetoric, but historical facts, which international law does
not ignore.

In the light of the recognition by the United Nations of the right of the Jewish people
to establish their State, and in the light of the recognition of the established Jewish State
by the family of nations, the connection between the Jewish people and the State of Israel constitutes an integral part of the law of nations....

* * *

...[B]ut may a new State, at all, try crimes that were committed before it was established? The reply to this question was given in *Katz-Cohen v. Attorney-General*...
wherein it was decided that the Israel courts have full jurisdiction to try offences committed before the establishment of the State, and that "in spite of the changes in sovereignty there subsisted a continuity of law." "I cannot see," said President Smoira, "why
that community in the country against whom the crime was committed should not demand the punishment of the offender solely because that community is now governed
by the Government of Israel instead of the Mandatory Power." [The "Mandatory
Power" referred to here is Great Britain].... Had the Mandatory legislator enacted at the
time an extraterritorial law for the punishment of war criminals...it is clear that the Israel Court would have been competent to try under such law offences which were committed abroad prior to the establishment of the State. The principle of continuity also
applied to the power to legislate: the Israel legislator is empowered to amend or supplement the mandatory legislation retroactively, by enacting laws applicable to criminal
acts which were committed prior to the establishment of the State.

Indeed, this retroactive law is designed to supplement a gap in the laws of
Mandatory Palestine, and the interests protected by the law had existed also during the
period of the Jewish National Home. The Balfour Declaration [of November 2, 1917,
that favored the establishment in Palestine of a homeland for the Jewish people, issued
by the British government] and the Palestine Mandate given by the League of Nations to
Great Britain constituted an international recognition of the Jewish people...the historical link of the Jewish people with Eretz Israel and their right to re-establish their National Home in that country. The Jewish people has actually made use of that right, and
the National Home has grown and developed until it reached a sovereign status.... The
Jewish "Yishuv" in Palestine constituted during that period a "State-on-the way," as it
were, which reached in due time a sovereign status. The want of sovereignty made it
impossible for the Jewish "Yishuv" in the country to enact a criminal law against the
Nazi crimes at the time of the commission thereof, but these crimes were also directed
against that "Yishuv" who constituted an integral part of the Jewish people, and the enactment with retroactive application of the law in question by the State of Israel filled
the need which had already existed previously.

* * *

39. We should add that the well-known judgment of the International Court of Justice at The Hague in the "Lotus Case" [P. C. I. J., ser. A., No. 10 (1927)] has ruled that
the principle of territoriality does not limit the power of the State to try crimes and,
moreover, any argument against such power must point to a specific rule in international law which negates that power. We have not guided ourselves by this which de-

volves, so to speak, the "onus of proof" upon him who contends against such power, but have preferred to base ourselves on positive reasons which establish the jurisdiction of the State of Israel.

40. The second contention of Learned Counsel was that the trial in Israel of the accused following upon his capture in a foreign land is in conflict with international law, and takes away the jurisdiction of the Court.... He summed up his contentions by submitting that the Court ought not to lend its support to an illegal act of the State, and that in these circumstances the Court has no jurisdiction to try the accused.

* * *

41. It is an established rule of law that a person standing trial for an offence against the laws of the land may not oppose his being tried by reason of the illegality of his arrest or of the means whereby he was brought to the area of jurisdiction of the country. The courts in England, the United States and Israel have ruled continuously that the circumstances of the arrest and the mode of bringing of the accused into the area of the State have no relevance to his trial, and they consistently refused in all cases to enter into the examination of these circumstances...

* * *

47. An analysis of these judgments reveals that the doctrine is not confined to the infringement of municipal laws, as distinct from international laws, but the principle is general and comprehensive...

* * *

It is hardly necessary to state,...that the accused is not at all a "political" criminal; the reverse is the case: The crimes which are attributed to the accused have been condemned by all nations as "abhorrent crimes" whose perpetrators do not deserve any asylum, "political" or other.

* * *

...There is considerable foundation for the view that the grant by any country of asylum to a person accused of a major crime of this type and the prevention of his prosecution constitute an abuse of the sovereignty of the country contrary to its obligation under international law.

* * *

To sum up, the contention of the accused against the jurisdiction of the Court by reason of his abduction from Argentina is in essence nothing but a plea for immunity by a fugitive offender on the strength of the refuge given him by a sovereign State. That contention does not avail the accused for two reasons: (a) According to the established rule of law there is no immunity for a fugitive offender save in the one and only case where he has been extradited by the country of asylum to the country applying for extradition by reason of a specific offence, which is not the offence tried in his case. The accused was not surrendered to Israel by Argentina and the State of Israel is not bound by any agreement with Argentina to try the accused for any other specific offence with which the Court is concerned in this case.

(b) The rights of asylum and immunity belong to the country of asylum and not to the offender, and the accused cannot compel a foreign sovereign country to give him protection against its will. The accused was a wanted war criminal when he escaped to Argentina by concealing his true identity. It was only after he was captured and brought to Israel that his identity has been revealed, and after negotiations between the two

Governments, the Government of Argentina thereby refused definitely to give the accused any sort of protection. The accused has been brought to trial before a Court of a State which accuses him of grave offences against its laws. The accused has no immunity against this trial, and must stand his trial in accordance with the Charge Sheet.

For all the above-mentioned reasons we have dismissed the second contention of Counsel and his prayer to hear witnesses on this point...

---

3. *Eichmann v. The Attorney-General of the Government of Israel*
Supreme Court of Israel, May 29, 1962
136 *International Law Reports* 277

JUDGMENT

Per Curiam:

...[As] to the retroactivity argument, the principle *nullum crimen sine lege, nulla poena sine lege* [no crime without a law, no punishment without a law] in so far as it negates penal legislation with retroactive effect, has not yet become a rule of customary international law....

It is true that in many countries [it] has been embodied in the Constitution of the State or in its criminal code, because of the considerable moral value inherent in it, and in such countries the Court may not depart from it by one iota.... But this rule of affairs is not universal. Thus, in the United Kingdom...there is no constitutional limitation of the power of the legislature to enact its criminal laws with retrospective effect, and should it do so the court will have no power to invalidate them.... [I]n those countries...the moral value in the principle...has become legally effective only to the extent that the maxim constitutes a rule of the interpretation of statutes—where there is doubt as to the intention of the legislature the court is directed not to construe the criminal statute under its consideration as to include within its purview an act that was committed prior to its enactment....

Therefore, if it is [contended] that we must apply international law as it is, and not as it ought to be from the moral point of view, then we must reply that precisely from a legal point of view there is no such provision in it; it follows automatically that the principle cannot be deemed to be part of the Israel municipal law by virtue of international law, but that the extent of its application in this country is the same as in England.

...[As] to the contention [that] the enactment of a criminal law applicable to an act committed in a foreign country by a foreign national conflicts with the principle of territorial sovereignty, here too we must hold that there is no such rule in international customary law.... This is established by the Judgment of the [Permanent Court of International Justice]...in the *Lotus* case.... It was held that the principle of territorial sovereignty merely requires that the State exercise its power to punish within its own borders, not outside them; that subject to this restriction every State may exercise a wide discretion as to the application of its laws and the jurisdiction of its courts in respect of acts committed outside the State; and that only in so far as it is possible to point to a specific rule prohibiting the exercise of this discretion...is a State prevented from exercising it. That view was based on the following two grounds: (1) It is precisely the conception of State sovereignty which demands the preclusion of any presumption that there is a restriction on its independence; (2) Even if it is true that the principle of the territorial character of criminal law is firmly established in various States, it is no less true that in almost all of such States criminal jurisdiction has been extended...so as to embrace offences committed outside its territory....

...[O]n the question of the jurisdiction of a State to punish persons who are not its nationals for acts committed beyond its borders, there is as yet no international accord....

It follows that in the absence of general agreement as to the existence of [such a] rule of international law,...there is, again, no escape from the conclusion that it cannot be deemed to be embodied in Israel municipal law, and therefore on that ground too, its contention fails.

* * *

There is no *prohibition* whatever by international law of the enactment of the law of 1950, [Nazis and Nazi Collaborators (Punishment) Law] either because it created *ex post facto* offences or because such offences are of an extraterritorial character.... [But] these contentions are unjustifiable even from a positive approach, namely, that when enacting the Law the Knesset only sought to apply the principle of international law and to realize its objections....

The crimes created by the Law and of which the appellant was convicted must be deemed today to have always borne the stamps of international crimes, banned by international law and entailing individual criminal liability. It is the particular universal character of these crimes that vests in each State the power to try and punish any one who assisted in their commission....

...As is well known, the rules of the law of nations are not derived solely from international treaties and crystallized international usage. In the absence of a supreme legislative authority and international codes the process of its evolution resembles that of the common law,...its rules are established from case to case, by analogy with the rules embodied in treaties and in international custom, on the basis of the "general principles of law recognized by civilised nations."... [C]ustomary international law is never stagnant, but is rather in a process of constant growth....

...[In relation to] the features which identify crimes that have long been recognized by customary international law...they constitute acts which damage vital international interests; they impair the foundations and security of the international community; they violate universal moral values and humanitarian principles which are at the root of the systems of the criminal law adopted by civilised nations. The underlying principle in international law that governs such crimes is that the individual who has committed any of them and who, at the time of his act, may be presumed to have had a thorough understanding of its heinous nature, must account in law for his behaviour. It is true that international law does not establish explicit and graduated criminal sanctions; that there is not as yet in existence either an International Criminal Court, or international machinery for the imposition of punishment. But, for the time being, international law surmounts these difficulties...by authorizing the countries of the world to mete out punishment for the violation of its provisions. This they do by enforcing these provisions either directly or by virtue of the municipal legislation which has adopted and integrated them....

* * *

In view of the characteristic traits of international crimes...and the organic development of the law of nations—a development that advances from case to case under the impact of the humane sentiments common to civilised nations, and under the pressure of the needs that are vital for the survival of mankind and for ensuring the stability of the world order—it definitely cannot be said that when the Charter of the Nuremberg International Military Tribunal was signed and the categories of "war crimes" and "crimes against humanity" were defined in it, this merely amounted to an act of legislation by the victorious countries....

...[T]he interest in preventing and imposing punishment for acts comprised in the category in question—especially when they were perpetrated on a very large scale—must necessarily extend beyond the borders of the State to which the perpetrators belong and which evinced tolerance or encouragement of their outrages; for such acts can undermine the foundations of the international community as a whole and impair its very stability....

If we are to regard customary international law as a developing progressive system, the criticism becomes devoid of value.... [E]ver since the Nuremberg Tribunal decided this question, that very decision must be seen as a judicial act which establishes a "precedent" defining the rule of international law. In any event, it would be unseemly for any other court to disregard such a rule and not to follow it....

If there was any doubt as to this appraisal of the "Nuremberg Principles" as principles that have formed part of customary international law "since time immemorial," such doubt has been removed by...the United Nations Resolution on the Affirmation of the Principles of International Law recognized by the Charter and Judgment of the Nuremberg Tribunal and that affirming that Genocide is a crime under international law...

...[T]he crimes established in the Law of 1950...must be seen today as acts that have always been forbidden by customary international law—acts which are of a "universal" criminal character and entail individual criminal responsibility.... [T]he enactment of the Law was not, from the point of view of international law, a legislative act that conflicted with the principle *nulla poena* or the operation of which was retroactive, but rather one by which the Knesset gave effect to international law and its objectives....

...[I]t is the universal character of the crimes in question which vests in every State the power to try those who participated in the preparation of such crimes, and to punish them...

One of the principles whereby States assume, in one degree or another, the power to try and punish a person for an offence he has committed is the principle of universality. Its meaning is, in essence, that the power is vested in every State regardless of the fact that the offence was committed outside its territory by a person who did not belong to it, provided he is in its custody at the time he is brought to trial. This principle has wide support and is universally acknowledged with respect to the offence of piracy *jure gentium*....

* * *

...[T] here is full justification for applying here the principle of universal jurisdiction since the international character of the "crimes against humanity" (in the wide meaning of the term) is, in this case, not in doubt, and the unprecedented extent of their injurious and murderous effect is not open to dispute at the present day....

[I]t was not the recognition of the universal jurisdiction to try and punish the person who committed "piracy" that justified the viewing of such an act as an international crime *sui generis*, but it was the agreed vital interest of the international community that justified the exercise of the jurisdiction in question....

* * *

We have also taken into consideration the possible desire of other countries to try the appellant in so far as the crimes...were committed in those countries or their evil effects were felt there.... But...we have not heard of a single protest by any of these countries against conducting the trial in Israel.... What is more, it is precisely the fact that the crimes...and their effects have extended to numerous countries that empties the territorial principle of its content in the present case, and justifies Israel in assuming criminal jurisdiction by virtue of the "universal" principle....

[In regard to Article 6 of the Genocide Convention regarding territorial boundaries, the Court went on to say]: Article 6 imposes upon the parties contractual obligations with future effect...obligations which bind them to prosecute for crimes of "genocide" which will be committed within their territories in the future. The obligation, however, has nothing to do with the universal *power* vested in every State to prosecute for crimes of this type committed in the past—a power which is based on *customary* international law.... The State of Israel was entitled, pursuant to the principle of universal jurisdiction and acting in the capacity of guardian of international law and agent for its enforcement, to try the appellant. This being so, it is immaterial that the State of Israel did not exist at the time the offences were committed....

* * *

...The appellant is a "fugitive from justice" from the point of view of the law of nations, since the crimes that were attributed to him are of an *international* character and have been condemned publicly by the civilised world...; therefore, by virtue of the principle of universal jurisdiction, every country has the right to try him. This jurisdiction was automatically vested in the State of Israel on its establishment in 1948 as a sovereign State. Therefore, in bringing the appellant to trial, it functioned as an organ of international law and acted to enforce the provisions thereof through its own law. Consequently, it is immaterial that the crimes in question were committed...when the State of Israel did not exist, and outside its territory.... The moment it is admitted that the State of Israel possesses criminal jurisdiction both according to local law and according to the law of nations, it must also be conceded that the Court is not bound to investigate the manner and legality of the...detention.... [The Court's opinion regarding "acts of State" and the "superior orders" defense are omitted].

Appeal dismissed.

---

4. Nicholas N. Kittrie, "A Post Mortem of the Eichmann Case—The Lessons for International Law"

58 *Journal of Criminal Law, Criminology and Police Science* 16; 18–26 (1964)
Reprinted by Special Permission of Northwestern University School of Law,
Journal of Criminal Law, Criminology and Police Science. © 1964

Two seconds before midnight, on May 30, 1962, a few short hours after his petition to the President of Israel for clemency was denied, Adolf Eichmann was hanged. Within hours, his body having been cremated pursuant to his own request, the ashes were taken up into the air by a military airplane and were spread upon the Mediterranean. Thus more than two years after his clandestine capture in Argentina and following a four-month televised trial, in which 111 surviving witnesses testified for the prosecution, came an end to the Third Reich's leading expert on the Final Solution to the Jewish Problem. The story of Eichmann's capture, Argentina's protest, the debate in the United Nations, the announcement of the trial, the terrible drama told in the courtroom... [made] this case one of the best recorded in the annals of world law.

* * *

Apparently there is nothing in international law that would prohibit an exercise of national jurisdiction following an illegal capture. In its final judgment the Israeli court in the Eichmann case discussed British and American decisions relating to this issue and indicated that Palestinian case law, which constitutes precedent for Israel, has adopted the unequivocal American view that a court may not inquire into the manner by which a prisoner was brought before it. Although legally the Israeli court's authority over Eichmann could not be challenged, a bad taste of justice achieved through an unlawful act still remained with those who firmly believe that the future of the world depends upon nations conforming in all instances with higher rules of international conduct. Others less sensitive to procedural proprieties have argued that the abduction was justified by the nature and extent of the crimes charged and by the impossibility of extradition of Nazis from Argentina. Indeed, they assert that in some extreme situations the strict standards of positive law must yield to the natural and moral law, and that the situation in this case called for a law akin to the natural law of self-defense.

* * *

To lawyers and students of international law, one of the most interesting aspects of the Eichmann case was the question of the jurisdiction of the Israeli court to try him for crimes committed outside the State of Israel and, indeed, before the state came into being. The question of jurisdiction can be divided into two separate phases: the first concerns the retroactive nature of Israel's 1950 law which provides for the punishment of Nazis and Nazi collaborators, the second relates to the extraterritorial jurisdiction of the Israeli court to try a person for crimes committed outside the national boundaries.

The legal literature dealing with the Eichmann trial revolves primarily around these points. Both the opinion of the District Court which tried Eichmann and the Supreme Court of Israel which heard the appeal devoted considerable space to the question of jurisdiction. It should be stated at the outset, however, that the question of jurisdiction was never properly before the Israeli courts. Israel does not have a written constitution. Since Israel's courts conform generally to the British judicial tradition, the American concept of judicial review is unknown. Consequently, once Israel's legislature has enacted statutes authorizing the courts to try and punish certain offenses, it is beyond the power of the courts to question the validity of such legislation. Lacking the power to overturn the law under which Eichmann was tried, the Israeli court, nevertheless, dealt with the issue quite directly, realizing that the manner of its resolution of the jurisdictional issue will have a bearing not only upon world opinion but also upon the development of Israel's domestic law and the growth of international law.

* * *

The statute under which Eichmann was tried was similar in scope to the provisions of the multi-national agreement establishing the International Military Tribunal at Nuremberg. In both instances, punishment was authorized for crimes hitherto ill-defined in international law "war crime," "crime against humanity," "crime against peace." In both instances, the specific laws under which the culprits were tried were not in effect at the time the crimes were committed. The Nuremberg court and, subsequently, the United Nations General Assembly in its affirmation of the Charter and judgment of the tribunal gave broad international recognition to the legality of such ex post facto legislation. A substantial school of legal scholars subscribes to the view that a penal statute need not be condemned merely because of its retroactive effect, as long as the crime penalized was obviously and undeniably prohibited under the laws of most civilized nations. It is the rationale of this position that in such cases "the law is retroactive in form, not in substance," and the punishment is not therefore, liberally speaking, retroactive. The validity of the law has also been defended on the ground that the terrible crimes of the Nazis required unusual penal provisions, "for no sane legislator *could* have contemplated such crime to be even possible and no tribunal could have been provided for its adjudication in advance." A compelling defense [by Woetzel] of the justice meted out at the Nuremberg trial states:

> "[I]f the act was a heinous violation of international law; if it was recognisable as such to the individual; if he could reasonably be expected to know that it was punishable; and if he intended to do the thing he did which was in violation of his duties and obligations under international law...there could be no violation of the maximum *nullum crimen nulla poena* in such a case."

* * *

It needs to be stressed that there is in actuality no binding prohibition in international law against retroactive criminal statutes in domestic law.... A nation enacting ex post facto laws will therefore not be in violation of positive international law, despite the fact that it may be condemned by world public opinion. Whether an international law statute, which the Nuremberg Charter may have been, providing retroactive penalties is illegal may be another question. It is noteworthy that regardless of its multi-national character, the Nuremberg Tribunal was established by the occupation forces then exercising sovereignty over Germany, and its jurisdiction indeed was claimed under both international law and domestic law. The Israeli court was, on the other hand, merely exercising its powers under domestic law. In both instances the tribunals were looking to the legal principles of other civilized nations and to international law for justification, moral support, permissive authority and precedent. It is in this light that the retroactive jurisdiction of the Nuremberg and Eichmann tribunals must be judged.

The Nuremberg Charter claimed to derive permissive authority from the General Pact for the Renunciation of War, popularly known as the Kellogg-Briand Pact, which was signed at Paris on August 27, 1928, and prohibited resort to war. Yet the Pact failed to proscribe criminal penalties for its violators. The Israeli court, similarly, based much of its claim for authority upon international enactments and precedent which, although dating prior to the adoption of the Israeli law, were nevertheless not effectuated until after the crimes were committed. Indeed, it is interesting to note that the acts with which Adolph Eichmann was charged may fall within the prohibition of positive international law as it is now recognized. "War crime" and "crime against humanity" have been specifically defined in the Charter annexed to the August 8, 1945, Agreement made in London among the United Kingdom, the United States, France and the USSR establishing the International Tribunal at Nuremberg. The principles of law embodied in the Charter and in the judgment of the Tribunal were affirmed as international law by a unanimous resolution of the United Nations General Assembly on December 11, 1946. Eichmann's terrible record of violence and atrocities also falls within the definition of genocide as contained in the United Nations Resolution on the Prevention and Punishment of the Crime of Genocide and in the text of the Convention adopted by the General Assembly on December 9, 1948.

* * *

...Despite the Jerusalem District Court's reiteration that there is not "any taint of *ex post facto*-ism in the law of murder*," still, the fear remains of abuses that could be made in the name of international law. There is always the fear that a victorious nation or group of nations will join together to define as criminal conduct such activities as they consider contrary to their own interests. There is always the fear that the winner may not be a nation with "right motives" but one with "wrong motives." The only solution is apparently in the drafting of an international code under which, and only under which, punishment is to be meted out—whether by domestic or international tribunals.

* * *

Shortly after Eichmann's capture, Brigadier General Telford Taylor, who previously served as a chief prosecutor at Nuremberg, voiced his concern that trying Eichmann in Israel, rather than in Germany, would be contrary to the traditions of the law. It was General Taylor's position that under the generally accepted principles of law a man is entitled to be tried where his offense is charged to have been committed, and he proceeded further to substantiate his view by arguing that "This right is guaranteed in the 6th Amendment to the Constitution and its origin antedates the Magna Charta where it is also found." Other writers have also concerned themselves with the question of Israel's jurisdiction to try Eichmann for crimes committed elsewhere, since the jurisdiction of nations is limited in cases to crimes committed within their national boundaries. Several exceptions have, however, been recognized. Nations, under a theory described as the "principle of active personality" or "nationality principle," often assume jurisdiction over criminal acts performed by their nationals in foreign countries. Likewise, the right of national jurisdiction has been recognized, under a theory described as the "principle of passive personality," in cases where crimes, although committed outside the national territory affected citizens of the trying nation. Also given recognition is the "principle of real protection" or "protective theory," permitting national jurisdiction in cases of crimes committed abroad against the most essential interest of the state. None of these specific exceptions applies in the case of Eichmann. The crimes were committed outside the territory of Israel, and, strictly speaking, the vital interests of the State of Israel, not being yet in existence, could not have been directly at stake.

Eichmann's council argued this point. He reiterated that there was an absence of a linking point between the crimes and Israel because territoriality was the only true basis of jurisdiction. The Israeli trial court responded vigorously to the suggestion that jurisdiction lay only in the countries of Europe where the crimes were committed....

* * *

The court could not understand anybody's failing to see the connection between Israel and the Nazi holocaust. "The connection between the State of Israel and the Jewish people needs no explanation," the court concluded.

Whether of not Israel's extraterritorial Nazi Punishment Law conforms with the standards of American constitutional law, its provisions are not contrary to the general legal practices in the world. There appears to exist no rule of international law governing the penal jurisdiction of national courts.

* * *

...International law has long recognized certain crimes as being universally reprehensible and has marked the offenders as *hostes generis humani* (enemies of the human race) and subject to trial any place. Piracy has been accorded this special status, both because piracy is everywhere made a crime and because piracy is often committed on the high seas over which no nation has jurisdiction. The punishment of brigands, like-wise, has been said to come within the rule of universality....

* * *

Could the same principle be extended to other crimes which are generally recog-nized? Could the principle be extended whenever a crime is committed in a territory or a country where no adequate judicial system is in existence—as was the case with Nazi Germany?

* * *

In asserting jurisdiction over Eichmann's crime, Israel was, in fact, not merely argu-ing for the extension of the rule of universality, but also claiming to have derived its right, at least in part, from its special relationship to a large portion of the victims—those of the Jewish heritage. Israel's court stressed that Israel's right to represent Jews who had no nationality or who were the victims of Nazi oppression was recognized by the Federal Republic of Germany in the 1952 Reparation Agreement between Israel and West Germany.... Indeed, one of the subtle thrusts of the judgment seems to be the as-sertion of Israel's sovereignty and right to protect the legal rights of Jewish people wher-ever they may be found.

* * *

It has long been recognized that the individual is not generally subject to interna-tional law. International law pertains to the rights and duties of nations or sovereigns, and it is only through the sovereign that the individual becomes indirectly involved.... Yet both in the Nuremberg Tribunal and in the Eichmann case individuals were on trial for what was commonly described as violations of international law. At Nuremberg a multi-national tribunal was asserting its jurisdiction under international law. In the Jerusalem courtroom it was a national tribunal dispensing domestic justice according to a law described to have been derived from the provisions of the law of nations. In both instances the motivators or active participants in the Third Reich's national policy were put on trial as individuals.

* * *

The Eichmann case will apparently serve further to establish the responsibility of the individual in international criminal law.... Obviously, there is a need for the exten-sion of international criminal law to individuals. The Nuremberg Tribunal correctly observed:

> "Crimes against international law are committed by men, not by abstract enti-ties, and only by punishing individuals who commit such crimes can the provi-sions of international law be enforced....

But however desirable it may be to see the ushering in of a system of international law which would protect the individual against the injustices of foreign powers as well as of his own sovereign, it is dubious whether this can be properly accomplished by permit-ting one nation to sit in judgment in an ad hoc fashion on actions performed under the authority of another nation. If certain rights of individuals are to be protected and cer-tain standards of national conduct are to be enforced, it is essential that these rights and standards be clearly and positively defined by the international community, to make certain that political interests and national prejudices do not take the place of interna-tional law.

———

5. *The State v. Schumann*

Ghana, Court of Appeal, Accra
November 4, 1966
39 *International Law Reports* 433

[The Federal Republic of Germany requested the Government of Ghana to extradite Dr. Horst Schumann on a charge of murder. The request was based on allegations that the defendant was involved in the deaths of more than 30,000 individuals who were patients in mental institutions located within two concentration camps in the Third Reich, along with the killing of a number of Jews at Auschwitz between 1942 and 1944 during experiments involving mass sterilization. Schumann had been a resident of Ghana since 1959 and was employed as a government Medical Officer in the country. He was arrested and appeared before a District Magistrate in Accra, who ordered him imprisoned to await surrender by Ghana to the Federal Republic of Germany under an extradition act in force between West Germany and Ghana. Schumann applied for a writ of habeas corpus to the High Court of Ghana on the grounds, among others, that the offense for which his extradition was requested was "political" in nature and thus was not extraditable under the Extradition Act of 1960. The High Court dismissed Shumann's application for habeas corpus and he now appeals to the Court of Appeal].

AKUFO-ADDO, C. J.: This is an appeal from the decision of the High Court, Accra, refusing to grant an application for a writ of Habeas Corpus made by the appellant, Dr. Horst Schumann, a German national resident in Ghana and who was on 25 August 1966 committed to Ussher Fort Prison to await orders for his extradition to the Federal Republic of West Germany to stand trial on a charge of murder.

The charge of murder brought against the appellant by the Federal Republic of West Germany arose out of the brutal excesses of the Nazi regime in the period of World War II in furthering their political ideology which called for, among other things, the extermination of the Jewish race.

The appellant has been resident in this country since 1959 and until 6 March 1966 has been in the employment of the Government as a Medical Officer. He was arrested on a Warrant issued by the District Magistrate, Accra, upon an order of the Government of Ghana made at the request of the Federal Republic of West Germany and brought before the said District Magistrate under the provisions of the Extradition Act, 1960,...

The appellant applied to the High Court, Accra, for the issue of a writ of Habeas Corpus directed to the Assistant Director (who is the Keeper) of the Ussher Fort Prison for his release on the ground that his committal to prison by the District Magistrate was wrong in law, that is, in breach of the requirements of the Extradition Act, 1960, and therefore his incarceration consequent upon that committal was unlawful. The appellant relied on a number of grounds in support of his application.... They are: (1) that the appellant was not given opportunity to tender evidence to prove that the offence wherewith he was charged was of a political character as he was by law entitled to do under section 9(2) of the Extradition Act, 1960; (2) that the appearance in the Magistrates' Court of a State Attorney representing the Government of the Federal Republic of West Germany offended against natural justice and rendered the proceedings from the viewpoint of the appellant "unfair and oppressive"; (3) that the charge was bad for duplicity; and (4) that there was not sufficient evidence before the Magistrate on which to find a *prima facie* case against the appellant.

The High Court heard the application on 16 September 1966, and found against the appellant on all points raised by him. That Court therefore dismissed the application.

In this Court the appellant's counsel has advanced practically the same points as he did in the Court below, with the addition of a further ground alleging that the statements of the various witnesses in West Germany which formed the main evidence of the West German Government were unsworn and their admission as evidence rendered the proceedings a nullity. This latest point may be disposed of in a few words. Extradition proceedings are by our law governed by the same principles and rules of procedure as committal proceedings in an indictable offence...and the law does not require that committal proceedings shall be based on sworn statements of witnesses...

* * *

The only complaint of the appellant's counsel which has engaged our serious attention is the one alleging that the appellant's counsel was not given the opportunity to call evidence...to prove that the offence charged was of a political character. And this because, while we do not sit on appeal from the findings of fact by the Magistrate, the question of the political character of the offence in extradition proceedings is one that goes to the Magistrate's jurisdiction over the entire matter. If therefore there are any facts that go to challenge the Magistrate's jurisdiction, it becomes, in our view, our duty even at this state to ascertain those facts.

* * *

As the question of the political character of the offence involved went to the very foundation of the Magistrate's jurisdiction...and since the Magistrate's decision that the offence was not of a political character was subject to review on Habeas Corpus..., we thought it desirable that we should give the appellant the opportunity to adduce evidence before us to prove his contention that the offence was of a political character. We therefore on 26 October 1966, on our own motion, granted the appellant leave to tender the evidence aforesaid, such evidence to include the appellant's own testimony if he so wished.... The appellant gave evidence himself and called no other witnesses nor tendered any other evidence.

The appellant's evidence, in sum, was that he committed the acts that form the basis of the charge of murder, but that he did so upon the specific command of Hitler, the Head of the German State and Government; that it was explained to him that the acts, namely, the killing of incurable lunatics and the sterilization of Jews were in accordance with Nazi political ideology which expressed itself in the notorious "euthanasia programme" and "the final solution of the Jewish problem," a euphemism for the total extermination of the Jewish race "not only," in the words of the appellant, "from Germany, but also from Europe..."; that at the time he committed the acts he believed he was doing the right thing, first, because he believed in obedience to the order of Hitler, and secondly, because he believed in the righteousness of the Nazi ideology, and finally, that he risked death or some severe punishment if he did not obey Hitler's orders.

Upon this evidence appellant's counsel argued that the offence was one of a political character, for the appellant's evidence summarized above contained, so counsel submitted, all the elements necessary to constitute the offence one of a political character. The offence, counsel submitted, was therefore not extraditable. [The Court then cites four English cases relating to the question of the "political character" of an offense and the principles deduced by that line of precedent. The opinion then notes]: that none of the facts stated in appellant's evidence fell within these principles.... [T]o constitute an offence of a political nature there must be some political disturbance or upheaval or there must be some physical struggle between two opposing political parties for the mastery of the government of the country, and that the crime in question must have been committed in furtherance of that disturbance or struggle....

It is clear beyond argument that the appellant's case is not covered by these principles. It is not his case that the poor helpless lunatics at the Munsungen Asylum or the Jews at Auschwitz had rebelled against the Nazi ideology and had thereby created some form of political disturbance which needed quelling, nor indeed does he claim to have committed the offence charged with a view to avoiding political persecution or prosecution.

The fact, however, that the appellant cannot bring his case within the principles enunciated...would not, at any rate in theory, seem to conclude the matter against him, for I do not think that the principles embodied in these [English] cases can be regarded as exhausting the category of "political crimes" for purposes of extradition. The appellant, however, has not put forward for consideration any other principle by which the political character of his acts may be ascertained, and I can think of no principle that places his acts in this category.

The appellant's case, as is clear from his evidence and also from his counsel's submissions, rests essentially on two grounds. First, that he acted in obedience to superior orders, that is, orders from the State, and his acts were in effect "acts of State" and that, therefore, he as an individual could not be punished for them; and, secondly, that the acts which constituted the offence with which he was charged were at the time of their commission in Germany not punishable at law.

The appellant must be particularly aware of the invalidity of these defences, for he said in his evidence before us that he escaped from Germany in 1951 to avoid being tried for his acts, because, although he had these defences to put up, the German courts would not accept them.

These defences appear to have been the stock defences of almost all the Nazi criminals in the numerous trials that followed in the wake of World War II, including the famous trials by the International Military Tribunal at Nuremberg. Needless to say, these defences have invariably been rejected. The principle that an official of a State cannot hide his crimes behind the façade of the theory of "Act of State" is too well established to require any further elaboration.

* * *

On the contention that the appellant's acts were at the time of their commission not punishable in Germany, I can only refer to and adopt, with respect, a dictum contained in the Judgment...of the District Court of Jerusalem in the case of *The Attorney-General of the Government of Israel v. Adolf Eichmann*, which is as follows:

"The courts in Germany, too, have rejected the contention that the crimes of the Nazis were not prohibited at the time and that their perpetrators did not have the requisite criminal intent. The judgment of the Supreme Federal Tribunal of January 29, 1952...declares that the expulsion of the Jews, the object of which was the death of the deportees, was a continuous crime of murder committed by the principal planners and executants, a matter of which all other executants must have been conscious, since it cannot be accepted that they were unaware of the basic principles on which human society is based and which are the common legacy of all civilized nations."

After referring to another judgment in 1960 of the German Supreme Federal Tribunal which dealt with the murder of mentally deranged persons on the order of Hitler, the victim goes on to say:

"…The judgment says…that in 1940 at the latest, it was clear to every person not too naïve, and certainly to all who were part of the leadership establishment, that the Nazi regime did not shrink from the commission of crimes, and that whoever took part in these crimes could not argue that he had mistakenly assumed that a forbidden act was permissible, when these crimes violated basic principles of the rule of law."

Moreover, we have it on record from the evidence of Dr. Jose Fabry, an official of the Ministry of Justice in West Germany and formerly a Public Prosecutor, that murder has always been a crime in Germany and it was a crime during the entire period of the Nazi regime. The fact that for political reasons murder of the type with which the appellant is charged was not punishable during the Nazi regime does not by any reason render its prosecution now unlawful. I am unable to accept as tenable any of the grounds advanced by the appellant's counsel in support of his submission that the offence involved in these proceedings is of a political character.

The offence of murder with which the appellant is charged is, having full regard to all the circumstances in which the offence was committed, no more of a political character than the offence of, say, robbery with violence or burglary committed by a political party activist in a desperate bid to seek means of replenishing the dwindling coffers of his political party.

Counsel for the appellant complains that the presence of a State Attorney prosecuting, in effect, on behalf of the West German Government offended against principles of International Law and Practice and that the proceedings at the Magistrate's Court were, for that reason, "unfair and oppressive" and that these proceedings should therefore be declared a nullity. It is enough to say that, according to the law of this country, criminal proceedings such as these proceedings could only be initiated either by or on behalf of the Attorney-General, that is, the State is the prosecutor, and there seems to be no reason why the State should not be represented by a State Attorney. Counsel has not been able to refer us to any authority which makes such a representation bad in law, nor has he been able to satisfy us how his client was in any way prejudiced.

* * *

I am satisfied that there was ample evidence before the Magistrate to justify his findings, and having decided that the offence with which the appellant is charged is not of a political character, it only remains for me to dismiss the appeal.

The appeal is accordingly dismissed. The appellant shall continue to remain in prison until his surrender by the National Liberation Council.

CRABBE, J. A.: I agree that this appeal should be dismissed and desire to make some few observations on the main points raised in the appeal.

* * *

In this appeal it is not disputed that the offence for which extradition is sought is murder,…. The charge against the appellant is therefore *prima facie* extraditable…. The following facts proved before the District Magistrate and upon which the committal order was founded are culled from his ruling:

"The particulars of the charges are that from 1939 to 1941, the accused acting in concert with others, and as director of the killing institutions at Grafeneck and Sonnenstein maliciously killed at least 30,000 human beings, inmates of medical establishments in respective concentration camps. Again, from 1942 till 1944 the accused, in common with others, killed a large number of prisoners in the concentration camp at Auschwitz by unskillful performance of X-ray-therapy and operations in experiments for finding out a quick and simple method suitable for mass-sterilization.

"Exhibit 'B1' also reveals that shortly before the outbreak of World War II Hitler gave the order to his escort physician and others to organize the extermination of the 'Lebensunwerten Lebens' ('of life unworthy to live') according to the National-Socialist Point of View. Various types of patients in medical establishments fell in this class for extermination. The mass killings of about 30,000 human beings for which the accused is sought form part of the so-called mercy killing. It is further alleged that in 1941 the then Reich Leader S. S. Himmler and his staff were occupied with the question of prevention of propagation of the 'Erbuntuchtigen' ('incapable of inheriting') in accordance with National-Socialist or Nazi ideology. In the foreground stood first of all the 'elimination' of the entire Jewish population in Germany and in the territories occupied by the German armed forces. A programme for mass sterilization was worked out and experiments in Rontgen castration were carried out. Material for Rontgen castration was installed at Auschwitz concentration camp and the accused was induced to experiment on both males and females. There is abundant evidence in the depositions of the accused's active participation in the mass killings in the Gas Chamber and also of the fatal experiments he carried out, the details of which are blood-chilling."

* * *

The weight of authority inclines me to the view that a crime can be classified as a political offence if it is committed in the course of a dispute, not necessarily a civil commotion, between the ruling part in the State, on the one hand, and another political party or movement within the State, on the other hand, with the view solely to advance the cause or further the purpose of the political party or movement concerned.

* * *

It is clear, as the evidence seems to me, that the dominant motive of the appellant in killing these thousands of lunatics and Jews was anything but political. There was no political rivalry in Nazi Germany, and the appellant has not contended that fear of prosecution for a political offence or political persecution led him to commit the offences with which he is charged.... In my judgment the appellant is a "fugitive from justice" and must be surrendered for trial.

For the above reasons I would, therefore, dismiss the appeal.

[Another even more notorious Nazi and the last surviving member of Adolf Hitler's inner circle was Richard Rudolf Hess. Born in 1894 in Alexandria, Egypt, Hess rose to the top ranks in the National Socialist hierarchy and served as Deputy Führer from 1933 to 1941. In a bizarre turn of events in that latter year, Hess flew a specially-equipped Messerschmidt alone to England, apparently on a self-styled mission to promote peace between the Third Reich and Great Britain. His aircraft eventually gave out of fuel over Scotland and he managed to parachute to safety with only minor injuries. He was arrested and spent the duration of World War II in a British prison. After the conclusion of the war in Europe, Hess was taken to Nuremberg to stand trial as a major war criminal. The IMT-Nuremberg convicted Hess of "crimes against peace" and sentenced him to life imprisonment. From 1947 to the date of the following case in 1980, and after, Hess was held captive in the Allied Military Prison at Spandau-Berlin, an institution established and operated pursuant to arrangements between the four victorious Powers that occupied Germany for some years after her defeat in May, 1945. In 1952, the Federal Republic of Germany (West Germany) assumed the costs of running Spandau Prison. Spandau at one time held a total of seven Nazis who had been sentenced to prison terms by the IMT-Nuremberg. All except Rudolf Hess had been released by 1966. The Soviet Union, however, refused to even consider any suggestion that Hess be released, regardless of his personal circumstances. Nonetheless, Hess, his family and various support groups made repeated attempts to secure his freedom. These entreaties were made not only to the government of the Federal Republic, but also to the European Commission of Human Rights and to the Secretary-General of the United Nations. All were unsuccessful. In June, 1977, Hess initiated proceedings before a West German administrative court seeking a ruling requiring the Federal Republic of Germany to take more aggressive diplomatic steps to secure his release. That application was rejected. A further appeal taken to the West German Federal Administrative Court was pending at the time of the case reported below.

A constitutional complaint was then lodged by the complainant in the Federal Constitutional Court against the Federal Republic of Germany, seeking sundry relief, chief among which included (1) a plea to persuade the former Four Occupation Powers, especially the U.S.S.R., to agree to immediately release Hess on humanitarian grounds; (2) to refer complainant's case to the International Court of Justice at The Hague seeking to have that tribunal declare his confinement to be in violation of Article 107 of the United Nation's Charter; and (3) to rule that the failure of the West German Federal Administrative Court to fix a date certain for hearing his appeal violated complainant's constitutional right to effective judicial protection. What follows are excerpts from the judgment handed down by the West German Federal Constitutional Court].

---

6. *Rudolf Hess v. Federal Republic of Germany*
Federal Constitutional Court
Bundesnerfassungsgericht
December 16, 1980
90 *International Law Reports* 387

The Complainant was born in 1894 and from 1933 onwards was the "Deputy to the Führer of the National Socialist Party" and *Reichminister* without Portfolio. In May 1941 he flew to Scotland as "a parliamentarian acting on his own initiative" in order to promote a peaceful understanding between the German Reich and the United Kingdom. He was arrested there and, in October 1945, the British Government sent him to Nuremberg to be tried before the International Military Tribunal.

* * *

By a decision of 30 September and 1 October 1946, the Tribunal found the Complainant guilty of crimes against peace...and sentenced him to life imprisonment. He was acquitted of war crimes...and crimes against humanity.

For the enforcement of the decision of the Tribunal, the Allied Kommandatura for Berlin established, in accordance with the order of the Control Council for Germany, an Allied Prison at Spandau-Berlin. Supreme executive authority over the Prison was vested in the Allied Kommandatura itself. The quadripartite administration and supervision of the prison continued notwithstanding the withdrawal of the Soviet representative from the Kommandatura on 1 July 1948. Day-to-day administration of the prison remains as before in the hands of four governors, each of whom is the delegate of one of the four Occupying Powers in Berlin.

The Complainant was transferred to the Allied Prison in Spandau in July 1947 and has been imprisoned there ever since. Following the release of his last fellow prisoner on 1 October 1966, the Complainant is now the only inmate in the prison. His family members, his counsel and the "Support Group for the Release of Rudolf Hess," established in 1967 has made numerous, so far unsuccessful, applications to the authorities to obtain his release. An application by the wife of the Complainant against the United Kingdom made to the European Commission of Human Rights was declared inadmissible. A decision has apparently so far not been made on an application made by the Complainant in his own name to the Commission on 23 July 1979.

* * *

In June 1977 the Complainant instituted proceedings before the Administrative Court...of Cologne against the Federal Republic of Germany. He sought a ruling with regard to the duty of the Federal Republic of Germany to take specific diplomatic steps to obtain his immediate release. The Administrative Court rejected the application by a decision of 19 December 1977...

The Complainant appealed against the judgment of the Administrative Court. By a decision of 14 May 1979...the Superior Administrative Court...for the *Land* [State] of North Rhine-Westphalia dismissed the appeal. Leave to appeal further was granted...

The Federal Administrative Court...has not yet rendered a decision on the appeal against the judgment of the Superior Administrative Court...

By his constitutional complaint, the Complainant asks this Court:

I. To quash the judgment of the Superior Administrative Court...for the *Land* of North Rhine-Westphalia of 14 May 1979 and to order the Federal Republic of Germany, through its organs the Federal President, the Federal Chancellor, the Federal minister for Foreign Affairs and the Federal Minister for Justice:

(1) To clarify and publicize the fact that the continued detention of the claimant, Rudolf Hess, who is eighty-six years old and has already been imprisoned for thirty-eight years, of which the last thirteen have been in isolation, violates the binding rules of international law and fundamental human rights law;

(2) To take all possible initiatives to persuade the Four Occupying Powers to grant his immediate release and, in particular, to intercede with Great Britain as the Occupying Power which delivered Rudolf Hess to the International Military Tribunal in Nuremberg;

(3) To apply immediately to the United Nations in order to obtain:

(a) a Resolution of the General Assembly disapproving of and condemning the continued detention of the Complainant which has so far lasted for thirty-eight years, of which the last thirteen have been in isolation, as a violation of binding international law and fundamental human rights law; and

(b) an instruction from the General Assembly to the Four Occupying Powers to release the Complainant immediately.

(4) To apply to the European Court of Human Rights in Strasbourg for a decision disapproving of and condemning the detention of the Complainant for thirty-eight years, of which the last thirteen have been in isolation, as a violation of the European Convention for the Protection of Human Rights and Fundamental Freedoms;

(5) To refer the Complainant's case to the International Court of Justice in The Hague with the request that the Court should declare that the imprisonment of the Complainant cannot be justified by the provisions of Article 107 of the Charter of the

United Nations, and further to request that the Four Occupying Powers should be ordered to release the former *Reichminister* Rudolf Hess immediately from the Military Prison in Berlin-Spandau....

* * *

The Federal Republic of Germany is not responsible for the detention imposed on the Complainant, neither in its origin, nor for its duration, nor for the manner of its execution, either under constitutional law or under international law. Equally, the Federal Republic did not assume responsibility for the measure by taking over the liability to meet the costs of occupation in Berlin.

In any case the Occupying Powers did not perceive the powers which they exercised in enforcing the measures imposed against the Complainant as being derived from the Federal Republic of Germany.... The Federal Republic of Germany accepts the sanction imposed by the Tribunal, its enforcement and the occupation costs thereby incurred as the consequence of the defeat of Germany. Nevertheless the Federal Republic has cooperated in neither the continuation nor the conditions of the detention suffered by the Complainant. In these circumstances there has been no recognition under international law of either the sanction nor its execution. A refusal by the Federal Republic to take over responsibility for payment of the costs of the Allied Prison at Spandau would almost certainly not have altered the position in this regard.

The Federal Constitutional Court cannot therefore give a ruling in this connection on the question of whether, especially with regard to the Complainant's state of health and other circumstances, the continuation of his detention constitutes a violation of the international law of occupation or the minimum human rights standard binding under international law, as the Complainant alleges....

* * *

The Federal Government has maintained, in both the proceedings before the administrative courts and the constitutional complaint proceedings, that it has already undertaken the necessary steps to obtain the release of the Complainant, whose detention is a matter beyond its control. The Federal Government also wishes to continue to undertake further similar initiatives with the Occupying Powers. In so doing it is clearly aware of the Complainant's personal situation and the nature of his constitutional rights which are at issue. Indeed the Federal Government considers that the continued detention of the Complainant is wrong, bearing in mind his advanced age and his state of health.... The mere fact that the steps hitherto taken by the Federal Government have failed to produce the Complainant's release is certainly not, of itself, sufficient to give rise to a duty under constitutional law for the Federal Government to take specific further measures of possibility greater scope and consequence. It must be left to the Government to assess the foreign policy considerations in order to decide how far other measures are appropriate and necessary, bearing in mind the Complainant's interests as well as the interests of the community as a whole. Even from the constitutional standpoint it cannot be objected that the Federal Government has only brought humanitarian considerations and not legal grounds to the attention of the Occupying Powers in its efforts to obtain the release of the Complainant. The Government clearly starts from the premise that the Occupying Powers, and in Particular the Three Western Powers, are only approachable on humanitarian grounds and harbour objections in principle to the reopening of the question of the legality of the sentence and detention of the Complainant.... It can therefore remain a debatable point how this question should be decided in law and whether the Federal Government has made a correct assessment of the position.... The Superior Administrative Court...established in a constitutionally unobjectionable manner that the Federal Government considered the political significance of the decision at issue as essentially more important than the effect of legal arguments on the position of the Occupying Powers.

* * *

...In any case it is open to the Complainant to institute proceedings for preliminary legal protection on the basis of possible legal prejudice.

[On February 24, 1981, the Federal Administrative Court of West Germany announced its judgment on the appeal in the main proceedings, dismissing the appeal on grounds similar to that set forth in the above opinion by the Federal Constitutional Court. The European Commission on Human Rights in Strasbourg, France, declared inadmissible all three applications to it in regard to the continued confinement of Rudolf Hess. All remaining avenues of legal and diplomatic means to secure the release of the former Deputy *Führer* of the Third Reich became moot on August 17, 1987. On that date, the body of Rudolf Hess was discovered in a small summer house within the prison compound. An investigation revealed that the former *Reichminister* had committed suicide using a cord from a reading lamp attached to an overhead window latch. Although attempts to revive him were made, all were unsuccessful and he was pronounced dead at 4:10 p.m. (Berlin time). Hess's suicide thus closed one more protracted and gruesome legacy in twentieth century German history. Other prominent Nazis and Nazi sympathizers were tried in the final decades of the century. The following materials are illustrative cases of note in the United States, France and Canada].

---

7. *Handel v. Artukovic*
United States District Court
601 F. Supp. 1421 (C.D. Cal. 1985)

RYMER, District Judge.

Plaintiffs in this class action seek compensatory and punitive damages against defendant for his alleged involvement in the deprivations of life and property suffered by the Jews in Yugoslavia during World War II. The complaint...alleges that the defendant was the Commissioner of Public Security and Internal Administration and later the Minister of the Interior for the Independent State of Croatia, a puppet state of the German Reich established after its invasion of the Kingdom of Yugoslavia. In his official capacity, defendant oversaw and implemented Croatia's solution to "the Jewish question." The result of defendant's implementation of this policy was the passage of anti-Jewish legislation; the seizure of property owned by Croatian Jews; and the imprisonment and eventual execution of tens of thousands of Jewish men, women and children.

The complaint avers that defendant fled Croatia in 1945, and that he entered this country illegally in 1949. In May 1951, defendant was the subject of deportation proceedings. These proceedings eventually culminated in the grant to defendant in 1959 of a temporary stay of deportation, and defendant has remained in the United States until the present. Plaintiffs state that they were Jewish citizens of Yugoslavia in 1941, and each has close relatives who were murdered under the auspices of Croatian authority. All the plaintiffs are now United States citizens.

In their complaint, plaintiffs state four causes of action: (1) violation of the Hague Convention of 1907 and the Geneva Convention of 1929; (2) war crimes in violation of international law; (3) crimes against humanity in violation of international law; and (4) violation of Articles 100, 125, 141 and 145 of the Yugoslavian Criminal Code.

* * *

After having considered the briefs of the parties and the amici as well as the voluminous exhibits submitted in this case, the Court concludes that the international law claims should be dismissed under Fed.R.Civ.P. 12(b)(1) for lack of subject matter jurisdiction. The war crime and crime against humanity claims are also barred by the statute of limitations, and therefore fail to state a claim for relief.... The Court finds that the Yugoslavian law claim is barred by the applicable statute of limitations; and that to apply Yugoslavian substantive law as requested would in any event be unconstitutional under United States law as well as unenforceable under Yugoslavian and international law. The Yugoslavian law count therefore also fails to state a claim upon which relief can be granted.

I. Violation of the Hague and Geneva Conventions.

Pursuant to 18 U.S.C. §1331, the Court has jurisdiction over actions "arising under" the "Constitution, laws, or treaties" of the United States. In plaintiff's third count, they assert a cause of action under two United States treaties: the Convention Respecting the Laws and Customs of War on Land, Oct. 18, 1907, 36 Stat. 2277, T. S. No. 539 ("Hague Convention"); and the Convention Between the United States of America and other Powers Relating to Prisoners of War, July 27, 1929, Stat. 2021 (1932), *revised in* Geneva Convention Relative to the Treatment of Prisoners of War, Aug. 12, 1949, 6 U. S. T. 3316, T. I. A. S. 3364, 75 U. N. T. S. 135 ("Geneva Convention.") [The court then ruled that these two treaties above mentioned were not self-executing and therefore did not provide any judicially enforceable obligations. Neither treaty gave the plaintiffs a private right of action "arising under" said treaties and thus the first count must therefore be dismissed for want of jurisdiction].

II. Violation of Customary International Law.

Plaintiffs' second and third claims for relief are based on alleged violations of the laws of war and the laws of humanity. Two issues are presented by these claims: first, whether the Court has jurisdiction over such claims under section 1331; and second, if the Court does have jurisdiction, whether plaintiffs have stated a cognizable claim for relief under international law. The Court concludes that it does not have jurisdiction under section 1331, and, even if it did, plaintiffs fail to state a claim upon which relief may be granted.

A. Jurisdiction under Section 1331.

Plaintiffs' international law claims, like their treaty claims, must "arise under" the "laws of the United States" for jurisdiction to lie. It is clear that the law of nations "is part of our law, and must be ascertained and administered by the courts of justice of appropriate jurisdiction, as often as questions of right depending upon it are duly presented for their determination." *The Paquete Habana*, 175 U.S. 677, 700,... (1990). As Judge Kaufman stated in *Filartiga v. Pena-Irala*, 630 F. 2d 876 (2d Cir. 1980):

> The law of nations forms an integral part of the common law, and a review of the history surrounding the adoption of the Constitution demonstrates that it

became a part of the common law of the United States upon adoption of the Constitution....

The more difficult issue is whether plaintiffs have a claim "arising under" the law of nations. Plaintiffs contend that because international law is part of federal common law, the Court should find an explicit or implicit right of action for its enforcement. There are three possible sources for such a private right of action: an explicit grant of authority under 28 U.S.C. §1331; an implicit right derived from the law of nations; or an implicit right derived from federal common law.

Section 1331 does not provide plaintiffs with a right of action. Although two recent circuit court opinions, *Filartiga* and Judge Edwards' concurrence in *Tel-Oren*, have found that 28 U.S.C. §1350 creates a private right to sue for violations of the law of nations, it is clear that the result would be different if section 1331 rather than section 1350 were the applicable jurisdictional statute:

> Unlike section 1331, which requires that an action "arise under" the laws of the United States, section 1350 does not require that the action "arise under" the law of nations, but only mandates a "violation of the law of nations" in order to create a cause of action. The language of the statute is explicit on this issue: by its express terms, nothing more than a *violation* of the law of nations is required to invoke section 1350. Judge Bork nevertheless would propose to write into section 1350 an additional restriction that is not even suggested by the statutory language. Congress, of course, knew full well that it could draft section 1350 with "arising under" language, or the equivalent, to require a "cause of action" or "right to sue," but it chose not to do so.

Tel-Oren, 726 F. 2d at 779 (Edwards, J., concurring). Thus, while the "violation" language of section 1350 may be interpreted as explicitly granting a cause of action, the "arising under" language of section 1331 cannot be so interpreted. Section 1331, standing alone, does not give the Court jurisdiction over plaintiffs' claims.

Nor may plaintiffs urge that a right of action can be inferred from the law of nations. While international law may provide the substantive rule of law in a given situation, the enforcement of international law is left to individual states.... As Judge Edwards stated in *Tel-Oren*: "[T]he law of nations never has been perceived to create or define the civil actions to be made available by each member of the community of nations; by concensus, the states leave that determination to their respective municipal Laws." 726 F. 2d at 778.

It is important that this distinction be maintained for two reasons. First as a matter of policy, the distinction is a fundamental aspect of international law's accommodation to principles of national sovereignty. The Nuremberg tribunal articulated this interest in *United States v. Alstoetter* (The "Justice Case"),... when it stated:

> This universality and superiority of international law does not necessarily imply universality of its enforcement.... The law is universal, but such a state reserves unto itself the exclusive power within its boundaries to apply or withhold sanctions. Thus, notwithstanding the paramount authority of the substantive rules of common international law, the doctrine of national sovereignty have been preserved through the control of enforcement machinery.

Second, the distinction reflects the practical limits on enforcement of international law by municipal courts. The absence of a concensus on international law, particularly with respect to technical issues created by the wide array of legal systems of the world, makes it "hard even to imagine that harmony ever would characterize this issue." *Tel-Oren*, 726 F. 2d at 778 (Edwards, J., concurring).

Thus, although plaintiffs cite a number of jurists and commentators who described customary international law *substantively*, they have not pointed to any source, and the Court has found none, for the proposition that one looks to the law of nations to determine the *actionability* of conduct condemned by that body of law. The Court declines to rewrite a long-established rule based on sound policy concerns. The law of nations therefore does not provide plaintiffs with a private right of action in this municipal court.

The third possible source of a right of action, urged particularly by amicus ACLU, is federal common law. They argue that the present case is analogous to *Bivens v. Six Unknown Federal Narcotics Agents*, 403 U.S. 388,... (1971), in that "where federally protected rights have been invaded, it has been the rule from the beginning that courts will be alert to adjust their remedies so as to grant the necessary relief."... As amicus puts the argument, "the legal prohibition of such conduct entitles the plaintiffs to sue for damages, just as the rights guaranteed by treaties, statutes, and the Constitution may by their very nature justify private enforcement."...

However, the step encouraged by amicus fails to recognize the fundamental difference between municipal enforcement of municipal law and municipal enforcement of international law. The Supreme Court has noted that, under *Bivens*, there may be "special factors counseling hesitation in the absence of affirmative action by Congress."... In the present case, the "special factor" is the absence of any affirmative legislative action at all. Unlike violations of federal statutes or the United States Constitution, no American legislative body has acted in any way with respect to customary international law. To imply a cause of action from the law of nations would completely defeat the critical right of the sovereign to determine whether and how international rights should be enforced in that municipality. As stated in the Restatement (Second) Foreign Relations §3 (1965), a violation of international law gives to individual litigants such remedies or defenses in a forum of a state "*as are provided by its domestic law.*" Until Congress evinces an intent to give effect to international law, either by passing a jurisdictional statute or by incorporating international rights into the statutes of the United States, the Court declines to infer such an intent solely from the United States' membership in the community of nations.

B. Stating a Claim under International Law

Even assuming that the Court has jurisdiction over plaintiffs' customary international law claims, plaintiffs have not stated an actionable claim pursuant to Fed.R.Civ.P. 12(b)(6). Two issues are raised by plaintiffs' claims: first, whether the alleged acts constituted a violation of international law at the time they were committed; and second, whether the claims would be time barred.

It appears clear that the acts of genocide, torture, enslavement, and religious discrimination alleged in plaintiffs' complaint constituted violations of the laws of humanity at the time they were committed. In the late nineteenth century, occasional treaties began to reflect a growing consciousness of fundamental human rights. For example, in 1878, under the Treaty of Berlin, the people of Serbia, Montenegro, and Rumania were guaranteed freedom of religious practice.... Finally, at the Hague Conferences of 1899 and 1907, the signatory countries established detailed rules for land and naval warfare as well as for the treatment of prisoners of war.

Despite this increasing awareness of international human rights, at the end of World War I there was not a generalized recognition of the "laws of humanity." For example, the American delegates to the 1919 Paris Convention expressed considerable reservations regarding the condemnation of violations of "the laws of humanity" contained in the report of the Paris Commission on Responsibility of Authors of the War.

Nevertheless, international law continued to develop in the decades between the two world wars. Protection for minority groups received particular attention as multi-national kingdoms were replaced with nation states:

> On the one hand, with the disappearance of multi-national, non-racial states, such as the old Austro-Hungarian and Turkish Empires, almost every European nation came to be dominated by a single nationality which, without special measures of protection, might abuse its position at the expense of the minorities. On the other [hand], the ideal of self-determination itself presupposed a special concern to protect all national groups even if, for reasons of their geographical distribution, they were not able to enjoy that right in a direct form.... [citation omitted].

This concern for minority groups led to a League of Nations requirement that all new or substantially enlarged states, including Yugoslavia, assume obligations for the protection of their minorities as a condition of recognition of their independence or new frontiers.... The minority treaty signed by Yugoslavia as well as many other European countries placed members of racial, religious, or linguistic minorities "under the guarantee of the League of Nations," and "guaranteed such rights as freedom from discrimination in civil and political affairs, and the free exercise of speech and religion."...

The work of the League of Nations suggests that there was a general recognition of the rights of religious and ethnic minorities by the time of the outbreak of World War II. The existence of this concensus was confirmed by the Nuremberg court sitting immediately after World War II. That court, when faced with the issue of whether "crimes against humanity" were part of the law of nations prior to World War II, quoted with approval from Sir David Maxwell-Fyfe:

> With regard to "crimes against humanity," this at any rate is clear. The Nazis, when they persecuted and murdered countless Jews and political opponents in Germany, knew that what they were doing was wrong and that their actions were crimes which had been condemned by the criminal law of every civilized state. When these crimes were mixed with the preparation for aggressive war and later with the commission of war crimes in occupied territories, it cannot be a matter of complaint that a procedure is established for their punishment....

Although the law of nations was not codified until after the war, the court concluded that the notion of the "laws of humanity," put forward initially in the 1919 Paris Commission on Responsibility of Authors of the War, had clearly become an international concensus by the time of World War II.

It therefore seems clear that defendant's alleged actions constituted a violation of international law when they were committed. Turning to the second question raised by the plaintiffs' claim, namely, what is the applicable statute of limitations for this violation, plaintiffs urge the Court to look to international law, noting that "the incorporation of the law of nations into federal common law permits a federal court to determine an appropriate period of limitations without regard to the parochial interests of the forum state."... They further argue that in applying this federal common law, the universal concensus condemning defendant's behavior "requires this court to look to international standards before applying any limitations for actions of this nature."...

Assuming, *arguendo*, plaintiff's initial premise that federal rather than state law should provide the applicable rule of decision regarding the limitation of actions, there is no basis in the cases or commentaries for the conclusion that international law should govern the procedural aspects of plaintiffs' claim. Even plaintiffs' expert, Professor Almond, states that "the practice of states does not show that statutes of limitation have been established, as such, applicable as part of the international law shared among nations." ... It is therefore municipal, rather than international, law that must provide the rule of decision for plaintiffs' international law claims.

In ascertaining the federal law that should govern plaintiffs' claims, considerable energy has been expended by the parties on the issue of whether or not the United States has endorsed the statute of no limitation set forth in the Convention on the Non-Applicability of Statutes of Limitation to War Crimes and Crimes Against Humanity, *adopted and opened for signature, ... (entered into force* November 11, 1970). From the proceedings of the United Nations General Assembly, it appears that the United States did support the principle of a statute of no limitations. In Press Release US-UN 220 (1968), November 26, 1968, the United States delegation stated that

> the original purposes of the convention were—(1) to make clear that under international law there are no periods of limitation applicable to war crimes and crimes against humanity, and (2) to establish a new rule of international law by treaty that states which become parties to the convention should adopt necessary measures to abolish domestic statutes of limitation insofar as they might apply to war crimes and crimes against humanity.

The reasons enumerated by the delegation for opposing the draft convention do not suggest that the United States had any reservations about this initial purpose.... Thus, while the United States did not sign the resulting convention, it appears to recognize the principle that a statute of no limitation should be applied to the criminal prosecution of war crimes and crimes against humanity.

Regardless of what was the position of the United States, however, the period of limitations appropriate for criminal prosecutions does not suggest that a similar rule should be adopted for civil actions. In American jurisprudence, criminal and civil statutes of limitations have different conceptual underpinnings. For criminal violations, the common law rule was that there was no limitation as to the time within which offenses might be prosecuted.... Criminal statutes of limitations were therefore adopted at the will of the legislature, and were, in effect, an act of grace by which the sovereign surrendered its right to prosecute. Because these statutes are equivalent to acts of amnesty, the length of the statute of limitations bears a necessary relation to the heinousness of the crime. For example, in federal law, no statute of limitation exists for capital crimes, while non-capital crimes generally have a limitations period of five years.... Given the extreme nature of war crimes and crimes against humanity, the position of the American delegation that these violations should have no statute of limitations is consistent with the nature of criminal limitation statutes.

Civil statutes of limitations, by contrast, are viewed as a procedural requirement designed to protect against stale claims, and are unrelated to the underlying merits of the action.... This procedural concern with stale claims causes civil statutes of limitation to be divorced from the seriousness of the underlying allegations....

* * *

Considering these factors, plaintiffs' international law claims should have a shorter rather than a longer limitations period. First, like instances of wrongful death, crimes against humanity are immediately known to the victims and their families. Second, a claim of a crime against humanity is one that is particularly susceptible to the loss of evidence through the death or disappearance of witnesses and the loss of documents; it is unlike a claim for breach of a written contract, where the most critical evidence does not change with time. Finally, the gravity of international law violations mandates a reasonably short period to protect individuals from fraudulent claims.

In light of these considerations, the Court does not need to determine the precise limit applicable to plaintiff's cause of action in order to hold that thirty-five years is beyond the time within which plaintiffs should have brought their claims. The parties have not brought to the Court's attention any civil statute of limitations, either in domestic law or in an international forum, that comes close to the length of time involved here. While defendant's alleged activities shock the conscience, the gravity of this conduct does not play the role in civil limitation statutes that it fulfills in criminal statutes. Criminal prosecutions of crimes against humanity should be and are subject to a statute of no limitations; but civil actions cannot be subjected to this rule under American Law. [Plaintiffs' claims on alleged violations of the Yugoslav Criminal Code are omitted].

IT IS THEREFORE ORDERED that plaintiffs' complaint be dismissed with prejudice.

[We turn next to two late post-war trials in France involving men who committed criminal offenses in the name of the Third Reich. The trials of Klaus Barbie and Paul Touvier, for example, illustrate both the problems and the possibilities inherent in trying war crime cases of two individuals each some forty and fifty years after the fact. France, of course, suffered under the yoke of German occupation from the early summer of 1940 until the late summer of 1944. In that four-year time span, the French displayed a remarkable degree of both courage and resistance to Nazi tyranny as well as a notable accommodation by some to German fascism. Unlike the other Allied nations in World War II, France at the time was a state riven with political ineptness, military myopia and a disturbing degree of internal dissonance. It was a well-known fact that some Frenchmen openly admired Nazi policies and practices and actively promoted the tenets of National Socialism.

On June 20, 1940, at Compiegne, some fifty miles northeast of Paris, Adolf Hitler prepared a humiliating stage set for French capitulation. At Compiegne stood the historic railway car that had been the site of the November, 1918, surrender of Imperial Germany that concluded World War I and marked the end of the second Reich. In that car in 1918, Marshal Foch and French General Weygand had met with the German delegation to conclude World War I. Now, a generation later, in June, 1940, the Germans had draped a flag with a huge Swastika over the monument erected by the French to commemorate the glorious Allied and Associated Powers victory over the Kaiser and his minions. An inscription under that hated symbol of Nazi oppression read, in part: "Here on the eleventh of November 1918 succumbed the criminal pride of the German people..." The actual World War II armistice instrument was officially signed on Saturday, June 22, 1940. Thus, in the space of a mere six weeks, the German war machine with its *blitzkrieg* tactics, had defeated all the Western Allies on the European continent. To embarrass the French even more, Hitler ordered that the entire Compiegne site, including the 1918 victory monument, be razed so there would be no physical "identification" with the German surrender there in 1918. Horne, in his outstanding book on the fall of France,[8] writes that "[o]n July 17, the Grossdeutschland paraded in triumpth

8. Alistair Horne, *To Lose a Battle: France 1940* (1969).

through Paris, to hold a thanksgiving service at Notre Dame. The next day, a victory parade marched through the Brandenburger Tor [Brandenburg Gate] for the first time since 1871."[9]

As a result of the Franco-German armistice of June, 1940, France was divided into two zones of occupation—the heavily occupied zone in the northern half of the country, including Paris, and the sparsely occupied southern zone, including the City of Lyon. It was in this southern zone of occupation, known as Vichy France, that Germany allowed the aging World War I French hero, Marshal Henri Phillipe Pétain (1856–1951), to become Premier of the German Puppet government of Vichy from 1940 to 1944. By late 1943, however, German patience with the Pétain government grew thin and the Nazis abrogated their armistice agreement of 1940 and began, under the code name *Operation Attila*, to re-occupy southern France. It was in this particular region of the country that Klaus Barbie and Paul Touvier were alleged to have committed the offenses charged against them in their trials in 1985 and in 1994, respectively. We will first take up the Barbie case. A brief background summary may be instructive to place his trial in its proper context.

Barbie was the illegitimate son of Anna and Nicholas Barbie who lived in the small German hamlet of Udler in the Saarland. Morgan, in his book on Barbie and his times in Vichy France,[10] notes that Klaus "[h]aving been denied a conventional birth...was an untouchable.... Such was the accident of birth that gave Klaus Barbie feelings of personal worthlessness.... He was a man in search of something to erase his original flaw."[11]

Barbie joined the SS in September, 1935 which, for many German youth in that period, was a significant act of status elevation. After the fall of France, he was appointed to head Section Four (Repression of Political Crimes) of the *Kommando der SIPO und SD* (KDS) in Lyon, France. The KDS was an organization modeled on the infamous *Einsatzgruppen* that operated on the eastern front during the Polish and Russian campaigns. One of the chief missions of this organization was to round up and deport to the prison and death camps in the East, Jews, resistance fighters and other real or perceived enemies of the Third Reich. Barbie, because of his teutonic efficiency, was considered by many to be a "poor man's Eichmann"—an SS officer who, from 1942 until 1944, was responsible for sending a multitude of French Jews, members of the resistance and other "undesirables" into slave labor, annihilation, or both. At his trial, the prosecution charged Barbie with about thirty cases involving persons who were arrested, deported and/or tortured to death by the KDS, as well as four separate "operations" carried out under his instructions in Lyon involving the murder of a number of French railway workers; the torture and deportation of members of the Lyon *Union Gererale des Israelites de France*; a raid on the reception center for Jewish children wherein some forty-four children and seven staff members were taken into custody and deported by train to Auschwitz, where all but a handful were gassed; and the deportation of some 600-plus Jews and resistance partisans on the final deportee train to leave Lyon for Germany on August 11, 1944. Morgan[12] relates the escape of Barbie from Lyon in these words:

> As for Klaus Barbie, he was one of the last Germans to leave Lyon. On August 28 he was wounded in the left foot on the outskirts of the city during a

---

9. *Id.* at 586.

10. Ted Morgan, *An Uncertain Hour: The French, the Germans, the Jews, the Barbie Trial, and the City of Lyon, 1940–1945* (1990).

11. *Id.* at 203–204.

12. Morgan, *supra* note 11.

skirmish with the resistance. Barbie was taken to Croix-Rousse Hospital where he was operated on, on August 30. That same day he took the last train out of Lyon, eventually reaching a military hospital in Baden-Baden, Germany, where he recuperated. On May 9, 1945, the day that Germany capitulated, Barbie went underground].[13]

8. *Federation Nationale des Deportes et Internes Resistants et Patriotes and Others v. Barbie*

France, Court of Cassation (Criminal Chamber)
December 20, 1985
78 *International Law Reports* 125

[Klaus Barbie was the highest official in the Gestapo in Lyon, France, from November, 1942 to August, 1944. When World War II ended, the French authorities issued a warrant for his arrest and he was later found and taken into custody. He then disappeared. Subsequently, he was tried *in absentia*, found guilty, and sentenced to death by the *Tribuanl Permanent des Forces Armees de Lyon*, in two separate judgments handed down on April 29, 1952, and again on November 25, 1954.

The French government then discovered that Barbie had fled Europe and had taken up residence in and become a citizen of Bolivia. France sought extradition of Barbie, but the Supreme Court of Bolivia rejected the French extradition request citing the lack of an extradition treaty between the two countries. However, when a new Bolivian president was elected in December, 1982, Bolivia expelled Barbie for using "false identification" to obtain Bolivian citizenship.

Earlier, in February, 1982, new criminal proceedings had been filed against Barbie in Lyon. In those proceedings, the accused was charged with the crimes of murder, torture and arbitrary arrests as well as illegal detentions and imprisonments. The prosecution charged that in Lyon alone, Barbie was responsible for the murder of some 4,342 persons, the forced deportation of some 9,591 Jews along with the arrest and forced deportation of an additional 14, 311 members of the French resistance.

An examining Magistrate issued an arrest warrant in Lyon on November 3, 1982. Finally, on February 3, 1983, Barbie was expelled from Bolivia and placed upon an aircraft bound for French Guiana. Upon landing in French Guiana, he was arrested and put aboard an aircraft and flown to France where he was placed in the custody of the Examining Magistrate in Lyon. Once in French custody, Barbie argued that his arrest and detention were illegal because he was a victim of what he alleged was a "disguised extradition," thus voiding the entire proceeding against him. His application for release was rejected and he appealed.

In two prior appeals, the Court of Cassation, *held* on October 6, 1983, that (a) his expulsion from refuge in Bolivia was not an obstacle to the institution of a criminal prosecution against him on his return to France, provided he was given adequate rights of defense (b) that crimes against humanity did not fall under only French municipal law, but were subject to an international criminal order wherein the rules of extradition were not of paramount importance; and (c) that the offenses he was charged with were subject to a ten-year statutory limitation period under a French law of December 26,

---

13. *Id.* at 321.

1964. To prosecute him now for alleged crimes committed in the 1942–1944 time period would violate Article 55 of the French Constitution. The Court of Cassation rejected these arguments and Barbie appealed. In another hearing before the Court of Cassation on January 26, 1984, the appeal from the hearing of October 6, 1983, was dismissed. The Court of Cassation in its January 26, 1984, ruling *held* (a) that crimes against humanity are not subject to a statute of limitations under French law and that such an interpretation could be deduced from the Charter of the IMT-Nuremberg; (b) that neither the European Convention on Human Rights of 1950 nor the International Covenant on Civil and Political Rights of 1966, gave rise to any derogation from the rule that the prosecution of crimes against humanity was not subject to a statute of limitation. The initial list of charges in the indictment against Barbie included eleven sets of charges relating to the detention, torture, murder and deportation to death camps of some 1,500 persons during 1943 and 1944. These were new charges that were separate from those for which Barbie had already been tried *in absentia* in 1952 and in 1954. Upon the drafting of the final indictment, the Examining Magistrate of Lyon took the position that only the acts of the persecution of innocent Jews, on racial or religious grounds, carried out in furtherance of the "final solution" constituted crimes against humanity which were *not* subject to statutory limitation for which Barbie could still be prosecuted.

At that point, various individuals and organizations who alleged they were victims of Nazi oppression and some former members of the French Resistance appealed this decision by the Examining Magistrate. On October 4, 1985, the Court of Appeal of Lyon *upheld* the position taken by the Examining Magistrate. In effect, the Court of Appeal *held* that torture, deportation and the murder of members of the French Resistance, even if they were Jews, could be classified *only as war crimes* whose prosecution was statute-barred. The appellants then appealed again to the Court of Cassation.

On December 20, 1985, the Court of Cassation allowed the appeal and quashed the judgment of the Court of Appeal of Lyon in part and the case was then remitted to the Court of Appeal of Paris to consider which charges should be added to the indictment against Barbie, in light of the definition of crimes against humanity given by the Court of Cassation. The Court of Appeal of Paris *held*: (a) that war crimes could not be treated in the same manner as crimes against humanity and that thus, war crimes *were subject* to time-limits imposed by statute; (b) that crimes against humanity were *not* subject to statutory limitations even if they could also be classified as "war crimes" within the meaning of the Charter of the IMT, Article 6(b) and (c) and it was *error* to exclude from the category of crimes against humanity all acts imputed to the accused which had been committed against members or possible members of the French Resistance.

The following is selected text from the judgment of the Court of Cassation of December 20, 1985]:

BRAUNSCHWEIG, *President*; LE GUNEHEC, *Rapporteur*; DONTENWILLE, *Advocate General*

The Court has considered Article 575, second paragraph, subparagraph 3, of the Code of Criminal Procedure, by virtue of which these appeals are admissible.

On the first ground of cassation put forward by the Association Nationale des Anciens Combattants de la Resistance (ANACR) — This ground is based on violation of Articles 2 to 4, 7, 573(3) and 593 of the Code of Criminal Procedure, the Moscow Declaration of 30 October 1943, Article 6 of the Charter of the Nuremberg International Tribunal of 8 August 1945, the interpretation given on 19 June 1979 by the Minister of Foreign Affairs of the United Nations Resolution of 13 February 1946, Article 7 of the European Convention for the Protection of Human Rights and Fundamental Freedoms and Article 15(2) of the International Covenant on Civil and Political Rights"].

The appellant Association has wrongly contended that war crimes, to the extent that they are also defined in Article 6 of the Charter of the International Military Tribunal of Nuremberg annexed to the London Agreement of 8 August 1945, are to be treated as crimes against humanity for the purposes of the principle of not being subject to statutory limitations.

In fact, in contrast to crimes against humanity, war crimes are directly connected with the existence of a situation of hostilities declared between the respective States to which the perpetrators and the victims of the acts in question belong. Following the termination of hostilities, it is necessary that the passage of time should be allowed to blur acts of brutality which may have been committed in the course of armed conflict, even if those acts constituted violations of the laws and customs of war or were not justified by military necessity, provided that those acts were not of such a nature as to deserve the qualification of crimes against humanity. There is no principle of law with authority superior to that of French law which would allow war crimes, either within the meaning of the London Agreement which preceded it, to be declared not subject to statutory limitation. Article (2)(4) of the Code of Criminal Procedure...has no effect in this regard since its provisions are applicable only to proceedings concerning war crimes in respect of which the time-limit for statutory limitation has not been reached. This ground of cassation cannot therefore be accepted.

[The Court then set out and joined three grounds of cassation put forward by organizations seeking to be admitted in the proceedings *as civil parties*, in reliance on acts committed by the defendant when he was tried and sentenced to death *in absentia* in 1952 and in 1954. The Court *held* that a civil suit was inadmissible provided that it related to acts for which the defendant had already been tried, even if the subject trial had been *in absentia*.

Several other French organizations requested joinder in the prosecution against Klaus Barbie. The Court then continued]:

The following acts constitute crimes against humanity within the meaning of Article 6(c) of the Charter of the Nuremberg International Military Tribunal annexed to the London Agreement of 8 August 1945, which are not subject to statutory limitation of the right of prosecution, even if they are crimes which could also be classified as war crimes within the meaning of Article 6(b) of the Charter: inhumane acts and persecution committed in a systematic manner in the name of a State practicing a policy of ideological supremacy not only against persons by reason of their membership of a racial or religious community, but also against the opponents of that policy, whatever the form of their opposition.

The indictment which is the subject of the judgment under appeal lists various counts of crimes against humanity, arising from a series of acts which are indisputably quite separate from those for which Klaus Barbie was convicted *in absentia* by judgments handed down in 1952 and 1954. These acts as detailed by the judges of the lower court, consisted in the arrest and illegal imprisonment of numerous persons, followed by brutality and physical torture or deportation to concentration camps normally resulting in the death of the victims. These acts were allegedly committed in 1943 and 1944 by or on the orders of Klaus Barbie, in his capacity as SS Lieutenant and head of the Gestapo of Lyon, which was responsible for the suppression of crimes and political offences. One of the five sections of the Gestapo of Lyon specialized in the fight against communism and sabotage whilst another was responsible for the fight against Jews. The judgment under appeal lists about thirty cases of persons arrested and subsequently tortured to death or deported or, more frequently, persons who died in the course of deportation. That judgment also lists four complete operations carried on the instructions of the accused and with his participation. [These were noted in the discussion prior to this opinion].

* * *

The *Chambre d'accusation*, having analyzed Article 6 of the Charter of the Nuremberg International Military Tribunal, stated that

> Only the persecution of persons who are noncombatants, committed in furtherance of a deliberate State policy and for racial, religious or political motives, is of such a nature as to constitute a crime against humanity whose prosecution is not subject to statutory limitation. On the other hand a war crime, even if it may be committed by the same means, is characterized, in contrast to a crime against humanity, by the fact that it appears to assist the conduct of the war.

By application of these principles, the *Chambre d'accusation* ordered that an indictment should be drawn up against Klaus Barbie and he should be sent for trial by the *Cour d'assises* for crimes against humanity, but only for those acts established by the examining magistrate which constituted "persecution against innocent Jews," carried out for racial and religious motives with a view to their extermination, that is to say in furtherance of the "final solution" sought by the leaders of the Nazi regime. In this regard, the judgment under appeal is final since no appeal has been lodged against its provisions seising the trial court.

In addition the judgment under appeal, in considering the appeal of civil parties, confirmed the order of the examining magistrate by which he held that:

> …the prosecution is barred by statutory limitation to the extent that it relates to the unlawful imprisonment without judgment, torture, deportation and death of combatants who were member of the Resistance, or persons whom Barbie supposed to be members of the Resistance, even if they were Jewish. Even it such acts were heinous and were committed in violation of human dignity and the law of war, they could only constitute war crimes, whose prosecution was barred by statutory limitation.

Finally, the judgment under appeal adds that the deportation of persons with regard to whom there was information allowing Barbie to think that they were members of the Resistance was to be considered as a war crime whose prosecution was barred by statutory limitation and not as a crime against humanity, in the absence of the element of intention necessary for the latter crime.…

[This Court considers] however that the judgment under appeal states that the "heinous" crimes committed systematically or collectively against persons who were members or could have been members of the Resistance were presented, by those in whose name they were perpetrated, as justified politically by the national socialist ideology. Neither the driving force which motivated the victims, nor their possible membership [in] the Resistance, excludes the possibility that the accused acted with the element of intent necessary for the commission of crimes against humanity. In pronouncing as it did and excluding from the category of crimes against humanity all the acts imputed to the accused committed against members or possible members of the Resistance, the

Chambre d'accusation misconstrued the meaning and the scope of the provisions listed in these grounds of appeal.

The judgment under appeal therefore also incurs cassation on this ground.

For these reasons the Court:

(1)   — Quashes and annuls those provisions of the judgment of the *Chambre d'ac-cusation* of the Court of Appeal of Lyon, of 4 October 1985, by which it was held that the right of prosecution was extinguished in relation to those crimes which had been the subject of judgments *in absentia* pronounced against Klaus Barbie by the *Tribunal Permanent des Forces Armees* of Lyon, on 29 April 1952 and 25 November 1954;

   — Holds that there is no reason to remit the case for further consideration on this point since the *Chambre d'accusation* had no jurisdiction over those crimes;

(2)   — Quashes and annuls those provisions of the judgment of the Court of Ap-peals by which the prosecution of certain acts committed by Klaus Barbie was declared barred by statutory limitation on the ground that those acts constituted war crimes, the victims being members or possible members of the Resistance. With regard to these facts a fresh judgment shall be given in accordance with the law and within the limits of this order for cassation;

   — Remits the case and the parties to the *Chambre d'accusation* of the Court of Appeal of Paris designated for the purpose by special decision of the *Chambre du Conseil;*

   — Orders the *Chambre d'accusation* to send Klaus Barbie for trial before the *Cour d'assises* of the Department of the Rhone, if the *Chambre d'accusation* finds that there are sufficient charges against Klaus Barbie in relation to this head of the indict-ments against him...

[The following excerpts are taken from the text of the last part of the submissions made to the Court by *Advocate General* Dontenwille]:

...It was my intention to demonstrate that the *Chambre d'accusation* of Lyon...did not take account of certain essential factors...and therefore failed to draw the conclu-sions which ought to have resulted from its examination of the case.

The *Chambre d'accusation* remained aloof from the historic implications of the prob-lem before it.

I also believe that the judgment under appeal, faced with the task of determining the scope of the crimes against humanity with which Klaus Barbie could be charged, adopted an approach which was too restrictive and even altered the definition of such crimes.

It is certainly true that the notion of crimes against humanity is difficult to trace, the abominable nature of the crime being merely a function of the depths to which civiliza-tion has sunk in the course of time...I freely admit that it was a thankless task to have to deduce a rule, just as it is a thankless task for this Court today to fix the principle!

* * *

In fact the idea of the protection of humanity only really came to life in concrete form after the 1914–18 war.... But it was only the calculated, systematic atrocities of the last war [World War II] which really caused the world community to react. That re-action came first in the form of the voices of several Heads of State including Churchill who, from 1942 onwards, raised his voice in solemn warning against the "inhuman acts" committed in occupied countries.

These raised voices were in fact the preliminaries to the London Agreements which were concerned with the establishment of an international tribunal and the often laborious task of drawing up legal texts to serve as a basis for prosecution.... [I]t should be underlined...that it is necessary to place this "conception" [i. e., crimes against humanity] in the full sense of that term into the context of the period, as a new construction integrated into international law which until then did not extend to criminal law....

I believe that this factor must be taken into account together with a second fact, even more important to our purposes. The problem of statutory limitation of prosecution, at that time unknown in many States, did not arise and it was therefore unnecessary to draw a particularly fine distinction between war crimes and crimes against humanity. In fact such a distinction was hardly thought of. The universally accepted reference at the time was to "The Trial of the Major War Criminals." This terminology, which has long been implanted into our language, was employed on numerous occasions in the course of the proceedings at Nuremberg.

But it must not be strictly adhered to today if the wrong conclusions are not to be drawn. The "major war crimes" include crimes against peace and crimes against humanity, as well as war crimes in the strict sense of that term....

The international community, which certainly never reacts until thunder has struck, has never substantially modified the content of that Charter, at least in so far as crimes against humanity are concerned.

The Charter, in Article 6, contains two definitions with regard to war crimes and crimes against humanity. I am hesitant to return to them because they have already been cited, elaborated and commented upon at length in this hearing. Their text is familiar to you and it would be wrong for me to recall it once more...I shall limit myself to making just two remarks which help to direct my train of thought.

The first, please excuse me, is a list which is almost unbearable but is nevertheless necessary because it unfortunately evinces a hierarchy of horror.

Article 6(b) gives the following description of war crimes:

Murder, ill-treatment or deportation to slave labour...killing of hostages, plunder... destruction...devastation...

Article 6(c) which deals with crimes against humanity covers specifically:

Murder, extermination, enslavement, deportation and other inhumane acts...or persecutions...

...The careful choice of each term used surely makes it clear that the intention of those who drafted this text was to make a distinction between brutality which is unfortunately inherent in many wars and a major, orchestrated attack on the very dignity of man.

My second remark constitutes a linchpin in my argument...

Article 6(c) uses a series of terms defining a certain number of atrocities without making them subject to any particular condition and it is only after the conjunction "or" that political, racial or religious grounds are mentioned and tied, it is true, to the word "persecution."

This break in the sentence is of vital importance because it implies two distinct categories of crimes against humanity, acts which are inhuman in themselves and acts of clearly directed persecution.

One could give an infinite number of glosses but I prefer to rely on the text itself…
because despite the uneasy compromise which influenced its drafting, it is nevertheless
the common denominator of the conscience of mankind.…

How, and according to what lines, was this test applied by the Nuremberg Tribunal?

A constant theme emerges from their deliberations. The exacerbation in the methods
used, their systematic nature and the fact that the victims came from all horizons often
led to the conclusion that crimes against humanity exceeded the classical notion of war
crimes, of which they constituted an aggravated form.

Everyone has in mind the phrase of M. de Menthon [the Chief French Prosecutor at
Nuremberg] which has so often been cited and which so aptly describes the escalating
nature of the crime.…I refer to it again…

> The most frightful aspect of these crimes is perhaps the deliberate moral
> degradation, the debasement of those detained to the point of making them
> lose, if that were possible, all character as human beings…

> The terrible accumulation and confused tangle of crimes against humanity at
> once includes and surpasses the two more precise legal notions of crimes
> against peace and war crimes…

Surely these lines constitute a statement of the essential overlap of the different crimes,
which the civil parties have criticized the judgment under appeal for failing to perceive.

Since Nuremberg the matter has been clouded over. The courts of several countries
have examined, prosecuted and convicted the perpetrators of such acts without finding
it necessary to trace the delicate dividing line which this Court is called upon to establish today.

* * *

Crimes against humanity in fact transcend our three traditional notions:

— the perpetrator and his motivation;

— the act;

— the victim…

The perpetrator, beyond the accused himself, is the "system" which he represents
and personifies, that system in its totality…

The judgment under appeal, whilst presenting that system in giving the reasons for
its decision, failed to take account in the operative part of the judgment of the ambiva-
lence of the role of that system. Everyone agrees that crimes against humanity presume
the establishment of an orchestrated State Policy. Indeed that programme was orchestrated by a single hand.… A parallel which brings us back to classic criteria may be
drawn with premeditation,…

Crimes against humanity are to war crimes what assassination is to murder. The premeditation involved is simply of another order. On one side stands not simply an individual but a State with all its resources. On the other side is not merely a single victim
but humanity. The deliberate intention to destroy is also of this order.

…The criminal act, savage as it is, assumes an additional element in order to be designated as a crime against humanity. That element is the insertion of the act at issue
into a method which has been systematically established and the use of means permitting not merely the suppression of a person but the denial of his very humanity. Debasement, collective degradation, as it occurred in the concentration camps…

I have already let it be known that in my view the appropriate criteria should be determined by the fate of the victim, in this case deportation. Here also the judgment under appeal does not appear to have given sufficient weight to the terrible nature of deportation, in drawing the distinction which it made between men vowed to the same procedures of annihilation, that is to say barbarity. Their human stature was the same! And that is not a hollow statement.

* * *

Turning finally to the victim, it is certainly here that I must separate myself most from the judgment under appeal and from opinions which have frequently been accepted.

I consider that a crime against humanity is established once the elements which I have specified are present, that is to say the perpetrator (in the broad sense), his intention (his ideology, his system) and the abominable means of action which I just described have been used.

I cannot accept, once such a stage is reached, that a legal choice should be made between different victims. To accept a distinction between the victims would be to play the game of the perpetrator of the crime in the arbitrary discrimination which he operated in relation to the human race. Are we, tomorrow, to listen to the accused Klaus Barbie request before the *Cour c'assises* that a civil party should prove that he is Jewish!

It matters little in my view, faced with an orchestrated and collective programme of action which denies civilization as such, whether the victim was a member of a group, whether or not he was "useful for the war" to his enemies, whether he espoused a particular political persuasion, or even whether he belonged to a particular race…

Crimes against humanity are not to be confused with genocide which is merely one abominable aspect of such crimes. The only relevant membership, of a victim of action which has reached such a level of horror that it is no more than a mechanism of negation, is his membership of the human race…. This Supreme Court is not judging Klaus Barbie and we are not in Lyon. The Court has another mission to fulfill, more permanent and more universal, to deduce a principle…. The distance from the events at issue and the gravity of the task require you to give a definition which is transplantable to the present and of such a nature as to protect the future. You must interpret…. Did crimes against humanity disappear forty years ago? It is not for me to say.

Your judgment, gentlemen, is awaited well beyond the frontiers of France. To my knowledge it is the first occasion when a supreme court anywhere in the world has been called up to give a precise definition of crimes against humanity. The impact of your decision will be considerable…I conclude by proposing that the judgment under appeal which has been referred to you should be quashed…

[The *Chambre d'accusation* of the Court of Appeal of Paris then took under consideration what additional charges, if any, should be appended to the indictments against Barbie regarding the definition of "crimes against humanity" set forth by the Court of Cassation.

After an investigation, the *Chambre d'accusation* ruled that three additional charges should be added to the indictment as crimes against humanity, namely, the torture and death in confinement of a Professor Gompel, a Jewish member of the French resistance in 1944; the arrest and deportation to Germany of French resistance members in both 1943 and 1944, and the deportation, and, in many cases, the deaths of resistance personnel deported from France on the last train to leave Lyon before that city was liberated by the Allies, namely, on August 11, 1944. It was determined by the *Chambre d'ac-*

cusation that Klaus Barbie should stand trial for these additional crimes against humanity and his case was then remitted to the *Cour d'Assises du Rhone*. The trial before the *Cour d'Assises du Rhone* (Judge Cerdini, President), began on May 11, 1987. Less than two months later, on July 4, 1987, that tribunal found Klaus Barbie guilty on all 340 counts of the seventeen crimes against humanity with which he was charged. Finding no extenuating circumstances, the court sentenced Barbie to life imprisonment].

* * *

[Another collaborator with the Germans in Vichy France was Paul Touvier. Touvier was an officer in the *Milice*, a paramilitary police force organized to combat enemies of the Vichy government, with a special emphasis on eradicating the French Resistance. In addition, the Milice also had violent anti-Semitic tendencies and often engaged in the harassment of Jews and the plundering of Jewish property. At the conclusion of World War II, members of the Milice, along with other Nazi collaborators were purged, as far as possible, from French life and culture. Had Paul Touvier not been successful in going underground when he did, he surely would have faced execution had he been caught and tried shortly after the end of the war. As it was, Touvier escaped capture by seeking initial refuge with Father Stephane Vautherin, a Catholic priest who was the unofficial chaplain to the Milice in Lyon. For the next forty-five years, Touvier managed to evade arrest and trial through the good offices of friendly clerics and the able assistance of the Catholic right-wing underground network in France. Like Klaus Barbie, Touvier was twice tried *in absentia* for war crimes and sentenced to death in both cases; once in Lyon on September 10, 1946 and the other in Chambery, on March 4, 1947. After a controversial pardon by then French President Georges Pompidou in November, 1971, and the resultant public outcry, Touvier was subsequently re-charged under a 1964 French statute on charges alleging that he committed crimes against humanity which were exempt from statutory prescription. Finally, in May, 1989, he was caught while hiding in yet another Catholic sanctuary. At the time, Paul Touvier was seventy-nine years of age. The following excerpts from the excellent law review commentary by Wexler provide a general overview of the somewhat complicated case marshaled by the French against this former member of the Lyon Milice].

---

9. The Case of Paul Touvier

Leila Sadat Wexler, "Reflections on the Trial of Vichy Collaborator Paul Touvier for Crimes against Humanity in France"

20 *Law and Social Inquiry* 191; 192; 196–197; 199; 200–211; 213–214 (1995)
Reproduced with permission from 20 *Law and Social Inquiry* 191 (1995)
and Leila Sadat Wexler. © The University of Chicago Press (1995)

On 29 June 1944, at Rillieux-la-Pape, a small suburb of Lyon, France, seven men were murdered by members of the French *Milice* because they were Jewish. Fifty years later, the man ostensibly responsible for the killings, Paul Touvier, was sentenced to life imprisonment by a French court for his role in their deaths.... Based as it was on the Nuremberg Charter, the trial raised many fascinating legal issues and is significant as one of the few successful attempts by any country to apply the Nuremberg principles to its own citizens.

* * *

To the extent that Touvier's trial focused on the Vichy regime, it was necessarily political, for Vichy not only pitted family members against each other but put in question political ideologies as well. After the invasion of France by the Germans in the summer of 1940, "Work, family, fatherland" ("Travail, famille, patrie") replaced "liberty, equality, brotherhood" as the country 's new moto under the leadership of... Pétain. On the basis of these ideas, the "Constitution" of 1875 and the Third Republic fell by the stroke of a pen as the National Assembly granted all power, including the right to promulgate a new constitution, to [Pétain]. The town of Vichy was chosen as the site for the new French government, and although historians debate the extent to which Vichy became a vassal state of Nazi Germany, two general observations are in order. First, the Vichy regime cooperated extensively with the Nazis.... Second, the new regime clearly represented a significant shift to the right and was ready to take up arms against "nonbelievers" (Jews, members of the Resistance, communists) to pursue its moral reformation of France.

Among those most vigorous in their pursuit of the new state's ideals were members of the Milice. A special paramilitary force, separate from the normal civil authorities (the police and the judiciary), the Milice was established to combat the Resistance and other enemies of the Vichy government through propaganda and violence, if necessary. It was also violently anti-Semitic. Indeed, the organization's motto included a pledge to "struggle against the Jewish leper and for French purity." Often involved in theft and extortion, Milicians confiscated and plundered the apartments of Jews. They also arrested, tortured, and sometimes murdered those thought to be opponents of the new order.

* * *

After the war, a violent purge... of collaborators occurred in practically every sector of French life, during which members of the Milice were particularly singled out for punishment. Many were executed.... Yet the purge did not resolve many of the enmities bred by the war and the occupation years, and the Vichy period remains an open wound in France.

* * *

... Touvier never served any sentence for his activities during the war. Captured on 3 July 1947, he escaped shortly thereafter under mysterious circumstances. By 1967, his death sentence had prescribed, and no longer afraid of being executed, he engaged in a vigorous campaign (while still in hiding) to be pardoned for his wartime activities. Several prominent clergymen came to his aid and successfully interceded on his behalf with the government. On 28 November 1971 he was pardoned by President Pompidou, despite a report by Police Commissioner Jacques Delarue which concluded that Touvier's behavior during the war had been "nefarious, unscrupulous and inexcusable" ("nefaste, crapuleuse, et san excuse.")

Touvier's pardon would ultimately be his downfall, however. When revealed to the republic, it brought him to the attention of victims of the war who remembered his activities. To pursue Touvier, they relied on a 1964 law exempting "crimes against humanity" from the prescriptive period normally applicable to war crimes and in 1973 and 1974 lodged criminal complaints against him.

The case was stalled in the French court system for the next 20 years, primarily due to various procedural hurdles raised by Touvier's lawyers and foot-dragging by the government (both prosecutors and judges). It was only with the successful prosecution of Klaus

Barbie, a German, for crimes against humanity and the appointment of Judge Getti, a *juge d'instruction* (investigating magistrate) determined to prosecute Touvier, that the *Touvier* case was finally able to shake off its inertia. Touvier was tracked to his hiding place in a monastery near Nice and arrested in 1989. On 29 October 1991, Judge Getti held that Touvier could be indicted on 5 of the 11 charges then lodged against him.

As required by French law in cases involving serious crimes, however, Touvier's indictment would not be final until an appellate chamber reviewed the thick file (*dossier d'instruction*) compiled by the *juge d'instruction*. On review, in an extraordinary 215-page decision that proved even more controversial than Pompidou's pardon of Touvier, the Indicting Chamber of the Paris Court of Appeals reversed Judge Getti and threw out the indictment. According to the upper court's reading of the file, the evidence with respect to 10 of the 11 counts was insufficient. With respect to the one crime for which Touvier's involvement was undeniable (the massacre at Rillieux), one of the requisite elements of a "crime against humanity" was missing. Relying on the decisions of the French Court of Cassation in the *Barbie* case, the Court of Appeals pointed out that the prosecution must prove that the accused intended to take part in a common plan by systematically committing inhumane acts and illegal persecutions in the name of a state practicing a hegemonic political ideology.

To determine whether this was so, the Paris Court of Appeals considered the "historical" record of the Vichy government: its policies toward the Jews and its relationship with the Germans then occupying France. Although agreeing that the Milice and the Vichy government exhibited certain anti-Semitic tendencies, in the court's view, Vichy France, unlike Nazi Germany was not a hegemonic state. Thus, Touvier could not, *as a matter of law*, have committed a crime against humanity in carrying out Vichy's orders. The court also rejected the idea that Touvier was not carrying out any German plan at Rillieux—it was entirely *"une affaire entre Francais"* (a French affair).

The decision of the Paris court was widely criticized as replete with errors, omissions, and even untruths. The historical record showed that the Milice specifically excluded Jews from their number and repeatedly targeted them for abuse.... Finally, Touvier himself admitted that the Milice carried out the Rillieux massacre under German orders. Indeed, this was his principal defense.

On 28 November 1992 the French Court of Cassation reversed the lower court in part without commenting on the Court of Appeals' revisionist account of the Vichy regime. In a somewhat convoluted opinion, the High Court held that Touvier, although French, could be tried for the massacre at Rillieux as an accomplice of the Gestapo. Following this decision, the Indicting Chamber of the Court of Appeals of Versailles, to whom the case had been remanded, indicted Touvier on 2 June 1993. The case was subsequently set for trial, some 20 years and dozens of court decisions after the original complaints were filed.

Touvier's trial opened on 17 March 1994. The case was tried to a Court of Assizes, a unique French institution used only for the trial of serious offenses. A child of the French Revolution, the modern Court of Assizes was created by the French constitution of 1791. Its chief distinguishing feature is that it combines three professional and nine lay jurors into a tribunal of mixed composition that deliberates together on the defendant's guilt of innocence and on his sentence. The jurors are chosen by lottery, although the defendant and the prosecution each have the right to recuse five and four jurors, respectively, for any reason (or no reason) at all. In keeping with the Revolutionary tradition that led to the adoption of the jury system for the trial of serious criminal cases, a conviction cannot be obtained without the vote of at least eight members of the entire tribunal meaning that at least five of the nine lay jurors must vote for the defendant's conviction. Although it is thus the jury that will determine a defendant's guilt or innocence, it is "the Court" (*la Cour*), or the three professional judges (who are not jurors), and in particular the president judge (*le President*) of the Court who control the proceedings.

Although essentially all felony cases are tried to a Court of Assizes in France, it was somehow particularly fitting that Touvier's case was heard by a jury. Throughout its history, the jury of the Court of Assizes has had a political cast, as various groups have sought to mold it to fit their particular ideology, whether it be as a voice of those holding power or of those seeking it. And indeed, in this very political trial, the significance of the jury cannot be underestimated, for to a large degree it was to the conscience of the jury (as the representatives of society at large), rather than the law of the case, that the lawyers appealed. . . .

Touvier's case was tried to a jury of eight men and one woman, the oldest of whom would have been only 13 at the time of the liberation. Presiding was Judge Heri Boulard. The trial lasted five and one-half weeks, during which more than 50 witnesses and experts, the civil parties themselves, and Touvier were heard. Theatrical and long awaited, the event was well attended by French journalists, although few from the international press were present. . . .

* * *

The defense availed itself of essentially four tactics. First, Touvier's attorney attacked various aspects of the procedure by making numerous evidentiary motions and objections. . . .

Second, Touvier's attorney, attempted what came to be characterized in the press as a sort of "Shindler defense." Touvier's argument had always been that he ordered the murder of the 7 men at Rillieux in self-defense because the Gestapo forced him to after the execution of Phillipe Henriot, a high-ranking Vinchy official, by the Resistance. But Touvier also claimed that Commandant Knab of the Gestapo had ordered the killing of 100 hostages; that Touvier's chief reduced that number to 30, and that only through Touvier's intervention was the number reduced to 7. Thus, according to his reckoning, he had saved the lives of 23 men. Although the press of the Far Right accepted this version of the story, very few others did. . . .

Third, the defense relied on Touvier's advancing age and the press's use of him as a scapegoat to portray him as a defenseless old man who had already suffered enough. His obvious illness and his family's favorable testimony might have allowed this strategy to succeed had Touvier not been his worst enemy. Evasive and unrepentant when questioned, he often appeared to be lying on the stand, particularly when he denied that he was in any way anti-Semitic. . . .

Finally, Tremolet de Villers [Touvier's attorney] attempted to appeal to the jury's sense of justice by pointing to the artificial legal construct on which Touvier's trial was based. One prong of this argument promoted the idea that Touvier was being prosecuted selectively and that many others who were guilty of crimes against humanity over the years had not been punished. Thus, Touvier's lawyer referred to the failure to prosecute the Russian perpetrators of the Katyn massacre in Poland and to the unsuccessful attempt to prosecute Frenchman George Boudarel for his alleged crimes against French soldiers in Indochina. This vein of argument did not appear to impress either the judge or the jury.

* * *

On Wednesday, 20 April 1994, after five and one-half hours of deliberation, the verdict was delivered at about 12:30 a.m. Touvier was pronounced guilty and sentenced to life imprisonment, and the symbolic one franc requested by the civil parties was granted.

* * *

If one accepts that punishment is generally an appropriate societal response to criminal behavior such as the murders at Rillieux, the only issue is whether there is any reason *not* to punish Touvier. The legal obstacles were put to rest through a series of French Supreme Court decisions issued from 1973 to 1992....

Modern theories of criminal justice generally justify the punishment of criminals either on the basis of some benefit society can expect to receive as a result—to deter other criminals or to rehabilitate or to incapacitate the offender (utilitarian theory) or because the criminal "deserves" punishment for the hurt he has inflicted on society (retributive theory). Considering Touvier's age (79), neither specific deterrence nor rehabilitation appear particularly relevant to his case. There is no suggestion that he needed to be punished to stop him from committing further crimes or to rehabilitate him. Although a strong argument can be made that he should be punished to deter repeat violations of the "laws of humanity" either in France or abroad, it is not clear that there is much empirical support for this position.

* * *

I am not suggesting that retribution is by itself a sufficient moral basis for punishment. But Touvier's trial did not merely "avenge" his victims; it honored their losses and restored to their descendants a sense of dignity and faith in society. Much of the testimony from the civil parties during his trial is to this effect. And while it may surprise American lawyers that the victims could themselves bring and participate in Touvier's criminal trial, in France this is not unusual. The French criminal code specifically permits private parties and certain groups to bring a civil action for damages (*action civile*) based on a criminal offense and to initiate a criminal prosecution if the state fails to do so. Thus, many of the prosecuting parties in Touvier's case were private, including several associations organized to combat crimes against humanity or to represent the rights of former deportees and members of the Resistance.

Given the facts of Touvier's case, it is almost unthinkable that he should not be held accountable. Already sentenced to death just after the war, Touvier was able to avoid punishment only by hiding from the French authorities. He did nothing in the way of contributing to or reinserting himself into society that one could argue had "earned" him his freedom.... Touvier was convicted on the basis of extensive eyewitness testimony, corroborated by his own admission of guilt. Finally, arguments that he should not be tried because other war criminals (either from World War II or otherwise) have not been prosecuted are misplaced. If this is problematic, the problem is the government's failure to pursue the other defendants, not its decision to prosecute Touvier.

[The *Finta* case from Canada concludes *Part Four*. The excerpts that follow are taken from the opinion of the Supreme Court of Canada handed down in March, 1994. Respondent, who emigrated to Canada in 1951, was charged with war crimes and crimes against humanity that were allegedly committed by him while he was a member of the Royal Hungarian Gendarmerie during the German occupation of Hungary in 1944. Finta, among others, was attempting to enforce the so-called "Baky Order"—the deporting of Hungarian Jews to Nazi concentration camps and the consequent plundering of their property.

Imre Finta was charged in a eight-count indictment preferred by the Attorney-General of Canada on August 18, 1988. The accused maintained that sec. 6(1.91) of the *Canadian Criminal Code*, under which he was charged, was, among other things, contrary to the provisions of the *Canadian Charter of Rights and Freedoms* on the grounds that it was retroactive. In reply, the Crown maintained that sec. 6(1.91) was not retroactive, but simply extended the jurisdiction of the Canadian courts to cover both war crimes and crimes against humanity that were committed outside of Canada. The Crown also argued that no new crimes had been created by this legislation because both war crimes and crimes against humanity existed at the time respondent had committed the charged offenses in Hungary. Continuing his attack on the entire process, respondent also averred that the charges against him were summary in nature and that the Canadian Criminal Code did not provide that they were indictable, hence they were prescribed by a six-month statute of limitation. Finta also argued that the Canadian legislation violated the principle of extraterritoriality and was thus *untra vires* the Canadian Parliament; that he had already been tried and found guilty *in absentia* in Hungary and argued that evidence coming to Canada from the latter country was highly suspect. Finally, Finta maintained that the indictment was too vague and that the time lapse between alleged charges and the Canadian indictment (1944–1988) had materially contributed to the difficulty in preparing an adequate defense.

The trial court ruled that the provisions of the Canadian Criminal Code were *retrospective* in application and not retroactive. The code provisions did not transform a previously innocent act into a criminal offense. The trial court was of the opinion that the Canadian legislation complained of was simply to extend the jurisdiction of Canadian courts to cover certain offenses that occurred beyond the territorial jurisdiction of the Commonwealth. The prosecution's argument here was that war crimes and crimes against humanity had existed as offences well before 1944 when the respondent had allegedly committed the acts and omissions at issue.

In point of fact, the charged crimes against respondent were (a) unlawful confinement; (b) robbery; (c) kidnapping; and (d) manslaughter. The trial court also held that the principle of extraterritoriality was not violated and was not *ultra vires* the power of the Canadian Parliament; and, furthermore, the legislation did not discriminate on the basis of national or ethnic origins. The lower court also was of the opinion that evidence from an "Eastern Bloc" country, a Communist State, was not, of itself, inherently unreliable. The trial court concluded, finally, that the indictment was sufficiently explicit and was not vague and that it was up to the trial judge, *ex mero motu*, to correct any prejudicial effects such a long delay may have had regarding the fairness of the proceedings].

---

10. *Regina v. Finta*

Supreme Court of Canada
March 24, 1994
104 *International Law Reports* 285

LAMER, C. J. C.: I have read the reasons of my colleagues, LaForest and Cory JJ. For reasons give by Corey, J., I would dismiss the appeal. This being so, I would dismiss the cross-appeal as being moot. [The facts are reported in the dissenting opinion by Justice La Forest]:

The accused, Imre Finta, was born in Kolosvar, Hungary (now a part of Romania) in 1912. During the 1930s, he lived and studied in the Royal Hungarian Military Academy and in January, 1939, he was commissioned as an officer in the Royal Hungarian Gendarmerie. The gendarmerie is the most accurately described as an armed paramilitary police force which served the Hungarian government by wielding political muscle in the country's more rural areas. By 1942, Mr. Finta had achieved the rank of captain in this notorious organization.

In March, 1944, Mr. Finta was posted to Szeged as commander of the investigative subdivision of the gendarmerie. That same month Hungary had been occupied by the forces of the Third Reich. Despite the fact that Hungary had joined the Axis powers in 1940, Germany proceeded to install an even more pro-German puppet government in the Hungarian capital of Budapest. Thus, throughout the relevant period, Hungary was a *de facto* occupied state. The Hungarian police and the gendarmerie came under the direct command of the German SS, and these two organizations were instrumental in administering the anti-Jewish laws adopted by the Nazi government of Germany and the Hungarian government under its control.

The charges against Mr. Finta stem from his time in Szeged. Mr. Finta is alleged to have been in charge of the "de-jewification" of Szeged during the spring of 1944. This activity was authorized by the so-called "Baky Order," the Hungarian Ministry of Interior order passed on April 7, 1944. In its essentials, the "Baky Order" called for the isolation, complete expropriation, ghettoization, concentration, entrainment and eventual deportation (primarily to Auschwitz and Birkenau) of all Hungarian Jews. Once there, these Jews faced either immediate extermination or forced labor followed by eventual extermination. The events at Szeged were duplicated in villages and towns across Hungary throughout that unfortunate spring. There can be no doubt that this process, which my colleague, Justice Cory, has described in all its horrific detail, was an integral part of what the Nazis themselves dubbed the "final solution" to the "Jewish problem," namely, the systematic slaughter of every last European Jew.

In 1947–48, Mr. Finta was tried and convicted, *in absentia*, by a Szeged court for "crimes against the people" relating to his role as a gendarmerie captain during the spring 1944 purge of Szeged's Jewish population. In 1951, Finta emigrated to Canada. In 1956, he became a Canadian citizen, and has lived in this country ever since.

Mr. Finta was charged with unlawful confinement, robbery, kidnapping and manslaughter of 8,617 Jews between May 16th and June 30, 1944, at or about Szeged, Hungary, thereby committing an offence under the definitions of these crimes in the *Criminal Code* existing at the time the offences were committed. The indictment added that such offences constituted crimes against humanity and war crimes under what is now s. 7(3.71) of the *Criminal Code*. The latter reference was added because prosecution for crimes committed abroad cannot ordinarily take place in Canada since criminal offences are generally confined to conduct that takes place in Canada (s.6 of the *Code*), and the conduct alleged here took place in Hungary: Section 7(3.71), however, permits prosecution for conduct outside Canada if such conduct constitutes a crime against humanity or a war crime and would have been a crime in Canada at the time it took place had it been committed here. As Corey J., states, the principal issue in this case concerns a proper understanding of this and related provisions permitting persons to be prosecuted in Canada for crimes against Canadian law if these crimes also constitute crimes against humanity or war crimes under international law.

* * *

…Following a pre-trial motion before the late Callaghan A. C. J. H. C. of the Ontario Court, General Division, to consider a number of constitutional issues regarding the validity of the legislation under the Charter; a trial was held before Campbell J. sitting with a jury. The accused was acquitted and the acquittal was affirmed by a majority of the Ontario Court of Appeal,.... From that decision, the Crown appealed to this court, raising seven grounds of appeal.

* * *

CORY, J....

Some facts, well known to all, must be set out. In September of 1939, the Second World War began in Europe. It ended on that continent with the surrender of Germany on May 8, 1945. Canada, as one of the allied powers, was at war with the axis countries (Germany and Italy) during the war. Hungary joined the axis powers in 1940, and was officially in armed conflict with Canada between December 7, 1941, and January 20, 1945.

Throughout the war, Germany was led by Adolf Hitler and the National Socialist German Workers' Party (the Nazi Party). The German government pursued a cruel and vicious policy directed against Jewish people. When the war broke out, this same cruel policy was extended to all the areas under German influence and occupation, including Hungary. The implementation of the "final solution" by the German government meant that Jews were deprived of all means of earning an income, of their property, and eventually deported to camps in eastern Europe, where they provided forced labour for the German war effort. In these dreadful camps, many were put to death.

In Hungary, between 1941 and 1944, a series of anti-Jewish laws were passed. They culminated in the promulgation of a law containing a formula for the identification of Jews and requiring them to wear the yellow star. The Jews were therefore an identifiable group for the purposes of Hungarian law.

In March, 1944, German troops invaded Hungary. The existing government was removed and an even more servile pro-German puppet government was installed. After the invasion, although Hungary appeared to exist as a sovereign state, it was in fact an occupied country. In order to obtain complete control over Hungary's economic and military resources, the German government established a command structure which flowed directly from Heinrich Himmler, the Reischfuehrer SS and chief of German police, through the German-appointed Higher SS and Police leader for Hungary in Budapest, and thence to the various German police and SS units that were stationed throughout the country, and from there to the Royal Hungarian Gendarmerie and the Hungarian police force.

The Royal Hungarian Gendarmerie was an armed paramilitary public security organization. It provided police services in rural areas and acted as a political police force. The German forces occupying Hungary were instructed not to disarm the gendarmerie as it was in the process of being restructured so that it would be available to the Hungarian Higher SS and the police leader. Following the German occupation, the new puppet government quickly passed a series of anti-Jewish laws and decrees. A plan for the purging of Jews from Hungary was incorporated in Ministry of Interior Order 6163/44, dated April 7, 1944. This was the infamous Baky Order: It was the only "authority" for the confinement of all Hungarian Jews, the confiscation of their property and their deportation.

* * *

Shortly after the issuance of the Baky Order; the six phases of the "final solution" were put into effect in Szeged. The Jewish people of the city were rounded up and forced into a fenced-in ghetto. Usually the Jews remained in the ghetto for a couple of weeks. They were then either transferred directly to a brickyard, or first to a sports field and then a few days later to the brickyard. By June 20, 1944, 8,617 Jews had been collected in the brickyard.

The brickyard was filthy, with grossly inadequate sanitary facilities. It consisted of a large open area containing an enormous kiln, a chimney and several buildings used for drying bricks. Jewish men, women and children were crowded together. They slept on the ground in the drying sheds, which had roofs but no walls. The compound was surrounded by a fence and guarded by gendarmes.

Announcements were repeatedly made over the loudspeaker ordering the Jews to surrender their remaining valuables, gold or jewellery: When the Jews were gathered for these announcements, a basket or hamper was presented for the collection of the valuables and the people were told that anyone who failed to comply with the orders would be executed.

In the days between June 24 and 30, 1944, the Jews in the brickyard were marched by the gendarmes to the Rokus train station. There they were forced into boxcars on three trains which took them from their homes in Hungary to the stark horror of the concentration camps.

Some 70 to 90 Jews together with their luggage were forced into each boxcar. These cars measured roughly eight metres by two metres. There was no artificial lighting in them. The crowding was so intense that most were forced to remain standing throughout the dreadful journey. The doors of the boxcars were padlocked shut. The only openings for air were small windows with grilles located in each of the four upper corners of the boxcar....

As a result of the intolerable conditions in the boxcars, some of the Jews, particularly the elderly, died during the journey. Neither the gendarmes nor the German guards permitted the bodies to be removed prior to the train's reaching its destination. The stench of decaying flesh was added to that of human excrement. Truly, these were nightmare journeys into hell.

* * *

The trial judge directed the jury that the Baky Order was unlawful as violating Hungarian law, including a number of principles of the Hungarian Constitution.

* * *

The Crown's case depended in large measure on the testimony of 19 witnesses who had been interned in the brickyard and deported on one of three trains. Some gave *viva voce* [oral testimony] evidence before the jury. Others were examined by way of commission evidence taken in Israel and Hungary and their evidence was then presented at trial on videotape. Additionally, the trial judge at the request of the defence, directed that the videotape of commission evidence of two other survivors be placed before the jury.

* * *

In addition to evidence of the survivors, the Crown relied on photographs, handwriting and fingerprint evidence to identify Finta as a captain in the gendarmerie at Szeged at the relevant time.

Expert and documentary evidence was tendered to establish the historical context of the evidence, the relevant command structure in place in Hungary in 1944, and the state of international law in 1944.

* * *

At trial, the Crown contended that Finta was the senior officer of the gendarmerie at the Szeged concentration centre and had effective control over the operation and guarding of the centre, thus committing the acts in question. Alternatively it was said that through his supervisory role, he procured, aided or abetted others who actually performed the acts alleged. Though acknowledging his presence at the time and place of the alleged offences, Finta denied that he was in a position of authority at the brickyard and stated that he was subject at the time to the command of the German SS. He denied responsibility for the alleged offences.

* * *

The jury acquitted Finta on all counts.

* * *

The jurisdiction of Canadian courts is, in part, limited by the principle of territoriality. That is, Canadian courts, as a rule, may only prosecute those crimes which have been committed within Canadian territory.... This rule reflects the principle of sovereign integrity, which dictates that a state has exclusive sovereignty over all persons, citizens or aliens and all property, real or personal, within its own territory.... However, there are exceptions to the principle of territoriality. [Here the Court accepts the principle of universality as a jurisdictional reality and then alludes to the so-called Deschenes Commission (the Commission of Inquiry on War Criminals), established in 1985, whose recommendations moved the Canadian Parliament to amend the *Criminal Code* to include section 7(3.71) to section (3.77)]. These provisions constitute an exception to the principle of territoriality found in s. 6(2) of the *Code*.

However, the jurisdiction of Canadian courts to try offences under s. 7(3.71) to (3.77) is carefully circumscribed. It is only when the following conditions are fulfilled that offences under s 7(3.71) may be prosecuted in Canada: (1) the act or omission was committed outside the territorial boundaries of Canada; (2) *the act or omission constitutes a crime against humanity or a war crime*; (3) the act or omission, had it been committed in Canada, would have constituted an offence against the laws of Canada in force at the time, and (4) in the words of the section at the time of the act or omission [the defendant was a Canadian citizen; a citizen of a state engaged in armed conflict against Canada; or the victim is either a Canadian citizen or a citizen of a state allied with Canada in an armed conflict; or (5) Canada could have exercised jurisdiction over the person on the basis of that person's presence in Canada].

* * *

It can be seen that the accused, in order to be convicted, must have committed an act that constituted a war crime or a crime against humanity *and* that the same act would constitute an offence against the laws of Canada in force at the time the act was committed.... In the mind of the public, those persons indicted for having committed crimes against humanity or war crimes stand charged with committing offences so grave that they shock the conscience of all right-thinking people. The stigma that must attach to a conviction for such a crime is overwhelming. Society simply cannot tolerate the commission of such crimes....

* * *

Thus, *with respect to crimes against humanity, the additional element is that the inhumane acts were based on discrimination against or the persecution of an identifiable group of people. With respect to war crimes, the additional element is that the actions constitute a violation of the laws of armed conflict.* These elements must be established both in order for a Canadian court to have jurisdiction to try the accused *and* in order to convict the accused of the offence.

ii. *The Mental Element or Mens Rea*

The "international element" of the s.7(3.71) offences is not comprised solely of the *actus reus* or of the physical quality of the actions. Canada acquires jurisdiction over actions performed in foreign territory only when those actions reach the level of an international crime or when they are "criminal" according to the general principles of international law. A crime is composed of both a physical and a mental element. As was noted by the Court of Appeals in the present case, the definition of war crimes and crimes against humanity found in s.7(3.76) do not expressly define the mental state which must accompany the facts or circumstances that bring an act within the definition of a war crime or a crime against humanity. Thus, a mental element must be read into those definitions.... Proof of this mental element is an integral part of determining whether the offences committed amount to a war crime or a crime against humanity and thus, whether the court has jurisdiction to try the case.

The appellant contends that the deeming mechanism in the *Code* provision presently under consideration is such that an accused charged under s.7(3.71) may be found guilty *not* of "war crimes" or "crimes against humanity" but of "ordinary" *Code* offenses such as manslaughter, confinement or robbery. It is further argued that proof of the *mens rea* with respect to the domestic offences provides the element of personal fault required for offences under s7(3.71). Thus, it is submitted, proof of further moral culpability is not required, since once the necessary *mens rea* to confine forcibly, rob or commit manslaughter has been proved, it becomes impossible to maintain that the accused was morally innocent.

I cannot accept that argument. What distinguishes a crime against humanity from any other criminal offence under the Canadian *Criminal Code* is that the cruel and terrible actions which are essential elements of the offence were undertaken in pursuance of a policy of discrimination or persecution of an identifiable group or race. With respect to war crimes, the distinguishing feature is that the terrible actions constituted a violation of the laws of war. Although the term laws of war may appear to be an oxymoron, such laws do exist. War crimes, like crimes against humanity, shock the conscience of all right-thinking people. The offences described in s.7(3.71) are thus very different from and far more grievous than any of the underlying offences.

For example, it cannot be denied that the crimes against humanity alleged in this case, which resulted in the cruel killing of thousands of people, are far more grievous than occasioning the death of a single person by an act which constitutes manslaughter in Canada. To be involved in the confinement, robbing and killing of thousands of people belonging to an identifiable group must, in any view of morality or criminality, be more serious than even the commission of an act which would constitute murder in Canada.

Therefore, while the underlying offences may constitute a base level of moral culpability, Parliament has added a further measure of blameworthiness by requiring that the act or omission constitute a crime against humanity or a war crime. If the jury is not satisfied that this additional element of culpability has been established beyond a reasonable doubt, then the accused cannot be found guilty of a war crime or a crime against humanity....

There can be no doubt that Canadians were revolted by the suffering inflicted upon millions of innocent people. It seems that the section was passed to bring to trial those who inflicted death and cruel suffering in a knowing, premeditated, calculated way. The essential quality of a war crime or a crime against humanity is that the accused must be aware of or willfully blind to the fact that he is inflicting untold misery on his victims.

The requisite mental element of a war crime or a crime against humanity should be based on a subjective test. I reach this conclusion for a number of reasons. First, the crime itself must be considered in context. Such crimes are usually committed during a time of war. Wars are concerned with death and destruction. Sweet reason is often among the first victims. The manipulation of emotions, often by the dissemination of false information and propaganda, is part and parcel of the terrible tapestry of war. False information and slanted reporting is so predominant that it cannot be automatically assumed that persons in units such as the Gendarmerie would really know that they were part of a plot to exterminate an entire race of people.

It cannot be forgotten that the Hungarian people were loyal to the Axis cause. There was strong pro-German sentiment throughout the country. This was a time of great stress and anxiety as the Russian advance pushed back the German armies towards the borders of Hungary....

Section 7(3.71) cannot be aimed at those who killed in the heat of battle or in defence of their country. It is aimed at those who inflicted immense suffering with foresight and calculated malevolence.

* * *

...The degree of moral turpitude that attaches to crimes against humanity and war must exceed that of domestic offences of manslaughter or robbery. It follows that the accused must be aware of the conditions which render his or her actions more blameworthy than the domestic offence....

Thus, for all of the reasons set out earlier, I am in agreement with the majority of the Court of Appeal's assessment that the mental element of a crime against humanity must involve an awareness of the facts or circumstances which would bring the acts within the definition of a crime against humanity. However, I emphasize it is *not* necessary to establish that the accused knew that his or her actions were inhumane. As the majority stated at p. 116 [D.L.R.]:

> ...If the jury accepted the evidence of the various witnesses who described the conditions in the boxcars which transported the Jews away from Szeged, the jury would have no difficulty concluding that the treatment was "inhumane" within the definition of that word supplied by the trial judge. The jury would then have to determine whether Finta was aware of those conditions. If the jury decided that he was aware of the relevant conditions, the knowledge requirement was established regardless of whether Finta believed those conditions to be inhumane.

Similarly, for war crimes, the Crown would have to establish that the accused knew or was aware of the facts or circumstances that brought his or her actions within the definition of a war crime. That is to say that the accused would have to be aware that the facts or circumstances of his or her actions were such that, viewed objectively, they would shock the conscience of all right-thinking people.

Alternatively, the *mens rea* requirement of both crimes against humanity and war crimes would be met if it were established that the accused was willfully blind to the facts or circumstances that would bring his or her actions within the provisions of these offences.

* * *

...I am of the view that...the challenged provisions of the *Criminal Code* do not violate the Charter [i. e., the *Canadian Charter of Rights and Freedoms*].

MCLACHLIN, J. concurs with LAFOREST J.

MAJORS J. concurs with CORY J.

Suggestions for Further Reading

(1) Abarinov, Vladimir, *The Murderers of Katyn.* New York: Hippocrene Books (1993).

(2) Aly, Gotz & Susanne Heim, *Architects of Annihilation: Auschwitz and the Logic of Destruction.* London: Orion (2002).

(3) Arendt, Hannah, *Eichmann in Jerusalem: A Report on the Banality of Evil.* New York: Penguin Books (1977).

(4) Baade, Hans W., "The Eichmann Trial: Some Legal Aspects," 1961 *Duke Law Journal* 400.

(5) Bassiouni, M. Cherif, *Crimes Against Humanity in International Criminal Law*, 2d rev. ed. The Hague: Kluwer Law International (1999).

(6) Binder, Guyora, "Representing Nazism: Advocacy and Identity at the Trial of Klaus Barbie," 99 *Yale Law Journal* 1321 (1989).

(7) Braham, Randolph L., *The Eichmann Case: A Source Book.* New York: World Federation of Hungarian Jews (1969).

(8) Corni, Gustavo, *Hitler's Ghettos: Voices from a Beleagued Society 1939–1944* (Nicola R. Iannelli trans.). London: Arnold (2002).

(9) Cowles, Willard B., "Universality of Jurisdiction Over War Crimes," 33 *California Law Review* 177 (1945).

(10) Fawcett, J. E. S., "The Eichmann Case," 38 *British Yearbook of International Law* 181 (1962).

(11) Feig, Konnilyn G., *Hell on Earth: A Holocaust Bibliography.* San Francisco: Multilith (1981).

(12) Finkielkraut, Alian, *Remembering in Vain: The Klaus Barbie Trial and Crimes Against Humanity* (Roxanne Lipidus & Sima Godfrey trans.). New York: Columbia University Press (1992).

(13) Green, Leslie C., "The Eichmann Case," 23 *Modern Law Review* 507 (1960).

(14) Heazlett, Elizabeth, Note, "Eichmann—International Law,?" 24 *University of Pittsburgh Law Review* 116 (1962).

(15) Horne, Alistair, *To Lose a Battle: France 1940.* Boston: Little, Brown (1969).

(16) Komarow, Gary, "Individual Responsibility Under International Law: The Nuremberg Principles in Domestic Legal Systems," 29 *International and Comparative Law Quarterly* 21 (1980).

(17) Lippmann, Matthew, "The Trial of Adolf Eichmann and the Quest for Global Justice," 8 *Buffalo Human Rights Law Review* 45 (2002).

(18) Marrus, Michael R., *The Holocaust in History*. New York: Penguin Books (1987).

(19) Massey, Stephen J., "Individual Responsibility for Assisting the Nazis Persecuting Civilians," 71 *Minnesota Law Review* 97 (1986).

(20) Merkl, Peter H., *Political Violence Under the Swastika*. Princeton, NJ: Princeton University Press (1975).

(21) Morgan, Ted, *An Uncertain Hour: The French, the Germans, the Jews, the Klaus Barbie Trial, and the City of Lyon, 1940–1945*. New York: Arbor/Morrow (1990).

(22) Musmanno, Michael A., *The Eichmann Kommandos*. Philadelphia: Macrae Smith (1961).

(23) Papadatos, Peter, *The Eichmann Trial*. New York: Praeger (1964).

(24) Paris, Erna, *Unhealed Wounds: France and the Klaus Barbie Affair*. New York: Grove Press (1985).

(25) Parsons,Geoge., Jr., Note, "Interntational Law: Jurisdiction Over Extraterritorial Crime: Universality Principle: War Crimes: Crimes Against Humanity: Piracy, Israel's Nazi and Nazi Collaborators (Punishment) Law," 46 *Cornell Law Quarterly* 326 (1961).

(26) Pearlman, Moshe, *The Capture and Trial of Adolf Eichmann*. London: Weidenfeld & Nicolson (1963).

(27) Peeler, Calvin, "The Politics of Memory: Restructuring Vichy and the Past the French Chose to Forget," 19 *Whittier Law Review* 353 (1997).

(28) Randall, Kenneth C., "Universal Jurisdiction Under International Law," 66 *Texas Law Review* 785 (1988).

(29) Robinson, Jacob, *And the Crooked Shall be Made Straight: The Eichmann Trial, the Jewish Catastrophe, and Hannah Arendt's Narrative*. New York:; Macmillian (1965).

(30) Schwarzenberger, Georg, "The Eichmann Judgment: An Essay in Censorial Jurisprudence," 15 *Current Legal Problems* 250 (1962).

(31) Tigar, Michael E., Susan S. Casey, Isabelle Giordani & Sivakumaren Mardemootoo, "Paul Touvier and the Crime Against Humanity," 30 *Texas International Law Journal* 285 (1995).

(32) Treves, Vanni E., "Jurisdictional Aspects of the Eichmann Trial," 47 *Minnesota Law Review* 557 (1963).

(33) Weinberg, Gerhard L., "Germany's War for World Conquest and the Extermination of the Jews," 10 *Holocaust and Genocide Studies* 119 (1996).

(34) Wexler, Lelia Sadat, "Reflections on the Trial of Vichy Collaborator Paul Touvier for Crimes against Humanity in France," 20 *Law and Social Inquiry* 191 (1995).

Part Five

SEATO Treaty; Vietnam War; Gulf of Tonkin Resolution; Peers Commission Report; *Medina and Calley* Cases; Commentary on My Lai; U.S. District Court Cases on Legality of Vietnam Conflict (1964–1975)

Editorial Commentary

Foreign military operations by the United States armed forces have taken a variety of forms. The United States-North Vietnam conflict in former French Indochina is certainly no exception, but for the fact that the Vietnam War was the first twentieth century foreign encounter involving a large-scale dual military and civilian insurgency. On the American side there were a number of low-visibility and unremarked run-of-the-mill courts-martials conducted by military commanders throughout South Vietnam under the authority of the *Uniform Code of Military Justice* (UCMJ). These involved a congeries of alleged violations of the UCMJ by American GIs against both civilian and military personnel. We will not dwell on these events in *Part Five*. Instead, we will focus attention on two cases that garnered widespread national and international attention—the *Medina* and *Calley* decisions tried in the United States—that involved violations of both the UCMJ and international law as well. We will also report two decisions from United States district courts that dealt with questions regarding the constitutional legitimacy of the Vietnam War coming to the legal forefront during the last phases of that conflict.

Before presenting selected case excerpts, we will reprint portions of a widely-acclaimed book on the Vietnam War by Belknap[1] that sets the stage for the American Vietnam morass and the military culture that was partially responsible for events

---

1. Michal R. Belknap, *The Vietnam War on Trial: The My Lai Massacre and the Court-Martial of Lieutenant Calley* (2002).

such as the My Lai killings. After the Belknap commentary, we will present the provisions of the 1954 SEATO agreement hammered out by then Secretary of State, John Foster Fulles, the United States government's legal justification for intervention in Vietnam via a State Department *Bulletin*, the Gulf of Tonkin Resolution by the United States Congress in 1964, and finally excerpts from the *Peers Commission Report* of 1970—the official United States Army internal investigation surrounding the My Lai incident. Subsequent to the *Peers* material, we will include excerpts from both the military and federal court proceedings implicating Captain Medina and Lieutenant Calley in the My Lai massacre. Additional commentary on both My Lai and the Vietnam War will be included among the various opinions in *Medina* and *Calley.*

We conclude *Part Five* with excerpts from two United States District Court opinions detailing their respective reasoning on the non-justiciability of the Vietnam War coming to them for resolution in the waning years of the Johnson Administration and early years of the Nixon Administration. These cases, in part, reflect the traditional reluctance of the federal judiciary to become embroiled in what, to it, was a particularly volatile and sensitive national issue unsuited to judicial resolution.

The Vietnam War was a somewhat unique martial encounter in the annals of American military and international relations history. To date, it remains the longest war in terms of years ever fought by this nation. Depending upon the time-line selected, one could argue that the Vietnamese conflict with the United States actually began as far back as 1954 when the French were roundly defeated and driven out of their Indochina colony by Ho Chi Minh's communist Vietminh at the battle of Dienbienphu in May, 1954. On July 21, 1954, a peace conference held in Geneva, Switzerland, agreed upon a cease-fire and the division of Vietnam into two relatively equal zones at the seventeenth parallel—the French South and the Vietminh North. The United States was not a signatory to these so-called Geneva Accords, but Secretary of State John Foster Dulles promoted the drafting of the Southeast Asia Treaty Organization (SEATO) to be a force in assisting those nations in the region to resist communist encroachments and provide a defense shield to protect countries such as Cambodia, Thailand, Laos and South Vietnam from the geopolitical designs of Communist China and North Vietnam. For all practical purposes, the communists insurgents loyal to Ho Chi Minh disregarded those provisions of the Geneva Accords that had set a timetable for domestic democratic elections and a democratic government for all of Vietnam. Their avowed aim was to remove, by force if necessary, all remnants of Western democratic influence in that part of the world. During the presidency of Dwight D. Eisenhower (1953–1961), the United States began the incremental support of the South Vietnamese government by dispatching members of MAAG (Military Assistance Advisory Group) to that country. By the year 1956, there were in place in South Vietnam more than 600 MAAG personnel. In his book on the Vietnam War and the trial of Lieutenant William Calley, Belknap presents an excellent summary of events leading up to the massive United States involvement in Vietnam. Belknap's narrative succinctly describes the historical antecedents that ultimately led to the subsequent trials of both Medina and Calley. We quote directly from *The Vietnam War on Trial.*

———————

1. Michal R. Belknap, *The Vietnam War on Trial*
8–12; 15; 17–18; 20; 22 (2002)
From *The Vietnam War on Trial*, by Michal R. Belknap,
© 2002 by the University Press of Kansas

…The United States was heavily involved in preventing a Communist takeover of South Vietnam when John F. Kennedy became president in 1961. "Inheriting from Eisenhower an increasingly dangerous if still limited commitment," historian George Herring writes, "he plunged deeper into the morass." Like most Americans, Kennedy believed the Cold War between the United States and the Soviet Union was a global struggle and consequently that Communist revolutionaries in Third World countries were direct threats to American interests. In his first year in office, he sent 100 more MAGG advisors to South Vietnam, along with 400 Special Forces troops to provide training in counterinsurgency techniques. Kennedy also approved an additional $42 million to support expansion of Diem's army. The CIA initiated a program designed to help villagers defend themselves against Communists and sent clandestine teams of South Vietnamese into the North to engage in sabotage and disruption. Despite these initiatives, the Vietcong stepped up military operations, infiltration accelerated, and the Diem regime grew increasingly unpopular. In late 1961, after visiting Vietnam, two of Kennedy's aides, General Maxwell Taylor and Professor Walt Rostow, recommended sending not only more military equipment and advisors but also American troops, ostensibly to assist in repairing flood damage in the Mekong Delta but actually to demonstrate the strength of America's commitment and provide a military reserve that could be employed if the situation deteriorated further. Secretary of Defense Robert McNamara and the Joint Chiefs of Staff supported their proposal, but other presidential advisers feared a deeper military involvement in Vietnam. Some even advocated negotiating an end to the conflict.

In the end Kennedy rejected the idea of introducing American ground forces. He opted instead for more of the same, authorizing significant increases in aid and advisers. The number of American military personnel in South Vietnam rose from 3,205 in December 1961 to more than 9,000 by the end of 1962. Many of the Americans did more than just advise. Special Forces "Green Berets" conducted civic action programs among Montagnard tribesmen in the Central Highlands, while other U.S. servicemen flew helicopters on combat support missions and even substituted for South Vietnamese aviators on bombing and strafing runs. The massive infusion of American men and weapons improved the military situation temporarily but by late 1962 the Vietcong had regained the initiative. Furthermore, the political situation was deteriorating toward chaos, as Buddhists mounted widespread demonstrations against the Catholic Diem, and his own generals plotted a coup. On 1 November 1963, they overthrew and murdered him.

Three weeks later Kennedy, too, was assassinated. Within less than two years after replacing him, his vice president, Lyndon Johnson, managed, as Herring explains, "to transform a limited commitment to assist the South Vietnamese government into an open-ended commitment to preserve an independent, non-Communist South Vietnam." Johnson did not set out to change his predecessors' policies. He and his advisers firmly believed, however, that the United States must stand firm in Vietnam in order to deter Chinese Communist aggression in Southeast Asia….

Intent on winning the 1964 presidential election, however, Johnson was unwilling to run the political risk that abandoning South Vietnam would entail. Rather than seek a diplomatic resolution of the conflict, he decided, after a major policy review in mid-March, to do more of the same, but to do it more efficiently.

Emphasizing that the essential U.S. goal was the maintenance of an independent, non-Communist South Vietnam, LBJ increased the number of American military "advisers" in the country from 16,300 to 23,300 during his first nine months in office and dispatched a hard-charging paratrooper, General William Westmoreland, to command them. The Johnson administration also boosted economic assistance to South Vietnam by $50 million. While most of its initiatives in the spring of 1964 were really just extensions of existing policies, it did opt for a new and more aggressive posture toward North Vietnam. Hoping to signal to Hanoi that the price for continued intervention in the South would be high, the United States expanded covert operations above the seventeenth parallel. These entailed intelligence overflights and the dropping of propaganda leaflets. They also included commando raids along the North Vietnamese coast, carried out by South Vietnamese personnel, acting pursuant to an operations plan known as 34A.

The 34A raids led to the Gulf of Tonkin incident in August 1964, which provided both a justification for stepping up the war and the occasion for congressional endorsements of Johnson's efforts to save South Vietnam from communism by military means....

[I]n the early morning hours of 2 August 1964, the U.S. destroyer *Maddox*, while conducting patrols in the Gulf of Tonkin in support of the 34A raids, came under attack by North Vietnamese PT boats eleven miles off the coast. North Vietnam claimed its territorial waters extended twelve miles; according to the United States, no country could exercise jurisdiction over more than three miles of ocean. Thus, it was debatable whether the *Maddox* had been the victim of aggression in international waters or whether the vessels that shot at the destroyer were merely defending North Vietnamese territory. Two nights later and much farther off the coast, the commander of the *Maddox's* sister ship, the *C. Turner Joy*, concluding (probably erroneously) that it, too, had come under attack, ordered his gunners to return fire. They hit nothing. Despite the ambiguities surrounding the two "attacks" in the Gulf of Tonkin, President Johnson responded with retaliatory air strikes against North Vietnamese bases.

He also seized upon the Gulf of Tonkin incidents as a justification for requesting enactment of the congressional resolution his advisers had drafted in May. Secretary McNamara told Congress that both American destroyers had been attacked. He failed to mention their involvement in the 34A commando raids against North Vietnam. Nor did he say how far off the coast the *Maddox* had been; instead, he declared it had been carrying out a "routine patrol" when it was attacked in "international waters." Deceived by the administration about precisely what had happened in the Gulf of Tonkin, Congress rallied behind the president, giving him on 7 August 1964 the show of unity in support of standing firm in Vietnam that he wanted. The House passed the Gulf of Tonkin Resolution unanimously, and only two senators voted against it. The closest thing there would ever be to a declaration of war in Vietnam, the resolution expressed congressional approval and support for the "determination of the President...to take all necessary measures to repel any armed attack against the forces of the United States and to prevent further aggression."...

* * *

Despite the growing doubts about where the Johnson administration was headed, it continued to muddle deeper in a military morass. The number of American troops in

Vietnam climbed steadily, rising from 23,000 at the beginning of 1965 to 184,000 only one year later. By the end of 1966, the number had climbed to 385,000. Early in 1968 it reached 535,000.

* * *

...Ninety-six percent of battles with the Vietcong and the North Vietnamese involved units of company size (around 200 men) or smaller. Although guerrilla warfare tactics would probably have produced the best results in such engagements, U.S. forces generally eschewed those in favor of the same reliance on firepower and helicopter mobility that characterized major operations. That held down American causalities, but with so much fighting going on and so many U.S. Army and Marine Corps troops involved, it did not eliminate them. During 1967 the number of U.S. personnel killed in action rose to over 200 each week, while the number wounded neared 1,400.

* * *

...The North Vietnamese relied heavily on ambushes and hit-and-run operations, seeking to initiate small fights at close quarters, in which the Americans could not make much use of their artillery and airpower. Their strategic objective was to draw U.S. forces away from populated areas, where the Vietcong could then operate freely.

Westmorland's search and destroy strategy played into the enemy's hands. It also gave American operations a dubious objective. The mission was simply to kill people. In the war of attrition Westmoreland was fighting, there were no "front lines" to be advanced, and the seizure of territorial objectives was at most a means to the end of annihilating the enemy. The measure of success became the "body count."

* * *

Diplomatically as well as militarily, the United States was getting nowhere. By the end of 1966, McNamara had become convinced the war was stalemated. He had concluded that no matter how much military pressure is applied, the United States could never break the will of the North Vietnamese. Throughout 1967 he pressed quietly for basic policy changes. The secretary of defense was not alone. During 1966, opposition to further escalation of the war increased among Johnson's civilian advisers. Eventually, some of them, such as Bill Moyers at the White House and George Ball at the State Department, became so alienated that they quietly resigned. By the spring of 1967, some presidential advisers were openly advocating the abandonment of policies they had become convinced were completely bankrupt.

* * *

Among the hundreds of thousands who would be sent off to Southeast Asia to risk their lives in this long, futile, and increasingly controversial military struggle was Lieutenant William Calley. On 15 September 1967 Calley completed OCS (Officer Candidate School) at Fort Benning. Now pinned on each shoulder of his uniform was the single gold bar that identified him as a second lieutenant. His new rank insignia required enlisted men to salute him. It was the army's certification that he was qualified to lead them into battle. The gold bar lied. Lieutenant Calley was not ready for the hell that awaited him in Vietnam.

———————

2. Southeast Asia Collective Defense Treaty

(SEATO) (1954)

Signed at Manila, September 8, 1954, entered into force as to the United States,
February 19, 1955 6 U.S. Treaties 81, T. I. A. S., No. 3170

60 *American Journal of International Law* 646 (1966)

Reproduced with permission from 60 *American Journal of International Law*
646 (1966). © The American Society of International Law

The parties to this Treaty,

Recognizing the sovereign equality of all the parties,

Reiterating their faith in the purposes and principles set forth in the Charter of the United Nations and their desire to live in peace with all peoples and all governments,

Reaffirming that, in accordance with the Charter of the United Nations, they uphold the principle of equal rights and self-determination of peoples, and declaring that they will earnestly strive by every peaceful means to promote self-government and to secure the independence of all countries whose peoples desire it and are able to undertake its responsibilities,

Desiring to strengthen the fabric of peace and freedom and to uphold the principles of democracy, individual liberty and the rule of law, and to promote the economic well-being and development of all peoples in the treaty area,

Intending to declare publicly and formally their sense of unity, so that any potential aggressor will appreciate that the parties stand together in the area, and

Desiring further to coordinate their efforts for collective defense for the preservation of peace and security,

Therefore agree as follows:

Article I

The parties undertake, as set forth in the Charter of the United Nations, to settle any international disputes in which they may be involved by peaceful means in such a manner that international peace and security and justice are not endangered, and to refrain in their international relations from the threat or use of force in any manner inconsistent with the purposes of the United Nations.

Article II

In order more effectively to achieve the objectives of this Treaty, the parties, separately and jointly, by means of continuous and effective self-help and mutual aid will maintain and develop their individual and collective capacity to resist armed attack and to prevent and counter subversive activities directed from without against their territorial integrity and political stability.

Article III

The parties undertake to strengthen their free institutions and to cooperate with one another in the further development of economic measures, including technical assistance, designed both to promote economic progress and social well-being and to further the individual and collective efforts of governments toward these ends.

Article IV

1. Each party recognizes that aggression by means of armed attack in the treaty area against any of the parties or against any state or territory which the parties by unanimous agreement may hereafter designate, would endanger its own peace and safety, and agrees that it will in that event act to meet the common danger in accordance with its constitutional processes. Measures taken under this paragraph shall be immediately reported to the Security Council of the United Nations.

2. If, in the opinion of any of the parties, the inviolability or the integrity of the territory or the sovereignty or political independence of any party in the treaty area or of any other state or territory to which the provisions of paragraph 1 of this article from time to time apply is threatened in any way other than by armed attack or is affected or threatened by any fact or situation which might endanger the peace of the area, the Parties shall consult immediately in order to agree on the measures which should be taken for the common defense.

3. It is understood that no action on the territory of any state designated by unanimous agreement under paragraph 1 of this article or on any territory so designated shall be taken except at the invitation or with the consent of the government concerned.

Article V

The parties hereby establish a Council, on which each of them shall be represented, to consider matters concerning the implementation of this Treaty. The Council shall provide for consultation with regard to military and any other planning as the situation obtaining in the treaty area may from time to time require. The Council shall be so organized as to be able to meet at any time.

Article VI

This Treaty does not affect and shall not be interpreted as affecting in any way the rights and obligations of any of the parties under the Charter of the United Nations or the responsibility of the United Nations for the maintenance of international peace and security. Each party declares that none of the international engagements now in force between it and any other of the parties or any third party is in conflict with the provisions of this Treaty, and undertakes not to enter into any international engagement in conflict with this Treaty.

Article VII

Any other state in a position to further the objectives of this Treaty and to contribute to the security of the area may, by unanimous agreement of the parties, be invited to accede to this Treaty. Any state so invited may become a party to the Treaty by depositing its instrument of accession with the Government of the Republic of the Philippines. The Government of the Republic of the Philippines shall inform each of the parties of the deposit of each such instrument of accession.

Article VIII

As used in this Treaty, the "treaty area" is the general area of Southeast Asia, including also the entire territories of the Asian parties, and the general area of the Southwest Pacific not including the Pacific area north of 21 degrees 30 minutes north latitude. The parties may, by unanimous agreement, amend this article to include within the treaty area the territory of any state acceding to this Treaty in accordance with Article VII or otherwise to change the treaty area.

Article IX

1. This Treaty shall be deposited in the archives of the Government of the Republic of the Philippines. Duly certified copies thereof shall be transmitted by that government to the other signatories.

2. The Treaty shall be ratified and its provisions carried out by the parties in accordance with their respective constitutional processes. The instruments of ratification shall be deposited as soon as possible with the Government of the Republic of the Philippines, which shall notify all of the other signatories of such deposit.

3. The Treaty shall enter into force between the states which have ratified it as soon as the instruments of ratification of a majority of the signatories shall have been deposited, and shall come into effect with respect to each other state on the date of the deposit of its instrument of ratification.

Article X

This Treaty shall remain in force indefinitely, but any party may cease to be a party one year after its notice of denunciation has been given to the Government of the Republic of the Philippines, which shall inform the governments of the other parties of the deposit of each notice of renunciation. [Article XI omitted].

Understanding of the United States of America

The United States of America in executing the present Treaty does so with the understanding that its recognition of the effect of aggression and armed attack and its agreement with reference thereto in Article IV, paragraph 1 apply only to communist aggression but affirms that in the event of other aggression or armed attack it will consult under the provisions of Article IV, paragraph 2.

In witness whereof, the undersigned Plenipotentiaries have signed this Treaty. [Signatures not listed].

Done at Manila, this eighth day of September, 1954.

Protocol to the Southeast Asia Collective Defense Treaty
Signed at Manila, September 8, 1954; entered into force
As to the United States, February 19, 1955

Designation of States and Territory As to which Provisions of
Article IV and Article III Are To Be Applicable

The parties to the Southeast Asia Collective Defense Treaty unanimously designate for the purposes of Article IV of the Treaty the States of Cambodia and Laos and the free territory under the jurisdiction of the state of Vietnam.

The parties further agree that the above mentioned states and territory shall be eligible in respect of the economic measures contemplated by Article III.

This Protocol shall enter into force simultaneously with the coming into force of the Treaty.

IN WITNESS WHEREOF, the undersigned Plenipotentiaries have signed this Protocol to the Southeast Asia Collective Defense Treaty. [Signatures not listed].

Done at Manila, this eighth day of September, 1954.

---

3. The Legality of United States Participation in the Defense of Viet-Nam

54 Department of State *Bulletin* 474 (1966);
Cong. Rec., March 10, 1966, p. 5274;
60 *American Journal of International Law* 565 (1966)
Reproduced with permission from 60 *American Journal of International Law*
565 (1966). © The American Society of International Law

1. The United States and South Viet-Nam Have the Right under International Law to Participate in the Collective Defense of South Viet-Nam against Armed Attack

In response to requests from the Government of South Viet-Nam, the United States has been assisting that country in defending itself against armed attack from the Communist North. This attack has taken the forms of externally supported subversion, clandestine supply of arms, infiltration of armed personnel, and most recently the sending of regular units of the North Vietnamese army into the South.

International law has long recognized the right of individual and collective self-defense against armed attack. South Viet-Nam and the United States are engaging in such collective defense consistently with international law and with United States obligations under the United Nations Charter.

A. South Viet-Nam is Being Subjected to Armed Attack by Communist North Viet-Nam

The Geneva accords of 1954 established a demarcation line between North Viet-Nam and South Viet-Nam. They provided for withdrawals of military forces into the respective zones north and south of this line. The accords prohibited the use of either zone for the resumption of hostilities or to "further an aggressive policy."

During the 5 years following the Geneva conference of 1954, the Hanoi regime developed a covert political-military organization in South Viet-Nam based on Communist cadres it had ordered to stay in the South, contrary to the provisions of the Geneva accords. The activities of this covert organization were directed toward the kidnapping and assassination of civilian officials—acts of terrorism that were perpetrated in increasing numbers.

In the 3-year period from 1959 to 1961, the North Viet-Nam regime infiltrated an estimated 10,000 men into the South. It is estimated that 13,000 additional personnel were infiltrated in 1962, and, by the end of 1964, North Viet-Nam may well have moved over 40,000 armed and unarmed guerrillas into South Viet-Nam.

The International Control Commission reported in 1962 the findings of its Legal Committee:

> …there is evidence to show that arms, armed and unarmed personnel, munitions and other supplies have been sent from the Zone in the North to the

Zone in the South with the objective of supporting, organizing and carrying out hostile activities, including armed attacks, directed against the Armed Forces and Administration of the Zone in the South.

...there is evidence that the PAVIN [People's Army of Viet Nam] has allowed the Zone in the North to be used for inciting, encouraging and supporting hostile activities in the Zone in the South, aimed at the overthrow of the Administration in the South.

Beginning in 1964, the Communist apparently exhausted their reservoir of Southerners who had gone North. Since then the greater number of men infiltrated into the South have been native-born North Vietnamese. Most recently, Hanoi has begun to infiltrate elements of the North Vietnamese army in increasingly larger numbers. Today, there is evidence that nine regiments of regular North Vietnamese forces are fighting in organized units in the South.

In the guerrilla war in Viet-Nam, the external aggression from the North is the critical military element of the insurgency, although it is unacknowledged by North Viet-Nam. In these circumstances, an "armed attack" is not as easily fixed by date and hour as in the case of traditional warfare. However, the infiltration of thousands of armed men clearly constitutes an "armed attack" under any reasonable definition. There may be some question as to the exact date at which North Viet-Nam's aggression grew into an "armed attack," but there can be no doubt that it had occurred before February 1965.

B. International Law Recognizes the Right of Individual and Collective Self-Defense against Armed Attack

International law has traditionally recognized the right of self-defense against armed attack. This proposition has been asserted by writers on international law through the several centuries in which the modern law of nations has developed. The proposition has been acted on numerous times by governments throughout modern history. Today the principle of self-defense against armed attack is universally recognized and accepted.

The Charter of the United Nations, concluded at the end of World War II, imposed an important limitation on the use of force by United Nations members. Article 2, paragraph 4, provides:

All Members shall refrain in their international relations from the threat or use of force against the territorial integrity or political independence of any state, or in any other manner inconsistent with the Purposes of the United Nations.

In addition, the charter embodied a system of international peace-keeping through the organs of the United Nations. Article 24 summarizes these structural arrangements in stating that the United Nations members:

...confer on the Security Council primary responsibility for the maintenance of international peace and security, and agree that in carrying out its duties under this responsibility the Security Council acts on their behalf.

However, the charter expressly states in Article 51 that the remaining provisions of the charter—including the limitation of article 2, paragraph 4, and the creation of United Nations machinery to keep the peace—in no way diminish the inherent right of self-defense against armed attack. Article 51 provides:

Nothing in the present Charter shall impair the inherent right of individual or collective self-defense if an armed attack occurs against a Member of the United Nations, until the Security Council has taken the measures necessary to maintain international peace and security. Measures taken by Members in the exercise of this right of self-defense shall be immediately reported to the Security Council and shall not in any way affect the authority and responsibility of the Security Council under the present Charter to take at any time such action as it deems necessary in order to maintain or restore international peace and security.

Thus, article 51 restates and preserves, for member states in the situations covered by the article, a long-recognized principle of international law. The article is a "saving clause" designed to make clear that no other provision in the charter shall be interpreted to impair the inherent right of self-defense referred to in article 51.

Three principal objections have been raised against the availability of the right of individual and collective self-defense in the case of Viet-Nam: (1) that this right applies only in the case of an armed attack on a United Nations member; (2) that it does not apply in the case of South Viet-Nam because the latter is not an independent sovereign state; and (3) that collective self-defense may be undertaken only by a regional organization operating under Chapter VIII of the United Nations Charter. These objections will now be considered in turn.

C. The Right of Individual and Collective Self-Defense Applies in the Case of South Viet-Nam Whether or Not That Country Is a Member of the United Nations

1. South Viet-Nam enjoys the right of self-defense

The argument that the right of self-defense is available only to members of the United Nations mistakes the nature of the right of self-defense and the relationship of the United Nations Charter to international law in this respect. As already shown, the right of self-defense against armed attack is an inherent right under international law. The right is not conferred by the Charter, and, indeed, article 51 expressly recognizes that the right is inherent.

The charter nowhere contains any provision designed to deprive non-members of the right of self-defense against armed attack. Article 2, paragraph 6, does charge the United Nations with responsibility for insuring that nonmember states act in accordance with United Nations "Principles so far as may be necessary for the maintenance of international peace and security." Protection against aggression and self-defense against armed attack are important elements in the whole charter scheme for the maintenance of international peace and security. To deprive nonmembers of their inherent right of self-defense would not accord with the principles of the organization, but would instead be prejudicial to the maintenance of peace. Thus article 2, paragraph 6 — and, indeed, the rest of the charter — should certainly not be construed to nullify or diminish the inherent defensive rights of nonmembers.

2. The United States has the right to assist in the defense of South Viet-Nam although the latter is not a United Nations member

The cooperation of two or more international entities in the defense of one or both against armed attack is generally referred to as collective self-defense. United States participation in the defense of South Viet-Nam at the latter's request is an example of collective self-defense.

The United States is entitled to exercise the right of individual or collective self-defense against armed attack, as that right exists in international law, subject only to treaty limitations and obligations undertaken by this country.

It has been urged that the United States has no right to participate in the collective defense of South Viet-Nam because article 51 of the United Nations Charter speaks only of the situation "if an armed attack occurs *against a Member of the United Nations.*" This argument is without substance. In the first place, article 51 does not impose restrictions or cut down the otherwise available rights of United Nations members. By its own terms, the article preserves an inherent right. It is, therefore, necessary to look elsewhere in the charter for any obligation of members restricting their participation in collective defense of an entity that is not a United Nations member.

Article 2, paragraph 4, is the principal provision of the charter imposing limitations on the use of force by members. It states that they:

> ...shall refrain in their international relations from the threat or use of force against the territorial integrity or political independence of any state, or in any other manner inconsistent with the Purposes of the United Nations.

Action taken in defense against armed attack cannot be characterized as falling within this proscription. The record of the San Francisco conference [which established the U.N.] makes clear that article 2, paragraph 4, was not intended to restrict the right of self-defense against armed attack.

One will search in vain for any other provision in the charter that would preclude United States participation in the collective defense of a nonmember. The fact that article 51 refers only to armed attack "against a Member of the United Nations" implies no intention to preclude members from participating in the defense of nonmembers. Any such result would have seriously detrimental consequences for international peace and security and would be inconsistent with the purposes of the United Nations as they are set forth in article 1 of the charter. The right of members to participate in the defense of nonmembers is upheld by leading authorities on international law.

D. The Right of Individual and Collective Self-Defense Applies Whether or Not South Viet-Nam Is Regarded as an Independent Sovereign State

1. *South Viet-Nam enjoys the right of self-defense*

It has been asserted that the conflict in Viet-Nam is "civil strife" in which foreign intervention is forbidden. Those who makes this assertion have gone so far as to compare Ho Chi Minh's actions in Viet-Nam with the efforts of President Lincoln to preserve the Union during the American Civil War. Any such characterization is an entire fiction disregarding the actual situation in Viet-Nam. The Hanoi regime is anything but the legitimate government of an unified country in which the South is rebelling against lawful national authority.

The Geneva accords of 1954 provided for a division of Viet-Nam into two zones at the 17th parallel. Although this line of demarcation was intended to be temporary, it was established by international agreement, which specifically forbade aggression by one zone against the other.

The Republic of Viet-Nam in the South has been recognized as a separate international entity by approximately 60 governments the world over. It has been admitted as a member of a number of the specialized agencies of the United Nations. The United Nations General Assembly in 1957 voted to recommend South Viet-Nam for membership in the organization, and its admission was frustrated only by the veto of the Soviet Union in the Security Council.

In any event there is no warrant for the suggestion that one zone of a temporarily divided state—whether it be Germany, Korea, or Viet-Nam—can be legally overrun by armed forces from the other zone, crossing the internationally recognized line of demarcation between the two. Any such doctrine would subvert the international agreement establishing the line of demarcation, and would pose grave dangers to international peace.

2. The United States is entitled to participate in the collective defense of South Viet-Nam whether or not the latter is regarded as an independent sovereign state

As stated earlier, South Viet-Nam has been recognized as a separate international entity by approximately 60 governments. It has been admitted to membership in a number of the United Nations specialized agencies and has been excluded from the United Nations Organization only by the Soviet veto.

There is nothing in the charter to suggest that United Nations members are precluded from participating in the defense of a recognized international entity against armed attack merely because the entity may lack some of the attributes of an independent sovereign state. Any such result would have a destructive effect on the stability of international engagements such as the Geneva accords of 1954 and on internationally agreed lines of demarcation. Such a result, far from being in accord with the charter and the purposes of the United Nations, would undermine them and would create new dangers to international peace and security.

* * *

F. The United States Has Fulfilled Its Obligations to the United Nations

A further argument has been made that the members of the United Nations have conferred on United Nations organs—and, in particular, on the Security Council—exclusive power to act against aggression. Again, the express language of article 51 contradicts that assertion. A victim of armed attack is not required to forego individual or collective defense of its territory until such time as the United Nation organizes collective action and takes appropriate measures. To the contrary, article 51 clearly states that the right of self-defense may be exercised "*until* the Security Council has taken the measures necessary to maintain international peace and security."

As indicated earlier, article 51 is not literally applicable to the Viet-Nam situation since North Vietnam is not a member. However, reasoning by analogy from article 51 and adopting its provisions as an appropriate guide for the conduct of members in a case like Viet-Nam, one can only conclude that United States actions are fully in accord with this country's obligations as a member of the United Nations.

Article 51 requires that:

> Measures taken by Members in the exercise of this right of self-defense shall be immediately reported to the Security Council and shall not in any way affect the authority and responsibility of the Security Council under the present Charter to take at any time such action as it deems necessary in order to maintain or restore international peace and security.

The United States has reported to the Security Council on measures it has taken in countering the Communist aggression in Viet-Nam. In August 1964 the United States asked the Council to consider the situation created by North Vietnamese attacks on United States destroyers in the Tonkin Gulf. The Council thereafter met to debate the question, but adopted no resolutions. Twice in February 1965 the United States sent additional reports to the Security Council on the conflict in Viet-Nam and on the additional measures taken by the United States in the collective defense of South Viet-Nam. In January 1966 the United States formally submitted the Viet-Nam question to the Security Council for its consideration and introduced a draft resolution calling for discussions looking toward a peaceful settlement on the basis of the Geneva accords.

At no time has the Council taken any action to restore peace and security in Southeast Asia. The Council has not expressed criticism of United States actions. Indeed, since the United States submission of January 1966, members of the Council have been notably reluctant to proceed with any consideration of the Viet-Nam question.

The conclusion is clear that the United States has in no way acted to interfere with United Nations consideration of the conflict in Viet-Nam. On the contrary, the United States has requested United Nations consideration, and the Council has not seen fit to act.

G. International Law Does Not Require a Declaration of War As a Condition Precedent to Taking Measures of Self-Defense against Armed Attack

The existence or absence of a formal declaration of war is not a factor in determining whether an international use of force is lawful as a matter of international law. The United Nations Charter's restrictions focus on the manner and purpose of its use and not on any formalities of announcement.

It should also be noted that a formal declaration of war would not place any obligations on either side in the conflict by which that side would not be bound in any event. The rules of international law concerning the conduct of hostilities in an international armed conflict apply regardless of any declaration or war.

* * *

II. The United States Has Undertaken Commitments to Assist South Viet-Nam in Defending Itself against Communists Aggression from the North

* * *

B. The United States Undertook an International Obligations to Defend South Viet-Nam in the SEATO Treaty

Later in 1954 the United States negotiated with a number of other countries and signed the Southeast Asia Collective Defense Treaty.

* * *

Thus, the obligations of article IV, paragraph 1, [of the SEATO Treaty, *supra*] dealing with the eventuality of armed attack, have from the outset covered the territory of South Viet-Nam. The facts as to the North Vietnamese armed attack against the South have been summarized earlier, in the discussion of the right to self-defense under international law and the Charter of the United Nations. The term "armed attack" has the same meaning in the SEATO treaty as in the United Nations Charter.

Article IV, paragraph 1, places an obligation on each party to the SEATO treaty to "act to meet the common danger in accordance with its constitutional processes" in the event of an armed attack. The treaty does not require a collective determination that an armed attack has occurred in order that the obligation of article IV, paragraph 1 become operative. Nor does the provision require collective decision on actions to be taken to meet the common danger. As Secretary Dulles pointed out when transmitting the treaty to the President, the Commitment in article IV, paragraph 1, "leaves to the judgment of each country the type of action to be taken in the event an armed attack occurs."

The treaty was intended to deter armed aggression in Southeast Asia. To that end it created not only a multilateral alliance but also a series of bilateral relationships. The obligations are placed squarely on "each Party" in the event of armed attack in the treaty area — not upon "the Parties," a wording that might have implied a necessity for collective decisions. The treaty was intended to give the assurance of United States assistance to any party or protocol state that might suffer a Communist armed attack, regardless of the views or actions of other parties. The fact that the obligations are individual, and may even to some extent differ among the parties to the treaty, is demonstrated by the United States understanding, expressed at the time of signature, that its obligations under article IV, paragraph 1, apply only in the event of *Communist* aggression, whereas the other parties to the treaty were unwilling so to limit their obligations to each other.

Thus, the United States has a commitment under article IV, paragraph 1, in the event of an armed attack, independent of the decision or action of other treaty parties. A joint statement issued by Secretary Rusk and Foreign Minister Thanat Khoman of Thailand on March 6, 1962, reflected this understanding:...

Most of the SEATO countries have stated that they agreed with this [Rusk-Khoman] interpretation. None has registered objection to it.

When the Senate Committee on Foreign Relations reported on the Southeast Asia Collective Defense Treaty, it noted that the treaty area was further defined so that the "Free Territory of Vietnam" was an area "which if attacked, would fall under the protection of the instrument." In its conclusion the committee stated:

> The committee is not impervious to the risks which the treaty entails. It fully appreciates that acceptance of these additional obligations commits the United States to a course of action over a vast expanse of the Pacific. Yet these risks are consistent with our own highest interests.

The Senate gave its advice and consent to the treaty by a vote of 82 to 1.

* * *

III. Actions by the United States and South Viet-Nam Are Justified under the Geneva Accords of 1954

A. Description of the Accords

The Geneva accords of 1954 established the date and hour for a cease-fire in Viet-Nam, drew a "provisional military demarcation line" with a demilitarized zone on both sides, and required an exchange of prisoners and the phased regroupment of Viet Minh forces from the south to the north and of French Union forces from the north to the south. The introduction into Viet-Nam of troop reinforcements and new military equipment (except for replacement and repair) was prohibited. The armed forces of each party were required to respect the demilitarized zone and the territory of the other zone. The adherence of either zone to any military alliance, and the use of either zone for the resumption of hostilities or to "further an aggressive policy," were prohibited. The International Control Commission was established composed of India, Canada and Poland, with India as chairman. The task of the Commission was to supervise the proper execution of the provisions of the cease-fire agreement. General elections that would result in reunification were required to be held in July 1956 under the supervision of the ICC.

B. North Viet-Nam Violated the Accords From the Beginning

From the very beginning, the North Vietnamese violated the 1954 Geneva accords. Communist military forces and supplies were left in the South in violation of the accords. Other Communist guerrillas were moved north for further training and then were infiltrated into the South in violation of the accords.

C. The Introduction of United States Military Personnel and Equipment Was Justified

The accords prohibited the reinforcement of foreign military forces in Viet-Nam and the introduction of new military equipment, but they allowed replacement of existing military personnel and equipment. Prior to late 1961 South Viet-Nam had received considerable military equipment and supplies from the United States, and the United States had gradually enlarged its Military Assistance Advisory Group to slightly less than 900 men. These actions were reported to the ICC and were justified as replacements for equipment in Viet-Nam in 1954 and for French training and advisory personnel who had been withdrawn after 1954.

As the Communist aggression intensified during 1961, with increased infiltration and a marked stepping up of a Communist terrorism in the South, the United States found it necessary in late 1961 to increase substantially the numbers of our military personnel and the amounts and types of equipment introduced by this country into South Viet-Nam. These increases were justified by the international law principle that a material breach of an agreement by one party entitles the other at least to withhold compliance with an equivalent, corresponding, or related provision until the defaulting party is prepared to honor its obligations.

In accordance with this principle, the systematic violation of the Geneva accords by North Viet-Nam justified South Viet-Nam in suspending compliance with the provision controlling entry of foreign military personnel and military equipment.

* * *

IV. The President Has Full Authority to Commit United States
Forces in the Collective Defense of South Viet-Nam

There can be no question in present circumstances of the President's authority to commit United States forces to the defense of South Viet-Nam. The grant of authority to the President in article II of the Constitution extends to the actions of the United States currently undertaken in Viet-Nam. In fact, however, it is unnecessary to determine whether this grant standing alone is sufficient to authorize the actions taken in Viet-Nam. These actions rest not only on the exercise of Presidential powers under article II but on the SEATO treaty—a treaty advised and consented to by all the Senate—and on actions of the Congress, particularly the joint resolution of August 10, 1964 [the Gulf of Tonkin Resolution]. When these sources of authority are taken together—article II of the Constitution, the SEATO treaty, and actions by the Congress—there can be no question of the legality under domestic law of United States actions in Viet-Nam.

A. The President's Power Under Article II of the Constitution Extends to the Actions Currently Undertaken in Viet-Nam

Under the Constitution, the President, in addition to being Chief Executive, is Commander in Chief of the Army and Navy. He holds the prime responsibility for the conduct of United States foreign relations. These duties carry very broad powers, including the power to deploy American forces abroad and commit them to military operations when the President deems such action necessary to maintain the security and defense of the United States.

* * *

Since the Constitution was adopted there have been at least 125 instances in which the President has ordered the armed forces to take action or maintain positions abroad without obtaining prior congressional authorization, starting with the "undeclared war" with France (1798–1800). For example, President Truman ordered 250,000 troops to Korea during the Korean war of the early 1950s. President Eisenhower dispatched 14,000 troops to Lebanon in 1958.

The Constitution leaves to the President the judgment to determine whether the circumstances of a particular armed attack are so urgent and the potential consequences so threatening to the security of the United States that he should act without formally consulting the Congress.

B. The Southeast Asia Collective Defense Treaty Authorizes the President's Actions

Under article VI of the United States Constitution, "all Treaties made, or which shall be made, under the Authority of the United States, shall be the supreme Law of the Land." Article IV, paragraph 1, of the SEATO treaty establishes as a matter of law that a Communist armed attack against South Viet-Nam endangers the peace and safety of the United States. In this same provision the United States has undertaken a commitment in the SEATO treaty to "act to meet the common danger in accordance with its constitutional processes" in the event of such an attack.

Under our Constitution it is the President who must decide when an armed attack has occurred. He has also the constitutional responsibility for determining what measures of defense are required when the peace and safety of the United States are endangered. If he considers that deployment of U.S. forces in South Viet-Nam is required, and that military measures against the source of Communist aggression in North Vietnam are necessary, he is constitutionally empowered to take those measures.

It has recently been argued that the use of land forces in Asia is not authorized under the treaty because their use to deter armed attack was not contemplated at the time the treaty was considered by the Senate. Secretary Dulles testified at that time that we did not intend to establish (1) a land army in Southeast Asia capable of deterring Communist aggression, or (2) an integrated headquarters and military organization like that of NATO; instead, the United States would rely on "mobile striking power" against the sources of aggression, However, the treaty obligations in article IV, paragraph 1, to meet the common danger in the event of armed aggression, is not limited to particular modes of military action. What constitutes an adequate deterrent or an appropriate response, in terms of military strategy, may change; but the essence of our commitment to act to meet the common danger, as necessary at the time of an armed aggression, remains. In 1954 the forecast of military judgment might have been against the use of substantial United States ground forces in Viet-Nam. But that does not preclude the President from reaching a different military judgment in different circumstances, 12 years later.

C. The Joint Resolution of Congress of August 10, 1964, Authorizes United States Participation in the Collective Defense of South Viet-Nam

* * *

Following the North Vietnamese attacks in the Gulf of Tonkin against United States destroyers, Congress adopted, by a Senate vote of 88–2 and a House vote of 416–0, a joint resolution containing a series of important declarations and provisions of law [*infra*].

* * *

Congressional realization of the scope of authority being conferred by the joint resolution is shown by the legislative history of the measure as a whole....

* * *

The August 1964 joint resolution continues in force today [1966]. Section 2 of the resolution provides that it shall expire "when the President shall determine that the peace and security of the area is reasonably assured by international conditions created by action of the United Nations or otherwise, except that it may be terminated earlier by concurrent resolution of the Congress." The President has made no such determination, nor has Congress terminated the joint resolution.

Instead, Congress in May 1965 approved an appropriation of $700 million to meet the expense of mounting military requirements in Viet-Nam.... The President's message asking for this appropriation stated that this was "not a routine appropriation. For each Member of Congress who supports this request is also voting to persist in our efforts to halt Communist aggression in South Vietnam." The appropriation act constitutes a clear congressional endorsement and approval of the actions taken by the President.

On March 1, 1966, the Congress continued to express its support of the President's policy by approving a $4.8 billion supplemental military authorization by votes of 392–4 and 93–2. An amendment that would have limited the President's authority to commit forces to Viet-Nam was rejected in the Senate by a vote of 94–2.

---

4. The Gulf of Tonkin Resolution

Joint Resolution
To promote the maintenance of international
peace and security in southeast Asia
Pub. Law 88–408, August 10, 1964, 78 *Stat.* 384

Whereas naval units of the Communist regime in Vietnam, in violation of the principles of the Charter of the United Nations and of international law, have deliberately and repeatedly attacked United States naval vessels lawfully present in international waters, and have thereby created a serious threat to international peace; and

Whereas these attacks are part of a deliberate and systematic campaign of aggression that the Communist regime of North Vietnam has been waging against its neighbors and the nations joined with them in the collective defense of their freedom; and

Whereas the United States is assisting the peoples of southeast Asia to protect their freedom and has no territorial, military or political ambitions in that area, but desires only that these peoples should be left in peace to work out their own destinies in their own way: Now, therefore, be it.

Resolved by the Senate and House of Representatives of the United States of America in Congress assembled, That the Congress approves and supports the determination of the President, as Commander in Chief, to take all necessary measures to repel any armed attack against the forces of the United States and to prevent further aggression.

Sec. 2. The United States regards as vital to its national interest and to world peace the maintenance of international peace and security in southeast Asia. Consonant with the Constitution of the United States and the Charter of the United Nations and in accordance with its obligations under the southeast Asia Collective Defense Treaty, the United States is, therefore, prepared, as the President determines, to take all necessary steps, including the use of armed force, to assist any member or protocol state of the Southeast Asia Collective Defense Treaty requesting assistance in defense of its freedom.

Sec. 3. This resolution shall expire when the President shall determine that the peace and security of the area is reasonably assured by international conditions created by action of the United Nations or otherwise, except that it may be terminated earlier by concurrent resolution of Congress.

Approved August 10, 1964.

---

5. Headquarters

United States Military Assistance Command, Vietnam
APO San Francisco 96222

[MACV]

DIRECTIVE   18 May 1968

NUMBER 20-4   (MACJA)

INSPECTIONS AND INVESTIGATIONS
WAR CRIMES

1. PURPOSE. To provide uniform procedures for the collection and perpetuation of evidence relative to war crimes incidents and to designate the agencies responsible for the conduct of investigations for alleged or possible violations of the Geneva Conventions of 12 August 1949 For the Protection of War Victims.

2. APPLICABILITY. This directive is applicable to all alleged or possible war crimes violations of the subject Geneva Conventions, inflicted by hostile forces upon US military or civilian personnel assigned in Vietnam, or by US military personnel upon hostile military or civilian personnel.

3. DEFINITIONS.

a. War Crime. Every violation of the law of war is a war crime (Chapter 8, DA Field Manual 27-10, The Law of the Land Warfare, July 1956).

b. Grave Breach. A grave breach of the Geneva Conventions is the most serious type of war crime. Examples of grave breaches are: willful killing, torture or inhuman treatment, including biological experiments, willfully causing great suffering or serious injury to body or health, taking of hostages, compelling a prisoner of war to serve in the forces of the hostile power.

c. Other War Crimes. Examples are: making use of poisoned or otherwise forbidden arms or ammunition, treacherous request for quarter, maltreatment of dead bodies, firing on localities which are undefended and without military significance, abuse of or firing on the flag of truce, misuse of the Red Cross emblem, use of civilian clothing by troops to conceal their military character during battle, poisoning of wells or streams, pillage or purposeless destruction, improper use of buildings for military purposes, compelling prisoners of war to perform prohibited labor, killing spies or other persons who have committed hostile acts without trial, compelling civilians to perform prohibited labor, and violations of surrender terms.

4. COORDINATION. Investigations of alleged or possible war crimes will be coordinated with the Staff Judge Advocate, MACV.

5. RESPONSIBILITIES.

a. It is the responsibility of all military personnel having knowledge or receiving a report of an incident or of an act thought to be a war crime to make such incident known to his commanding officer as soon as practicable. Personnel performing investigative, intelligence, police, photographic, grave registration, or medical functions, as well as those in contact with the enemy, will, in the normal course of their duty, make every effort to detect the commission of war crimes and will report the essential facts to their commanding officer. Persons discovering war crimes will take all reasonable action under the circumstances to preserve physical evidence, to note identity of witnesses present, and to record (by photograph, sketch, or descriptive notes) the circumstances and surroundings.

b. Commanders and MACV staff sections receiving reports of probable war crimes will, in addition to any other required reports, report the facts as soon as practicable to the Staff Judge Advocate, MACV, and will make pertinent collateral information available to the appointing authority and investigating officers.

c. The Staff Judge Advocate, MACV, will:

(1) Immediately notify the appropriate appointing authority (see paragraph 5d, below) of the receipt of a report of an alleged or possible war crime.

(2) Assist and advise the appointed investigating officer, in coordination with the Staff Judge Advocate or Legal Officer of the appointing authority.

(3) Receive and review completed and approved investigations from the appointing authority.

(4) Maintain a file on all war crime investigations.

(5) Make appropriate recommendations to COMUSMACV concerning use of the evidence obtained and disposition of the report of investigation.

d. Appointing authority:

(1) Appoint an investigating officer and, if appropriate, designate a qualified criminal investigator as technical assistant. Upon receipt of notification of an alleged or possible war crime concerning a member of his command, one of the following appointing authorities will, with all dispatch, appoint an investigating officer to prepare and transmit to him a report of investigation. [Here the DIRECTIVE lists the individuals designated as appointing authorities for the United States Army, Navy, Air Force, Marine Corps and Coast Guard].

* * *

(2) If two or more appointing authorities are concerned with the same incident, they will agree upon the appointment of one investigating officer, with such additional assistants as may be necessary, to make inquiry on behalf of all concerned.

(3) When the complete report of Investigation (ROI) has been submitted to the appointing authority by the investigating officer, the appointing authority will receive, review, and, if appropriate, approve the report. Three copies of the ROI will be transmitted to COMUSMACV, ATTN: MACJA.

* * *

FOR THE COMMANDER:

WALTER T. KERWIN, JR.
Major General, USA
Chief of Staff

SIDNEY GRITZ

Colonel, USA

Adjutant General

---

6. Jeffrey P. Addicott & William A. Hudson, Jr., "The Twenty-Fifth Anniversary of My Lai: A Time to Inculcate the Lessons"

139 Military Law Review 153;
151–161 (1993)
Reproduced with permission from 139 Military Law Review 153 (1993)

* * *

The Facts of My Lai

The hard facts relating to the My Lai massacre are now fairly certain, thanks to a thorough criminal investigation aimed at the perpetrators of the crime and a collateral administrative investigation ordered by the Secretary of the Army and headed by Lieutenant General W. R. Peers. Despite the initial cover-up by some of those associated with the crime, the enormity of the atrocity diminished the likelihood that it long could be kept secret. Nevertheless, for well over a year, the general public knew nothing of the incident.

On March 16, 1968, an American combat task force of the 23d Infantry division (the Americal Division) launched an air-mobile assault into the village complex of Son My in the province of Quang Ngai, South Vietnam. Like all such operations, the attack was executed only after the commander of the task force, Lieutenant Colonel Frank Barker, had assembled his key junior commanders for a final review of the details of the combat operation. This briefing, which took place on March 15, 1968, involved discussions on the positioning of helicopters, the conduct of artillery preparation, and the specific assignments of the three companies that comprised what became known as *Task Force "Barker."* While the other two companies provided blocking and support functions, Charlie Company, commanded by Captain Ernest Medina, would take the primary responsibility for battling any enemy resistance encountered in the village.

At the briefing, Lieutenant Colonel Barker reminded his commanders that intelligence reports had indicated that the village complex was a staging area for the 48th Viet Cong local force battalion and that the Americans could expect an enemy force of up to

250 soldiers. Accordingly, the American soldiers anticipated that they would be out-numbered by the enemy. Still, having yet to engage any enemy forces in direct combat, *Task Force Barker* saw the operation as an opportunity finally to fight the ever-elusive Viet Cong in the open.

The intelligence on a large enemy force, however, proved to be incorrect. When the American combat forces landed, they soon found that the village was occupied almost totally by noncombatants. Although the civilians offered no resistance whatsoever, some of the members of Charlie Company went on a command-directed killing spree. Under the direct supervision of several company grade officers—First Lieutenant William L. Calley, Jr., being the most notorious—American troops murdered well over 200 unarmed South Vietnamese civilians.

The largest killing of civilians occurred in the hamlet of My Lai, known to the Americans by the nickname of "Pinkville," which was part of the Son My complex. The murdered consisted primarily of women, children, and old men; some were shot in small groups, others were fired upon as they fled. At My Lai, most of the civilians methodically had been herded into groups and then gunned down. The largest group was killed under the direct supervision of Lieutenant Calley.

In addition to the unlawful killing of civilians, the soldiers destroyed most of the homes and killed most of the domestic animals in the village. Several cases of rape also were reported to have taken place during the massacre. When it was all over, the statistics told the story: one American soldier in Charlie Company had been wounded by friendly fire and hundreds of South Vietnamese women, children, and elderly men were dead.

Perhaps the only redeeming aspect of the incident was the fact that some of the American soldiers either had refused to participate or openly attempted to halt the killings. Chief Warrant Officer Hugh C. Thompson, Jr., was one of those who took specific actions to halt the killings. Tasked with piloting one of the helicopters during the operation, Chief Thompson testified that he noticed large numbers of "wounded and dead civilians everywhere." Assuming that the Americans on the ground would assist those who were wounded, which was the standard procedure, Chief Thompson began to mark the location of the wounded Vietnamese civilians with smoke canisters as he flew overhead. To his horror, he witnessed the exact opposite. Drawn to the smoke, American soldiers were shooting the wounded that Chief Thompson had marked so accurately. Still only partially realizing the full impact of what was happening on the ground, Chief Thompson immediately headed his helicopter into My Lai, and landed near a large drainage ditch filled with dead and dying civilians. As he began to assist the Vietnamese who were still alive, Lieutenant Calley and a handful of troops approached.

When Chief Thompson asked for assistance in caring for the civilians, Lieutenant Calley clarified his intentions to kill the remaining noncombatants. Chief Thompson recalled that Lieutenant Calley said of the civilians, "The only way you'll get them out is with a hand grenade." Instead of backing down from the clear designs of a superior officer, however, Chief Thompson quickly ordered his M60 machine gunner, Private First Class Lawrence Colburn, to open fire on the United States soldiers if they came any closer to the remaining civilians. Chief Thompson then placed the civilians he could on his helicopter and ferried them to safety.

The initial attempts to cover up the crime could not quell the nightmares of those who had witnessed the slaughter. Rumors of the massacre persisted, coming to a boiling point when an ex-serviceman named Ron Ridenhour sent a second-hand account of the massacre to President Richard Nixon, "twenty three members of Congress, the Secretaries of State and Defense, the Secretary of the Army, and the Chairman of the Joint Chiefs of Staff." Ridenhour had written a four-page letter that chronicled detailed information from several of the soldiers who either had taken part in the bloody massacre or had witnessed it first hand.

* * *

Ron Ridenhour's letter received prompt attention both in the media and in the legislative and executive branches of the federal government. The initial military reaction was one of disbelief. No one believed that a massacre of that magnitude could have been committed by American soldiers or that the massacre "could have remained hidden for so long."

* * *

Charges were preferred against four officers [for murder: Captain Ernest L. Medina, Captain Eugene M. Kotouc, First Lieutenant William L. Calley, Jr. and First Lieutenant Thomas K. Willingham] and nine enlisted personnel [for murder: Sergeant Kenneth L. Hodges, Sergeant Charles E. Hutto, Sergeant David Mitchell, Sergeant Escquiel Torres, Specialist Four William F. Doherty, Specialist Four Robert W. T'Souvas, Corporal Kenneth Schiel, Private Max Hutson and Private Gerald A. Smith. Before the formal Army investigation began, Lieutenant Steven Brooks and Colonel Frank Barker had been killed in action in Vietnam. Each of these men, apparently, had played a key role in the My Lai affair]. In addition, twelve other officers were charged with military offenses associated with the cover-up. Of these twenty-five accused soldiers, only Lieutenant William Calley was convicted. The other officers and enlisted men either successfully moved to have the charges against them dismissed or were found not guilty at their courts-martial.

Tried before a military panel composed of six officers, Lieutenant Calley was found guilty of the premeditated murder of twenty-two noncombatants and of assault with intent to murder a two-year old child. Although Calley was sentenced to a dismissal and confinement at hard labor for life, the convening authority reduced this sentence to a dismissal and twenty years at hard labor. Subsequent to the convening authority's action, the Secretary of the Army further reduced the sentence to a dismissal and ten years at hard labor. [Further appellate and administrative review of the sentence had the effect of eventually releasing Calley from confinement at the United States Disciplinary Barracks, Fort Leavenworth, Kansas, and he was never returned to that institution because of a decision by the Secretary of the Army to parole him in 1975].

7. Michael Bilton & Kevin Sim, *Four Hours in My Lai*
1–5 (1992)
From FOUR HOURS IN MY LAI by Michael Bilton and Kevin Sim,
Copyright © 1992 by Michael Bilton and Kevin Sim. Used by permission
of Viking Penguin, a division of Penguin Group (USA) Inc.

1. Introduction

At 5:45 PM every working day, in Columbus, Georgia, a middle-aged businessman locks up his jewelry store, strolls across the parking lot to his Mercedes sedan, and heads for home.

This small, paunchy figure who keeps such regular habits is America's most infamous war criminal. His name is William Laws "Rusty" Calley, the same Lieutenant Calley whose name was once inseparable from the massacre at My Lai. It was of him that Brigadier-General Al Haig warned in a memo to White House staff concerning the case: "There is no individual under investigation charged or convicted in any case [resulting from the Vietnam War] whose crime can *even remotely* be said to equal that of Calley" (original italics). It was Calley who, weeks before My Lai, threw a defenseless old man down a well and shot him. It was Calley who, seeing a baby at My Lai crawling away from a ditch already filled with dead and dying villagers, seized the child by the leg threw it back in the pit, and shot it.

"No one," Haig's White House memo concluded, "should undertake to advise the President, who is not fully informed of the sordid facts."

Calley was by no means the only one responsible for the massacre at My Lai—but he was the only man ever found guilty of any offense committed there. In 1971, he was sentenced to life imprisonment with hard labor. Within three days, President Nixon ordered that he should be released from jail pending appeal.

Following this presidential intervention, Calley became the most privileged prisoner in America. He spent the next thirty-five months in his "bachelor apartment" at Fort Benning accompanied, it was reported at the time, by his dog, his myna bird, and a tankful of tropical fish....

In 1974, Calley was released on parole. Judge Robert Elliott, explaining this decision, observed: "War is war and it's not unusual for innocent civilians such as the My Lai victims to be killed." By way of further elaboration, the judge explained that when Joshua took the city of Jericho in biblical times, no charges had been brought against him for the slaughter of the civilian population.

On his release, Calley moved into a new apartment in Columbus, Georgia. He drove around the streets in a white Mercedes sports car on loan from a sympathizer.... In 1976 he married—not the girlfriend of his captivity, but Penny Vick, the 29-year-old daughter of a local jeweler. "I don't want to talk about the past," he told reporters at the wedding....

The three days Calley spent in the stockade at Fort Benning, together with the weeks he spent much later imprisoned at Fort Leavenworth, were the harshest punishment served by anyone connected with the My Lai massacre. Everyone else responsible for the most inexcusable act of American arms during this [twentieth] century had got clean away with it. No one remembers them. And now the jeweler from Columbus would also like to forget.

* * *

...At the time of the massacre, Charlie Company, a unit of the Americal Division's 11th Light Infantry Brigade, had been in Vietnam for just over three months. On March 16, 1968, they entered an undefended village on the coast of Central Vietnam and murdered around five hundred old men, women, and children in cold blood. The killings took place, part maniacally, part methodically, over a period of about four hours. They were accompanied by rape, sodomy, mutilations, and unimaginable random cruelties. "It was this Nazi kind of thing," we were told again and again by men who were there—an observation underscored by a single unassimilable thought: How could we have behaved like Nazis?

* * *

My Lai is now almost forgotten, erased almost entirely from national consciousness. What once was an image of incandescent horror has become at most a vague recollection of something unpleasant that happened during the Vietnam War. Even in the newspapers of the time, a process of eclipse can be traced clearly. What was first a "massacre" quickly became a "tragedy" and was then referred to as an "incident." General Peers, whose exhaustive inquiry into the events at My Lai remains the best source for what really happened there, was warned by his superiors not to use the word "massacre" at the press conference held on the publication of his report.

After the initial shocked outcry, My Lai soon became a political and ideological football—with bizarre results. By the time William Calley, the only man found guilty of crimes committed at My Lai, was put on trial before a court-martial of his military peers, public opinion had swung overwhelmingly in his favor. Reporters at the later trial of his immediate superior, Captain Ernest Medina, were agreed that the whole procedure had simply been tedious. The massacre had outlived the nation's attention span....

---

8. The Peers Commission Report

Report of the Department of the Army of the Preliminary Investigations into the My Lai Incident: vol. 1; The Report of the Investigations, William R. Peers, U.S. Department of the Army 1-6; 12-1-4; 12-7; 12-9; 12-29-30; 12-32-33 Washington, DC: U.S. Government Printing Office (1974)

(a) DEPARTMENT OF THE ARMY
Washington, D. C. 20310

26 November 1969

MEMORANDUM FOR LIEUTENANT GENERAL WILLIAM R. PEERS
218-34-7474

SUBJECT: Directive of Investigation

Confirming oral instructions given you on 24 November 1969, you are directed to explore the nature and the scope of the original U.S. Army investigation(s) of the alleged My Lai (4) incident which occurred 16 March 1968 in Quang Ngai Province, Republic of Vietnam. Your investigation will include a determination of the adequacy of the investigation(s) or inquiries on this subject, their subsequent reviews and reports within the chain of command, and possible suppression or withholding of information by persons involved in the incident.

Your investigation will be concerned with the time period beginning March 1968 until Mr. Ronald L. Ridenhour sent his letter, dated 29 March 1969, to the Secretary of Defense and others. The scope of your investigation does not include, nor will it interfere with, ongoing criminal investigations in progress.

The procedures contained in AR 15-6 are authorized for such use as may be required.

You are authorized to select and use on a full-time basis officer and civilian members of the Army whom you deem necessary for the conduct of the investigation. Your deputy is designated as Mr. Bland West, Assistant General Counsel, Department of the Army. Should you require other assistance, please let us know.

You will inform us at an early date of the expected completion date of your report.

/s/ W. C. Westmoreland

/s/ Stanley R. Resor

General, U.S. Army

Secretary of the Army

Chief of Staff

———————

(b) DEPARTMENT OF THE ARMY
Washington, D. C., 20310

CS (Peers Inquiry)

14 March 1970

MEMORANDUM FOR: SECRETARY OF THE ARMY

CHIEF OF STAFF, US ARMY

SUBJECT: Letter of Transmittal

1. Pursuant to your directive of 26 November 1969, I have completed the investigation of facts and circumstances surrounding the original Army investigation of incidents which occurred during the period 16–19 March 1968 in Son My village, Quant Ngai Province, Republic of Vietnam.

2. Forwarded herewith is the final report of investigation.

1 incl

/s/ W. R. Peers

as

Lieutenant General, USA

———————

(c) FINDINGS AND RECOMMENDATIONS
(Peers Commission Report)

A. CONCERNING EVENTS SURROUNDING THE SON MY OPERATION OF 16–19 MARCH 1968

1. During the period 16–19 March 1968, US Army troops of TF Barker, 11th Brigade, Americal Division, massacred a large number of noncombatants in two hamlets of Son My village, Quang Ngai Province, Republic of Vietnam. The precise number of Vietnamese killed cannot be determined but was at least 175 and may exceed 400.

2. The massacre occurred in conjunction with a combat operation which was intended to neutralize Son My village as a logistical support base and staging area, and to destroy elements of an enemy battalion thought to be located in the Son My area.

3. The massacre resulted primarily from the nature of the orders issued by persons in the chain of command within TF Barker.

4. The task force commander's order and the associated intelligence estimate issued prior to the operation were embellished as they were disseminated through each lower level of command, and ultimately presented to the individual soldier a false and misleading picture of the Son My area as an armed enemy camp, largely devoid of civilian inhabitants.

5. Prior to the incident, there had developed within certain elements of the 11th Brigade a permissive attitude toward the treatment of safeguarding of noncombatants which contributed to the mistreatment of such persons during the Son My operation.

6. The permissive attitude in the treatment of the Vietnamese was, on 16–19 March 1968, exemplified by an almost total disregard for the lives and property of the civilian population of Son My Village on the part of commanders and key staff officers of TF Barker.

7. On 16 March, soldiers at the squad and platoon level, within some elements of TF Barker, murdered noncombatants while under the supervision and control of their immediate superiors.

8. A part of the crimes visited on the inhabitants of Son My Village included individual and group acts of murder, rape, sodomy, maiming, and assault on noncombatants and the mistreatment and killing of detainees. They further included the killing of livestock, destruction of crops, closing wells, and the burning of dwellings within several sub-hamlets.

9. Some attempts were made to stop the criminal acts in Son My Village on 16 March; but with few exceptions, such efforts were too feeble or too late.

10. Intensive interrogation has developed no evidence that any members of the units engaged in the Son My operation was under the influence of marijuana or other narcotics.

B. CONCERNING THE ADEQUACY OF REPORTS, INVESTIGATIONS AND REVIEWS

11. The commanders of TF Barker and the 11th Brigade had substantial knowledge as to the extent of the killing of noncombatants but only a portion of their information was ever reported to the Commanding General of the American Division.

12. Based on his observations, W01 Thompson made a specific complaint through his command channels that serious war crimes had been committed but through a series of inadequate responses at each level of command, action on his complaint was delayed and the severity of his charges considerably diluted by the time it reached the Division Commander.

13. Sufficient information concerning the highly irregular nature of the operations of TF Barker on March 1968 reached the Commanding General of the American Division to require that a thorough investigation be conducted.

14. An investigation by the Commanding General of the American Division, was little more than a pretense and was subsequently misrepresented as a thorough investigation to the CG, American Division in order to conceal from him the true enormity of the atrocities.

15. Patently inadequate reports of investigation submitted by the Commander of the 11th Brigade were accepted at face value and without an effective review by the CG, American Division.

16. Reports of alleged war crimes, noncombatant casualties, and serious incidents concerning the Son My operation of 16 March were received at the headquarters of the American Division but were not reported to higher headquarters despite the existence of directives requiring such action.

17. Reports of alleged war crimes relating to the Son My operation of 16 March reached Vietnamese government officials, but those officials did not take effective action to ascertain the true facts.

18. Efforts of the ARVIN/GVN officials discreetly to inform the US commanders of the magnitude of the war crimes committed on 16 March 1968 met with no affirmative response.

C. CONCERNING ATTEMPTS TO SUPPRESS INFORMATION

19. At every command level within the American Division, actions were taken, both wittingly and unwittingly, which effectively suppressed information concerning the war crimes committed at Son My Village

20. At the company level there was a failure to report the war crimes which had been committed. This, combined with instructions to members of one unit not to discuss the events of 16 March, contributed significantly to the suppression of information.

21. The task force commander and at least one, and probably more, staff officers of TF Barker may have conspired to suppress information and to mislead higher headquarters concerning the events of 16–19 March 1968.

22. At the 11th Brigade level, the commander and at least one principal staff officer may have conspired to suppress information to deceive the division commander concerning the true facts of the Son My operation of 16–19 March.

23. A reporter and a photographer from the 11th Brigade observed many war crimes committed by C/1-20 Inf on 16 March. Both failed to report what they had seen; the reporter submitted a misleading account of the operation; and the photographer withheld and suppressed (and wrongfully misappropriated upon his discharge from the service) photographic evidence of such war crimes.

24. Efforts within the 11th Brigade to suppress information concerning the Son My operation were aided in varying degrees by members of US Advisory teams working with ARVN and GVN officials.

25. Within the American Division headquarters, actions taken to suppress information concerning what was purportedly believed to be the inadvertent killing of 20 to 28 noncombatants effectively served to conceal the true nature and scope of the events which had taken place in Son My Village on 16–19 March 1968.

26. Failure of the American Division headquarters to act on reports and information received from GVN/ARVAN officials in mid-April served effectively to suppress the true nature and scope of the events which had taken place in Son My Village on 16–19 March 1968.

27. Despite an exhaustive search of the files of the 11th Brigade, American Division, GVN/ARVN advisory team files, and records holding centers, with few exceptions, none of the documents relating to the so-called investigation of the events of 16–19 March were located.

D. WITH RESPECT TO INDIVIDUALS

[The *Report* here dealt with a total of thirty individuals implicated in the My Lai operation. We reprint that portion of the *Report* implicating Captain Ernest L. Medina and Lieutenant William L. Calley, Jr.].

* * *

1. During the period March–June 1968 a number of persons assigned to the American Division and to US Advisory elements located in Quang Ngai Province had information as to the killing of noncombatants and other serious offenses committed by members of TF Barker during the Son My operation in March 1968 and did one or more of the following:

    a.   Failed to make such official report thereof as their duty required them to make;

b. Suppressed information concerning the occurrence of such offenses acting singly or in concert with others;

c. Failed to order a thorough investigation and to insure that such was made, or failed to conduct an adequate investigation, or failed to submit an adequate report of investigation, or failed to make an adequate review of a report of investigation, as applicable;

Or committed other derelictions related to the events of the Son My operation, some constituting criminal offenses.

* * *

3. Evidence adduced in this inquiry also indicates that numerous serious offenses in violation of the Uniform Code of Military Justice and the law of war may have been committed by military personnel who participated in the TF Barker operation in Son My during the period 16–19 March 1968. Evidence of these suspected offenses has been furnished to representatives of the Provost Marshal General of the Army for further investigation.

4. Some of the officers and enlisted men concerned fulfilled their minimum obligation to report their knowledge of crimes committed during the Son My operation to their commanding officers. However, had they exhibited deeper concern for their units, the United States Army and the Nation by taking action beyond that which was technically required, it is probable that the details of the Son My incident would have come to light promptly. Those who failed to do so have contributed to a serious obstruction of justice.

OMMISSIONS AND COMMISSIONS BY INDIVIDUALS

Following is a listing of individuals and the omissions and commissions of which they are suspected pertaining to the planning, conduct, reporting, and investigation of the operation by TF Barker in the Son My area and the related incidents. The terms omissions and commissions are used here to denote, respectively, instances in which an individual may have failed to perform his duty or may have performed his duty improperly, measured in terms of those responsibilities which were reasonably his under the attendant circumstances. It is recognized that some of the omissions and commissions may involve criminal offenses.

* * *

19. CPT ERNEST L. MEDINA

a. He informed the men of C/1-20 Inf that nearly all the civilian residents of the hamlets in Son My Village would be gone to market by 0700, 16 March 1968, and that any who remained would be VC [Viet Cong] or VC sympathizers. This caused many of the men in C/1-20 Inf to believe that they would find only armed enemy in the hamlets and directly contributed to the killing of noncombatants which followed.

b. He planned, ordered, and supervised the execution by his company of an unlawful operation against inhabited hamlets in Son My Village which included the destruction of houses by burning, killing of livestock, and the destruction of crops and other foodstuffs, and the closing of wells; and impliedly directed the killing of any persons found there.

c. There is evidence that he possibly killed as many as three noncombatants in My Lai (4).

d. He probably conspired with LTC Barker and others to suppress information concerning the killing of noncombatants during the Son My operation.

e. He actively suppressed information concerning the killing of noncombatants in Son My Village on 16 March 1968 by:

1. Telling the men of C/1-20 Inf not to talk about what happened in Son My Village on 16 March.

2. Advising at least one member of his company not to write to his Congressman.

3. Giving false reports as to the number of noncombatants killed by the men of C/1-20 Inf and the cause of death.

f. He failed to report the killings in and around My Lai (4) as a possible war crime as required by MACV Directive 20-4.

g. If he in fact believed that 20–28 civilians had been killed in My Lai (4) by artillery or gunship fire, he failed to request an artillery incident investigation.

h. He obstructed an inquiry into the killing of civilians in My Lai (4) by objecting to orders to return C/1-20 Inf to the hamlet for that purpose.

i. He failed to prevent the killing of VC suspects by the RVN [Republic of Vietnam] National Police on 16 March 1968 and subsequently failed to report these killings as required in MACF Directive 20-4.

j. He personally mistreated a VC suspect during an interrogation on 17 March 1968 by striking him on the head and repeatedly firing an M-16 close to the prisoner's head to induce him to talk.

k. He failed to determine the cause of death of the 20–24 people whose bodies he admitted seeing on the trial leading south from My Lai (4).

l. He gave false testimony before this Inquiry in a manner calculated to be misleading when he stated that:

1. He did not see any bodies or wounded as he moved within my Lai (4).

2. Only 20 to 28 civilians were killed by C/1-20 Inf in and around My Lai (4) on 16 March 1968.

3. He questioned his platoon leaders about killing of civilians in My Lai (4).

* * *

23. 1LT (then 2LT)   WILLIAM L. CALLEY [JR.]

a. He ordered the execution by his platoon of an unlawful operation against inhabited hamlets in Son My Village, which included the destruction of houses by burning, killing of livestock, the destruction of crops and other foodstuffs, and the closing of wells; and expressly ordered the killing of persons found there.

b. He directed and supervised the men of his platoon in the systematic killing of many noncombatants in and around My Lai (4).

c. He personally participated in the killing of some noncombatants in and around My Lai (4).

d. He failed to report the killings of noncombatants in and around My Lai (4) as a possible war crime as required by MACF Directive 20-4.

9. *Medina v. Resor*

United States Court of Military Appeals
20 U.S.C.M.A. 403, 43 C. M. R. 243 (1971)
(Miscellaneous Docket No. 71-12)

On petition for Writ of Mandamus and/or Prohibition and/or Other
Appropriate Relief. Petition dismissed.

Memorandum Opinion of the Court

This petition for Writ of Mandamus and/or Prohibition and/or Other Appropriate Extraordinary Relief has been filed by Captain Ernest L. Medina, presently assigned to duty at Headquarters, United States Army Garrison, Fort McPherson, Georgia.

Petitioner represents that:

(A) Charges alleging murder, maiming, and aggravated assault have been preferred against him and have been investigated pursuant to Article 32, Uniform Code of Military Justice, 10 USC §832.

(B) Petitioner "believes and therefore alleges that the respondents herein have conspired and are conspiring to deny him a fair trial and impartial trial in violation of the due process and equal protection clauses of the United States Construction."

I. (C) During the investigation, pursuant to Article 32, Code, supra, the investigating officer admitted into evidence, over the objection of the petitioner, many unsworn statements.

B. (D) In the trial of United States v. Lieutenant William L. Calley, Jr., presently being conducted at Fort Benning, Georgia, that accused has claimed that his alleged criminal conduct was occasioned by the direct order of the petitioner. Petitioner is ready, willing, and able to testify on behalf of the United States Army in direct refutation of Lieutenant Calley's testimony. Petitioner believes and therefore he alleges that Respondent Captain Aubrey Daniel, III, trial counsel of the general court-martial to which Calley's trial has been referred, wishes to call petitioner as a rebuttal witness. However, there allegedly exists a written directive, dated on or about February 26, 1971, from Respondent Colonel Robert M. Lathrop, Staff Judge Advocate, Fort Benning, reflecting the prohibitive order negating Daniel's desire to call the petitioner as a rebuttal witness. Petitioner avers that there exists a special reason which substantiates Daniel's belief in the petitioner's credibility and his desire to use the latter's testimony in rebuttal.

(E) The conspiracy among the respondents to deprive the petitioner of a fair trial in violation of his constitutionally guaranteed rights to due process and equal protection is further manifested by:

"A. The deliberate chronology of Lieutenant Calley's testimony incriminatory towards Petitioner, the directive not to call Petitioner in rebuttal, and the imminent referral of charges against Petitioner to general court-martial, gives rise to a prejudicial presumption of Petitioner's criminal liability."

"B. The refusal of Respondent Eckhardt, Prosecutor of Sergeant Charles Hutto, to utilize the available rebuttal testimony of Petitioner in the court-martial of said Hutto, which proceedings resulted in an acquittal."

Petitioner prays that:

"1. Respondents Resor, Connor, Eckhardt, and all other appropriate agents of said respondents be temporarily prohibited from referring for court-martial any charges against Petitioner.

"2. Said respondents be permanently prohibited from so acting.

"3. Respondents Resor, Hodson and Lathrop be prohibited from interfering with the administration of justice particularly as it pertains to your Petitioner's available testimony in the Calley court-martial.

"4. An evidentiary hearing be held as soon as is convenient to this Honorable Court affording your Petitioner the opportunity to present evidence, testimonial and other wise, in support of his allegations and prayers therein...."

The petitioner's request for a writ of prohibition enjoining the named respondents temporarily and permanently from referring for court-martial any charges against the petitioner...is dismissed.

The nature, source, or possible effect of unsworn statements upon the investigating officer's findings and recommendations are not set out or otherwise described in the petition, nor is there any indication that the rulings of the investigating officer were encompassed within or in any way related to the "conspiracy" of which he complains. The allegation expresses simply the subjective conclusion of the petitioner and, considered alone or in conjunction with other allegations, is insufficient basis for affirmative relief.... Also, there is no indication that, assuming the charges are referred to trial by court-martial, the ordinary course of the proceedings against him through trial and appellate channels is not an adequate source of relief for any pre-trial defects of this nature....

* * *

The petitioner's request for a writ of prohibition enjoining the named respondents from interfering with the administration of justice particularly as it pertain to the petitioner's availability in the Calley court-martial...is also dismissed.

Primary responsibility for the appearance of witnesses before courts-martial rests upon the trial counsel. That officer is required to consider whether the evidence which the witness is expected to give is material and necessary before deciding whether the presence of any particular witness is necessary.... Since the responsibility for the prosecution of any case rests upon him, the means for discharging that responsibility, within the law, are his to choose. This includes the right to call all witnesses necessary to the proof of any case referred to him as prosecutor. The creditability of any witness is a matter for determination by the members of the court.

Fundamental to the problem posed by this petition is the fact that neither the actions nor the rights of petitioner are involved in the Calley trial in such a way as to affect the outcome of petitioner's trial, should such trial be ordered. Whatever the outcome of Calley's trial may be, that result can in no way be used for or against this petitioner at his possible future trial.

* * *

The petitioner's request for an evidentiary hearing affording him the opportunity to present evidence, testimonial or otherwise, in support of his allegations and prayers... is similarly dismissed....

Accordingly, since the petition sets forth no basis for the relief sought, it is dismissed.

10. Norman G. Cooper,
"My Lai and Military Justice — To What Effect?"

59 *Military Law Review* 93; 116–117 (1973)
Reproduced with permission from 59 *Military Law Review* 93 (1993)

D. MEDINA V. RESOR

Undoubtedly the most unusual petition filed by a My Lai accused was the one filed by Captain Ernest L. Medina. Considering the many roles of Captain Medina in the My Lai cases, it is perhaps appropriate that his search for extraordinary relief was the most ambitious. Essentially the several prayers for relief…embodied allegations that a conspiracy to deprive him of a fair trial existed among the several individuals charged with the administration of military justice within the Army command structure. The respondents named included the Secretary of the Army, the Judge Advocate General, the General Court-Martial Convening Authority, the Staff Judge Advocate, the Trial Counsel, and the Staff Judge Advocate and Trial Counsel in the *Calley* case. In particular, the allegations concerned the alleged admission of the unsworn statements into evidence at Captain Medina's Article 32 investigation, the absence of Captain Medina's government witness in the court-martial of Sergeant Charles Hutto which resulted in an acquittal, and a decision not to call him as a government rebuttal witness in the *Calley* case on the issue of orders alleged to have been given by him prior to the assault of his company at My Lai.

The Court of Military Appeals held that the accused had failed to sufficiently set forth the nature, source, or possible effect of the unsworn statements, and that there was no showing that "the ordinary course of proceedings against him through trial and appellate channels is not an adequate source of relief for any pretrial defects of this nature."… The Court…denied any relief with regard to the accused's appearance as a witness at the *Calley* court-martial. Citing paragraph 44f, Manual for Courts-Martial, United States 1969 (Revised Edition), the Court noted that the trial counsel has the primary responsibility for prosecution of a case, including the calling of witnesses. The means of fulfilling that responsibility are left to him. Finally, the Court concluded that the result of the *Calley* trial "can in no way be used for or against this petitioner at his possible future trial."… Further, the Court expressed "no opinion on the question of whether an uncalled witness may compel a party to produce his testimony at a given trial." In its decision the Court found no basis for extraordinary relief being granted to a My Lai defendant, thereby avoiding the unique and potentially embarrassing issues raised by Captain Medina's petition.

11. *United States v. Calley*
United States Court of Military Appeals
22 U.S.C.M.A. 534, 48 C. M. R. 19 (1973)

QUINN, Judge.

First Lieutenant Calley stands convicted of the premeditated murder of 22 infants, children, women and old men, and of assault with intent to murder a child of about 2 years of age. All of the killings and the assault took place on March 16, 1968 in the area of the village of My Lai in the Republic of South Vietnam. The Army Court of Military Review affirmed the findings of guilty and the sentence, which, as reduced by the convening authority, includes dismissal and confinement at hard labor for 20 years. The accused petitioned this Court for further review, alleging 30 assignments of error. We granted three of these assignments.

We consider first whether the public attention given the charges was so pernicious as to prevent a fair trial for the accused. At the trial, defense counsel moved to dismiss all the charges on the ground that the pretrial publicity made it impossible for the Government to accord the accused a fair trial. The motion was denied. It is contended that the ruling was wrong.

The defense asserts, and the Governments concedes, that the pretrial publicity was massive. The defense perceives the publicity as virulent and vicious. At trial, it submitted a vast array of newspaper stories, copies of national news magazines, transcripts of television interviews, and editorial comment. Counsel also referred to comments by the President in which he alluded to the deaths as a "massacre" and to similar remarks by the Secretary of State, the Secretary of Defense, the Secretary of the Army, and various members of Congress. Before us, defense counsel contend that the decision of the United States Supreme Court in Marshall v. United States, 360 U.S. 310 (1959), Irvin v. Dowd, 366 U.S. 717 (1961), and Sheppard v. Maxwell, 384 U.S. 333 (1966) require reversal of this conviction. In our opinion, neither the cited cases, nor others dealing with pretrial publicity and its effect upon an accused's constitutional right to a fair trial, mandate that result.

Under our constitutional system of government and individual rights, the exercise of a constitutional right by one person can affect the constitutional right of another. Thus, the First Amendment guarantees to the public and the news media the right to comment on and discuss impending or pending criminal prosecutions. The content of the comment can pose a danger to the right of an accused to the fair trial assured by the Due Process clause of the Fifth Amendment. The accommodation of such competing rights has been, and will continue to be, a challenge to the courts. As we construe the Supreme Court's decisions in this area, the trier of the facts, and more particularly, a juror, is not disqualified just because he has been exposed to pretrial publicity or even has formulated an opinion as to the guilt or innocence of an accused on the basis of his exposure. "[I]f the juror can lay aside his impression or opinion and render a verdict based on the evidence presented in court," he is qualified to serve. Irvin v. Dowd, supra at 723. The difficulty is that sometimes the impact of the quantity and character of pretrial publicity is so patently profound that the juror's personal belief in his impartiality is not sufficient to overcome the likelihood of bias.... Our task, therefore, is not merely to ascertain that there was widespread publicity adverse to the accused, but to judge whether it was of a kind that inevitably had to influence the court members against the accused, irrespective of their good-faith disclaimers that they could, and would, determine his guilt from the evidence presented to them in open court, fairly and impartially.

We have reviewed the material submitted to support the defense argument on the issue. In contrast to the publicity in some of the cases cited, most of the matter is factual and impersonal in the attribution of guilt. Many accounts note that the accused had not been tried and the question of his culpability remained undetermined by the standard of American law. A number of editorials appear to regard the tragedy as another reason to deplore or oppose our participation in the war in Vietnam. A considerable amount of material is favorable to Lieutenant Calley; some stories were largely expressions of sympathy.

First official government statements were to the effect that a full investigation would be conducted to determine where the killings took place and, if so, to establish the identity of those responsible. Later statements described what occurred at My Lai as a massacre and promised that those who perpetrated it would be brought to justice. By the time of the trial few persons in the United States who read, watched or listened to the daily news would not have been convinced that many Vietnamese civilians, including women and children, had been killed during the My Lai operation. It is by no means certain, however, that the conviction that people had died included a judgment that Lieutenant Calley was criminally responsible for those deaths. Our attention has not been called to any official statement or report that demanded Lieutenant Calley's conviction as the guilty party.

Unlike the situation in the Sheppard case, neither the trial judge nor government counsel ignored the potentially adverse effect of the extensive publicity. In pretrial proceedings, the prosecution labored jointly with the defense to minimize the effects of the publicity. The military judge issued special orders to prospective witnesses to curb public discussion of the case and to insulate them from the influence of possible newspaper, magazine, radio and television reports of the case. At trial, the judge was exceedingly liberal in the scope of the voir dire of the court members and in bases for challenge for cause, but defense counsel challenged only two members because of exposure to the pretrial publicity.

We have carefully examined the extensive voir dire of the court members in the light of the pretrial materials submitted to us and we are satisfied that none of the court members had formed unalterable opinions about Lieutenant Calley's guilt from the publicity to which they had been exposed and that the total impact of that publicity does not oppose the individual declaration by each member retained on the court that he could, fairly and impartially, decide whether Lieutenant Calley was guilty of any crime upon the evidence presented in open court.... We conclude that this assignment of error has no merit.

In his second assignment of error the accused contends that the evidence is insufficient to establish his guilt beyond a reasonable doubt. Summarized, the pertinent evidence is as follows:

Lieutenant Calley was a platoon leader in C. Company, a unit that was part of an organization known as Task Force Barker, whose mission was to subdue and drive out the enemy in an area in the Republic of Vietnam known popularly as Pinkville. Before March 16, 1968, this area, which included the village of My Lai 4, was a Viet Cong stronghold. C Company had operated in the area several times. Each time the unit had entered the area it had suffered casualties by sniper fire, machine gun fire, mines, and other forms of attack. Lieutenant Calley had accompanied his platoon on some of the incursions.

On March 15, 1968, a memorial service for members of the company killed in the area during the preceding weeks was held. After the service Captain Ernest L. Medina, the commanding officer of C Company, briefed the company on a mission in the Pinkville area set for the next day. C Company was to serve as the main attack formation for Task Force Barker. In that role it would assault and neutralize My Lai 4, 5, and 6 and then mass for an assault on My Lai 1. Intelligence reports indicated that the unit would be opposed by a veteran enemy battalion, and that all civilians would be absent from the area. The objective was to destroy the enemy. Disagreement exists as to the instructions on the specifics of destruction.

Captain Medina testified that he instructed his troops that they were to destroy My Lai 4 by "burning the hootches, to kill the livestock, to close the wells and to destroy the food crops." Asked if women and children were to be killed, Medina said he replied in the negative, adding that, "You must use common sense. If they have a weapon and are trying to engage you, then you can shoot back, but you must use common sense." However, Lieutenant Calley testified that Captain Medina informed the troops they were to kill every living thing—men, women, children, and animals—and under no circumstances were they to leave any Vietnamese behind them as they passed through the villages enroute to their final objective. Other witnesses gave more or less support to both versions of the briefing.

On March 16, 1968, the operation began with interdicting fire. C Company was then brought to the area by helicopters. Lieutenant Calley's platoon was on the first lift. This platoon formed a defense perimeter until the remainder of the force was landed. The unit received no hostile fire from the village.

Calley's platoon passed the approaches to the village with his men firing heavily. Entering the village, the platoon encountered only unarmed, unresisting men, women, and children. The villagers, including infants held in their mothers' arms, were assembled and moved in separate groups to collection points. Calley testified that during this time he was radioed twice by Captain Medina, who demanded to know what was delaying the platoon. On being told that a large number of villagers had been detained, Calley said Medina ordered him to "waste them." Calley further testified that he obeyed orders because he had been taught the doctrine of obedience throughout his military career. Medina denied that he gave any such order.

One of the collection points for the villagers was in the southern part of the village. There, Private First Class Paul D. Meadlo guarded a group of between 30 to 40 old men, women, and children. Lieutenant Calley approached Meadlo and told him, "You know what to do," and left. He returned shortly and asked Meadlo why the people were not yet dead. Meadlo replied he did not know that Calley had meant that they should be killed. Calley declared that he wanted them dead. He and Meadlo then opened fire on the group, until all but a few children fell. Calley then personally shot these children. He expended 4 or 5 magazines from his M-16 rifle in the incident.

Lieutenant Calley and Meadlo moved from this point to an irrigation ditch on the east side of My Lai 4. There, they encountered another group of civilians being held by several soldiers. Meadlo estimated that this group contained from 75 to 100 persons. Calley stated, "We got another job to do. Meadlo," and he ordered the group into the ditch. When all were in the ditch, Calley and Meadlo opened fire on them. Although ordered by Calley to shoot, Private First Class James J. Dursi refused to join in the killings, and Specialist Four Robert E. Maples refused to give his machine gun to Calley for use in the killings. Lieutenant Calley admitted that he fired into the ditch, with the muzzle of his weapon within 5 feet of people in it. He expended between 10 to 15 magazines of ammunition on this occasion.

With his radio operator, Private Charles Sledge, Calley moved to the north end of the ditch. There, he found an elderly Vietnamese monk whom he interrogated. Calley struck the man with his rifle butt and then shot him in the head. Other testimony indicates that immediately afterwards a young child was observed running toward the village. Calley seized him by the arm, threw him into the ditch, and fired at him. Calley admitted interrogating and striking the monk, but denied shooting him. He also denied the incident involving the child.

Appellate defense counsel contend that the evidence is insufficient to establish the accused's guilt. They do not dispute Calley's participation in the homicides, but they argue that he did not act with the malice or mens rea essential to a conviction of murder; that the orders he received to kill everyone in the village were not palpably illegal; that he was acting in ignorance of the laws of war; that since he was told that only "the enemy" would be in the village, his honest belief that there were no innocent civilians in the village exonerates him of criminal responsibility for their deaths; and, finally, that his actions were in the heat of passion caused by reasonable provocation.

In assessing the sufficiency of the evidence to support the findings of guilty, we cannot reevaluate the credibility of the witnesses or resolve conflicts in their testimony and thus decide anew whether the accused's guilt was established beyond a reasonable doubt. Our function is more limited; it is to determine whether the record contains enough evidence for the triers of fact to find beyond a reasonable doubt each element of the offenses involved....

The testimony of Meadlo and others provided the court members with ample evidence from which to find that Lieutenant Calley directed and personally participated in the intentional killing of men, women, and children, who were unarmed and in the custody of armed soldiers of C Company. If the prosecution's witnesses are believed, there is also ample evidence to support a finding that the accused deliberately shot the Vietnamese monk whom he interrogated, and that he seized, threw into a ditch, and fired on a child with intent to kill.

Enemy prisoners are not subject to summary execution by their captors. Military law has long held that the killing of an unresisting prisoner is murder....

Conceding for the purposes of this assignment of error that Calley believed the villagers were part of the "the enemy," the uncontradicted evidence is that they were under the control of armed soldiers and were offering no resistance. In his testimony, Calley admitted he was aware of the requirement that prisoners be treated with respect. He also admitted he knew that the normal practice was to interrogate villagers, release those who could satisfactorily account for themselves, and evacuate the suspect among them for further examination. Instead of proceeding in the usual way, Calley executed all, without regard to age, condition, or possibly of suspicion. On the evidence, the court-martial could reasonably find Calley guilty of the offenses before us.

At trial, Calley's principal defense was that he acted in execution of Captain Medina's order to kill everyone in My Lai 4.... Captain Medina denied that he issued any such order, either during the previous day's briefing or on the date the killings were carried out. Resolution of the conflict between his testimony and that of the accused was for the triers of the facts.... The general findings of guilty, with exceptions as to the number of persons killed, does not indicate whether the court members found that Captain Medina did not issue the alleged order to kill, or whether, if he did, the court members believed that the accused knew the order was illegal. For the purpose of the legal sufficiency of the evidence, the record supports the findings of guilty.

In the third assignment of error, appellate defense counsel assert gross deficiencies in the military judge's instructions to the court members. Only two assertions merit discussion. One contention is that the judge should have, but did not, advise the court members of the necessity to find the existence of "malice aforethought" in connection with the murder charges; the second allegation is that the defense of compliance with superior orders was not properly submitted to the court members.

The existence vel non of malice, say appellate defense counsel, is the factor that distinguishes murder from manslaughter.... They argue that malice is an indispensable element of murder and must be the subject of a specific instruction....

* * *

...In enactment of the Uniform Code of Military Justice, Congress eliminated malice as an element of murder by codifying the common circumstances under which that
state of mind was deemed to be present.... One of the stated purposes of the Code was
the "listing and definition of offenses, redrafted and rephrased in modern legislative
language."... That purpose was accomplished by defining murder as the unlawful
killing of a human...being, without justification or excuse. Article 118 [UCMJ] also
provides that murder is committed if the person, intending to kill or inflict grievous
bodily harm, was engaged in an inherently dangerous act, or was engaged in the perpetration or attempted perpetration of certain felonies.... The Code language made it unnecessary that the court members be instructed in the earlier terminology of "malice
aforethought." Now, the conditions and states of mind that must be the subject of instructions have been declared by Congress; they do not require reference to malice itself....

The trial judge delineated the elements of premeditated murder for the court members in accordance with the statutory language. He instructed them that to convict Lieutenant Calley, they must be convinced beyond a reasonable doubt that the victims were
dead; that there respective deaths resulted from specified acts of the accused; that the
killings were unlawful; and that Calley acted with a premeditated design to kill....
These instructions comported fully with requirements of existing law for the offense of
premeditated murder, and nether statute nor judicial precedent requires that reference
also be made to the pre-Code concept of malice.

We turn to the contention that the judge erred in his submission of the defense of superior orders to the court. After fairly summarizing the evidence, the judge gave the following instructions pertinent to the issue:

> The killing of resisting or fleeing enemy forces is generally recognized as a jus-
> tifiable act of war, and you may consider any such killings justifiable in this
> case. The law attempts to protect those persons not actually engaged in war-
> fare, however, and limits the circumstances under which their lives may be
> taken.

> Both combatants captured by and noncombatants detained by the opposing
> forces, regardless of their loyalties, political views, or prior acts, have the right
> to be treated as prisoners until released, confined, or executed, in accordance
> with law and established procedures, by competent authority sitting in judg-
> ment of such detained or captured individual. Summary executions of de-
> tainees or prisoners is forbidden by law. Further, it's clear under the evidence
> presented in this case, that hostile acts or support of the enemy North Viet-
> namese or Viet Cong forces inhabitants of My Lai (4) at some time prior to 16
> March 1968, would not justify the summary execution of all or part of the oc-
> cupants of My Lai (4) on 16 March, nor would hostile acts committed that day,
> if, following the hostility, the belligerents surrendered or were captured by our
> forces. I therefore instruct you, as a matter of law, that if unresisting human
> beings were killed at My Lai (4) while within the effective custody and control
> of our military forces, their deaths cannot be considered justified, and any
> order to kill such people would be, as a matter of law, an illegal order. Thus, if
> you find that Lieutenant Calley received an order directing him to kill unresist-
> ing Vietnamese within his control or within the control of his troops, that
> order would be an illegal order. A determination that an order is illegal does

not, of itself, assign criminal responsibility to the person following the order for acts done in compliance with it. Soldiers are taught to follow orders, and special attention is given to obedience of orders on the battlefield. Military effectiveness depends upon obedience to orders. On the other hand, the obedience of a soldier is not the obedience of an automaton. A soldier is a reasoning agent, obliged to respond, not as a machine, but as a person. The law takes these factors into account in assessing criminal responsibility for acts done in compliance with illegal orders.

The acts of a subordinate done in compliance with an unlawful order given him by his superior are excused and impose no criminal liability upon him unless the superior's order is one which a man of ordinary sense and understanding would, under the circumstances, know to be unlawful, or if the order in question is actually known to the accused to be unlawful.

* * *

...In determining what orders, if any, Lieutenant Calley acted under, if you find him to have acted, you should consider all of the matters which he has testified reached him and which you can infer from other evidence that he saw and heard. Then, unless you find beyond a reasonable doubt that he was not acting under orders directing him in substance and effect to kill unresisting occupants of My Lai (4), you must determine whether Lieutenant Calley actually knew those orders to be unlawful.... In determining whether or not Lieutenant Calley had knowledge of the unlawfulness of any orders found by you to have been given, you may consider all relevant facts and circumstances, including Lieutenant Calley's rank; educational background; OCS schooling; other training while in Hawaii and Vietnam; his experience on prior operations involving contact with hostile and friendly Vietnamese; his age; and any other evidence tending to prove or disprove that on 16 March 1968, Lieutenant Calley knew the order was unlawful. If you find beyond a reasonable doubt, on the basis of all the evidence, that Lieutenant Calley actually knew the order under which he asserts he operated was unlawful, the fact that the order was given operates as no defense....

* * *

Appellate defense counsel contend that these instructions are prejudicially erroneous in that they require the court members to determine that Lieutenant Calley knew that an order to kill human beings in the circumstances under which he killed was illegal by the standard of whether "a man of ordinary sense and understanding" would know the order was illegal. They urge us to adopt as the governing test whether the order is so palpably or manifestly illegal that a person of "the commonest understanding" would be aware of its illegality. They maintain the standard stated by the judge is too strict and unjust; that it confronts members of the armed forces who are not persons of ordinary sense and understanding with the dilemma of choosing between the penalty of death for disobedience of an order in time of war on the one hand and the equally serious punishment for obedience on the other. Some thoughtful commentators on military law have presented much the same argument.

* * *

The "ordinary sense and understanding" standard is set forth in the present Manual for Courts-Martial, United States 1969 (Rev) and was the standard accepted by this Court...

* * *

Colonel William Winthrop, the leading American commentator on military law, notes:...

> Where the order is apparently regular and lawful on its face, he is not to go behind it to satisfy himself that his superior has proceeded with authority, but is to obey it according to its terms, the only exceptions recognized to the rule of obedience being cases of orders so manifestly beyond the legal power or discretion of the commander as to admit of no rational doubt of their unlawfulness....

> Except in such instances of palpable illegality, which must be of rare occurrence, the inferior should presume that the order was lawful and authorized and obey it accordingly, and in obeying it can scarcely fail to be held justified by a military court.

In the stress of combat a member of the armed forces cannot reasonably be expected to make a refined legal judgment and be held criminally responsible if he guesses wrong on a question as to which there may be considerable disagreement. But there is no disagreement as to the illegality of the order to kill in this case. For 100 years it has been a settled rule of American law that even in war the summary killing of an enemy, who has submitted to, and is under, effective physical control, is murder. Appellate defense counsel acknowledged that rule of law and its continued viability, but they say that Lieutenant Calley should not be held accountable for the men, women and children he killed because the court-martial could have found that he was a person of "commonest understanding" and such a person might not know what our law provides; that his captain had ordered him to kill these unarmed and submissive people and he only carried out that order as a good disciplined soldier should.

Whether Lieutenant Calley was the most ignorant person in the United States Army in Vietnam, or the most intelligent, he must be presumed to know that he could not kill the people involved here. The United States Supreme Court has pointed out that "[t]he rule that 'ignorance of the law will not excuse' [a positive act that constitutes a crime]... is deep in our law." Lambert v. California, 355 U.S. 225, 228 (1957). An order to kill infants and unarmed civilians who were so demonstrably incapable of resistance to the armed might of a military force as were those killed by Lieutenant Calley is, in my opinion, so palpably illegal that whatever conceptual difference there may be between a person of "commonest understanding" and a person of "common understanding," that difference could not have had any "impact on a court of lay members receiving the respective wordings in instructions," as appellate defense counsel contend. In my judgment, there is no possibility of prejudice to Lieutenant Calley in the trial judge's reliance upon the establishment standard of excuse of criminal conduct, rather than the standard of "commonest understanding" presented by the defense, or by the new variable test postulated in the dissent, which, with the inclusion of such variable factors for consideration as grade and experience, would appear to exact a higher standard of understanding from Lieutenant Calley than that of the person of ordinary understanding.

In summary, as reflected in the record, the judge was capable and fair, and dedicated to assuring the accused a trial on the merits as provided by law; his instructions on all issues were comprehensive and correct. Lieutenant Calley was given every consideration to which he was entitled, and perhaps more. We are impressed with the absence of bias or prejudice on the part of the court members. They were instructed to determine the truth according to the law and this they did with due deliberation and full consideration of the evidence. Their findings of guilty represent the truth of the facts as they determined them to be and there is substantial evidence to support those findings. No mistakes of procedure cast doubt upon them.

Consequently, the decision of the Court of Military Review is affirmed.

DUNCAN, Judge (concurring in the result)

DARDEN, Chief Judge (dissenting).

---

12. *Calley v. Callaway*

United States Court of Appeals
519 F. 2d 184 (5th Cir. 1975)

Appeal from the United States District Court for the Middle District of Georgia.

AINSWORTH, Circuit Judge:

In this habeas corpus proceeding we review the conviction by military court-martial of Lieutenant William L. Calley, Jr., the principal accused in the My Lai incident in South Vietnam, where a large number of defenseless old men, women and children were systematically shot and killed by Calley and other American soldiers in what must be regarded as one of the most tragic Chapters in the history of the nation's armed forces.

Petitioner Calley was charged on September 5, 1969, under the Uniform Code of Military Justice…with the premeditated murder on March 16, 1968 of not less than 102 Vietnamese civilians at My Lai (4) hamlet, Song My village, Quang Ngai province, Republic of Vietnam. The trial by general court-martial began on November 12, 1970, at Fort Benning, Georgia, and the court members received the case on March 16, 1971. (The function of court members in a military court-martial is substantially equivalent to that of jurors in a civil court.) On March 29, 1971, the court-martial, whose members consisted of six Army officers, found Calley guilty of the premeditated murder of not fewer than 22 Vietnamese civilians of undetermined age and sex, and of assault with intent to murder one Vietnamese child. Two days later, on March 31, 1971, the court members sentenced Calley to dismissal from the service, forfeiture of all pay and allowances, and to confinement at hard labor for life. On August 20, 1971, the convening authority, the Commanding General of Fort Benning, Georgia, approved the findings and sentence except as to the confinement period which was reduced to twenty years…. The Army Court of Military Review then affirmed the conviction and sentence…. The United States Court of Military Appeals granted a petition for review as to certain of the assignments of error, and then affirmed the decision of the Court of Military Review…. The Secretary of the Army reviewed the sentence as required by Art. 71(b), U. C. M. J.,…approved the findings and sentence, but in a separate clemency action commuted the confinement portion of the sentence to ten years. On May 3, 1974, President Richard Nixon notified the Secretary of the Army that he had reviewed the case and determined that he would take no further action in the matter.

On February 11, 1974, Calley filed a petition for a writ of habeas corpus in the United States District Court for the Middle District of Georgia against the Secretary of the Army and the Commanding General, Fort Benning, Georgia. At that time, the district court enjoined respondents from changing the place of Calley's custody or increasing the conditions of his confinement. On February 27, 1974, the district court ordered that Calley be released on bail pending his habeas corpus application. On June 13, 1974, this Court reversed the district court's orders, returning Calley to the Army's custody.... On September 25, 1974, District Judge Elliott granted Calley's petition for a writ of habeas corpus and ordered his immediate release [from his custody at Fort Benning]. The Army appealed and Calley cross-appealed. At the Army's request a temporary stay of the district judge's order of immediate release was granted by a single judge of this Court.... This Court subsequently met en banc, upheld the release of Calley pending appeal, and ordered en banc consideration of the case. We reverse the district court's order granting a writ of habeas corpus and reinstate the judgment of the court-martial.

* * *

Military court-martial convictions are subject to collateral review by federal civil courts on petitions for writs of habeas corpus where is asserted that the court-martial acted without jurisdiction, or that substantial constitutional rights have been violated, or that exceptional circumstances have been presented which are so fundamentally defective as to result in a miscarriage of justice. Consideration by the military of such issues will not preclude judicial review for the military must accord to its personnel the protections of basic constitutional rights essential to a fair trial and the guarantee of due process of law. The scope of review for violations of constitutional rights, however, is more narrow than in civil cases. Thus federal courts should differentiate between questions of fact and law and review only questions of law which present substantial constitutional issues. Accordingly, they may not retry the facts or reevaluate the evidence, their function in this regard being limited to determining whether the military has fully and fairly considered contested factual issues. Moreover, military law is a jurisprudence which exists separate and apart from the law governing civilian society so that what is permissible within the military may be constitutionally impermissible outside it. Therefore, when the military courts have determined that factors peculiar to the military require a different application of constitutional standards, federal courts are reluctant to set aside such decisions.

[The Court then took up, *seriatim*, the issues raised by defense counsel in this case, namely: (1) Pretrial publicity; (2) compulsory process; (3) discovery of Congressional testimony; (4) notice and double jeopardy; and (5) Calley's cross-appeal that raised the issue of the accused's retention on active duty in the United States Army beyond his scheduled separation date of September 6, 1969. The following excerpts set forth the Courts ruling on each of these issues].

[On pretrial publicity]: The critical issue is the actual or probable effect of the pretrial publicity on the trial itself and, more precisely, on those who sat in judgment of Calley. A careful review of the exhaustive voir dire conducted at trial indicates that there is no likelihood that pretrial publicity prejudiced Lieutenant Calley such as to deny him a fair trial....

* * *

The military court should not be criticized for refusing to do what was in all probability constitutionally impermissible controlling or imposing prior restraints on the news media.... Thus, we find no error in the actions taken by the military court which were fully consistent with the requirements of the Sixth Amendment and the limitations of the First Amendment.

[On compulsory process]: Prior to trial, defense counsel sought unsuccessfully to have subpoenaed the following persons: Secretary of Defense Melvin Laird, Secretary of the Army Stanley R. Resor, and Chief of Staff of the Army William Westmoreland. The defense stated that these individuals were essential to establish Calley's defense that all charges against him should be dismissed because "command influence and control had permeated the processing of the charges against the petitioner." The military judge declined to require the appearance of these witnesses. The district court held that the failure to compel the attendance of these witnesses deprived petitioner of his Sixth Amendment right "to have compulsory process for obtaining witnesses in his favor...." We conclude, however, that the district court's holding was erroneous and exceeded the proper scope of review.

* * *

...The military judge conducted an extensive hearing on Calley's [compulsory process] contentions. He found there was no evidence to support the accusations of command influence.... We hold that the conclusions of the military judge, which were fully and fairly considered and reaffirmed by the Court of Military Review, amply support the decision not to subpoena the witnesses in question.

* * *

[On discovery of Congressional testimony]: A congressional investigation subcommittee, chaired by Congressman F. Edward Hebert, conducted an investigation into the My Lai case, interviewed 152 witnesses, took some 1,812 pages of sworn testimony, looked at hundreds of documents and took some 3,045 pages of witness statements. The hearing lasted for some sixteen days. Once the subcommittee report had been made, Calley's defense team moved to obtain production of "(a)11 witness testimony and documentary evidence in the custody and control of the House of Representatives of the United States." The prosecutor made an informal inquiry of Congressman Hebert whether the materials from the subcommittee's hearing might be furnished. The Congressman replied, in effect, that it was the position of the subcommittee that the requested documents were neither within the purview of Brady v. Maryland, 373 U.S. 83...(1963) nor were they subject to disclosure under the provisions of the Jencks Act, 18 U. S. C §3500. Nonetheless, a list of the persons who had testified before the Hebert subcommittee was provided counsel. On October 13, 1970, Judge Kennedy (the trial judge) denied the general discovery request pertaining to all material in the possession of the House subcommittee].

* * *

... [T]here was no Brady due process problem in this case. The testimony in question was never available to the prosecution, which not only did not benefit from the information, but was not responsible for its nonproduction. This fact distinguishes the present case from other Brady cases, because the defense contention in the present case is that Brady or the Due Process Clause entitles the defense to obtain evidence unavailable to the prosecution and beyond the power of the prosecution to obtain.

The holding of the Brady case...is that "the suppression by the prosecution" of certain kinds of evidence violates due process. The basic import of Brady is not that there is an abstract right on the part of the defendant to obtain all evidence possibly helpful to his case, but rather that there is an obligation on the part of the prosecution to produce certain evidence actually or constructively in its possession or accessible to it in the interest of inherent fairness.

* * *

There is no prosecutorial dereliction in this case.

* * *

... The prosecution clearly did not have "exclusive access" to the testimony in question, it had no access at all. To this date there has been no holding that Brady confers on the defense a right to receive information or evidence greater than that possessed by the prosecution, and we decline to so hold now.

[On the Jencks Act allegation, the Court noted the following]: The Jencks Act provides that after a witness "called by the United States" has given testimony, the "United States" must produce to the defense any prior statement of the witness "in the possession of the United States" relevant to the subject matter of the witness' testimony. 18 U.S.C. §3500(b). If such statements are not provided, the trial court may strike the testimony or, if necessary, declare a mistrial. 18 U.S.C. §3500(d). Both sides agree that the Jencks Act applies to military proceedings. The question here is the application of the Act where certain statements of prosecution witnesses are possessed by Congress but withheld from both the prosecution and the defense. If the "United States" (the prosecution) calls a witness, are statements retained by the Congress "in the possession of the United States" so as to require furnishing the defense with the statements even though the prosecution does not possess and cannot obtain the statements?...

The district court held that under the Jencks Act "the statement need not be made to or held by the prosecution; any statement held by any part of the United States Government is covered." 382 F. Supp at 700.... The narrower issue is whether the failure to furnish the testimony created a defect of constitutional magnitude in the court-martial proceeding.

[The Court then cited the decision of *United States v. Augenblick*, 393 U.S. 348 (1969). It then continued]: The Supreme Court decision in United States v. Augenblick controls our decision in this case, as it demonstrates that no error of constitutional proportions is raised by the failure to provide the defense with the prior testimony of the witnesses in question.

* * *

... Thus under the authority of Augenblick, there was no constitutional error in the failure to provide the testimony of the witnesses here.

* * *

[On Petitioner Calley's Cross Appeal]: Calley [contended] that the Army lacked jurisdiction over his person because he was improperly retained on active duty by the Army beyond his scheduled separation date of September 6, 1969, and that the military had no authority to court-martial a serviceman after the date of his scheduled separation by so retaining him on active duty. We agree, however, with the Government that Calley was lawfully retained in active duty status, and that military jurisdiction having properly attached prior to September 6, 1969, it continued until disposition of the case.

* * *

This Court is convinced that Lieutenant Calley received a fair trial from the military court-martial which convicted him for the premeditated murder of numerous Vietnamese civilians at My Lai. The military courts have fully and fairly considered all of the defenses made by him and have affirmed that he is guilty. We are satisfied after a careful and painstaking review of this case that no violation of Calley's constitutional or fundamental rights has occurred, and that the findings of guilty were returned by impartial members on the evidence presented at a fairly conducted trial.

There is no valid reason then for the federal courts to interfere with the military judgment, for Calley has been afforded every right under our American system of criminal justice to which he is entitled.

Accordingly, the order of the district court granting a writ of habeas corpus to Calley is Reversed.

BELL, Circuit Judge, with whom GEWIN, THORNBERRY, MORGAN and CLARK, Circuit Judges, join (dissenting).

---

13. Kenneth A. Howard, "Command Responsibility for War Crimes"

21 *Journal of Public Law* 7, 13–15; 17, 19–20 (1972)
Reproduced with permission from Kenneth A. Howard, *Command Responsibility for War Crimes*, 21 J. Pub. L. 7 (1972)

* * *

...[S]ince the Nuremberg Trials and the International Tribunal in the Far East following World War II, any defense to a war crime based upon obedience to orders has been of questionable value to the defendant.

Of equal concern is the question of legal responsibility of a commander for the actions of subordinates under his command. It has long been a custom of the armed services of civilized nations that, in general, a commander is responsible for the actions of his subordinates in the performance of their duties. This, of course, does not contemplate their personal and individual actions not involving the performance of their assigned duties.... [T]he various publications that furnish guidance to members of the Army establishment in the exercise of their command duties place a clear supervisory responsibility upon the unit commander. These Field Manuals announce the policies of the United States in the exercise of its military functions and have the force and effect of law unless in derogation of the Constitution, statute, or treaty.

* * *

...[C]ommand responsibility does not extend to criminal responsibility for the individual crimes of military personnel, unless the commander knowingly participates in the criminal acts of his men, consciously fails to intervene in such activities, or declines to take appropriate action against violators after having gained knowledge of such unlawful activities. This principle of shared responsibility is not controversial when one considers the routinely accepted law of principals. There can be no argument with a concept of criminal responsibility where facts clearly demonstrate that a commander ordered his troops to commit obviously unlawful acts and thereafter joins in and participates in the commission of those very acts.

* * *

...Article 77 of the Uniform Code of Military Justice modernizes the common law by making criminally liable as a principal anyone who actually commits an offense punishable by the Code or anyone who aids, abets, counsels, commands, or procures the commission of an offense or who causes an act to be done which if directly performed by him would be punishable under the Uniform Code of Military Justice.

The Army Field Manual dealing with the subject of the Law of Land Warfare [Field Manual 27-10)] recognizes this principle. It provides:

> [W]hen troops commit massacres and atrocities against the civilian population of occupied territory or against prisoners of war, the responsibility may rest not only with the actual perpetrators but also with the commander. Such a responsibility arises directly when the acts in question have been committed in pursuance of an order of the commander concerned. The commander is also responsible if he has actual knowledge, or should have knowledge, through reports received by him or through other means, that troops or other persons subject to his control are about to commit or have committed war crimes and he fails to take the necessary and reasonable steps to insure compliance with the law of war or to punish violators thereof. [FM 27-19, §501, at 178–179].

* * *

...A combat commander has a duty both as an individual and as a commander to ensure humane treatment of noncombatants and surrendering or wounded combatants. Article 3 of the Geneva Convention Relative to the Treatment of Prisoners of War specifically prohibits violence to life and person, particularly murder, mutilation, cruel treatment, and torture. Also prohibited are the taking of hostages, outrages against personal dignity, and summary judgment and sentence. It also demands that the wounded and sick be extended treatment. These same provisions are found in the Geneva Convention Relative to the Protection of Civilian Persons in Time of War.

Though the cases are less in number and the principle less often invoked, the attachment of criminal responsibility based on mere presence under particular circumstances is an accepted legal premise. Simply stated, it is the principle that criminal liability may attach because of noninterference when there is an affirmative duty to act.... From such noninterference, under appropriate circumstances, it could well be inferred that his noninterference was designed by him to operate and did operate as an encouragement to or protection of the perpetrator, therefore rendering the defendant a principal.

* * *

...As the provisions of the Law of Land Warfare provide: "The commander is also responsible [for the acts of subordinates] if he has actual knowledge...that troops or other persons subject to his control are about to commit or have committed a war crime, and he fails to take the necessary and reasonable steps to insure compliance with the law of war or to punish violators thereof."

* * *

...Direct responsibility for criminal acts by troops totally out of control and not responsive to the commander's orders, surely should not be attributable to the commander as a form of vicarious responsibility. However, where competent evidence reflects that troops are under the control of their commander and commit war crimes under the mistaken belief that they are carrying out the commander's orders, then a different result should attach.

Under appropriate international law, a commander must take necessary and reasonable steps to prevent the commission of war crimes. If by his failure to intervene his troops continue to commit war crimes, then a new proximate cause, in fact, arises, namely the negligence of the commander. For instance, culpable negligence is a degree of negligence accompanied by a gross, reckless, deliberate or wanton disregard for the foreseeable consequences to others of that omission: it is an omission showing a disregard for human safety. The essence of wanton or reckless conduct is intentional conduct by way of omission where there is a duty to act, which conduct involves a high degree of likelihood that substantial harm will result to others.

* * *

The anomaly is that in the case of unlawful homicide, for instance, the subordinate may be guilty of premeditated murder whereas the commander may be guilty only of the lesser offense of involuntary manslaughter. This is so since the punishable act in the case of the subordinate is the unlawful death of the protected person whereas in the case of the commander the punishable act is the negligent omission of the commander to restrain the act of the subordinate which results in the death of the protected person.

14. The Constitution, International Law and Vietnam

(a) Jonathan M. Fredman, "American Courts, International Law and the War in Vietnam"

18 *Columbia Journal of Law and Social Problems*
295; 296–299; 302, 307–309; 312–314 (1984)
Reproduced with permission from Jonathan M. Fredman,
American Courts, International Law and the War in Vietnam,
18 Colum. J. L. & Soc. Probs. 295 (1984)

During the Vietnam War, many American citizens sought to block government action by invoking international legal principles they claimed to be superior to domestic law. Throughout the Vietnam conflict, however, the courts refused to evaluate official actions according to international criminal law. Judges did not discuss the possibility that the due process clause of the fifth amendment incorporates the international legal obligations of the individual into United States law, a possibility that would result in a constitutional prohibition against official actions that flout international law.

In addition, the courts occasionally held that the antiwar claims were barred by the unconsented-suit doctrine, found ripeness or remoteness barriers to their prosecution, or declared that the cases involved political questions not susceptible to judicial resolution. In rejecting the attacks, the courts consistently refused to consider the merits of arguments founded upon the individual's obligation, recognized by this in the Nuremberg Charter, not to participate in crimes against peace, war crimes, and crimes against humanity.

* * *

...American judges have acknowledged the legitimacy of international legal obligations, and the courts have declared that they might at some time decide a challenge to government action according to the Nuremberg law. These courts, nevertheless, found the international obligations to be irrelevant to the particular controversies before them, and upheld the government's actions.

* * *

...Why did the judges consistently find reasons to avoid rendering a Nuremberg-based decision? While most of the Vietnam-era opinions involving Nuremberg claims presented thorough and well-reasoned legal arguments, the diversity of rationales cited for the judgments and the consistent failure of the litigants suggest that the motivations behind the judgments included several that were rarely, if ever, articulated.

It is perhaps clear as a matter of common sense that no American court sitting during wartime will declare its government's policies to be fundamentally criminal under international law.

* * *

... [T]he typical Vietnam-era case revolved around an individual's argument that to pay taxes, to submit to induction, or to report for shipment to the battle area would make that individual guilty of providing aid for war crimes such as murder, torture, or mutilation, and would require his or her criminal assistance in crimes against peace. Consequently, to obey the challenged mandate would violate a duty to refrain under international law. In order to assert these arguments in domestic courts, the challenger must establish that the Nuremberg doctrines constitute enforceable American law.

* * *

... [C]ase law demonstrates that a United States citizen may be tried in American courts for violation of the international laws of war. Consequently, if Nuremberg defines certain laws of war, its strictures should be enforced by American judges. That Nuremberg defines various laws of war should be clear. During the Second World War, the Supreme Court stated in *Ex parte Quirin* [317 U.S. 1 (1942) *infra*] that "[f]rom the very beginning of its history this Court has recognized and applied the law of war as including that part of the law of nations which prescribes, for the conduct of war, the status, rights and duties of enemy nations as well as of enemy individuals." If this analysis is correct, the law set forth at Nuremberg should be found to constitute enforceable American law, and should be upheld by domestic courts.

* * *

Despite the Nuremberg decisions, which declared that individuals have obligations transcending their duties of loyalty to any particular state, and despite the arguments supporting a finding that the international standards have been incorporated into United States law, the American recognition of international law is effective only in the absence of a "contrary [treaty,] executive or legislative act or judicial decision." [*The Paquete Habana*, 175 U.S. 677, 700 (1900)]. Under American law, the presence of any of these would explicitly negate the application of Nuremberg principles in United States courts, despite the contrary dictates of the Nuremberg tribunal.

An implicit negation of international obligations may occur as well through the basic judicial reluctance to employ international law, or by judicial findings that particular national laws govern specific circumstances. In that event, the international obligations, still recognized as valid, would be deemed irrelevant to the decision of the particular case. Such as interpretation of national directive between the citizen and international law, precluding an examination of American actions in light of international principles just as effectively as would explicit negation, was frequently cited by judges during the Vietnam War.

* * *

This is not to suggest, or course, that certain war crimes, such as the indiscriminate murder of noncombatants, [as happened at My Lai] would ever be quietly sanctioned by United States courts. Rather, judges found an implicit congressional preemption of international standards when challenges were brought against the international legality of the methods by which the Vietnam War was being conducted.

* * *

Even though there never has been an explicit American negation of Nuremberg law, then, its practical utility in American courts during the Vietnam War was greatly attenuated by the judges' refusal to consider it when domestically enacted statutes could be found to govern the relationship between an individual and the government. This technique of implicit negation by interposition provided courts trying cases during those times of grave internal dissension with a means to avoid an absolute renunciation of Nuremberg law, while sustaining for the moment contemporary national policies.

* * *

Unlike the negation cases, in which the individual was implicitly held to lack standing to invoke international standards on a particular issue because of an interposition of domestic law, other cases demonstrated the judges' explicit use of jurisdictional bases to deny claimants any opportunity to litigate the particular issue upon which international law was alleged to bear. At times the individual was found to be challenging an activity wholly distinct from that producing the allegedly unlawful results; at other times the issues were found to be unripe, or the potential harm too remote to support adjudication, so that the questions of incorporation or interposition never had to be reached at all. On other occasions, the underlying controversies were held to be political questions, the resolution of which was committed to another branch of government, especially since the conduct of foreign affairs was often involved. Courts also held themselves unsuited to decide the merits of claims presented to them, or doubted the efficacy that their judgment would have, and cited those doubts as reasons to refuse to decide.

Whatever the jurisdictional or institutional grounds cited by judges in this field, the net effect was largely similar to that of interposition: Litigants challenging perceived abuses were denied relief without review by the judiciary of the merits of their claims.... [T]he courts "can literally manipulate [such doctrines as] 'standing to sue,' stare decisis, 'political' questions and all other aspects of constitutional law." Given the charged nature of American society during the Vietnam War, it may be that the ends desired by those who judged necessarily colored the results that they attained; the uniformity with which consideration of international legal claims was foreclosed during the Vietnam era appears not to have been a coincidental outcome.

[The following federal cases are illustrative of some of the ways judges sidestepped a decision on the merits of cases brought before them by individuals or groups alleging the illegality of the Vietnam War as noted by Fredman in the preceding discussion. The *Berrigan* decision was a criminal prosecution involving interference by the accused and others with United States Selective Service System operations which involved damage and destruction to draft records. The *Berk* decision involved an action by an enlisted member of the United States Army that challenged the constitutional basis for the presence of United States forces in Vietnam, coincident with seeking an injunction prohibiting the complainant from being sent to Vietnam. Both the United States district court in Maryland (*Berrigan*) and the United States district court in New York (*Berk*) dismissed the lawsuits].

(b) *United States v. Berrigan*

United States District Court
283 F. Supp. 336 (D. Md. 1968)

NORTHROP, District Judge.

The defendants before this court are charged in three counts that they did willfully

1. Injure property of the Untied States; 2. Mutilate records filed in a public office of the United states; and 3. Hinder the administration of the Military Selective Service Act.

Defendants wish to proffer an opening statement to the jury as to what they would present for their defense. Specifically, they contend that, by virtue of what they have read, heard and seen, the war in Vietnam is immoral and illegal; and that the United States, in carrying on the war in Vietnam, is violating certain precepts of international law, constitutional law, and judgments which were handed down at Nuremberg.

To serve as a foundation and a basis for their beliefs, defendants wish to produce in court, among other evidence, 'the outstanding experts' on international law who would testify that the acts of the United States government in Vietnam are illegal. Their conduct, they say, was prompted by their belief that the United States is acting illegally and was intended to prevent criminal acts from being committed. Because this belief prompted their acts, they argue that the necessary mens rea is lacking.

Initially, it must be pointed out that in law once the commission of a crime is established—the doing of a prohibited act with the necessary intent—proof of a good motive will not save the accused from conviction. In a long line of cases, the courts have consistently reiterated that 'One is criminally responsible who does an act which is prohibited by a valid criminal statute, though the one who does this act may do it under a deep and sincere religious belief that the doing of the act was not only his right but also his duty.' Baxley v. United States, 134 F. 2d 937, 938 (4th Cir. 1943).

This point is best illustrated and highlighted by those cases where a defendant has been found guilty of murder even though the motive advanced for justification was of the highest and most selfless level. For example, a man drowns his children because he loves them and wants to prevent their suffering in poverty; and a man poisons his wife, at her request, to end her agony from an incurable disease....

Counsel for defendants candidly admit that there is not precedent for the proposition advanced here, namely that any citizen is justified in mutilating and damaging government property and interfering with vital government functions—all acts specifically prohibited by penal statutes—if he reasonably believes that the government is acting illegally under international and possibly constitutional law.

The defense, as proffered, is analogous to the common-law right or privilege of one to use force to prevent the commission or consummation of a felony or of a misdemeanor amounting to a breach of the peace. But the defense of justification is not as broad as stated by counsel. Historically, it has been limited to well-recognized situations,...and well-defined areas of the law. More recently, it has been further limited by courts which have realized that in certain respects the doctrine of justification is outdated in our modern society because of the potential danger to society itself and because of the availability of other more civilized remedies....

That there is no legal precedent for defendants' proposition is not surprising. No civilized nation can endure where a citizen can select what law he would obey because of his moral or religious belief. It matters not how worthy his motives may be. It is axiomatic that chaos would exist if an individual were permitted to impose his transgression of a duly-enacted law.

* * *

The reasonableness of the belief of these defendants that the government is acting illegally in Vietnam is irrelevant to the present case; for, even if it were demonstrable that the United States is committing violations of international law, this violation by itself would afford the defendants no justifiable basis for their acts.

More specifically, no matter how reasonably, sincerely, or deeply these defendants believed that the government was acting illegally does not go to the question whether they sincerely and honestly believed that their acts were lawful and thus negates the specific intent necessary for conviction, namely willfulness. Thus, the proposition presented here is to be distinguished from a case where a defendant believed that he was acting within the law, although subsequently it turns out that he was mistaken as to the applicable law. United States v. Murdock, 290 U.S. 389...(1933).

In essence, the defendants are arguing not that they were legally justified in acting the way they chose to, or that they had a bona fide belief that they were legally justified, but that their lofty motives and sincerely-held convictions negate criminal intent.

Counsel also contends that the defendants' acts are symbolic expressions of speech which are protected by the First Amendment of the United States Constitution and thus [they are] entitled to offer this defense before the jury. In Dennis v. United States, 341 U.S. 497, 513...(1951), the Court said:

'Whether the First Amendment protects the activity which constitutes the violation of the statute must depend upon a judicial determination of the scope of the First Amendment applied to the circumstances of the case.'

* * *

It embraces two concepts: Freedom of belief, opinion and communication, and freedom to act.

'The first is absolute but, in the nature of things, the second cannot be. Conduct remains subject to regulation for the protection of society.' Cantwell v. State of Connecticut, 310 U.S. 296...(1940).

Now, in this particular instance, it cannot be seriously argued that the violation of the statutes charged to these defendants are premised upon speech or any type of expression in its pristine form. On the contrary, what is sought to be prohibited by these criminal statutes and what the defendants are charged with is activity or conduct which results in the disruption of a valid and vital governmental function and the depredation and destruction of government property and files.

It is true that some types of conduct are classified as symbolic speech and have been afforded the protection of freedom of speech because symbolism in the form of a flag, a salute, or picketing...has been recognized as 'a primitive but effective way of communicating ideas.' West Virginia State Board of Education v. Barnette, 319 U.S. 624...(1943). But, in Cox v. State of Louisiana, 379 U.S. 559...(1965), it was held that not all kinds of communicative acts are examples of symbolic speech and not all acts are afforded the protection of the First Amendment.

There can be no doubt that the First Amendment protects speech in opposition to national policy in Vietnam and to the Selective Service System.... But this protection does not shield conduct which collides with a valid criminal statute. And it makes no difference, as this court has pointed out before, that the defendants acted out of the sincerest of motives and the deepest of conviction, be that religion, moral, or political....

It was said by Mr. Justice Cardozo in connection with religious convictions: "The conscientious objector, if his liberties were to be thus extended, might refuse to contribute taxes in furtherance of a war, whether for attack or for defense, or in furtherance of any other end condemned by his conscience as irreligious or immoral. The right of private judgment has never yet been so exalted above the powers and the compulsion of the agencies of government. One who is a martyr to a principle—which may turn out in the end to be a delusion or an error—does not prove by his martyrdom that he has kept within the law." Hamilton v. Regents of the University of California, 293 U.S. 245...(1934).

This court finds that under the circumstances of this case the conduct which is charged in the indictment is not afforded the protections of the First Amendment and a conviction under these criminal statutes would not deny to these defendants any of the guarantees of that Amendment.

Finally, counsel contends that these defendants should be allowed to present to the jury what is popularly known as the 'Nurnberg Defense.' The trial of the Nazi war criminals at Nurnberg was premised on the generally accepted view that there are, as a part of international law, certain crimes against peace and humanity which are punishable.... It is urged here that the belief of these defendants that the United States was waging a war of aggression, and thus committing a crime against peace, justified the acts charged.

It is not clear what standing these defendants have to raise the legality of this country's involvement in Vietnam when they have not been called to serve in the armed forces, are not directly affected by our government's actions in that country, and are not even directly affected by the Selective Service apparatus....

* * *

The important element in this defense, assuming its applicability in an American court, is the individual responsibility which is necessary before it can be raised. These defendants do not have standing to raise the validity of governmental actions, either under international law or constitutional law, on the grounds that the rights of parties not before this court are violated....

* * *

Buy irrespective of the lack of standing of these defendants to raise the issue of the legality of the government's actions as they relate to the Vietnam situation, the proffered defense suffers from a more fundamental bar. It is clear that there are certain questions of substantive law, that is, 'political questions,' which are not cognizable in our courts because of the nature of our governmental system which is based upon a separation of functions among different branches of the government. The doctrine "is one of 'political questions,' not one of 'political cases.' The courts cannot reject as 'no law suit' a bona fide controversy as to whether some action denominated 'political' exceeds constitutional authority." Baker v. Carr, 369 U.S. 186, 217...(1962). Certain clearly defined areas have traditionally and necessarily been left to other departments of the government, free from interference by the judiciary. One such area is foreign relations.

It is true that not every case which touches the foreign-relations power of the country is necessarily a 'political question.' Courts have usually decided the constitutional questions concerning international agreements...but the corresponding question of international law has been treated as a 'political question.'

The activities of these defendants were directed towards the Selective Service System, which system counsel has admitted is not criminal or illegal in and of itself. What is called into question here is the utilization of the armed forces by the executive and legislative branches. It cannot be disputed that the recognition of belligerency abroad, and the measures necessary to meet a crisis to preserve the peace and safety of this country, is uniquely an executive and a legislative responsibility. Whether the actions by the executive and the legislative branches in utilizing our armed forces are in accord with international law is a question which necessarily must be left to the elected representatives of the people and not to the judiciary. This is so even if the government's actions are contrary to valid treaties to which the government is a signatory. And the Supreme Court has held that Congress may constitutionally override treaties by later enactment of an inconsistent statute, even though the subsequent statute is in violation of international law.

The categorization of this defense as a 'political question' is not an abdication of responsibility by the judiciary. Rather, it is a recognition that the responsibility is assumed by that level of government which under the Constitution and international law is authorized to commit the nation.

The 'Nurnberg Defense' is premised on a finding that the government is acting in violation of international law in waging an aggressive war, and, as such, cannot be raised here because the question of violations of international law by the government is uniquely a 'political' question.

(c) *Berk v. Laird*

United Stats District Court
317 F. Supp. 715 (E. D. New York 1970)

JUDD, District Judge.

An action for an injunction against sending an enlisted Army man to Vietnam challenges the constitutional basis for the presence of United States armed forces in South Vietnam. The case is before the court on defendants' motion to dismiss on the three grounds of lack of jurisdiction, failure to state a valid claim, and summary judgment for lack of genuine issues of material fact.

General Outline

The following controlling conclusions seem appropriate on the basis of the pleadings, affidavits, memoranda and public documents which the court has studied:

1. From the early days of our republic, there has been a recognized distinction between a "perfect war" or total war, initiated by a formal declaration of war, and an "imperfect war" or partial war, which involve military action authorized by Congress without a formal declaration of war.

2. There is no doubt that Congress has authorized the President to send members of the armed forces to South Vietnam to engage in hostilities.

3. The question whether Congress should declare total war or rely on some other mode of authorizing military action is a political question, on which a court should not overrule Congress' determination.

4. The controversies between the parties raise only questions of law, and no disputes of any material fact....

The Posture of the Case

At an earlier state, this court denied a motion for preliminary injunction, on the ground that, among others, that prior court decisions indicated that the power of the President as Commander-in-Chief to send the armed forces abroad was a political question, which courts should not decide.

An appeal was taken and decided by the Court of Appeals on June 19, 1970 [2d Cir., 429 F. 2d 302]. The Court of Appeals affirmed the denial of a preliminary injunction, but held that the question of the President's power to commit the armed forces to action involved a justiciable question, and remanded the case for further proceedings.

The Court of Appeals recognized that even a justiciable claim may not be decided if it involves a political question without "judicially discoverable and manageable standards for resolving it." The quotation was taken from Baker v. Carr, 369 U.S. 186, 217... (1962). After referring to Congress' actions concerning the Vietnam hostilities, "in part expressly through the Gulf of Tonkin Resolution and impliedly through appropriations and other acts in support of the project over a period of years," the Court of Appeals left it open for plaintiff's counsel "to suggest a set of manageable standards and escape the likelihood that his particular claim about this war at this time is a political question." 429 F. 2d 302, p. 305.

[The court then reviewed in detail the proposed "manageable standards" proffered by counsel for the plaintiffs, the plaintiff's proposed expert testimony and what their testimony would reveal, the legal issues surrounding the power to declare war and the congressional appropriation record over the years since the early 1960s relative to the Vietnam conflict. The following are excerpts regarding congressional appropriations and the concluding remarks by the district judge granting summary judgment for the defendants and dismissing plaintiff's complaint]:

By the end of 1967, there were 475,000 American military men in Vietnam, and the military command regarded this number as insufficient.

Plaintiff asserts that the President was always ahead of Congress in sending troops, and that Congress was always presented with a fait accompli which it was compelled to ratify. The course of events described above is more consistent with Congress and the President moving in concert.

Authorized expenditures for Vietnam increased from $21.9 billion in 1967 to $25.8 billion in 1968 and $28.8 billion in 1969, declining to 25.4 billion in 1970.

* * *

The Supreme Court has held that powers can be conferred on the President by appropriations acts.... Of course, there are instances where appropriations do not confer authority or ratify action—as where there is an appropriation to support an agency without proof that Congress knew what the agency was doing.

An appropriations act is like any other act of Congress. It must be introduced by a member of Congress, and obtain a majority vote in both House and Senate. The Constitution is not concerned with boundaries between the jurisdiction of appropriations sub-committees and substantive committees. Rules limiting amendment, even if enforced, are not of constitutional significance....

* * *

Plaintiff contends that any authorizations for Vietnam hostilities are not sufficiently explicit. This argument puts too narrow a limit on Congress' manner of expressing its will. The entire course of legislation shows that Congress knew what it was doing, and that it intended to have American troops fight in Vietnam.... Having found that Congress authorized the sending of American troops to Vietnam, the court would be entering the realm of politics in saying that the authorization should have been couched in difference language.

* * *

In connection with the Vietnam conflict, Congress may also have had reasons for acting in a manner short of an express declaration of war. A declaration of war might have consequences far beyond North Vietnam, and might trigger unknown responses from Communist China and the Soviet Union. Congress may also have considered the well-known fact that many of our friends in the free world look askance at our Vietnam adventure. To change the professed character of the conflict from a defense of South Vietnam against aggression to a declared war against North Vietnam might affect our relations with friendly powers abroad, and with non-aligned nations.

Respect for the Congressional judgment is also supported by the opinion of the Court of Appeals for the District of Columbia, which dismissed a suit to declare the Vietnam military action unconstitutional with the statement that: "It would be difficult to think of an area less suited for judicial action," Luftig v. McNamara, 126 U.S. App. D. C. 4, 373 F. 2d 664, 665 (1967). *cert. den.* 387 U.S. 945...(1967).

A similar conclusion was reached by Judge Wyzanski on a preliminary motion in United States v. Sisson, 294 F. Supp 511 (D. Mass. 1968). After finding that there was joint action by the President and Congress, without a declaration of war, he ruled that the method of collaboration between Congress and the Executive is a political question, saying (p. 515): "*** the distinction between a declaration of war and a cooperative action by the legislative and executive with respect to military activities in foreign countries is the very essence of what is meant by a political question. It involves just the sort of evidence, policy considerations, and constitutional principles which elude the normal process of the judiciary and which are far more suitable for determination by coordinate branches of the government."

* * *

The present case presents at least one of the elements which the Supreme Court has held to involve a political question. The combination of Congress' power to declare war and the President's power to direct the armed forces as Commander-in-Chief, provide a "textually demonstrable constitutional commitment of the issue to a coordinate political department" other than the judiciary Baker v. Carr, 369 U.S. 186, 217... (1962).

Nothing which plaintiff has offered in this case requires a departure from Judge Dooling's conclusion (317 F. Supp. 1019) that "political expediency may have counseled the Congress's choice of the particular forms and modes by which it has united with the presidency in prosecuting the Vietnam combat activities, but the reality of the collaborative action of the executive and the legislative required by the Constitution has been present from the earliest stages."

* * *

This court will not deal with the question whether South Vietnam or the United States violated the provisions of the Geneva Agreements concerning general elections in Vietnam. That question does not affect the authority given to the President by Congress.

Interpretation of the SEATO Treaty or other international agreements cited by the parties is also unnecessary to the decision of the question of United States "municipal law" whether Congress has authorized American troops to fight in Vietnam.

The Congress repeatedly and unmistakably authorized the use of armed forces of the United States to fight in Vietnam. Whether this was a prudent course of action or a tragic diversion of men and money, is immaterial. The Vietnam conflict cannot be blamed on usurpation by either of the Presidents who have held office from 1964 to date. Having reached that decision, the court's function is ended.

It is ORDERED that defendant's motion for summary judgment be granted, and that the Clerk enter judgment dismissing the complaint without costs.

Suggestions for Further Reading

(1) Addicott, Jeffrey F. & William A. Hudson, Jr., "The Twenty-Fifth Anniversary of My Lai: A Time to Inculcate the Lessons," 139 *Military Law Review* 153 (1993).

(2) Armistead, J. Holmes, Jr., "The United States vs. William Calley: An Opportunity Missed," 10 *Southern University Law Review* 205 (1984).

(3) Baird, Jay W., *From Nuremberg to My Lai*. Lexington, MA: Heath (1972).

(4) Belknap, Michal R., *The Vietnam War on Trial: The My Lai Massacre and the Court-Martial of Lieutenant Calley*. Lawrence, KS: University Press of Kansas (2002).

(5) Bilton, Michael & Kevin Sim, *Four Hours in My Lai*. New York: Viking Press (1992).

(6) Clark, Roger S., "Medina: An Essay on the Principles of Criminal Liability for Homicide," 5 *Rutgers-Camden Law Review* 59 (1973).

(7) D'Amato, Anthony C., Harvey L. Gould & Larry D. Woods, "War Crimes and Vietnam: The 'Nuremberg Defense' and the Military Service Register," *California Law Review* 1055 (1969).

(8) Daniel, Aubrey M., III, "The Defense of Superior Orders," 57 *University of Richmond Law Review* 477 (1973).

(9) Dinstein, Yoram, *The Defense of 'Obedience to Superior Orders' in International Law*. Leyden: A. W. Sijthoff (1965).

(10) *Facing My Lai: Moving Beyond the Massacre* (David L. Anderson ed.). Lawrence, KS: University Press of Kansas (1998).

(11) Faulkner, Stenley, "War Crimes: Responsibilities of Individual Servicemen and Superior Officers," 31 *National Lawyers Guild Practitioner* 131 (1974).

(12) Ferencz, Benjamin B., "War Crimes Law and the Vietnam War," 17 *American University Law Review* 403 (1968).

(13) Firmage, Edwin B., "Law and the Indo-China War: A Retrospective View," 1 *Utah Law Review* 1 (1974).

(14) Friedmann, Wolfgang, Note, "Law and Politics in the Vietnam War: A Comment," 61 *American Journal of International Law* 776 (1967).

(15) Henkin, Louis, "Viet-Nam in the Courts of the United States: 'Political Questions,'" 63 *American Journal of International Law* 285 (1969).

(16) Hersh, Seymour, *Cover-Up: The Army's Secret Investigation of the Massacre at My Lai.* New York: Random House (1972).

(17) Landsberg, Brian K., Comment, "The United States in Vietnam: A Case Study in the Law of Intervention," 50 *California Law Review* 515 (1962).

(18) McCarthy, Mary, *Medina.* New York: Harcourt, Brace, Jovanovich (1972).

(19) Mann, Robert, *The Grand Delusion: America's Descent Into Vietnam.* New York: Basic Books (2001).

(20) Moore, John N., "The Lawfulness of Military Assistance to the Republic of Viet-Nam," 61 *American Journal of International Law* 1 (1967).

(21) Morrison, Wilbur H., *The Elephant and the Tiger: The Full Story of the Vietnam War.* Central Point, OR: Hellgate Press (2001).

(22) O'Brien, James V., "The Law of War: Command Responsibility and Vietnam," 60 *Georgetown Law Journal* 605 (972).

(23) Paust, Jordan J., "My Lai and Vietnam: Norms, Myths and Leader Responsibility," 57 *Military Law Review* 99 (1972).

(24) Taylor, Telford, *Nuremberg and Vietnam: An American Tragedy.* Chicago: Quadraugle Books (1970).

Part Six

A Postscript on Twentieth Century Impunity; Selected ICTY and ICTR cases; International Criminal Court and the Rome Statute; Military Commission Controversy: History, Cases and Commentary; the *Hamdi* and *Padilla* Cases and the U.S. Supreme Court; Citizen Terrorists and the Constitution; Political Ethics and Terrorism (1990–2004)

Editorial Commentary

Part six of this work will concentrate on several international criminal justice events of signal importance that emerged during the final decade of the twentieth century and early years of the twenty-first. First, however, we reflect upon war crimes, genocide and other international delicts committed with *impunity*, that is, without trial or punishment, by notorious malefactors throughout the century just past. Their crimes, singly or in combination, never produced sufficient political and/or geopolitical critical mass to move the international criminal justice apparatus to action.

For example, the unpunished Soviet massacres ordered by Vladimir Lenin and Josef Stalin in the 1920s and 1930s; the failure of the Allies to prosecute Italian Axis war criminals after the Second World War; the failure to bring to justice those in the Chinese Communist regime of Mao Tse-tung, Chairman of the People's Republic of China (1949–1959), who ordered mass genocide in China during the consolidation of the communist state; the unpunished and little-remarked mid-1960s massacres in Indonesia; the horrific late 1970s genocide in Cambodia by the Pol Pot regime; and war crimes and genocide perpetrated by the Iraqi regime of Saddam Hussien both during and after the conclusion of the first Gulf War in 1991. These represent a catalog of some of the more gruesome offenses which, to date, have been forgotten, unremarked or simply ignored for a variety of reasons. Illegal activities such as these and others raise the question as to what extent the "Nuremberg Principles" are still a viable set of international criminal justice ukases in the early twenty-first century, especially set against the new spectre of transnational terrorism practiced by those nihilistic persons and groups who live beyond the pale of traditional international criminal law proscriptions.

The ad hoc international criminal tribunals for the Former Yugoslavia and for Rwanda were established by the U. N. Security Council in 1993 and 1994, respectively. The ICTY (International Criminal Tribunal Yugoslavia) came into being on May 15, 1993, under the auspices of Security Council Resolution 827.[1] Resolution 827 established the Tribunal's structure, its jurisdiction and its procedures. The first indictment preferred by the ICTY prosecutor was against Dusko Tadic in February, 1995.[2] Subsequently, other defendants involved in the Yugoslav crimes have been brought to trial by the ICTY at The Hague, and we report (besides the *Tadic* case), excerpts from the cases of *Prosecutor v. Erdemovic* and *Prosecutor v. Blaskic*, as examples. The ICTY trials of additional defendants are still-on going with perhaps the most notorious defendant, Slobodan Milosevic, currently in the dock at the Hague as this book goes to press.

The ICTR (International Criminal Tribunal Rwanda) was established on November 8, 1994, by U. N. Security Council Resolution 955.[3] Like Resolution 827 establishing the ICTY, Resolution 955 sets forth the structure, jurisdiction and procedures for the ICTR. The full title of the ICTR is the "International Tribunal for Prosecution of Persons Responsible for Genocide and Other Serious Violations of International Humanitarian Law Committed in the Territory of Rwanda and Rwandan Citizens Responsible for Genocide and Other Such Violations Committed in the Territory of Neighboring States, between 1 January 1994 and 31 December 1994." Thus, from the above caption, one can discern that the ICTR operates under a truncated jurisdictional time-frame limitation. Its sister tribunal at The Hague enjoys a wider jurisdictional time-frame in which to prosecute Balkan suspects which extends as far back as 1991. Two ICTR cases will be reported: *Prosecutor v. Akayesu* (1998) and *Prosecutor v. Rutaganda* (1999).

The historical and cultural antecedents surrounding the genocides in both the former Yugoslavia and in Rwanda are complex and somewhat convoluted and difficult to disentangle. Selected commentary and case opinions will clarify, to some degree, both the historical and cultural antinomies which bred the hatred, violence and killings in each of these two regions of the world.

In terms of international law development, the most significant benchmark in the 1990s, and, indeed, perhaps in the entire twentieth century, was the passage in 1998 in Rome of the statute establishing the first *permanent* International Criminal Court in the history of international law. This was a wetherbell event because as far back as the 1920s, there were calls for the establishment of such a court by leading international

---

1. U. N. SCOR, 48th Sess. 3217 mtg., U. N. Doc S/RES/827.
2. *Prosecutor v. Tadic*, Case No. IT-94-I-T (May 7, 1997).
3. U. N. SCOR, 6 U. N. Doc. S/RES/955 (1994).

lawyers and academic commentators as well as by politicians who envisaged such a body to be an important step in international criminal justice enforcement and conflict resolution. We will set out selections from the ICC statute and will include selected commentary on the court itself and the position of the United States government on this development in international criminal jurisprudence.

Part Six will conclude with an overview of the military commission and its use by the United States from the American Civil War up to and including the Presidency of George W. Bush. Within this historical frame of reference, we will include excerpts from eight federal court opinions that touch and concern the operations and legality of the military commission issue, commencing with *Ex parte Milligan* in 1867 and concluding with the post-9/11 case of *Al Odah v. United States* in 2003. Closing commentary will focus on the employment of military commissions to try and sentence those held in captivity as a result of the attack on the United States on September 11, 2001, as well as the summer, 2004, U.S. Supreme Court decisions addressing the proper forum to try and sentence American citizens who have allied themselves with international terrorism. An *Epilogue* on political ethics and terrorism concludes the book.

---

1. Twentieth Century Impunity

(a) Yves Beigbeder, *Judging War Criminals: The Politics of International Justice*

87–92 (1999) Copyright © Yves Beigbeder from: *Judging War Criminals: The Politics of International Justice* by Yves Beigbeder, reprinted with permission of Palgrave Macmillan

(i) The Unpunished Soviet Massacres

The number of Soviet victims who died as a result of decisions and orders given by Lenin and Stalin is estimated at 20 million. The Bolshevicks created a totalitarian one-party system, without institutional counter-powers, which effectively prevented the exercise of most individual rights and freedoms. A regime of terror subjected all Soviet citizens to the arbitrary decision-making power of the supreme Communist leader and his close associates in the name of the people. The Marxist-Leninist utopia was to create a new egalitarian society, which implied the destruction of the former social order, of the former elites, of 'counter-revolutionaries' and of 'enemies to the people,' an ill-defined group that could include whoever the new power had decided to eliminate. The creation of a new Socialist world, a world of political and social progress which was to replace decadent and corrupt capitalist and social-democratic countries, justified all human sacrifices. Most of the reality—political repression, famines, deportations to concentration camps (the gulags), executions without judgment, forced confessions and condemnations in well-scripted trials, torture and forced conformity with the official dogma—was carefully hidden from the Soviet population and from the outside world through propaganda and disinformation, with the loyal support, in foreign countries, of local Communist Party leaders and members and convinced fellow-travelers.

For its apologists, the first Red Terror was initiated by Lenin in order to save the October 1917 Revolution from internal counter-revolutionaries and external attacks against the Soviet Union. From 1918 to 1922, the Tcheka, the political police, was granted, and used, all powers to search private homes, and to arrest and shoot—individually or in groups—all persons suspected of opposition to the new regime, with or without judgment. In the case of judgment, the sentence is almost always the death penalty, labeled as the 'supreme measure of social protection.' The repression caused hundreds of thousands of deaths. The Red Terror and the civil war were in part 'natural' measures of self-defence against counter-revolutionary violence and external intervention.

According to Medvedev:

> The terror was also intimately connected with serious errors on the part of the first Soviet government in the implementations of important economic and political measures. Government actions provoked opposition and resistance among an overwhelming majority of the petty bourgeois masses of Russia, bringing Soviet power to the brink of catastrophe and compelling those in charge to resort to mass terror.

Medvedev adds that the excesses of this terror were without any justification, although it is 'inevitably misleading to judge a revolutionary epoch or wartime situation by the laws and customs normally applicable to peacetime.'

Stalin admitted to Churchill, in August 1942, that 10 million peasants had been killed or deported during the forced collectivization of the early 1930s. The well-to-do peasants, the kulaks, were class enemies who had to be eliminated through killings or deportations. Stalin was responsible for the Ukrainian famine genocide. The nationalist Ukrainians were subjected to harsh dekulakization and collectivization: their social base, the individual land holdings, had to be destroyed. Grain quotas and levels of requisition were set at impossible levels. Outside help was prevented. Conquest estimates that, from 1928 to 1932, 1.5–2.0 million Ukrainians were deported and 500 000 killed locally as kulaks. From the spring 1932, at the beginning of the famine, until February 1933, when Stalin stopped the requisitions, out of 20·5 million Ukrainian peasants, approximately 5 million died of famine. The Soviet authorities denied to their own people and to the West that any famine was taking or had taken place. The overall death toll of peasants in the USSR in the period 1930–7 has been estimated by Conquest at 14.5 million.

The Great Purge of 1936–8 adds millions of victims to previous counts. The number of arrests of innocent victims is estimated at 7 million, including about half a million death sentences. For the period 1936–50, an estimated average of 8 million detained in camps, with a 10% death rate per annum, produces a total casualty figure of 12 million dead. The 'gulags' were maintained until 1987. Whole nations were deported without any military or other justification:

1. in August 1941, approximately 1 225 000 ethnic Germans living in the USSR were deported to Siberia and Kazakhstan;

2. in December 1943, all the Karachai and Kalmyk peoples were deported—the autonomous Kalmyk Republic was liquidated;

3. in March 1944, all the Chechen and Ingush peoples were deported and the Chechen-Ingush Autonomous Republic was abolished;

4. in April 1944, all Balkars were deported;

5. in May 1944, 194 000 Tatars are deported from the Crimea and 86 000 from Georgia.

Of the 2.3 million Soviet prisoners of war detained in Germany and repatriated to the USSR, 80% were deported, exiled or killed.

Stalin's Crimes Disclosed

Stalin's crimes were finally officially disclosed by Nikita Khrushchev in his secret speech to the Twentieth Communist Party Congress on 24 and 25 February 1956. Khrushchev blamed Stalin for having used extreme methods and mass repressions when the Revolution was already victorious.... He had annihilated many military commanders and political workers during 1937–41 because of his suspiciousness and through slanderous accusations. The mass deportations from their native places of whole nations initiated by Stalin were [in Khrushchev's words] 'rude violations of the basic Leninist principles of the nationality policy of the Soviet state.' Stalin himself had encouraged the cult of personality.

* * *

Khrushchev's 1956 speech was approved by the Twentieth Congress, which instructed the Central Committee 'consistently to carry out measures with the object of fully overcoming the cult of personality, which is alien to the principles of Marxism-Leninism, and eliminating the consequences in every aspect of Party, state and ideological activity.' After Stalin's death in March 1953, Beria—former chief of the political police and vice-President of the Council of Ministers—had been arrested and executed after a secret trial in the same year. After his execution, his closest associates were put on trial in various cities, but Stalin's name was never mentioned in these trials, and the entire responsibility for lawlessness was attributed to the NKVD.

Khrushchev himself and many other senior members of the Central Committee and the Presidium shared responsibility in the implementation of Stalin's policies and decisions, if not in the decision-making process itself, decisions which caused massive losses of life and great suffering. However, no systematic investigations or organized prosecutions of those responsible at various levels for the violations of human rights were ever initiated. In fact, Khrushchev's speech had only attacked Stalin's deviations from Marxism-Leninism, not the Soviet ideology that was at the root of these deviations. The Party's structure and its officials, who had benefited from privileges linked to their status and who undoubtedly also shared responsibility in the implementation of Stalin's decisions, were still in power and would have resisted any attempt to probe and reveal unpleasant facts, without even speaking of prosecutions and punishment.

* * *

As seen in many other countries, the investigation of old crimes and opening of old wounds is a particularly difficult task; it may be an impossible task in Russia when the demise of the USSR has essentially left, in positions of political, military and economic power, the same persons who held important positions in the Soviet Union Communist hierarchy. It is therefore unlikely that the main senior Soviet officials responsible for genocide, other massacres and exactions inflicted on their own population, if still alive, will ever be prosecuted, judged and punished.

By reference to the Genocide Convention, the Ukrainian famine, initiated and planned by Stalin, carried out and finally stopped under his orders, may be classified as a genocide with intent to destroy, in whole or in part, a national or ethnic group. The other enormous losses of population may be considered as political 'class' genocides, in view of their ideological motivation, linked, in some cases, to ignorance of the economic consequences of political decisions, or voluntary neglect of such considerations.

(b) M. Cherif Bassiouni, *Crimes against Humanity in International Criminal Law*

2d Rev. ed. 547–549 (1999) Reproduced with permission of Brill Academic Publishers NV, M. Cherif Bossiouni, *Crimes Against Humanity in International Criminal Law*, 2d rev. ed. © 1999 Kluwer Law International

(i) Selective Enforcement

While this [twentieth] century has seen some individuals held responsible under international criminal law, there have been all too many instances where prosecution did not occur....

Among the most notable examples of selective enforcement was the case of accused Italian war criminals of the 1930s and 1940s.

...[T]he UNWCC [United Nations War Crimes Commission] listed 750 Italian war criminals, accusing them, *inter alia*, of using poison and mustard gas against the Ethiopians during that aggressive war in 1936 in violation of the 1925 Protocol for the Prohibition of the Use in War of Asphyxiating, Poisonous or other Gases, and of Bacteriological Methods of Warfare. The accused also were charged with killing prisoners of war, bombarding hospitals and committing other violations of the customary law of armed conflicts. Also during World War II, several war crime violations were documented by Yugoslavia and Greece against their Italian occupiers relating to the mistreatment of prisoners of war, the killing of innocent civilians and the destruction of civilian property. Libya also advanced similar claims during Italy's occupation of that country. The 1943 Moscow Declaration provided that countries in which such violations were committed had the right to prosecute offenders. The Instrument of Surrender of Italy, Article 45, provided that Italy had a duty to extradite any one of its nationals charged with war crimes. Yugoslavia, Ethiopia, and Greece repeatedly requested extradition of a number of Italian war criminals, which included Marshall Badoglio and General Ambrosio, for war crimes committed in the Balkans. Libya also asked for Badoglio and Grazinani, but Italy turned a deaf ear, with United States and British assent, and never surrendered anyone accused of war crimes.

The UNWCC specifically referred to the use of prohibited gas in Ethiopia and to the bombardment of Red Cross hospitals by troops under the command of Badoglio and Graziani, as well as eight other officers. At first, the United States and the United Kingdom, being the Allies in control of Italy, ignored the extradition requests of Yugoslavia, Greece and Ethiopia and also ignored their repeated protests. Subsequently, as stated above, the Italian government also refused their extradition. Thus, the United States and the United Kingdom violated the terms of the 1943 Moscow Declaration and the provisions of the Italian Armistice Agreement. Thereafter the U.S. and the U.K. formally renounced their rights to try Italian war criminals under Article 45 of the Armistice Agreement. Italian governments since 1946 have also refused extradition to these same requesting countries. Only one Italian officer, General Bellomo, was prosecuted for war crimes committed outside of Italy. He was convicted and sentenced to death. Interestingly, he was not a fascist. None of the fascist generals were ever prosecuted for war crimes committed outside of Italy. It is commonly assumed that this benign attitude toward Italian fascist war criminals ·was due to the fact that, in 1943 Marshal Badoglio headed a provisional government for Italy while it was still occupied by Germany. He made a separate Armistice with the Allies who were particularly eager to neutralize the Italian navy in the Mediterranean and wanted to attract as many as possible from the Italian military to fight alongside the Allies against Germany. Thereafter, it was the belief of United States and United Kingdom senior officials that the future stability of Italy required the cooperation of the fascists into the democratic process to oppose what they feared was a communist onslaught in that country.

(c) Yves Beigbeder, *Judging War Criminals, The Politics of International Justice*

92–95; 98, 101 (1999) Copyright © Yves Beigbeder from:
Judging War Criminals: The Politics of International Justice by Yves Beigbeder, reprinted with permission of Palgrave-Macmillan

(i) Indonesia: The 1965 Massacre

The former Dutch Indies became independent in 1949 as Indonesia, under the leadership of Sukarno, its first President and one of the leaders of the Third World. It is composed of more than 3000 islands, with a population of over 185 million and a large diversity of languages (more than 250), ethnic groups (3% are Chinese) and—religions 90% Muslim, 3.5% Christian, 2% Buddhist and the remainder being Hindu and animists. By 1957, efforts to establish parliamentary rule had collapsed, and there was widespread rebellion. The army took power, and in 1959 Sukarno re-emerged as head of state in alliance with the Indonesian Communist Party (PKI) and the army under the banner of 'Guided Democracy.' With 10 million members in 1965, the Communist Party began to push for radical land reform and rent reduction, alarming many traditional elites. The army was opposed to the Party because of its influence with Sukarno and because of its penetration of part of the air force and the navy. The Communist Party was also perceived as a threat to landowners because of its collective plans, to Muslims because of its atheist and anti-religious doctrine, and to the USA, concerned about Communist designs for assuming power in Southeast Asian countries.

On the night of 30 September/1 October 1965, a group of junior officers murdered six senior generals in an attempted coup, claiming to overthrow Sukarno's leadership. The failed coup was officially interpreted as a Communist plot to seize power, although the purpose and sponsorship of the coup have not been clarified. The army, under the direction of General Suharto and with the support of the CIA, then took power. It initiated and encouraged the savage killing of Communist Party leaders, members and supporters, with the aid of bands of youths and of the local population. In a holy war, fanatical Muslims slaughtered atheists. The victims included many thousands of Chinese, suspected because China had become Communist, but also targets of long-standing ethnic resentment in view of their domination of commerce and trade. Possessions were looted and houses burned. Eventually, the army reestablished order. The number killed is estimated at about 500 000 for the period December 1965 to mid-1966, and the number of those arrested also at 500,000. Most were detained without judgment and were only released in 1978. The massacres had first an internal political motivation: to eliminate the Communist threat from Indonesian politics, within the context of the East-West confrontation that provided US support to the Indonesian political and military leaders.... The primary political motivation should identify the massacres as a genocide, even if the present terms of the [Genocide] Convention do not include this category. The secondary and perhaps accidental destruction of members of ethnic, racial and religious groups was genocidal, although not intended as a total extermination of these groups and limited in time.

General Suharto became President in 1968 and was still Chief of State in 1997. Indonesia is a police state, which suppresses free expression, and jails and tortures political opponents. Those who initiated and condoned the massacres of 1965 are still in power. Failing a democratic revolution, the perpetrators of the massacres will not be prosecuted or sanctioned.

(ii) China

According to Rummel, the number of deaths caused by the Chinese Communist regime amongst its own population may be estimated as follows:

The Totalization Period:	8 427 000
Collectivization and 'The Great Leap Forward'	7 474 000
The Great Famine and Retrenchment Period	10 729 000
The 'Cultural Revolution'	7 731 000
Liberalization	874 000
TOTAL	35 235 000

These human losses were related to, and caused by, an ideological drive aimed at transforming the traditional Chinese political and social system into a Communist society, initially on the Soviet model. The first enemies were the counter-revolutionaries, nationalist sympathizers and other political opponents. Then, landlords, rich peasants, the gentry and the bourgeoisie as class enemies were to be re-educated or exterminated. The Communist Party and the army were periodically purged. The collectivization of the peasants and the 'Great Leap Forward' caused the world's greatest recorded famine. Unlike the Ukraine famine willed by Stalin, the Chinese famine was 'only' the result of erroneous decisions by the Great Helmsman. The succession of massacres, either intentional or accidental, was caused by political leaders intent on creating a 'new society' and a 'new (Communist) man' without any consideration for the human consequences. Notwithstanding its political motivation, the extent of human losses and suffering should justify the charge of genocide, even if the present text of the Convention has excluded this category.

China is still a one-party Communist dictatorship, in absolute power, in spite of its economic evolution. Only dissidents are punished; none of the past or present Communist leadership is liable to be considered responsible and accountable for the criminal consequences of their political and economic decisions.

(iii) The Khmer Rouge Genocide

Even if terror cannot be rated in number of victims, types of atrocities or the duration of a genocide or massacres, the killings, torture and associated suffering inflicted by the Khmer Rouge upon their own population in a small country [Cambodia] between 1975 and 1978 appear particularly monstrous. The Marxist real-life (or real-death) 'scientific' social experiment resulted in approximately 1.7 million deaths amongst its eight million people. A despotic, dogmatic group made use of the worst sadistic instincts of indoctrinated youths to destroy a traditional society, eliminate the elites and ethnic groups, break up families, condemn the masses to hard labour under starvation conditions and transform a country into a prison camp under high security, an immediate death sentence being applied to any suspected deviations from the ortho-dox ideology.

* * *

…Mixed political alliances and supports during the Cold War led to more confusion and prevented the genocide from being brought formally to the United Nations Security Council. China was supporting the Khmer Rouge for ideological reasons and as a coun-terweight to Vietnam, the assertive regional power with the hegemonic ambition of recreating an Indochinese federation. The USA kept their own support for the Khmer Rouge after the Vietnamese intervention [in Cambodia] out of their own humiliation after having lost the Vietnam war. The USSR was supporting Socialist Vietnam. Any draft resolution condemning the Khmer Rouge government would have been vetoed in the Security Council. No military intervention by Western countries could have been envisaged: France had not yet recovered from its own Vietnamese colonial defeat, and the USA was clearly not ready for another Asian intervention.

* * *

On 21 June 1997, Prince Norodom Ranariddh and Hun Sen, respectively First and Second Prime Ministers, asked for the assistance of the UN and the international com-munity in bringing to justice those persons responsible for the genocide and crimes against humanity during the rule of the Khmer Rouge from 1975 to 1979. As Cambodia did not have the resources or expertise to conduct this procedure, UN assistance was necessary on the basis of similar efforts to respond to genocide and crimes against hu-manity in Rwanda and the former Yugoslavia. It is, however, unlikely that the UN and the international community will respond positively to this request by creating another *ad hoc* International Tribunal. It is also clear that the present Cambodian government, headed by a former Khmer Rouge member, is both unwilling and incapable of holding a fair and well-documented trial of Pol Pot and his main associates….

[Beigbeder's prediction was accurate. U. N. Secretary-General Kofi Annan recom-mended an international criminal tribunal be established for Cambodia and the U. N. Secretariat commenced plans in late 1999 to establish such a court. However, by then, Western governments were preoccupied with the situation in Kosovo and their previous interests in seeing another *ad hoc* tribunal being created waned. As a result, States who had the power and resources to move a Cambodian tribunal into being failed to per-suade the Cambodian authorities of the need for such a court].

―――――――――

(d) M. Cherif Bassiouni, *Crimes against Humanity in International Criminal Law*

2d rev. ed., 552–555 (1999) Reproduced with permission of Brill Academic Publishers NV, M. Cherif Bossiouni, *Crimes Against Humanity in Interna-tional Criminal Law*, 2d rev. ed. © 1999 Kluwer Law International

…[T]he precedents [of World War II]…all involved prosecutions of the defeated by the victorious…. These prosecutions were, nevertheless, justified. The fact that only a few prosecutions of personnel belonging to the Victorious powers occurred (mostly by their own courts-martial), does not diminish the legal validity of the prosecutions that did take place. But, more importantly, the concept of one-sided justice does reveal the still arbitrary *ad hoc* nature of the international legal system. Germany, during World War I and World War II, had records of Allied violations of the very laws and rules with which the Allies charged Germany with violating. The German documentation of the World War I Allies' violations against Germany even escaped public attention and no significant trace of World War II Allied violations against Germany and against Germans and others appears in the recollection of world public opinion. Some exceptions exist, however, such as the dreadful firebombing of Dresden [called the "Florence of the Elbe"], a city of no strategic importance, after the war had been won.[4] This event remains in the world's consciousness as a symbol of the terrible and unnecessary suffering inflicted upon the German civilian population. It is also shocking that the wholesale violation of conventional and customary rules of war against German prisoner of war by the USSR have escaped international public attention. An equal disregard applied to the Allies' violations against the Japanese, the worst example of which is the world community's apparent approval of the use of two atomic bombs in 1945 against the cities of Hiroshima and Nagasaki, killing and injuring hundreds of thousands of civilians. Had Japan or Germany so bombed an Allied power, there is no doubt that its perpetrators, from the decision-makers to the crews of the planes that dropped the bombs, would have been tried and convicted of war crimes. These horrible events deserve the same equally forceful condemnation as that visited upon the perpetrators of similar acts performed by the defeated.

What must also not escape attention is the fact that since World War II many regional and national conflicts have occurred. Korea, Vietnam, Palestine, Pakistan-Bangladesh-India, Cyprus, Lebanon, and the Persian Gulf are among the regional armed conflicts with an international character, while Biafra and Cambodia are among those national conflicts that engulfed entire populations. In all of these conflicts, there have been violations that constitute war crimes and/or "crimes against humanity," but in no instance were the perpetrators prosecuted. Only Bangladesh...considered setting up a war crimes tribunal to prosecute Pakistan's military personnel, but then dropped the initiative for a variety of political and diplomatic considerations.

Germany lost both World War I and World War II and some of its officials were prosecuted. The same was true for Japan after World War II, but not Italy, which was part of the Axis. Neither did Turkey, which was an ally of Germany in World War I and whose officials were accused of killing an estimated one million Armenians and of deporting a large number of non-Turkish nationals and other minorities, particularly Greeks, incur that fate, though it came close to it with the Treaty of Sevres [1920, but never ratified]. The USSR, whose troops committed war crimes in World War II, some of which, such as the Katyn massacre of some 14,700 Polish prisoners of war, it falsely charged Germany with and was never even officially reproached for such war crimes.... These and other related national conflicts evidence the need to reformulate and broaden the concepts of "crimes against humanity" to include such violations that might otherwise fall outside the ambit of the Article 6(c) definition, and which are not covered by the Geno-

---

4. [Dresden was firebombed by British RAF Bomber Command on the night of February 13–14, 1945, and that single raid killed between 50,000 and 100,000 persons, most of whom were civilians. On March 2, 1945, the city was again attacked, this time by the United States 8th Air Force. For a detailed and gripping account of these raids, see David Irving, *Apocalypse 1945: The Destruction of Dresden* (1995)].

cide Convention. Such reformulation could also limit the impact of short-term and near-sighted political expedients.

In the midst of two cities in ruins by Allied hands, Nuremberg and Tokyo, Allied tribunals sat in legal, moral and ethical judgment. These prosecutions and judgments became a beacon of higher values, standards and rules of conduct for those entrusted with the power to govern (and potentially to harm) others. Lamentably, the light they produced was not that of a beacon that spreads widely and evenly. Instead, the light was narrow, as though emitted through a tunnel. The moral tunnel condemned the Germans and the Japanese, but ignored Italian and Allied violations. Nuremberg and Tokyo, like the Leipzig trials after World War I, left many unanswered questions but they did, at least, provide partial answers. To be sure, the post-World War I and II prosecutions were not unjust, nor were the prosecutions, in the main, unfair, considering the crimes committed and the legal standards of the time. It is more the missed opportunities to advance a more permanent and more universal "Rule of Law" that one cannot help but deeply regret, as the search for solutions continues.

International Criminal prosecutions were never easy. They occurred only on a very small way after WWI owning to the pressures of the Allies on Germany. What occurred then may be described as tokenism. After WWII, the victorious Allies simply imposed their will on the defeated, while totally absolving themselves. This is not to say that those who were prosecuted did not deserve it, but rather that on the Allies' side there were many similar crimes that warranted prosecution, but were conveniently overlooked.

When political considerations required it, the Allies after WWI failed to pursue any prosecution of their own. They also looked the other way as to Italians charged with war crimes. By 1953 almost all of those who were convicted and sentenced in the Far East trials (that spanned the period (1946–1951) were released. Between 1945 and 1998 some 250 conflicts took place, and along with tyrannical regime victimization, these have caused an estimated 170 million casualties. Yet almost all the perpetrators of these crimes have benefited from impunity. The ICTY and ICTR had different beginnings, and have only dealt with a few cases. For the time being at least, they are not likely to deal with many more, and it is still doubtful whether they will be able to prosecute the major decision-makers. The ICTY more so than the ICTR will be particularly affected by the political climate in the region as has been consistently evident. Conversely, the ICTR, whose situation is different from the political perspective, has been the subject of mismanagement and neglect for its first three years.

Nevertheless, the ICTY and recently the ICTR have overcome many problems and difficulties, and have proven that the combination of dedicated judges, prosecutors and staff, and the support of NGOs and civil society throughout the world is a force that *realpolitik* must reckon with....

---

2. *Statute of the International Tribunal for the Former Yugoslavia*

UN Doc. S/25704, 3 May 1993, Annex, at 36–48

Having been established by the Security Council acting under Chapter VII of the Charter of the United Nations, the International Tribunal for the Prosecutions of Persons Responsible for Serious Violations of International Humanitarian Law Committed in the Territory of the Former Yugoslavia since 1991...shall function in accordance with the provisions of the present statute.

Article 1
Competence of the International Tribunal

The International Tribunal shall have the power to prosecute persons responsible for serious violations of international humanitarian law committed in the territory of the former Yugoslavia since 1991 in accordance with the provisions of the present Statute.

Article 2
Grave breaches of the Geneva Conventions of 1949

The International Tribunal shall have the power to prosecute persons committing or ordering to be committed grave breaches of the Geneva Conventions of 12 August 1949, namely the following acts against persons or property protected under the provisions of the relevant Geneva Convention:

(a) wilful killing;

(b) torture or inhuman treatment, including biological experiments;

(c) wilfully causing great suffering or serious injury to body or health;

(d) extensive destruction and appropriation of property, not justified by military necessity and carried out unlawfully and wantonly:

(e) compelling a prisoner of war or a civilian to serve in the forces of a hostile power;

(f) wilfully depriving a prisoner of war or a civilian of the rights of fair and regular trial;

(g) unlawful deportation or transfer or unlawful confinement of a civilian;

(h) taking civilians as hostages.

Article 3
Violations of the laws or customs of war

The International Tribunal shall have the power to prosecute persons violating the laws or customs of war. Such violations shall include, but not be limited to:

(a) employment of poisonous weapons or other weapons calculated to cause unnecessary suffering;

(b) wanton destruction of cities, towns or villages, or devastation not justified by military necessity;

(c) attack, or bombardment, by whatever means, of undefended towns, villages, dwellings, or buildings;

(d) seizure of, destruction or wilful damage done to institutions dedicated to religion, charity and education, the arts and sciences, historic monuments and works of art and science;

(e) plunder of public or private property.

Article 4
Genocide

1. The International Tribunal shall have the power to prosecute persons committing genocide as defined in paragraph 2 of this article or of committing any of the other acts enumerated in paragraph 3 of this article.

2. Genocide means any of the following acts committed with intent to destroy, in whole or in part, a national, ethical, racial or religious group, as such:

(a) killing members of the group;

(b) causing serious bodily or mental harm to members of the group;

(c) deliberately inflicting on the group conditions of life calculated to bring about its physical destruction in whole or in part;

(d) imposing measures intended to prevent births within the group;

(e) forcibly transferring children of the group to another group.

3. The following acts shall be punishable:

(a) genocide;

(b) conspiracy to commit genocide;

(c) direct and public incitement to commit genocide;

(d) attempt to commit genocide;

(e) complicity in genocide.

Article 5
Crimes against Humanity

The International Tribunal shall have the power to prosecute persons responsible for the following crimes when committed in armed conflict, whether international or internal in character, and directed against any civilian population:

(a) murder;

(b) extermination;

(c) enslavement;

(d) deportation;

(e) imprisonment;

(f) torture;

(g) rape;

(h) persecutions on political, racial and religious grounds

(i) other inhumane acts.

Article 6
Personal jurisdiction

The International Tribunal shall have jurisdiction over natural persons pursuant to the provisions of the present Statute.

Article 7
Individual Criminal responsibility

1. A person who planned, instigated, ordered, committed, or otherwise aided and abetted in the planning, preparation or execution of a crime referred to in articles 2 to 5 of the present Statute, shall be individually responsible for the crime.

2. The official position of any accused person, whether as Head of State or Government or as a responsible Government official, shall not relieve such person of criminal responsibility nor mitigate punishment.

3. The fact that any of the acts referred to in articles 2 to 5 of the present Statute was committed by a subordinate does not relieve his superior of criminal responsibility if he knew or had reason to know that the subordinate was about to commit such acts or had done so and the superior failed to take the necessary and reasonable measures to prevent such acts or to punish the perpetrators thereof.

4. The fact that an accused person acted pursuant to an order of a Government or of a superior shall not relieve him of criminal responsibility, but may be considered in mitigation of punishment if the International Tribunal determines that justice so requires.

Article 8
Territorial and temporal jurisdiction

The territorial jurisdiction of the International Tribunal shall extend to the territory of the former Socialist Federal Republic of Yugoslavia, including its land surface, airspace and territorial waters. The temporal jurisdiction of the International Tribunal shall extend to a period beginning on 1 January 1991.

Article 9
Concurrent jurisdiction

1. The International Tribunal and national courts shall have concurrent jurisdiction to prosecute persons for serious violations of international humanitarian law committed in the territory of the former Yugoslavia since 1 January 1991.

2. The International Tribunal shall have primacy over national courts. At any state of the procedure, the International Tribunal may formally request national courts to defer to the competence of the International Tribunal in accordance with the present Statute and the Rules of Procedure and Evidence of the International Tribunal.

Article 10
Non-bis-in-idem

1. No person shall be tried before a national court for acts constituting serious violations of international humanitarian law under the present Statute, for which he or she has already been tried by the International Tribunal.

2. A person who has been tried by a national court for acts constituting serious violations of international humanitarian law may be subsequently tried by the International Tribunal only if:

(a) the act for which he or she was tried was characterized as an ordinary crime; or

(b) the national court proceedings were not impartial or independent, were designed to shield the accused from international criminal responsibility, or the case was not diligently prosecuted.

3. In considering the penalty to be imposed on a person convicted of a crime under the present Statute, the International Tribunal shall take into account the extent to which any penalty imposed by a national court on the same person for the same act has already been served.

Article 11
Organization of the International Tribunal

The International Tribunal shall consist of the following organs:

(a) The Chambers, comprising two Trial Chambers and an Appeals Chamber;

(b) The Prosecutor, and

(c) A Registry, servicing both the Chambers and the Prosecutor.

Article 12
Composition of the Chambers

The Chambers shall be composed of eleven independent judges, no two of whom may be nationals of the same State, who shall serve as follows:

(a) Three judges may serve in each of the Trial Chambers;

(b) Five judges shall serve in the Appeals Chamber.

Article 14
Officers and members of the Chambers

1. The judges of the International Tribunal shall elect a President.

2. The President of the International Tribunal shall be a member of the Appeals Chamber and shall preside over its proceedings.

3. After consultation with the judges of the International Tribunal, the President shall assign the judges to the Appeals Chamber and to the Trial Chambers. A judge shall serve only in the Chamber to which he or she was assigned.

4. The judges of each Trial Chamber shall elect a Presiding Judge, who shall conduct all of the proceedings of the Trial Chamber as a whole.

Article 15
Rules of procedure and evidence

The judges of the International Tribunal shall adopt rules of procedure and evidence for the conduct of the pre-trial phase of the proceedings, trials and appeals, the admission of evidence, the protection of victims and witnesses and other appropriate matters.

1. The Prosecutor shall be responsible for the investigation and prosecution of persons responsible for serious violations of international humanitarian law committed in the territory of the former Yugoslavia since 1 January 1991.

2. The Prosecutor shall act independently as a separate organ of the International Tribunal. He or she shall not seek or receive instructions from any Government or from any source.

3. The Office of the Prosecutor shall be composed of a Prosecutor and such other qualified staff as may be required.

4. The Prosecutor shall be appointed by the Security Council on nomination by the Secretary-General. He or she shall be of high moral character and possess the highest level of competence and experience in the conduct of investigations and prosecutions of criminal cases. The Prosecutor shall serve for a four-year term and be eligible for reappointment. The terms and conditions of service of the Prosecutor shall be those of an Under-Secretary-General of the United Nations.

5. The staff of the Office of the Prosecutor shall be appointed by the Secretary-General on the recommendation of the Prosecutor.

Article 17
The Registry

1. The Registry shall be responsible for the administration and servicing of the International Tribunal.

2. The Registry shall consist of a Registrar and such other staff as may be required.

3. The Registrar shall be appointed by the Secretary-General after consultation with the President of the International Tribunal. He or she shall serve for a four-year term and be eligible for reappointment. The terms and conditions of service of the Registrar shall be those of an Assistant Secretary-General of the United Nations.

4. The staff of the Registry shall be appointed by the Secretary-General on the recommendation of the Registrar.

Article 18
Investigation and preparation of indictment

1. The Prosecutor shall initiate investigations ex-officio or on the basis of information obtained from any source, particularly from Governments, United Nations organs, intergovernmental and non-governmental organizations. The Prosecutor shall assess the information received or obtained and decide whether there is sufficient basis to proceed.

2. The Prosecutor shall have the power to question suspects, victims and witnesses, to collect evidence and to conduct on-site investigations. In carrying out these tasks, the Prosecutor may, as appropriate, seek the assistance of the State authorities concerned.

3. If questioned, the suspect shall be entitled to be assisted by counsel of his own choice, including the right to have legal assistance assigned to him without payment by him in any such case if he does not have sufficient means to pay for it, as well as to necessary translation into and from a language he speaks and understands.

4. Upon a determination that a prima facie case exists, the Prosecutor shall prepare an indictment containing a concise statement of the facts and the crime or crimes with which the accused is charged under the Statute. The indictment shall be transmitted to a judge of the Trial Chamber.

Article 19
Review of the indictment

1. The judge of the Trial Chamber to whom the indictment has been transmitted shall review it. If satisfied that a prima facie case has been established by the Prosecutor, he shall confirm the indictment. If not so satisfied, the indictment shall be dismissed.

2. Upon confirmation of an indictment, the judge may, at the request of the Prosecutor, issue such orders and warrants for the arrest, detention, surrender or transfer of persons, and any other orders as may be required for the conduct of the trial.

Article 20
Commencement and conduct of trial proceedings

1. The Trial Chambers shall ensure that a trial is fair and expeditious and that proceedings are conducted in accordance with the rules of procedure and evidence, with full respect for the rights of the accused and due regard for the protection of victims and witnesses.

2. A person against whom an indictment has been confirmed shall, pursuant to an order or an arrest warrant of the International Tribunal, be taken into custody, immediately informed of the charges against him and transferred to the International Tribunal.

3. The Trial Chamber shall read the indictment, satisfy itself that the rights of the accused are respected, confirm that the accused understands the indictment, and instruct the accused to enter a plea. The Trial Chamber shall then set the date for trial.

4. The hearings shall be public unless the Trial Chamber decides to close the proceedings in accordance with its rules of procedure and evidence.

Article 21
Rights of the accused

1. All person shall be equal before the International Tribunal.

2. In the determination of charges against him, the accused shall be entitled to a fair and public hearing, subject to article 22 of the Statute.

3. The accused shall be presumed innocent until proved guilty according to the provisions of the present Statite.

4. In the determination of any charge against the accused pursuant to the present Statute, the accused shall be entitled to the following minimum guarantees, in full equality:

(a) to be informed promptly and in detail in a language which he understands of the nature and cause of the charge against him;

(b) to have adequate time and facilities for the preparation of his defence and to communicate with counsel of his own choosing;

(c) to be tried without undue delay;

(d) to be tried in his presence, and to defend himself in person or through legal assistance of his own choosing; to be informed, if he does not have legal assistance, of this right; and to have legal assistance assigned to him, in any case where the interests of justice so require, and without payment by him in any such case if he does not have sufficient means to pay for it;

(e) to examine, or have examined, the witnesses against him and to obtain the attendance and examination of witnesses on his behalf under the same conditions as witnesses against him;

(f) to have the free assistance of an interpreter if he cannot understand or speak the language used in the International Tribunal;

(g) not to be compelled to testify against himself or to confess guilt.

Article 23
Judgement

1. The Trial Chambers shall pronounce judgments and impose sentences on persons convicted of serious violations of international humanitarian law.

2. The judgment shall be rendered by a majority of the judges of the Trial Chamber, and shall be delivered by the Trial Chamber in public. It shall be accompanied by a reasoned opinion in writing, to which separate or dissenting opinions may be appended.

Article 24
Penalties

1. The penalty imposed by the Trial Chamber shall be limited to imprisonment. In determining the terms of imprisonment, the Trial Chambers shall have recourse to the general practice regarding prison sentences in the courts of the former Yugoslavia.

2. In imposing the sentences, the Trial Chambers should take into account such factors as the gravity of the offence and the individual circumstances of the convicted person.

3. In addition to imprisonment, the Trial Chambers may order the return of any property and proceeds acquired by criminal conduct, including by means of duress, to their rightful owners.

Article 25
Appellate proceedings

1. The Appeals Chamber shall hear appeals from persons convicted by the Trial Chambers or from the Prosecutor on the following grounds:

    (a) an error on a question of law invalidating the decision; or

    (b) an error of fact which has occasioned a miscarriage of justice.

2. The Appeals Chamber may affirm, reverse or revise the decisions taken by the Trial Chambers.

Article 26
Review proceedings

Where a new fact has been discovered which was not known at the time of the proceedings before the Trial Chambers or the Appeals Chamber and which could have been a decisive factor in reaching the decision, the convicted person or the Prosecutor may submit to the International Tribunal an application for review of the judgment.

Article 27
Enforcement of Sentences

Imprisonment shall be served in a State designated by the International Tribunal from a list of States which have indicated to the Security Council their willingness to accept convicted persons. Such imprisonment shall be in accordance with the applicable law of the State concerned, subject to the supervision of the International Tribunal.

Article 28
Pardon or commutation of sentences

If, pursuant to the applicable law of the State in which the convicted person is imprisoned, he or she is eligible for pardon or commutation of sentence, the State concerned shall notify the International Tribunal accordingly. The President of the International Tribunal, in consultation with the judges, shall decide the matter on the basis of the interests of justice and the general principles of law.

Article 31
Seat of the International Tribunal

The international Tribunal shall have its seat at The Hague.

3. The *Tadic* Judgment of the ICTY

[Dusko Tadic, a Bosnian Serb, was one of the many participants in so-called "ethnic cleansing" operations against Bosnian Muslims in the Prijedor region of Bosnia and Herzegovina during the year 1992. The forty-year-old defendant was a karate expert and former café owner who was charged with both torture and murder in and around three Serbian concentration camps in northeast Bosnia in 1992. The *Tadic* trial's 301-page ruling by the ICTY was the first such verdict announced by an *ad hoc* international criminal tribunal since the decisions of the military tribunals at Nuremberg and Tokyo in the 1940s.

Dusko Tadic's trial was the opening round in a series of trials conducted (and still continuing) under United Nations auspices at The Hague. Since June, 1991, an ethnic conflict of serious proportion had erupted in the former communist Socialist Federal Republic of Yugoslavia. In 1993, the United Nations Security Council established the ICTY to prosecute those individuals found to be significantly involved in violations of international law in the territory of the former Yugoslav state. Both the European Community and the United Nations had, up until the establishment of the ICTY, tried unsuccessfully to mediate a peaceful diplomatic solution to the Balkan crisis. Impelled by mounting evidence of massive and widespread violations of international humanitarian law and the laws and customs of war, however, the U. N. Security Council finally acted. The history of this most recent Balkan conflict is replete with confusing allegiances, visages of past atrocities and political instability that has haunted this region since World War I. There are several excellent summations of the events that precipitated the late twentieth century Balkan strife. We will preface excerpts from the *Tadic* opinion with selected commentary from the following *Note* in the *Vanderbilt Journal of Transnational Law* that places the ICTY cases in historical perspective].

(a) Karl A. Hockhammer, *Note*, "The Yugoslav War Crimes Tribunal: The Compatibility of Peace, Politics, and International Law"

28 Vanderbilt Journal of Transnational Law 119, 125–130 (1995)
Reproduced with permission from Karl A. Hockhammer,
The Yugoslav War Crimes Tribunal: The Compatibility of Peace, Politics, and International Law, 28 Vand. J. Transnat'l L. 119 (1995)

* * *

II. A Brief Chronology of the Break-Up of Yugoslavia

The Socialist Federal Republic of Yugoslavia (SFRY) was formed from the rubble of the Austro-Hungarian Empire after World War I. Prior to its dissolution in 1991, the SFRY consisted of six republics—Slovenia, Croatia, Serbia, Bosnia-Herzegovina, Montenegro, and Macedonia—and two autonomous regions—Kosovo and Vojvodina.

Political instability and ethnic tension plagued the SFRY from its inception until Marshall Tito established a communist government in 1947. In 1980, after the death of Tito, tension among three major ethnic groups in the SFRY—the Croats, Bosnian Muslims, and Serbs—resurfaced. The ethnic unrest contributed to the decentralization of the federal government as the more prosperous republics of Croatia and Slovenia objected to subsidizing the economies of less industrialized republics like Serbia, while Serbia wanted to retain control over the federal government to ensure that economic support.

While the Republic of Serbia consolidated political control over the remaining republics by the late 1980s, the SFRY's governing party—the League of Communists of Yugoslavia—had begun to disintegrate because of inter-ethnic squabbling. In January

1990, in an attempt to save itself, the League voted to end its monopoly on political power and instituted multi-party elections in the republics. In these elections, the Communists lost control of the Slovenian government. By the end of 1990, the Communists had also lost power in the Republic of Croatia, Bosnia-Herzegovina, and Macedonia.

These shifts in political power precipitated the dissolution of the SFRY. In June 1990, the Republic of Slovenia declared itself fully sovereign, and on September 27, 1990, it became the first republic to renounce the supremacy of federal law within its territory. In a December 23, 1990 referendum, Slovenian citizens voted heavily in favor of independence. Meanwhile, on December 22, 1990, the parliament in the Republic of Croatia also declared federal legislation inferior to its own.

Although Serbia, Slovenia, and Croatia attempted to agree on a future form of government for the SFRY, the effort failed when Slovenia and Croatia advocated a loose confederation that would have limited Serbia's control. Displeased with the proposal, Serbia severed negotiations and, claiming that the internal borders of Yugoslavia were purely administrative, asserted it would seek to create a Greater Serbia. On March 18, 1991, the Serbian leadership, through the Yugoslav People's Army—and in flagrant disregard of the Yugoslav Constitution—imposed martial law over the SFRY.

The final blow to the SFRY occurred on May 15, 1991, when Serbia and Montenegro blocked the election of Strip Mesic of Croatia to the Chair of the Presidency. On June 25, 1991, after further negotiations had failed, Slovenia and Croatia declared their independence. Two days later, civil war erupted when the Serb-controlled Yugoslav People's Army attacked Slovenia. Slovenia declared war against the rump Yugoslavia (Serbia, Montenegro, Kosovo, and Vojvodina) controlled by Serbia, and requested international mediation. Shortly into the war, ethnic Serbs living in Croatia began a policy of ethnic cleansing, slaughtering Muslims and Croats in parts of Croatia, and the Serb population of Bosnia-Herzegovina began its initial attempt to consolidate the territory under its control.

As the war escalated, still other republics of the SFRY declared their independence. Bosnia-Herzegovina's Muslims and Croats held a referendum on independence in March 1992. Bosnian Serbs boycotted the referendum and sought to establish their own independent state within Bosnia-Herzegovina. Shortly after the referendum, on April 6, 1992, the European Community recognized Bosnia-Herzegovina as an independent state; the United States and Croatia followed suit the next day. Full-scale war broke out among the Serbs, Muslims, and Croats when the Bosnian Serbs declared their own independent Serbian Republic of Bosnia-Herzegovina on April 7, 1992. Ten days later, the republics of Serbia and Montenegro declared a new "Federal Republic of Yugoslavia." Although fighting among the fledgling nations began as a virtual free-for-all, by June 20, 1992, Bosnia had cemented an alliance with Croatia, which was also fighting ethnic Serbs within its own territory, and declared a state of war. Since then, the majority of the fighting has been confined to Bosnia and parts of Croatia.

The United Nations reaction to the Yugoslav conflict typified the world's rush to condemn Serbian aggression, but reluctance to intervene. Fighting in the former Yugoslavia proceeded for several months before the United Nations took action. The Security Council left the task of trying to resolve the conflict initially to the European Community, and later to NATO. Eventually, on September 25, 1991, the UN Security Council intervened by passing Resolution 713, which established an arms embargo against all combatants. Finally, in February, 1992, the United Nations dispatched the UN Peacekeeping Force pursuant to Security Council Resolution 721.

Since the beginning of the armed conflict in 1991, the Bosnian government, the Bosnian Serbs, and Croatia have repeatedly rejected peace proposals drafted by the European Community and the United Nations. The Serbs maintain past injustices justify the current round of killings, and other combatants have replied in kind. At the time of this writing [1995], the United Nations strategy has been to use the weapons of poverty and isolation to force ethnic Serbs toward a peace settlement....

[The Dayton Accords, signed at Dayton, Ohio, in December 1995, brought the fighting in the former Yugoslavia to an end. One of the provisos of the Dayton agreement obligated all parties to the Balkan conflict to cooperate in the apprehension and prosecution of offenders brought before the ICTY. The Accords, however, failed to lay out a role for the 60,000-strong NATO Implementing Force (IFOR) in searching out and arresting indicted war criminals. This was a major defect in the peace agreement, but the reality of the situation was such that had NATO been obligated by the Dayton Accords to be both a peace-keeping and law enforcement force, there was little reason to believe that it would have been signed and implemented. As a result, there are still today numerous indicted war criminals and those who have violated international humanitarian law still at large in the former Yugoslavia. Unlike the post-World War II trials of the Germans and the Japanese by the Allied Powers who had complete military, political and economic control over those vanquished nations, the military, political and economic situation in the former Yugoslavia since the Dayton Accords militates against a World War II-like approach in the Balkans. Thus, we see only a minimalist approach to apprehending and bringing alleged criminal perpetrators to international justice. In a word, the ICTY apparently sees its mandate as being simply to adjudicate the cases presented to it; not a tribunal whose high mission it is to mold the rule of law in the Balkans for a wider audience who, in generations to come, would view the Tribunal's handiwork as a foundational element in Western-style democratic self-government. We present two separate parts of the very lengthy Tadic case. The Trial Chamber (by a 2–1 majority) found Dusko Tadic not guilty of violating the "grave breaches" provisions of the 1949 Geneva Conventions. On the other hand, he was found guilty on eleven of the thirty-one other counts. Tadic was not charged with "genocide" but was convicted of "persecution" and a total of fourteen assaults (designated as "crimes against humanity") plus five separate violations of the laws and customs of war. He was sentenced to a twenty-year prison term for, among other things, his "discriminatory animus" towards his victims. The first selected excerpt from Tadic comes from Judge Cassese's opinion on a defense motion for an interlocutory appeal on the issue of the tribunal's jurisdiction. The second selection presents excerpts from the final judgment of the Tribunal handed down on May 7, 1997].

(b) *Prosecutor v. Tadic*

International Criminal Court for the Former Yugoslavia
October 2, 1995
4 IT-94-1-AR 72

[Decision on Defense Motion for Interlocutory Appeal on Jurisdiction].

CASSESE, J.

79. Article 2 of the Statute of the International Tribunal provides:

"The International Tribunal shall have the power to prosecute persons committing or ordering to be committed grave breaches of the Geneva Conventions of 12 August 1949...."

By its explicit terms, and as confirmed in the Report of the Secretary-General, this Article of the Statute is based on the Geneva Conventions of 1949 and, more specifically, the provisions of those Conventions relating to "grave breaches" of the Conventions. Each of the four Geneva Conventions of 1949 contains a "grave breaches" provision, specifying particular breaches of the Convention for which the High Contracting Parties have a duty to prosecute those responsible. In other words, for these specific acts, the Conventions create universal mandatory criminal jurisdiction among contracting States. Although the language of the Conventions might appear to be ambiguous and the question is open to some debate...it is widely contended that the grave breaches provisions establish universal mandatory jurisdiction only with respect to those breaches of the Conventions committed in international armed conflicts. Appellant argues that, as the grave breaches enforcement system only applied to international armed conflicts, reference in Article 2 of the Statute to the grave breaches provisions of the Geneva Conventions limits the International Tribunal's jurisdiction under that Article to acts committed in the context of an international armed conflict.

The Trial Chamber has held that Article 2 [of the Statute of the Tribunal]:

["H]as been so drafted as to be self-contained rather than referential, save for the identification of the victims of enumerated acts; that identification and that alone involves going to the Conventions themselves for the definition of 'persons or property protected'....

[T]he requirement of international conflict does not appear on the face of Article 2. Certainly, nothing in the words of the Article expressly require its existence; once one of the specified acts is allegedly committed upon a protected person the power of the International Tribunal to prosecute arises if the special and temporal requirements of Article 1 are met....

80. With all due respect, the Trial Chamber's reasoning is based on a misconception of the grave breaches provisions and the extent of their incorporation into the Statute of the International Tribunal. The grave breaches system of the Geneva Conventions establishes a twofold system: there is on the one hand an enumeration of offences that are regarded so serious as to constitute "grave breaches," closely bound up with this enumeration a mandatory enforcement mechanism is set up, based on the concept of a duty and right of all Contracting States to search for and try or extradite persons allegedly responsible for "grave breaches." The international armed conflict element generally attributed to the grave breaches provisions of the Geneva Conventions is merely a function of the system of universal mandatory jurisdiction that those provisions create. The international armed conflict requirement was a necessary limitation on the grave breaches system in light of the intrusion on State sovereignty that such mandatory universal jurisdiction represents. State parties to the 1949 Geneva Conventions did not want to give other states jurisdiction over serious violations of international humanitarian law committed in their internal armed conflicts—at least not the mandatory universal jurisdiction involved in the grave breaches system.

81. The Trial Chamber is right in implying that the enforcement mechanism has of course not been imported into the Statute of the International Tribunal, for the obvious reason that the International Tribunal itself constitutes a mechanism for the prosecution and punishment of the perpetrators of "grave breaches." However, the Trial Cham-

ber has misinterpreted the reference to the Geneva Conventions contained in the sentence of Article 2: "persons or property protected under the provisions of the relevant Geneva Conventions."... For the reasons set out above, this reference is clearly intended to indicate that the offences listed under Article 2 can only be prosecuted when perpetrated against persons or property regarded as "protected" by the Geneva Conventions under the strict conditions set out by the Conventions themselves.... Clearly, these provisions of the Geneva Conventions apply to persons or objects protected only to the extent that they are caught up in an international armed conflict. By contrast, those provisions do not include persons or property coming within the purview of common Article 3 of the four Geneva Conventions.

83. We find that our interpretation of Article 2 is the only one warranted by the text of the [ICTY] Statute and the relevant provisions of the Geneva Conventions, as well as by a logical construction of their interplay as dictated by Article 2. However, we are aware that this conclusion may appear not to be consonant with recent trends of both State practice and the whole doctrine of human rights—which, as pointed out below (see paras. 97–127), tend to blur in many respects the traditional dichotomy between international wars and civil strife. In this connection the Chamber notes with satisfaction the statement in the *amicus curiae* [friend of the court] brief submitted by the Government of the United States, where it is contended that:

"the 'grave breaches' provisions of Article 2 of the International Tribunal Statute apply to armed conflicts of a non-international character as well as those of an international character." (U.S. Amicus Curiae Brief, at 35.)

This statement, unsupported by any authority, does not seem to be warranted as to the interpretation of Article 2 of the [ICTY] Statute. Nevertheless, seen from another viewpoint, there is no gainsaying its significance: The statement articulates the legal views of one of the permanent members of the Security Council on a delicate legal issue; on this score it provides the first indication of a possible change in *opinio juris* of States. Were other States and international bodies to come to share this view, a change in customary law concerning the scope of the "grave breaches" system might gradually materialize.... In addition, attention can be drawn to the Agreement of 1 October 1992 entered into by the conflicting parties in Bosnia-Herzegovina. Articles 3 and 4 of this Agreement implicitly provided for the prosecution and punishment of those responsible for grave breaches of the Geneva Conventions and Additional Protocol I. As the agreement was clearly concluded within a framework of an internal armed conflict...it may be taken as an important indication of the present trend to extend the grave breaches provisions to such categories of conflicts.

Notwithstanding the foregoing, the Appeals Chamber must conclude that, in the present state of development of the law, Article 2 of the [ICTY] Statute only applies to offences committed within the context of international armed conflict.

LI, J. (concurring in part)

* * *

7. Professor Meron states the customary international law of war crimes very correctly and clearly in the following terms:

"Whether the conflicts in Yugoslavia are characterized as internal or international is critically important. The Fourth Hague Convention of 1907, which codified the principal laws of war and served as the normative core for the post-World War II war crimes prosecutions, applies to international wars only. The other principal prong of the penal laws of war, the grave breaches provisions of the Geneva Conventions and Protocol I, is also directed to international wars. Violations of common Article 3 of the Geneva Conventions, which concerns internal wars, do not constitute grave breaches giving rise to universal criminal jurisdiction. Were any part of the conflict deemed internal rather than international, the perpetrators of even the worst atrocities might try to challenge prosecutions for war crimes or grave breaches, but not for genocide or crimes against humanity." (Meron, *War Crimes in Yugoslavia and the Development of International Law* 88 AJIL 78, 80 (1994)).

8. The Final Report of 27 May 1994 of the Commission of Experts established pursuant to Security Council resolution 780 (1992) takes the same view as Professor Meron:

"If a conflict is classified as international, then, the grave breaches of the Geneva Conventions, including Additional Protocol I, apply as well as violations of the laws and customs of war. The treaty and customary law applicable to international armed conflict is well-established. The treaty law designed for international armed conflict is in common [A]rticle 3 of the Geneva Conventions, Additional Protocol II of 1977, and [A]rticle 19 of the 1954 Hague Convention for the Protection of Cultural Property in the Event of Armed Conflict. These legal sources do not use the terms 'grave breaches' or 'war crimes.' Further, the content of customary law applicable to internal armed conflict is debatable. As a result, in general, unless the parties to an internal armed conflict agree otherwise, the only offences committed in internal armed conflict for which universal jurisdiction exists are 'crimes against humanity' and genocide, which apply irrespective of the conflicts' classification." (S/1994/674, p. 13, para. 42.}

ABI-SAAB, J., (concurring in part)

* * *

Admittedly, the traditional view, as far as the interpretation of the Geneva Conventions is concerned, has been that the "grave breaches" regime does not apply to internal armed conflicts. But the minority view that it does is not devoid of merit if we go by the texts alone and their possible teleological interpretation.

Regardless, however, of the outcome of this initial debate, if we consider the recent developments which are aptly presented in the Decision, we can draw two conclusions from them. The first is that a growing practice and *opinio juris* both of States and international organizations, has established the principle of personal criminal responsibility for the acts figuring in the grave breaches articles as well as for the other serious violations of the *jus in bello*, even when they are committed in the course of an internal armed conflict. The second conclusion is that in much of this accumulating practice and *opinio juris*, the former acts are expressly designated as "grave breaches"...

This is not a mere question of semantics, but of proper legal classification of this accumulated normative substance, with a view to introducing a modicum of order among the categories of crimes falling within the substantive jurisdiction of the Tribunal....

[Under the provisions of the 1949 Geneva Conventions, so-called "grave breaches" consist of such acts as (a) willful killing, (b) torture, (c) inhumane treatment and other enumerated acts against persons protected under the Conventions. In Article 2 of the ICTY Statute, this list of "grave breaches" is reproduced. A key element that is a condition precedent to proving grave breaches under the ICTY Statute is the existence of an *international armed conflict*. Because of the complexity in the collapse of the Socialist Federal Republic of Yugoslavia, the task of proving an armed conflict of international proportion has been somewhat difficult for the prosecution.

In the opinion of the Appeals Chamber in the above interlocutory appeal, it found that Article 2 of the ICTY has applicability only to those offenses committed during the course of an *international* armed conflict. Nonetheless, from a reading of the various opinions by the judges, it can be assumed that they were sensitive to the counter-argument that the "grave breaches" provisos of the 1949 Geneva Conventions did, in fact, apply to the atrocities found to have been committed in the former Yugoslavia. The Appeals Chamber found, in essence, that the conflict in Bosnia-Herzegovina was "mixed" in nature—the result being that the prosecution must, in each particular case, establish the character of the armed conflict in question, be it "internal" or "international" before alleging a "grave breaches" allegation under Article 2 of the ICTY Statute.

The Trial Chamber eventually concluded (by a 2–1 majority) that Dusko Tadic was *not* guilty of those counts in the indictment which charged him with "grave breaches" because the prosecution had not satisfactorily shown that the victims involved in Tadic's crimes in Bosnia-Herzegovina were "protected persons" within the meaning of the 1949 Geneva Convention Relative to the Protection of Civilian Persons in Time of War. The Trial Chamber apparently concluded that since Tadic's alleged victims were of the *same nationality* as their captors and since these captors were not being directed by a *foreign government*, the conflict in question was thus not of an "international character," hence the grave breaches provisions of the 1949 Geneva Conventions did not apply. The entire grave breaches issue in the *Tadic* case and others have come in for some serious criticism. By 1997, the ICTY prosecution began amending some indictments by omitting any charges of grave breaches of the 1949 Conventions. What follows are excerpts from the final judgment in *Prosecutor v. Tadic*].

(c) *Prosecutor v. Dusko Tadic*

International Criminal Court for the Former Yugoslavia
May 7, 1997
112 *International Law Reports* 2

McDONALD, P.J., STEPHEN AND VOHRAH, JJ.

* * *

(1) With regard to paragraph 6 of the indictment (counts 5 to 11, it was proved beyond reasonable doubt that the accused took part in beatings of great severity and other grievous acts of violence inflicted upon the five named prisoners and a sixth prisoner, all of whom were Muslims and none of whom were taking an active part in the hostilities, that these acts were committed in the course of, and in close connection with, an armed conflict and that the perpetrators intended to inflict suffering upon the prisoners concerned. The accused was, in some instances, the perpetrator of these acts. On other occasions he was present when the acts occurred and intentionally assisted directly and substantially in the common purpose of inflicting physical suffering. These beatings were inflicted as part of a widespread or systematic attack on a civilian population and with discriminatory intent. The prosecution had, however, failed to prove beyond reasonable doubt that any of the victims died from their injuries...

(2) With regard to paragraph 7 of the indictment (counts 12 to 14), while there was no direct evidence that the accused physically participated in the beating of the Muslim prisoner or was present when the prisoner was beaten, it had been proved beyond reasonable doubts that he intentionally assisted directly and substantially in the common

purpose of a group to inflict great suffering upon the prisoner, who was a Muslim taking no part in the hostilities. The beating constituted cruel treatment and was inflicted
with the intention of causing suffering. The beating occurred in the context of, and in
close connection with, an armed conflict. It was inflicted as part of a widespread or systematic attack on a civilian population and with discriminatory intent...

* * *

(6) With regard to paragraph 11 of the indictment (counts 24 to 28), although the
accused had been present and had participated in calling out from the column of prisoners, it had not been proved beyond reasonable doubt that the four persons named in
this paragraph of the indictment had been killed...

(7) With regard to paragraph 12 of the indictment (counts 29–34), it had been proved
beyond reasonable doubt that the accused had participated in the removal and beating of
certain men. The treatment of the victims amounted to cruel treatment which the accused had intentionally inflicted in the context of, and in close connection with, an armed
conflict. Other allegations contained in these counts had not, however, been proven...

(8) With regard to paragraph 4 of the indictment (count 1), which charged persecution, it had been proved beyond reasonable doubt that the accused had committed a
number of the acts specified in this paragraph of the indictment, including participating in the attack on Kozarac and the surrounding area, the collection and forced transfer of civilians to detention camps, the beating and ill-treatment of some of those civilians and the murder of two Muslim policemen. It had also been proved that he
participated in acts of violence against prisoners at the Omarska and Keraterm camps
and had been present at the Trnopolje camp when beatings occurred. He had participated in these acts as part of a widespread or systematic attack upon a civilian population singled out on racial grounds with the intention of creating a "greater Serbia."

* * *

(5) The provisions of Article 7(1) of the Statute on individual criminal responsibility
reflected customary international law. The parameters of individual criminal responsibility were that the accused had to have the necessary intent and his act must have contributed directly and substantially to the commission of the crime. The requirement of
intent meant that knowledge, actual or inferred, was essential but it was not necessary
to prove that there was a pre-arranged plan, to which the accused was a part, to engage
in any specific conduct. The requirement of a direct and substantial contribution was
wide enough to extend to a person who aided and abetted the commission of an offence
by acts or words which lent encouragement or support. Presence at the commission of a
crime was insufficient if it was an ignorant or unwilling presence but if that presence
could be shown to be knowing and to have had a direct and substantial effect then it
was a sufficient basis on which to found a finding of participation...

(6) Persecution, as charged in count 1, was a crime against humanity. It required
some form of discrimination which was intended to be, and actually resulted in, an infringement of an individual's fundamental rights. It was not necessary to have a specific
inhumane act; the discrimination itself made the act inhumane. The acts which were
capable of constituting persecution included not only the specific acts mentioned elsewhere in Article 5 of the Statute but also other acts of varying severity, including systematic plunder of property and other economic measures...

[The Court held Tadic guilty of crimes against humanity in certain specific cases,
guilty of violations of the laws and customs of war in specific instances, and acquitted

him on twenty counts, including all nine charges of murder. In addition, the Court ruled that the prosecution had failed to prove that Tadic's victims came under the "protected persons" rubric of the 1949 Geneva Conventions. Collectively, on the findings of guilt, the accused was sentenced to a twenty-year prison term. In looking back at the *Tadic* judgment, Alvarez[5] voiced a well-known truism that affects international criminal justice when he wrote that

> ...From Rwanda to the Balkans, from Argentina to El Salvador and South Africa, we have considerable evidence that the peoples and governments of the world, when faced with mass atrocities, equivocate not only about whether to impose criminal liability but also about whom to indict. Punishment for mass atrocities is and always has been undoubtedly selective at both the international and national levels. National courts have varied tremendously with respect to their reactions to violations of humanitarian law by their own nationals. Selective national prosecutions for such crimes appear to be the norm.... The lack of concensus on such issues should hardly surprise. We ought to expect debates about whether the failures of political will that render difficult the arrests of suspects or make impossible the imposition of sanctions on states who fail to cooperate with the tribunals make those trials that do proceed illegitimate.... The lack of concensus on whom to prosecute reflects the lack of agreement on those other issues as well.... Moreover, the U.N. has seen fit to establish tribunals only for the former Yugoslavia and Rwanda but not for Haiti, Iraq, Cambodia, or a number of other places.[6]

Thus, selective tribunals enforcing selective prosecutions against selected defendants will continue to be a common practice in international criminal justice administration unless the ICC's presence changes that. The geopolitical realities of the twenty-first century that mirror the "state" and "sovereignty" constructs of the twentieth and earlier centuries will militate against anything but a partial closure to those victimized by international criminal depradations. The following excerpts are from the Trial Chamber opinion in the *Erdemovic* case].

---

4. *Prosecutor v. Erdemovic*

International Criminal Tribunal for the Former Yugoslavia
November 29, 1996
108 *International Law Reports* 180

JORDA, P.J., BENITO AND RIAD, JJ.

* * *

1. On 28 March 1996, Judge Fouad Riad, pursuant to the provisions of Rule 90 *bis* of the Rules of Procedure and Evidence (hereinafter "the Rules") ordered the transfer and provisional detention in the Detention Unit of the International Tribunal for the Former Yugoslavia...of Drazen Erdomovic then being held by the authorities of the Federal Republic of Yugoslavia (Serbia and Montenegro) in connection with a criminal investigation into the war crimes committed against the civilian population in July 1995 in Srebrenica and its surroundings. Judge Riad thus granted an application from

---

5. Jose E. Alvarez, *Rush to Closure: Lessons of the Tadic Judgment*, 96 *Mich. L. Rev.* 2031 (1998).
6. *Id.* at 2089–2090.

the Prosecutor of the International Tribunal who considered that Drazen Erdemovic could provide additional evidence in the cases against Radovan Karadzic and Ratko Mladic.

2. On 29 May 1996, the Prosecutor of the International Tribunal, pursuant to Article 18 of the Statute, submitted to the reviewing Judge an indictment against Drazen Erdemovic. The latter is accused of having committed a crime against humanity (Article 5 of the Statute) or a violation of the laws and customs of war (Article 3 of the Statute) for the following: Drazen Erdemovic, born of 25 November 1971, in the municipality of Tuzla in Bosnia and Herzegovina was a member of the 10th Sabotage Detachment of the Bosnian Serb army. On 16 July 1995, he was sent with other members of his unit to the Branjevo collective farm near Pilica, north-west of Zvornik. Once there, they were informed that later that day Muslim men from 17 to 60 years of age would be brought to the farm in buses. These men were unarmed civilians who had surrendered to the members of the Bosnian Serb army or police after the fall of the United Nations "safe area" at Srebrenica. Members of the military police took the civilians off the buses in groups of ten and escorted them to a field next to the farm buildings, where they were lined up with their backs to a firing squad. The men were then killed by Drazen Erdemovic, and other members of his unit with the help of soldiers from another brigade.

On 29 May 1996, Trial Chamber II requested the Government of the Federal Republic of Yugoslavia (Serbia and Montenegro) to order its national courts to defer all investigations and criminal proceedings against Drazen Erdemovic to the International Tribunal.

3. On the same date, pursuant to Article 19 of the Statute and Rule 47 of the Rules, Judge Rustam S. Sidhwa confirmed the indictment.

On 31 May 1996, Drazen Erdemovic appeared for the first time before the Trial Chamber. At the hearing, he pleaded guilty to Count No. 1, "crime against humanity," of the Indictment. Having verified that the accused had entered his plea fully cognizant of what he was doing, and having heard his additional statements, the Trial Chamber decided to accept as final Drazen Erdemovic's guilty plea. Accordingly, with the consent of the Parties, the Trial Chamber also decided that, for the remainder of the proceedings, it would dismiss the second count, "violation of the laws and customs of war," which had been charged as an alternative to the first. Further, the Trial Chamber ordered a psychological and psychiatric examination of the accused. It entrusted this task to a commission of three experts,...

* * *

8. In its report submitted on 17 October 1996, the commission of experts declared Drazen Erdemovic competent to stand trial...

* * *

...Drazen Erdemovic pleaded guilty, pursuant to the provisions of Article 20(3) of the Statute and Rule 62 of the Rules, to the count of a crime against humanity and stated his consent to the version of the events as set forth briefly by the Prosecutor. He added the following, however:

Your Honour, I had to do this. If I had refused, I would have been killed together with the victims. When I refused, they told me: "If you're sorry for them, stand up, line up with them and we will kill you too." I am not sorry for myself but for my family, my wife and son who then had nine months, and I could not refuse because then they would have killed me.

* * *

14. ...In order to explain his conduct, the accused argued both an obligation to obey the orders of his military superior and physical and moral duress stemming from his fear for his own life and that of his wife and child. In and of themselves, these factors may mitigate the penalty. Depending on the probative value and force which may be given to them, they may also be regarded as a defence for the criminal conduct which might go so far as to eliminate the *mens rea* of the offence and therefore the offence itself. In consequence, the plea would be invalidated. The Trial Chamber considers that it must examine the possible defence for the elements invoked.

15. The defence of obedience to superior orders has been addressed expressly in Article 7(4) of the Statute. This defence does not relieve the accused of criminal responsibility. The Secretary-General's report which proposed the Statute of the International Tribunal and which was approved by Security Council Resolution 827 of 25 May 1993...clearly stated in respect of this provision that, at most, obedience to superior orders may justify a reduced penalty "should the International Tribunal determine that justice so requires" (S/25704, para. 57).

16. In respect of the physical and moral duress accompanied by the order from a military superior (sometimes referred to as "extreme necessity"), which has been argued in this case, the Statute provides no guidance. At most, the Secretary-General refers to duress in paragraph 57 of his report and seems moreover to regard it as a mitigating circumstances.

17. A review of the United Nations War Crimes Commission of the post-World War II international military case-law, as reproduced in the 1996 report of the International Law Commission...shows that post-World War II military tribunals of nine nations considered the issue of duress as constituting a complete defence. After an analysis of some 2,000 decisions by these military tribunals, the United Nations Commission cited three features which were always present and which it laid down as essential conditions for duress to be accepted as a defence for a violation of international humanitarian law:

(i)   the act charged was done to avoid an immediate danger both serious and irreparable;

(ii)   there was no adequate means of escape;

(iii) the remedy was not disproportionate to the evil...

These criteria have already been identified in the *Krupp* case.[7]

18. The Trial Chamber notes that these military tribunals have on occasion characterized the said criteria in different ways. The variations in the criteria have defined them more precisely. In addition, some of the decisions set forth other criteria and therefore further narrow the scope of that defence.

The absence of moral choice was recognized on several occasions as one of the essential components for considering duress as a complete defence. A soldier may be considered as being deprived of his moral choice in the face of imminent physical danger. This physical threat, understood in the case-law as a danger of death or serious bodily harm, must in some cases also meet the following conditions: it must be "clear and present" or else be "imminent, real, and inevitable."

---

7. *Trial of Alfried Felix Alwyn Krupp von Bohlen und Halbach and eleven others*, US Military Tribunal, Nuremberg, 17 November 1947–30 June 1948, Case No. 58. 10 LRTWC 147 (1949).

These tribunals also took into account the issue of voluntary participation in an enterprise that leaves no doubt as to its end results in order to determine the individual responsibility of the accused members of the armed forces or paramilitary groups. The rank held by the soldier giving the order and by the one receiving it has also been taken into account in assessing the duress a soldier may be subject to when forced to execute a manifestly illegal order.

Although the accused did not challenge the manifestly illegal order he was allegedly given, the Trial Chamber would point out that according to the case-law referred to, in such an instance, the duty was to disobey rather than obey. This duty to disobey could only recede in the face of the most extreme duress.

19. Accordingly, while the complete defense based on moral duress and/or a state of necessity stemming from superior orders is not ruled out absolutely, its conditions of application are particularly strict. They must be sought not only in the very existence of a superior order—which must first be proven—but also and especially in the circumstances characterizing how the order was given and how it was received. In this case-by-case approach—the one adopted by these post-war tribunals—when it assesses the objective and subjective elements characterizing duress or the state of necessity, it is incumbent on the Trial Chamber to examine whether the accused in his situation did not have the duty to disobey, whether he had the moral choice to do so or to try to do so. Using this rigorous and restrictive approach, the Trial Chamber relies not only on general principles of law as expressed in numerous national laws and case-law, but would also like to make clear through its unfettered discretion that the scope of its jurisdiction requires it to judge the most serious violations of international humanitarian law.

With regard to a crime against humanity, the Trial Chamber considers that the life of the accused and that of the victim are not fully equivalent. As opposed to ordinary law, the violation here is no longer directed at the physical welfare of the victim alone but of humanity as a whole.

20. On the basis of the case-by-case approach and in light of all the elements before it, the Trial Chamber is of the view that proof of the specific circumstances which would fully exonerate the accused of his responsibility has not been provided. Thus, the defense of duress accompanying the superior order will, as the Secretary-General seems to suggest in his report, be taken into account at the same time as other factors in the consideration of mitigating circumstances.

In conclusion, the Trial Chamber, for all the reasons of fact and law surrounding Drazen Erdemovic's guilty plea, considers it valid.

* * *

83. The Trial Chamber reaffirms that there is no valid reason for discussing the charge of crime against humanity since Drazen Erdemovic pleaded guilty to this count. Furthermore, all the facts relating to the fall of Srebrenica in which the accused played a part were characterized as a crime against humanity...

* * *

...[T]he Trial Chamber considers that in view of the intrinsic gravity of his crime and the individual circumstances which surrounded its commission, it is appropriate to grant Drazen Erdemovic the benefit of mitigating circumstances based on the following elements:

   — his age at the time of the events and his subordinate level in the military hierarchy;

— the remorse he has shown, his desire to surrender to the International Tribunal, his guilty plea and his cooperation with the Office of the Prosecutor;

— the fact that he now does not constitute a danger and the corrigible character of his personality;

and the fact that the sentence pronounced will be served in a prison far from his own county.

In his closing statement, the Prosecutor suggest that the Trial Chamber hand down a prison sentence not exceeding 10 years.

The Defence argued principally for a remission of the penalty and in the alternative a mitigation of the sentence down to one year.

The Trial Chamber considers that in light of all the legal and factual elements which it has reviewed and accepted, it is appropriate to sentence Drazen Erdemovic as punishment for the crime against humanity for which he admitted guilt to a prison sentence of 10 years with credit to be given for previous periods spent in custody, pursuant to Sub-rule 101(E) of the Rules.

HAVING HEARD the Closing Statements of the Prosecution and of the Defense,

IN PUNISHMENT OF SAID CRIME,

SENTENCES Drazen Erdemovic

born on 25 November 1971 at Tuzla,

to ten years' imprisonment;...

* * *

RULES that this judgment shall be enforceable immediately.

---

5. The Concept of Ethnic Cleansing

[The term "ethnic cleansing' emerged on the international criminal justice scene in the 1990s to describe a practice that had periodically erupted in the twentieth century as far back as 1915. In that year, during the midst of World War I, Great Britain, France and Czarist Russia denounced the wholesale massacres of the Christian Armenian minority by the Ottoman Turks. These nations characterized those killings and deportations as "crimes against civilization and humanity" and vowed to hold the Turkish government responsible. In the Peace Treaty of Sevres in 1920, Article 230 of that instrument prescribed criminal conduct regarding the "massacres," but no mention was made of the words "civilization" or "humanity." Turkey never ratified the Treaty of Sevres and the subsequent Treaty of Lausanne, signed in 1923, failed to mention the Armenian genocide at all. The Allied and Associated Powers, fresh from the experience of the Leipzig Trials debacle in Germany, dropped any further thought of trying the offending Turks. Next, of course, came the genocides and butchery of civilian populations in the Soviet Union in the 1930s and in Europe and European Russia and the Far East during the Second World War, followed by the notorious Cambodian and Iraqi massacres in the last quarter of the century. Out of the internecine strife in the Balkans, particularly, emerged a new phrase—"ethnic cleansing"—to describe an old and tragically familiar practice. The following two excerpts give varied perspectives on this too often repeated phenomenon].

(a) L.C. Green, *Notes and Comments:*
"The Rule of Law and Human Rights in the Balkans"

37 *The Canadian Yearbook of International Law* 223; 236–237 1999
Reproduced with permission from L.C. Green, "The Rule of Law and
Human Rights in the Balkans," 37 *The Canadian Yearbook of
International Law* 223 © UBC Press (2000)

Ethnic cleansing as practiced in the Balkans, particularly since the break-up of the former Yugoslavia, involves mass expulsion under threat, often accompanied by the massacre of large numbers of minority groups.... In Bosnia, Croatia, and Serbia, there have been mass expulsions of minority groups, accompanied in many cases by the destruction of the homes and property of the persons affected. However, in many of these cases, the actual physical destruction of the individuals has not been an inherent part of the operation, although there have been trials before the special tribunal at the Hague of some individuals in which genocide has been alleged on account of their having ordered or participated in the actual killings of members of minority groups. [The *Erdemovic* trial, for example]. While there have been no reports of the sterilization of minority persons, there have been numerous instances of the rape of Muslim women by, in particular, non-Muslim Serbs. Since a raped woman, whether she became pregnant or not, is regarded as "damaged goods" and is unlikely to find a Muslim husband, this activity, together with those instances in which the rape has been accompanied by statements that "you will give birth to a non-Muslim child," are clearly directed at the prevention of further births within the group attacked.

In so far as ethnic cleansing in the Kosovo province of Serbia is concerned, expulsions of the Albanian population took place at extremely short notice with the victims being forced to make their own way, often on foot and without food or water, over long distances to the Albanian, Montenegran and Macedonian border. No shelter was available during their flight over inhospitable terrain, and the journey often took place in highly inclement weather. Regardless whether the intention was to destroy such fugitives, it must have been clear to those instituting or enforcing the policy that what would ensue would, in the words of the Genocide Convention, "cause serious bodily or mental harm... [and] inflict on the group conditions of life calculated to bring about its physical destruction in whole or in part." It would seem, therefore, that "ethnic cleansing" is nothing but a less emotional synonym for "genocide."

* * *

Genocide is not normally a crime that can be committed by "private enterprise." It is invariably committed by order of, or with the collusion or tolerance of, the authority to which the offender owes allegiance. It is perhaps somewhat unrealistic, therefore, to expect that any trials other than those dealing with "rebels" or captured government personnel would ever take place and that these trials would more likely be based on vengeance rather than on justice. On the other hand, it is becoming clear that the international community, especially those non-governmental organizations committed to the propagation of human rights, is increasingly concerned with the numerous reports of horrors committed during non-international conflicts throughout the world, although governments have tended to be somewhat eclectic in their choice of which conflicts necessitate international action beyond verbal condemnation. In addition, one must bear in mind that the right of a government to treat its nationals as it pleases has long been regarded as a matter of domestic jurisdiction—a view that is confirmed by the Charter of the United Nations as well as by Article 3 of Additional Protocol II [of the Geneva Conventions of June 8, 1997].

(b) John Quigley, "State Responsibility for Ethnic Cleansing"

32 *University of California-Davis Law Review* 341, 343–346 (1999)
Reproduced with permission from John Quigley, "State Responsibility for Ethnic Cleansing," 32 *U.C. Davis L. Rev.* 341 (1999)

Introduction

Criminal trials at The Hague for atrocities committed in the former Yugoslavia have focused public attention on legal liability for what has come to be called "ethnic cleansing." These trials involve the responsibility of individuals. The liability of states for ethnic cleansing has received less public attention. Through their command of resources and personnel, states have the potential to organize ethnic cleansing on a large scale. If the international legal community is to be effective in combating ethnic cleansing, it must focus on the responsibility of states.

States may be involved in ethnic cleansing in a variety of ways. They may perpetrate it directly. They may give arms or advice to a state or to a nonstate party that is perpetrating ethnic cleansing. States may be aware of ethnic cleansing being perpetrated without their involvement while possibly being in a position to stop it....

I. Acts That Constitute Ethnic Cleansing

The term "ethnic cleansing" is of recent origin. Terminology referring to rendering a territory "clean" of a population group was, of course, used in Nazi Germany, with the term *Judenrein*, meaning "clean of Jews." The term "ethnic cleansing," however, entered the vocabulary of diplomacy only in the 1990s, in connection with events in the former Yugoslavia. One finds the term in resolutions of international organizations. It is an umbrella term that covers a variety of delictual acts aimed at driving members of an ethnic group from their home area in order to reduce the number of members of that group. The term "ethnic cleansing," as used by Nazi Germany, was intended to make the activity seem benign (i.e., rendering clean something that, presumably, was previously dirty). In its more recent usage it has had a distinctly pejorative connotation.

Much of the learning on ethnic cleansing comes from the United Nations ("U. N.") Security Council. The U. N. Security Council called for the prosecution of individuals who participated in acts of ethnic cleansing during the early 1990s in the former Yugoslavia for breaches of humanitarian law. To that end, the Security Council established a commission of experts to analyze the facts and prepare for prosecutorial proceedings. The Security Council asked the Commission to investigate the practice of ethnic cleansing.

* * *

The Commission in its interim report defined ethnic cleansing as "rendering an area ethnically homogeneous by using force or intimidation to remove persons of given groups from the area." In its final report, the Commission called it "a purposeful policy designed by one ethnic or religious group to remove by violent and terror-inspiring means the civilian populations of another ethnic or religious group from certain geographic areas."[8]

As developed in U. N. practice, the term "ethnic cleansing" does not seem to be a category of legal wrong. Rather, it seems to be a term which encompasses a variety of acts which either a state or an individual may commit, and that violate other legal prohibitions. In the case of a state, these violations entail state responsibility.

Any mistreatment of an ethnic group may lead members of the group to emigrate. The U. N. Commission on Human Rights has criticized policies of intolerance towards ethnic groups as a cause of "forced migratory movements." In 1991, upwards of one million Iraqis fled Iraq into neighboring Turkey and Iran as Iraqi government forces put down an uprising [at the conclusion of the first Gulf War]. The Security Council condemned Iraq for acts of suppression that precipitated the flight, and troops operating under the U. N. facilitated the emigrants' return to Iraq.

It would seem that only when mistreatment of an ethnic group evidences an effort to induce emigration is the term ethnic cleansing applied. The killings of Tutsis in Rwanda in 1994, for example, would seem to show an effort to induce emigration. The killings were inspired by members of the predominantly Hutu government against Tutsis, and against Hutus who sympathized with Tutsis. The killings took place in the context of a civil war in which a Tutsi-led rebel movement challenged the Hutu-led government. While the Hutu government never acknowledged inducing flight, the magnitude of the killings, approximately one half million victims, suggested an effort to frighten Tutsis into departing.

One other circumstance would seem to constitute ethnic cleansing. If a state undertakes to kill a given population, not so much with the intent of inducing flight, but with the intent of killing as many people as possible, perhaps all of them, this too would qualify.

Many of the means by which ethnic cleansing is carried out are cognizable as international wrongs that either an individual or a state can commit. In a resolution on Bosnia, the U. N. Commission on Human Rights stated that rape and other abuses of women were "a deliberate weapon of war in fulfilling the policy of ethnic cleansing carried out by Serbian forces in the Republic of Bosnia and Herzegovina." The Security Council's Commission of Experts said that ethnic cleansing was carried out "by means of murder, torture, arbitrary arrest and detention, extra-judicial executions, rape and sexual assault, confinement of civilian population in ghetto areas, forcible removal, displacement and deportation of civilian population, deliberate military attacks or threats of attacks on civilians and civilian areas, and wanton destruction of property."

The [U. N.] Committee on the Elimination of Racial Discrimination condemned ethnic cleansing, which it said was being carried out in Bosnia, as including "forced population transfers, torture, rape, summary executions, the blockading of international humanitarian aid and the commission of atrocities for the purpose of instilling terror among the civilian population." The Committee said these violations were being committed "on the basis of 'ethnic identity' for the purpose of attempting to create ethnically pure States."

---

8. *Final Report of the Commission of Experts Established Pursuant to Security Council Resolution* 780 (1992), U. N. SCOR, Annex 1, at 33, U. N. Doc E/1995/23, E/CN.4/1995/176 (1995).

6. *Prosecutor v. Blaskic*[*]

International Criminal Tribunal for the Former Yugoslavia
March 3, 2000
122 *International Law Reports* 2

JORDA, P. J., RODRIGUES AND SHAHABUDDEEN, JJ.

* * *

17. Following Judge McDonald's confirmation of the initial indictment on 10 November 1995, the warrants of arrest ordering the transfer of the accused were sent to the authorities of the Federation of Bosnia-Herzegovina of the Republic of Croatia. Copies of the indictments and warrants of arrest were subsequently sent to IFOR upon an Order of Judge Jorda. Lastly, Judge Vohrah issued a warrant of arrest ordering the transfer of Tihomir Blaskic to the Kingdom of The Netherlands on 28 March 1996.

18. Tihomir Blaskic voluntarily gave himself up to the International Tribunal on 1 April 1996 and, pursuant to Rule 62 of the Rules, his initial appearance hearing was held on 3 April 1996 before Trial Chamber I composed of Judge Jorda, presiding, Judge Deschenes and Judge Riad. The accused pleaded "not guilty" to all counts brought against him in the initial indictment. On 4 December 1996, Tihomir Blaskic pleaded "not guilty" to the new counts confirmed against him following the first amendment of the indictment on 22 November 1996. The second amendment of the indictment on 25 April 1997 did not bring any new counts against the accused who, for that reason, did not have to enter a new plea.

19. The proceedings against Tihomir Blaskic before the Tribunal were complex and at each stage gave rise to many questions, often without precedent. Accordingly, during the fourteen-month pre-trial phase, the Tribunal rendered eighty-two interlocutory decisions. The trial proper commenced on 24 June 1997 and lasted a little over two years, closing on 30 July 1999. During this stage of the proceedings, seventy-eight interlocutory Decisions were rendered, 158 witnesses heard and more than one thousand three hundred exhibits filed....

* * *

75. The legal criteria which allow the international nature of an armed conflict to be demonstrated were set out in great detail by the Appeals Chamber in its Judgment of 15 July 1999 in the *Tadic* case. The Trial Chamber, which agrees with the conclusions in that Judgment, does not intend to reproduce the lengthy analysis set forth therein. It prefers to limit itself to drawing on those essential elements necessary for ruling on the present case.

76. An armed conflict which erupts in the territory of a single State and which is thus at first sight internal may be deemed international where the troops of another State intervene in the conflict or even where some participants in the internal armed conflict act on behalf of this other State. The intervention of a foreign State may be proved factually. Analysing this second hypothesis is more complex. In this instance, the legal criteria allowing armed forces to be linked to a foreign power must be determined. This link confers an international nature upon an armed conflict which initially appears internal.

---

[*] [General Blaskic's conviction was overturned on July 29, 2004, by the Appeals Chamber of the ICTY in a 289-page ruling and the Bosnian-Croat general was released from custody to return to Zagreb, Croatia, on August 2, 2004].

* * *

175. The Prosecution contended that the provisions of the Regulations annexed to the Hague Convention IV of 1907 constitute international customary rules which were restated in Article 6(b) of the Nuremberg Statute. Violations of these provisions incur the individual criminal responsibility of the person violating the rule. Conversely, the Defence did not acknowledge that violations of the laws and customs of war within the meaning of Common Article 3 of the Geneva Conventions had ever been upheld to impose criminal sanctions upon individuals.

176. The Trial Chamber recalls that violations of Article 3 of the Statute which include violations of the Regulations of The Hague and those of Common Article 3 are by definition serious violations of international humanitarian law within the meaning of the Statute. They are thus likely to incur individual criminal responsibility in accordance with Article 7 of the Statute. The Trial Chamber observes moreover that the provisions of the criminal code of the SFRY, adopted by Bosnia-Herzegovina in April 1992, provide that war crimes committed during internal or international conflicts incur individual criminal responsibility. The Trial Chamber is of the opinion that, as was concluded in the *Tadic* Appeal Decision, customary international law imposes criminal responsibility for serious violations of Common Article 3.

* * *

IV. FINAL CONCLUSIONS

744. The Trial Chamber concludes that the acts ascribed to Tihomir Blaskic occurred as part of an international armed conflict because the Republic of Croatia exercised total control over the Croatian Community of Herceg-Bosna and the HVO [Bosnian-Croat armed forces] and exercised general control over the Croatian political and military authorities in central Bosnia.

745. The accused was appointed by the Croatian military authorities. Following his arrival in Kiseljak in April 1992, he was designated chief of the Central Bosnia Operative Zone on 27 June 1992 and remained there until the end of the period covered by the indictment. From the outset, he shared the policy of the local Croatian authorities. For example, he outlawed the Muslim Territorial Defence forces in the municipality of Kiseljak.

746. From May 1992 to January 1993, tensions between Croats and Muslims continued to rise. At the same time, General Blaskic reinforced the structure of the HVO armed forces with the agreement of the Croatian political authorities.

747. In January 1993, the Croatian political authorities sent an ultimatum to the Muslims, *inter alia*, so as to force them to surrender their weapons. They sought to gain control of all the territories considered historically Croatian, in particular the Lasva Valley. Serious incidents then broke out in Busovaca and Muslim houses were destroyed. After being detained, many Muslim civilians were forced to leave the territory of the municipality.

748. Despite the efforts of international organizations...the atmosphere between the communities remained extremely tense.

749. On 15 April 1993, the Croatian military and political authorities, including the accused, issued a fresh ultimatum. General Blaskic met with the HVO, military police and Vitezovi commanders and gave them orders which the Trial Chamber considers to be genuine attack orders. On 16 April 1993, the Croatian forces, commanded by General Blaskic, attacked in the municipalities of Vitez and Busovaca.

750. The Croatian forces, both the HVO and independent units plundered and burned to the ground the houses and stables, killed the civilians regardless of age or gender, slaughtered the livestock and destroyed or damaged the mosques. Furthermore, they arrested some civilians and transferred them to detention centres where the living conditions were appalling and forced them to dig trenches, sometimes also using them as hostages or human shields. The accused himself stated that twenty or so villages were attacked according to a pattern which never changed. The village firstly was "sealed off." Artillery fire opened the attack and assault search forces organized into groups of five to ten soldiers then "cleansed" the village. The same scenario was repeated in the municipality of Kiseljak several days later. The Croatian forces acted in perfect co-ordination. The scale and uniformity of the crimes committed against the Muslim population over such a short period of time has enabled the conclusion that the operation was, beyond all reasonable doubt, planned and that its objective was to make the Muslim population take flight.

751. The attacks were thus widespread, systematic and violent and formed a part of a policy to persecute the Muslim populations.

752. To achieve the political objectives to which he subscribed, General Blaskic used all the military forces on which he could rely, whatever the legal nexus subordinating them to him.

753. He issued the orders sometimes employing national discourse and with no concern for their possible consequences. In addition, despite knowing that some of the forces had committed crimes, he redeployed them for other attacks.

754. At no time did he even take the most basic measure which any commander must at least take when he knows that crimes are about to be or have actually been committed. The end result of such an attitude was not only the scale of the crimes, which the Trial Chamber has explained, but also the realization of the Croatian nationalists' goals—the forced departure of the majority of Muslim population in the Lasva Valley after the death and wounding of its members, the destruction of its dwellings, the plunder of property and the cruel and inhuman treatment meted out to many.

* * *

759. Keeping in mind the...provisions [of the ICTY Statute], the Trial Chamber has recourse to the general practice regarding prison sentences in the courts of the former Yugoslavia. Reference to the practice is only indicative and not binding. Whenever possible, the Tribunal examines the texts and relevant judicial practice of the former Yugoslavia. However, it could not be legally bound by them in determining the sentences and sanctions it imposes for crimes falling under its jurisdiction.

760. The practice for determining prison sentences in the courts of the former Yugoslavia is based on the provisions of Chapter 16 and Article 41(1) of the SFRY criminal code. Nonetheless, the Trial Chamber is not limited by the practice of the courts of the former Yugoslavia and it may draw upon other legal sources in order to determine the appropriate sentence.

* * *

765. The factors taken into account in the various Judgments of the two International Tribunals to assess the sentence must be interpreted in the light of the type of offence committed and the personal circumstances of the accused. This explains why it is appropriate to identify the specific material circumstances directly related to the offence in order to evaluate the gravity thereof and also the specific personal circumstances in

order to adapt the sentence imposed to the accused's character and potential for rehabilitation. Notwithstanding this, in determining the sentence, the weight attributed to each type of circumstance depends on the objective sought by international justice. Keeping in mind the mission of the Tribunal, it is appropriate to attribute a lesser significance to the specific personal circumstances. Although they help explain why the accused committed the crimes they do not in any event mitigate the seriousness [of such crimes].

* * *

788. In the case-law of the two Tribunals, there can be no doubt that command position may justify a harsher sentence, which must be that much harsher because the accused held a high position within the civilian or military command authority alone. The Judgments of the ICTR on the issue are of particular importance in view of the high level of command authority held by some of the accused. The Trial Chambers observed that the case-law of the Tribunal classifies command position as an aggravating circumstance....

789. Therefore, when a commander fails in his duty to prevent the crime or to punish the perpetrator thereof he should receive a heavier sentence than the subordinate who committed the crime insofar as the failing conveys some tolerance or even approval on the part of the commander towards the commission of crimes by his subordinates and thus contributes to encouraging the commission of new crimes. It would not in fact be consistent to punish a simple perpetrator with a sentence equal or greater to that of the commander. From this viewpoint, the Trial Chamber recalls that in the *Tadic* case the Appeals Chamber found that a prison sentence above twenty years would be excessive given the relatively low rank of Dusko Tadic within the command structure. Command position must therefore systematically increase the sentence or at least lead the Trial Chamber to give less weight to the mitigating circumstances, independently of the issue of the form of participation in the crime. The Trial Chamber observes that as commander of the Central Bosnia Operative Zone at the time of the facts, Tihomir Blaskic held a senior command position. As indicated above, the Trial Chamber is of the opinion that the accused had more than a constructive knowledge of the crimes. It is satisfied beyond all reasonable doubt that General Blaskic ordered attacks which targeted the Muslim civilian population and thereby incurred responsibility for crimes committed during these attacks or at least made himself an accomplice thereto and, as regards those crimes not ensuing from such orders, he failed in his duty to prevent them and did not take the necessary measures to punish their perpetrators after they had been committed.

* * *

795. Neither the Statute nor the Rules lays down expressly a scale of sentences applicable to the crimes falling under the jurisdiction of the Tribunal. Article 24(2) of the Statute draws no distinction between crimes when determining the sentence. The Trial Chamber passes only prison sentences, the maximum being life imprisonment pursuant to Sub-rule 101(A) of the Rules.

796. However, the principle of proportionality, a general principle of criminal law, and Article 24(2) of the Statute call on the Trial Chamber to bear in mind the seriousness of the offence and could consequently constitute the legal basis for the scale of sentences....

* * *

800. A hierarchy of crimes seems to emerge from the case-law of the ICTR. The Trial Chamber seised of the *Kambanda* case established a complete scale of seriousness of the crimes which was taken up in the subsequent Judgments of the ICTR. The following hierarchy of crimes falling under the jurisdiction of the Tribunal may therefore be compiled:

(1) "The crime of crimes": genocide

(2) Crimes of an extreme seriousness: crimes against humanity

(3) Crimes of lesser seriousness: war crimes

The ICTR has thus supposedly established a genuine hierarchy of crimes and this has been used in determining sentences as witnessed by the fact that the crime of genocide was punished by life imprisonment.

801. The ICTY has not yet transported this hierarchy of crimes to the sentencing phase. Until now only the *Tadic* case has the distinctive feature whereby the accused has been found guilty of crimes against humanity *and* war crimes for the same acts and was sentenced separately for each characterization specified. In view of this, it should also be noted that the sentences imposed for crimes against humanity were systematically one year longer than those of war crimes. Even in the *Erdemovic* case, the Appeals Chamber did not clearly use the hierarchy of offences as established in the Judgment, in order to determine the corresponding applicable sentence. Recently in the *Tadic* case, the Appeals Chamber noted that in determining the sentence there is no distinction in law between the seriousness of a crime against humanity and that of a war crime. In setting the sentence, the Chamber indicated:

[t]he authorized penalties are also the same, the level in any particular case being fixed by reference to the circumstances of the case.

802. Ultimately, it appears that the case-law of the Tribunal is not fixed. The Trial Chamber will therefore confine itself to assessing seriousness based on the circumstances of the case.

803. The objective method for assessing the seriousness of a crime is linked to the intrinsic seriousness of the crime's legal characterization. It is not the seriousness of the crime committed in the case in point which is borne in mind but the seriousness of the characterization specified. The subjective method for assessing the seriousness relates to the seriousness *in personam* of the crime.

804. In addition to the seriousness *per se* of the crime, it is also appropriate to take into account its seriousness *in personam*. Although the subjective seriousness is not taken into account in the scale of seriousness of the crimes, it is a factor in the second phase of determining the sentence and thereby ensures that the circumstances of the case may be duly taken into account in setting the sentence to rely on a scale of seriousness, if relevant, and the subjective seriousness of the crimes. It is understood that the weight of the second factor, that is the subjective seriousness, should not, other than in exceptional circumstances, cancel out the first factor, that is the objective seriousness. Furthermore and where necessary, the imposition of a minimum sentence to be served would give some scope for the sentence to be fined-tuned. However, the Trial Chamber notes that this notion is not universally accepted in the various legal systems.

805. The Trial Chamber is of the view that the provisions of Rule 101 of the Rules do not preclude the passing of a single sentence for several crimes. In this regard, the Trial Chamber takes note that although until now the ICTY Trial Chambers have rendered

Judgments imposing multiple sentences, Trial Chamber I of the ICTR imposed single sentences in the *Kambanda* and *Serushago* cases.

806. Moreover, the Trial Chamber recalls that in the cases brought before the military Tribunals at Nuremberg and Tokyo, a single sentence was passed even for multiple crimes.

807. Here, the crimes ascribed to the accused have been characterized in several distinct ways but form a part of a single set of crimes committed in a given geographic region during a relatively extended time-span, the very length of which served to ground their characterization as a crime against humanity, without its being possible to distinguish criminal intent from motive. The Trial Chamber further observes that crimes other than the crime of persecution brought against the accused rest fully on the same facts as those specified under the other crimes for which the accused is being prosecuted. In other words. it is impossible to identify which acts would relate to which of the various counts—other than those supporting the prosecution for and conviction of persecution under count I which, moreover, covers a longer period of time than any of the other counts. In light of this overall consistency, the Trial Chamber finds that there is reason to impose a single sentence for all the crimes of which the accused has been found guilty.

808. In conclusion, the Trial Chamber holds that in this case, the aggravating circumstances unarguably outweigh the mitigating circumstances and that the sentence pronounced accurately reflects the degree of seriousness of the crimes perpetrated and the faults of the accused given his character, the violence done to the victims, the circumstances at the time and the need to provide a punishment commensurate with the serious violations of international humanitarian law which the Tribunal was set up to punish according to the accused's level of responsibility.

FOR THE FOREGOING REASONS, THE TRIAL CHAMBER, in a unanimous ruling of its members,

FINDS Tihomir Blaskic GUILTY:

of having ordered a crime against humanity, namely persecutions against the Muslim civilians of Bosnia, in the municipalities of [here the Tribunal lists three] and, in particular, in the towns and villages of [here the Tribunal lists twenty-two] between 1 May 1992 and 31 January 1994 (count 1) for the following acts:

— attacks on towns and villages;

— murder and serious bodily injury;

— the destruction and plunder of property and, in particular, of institutions dedicated to religion and education;

— inhuman and cruel treatment of civilians and, in particular, their being taken hostage and used as human shields;

— the forcible transfer of civilians

and by these same acts, in particular, as regards an international armed conflict, General Blaskic committed: [here the Tribunal lists eighteen sundry violations of both the ICTY Statute and various provisions of the Geneva Conventions].

* * *

In any event, as a commander, he failed to take the necessary and reasonable measures which would have allowed these crimes to be prevented or the perpetrators thereof to be punished, and

NOT GUILTY of counts 3 and 4 in relation to the shelling of the town of Zenica,

and therefore,

SENTENCES Tihomir Blaskic for forty-five years in prison;

STATES that the length of time he has been detained for the Tribunal, that is the period from 1 April 1996 until the date of this Judgment, shall be deducted from the overall length of the sentence.

Judge Shahabuddeen appends a declaration to this Judgment. [Declaration is omitted].

---

7. The International Criminal Tribunal for Rwanda

[The Rwandan Tribunal's jurisdiction deals with a different set of circumstances than that of the ICTY. In Rwanda there occurred a variant set of international offenses in an entirely different culture with a different political system in place. Thus, the U. N. tribunal for Rwanda perhaps faces an even more daunting task than its sister tribunal for the former Yugoslavia. The genocide and other violations of international criminal law that took place in this African nation between the Hutus and the Tutsis will take some time to sort out. By 1998, for example, there were almost 90,000 detainees held in Rwanda awaiting trial. To expect all of these individuals to receive a full and fair trial on the merits of their cases is, in a word, sheer light-hearted optimism. In addition, there is the real fear in some quarters that even if a number of these detainees are convicted and sentenced, by either domestic courts or by the ICTR sitting in Arusha, Tanzania, instead of at The Hague, many of the victims of this admittedly large-scale civil war will remain unsatisfied and begrudged. While exact figures will probably never be known, there were horrific slaughters in Rwanda that have accounted for anywhere between 500,000 and 1 million deaths. In terms of absolute victims alone, the Rwandan genocide was an ethnic cleansing more irredeemably gruesome than that which befell the Balkans. The savagery and scale of the Rwandan slaughter raises the question whether any tribunal, domestic or international in character, will be able to eventually bestow a healing hand on this blighted nation. Another issue that intrudes into this scenario is the fact that the ICTR's jurisdiction is truncated. The Tribunal, of course, has been granted jurisdiction over genocidal offenses as well as over crimes against humanity and an expanded jurisdiction over war crimes not granted to the ICTY. Nonetheless, the Tribunal can hear and determine only those offenses brought before it that occurred in Rwanda *during the calendar year 1994*. This seemingly odd jurisdictional limitation was the result of an essentially political compromise between the Tutsi government in Rwanda at the time and the U. N. Security Council who was eager to establish another *ad hoc* court to address the international criminal depradations taking place in central Africa.

Legal scholars and defense lawyers, in particular, have complained and will apparently continue to voice complaints about the ultimate fairness of the Arusha proceedings. The U. N. Security Council ventured into uncharted international criminal law waters when it extended the ICTR's jurisdictional reach to include violations of Common Article Three of the 1949 Geneva Conventions as well as Article Four of the 1977 Additional Protocol II of the Geneva Conventions. In a nutshell, there are some international law commentators that reject the idea that the above two instruments constitute established customary international law. This effort by the Security Council in the Rwanda situation represents a watershed of sorts. It is the first time that Common Article Three of the 1949 Geneva Conventions has been employed as a baseline for establishing criminal responsibility of charged individuals. In his *Report* on the ICTR Statute, the U. N. Secretary General observed that the Security Council "Has elected to take a more expansive approach to the choice of the applicable law than the one underlying the statute of the Yugoslav Tribunal."[9] In the interest of taking a common legal approach to both the ICTY and the ICTR, Article 12(2) of the ICTR Statute [*infra*] mandates that those judges who are members of the ICTY Appeals Chamber "Shall also serve as members of the Appeals Chamber of the International Tribunal for Rwanda." Another significant difference between the Yugoslav and the Rwandan tribunals is that, unlike the ICTY Statute, the ICTR Statute, in defining crimes against humanity, omits the necessary linkage between those crimes and an *armed conflict*.

What follows are selected excerpts from an article by Carroll which places the Rwandan turmoil in proper historical perspective. This is followed by selective provisions from the ICTR Statute and excerpts from two ICTR cases: (a) *Prosecutor v. Akayesu* and (b) *Prosecutor v. Rutaganda*].

(a) Christina M. Carroll, "An Assessment of the Role and Effectiveness of the International Criminal Tribunal for Rwanda and the Rwandan National Justice System in Dealing with Mass Atrocities of 1994"

18 *Boston University International Law Journal* 163; 166–170 (2000)
Reproduced with permission from Christina M. Carroll, *An Assessment of the Role and Effectiveness of The International Criminal Tribunal for Rwanda and The Rwandan National Justice System in Dealing with Mass Atrocities of 1994*, 18 B.U. Int'l L. J. 163 (2000)

* * *

Since pre-colonial times, an ethnic, social, political, and economic rivalry has existed between the Hutus and the Tutsis in central Africa. In 1994, the Rwandan population was made up of eighty-four percent Hutu, fourteen percent Tutsi, and two percent other ethnic groups such as the Twa. The Hutus, who made up a majority of the population, are a Bantu people with physical characteristics resembling populations in Uganda and are predominantly agricultural peasants. The Tutsis, in comparison, are extremely tall and thin and traditionally were mainly cattle herders. Despite these differences, they shared a common language. Kinyarawanda, intermarriage was common, and the two groups did not exist as segregated tribes.

Yet ethnicity plays a significant role in Rwanda. For administrative purposes, the Belgian colonial rulers established a system of national identification cards with ethic classifications: Hutu, Tutsi, and Twa. The European colonizers accentuated ethnic differences and solidified group identities through this categorization. Following colonial policy, the Rwandan government of President Juvenal Habarimana of 1973 to 1994 classified people according to their ethnicity. Rwandans are considered to have the ethnicity of their father, despite the heritage of their mother. Additionally, ethnicity is recorded on Rwandan's identity cards and in the census.

---

9. UN DOC. S/1995/134, at 3–4, para. 12.

In the few years before Rwanda gained independence in 1962, Rwanda's Hutu majority rebelled against the minority Tutsi power structure. Hutus may have been resentful of the favoritism Europeans showed the Tutsis during colonial times. From the early 1960s, when the Hutu's gained power, to the 1990s, ethnic violence erupted periodically. Massacres occurred in 1959, 1963, 1966, and 1973. No one, however, was ever prosecuted or otherwise held accountable for those massacres. Many Tutsis were forced to flee the country and Tutsi groups in exile continually tried to invade Rwanda. Claiming that order must be established in Rwanda, Hutu Jevenal Habyarimana seized power in a 1973 coup d'etat and went on to rule as president for the next twenty-one years. Habyarimana, however, created a one-party system and did little to resolve ethnic divisions or establish peace in Rwanda. Rwandan Tutsis living in neighboring countries were denied repatriation to Rwanda.

In October of 1990, the Rwandan Patriotic Front ('REP'), made up of Tutsis in exile, attacked Rwanda. The Habyarimana regime, which had been losing political power due to negative economic conditions in the 1980s, took steps to preserve its power in the face of the latest Tutsi infiltration in the early 1990s. As a result, mass killings started occurring in 1990 through 1993. In 1992, groups affiliated with the Rwandan army of the Habyarimana regime established two militias—the Interahamwe and the Impuza-mugambi. These militias, which were trained and supplied by the Rwandan army, periodically attacked Rwandan Tutsis and eventually played an instrumental role in the 1994 atrocities. Many Tutsis and opponents of Habyarimana were arrested. The government also sponsored the broadest of hate propaganda against the Tutsis and government opponents.

In an attempt to halt the violence, on August 4, 1993, the Rwandan government and the RPF signed the Arusha Accords, a group of agreements and protocols negotiated between 1990 and 1993.... The United Nations Security Council established the United Nations Assistance Mission in Rwanda ('UNAMIR'), a peacekeeping force of 2,500, to oversee the implementation of the peace accords. The accords and the United Nations mission, however, did not result in peace. Many Hutu extremists, who did not believe that any compromises should be made between the Hutus and the Tutsis, disagreed with the peace process and thus were at odds with its implementation. In 1993, the United Nations and non-governmental organizations ('NGOs') began reporting serious human rights violations against the Tutsis in Rwanda, but the international community did little to stop the bloodshed.

The most serious human rights violations, however, did not occur until the spring of 1994. On April 6, 1994, a plane carrying President Habyarimana and the President of Burundi crashed outside Kigali. Habyarimana supporters immediately claimed that the RPF was responsible for their deaths. This event "was undoubtedly the spark" which triggered a campaign of genocide and crimes against humanity by the militias, presidential guard, and military against Tutsis and moderate Hutus. Instead of authorizing additional peacekeeping measures, the United Nations withdrew a majority of the peacekeepers of the UNAMIR force in April 1994. The remaining 400 peacekeepers did little to halt the violence. Between half a million and a million people out of a population of 7.5 million were killed in the four-month period following the plane crash. In addition, thousands of people were raped and tortured and over three million refugees were forced to flee the country.

* * *

Despite the killings of Tutsi by the Hutu government, the largely Tutsi RPF managed to seize control in July 1994. Consequently, over two million Rwandan refugees, mainly

Hutus fearing reprisals, eventually fled to Zaire, now the Democratic Republic of the Congo, and destabilized that country. In an attempt to appease the Hutu majority in 1994, Hutu RPF member, Pasteur Bizimungu, became president of Rwanda while the Tutsi RPF leader Paul Kagame became the vice-president and minister of defense. The Tutsis, however, have been in power since 1994, and Paul Kagame is now president of Rwanda.

In reflecting on the conflict and its causes, it is important to note that although the conflict in Rwanda resulted in large part from ethnic hatred, classification of the conflict as "ethnic" or "tribal" is too simplistic. The conflict is also political in that representatives of each ethnic group periodically used the elimination of the other ethnic group, and political opponents within their own group, as a mechanism for gaining or retaining power. In Rwanda, ethnicity was used as a political weapon to prevent power-sharing and democracy; incitement to ethnic hatred and violence was used as a method of power consolidation. Political leaders and their agents were considered above the law, and did not worry about being held criminally accountable for any human rights violations committed to further their power.

(b) *Statute of the International Criminal Tribunal for Rwanda*
U. N. Doc S/RES/955 (1994)

Article I
Competence of the International Tribunal for Rwanda

The International Tribunal for Rwanda shall have the power to prosecute persons responsible for serious violations of international humanitarian law committed in the territory of Rwanda and Rwandan citizens responsible for such violations committed in the territory of neighboring States, between 1 January 1994 and 31 December 1994, in accordance with the provisions of the present Statute.

Article 2
Genocide

1. The International Tribunal for Rwanda shall have the power to prosecute persons committing genocide as defined in paragraph 2 of this article or of committing any of the other acts enumerated in paragraph 3 of this article.

2. Genocide means any of the following acts committed with intent to destroy, in whole or in part, a national, ethnical, racial or religious group, as such:

(a) Killing members of the group;

(b) Causing serious bodily or mental harm to members of the group;

(c) Deliberately inflicting on the group conditions of life calculated to bring about its physical destruction in whole or in part;

(d) Imposing measures intended to prevent births within the group;

(e) Forcibly transferring children of the group to another group.

3. The following acts shall be punishable:

(a) Genocide;

(b) Conspiracy to commit genocide;

(c) Direct and public incitement to commit genocide;

(d) Attempt to commit genocide;

(e) Complicity in genocide.

Article 3
Crimes against humanity

The International Tribunal for Rwanda shall have the power to prosecute persons responsible for the following crimes when committed as part of a widespread or systematic attack against any civilian population on national, political, ethnic, racial or religious grounds:

(a) Murder;

(b) Extermination;

(c) Enslavement;

(d) Deportation;

(e) Imprisonment;

(f) Torture;

(g) Rape;

(h) Persecutions on political, racial and religious grounds;

(i) Other inhumane acts.

Article 4
Violations of Article 3 Common to the Geneva Conventions and of Additional Protocol II

The International Tribunal for Rwanda shall have the power to prosecute persons committing or ordering to be committed serious violations of Article 3 common to the Geneva Conventions of 12 August 1949 for the Protection of War Victims, and of Additional Protocol II thereto of 8 June 1977. These violations shall include, but shall not be limited to:

(a) Violence to life, health and physical or mental well-being of persons, in particular murder as well as cruel treatment such as torture, mutilation or any form of corporal punishment;

(b) Collective punishment;

(c) Taking of hostages;

(d) Acts of terrorism;

(e) Outrages upon personal dignity, in particular humiliating and degrading treatment, rape, enforced prostitution and any form of indecent assault;

(f) Pillage;

(g) The passing of sentences and the carrying out of executions without previous judgment pronounced by a regularly constituted court, affording all the judicial guarantees which are recognized as indispensable by civilized peoples;

(h) Threats to commit any of the following acts.

Article 5
Personal Jurisdiction

The International Tribunal for Rwanda shall have jurisdiction over natural persons pursuant to the provisions of the present Statute.

Article 6
Individual criminal responsibility

1. A person who planned, instigated, ordered, committed or otherwise aided and abetted in the planning, preparation, or execution of a crime referred to in articles 2 to 4 of the present Statute, shall be individually responsible for the crime.

2. The official position of any accused person, whether as Head of State or Government or as a responsible Government official, shall not relieve such person of criminal responsibility nor mitigate punishment.

3. The fact that any of the acts referred to in articles 2 to 4 of the present Statute was committed by a subordinate does not relieve his or her superior of criminal responsibility if he or she knew or had reason to know that the subordinate was about to commit such acts or had done so and the superior failed to take the necessary and reasonable measure to prevent such acts or punish the perpetrators thereof.

4. The fact that an accused person acted pursuant to an order of a Government or of a superior shall not relieve him or her of criminal responsibility, but may be considered in mitigation of punishment if the International Tribunal for Rwanda determines that justice so requires.

Article 7
Territorial and temporal jurisdiction

The territorial jurisdiction of the International Tribunal for Rwanda shall extend to the territory of Rwanda including land surface and airspace as well as to the territory of neighboring States in respect of serious violations of international humanitarian law committed by Rwandan citizens. The temporal jurisdiction of the International Tribunal for Rwanda shall extend to a period beginning on 1 January 1994 and ending on 31 December 1994.

Article 8
Concurrent jurisdiction

1. The International Tribunal for Rwanda and national courts shall have concurrent jurisdiction to prosecute persons for serious violations of international humanitarian law committed in the territory of Rwanda and Rwandan citizens for such violations committed in the territory of neighboring States, between 1 January 1994 and 31 December 1994.

2. The International Tribunal for Rwanda shall have primacy over the national courts of all States. At any stage of the procedure, the International Tribunal for Rwanda may formally request national courts to defer to its competence in accordance with the present Statute and the Rules of Procedure and Evidence of the International Tribunal for Rwanda.

Article 9
Non bis in idem

1. No person shall be tried before a national court for acts constituting serious violations of international humanitarian law under the present Statute, for which he or she has already been tried by the International Tribunal for Rwanda.

2. A persons who has been tried by a national court for acts constituting serious violations of international humanitarian law may be subsequently tried by the International Tribunal for Rwanda only if:

(a) The act for which he or she was tried was characterized as an ordinary crime; or

(b) The national court proceedings were not impartial or independent, were designed to shield the accused from international criminal responsibility, or the case was not diligently prosecuted.

3. In considering the penalty to be imposed on a person convicted of a crime under the present Statute, the International Tribunal for Rwanda shall take into account the extent to which any penalty imposed by a national court on the same person for the same act has already been served.

Article 10
Organization of the International Tribunal for Rwanda

The International Tribunal for Rwanda shall consist of the following organs:

(a) The Chambers, comprising two Trial Chambers and an Appeals Chamber;

(b) The Prosecutor; and

(c) A Registry.

Article 11
Composition of the Chambers

The Chambers shall be composed of eleven independent judges, no two of whom may be nationals of the same State, who shall serve as follows:

(a) Three judges shall serve in each of the Trial Chambers;

(b) Five judges shall serve in the Appeals Chamber.

Article 17
Investigation and preparation of indictment

1. The Prosecutor shall initiate investigations ex-officio or on the basis of information obtained from any source, particularly from Governments, United Nations organs, intergovernmental and non-governmental organizations. The Prosecutor shall assess the information received or obtained and decide whether there is sufficient basis to proceed.

2. The Prosecutor shall have the power to question suspects, victims and witnesses, to collect evidence and to conduct on-site investigations. In carrying out these tasks, the Prosecutor may, as appropriate, seek the assistance of the State authorities concerned.

3. If questioned, the suspect shall be entitled to be assisted by counsel of his or her own choice, including the right to have legal assistance assigned to the suspect without payment by him or her in any such case if he or she does not have sufficient means to pay for it, as well as to necessary translation into and from a language he or she speaks and understands.

4. Upon a determination that a prima facie case exists, the Prosecutor shall prepare an indictment containing a concise statement of the facts and the crime or crimes with which the accused is charged under the Statute. The indictment shall be transmitted to a judge of the Trial Chamber.

Article 18
Review of the indictment

1. The judge of the Trial Chamber to whom the indictment has been transmitted shall review it. If satisfied that a prima facie case has been established by the Prosecutor, he or she shall confirm the indictment. If not so satisfied, the indictment shall be dismissed.

2. Upon confirmation of an indictment, the judge may, at the request of the prosecutor, issue such orders and warrants for the arrest, detention, surrender or transfer of persons, and any other orders as may be required for the conduct of the trial.

Article 20
Rights of the accused

1. All persons shall be equal before the International Tribunal for Rwanda.

2. In the determination of charges against him or her, the accused shall be entitled to a fair and public hearing, subject to Article 21 of the Statute. [Protection of victims and witnesses].

3. The accused shall be presumed innocent until proved guilty according to the provisions of the present Statute.

4. In the determination of any charge against the accused pursuant to the present Statute, the accused shall be entitled to the following minimum guarantees, in full equality:

(a) To be informed promptly and in detail in a language which he or she understands of the nature and cause of the charge against him or her;

(b) To have adequate time and facilities for the preparation of his or her defence and to communicate with counsel of his or her own choosing;

(c) To be tried without undue delay;

(d) To be tried in his or her presence, and to defend himself or herself in person or through legal assistance of his or her own choosing; to be informed, it he or she does not have legal assistance, of this right; and to have legal assistance assigned to him or her, in any case where the interests of justice so require, and without payment by him or her in any such case if he or she does not have sufficient means to pay for it;

(e) To examine, or have examined, the witnesses against him or her and to obtain the attendance and examination of witnesses on his or her behalf under the same conditions as witnesses against him or her;

(f) To have the free assistance of an interpreter if he or she cannot understand or speak the language used in the International Tribunal for Rwanda;

(g) Not to be compelled to testify against himself or herself or to confess guilt.

Article 23
Penalties

1. The penalty imposed by the Trial Chamber shall be limited to imprisonment. In determining the terms of imprisonment, the Trial Chambers shall have recourse to the general practice regarding prison sentences in the courts of Rwanda.

2. In imposing the sentences, the Trial Chambers shall take into account such factors as the gravity of the offence and the individual circumstances of the convicted person.

3. In addition to imprisonment, the Trial Chambers may order the return of any property and proceeds acquired by criminal conduct, including by means of duress, to their rightful owners.

Article 24
Appellate proceedings

1. The Appeals Chamber shall hear appeals from persons convicted by the Trial Chambers or from the Prosecutor on the following grounds:

(a) An error on a question of law invalidating the decision; or

(b) An error of fact which has occasioned a miscarriage of justice.

2. The Appeals Chamber may affirm, reverse or revise the decisions taken by the Trial Chambers.

Article 26
Enforcement of sentences

Imprisonment shall be served in Rwanda or any of the States on a list of States which have indicated to the Security Council their willingness to accept convicted persons, as designated by the International Tribunal for Rwanda. Such imprisonment shall be in accordance with the applicable law of the State concerned, subject to the supervision of the International Tribunal for Rwanda.

(c) *Prosecutor v. Jean-Paul Akayesu*

International Criminal Tribunal for Rwanda
February 12, 1996
ICTR-96-4-I

[Selected excerpts from the *Akayesu* Indictment].

The Prosecutor of the International Criminal Tribunal for Rwanda, pursuant to his authority under Article 17 of the Statute of the Tribunal, charges:

JEAN PAUL AKAYESU

with GENOCIDE, CRIMES AGAINST HUMANITY and VIOLATIONS OF ARTICLE 3 COMMON TO THE GENEVA CONVENTIONS, as set forth below:

Background

1. On April 6, 1994, a plane carrying President Jevenal Habyarimana of Rwanda and President Cyprien Ntaryamira of Burundi crashed at Kigali airport, killing all on board. Following the deaths of the two Presidents, widespread killings, having both political and ethnic dimensions, began in Kigali and spread to other parts of Rwanda.

2. Rwanda is divided into 11 prefectures, each of which is governed by a prefect. The prefectures are further subdivided into communes which are placed under the authority of bourgmestres. The bourgmestre of each commune is appointed by the President of the Republic, upon the recommendation of the Minister of the Interior. In Rwanda, the bourgmestre is the most powerful figure in the commune. His *de facto* authority in the area is significantly greater than that which is conferred upon him *de jure*.

3. Jean Paul AKAYESU, born in 1953 in Murche sector, Taba commune, served as bourgmestre of that commune from April 1993 until June 1994. Prior to his appointment as bourgmestre, he was a teacher and school inspector in Taba.

4. As bourgmestre, Jean Paul AKAYESU was charged with the performance of executive functions and the maintenance of public order within his commune, subject to the authority of the prefect. He had exclusive control over the communal police, as well as any gendarmes put at the disposition of the commune. He was responsible for the execution of laws and regulations and the administration of justice, also subject only to the prefect's authority.

General Allegations

* * *

5. Unless otherwise specified, all acts and omissions set forth in this indictment took place between 1 January 1994 and 31 December 1994, in the commune of Taba, prefecture of Gitarama, territory of Rwanda.

6. In each paragraph charging genocide, a crime recognized by Article 2 of the Statute of the Tribunal, the alleged acts or omissions were committed with intent to destroy, in whole or in part a national, ethnical or racial group.

7. The victims in each paragraph charging genocide were members of a national, ethnical, racial or religious group.

8. In each paragraph charging crimes against humanity, crimes recognized by Article 3 of the Tribunal Statute, the alleged acts or omissions were committed as part of a widespread or systematic attack against a civilian population on national, political, ethnic or racial grounds.

9. At all times relevant to this indictment, a state of internal armed conflict existed in Rwanda.

10. The victims referred to in this indictment were, at all relevant times, persons not taking an active part in the hostilities.

11. The accused is individually responsible for the crimes alleged in this indictment. Under Article 6(1) of the Statute of the Tribunal, individual criminal responsibility is attributable to one who plans, instigates, orders, commits or otherwise aids and abets in the planning, preparation or execution of any of the crimes referred to in Articles 2 to 4 of the Statute of the Tribunal.

Charges

12. As bourgmestre, Jean Paul AKAYESU was responsible for maintaining law and public order in his commune. At least 2000 Tutsis were killed in Taba between April 7 and the end of June 1994, while he was still in power. The killings in Taba were openly committed and so widespread that, as bourgmestre, Jean Paul AKAYESU must have known about them. Although he had the authority and responsibility to do so, Jean Paul AKAYESU never attempted to prevent the killing of Tutsis in the commune in any way or called for assistance from regional or national authorities to quell the violence.

13. On or about 19 April 1994, before dawn, in Gisheyeshye sector, Taba commune, a group of men, one of whom was named Francois Ndimubanzi, killed a local teacher, Sylvere, because he was accused of associating with the Rwandan Patriotic Front

("RPF") and plotting to kill Hutus. Even though at least one of the perpetrators was turned over to Jean Paul AKAYESU, he failed to take measures to have him arrested.

14. The morning of April 19, 1994, following the murder of Sylvere Karera, Jean Paul AKAYESU led a meeting in Gishyeshye sector at which he sanctioned the death of Sylvere Karera and urged the population to eliminate accomplices of the RPF, which was understood by those present to mean Tutsis. Over 100 people were present at the meeting. The killing of Tutsis in Taba began shortly after the meeting.

* * *

19. On or about April 19, 1994, Jean Paul AKAYESU took 8 detained men from the Taba *bureau communal* and ordered militia members to kill them. The militia killed them with clubs, machetes, small axes and sticks. The victims had fled from Runda commune and had been held by Jean Paul AKAYESU.

20. On or about April 19, 1994, Jean Paul AKAYESU ordered local people and militia to kill intellectual and influential people. Five teachers from the secondary school of Taba were killed on his instructions.... The local people and militia killed them with machetes and agricultural tools in front of the Taba *bureau communal.*

* * *

Counts 1–3
(Genocide)
(Crimes against Humanity)

COUNT 1: GENOCIDE [Article 2(3)(a) of the Statute].

COUNT 2: Complicity in GENOCIDE [Article 2(3)(e) of the Statute].

COUNT 3: CRIMES AGAINST HUMANITY (extermination) [Article 3(b) of the Statute].

Count 4
(Incitement to Genocide)

COUNT 4: Direct and Public Incitement to Commit GENOCIDE [Article 2(3)(c) of the Statute].

Counts 5–6
(Crimes Against Humanity)

(Violations of Article 3 common to the Geneva Conventions)

COUNT 5: CRIMES AGAINST HUMANITY (murder) [Article 3(a) of the Statute].

COUNT 6: VIOLATIONS OF ARTICLE 3 COMMON TO THE GENEVA CONVENTIONS [incorporated by Article 4(a) (murder) or the Statute].

Counts 7–8
(Crimes Against Humanity)
(Violations of Article 3 common to the Geneva Conventions)

By his acts in relation to the murders of 8 detained men in front of the *bureau communal* in paragraph 19, Jean Paul AKAYESU committed:

COUNT 7: CRIMES AGAINST HUMANITY (murder) [Article 3(a) of the Statute].

COUNT 8: VIOLATIONS OF ARTICLE 3 COMMON TO THE GENEVA CONVEN-
TIONS (murder) [Article 4(a) of the Statute].

Counts 9–10
(Crimes Against Humanity)
(Violations of Article 3 common to the Geneva Conventions)

By his acts in relation [to] the murders of 5 teachers in front of the *bureau communal* as described in paragraph 20, Jean Paul AKAYESU committed:

COUNT 9: CRIMES AGAINST HUMANITY (murder) [Article 3(a) of the Statute]; and

COUNT 10: VIOLATIONS OF ARTICLE 3 COMMON TO THE GENEVA CONVEN-
TIONS (murder) [Article 4(a) of the Statute].

Counts 11–12
(Crimes Against Humanity)
(Violations of Article 3 Common to the Geneva Conventions)

By his acts in relation [to] the beatings of Victims [naming them by letter designations] as described in paragraphs [naming them by number], Jean Paul AKAYESU committed:

COUNT 11: CRIMES AGAINST HUMANITY (torture) [Article 3(f) of the Statute]; and

COUNT 12: VIOLATIONS OF ARTICLE 3 COMMON TO THE GENEVA CONVEN-
TIONS,

(Cruel treatment) [Article 4(a) of the Statute].

(d) *Prosecutor v. Jean-Paul Akayesu*

International Criminal Tribunal for Rwanda
September 2, 1998
ICTR-96-4-T

KAMA, P. J., ASPERGREN AND PILLAY, JJ.

* * *

12. Before rendering its findings on the acts with which Akayesu is charged and the applicable law, the Chamber is of the opinion that it would be appropriate, for a better understanding of the events alleged in the Indictment, to briefly summarise the history of Rwanda. To this end, it recalled the most important events in the country's history, from the pre-colonial period up to 1994, reviewing the colonial period and the "Revolution" of 1959 by Gregoire Kayibanda. The Chamber most particularly highlighted the military political conflict between the Rwandan Armed Forces (RAF) and the Rwandan Patriotic Front (FPF) and its armed wing, from 1990. This conflict led to the signing of the Arusha Peace Accords and the deployment of a United Nations peacekeeping force, UNAMIR.

13. The Chamber then considered whether the events that took place in Rwanda in 1994 occurred solely within the context of the conflict between the RAF and the RPF, as some maintain, or constituted genocide. To that end, and even if the Chamber later goes back on its definition of genocide, it should be noted that genocide means, as defined in the Convention for the Prevention and Punishment of the Crime of Genocide, as the act of committing certain crimes, including the killing of members of the group or causing serious physical or mental harm to members of the group with intent to destroy, in whole or in part, a national, ethnical, racial or religious group, as such.

14. Even though the number of victims is yet to be known with accuracy, no one can reasonably refute the fact that widespread killings took place during this period throughout the country. Dr. Zachariah, who appeared as an expert witness before this Tribunal, described the piles of bodies he saw everywhere, on the roads, on the footpaths and in rivers and, particularly, the manner in which all these people had been killed. He saw many wounded people who, according to him, were mostly Tutsi and who, apparently, had sustained wounds inflicted with machetes to the face, the neck, the ankle and also to the Achilles' tendon to prevent them from fleeing. Similarly, the testimony of Major-General Dallaire, former Commander of UNAMIR, before the Chamber indicated that, from 6 April 1994, the date of the crash that claimed the life of President Habyarimana, members of FAR and the Presidential Guard were going into houses in Kigali that had been previously identified in order to kill. Another witness, the British cameraman, Simon Cox, took photographs of bodies in various localities in Rwanda, and mentioned identity cards strewn on the ground, all of which were marked "Tutsi."

15. Consequently, in view of these widespread killings the victims of which were mainly Tutsi, the Trial Chamber is of the opinion that the first requirement for there to be genocide has been met, to wit, killing and causing serious bodily harm to members of a group. The second requirement is that these killings and serious bodily harm be committed with the intent to destroy, in whole or in part, a particular group targeted as such.

16. In the Opinion of the Chamber, many facts show that the intention of the perpetrators of these killings was to cause the complete disappearance of the Tutsi people. In this connection, Alison DesForges, a specialist historian on Rwanda, who appeared as an expert witness, stated as follows: "on the basis of the statements made by certain political leaders, on the basis of songs and slogans popular among the interahamwe, I believe that these people had the intention of completely wiping out the Tutsi from Rwanda so that—as they said on certain occasions—their children, later on, should not know what a Tutsi looked like, unless they referred to history books." This testimony given by Dr. DesForges was confirmed by two prosecution witnesses, who testified separately before the Tribunal that one Silas Kubwimana said during a public meeting chaired by the Accused himself that all the Tutsi had to be killed so that someday Hutu children would not know what a Tutsi looked like. Dr. Zachariah also testified that the Achilles' tendons of many wounded persons were cut to prevent them from fleeing. In the opinion of the Chamber, this demonstrates the resolve of the perpetrators of these massacres not to spare any Tutsi. Their plan called for doing whatever was possible to prevent any Tutsi from escaping and, thus, to destroy the whole group. Dr. Alison DesForges stated that numerous Tutsi corpses were systematically thrown into the River Nyabarongo, a tributary of the Nile, as seen, incidentally, in several photographs shown in court throughout the trial. She explained that the intent in the gesture was "to send the Tutsi back to their origin," to make them "return to Abyssinia," in accordance with the notion that the Tutsi are a "foreign" group in Rwanda, believed to have come from the Nilotic regions.

17. Other testimonies heard, especially that of Major-General Dallaire, also show that there was an intention to wipe out the Tutsi group in its entirety, since even new-born babies were not spared. Many testimonies given before the Chamber concur on the fact that it was the Tutsi as members of an ethnic group who were targeted in the massacres. General Dallaire, Doctor Zachariah and, particularly, the Accused himself, unanimously stated so before the Chamber.

18. Numerous witnesses testified before the Chamber that the systematic checking of identity cards, on which the ethnic group was mentioned, made it possible to separate the Hutu from the Tutsi, with the latter being immediately arrested and often killed, sometimes on the spot, at the roadblocks which were erected in Kigali soon after the crash of the plane of President Habyarimana, and thereafter everywhere in the country.

19. Based on the evidence submitted to the Chamber, it is clear that the massacres which occurred in Rwanda in 1994 had a specific objective, namely the extermination of the Tutsi, who were targeted especially because of their Tutsi origin and not because they were RPF fighters. In any case, the Tutsi children and pregnant women would, naturally, not have been among the fighters. The Chamber concludes that, alongside the conflict between the RAF and the RPF, genocide was committed in Rwanda in 1994 against the Tutsi as a group. The execution of this genocide was probably facilitated by the conflict, in the sense that the conflict with the RPF forces served as a pretext for the propaganda inciting genocide against the Tutsi, by branding RPF fighters and Tutsi civilians together through the notion widely disseminated, particularly by Radio Television Libre des Mille Collines (RTLM), to the effect that every Tutsi was allegedly an accomplice of the RPF soldiers or "Inkotanyi." However, the fact that the genocide occurred while the RAF were in conflict with the RPF, obviously, cannot serve as a mitigating circumstance for the genocide.

20. Consequently, the Chamber concludes from all the foregoing that it was, indeed, genocide that was committed in Rwanda in 1994, against the Tutsi as a group. The Chamber is of the opinion that the genocide appears to have been meticulously organized. In fact, Dr. Alison DesForges testifying before the Chamber on 24 May 1997, talked of "centrally organized and supervised massacres." Some evidence supports this view that the genocide had been planned. First, the existence of lists of Tutsi to be eliminated is corroborated by many testimonies. In this respect, Dr. Zachariah mentioned the case of patients and nurses killed in a hospital because a soldier had a list including their names.

21. The Chamber holds that the genocide was organized and planned not only by members of the RAF, but also by the political forces who were behind the "Hutu-power," that it was executed essentially by civilians including the armed militia and even ordinary citizens, and above all, that the majority of the Tutsi victims were non-combatants, including thousands of women and children....

* * *

37. Having made its factual findings, the Chamber analysed the legal definitions proposed by the Prosecutor for each of the facts. It thus considered the applicable law for each of the three crimes under its jurisdiction, which is all the more important since this is the very first Judgment on the legal definitions of genocide on the one hand, and of serious violations of Additional Protocol II of the Geneva Conventions, on the other. Moreover, the Chamber also had to define certain crimes which constitute offences under its jurisdiction, in particular, rape, because to date, there is no commonly accepted definition of this term in international law.

38. In the opinion of the Chamber, rape is a form of aggression the central elements of which cannot be captured in a mechanical description of objects and body parts. The Chamber also notes the cultural sensitivities involved in public discussion of intimate matters and recalls the painful reluctance and inability of witnesses to disclose graphic anatomical details of the sexual violence they endured. The Chamber defines rape as a physical invasion of a sexual nature, committed on a person under circumstances which

are coercive. Sexual violence, including rape, is not limited to physical invasion of the human body and may include acts which do not involve penetration or even physical contact. The Chamber notes in this context that coercive circumstances need not be evidenced by a show of physical force. Threats, intimidation, extortion, and other forms of duress which prey on fear or desperation may constitute coercion.

39. The Chamber reviewed Article 6(1) of its Statute, on the individual criminal responsibility of the accused for the three crimes constituting *ratione materiae* of the Chamber. Article 6(1) enunciates the basic principles of individual criminal liability which are probably common to most national criminal jurisdictions. Article 6(3), by contrast, constitutes something of an exception to the principles articulated in Article 6(1), an exception which derives from military law, particularly the principle of the liability of a commander for the acts of his subordinates or "command responsibility." Article 6(3) does not necessarily require the superior to have had knowledge of such to render him criminally liable. The only requirement is that he had reason to know that his subordinates were about to commit or had committed and failed to take the necessary or reasonable measure to prevent such acts or punish the perpetrators thereof.

40. The Chamber then expressed its opinion that with respect to the crimes under its jurisdiction, it should adhere to the concept of notional plurality of offences (cumulative charges) which would render multiple convictions permissible for the same act. As a result, a particular act may constitute both genocide and a crime against humanity.

41. On the crime of genocide, the Chamber recalls that the definition given by Article 2 of the Statute is echoed exactly by the Convention for the Prevention and Repression of the Crime of Genocide. The Chamber notes that Rwanda acceded, by legislative decree, to the Convention on Genocide on 12 February 1975. Thus, punishment of the crime of genocide did exist in Rwanda in 1994, at the time of the acts alleged in the Indictment, and the perpetrator was liable to be brought before the competent courts of Rwanda to answer for this crime.

42. Contrary to popular belief, the crime of genocide does not imply the actual extermination of a group in its entirety, but is understood as such once any one of the acts mentioned in Article 2 of the Statute is committed with the specific intent to destroy "in whole or in part" a national, ethnical, racial or religious group. Genocide is distinct from other crimes inasmuch as it embodies a special intent or *dolus specialis*. Special intent of a crime is the specific intention, required as a constitutive element of the crime, which requires that the perpetrator clearly seek to produce the act charged. The special intent in the crime of genocide lies in "the intent to destroy, in whole or in part, a national, ethical, racial or religious group, as such."

43. Specifically, for any of the acts charged under Article 2(2) of the Statute to be a constructive element of genocide, the act must have been committed against one or several individuals, because such individual or individuals were members of a specific group, and specifically because they belonged to this group. Thus, the victim is chosen not because of his individual identity, but rather on account of his being a member of a national, ethnical, racial or religious group. The victim of the act is therefore a member of a group, targeted as such; hence, the victim of the crime of genocide is the group itself and not the individual alone.

44. On the issue of determining the offender's specific intent, the Chamber considers that intent is a mental factor which is difficult, even impossible, to determine. This is the reason why, in the absence of a confession from the Accused, his intent can be inferred from a certain number of presumptions of fact. The Chamber considers that it is

possible to deduce the genocidal intent inherent in a particular act charged from the general context of the perpetration of other culpable acts systematically directed against that same group, whether these acts were committed by the same offender or by others. Other factors, such as the scale of the atrocities committed, their general nature, in a region or a country, or furthermore, the fact of deliberately and systematically targeting victims on account of their membership of a particular group, while excluding the members of other groups, can enable the Chamber to infer the genocidal intent of a particular act.

45. Apart from the crime of genocide, Jean-Paul Akayesu is charged with complicity in genocide and direct and public incitement to commit genocide.

46. In the opinion of the Chamber, an Accused is an accomplice in genocide if he knowingly aided and abetted or provoked a person or persons to commit genocide, knowing that this person or persons were committing genocide, even if the Accused himself lacked the specific intent of destroying in whole or in part, the national, ethnical, racial or religious group, as such.

47. Regarding the crime of direct and public incitement to commit genocide, the Chamber defines it mainly on the basis of Article 91 of the Rwandan Penal Code, as directly provoking another to commit genocide, either through speeches, shouting or threats uttered in public places or at public gatherings, or through the public display of placards or posters, or by any other means of audiovisual communication. The moral element of this crime lies in the intent to directly encourage or provoke another to commit genocide. It presupposes the desire of the guilty to create, by his actions, within the person or persons whom he is addressing, the state of mind which is appropriate to the commission of the crime. In other words, the person who is inciting to commit genocide must have the specific intent of genocide: that of destroying in whole or in part, a national, ethnical, racial or religious group, as such. The Chamber believes that incitement is a formal offence, for which the mere method used is culpable. In other words, the offence is considered to have been completed once the incitement has taken place and that it is direct and public, whether or not it was successful....

* * *

51. With regard to count one on genocide, the Chamber having regard, particularly, to the acts described in paragraphs 12(A) and 12(B) of the Indictment, that is, rape and sexual violence, the Chamber wishes to underscore the fact that in its opinion, they constitute genocide in the same way as any other act as long as they were committed with the specific intent to destroy, in whole or in part, a particular group, targeted as such. Indeed, rape and sexual violence certainly constitute infliction of serious bodily and mental harm on the victims.... In light of all the evidence before it, the Chamber is satisfied that the acts of rape and sexual violence...were committed solely against the Tutsi women, many of whom were subjected to the worst public humiliation, mutilated, and raped several times, often in public, in the Bureau Communal premises or in other public places, and often by more than one assailant. These rapes resulted in physical and psychological destruction of Tutsi women, their families and their communities. Sexual violence was an integral part of the process of destruction, specifically targeting Tutsi women and specifically contributing to their destruction and to the destruction of the Tutsi group as a whole.

52. The rape of Tutsi women was systematic and was perpetrated against all Tutsi women and solely against them. A Tutsi woman, married to a Hutu, testified before the Chamber that she was not raped because her ethnic background was unknown. As part

of the propaganda campaign geared to mobilizing the Hutu against the Tutsi, the Tutsi women were presented as sexual objects. Indeed, the Chamber was told, for an example, that before being raped and killed, Alexia, who was the wife of the Professor, Ntereye, and her two nieces, were forced by the Interahamwe to undress and ordered to run and do exercises "in order to display the thighs of Tutsi women." The Interahamwe who raped Alexia said, as he threw her on the ground and got on top of her, "let us now see what the vagina of a Tutsi woman tastes like." As stated above, Akayesu himself, speaking to the Interahamwe, who were committing the rapes, said to them: "don't ever ask again what a Tutsi women tastes like."

53. On the basis of the substantial testimonies brought before it, the Chamber finds that in most cases, the rapes of Tutsi women in Taba, were accompanied with the intent to kill those women. Many rapes were perpetrated near mass graves where the women were taken to be killed. A victim testified that Tutsi women caught could be taken away by peasants and men with the promise that they would be collected later to be executed. Following an act of gang rape, a witness heard Akayesu say "tomorrow they will be killed" and they were actually killed. In this respect, it appears clearly to the Chamber that the acts of rape and sexual violence, as other acts of serious bodily and mental harm committed against the Tutsi, reflected the determination to make Tutsi women suffer and to mutilate them even before killing them, the intent being to destroy the Tutsi group while inflicting acute suffering on its members in the process.

54. The Chamber has already established that genocide was committed against the Tutsi group in Rwanda in 1994, throughout the period covering the events alleged in the Indictment. Owing to the very high number of atrocities committed against the Tutsi, their widespread nature not only in the commune of Taba, but also throughout Rwanda, and to the fact that the victims were systematically and deliberately selected because they belonged to the Tutsi group, with persons belonging to other groups being excluded, the Chamber is also able to infer, beyond reasonable doubt, the genocidal intent of the accused in the commission of the above-mentioned crimes; to the extent that the actions and words of Akayesu during the period of the facts alleged in the Indictment, the Chamber is convinced beyond reasonable doubt, on the basis of evidence adduced before it during the hearing, that he repeatedly made statements more or less explicitly calling for the commission of genocide. Yet, according to the Chamber, he who incites another to commit genocide must have the specific intent to commit genocide: that of destroying in whole or in part, a national, ethnical, racial, or religious group, as such.

55. In conclusion, regarding Count One on genocide, the Chamber is satisfied beyond reasonable doubt that these various acts were committed by Akayesu with the specific intent to destroy the Tutsi group, as such. Consequently, the Chamber is of the opinion that the acts alleged in paragraphs 12, 12A, 12B, 16, 18, 19, 20, 22 and 23 of the Indictment, constitute the crimes of killing members of the Tutsi group and causing serious bodily and mental harm to members of the Tutsi group. Furthermore, the Chamber is satisfied beyond reasonable doubt that in committing the various acts alleged, Akayesu had the specific intent of destroying the Tutsi group as such.

———————

(e) Diane Marie Amann, "Prosecutor v. Akayesu, Case ICTR-96-4T, 'International Decisions'"

93 *American Journal of International Law* 195–199 (1999)
Reproduced with permission from 93 *American Journal of International Law* 195 (1999). ©The American Society of International Law

This pioneering opinion marks the first time an international criminal tribunal has tried and convicted an individual for genocide and international crimes of sexual violence. The case arose out of the massacres of perhaps a million Tutsi in Rwanda in 1994. At least two thousand died in Taba, a rural commune where defendant Jean-Paul Akayesu was mayor. A trial chamber of the International Criminal Tribunal for Rwanda concluded that, although Akayesu may at first have tried to prevent killings, he eventually donned a military jacket and participated in or ordered atrocities. The Tribunal found him guilty of one count each of genocide and incitement to commit genocide and seven counts of crimes against humanity. It acquitted Akayesu of five counts brought under common Article 3 of the 1949 Geneva Conventions and Protocol Additional II to those Conventions on the ground that he was not within the class of perpetrators contemplated by them.

* * *

Do the Tutsi, the Tribunal asked, constitute a group protected against genocide? Both the ICTR Statute and the Genocide Convention proscribe acts "committed with intent to destroy...a national, ethnical, racial or religious group." Hutu and Tutsi shared nationality, race and religion. They also partook of "a common language or culture," The Tribunal concluded that they were not, as a technical matter, separate ethnic groups.

The Tribunal nevertheless discerned from records of the Genocide Convention the intent to protect not just the four enumerated groups but "any group, similar...in terms of its stability and permanence." Such group membership must be "determined by birth," "in a continuous and often irremediable manner," in contrast with "the more 'mobile' groups which one joins through individual voluntary commitment, such as political and economic groups." Decades of discrimination—by custom of patrilineal descent and by laws, such as that requiring cards that identified each person by the *ethnie*, or ethnic group, of Hutu or Tutsi—had led the Tutsi to be regarded as a distinct, stable, permanent group. Victims were selected in 1994 not as individuals, but because of this perceived ethnic difference. In particular, Akayesu, through his speeches, orders and actions, had demonstrated a specific intent to destroy Tutsi as an ethnic group. Thus, he was found guilty of genocide for actually participating in beating, killings and rapes of Tutsi in some instances, and encouraging, abetting or ordering such acts in others.

Rape was not among the initial charges against Akayesu. After witnesses testified about sexual assaults, pressure by Judge Pillay, the sole woman on the panel, and by human rights groups resulted in further investigation and an amended indictment. The Tribunal was accordingly required to determine when sexual violence constitutes an international crime. It was recognized that municipal rape laws often depend on a "mechanical description" of specific methods of assault. Taking its lead, however, from the Convention against Torture, the Tribunal opted for a broader definition, "more useful in international law." Both torture and rape, it noted, are crimes that violate personal dignity and that often further specific purposes like "intimidation, degradation, humiliation, discrimination, punishment, control or destruction of a person." Indeed, rape committed with the aid of a public official is torture. The Tribunal thus defined "rape"—listed as a crime against humanity in the ICTR Statute—"as a physical invasion of a sexual nature, committed on a person under circumstances which are coercive." It defined "sexual violence"—a crime it derived from other provisions of the Statute—as "any act of a sexual nature which is committed on a person under circumstances which are coercive." Within the latter category are affronts like forcing a student to perform gymnastics naked. Coercion, the Tribunal stressed, includes not only "physical force," but also "[t]hreats, intimidation, extortion and other forms of duress," such as the existence of armed conflict and the presence of armed militants.

The Tribunal credited the testimony of several victims and eyewitnesses—each designated not by name but by letters—rather than Akayesu's "bare denial" that sexual violence had occurred. Thus, it found him guilty of crimes against humanity and genocide for aiding, abetting, ordering, or encouraging, and sometimes witnessing, more than two dozen rapes and other sexual assaults at the bureau communal where, by dint of his authority, he could have prevented them.

Akayesu's encouragement of crimes led to his conviction on an additional charge of direct and public incitement to commit genocide, proscribed both in the ICTR Statute and in the Genocide Convention. After a review of national laws in common law and civil law systems, the Tribunal held that the Statute is violated when a person, in a public place or through a mass medium, directly encourages or persuades another to commit genocide, with the specific intent that the person's acts contribute to the destruction of a protected group. It found Akayesu guilty of this crime for having publicly urged a crowd "to unite in order to eliminate what he termed the sole enemy," in a manner understood as a call "to kill the Tutsi," some of whom he named explicitly. As intended, his speech "did lead to the destruction of a great number of Tutsi in the commune of Taba."

The Prosecutor had also alleged that Akayesu had violated Article 4 of the ICTR Statute by committing serious violations of both common Article 3 of the 1949 Geneva Conventions and the 1977 Protocol Additional II to those Conventions. The Tribunal concluded that customary international law supported the inclusion of common Article 3 and the Protocol, designed to extend humanitarian protection to victims of internal armed conflicts, in its Statute. But it refrained from holding Akayesu criminally liable under the provisions. It reasoned that, because the provisions purport to protect victims of armed conflicts, they are designed to constrain the activity of "persons who by virtue of their authority, are responsible for the outbreak of, or are otherwise engaged in the conduct of hostilities." This would encompass all military personnel and some civilians. The latter, however, must have been "legitimately mandated and expected, as public officials or agents or persons otherwise holding pubic authority or *de facto* representing the Government, to support or fulfil the war efforts." Finding insufficient proof that Akayesu fell within this category, the Tribunal acquitted him of all charges under Article 4 of the ICTR Statute.

* * *

The Tribunal's ruling on sexual violence is but one of many intriguing international law issues addressed by this case. That the Tribunal extended protection to a group not among the four enumerated groups might surprise those familiar with the debates that led to the exclusion of other groups, particularly political or social groups, from the Genocide Convention. Yet the enumerated groups are not defined in either the Convention or the Statute; in particular, the scope of the term "ethnic" remains in dispute. Though Tutsi may not be an ethnic group within the strict definition, they share characteristics of the enumerated groups. Tutsi membership was defined at birth and, within the Rwandan social and legal system, remained for life. Both the victims and the perpetrators considered themselves to belong to separate ethnic groups. Tutsi identity was thus immutable, stable and permanent. The decision of the Tribunal to treat the Tutsi as if it were an enumerated group properly recognizes the role of socially imposed discrimination in establishing group identity. It evinces the kind of flexibility that drafters of the Convention, had, in fact, endorsed.

On the other hand, the decision is unlikely to bring political or economic groups within the ambit of genocide. Membership in those groups is mutable and is neither dependent on birth nor readily recognized by the larger society. Moreover, the text of the ICTR Statute links the protected groups to the specific intent of the defendant. Akayesu regarded Tutsi as a separate ethnic group and chose his victims out of a belief that to harm them would help destroy their group. These factors also justified his conviction for genocide.

The convictions for involvement in rapes and other sexual violence culminated a long campaign to have rape treated not as a "trophy" but as a crime of war. The development was particularly appropriate in this instance; testimony indicated that victims were chosen because of their group identity, in order to wreck destruction on the group as a whole. Likewise, the choice of a definition focusing on the concept of rape rather than on methodological detail properly reflects the aim of international humanitarian law to give full protection to the most vulnerable victims. By requiring proof of both physical, sexual invasion and coercion for a rape conviction, the Tribunal fashioned a standard that is sufficiently precise and within accepted definitions to give notice of forbidden conduct. The definition of "sexual violence" may be another matter. Unlike rape, this crime is not specified in the ICTR Statute. The Tribunal inferred it from proscriptions against "inhumane acts," acts causing "serious bodily or mental harm" and "outrages against personal dignity," terms themselves indefinite. Furthermore, the Tribunal included within the meaning of sexual violence "any act of a sexual nature" involving coercion. Though the sexual mistreatment described by witnesses cries out for punishment, a clear, established definition would have obviated any risk of the kind of criticism based on the principle of *nullum crimen sine lege* that dogged the Nuremberg trials.

Criminal punishment for incitement might, in the abstract, also give pause to civil libertarians. In this case, however, the Tribunal carefully applied elements drawn from the text of the Statute. It thus required that the words forming the gravaman of the crime were uttered in a public place, that the speaker had intended the words to provoke immediate, genocidal violence; and that the speaker had conveyed this intent to the listeners in a direct manner. Each element was proved; indeed, Akayesu's speech actually touched off killings and other assaults. Even according to U.S. Supreme Court doctrine [in the case of *Brandenburg v. Ohio*, 395 U.S. 444 (1969)], his words did not deserve protection.

The Tribunal itself voiced a concern based on *nullum crimen* respecting the prosecution's effort to hold Akayesu liable for violations of common Article 3 and Protocol Additional II. Its effort to accommodate the principles that civilians may be guilty of war crimes and that convictions ought to be based upon customary international law is admirable. But its standard for civilian liability is unduly high, in that it excludes Akayesu, an elected official who held chief executive power in his community, who was a local representative of the national Government, and who gave some assistance to the Government's war effort. In contrast, opinions of the Tribunal for the Former Yugoslavia in *Tadic* suggest that everyone may be held criminally liable. Unless the standard of the Rwanda Tribunal is relaxed on appeal, far too many civilians will escape responsibility for committing war crimes against non-combatants caught in the middle of internal armed conflict.

(f) *Prosecutor v. Georges Anderson Nderubumwe Rutaganda*

International Criminal Tribunal for Rwanda
February 12, 1996
ICTR-96-3-I

[Selected excerpts from the *Rutaganda* Indictment].

The Prosecutor of the International Criminal Tribunal for Rwanda pursuant to his authority under Article 17 of the Statute of the Tribunal, charges:

GEORGES ANDERSON NDERUBUMWE RUTAGANDA
with GENOCIDE, CRIMES AGAINST HUMANITY and VIOLATIONS OF ARTICLE
3 COMMON TO THE GENEVA CONVENTIONS, as set forth below:

Background

1. On April 6, 1994, a plane carrying President Juvenal Habyarimana of Rwanda and President Cyprien Ntaryamira of Burundi crashed at Kigali airport, killing all on board. Following the deaths of the two Presidents, widespread killings having both political and ethnic dimensions began in Kigali and spread to other parts of Rwanda.

The Accused

2. Georges RUTAGANDA, born in 1958 in Masango commune, Gitarama prefecture, was an agricultural engineer and businessman; he was general manager and proprietor of Rutaganda SARL. Georges RUTAGANDA was also a member of the National and Prefectoral Committees of the *Mouvement Republic National pour le Developpement et la Democratie* (hereinafter, "MRND") and a shareholder of *Radio Television Libre des Mille Collines*. On April 6, 1994, he was serving as the second vice president of the National Committee of the Interahamwe, the youth militia of the MRND.

General Allegations

3. Unless otherwise specified, all acts set forth in this indictment took place between 1 January 1994 and 31 December 1994 in the prefectures of Kigali and Gitarama, territory of Rwanda.

4. In each paragraph charging genocide, a crime recognized by Article 2 of the Statute of the Tribunal, the alleged acts were committed with intent to destroy, in whole or in part, a national, ethnical or racial group.

5. The victims in each paragraph charging genocide were members of a national, ethnical, racial or religious group.

6. In each paragraph charging crimes against humanity, crimes punishable by Article 3 of the Statute of the Tribunal, the alleged acts were committed as part of a widespread or systematic attack against a civilian population on political, ethnic or racial grounds.

7. At all times relevant to this indictment, a state of internal armed conflict existed in Rwanda.

8. The victims referred to in this indictment were, at all relevant times, persons taking no active part in the hostilities.

9. The accused is individually responsible for the crimes alleged in this indictment. Under Article 6(1) of the Statute of the Tribunal, individual criminal responsibility is

attributable to one who plans, instigates, orders, commits or otherwise aids and abets in the planning, preparation or execution of any of the crimes referred to in Articles 2 of the Statute of the Tribunal.

Charges

10. On or about April 6, 1994, Georges RUTAGANDA distributed guns and other weapons to Interahamwe members in Nyarugenge commune, Kigali.

11. On or about April 10, 1994, Georges RUTAGANDA stationed Interahamwe members at a roadblock near his office at the "Amgar" garage in Kigali. Shortly after he left the area, the Interahamwe members started checking identity cards of people passing the roadblock. The Interahamwe members ordered persons with Tutsi identity cards to stand on one side of the road. Eight of the Tutsis were then killed. The victims included men, women and an infant who had been carried on the back of one of the women.

12. In April 1994, on a date unknown, Tutsis who had been separated at a roadblock in front of the Amgar garage were taken to Georges RUTAGANDA and questioned by him. He thereafter directed that these Tutsis be detained with others at a nearby building. Later, Georges RUTAGANDA directed men under his control to take 10 Tutsi detainees to a deep, open hole near the Amgar garage. On Georges RUTAGANDA's orders, his men killed the 10 Tutsis with machetes and threw their bodies into the hole.

13. From April 7 to April 11, 1994, thousands of unarmed Tutsi men, and women children and some unarmed Hutus sought refuge at the Ecole Technique Officielle ("ETO school") in Kicukiro sector, Kicukiro commune. The ETO school was considered a safe haven because Belgian soldiers, part of the United Nations Assistance Mission for Rwanda forces, were stationed there.

14. On or about April 11, 1994, immediately after the Belgians withdrew from the ETO school, members of the Rwandan armed forces, the gendarmerie and militia, including the Interahamwe, attacked the ETO school and, using machetes, grenades and guns, killed the people who had sought refuge there. The Interahamwe separated Hutus from Tutsis during the attack, killing the Tutsis. Georges RUTAGANDA participated in the attack at the ETO school, which resulted in the deaths of a large number of Tutsis.

15. The men, women and children who survived the ETO school attack were forcibly transferred by Georges RUTAGANDA, members of the Interahamwe and soldiers to a gravel pit near the primary school of Nyanza. Presidential Guard members awaited their arrival. More Interahamwe members converged upon Nyanza from many directions and surrounded the group of survivors.

16. On or about April 12, 1994, the survivors who were able to show that they were Hutu were permitted to leave the gravel pit. Tutsis who presented altered identity cards were immediately killed. Most of the remainder of the group were attacked and killed by grenades or shot to death. Those who tried to escape were attacked by machetes. Georges RUTAGANDA, among others, directed and participated in these attacks.

17. In April of 1994, on dates unknown, in Masango commune, Georges RUTAGANDA and others known to the Prosecutor conducted house-to-house searches for Tutsis and their families. Throughout these searches, Tutsis were separated from Hutus

and taken to a river. Georges RUTAGANDA instructed the Interahamwe to track all the Tutsis and throw them into the river.

18. On or about April 28, 1994, Georges RUTAGANDA, together with Interahamwe members, collected residents from Kigali and detained them near the Amgar garage. Georges RUTAGANDA and the Interahamwe demanded identity cards from the detainees. A number of persons, including Emmanuel Kayitare, were forcibly separated from the group. Later that day, Emmanuel Kayitare attempted to flee from where he was being detained and Georges RUTAGANDA pursued him, caught him and struck him on the head with a machete and killed. him.

19. In June 1994, on a date unknown, Georges RUTAGANDA ordered people to bury the bodies of victims in order to conceal his crimes from international community.

Counts 1–2
(Genocide)
(Crimes Against Humanity)

COUNT 1: GENOCIDE [Article 1(3)(a) of the Statute].

COUNT 2: CRIMES AGAINST HUMANITY (extermination) [Article 3(b) of the Statute].

Counts 3–4
(Crimes Against Humanity)

COUNT 3: CRIMES AGAINST HUMANITY (murder) [Article 3(a) of the Statute]; and

COUNT 4: VIOLATIONS OF ARTICLE 3 COMMON TO THE GENEVA CONVENTIONS

[incorporated by Article 4(a) of the Statute].

Counts 5–6
(Crimes Against Humanity)
(Violations of Article 3 common to the Geneva Conventions)

By his acts in relation to the killings at the gravel pit in Nyanza, as described in paragraphs 15 and 16, Georges RUTAGANDA committed:

COUNT 5: CRIMES AGAINST HUMANITY (murder) [Article 3(a) of the Statute]; and

COUNT 6: VIOLATIONS OF ARTICLE 3 COMMON TO THE GENEVA CONVENTIONS

[incorporated by Article 4(a) (murder) of the Statute].

Count 7–8
(Crimes Against Humanity)
(Violation of Article 3 common to the Geneva Convention

By killing Emmanuel Kayitare, as described in paragraph 18, Georges RUTAGANDA committed:

COUNT 7: CRIMES AGAINST HUMANITY (murder) [Article 3(a) of the Statute]; and

COUNT 8: VIOLATION OF ARTICLE 3 COMMON TO THE GENEVA CONVENTIONS

[incorporated by Article 4(a) (murder) of the Statute].

(g) *Prosecutor v. Rutaganda*

International Criminal Tribunal for Rwanda
December 6, 1999
ICTR-96-3-T

KAMA, P. J., ASPERGREN AND PILLAY, JJ.

* * *

48. The Chamber accepts that the crime of genocide involves, firstly, that one of the acts listed under Article 2(2) of the Statute be committed; secondly, that such an act be committed against a national, ethnical, racial or religious group, specifically targeted as such; and, thirdly, that the "act be committed with the intent to destroy, in whole or in part, the targeted group."

The Acts Enumerated under Article 2(2)(a) to (e) of the Statute

49. Article 2(2) of the Statute, like the corresponding provisions of the Genocide Convention, refers to *"meurtre"* in the French version and to "killing" in the English version. In the opinion of the Chamber, the term "killing" includes both intentional and unintentional homicides, whereas the word *"meurtre"* covers homicide committed with the intent to cause death. Given the presumption of innocence, and pursuant to the general principles of criminal law, the Chamber holds that the version more favourable to the Accused should be adopted, and finds that Article 2(2)(a) of the Statute must be interpreted in accordance with the definition of murder in the Criminal Code of Rwanda, which provides, under Article 311, that "Homicide committed with intent to cause death shall be treated as murder."

50. For the purposes of interpreting Article 2(2)(b) of the Statute, the Chamber understands the words "serious bodily or mental harm" to include acts of bodily or mental torture, inhumane or degrading treatment, rape, sexual violence, and persecution. The Chamber is of the opinion that "serious harm" need not entail permanent or irremediable harm.

51. In the opinion of the Chamber, the words "deliberately inflicting on the group conditions of life calculated to bring about its physical destruction in whole or in part," as indicated in Article 2(2)(c) of the Statute, are to be construed "as methods of destruction by which the perpetrator does not necessarily intend to immediately kill the members of the group," but which are, ultimately, aimed at their physical destruction. The Chamber holds that the means...include subjecting a group of people to a subsistence diet, systematic expulsion from their homes and deprivation of essential medical supplies below a minimum vital standard.

52. For the purposes of interpreting Article 2(2)(d) of the Statute, the Chamber holds that the words "measures intended to prevent births within the group" should be construed as including sexual mutilation, enforced sterilization, forced birth control, forced separation of males and females, and prohibition of marriages. The Chamber notes that measures intended to prevent births within the group may be not only physical, but also mental.

53. The Chamber is of the opinion that the provisions of Article 2(2)(e) of the Statute, on the forcible transfer of children from one group to another, are aimed at

sanctioning not only any direct act of forcible physical transfer, but also any acts of threats or trauma which would lead to the forcible transfer of children from one group to another group.

Potential Groups of Victims of the Crime of Genocide

54. The Chamber is of the view that it is necessary to consider the issue of the potential groups of victims of genocide in light of the provisions of the Statute and the Genocide Convention, which stipulate that genocide aims at "destroy[ing], in whole or in part, a national, ethnical, racial or religious group, as such."

55. The Chamber notes that the concepts of national, ethnical, racial and religious groups have been researched extensively and that, at present, there are no generally and internationally accepted precise definitions thereof. Each of these concepts must be assessed in the light of a particular political, social and cultural context. Moreover, the Chamber notes that for the purposes of applying the Genocide Convention, membership of a group is, in essence, a subjective rather than an objective concept. The victim is perceived by the perpetrator of genocide as belonging to a group slated for destruction. In some instances, the victim may perceive himself/herself as belonging to the said group.

56. Nevertheless, the Chamber is of the view that a subjective definition alone is not enough to determine victim groups, as provided for in the Genocide Convention. It appears, from a reading of the *travaux preparatories* of the Genocide Convention, that certain groups, such as political and economic groups, have been excluded from the protected groups, because they are considered to be "mobile groups" which one joins through individual, political commitment. That would seem to suggest *a contrario* that the Convention was presumably intended to cover relatively stable and permanent groups.

57. Therefore, the Chamber holds that in assessing whether a particular group may be considered as protected from the crime of genocide, it will proceed on a case-by-case basis, taking into account both the relevant evidence proffered and the political and cultural context as indicated *supra*....

* * *

60. The *dolus specialis* is a key element of an intentional offence, which offence is characterized by a psychological nexus between the physical result and the mental state of the perpetrator. With regard to the issue of determining the offender's specific intent, the Chamber applies the following reasoning, as held in the *Akayesu Judgement*:

> "[…] intent is a mental factor which is difficult, even impossible, to determine. This is the reason why, in the absence of a confession from the accused, his intent can be inferred from a certain number of presumptions of fact. The Chamber is of the view that the genocidal intent inherent in a particular act charged can be inferred from the general context of the perpetration of other culpable acts systematically directed against the same group, whether these acts were committed by the same offender or by others. Other factors, such as the scale of the atrocities committed, their general nature, in a region or a country, or furthermore, the fact of deliberately and systematically targeting victims on account of their membership of a particular group, while excluding the members of other groups, can enable the Chamber to infer the genocidal intent of a particular act."

61. Similarly, in the *Jayishema* and *Ruzindana Judgement*, Trial Chamber II held that:

"[…] The Chamber finds that the intent can be inferred either from words or deeds and may be determined by a pattern of purposeful action. In particular, the Chamber considers such as […] the methodical way of planning, the systematic manner of killing. […]"

62. Therefore, the Chamber is of the view that, in practice, intent can be, on a case-by-case basis, inferred from the material evidence submitted to the Chamber, including the evidence which demonstrates a consistent pattern of conduct by the Accused.

* * *

Crimes Against Humanity Pursuant to Article 3 of the Statute of the Tribunal

65. Article 3 of the Statute confers on the Tribunal the jurisdiction to prosecute persons for various inhumane acts which constitute crimes against humanity. The Chamber concurs with the reasoning in the *Akayesu Judgement* that offences falling within the ambit of crimes against humanity may be broadly broken down into four essential elements, namely:

(a) the *actus reus* must be inhumane in nature and character, or serious injury to body or to mental or physical health.

(b) the *actus reus* must be committed as part of a widespread or systematic attack

(c) the *actus reus* must be committed against members of the civilian population

(d) the *actus reus* must be committed on one or more discriminatory grounds, namely, national, political, ethnic, racial or religious grounds.

The *Actus Reus* Must be Committed as Part of a Widespread or Systematic Attack

66. The Chamber is of the opinion that the *actus reus* cannot be a random inhumane act, but rather an act committed as part of an attack. With regard to the nature of this attack, the Chamber notes that Article 3 of the English version of the Statute reads "[…] as part of a widespread or systematic attack. […]" whilst the French version of the Statute reads "[…] *dans le cadre d'une attacque généralisee et systématique* […]." The French version requires that the attack be both of a widespread *and* systematic nature, whilst the English version requires that the attack be of a widespread *or* systematic nature and need not be both.

The Chamber notes that customary international law requires that the attack be either of a widespread *or* systematic nature and need not be both. The English version of the Statute conforms more closely with customary international law and the Chamber therefore accepts the elements as set forth in Article 3 of the English version of the Statute and follows the interpretation in other ICTR judgements namely: that the "attack" under Article 3 of the Statute, must be either of a widespread or systematic nature and need not be both.

67. The Chamber notes that "widespread," as an element of crimes against humanity, was defined in the *Akayesu Judgement*, as massive, frequent, large scale action, carried out collectively with considerable seriousness and directed against a multiplicity of victims, whilst "systematic" was defined as thoroughly organized action, following a regular pattern on the basis of a common policy and involving substantial public or private resources. The Chamber concurs with these definitions and finds that it is not essential

for this policy to be adopted formally as a policy of a State. There must, however, be some kind of preconceived plan or policy.

68. The Chamber notes that "attack," as an element of crimes against humanity, was defined in the *Akayesu Judgement*, as an unlawful act of the kind enumerated in Article 3(a) to (i) of the Statute, such as murder, extermination, enslavement, etc. an attack may also be non-violent in nature, like imposing a system of apartheid, which is declared a crime against humanity in Article 1 of the Apartheid Convention of 1973, or exerting pressure on the population to act in a particular manner may also come under the purview of an attack, if orchestrated on a massive scale or in a systematic manner. The Chamber concurs with this definition.

69. The Chamber considers that the perpetrator must have:

"[…] actual or constructive knowledge of the broader context of the attack, meaning that the accused must know his act(s) is part of a widespread or systematic attack on a civilian population and pursuant to some kind of policy or plan."

The Actus Reus Must be Directed against the Civilian Population

70. The Chamber notes that the *actus reus* must be directed against the civilian population, if it is to constitute a crime against humanity. In the *Akayesu Judgement*, the civilian population was defined as people who were not taking any active part in the hostilities. The fact that there are certain individuals among the civilian population who are not civilians does not deprive the population of its civilian character. The Chamber concurs with this definition.

The Enumerated Acts

* * *

76. The Chamber notes that in respect of crimes against humanity, the Accused is indicted for murder and extermination. The Chamber, in interpreting Article 3 of the Statute, will focus its discussion on these offences only.

Murder

77. Pursuant to Article 3(a) of the Statute, murder constitutes a crime against humanity. The Chamber notes that Article 3(a) of the English version of the Statute refers to "Murder," whilst the French version of the Statute refers to "*Assassinat.*" Customary International Law dictates that it is the offence of "Murder" that constitutes a crime against humanity and not "*Assassinat.*"

78. The *Akayesu Judgement* defined Murder as the unlawful, intentional killing of a human being. The requisite elements of murder are:

(a) The victim is dead;

(b) The death resulted from an unlawful act or omission of the accused or a subordinate;

(c) At the time of the killing the accused or a subordinate had the intention to kill or inflict grievous bodily harm on the deceased having known that such bodily harm is likely to cause the victim's death, and is reckless as to whether or not the death ensues;

(d) The victim was discriminated against on any one of the enumerated discriminatory grounds;

(e) The victim was a member of the civilian population; and

(f) The act or omission was part of a widespread or systematic attack on the civilian population.

79. The Chamber concurs with this definition of murder and is of the opinion that the act or omission that constitutes murder must be discriminatory in nature and directed against a member of the civilian population.

Extermination

80. Pursuant to Article 3(c) of the Statute, extermination constitutes a crime against humanity. By its very nature, extermination is a crime which is directed against a group of individuals. Extermination differs from murder in that it requires an element of mass destruction which is not a pre-requisite for murder.

81. The *Akayesu Judgment*, defined the essential elements of extermination as follows:

(a) the accused or his subordinate participated in the killing of certain named or described persons;

(b) the act or omission was unlawful and intentional;

(c) the unlawful act or omission must be part of a wide-spread or systematic attack;

(d) the attack must be against the civilian population; and

(e) the attack must be on discriminatory grounds, namely: national, political, ethnic, racial, or religious grounds.

82. The Chamber concurs with this definition of extermination and is of the opinion that the act or omission that constitutes extermination must be discriminatory in nature and directed against members of the civilian population. Further, this act or omission includes, but is not limited to the direct act of killing. It can be any act or omission, or cumulative acts or omissions, that cause the death of the targeted group of individuals.

* * *

[Regarding the *Rutaganda* Indictment and the issue of the trial of persons on "cumulative" charges, the Tribunal remarked]:

109. The Chamber notes, first of all, that the principle of cumulative charges was applied by the Nuremberg Tribunal, especially regarding war crimes and crimes against humanity.

* * *

111. Trial Chamber II of the Tribunal, in its *Kayishema and Ruzindana Judgment*, endorsed the…test of concurrence of crimes and found that it is only acceptable:

"(1) where offenses having differing elements, or (2) where the laws in question protect differing social interests."

112. Trial Chamber II ruled that the cumulative charges in the *Kayishema and Ruzindana Judgment* in particular were legally improper and untenable. It found that all elements including the *mens rea* element requisite to show genocide, "extermination" and "murder" in the particular case were the same, and the evidence relied upon to prove the crimes were the same. Furthermore, in the opinion of Trial Chamber II, the protected social interests were also the same. Therefore, it held that the Prosecutor should have charged the Accused in the alternative.

113. Judge Tafazzal H. Khan, one of the judges sitting in Trial Chamber II to consider the said case, dissented on the issue of cumulative charges. Relying on consistent jurisprudence he pointed out that the Chamber should have placed less emphasis on the overlapping elements of the cumulative crimes.

"What must be punished is culpable conduct; this principle applies to situations where the conduct offends two or more crimes, whether or not the factual situation also satisfies the distinct elements of the two or more crimes, as proven."

114. In his dissenting opinion, the Judge goes on to emphasize that the full assessment of charges and the pronouncement of guilty verdicts are important in order to reflect the totality of the accused's culpable conduct.

"[...] where the culpable conduct was part of a widespread and systematic attack specifically against civilians, to record a conviction for genocide alone does not reflect the totality of the accused's culpable conduct. Similarly, if the Majority had chosen to convict for extermination alone instead of genocide, the verdict would still fail to adequately capture the totality of the accused's conduct."

115. This Chamber fully concurs with the dissenting opinion thus entered. It notes that this position, which endorses the principle of cumulative charges, also finds support in various decisions rendered by the ICTY. In the case of the *Prosecutor v. Zoran Kupreskic and others*, the Trial Chamber of the ICTY in its decision on Defence challenges to the form of the indictment held that:

"The Prosecutor may be justified in bringing cumulative charges when the articles of the Statute referred to are designed to protect different values and when each article requires proof of a legal element not required by the others."

116. Furthermore, the Chamber holds that offences covered under the Statute — genocide, crimes against humanity and violations of Article 3 common to Geneva Conventions and of Additional Protocol II — have disparate ingredients and, especially, that their punishment is aimed at protecting discrete interests. As a result, multiple offences may be charged on the basis of the same acts, in order to capture the full extent of the crimes committed by an accused.

[Georges A. N. Rutaganda was convicted on one count of genocide and two additional counts of crimes against humanity and murder by Trial Chamber I on December 6, 1999. The ICTR deemed Rutaganda to have ordered, incited and carried out various murders and, additionally, to have been involved in causing serious bodily or mental harm to members of the Tutsi ethnic group. Thus, Rutaganda was convicted on three counts of the Indictment, but was found not guilty on five counts. Two counts charging the accused with crimes against humanity were subsumed within the genocide conviction and three Article 4 charges (in the ICTR Statute) for violation of Common Article 3 to the Geneva Conventions were not proven.

Trial Chamber I sentenced Rutaganda concurrently to life imprisonment for the genocide conviction and for conviction of a crime against humanity (extermination). Additionally, defendant was sentenced to fifteen years' incarceration for the crime against humanity (murder) conviction. By December 31, 1999, the ICTR had not convicted a single individual of war crimes which were charges preferred under Common Article 3 and Additional Protocol II for offenses committed during an internal armed conflict. The following excerpts by Judge McDonald, the past president of the ICTY, illustrate some of the contributions both tribunals have made to international law and international criminal justice].

(h) Gabrielle Kirk McDonald, "The International Criminal Tribunals: Crime and Punishment in the International Arena"

7 *ILSA Journal of International and Comparative Law* 667; 682–686 (2001)
Reproduced with permission from Gabrielle Kirk McDonald,
The International Criminal Tribunals: Crime and Punishment in the
International Arena, 7 ILSA J. Int'l & Comp. L. 667 (2001)

* * *

B. *General Contributions of the Tribunals*

Perhaps the most far-reaching contributions of the Tribunals is that their very establishment signaled the beginning of the end of the cycle of impunity. Those responsible for committing or ordering the commission of horrific acts of violence against innocent civilians, simply because of the happenstance of their birth, their ethnicity, their religious beliefs, or their gender, are now for the first time being called to account for their criminal deeds. By ensuring this accounting, the Tribunals concretely show that the international instruments guaranteeing basic human rights are more than merely as aspiration.

The Tribunals have also demonstrated that the rule of law has been an integral part of the peace process; expanded the jurisprudence of international humanitarian law; raised the international community's level of consciousness regarding the need of states to enforce international norms; and accelerated the development of the permanent International Criminal Court....

The Security Council's choice of a court of law as the measure to help bring about and maintain peace is a victory for the rule of law, the anchor of civil society.... Now, the goals of peace and international criminal justice are no longer seen as mutually exclusive. Rather, they are interdependent and complimentary.

Moreover, the trials in the Tribunals develop a historical record of what happened in the regions of conflict, thus guarding against revisionism. The judgments, which typically detail the factual circumstances of the crime charged, provide an incontrovertible record of the brutality engaged in by ethnic groups pitted against each other by incessant, virulent propaganda. The judgments also have made substantive findings on a myriad of legal issues, most of which have never been considered by a court. For example, the Geneva Conventions of 1949 establish a "grave breaches" regime that prohibits certain types of behavior directed against protected persons or property. The ICTY has held that Article 2 applies only in the context of an international armed conflict. Further, the victims must be regarded as "protected" by the Fourth Geneva Convention.

In the *Tadic* case, the Trial Chamber, by majority, found that the conflict in the Prijedor area of Bosnia was not international after May 19, 1992, the date of the purported withdrawal of the forces of the Federal Republic of Yugoslavia ("FRY"), the Yugoslavian military. The majority also found that the victims were not protected persons. The Appeals Chamber reversed on this point and after a lengthy discussion of the Nicaragua Decision from the International Court of Justice, construed it as requiring only that the

Bosnian Serb armed forces were acting "under the overall control of and on behalf of the FRY." Thus, the Bosnian victims were deemed to be in the hands of an armed force of a state of which they were not nationals and thus, were protected persons. The *Blaskic* Judgment follows this approach and has found that the "grave breaches" regime applied. The ICTY also construed broadly the laws and customs of war and held that this body of law, knows as the "Hague Law," applies to both international and internal armed conflicts. The judgments also have significantly advanced the jurisprudence relating to crimes of sexual violence, an area ignored in international law.

Additionally, the work of the Tribunals has significantly raised the awareness of the importance of enforcing international humanitarian law. It has given the many human rights instruments some real meaning and power. Since the establishment of the Tribunals, the awareness of the need to enforce human rights violations in armed conflicts and the actual prosecution of such crimes has increased. This is an important development because the ad hoc Tribunals cannot possibly handle all of the potential prosecutions growing out of the conflicts in the former Yugoslavia and in Rwanda. Because of limited resources, the Tribunals can simply apply law which has been ignored in a forum free from accusations of bias, thereby developing a body of jurisprudence that can be used by municipal courts in their own trials. Thus, by raising the consciousness of states and developing a body of law that states can apply, the Tribunals pass the torch to national courts which are, or may become, better equipped to handle large numbers of prosecutions.

* * *

III. CONCLUSION

The critical contributions of the Tribunals has been to foster and enhance the recognition by states of the need to enforce norms of international law prohibiting massive violations of human rights. Judicial mechanisms are now an established element of conflict resolution, and proposals under discussion around the world envision a range of international, national, and mixed Tribunals. Moreover, following the lead of the Tribunals, the culture of impunity is being challenged by states whose national courts are applying international law. Finally, the International Criminal Court would not be so close to reality...without the influence of both the ICTY and the ICTR.

The judgments of the Tribunals do more than determine the guilt or innocence of the accused. They do more than establish a historical record of what transpired. They do more than interpret international humanitarian law. Rather, the judgments of the Tribunals are evidence of actual enforcement of international norms. This is the best proof that the numerous conventions, protocols, and resolutions affirming human dignity are more than promises. Rather, the rule of law is an important component of the peace process.

It is clear then that we are living through tremendously encouraging times. Yet, how do we situate the progress over the past seven years in light of the amount of bloodshed that has gone unchecked from Iraq to the former Yugoslavia, to Somalia, through Rwanda, Afghanistan, Burundi, Liberia, Sierra Leone, Columbia, the Congo, Chechyna, Indonesia and the Sudan? The Tribunals have demonstrated that international criminal law is feasible. We have seen that the establishment of international courts of law is now being considered as a policy option to repond to humanitarian crises. No court can prevent all war, and the challenge of the twenty-first century is to utilize options to prevent wanton destruction of innocent civilians which was characteristic of the twentieth century.

(i) Michael P. Scharf, "The International Trial of Slobodan Milosevic: Real Justice or Realpolitik?"

8 *ILSA Journal of International & Comparative Law*
389; 390–392; 394–395; 397–398 (2002)
Reproduced with permission from Michael P. Scharf,
The International Trial of Slobodan Milosevic: Real Justice or Realpolitik?,
8 ILSA J. Int'l & Comp. L. 389 (2002)

I. INTRODUCTION: SCAPEGOAT OR WAR CRIMINAL?

There were disquieting echoes of Nuremberg at the arraignment of Slobodan Milosevic in The Hague on July 3, 2001. Standing before the three-judge panel, Milosevic challenged the Security Council-created War Crimes Tribunal's validity. "You are not a judicial institution; you are a political tool," Milosevic told the panel. Drawing on the commonly-accepted notion that the post-World War II Nuremberg Trials were tainted by "victor's justice," Milosevic's initial trial strategy was to attempt to discredit the Yugoslavia Tribunal's legitimacy and impartiality.

Will history remember Milosevic as a victim of victor's justice, a scapegoat tried in a show trial before a one-sided court? Or will the Milosevic trial be seen as fair and free of political influence? More than anything else, the answer to these questions may dictate the ultimate success or failure of the proceedings.

If viewed as legitimate, the trial of Milosevic could potentially serve several important functions in the Balkan peace process. By pinning prime responsibility on Milosevic and disclosing the way the Yugoslav people were manipulated by their leaders into committing acts of savagery on a mass scale, the trial would help break the cycle of violence that has long plagued the Balkans. While this would not completely absolve the underlings for their acts, it would make it easier for victims to eventually forgive, or at least, reconcile with former neighbors who had been caught up in the institutionalized violence. This would also promote a political catharsis in Serbia, enabling the new leadership to distance themselves from the discredited nationalistic policies of the past. The historic record generated from the trial would educate the Serb people, long subject to Milosevic's propaganda, about what really happened in Kosovo and Bosnia, and help ensure that such horrific acts are not repeated in the future.

On the other hand, a trial that is seen as "victor's justice" would undermine the goal of fostering reconciliation between ethnic groups living in the former Yugoslavia. The historic record developed by the trial would forever be questioned. The trial would add to the Serb martyrdom complex, amounting to another grievance requiring vengeance. In addition, the judicial precedent would be tainted. For any real advance to be made in the long march toward the establishment of a permanent international criminal court, Milosevic's trial must be seen to be more about real justice than realpolitik.

II. THE MISTAKES OF THE PAST

History's first international criminal court was the Nuremberg Tribunal, created by the victorious Allies after World War II to prosecute the major German war criminals. Although Adolf Hitler escaped prosecution by committing suicide, many of the most notorious German leaders were tried before the Nuremberg Tribunal. After a trial that lasted 284 days, nineteen of the twenty-two German officials tried at Nuremberg were found guilty, and twelve were sentenced to death by hanging. As the former Serb president, himself, is keenly aware, Nuremberg provides a compelling benchmark for assessing the legitimacy of the trial of Slobodan Milosevic....

In the years following the judgment, there have been three main criticisms levied on the Nuremberg Tribunal;: first, that it was a victor's tribunal before which only the vanquished were called to account for violations of international humanitarian law committed during the war; second, that the defendants were prosecuted and punished for crimes expressly defined for the first time in an instrument adopted by the victors at the conclusion of the war; and third, that the Nuremberg Tribunal functioned on the basis of limited procedural rules that inadequately protected the rights of the accused.

While the Nuremberg Tribunal deserves praise as a novel endeavor that paved the way for future war crimes tribunals and the development of international criminal law, these criticisms are not without foundation. It was true, for example, that only the leading victorious nations—the United States, United Kingdom, France, and the Soviet Union—were represented on the Nuremberg Tribunal's bench. There were no judges from neutral states, and the defendants were confined to German political and military leaders. None of the Allied commanders had to answer for similar crimes.

Moreover, the Nuremberg judges oversaw the collection of evidence and judged the defendants in a necessarily political arena, thereby raising questions about their ability to objectively preside over the trials. Most astonishing of all, however, was the fact that two of the Judges of the Nuremberg Tribunal (General Nikitchenko (Soviet Union) and Robert Falko (Alternate, France), served earlier as members of the committee that had drafted the Nuremberg Charter and the indictments. Having written the law to be applied and selected the defendants to be tried, it is hard to believe they could be sufficiently impartial and unbiased. And yet, they were insulated from challenge since the Nuremberg Charter stipulated that neither the Court, nor its members, could be challenged by the prosecution or the defendants.

In addition, the States which tried the Nuremberg defendants were arguably guilty of many of the same sorts of crimes for which they sat in judgment over their former adversaries. Had Germany and Japan won the war, American leaders could just as easily have been prosecuted for crimes against humanity in relation to the dropping of the atomic bombs, firebombing civilian centers, and conducting unrestricted submarine warfare. Soviet leaders could have been prosecuted for waging aggressive war and mistreatment of prisoners with respect to the forcible Soviet annexation of the Baltic States and the appalling record of the Soviets regarding the treatment of prisoners of war. Most reprehensible of all, however, was the Soviet Union's insistence that the German defendants be charged with responsibility for the Katyn Forest Massacre, in which 14,700 Polish prisoners of war were murdered in 1941—when the true perpetrators of this atrocity, we now know, were the Soviets and not the Germans.

Perhaps the most often-heard criticism of Nuremberg was its application of *ex post facto* laws, by holding individuals responsible for the first time in history for waging a war of aggression and by applying the concept of conspiracy which had never before been recognized in continental Europe. One of the first to voice this criticism was Senator Robert Taft of Ohio in 1946, but it was not until John F. Kennedy reproduced Taft's speech in Kennedy's Pulitzer Prize-winning 1956 book, *Profiles of Courage*, that this criticism became part of the public legacy of Nuremberg....

*　*　*

V. VICTORS JUSTICE

If Milosevic's goal is not to obtain a dismissal but to publicly discredit the Tribunal, he may have a greater chance of success with his argument that the Yugoslavia Tribunal, like Nuremberg, represents "victor's justice."

In contrast to Nuremberg, however, the Yugoslavia Tribunal was created neither by the victors nor by the parties involved in the conflict, but rather by the United Nations, representing the international community of States. The judges of the Yugoslavia Tribunal come from all parts of the world, and are elected by the General Assembly, in which each of the world's 188 countries gets an equal vote. Moreover, the message of the International Tribunal's indictments, prosecutions, and convictions to date [2002] of Muslims and Croats, as well as Serbs, has been that a war crime is a war crime, whoever it is committed by. The Tribunal has taken no sides.

On the other hand, the decision to establish the Yugoslavia Tribunal was made by the United Nations Security Council, which cannot truly be characterized as a neutral third party; rather, it has itself become deeply involved and taken sides in the Balkan conflict. The Security Council has, for example, imposed sanctions on Milosevic's Serbia, which it felt was most responsible for the conflict and atrocities. Throughout the conflict, the Security Council has been quite vocal in its condemnation of Serb atrocities, but its criticisms of those committed by Muslims and Croats were comparatively muted. And, most problematic of all, three of the Permanent Members of the Council—the United States, France and the United Kingdom—led the 78-day bombing campaign against Milosevic and Serbia in 1999.

While both the Prosecutor and the Judicial Chamber of the Yugoslavia Tribunal were conceived to be independent from the Security Council, one cannot ignore the fact that the [ICTY] Statute provides that the Tribunal's Prosecutor is selected by the Security Council. The Judges are selected by the General Assembly from a short list proposed by the Security Council, and they have to stand for re-election after a four-year-term. Moreover, the operation of the Tribunal has been dependent on hundreds of millions of dollars in contributions from the United Sates and its Western allies. And most of the staff of the office of the International Prosecutor are on loan from NATO countries.

Although a creature of the United Nations, the Tribunal has, according to its former president, Antonio Cassese, tended to "take into account the exigencies and tempo of the international community." There are those who would argue that this means that the Tribunal has yielded to the objectives of the United States and other NATO powers, without whose financial and military support the Tribunal could not function.

*　*　*

VIII. UNCLEAN HANDS

To further illustrate the Tribunal's politicization, Milosevic will attempt to force the Tribunal to face the *tu quoque* argument (literally meaning "you too"). First, Milosevic may point out that Franjo Tudjman, the former leader of Croatia, was never indicted by the Tribunal for the mass atrocities that Croatian troops committed against the Serbs in re-taking Serb-controlled areas of eastern Croatia. In fact, Tudjman was welcomed to the United States for cancer treatment at Walter Reed Hospital in Washington, D. C., a few months before his death in 1999.

Next, Milosevic will raise the issue of NATO war crimes. When several respected human rights organizations urged the Tribunal to investigate the possibility that NATO had committed war crimes during the 1999 intervention, the then Prosecutor, Louise Arbour (from Canada, a NATO country), assigned the task to her Legal Advisor, William Fenrick. Fenrick is an ex-NATO lawyer, who went to the Tribunal directly from his post as director of law for operations and training in the Canadian Department of Defense. Not surprisingly, Fenrick's report, which was released in June 2000, concluded that NATO had committed no indictable offenses. But critics have been quick to seize upon the clause of the report that notes that the review of NATO's actions relied primarily on public documents produced by NATO, and that the authors of the report "tended to assume that the NATO and NATO countries' press statements are generally reliable and that explanations have been honestly given."

Finally, Milosevic may argue that the United States opposition to a permanent international criminal court has undermined its moral right to participate in any way in the trial of Milosevic. According to United States officials, such international tribunals are prone to politicization—the very argument that Milosevic has made about the Yugoslav Tribunal.

There are several answers to Milosevic's *tu quoque* arguments. First, whatever Franjo Tudjman and NATO have done, their actions do not excuse what Milosevic did. Second, the Tribunal's Prosecutor at the time of the Milosevic indictment, Louise Arbour, has stated that she was about to issue an indictment for Franjo Tudjman just before the Croatian President passed away, demonstrating that the Tribunal was striving to be evenhanded. Third, whether or not one believes NATO violated the laws of war during the 1999 bombing campaign, NATO did not systematically set out to kill and torture civilians on a mass scale—the crimes of which Milosevic has been accused. The alleged NATO offenses are just not in a league with those of which Milosevic is charged. Fourth, established democracies have mechanisms (a free press, political opposition, and an independent judiciary) to examine publicly their own past: for example, America's actions in Vietnam or France's use of torture in Algeria. While Serbia was willing to try Milosevic for corruption, the Yugoslav Tribunal is the only venue in which his war crimes and crimes against humanity could be exposed.

Finally these arguments might suggest that the Tribunal's Prosecutors have been out to get Milosevic. But selective prosecution is never a valid defense, even in domestic trials. Milosevic's ultimate fate is in the hands of the Tribunal's judges, not its prosecutor. As long as the bench is impartial, and the procedures are equitable, the trial of Milosevic will be considered credible.

8. The International Criminal Court,
The Rome Statute and Commentary

(a) *The Statute of the International Criminal Court*
as quoted in ch. 7, "International Prosecutorial Efforts
and Tribunals," in *International Criminal Law:*
Cases & Materials

(Jordan J. Paust et. al., eds.) 708–711 (2000),
from *International Criminal Law: Cases & Materials* (Jordan J. Paust et al.
eds.), Copyright © 2000 by Jordan J. Paust et al.
Used by permission of Carolina Academic Press

In 1948, the United Nations General Assembly invited the International Law Commission (ILC) "to study the desirability and possibility of establishing an international judicial organ for the trial of persons charged with genocide or other crimes over which jurisdiction will be conferred upon that organ by international conventions." After considering the matter, the ILC concluded that the establishment of such an organ was both desirable and possible. As a result, in 1950, the General Assembly set up a Committee on International Criminal Jurisdiction consisting of representatives of seventeen member states. The Committee was charged with preparing concrete proposals on the establishment of an international criminal court that could administer the Code of Crimes Against the Peace and Security of Mankind, which the International Law Commission was simultaneously drafting. The Committee submitted a draft statute in 1951, which was amended by a Second Committee in 1953.

The 1953 Draft Statute was permanently shelved due to the absence of an internationally accepted definition of the crime of "aggression" and the resulting inability to complete the Draft Code of Crimes Against the Peace and Security of Mankind, which was to define the subject matter jurisdiction of the International Criminal Court. The General Assembly adopted a definition of "aggression" in 1974, but it would be almost twenty years before the United Nations would return to the project of creating an international criminal court. There are several reasons why the initial efforts of the United Nations to create an international criminal court never got off the ground. First, since World War II, there has not been a repeat of the unique circumstances that made the Nuremberg and Tokyo Tribunals possible; that is, there have been no wars in which a coalition broadly supported by other members of the international community has defeated an aggressor and violator of the laws of war and humanity so decisively as to bring about its complete defeat and subjugation. Second, an international criminal court whose goals included the punishment of aggressive warfare was seen in the context of the cold war as a threat to national sovereignty. For the major powers in particular, the power to review the legitimacy of the use of force or to supersede the criminal jurisdiction of national courts was more than they were willing to cede. Finally, the formulation of the United Nations Draft Statute for an International Criminal Court in 1953 had the paradoxical effect of setting back the effort to create such a court. Once the document was drafted, the debate shifted from whether to establish an international criminal court to whether to adopt the 1953 Draft Statute, which was extremely ambitious in the powers it conferred on the court with respect to states. In addition, the Draft Statute was tied inextricably to the Draft Code of Crimes Against the Peace and Security of Mankind, which was strongly opposed by many countries.

With the end of the cold war in the late 1980s, the United Nations returned to its project to create a permanent international criminal court. In 1989, the issue was reintroduced in the agenda of the General Assembly at the urging of a coalition of sixteen Caribbean and Latin American nations led by Trinidad and Tobago, who saw such a court as a way to solve the difficulties which they encounter in prosecuting or extraditing narco-terrorist. The General Assembly acted on the Trinidadian initiative by requesting the International Law Commission to study the issue and report back with its recommendations.

As requested, at the completion of its forty-second session in 1990, the ILC submitted an interim report to the General Assembly on the issue of establishing an international criminal court. The report surveys previous international efforts concerning the establishment of an international criminal court, and contains a cursory discussion of some of the potential benefits and obstacles to establishing such a court. The interim report was primarily devoted to identifying various issues, namely: (1) the jurisdiction and competence of the court; (2) the structure of the court; (3) the legal force of the court's judgments; (4) other questions relating to, *inter alia*, penalties, implementation of judgments and financing; and (5) possible international trial mechanisms other than an international tribunal.

The General Assembly responded to the interim report by requesting the ILC to further consider the issues raised and to make concrete proposals for resolving them. To this end, during its forty-third session, the ILC formed a working group on the question of an international criminal jurisdiction, chaired by Abdul Koroma of Sierra Leone. The Working Group produced a more detailed point-by-point analysis of the key issues, in some cases with recommended resolutions and in others with a choice of options. The Report of the Working Group greatly refined the ILC's earlier conception of an international criminal court. The Working Group recommended that the court should be a "flexible and supplementary facility" for states parties to its statute and that it should not have exclusive jurisdiction. As so envisioned, the court would provide a third alternative for states currently faced with only two choices when international criminals are found within their territory—to prosecute the individuals or to extradite them to another state. Parties to the Court's statute would select from a list of international offenses those for which they would be bound to provide assistance to the Court. The Court would not be a full-time body, but rather an established structure which could be called into operation when required. On the basis of the Working Group's proposals, on November 25, 1992, the General Assembly adopted by concensus a resolution calling for an International Criminal Court "as a matter of urgency."

The steps taken by the Security Council to address the war crimes and other atrocities committed in the former Yugoslavia added a new significance and a sense of urgency to the efforts of the General Assembly to create a permanent international criminal court. The Security Council's establishment of the Yugoslavia Tribunal in May 1993 removed any question as to the political and legal feasibility of creating an international criminal court in the latter half of the twentieth century. Most of the complex legal and practical issues that had been identified as barriers to a permanent international criminal court had been successfully met by the Secretary-General's draft statute, adopted by the Security Council, which had been based on the views and proposals of various states and organizations. Thus, the members of the international community were hard pressed to find any justification for continuing the delay in the creation of a permanent court.

As its forty-fifth session, in 1993, the International Law Commission reconvened its Working Group on an international criminal court which, borrowing liberally from the Statute of the newly-established Yugoslavia Tribunal, completed a preliminary 67-article draft statute for a permanent court. At its forty-sixth session, in 1994, the Working Group, under the chairmanship of James Crawford of Australia, refined the draft statute, consisting of 60 articles and an annex enumerating treaty crimes over which the Court would have jurisdiction. Thereafter, the International Law Commission submitted the statute to the General Assembly for consideration, and recommended that an international conference be convened to adopt the statute in the form of a treaty.

The final Statute of the International Criminal Court was adopted at a conference in Rome in 1998.

(b) The Rome Conference and the ICC Statute
"The Rome Conference — 15 June–7 July 1998,"
as quoted in Yves Beigbeder, *Judging War Criminals: The Politics of International Justice*

195–199 (1999)
Copyright © Yves Beigbeder from: *Judging War Criminals: The Politics of International Justice* by Yves Beigbeder.
Reprinted with permission of Palgrave Macmillan

On 17 July 1998, the UN Diplomatic Conference held in Rome decided to establish a permanent International Criminal Court by adopting its Statute by a vote of 120 in favour to 7 against, with 21 abstentions. The USA, together with China, Israel, Libya, Iraq, Qatar and Yemen, voted against the establishment of the Court. [Israel subsequently changed its mind and voted in favor of the Statute]. UN Secretary-General Kofi Annan declared that this was a 'giant step forward in the march towards universal human rights and the rule of law.' The Statute will enter into force following the ratification, acceptance, approval or accession of 60 States.

The vote, after five weeks of difficult, at times acrimonious, negotiations, was introducing radically important innovations into relations between States, eroding their sovereign prerogatives and establishing a new relationship between the national courts and international justice. The Statute was the final result of battles and compromises between the determination of many 'like-minded' countries to set up an independent court, with the strong support of NGOs, [non-governmental organizations] the fears of the US and France that their military personnel on peacekeeping missions might be indicted for war crimes by an overly independent court, the frustrated wishes of some countries to include nuclear weapons among banned weapons (India), or to add the crime of terrorism among core crimes (Sri Lanka). Some countries protested against the powers granted to the Prosecutor (China), or against the non-inclusion of the death penalty (Singapore). Most non-aligned and Arab countries opposed the creation of the Court. The US delegates objected to two key points in the Statute: the prosecutor's power to initiate investigations and the court's jurisdiction over crimes committed by citizens of non-signatory countries. After the vote, American officials promised active opposition to the ratification of the Statute by other countries and to the eventual operations of the court, in a cynical reversal of their earlier support for the punishment of genociders and war criminals, and in total contradiction to the decisive role of the USA in the creation of and support for the Nuremberg, Tokyo, ex-Yugoslavia and Rwanda Tribunals.

- The Court will be a permanent institution with the power to exercise jurisdiction over persons for the most serious crimes of international concern, and is to be complementary to national criminal jurisdictions. National courts have primacy in investigating and prosecuting crimes, unless the State is unwilling or genuinely unable to carry out the investigation or prosecution.
- The Court will not be part of the UN: it will be brought into relationship with the UN through an agreement. Its seat will be in The Hague.
- Its jurisdiction will be limited to four crimes: genocide, crimes against humanity, war crimes and the crime of aggression:...

Although the Preamble of the Statute refers to an 'independent' Court, a number of qualifications limits its powers.

1. The Court may exercise its jurisdiction only for crimes committed on the territory of a State Party to the Statute, or of a State which has accepted to jurisdiction of the Court, or for crimes committed by a person who is a national of such a state.

2. The Prosecutor's investigation has to be authorized by a Pre-Trail Chamber of the Court.

3. As another limitation to the Prosecutor's powers, no investigation or prosecution may be commenced or proceeded with for a period of 12 months after the Security Council, in a resolution adopted under Chapter VII of the UN Charter, has requested the Court to that effect—that request may be renewed by the Council under the same conditions. This reflected the Singapore compromise, which was previously rejected by the USA (Art. 12, 15, 16).

The general principles of criminal law are confirmed: *ne bis in idem, nullum crimen sine lege, nulla poena sine lege* and non-retroactivity *ratione personae* (Art. 20, 22, 23, 24). The accused 'shall be present during the trial': no trial *in absentia* is allowed except when the accused 'continues to disrupt the trial.' The presumption of innocence and the rights of the accused are confirmed (Art. 63, 66, 67).

The Court is composed of the following organs: the Presidency—an Appeals Division, a Trial Division and a Pre-Trial Division—the Office of the Prosecutor and the Registry.

As recommended by Bassiouni, Joinet and van Boven, the Court will establish principles relating to reparations to, or in respect of, victims, including restitution, compensation and rehabilitation. The Court may make an order directly against a convicted person specifying appropriate reparations to, or in respect of, victims (Art. 75). Applicable penalties include imprisonment not to exceed a maximum of 30 years, life imprisonment when justified by the extreme gravity of the crime and the individual circumstances of the convicted person—and, in addition, as applicable, a fine, a forfeiture of proceeds, property and assets derived directly or indirectly from the crime, without prejudice to the rights of bona fide third parties (Art. 77). Sentences are subject to appeal by the Prosecutor or the convicted person—either party may apply to the Appeals Chamber to revise a final judgment of conviction or sentence on established grounds (Art. 81, 84). States Parties have a general obligation to cooperate fully with the Court in its investigation and prosecution of crimes within the jurisdiction of the Court (Art. 86).

The expenses of the Court and the Assembly of States Parties will be provided by as-sessed contributions made by States Parties—based on the UN scale of assessment for its regular budget—in addition to funds provided by the UN in particular in relation to the expenses incurred due to referrals by the Security Council, and to voluntary contri-butions (Art. 115, 116, 117).

Article 124 includes a controversial transitional provision, introduced as a demand by the French delegation, itself under pressure by its military: a State, on becoming a party to the Statute, may declare that, for a period of seven years after the entry into force of the Statute for the State concerned, it does not accept the jurisdiction of the Court with respect to war crimes when a crime is alleged to have been committed by its nationals or on its territory: as stated by Amnesty International at the conclusion of the Conference, 'a few powerful countries…were all along more concerned to shield possi-ble criminals from trials rather than producing a charter for victims.'

CONCLUSION

The approval of the Statute of an International Criminal Court in July 1998 by 120 countries is a historical achievement for the world. It is due to those States which led the determined campaign, with the strong support of many NGOs, to create an indepen-dent Court, in order to fight against the all-too-frequent impunity of those leaders re-sponsible for genocide, crimes against humanity, war crimes and crimes of aggression, to respond to the suffering of millions of victims, and, hopefully, to act as a deterrent for more violence and violations of international human rights and humanitarian law.

The Rome Conference was a success, in overcoming the many substantial and proce-dural objections raised by powerful and other countries on different grounds. The ap-proved Statute, which benefited from the experience acquired by the ex-Yugoslavia and Rwanda Tribunals, ensures a fair degree of independence to the Court and its Prosecu-tor while retaining a role for the Security Council, a compromise between idealists and realists. It is unfortunate that two permanent members of the Security Council, the USA and China, have voted against the creation of the Court, as their cooperation and participation, particularly those of the USA, would be needed in the planning, in-stalling and developing the Court. It is to be hoped that the US government and Senate will later adhere to the Statute, after the Court has gained some experience and showed its capacity.

The new Court, like the Yugoslavia and Rwanda Tribunals, will lack its own police force. In this respect, the Court will be dependent on governments' respect of their com-mitments, on their good faith and goodwill, to obtain custody of indicted individuals.

When the Statute of the Court enters into force, which will require a number of years, more years will, again, be needed to assess its usefulness and 'effectiveness' on two points:

1. Has the Court been allowed by governments or by the Security Counsil to in-dict, obtain custody of and judge the main perpetrators of the 'most serious crimes of concern to the international community as a whole'?

2. A more difficult and uncertain assessment will be to determine whether the Court's mere existence and/or its judgments have acted as a deterrent to more grave violations of international humanitarian law. While it would be unwise to set high expectations on the potential capacity of the future Court to act as such a deterrent, the creation of the ICC is in itself an impressive progress in international criminal law by providing, at the global level, an international ju-

diciary mechanism to prosecute and judge individuals alleged to have committed the 'most serious crimes of international concern.'

(c) Ceremony for the Opening for Signature of the Convention on the Establishment of an International Criminal Court, Rome, "Il Campidoglio"

18 July 1998

Statement of Professor M. Cherif Bassiouni Chairman, Drafting Committee

United Nations Diplomatic Conference on the Establishment of an International Criminal Court, Rome, 15 June–17 July 1998
M. Cherif Bassiouni, *Crimes against Humanity in International Criminal Law*, 2d rev. ed. 555–556 (1999)
Reproduced with permission of Brill Academic Publishers, NV, M. Cherif Bassiouni, *Crimes Against Humanity in International Criminal Law*, 2d rev. ed. © 1999 Kluwer Law International

The world will never be the same after the establishment of the International Criminal Court. Yesterday's adoption of the Final Act of the United Nations Diplomatic Conference and today's opening of the Convention for signature marks both the end of a historical process that started after World War I, as well as the beginning of a new phase in the history of international criminal justice.

The establishment of the ICC symbolizes and embodies certain fundamental values and expectations shared by all peoples of the world and is, therefore, a triumph for all peoples of the world. The ICC reminds governments that *realpolitik*, which sacrifices justice at the altar of political settlements, is no longer accepted. It asserts that impunity for the perpetrator's of "genocide," "crimes against humanity" and "war crimes" is no longer tolerated. In that respect it fulfills what Prophet Mohammad said, that "wrongs must be righted." It affirms that justice is an integral part of peace and thus reflects what Pope Paul VI once said, "If you want peace, work for justice." These values are clearly reflected in the ICC's Preamble.

The ICC will not be a panacea for all the ills of humankind. It will not eliminate conflicts, nor return victims to life, nor restore survivors to their prior conditions of well-being and it will not bring all perpetrators of major crimes to justice. But it can help avoid some conflicts, prevent some victimization and bring to justice some of the perpetrators of these crimes. In so doing, the ICC will strengthen world order and contribute to world peace and security. As such, the ICC, like other international and national legal institutions, will add its contributions to the humanization of our civilization.

The ICC also symbolizes human solidarity, for as John Donne so eloquently stated, "No man is an island, entire of itself; each man is a piece of the continent, a part of the main…. Any man's death diminishes me because I am involved in mankind." Lastly, the ICC will remind us not to forget these terrible crimes so that we can heed the admonishment so aptly recorded by George Santayana, that those who forget the lessons of the past are condemned to repeat their mistakes.

Ultimately, if the ICC saves but one life, as it is said in the *Talmud*, it will be as if it saved the whole of humanity.

From Versailles to Rwanda, and now to the "Treaty of Rome," many have arduously labored for the establishment of a system of international criminal justice. Today our generation proudly, yet humbly, passes that torch on to future generations. Thus, the long relay of history goes on, with each generation incrementally adding on to the accomplishments of its predecessors. But today, I can say to those who brought about this historic result, the government delegates in Rome, those who preceded them in New York since 1995, the United Nations staff, members of the Legal Office, the non-governmental organizations and here in Rome the staff of the Italian Ministry of Foreign Affairs, what Winston Churchill once said about heroes of another time, "Never have so many, owed so much, to so few."

(d) *Statute of the International Criminal Court*
UN Doc.A/CONF 183/9, July 17, 1998

[The Rome Statute entered into force on July 1, 2002. The Rome Conference was officially known as "The United Nations Diplomatic Conference of Plenipotentiaries on the Establishment of an International Criminal Court."]

Article 1
The Court

An International Criminal Court ("the Court") is hereby established. It shall be a permanent institution and shall have the power to exercise its jurisdiction over persons for the most serious crimes of international concern, as referred to in this Statute, and shall be complementary to national criminal jurisdictions. The jurisdiction and functioning of the Court shall be governed by the provisions of this Statute.

Article 2
Relationship of the Court with the United Nations

The Court shall be brought into relationship with the United Nations through an agreement to be approved by the Assembly of States Parties to this Statute and thereafter concluded by the President of the Court on its behalf.

Article 3
Seat of the Court

1. The seat of the Court shall be established at The Hague in the Netherlands (the "host State.")

2. The Court shall enter into a headquarters agreement with the host State, to be approved by the Assembly of States Parties and thereafter concluded by the President of the Court on its behalf.

Article 4
Legal Status and Powers of the Court

1. The Court shall have international legal personality. It shall also have such legal capacity as may be necessary for the exercise of its functions and the fulfillment of its purposes.

2. The Court may exercise its functions and powers, as provided in this Statute, on the territory of any State Party and, by special agreement, on the territory of any other State.

Article 5
Crimes within the Jurisdiction of the Court

1. The jurisdiction of the Court shall be limited to the most serious crimes of concern to the international community as a whole. The Court has jurisdiction in accordance with this Statute with respect to the following crimes:

(a) The crime of genocide;

(b) Crimes against humanity;

(c) War crimes;

(d) The crime of aggression.

2. The Court shall exercise jurisdiction over the crime of aggression once a provision is adopted in accordance with articles 121 and 123 defining the crime and setting out the conditions under which the Court shall exercise jurisdiction with respect to this crime. Such a provision shall be consistent with the relevant provisions of the Charter of the United Nations.

Article 6
Genocide

For the purpose of this Statute, "genocide" means any of the following acts committed with intent to destroy, in whole or in part, a national, ethnical, racial or religious group, as such:

(a) Killing members of the group;

(b) Causing serious bodily or mental harm to members of the group;

(c) Deliberately inflicting on the group conditions of life calculated to bring about its physical destruction in whole or in part

(d) Imposing measures intended to prevent births within the group;

(e) Forcibly transferring children of the group to another group.

Article 7
Crimes Against Humanity

1. For the purpose of this statute, "crimes against humanity" means any of the following acts when committed as part of a widespread or systematic attack directed against any civilian population, with knowledge of the attack;

(a) Murder;

(b) Extermination;

(c) Enslavement;

(d) Deportation or forcible transfer of population;

(e) Imprisonment or other severe deprivation of physical liberty in violation of fundamental rules of international law;

(f) Torture;

(g) Rape, sexual slavery, enforced prostitution, forced pregnancy, enforced sterilization, or any other form of sexual violence of comparable gravity;

(h) Persecution against any identifiable group or collectivity on political, racial, national, ethnic, cultural, religious, gender as defined in paragraph 3, or other grounds that are universally recognized as impermissible under international law, in connection with any act referred to in this paragraph or any crime within the jurisdiction of the Court;

(i) Enforced disappearance of persons;

(j) The crime of apartheid;

(k) Other inhumane acts of a similar character intentionally causing great suffering, or serious injury or to mental or physical health.

2. For the purpose of paragraph 1:

(a) "Attack directed against any civilian population" means a course of conduct involving the multiple commission of acts referred to in paragraph 1 against any civilian population, pursuant to or in furtherance of a State or organizational policy to commit such attack;

(b) "Extermination" includes the intentional infliction of conditions of life, inter alia the deprivation of access to food and medicine, calculated to bring about the destruction of a part of a population;

(c) "Enslavement" means the exercise of any or all of the powers attaching to the right of ownership over a person and includes the exercise of such power in the course of trafficking in persons, in particular women and children;

(d) "Deportation or forcible transfer of population" means forced displacement of the persons concerned by expulsion or other coercive acts from the area in which they are lawfully present, without grounds permitted under international law;

(e) "Torture" means the intentional infliction of severe pain or suffering, whether physical or mental, upon a person in the custody or under control of the accused; except that torture shall not include pain or suffering arising only from, inherent in or incidental to, lawful sanctions;

(f) "Forced pregnancy" means the unlawful confinement, of a woman forcibly made pregnant, with the intent of affecting the ethnic composition of any population or carrying out other grave violations of international law. This definition shall not in any way be interpreted as affecting national laws relating to pregnancy.

(g) "Persecution" means the intentional and severe deprivation of fundamental rights contrary to international law by reason of the identity of the group or collectivity;

(h) "The crime of apartheid" means inhumane acts of a character similar to those referred to in paragraph 1, committed in the context of an institutionalized regime of systematic oppression and domination by one racial group over any other racial group or groups and committed with the intention of maintaining that regime;

(i) "Enforced disappearance of persons" means the arrest, detention or abduction of persons by, or with the authorization, support or acquiescence of, a State or a political organization, followed by a refusal to acknowledge that deprivation of freedom or to give information on the fate or whereabouts of those persons, with the intention of removing them from the protection of the law for a prolonged period of time.

3. For the purpose of this Statute, it is understood that the term "gender" refers to the two sexes, male and female, within the context of society. The term "gender" does not indicate any meaning different from the above.

Article 8
War Crimes

1. The Court shall have jurisdiction in respect of war crimes in particular when committed as a part of a plan or policy or as part of a large-scale commission of such crimes.

2. For the purposes of this Statute, "war crimes" means:

(a) Grave breaches of the Geneva Conventions of 12 August 1949, namely, any of the following acts against persons or property protected under the provisions of the relevant Geneva Convention:

(i) Wilful Killing;

(ii) Torture or inhumane treatment, including biological experiments;

(iii) Wilfully causing great suffering, or serious injury to body or health;

(iv) Extensive destruction and appropriation of property, not justified by military necessity and carried out unlawfully and wantonly;

(v) Compelling a prisoner of war or other protected person to serve in the forces of a hostile Power;

(vi) Wilfully depriving a prisoner of war or other protected person of the rights of fair and regular trial;

(vii) Unlawful deportation or transfer or unlawful confinement;

(viii) Taking of hostages.

(b) Other serious violations of the laws and customs applicable in international armed conflict, within the established framework of international law, namely, any of the following acts:

(i) Intentionally directed attacks against the civilian population as such or against individual civilians not taking direct part in hostilities;

(ii) Intentionally directing attacks against civilian objects, that is, objects which are not military objectives;

(iii) Intentionally directing attacks against personnel, installations, material, units or vehicles involved in a humanitarian assistance or peacekeeping mission in accordance with the Charter of the United Nations, as long as they are entitled to the protection given to civilians or civilian objects under the international law of armed conflict;

(iv) Intentionally launching an attack in the knowledge that such attack will cause incidental loss of live or injury to civilians or damage to civilian objects or widespread, long-term and severe damage to the natural environment which would be clearly excessive in relation to the concrete and direct overall military advantage anticipated;

(v) Attacking or bombarding, by whatever means, towns, villages, dwellings or buildings which are undefended and which are not military objectives;

(vi) Killing or wounding a combatant who, having laid down his arms or having no longer means of defence, has surrendered at discretion;

(vii) Making improper use of a flag of truce, of the flag or of the military insignia and uniform of the enemy or of the United Nations, as well as of the distinctive emblems of the Geneva Conventions, resulting in death or serious personal injury;

(viii) The transfer, directly or indirectly, by the Occupying Power of parts of its own civilian population into the territory it occupies, or the deportation or transfer of all or parts of the population of the occupied territory within or outside this territory.

(ix) Intentionally directing attacks against buildings dedicated to religion, education, art, science or charitable purposes, historic monuments, hospitals and places where the sick and wounded are collected, provided they are not military objectives;

(x) Subjecting persons who are in the power of an adverse party to physical mutilation or to medical or scientific experiments of any kind which are neither justified by the medical, dental or hospital treatment of the person concerned nor carried out in his or her interest, and which cause death to or seriously endanger the health of such person or persons;

(xi) Killing or wounding treacherously individual belonging to the hostile nation or army;

(xii) Declaring that no quarter will be given;

(xiii) Destroying or seizing the enemy's property unless such destruction or seizure be imperatively demanded by the necessities of war;

(xiv) Declaring abolished, suspended or inadmissible in a court of law the rights and actions of the nationals of the hostile party;

(xv) Compelling the nationals of the hostile party to take part in the operations of war directed against their own country, even if they were in the belligerent's service before the commencement of the war;

(xvi) Pillaging a town or place, even when taken by assault;

(xxiii) Employing poison or poisoned weapons;

(xviii) Employing asphyxiating, poisonous or other gases, and all analogous liquids, materials or devices;

(xix) Employing bullets which expand or flatten easily in the human body, such as bullets with a hard envelope which does not entirely cover the core or is pierced with incisions;

(xx) Employing weapons, projectiles and materials and methods of warfare which are of a nature to cause superfluous injury or unnecessary suffering or which are inherently indiscriminate in violation of the international law of armed conflict, provided that such weapons, projectiles and material and methods of warfare are the subject of a comprehensive prohibition and are included in an annex to this Statute, by an amendment in accordance with the relevant provisions set forth in articles 121 and 123;

(xxi) Committing outrages upon personal dignity, in particular humiliating and degrading treatment;

(xxii) Committing rape, sexual slavery, enforced prostitution, forced pregnancy, as defined in article 7, paragraph 2(f), enforced sterilization, or any other form of sexual violence also constituting a grave breach of the Geneva Conventions;

(xxiii) Intentionally directing attacks against buildings, material, medical units and transport, and personnel using the distinctive emblems of the Geneva Conventions in conformity with international law;

(xxv) Intentionally using starvation of civilians as a method of warfare by depriving them of objects indispensable to their survival, including willfully impeding relief supplies as provided for under the Geneva Conventions;

(xxvi) Conscripting or enlisting children under the age of fifteen years into the national armed forces or using them to participate actively in hostilities.

[The above list of war crime offenses gives an idea of the reach of the ICC Statute in this particular context. For further war crimes provisions and provisions of the entire Statute, go to the United Nations cite above Article 1 (*supra.*) or see 37 ILM 999 (1998) or *www.un.org/icc*].

* * *

Article 29
Non-applicability of Statute of Limitations

The crimes within the jurisdiction of the Court shall not be subject to any statute of limitations.

Article 30
Mental Element

1. Unless otherwise provided, a person shall be criminally responsible and liable for punishment for a crime within the jurisdiction of the Court only if the mental elements are committed with intent and knowledge.

2. For purposes of this article, a person has intent where:

(a) In relation to conduct, that person means to engage in that conduct;

(b) In relation to a consequence, that person means to cause that consequence or is aware that it will occur in the ordinary course of events.

3. For purposes of this article, "knowledge" means awareness that a circumstance exists or a consequence will occur in the ordinary course of events. "Know" and "knowingly" shall be construed accordingly.

Article 33
Superior Orders and Prescription of Law

1. The fact that a crime within the jurisdiction of the Court has been committed by a person pursuant to an order of an Government or of a superior, whether military or civilian, shall not relieve that person of criminal responsibility unless:

(a) The person was under a legal obligation to obey orders of the Government or the superior in question;

(b) The person did not know that the order was unlawful; and

(c) The order was not manifestly unlawful.

2. For the purposes of this article, orders to commit genocide or crimes against humanity are manifestly unlawful.

Article 124
Transitional Provision

Notwithstanding article 12, paragraphs 1 and 2, a State, on becoming a party to the Statute, may declare that, for a period of seven years after the entry into force of this Statute for the State concerned, it does not accept the jurisdiction of the Court with respect to the category of crimes referred to in article 8 when a crime is alleged to have been committed by its nationals or on its territory. A declaration under this article may be withdrawn at any time.

––––––––––––

(e) Michael P. Scharf, "The United States and the International Criminal Court: A Recommendation for the Bush Administration"

7 ILSA Journal of International and Comparative Law 385; 385–389 (2001) Reproduced with permission from Michael P. Scharf, The United States and the International Criminal Court: A Recommendation for the Bush Administration, 7 ISLA J. Int'l & Comp. L. 385 (2001)

1. Introduction

In the waning days of his presidency, William J. Clinton authorized the United States signature on the Rome Treaty establishing an International Criminal Court (ICC), making the United States the 138th country to sign the treaty by the December 30th deadline. According to the ICC Statute, after December 31, 2000, States must accede to the Treaty, which requires full ratification— something that was not likely for the United States in the near term given the current level of Senate opposition to the Treaty. While signature is not equivalent to ratification, it sets the stage for United States support of Security Council referrals to the International Criminal Court, as well as other forms of United States cooperation with the Court. In addition, it enables the United States to continue to seek additional provisions to protect American personnel from the court's jurisdiction.

Clinton's action drew immediate reaction from Senator Helms, Chairman of the United States Senate Foreign Relations Committee, who has been one of the treaty's greatest opponents. In a Press Release, Helms stated: "Today's action is a blatant attempt by a lame-duck President to tie the hands of his successor. Well, I have a message for the outgoing President. This decision will not stand. I will make reversing this decision, and protecting America's fighting men and women from the jurisdiction of this international kangaroo court, one of my highest priorities in the new Congress."

During the 107th Congress, Helms is likely to resurrect the "Servicemembers' Protection Act," Senate Bill 2726, which he initially introduced in June 2000. The Act would prohibit any United States Government cooperation with the ICC, and cut off United States Military assistance to any country that has ratified the ICC Treaty (with the exception of major United States allies), as long as the United States has not ratified the Rome Treaty. Further, the proposed legislation provides that United States Military personnel must be immunized from ICC jurisdiction before the United States participates in any United Nations peacekeeping operation. The proposed legislation also authorizes the President to use all means necessary to release any United States or allied personnel detained on behalf of the Court.

II. Influential Insider or Hostile Outsider?

The inescapable reality for the United States is that the ICC will soon enter into force with or without United States support. As this is being written, thirty countries have already ratified the treaty, and 139 have signed it indicating their intention to ratify. Sixty ratifications are necessary to bring it into force [which was accomplished on July 1, 2002]. The Signatories include every North Atlantic Treaty Organization (NATO) State except Turkey. Three of the Permanent Members of the Security Council (France, Russia, and the United Kingdom) have signed it. Both of the United States' closest neighbors (Mexico and Canada) have signed it. And even Israel, which was the only Western country to join the United States in voting against the ICC Treaty in Rome in 1998, later changed its position and signed the Treaty.

The question facing the Bush Administration, then, is whether its interests are better served by playing the role of hostile outsider (as embodied in Jesse Helms' "American Servicemembers' Protection Act") or by playing the role of an influential insider (as it has done for example with the Yugoslavia Tribunal). In deciding on a course of action, the Bush Administration must recognize the consequences that would flow from the hostile approach.

First, the hostile approach would transform American exceptionalism into unilateralism and/or isolationism by preventing the United States from participating in United Nations peacekeeping operations and cutting off aid to many countries vital to United States national security. Further, overt opposition to the ICC would erode the moral legitimacy of the United States, which has historically been as important to achieving United States foreign policy goals as military and economic might. Perversely, the hostile approach may even turn the United States into a safe haven for international war criminals, since the United States would be prevented from surrendering them directly to the ICC or indirectly to another country which would surrender them to the ICC.

Second, the United States would be prevented from being able to take advantage of the very real benefits of the ICC. The experience with the Yugoslavia Tribunal has shown that, even absent arrests, an international indictment has the effect of isolating rogue leaders, strengthening domestic opposition, and increasing international support for sanctions and even use of force. The United States has recognized these benefits in pushing for the subsequent creation of the *ad hoc* tribunals for Rwanda and Sierra Leone, as well as proposing the establishment of tribunals for Cambodia and Iraq. But the establishment of the ICC will signal the end of the era of *ad hoc* tribunals. Under the hostile approach, when the next Rwanda-like situation occurs, the United States will not be able to employ the very useful tool of international criminal justice.

The United States opponents of the ICC have suggested that without United States support, the ICC is destined to be impotent because it will lack the power of the Security Council to enforce its arrest orders. But as the *ad hoc* Tribunals for Rwanda and Sierra Leone indicate, in most cases where an ICC is needed, the perpetrators are no longer in power and are in the custody of a new government or nearby states which are perfectly willing to hand them over to an ICC absent Security Council action. Moreover, the Security Council has been prevented (by Russian veto threats) from taking any action to impose sanctions on States that have not cooperated with the Yugoslavia Tribunal despite repeated pleas from the Tribunal's Prosecutor and Judges that it do so. Indeed, in the Yugoslavia context, where the perpetrators were still in power when the Tribunal was established, it was not action by the Security Council, but rather the withholding of international loans that have induced Croatia and Serbia to hand over two dozen indictees. This indicates that, unlike the League of Nations (which United States opponents of the ICC have frequently referred to in this context), the ICC is likely to be a thriving institution even without United States participation. In other words, the United States may actually need the ICC more than the ICC needs the Untied States.

The third problem with the hostile approach is that the United States achieves no real protection from the ICC by remaining outside the ICC regime. This is because Article 12 of the Rome Statute empowers the ICC to exercise jurisdiction over nationals of non-party States who commit crimes in the territory of State Parties. Opponents of the ICC have attempted to negate this problem by arguing that international law prohibits the ICC from exercising jurisdiction over the nationals of non-parties. In a lengthy article in *Law and Contemporary Problems* ["The ICC's Jurisdiction over the Nationals of Non-Party States: A Critique of the U.S. Position," 64 *Law & Contemp. Probs.* 67 (2001)], I provide a detailed critique of this legal argument, pointing out that it is not supported by the historic record or guiding precedents. But far more important than what I have to say is the fact that the representatives at the ICC Prep. Con. [sic.] have rejected the argument, indicating that the ICC Assembly of State Parties and the ICC itself are extremely unlikely to accept it.

If United States officials can be indicted by the ICC whether or not the United States is a party to the Rome Treaty, then the United States preserves very little by remaining outside the treaty regime, and could protect itself better by signing the treaty. This has been proven to be the case with the Yugoslavia Tribunal, which the United States has supported with contributions exceeding $15 million annually, the loan of top-ranking investigators and lawyers from the federal government, the support of troops to permit the safe exhumation of mass graves, and even the provision of U-2 surveillance photographs to locate the places where Serb authorities had tried to hide the evidence of its wrongdoing.

This policy bore fruit when the International Prosecutor opened an investigation into allegations of war crimes committed by NATO during the 1999 Kosovo intervention. Despite the briefs and reports of reputable human rights organizations arguing that NATO had committed breaches of international humanitarian law, on June 8, 2000 the International Prosecutor issued a report concluding that charges against NATO personnel were not warranted. I am not suggesting that the United States co-opted the Yugoslavia Tribunal, but when dealing with close calls regarding application of international humanitarian law it is obviously better to have a sympathetic Prosecutor and Court than a hostile one.

III. A Recommendation Based on Real Politick Considerations

I served as Attorney-Advisor for Law Enforcement and Intelligence and Attorney-Advisor for United Nations Affairs at the State Department under the first President Bush. Unlike much of the commentary on both sides of this issue, which is clouded by emotionalism and idealism, I have sought here to provide a detached risk-benefit analysis of the foreign policy and national security consequence of the question facing the new [Bush] administration.

The risks to the United States servicemembers presented by the ICC Treaty have been seriously underrated. But to the extent that such fears are valid, United States opposition to the ICC will only increase the likelihood that the ICC will be more hostile than sympathetic to United States positions. And, ironically, by opposing the Court, the

United States would likely engender more international hostility toward United States foreign policy than could result from an indictment by the Court. Thus, whether or not the United States is able to achieve additional safeguards to prevent the ICC from exercising jurisdiction over United States personnel, it will be in the interest of United States national security foreign policy to support, rather than oppose, the ICC. This does not require immediate ratification. Perhaps it is better to let the Court prove itself over a period of years before sending the treaty to the Senate. But when the next Rwanda-like situation comes along, the Bush Administration will find value in having the option of Security Council referral to the ICC in its arsenal of foreign policy responses.

(f) "U.S. Policy and the International Criminal Court," Comments by Ambassador David J. Scheffer, U.S. Ambassador-at-Large for War Crimes Issues

Before the International Military Operations and Law Conference, Honolulu, Hawaii, Feb 23, 1999, 23 *Maryland Journal of International Law and Trade* 1; 8–13 (1999)

Reproduced with permission from *U.S. Policy and The International Criminal Court*, 23 Md. J. Int'l. L. & Trade 1 (1999)

The United States has had and will continue to have a compelling interest in the establishment of a permanent international criminal court (ICC). Such as international court, so long contemplated and so relevant in a world burdened with mass murderers, can both deter and punish those who might escape justice in national courts. As head of the U.S. delegation to the ICC talks since mid-1997, I can confirm that the United States has had an abiding interest in what kind of court the ICC would be in order to operate efficiently, effectively and appropriately within a global system that also requires our constant vigilance to protect international peace and security. Our refusal to support the final draft of the treaty in Rome last summer was grounded in law and in the reality of our international system.

On December 8, 1998, we joined consensus in the UN General Assembly to adopt a resolution creating the Preparatory Commission on the ICC which is meeting now in New York under the expert leadership of Philippe Kirsch, the Legal Advisor of the Canadian Ministry of Foreign Affairs. I recently led the U.S. delegation in the critical work of the PrepCom to develop the elements of crimes and the rules of evidence and procedure. The United States has taken the lead in the elements discussions. This summer the PrepCom will afford opportunity for concerns we and others have had about the effectiveness and acceptance of the Court to be addressed. This is an important opportunity to correct the Treaty. We believe the problem in the treaty which prevent us from signing it can be solved, and that it is in the interest of all governments to address those problems now so that we can all be active partners in the ICC. There is far more to lose in the effectiveness of the ICC if the United States is not a treaty partner than there is to gain from its current dubious regime of jurisdiction. As I said at the United Nations in October, we do not pretend to know all the answers. We hope some creative thinking can be generated in the months ahead.

At the Rome conference last summer [1998], the U.S. delegation worked with other delegations, many of whose governments are sitting in this room today, to achieve important objectives. One major objective was a strong complementarity regime, namely, deferral to national jurisdiction. A key purpose of the international criminal court should be to promote observance and enforcement of international humanitarian law by domestic legal systems. Therefore, we were pleased to see the adoption of Article 18 (preliminary ruling regarding admissibility), which is drawn originally from an American proposal, and its companion Articles 17 and 19. We considered it only logical that, when an investigation of an overall situation is initiated, relevant and capable national governments be given an opportunity under reasonable guidelines that respect the authority of the court to take the lead in investigating their own nationals or others within their jurisdiction.

Our negotiators struggled, successfully, to preserve appropriate sovereign decision-making in connection with obligations to cooperate with the court. Some delegates were tempted to require unqualified cooperation by states parties with all court orders, notwithstanding national judicial procedures that would be involved in any event. Such obligations of unqualified cooperation were unrealistic and would have raised serious constitutional issues not only in the United States but in many other jurisdictions. Part 9 of the statute represents hard-fought battles in this respect. The requirement that the actions of states parties be taken "in accordance with national procedural law" or similar language is pragmatic and legally essential for the successful operation of the court.

The U.S. experience with the Yugoslav Tribunal has shown that some sensitive information collected by a government could be made available as lead evidence to the prosecutor, provided that detailed procedures were strictly followed. We applied years of experience with the Yugoslav Tribunal to the challenge of similar cooperation with a permanent court. It was not easy. Some delegations argued that the court should have the final determination on the release of all national security information requested from a government. Our view prevailed in Article 72: a national government must have the right of final refusal if the request pertains to its national security. In the case of a government's refusal, the court may seek a remedy from the Assembly of States Parties or the Security Council.

The United States helped lead the successful effort to ensure that the ICC's jurisdiction over crimes against humanity included acts in internal armed conflicts and acts in the absence of armed conflict. We also argued successfully that there had to be a reasonably high threshold for such crimes.

U.S. lawyers insisted that definitions of war crimes be drawn from customary international law and that they respect the requirements of military objectives during combat and of genuine intent. We had long sought a high threshold for the court's jurisdiction over war crimes, since individual soldiers often commit isolated war crimes that by themselves should not automatically trigger the massive machinery of the ICC. We believe the definition arrived at serves our purposes well: "The Court shall have jurisdiction in respect of war crimes in particular when committed as a part of a plan or policy or as part of a large-scale commission of such crimes."

A major achievement of Article 8 of the treaty is its application to war crimes committed during internal armed conflicts. In order to widen acceptance of the application of the statute to war crimes committed during internal armed conflicts, the United States helped broker language that excludes situations of internal disturbances and tensions, such as riots, isolated and sporadic acts of violence, and other acts of a similar nature.

One of the more difficult, but essential, issues to negotiate was the coverage of crimes against women, in particular either as a crime against humanity or as a war crime. The U.S. delegation worked hard to include explicit reference to crimes relating to sexual assault in the text of the statute. Rape, sexual slavery, enforced prostitution, forced pregnancy, enforced sterilization, and any other form of sexual violence of significant magnitude were included as crimes.

As I mentioned earlier, our emphasis on the elements of crimes resulted in Article 9 of the treaty, which requires their preparation; a task that governments are now undertaking in New York. We also were instrumental in creating acceptable definitions of command responsibility and the defense of superior orders.

These accomplishments and others in the Rome Treaty are significant. But the U.S. delegation was not prepared at any time during the Rome Conference to accept a treaty text that represented a political compromise on fundamental issues of international criminal law and international peace and security. We could not negotiate as if certain risks could be easily dismissed or certain procedures of the permanent court would be infallible. We could not bargain away unique security requirements or our need to uphold basic principles of international law even if some of our closest allies reached their own level of satisfaction with the final treaty text. The United States made compromises throughout the Rome process, but we always emphasized that the issue of jurisdiction had to be resolved satisfactorily or else the entire treaty and the integrity of the court would be imperiled.

The theory of universal jurisdiction for genocide, crimes against humanity and war crimes seized the imagination of many delegates negotiating the ICC treaty. They appeared to believe that the ICC should be empowered to do what some national governments have done unilaterally, namely, to enact laws that empower their courts to prosecute any individuals, including non-nationals, who commit one or more of these crimes. Some governments have enacted such laws, which theoretically, but rarely in practice, make their courts arenas for international prosecutions. Of course, the catch for any national government seeking to exercise universal jurisdiction is to exercise personal jurisdiction over the suspect. Without custody, or the prospect of it through an extradition proceeding, a national court's claim of universal jurisdiction necessarily and rightly is limited.

The ICC is designed as a treaty-based court with the unique power to prosecute and sentence individuals, but also to impose obligations of cooperation upon the contracting states. A fundamental principle of international treaty law is that only states that are party to a treaty should be bound by its terms. Yet Article 12 of the ICC treaty reduces the need for ratification of the treaty by national governments by providing the court with jurisdiction over nationals of a non-party state. Under Article 12, the ICC may exercise such jurisdiction over anyone anywhere in the world, even in the absence of a referral by the Security Council, if either the state of the territory where the crime was committed or the state of nationality of the accused consents. Ironically, the treaty exposes non-parties in ways that parties are not exposed.

Why is the United States so concerned about the status of non-party states under the ICC treaty? Why not, as many have suggested, simply sign and ratify the treaty and thus eliminate the problem of non-party status? First, fundamental principles of treaty law still matter and we are loath to ignore them with respect to any state's obligations vis-à-vis a treaty regime. While certain conduct is prohibited under customary international law and might be the object of universal jurisdiction by a national court, the establishment of, and a state's participation in, an international criminal court are not derived from custom but, rather, from the requirements of treaty law.

Second, even if the Clinton Administration were in a position to sign the treaty, U.S. ratification could take many years and stretch beyond the date of entry into force of the treaty [which, in fact, is exactly what has happened, since the Treaty came into force on July 1, 2002. Ratification of the ICC Treaty remains a non-issue given the political climate extant in the second Bush Administration]. Thus, the United States could have non-party status under the ICC treaty for a significant period of time. The crimes within the court's jurisdiction also go beyond those arguably covered by universal jurisdiction, and court decisions or future amendments could effectively create "new" and unacceptable crimes. Moreover, the ability to withdraw from the treaty, should the court develop in unacceptable ways, would be negated as an effective protection.

Equally troubling are the implications of Article 12 for the future willingness of the United States and other governments to take significant risks to intervene in foreign lands in order to save human lives or to restore international or regional peace and security. The illogical consequence imposed by Article 12, particularly for non-parties to the treaty, will be to limit severely those lawful, but highly controversial and inherently risky, interventions that the advocates of human rights and world peace so desperately seek from the United States and other military powers. There will be significant new legal and political risks in such interventions, which up to this point have been mostly shielded from politically motivated charges.

In Rome, the U.S. delegation offered various proposals to break the back of the jurisdiction problem. The other permanent members of the Security Council joined us in a compromise formula during the last week of the Rome conference. One of our proposals was to exempt from the court's jurisdiction conduct that arises from the official actions of a non-party state acknowledged as such by that non-party. This would require a non-party state to acknowledge responsibility for an atrocity in order to be exempted, an unlikely occurrence for those who usually commit genocide or other serious violations of international humanitarian law. Regrettably, our proposed amendments to Article 12 were rejected on the premise that the proposed take it or leave it draft of the treaty was so fragile that, if any part were reopened, the conference would fall apart.

The final text of the treaty includes the crime of aggression, albeit undefined until a Review Conference seven years after entry into force of the treaty when only states parties to the treaty at that time determine the meaning of aggression. This political concession to the most persistent advocates of a crime of aggression without a consensus definition and without the linkage to a prior Security Council determination that an act of aggression has occurred, should concern all of us. The Preparatory Commission is addressing the issue, however, and we hope it will proceed responsibly in the years ahead. If handled poorly, this issue alone could fatally compromise the ICC's future credibility.

I will not belabor the final hours of the conference except to say that it could have been done differently and the outcome might have been far more encouraging. While we firmly believe that the true intent of national governments cannot be that which now appears reflected in a few key provisions of the Rome treaty, the political will remains within the Clinton Administration to support a treaty that is fairly and realistically constituted. We hope developments will unfold in the future so that the considerable support that the United States could bring to a properly constituted international criminal court can be realized.

(g) Alison M. McIntire, *Comment,* "Be Careful What You Wish for Because You Just Might Get It: The United States and the International Criminal Court"

25 *Suffolk Transnational Law Review* 249; 251–267; 270–272 (2001)
Reproduced with permission from Alison M. McIntire, *Be Careful What you Wish For Because You Just Might Get It: The United States and the International Criminal Court*, 25 Suffolk Transnat'l L. Rev. 249 (2001)

* * *

II. Predecessors of the ICC and the Conference in Rome

The desire to establish a permanent tribunal for international crimes coalesced most visibly at the beginning of the twentieth century. Following World War I, the Allies signed the Treaty of Versailles, which included provisions for prosecuting the former emperor of Germany. A commission of the Allied powers relied on the 1907 Hague Convention on the regulation of armed conflict to charge the Kaiser with what would today be the crime of aggression. The victors of World War II created similar provisions in the Charter of the International Military Tribunal in Nuremberg for prosecuting war crimes, crimes against peace, and crimes against humanity. The Allies in each of the four zones of occupation again had authority to prosecute those they arrested within their zone. The world's witness of horrific, genocidal atrocities almost fifty years later in the Rwandan and Bosnian civil wars resulted in the United Nations Security Council establishing two more tribunals.

Problems encountered as a result of the tribunals' ad hoc creation provided the motivation for creating a permanent ICC. For example, criminals subject to indictment often see the tribunals as illegitimate victors' courts because Western powers are not prosecuted for similar acts committed during the same conflicts. The United Nations Secretary-General also highlighted the lack of funding and resources for the Rwandan Tribunal in a report to the General Assembly and the Security Council.... Many international lawyers therefore argue that a permanent ICC would create more consistency and reliability in international law, be more cost-efficient, and facilitate justice for those with legitimate claims.

In 1993, the experiences of the ad hoc tribunals served as a catalyst to the United Nations General Assembly request that the International Law Commission (ILC) draft a statute creating a permanent ICC. The United Nations General Assembly subsequently passed a resolution creating the United Nations Preparatory Committee on the Establishment of an ICC (PrepCom) in 1995. The General Assembly mandated that PrepCom use the ILC's preliminary draft to fashion a widely acceptable document for an ICC. PrepCom held meetings once a year from 1996 to 1998, during which state delegations participated in committees dedicated to composing the Statute. The delegations completed the draft in April [1998] and then submitted it to the Rome Conference.

In July of 1998, 160 countries convened for five weeks to negotiate provisions for an international criminal justice system. Attendees organized into a General Committee of thirty-four and a Drafting Committee of twenty-five, composed of regional groups representing Africa, Asia, Eastern Europe, Latin America, the Caribbean, Western Europe, and other nations. The decision-making process ensured that "all matters of substance were settled first and foremost by general agreement," with a voting procedure utilized only where agreement could not be reached. Consensus existed from the beginning as to the core issues, which included the definition of crimes, jurisdiction, the prosecutor's authority, and the composition and administration of the court. In the end, 121 states voted in favor of the final draft of the Statute, with seven against, and 21 abstaining.

III. Provisions of the Rome Statute and the United States' Response

The Conference resulted in the Rome Statute, which is both legislation and constitution. The Statute includes provisions for the ICC's governance, administration, structure, financing, and fundamental procedures. The Statute becomes effective when sixty countries ratify it.

Three main principles guide the Statute's provisions. First, the principle of complementarity permits the ICC jurisdiction only when the accused's national legal system is unable or unwilling to prosecute. Second, the Statute only addresses the most serious crimes affecting the international community as a whole, including genocide, crimes against humanity, and war crimes. Finally, the drafters attempted to utilize concepts of customary international law wherever possible to increase the likelihood of state support.

Though President Clinton signed the Statute on December 31, 2000, the United States' delegation did not initially support the final draft. The United States successfully lobbied against the ICC's exercise of universal jurisdiction because U.S. officials feared the Statute's jurisdictional provisions would extend to nationals of non-party states. The United States argued that subjecting a non-party state to the terms of the Statute is contrary to established treaty law. The U.S. delegation also sought a longer period in which to judge the ICC's effectiveness and impartiality prior to accepting its jurisdiction. Some government officials also expressed concerned [sic.] about the power of the ICC's prosecutor, who may initiate investigations without referral from a signatory state or the United Nations Security Council. The United States initially refused to sign a treaty that left the crime of aggression undefined and that presented potentially troubling constitutional questions.

Other states and many non-governmental organizations (NGO's) campaigned strongly in favor of signing the Rome Statute. Proponents of the Statute view it as a representation of American values, a deterrent to future international crimes, a contributor to stable international order, and reaffirmation of international law. The Statute reflects a reference to national sovereignty through its role as a court of last resort that has jurisdiction over only the most heinous crimes. Proponents argue that the United States should realize its inability to control every aspect of the ICC process because the international community will create the court whether or not the United States ratifies the Statute.

IV. Why Detractors' Arguments Regarding ICC Jurisdiction, Crimes, Prosecutorial Power, and the Nature of the Court Fail

Opposing views surrounding the drafting of the Statute's provisions for jurisdiction, crimes, prosecutorial powers, and court procedure illustrate the primary issues in the debate as to whether the Statute sufficiently codifies the ICC. ICC jurisdiction is of foremost importance to the United States because it potentially restricts American military operations and endangers U.S. service personnel. Opponents also contest the elements of crimes the ICC may adjudicate because some of the definitions do not originate in customary international law. Additionally, opponents fear politically motivated prosecutions may result if the prosecutor can make referrals to the ICC. Finally, procedural aspects of the court provoke questions as to the ICC's constitutionality. Opponents demonstrate an unwillingness to face the reality of globalization and accept a changing concept of sovereignty. ICC supporters, however, seek to expand the role of international law and establish enforcement mechanisms to ensure the preservation of human rights.

A. Jurisdiction

* * *

States and leaders opposed to the jurisdictional provisions of the Statute maintain that Articles Twelve and Thirteen contradict established treaty law because the articles purport to gain jurisdiction over non-party states. Opponents argue that ICC jurisdiction threatens America's ability to protect foreign policy interests through military operations. Further, detractors complain the Statute dilutes the Security Council's power because a state party may refer a case without Security Council approval. ICC opponents hold that its expansive jurisdiction will diminish U.S. sovereignty because of the possibility that a foreign court may try American nationals.

Conversely, proponents of the Statute argue the ICC merely allows for an option when state governments act to shield individuals from national courts. The Statute also contains provisions impeding prosecution of troops stationed abroad who stand accused of serious human rights crimes. Proponents point to the complemantarity principle, which gives nations original jurisdiction over crimes they choose to try. The Statute upholds sovereign countries' well-established right to determine the adjudication of crimes occurring within their territory. The Security Council may also defer investigations and prosecutions. Finally, Statute provisions forbidding amendments for at least seven years and requiring consensus among signatories dispel opponents' preoccupation that the ICC's jurisdiction will rapidly expand and present an immediate threat to national sovereignty.

While proponents of the Statute's text present more persuasive arguments, at first glance, the jurisdictional language of Article 12 could disconcert any student of customary international law because it purports to bind the Statute's non-signatories. Treaties are international law's equivalent to contracts between countries and thus may only bind those who agree to their terms. Article 12 explicitly states that the court will have jurisdiction under the Statute as long as the conduct complained of occurred in a state which is a party to the Statute. In application, however, the provision is indistinguishable from a situation in which another country tries a United State's citizen who breaks that country's laws, illustrating a principle of territorial jurisdiction long-accepted by the United States.

Despite Ambassador Scheffer and other like-minded participants' espousal of the importance of American involvement internationally, their view overlooks the evolution of international networks of authority. The jurisdictional powers of the ICC must necessarily be broad because of international law's movement away from state-centered approaches towards a more international human rights approach. Any insistence on strict boundaries of sovereignty or attempts to create exceptions for the United States enhances the credibility of rogue leaders who accuse the United States of hypocrisy.

The United States participation in the ICC as well as its guidance in the court's direction during the early years will assist in institutionalizing the rule of international law and provide further influence in establishing international precedent. Controversy over the ICC illustrates the divide between those interested in wielding significant power with few consequences and those dedicated to establishing a body of international law that punishes arbitrary uses of national force.

B. Crimes

Currently the ICC may adjudicate genocide, crimes against humanity, and war crimes. The Statute also leaves open the possibility of ICC jurisdiction over the crime of aggression, which is presently undefined because of disagreement among the delegates at the conference. The polemic regarding provisions defining crimes epitomizes the United States' unwillingness to place any domestic authority in the control of an international institution.

Opponents of the Rome Statute claim the United States should not ratify a treaty that has jurisdiction over undefined crimes because of the potentially broad application to state-sanctioned conduct. Various proposals for defining the crime of aggression include the planning, preparing, initiating, and carrying out of a war of aggression such to threaten international peace and security; the blockade of a State's ports or coasts by the armed forces of another; and using armed force against the territory of another State. Dissenters worry the ICC would significantly restrict United States foreign policy options because of the lack of specificity and broad nature of the proposals. The Statute's critics warn that the standards of proof for war crimes and the crime of aggression could allow a country with animosity towards the United States to bring charges against a United States President.

Articles 6–8, which define the crimes within the court's jurisdiction and provide the standards of proof necessary to determine guilt, undermine opponents' statements. Article 6 of the Statute lists acts chargeable as genocide if "committed with intent to destroy, in whole or in part, a national, ethnical, racial or religious group." Article 7 considers conduct a crime against humanity "when [it is] committed as part of a widespread or systematic attack directed against any civilian population, with knowledge of the attack." As defined in Article 8, a war crime requires the conduct to be "committed as part of a plan or policy or as part of a large-scale commission of such crimes." The Statute further requires the prosecutor prove the perpetrator committed the crime with knowledge and intent. Examination of the Statute's language thus proves that an isolated act committed recklessly or negligently that was not part of a larger state plan would fail to meet the high standards of proof necessary for conviction in the ICC.

Proponents of the Statute emphasize the onerous amendment procedures, which preclude a change in the text without consensus. Any amendment to the treaty cannot be inconsistent with the U. N. Charter, thus ensuring that the Statute will not lessen the role of the Security Council or the influence of the United States in maintaining international peace. Further, any party may withdraw prior to the Statute going into force if the state disagrees with the amendment language.

Controversy over crimes within the court's jurisdiction further exemplifies each side's opinion as to the power an international organization should assume in enforcing the rule of law. The Statute's amendment procedures and withdrawal options cast doubt on opponents' position that the crime of aggression will automatically include elements subverting United States' foreign policy. Further, the Statute's high burdens of proof undermine challengers' arguments regarding the potentially broad application to United States' presidents and military operations. Statute supporters thus persuasively argue that crimes over which the ICC has jurisdiction present no significant threat to diminishment of United States' sovereignty or Security Council influence.

* * *

D. The Nature of the ICC and Other Procedural Issues

The controversy over the Rome Statute extends to a debate over the nature of the court itself. ICC challengers characterize the court as contrary to the United States Constitution. Statute supporters accurately cite provisions explicitly providing that which opponents claim the Statute takes away. Detractors' accusations that the ICC is unconstitutional illustrate a desire to preclude United States' involvement in an international organization holding all nations to the same rule of law, regardless of their position in the world community.

ICC opponents maintain that the United States' participation in the ICC is unconstitutional because of its status as a foreign court. Opponents interpret the Statute as circumventing rights familiar to American citizens, specifically the right to a jury trial, the right to confront witnesses, and the right against double jeopardy. Opponents therefore conclude that the Senate may not ratify a treaty that surrenders American citizens' constitutional rights. Alternatively, ICC detractors argue the court is de facto unconstitutional because it consists of foreign judges who are unaccountable to United States' laws. The majority of Congress holds a similar view,…as…in the…reasons for the bill to protect American Servicemen abroad.

A closer reading of the Statute reveals that it in fact preserves the constitutionally protected rights meant to ensure a "fair hearing conducted impartially." The rights include the presumption of innocence for the accused and the requirement that guilt be proven beyond a reasonable doubt. Any person brought before the ICC has a right to be given notice of the charges against him and to be tried without unnecessary delay. The accused may also "examine…witnesses against him or her." In direct contradiction to some opponents' views, the Statute explicitly states that the court shall not compel any witnesses to confess his guilt nor will the court consider a witness' decision to remain silent when evaluating guilt or innocence. Finally, Article 20 specifically prohibits double jeopardy.

Proponents contend the ICC's formation and operation are in accord with all nations' sovereign domestic jurisdiction, as established by their respective constitutions. The characterization of the ICC as a foreign national court fails because states voluntarily created the ICC through democratic participation in the Rome Conference process. Further, claims that the ICC conflicts with the United States Constitution based on the absence of the concept of international criminal jurisdiction at the framing of the [U.S.] Constitution, must fail because the concept is novel to most states' formative documents. Finally, the absence of a provision prohibiting the United States' participation in an international tribunal definitely undermines arguments against the ICC's constitutionality.

[On June 14, 2000, United States Senator Jesse Helms of North Carolina introduced a bill in the Senate titled the *American Servicemembers' Protection Act* (S.2726). This bill and its U.S. House companion legislation (H.R. 4654) were opposed by both the Department of State and the United States Department of Defense. The bill's language forbids any United States government agency from cooperating with the ICC as long as the United States is not a signatory to the treaty and it correspondingly criticizes the Rome Statute because it would, according to Helm's bill, deny to personnel in the American armed forces "many of the procedural protections to which all Americans are entitled under the Bill of Rights." Having so stated, the bill then lists only three "rights" it says are denied American service personnel by the Rome Statute: (1) right of trial by jury; (2) the right against compulsory self-incrimination; and (3) the right to confront and cross-examine witnesses.

It should be noted, however, that the constitutional right to a jury trial in the common law sense of that term is not available to members of the United States armed forces and is specifically excepted from coverage by the language of the Fifth Amendment. Legal commentators have also generally assumed that this self-same exception applies under the Sixth Amendment. The other two rights mentioned in the Helms' bill (self-incrimination and confrontation and cross-examination) are guaranteed by express language contained in the ICC statute. In addition, there are a number of other procedural rights written into the Rome Statute that are even more detailed in their provisos than the language contained in the American Bill of Rights. Thus, upon careful examination of the ICC Statute, the allegations that United States military personnel would be short-changed by being denied basic due process under the provisions of that law is both disingenuous and misplaced. In comparing rights guaranteed to military personnel by the U.S. Constitution with those self-same rights guaranteed under the ICC Statute, the ICC Statute stands up very well when juxtaposed with those found within the basic American canon of government. Senator Helms' concerns clearly hit a nerve in the minds of some conservative politicians and the second Bush Administration is distracted by many other geopolitical and domestic problems to seriously consider sending the Rome Treaty up to the United States Senate for ratification as this book goes to press. The caveats and cautions expressed by Senator Helms are reflected in the language of the *American Servicemembers' Protections Act of 2002*].

(h) *American Servicemembers' Protection Act*

P.L. 107-206, 116 STAT. 899, Aug. 2, 2002

SEC. 2002. Findings.

Congress makes the following findings:

(1) On July 17, 1998, the United Nations Diplomatic Conference of Plenipotentiaries on the Establishment of an International Criminal Court, meeting in Rome, Italy, adopted the "Rome Statute of the International Criminal Court." The vote on whether to proceed with the statute was 120 in favor to 7 against, with 21 countries abstaining. The United States voted against the final adoption of the Rome Statute.

(2) As of April 30, 2001, 139 countries had signed the Rome Statute and 30 had ratified it. Pursuant to Article 126 of the Rome Statute, the statute will enter into force on the first day of the month after the 60th day following the date on which the 60th country deposits an instrument ratifying the statute.

(3) Since adoption of the Rome Statute, a Preparatory Commission for the International Criminal Court has met regularly to draft documents to implement the Rome Statute, including Rules of Procedure and Evidence, Elements of Crimes, and a definition of the Crime of Aggression.

(4) During testimony before the Congress following the adoption of the Rome Statute, the lead United States negotiator, Ambassador David Scheffer stated that the United States could not sign the Rome Statute because certain critical negotiating objectives of the United States had not been achieved. As a result, he stated: "We are left with consequences that do not serve the cause of international justice."

(5) Ambassador Scheffer went on to tell the Congress that: "Multinational peacekeeping forces operating in a country that has joined the treaty can be exposed to the Court's jurisdiction even if the country of the individual peacekeeper has not joined the treaty. Thus, the treaty purports to establish an arrangement whereby

United States armed forces operating overseas could be conceivably prosecuted by the international court even if the United States has not agreed to be bound by the treaty. Not only is this contrary to the most fundamental principles of treaty law, it could inhibit the ability of the United States to use its military to meet alliance obligations and participate in multinational operations, including humanitarian interventions to save civilian lives. Other contributors to peacekeeping operations will be similarly exposed."

(6) Notwithstanding these concerns, President Clinton directed that the United States sign the Rome Statute on December 31, 2000. In a statement issued that day, he stated that in view of the unremedied deficiencies of the Rome Statute, "I will not, and do not recommend that my successor submit the Treaty to the Senate for advice and consent until our fundamental concerns are satisfied."

(7) Any American prosecuted by the International Criminal Court will, under the Rome Statute, be denied procedural protections to which all American are entitled under the Bill of Rights to the United States Constitution, such as the right to trial by jury.

(8) Members of the Armed Forces of the United States should be free from the risk of prosecution by the International Criminal Court, especially when they are stationed or deployed around the world to protect the vital national interest of the United States. The United States Government has an obligation to protect the members of its Armed Forces, to the maximum extent possible, against criminal prosecutions carried out by the International Criminal Court.

(9) In addition to exposing members of the Armed Forces of the United States to the risk of international criminal prosecution, the Rome Statute creates a risk that the President and other senior elected and appointed officials of the United States Government may be prosecuted by the International Criminal Court. Particularly if the Preparatory Commission agrees on a definition of the Crime of Aggression over United States objections, senior United States officials may be at risk of criminal prosecution for national security decisions involving such matters as responding to acts of terrorism, preventing the proliferation of weapons of mass destruction, and deterring aggression. No less than members of the Armed Forces of the United States, senior officials of the United States Government should be free from the risk of prosecution by the International Criminal Court, especially with respect to official actions taken by them to protect the national interest of the United States.

(10) Any agreement within the Preparatory Commission on a definition of the Crime of Aggression that usurps the prerogative of the United Nations Security Council under Article 39 of the charter of the United Nations to "determine the existence of any...act of aggression" would contravene the charter of the United Nations and undermine deterrence.

(11) It is a fundamental principle of international law that a treaty is binding upon its parties only and that it does not create obligations for nonparties without their consent to be bound. The United States is not a party to the Rome Statute and will not be bound by any of its terms. The United States will not recognize the jurisdiction of the International Criminal Court over United States nationals.

* * *

SEC. 2004. Prohibition on cooperation with the International Criminal Court

(a) **Application.** The provisions of this section—

(1) apply only to cooperation with the International Criminal Court and shall not apply to cooperation with an ad hoc international criminal tribunal established by the United Nations Security Council before or after the date of the enactment of this Act [enacted Aug. 2, 2002] to investigate and prosecute war crimes committed in a specific country or during a specific conflict; and

(2) shall not prohibit—

(A) any action permitted under section 2008; or

(B) communication by the United States of its policy with respect to a matter.

(b) **Prohibition on responding to requests for cooperation.** Notwithstanding section 1782 of title 28, United States Code, or any other provision of law, no United States Court, and no agency or entity of any State or local government, including any court, may cooperate with the International Criminal Court in response to a request for cooperation submitted by the International Criminal Court pursuant to the Rome Statute.

(c) **Prohibition on transmittal of letters rogatory from the International Criminal Court.** Notwithstanding section 1781 of title 28, United States Code, or any other provision of law, no agency of the United States Government may transmit for execution any letter rogatory issued, or other request for cooperation made, by the International Criminal Court to the tribunal, officer, or agency in the United States to whom it is addressed.

(d) **Prohibition on extradition to the International Criminal Court.** Notwithstanding any other provision of law, no agency or entity of the United States Government or of any State or local government may extradite any person from the United States to the International Criminal Court, nor support the transfer of any United States citizen or permanent resident alien to the International Criminal Court.

(e) **Prohibition on provision of support to the International Criminal Court.** Notwithstanding any other provision of law, no agency or entity of the United States Government or of any State or local government, including any court, may provide support to the International Criminal Court.

(f) **Prohibition on use of appropriated funds to assist the International Criminal Court.** Notwithstanding any other provision of law, no funds appropriated under any provision of law may be used for the purpose of assisting the investigation, arrest, detention, extradition, or prosecution of any United States citizen or permanent resident alien by the International Criminal Court.

(g) **Restriction on assistance pursuant to mutual legal assistance treaties.** The United States shall exercise its rights to limit the use of assistance provided under all treaties and executive agreements for mutual legal assistance in criminal matters, multilateral conventions with legal assistance provisions, and extradition treaties, to which the United States is a party, and in connection with the execution or issuance of any letter rogatory, to prevent the transfer to, or other use by, the International Criminal Court of any assistance provided by the United States under such treaties or letters rogatory.

(h) **Prohibition on investigative activities of agents.** No agent of the International Criminal Court may conduct, in the United States or any territory subject to the jurisdiction of the United States, any investigative activity relating to a preliminary inquiry, investigation, prosecution, or other proceedings at the International Criminal Court.

* * *

SEC. 2008.   Authority to free members of the Armed Forces of the United States and certain other persons detained or imprisoned by or on behalf of the International Criminal Court.

(a) **Authority.** The president is authorized to use all means necessary and appropriate to bring about the release of any person described in subsection (b) who is being detained or imprisoned by, or on behalf of, or at the request of the International Criminal Court.

(b) Persons authorized to be freed. The authority of subsection

(a) **Shall extend to the following persons:**

(1) Covered United States persons.

(2) Covered Allied persons.

(3) Individuals detained or imprisoned for official actions taken while the individual was a covered United States person or a covered allied person, and in the case of a covered allied person, upon request of such government.

(c) **Authorization of legal assistance.** When any person described in subsection (b) is arrested, detained, investigated, prosecuted, or imprisoned by, on behalf of, or at the request of the International Criminal Court, the President is authorized to direct any agency of the United States Government to provide—

(1) legal representation and other legal assistance to that person (including, in the case of a person entitled to assistance under section 1037 of title 10, United States Code, representation and other assistance in the manner provided in that section):

(2) exculpatory evidence on behalf of that person; and;

(3) defense of the interests of the United States through appearance before the International Criminal Court pursuant to Article 18 or 19 of the Rome Statute, or before the courts or tribunals of any country.

(d) **Bribes and other inducements not authorized.** This section does not authorize the payment of bribes or the provisions of other such incentives to induce the release of a person described subsection (b).

SEC. 2009. Alliance command arrangements

(a). **Report on alliance command arrangements.** Not later than 6 months after the date of the enactment of this Act [enacted Aug. 2, 2002], the President should transmit to the appropriate congressional committees a report with respect to each military alliance to which the United States is a party—

(1) describing the degree to which members of the Armed Forces of the United States may, in the context of military operations undertaken by or pursuant to that alliance, be placed under the command or operational control of foreign military officers subject to the jurisdiction of the International Criminal Court because they are nationals of a party to the International Criminal Court; and

(2) evaluating the degree to which members of the Armed Forces of the United States engaged in military operations undertaken by or pursuant to that alliance may be exposed to greater risks as a result of being placed under the command or operational control of foreign military officers subject to the jurisdiction of the International Criminal Court.

(b) **Description of measures to achieve enhanced protection for members of the Armed Forces of the United States.** Not later than 1 year after the date of the enactment of this Act, the President should transmit to the appropriate congressional committees a description of modifications to command and operational control arrangements within military alliances to which the United States is a party that could be made in order to reduce any risks to members of the Armed Forces of the United States identified pursuant to subsection (a) (2).

* * *

SEC. 2015 Assistance to international efforts

Nothing in this title shall prohibit the United States from rendering assistance to international efforts to bring to justice Saddam Hussein, Slobodan Milosovic, Osama bin Laden, other members of Al Queda, leaders of Islamic Jihad, and other foreign nationals accused of genocide, war crimes or crimes against humanity.

---

9. International Criminal Justice, Asymmetrical Warfare and the Military Commission Controversy

(a) *Public Law* 107-39, 107th Congress

Sept. 18, 2001

Joint Resolution

Whereas on September 11, 2001, terrorists hijacked and destroyed four civilian aircraft, crashing two of them into the towers of the World Trade Center in New York City, and a third into the Pentagon outside Washington, D. C.:

Whereas thousands of innocent Americans were killed and injured as a result of these attacks, including the passengers and crew of the four aircraft, workers in the World Trade Center and in the Pentagon, rescue workers, and bystanders;

Whereas these attacks destroyed both towers of the World Trade Center, as well as adjacent buildings, and seriously damaged the Pentagon; and

Whereas these attacks were by far the deadliest terrorists attacks ever launched against the United States, and, by targeting symbols of American strength and success, clearly were intended to intimidate our Nation and weaken its resolve: Now, therefore, be it

Resolved by the Senate and House of Representatives of the United States of America in Congress assembled, That Congress—

(1) condemns in the strongest possible terms the terrorists who planned and carried out the September 11, 2001, attacks against the United States, as well as their sponsors;

(2) extends its deepest condolences to the victims of these heinous and cowardly attacks, as well as to their families, friends, and loved ones;

(3) is certain that the people of the United States will stand united as our Nation begins the process of recovering and rebuilding in the aftermath of these tragic acts;

(4) commends the heroic actions of the rescue workers, volunteers, and State and local officials who responded to these tragic events with courage, determination, and skill;

(5) declares that these premeditated attacks struck not only at the people of America, but also at the symbols and structures of our economic and military strength, and that the United States is entitled to respond under international law;

(6) thanks those foreign leaders and individual who have expressed solidarity with the United States in the aftermath of the attacks, and asks them to continue to stand with the United States in the war against international terrorism;

(7) commits to support increased resources in the war to eradicate terrorism;

(8) supports the determination of the President, in close consultation with Congress, to bring to justice and punish the perpetrators of these attacks as well as their sponsors; and

(9) declares that September 12, 2001, shall be a National Day of Unity and Mourning, and that when Congress adjourns today, it stands adjourned out of respect to the victims of the terrorist attacks.

Approved September 18, 2001.

(b) *Public Law* 107-40, 107th Congress

Sept. 18, 2001

Joint Resolution

Whereas on September 11, 2001, acts of treacherous violence were committed against the United States and its citizens; and

Whereas, such acts render it both necessary and appropriate that the United States exercise its rights to self-defense and to protect United States citizens both at home and abroad; and

Whereas, in light of the threat to the national security and foreign policy of the United States posed by these grave acts of violence; and

Whereas, such acts continue to pose an unusual and extraordinary threat to the national security and foreign policy of the United States; and

Whereas, the President has authority under the Constitution to take action to deter and prevent acts of international terrorism against the United States: Now, therefore, be it

Resolved by the Senate and House of Representatives of the United States of America in Congress assembled,

Section 1. Short Title.

This joint resolution may be cited as the "Authorization for Use of Military Force."

* * *

(a) In General—That the President is authorized to use all necessary and appropriate force against those nations, organizations, or persons he determines planned, authorized, committed, or aided the terrorist attacks that occurred on September 11, 2001, or harbored such organizations or persons, in order to prevent any future acts of international terrorism against the United States by such nations, organizations or persons.

(b) War Powers Resolution Requirements—

(1) Specific Statutory Authorization—Consistent with section 8(a)(1) of the War Powers Resolution, the Congress declares that this section is intended to constitute specific statutory authorization within the meaning of section 5(b) of the War Powers Resolution.

(2) Applicability of Other Requirement.—Nothing in this resolution supercedes any requirement of the War Powers Resolution.

Approved September 18, 2001.

(c) W. Michael Reisman, *Editorial Comment,* "In Defense of World Public Order"

95 *American Journal of International Law* 833; 833–835 (2001)
Reproduced with permission from 95 *American Journal of International Law,* 833 (2001). © The American Society of International Law

With the end of the Cold War, many in America and throughout the industrialized world came to take national security for granted and to view military action as essentially optional. The lawfulness and wisdom of prospective interventions—in Kuwait, Somalia, Bosnia-Herzegovina, Kosovo, East Timor, or Macedonia—could be debated in terms of humanitarianism, "just war" theories, or the degree of national interest at stake, and stringent pre-conditions for engagement, such as alliance support, projected casualty rates, and carefully defined "exit strategies," could be exacted. Many countries drastically reduced their military budgets. The attacks on September 11, 2001, not only killed thousands of Americans and foreign nationals and tore holes in New York and Washington; they shattered the world view and, quite possibly, the emotional foundation on which that sense of security rested.

All terrorism is unlawful, but the attacks on New York and Washington, whether they prove to have been initiated by groups of individuals or by governments, are different from those that have plagued London, Belfast, Madrid, and Moscow. Those unlawful acts were designed to change a particular policy, but not to destroy a social organization. The ambition, scope, and intended fallout of the acts of September 11 make them an aggression, initially targeting the United States but aimed, through these and subsequent acts, at destroying the social and economic structures and values of a system of world public order, along with the international law that sustains it. Not just the United States, but all peoples who value freedom and human rights have been forced into a war of self-defense.

These implications were quickly and widely recognized. Within a day, NATO's North Atlantic Council agreed that

> if it is determined that this attack was directed from abroad against the United States, it shall be regarded as an action covered under *Article 5* of the Washington Treaty, which states that an armed attack against one or more of the Allies in Europe or North America shall be considered an attack against them all.

The council explained that "[t]he commitment to collective self-defence embodied in the Washington Treaty was first entered into in circumstances very different from those that exist now, but it remains no less valid and no less essential today, in a world subject to the scourge of international terrorism." [Statement of the North Atlantic Council (Sept. 12, 2001)]. On October 2, Lord Robertson, the secretary general of NATO, reported that "it has now been determined that the attack against the United States on 11 September was directed from abroad" and that it would "therefore be regarded as an action covered by Article 5 of the Washington Treaty." [Statement by NATO Secretary General Lord Robertson, Brussels, Belgium (Oct. 2, 2001)].

Meanwhile, on September 12, the United Nations Security Council had issued Resolution 1368, by which the Council,

Recognizing the inherent right of individual or collective self-defence in accordance with the Charter,

1. *Unequivocally condemns* in the strongest terms the horrifying terrorist attacks which took place on 11 September 2001 in New York, Washington, D. C. and Pennsylvania and *regards* such acts, like any other act of international terrorism, as a threat to international peace and security;

...

3. *Calls* on all States to work together urgently to bring to justice the perpetrators, organizers and sponsors of these terrorist attacks and *stresses* that those responsible for aiding, supporting or harbouring the perpetrators, organizers and sponsors of these acts will be held accountable;

...

5. *Expresses* it readiness to take all necessary steps to respond to the terrorist attacks of 11 September 2001, and to combat all forms of terrorism, in accordance with its responsibilities under the Charter of the United Nations.

Many other governments have expressed willingness to assist the United States in this common defense.

This rapidly and almost spontaneously formed coalition evidences the shared perception of a common danger, not simply to individual states, but to a system of world public order. How much cooperation will materialize in the implementation of military and economic strategies in the coming months and years remains to be seen. All the parties have their own concerns and interests, which could diffuse the immediate objectives or simply prove to be incompatible with them. In strategic matters, the efficiency of forceful unilateral action can sometimes outweigh the political advantages and moral strengths of multilateralism. This is why executive committees operate at every level of social organization as unilateral instruments for the implementation of multilateral policy. What is now clear, however, is that the executive committee, whatever its membership, will operate with wide international authority and broad support.

The United States, perforce the leader in this war of self-defense, commands the most powerful military force in the world. The fact that the enemy has no comparable arsenal should not lull observers into the comfortable illusion that victory is assured. For one thing, the enemy has chosen a form of warfare that makes it inaccessible to many current weapons and practices. Moreover, the real sources of strength of the free world—open societies, constitutional safeguards, and a science-based and technological civilization—present the enemy with innumerable vulnerable targets and, often, with the very weapons to attack them, wrecking horrible damage. Using terror, small but radical and ruthless forces, such as Sendero Luminoso and Tamil Eelam, have demonstrated that they can sow violence and destruction and bring large communities to a standstill.

Democracy's arsenal will have to develop new offensive and defensive weapons and new modes of warfare that can destroy the enemy's capacity without destroying democracy itself. The international law about using those weapons will also have to be developed. The different circumstances of each new conflict will require different adaptations, which, while faithful to the policies and principles of humanitarian law, will ensure their continuing relevance in new contexts. For example, the enemy has chosen to infiltrate or conceal itself in apparently neutral countries from which it can conduct a dirty war, targeting and reveling in massive civilian destruction. New methods of response may have to be devised to reach the enemy, even in the territory of states that are unwilling or unable to exercise the control required by international law. Security Council Resolution 1373, adopted on September 28, 2001, spells out many of the specific controls required to defeat the enemy.

Precisely because of who they are, societies that cherish human dignity anguish over every decision about using force, seek to ensure that the law of armed conflict is observed, and, above all, search for avenues of accommodation and settlement. But the United Nations and all people committed to a public order of human dignity must keep in mind that this time they are not engaged in a elective or optional conflict. They are under mortal attack and in a war of self-defense, they must choose between only two possible exit strategies: either victory or defeat.

[Reisman alludes to some of the concepts that comprise so-called "asymmetrical" warfare. The terrorists and the terrorist organizations, for example, that planned and put into execution the September 11th attacks on the United States are outside the definition of "combatants:" who are entitled to the benefits of POW status under international treaties and protocols. Furthermore, the tactics employed in those attacks do not fit neatly into the generally accepted canons of armed conflict. Reisman speaks also of "new modes of warfare" that must be employed in the international war on terror, as well as "[n]ew methods of response…" In short, a virtual sea change is upon us that demands creative ideas and steadfast resolve in fighting a foe that is virtually nihilistic and brazenly suicidal. Traditional military tactics, while still necessary in some contexts, must be re-thought and revised to deal with a threat far more dangerous than any that has faced either the United States or the international community as a whole. The new world order terrorists fail most, if not all, the international law requirements of conducting their operations in accordance with the time-honored laws and customs of war. Their penchant for employing civilians as both the means and ultimately the targets of their attacks flies in the face of international rules and regulations developed over the past century to deal with armed conflict. This is "asymmetrical" warfare in its most destructive and virulent manifestation].

––––––––––

(d) Detlev F. Vagts, *Editorial Comments,* "Hegemonic International Law"

95 *American Journal of International Law* 843; 845–848 (2001)
Reproduced with permission from 95 *American Journal of International Law* 843 (2001). © The American Society of International Law

One increasingly sees the United States designated as the hegemonic (or indispensable, dominant, or preeminent) power. Those employing this terminology include former officials of high rank as well as widely read publicists. The French, for their part, use the term "hyper-power." A passage by Charles Krauthammer in *Time* best captures the spirit: "America is no mere international citizen. It is the dominant power in the world, more dominant than any since Rome. Accordingly, America is in a position to reshape norms, alter expectations and create new realities. How? By unapologetic and implacable demonstrations of will."

The idea of hegemony has begun to work its way into the world of international law to the point where a session of the annual meeting of the American Society of International Law in 2000 was dedicated to "the single superpower." A new undersecretary of state, John Bolton, while still at the American Enterprise Institute, wrote an article entitled *Is There Really "Law" in International Affairs?* that we "should be unashamed, unapologetic, uncompromising American constitutional hegemonists." Since the terrorist attacks of September 11, 2001, the shapers of America foreign policy are showing some signs of second thoughts about the U.S. hegemonic position or at least of thinking of hegemony as a form of leadership rather than command. But it is still appropriate to ask whether there is such a thing as hegemonic international law (HIL) and what it would look like. Bolton answers in the negative, but this Editorial maintains that there can be, and has been, such a thing as HIL. It does not take a position as to whether the United States is or should be a hegemon but merely addresses the lawyer's question of what the legal implications would be if it is.

* * *

II. HIL as Normative

The received body of international law is based on the idea of the equality of states. The United Nations Charter in Article 2(1) proclaims that it is "based on the principle of the sovereign equality of all its Members." In 1979 the General Assembly reinforced that idea by passing a resolution entitled "Inadmissibility of the Policy of Hegemonism in International Relations" (which the United States and three other members opposed). To get to HIL, one must discard or seriously modify this principle. Note that equality is questioned by another influential body of international law thinking, the one that asserts that a different law prevails among liberal democracies than in the rest of the world. HIL advocates would also say that norms cannot stray too far from reality and must therefore recognize inequalities of power.... Even classical publicists of international law acknowledge the role that power, and disparities in power, played in their subject. In the scholarship of international relations, power has been a central object of study ever since the work of Hans Morgenthau.

One might thus conclude that no law graces the Hegemon's universe and this is what Bolton seems to say. But the historical record shows that it can be convenient for the hegemon to have a body of law to work with, provided that it is suitably adapted. Moreover, those subject to its domination may need clear indications of what is expected of them. The hegemon is also a trading party and the world of trade needs rules. While Bolton's national security world may be rather free of rules, his colleague, Special Trade Representative Robert Zoellick, has to operate in the highly legalized universe of the World Trade Organization.

III. HIL and Intervention

A shift to HIL most specially requires setting aside the norm of nonintervention into the internal affairs of states. Indeed, Bolton's objection to international law centers particularly on its attempted use to hamper unilateral intervention by the United States.

German thinking about hegemony centered on defending the legitimacy of German intervention within Europe for such purposes as protecting persons of German origin and attacking the appropriateness of intervention by nations outside the continent. The United States, as all students of history know, openly asserted through the Monroe Doctrine the right to exclude other powers from the Western Hemisphere. It is less generally remembered that the United States also assumed for itself the right to intervene militarily within that territory.

* * *

... Since President Franklin D. Roosevelt withdrew the marines from Haiti and Nicaragua, we have been more circumspect about intervention but have not ceased the practice. Indeed, even without United Nations blessings we have projected military force into areas outside Latin America such as Sudan, Afghanistan, Libya, and the former Yugoslavia. A true hegemon would have reverted to the practice of over intervention and would have demonstrated its unapologetic and implacable will by not canceling air cover for the Bay of Pigs invasion. Whatever changes that would require in international law would have been made.

* * *

V. HIL and Customary International Law

A hegemon confronts customary international law differently from other countries. In terms of the formation of customary law, such a power can by its abstention prevent the emerging rule from becoming part of custom.... [A] customary rule against executing those who commit crimes while under eighteen cannot be confirmed if it is not joined in by the United States—not to mention it sympathizers, such as Iran and Iraq. This implies that, whereas a lesser state might find itself bound by custom even if it failed to sign a treaty that had gained overwhelming assent, a hegemon could safely abstain. If custom has crystallized, the hegemon can disregard it more safely than a treaty rule and have its actions hailed as creative. Bolton finds it even easier to dispose of customary international law than treaties:

> Customary international law changes under this definition when state practice changes, which led former Attorney General Bill Barr to opine: "Well, as I understand it, what you're saying is the only way to change international law is to break it." This telling remark shows the incoherence of treating "customary international law" as law.

Attorney General Barr will be remembered as the author of the policy of extraterritorial abductions in lieu of extradition...

VI Conclusion

This brief survey sketches what HIL might become if international relations move in that direction. Hegemony can obviously vary in degree, ranging from empire to first among equals. The process of adapting present international law to a move toward hegemony would be technically manageable but would highlight features of the hegemonic order that many would find unattractive. Moreover, it would force people who do find the idea of American hegemony attractive to confront its implications in a concrete way.

Just a few years before Britain plunged into World War I and lost its imperial version of hegemony, its most popular poet wrote some lines about publicists and hegemony that are worth recalling when one ponders the relations between states, law, and power.

If, drunk with sight of power, we loose
Wild tongues that have not Thee in awe,
Such boasting as the Gentiles use,
Or lesser breeds without the law—
Lord God of Hosts, be with us yet,
Lest we forget—lest we forget!

For heathern heart that puts her trust
In reeking tube and iron shard,
All valiant dust that builds on dust,
And, guarding, calls not Thee to guard,
For frantic boast and foolish word—
Thy mercy on Thy People, Lord.

Rudyard Kipling, "Recessional" (1897).

(e) United States Department of the Army

FM 27-10, The Law of: Land Warfare 180–81 para. 505d (1956)

d. **How Jurisdiction Exercised.** War crimes are within the jurisdiction of general courts-martial (UCMJ, Art. 18), military commissions, provost courts, military government courts, and other military tribunals (UCMJ, Art. 1) of the United States, as well as of international tribunals.

(f) (1) United States Code

18 USC §2441 (2001)

§2441. War crimes

(a) **Offense**—Whoever, whether inside or outside the United States, commits a war crime, in any of the circumstances described in subsection (b) shall be fined under this title or imprisoned for life or any term of years, or both, and if death results to the victim, shall also be subject to the penalty of death

(b) **Circumstances**—The circumstances referred to in subsection (a) are that the person committing such war crime or the victim of such war crime is a member of the Armed Forces of the United States or a national of the United States...

(c) **Definition**—As used in this section, the term "war crime" means any conduct—

(1) defined as a grave breach in any of the international conventions signed at Geneva 12 August 1949, or any protocol to such convention to which the United States is a party;

(2) prohibited by Article 23, 25, 27, or 28 of the Annex to the Hague Convention IV, Respecting the Laws and Customs of War on land, signed 18 October 1907;

(3) which constitutes a violation of common Article 3 of the international conventions signed at Geneva, 12 August 1949, or any protocol to such convention to which the United States is a party and which deals with non-international armed conflict; or

(4) of a person who, in relation to an armed conflict and contrary to the provisions of the Protocol on Prohibition or Restrictions on the Use of Mines, Booby-Traps and

Other Devices as amended at Geneva on 3 May 1996 (Protocol II as amended on 3 May 1996), when the United states is a party to such Protocol, willfully kills or causes serious injury to civilians.

(g) (2) United States Code

10 USC §836 (2003)

§836. President prescribes rules

(a) Pretrial, trial, and post-trial procedures, including modes of proof, for cases arising under this chapter triable in courts-martial, military commissions and other military tribunals, and procedures for courts of inquiry, may be prescribed by the President by regulations which shall, so far as he considers practicable, apply the principles of law and the rules of evidence generally recognized in the trial of criminal cases in the United States district courts...

(h) *Ex parte Milligan*

Supreme Court of the United States
71 U.S. (4 Wall.) 2 (1867)

MR. JUSTICE DAVIS delivered the opinion of the court.

On the 10th day of May, 1865, Lambdin P. Milligan presented a petition to the Circuit Court of the United States of the District of Indiana, to be discharged from an alleged unlawful imprisonment. The case made by the petition is this: Milligan is a citizen of the United States; has lived for twenty years in Indiana; and, at the time of the grievances complained of, was not, and never had been in the military or naval service of the United States. On the 5th day of October, 1864, while at home, he was arrested by order of General Alvin P. Hovey, commanding the military district of Indiana; and has ever since been kept in close confinement. [Milligan was an Indiana "Copperhead," a term of opprobrium that designated those persons in the North who had strong pro-southern allegiances. He had assisted in organizing a group called the Order of the American Knights who allegedly had plotted an armed uprising in Indiana and, coincident with such plot, had asked for military assistance from the Confederacy].

On the 21st day of October, 1864, he was brought before a military commission, convened at Indianapolis, by order of General Hovey, tried on certain charges and specifications; found guilty, and sentenced to be hanged; and the sentence ordered to be executed on Friday, the 19th day of May, 1865.

On the 2d day of January, 1865, after the proceedings of the military commission were at an end, the Circuit Court of the United States for Indiana met in Indianapolis and empanelled a grand jury, who were charged to inquire whether the laws of the United States had been violated; and, if so, to make presentments. The court adjourned on the 27th day of January, having, prior thereto, discharged from further service the grand jury, who did not find any bill of indictment or make any presentment against Milligan for any offence whatever; and, in fact, since his imprisonment, no bill of indictment has been found or presentment made against him by any grand jury of the United States.

Milligan insists that said military commission had no jurisdiction to try him upon the charges preferred, or upon any charges whatever; because he was a citizen of the United States and the State of Indiana, and had not been, since the commencement of the late Rebellion, a resident of any of the States whose citizens were arrayed against the government, and that the right of trial by jury was guaranteed to him by the Constitution of the United States.

The prayer of the petition was, that under the act of Congress, approved March 3d, 1863, entitled, "An act relating to *habeas corpus* and regulating judicial proceedings in certain cases," he may be brought before the court, and either turned over to the proper civil tribunal to be proceeded against according to the law of the land or discharged from custody altogether.

With the petition were filed the order for the commission, the charges and specifications, the findings of the court, with the order of the War Department reciting that the sentence was approved by the President of the United States, and directing that it be carried into execution without delay. The petition was presented and filed in open court by the counsel for Milligan; at the same time the District Attorney of the United States for Indiana appeared, and, by the agreement of counsel, the application was submitted to the court. The opinions of the judges of the Circuit Court were opposed on three questions, which are certified to the Supreme Court:

1st. "On the facts stated in said petition and exhibits, ought a writ of *habeas corpus* to be issued"?

2d. On the facts stated in said petition and exhibits, ought the said Lambdin P. Milligan to be discharged from custody as in said petition prayed"?

3d "Whether, upon the facts stated in said petition and exhibits, the military commission mentioned therein had jurisdiction legally to try and sentence said Milligan in manner and form as in said petition and exhibits as stated"?

The importance of the main question presented by this record cannot be overstated; for it involves the very framework of the government and the fundamental principles of American liberty.

During the late wicked Rebellion, the temper of the times did not allow that calmness in deliberation and discussion so necessary to a correct conclusion of a purely judicial question. *Then,* considerations of safety were mingled with the exercise of power; and feelings and interests prevailed which are happily terminated. *Now* that the public safety is assured, this question as well as all others, can be discussed and decided without passion or the admixture of any element not required to form a legal judgment. We approach the investigation of this case, fully sensible of the magnitude of the inquiry and the necessity of full and cautious deliberation.

* * *

In interpreting a law, the motives which must have operated with the legislature in passing it are proper to be considered. This law was passed in a time of great national peril, when our heritage of free government was in danger. An armed rebellion against the national authority, of greater proportions than history affords an example of, was raging; and the public safety required that the privilege of the writ of *habeas corpus* should be suspended.

* * *

…The privilege of this great writ had never before been withheld from the citizen; and as the exigence of the times demanded immediate action, it was of the highest importance that the lawfulness of the suspension should be fully established. It was under these circumstances, which were such as to arrest the attention of the country, that this law was passed. The President was authorized by it to suspend the privilege of the writ of *habeas corpus*, whenever, in his judgment, the public safety required; and he did, by proclamation, bearing date of 15th of September, 1863, reciting, among other things, the authority of this statute, suspend it. The suspension of the writ does not authorize the arrest of any one, but simply denies to one arrested the privilege of this writ in order to obtain his liberty.

It is proper, therefore, to inquire under what circumstances the courts could rightfully refuse to grant this writ, and when the citizen was at liberty to invoke its aid.

* * *

The controlling question in this case is this: Upon the *facts* stated in Milligan's petition, and the exhibits filed, had the military commission mentioned in it *jurisdiction*, legally, to try and sentence him? Milligan, not a resident of one of the rebellious states, or a prisoner of war, but a citizen of Indiana for twenty years past, and never in the military or naval service, is, while at his home, arrested by the military power of the United States, imprisoned, and, on certain criminal charges preferred against him, tried, convicted, and sentenced to be hanged by a military commission, organized under the direction of the military commander of the military district of Indiana. Had this tribunal the *legal* power and authority to try and punish this man?

No graver question was ever considered by this court, nor one which more nearly concerns the rights of the whole people; for it is the birthright of every American citizen when charged with crime, to be tried and punished according to law.... If there was law to justify this military trial, it is not our province to interfere; if there was not, it is our duty—to declare the nullity of the whole proceedings.

* * *

Time has proven the discernment of our ancestors;... Those great and good men foresaw that troublous times would arise, when rulers and people would become restive under restraint, and see by sharp and decisive measures to accomplish ends deemed just and proper; and that the principles of constitutional liberty would be in peril, unless established by irrepealable law. The history of the world had taught them that what was done in the past might be attempted in the future. The Constitution of the United States is a law for rulers and people, equally in war and in peace, and covers with the shield of its protection all classes of men, at all times, and under all circumstances. No doctrine, involving more pernicious consequences, was ever invented by the wit of man than that any of its provisions can be suspended during any of the great exigencies of government. Such a doctrine leads directly to anarchy or despotism, but the theory of necessity on which it is based is false; for the government, within the Constitution, has all the powers granted to it, which are necessary to preserve its existence; as has been happily proved by the result of the great effort to throw off its just authority.

Have any of the rights guaranteed by the Constitution been violated in the case of Milligan? and if so, what are they?

Every trial involves the exercise of judicial power; and from what source did the military commission that tried him derive their authority? Certainly no part of the judicial power of the country was conferred on them; because the Constitution expressly vests it "in one supreme court and such inferior courts as the Congress may from time to time ordain and establish," and it is not pretended that the commission was a court ordained and established by Congress. They cannot justify on the mandate of the President; because he is controlled by law, and has his appropriate sphere of duty, which is to execute, not to make, the laws; and there is "no unwritten criminal code to which resort can be had as a source of jurisdiction."

But it is said that the jurisdiction is complete under the "laws and usages of war."

It can serve no useful purpose to inquire what those laws and usages are, whence they originated, where found, and on whom they operate; they can never be applied to citizens in states which have upheld the authority of the government, and where the courts are open and their process unobstructed. This court has judicial knowledge that in Indiana the Federal authority was always unopposed, and its courts always open to hear criminal accusations and redress grievances; and no usage of war could sanction a military trial there for any offence whatever of a citizen in civil life, in nowise connected with the military service. Congress could grant no such power; and to the honor of our national legislature be it said, it has never been provoked by the state of the country even to attempt its exercise. One of the plainest constitutional provisions was, therefore, infringed when Milligan was tried by a court not ordained and established by Congress, and not composed of judges appointed during good behaviour.

* * *

The discipline necessary to the efficiency of the army and navy, required other and swifter modes of trial than are furnished by the common law courts; and, in pursuance of the power conferred by the Constitution, Congress has declared the kinds of trial, and the manner in which they shall be conducted, for offences committed while the party is in the military or naval service. Every one connected with these branches of the public service is amenable to the jurisdiction which Congress has created for their government, and, while thus serving, surrenders his right to be tried by the civil courts. *All other persons*, citizens of states where the courts are open, if charged with crime, are guaranteed the inestimable privilege of trial by jury. This privilege is a vital principle, underlying the whole administration of criminal justice; it is not held by sufferance, and cannot be frittered away on any plea of state or political necessity....

* * *

This nation, as experience has proved, cannot always remain at peace, and has no right to expect that it will always have wise and humane rulers, sincerely attached to the principles of the Constitution. Wicked men, ambitious of power, with hatred of liberty and contempt of law, may fill the peace once occupied by Washington and Lincoln; and if this right is conceded, and the calamities of war again befall us, the dangers to human liberty are frightful to contemplate. If our fathers had failed to provide for just such a contingency, they would have been false to the trust reposed in them. They knew—the history of the world told them—the nation they were founding, be its existence short or long, would be involved in war; how often or how long continued, human foresight could not tell; and that unlimited power, wherever lodged at such a time, was especially hazardous to freemen. For this, and other equal*ly* weighty reasons, they secured the inheritance they had fought to maintain, by incorporating in a written constitution the safeguards which *time* had proved were essential to its preservation. Not one of these safeguards can the President, or Congress, or the Judiciary disturb, except the one concerning the writ of *habeas corpus.*

* * *

To the third question, then, on which the judges below were opposed in opinion, an answer in the negative must be returned.

* * *

The two remaining questions in this case must be answered in the affirmative. The suspension of the privilege of the writ of *habeas corpus* does not suspend the writ itself. The writ issues as a matter of course; and on the return made to it the court decides whether the party applying is denied the right of proceedings any further with it.

* * *

...Milligan avers he was a citizen of Indiana, not in the military or naval service, and was detained in close confinement, by order of the President, from the 5th day of October, 1864, until the 2d of January, 1865, when the Circuit Court for the District of Indiana, with a grand jury, convened in session at Indianapolis; and afterwards, on the 27th day of the same month, adjourned without finding an indictment or presentment against him. If these averments were true (and their truth is conceded for the purposes of this case), the court was required to liberate him on taking certain oaths prescribed by the law, and entering into recognizance for his good behaviour.

[The *Milligan* decision was a landmark ruling that placed limits on the jurisdiction of military commissions. A large segment of the opinion dealt with the granting or withholding of the writ of *habeas corpus*. *Habeas corpus* is a procedural devise whose function it is to determine the legality or illegality of an individual's incarceration. Milligan was being detained in military custody at the time his lawyer sought the writ. If it is established that one's imprisonment does not conform to the law, the prisoner is entitled to immediate release from custody. For over 140 years, Abraham Lincoln's decision in 1863 to *suspend* (not abrogate) the writ of *habeas corpus* has been a source of controversy producing a multitude of contending arguments by publicists of all persuasions.

Ex parte Milligan stood for the proposition that the writ of *habeas corpus* could lawfully be suspended, but that the *source* of such a suspension must originate in the Congress, not with the President. Furthermore, the Court was quite explicit in ruling that civilian citizen detainees could not be tried before a military commission in a jurisdiction loyal to the federal government in which its domestic courts were open and functioning. This, despite the fact that there was ample evidence suggesting that Milligan was complicit in fomenting armed rebellion against the United States during the Civil war.

The late Chief Justice of the United States, William H. Rehnquist, wrote that "[t]he *Milligan* decision is justly celebrated for its rejection of the government's position that the Bill of Rights has no application in wartime."[10] Military tribunals were also convened during the Civil War in those parts of the South occupied by Union armed forces. At the conclusion of hostilities, military courts were established in various Southern states during some portions of the Reconstruction era as a result of the passage of the *Military Reconstruction Act* of March 2, 1867. However, by 1877, all military commissions had ceased operations within the states of the former Confederacy. Williams[11] provides an excellent historical and legal insight into the various countervailing currents surrounding Lincoln's decision to suspend the writ of *habeas corpus* in 1863.

---

10. William H. Rehnquist, *All the Liberties But One: Civil Liberties in Wartime* 137 (1998).

11. Frank J. Williams, *Abraham Lincoln, Civil Liberties and the Corning Letter*, 5 *Roger Williams U. L. Rev.* 319 (2000).

During World War I, a lieutenant in the German Navy, one Lothar Witzke, was arrested in Arizona in 1918 after he had entered the United States from Mexico dressed in civilian clothes. Witzke was charged with spying for Imperial Germany, tried by a secret United States Army courts-martial, convicted and sentenced to be hanged. Subsequently, in 1920, President Woodrow Wilson commuted Witzke's sentence to life imprisonment after he had rescued several inmates in a prison fire. He was eventually released from custody in 1923 and was returned to Germany where he was decorated with two Iron Cross medals.

Some seventy-six years after *Milligan* and twenty-four years after the *Witzke* courts-martial, the Supreme Court of the United States once again had occasion to consider the issue of *habeas corpus*, military commissions and the federal government's handling of eight German saboteurs who, during World War II, landed surreptitiously in the United States on Long Island, New York, and on the northern coast of Florida in June, 1942. Trained at the secret Quenz Lake camp for saboteurs in East Prussia on an estate confiscated from a wealthy Jewish landowner by the Nazis, the members of code-named "Operation Pastorius" consisted of eight men transported in two four-man teams to the United States on two separate U-boats. Their names, in alphabetical order were: Ernest Peter Burger, George John Dasch, Herbie Haupt, Heinrich Heinck, Edward Kerling, Hermann Neubauer, Richard Quirin and Werner Thiel. They came ashore wearing German military uniforms under cover of darkness, but quickly changed into civilian dress, buried their uniforms, munitions and other devices, and headed inland with a large amount of United States currency in their possession for a planned rendevous to make plans for carrying out their assigned tasks. Their plan was never put into operation. They were arrested by the FBI less than three weeks after their clandestine arrival in the United States, largely due to information personally supplied to the FBI by George John Dasch, who, in his later testimony, stated he never intended to carry out his part of the operation.

President Franklin D. Roosevelt, once he was notified of the arrests of all eight members of "Operation Pastorius," concluded that they must be swiftly tried, sentenced and executed in order to send a message to Nazi Germany that they should seriously reconsider whether they should again send saboteurs to American shores. News of the Germans' arrests was not well received by Adolph Hitler. In his outstanding historical narrative of "Operation Pastorius" and the *Quirin* case, Dobbs[12] writes:

> News of the saboteur debacle reached Hitler at the Wolf's Lair in eastern Prussia as he was preparing a new offensive in the Crimea. In the early morning hours of Sunday, June 28, [1942] Berlin time, American radio stations started carrying reports of the arrest of all the participants in Operation Pastorius. The detail contained in the reports — the names of the V-men, as well as an account of how they received training at a sabotage school outside Berlin — left no room for doubt that the operation had been a complete fiasco.
>
> The Führer was livid. He summoned the Abwehr [German Intelligence] chiefs, Canaris and Lahousen, to appear at Wolfsschanze the following Tuesday. Once again, they took a military plane from Berlin to Rastenburg, and then a staff car through the woods to Hitler's military headquarters. That afternoon, Hitler subjected them to one of his most withering tirades, complaining that the Americans had achieved a huge propaganda victory....

---

12. Michael Dobbs, *Saboteurs: The Nazi Raid on America* (2004).

Canaris tried to shift the blame onto the Nazi Party, arguing that the sabo-teurs had not been "trained Abwehr agents," but Nazi loyalists selected by the party. This only made Hitler more angry.

"Why didn't you use Jews for that?" he yelled at the stocky admiral....

The commander in chief of the submarine fleet, Admiral Dönitz, was also infuriated by the news from America. He had little confidence in either the Ab-wehr or the Nazi Party's Ausland Institut, which had screened the agents in the first place. He had opposed the use of U-boats for transporting saboteurs, and had only agreed to Operation Pastorius after being assured by the Abwehr that the V-men were all "high-class intelligence agents." This was obviously not the case, and Dönitz angrily withdrew his consent for follow-up operations.[13]

The trial of the saboteurs began promptly at 10:00 a.m. on July 8, 1942, in a special room set aside for that purpose on the fifth floor of the Department of Justice building in Washington, D. C. amid tight security. The defense attorneys assigned to the case, Kenneth C. Royall and Cassius M. Dowell, both Army colonels, immediately sensed that the Military Commission convened to hear these proceedings would not allow them to argue certain points of constitutional law that would have been relevant if pre-sented in a United States District Court and even, perhaps, in a general courts-martial. During the course of the trial, therefore, defense counsel felt an obligation to challenge the legality of the commission itself. They eventually persuaded all members of the United States Supreme Court, most of whom were on vacation at the time, to convene in emergency session to hear their arguments challenging the legality of the military proceedings continuing apace in the Justice Department. Defense lawyers Royall and Dowell also wanted to mount a full legal challenge to President Roosevelt's proclama-tion establishing procedures to try the Germans. A petition for a writ of *habeas corpus* was first filed in the United States District Court for the District of Columbia. When Judge James W. Morris summarily rejected the petitions, in the words of Dobbs, "[t]he stage was now set for a landmark Supreme Court hearing"[14].

(i) *Ex parte Quirin*

Supreme Court of the United States
317 U.S. 1 (1942)
[Full Opinion filed, October 29, 1942]

MR. CHIEF JUSTICE STONE delivered the opinion of the Court.

These cases are brought here by petitioners' several applications for leave to file peti-tions for habeas corpus in this Court, and by their petitions for certiorari to review or-ders of the District Court for the District of Columbia, which denied their applications for leave to file petitions for habeas corpus in that court.

The question for decision is whether the detention of petitioners by respondent for trial by Military Commission, appointed by Order of the President of July 2, 1942, on charges preferred against them purporting to set out their violations of the law of war and of the Articles of war, is in conformity to the laws and Constitution of the United States.

---

13. *Id.* at 201–202.
14. *Id.* at 237.

After denial of their application by the District Court,... petitioners' ask leave to file petitions for habeas corpus in this Court. In view of the public importance of the questions raised by their petitions and of the duty which rests on the courts, in time of war as well as in time of peace, to preserve unimpaired the constitutional safeguards of civil liberty, and because in our opinion the public interest required that we consider and decide those questions without any avoidable delay, we directed that petitioners' applications be set down for full oral argument at a special term of this Court, convened on July 29, 1942. The applications for leave to file the petitions were presented in open court on that day and we heard on the petitions, the answers to them of respondent, a stipulation of facts by counsel, and the record of the testimony given before the Commission.

While the argument was proceeding before us, petitioners perfected their appeals from the orders of the District Court to the United States Court of Appeals for the District of Columbia and thereupon filed with this Court petitions for certiorari to the Court of Appeals before judgment, pursuant to §240(a) of the Judicial Code, 28 U.S.C. §347(a). We granted certiorari before judgment for the reasons which moved us to convene the special term of Court. In accordance with the stipulation of counsel we treat the record, briefs and arguments in the habeas corpus proceedings in this Court as the record, briefs and arguments upon the writs of certiorari.

On July 31, 1942, after hearing argument of counsel and after full consideration of all questions raised, this Court affirmed the orders of the District Court and denied petitioners' application for leave to file petitions for habeas corpus. By per curiam opinion we announced the decision of the Court, and that the full opinion in the causes would be prepared and filed with the Clerk.

The following facts appear from the petitions or are stipulated. Except as noted they are undisputed.

All the petitioners were born in Germany; all have lived in the United States. All returned to Germany between 1933 and 1941. All except petitioner Haupt are admittedly citizens of the German Reich, with which the United States is at war. Haupt came to this country with his parents when he was five years old; it is contended that he became a citizen of the Untied States by virtue of the naturalization of his parents during his minority and that he has not since lost his citizenship. The Government, however, takes the position that on attaining his majority he elected to maintain German allegiance and citizenship, or in any case that he has by his conduct renounced or abandoned his United States citizenship.... For reasons presently to be stated we do not find it necessary to resolve these contentions.

After the declaration of war between the United States and the German Reich, petitioners received training at a sabotage school near Berlin, Germany, where they were instructed in the use of explosives and in methods of secret writing. Thereafter petitioners, with a German citizen, Dasch, proceeded from Germany to a seaport in Occupied France, where petitioners Burger, Heinck, and Quirin, together with Dasch, boarded a German submarine which proceeded across the Atlantic to Amagansett Beach on Long Island, New York. The four were then landed from the submarine in the hours of darkness, on or about June 13, 1942, carrying with them a supply of explosives, fuses, and incendiary and timing devices. While landing they wore German Marine Infantry uniforms or parts of uniforms. Immediately after landing they buried their uniforms and other articles mentioned, and proceeded in civilian dress to New York City.

The remaining four petitioners at the same French port boarded another German submarine, which carried them across the Atlantic to Ponte Vedra Beach, Florida. On or about June 17, 1942, they came ashore during the hours of darkness, wearing caps of the German Marine Infantry and carrying with them a supply of explosives, fuses, and incendiary and timing devices. They immediately buried their caps and other articles mentioned, and proceeded in civilian dress to Jacksonville, Florida, and thence to various points in the United States. All were taken into custody in New York or Chicago by agents of the Federal Bureau of Investigation. All had received instructions in Germany from an officer of the German High Command to destroy war industries and war facilities in the United States, for which they or their relatives in Germany were to receive salary payments from the German Government. They also had been paid by the German Government during their course of training at the sabotage school and had received substantial sums in United States currency, which were in their possession when arrested. The currency had been handed to them by an officer of the German High Command, who had instructed them to wear their German uniforms while landing in the United States.

The President, as President and Commander in Chief of the Army and Navy, by Order of July 2, 1942, appointed a Military Commission and directed it to try petitioners for offenses against the law of war and the Articles of War, and prescribed regulations for the procedure on the trial and for review of the record of the trial and of any judgment or sentence of the Commission. On the same day, by Proclamation, the President declared that "all persons who are subjects, citizens or residents of any nation at war with the United States or who give obedience to or act under the direction of any such nation, and who during time of war enter or attempt to enter the United States... through coastal or boundary defenses, and are charged with committing or attempting or preparing to commit sabotage, espionage, hostile or warlike acts, or violations of the law of war, shall be subject to the law of war and to the jurisdiction of military tribunals." [7 Federal Register 5101].

The Proclamation also stated in terms that all such persons were denied access to the courts.

Pursuant to the direction of the Attorney General, the Federal Bureau of Investigation surrendered custody of petitioners to respondent, Provost Marshall of the Military District of Washington, who was directed by the Secretary of War to receive and keep them in custody, and who thereafter held petitioners for trial before the Commission.

On July 3, 1942, the Judge Advocate General's Department of the Army prepared and lodged with the Commission the following charges against petitioners, supported by specifications:

1. Violation of the law of war.

2. Violation of Article 81 of the Articles of War, defining the offense of relieving or attempting to relieve, or corresponding with or giving intelligence to, the enemy.

3. Violation of Article 82, defining the offense of spying.

4. Conspiracy to commit the offenses alleged in charges 1, 2 and 3.

The Commission met on July 8, 1942, and proceeded with the trial, which continued in progress while the causes were pending in this Court. On July 27th, before petitioners' applications to the District Court, all the evidence for the prosecution and the defense had been taken by the Commission and the case had been closed except for arguments of counsel. It is conceded that ever since petitioners' arrest the state and federal courts in Florida, New York, and the District of Columbia, and in the states in which each of the petitioners was arrested or detained, have been open and functioning normally.

* * *

Petitioners' main contention is that the President is without any statutory or constitutional authority to order the petitioners to be tried by military tribunal for offenses with which they are charged; that in consequence they are entitled to be tried in the civil courts with the safeguards, including trial by jury, which the Fifth and Sixth Amendments guarantee to all persons charged in such courts with criminal offenses. In any case it is urged that the President's Order, in prescribing the procedure of the Commission and the method for review of its findings and sentence, and the proceedings of the Commission under the Order, conflict with Articles 38, 43, 46, 50 and ½ and 70 — are illegal and void.

The Government challenges each of these propositions. But regardless of their merits, it also insists that petitioners must be denied access to the courts, both because they are enemy aliens or have entered our territory as enemy belligerents, and because the President's Proclamation undertakes in terms to deny such access to the class of persons defined by the Proclamation, which aptly describes the character and conduct of petitioners. It is urged that if they are enemy aliens or if the Proclamation has force, no court may afford the petitioners a hearing. But there is certainly nothing in the Proclamation to preclude access to the courts for determining its applicability to the particular case. And neither the Proclamation nor the fact that they are enemy aliens forecloses consideration by the courts of petitioners' contentions that the Constitution and laws of the United States constitutionally enacted forbid their trial by military commission. As announced in our per curiam opinion, we have resolved those questions by our conclusion that the Commission has jurisdiction to try the charge preferred against petitioners. There is therefore no occasion to decide contentions of the parties unrelated to this issue. We pass at once to the consideration of the basis of the Commission's authority.

We are not here concerned with any questions of the guilt or innocence of petitioners. Constitutional safeguards for the protection of all who are charged with offenses are not to be disregarded in order to inflict merited punishment on some who are guilty.... But the detention and trial of petitioners — ordered by the President in the declared exercise of his powers as Commander in Chief of the Army in time of war and of grave public danger — are not to be set aside by the courts without the clear conviction that they are in conflict with the Constitution or laws of Congress constitutionally enacted.

Congress and the President, like the courts, possess no power not derived from the Constitution. But one of the objects of the Constitution, as declared by its preamble, is to "provide for the common defense."

* * *

The Constitution thus invests the President, as Commander in Chief, with the power to wage war which Congress has declared, and to carry into effect all laws passed by Congress for the conduct of war and for the government and regulation of the Armed Forces, and all laws defining and punishing offenses against the law of nations, including those whose pertain to the conduct of war.

By the Articles of War, 10 U.S.C. §§1471–1593, Congress has provided rules for the government of the Army. It has provided for the trial and punishment, by courts martial, of violations of the Articles by members of the armed forces and by specified classes of persons associated or serving with the Army.... But the Articles also recognize the "military commission" appointed by military command as an appropriate tribunal for the trial and punishment of offenses against the law of war not ordinarily tried by courts[s] martial.... Articles 38 and 46 authorize the President, with certain limitations, to prescribe the procedure for military commissions....

* * *

Similarly the Espionage Act of 1917, which authorizes trial in the district courts of certain offenses that tend to interfere with the prosecution of war, provides that nothing contained in the act "shall be deemed to limit the jurisdiction of the general courts-martial, military commissions, or naval courts-martial." 50 U.S.C. §38.

From the very beginning of its history this Court has recognized and applied the law of war as including that part of the law of nations which prescribes, for the conduct of war, the status, rights and duties of enemy nations as well as enemy individuals. By the Articles of War, and especially Article 15, Congress has explicitly provided, so far as it may constitutionally do so, that military tribunals shall have jurisdiction to try offenders or offenses against the law of war in appropriate cases. Congress, in addition to making rules for the government of our Armed Forces, has thus exercised its authority to define and punish offenses against the law of nations by sanctioning, within constitutional limitations, the jurisdiction of military commissions to try persons for offenses which, according to the rules and precepts of the law of nations, and more particularly the law of war, are cognizable by such tribunals. And the President, as Commander in Chief, by his Proclamation in time of war has invoked that law. By his Order creating the present Commission he has undertaken to exercise the authority conferred upon him by Congress, and also such authority as the Constitution itself gives the Commander in Chief, to direct the performance of those functions which may constitutionally be performed by the military arm of the nation in time of war.

* * *

By universal agreement and practice, the law of war draws a distinction between the armed forces and the peaceful populations of belligerent nations, and also between those who are lawful and unlawful combatants. Lawful combatants are subject to capture and detention as prisoners of war by opposing military forces. Unlawful combatants are likewise subject to capture and detention, but in addition they are subject to trial and punishment by military tribunals for acts which render their belligerency unlawful.... [A]n enemy combatant who without uniform comes secretly through the lines for the purpose of waging war by destruction of life or property, are familiar examples of belligerents who are generally deemed not to be entitled to the status of prisoners of war, but to be offenders against the law of war subject to trial and punishment by military tribunals....

Such was the practice of our own military authorities before the adoption of the Constitution, and during the Mexican and Civil Wars.

* * *

...The definition of lawful belligerents by Paragraph 9 is that adopted by Article 1, Annex to Hague Convention No. IV of October 18, 1907, to which the United States was a signatory and which was ratified by the Senate in 1909.... The preamble to the Convention declares:

"Until a more complete code of the laws of war has been issued, the High Contracting Parties deem it expedient to declare that, in cases not included in the Regulations adopted by them, the inhabitants and the belligerents remain under the protection and the rule of the principles of the law of nations, as they result from the usages established among civilized peoples, from the laws of humanity, and the dictates of public conscience."

Our Government, by thus defining lawful belligerents entitled to be treated as prisoners of war, has recognized that there is a class of unlawful belligerents not entitled to that privilege, including those who, though combatants, do not wear "fixed and distinctive emblems." And by Article 15 of the Articles of War Congress has made provision for their trial and punishment by military commission, according to "the law of war."

By a long course of practical administrative construction by its military authorities, our Government has likewise recognized that those who during time of war pass surreptitiously from enemy territory into our own, discarding their uniforms upon entry, for the commission of hostile acts involving destruction of life or property, have the status of unlawful combatants punishable as such by military commission. This precept of the law of war has been so recognized in practice both here and abroad, and has so generally been accepted as valid by authorities on international law, that we think it must be regarded as a rule or principle of the law of war recognized by this Government by its enactment of the Fifteenth Article of War.

* * *

The law of war cannot rightly treat those agents of enemy armies who enter our territory, armed with explosives intended for the destruction of war industries and supplies, as any the less belligerent enemies than are agents similarly entering for the purpose of destroying fortified places or our Armed Forces. By passing our boundaries for such purposes without uniform or other emblem signifying their belligerent status, or by discarding that means of identification after entry, such enemies become unlawful belligerents subject to trial and punishment.

Citizenship in the United States of an enemy belligerent does not relieve him from the consequences of belligerency which is unlawful because in violation of the law of war. Citizens who associate themselves with the military arm of the enemy government, and with its aid, guidance and direction enter this country bent on hostile acts, are enemy belligerents within the meaning of the Hague Convention and the law of war.... It is as an enemy belligerent that petitioner Haupt is charged with entering the United States, and unlawful belligerency is the gravamen of the offense of which he is accused.

* * *

...We have no occasion now to define with meticulous care the ultimate boundaries of the jurisdiction of military tribunals to try persons according to the law of war. It is enough that petitioners here, upon the conceded facts, were plainly within those boundaries, and were held in good faith for trial by military commission, charged with being enemies who, with the purpose of destroying war materials and utilities, entered, or after entry remained in, our territory without uniform—an offense against the law of war. We hold only that those particular acts constitute an offense against the law of war which the Constitution authorizes to be tried by military commission.

* * *

Accordingly, we conclude that Charge I, on which petitioners were detained for trial by the Military Commission, alleged an offense which the President is authorized to order tried by military commission; that his Order convening the Commission was a lawful order and that the Commission was lawfully constituted; that the petitioners were held in lawful custody and did not show cause for their discharge. It follows that the orders of the District Court should be affirmed, and that leave to file petitions for habeas corpus in this Court should be denied.

MR. JUSTICE ROBERTS took no part in the consideration or decision of these cases.

(j) *Duncan v. Kahanamoku*

Supreme Court of the United States
327 U.S. 304 (1946)

MR. JUSTICE BLACK delivered the opinion of the Court.

These petitioners in these cases were sentenced to prison by military tribunals in Hawaii. Both are civilians. The question before us is whether the military tribunals had power to do this. The United States district court for Hawaii in habeas corpus proceedings held that the military tribunals had no such power and ordered that they be set free. The circuit court of appeals reversed, and ordered that the petitioners be returned to prison.... Both cases thus involve the rights of individuals charged with crime and not connected with the armed forces to have their guilt or innocence determined in courts of law which provide established procedural safeguards, rather than by military tribunals which fail to afford many of these safeguards. Since these judicial safeguards are prized privileges of our system of government we granted certiorari.

The following events led to the military tribunals' exercise of jurisdiction over the petitioners. On December 7, 1941, immediately following the surprise air attack by the Japanese on Pearl Harbor, the Governor of Hawaii by proclamation undertook to suspend the privilege of the writ of habeas corpus and to place the Territory under "martial law." Section 67 of the Hawaiian Organic Act...authorizes the Territorial Governor to take this action "in case of rebellion or invasion, or imminent danger thereof, when the public safety requires it..." His action was to remain in effect only "until communication can be had with the President and his decision thereon made known." The President approved the Governor's action on December 9th. The Governor's proclamation also authorized and requested the Commanding General, "during the...emergency and until danger of invasion is removed, to exercise all the powers normally exercised" by the Governor and by the "judicial officers and employees of this territory."

Pursuant to this authorization the commanding general immediately proclaimed himself Military Governor and undertook the defense of the Territory and the maintenance of order. On December 8th, both civil and criminal courts were forbidden to summon jurors and witnesses and to try cases. The Commanding General established military tribunals to take the place of the courts. These were to try civilians charged with violating the laws of the United States and of the Territory, and rules, regulations, orders or policies of the Military Government. Rules of evidence and procedure of courts of law were not to control the military trials. In imposing penalties the military tribunals were to be "guided by, but not limited to the penalties authorized by the courts martial manual, the laws of the United States, the Territory of Hawaii, the District of Columbia, and the customs of war in like cases." The rule announced was simply that punishment was to be "commensurate with the offense committed" and that the death penalty might be imposed "in appropriate cases." Thus the military authorities took over the government of Hawaii. They could and did, by simply promulgating orders, govern the day to day activities of civilians who lived, worked, or were merely passing through there. The military tribunals interpreted the very orders promulgated by the military authorities and proceeded to punish violators. The sentences imposed were not subject to direct appellate court review, since it had long been established that military tribunals are not part of our judicial system *Ex parte Vallandigham*, 1 Wall. 243.

The military undoubtedly assumed that its rule was not subject to any judicial control whatever, for by orders issued on August 25, 1943, it prohibited even accepting of a petition for writ of habeas corpus by a judge or judicial employee or the filing of such a petition by a prisoner or his attorney. Military tribunals could punish violators of these orders by fine, imprisonment or death.

White, the petitioner in No. 15, was s stockbroker in Honolulu. Neither he nor his business was connected with the armed forces. On August 20, 1942, more than eight months after the Pearl Harbor attack, the military police arrested him. The charge against him was embezzling stock belonging to another civilian in violation of Chapter 183 of the Revised Laws of Hawaii. Though by the time of White's arrest the courts were permitted "as agents of the Military Governor" to dispose of some non-jury civil cases, they were still forbidden to summon jurors and to exercise criminal jurisdiction. On August 22nd, White was brought before a military tribunal designated as a "provost Court." The "Court" orally informed him of the charge. He objected to the tribunal's jurisdiction but the objection was overruled. He demanded to be tried by a jury. This request was denied. His attorney asked for additional time to prepare the case. This was refused. On August 25th he was tried and convicted. The Tribunal sentenced him to five years imprisonment. Later the sentence was reduced to four years.

Duncan, the petitioner in No. 14, was a civilian shipfitter employed in the Navy Yard at Honolulu. On February 24, 1944, more than two years and two months after the Pearl Harbor attack, he engaged in a brawl with two armed Marine sentries at the yard. He was arrested by the Military authorities. By the time of his arrest the military had to some extent eased the stringency of military rule. Schools, bars and motion picture theatres had been reopened. Courts had been authorized to "exercise their normal jurisdiction." They were once more summoning jurors and witnesses and conducting criminal trials. There were important exceptions however. One of these was that only military tribunals were to try "Criminal prosecutions for violations of military orders." As the record shows, these military orders still covered a wide range of day to day civilian conduct. Duncan was charged with violating one of these orders, paragraph 8.01, Title S., of General Order No. 2, which prohibited assault on military or naval personnel with intent to resist or hinder them in the discharge of their duty. He was, therefore, tried by a military tribunal rather than the territorial court, although the general laws of Hawaii made assault a crime.... A conviction followed and Duncan was sentenced to six months imprisonment.

Both White and Duncan challenged the power of the military tribunals to try them by petitions for writs of habeas corpus filed in the district court for Hawaii on March 14 and April 14, 1944, respectively. Their petitions urged both statutory and constitutional grounds. The court issued orders to show cause. Returns to these orders contended that Hawaii had become part of an active theatre of war constantly threatened by invasion from without; that the writ of habeas corpus had therefore properly been suspended and martial law had validly been established in accordance with the provisions of the Organic Act; that consequently the district court did not have jurisdiction to issue the writ; and that the trials of petitioners by military tribunals pursuant to orders by the Military Governor issued because of military necessity were valid. Each petitioner filed a traverse to the returns. which traverse challenged among other things the suspension of habeas corpus, the establishment of martial law and the validity of the Military Governor's orders, asserting that such action could not be taken except when required by military necessity due to actual or threatened invasion, which even if it did exist on December 7, 1941, did not exist when the petitioners were tried; and that, whatever the necessity for martial law, there was no justification for trying them in military tribunals rather than the regular courts of law. The district court, after separate trials, found in each case, among other things, that the courts had always been able to function but for the military orders closing them, and that consequently there was no military necessity for the trial of petitioners by military tribunals rather than regular courts. It accordingly held the trials void and ordered the release of the petitioners.

The circuit court of appeals, assuming without deciding that the district court had jurisdiction to entertain the petitions, held the military trials valid and reversed the ruling of the district court. 146 F.2d 576. It held that the military orders providing for military trials were fully authorized by §67 of the Organic Act and the Governor's actions taken under it. The court relied on that part of the section which, as we have indicated, authorizes the Governor with the approval of the President to proclaim "martial law" whenever the public safety requires it. The circuit court thought that the term "martial law" as used in the Act denotes among other things the establishment of a "total military government" completely displacing or subordinating the regular courts, that the decision of the executive as to what the public safety requires must be sustained so long as that decision is based on reasonable grounds and that such reasonable grounds did exist.

In presenting its argument before this Court the Government…abandons its contention as to the suspension of the writ of habeas corpus and advances the argument employed by the circuit court for sustaining trials and convictions of petitioners by military tribunals. The petitioners contend that "martial law" as provided for by §67 did not authorize the military to try and punish civilians such as petitioners and urge further that if such authority should be inferred from the Organic Act, it would be unconstitutional. We need decide the constitutional question only if we agree with the Government that Congress did authorize what was done here.

Did the Organic Act during the period of martial law give the armed forces power to supplant all civilian laws and to substitute military for judicial trials under the conditions that existed in Hawaii at the time these petitioners were tried? The relevant conditions, for our purposes, were the same when both petitioners were tried. The answer to the question depends on a correct interpretation of the Act. But we need not construe the Act, insofar as the power of the military might be used to meet other and different conditions and situations. The boundaries of the situation with reference to which we do interpret the scope of an Act can be more sharply defined by stating at this point some different conditions which either would or might conceivably have affected to a greater or lesser extent the scope of the authorized military power. We note first that at the time the alleged offenses were committed the dangers apprehended by the military were not sufficiently imminent to cause them to require civilians to evacuate the area or even to evacuate any of the buildings necessary to carry on the business of the courts. In fact, the buildings had long been open and actually in use for certain kinds of trials. Our question does not involve the well-established power of the military to exercise jurisdiction over members of the armed forces, those directly connected with such forces, or enemy belligerents, prisoners of war, or others with violating the laws of war. We are not concerned with the recognized power of the military to try civilians in tribunals established as a part of a temporary military government over occupied enemy territory or territory regained from an enemy where civilian government cannot and does not function. For Hawaii since annexation has been held by and loyal to the United States. Nor need we here consider the power of the military simply to arrest and detain civilians interfering with a necessary military function at a time of turbulence and danger from insurrection or war. And, finally, there was no specialized effort of the military, here, to enforce orders which related only to military functions, such as, for illustration, curfew rules or blackouts. For these petitioners were tried before tribunals set up under a military program which took over all government and superseded all civil laws and courts. If the Organic Act, properly interpreted, did not give the armed forces this awesome power, both petitioners are entitled to their freedom.

I.

In interpreting this act we must first look to its language. Section 67 makes it plain that Congress did intend the Governor of Hawaii, with the approval of the President, to invoke military aid under certain circumstances. But Congress did not specifically state to what extent the army could be used or what power it could exercise. It certainly did not explicitly declare that the Governor in conjunction with the military could for days, months or years close all the courts and supplant them with military tribunals.... If a power thus to obliterate the judicial system of Hawaii can be found at all in the Organic Act, it must be inferred from §67's provision for placing the Territory under "martial law." But the term "martial law" carries no precise meaning. The Constitution does not refer to "martial law" at all and no Act of Congress has defined the term. It has been employed in various ways by different people and at different times. By some it has been identified as "military law" limited to members of, and those connected with, the armed forces. Others have said that the term does not imply a system of established rules but denotes simply some kind of day to day expression of a general's will dictated by what he considers the imperious necessity of the moment.... In 1857 the confusion as to the meaning of the phrase was so great that the Attorney General in an official opinion had this to say about it: "The common law authorities and commentators afford no clue to what martial law, as understood in England, really is... In this country it is still worse."... What was true in 1857 remains true today. The language of §67 thus fails to define adequately the scope of the power given to the military and to show whether the Organic Act provides that courts of law be supplanted by military tribunals.

II.

Since the Act's language does not provide a satisfactory answer, we look to the legislative history for possible further aid in interpreting the term "martial law" as used in the statute. The Government contends that the legislative history shows that Congress intended to give the armed forces extraordinarily broad powers to try civilians before military tribunals. Its argument is as follows: That portion of the language of §67 which prescribes the prerequisites to declaring martial law is identical with a part of the language of the original Constitution of Hawaii. Before Congress enacted the Organic Act the supreme court of Hawaii had construed that language as giving the Hawaiian President power to authorize military tribunals to try civilians charged with crime whenever the public safety required it. *In re Kalanianaole*, 10 Hawaii 29. When Congress passed the Organic Act it simply enacted the applicable language of the Hawaiian Constitution and with it the interpretation of that language by the Hawaiian supreme court.

In disposing of this argument we wish to point out at the outset that even had Congress intended the decision in the *Kalanianaole* case to become part of the Organic Act, that case did not go so far as to authorize military trials of the petitioners for these reasons. There the defendants were insurrectionists taking part in the very uprising which the military were to suppress, while here the petitioners had no connection with any organized resistance to the armed forces or the established government. If, on the other hand, we should take the *Kalanianaole* case to authorize the complete supplanting of courts by military tribunals, we are certain that Congress did not wish to make that case part of the Organic Act....

* * *

...[M]ilitary trials of civilians charged with crime, especially when not made subject to judicial review, are so obviously contrary to our political traditions and our institutions of jury trials in courts of law, that the tenuous circumstance offered by the Government can hardly suffice to persuade us that Congress was willing to enact a Hawaiian supreme court decision permitting such a radical departure from our steadfast beliefs.

* * *

...[W]hen the Organic Act is read as a whole and in light of its legislative history it becomes clear that Congress did not intend the Constitution to have a limited application to Hawaii.... Even when Hawaii was first annexed Congress had provided that the Territory's existing laws should remain in effect unless contrary to the Constitution.

* * *

It follows that civilians in Hawaii are entitled to the constitutional guarantee of a fair trial to the same extent as those who live in any other part of our country.... Extraordinary measures in Hawaii, however necessary, are not supportable on the mistaken premise that Hawaiian inhabitants are less entitled to constitutional protection than others.... The people of Hawaii are therefore entitled to constitutional protection to the same extent as the inhabitants of the 48 States....

III.

* * *

People of many ages and countries have feared and unflinchingly opposed the kind of subordination of executive, legislative and judicial authorities to complete military rule which, according to the Government, Congress has authorized here. In this country that fear has become part of our cultural and political institutions. The story of that development is well known as we see no need to retell it all. [The Court then discusses some examples of martial law use in other situations in American history].

* * *

Courts and their procedural safeguards are indispensable to our system of government. They were set up by our founders to protect the liberties they valued. *Ex parte Quirin*, 317 U.S. 1, 19. Our system of government clearly is the antithesis of total military rule and the founders of this country are not likely to have contemplated complete military dominance within the limits of a territory made part of this country and not recently taken from an enemy. They were opposed to governments that placed in the hands of one man the power to make, interpret, and enforce the laws. Their philosophy has been the people's throughout our history.... We have always been especially concerned about the potential evils of summary criminal trials and have guarded against them by provisions embodied in the Constitution itself.... Legislatures and courts are not merely cherished American institutions; they are indispensable to our Government.

Military tribunals have no such standing. For as this Court has said before: "...the military should always be kept in subjection to the laws of the country to which it belongs, and that he is no friend to the Republic who advocates to the contrary. The established principle of every free people is, that the law shall alone govern; and to it the military must always yield." *Dow v. Johnson*, 100 U.S. 158, 169.

* * *

We believe that when Congress passed the Hawaiian Organic Act and authorized the establishment of "martial law" it had in mind and did not wish to exceed the boundaries between military and civilian power,.... The phrase "martial law" as employed in that Act...was not intended to authorize the supplanting of courts by military tribunals.... We hold that both petitioners are now entitled to be released from custody.

(k) *Johnson v. Eisentrager*

> Supreme Court of the United States
> 339 U.S. 763 (1950)

MR. JUSTICE JACKSON delivered the opinion of the Court.

The ultimate question in this case is one of jurisdiction of civil courts of the United States *vis-à-vis* military authorities in dealing with enemy aliens overseas. The issue comes here in this way:

Twenty-one German nationals petitioned the District Court of the District of Columbia for writs of *habeas corpus*. They alleged that, prior to May 8, 1945, they were in the service of German armed forces in China. They amended to allege that their employment there was by civilian agencies of the German Government. Their exact affiliation is disputed, and, for our purposes, immaterial. On May 8, 1945, the German High Command executed an act of unconditional surrender, expressly obligating all forces under German control at once to cease active hostilities. These prisoners have been convicted of violating laws of war, by engaging in, permitting or ordering continued military activity against the United States after surrender of Germany and before surrender of Japan. Their hostile operations consisted principally of collecting and furnishing intelligence concerning American forces and their movements to the Japanese armed forces. They, with six others who were acquitted, were taken into custody by the United States Army after the Japanese surrender and were tried and convicted by a Military Commission constituted by our Commanding General at Nanking by delegation from the Commanding General, United States Forces, China Theatre, pursuant to authority specifically granted by the Joint Chiefs of Staff of the United States. The Commission sat in China, with express consent of the Chinese Government. The proceedings were conducted wholly under American auspices and involved no international participation. After conviction, the sentences were duly reviewed and, with immaterial modification, approved by military reviewing authority.

The prisoners were repatriated to Germany to serve their sentences. Their immediate custodian is Commandant of Landsberg Prison, an American Army officer under the Commanding General, Third United States Army, and the Commanding General, European Command. He could not be reached by process from the District Court. Respondents named in the petition are Secretary of Defense, Secretary of the Army, Chief of Staff of the Army, and the Joint Chiefs of Staff of the United States.

The petition alleges and respondents denied, that the jailer is subject to their direction. The Court of Appeals assumed, and we do likewise, that, while prisoners are in immediate physical custody of an officer or officers not parties to the proceeding, respondents named in the petition have lawful authority to effect their release.

The petition prays an order that the prisoners be produced before the District Court, that it may inquire into their confinement and order them discharged from such offenses and confinement. It is claimed that their trial, conviction and imprisonment violate Articles I and III of the Constitution, and the Fifth Amendment thereto, and other provisions of the Constitution and laws of the United States and provisions of the Geneva Convention governing treatment of prisoners of war.

A rule to show cause issued, to which the United States made return. Thereupon the petition was dismissed on authority of *Ahrens v. Clark*, 335 U.S. 188.

The Court of Appeals reversed and, reinstating the petition, remanded for further proceedings. 84 U.S. App. D. C. 396, 174 F.2d 961. It concluded that any person, including an enemy alien, deprived of his liberty anywhere under any purported authority of the United States is entitled to the writ if he can show that extension to his case of any constitutional rights or limitations would show his imprisonment illegal; that, although no statutory jurisdiction of such cases is given, courts must be held to possess it as part of the judicial power of the United States; that where deprivation of liberty and an official act occurs outside the territorial jurisdiction of any District Court, the petition will lie in the District Court which has territorial jurisdiction over officials who have directive power over the immediate jailer.

The obvious importance of these holdings to both judicial administration and military operations impelled us to grant certiorari.... The case is before us only on issues of law. The writ of *habeas corpus* must be granted "unless it appears from the application" that the applicants are not entitled to it. 28 U.S.C. §2243.

We are cited to no instance where a court, in this or any other country where the writ is known, has issued it on behalf of an alien enemy who, at no relevant time and in no stage of his captivity, has been within its territorial jurisdiction. Nothing in the text of the Constitution extends such a right, nor does anything in our statutes. Absence of support from legislative or juridical sources is implicit in the statement of the court below that "The answers stem directly from fundamentals. They cannot be found by casual reference to statutes or cases." The breadth of the court's premises and solution requires us to consider questions basic to alien enemy and kindred litigation which for some years have been beating upon our doors.

* * *

The alien, to whom the United States has been traditionally hospitable, has been accorded a generous and ascending scale of rights as he increases his identity with our society....

* * *

But in extending constitutional protections beyond the citizenry, the Court has been at pains to point out that it was the alien's presence within its territorial jurisdiction that gave the Judiciary power to act. In the pioneer case of *Yick Wo v. Hopkins*, the Court said of the Fourteenth Amendment, "These provisions are universal in their application, *to all persons within the territorial jurisdiction*, without regard to any differences in race, of color, or of nationality;..." (Italics supplied.) 118 U.S. 356, 369. And in the *Japanese Immigrant Case*, the Court held its processes available to "an alien, who has entered the country, and has become subject in all respects to its jurisdiction, and a part of its population, although alleged to be illegally here." 180 U.S. 86, 101.

* * *

II.

We are here confronted with a decision [by the Circuit Court of Appeals] whose basic premise is that these prisoners are entitled, as a constitutional right, to sue in some court of the United States for a writ of *habeas corpus*. To support that assumption we must hold that a prisoner of our military authorities is constitutionally entitled to the writ, even though he (a) is an enemy alien; (b) has never been or resided in the United States; (c) was captured outside of our territory and there held in military custody as a prisoner of war; (d) was tried and convicted by a Military Commission sitting outside the United States; (e) for offenses against the laws of war committed outside the United States; (f) and is at all times imprisoned outside the United States.

We have pointed out that the privilege of litigation has been extended to aliens, whether friendly or enemy, only because permitting their presence in the country implied protection. No such basis can be invoked here, for these prisoners at no relevant time were within any territory over which the United States is sovereign, and the scenes of their offense, their capture, their trial and their punishment were all beyond the territorial jurisdiction of any court of the United States.

... [T]hese prisoners were actual enemies, active in the hostile service of an enemy power. There is no fiction about their enmity. Yet the decision below confers upon them a right to use our courts, free even of the limitation we have imposed upon resident alien enemies, to whom we deny any use of our courts that would hamper our war effort or aid the enemy.

A basic consideration in *habeas corpus* practice is that the prisoner will be produced before the court. This is the crux of the statutory scheme established by the Congress; indeed, it is inherent in the very term *"habeas corpus."* And though production of the prisoner may be dispensed with where it appears on the face of the application that no cause for granting the writ exists,... we have consistently adhered to and recognized the general rule.... To grant the writ to these prisoners might mean that our army must transport them across the seas for hearing....

* * *

Moreover, we could expect no reciprocity for placing the litigation weapon in unrestrained enemy hands. The right of judicial refuge from military action, which it is proposed to bestow on the enemy, can purchase no equivalent for benefit of our citizen soldiers. Except in England, whose law appears to be in harmony with the views we have expressed, and other English-speaking peoples in whose practice nothing has been cited to the contrary, the writ of *habeas corpus* is generally unknown.

The prisoners rely, however, upon two decisions of this Court to get them over the threshold—*Ex parte Quirin*,...and *In re Yamashita*...Reliance on the *Quirin* case is clearly mistaken. Those prisoners were in custody in the District of Columbia. One was, or claimed to be, a citizen. They were tried by a Military Commission sitting in the District of Columbia at the time when civil courts were open and functioning normally. They were arrested by civil authorities and the prosecution was personally directed by the Attorney General, a civilian prosecutor, for acts committed in the United States.

* * *

Nor can the Court's decision in the *Yamashita* case aid the prisoners. This Court refused to receive Yamashita's petition for a writ of *habeas corpus*. For hearing and opinion, it was consolidated with another application for a writ of certiorari to review the refusal of *habeas corpus* by the Supreme Court of the Philippines over whose decisions the statute then gave this Court a right of review.... By reason of our sovereignty at that time over these insular possessions, Yamashita stood much as did Quirin before American courts. Yamashita's offenses were committed on our territory, he was tried within the jurisdiction of our insular courts and he was imprisoned within territory of the United States. None of these heads of jurisdiction can be invoked by these prisoners.

III.

The Court of Appeals dispensed with all requirements of territorial jurisdiction based on place of residence, captivity, trial, offense, or confinement. It could not predicate relief upon any intraterritorial contact of these prisoners with our laws or institutions. Instead, it gave our Constitution an extraterritorial application to embrace our enemies in arms.

* * *

The Court of Appeals has cited no authority whatever for holding that the Fifth Amendment confers rights upon all persons whatever their nationality, wherever they are located and whatever their offenses, except to quote extensively from a dissenting opinion in *In re Yamashita*.... The holding of the Court in that case is, of course, to the contrary.

If this Amendment invests enemy aliens in unlawful hostile action against us with immunity from military trial, it puts them in a more protected position than our own soldiers. American citizens conscripted into the military service are thereby stripped of their Fifth Amendment rights and as members of the military establishment are subject to its discipline, including military trials for offenses against aliens or Americans.

* * *

IV.

* * *

The jurisdiction of military authorities, during or following hostilities, to punish those guilty of offenses against the laws of war is long-established. By the Treaty of Versailles, "The German Government recognizes the right of the Allied and Associated Powers to bring before military tribunals persons accused of having committed acts in violation of the laws and customs of war." Article 228. This Court has characterized as "well-established" the "power of the military to exercise jurisdiction over members of the armed forces, those directly connected with such forces, or enemy belligerents, prisoners of war, or others charged with violating the laws of war." *Duncan v. Kahanamoka*, 327 U.S. 304, 312, 313–314. And we have held in the *Quirin* and *Yamashita* cases...that the Military Commission is a lawful tribunal to adjudge enemy offenses against the laws of war.

It is not for us to say whether these prisoner were or were not guilty of a war crime, or whether if we were to retry the case we would agree to the findings of fact or the application of the laws of war made by the Military Commission. The petition shows that these prisoners were formally accused of violating the laws of war and fully informed of particulars of these charges. As we observed in the *Yamashita* case, "If the military tribunals have lawful authority to hear, decide and condemn, their action is not subject to judicial review merely because they have made a wrong decision on disputed facts. Correction of their errors of decision is not for the courts but for the military authorities which are alone authorized to review their decisions."...

V.

The District Court dismissed this petition on authority of *Ahrens v. Clark*, 335 U.S. 188. The Court of Appeals considered only questions which it regarded as reserved in that decision and in *Ex parte Endo*, 323 U.S. 283. Those cases dealt with persons both residing and detained within the United States and whose capacity and standing to invoke the process of federal courts somewhere was unquestioned. The issue was where.

Since in the present application we find no basis for invoking federal judicial power in any district, we need not debate as to where, if the case were otherwise, the petition should be filed.

For reasons stated, the judgment of the Court of Appeals is reversed and the judgment of the District Court dismissing the petition is affirmed.

Reversed.

MR. JUSTICE BLACK, with whom MR. JUSTICE DOUGLAS and MR. JUSTICE BURTON concur, dissenting.

(l) *Reid v. Covert*

Supreme Court of the United States
354 U.S. 1 (1957)

MR. JUSTICE BLACK announced the judgment of the Court and delivered and opinion, in which THE CHIEF JUSTICE, MR. JUSTICE DOUGLAS, AND MR. JUSTICE BRENNAN join.

These cases raise basic constitutional issues of the utmost concern. They call into question the role of the military under our system of government. They involve the power of Congress to expose civilians to trial by military tribunals, under military regulations and procedures, for offenses against the United States thereby depriving them of trial in civilian courts, under civilian laws and procedures and with all the safeguards of the Bill of Rights. These cases are particularly significant because for the first time since the adoption of the Constitution wives of soldiers have been denied trial by jury in a court of law and forced to trial before courts-martial.

In No. 701 Mrs. Clarice Covert killed her husband, a sergeant in the United States Air Force, at an airbase in England. Mrs. Covert, who was not a member of the armed services, was residing on the base with her husband at the time. She was tried by a court-martial for murder under Article 118 of the Uniform Code of Military Justice (UCMJ). The trial was on charges preferred by Air Force personnel and the court-martial was composed of Air Force officers. The court-martial asserted jurisdiction over Mrs. Covert under Article 2(11) of the UCMJ, which provides:

"The following persons are subject to this code:

"(11) Subject to the provisions of any treaty or agreement to which the United States is or may be a party or to any accepted rule of international law, all persons serving with, employed by, or accompanying the armed forces without the continental limits of the United States...."

Counsel for Mrs. Covert contended that she was insane at the time she killed her husband, but the military tribunal found her guilty of murder and sentenced her to life imprisonment. The judgment was affirmed by the Air Force Board of Review, 16 CMR

465, but was reversed by the Court of Military Appeals, 6 USCMA 48, because of prejudicial errors concerning the defense of insanity. While Mrs. Covert was being held in this country pending a proposed retrial by court-martial in the District of Columbia, her counsel petitioned the District Court for a writ of habeas corpus to set her free on the ground that the Constitution forbade her trial by military authorities. Construing this Court's decision in *United States ex rel. Toth v. Quarles,* 350 U.S. 11, as holding that "a civilian is entitled to a civilian trial" the District Court held that Mrs. Covert could not be tried by court-martial and ordered her released from custody. The Government appealed directly to this Court under 28 U.S.C. §1252. See 350 U.S. 985.

In No. 713 Mrs. Dorothy Smith killed her husband, an Army officer, at a post in Japan where she was living with him. She was tried for murder by a court-martial and despite considerable evidence that she was insane was found guilty and sentenced to life imprisonment. The judgment was approved by the Army Board of Review, 10 CMR 350, 13 CMR 307, and the Court of Military Appeals, 5 USCMA 314. Mrs. Smith was then confined in a federal penitentiary in [Alderson,] West Virginia. Her father, respondent here, filed a petition for habeas corpus in a District Court for West Virginia. The petition charged that the court-martial was without jurisdiction because Article 2(11) of the UCMJ was unconstitutional insofar as it authorized the trial of civilian dependents accompanying servicemen overseas. The District Court refused to issue the writ, 137 F. Supp. 806, and while an appeal was pending in the Court of Appeals for the Fourth Circuit we granted certiorari at the request of the Government, 350 U.S. 986.

The two cases were consolidated and argued last Term and a majority of the Court, with three Justices dissenting and one reserving opinion, held that military trial of Mrs. Smith and Mrs. Covert for their alleged offenses was constitutional. 351 U.S. 470, 487. The majority held that the provisions of Article III and the Fifth and Sixth Amendments which require that crimes be tried by a jury after indictment by a grand jury did not protect an American citizen when he was tried by the American Government in foreign lands for offenses committed there and that Congress could provide for the trial of such offenses in any manner it saw fit so long as the procedures established were reasonable and consonant with due process.

* * *

Subsequently, the Court granted a petition for rehearing, 352 U.S. 901. Now, after further argument and consideration, we conclude that the previous decisions cannot be permitted to stand. We hold that Mrs. Smith and Mrs. Covert could not constitutionally be tried by military authorities.

I.

At the beginning we reject the idea that when the United States acts against citizens abroad it can do so free of the Bill of Rights. The United States is entirely a creature of the Constitution. Its power and authority have no other source. It can only act in accordance with all the limitations imposed by the Constitution. When the Government reaches out to punish a citizen who is abroad, the shield which the Bill of Rights and other parts of the Constitution provide to protect his life and liberty should not be stripped away just because he happened to be in another land. This is not a novel concept. To the contrary, it is as old as government. It was recognized long before [Saint] Paul successfully invoked his right as a Roman citizen to be tried in strict accordance with Roman law.

* * *

The rights and liberties which citizens of our country enjoy are not protected by custom and tradition alone, they have been jealously preserved from the encroachments of Government by express provisions of our written Constitution. [Here the Court quotes Article III, §2, and the provisions of the Fifth and Sixth Amendments].

The language of Art. III, §2 manifests that constitutional protections for the individual were designed to restrict the United States Government when it acts outside of this country, as well as here at home. After declaring that *all* criminal trials must be by jury, the section states that when a crime is "not committed within any State, the Trial shall be at such Place or Places as the Congress may by Law have directed." If this language is permitted to have its obvious meaning, §2 is applicable to criminal trials outside of the States as a group without regard to where the offense is committed or the trial held. From the very first Congress, federal statutes have implemented the provisions of §2 by providing for trial of murder and other crimes committed outside the jurisdiction of any State "in the district where the offender is apprehended, or into which he may first be brought." The Fifth and Sixth Amendments, like Art. III, §2, are also all inclusive with their sweeping references to "no person" and to "all criminal prosecutions."

This Court and other federal courts have held or asserted that various constitutional limitations apply to the Government when its acts outside the continental United States. While it has been suggested that only those constitutional rights which are "fundamental" protect Americans abroad, we can find no warrant, in logic or otherwise, for picking and choosing among the remarkable collection of "Thou shall nots" which were explicitly fastened on all departments and agencies of the Federal Government by the Constitution and its Amendments. Moreover, in view of our heritage and the history of the adoption of the Constitution and the Bill of Rights, it seems peculiarly anomalous to say that trial before a civilian judge and by an independent jury picked from the common citizenry is not a fundamental right. As Blackstone wrote in his Commentaries:

> "…the trial by jury has ever been, and I trust ever will be, looked upon as the glory of the English law. And if it has so great an advantage over others in regulating civil property, how much must that advantage be heightened when it is applied to criminal cases!… [I]t is the most transcendent privilege which any subject can enjoy, or wish for, that he cannot be affected either in his property, his liberty, or his person, but by the unanimous consent of twelve of his neighbors and equals."

Trial by jury in a court of law and in accordance with traditional modes of procedure after an indictment by grand jury has served and remains one of our most vital barriers to governmental arbitrariness. These elemental procedural safeguards were embedded in our Constitution to secure their inviolateness and sanctity against the passing demands of expediency or convenience.

* * *

II.

At the time of Mrs. Covert's alleged offense, an executive agreement was in effect between the United States and Great Britain which permitted United States' military courts to exercise exclusive jurisdiction over offenses committed in Great Britain by American servicemen or their dependents. For its part, the United States agreed that these military courts would be willing and able to try and to punish all offenses against the laws of Great Britain by such persons. In all material respects, the same situation existed in Japan when Mrs. Smith killed her husband. Even though a court-martial does not give an accused trial by jury and other Bill of Rights protections, the Government contends that Art. 2 (11) of the UCMJ, insofar as it provides for the military trial of dependents accompanying the armed forces in Great Britain and Japan, can be sustained as legislation which is necessary and proper to carry out the United States' obligations under the international agreements made with these countries. The obvious and decisive answer to this, of course, is that no agreement with a foreign nation can confer power on Congress, or on any branch of Government, which is free from the restraints of the Constitution.

Article VI, the Supremacy Clause of the Constitution, declares:

> "This Constitution, and the laws of the United States which shall be made in Pursuance thereof; and all Treaties made, or which shall be made, under the Authority of the United States, shall be the supreme Law of the Land;..."

There is nothing in this language which intimates that treaties and laws enacted pursuant to them do not have to comply with the provisions of the Constitution. Nor is there anything in the debates which accompanied the drafting and ratification of the Constitution which even suggest such a result.

* * *

There *is* nothing new or unique about what we say here. This Court has regularly and uniformly recognized the supremacy of the Constitution over a treaty.

* * *

This Court has also repeatedly taken the position that an Act of Congress, which must comply with the Constitution, is on a full parity with a treaty, and that when a statute which is subsequent in time is inconsistent with a treaty, the statute to the extent of conflict renders the treaty null. It would be completely anomalous to say that a treaty need not comply with the Constitution when such an agreement can be overridden by a statute that must conform to that instrument.

* * *

III.

Article I, §8, cl. 14 empowers Congress "To make Rules for the Government and Regulation of the land and naval Forces." It has been held that this creates an exception to the normal method of trial in civilian courts as provided by the Constitution and permits Congress to authorize military trial of members of the armed services without all the safeguards given an accused by Article III and the Bill of Rights. But if the language of Clause 14 is given its natural meaning, the power granted does not extend to civilians— even though they may be dependents living with servicemen on a military base. The term "land and naval Forces" refers to persons who are members of the armed services and not to their civilian wives, children and other dependents. It seems inconceivable that Mrs. Covert or Mrs. Smith could have been tried by military authorities as members of the :land and naval Forces: had they been living on a military post in this country. Yet this constitutional term surely has the same meaning everywhere. The wives of servicemen are no more members of the "land and naval Forces" when living at a military post in England or Japan than when living at a base in this country or in Hawaii or Alaska.

* * *

Just last Term, this Court held in *United States ex rel. Toth v. Quarles*, 350 U.S. 11, that military courts could not constitutionally try a discharged serviceman for an offense which he had allegedly committed while in the armed forces. It was decided (1) that since Toth was a civilian he could not be tried by military court-martial, and (2) that since he was charged with murder, a "crime" in the constitutional sense, he was entitled to indictment by a grand jury, jury trial, and other protections contained in Art. III, §2 and the Fifth, Sixth, and Eighth Amendments. The Court pointed out that trial by civilian courts was the rule for persons who were not members of the armed forces.

There are no supportable grounds upon which to distinguish the *Toth* case from the present cases. Toth, Mrs. Covert, and Mrs. Smith were all civilians. All three were American citizens. All three alleged crimes were committed in a foreign country.

* * *

The *Milligan, Duncan* and *Toth* cases recognized and manifested the deeply rooted and ancient opposition in this country to the extension of military control over civilians. In each instance an effort to expand the jurisdiction of military courts to civilians was repulsed.

There have been a number of decisions in the lower federal courts which have upheld military trial of civilians performing services for the armed forces "in the field" during *time of war*. To the extent that these cases can be justified, insofar as they involved trial of persons who were not "members" of the armed forces, they must rest on the Government's "war powers." In the face of an actively hostile enemy, military commanders necessarily have broad powers over persons on the battlefront. From a time prior to the adoption of the Constitution the extraordinary circumstances present in an area of actual fighting have been considered sufficient to permit punishment of some civilians in that area by military courts under military rules. But neither Japan nor Great Britain could properly be said to be an area where active hostilities were under way at the time Mrs. Smith and Mrs. Covert committed their offenses or at the time they were tried.

* * *

... [W]e reject the Government's argument that present threats to peace permit military trial of civilians accompanying the armed forces overseas in an area where no actual hostilities are under way. The exigencies which have required military rule on the battlefront are not present in areas where no conflict exists. Military trial of civilians "in the field" is an extraordinary jurisdiction and it should not be expanded at the expense of the Bill of Rights.

* * *

Courts-martial are typically *ad hoc* bodies appointed by a military officer from among his subordinates. They have always been subject to varying degrees of "command influence." In essence, these tribunals are simply executive tribunals whose personnel are in the executive chain of command. Frequently, the members of the court-martial must look to the appointing officer for promotions, advantageous assignments and efficiency ratings—in short, for their future progress in the service. Conceding to military personnel that a high degree of honesty and sense of justice which nearly all of them undoubtedly have, the members of a court-martial, in the nature of things, do not and cannot have the independence of jurors drawn from the general public or civilian judges.

* * *

We should not break faith with this Nation's tradition of keeping military power subservient to civilian authority, a tradition which we believe is firmly embodied in the

Constitution. The country has remained true to that faith for almost one hundred and seventy years.

* * *

Ours is a government of divided authority on the assumption that in division there is not only strength but freedom from tyranny. And under our Constitution courts of law alone are given power to try civilians for their offenses against the United States. The philosophy expressed by Lord Coke, speaking long ago from a wealth of experience, is still timely:

> "God send me never to live under the Law of Conveniency or Discretion. Shall the Souldier and Justice Sit on one Bench, the Trumpet will not let the Cryer speak in *Westminster-Hall.*"

In No. 701, the judgment of the District Court directing that Mrs. Covert be released from custody [in the District of Columbia jail] is

Affirmed.

In No. 713, *Kinsella v. Krueger*, the judgment of the District Court is reversed and the case is remanded with instructions to [the Warden of the U.S. Penitentiary for Women at Alderson, West Virginia, to] order Mrs. Smith released from Custody.

Reversed and remanded.

MR. JUSTICE WHITTAKER took no part in the consideration or decision of these cases.

MR. JUSTICE FRANKFURTER, concurring in the result.

(m) Proclamation 7463 of September 14, 2001

Federal Register, vol. 66, No.181
Tuesday, September 18, 2001

THE PRESIDENT: DECLARATION OF NATIONAL EMERGENCY BY REASON OF CERTAIN TERRORISTS ATTACKS

By the President of the United States of America

A Proclamation

A national emergency exists by reason of the terrorist attacks at the World Trade Center, New York, New York, and the Pentagon, and the continuing and immediate threat of further attacks on the United States.

NOW, THEREFORE, I, GEORGE W. BUSH, President of the United States of America, by virtue of the authority vested in me as President by the Constitution and the laws of the United States, I hereby declare that the national emergency has existed since September 11, 2001, and, pursuant to the National Emergencies Act (50 U.S.C. 1601 *et seq.*), I intend to utilize the following statutes: sections 123, 123a, 527, 2201(c), 122006 and 12302 of title 10, United States Code, and sections 331, 359, and 367 of title 14, United States Code.

This proclamation immediately shall be published in the **Federal Register** or disseminated through the Emergency **Federal Register**, and transmitted to the Congress.

This proclamation is not intended to create any right or benefit, substantive or procedural, enforceable at law by a party against the United States, its agencies, its officers, or any person.

IN WITNESS WHEREOF, I have hereunto set my hand this fourteenth day of September, in the year of our Lord two thousand one and of the Independence of the United States of America the two hundred twenty-sixth.

/s/ George W. Bush

[The attack by Islamic Jihadists on the twin towers of the World Trade Center in New York City and the Pentagon in Washington, D. C., plus the crash of a third plane in rural Pennsylvania now thought to be aimed at the United States Capitol Building, was the worst single act of violence against the United States in its 225-year history. Acts of terrorism had, of course, plagued many other countries of the world long before September 11, 2001, but there was still a sense by many both inside and outside the government of the United States that we were relatively immune from this new form of warfare conducted by religious militants. September 11th forced a true paradigm shift in our thinking about the state of the world in the new twenty-first century. With the collapse of the Soviet Union in the early 1990s, the bi-polarity in international relations that had existed shortly after the end of the Second World War in 1945 came to a welcomed end. There was widespread hope that, at last, a new century would usher in a stable world order free from the carnage wrought by "symmetrical" warfare throughout so much of the twentieth century. However, portents of things to come had already reared their ugly head during the last decade of the century. For example, in the decade preceding the attack on the United States the international community had already witnessed at least seven conflicts that cast a shadow on things to come: Iraq; Bosnia; Kosovo; Somalia; Rwanda; Chechnia; East Timor; and the India-Pakistani dispute. Along with these, there was continuing concern about North Korea, Iran and Syria. Overlapping all of this was the decades-long conflict between the State of Israel and the Palestinians—a seemingly unsolvable international relations "tar baby" that has continued to create international dissonance since 1948.

One week after the 9/11 attacks on the United States, the Congress of the United States adopted a joint resolution (*supra*) that authorized President Bush to "[u]se all necessary and appropriate force" against those who had planned and carried out the attacks on the United States. On October 7, 2001, the United States military launched aerial attacks on Osama bin Laden's training camps in Afghanistan and also on al Qaeda's surrogates in that country—the Taliban. On October 19–20, 2001, American military forces initiated ground operations with special forces troops in Afghanistan. Since that date, the United States has expanded its military operation in Afghanistan, defeated the Taliban in most parts of the country and installed a new Afghan president who seeks a democratic style of government for that war-torn land.

As an international terrorist organization, Osama bin Laden's al Qaeda had already placed its bloody fingerprints on a series of terrorists acts against the United States and other nations for at least a decade before the 9/11 attacks. For example, the United States State Department alleges that al Qaeda was involved in the attempted assassination of the Pope, President Clinton, and the blowing up of dozens of passenger aircraft while in flight. In addition, al Qaeda operatives were heavily involved in the 1993 bombing of the World Trade Center in New York City and the attack, in that same year, on United States special forces in Somalia. In 1998 came the East African embassy bombings in Nairobi and Dar-es-Salaam, while in the year 2000, the United States naval vessel, *U. S. S. Cole* was attacked in Yemen and an al Qaeda plot to attack tourist in Jordan during the millennium celebrations was uncovered. Thus, the United States was on notice that a violently militant, nihilistic, religiously-driven network of international killers were on the loose long before the tragedy that befell this nation on September 11, 2001. On September 20, 2001, the President of the United States issued an ominous warning to the world community: "[e]ither you are with us, or you are with the terrorists. From this day forward, any nation that continues to harbor or support terrorism will be regarded by the United States as a hostile regime"[15]].

(n) Military Order of November 13, 2001

Federal Register, vol. 66, No. 222
Friday, November 16, 2001

THE PRESIDENT: DETENTION, TREATMENT, AND TRIAL OF CERTAIN NON-CITIZENS IN THE WAR AGAINST TERRORISM

By the authority vested in me as President and as Commander in Chief of the Armed Forces of the United States by the Constitution and the laws of the United States of America, including the Authorization for Use of Military Force Joint Resolution (Public Law 107-40. 115 Stat. 224) and sections 821 and 836 of title 10 United States Code, it is hereby ordered as follows:

Section 1. *Findings*

(a) International terrorists, including members of al Qaeda, have carried out attacks on United States diplomatic and military personnel and facilities abroad and on citizens and property within the United States on a scale that has created a state of armed conflict that requires the use of the United States Armed Forces.

(b) In light of grave acts of terrorism and threats of terrorism, including the terrorist attacks on September 11, 2001, on the headquarters of the United States Department of Defense in the national capital region, on the World Trade Center in New York, and on civilian aircraft such as in Pennsylvania, I proclaimed a national emergency on September 14, 2001...

(c) Individuals acting alone and in concert involved in international terrorism posses both the capability and the intention to undertake further terrorist attacks against the United States that, if not detected and prevented, will cause mass deaths, mass injuries, and massive destruction of property, and may place at risk the continuity of the operations of the United States Government.

(d) The ability of the United States to protect the United States and its citizens, and to help its allies and other cooperating nations protect their nations and their citizens, from such further terrorist attacks depends in significant part upon using the United States Armed Forces to identify terrorists and those who support them, to disrupt their activities, and to eliminate their ability to conduct or support such attacks.

---

15. President George W. Bush, Address Before a Joint Session of the Congress on the United States Response to the Terrorist Attacks on September 11, 37 WEEKLY COMP. PRES. DOC. 1347 (Sept. 20, 2001).

(e) To protect the United States and its citizens, and for the effective conduct of military operations and prevention of terrorist attacks, it is necessary for individuals subject to this order pursuant to section 2 hereof to be detained, and, when tried, to be tried for violations of the laws of war and other applicable laws by military tribunals.

(f) Given the danger to the safety of the United States and the nature of international terrorism, and to the extent provided by and under this order, I find consistent with section 836 of title 10, United States Code, that it is not practicable to apply in military commissions under this order the principles of law and rules of evidence generally recognized in the trial of criminal cases in the United States district courts.

(g) Having fully considered the magnitude of the potential deaths, injuries, and property destruction that would result from potential acts of terrorism against the United States, and the probability that such acts will occur, I have determined that an extraordinary emergency exists for national defense purposes, that this emergency constitutes an urgent and compelling government interest, and that issuance of this order is necessary to meet the emergency.

Section 2. *Definition and Policy.*

(a) The term "individual subject to this order" shall mean any individual who is not a United States Citizen with respect to whom I determine from time to time in writing that:

(1) there is reason to believe that such individual, at the relevant times,

(i) is or was a member of the organization known as al Qaeda;

(ii) has engaged in, aided or abetted, or conspired to commit, acts of international terrorism, or acts in preparation therefor, that have caused, threaten to cause, or have as their aim to cause, injury to or adverse effects on the United States, its citizens, national security, foreign policy, or economy; or

(iii) has knowingly harbored one or more individuals described in subparagraphs (i) or (ii) of subsection 2(a)(1) of this order; and

(2) it is in the interest of the United States that such individual be subject to this order.

(b) It is the policy of the United States that the Secretary of Defense shall take all necessary measures to ensure that any individual subject to this order is detained in accordance with section 3, and, if the individual is to be tried, that such individual is tried only in accordance with section 4.

Section 3. *Detention Authority of the Secretary of Defense.* Any individual subject to this order shall be—

(a) detained at an appropriate location designated by the Secretary of Defense outside or within the United States;

(b) treated humanely, without any adverse distinction based on race, color, religion, gender, birth, wealth, or any similar criteria;

(c) afforded adequate food, drinking water, shelter, clothing, and medical treatment;

(d) allowed the free exercise of religion consistent with the requirements of such detention; and

(e) detained in accordance with such other conditions as the Secretary of Defense may prescribe.

Section 4. *Authority of the Secretary of Defense Regarding Trials of Individuals Subject to this Order.*

(a) Any individual subject to this order shall, when tried, be tried by military commission for any and all offenses triable by military commission that such individual is alleged to have committed, and may be punished in accordance with the penalties provided under applicable law, including life imprisonment or death.

(b) As a military function and in light of the findings in section 1, including subsection (f) thereof, the Secretary of Defense shall issue such orders and regulations, including orders for the appointment of one or more military commissions, as may be necessary to carry out subsection (a) of this section.

(c) Orders and regulations issued under subsection (b) of this section shall include, but not be limited to, rules for the conduct of the proceedings of military commissions, including pretrial, trial, and post-trial procedures, modes of proof, issuance of process, and qualifications of attorneys, which shall at a minimum provide for—

> (1) military commissions to sit at any time and any place, consistent with such guidance regarding time and place as the Secretary of Defense may provide:

> (2) a full and fair trial, with the military commission sitting as the triers of both fact and law;

> (3) admission of such evidence as would, in the opinion of the presiding officer of the military commission (or instead, if any other member of the commission so requests at the time the presiding officer renders that opinion, the opinion of the commission rendered at that time by a majority of the commission), have probative value to a reasonable person;

> (4) in a manner consistent with the protection of information classified or classifiable under Executive Order 12958 of April 17, 1995, as amended, or any successor Executive Order, protected by statute or rule from unauthorized disclosure, or otherwise protected by law, (A) the handling of, admission into evidence of, and access to materials and information, and (B) the conduct, closure of, and access to proceedings;

> (5) conduct of the prosecution by one or more attorneys designated by the Secretary of Defense and conduct of the defense by attorneys for the individual subject to this order;

> (6) conviction only upon the concurrence of two-thirds of the members of the commission present at the time of the vote, a majority being present.

> (7) sentencing only upon the concurrence of two-thirds of the members of the commission present at the time of the vote, a majority being present; and

> (8) submission of the record of the trial, including any conviction or sentence, for review and final decision by me or by the Secretary of Defense if so designated by me for the purpose.

* * *

Section 7. *Relationship to Other Law and Forums.*

(a) Nothing in this order shall be construed to—

> (1) authorize the disclosure of state secrets of any person not otherwise authorized to have access to them;

(2) limit the authority of the President as Commander in Chief of the Armed Forces or the power of the President to grant reprieves and pardons; or

(3) limit the lawful authority of the Secretary of Defense, any military commander, or any other officer or agent of the United States or of any State to detain or try any person who is not an individual subject to this order.

(b) With respect to any individual subject to this order—

(1) military tribunals shall have exclusive jurisdiction with respect to offenses by the individual; and

(2) the individual shall not be privileged to seek any remedy or maintain any proceeding, directly or indirectly, or to have any such remedy or proceeding sought on the individual's behalf, in (i) any court of the United States, or any State thereof, (ii) any court of any foreign nation or (iii) any international tribunal.

(c) This order is not intended to and does not create any right, benefit, or privilege, substantive or procedural, enforceable at law or equity by any party, against the United States, its departments, agencies, or other entities, its officers or employees or any other person.

(d) For purposes of this order, the term "State" includes any State, district, territory, or possession of the United States.

(e) I reserve the authority to direct the Secretary of Defense, at any time hereafter, to transfer to a governmental authority control of any individual subject to this order. Nothing in this order shall be construed to limit the authority of any such governmental authority to prosecute any individual for whom control is transferred.

/s/ George W. Bush

THE WHITE HOUSE
November 13, 2001

(o) *Coalition of Clergy v. Bush*

United States District Court
189 F. Supp.2d 1036 (C. D. Cal. 2002)

MATZ, District Judge.

I.

PROCEDURAL BACKGROUND AND SUMMARY OF RULING

This case results from the sudden attacks on the United States on September 11, 2001, resulting in the deaths of thousands of innocent civilians. Within a few days, the President, with the approval of Congress…commanded the Armed Forces of the United States to use all necessary and appropriate force against the persons responsible for those attacks, who soon came to be known as the "Al Qaeda terrorist network." The President dispatched American forces to Afghanistan, where that group was believed to be functioning with the active support of the "Taliban" government then in power in that country. In the course of combat operations, American forces, as well as other nations allied with the United States, captured or secured the surrender of thousands of persons. Beginning in early January 2002, the Armed Forces transferred scores of these captives to the United States Naval Base at Guantanamo Bay, Cuba ("Guantanamo"). Their confinement in Guantanamo led to this action.

Petitioners are a group referring to themselves as the "Coalition of Clergy, Lawyers, and Professors." They include at least two journalists; ten lawyers; three rabbis; and a Christian pastor. Some of these individuals are prominent professors at distinguished law schools or schools of journalism. One is a former Attorney-General of the United States. On January 20, 2002, they filed a Verified Petition for Writ of Habeas Corpus on behalf of "Persons Held Involuntarily at Guantanamo Naval Air Base, Cuba." In substance, the petition alleges that the captives held at Guantanamo (the "detainees") are in custody in violation of the Constitution or the laws or treaties of the United States, in that they: (1) have been deprived of their liberty without due process of law, (2) have not been informed of the nature and cause of the accusations against them and (3) have not been afforded the assistance of counsel. The petition also suggests, somewhat elliptically, that the detainees have rights under the Geneva Convention that have been violated such as "prohibition of [sic] transferring persons taken prisoner in [sic] war from the country of their capture."

Petitioners allege that "[b]ecause the persons for whom relief is sought appear to be held incommunicado and have been denied access to legal counsel, application properly is made by petitioners acting on their behalf. 28 U.S.C. 2242…"

The relief that petitioners seek is a writ or order to show cause (1) directing the respondents to "identify by full name and country of domicile and all other identifying information in their possession each person held by them within three days," (2) directing respondents "to show the true cause(s) of the detention of each person," and (3) directing respondents to produce the detainees at a hearing in this court.

The persons named as respondents are President George W. Bush; Secretary of Defense Donald H. Rumsfeld; Richard R. Myers, the Chairman of the Joint Chiefs of Staff; Gordon R. England, the Secretary of Navy; and five other named individuals and "1000 Unknown Named United States Military Personnel," all of whom are alleged to be military officers responsible for the operations at the Guantanamo Naval Base.

On January 22, 2002, two days after the petition was filed, the Court presided over a brief hearing at which it expressed strong doubts that it had jurisdiction to entertain the petition. The Court ordered the parties to address that threshold question in written briefs. They have done so and appeared at a second hearing today.

Having reviewed and considered all the arguments and conducted additional research on its own, the Court rules as follows:

1. Petitioners do not have standing to assert claims on behalf of the detainees.

2. Even if petitioners did have standing, this court lacks jurisdiction to entertain those claims.

3. No federal court would have jurisdiction over petitioner's claims, so there is no basis to transfer this matter to another federal district court.

4. The petition must be dismissed.

II.

THE WRIT OF HABEAS CORPUS

Given the importance of the issues that petitioners proclaim are at stake in this case, a decidedly abbreviated description of the writ of habeas corpus is appropriate. The writ of habeas corpus, providing a means by which the legal authority under which a person is detained can be challenged, is of immemorial antiquity.... The precise origin of the writ...is not certain, but as early as 1220 A. D. the words *"habeas corpora"* are to be found in an order directing an English sheriff to produce parties to a trespass action before the Court of Common Pleas.... Today it is regarded as "perhaps the most important writ known to the constitutional law of England...."

> Its significance in the United States has been no less great. Article I, §9 of the Constitution gives assurance that the privilege of the writ of habeas corpus shall not be suspended, unless when in cases of rebellion or invasion the public safety may require it, and its use by the federal courts was authorized [as long ago as in]...the Judiciary Act of 1789.

WRIGHT, MILLER AND COOPER, FEDERAL PRACTICE AND PROCEDURE: JURISDICTION 2D §4261 and n. 3 (citations omitted).

The statutory authorization for a federal judge to issue a writ of habeas corpus currently is set forth in 28 U.S.C. §2241, *et seq.* In essence, when a judge issues such a writ, the authorities responsible for the petitioner's custody are required to demonstrate that he is being detained lawfully. As Mr. Justice Black put it, the "grand purpose" of the writ of habeas corpus is "the protection of individuals against erosion of their right to be free from wrongful restraints upon their liberty." *Jones v. Cunningham,* 371 U.S. 236, 243 (1963).

Although the writ of habeas corpus plays a central role in American jurisprudence, there are many limitations on a court's authority to issue such a writ. Here, in urging the court to dismiss the petition—*i. e.,* effectively refuse to issue a writ—respondents invoke three such limitations. They contend: (1) petitioners lack "standing" to come to this court—*i. e.,* they are not entitled to ask the court on the detainees' behalf to order respondents to justify the detention of the detainees; (2) this particular federal court lacks jurisdiction to entertain the petition; and (3) no federal district court anywhere has jurisdiction. Respondents are correct as to all three contentions.

III.

PETITIONERS DO NOT HAVE STANDING

Respondents argue that petitioners lack standing to assert claims on behalf of the detainees. Whether a plaintiff (or, in the case of a habeas proceeding, a petitioner) has standing "is the threshold question in every federal case, determining the power of the court to entertain the suit.... The Art. III judicial power exists only to redress or otherwise to protect against injury to the complaining party, even though the court's judgment may benefit others collaterally...." *Warth v. Seldin,* 422 U.S. 490, 498–499... (1975).

28 U.S.C. §2242 provides that "[a]pplication for a writ of habeas corpus shall be in writing signed and verified by the person for whose relief it is intended *or by someone acting in his behalf.*" (Emphasis added). Courts use the term "next friend" to describe the person who acts on behalf of another person (the "real party in interest") for whom the relief is sought. The "next friend" has the burden "clearly to establish the propriety of his status and thereby justify the jurisdiction of the court." *Whitmore v. Arkansas,* 495 U.S. 149...(1990).

A number of courts have allowed habeas petitions to be filed by "next friends," although in circumstances different from those here. [citing cases].

* * *

IV.

THIS COURT LACKS JURISDICTION TO ISSUE THE WRIT BECAUSE NO CUSTODIAN IS WITHIN THE TERRITORIAL JURISDICTION OF THE COURT

Respondents argue that even if petitioners have standing this court lacks jurisdiction to entertain the petition because no custodian responsible for the custody of the detainees is present in the territorial jurisdiction of this district. Respondents are correct.

* * *

It is clear, then that because there is no showing or allegation that any named respondent is within the territorial jurisdiction of the Central District of California, this court lacks jurisdiction to issue the writ requested by petitioners. [Judge Matz then turned to the question of whether or not the United States District Court for the District of Columbia could entertain jurisdiction of petitioner's writ since all respondents named are resident within the District of Columbia].

* * *

Transfer to the United States District Court for the District of Columbia is appropriate if three conditions are met: (1) the transferring court lacks jurisdiction; (2) the transferee court could have exercised jurisdiction at the time the action was filed, and (3) the transfer is in the interest of justice.... As to condition (1), this Court has already found that it lacks jurisdiction. As to condition (3), a court is required to construe a habeas petition in the light most favorable to the petitioners. That requires this court to assume, without actually finding, that the allegations in this petition that the detainees' right have been violated are true. Construing the petition that way, transfer would be in the interests of justice, for it would avoid a "'time-consuming'" and "'justice defeating'" dismissal.

What remains for determination, therefore, is whether even though respondents are within the jurisdiction of another court—the District of Columbia—that court (or any federal court) has the authority to exercise jurisdiction over the parties and claim asserted in this petition. It is to that question that the Court will now turn.

V.

NO DISTRICT COURT HAS JURISDICTION OVER THIS PETITION

A. *Johnson v. Eisentrager* Compels Dismissal If the Detainees Are Outside the Sovereign Territory of the United States.

As this Court suggested in its previous order, the key case is *Johnson v. Eisentrager*, 339 U.S. 763...(1950). [*supra*]. Because the Supreme Court's holding in *Johnson* is controlling here, the decision warrants careful review. [The Court then reviews the facts developed in *Eisentrager*. After reviewing the facts and circumstances surrounding the *Eisentrager* case, the Court continued]:

Although there has been no decision since *Johnson* that involves facts comparable to those in this case, other courts have either followed *Johnson* or acknowledged its precendential authority. [Citing *Zadvydas v. Davis*, 533 U.S. 678…(2001); *United States v. Verdugo-Urquidez*, 494 U.S. 259 (1990)].

* * *

In all key respects, the Guantanamo detainees are like the petitioners in *Johnson*: They are aliens; they were enemy combatants; they were captured in combat; they were abroad when captured; they are abroad now; since their capture, they have been under the control of only the military; they have not stepped foot on American soil; and there are no legal or judicial precedents entitling them to pursue a writ of habeas corpus in an American civilian court. Moreover, there are sound practical reasons, such as legitimate security concerns, that make it unwise for this or any other court to take the unprecedented step of conferring such a right on these detainees.

Petitioners nevertheless argue that *Johnson* "is both factually and legally inapposite for numerous reasons." Petitioners' first supposed distinction is that in *Johnson* the petitioners already had been given access to American courts. Not so, the tribunal in *Johnson* was a Military Commission functioning in China; the petitioners there, as here, were seeking to get *into* a federal court. Next, petitioners argue that there are issues of fact that underlie jurisdiction which must be resolved before dismissal. Petitioners do not state what those supposed issues are and in any event the question before this court *is* a purely legal one, as in *Johnson*. Finally, as petitioner put it, "[m]ost importantly the detainees are 'present' in the United States of America, because Guantanamo Naval Base is, as a matter of both fact and law, the United States of America."

B. Detainees were seized and at all times have been held outside the sovereign territory of the United States.

Johnson establishes that whether the Guantanamo detainees can establish jurisdiction in any district court depends not on the nature of their claims but whether the Naval Base at Guantanamo Bay is under the sovereignty of the United States. Petitioners argue that the detainees are now within the territorial jurisdiction of the United States and thus are entitled to a writ of habeas corpus. But there is a difference between territorial jurisdiction and sovereignty, and it is the latter concept that is key. *See United States v. Spelar*, 338 U.S. 217…(1949), in which the Supreme Court observed, "We know of no more accurate phrase in common English usage than 'foreign country' to denote territory subject to the sovereignty of another nation." The Court finds that Guantanamo Bay is *not* within the sovereign territory of the United States and therefore rejects petitioners' argument.

The legal status of Guantanamo Bay is governed by a lease agreement entered into by the United States and Cuba in 1903 and extended by those countries in 1934…. The 1903 agreement provides that the United States shall lease Guantanamo Bay from the Republic of Cuba for use as a coaling or naval station…. Article III of the 1934 Treaty provides that the 1903 lease shall "continue in effect" until the parties agree to modify or abrogate it.

As to the legal status of Guantanamo Bay so long as it is leased to the U.S., the 1903 agreement states:

> While on the one hand the United States recognizes the continuance of the ultimate sovereignty of the Republic of Cuba over the above described areas of land and water, on the other hand the republic of Cuba consents that during the period of occupation by the United States of said areas under the terms of this agreement the United States shall exercise complete jurisdiction and control over and within said areas.

Lease Agreement, art. III.

It is telling that in their brief petitioners do not even mention the first clause of the 1903 agreement, which provides that Cuba explicitly retained sovereignty. The omission suggests that they realize that sovereignty is the dispositive value.

Relying instead only on the second clause, petitioners argue that because the Lease Agreement provides that Guantanamo Bay is under the "complete jurisdiction and control" of the United States, the detainees effectively are being held within United States territory and thus are entitled to the writ of habeas corpus.

One need only read the lease to realize that petitioners' argument that "jurisdiction and control" is equivalent to "sovereignty" is wrong. The agreement explicitly distinguishes between the two in providing that Cuba retains "sovereignty" whereas "jurisdiction and control" are exercised by the United States. Cuba and the United States defined the legal status of Guantanamo Bay, and this court has no basis, much less authority, to ignore their determination....

In addition to the express terms of the Lease Agreement, the only federal courts that have addressed the issue have held that Guantanamo Bay is not within the sovereign territory of the United States and is not the functional equivalent of United States sovereign territory. In *Cuban American Bar Association v. Christopher*, 43 F.3d 1412, 1425 (11th Cir. 1995), *cert. denied*, 515 U.S. 1142...(1995), the Eleventh Circuit had to determine whether Cuban and Haitian migrants temporarily detained at the Guantanamo Bay Naval Base could assert rights under various United States statutes and the United States Constitution.... Citing the language of the Lease Agreement quoted above, the Court of Appeals stated "the district court erred in concluding that Guantanamo Bay was a 'United States Territory.' We disagree that control and jurisdiction is equivalent to sovereignty."... The Court of Appeals then went on to reject the argument that United States military bases which are leased abroad and remain under the sovereignty of foreign nations are "'functionally equivalent' to being...within the United States."...

For the foregoing reasons, the court finds that sovereignty over Guantanamo Bay remains with Cuba. The court therefore holds that petitioners' claim that the Guantanamo detainees are entitled to a writ of habeas corpus is foreclosed by the Supreme Court's holding in *Johnson*.

VI.

CONCLUSION

The Court understands that many concerned citizens, here and abroad, believe this case presents the question of whether the Guantanamo detainees have any rights at all that the United States is bound, or willing, to recognize. That question is *not* before this Court and nothing in this ruling suggests that the captives are entitled to no legal protection whatsoever.

* * *

For the foregoing reasons, the Verified Petition For Writ of Habeas Corpus and the Verified First Amended Petition are both DISMISSED with prejudice.

IT IS SO ORDERED.

(p) *Rasul v. Bush*

United States District Court

215 F. Supp.2d 55 (D. D. C 2002)

MEMORANDUM OPINION

KOLLAR-KOTELLY, District Judge.

1. INTRODUCTION

Presently before the Court are two cases involving the federal government's detention of certain individuals at the United States Naval Base at Guantanamo Bay, Cuba. The question presented to the Court by these two cases is whether aliens held outside the sovereign territory of the United States can use the courts of the United States to pursue claims brought under the United States Constitution. The Court answers that question in the negative and finds that it is without jurisdiction to consider the merits of these two cases. Additionally, as the Court finds that no court would have jurisdiction to hear these actions, the Court shall dismiss both suits with prejudice.

Throughout their pleadings and at oral argument, Petitioners and Plaintiffs contend that unless the Court assumes jurisdiction over their suits, they will be left without any rights and thereby be held *incommunicado*. In response to this admittedly serious concern, the government at oral argument, conceded that "there's a body of international law that governs the rights of people who are seized during the course of combative activities."... It is the government's position that "the scope of those rights are for the military and political branches to determine and certainly that reflects the idea that other countries would play a role in that process."... Therefore, the government recognizes that these aliens fall within the protection of certain provisions of international law and that diplomatic channels remain an ongoing and viable means to address the claims raised by these aliens. While these two cases provide no opportunity for the Court to address these issues, the Court would point out that the notion that these aliens could be held *incommunicado* from the rest of the world would appear to be inaccurate.

After viewing the extensive briefings in these cases, considering the oral arguments of the parties and their oral responses to the Court's questions, and reflecting on the relevant case law, the Court shall grant the government's motion to dismiss in both cases on the ground that the Court is without jurisdiction to entertain these claims.

[The "two cases" mentioned by Judge Kollar-Kotelly that are consolidated here, along with additional petitioners, are captioned *Rasul v. Bush* and *Odah v. United States*. Besides Shafig Rasul and Khaled Al Odah, other petitioners include one David Hicks who was apparently captured in Afghanistan by the Afghan Northern Alliance and thence turned over to the United States, along with a petitioner named Iqbal (no other name given), along with twelve Kuwaiti nationals, including Khaled Al Odah. Petitioner Iqbal was captured by forces working in opposition to the United States, and subsequently captured by American forces. The twelve Kuwaiti nationals in custody were in both Pakistan and Afghanistan before and after the September 11, 2001, attacks on the United States. When they were taken into American custody, they claimed to be Kuwaiti volunteers for charitable organizations in that region of the world].

* * *

The Court...considers both cases as petitions for writs of habeas corpus on behalf of aliens detained by the United States at the military base at Guantanamo Bay, Cuba. In viewing both cases from this perspective, the Court concludes that the Supreme Court's ruling in *Johnson v. Eisentrager*...and its progency are controlling and bars the Court's consideration of the merits of these two cases....

* * *

VI. CONCLUSION

The Court concludes that the military base at Guantanamo Bay, Cuba is outside the sovereign territory of the United States; Given that under *Eisentrager*, writs of habeas corpus are not available to aliens held outside the sovereign territory of the United States, this Court does not have jurisdiction to entertain the claims made by Petitioners in *Rasul* or Plaintiffs in *Odah*. Of course, just as the *Eisentrager* Court did not hold "that these prisoners have no right which the military authorities are bound to respect," *Eisentrager*, 339 U.S. at 789 n. 14,...this opinion, too, should not be read as stating that these aliens do not have some form of rights under international law. Rather, the Court's decision solely involves whether it has jurisdiction to consider the constitutional claims that are presented to the Court for resolution.

* * *

...Accordingly, both cases shall be dismissed for want of jurisdiction.

* * *

ORDERED that *Rasul v. Bush*,...and *Odah v. United States*,...are DISMISSED WITH PREJUDICE.

SO ORDERED.

(q) *Al Odah v. United States*

United States Court of Appeals
321 F. 3d 1134 (D. C. Cir. 2003)

Before: RANDOLPH and GARLAND, Circuit Judges, and WILLIAMS, Senior Circuit Judge.

RANDOLPH, Circuit Judge:

Through their "next friends," aliens captured abroad during hostilities in Afghanistan and held abroad in United States military custody at the Guantanamo Bay Naval Base in Cuba brought three actions contesting the legality and conditions of their confinement. The ultimate question presented in each case is whether the district court had jurisdiction to adjudicate their actions.

* * *

In response to the attacks on September 11, 2001, and in the exercise of its constitutional powers, Congress authorized the President "to use all necessary and appropriate force against those nations, organizations, or persons he determines planned, authorized, committed, or aided" the attacks and recognized the President's "authority under the Constitution to take action to deter and prevent acts of international terrorism against the United States." Authorization for Use of Military Forces, Pub.L. No. 107-40, 115 Stat. 224, 224 (2001). The President declared a National Emergency...(Sept. 14, 2001), and, as Commander in Chief, dispatched armed forces to Afghanistan to seek out and subdue the al Qaeda terrorist network and the Taliban regime that had supported and protected it. During the course of the Afghanistan campaign, the United States and its Allies captured the aliens whose next friends bring these actions.

In one of these cases (*Al Odah v. United States,...*), fathers and brothers of twelve Kuwaiti nationals detained at Camp X-Ray in Guantanamo Bay brought action in the form of a complaint against the United States, President George W. Bush, Secretary of Defense Donald H. Rumsfeld, Chairman of the Joint Chiefs of Staff Gen. Richard B. Myers, Brig. Gen. Rick Baccus, whom they allege is the Commander of Joint Task Force 160, and Col. Terry Carrico, the Commandant of Camp X-Ray/Camp Delta. None of the plaintiffs' attorneys have communicated with the Kuwaiti detainees. The complaint alleges that the detainees were in Afghanistan and Pakistan as volunteers providing humanitarian aid; that local villagers seeking bounties seized them and handed them over to United States forces; and that they were transferred to Guantanamo Bay sometime between January and March 2002. A representative of the United States Embassy in Kuwait informed the Kuwaiti government of their whereabouts. Invoking the Great Writ, 28 U.S.C. §§2241–242; the Alien Tort Act, 28 U.S.C. §1350; and the Administrative Procedure Act, the *Al Odah* plaintiffs claim a denial of due process under the Fifth Amendment, tortuous conduct in violation of the law of nations and a treaty of the United States, and arbitrary and unlawful governmental conduct. They seek a declaratory judgment and an injunction ordering that they be informed of any charges against them and requiring that they be permitted to consult with counsel and meet with their families.

Rasul v. Bush...is styled a petition for a writ of habeas corpus on behalf of three detainees, although it seeks other relief as well. The next friends bringing the petition are the father of an Australian detainee, and the mother of another British detainee. Respondents are President Bush, Secretary Rumsfeld, Col. Carrico, and Brig. Gen. Michael Lehnert, who is alleged to be the Commander of Joint Task Force 160. The petition claims that the Australian detainee was living in Afghanistan when the Northern Alliance captured him in early December 2001; that one of the British detainees traveled to Pakistan for an arranged marriage after September 22, 2001; and that the other British detainee went to Pakistan after that date to visit relatives and continue his computer education. The next friends learned of their sons' detention at Guantanamo Bay from their respective governments. The *Rasul* petitioners claim violations of due process under the Fifth and Fourteenth Amendments, international law, and military regulations; a violation of the War Powers Clause; and a violation of Article I of the Constitution because of the President's alleged suspension of the writ of habeas corpus. They seek a writ of habeas corpus, release from unlawful custody, access to counsel, and end to interrogations, and other relief.

Habib v. Bush...is also in the form of a petition for writ of habeas corpus and is brought by the wife of an Australian citizen, acting as his next friend. Naming President Bush, Secretary Rumsfeld, Brig. Gen Baccus, and Lt. Col. William Cline as defendants, the petition alleges that Habib traveled to Pakistan to look for employment and a school for his children; that after Pakistani authorities arrested him in October 2001, they transferred him to Egyptian authorities, who handed him over to the United States military; and that the military moved him from Egypt to Afghanistan and ultimately to Guantanamo Bay in May 2002. Australian authorities visited Guantanamo and issued a press release confirming Habib's presence there. The *Habib* petition, like the other two cases, invokes the Due Process Clause of the Fifth Amendment and other constitutional provisions, the Alien Tort Act, the Administrative Procedure Act, due process under international law, and United States military regulations. Habib seeks a writ of habeas corpus, legally sufficient process to establish the legality of his detention, access to counsel, and end to all interrogations of him, and other relief.

The district court held that it lacked jurisdiction. Believing no court would have jurisdiction, it dismissed the complaint and the two habeas corpus petitions with prejudice. *Rasul v. Bush*, 215 F. Supp.2d 55, 56 (D. D. C. 2002). (supra). In the Court's view all the detainee's claims went to the lawfulness of their custody and thus were cognizable only in habeas corpus.... Relying on *Johnson v. Eisentrager*,...the court ruled that it did not have jurisdiction to issue writs of habeas corpus for aliens detained outside the sovereign territory of the United States.

II.

While these cases were pending, the Ninth Circuit affirmed an order dismissing a habeas corpus petition for all Guantanamo detainees on the ground that those bringing the action—clergy, lawyers, and law professors—were not proper "next friends." *Coalition of Clergy v. Bush*, 310 F.3d 1153, 1165 (9th Cir. 2002). (supra).

* * *

In each of the three cases, the detainees deny that they are enemy combatants, or *enemy* aliens.

* * *

...[N]o court in this country has jurisdiction to grant habeas relief, under 28 U.S.C. §2241, to the Guantanamo detainees, even if they have not been adjudicated enemies of the United States. We cannot see why, or how, the writ may be made available to aliens abroad when basic constitutional protections are not. This much is at the heart of *Eisentrager*. If the Constitution does not, they cannot invoke the jurisdiction of our courts to test the constitutionality or the legality of restraints on their liberty. *Eisentrager* itself directly tied jurisdiction to the extension of constitutional provisions: "in extending constitutional protections beyond the citizenry, the Court has been at pains to point out that it was the alien's presence within its territorial jurisdiction that gave the Judiciary power to act." 339 U.S. at 771.... Thus, the "privilege of litigation has been extended to aliens, *whether friendly or enemy,* only because permitting their presence in the country implied protection." *Id.* at 777–78...(emphasis added).

* * *

We have thus far assumed that the detainees are not "within any territory over which the United States is sovereign." *Eisentrager*, 339 U.S. at 778,.... The detainees dispute the assumption. They say the military controls Guantanamo Bay, that it is in essence a territory of the United States, that the government exercises sovereignty over it, and that in any event, *Eisentrager* does not turn on technical definitions of sovereignty or territory. [The Court then discusses the leasehold agreement with the Republic of Cuba in the same fashion as did Judge Matz in *Coalition of Clergy v. Bush (supra)*].

* * *

We also disagree with the detainees that the *Eisentrager* opinion interchanged "territorial jurisdiction" with "sovereignty," without attaching any particular significance to either term. When the Court referred to "territorial jurisdiction," it meant the territorial jurisdiction of the United States courts. The United States has sovereignty over the geographic area of the States and, as the *Eisentrager* Court recognized, over insular possessions...Guantanamo Bay fits within neither category.

* * *

...But as we have decided, the detainees are in all relevant respects in the same position as the prisoners in *Eisentrager*. They cannot seek release based on violations of the Constitution or treaties or federal law; the courts are not open to them. Whatever other relief the detainees seek, their claims necessarily rest on alleged violations of the same category of laws listed in the habeas corpus statute, and are therefore beyond the jurisdiction of the federal courts. Nothing in *Eisentrager* turned on the particular jurisdictional language of any statute; everything turned on the circumstances of those seeking relief, on the authority under which they were held, and on the consequences of opening the courts to them. With respect to the detainees, those circumstances, that authority and those consequences differ in no material respect from *Eisentrager*.

IV.

We have considered and rejected the other arguments the detainees have made to the court. The judgment of the district court dismissing the complaint in [*Al Odah*] and the petitions for writs of habeas corpus in [*Habib*] and [*Rasul*] for lack of jurisdiction is

Affirmed.

(r) Kenneth Anderson, "What to Do With Bin Laden and Al Qaeda Terrorists? A Qualified Defense of Military Commissions and United States Policy on Detainees at Guantanamo Bay Naval Base"

25 *Harvard Journal of Law and Public Policy*
591; 592–594; 596–597; 609–619; 725–634 (2002)
Reproduced with permission from Kenneth Anderson, *What to Do with Bin Laden and Al Qaeda Terrorists? A Qualified Defense of Military Commissions and United States Policy on Detainees at Guantanamo Bay Naval Base*, 25 Harv. J.L. & Pub. Pol'y 591 (2002)

I. INTRODUCTION

* * *

Proposals for how to treat the most serious category of suspects—those believed to have been involved in the planning or execution of the September 11 attacks—have fallen into three main camps. The first group has called for having them tried by international tribunals. Such proposals have included: extending the jurisdiction of the current Yugoslavia tribunal to cover the September 11 attacks and its Al Qaeda sponsors, establishing a new ad hoc tribunal under the authority of the Security Council or amending the terms of the...International Criminal Court to allow it to begin hearing terrorist cases. Second, many commentators, especially in the United States, have called for terrorist suspects, no matter where they are found, to be tried in the United States district courts for applicable violations of United States and international criminal law. Third, the Bush Administration has announced plans, pursuant to a Military Order signed by the President in his capacity as Commander in Chief, to create the option of trying non-citizen suspects in specially created "military commissions."

The Military Order has provoked a storm of protest from various civil libertarians, civil and human rights organizations, newspaper editorialists, academics, members of Congress, and sundry others, mostly on the political left, but including some prominent conservatives such as *New York Times* columnist William Safire and Rep. Bob Barr (R-Ga.). Combined with related criticism of other domestic security measures enacted by Congress in the wake of the attacks or put in place by the Bush Administration largely through actions by Attorney General John Ashcroft, protest over military tribunals and other perceived restrictions of civil liberties has constituted most of the domestic dissent from the Bush Administration's conduct in the wake of September 11.

Seemingly surprised by the criticism, the Bush Administration has moved to mollify opponents by promising additional regulations outlining the actual procedures for the military commissions (to be drafted by the General Counsel of the Department of Defense). The regulations apparently will provide for greater procedural protection that the original order requires. The Bush Administration has also moved, however, to challenge critics on grounds of national security and war-time exigency. In hearings before the Senate Judiciary Committee, for example, Attorney General John Ashcroft "bluntly [told] lawmakers that their 'power of oversight is not without limit,' and that, in some areas, 'I cannot and will not consult with you.'"

* * *

Yet, imperfect as the Military Order is…the fundamental concept of using military commissions is morally, politically, and legally justified. They can be shaped and made to work consistent with the Constitution, international law, and particularly the Geneva Conventions, to which the United States and its military are deeply and correctly committed. They—not international tribunals nor even ordinary United States district courts—ought to be the vehicle for the trial and punishment of at least the most serious categories of alleged terrorist, i. e., those who by their conduct and ideology have made themselves not merely criminals but our enemies.

* * *

…Whatever the outcome of the grand argument between liberal internationalism and democratic sovereignty, it is both the privilege and the awful responsibility of the United States to deal with those alleged to have planned or participated in the September 11 attacks. The tragedy certainly involved universally reprehensible crimes, such as making civilians both the means and object of attack. But fundamentally, September 11 was *not* an attack upon the whole world; it was an attack upon the United States, its territory, property, and people. A democratic polity owes to its members and citizens a good faith effort to protect them and do justice on their behalf, and it would be morally wrong for the United States, in a misguided attempt to provide "universal" justice through supposedly "universal" institutions, to seek to avoid this burden and refer it to international institutions.

Nor should the United States be swayed by arguments that only international bodies can provide "impartiality" and the appearance of "impartial" justice. Even accepting for argument's sake that international tribunals could provide more impartial justice than United States courts would, the United States as a democratic polity owes its citizens, its people, and particularly those who died and lost loved ones, justice according to *United States* traditions. It owes *our* people *our* justice, and should see that our justice is done to those who have attacked us. This principle is the genuine lesson of the Nuremberg Trials, not the anodyne universalism of liberal internationalists. It would have been morally contemptible for the Second World War Allies to have proclaimed, in a fit of political correctness, that they should turn the judgment of the Nazi leaders over to those countries which were neutral and impartial to have them tried in a genuinely unbiased manner.

On the contrary, partiality can be a moral badge of honor and goodness. Partiality entitled countries to sit in judgment after World War II, because it evidenced having fought for the good rather than letting evil flourish and go unpunished. If there were to be trials at all, the Allies owed a solemn obligation to their own and all victims to conduct such procedures themselves. They earned the right and obligation to conduct such trials not only because of victory, but also because of their own payment in blood. This principle remains true today. The United States owes *its* democratic community victory in this war, and the imposition of *its* justice upon those who would bring war and crime to its territory and people.

* * *

III

B. Criminals and Enemies

...The perpetrators of September 11 and other terrorist attacks are not morally and legally analogous to the perpetrators of domestic crime in a settled domestic society.

* * *

...The ability to prosecute domestic crime, and the necessity of providing constitutional standards of due process, including the extraordinarily complex rules of evidence, suppression of evidence, right to counsel, and the rights against self-incrimination have developed *within* a particular political community, and fundamentally reflect decisions about rights within a fundamentally domestic, democratic setting in which all of us have a stake in both sides of the equation, as prosecutors and prosecuted, because we are part of the political community which must consider both individual rights and collective security.

It is a system, in other words, that fundamentally treats crime as a *deviation from* the domestic legal order, not fundamentally as *attack upon* the very basis of that order. Terrorists who come from outside this society for the purpose of destroying it, cannot be assimilated into the structure of the ordinary criminal trial. True enough, citizenship alone is enough to qualify a person to be tried for attacks upon that order, as in the case of a domestic terrorist such as Timothy McVeigh. But, in fact, the domestic legal system strains to acknowledge the awfulness of what someone like McVeigh has done: his crimes are *not* reducible to so many murders, so many injured victims, so much destruction of property, and so on in the way one thinks of ordinary criminals. The actual charges available to prosecutors in his trial, and hence the conduct of the trial itself, in a curious but profound way, missed the point of his act, which was not merely to murder people, but to make war upon the United States, McVeigh, like bin Laden and Al Qaeda, undertook not a deviation from the domestic order, but an attack upon it. McVeigh's membership in the political community through citizenship was enough to grant him trial as though his acts were merely crimes and not attacks, but the moral reality is that McVeigh had transformed himself into a true outsider, not merely a deviant. He was not merely a criminal, but also an *enemy*. Al Qaeda has the same status—but the U.S. district courts are, by constitutional design, for criminals and not for those who are at once criminals and enemies. U.S. district courts are eminently unsuited by practicality but also by concept for the task of addressing those who planned and executed September 11.

IV. Military Commissions

A. *Constitutional Questions*

The fundamental problem, of course, is that while it is easy to accept the distinction between domestic criminals, deviating from the domestic order, on the one hand, and those who are at once criminals and enemies of it, on the other, the question remains who shall make that essential determination in any particular case.... The Military Order is deeply flawed...and I leave it to others to detail its problems. It is more useful instead to set out markers of what is constitutionally defensible, in conceptual terms.

First, the U.S. Constitution is not a document for the entire world. It is not a pact with the world, or a pact among people generally in the world. It is a document as among the members of a particular political community, and its burdens and benefits accrue to them. Particularly those in the international human rights community who now complain that the United States does not propose to extend full constitutional protections to categories of non-U.S. citizens on the ground that these protections are somehow required by notions of universal justice and due process seem to forget that this same human rights community has been careful to construct international tribunals, such as the Yugoslavia tribunal, which make no pretense of adhering to America's far more rigorous notions of procedure, due process, and evidentiary rules....

Second, the fundamental parameters of the United States political community are twofold: citizenship and territory. The case for full U.S. constitutional protection is strongest when dealing with U.S. citizens on the territory of the United States—even including McVeigh—while the weakest case is a non-U.S. citizen on foreign territory, such as non-citizen Al Qaeda suspects captured in Afghanistan. Even the McVeighs deserve U.S. constitutional protects in regular U.S. courts (and have received them), while aliens abroad have not: this is all ordinary jurisprudence, and is reflected in the Military Order insofar as only (certain) aliens may be tried by military commission. The questions arise in the mixed cases.

Third, in my understanding, permanent residents of the United States, like citizens, are accorded full constitutional protection. This view is at odds with the Military Order, however, which fails to treat alien permanent residency as a separate and protected category of non-citizen. Federal courts, however, have and, in my estimation, would continue to read the language of the Sixth Amendment, "In all criminal prosecutions, the accused shall enjoy the right to a speedy and public trial, by an impartial jury," for example, as applicable to permanent residents. Quoting Harvard Law School professor Laurence Tribe, "[N]ot even Congress could empower a president to subject any resident alien to trial by tribunal whenever the president claims reason to believe that the accused ever aided or abetted what the president deems international terrorism."

Fourth, in my view, territoriality ought to be decisive in the case of nonresident aliens *lawfully* on the territory of the United States. For example, alien students present on student visas for legitimate reasons would not be subject to military commissions, on the simple but intuitively persuasive ground that military commissions, as so many commentators have pointed out *are* constitutionally dangerous creatures and that territoriality is one way of limiting the damage they can do. On the other hand, someone who entered the United States on allegedly valid papers, such as a student visa, but with the intent of committing terrorism, would not be present "lawfully" in the United States, and so would be subject to a military tribunal. On the other hand, a permanent resident who had entered the country lawfully, perhaps many years before, and who, for example, underwent a conversion to doctrines of terrorism, ought not to be subject to military commission. Neither of these situations, however is consistent with the Military Order, which makes no such distinctions. On the other hand, White House counsel Alberto Gonzales, in what amounts to a reversal of portions of the Military Order and not merely an interpretation of them—has stated that an individual "arrested, detained, or tried in the United States" by military commission will be able to "challenge the lawfulness of the commission's jurisdiction through a habeas corpus proceeding in a federal court." Habeas can serve as the protection for those nonresident aliens with facially valid papers, present in the United States, but accused of terrorist intentions.

B. *International Law and Military Commissions*

If these basic markers of constitutionally acceptable jurisdiction of military commissions are provisionally accepted, so that persons who fall under the jurisdiction are acknowledged not to benefit from U.S. constitutional protection, then the question is to what procedural and due process protections they are entitled under international law. In the circumstances of armed conflict in which the United States is now embroiled, the applicable law is international humanitarian law. It is worth beginning with the observation that international humanitarian law applies when the facts indicate that an armed conflict is underway, as is now the case for the United States. It is not necessarily the case that at some point in the future the United States would continue to be at war in the *actual* sense of armed conflict, the actual conduct of hostilities, as distinguished from "war" in a metaphorical sense, such as the "war on drugs." The reason this distinction of actual armed conflict is relevant is that a different set of international laws might then apply outside the context of actual armed conflict, rather than international humanitarian law, including such agreements as the International Covenant on Civil and Political Rights.

In the present situation of armed conflict, however, the applicable laws are the Geneva Conventions, on the other hand, and customary international law, the so-called "laws and customs of war," on the other. The Third Geneva Convention covers the treatment of prisoners of war (POW), including the definition of who constitutes a bona fide POW and procedures for criminal proceedings against POW's.

It provides at Article 4 a definition of a lawful combatant, who thus benefits from the so-called "combatant's privilege," which provides: first, immunity from prosecution for such acts as killings and destruction that would, under other circumstances, be considered criminal acts, provided that they are carried out under the requirements of the laws of war; second, the privilege of surrender and quarter, and, third, the right to be treated as a POW in case of capture by the enemy. Article 4 provides, in part, that POW's include persons "who having fallen into the hands of the enemy," as:

> Members of other militias and members of other volunteer corps, including those of organized resistance movements, belonging to a Party to the conflict and operating in or outside their own territory, even if this territory is occupied, provided that such militias or volunteer corps, including such organized resistance movements, fulfill the following conditions: that of being commanded by a person responsible for his subordinates; that of having a fixed distinctive sign recognizable at a distance; that of carrying arms openly; that of conducting their operations in accordance with the laws and customs of war.

Protocol I also provides rules about the definition of a combatant entitled to POW treatment; Article 44(3) states in part:

[A combatant] shall retain his status as a combatant, provided that…he carries his arms openly: (a) during each military engagement, and (b) during such time as he is visible to the adversary while he is engaged in a military deployment preceding the launching of an attack in which he is to participate.

The United States, however, has never accepted this extended definition of a combatant in Protocol I, on the grounds that it lessens, rather than increases, protections for the civilian population. It has specifically named this article of Protocol I as a reason why it refuses to ratify Protocol I, and it will not be bound by it in the current circumstances.

The point, however, is that the terrorists and organizations which planned and executed the September 11 attacks do not fit the definition of combatants entitled to receive POW benefits. Apart from the requirements of carrying arms openly and bearing a fixed distinctive sign visible at a distance, and apart from any theoretical controversy over the extended definition of a combatant under Protocol I not accepted by the United States, it is patently clear that the September 11 terrorists fail the requirement of conducting their operations in accordance with the laws and customs of war. They failed this requirement, of course, by using civilians as both the means and targets of their attacks, among other things.

What is the consequence of failing to quality as a POW? It is not that a POW is entirely immune from prosecution. POW's are liable to prosecution, including by the forces holding them, for violations of the laws and customs of war—war crimes and grave breaches of the Geneva Conventions. Moreover, a national of a "party to a conflict" who is captured by his own sovereign government—a rebel fighter in a civil war captured by government forces, or even more to the point, an American citizen such as John Philip Walker Lindh, a Taliban fighter captured while engaged in combat against U.S. forces—is liable to prosecution for treason, murder, and other national laws by his own government. The significance is that a POW may only be tried according to the rules laid out in the Third Geneva Convention, which provide for basic due process. Those rules, found at Articles 99–108 of the Third Geneva Convention, do not provide for extensive due process on their own.

* * *

…[I]f a member of Al Qaeda or some other accused terrorist *was* determined to be a bona fide POW, then the procedures required to try him would be those under which an equivalent U.S. serviceman or woman would be tried. Those procedures would be under the United States Uniform Code of Military Justice (UCMJ), which in nearly every respect provides for the same constitutional rights for military personnel tried under courts-martial that a civilian would have in civilian courts….

If a person accused of terrorist activity does *not*, however, meet the requirements of the Third Geneva Convention as a POW, does he then benefit from any protection under international humanitarian law? Such people would be counted, at that point, as what the Bush Administration has declared them to be, "unqualified belligerents' or "unqualified combatants"—combatants who do not meet the legal requirements to be POWs and hence are liable to prosecution under national and international law for any belligerent actions they may have participated or conspired in. They are to be militarily as unqualified combatants, but if captured, treated as criminals.

Although unqualified belligerents benefit in international humanitarian law from some minimal procedural and due process protections, not even unqualified belligerents, spies, or civilian saboteurs may be dealt with summarily—that is, without benefit of a hearing to determine their status and fate. Article 75 of Protocol I lays out a roadmap to minimal procedural fairness accorded to such persons, and it states in part:

No sentences may be passed and no penalty may be executed on a person found guilty of a penal offense related to the armed conflict except pursuant to a conviction pronounced by an impartial and regularly constituted court respecting the general principles of regular judicial procedures....

* * *

It is worth noting what is *not* required by Article 75.... It does require that a person charged with an offense is presumed innocent until proven guilty. The Military Order is grievously wrong in this regard. Moreover, Article 78 does provide for notice, a right to be heard, conviction only for personal penal responsibility rather than collective punishment, the right to be present in the hearing, the right to examine witnesses against one and put on one's own witnesses under the same circumstances as witnesses against one, for public pronouncement of the judgment, and the right to be advised of post conviction remedies. Further, Article 75 prohibits prosecutions for ex post facto crimes. But Article 75 does not mention a right to counsel, let alone a right to counsel of one's choice. It does not provide for a public trial; only that it is a right of the convicted to have the judgment pronounced publicly. Nor does it provide for judicial review either by higher military or civilian authorities. It does not require any special procedures for reaching a capital verdict.

Article 75 of Protocol I is thus nearly void of procedural protections, yet it is the minimum due process required by international humanitarian law for persons, such as unprivileged combatants, who do not benefit from other protections of law. It is frankly far below what the United States has announced will be the procedural protections of the military commissions. Those protections ought to be far higher than announced in the Military Order, but the point is that the United States can and should frame these military commissions as consistent with international humanitarian law in this time of actual hostilities.

The final question, however, with respect to international humanitarian law, is who has the power to determine whether a person is an unprivileged combatant subject to Article 75 of Protocol I or is instead a POW who benefits from the Third Geneva Convention. The United States, thus far, appears to have taken the position that those persons involved in the September 11 attacks are, by definition, unprivileged combatants because of the nature of the attacks themselves and their violation of the laws and customs of war, and that this determination can be made under the power of the commander in chief. The Bush Administration has accepted, in addition, at least according to the White House counsel, Alberto Gonzales, a right of habeas corpus to determine jurisdiction and status for persons "arrested, detained, or tried *in the United States*" by military commission that would otherwise make a final determination of the question of POW status.

* * *

A much more serious issue is the question of how long detention might run. Here too, however, the issue of whether a detainee is a POW under the Third Geneva Convention is important but not the only consideration. It is true that bona fide POW's must be repatriated at the "cessation of active hostilities" (although prisoners serving sentences validly pronounced for war crimes or other crimes may be compelled to serve them). However, even if the detainees were not covered by the Third Geneva Convention, a person may not be held forever without charges or trial. At some point, in some manner, whether through the vehicle of the international law of war or some other avenue, the question of indefinite and possibly permanent detention without trail must eventually arise.

That having been said, even if the Third Geneva Convention applied, at least at this moment, active hostilities in Afghanistan continue. Detention and internment, even of civilians and non-combatants, let alone combatants, under the Third and Fourth Geneva Conventions are quite acceptable, so long as certain procedures for their protection are in place. Not only fighters, but under certain criteria, even non-combatant civilians may be deemed a security risk and interned; there are limits to this power, but the Fourth Geneva Convention grants a certain level of discretion to the security needs of a party to a conflict. Moreover, one could argue—decisively in my view—that as long as operations are being carried out against Al Qaeda, the organization whose destruction is one of the war aims of the United States, the United States is perfectly entitled under the Third Geneva Convention to detain fighters whom it determines to be a security risk in connection with that organization, not merely in Afghanistan, but elsewhere. The theatre of war is wider than Afghanistan. It probably could not do so with respect to an endless and essentially metaphorical "war on terrorism" dealing with targets unrelated to Al Qaeda—a war which might indeed have no end—but it is certainly entitled to do so with fighters or civilians connected even loosely with Al Qaeda, wherever they may be. Absent the application of the Third Geneva Convention, the United States, while it must eventually bring charges and have some kind of trial, even if only a military tribunal..., has considerable latitude in the timing and preparation of those trials. They need not happen on a timetable to suit Amnesty International, Human Rights Watch, or the governments of the European Union.

Ultimately, of course, the outcomes of many of the issues raised above hinge largely, although not completely, on whether a detainee is regarded as a bona fide POW under the Third Geneva Convention or not. Three positions have emerged on this issue. First, the Bush Administration has asserted strongly that the detainees are not entitled to *any* application of the Third Geneva Convention, not even to determine their status as POW's or, instead, as unlawful combatants, as discussed above.... The point made by the Bush Administration is that Al Qaeda is not a military force at all, even if *the* forces seeking to destroy it are U.S. military forces. It is instead, in this view, a criminal organization pure and simple, and its fighters are not legal combatants, nor are they entitled to a determination under the Third Geneva Convention to ascertain whether they are....

Although this position has been defended generally on grounds that the Geneva Conventions are simply inapplicable to criminal terrorists, it is worth noting that a principled argument to the same end can be made on the basis of the Third Geneva Convention itself. Critics of the Bush Administration's position have focused, logically enough, on the language of Article 5 which provides that in cases of doubt, the matter shall be resolved by a "competent tribunal." I have argued...that a competent tribunal may perfectly well be a military commission operating in conformity with Article 75 of Protocol I insofar as it embodies customary international law, rather than either civilian courts or a regular court martial. The text of Article 5, however, states a threshold before anything need be resolved by a "competent tribunal;" namely, a competent tribunal is required only "should any doubt arise" with respect to the status of detainees. Article 5 contains no requirement whatsoever that the question for a "competent tribunal" versus a determination by military authorities as such. Thus, Secretary of Defense Rumsfeld could and has asserted that there is no doubt as to their status—"[t]here is no ambiguity in this case"—and hence no requirement to hold a tribunal.

Despite the fact that one recoils at the implication that, in theory at least, every drug operation conducted by the U.S. military might require some kind of tribunal to determine POW status, and despite the fact that a principled argument can be made from the text of the Third Geneva Convention itself in Article 5, the Bush Administration's position is ultimately not persuasive. It is not persuasive principally for the reason that irrespective of such niceties as declaring war, by any understanding of the international law of war, the United States has and continues to be engaged in armed conflict. It is using its full military machinery to wage war. After all, what distinguishes the Bush strategy against terrorism from the Clinton-era strategy of law enforcement? It is emphatically *not* that law enforcement activities are being "supported" by military action. The United States went down that path, to its sorrow, in Somalia in 1993. The fundamental difference between the current war and law enforcement is not the participation of U.S. military acting as a posse sent out to arrest the bad guys. It is, rather, that Bush announced that the United States would *not distinguish* between terrorists and states that harbor them, and would bring down either as necessary. Announcing aims that deliberately link non-state actors and states means, if you use the weapons of modern war, that politically, morally, and legally, you are at war. In this instance, then, Human Rights Watch is correct in its assessment:

> The United States government could have pursued terrorist suspects by traditional law enforcement means, in which case the Geneva Conventions would not apply.... But since the United States government engaged in armed conflict in Afghanistan—by bombing and undertaking other military operations—the Geneva Conventions clearly do apply to that conflict.

The second position is that espoused at least occasionally by Amnesty International officials and a handful of other commentators. According to the Washington Post, although "Amnesty International has not taken a formal stand on the POW question... officials with the human rights group say they believe Al Qaeda fighters qualify as POWS's because they were at the time intermingled with regular Taliban forces in Afghanistan." The argument appears to be that by being "intermingled" with regular Taliban fighters, Al Qaeda fighters were somehow assimilated into Taliban command structure and so (presuming that Taliban fighters are entitled to regular POW status) they overcame the problem of Al Qaeda not adhering to the laws of war by being part of an organization that (presumably) did, at least enough for its fighters to qualify as legal combatants.

This second position appears dubious at best. It is not in the least bit obvious that by being an Al Qaeda fighter, someone who has come typically from outside Afghanistan to train and fight, becomes "part" of a "legal" organization by intermingling with them. The issue is command and control. It is simply a fact of international law that one's status as a legal or illegal combatant under the Third Geneva Convention depends in part on the nature of the *organization* for which one fights. If the organization collectively fails the test of the Third Geneva Convention, its fighters individually are not POW's, irrespective of whether they have individually committed war crimes or not: This is the meaning of Article 4(a)(2)(d) of the Third Geneva Convention requiring that those who are not members of "regular" armed forces be part of an organization capable of adhering to the laws of war. Al Qaeda plainly does not meet that test. Whether the Taliban meet that test is an open question, given that the Taliban was recognized as a government by no more than three states in the world and that it came to power through civil war that did not necessarily convey any status of a successor state. Even if the Taliban did meet that standard, however, merely being with them does not constitute being part of them in the relevant sense of command and control. On the contrary, it is far easier to argue that whatever legal status the Taliban enjoyed was instead vitiated by the incorporation of obviously illegal combatants into its ranks. It is far more persuasive to think that the Taliban weakened the claim of its fighters to POW status by fighting with Al Qaeda than that Al Qaeda fighters strengthened their claims by fighting with the Taliban.

The third, and most persuasive position, is that currently being enunciated by the U.S. State Department in discussions within the Bush Administration taking place. Under this view, the detainees are covered by the Third Geneva Convention in the sense that they are entitled individually to a hearing by a "competent tribunal" to determine their status as either bona fide POW's or else unlawful combatants. The question of their status, however, is determined by their membership or participation in an organization, Al Qaeda, that does not meet the requirements of the Third Geneva Convention. The sole issue for a tribunal is to determine their connection to organizations not meeting those requirements (and, significantly, whether they fought *for* some organization that met the requirements—fighting "solo" so to speak, also flunks the Third Geneva Convention tests). If they cross that legal threshold, they are treated as POW's and if not, they are illegal combatants. At some point, even as illegal combatants, they must be charged and tried, but they would receive no greater protections than the customary law provisions already outlined under the discussion of Article 75 of Protocol I.

The question then remains of what constitutes a "competent tribunal" within the meaning of the Third Geneva Convention. At that point, the legal analysis re-joins that already discussed with respect to military commissions. A competent tribunal need *not* be a tribunal convened with full POW protections and the Third Geneva Convention. The argument that providing provisional POW protections to a detainee in respect of treatment further means that a "competent tribunal" must also be a court martial under the Third Geneva Convention itself fatally ignores the specific provisions of Article 75, which—drafted some thirty years after the 1949 Conventions and fully cognizant of them—affirmatively establish a lower standard of process. To require that every hearing be under the Third Geneva Convention POW standard would render pointless the lesser procedures specifically established under Article 75 and customary law for dealing with those accused of abusing their civilian status, such as spies, saboteurs, and other illegal combatants. Rather, all that is required is what has already been stated under Article 75. It is a procedure which does not require an open trial, does not require counsel, and does not even require an appeals process although, as earlier stated, I believe the United States ought to provide for one.

In my view, the best way for the United States to proceed with the detainees at Guantanamo Bay Naval Base would be under the terms of its own regulations dating from 1997 and contemplating exactly this situation. The determination of POW or illegal combatant status should be done by a three officer tribunal, using a majority vote, and a standard of the preponderance of the evidence.

What kind of evidence should a panel consider, given that Al Qaeda is not an organization handing out membership cards? Among the factors to be considered ordinarily dispositive with respect to the fighters taken from Afghanistan to Guantanamo would at least figure whether the fighter had trained in Al Qaeda camps. Similarly ordinarily dispositive ought to be nationality: although there may well be Afghan Al Qaeda, foreigners fighting in Afghanistan should be regarded as Al Qaeda. Such tribunals could be convened quickly and efficiently. If conjoined with a limited appeals process made solely to a military tribunal (but during which time the United States would be free to treat the detainee as an illegal combatant subject to reversal by the appellate panel), the interests of a fair procedure under international law and the pursuit of illegal combatants could both be accommodated. Some level of infra-military appeals process also has the important political virtue of allowing a quick initial panel with an appeals panel (no counsel at any level, consistent with Article 75) that can consider appeals more slowly while still treating the detainees as formally adjudged illegal combatants. The political risk of not having an appeals process is that any initial trial panel would inevitably be denounced as a kangaroo court, and in order to respond to criticism—especially coming from so many erstwhile "allies" with nationals in custody—the Bush Administration would enevitably slow down the process and complicate the procedure. Better instead to have an appeals process, strictly within the military. Beyond that, it should ignore the shrill voices of those whose policy amounts to a tender solicitude for the alleged rights of anyone, just so long as they are not American.

VI. Conclusion

Nevertheless, a serious moral lacuna remains. The Military Order provides for trial by military commission on charges of "violations of the laws of war and other applicable laws" White House counsel Gonzales says that those tried "must be chargeable with offenses against the international laws of war, like targeting civilians or hiding in civilian populations and refusing to bear arms openly." The same substantive terms would apply to an international tribunal or to a U.S. district court trial. Yet it somehow misses the point.

If we were to elaborate the crimes with which the perpetrators of September 11 should be charged in any of these fora, we would include murder, conspiracy to murder, destruction of property, and others. Under international humanitarian law, they should also be charged with violations of the laws and customs of war, including the targeting of civilians and using prohibited means and methods of attack. Others would even add a charge for crimes against humanity. Yet, this does not quite satisfy us, because beyond the methods of warfare, in the traditional sense of *jus in bello*, we Americans also want to punish them, in the categorical, not narrowly legal, sense, for their aggression against the United States. We want retribution not just for crimes against individuals, but for aggression against the United States of America.

Liberal internationalists, it is true, have an easy solution to this conundrum. They would simply make such aggression an international crime and give it an international forum for trial. The ICC statute, for example, opens the possibility for the ICC to have jurisdiction over crimes of aggression—the traditional category of *jus ad bellum*, the law governing the resort to force rather than simply the law governing the conduct of combatants. But this would require agreement as to the substance, as well as the justiciability, of aggression. This enterprise, for many sound reasons, has failed since Nuremberg. The nascent United Nations, through its Charter, left the determination of what constitutes a threat to international peace and security solely to the political discretion of the Security Council, thus wiping out what the American prosecutor at Nuremberg, Justice Jackson, thought was his finest achievement in making the crime of aggression judicially cognizable. In addition to the Security Council, a state under both the U. N. Charter and customary international law retains its customary right of self-defense and, by implication, at least partly its independent judgment as to what constitutes aggression requiring self-defense. This independent determination, also valid under customary law of self-defense, underlies the U.S. basis for armed action in this conflict.

Given the existence of sound reasons for not judicially criminalizing aggression, its punishment becomes harder to conceive—at least in a world in which people are conditioned to believe that punishment must always be *judicially* mandated. With respect to those who we capture who are, as I argued earlier, criminals as well as our enemies—those who are criminals, but not criminals within the sense of a domestic or political order, and who by their actions and ideology have made themselves our enemies—we are left in a moral quandary. If our enemies were destroyed in battle, then that may be taken as punishment enough. Aggression defeated and punished in the same action. But what about those whom we capture? We try them for crimes, war crimes and domestic crimes, that do not wholly satisfy our sense of their evil acts, and yet we do not believe, either, that those who are outside of our domestic political arrangements ought to be treated as ordinary criminals.

This is part of the moral argument that takes us to military commissions, because they permit us to treat these accused with a form of due process, but which is a process unlike that given to ordinary criminals. If what is most objected to, at bottom, in the establishment of military commissions under the Military Order, is that they leave to the political determination of the President and his political appointees which individuals within certain categories, may be subjected to them—well, that is also a moral virtue. The determination of who is not merely a criminal but a criminal who is *also* an enemy is, and ought to remain, a fundamentally political decision. It requires a finding of criminality by a court— criminality in the sense of ordinary crimes or war crimes. This judicial finding of criminality, however, is a determination to be made by the military commission *after* it has received a suspect by referral from the President. And while the President ought to make a referral in part because he has a serious reason to think that domestic or international law of war has been violated, in part the President should act only because he has determined that this person has committed aggression against the United States, and is therefore an enemy of the United States. The procedure for a referral to a military commission does not treat aggression as a justiciable crime, but neither does it simply ignore the moral reality of it.

It is incontrovertible that commissions grant great power to the Presidency, to the Commander in Chief, and therefore ought to be exercised with great caution. But they do have the virtue of addressing a great moral gap. It is one we lived with in punishing McVeigh because, in the end, he was both an enemy and one of "ours." With Al Qaeda suspects who are not citizens and who are either unlawfully in the United States or beyond our shores, we have little, indeed no, reason to do so.

A military commission must be free to determine whether or not allegations of criminality are true or not, impartially and dispassionately, and what punishment, if any, might be deserved. But the determination that someone is an *enemy* of the United States, and therefore subject to this forum for trying their alleged criminality—is a political, not a judicial, decision. Judges determine who is guilty of a crime. Political authorities determine the identity of our nation's enemies. Military commissions must be invoked with vigilance for their propensity to threaten civil liberties, but the initial judgment of who—standing outside the embrace of the Constitution and on account of aggression—is an enemy of the United States is finally and properly one for the political branches of democratic government.

[On April 28, 2004, the Supreme Court of the United States heard oral arguments in dual consolidated appeals: *Hamdi v. Rumsfeld and Rumsfeld v. Padilla*. They involved two American *citizens* held in military captivity as a result of post-9/11 events in the war on terrorism. Yaser Esam Hamdi is a Baton Rouge, Louisiana-born, Saudi-American who, according to the United States government, was fighting on the side of the Taliban regime in Afghanistan when captured by the Northern Alliance and turned over to the U.S. military. Jose Padilla, a native of Brooklyn, New York, and a former Chicago gang member, was taken into custody by federal agents in Chicago at O'Hare International Airport and charged with plotting with various al Qaeda terrorists to denotate a so-called "dirty" radioactive device somewhere in the United States. Both Hamdi and Padilla are in custody at a United States Navy brig in Charleston, South Carolina. The Supreme Court addressed the merits in *Hamdi*, but in *Padilla*, it avoided a decision on the merits and dismissed Padilla's appeal on a jurisdictional point without prejudice. Padilla's lawyer appeared before the 4th Circuit U.S. Court of Appeals in July, 2005, and demanded that the United States government either charge his client with a crime, or set him free].

(s) The *Hamdi* and *Padilla* Appeals: Citizen Terrorists and the Constitution
(2004)

(i) *Hamdi et al. v. Rumsfeld*
Supreme Court of the United States
542 U.S. _____ (2004)
159 L. Ed. 2d 578

JUSTICE O'CONNOR announced the judgment of the Court and delivered an opinion in which THE CHIEF JUSTICE, JUSTICE KENNEDY, and JUSTICE BRYER join.

At this difficult time in our Nation's history, we are called upon to consider the legality of the Government's detention of a United States citizen on United States soil as an "enemy combatant" and to address the process that is constitutionally owed to one who seeks to challenge his classification as such. The United States Court of Appeals for the Fourth Circuit held that petitioner's detention was legally authorized and that he was entitled to no further opportunity to challenge his enemy-combatant label. We now vacate and remand. We hold that although Congress authorized the detention of combatants in the narrow circumstances alleged here, due process demands that a citizen held in the United States as an enemy combatant be given a meaningful opportunity to contest the factual basis for the detention before a neutral decisionmaker.

I.

On September 11, 2001, the al Qaeda terrorist network used hijacked commercial airliners to attack prominent targets in the United States. Approximately 3,000 people were killed in those attacks. One week later, in response to these "acts of treacherous violence," Congress passed a resolution authorizing the President to "use all necessary and appropriate force against those nations, organizations, or persons he determines planned, authorized, committed, or aided the terrorist attacks" or "harbored such organizations or persons, in order to prevent any future acts of international terrorism against the United States by such nations, organizations or persons."... Soon thereafter the President ordered United States Armed Forces to Afghanistan, with a mission to subdue al Qaeda and quell the Taliban regime that was known to support it.

This case rises out of the detention of a man whom the Government alleges took up arms with the Taliban during this conflict. His name is Yaser Esam Hamdi. Born an American citizen in Louisiana in 1980, Hamdi moved with his family to Saudi Arabia as a child. By 2001, the parties agree, he resided in Afghanistan. At some point that year, he was seized by members of the Northern Alliance, a coalition of military groups opposed to the Taliban government, and eventually was turned over to the United States military. The Government asserts that it initially detained and interrogated

Hamdi in Afghanistan before transferring him to the United States Naval Base in Guantanamo Bay in January 2002. In April 2002, upon learning that Hamdi is an American citizen, authorities transferred him to a naval brig in Norfolk, Virginia, where he remained until a recent transfer to a brig in Charleston, South Carolina. The Government contends that Hamdi is an "enemy combatant," and that this status justifies holding him in the United States indefinitely—without formal charges or proceedings—unless and until it makes the determination that access to counsel or further process is warranted.

In June 2002, Hamdi's father, Esam Fouad Hamdi, filed the present petition for a writ of habeas corpus under 28 U.S.C. §2241 in the Eastern District of Virginia, naming as petitioners his son and himself as next friend. The elder Hamdi alleges in the petition that he has had no contact with his son since the Government took custody of him in 2001, and that the Government has held his son "without access to legal counsel or notice of any charges pending against him."... The petition contends that Hamdi's detention was not legally authorized.... It argues that, "[a]s an American citizen,...Hamdi enjoys the full protection of the Constitution," and that Hamdi's detention in the United States without charges, access to an impartial tribunal, or assistance of counsel "violated and continue[s] to violate the Fifth and Fourteenth Amendments to the United States Constitution."... The habeas petition asks that the court, among other things, (1) appoint counsel for Hamdi; (2) order respondents to cease interrogating him; (3) declare that he is being held in violation of the Fifth and Fourteenth Amendments; (4) "[t]o the extent Respondents contest any material factual allegations in this Petition, schedule an evidentiary hearing, at which Petitioners may adduce proof in support of their allegations"; and (5) order that Hamdi be released from his "unlawful custody."... Although his habeas petition provides no details with regard to the factual circumstances surrounding his son's capture and detention, Hamdi's father has asserted in documents found elsewhere in the record that his son went to Afghanistan to do "relief work," and that he had been in that country less than two months before September 11, 2001, and could not have received military training.... The 20-year-old was traveling on his own for the first time, his father says, and "[b]ecause of his lack of experience, he was trapped in Afghanistan once that military campaign began."

The District Court found that Hamdi's father was a proper next friend, appointed the federal public defender as counsel for the petitioners, and ordered that counsel be given access to Handi.... The United States Court of Appeals for the Fourth Circuit reversed that order, holding that the District Court had failed to extend appropriate deference to the Government's security and intelligence interests. 296 F.3d 278, 279, 283 (2002). It directed the District Court to consider "the most cautious procedures first,"...and to conduct a deferential inquiry into Hambi's status,.... It opined that "if Hamdi is indeed an 'enemy combatant' who was captured during hostilities in Afghanistan, the government's present detention of him is a lawful one."...

On remand, the Government filed a response and a motion to dismiss the petition. It attached to its response a declaration from one Michael Mobbs (hereinafter"Mobbs Declaration"), who identified himself as Special Advisor to the Under Secretary of Defense for Policy. Mobbs indicated that in this position, he has been "substantially involved with matters related to the detention of enemy combatants in the current war against the al Qaeda terrorists and those who support and harbor them (including the Taliban.)"... He expressed his "familiar[ity]" with Department of Defense and United States military policies and procedures applicable to the defendant, control, and transfer of al Qaeda and Taliban personnel, and declared that "[b]ased upon my review of relevant records and reports, I am also familiar with the facts and circumstances related to the capture of...Hamdi and his detention by U.S. military forces."...

Mobbs then set forth what remains the sole evidentiary support that the Government has provided to the courts for Hamdi's detention. The declaration states that Hamdi "traveled to Afghanistan" in July or August 2001, and that he thereafter "affiliated with a Taliban military unit and received weapons training."... It asserts that Hamdi "remained with his Taliban unit following the attacks of September 11" and that, during the time when Northern Alliance forces were "engaged in battle with the Taliban," "Hamdi's Taliban unit surrendered" to those forces, after which he "surrender[ed] his Kalishnikov assault rifle" to them.... The Mobbs Declaration also states that, because al Qaeda and the Taliban "were and are hostile forces engaged in armed conflict with the armed forces of the United States," "individuals associated with those groups "were and continue to be enemy combatants."... Mobbs states that Hamdi was labeled an enemy combatant "[b]ased upon his interviews and in light of his association with the Taliban."... According to the declaration, a series of "U.S. military screening team[s]" determined that Hamdi met "the criteria for enemy combatants," and "a subsequent interview of Hamdi has confirmed that he surrendered and gave his firearm to Northern Alliance forces, which supports his classification as an enemy combatant."...

After the Government submitted this declaration, the Fourth Circuit directed the District Court to proceed in accordance with its earlier ruling and, specifically, to "consider the sufficiency of the Mobbs Declaration as an independent matter before proceeding further." 316 F.3d at 450, 462 (2003). The District Court found that the Mobbs Declaration fell far short of supporting Hamdi's detention.... It criticized the generic and hearsay nature of the affidavit, calling it "little more than the government's say-so.'"... It ordered the Government to turn over numerous materials for *in camera* review, including copies of all of Hamdi's statements and the notes taken from interviews with him that related to his reasons for going to Afghanistan and his activities therein; a list of all interrogators who had questioned Hamdi and their names and addresses; statements by members of the Northern Alliance regarding Hamdi's surrender and capture; a list of the dates and locations of his capture and subsequent detention; and the names and titles of the United States Government officials who made the determinations that Hamdi was an enemy combatant and that he should be moved to a naval brig.... The court indicated that all of these materials were necessary for "meaningful judicial review" of whether Hamdi's detention was legally authorized and whether Hamdi had received sufficient process to satisfy the Due Process Clause of the Constitution and relevant treaties or military regulations....

The Government sought to appeal the production order, and the District Court certified the question of whether the Mobbs Declaration, "standing alone, is sufficient as a matter of law to allow meaningful judicial review of [Hamdi's] classification as an enemy combatant." 316 F.3d at 462. The Fourth Circuit reversed, but did not squarely answer the certified question. It instead stressed that, because it was "undisputed that Hamdi was captured in a zone of active combat in a foreign theater of conflict," no factual inquiry or evidentiary hearing allowing Hamdi to be heard or to rebut the Government's assertions was necessary or proper.... Concluding that the factual averments in the Mobbs Declaration, "if accurate," provided a sufficient basis upon which to conclude that the President had constitutionally detained Hamdi pursuant to the President's war powers, it ordered the habeas petition dismissed.... The Fourth Circuit emphasized that the "vital purposes" of the detention of uncharged enemy combatants—preventing those combatants from rejoining the enemy while relieving the military of the burden of litigating the circumstances of wartime captures halfway around the globe—were interests "directly derived from the war powers of Articles I and II."... In that court's view, because "Article III contains nothing analogous to the specific powers of war so carefully enumerated in Articles I and II,"...separation of powers principles prohibited a federal court from "delv[ing] further into Hamdi's status and capture,".... Accordingly, the District Court's more vigorous inquiry "went far beyond the acceptable scope of review."...

On the more global question of whether legal authorization exists for the detention of citizen enemy combatants at all, the Fourth Circuit rejected Hamdi's arguments that 18 U.S.C. §4001(a) and Article 5 of the Geneva Convention rendered any such detentions unlawful. The court expressed doubt as to Hamdi's argument that §4001(a), which provides that "[n]o citizen shall be imprisoned or otherwise detained by the United States except pursuant to an Act of Congress," required express congressional authorization of detentions of this sort. But it held that, in any event, such authorization was found in the post-September 11 Authorization for Use of Military Force. 316 F.3d at 467. Because "capturing and detaining enemy combatants is an inherent part of warfare," the court held, "the 'necessary and appropriate force' referenced in the congressional resolution necessarily includes the capture and detention of any and all hostile forces arrayed against our troops."... The court likewise rejected Hamdi's Geneva Convention claim, concluding that the convention is not self-executing and that, even if it were, it would not preclude the Executive from detaining Hamdi until the cessation of hostilities. 316 F.3d at 468–469.

Finally, the Fourth Circuit rejected Hamdi's contention that its legal analyses with regard to the authorization for the detention scheme and the process to which he was constitutionally entitled should be altered by the fact that he is an American citizen detained on American soil. Relying on *Ex Parte Quirin*, 317 U.S. 1 (1942), the court emphasized that "[o]ne who takes up arms against the United States in a foreign theater of war, regardless of his citizenship, may properly be designated an enemy combatant and treated as such." 316 F.3d at 475. "The privilege of citizenship," the court held, "entitles Hamdi to a limited judicial inquiry into his detention, but only to determine its legality under the war powers of the political branches. At least where it is undisputed that he was present in a zone of active combat operations, we are satisfied that the Constitution does not entitle him to a searching review of the factual determinations underlying his seizure there."...

The Fourth Circuit denied rehearing en banc, 337 F.3d 335 (2003), and we granted certiorari. 540 U.S. _____ (2004). We now vacate the judgment below and remand.

II

The threshold question before us is whether the Executive has the authority to detain citizens who qualify as "enemy combatants." There is some debate as to the proper scope of this term, and the Government has never provided any court with the full criteria that it uses in classifying individuals as such. It has made clear, however, that, for purposes of this case, the "enemy combatant" that it is seeking to detain is an individual who, it alleges, was "part of or supporting forces hostile to the United States or coalition partners" in Afghanistan and who "engaged in an armed conflict against the United States" there.... We therefore answer only the narrow question before us: whether the detention of citizens falling within that definition is authorized.

The Government maintains that no explicit congressional authorization is required, because the Executive possesses plenary authority to detain pursuant to Article II of the

Constitution. We do not reach the question whether Article II provides such authority, however, because we agree with the Government's alternative position, that Congress has in fact authorized Hamdi's detention, through the AUMF. [Authorization of Use of Military Force].

* * *

...[W]e conclude that the AUMF is explicit congressional authorization for the detention of individuals in the narrow category we describe (assuming, without deciding, that such authorization is required), and that the AUMF satisfied 4001(a)'s requirement that a detention be "pursuant to an Act of Congress" (assuming, without deciding, that §4001(a) applies to military detentions).

The AUMF authorizes the President to use "all necessary and appropriate force" against "nations, organizations, or persons" associated with the September 11, 2001, terrorist attacks.... There can no doubt that the individuals who fought against the United States in Afghanistan as part of the Taliban, an organization known to have supported the al Qaeda terrorist network responsible for those attacks, are individuals Congress sought to target in passing the AUMF. We conclude that detention of individuals falling into the limited category we are considering, for the duration of the particular conflict in which they were captured, is so fundamental and accepted an incident to war as to be an exercise of the "necessary and appropriate force" Congress has authorized the President to use.

The capture and detention of lawful combatants and the capture, detention, and trial of unlawful combatants, by "universal agreement and practice," are "important incidents of war." *Ex Parte Quirin*, 317 U.S. at 28. The purpose of detention is to prevent captured individuals from returning to the field of battle and taking up arms again.... ("[C]aptivity in war is 'neither revenge, nor punishment, but solely protective custody, the only purpose of which is to prevent the prisoners of war from further participation in the war'" (quoting decision of Nuremberg Military Tribunal, reprinted in 41 Am. J. Int'l L. 172, 229 (1947));...

* * *

There is no bar to this Nation's holding one of its own citizens as an enemy combatant. In *Quirin*, one of the detainees, Haupt, alleged that he was a naturalized United States citizen.... We held that "[c]itizens who associate themselves with the military arm of the enemy government, and with its aid, guidance and direction enter this country bent on hostile acts, are enemy belligerents within the meaning of...the law of war."... While Haupt was tried for violations of the law of war, nothing in *Quirin* suggests that his citizenship would have precluded his mere detention for the duration of the relevant hostilities.... A citizen, no less than an alien, can be "part of or supporting forces hostile to the United States or coalition partners" and "engaged in an armed conflict against the United States,"...; such a citizen, if released, would pose the same threat of returning to the front during the ongoing conflict.

In light of these principles, it is of no moment that the AUMF does not use specific language of detention. Because detention to prevent a combatant's return to the battlefield is a fundamental incident of waging war, in permitting the use of "necessary and appropriate force," Congress has clearly and unmistakenly authorized detention in the narrow circumstances considered here.

Hamdi objects, nevertheless, that Congress has not authorized the *indefinite* detention to which he is now subject. The Government responds that "the detention of enemy combatants during World War II was just as 'indefinite' while that war was being fought."... We take Hamdi's objection to be not to the lack of certainty regarding the date on which the conflict will end, but to the substantial prospect of perpetual detention. We recognize that the national security underpinnings of the "war on terror," although crucially important, are broad and malleable.

* * *

It is a clearly established principle of the law of war that detention may last no longer than active hostilities....

* * *

Hamdi contends that the AUMF does not authorize indefinite or perpetual detention. Certainly, we agree that indefinite detention for the purpose of interrogation is not authorized. Further, we understand Congress' grant of authority for the use of "necessary and appropriate force" to include the authority to detain for the duration of the relevant conflict, and our understanding is based on long-standing law-of-war principles. If the practical circumstances of a given conflict are entirely unlike those of the conflicts that informed the development of the law of war, that understanding may unravel. But that is not the situation we face as of this date. Active combat operations against Taliban fighters apparently are ongoing in Afghanistan.

* * *

...The United States may detain, for the duration of these hostilities, individuals legitimately determined to be Taliban combatants who "engaged in an armed conflict against the United States." If the record establishes that United States troops are still involved in active combat in Afghanistan, those detentions are part of the exercise of "necessary and appropriate force," and therefore are authorized by the AUMF.

* * *

A

Though they reach radically different conclusions on the process that ought to attend the present proceeding, the parties begin on common ground. All agree that, absent suspension, the writ of habeas corpus remains available to every individual detained within the United States. U.S. Const., Art I, §9, cl. 2 ("The Privilege of the Writ of Habeas Corpus shall not be suspended, unless when in Cases of Rebellion or Invasion the public Safety may require it"). Only in the rarest of circumstances has Congress seen fit to suspend the writ. *See, e. g.,* Act of Mar 3, 1863, ch. 81, §1, 12 Stat. 755; Act of April 20, 1871, ch. 22, 4, 17 Stat. 14. At all other times, it has remained a critical check on the Executive, ensuring that it does not detain individuals except in accordance with law.... All agree suspension of the writ has not occurred here. Thus, it is undisputed that Hamdi was properly before an Article III court to challenge his detention under 28 U.S.C. §2241.

* * *

B

First, the Government urges the adoption of the Fourth Circuit's holding below—that because it is "undisputed" that Hamdi's seizure took place in a combat zone, the habeas determination can be made purely as a matter of law, with no further hearing or factfinding necessary. This argument is easily rejected. As the dissenters from the denial of rehearing en banc noted, the circumstances surrounding Hamdi's seizure cannot in any way be characterized as "undisputed," as "those circumstances are neither conceded in fact, nor susceptible to concession in law, because Hamdi has not been permitted to speak for himself or even through counsel as to those circumstances." 337 F.3d 335, 357 (CA4 2003) (Luttig, J. dissenting from denial of rehearing en banc);... Under the definition of enemy combatant that we accept today as falling within the scope of Congress' authorization, Hamdi would need to be "part of or supporting forces hostile to the United States or coalition partners" and "engaged in an armed conflict against the United States" to justify his detention in the United States for the duration of the relevant conflict.... An assertion one *resided* in a country in which combat operations are taking place is not a concession that one was "*captured* in a zone of active combat operations in a foreign theater of war," 316 F.3d at 459 (emphasis added), and certainly is not a concession that one was "part of or supporting forces hostile to the United States or coalition partners" and "engaged in an armed conflict against the United States." Accordingly, we reject any argument that Hamdi has made concessions that eliminate any right of further process.

* * *

C

The Government's second argument requires closer consideration. This is the argument that further factual exploration is unwarranted and inappropriate in light of the extraordinary constitutional interests at stake.

* * *

...At most, the Government argues, courts should review its determination that a citizen is an enemy combatant under a very deferential "some evidence" standard....

* * *

...Under this review, a court would assume the accuracy of the Government's articulated basis for Hamdi's detention, as set forth in the Mobbs Declaration, and assess only whether that articulated basis was a legitimate one....

In response, Hamdi emphasizes that this Court consistently has recognized that an individual challenging his detention may not be held at the will of the Executive without recourse to some proceeding before a neutral tribunal to determine whether the Executive's asserted justifications for that detention have basis in fact and warrant in law.... He argues that the Fourth Circuit inappropriately "ceded power to the Executive during wartime to define the conduct for which a citizen may be detained, judge whether that citizen has engaged in the proscribed conduct, and imprison that citizen indefinitely,"...and that due process demands that he receive a hearing in which he may challenge the Mobbs Declaration and adduce his own counter evidence. The District Court, agreeing with Hamdi, apparently believed that the appropriate process would approach the process that accompanies a criminal trial. It therefore disapproved of the hearsay nature of the Mobbs Declaration and anticipated quite extensive discovery of various military affairs. Anything less, it concluded, would not be "meaningful judicial review."

Both of these positions highlight legitimate concerns. And both emphasize the tension that often exists between the automony that the Government asserts is necessary in order to pursue effectively a particular goal and the process a citizen contends he is due before he is deprived of a constitutional right. The ordinary mechanism that we use for balancing such serious competing interests, and for determining the procedures that are necessary to ensure that a citizen is not "deprived of life, liberty, or property, without due process of law...is the test that we articulated in *Mathews v. Eldridge*, 424 U.S. 319 (1976)....*Mathews* dictates that the process due in any given instance is determined by weighing "the private interest that will be affected by the official action: against the Government's asserted interest, including the function involved" and the burdens the Government would face in providing process.... The *Mathews* calculus then contemplates a judicious balancing of these concerns, through an analysis of "risk of an erroneous deprivation" of the private interest if the process were reduced and the "probable value, if any, of additional or substitute safeguards."...

* * *

3

Striking the proper constitutional balance here is of great importance to the Nation during this period of on-going combat. But it is equally vital that our calculus not give short shrift to the values that this country holds dear or to the privilege that is American citizenship. It is during our most challenging and uncertain moments that our Nation's commitment to due process is most severely tested; and it is in those times that we must preserve our commitment at home to the principles for which we fight abroad.

* * *

With due recognition of these competing concerns, we believe that neither the process proposed by the Government nor the process apparently envisioned by the District Court below strikes the proper constitutional balance when a United States citizen is detained in the United States as an enemy combatant. That is, "the risk of erroneous deprivation" of the detainee's liberty interest is unacceptably high under the Government's proposed rule, while some of the "additional or substitute procedural safeguards" suggested by the District Court are unwarranted in light of their limited "probable value" and the burdens they may impose on the military in such cases....

* * *

We therefore hold that a citizen-detainee seeking to challenge his classification as an enemy combatant must receive notice of the factual basis for his classification, and a fair opportunity to rebut the Government's factual assertions before a neutral decisionmaker.

* * *

At the same time, the exigencies of the circumstances may demand that, aside from these core elements, enemy combatant proceedings may be tailored to alleviate their uncommon potential to burden the Executive at a time of ongoing military conflict. Hearsay, for example, may need to be accepted as the most reliable available evidence from the Government in such a proceeding. Likewise, the Constitution would not be offended by a presumption in favor of the Government's evidence, so long as that presumption remained a rebuttable one and fair opportunity for rebuttal were provided. Thus, once the Government puts forth credible evidence that the habeas petitioner meets the enemy-combatant criteria, the onus could shift to the petitioner to rebut that evidence with more persuasive evidence that he falls outside the criteria. A burden-shifting scheme of this sort would meet the goal of ensuring that the errant tourist, embedded journalist, or local aid worker has a chance to prove military error while giving due regard to the Executive once it has put forth meaningful support for its conclusion that the detainee is in fact an enemy combatant.

* * *

We think it unlikely that this basic process will have the dire impact on the central functions of warmaking that the Government forecasts. The parties agree that initial captures on the battlefield need not receive the process we have discussed here; that process is due only when the determination is made to *continue* to hold those who have been seized. The Government has made clear in its briefing that documentation regarding battlefield detainees already is kept in the ordinary course of military affairs.... Any factfinding imposition created by requiring a knowledgeable affiant to summarize these records to an independent tribunal is a minimal one.

* * *

In sum, while the full protections that accompany challenges to detentions in other settings may prove unworkable and inappropriate in the enemy-combatant setting, the threats to military operations posed by a basic system of independent review are not so weighty as to trump a citizen's core rights to challenge meaningfully the Government's case and to be heard by an impartial adjudicator.

* * *

...Likewise, we have made clear that, unless Congress acts to suspend it, the Great Writ of habeas corpus allows the Judicial Branch to play a necessary role in maintaining this delicate balance of governance, serving as an important judicial check on the Executive's discretion in the realm of detentions.... Thus, while we do not question that our due process assessment must pay keen attention to the particular burdens faced by the Executive in the context of military action, it would turn our system of checks and balances on its head to suggest that a citizen could not make his way to court with a challenge to the factual basis for his detention by his government, simply because the Executive opposes making available such a challenge. Absent suspension of the writ by Congress, a citizen detained as an enemy combatant is entitled to this process.

Because we conclude that due process demands some system for a citizen detainee to refute his classification, the proposed "some evidence" standard is inadequate. Any process in which the Executive's factual assertions go wholly unchallenged or are simply presumed correct without any opportunity for the alleged combatant to demonstrate otherwise falls constitutionally short.

* * *

The judgment of the United States Court of Appeals for the Fourth Circuit is vacated, and the case is remanded for further proceedings.

It is so ordered.

JUSTICE SCALIA, with whom JUSTICE STEVENS joins, dissenting.

Petitioner, a presumed American citizen, has been imprisoned without charge or hearing in the Norfolk and Charleston Naval brigs for more than two years, on the allegation that he is an enemy combatant who bore arms against his country for the Taliban. His father claims to the contrary, that he is an inexperienced aid worker caught in the wrong place at the wrong time. This case brings into conflict the competing demands of national security and our citizens' constitutional right to personal liberty. Although I share the Court's evident unease as it seeks to reconcile the two, I do not agree with its resolution.

Where the Government accuses a citizen of waging war against it, our constitutional tradition has been to prosecute him in federal court for treason or some other crime.

Where the exigencies of war prevent that, the Constitution's Suspension Clause, Art. I, §9, cl. 2, allows Congress to relax the usual protections temporarily. Absent suspension, however, the Executive's assertion of military exigency has not been thought sufficient to permit detention without charge. No one contends that the congressional Authorization for the Use of Military Force, on which the Government relies to justify its actions here, is an implementation of the Suspension Clause. Accordingly, I would reverse the decision below.

* * *

II

The allegations here, of course, are no ordinary accusations of criminal activity. Yaser Esam Hamdi has been imprisoned because the Government believes he participated in the waging of war against the United States. The relevant question, then, is whether there is a different, special procedure for imprisonment of a citizen accused of wrongdoing *by aiding the enemy in wartime.*

A

JUSTICE O'CONNOR, writing for the plurality of this Court, asserts that captured enemy combatants (other than those suspected of war crimes) have traditionally been detained until the cessation of hostilities and then released.... That is probably an accurate description of wartime practice with respect to enemy *aliens*. The tradition with respect to American citizens, however, has been quite different. Citizens aiding the enemy have been treated as traitors subject to the criminal process.

As early as 1350, England's Statute of Treasons made it a crime to "levy War against our Lord the King in his Realm, or be adherent to the King's Enemies in his Realm, giving to them Aid and Comfort, in the Realm, or elsewhere." 25 Edw. 3, Stat. 5, c. 2....

* * *

Subjects accused of levying war against the King were routinely prosecuted for treason.... The Founders inherited the understanding that a citizen's levying war against the Government was to be punished criminally. The Constitution provides: "Treason against the United States, shall consist only in levying War against them, or in adhering to their Enemies, giving them Aid and Comfort"; and establishes a heightened proof requirement (two witnesses) in order to "convic[t]" of that offense. Art. III, §3, cl. 1.

In more recent times, too, citizens have been charged and tried in Article III courts for acts of war against the United States, even when their noncitizen co-conspirators were not....

* * *

The modern treason statute is 18 U.S.C. §2381; it basically tracks the language of the constitutional provision. Other provisions of Title 18 criminalize various acts of war-making and adherence to the enemy.

* * *

...The only citizen other than Hamdi known to be imprisoned in connection with military hostilities in Afghanistan against the United States *was* subject to criminal process and convicted upon a guilty plea. See *United States v. Lindh*, 212 F. Supp. 2d 541 (ED Va. 2002) (denying motions for dismaissal);...

* * *

The Suspension clause was by design a safety valve, the Constitution's only "express provision for exercise of extraordinary authority because of a crisis," *Youngstown Sheet & Tube Co. v. Sawyer*, 343 U.S. 579, 650 (1952) (Jackson, J., concurring). Very early in the Nation's history, President Jefferson unsuccessfully sought a suspension of habeas corpus to deal with Aaron Burr's conspiracy to overthrow the Government.... During the Civil War, Congress passed its first Act authorizing Executive suspension of the writ of habeas corpus, see Act of Mar. 3, 1863, 12 Stat. 755, to the relief of those many who thought President's Lincoln's unauthorized proclamations of suspension...unconstitutional.... During reconstruction, Congress passed the Ku Klux Klan Act, which included a provision authorizing suspension of the writ, invoked by President Grant in quelling a rebellion in nine South Carolina counties. See Act of Apr. 20, 1871, ch. 22, &4, 17 Stat. 14...

Two later Acts of Congress provided broad suspension authority to governors of U.S. possessions. The Philippine Civil Government Act of 1902 provided that the Governor of the Philippines could suspend the writ in case of rebellion, insurrection, or invasion.... The Hawaiian Organic Act of 1900 likewise provided that the Governor of Hawaii could suspend the writ in case of rebellion or invasion (or threat thereof).

* * *

...Even if suspension of the writ on the one hand, and committal for criminal charges on the other hand, have been the only *traditional* means of dealing with citizens who levied war against their own country, it is theoretically possible that the Constitution does not *require* a choice between these alternatives.

I believe, however, that substantial evidence does refute that possibility. First, the text of the 1679 [English] Habeas Corpus Act makes clear that indefinite imprisonment on reasonable suspicion is not an available option of treatment for those accused of aiding the enemy, absent a suspension of the writ. In the United States, this Act was read as "enforce[ing] the common law," *Ex parte Watkins*, 3 Pet. 193, 202 (1830), and shaped the early understanding of the scope of the writ.

* * *

Writings from the founding generation also suggest that, without exception, the only constitutional alternatives are to charge the crime or suspend the writ.

* * *

The proposition that the Executive lacks indefinite wartime detention authority over citizens is consistent with the Founders' general mistrust of military power permanently at the Executive's disposal. In the Founders' view, the "blessings of liberty" were threatened by "those military establishments which must gradually poison its very foundation." The Federalist No. 45, p. 238 (J. Madison).

* * *

IV

The Government argues that our more recent jurisprudence ratifies its indefinite imprisonment of a citizen within the territorial jurisdiction of federal courts. It places primary reliance upon *Ex parte Quirin*, 317 U.S. 1 (1942), a World War II case upholding the trial by military commission of eight German saboteurs, one of whom, Hans Haupt, was a U.S. Citizen. The case was not this Court's finest hour. The Court upheld the commission and denied relief in a brief *per curium* issued the day after oral argument concluded...; a week later the Government carried out the commission's death sentence upon six saboteurs, including Haupt. The Court eventually explained its reasoning in a written opinion issued several months later.

* * *

...In *Quirin*, it was uncontested that the petitioners were members of enemy forces. They were "*admitted* enemy invaders," 317 U.S. at 47 (emphasis added), and it was "undisputed" that they had landed in the United States in service of German forces,.... The specific holding of the Court was only that, "upon the *conceded* facts," the petitioners were "plainly within [the] boundaries" of military jurisdiction,...(emphasis added). But where those jurisdictional facts are *not* a belligerent—*Quirin* left the pre-existing law in place. Absent suspension of the writ, a citizen held where the courts are open is entitled either to criminal trial or to a judicial decree requiring his release.

* * *

It follows from what I have said that Hamdi is entitled to a habeas corpus decree requiring his release unless (1) criminal proceedings are promptly brought, or (2) Congress has suspended the writ of habeas corpus. A suspension of the writ could, of course, lay down conditions for continued detention, similar to those that today's opinion prescribes under the Due Process Clause.... But there is a world of difference between the people's representatives' determining the need for that suspension (and prescribing the conditions for it), and this Court's doing so.

The plurality finds justification for Hamdi's imprisonment in the Authorization for Use of Military Force, 115 Stat. 224.... [quoting the AUMF]...

* * *

This [AUMF] is not remotely a congressional suspension of the writ, and no one claims that it is. Contrary to the plurality's view, I do not think this statute even authorizes detention of a citizen with the clarity necessary to satisfy the interpretive canon that statutes should be construed as as to avoid grave constitutional concerns, see *Edward J. DeBartolo Corp. v. Florida Gulf Coast Building & Constr. Trades Council*, 485 U.S. 568, 575 (1988); with the clarity necessary to comport with cases such as *Ex parte Endo*, 323 U.S. 283, 300 (1944), and *Duncan v. Kahanamoku*, 327 U.S. 304, 314–316, 324 (1946); or with the clarity necessary to overcome the statutory prescription that "[n]o citizen shall be imprisoned or otherwise detained by the United States except pursuant to an Act of Congress." 18 U.S.C. §4001(a). But even if it did, I would not permit it to overcome Hamdi's entitlement to habeas corpus relief. The Suspension Clause of the Constitution, which carefully circumscribes the conditions under which the writ can be withheld, would be a sham if it would be evaded by congressional prescription of requirements *other than the common law requirement of committal for criminal prosecution* that renders the writ, though available, unavailing. If the Suspension Clause does not guarantee the citizen that he will either be tried or released, unless the conditions for suspending the writ exist and the grave action of suspending the writ has been taken; if it merely guarantees the citizen that he will not be detained unless Congress by ordinary legislation says he can be detained; it guarantees him very little indeed.

It should not be thought, however, that the plurality's evisceration of the Suspension Clause augments, principally, the power of Congress. [*sic*]. As usual, the major effect of its constitutional improvisation is to increase the power of the Court. Having found a congressional authorization for detention of citizens where none clearly exists; and having discarded the categorical procedural protection of the Suspension Clause; the plurality then proceeds, under the guise of the Due Process Clause, to prescribe what procedural protections it thinks appropriate. It "weigh[s] the private interest...against the Government's asserted interests,"...and—just as though writing a new Constitution—comes up with an unheard-of system in which the citizen rather than the Government bears the burden of proof, testimony is by hearsay rather than live witnesses, and the presiding officer may well be a "neutral" military officer rather than a judge or jury.... It claims authority to engage in this sort of "judicious balancing" from *Mathews v. Eldridge,* 424 U.S. 319 (1976), a case involving...the *withdrawal of disability benefits!* Whatever the merits of this new technique when newly recognized property rights are at issue (and even there they are questionable), it has no place where the Constitution and the common law already supply an answer.

Having distorted the Suspension Clause, the plurality finishes up by transmogrifying the Great Writ—disposing of the present habeas petition by remanding for the District Court to "engag[e] in a factfinding process that is both prudent and incremental,"..."in the absence of [the Executive's prior provisions of procedures that satisfy due process]...a court that receives a petition for a writ of habeas corpus from an alleged enemy combatant must itself ensure that the minimum requirements of due process are achieved."... This judicial remediation of executive default is unheard of.

* * *

...If Hamdi is being imprisoned in violation of the Constitution (because without due process of law), then his habeas petition should be granted; the Executive may then hand him over to the criminal authorities, whose detention for the purpose of prosecution will be lawful, or else must release him.

* * *

Many think it not only inevitable but entirely proper that liberty give way to security in times of national crisis—that, at the extremes of military exigency, *inter arma silent leges.* Whatever the general merits of the view that war silences law or modulates its voice, that view has no place in the interpretation and application of a Constitution designed precisely to confront war and, in a manner that accords with democratic principles, to accommodate it. Because the Court has proceeded to meet the current emergency in a manner the Constitution does not envision, I respectfully dissent.

(ii) *Rumsfeld v. Padilla*

Supreme Court of the United States
542 U.S. _____ (2004)
159 L. Ed. 2d 513

CHIEF JUSTICE REHNQUIST delivered the opinion of the Court.

Respondent Jose Padilla is a United States citizen detained by the Department of Defense pursuant to the President's determination that he is an "enemy combatant" who conspired with al Qaeda to carry out terrorist attacks in the United States. We confront two questions: First, did Padilla properly file his habeas petition in the Southern District of New York; and second, did the President possess authority to detain Padilla militarily. We answer the threshold question in the negative and thus do not reach the second question presented.

Because we do not decide the merits, we only briefly recount the relevant facts. On May 8, 2002, Padilla flew from Pakistan to Chicago's O'Hare International Airport. As he stepped off the plane, Padilla was apprehended by federal agents executing a material witness warrant issued by the United States District Court for the Southern District of New York (Southern District) in connection with its grand jury investigations into the September 11th terrorist attacks. Padilla was then transported to New York, where he was held in federal criminal custody. On May 22, acting through appointed counsel, Padilla moved to vacate the material witness warrant.

Padilla's motion was still pending when, on June 9, the President issued an order to Secretary of Defense Donald H. Rumsfeld designating Padilla an "enemy combatant" and directing the Secretary to detain him in military custody.... In support of this action, the President invoked his authority as "Commander in Chief of the U.S. armed forces" and the Authorization for the Use of Military Force Joint Resolution, Pub. L. 107-40, 115 Stat. 224 (AUMF), enacted by Congress on September 18, 2001.... The President also made several factual findings explaining his decision to designate Padilla as an enemy combatant. Based on these findings, the President concluded that it is "consistent with U.S. law and the laws of war for the Secretary of Defense to detain Mr. Padilla as an enemy combatant."...

That same day, Padilla was taken into custody by Department of Defense officials and transported to the Consolidated Naval Brig in Charleston, South Carolina. He has been held there ever since.

On June 11, Padilla's counsel, claiming to act as his next friend, filed in the Southern District a habeas corpus petition under 28 U.S.C. §2241. The petition, as amended, alleged that Padilla's military detention violates the Fourth, Fifth, and Sixth Amendments and the Suspension Clause...of the United States Constitution. The amended petition named as respondents President Bush, Secretary Rumsfeld, and Melanie A. Marr, Commander of the Consolidated Naval Brig.

The Government moved to dismiss, arguing that Commander Marr, as Padilla's immediate custodian, is the only proper respondent to his habeas petition, and that the District Court lacks jurisdiction over Commander Marr because she is located outside the Southern District. On the merits, the Government contended that the President has authority to detain Padilla militarily pursuant to the Commander in Chief Clause of the Constitution, Art. II, §2, cl. 1, the congressional AUMF, and this Court's decision in *Ex parte Quirin*, 317 U.S. 1 (1942).

* * *

[The District Court for the Southern District of New York ruled that the Secretary of Defense was "a proper respondent to Padilla's habeas petition," and, on the merits, held that the President of the United States has the authority to detain a citizen as an "enemy combatant" who was captured on American soil during a time of war. The Court of Appeals for the Second Circuit reversed the District Court, agreeing that the Secretary of Defense was a proper respondent, but, on the merits, ruled that President Bush lacked legal authority to detain Padilla in military custody. Absent explicit congressional authorization, the Court of Appeals found that there existed a strong presumption *against* domestic military detention of a United States citizen and granted the writ, directing Secretary Rumsfeld to release Padilla from military confinement within a 30-day time span. Chief Justice Rehnquist then continues]:

* * *

We granted the Government's petition for certiorari to review the Court of Appeals' ruling with respect to the jurisdictional and the merits issues, both of which raise important questions of federal law....

The question of whether the Southern District has jurisdiction over Padilla's habeas petition breaks down into two related subquestions. First, who is the proper respondent to that petition? And second, does the Southern District have jurisdiction over him or her? We address these questions in turn.

I

The federal habeas statute straightforwardly provides that the proper respondent to a habeas petition is "the person who has custody over [the petitioner]." 28 U.S.C. §2242;... The consistent use of the definite article in reference to the custodian indicates that there is generally only one proper respondent to a given prisoner's habeas petition. This custodian, moreover, is "the person" with the ability to produce the prisoner's body before the habeas court.

* * *

...Padilla was moved from New York to South Carolina before his lawyer filed a habeas petition on his behalf.

* * *

...District courts are limited to granting habeas relief "within their respective jurisdictions." 28 U.S.C. §2241(a). We have interpreted this language to require "nothing more than that the court issuing the writ have jurisdiction over the custodian."... Thus, jurisdiction over Padilla's habeas petition lies in the Southern District only if it has jurisdiction over Commander Marr. We conclude it does not.

* * *

...Accordingly, with respect to habeas petitions "designed to relieve an individual from oppressive confinement," the traditional rule has always been that the Great Writ is "issuable only in the district of confinement." [*Carbo v. United States*, 364 U.S. 611, at 618 (1961)].

* * *

...Padilla seeks to challenge his present physical custody in South Carolina. Because the immediate-custodian rule applies in such habeas challenges, the proper respondent is Commander Marr, who is also present in South Carolina. There is thus no occasion to designate a "nominal" custodian [*i. e.*, Secretary Rumsfeld] and determine whether he or she is "present" in the same district as petitioner.... Padilla must file his habeas action in South Carolina.

* * *

...Whenever a §2241 habeas petitioner seeks to challenge his present physical custody within the United States, he should name his warden as respondent and file the petition in the district of confinement....

* * *

The District of South Carolina, not the Southern District of New York, was the district court in which Padilla should have brought his habeas petition. We therefore reverse the judgment of the Court of Appeals and remand the case for entry of an order of dismissal without prejudice.

It is so ordered.

[The final opinion in the trilogy of decisions handed down on June 28, 2004, is captioned *Rasul v. Bush*, coming to the United States Supreme Court on certiorari from the United States Court of Appeals for the District of Columbia Circuit. The majority opinion in *Rasul* was written by Justice John Paul Stevens and joined by Justices O'Connor, Souter, Ginsberg and Bryer, with Justice Kennedy filing a concurring opinion. Justice Scalia and Thomas dissented. The *Rasul* case deals not with alleged citizen-terrorists, but rather with the legal status of foreign nationals held in military captivity at the United States Naval Base at Quantanamo Bay, Cuba. In both *Hamdi* and *Rasul*, the Supreme Court refused to endorse one of the central post-9/11 claims of the Bush Administration, namely, that the United States Government has unreviewable plenary authority to detain non-citizen suspects, most of whom are from Afghanistan, Iraq or Iran, for an open-ended period of time, holding them incommunicado and thus denying them access to counsel and a hearing to determine the legality of their detention.].

(t) *Rasul v. Bush*

Supreme Court of the United States
542 U.S. _____ (2004)
159 L. Ed. 2d 548

JUSTICE STEVENS delivered the opinion of the court.

These two cases [*Al Odah* consolidated with *Rasul*] present the narrow but important question whether United States courts lack jurisdiction to consider challenges to the legality of the detention of foreign nationals captured abroad in connection with hostilities and incarcerated at the Guantanamo Bay Naval Base, Cuba.

I

On September 11, 2001, agents of the al Qaeda terrorist network hijacked four commercial airliners and used them as missiles to attack American targets. While one of the four attacks was foiled by the heroism of the plane's passengers, the other three killed approximately 3,000 innocent civilians, destroyed hundreds of millions of dollars of property, and severely damaged the U.S. economy. In response to the attacks, Congress passed a joint resolution authorizing the President to use "all necessary and appropriate force against those nations, organizations, or persons he determines planned, authorized, committed, or aided the terrorist attacks…or harbored such organizations or persons."… Acting pursuant to that authorization, the President sent U.S. Armed Forces into Afghanistan to wage a military campaign against al Qaeda and the Taliban regime that had supported it.

Petitioners in these cases are 2 Australian citizens and 12 Kuwaiti citizens who were captured abroad during hostilities between the United States and the Taliban. Since early 2002, the U.S. military has held them—along with, according to the Government's estimate, approximately 640 other non-Americans captured abroad—at the Naval Base at Quantanamo Bay.… The United States occupies the Base, which comprises 45 square miles of land and water along the southeast coast of Cuba, pursuant to a 1903 Lease Agreement executed with the newly independent Republic of Cuba in the aftermath of the Spanish-American War. Under the Agreement, "the United States recognizes the continuance of the ultimate sovereignty of the Republic of Cuba over the [leased areas]," while the Republic of Cuba consents that during the period of the occupation by the United States…"the United States shall exercise complete jurisdiction and control over and within said areas." In 1934, the parties entered into a treaty providing that absent an agreement to modify or abrogate the lease, the lease would remain in effect "[s]o long as the United States of America shall not abandon the…naval station at Guantanamo."

In 2002, petitioners, through relatives acting as their next friends, filed various actions in the U.S. District Court for the District of Columbia challenging the legality of their detention at the Base. All alleged that none of the petitioners has ever been a combatant against the United States or has ever engaged in any terrorist acts. They also allege that none has been charged with any wrongdoing, permitted to consult with counsel, or provided access to the courts or any other tribunal….

The two Australians, Mamdouh Habib and David Hicks, each filed a petition for writ of habeas corpus, seeking release from custody, access to counsel, freedom from interrogations, and other relief…. Fawzi Khalid Abdullah Fahad Al Odah and the 11 other Kuwaiti detainees filed a complaint seeking to be informed of the charges against them, to be allowed to meet with their families and with counsel, and to have access to the courts or some other impartial tribunal…. They claimed that denial of these rights violates the Constitution, international law, and treaties of the United States. Invoking the court's jurisdiction under 28 U.S.C. §§1331 and 1350, among other statutory bases, they asserted causes of action under the Administrative Procedure Act, 5 U.S.C. §§555, 702, 706; the Alien Tort Statute, 28 U.S.C. §1350; and the general federal habeas corpus statute, §§2241–2243….

Construing all three actions as petitions for writs of habeas corpus, the District Court dismissed them for want of jurisdiction. The court held, in reliance on our opinion *Johnson v. Eisentrager*, 339 U.S. 763 (1950), that "aliens detained outside the sovereign territory of the United States (may not) invok[e] a petition for a writ of habeas corpus." 215 F. Supp.2d 55, 68 (DC 2002). The Court of Appeals affirmed. Reading *Eisentrager* to hold that "the privilege of litigation does not extend to aliens in military custody who have no presence in 'any territory over which the United States is sovereign,'" 321 F.3d 1134, 1144 (CADC 2003) (quoting *Eisentrager*, 339 U.S. at 777–778), it held that the District Court lacked jurisdiction over petitioners' habeas actions, as well as their remaining federal statutory claims that do not sound in habeas. We granted certiorari, 540 U.S. 1003 (2003), and now reverse.

II

Congress has granted federal district courts, "within their respective jurisdictions," the authority to hear applications for habeas corpus by any person who claims to be held "in custody in violation of the Constitution or laws or treaties of the United States." 28 U.S.C. §§2241(a), (c)(3). The statute traces its ancestry to the first grant of federal court jurisdiction: Section 14 of the Judiciary Act of 1789 authorized federal courts to issue writs of habeas corpus to prisoners "in custody, under or by colour of the authority of the United States, or committed for trial before some court of the same." Act of September 24, 1789, ch. 20, §14, 1 Stat. 82. In 1867, Congress extended the protections of the writ to "all cases where any person may be restrained of his or her liberty in violation of the constitution, or of any treaty or law of the United States." Act of Feb. 5, 1867, ch. 28, 14 Stat. 385….

Habeas corpus is, however, "a writ antecedent to statute,…throwing its root deep into the genius of our common law," *Williams v. Kaiser*, 323 U.S. 471, 484, n.2 (1945) (internal quotation marks omitted). The writ appeared in English law several centuries ago, became "an integral part of our common-law heritage" by the time the Colonies achieved independence, *Preiser v. Rodriguez*, 411 U.S. 475, 485 (1972), and received explicit recognition in the Constitution, which forbids suspension of "[t]he Privilege of the Writ of Habeas Corpus...unless when in Cases of Rebellion or Invasion the public Safety may require it," Art. I, §9, c. 2.

As it has evolved over the past two centuries, the habeas statute clearly has expanded habeas corpus "beyond the limits that obtained during the 17th and 18th centuries." *Swain v. Pressley*, 430 U.S. 372, 380, n. 13 (1977). But "[a]t its historical core, the writ of habeas corpus has served as a means of reviewing the legality of Executive detention, and it is in that context that its protections have been strongest." *INS v. St. Cyr*, 533 U.S. 289, 301 (2001). See also *Brown v. Allen*, 344 U.S. 443, 533 (1953) (Jackson, J. concurring in result) ("The historic purpose of the writ has been to relieve detention by executive authorities without judicial trial.") As Justice Jackson wrote in an opinion respecting the availability of habeas corpus to aliens in U.S. custody:

> "Executive imprisonment has been considered oppressive and lawless since John, at Runnymede, pledged that no free man should be imprisoned, dispossessed, outlawed, or exiled save by the judgment of his peers or by the law of the land. The judges of England developed the writ of habeas corpus largely to preserve these immunities from executive restraint." *Shaughnessy v. United States ex rel. Mezei,*345 U.S. 206, 218–219 (1953) (dissenting opinion).

Consistent with the historic purpose of the writ, this Court has recognized the federal courts' power to review applications for habeas relief in a wide variety of cases involving Executive detention, in wartime as well as in times of peace. The Court has, for example, entertained the habeas petitions of an American citizen who plotted an attack on military installations during the Civil War, *Ex parte Milligan*, 4 Wall. 2 (1866), and of admitted enemy aliens convicted of war crimes during a declared war and held in the United States, *Ex parte Quirin*, 317 U.S. 1 (1942), and its insular possessions, *In re Yamashita* 327 U.S. 1 (1946).

The question now before us is whether the habeas statute confers a right to judicial review of the legality of Executive detention of aliens in a territory over which the United States exercises plenary and exclusive jurisdiction, but not "ultimate sovereignty." [1903 Lease Agreement with the Republic of Cuba Art. III.].

III

Respondents' primary submission is that the answer to the jurisdictional question is controlled by our decision in *Eisentrager*. In that case we held that a Federal District Court lacked authority to issue a writ of habeas corpus to 21 German citizens who had been captured by U.S. Forces in China, tried and convicted of war crimes by an American military commission headquartered in Nanking, and incarcerated in the Landsberg Prison in occupied Germany [after World War II].

* * *

Petitioners in these cases differ from the *Eisentrager* detainees in important respects: They are not nationals of countries at war with the United States, and they deny that they have engaged in or plotted acts of aggression against the United States; they have never been afforded access to any tribunal, much less charged with and convicted of wrongdoing; and for more than two years they have been imprisoned in territory over which the United States exercises exclusive jurisdiction and control.

Not only are petitioners differently situated from the *Eisentrager* detainees, but the Court in *Eisentrager* made quite clear that all six of the facts critical to its disposition were relevant only to the question of the prisoners' *constitutional* entitlement to habeas corpus.... The Court had far less to say on the question of the petitioners' *statutory* entitlement to habeas review....

IV

...By the express terms of its agreements with Cuba, the United States exercises "complete jurisdiction and control" over the Guantanamo Bay Naval Base, and may continue to exercise such control permanently if it so chooses.... Respondents themselves concede that the habeas statute would create federal-court jurisdiction over the claims of an American citizen held at the base.... Considering that the statute draws no distinction between American and aliens held in federal custody, there is little reason to think that Congress intended the geographical coverage of the statute to vary depending on the detainee's citizenship. Aliens held at the base, no less than American citizens, are entitled to invoke the federal courts' authority under §2241.

Application of the habeas statute to persons detained at the base is consistent with the historical reach of the writ of habeas corpus. At common law, courts exercised habeas jurisdiction over the claims of aliens detained within sovereign territory of the realm, as well as the claims of persons detained in the so-called "exempt jurisdiction," where ordinary writs did not run, and all other dominions under the sovereign's control. As Lord Mansfield wrote in 1759, even if a territory was "no part of the realm" there was "no doubt" as to the court's power to issue writs of habeas corpus if the territory was "under the subjection of the Crown." *King v. Cowle,* 2 Burr. 834, 164-855, 97 Eng. Rep. 587, 598–599 (K. B.). Later cases confirmed that the reach of the writ depended not on formal notions of territorial sovereignty, but rather on the practical question of "the exact extent and nature of the jurisdiction or dominion exercised in fact by the Crown." *Ex parte Mwenya,* [1960] 1 Q. B. 241, 303 (C. A.) (Lord Evershed, M. R.).

In the end, the answer to the question presented is clear. Petitioners contend that they are being held in federal custody in violation of the laws of the United States.... We therefore hold that §2241 confers on the District Court jurisdiction to hear petitioners' habeas corpus challenges to the legality of their detention at the Guantanamo Bay Naval Base.

* * *

Whether and what further proceedings may become necessary after respondents make their response to the merits of petitioners' claims are matters that we need not address now. What is presently at stake is only whether the federal courts have jurisdiction to determine the legality of the Executive's potentially indefinite detention of individuals who claim to be wholly innocent of wrongdoing. Answering that question in the affirmative, we reverse the judgment of the Court of Appeals and remand for the District Court to consider in the first instance the merits of petitioners' claims.

It is so ordered

10. Epilogue: Michael Ignatieff, *The Lesser Evil: Political Ethics in an Age of Terror*

1–10; 21; 23–24 (2004) IGNATIEFF, MICHAEL (ed.); THE LESSER EVIL: POLITICAL ETHICS IN AN AGE OF TERROR. Princeton University Press. Reprinted by permission of Princeton University Press

I

What lesser evils may a society commit when it believes it faces the greater evil of its own destruction? This is one of the oldest questions in politics and one of the hardest to answer. The old Roman adage—the safety of the people is the first law—set few limits to the claims of security over liberty. In the name of the people's safety, the Roman republic was prepared to sacrifice all other laws. For what laws would survive if Rome itself perished? The suspension of civil liberties, the detention of aliens, the secret assassination of enemies: all this might be allowed, as a last resort, if the life of the state were in danger. But if law must sometime compromise with necessity, must ethics surrender too? Is there no moral limit to what a republic can do when its existence is threatened? As Edward Gibbon retold the story of how the Romans slaughtered defenseless aliens in their eastern cities in 395 C. E. as a preemptive warning to the barbarians massing at the gates of their empire, he declined to consider whether actions that political necessity might require could still remain anathema to moral principle. But the question must not only be asked. It must be answered.

If the society attacked on September 11, 2001, had been a tyranny, these ancient questions might be relevant. For a tyranny will allow itself anything. But the nation attacked on that bright morning was a liberal democracy, a constitutional order that sets limits to any government's use of force. Democratic constitutions do allow some suspensions of rights in states of emergency. Thus rights are not always trumps. But neither is necessity. Even in times of real danger, political authorities have to prove the case that abridgments of rights are justified. Justifying them requires a government to submit them to the test of adversarial review by the legislature, the courts, and a free media. A government seeking to respond to an attack or an expected danger is required to present the case for extraordinary measures to a legislature, to argue for them with reasons that might convince a reasonable person, and to alter the measures in the face of criticism. Even after extraordinary measures receive legislative approval, they will still come under review by the courts.

The first challenge that a terrorist emergency poses to democracy is to this system of adversarial justification. The machinery of legislative deliberation and judicial review grinds slowly. Emergencies demand rapid action. Hence they require the exercise of prerogative. Presidents and prime ministers have to take action first and submit to questions later. But too much prerogative can be bad for democracy itself.

In emergencies, we have no alternative but to trust our leaders to act quickly, when our lives may be in danger, but it would be wrong to trust them to decide the larger question of how to balance liberty and security over the long term. For these larger questions, we ought to trust to democratic deliberation through our institutions. Adversarial justification is an institutional response, developed over centuries, to the inherent difficulty of making appropriate public judgments about these types of conflicts of values. Citizens are bound to disagree about how far the government is entitled to go in any given emergency. Because we disagree deeply about these matters, democracy's institutions provide a resolution, through a system of checks and balances, to ensure that no government's answer has the power to lead us either straight to anarchy or to tyranny.

In a terrorist emergency, we disagree, first of all, about the facts: chiefly, what type and degree of risk the threat of terrorism actually presents. It would make life easy if these facts were clear, but they rarely are. Public safety requires extrapolations about future threats on the basis of disputable facts about present ones. Worse, the facts are never presented to the public simply as neutral propositions available for dispassionate review. They come to us packaged with evaluation. They are usually stretched to justify whatever case for action is being made. Those who want coercive measures construe the risk to be great; those who oppose them usually minimize the threat. The disagreements don't end there. Even when we agree about the facts, we may still disagree whether the risks justify abridgments of liberty.

These disagreements extend to the very meaning of democracy itself. For most Americans, democracy simply means what Abraham Lincoln said it was: government of the people, by the people, for the people. In this account, democracy is a synonym for majority rule. Popular sovereignty, through elected representatives, has to be the final arbiter of what the government can be allowed to get away with when it is trying to defend our freedoms and our lives. Democracies do have bills of rights but these exist to serve vital majority interests. When the executive branch of government suspends rights, for example, it does so in the interest of the majority of citizens. The public interests that these rights defend are defined by the elected representatives of the people, and courts must interpret what these rights mean in obedience to what legislatures and the people say the rights mean. Defending a right of an individual, for example, to freedom of association in times of safety protects the liberty of all. But protecting that same individual in a time of emergency may do harm to all. A terrorist emergency is precisely a case where allowing individual liberty—to plan, to plot, to evade detection—may threaten a vital majority interest. A democracy has no more important purpose than the protection of its members, and rights exist to safeguard that purpose. Civil liberty, the chief justice of the U.S. Supreme Court has written, means the liberty of a citizen, not the abstract liberty of an individual in a state of nature. Such freedom, therefore, must depend on the survival of government and must be subordinate to its preservation.

What prevents such a system from falling prey to the tyranny of the majority is the system of checks and balances and, more broadly, the democratic process of adversarial justification itself. While injustice can always be justified if you have to justify it only to yourself, it is less easy when you have to justify it to other democratic institutions, like courts and legislatures or a free press. Thus presidents or prime ministers may not see anything wrong in a stringent measure, but if they knew that this measure will have to get by the courts and the legislature, they may think twice.

Besides these constitutional checks and balances, there would also be the democratic check of competing social, religious, and political interests in the nation at large. One of the most lucid versions of this argument is to be found in *Federalist* No. 51, where in discussing the federal system's balance of federal and state power, the authors go on to say that while all authority in the United States will be derived from the power of the majority,

> the society itself will be broken into so many parts, interests, and classes of citizens, that the rights of individuals, or of the minority, will be in little danger from interested combinations of the majority. In a free government, the secu-

rity for civil rights must be the same as that for religious rights. It consists in the one case in the multiplicity of interests and sects; and this may be presumed to depend on the extent of country and the number comprehended under the same government.

Against this *pragmatic* view there is a *moral* view of democracy which maintains that it is something more than majority rule disciplined by checks and balances. It is also an order of rights that puts limits to the power of the community over individuals. These limits are not there just for prudential reasons, to prevent governments from riding roughshod over individuals. The rights are also there to express the idea that individuals matter intrinsically. Democracies just don't serve majority interests, they accord individuals intrinsic respect. This respect is expressed in the form of rights that guarantee certain freedoms. Freedom matters, in turn, because it is a precondition for living in dignity. Dignity here means simply the right to shape your life as best you can, within the limits of the law, and to have a voice, however small, in the shaping of public affairs. Government for the people, in other words, is something more than government for the happiness and security of the greatest number. The essential constraint of democratic government is that it must serve majority interests without sacrificing the freedom and dignity of the individuals who comprise the political community to begin with and who on occasion may oppose how it is governed. Rights certainly owe their origin to the sovereignty of the people, but the people—and their representatives—must steer majority interests through the constraints of rights.

* * *

…Those who think of democracy primarily in terms of majority interest point to the frequent abridgments of liberty in national emergencies past—from Lincoln's suspension of habeas corpus during the Civil War to the detention of illegal aliens after 9/11—and argue that democracies survive in part because they do not let rights stand in the way of robust measures. Moreover, robust measures do not prevent rights' returning in times of safety. Temporary measures are just that and they need not do permanent damage to a democracy's constitutional fabric. Those who put rights first will reply that yes, democracy survives, but rights infringements needlessly compromise the democracy's commitment to dignity and freedom. The detention of Japanese Americans during World War II would qualify as an example of majoritarian tyranny and misuse of executive prerogative, driven by fear and racial bias. One side in the debate worries that caring overmuch about rights will tie the hands of the democracy, while the other insists that if rights are abridged, even for a few individuals, then democracy betrays its own identity.

Civil libertarians think civil liberties define what a democracy is. But the recurrently weak and shallow public support for civil liberties positions suggest that many American disagree. They believe that the majority interests should trump the civil liberties of terrorist suspects. For these democratics, rights are prudential limits on government action, revocable in times of danger; for civil libertarians, they are foundational commitments to individual dignity that ought to limit government action in times of safety and danger alike. For one side, what matters fundamentally is that democracies prevail. For the other, what matters more is that democracies prevail without betraying what they stand for.

A further disagreement arises over the question of whether a country facing a terrorist emergency should base its public policy exclusively on its own constitution and its own laws, or whether it has any duty to pay attention to what other states have to say and what international agreements and conventions require. Some maintain that a democracy's commitments to dignity are confined to its own citizens, not its enemies. Others point out that a democracy is not a moral island, sufficient unto itself. Thus, as many scholars have pointed out, the U.S. Constitution extends its protection to "persons" and not just to citizens. Hence aliens have rights under U.S. law—as well as, of course, under international conventions to which the United States is a signatory. Enemy combatants have rights under the Geneva Conventions, and even terrorists retain their *human* rights, since these are inherent in being human and hence irrevocable. Others think this approach values consistency more than justice. Justice—to the victims of terrorists outrages—requires that terrorists be treated as "enemies of the human race" and hunted down without any regard to their human rights.

When citizens of a democracy insist that what matters most in a terrorist emergency is the safety of the majority, they are usually saying that rights are at best a side constraint, at worst a pesky impediment to robust and decisive action. Those who think this are also likely to believe that international agreements, like the Geneva Conventions or the Torture Convention, should not limit what the United States can do in a war on terror. Since the threat is primarily directed at the United States, it must respond according to its own system of law, not according to anyone else's standards. To take this position, however, is to assume that the lives of your own citizens matter more than the lives of people in other countries. It is, as Ronald Dworkin has pointed out, to base policy on the premise that Americans come first. Those who disagree will usually be committed to the idea that a democracy's ethical commitments are universal and apply both to its own citizens and to its enemies.

* * *

A lesser evil position holds that in a terrorist emergency, neither rights nor necessity should trump. A democracy is committed to both the security of the majority and the rights of the individual. Neither a morality of consequences nor a morality of dignity can be allowed exclusive domain in public policy decisions. If each of these ethical principles has legitimate claims, the resulting framework is going to be complex, to say the least. In it, there are not trump cards, no table-clearing justifications or claims. What works is not always right. What is right doesn't always work. Rights may have to bow to security in some instances, but there had better be good reasons, and there had better be clear limitations to rights abridgments; otherwise, rights will soon lose all their value. At the same time, a constitution is not a suicide pact: rights cannot so limit the exercise of authority as to make decisive action impossible. Finally, international standards matter. Nations are not moral islands: they should conform to international standards, both to comply with the treaties and conventions that nations have signed and to pay what Thomas Jefferson called "decent respect for the opinions of mankind."

A lesser evil morality is designed for skeptics, for people who accept that leaders will have to take decisive action on the basis of less than accurate information; who think that some sacrifice of liberty in times of danger may be necessary; who want a policy that works but are not prepared to make what works the sole criterion for deciding what to do. Such an ethics is a balancing act seeking to adjudicate among the claims of risk, dignity, and security in a way that actually addresses particular cases of threat. An ethics of balance cannot privilege rights above all, or dignity above all, or to public safety above all.... They all are important principles—all must be weighed in the balance equally—and nothing trumps.

This is an ethics of prudence rather than first principles, one that assesses what to do in an emergency with a conservative bias against infringements of established standards of due process, equal protection, and basic dignity. A conservative bias assumes that in terrorist emergencies, the first response is usually wrong. Tried and tested standards of due process should not be hastily discarded. These standards are more than procedures, anchored in legal tradition. They reflect important commitments to individual dignity. Protection of the law means, concretely, that no one should be held indefinitely, without charge, without access to counsel or judicial review. Moreover, persons detained only for what they have done, not for who they are or for what they think, profess, or believe. A key conservative principle would be that blanket detentions and broad roundups of suspects are always a mistake, because they violate the law's principle of individuality of guilt. Any detention policy must be targeted to individuals against whom probable cause can eventually be demonstrated. By these standards, the United States failed the test in its detention of nearly five thousand aliens, mostly single males of Muslim or Arab origin, after September 11. None have been found to merit charging with terrorist offenses. In retrospect, the whole exercise seems to have been as unnecessary as it was unjust.

While a conservative bias will enable us to see through most of the overhasty reactions to terrorists emergencies, it may not be adequate when we have to face terrorists who control weapons of mass destruction. If the threat is sufficiently great, preemptive detention of suspects, together with military or police action to disarm, disable, or neutralize the threat, may be necessary. It is unrealistic to think that commitments to dignity, coupled with a conservative bias against departing from tried legal standards, will be sufficient to cope with any eventuality in the future. In the wake of another mass casualty terrorist attack, on or above the scale of September 11, most bets—and—gloves would be off. Even extreme necessity, however, cannot override democratic processes and the obligation to balance strong measures with basic commitments to full public justification.

* * *

A lesser evil morality is antiperfectionist in its assumptions. It accepts as inevitable that it is not always possible to save human beings from harm without killing other human beings; not always possible to preserve full democratic disclosure and transparency in counterterrorist operations; not always desirable for democratic leaders to avoid deception and perfidy; not always possible to preserve the liberty of the majority without suspending the liberties of a minority; not always possible to anticipate terrible consequences of well-meant acts, and so on. Far from making ethical reflection irrelevant, these dilemmas make ethical realism all the more essential to democratic reflection and good public policy. The fact that liberal democratic leaders may order the surreptitious killing of terrorist, may withhold information from their voters, may order the suspension of civil liberties need not mean that "anything goes." Even if liberties must be suspended, their suspension can be made temporary; if executives must withhold information from a legislature in public, they can be obliged to disclose it in private session or at a later date. Public disinformation whose whole purpose is to deceive the enemy might be justified, but deliberately misleading a democratic electorate with a view to exaggerating risk or minimizing hazard can never be. The same balancing act needs to be observed in other cases. If the targeted killing of terrorist proves necessary, it can be constrained by strict rules of engagement and subjected to legislative oversight and review. The interrogation of terrorist suspects can be kept free of torture. Drawing these lines means keeping in clear sight the question of whether these means reinforce or betray the democratic identity they are supposed to defend.

* * *

...I would propose the following test for policy makers. First, a democratic war on terror needs to subject all coercive measures to *the dignity test*—do they violate individual dignity? Foundational commitments to human rights should always preclude cruel and unusual punishment, torture, penal servitude, and extrajudicial execution, as well as rendition of suspects to right-abusing countries. Second, coercive measures need to pass *the conservative test*—are departures from existing due process really necessary? Do they damage our institutional inheritance? Such a standard would bar indefinite suspension of habeas corpus and require all detention, whether by civil or military authorities, to be subject to judicial review. Those deprived of rights—citizens and non-citizens—must never lose access to counsel. A third assessment of counterterror measures should be consequentialist. Will they make citizens more or less secure in the long run? This *effectiveness* test needs to focus not just on the short term, but on the long-term political implications of measures. Will they strengthen or weaken political support for the state undertaking such measures? A further consideration is *the last resort test:* have less coercive measures been tried and failed? Another important issue is whether measures have passed the test of *open adversarial review* by legislative and judicial bodies, either at the time, or as soon as necessity allows. Finally, "decent respect for the opinions of mankind," together with the more pragmatic necessity of securing the support of other nations in a global war on terror, requires any state fighting terrorism to respect its international obligations as well as the considered opinions of its allies and friends. If all of this adds up to a series of constraints that tie the hands of our governments, so be it. It is the very nature of a democracy that it not only does, but should, fight with one hand behind its back. It is also in the nature of democracy that it prevails against its enemies precisely because it does.

Suggestions for Further Reading

(1) Akhaven, Payam, "Beyond Impunity: Can International Criminal Justice Prevent Future Atrocities,?" 95 *American Journal of International Law* 7 (2001).

(2) _____, "Punishing War Criminals in the Former Yugoslavia: A Critical Juncture for the New World Order," 15 *Human Rights Quarterly* 262 (1993).

(3) _____, "The International Criminal Tribunal for Rwanda: The Politics and Pragmatics of Punishment," 90 *American Journal of International Law* 501 (1996).

(4) Allen, Beverly, *Rape Warfare: The Hidden Genocide in Bosnia-Herzegovina and Croatia.* Minneapolis, MN: University of Minnesota Press (1996).

(5) Alvarez, Jose E., "Rush to Closure: Lessons of the Tadic Judgment," 96 *Michigan Law Review* 2031 (1998).

(6) Bassiouni, M. Cherif, "Combating Impunity in International Crimes," 71 *University of Colorado Law Review* 414 (2000).

(7) Beard, Jack M., "America's New War on Terror: The Case for Self-Defense Under International Law," 25 *Harvard Journal of Law and Public Policy* 559 (2002).

(8) Bell-Falkoff, Andrew, *Ethnic Cleansing.* New York: St. Martin's Press (1996).

(9) Bolton, John R., "The Risks and Weaknesses of the International Criminal Court from America's Perspective,:" 41 *Virginia Journal of International Law* 186 (2000)

(10) Cramer, Myron C., "Military Commissions: Trial of the Eight Saboteurs," 17 *Washington Law Review* 247 (1942).

(11) David, Marcella, "Grotius Repudiated: The American Objections to the International Criminal Court and the Commitment to International Law," 20 *Michigan Journal of International Law* 337 (1999).

(12) Dextexhe, Alain, *Rwanda and Genocide in the Twentieth Century*. London/East Haven, CT: Pluto Press (1995).

(13) Dobbs, Michael, *Saboteurs: The Nazi Raid on America*. New York: Knopf (2004).

(14) Greenwood, Christopher, "International Law and the War against Terrorism," 78 *International Affairs* 301 (2002).

(15) Hagan, John, *Justice in the Balkans: Prosecuting War Crimes in the Hague Tribunal*. Chicago: The University Chicago Press (2003).

(16) Hannum, Hurst, "International Law and the Cambodian Genocide: The Sounds of Silence," 11 *Human Rights Quarterly* 82 (1989).

(17) *International Law and the War on Terror: International Law Studies*. (vol. 79), (Fred L. Borch & Paul S. Wilson eds.). Newport, RI: Naval War College (2003).

(18) Kaplan, Naomi, "A Failure of Perspective: Moral Assumptions and Genocide," 23 *Boston College Third World Law Journal* 359 (2003).

(19) Keane, Fergal, *Seasons of Blood: A Rwandan Journey*. New York: Viking Press (1995).

(20) Kresock, David M., "Ethnic Cleansing in the Balkans: The Legal Foundation of Foreign Intervention," 27 *Cornell International Law Journal* 203 (1994).

(21). Lipman, Matthew, "Genocide: The Crime of the Century. The Jurisprudence of Death at the Dawn of the New Millenium," 23 *Houston Journal of International Law* 467 (2001).

(22) Meron, Theodor, "International Criminalization of Internal Atrocities," 89 *American Journal of International Law* 554, (1995).

(23) Murphy, John F., "The Quivering Gulliver: U.S. Views on the Permanent International Criminal Court," 34 *International Lawyer* 45 (2000).

(24) Myjer, Eric & Nigel White, "The Twin Towers Attack: An Unlimited Right to Self-Defense," 7 *Journal of Conflict and Security Law* 1 (2002).

(25) Paust, Jordan J., "Antiterrorism Military Commissions: Courting Illegality," 23 *Michigan Journal of International Law* 1 (2001).

(26) Quigley, John, "State Responsibility for Ethnic Cleansing," 32 *University of California-Davis Law Review* 341 (1999).

(27) Scharf, Michael P., "The Case for an International Trial of the al Qaeda and Taliban Perpetrators of the 9/11 Attacks," 36 *New England Law Review* 911 (2002).

(28) Shamsey, John, "80 Years Too Late: The International Criminal Court and the 20th Century's First Genocide," 11 *Journal of Transnational Law and Policy* 327 (2002).

(29) *The International Criminal Court: The Making of the Rome Statute, Issues, Negotiations, Results* (Roy S. Lee ed.). The Hague: Kluwer Law International (1999).

(30) *The Specter of Genocide: Mass Murder in Historical Perspective* (Robert Gellately & Ben Kiernan eds.). New York: Cambridge University Press (2003).

(31) Travalio, Gregory, "Terrorism, International Law, and the Use of Military Force,"
      8 *Wisconsin International Law Journal* 165 (2000).

Appendices

Appendix A

General Orders No. 100[*]
[The Lieber Code]

GENERAL ORDERS

War Dept.
ADJT. GENERAL' OFFICE
Washington, April 24, 1863

No. 100.

The following "Instructions for the Government of Armies of the United States in the Field," prepared by Francis Lieber, LL.D., and revised by a board of officers, of which Maj. Gen. F. A. Hitchcock is president, having been approved by the President of the United States, he commands that they be published for the information of all concerned.

By order of the Secretary of War:

E.D. TOWNSEND
Assistant Adjutant-General

Instructions for the Government of Armies of the United States in the Field

Section I. *Martial law — Military jurisdiction — Military necessity — Retaliation*

1. A place, district, or country occupied by an enemy stands, in consequence of the occupation, under the martial law of the invading or occupying army, whether any proclamation declaring martial law, or any public warning to the inhabitants has been issued or not. Martial law is the immediate and direct effect and consequence of occupation or conquest.

The presence of a hostile army proclaims its martial law.

2. Martial law does not cease during the hostile occupation, except by special proclamation, ordered by the commander-in-chief, or by special mention in the treaty of peace concluding the war, when the occupation of a place or territory continues beyond the conclusion of peace as one of the conditions of the same.

---

[*] *Instructions For The Government of Armies of The United States in The Field,* General Orders No. 100, 24 April 1863, War Department, Washington, DC.

3. Martial law in a hostile country consists in the suspension by the occupying military authority of the criminal and civil law, and of the domestic administration and government in the occupied place or territory, and in the substitution rule and force for the same, as well as in the dictation of general laws as far as military necessity requires this suspension, substitution, or dictation.

The commander of the forces may proclaim that the administration of all civil and penal law shall continue either wholly or in part, as in time of peace, unless otherwise ordered by the military authority.

4. Martial law is simply military authority exercised in accordance with the laws and usages of war. Military oppression is not martial law; it is the abuse by military force, it is incumbent upon those who administer it to be strictly guided by the principles of justice, honor, and humanity—virtues adorning a soldier even more than other men, for the very reason that he possesses the power of his arms against the unarmed.

5. Martial law should be less stringent in places and countries fully occupied and fairly conquered. Much greater severity may be exercised in places or regions where actual hostilities exist or are expected and must be prepared for. Its most complete sway is allowed—even in the commander's own country—when face to face with the enemy, because of the absolute necessities of the case, and of the paramount duty to defend the country against invasion.

To save the country is paramount to all other considerations.

6. All civil and penal law shall continue to take its unusual course in the enemy's places and territories under martial law, unless interrupted or stopped by order of the occupying military power; but all the functions of the hostile government—legislative, executive, or administrative—whether of a general provincial, or local character, cease under martial law, or continue only with the sanction, or, if deemed necessary, the participation of the occupier or invader.

7. Martial law extends to property, and to persons, whether they are subjects of the enemy or aliens to the government.

* * *

11. The law of war does not only disclaim all cruelty and bad faith concerning engagements concluded with the enemy during the war, but also the breaking of stipulations solemnly contracted by the belligerents in time of peace, and avowedly intended to remain in force in case of war between the contracting powers.

It disclaims all extortions and other transactions for individual gain; all acts of private revenge, or connivance at such acts.

Offenses to the contrary shall be severely punished, and especially so if committed by officers.

12. Whenever feasible, martial law is carried out in cases of individual offenders by military courts; but sentences of death shall be executed only with the approval of the chief executive, provided the urgency of the case does not require a speedier execution, and then only with the approval of the chief commander.

13. Military jurisdiction is of two kinds: First, that which is conferred and defined by statute; second, that which is derived from the common law of war. Military offenses under the statute law must be tried in the manner therein directed; but military offenses which do not come within the statute must be tried and punished under the common

law of war. The character of the courts which exercise these jurisdictions depends upon the local laws of each particular country.

In the armies of the United States the first is exercised by courts-martial; while cases which do not come within the Rules and Articles of War, or the jurisdiction conferred by statute on courts-martial, are tried by military commissions.

14. Military necessity, as understood by modern civilized nations, consists in the necessity of those measures which are indispensable for securing the ends of the war, and which are lawful according to the modern law and usages of war.

* * *

17. War is not carried on by arms alone. It is lawful to starve the hostile belligerents, armed and unarmed, so that it leads to a speedier subjection of the enemy.

18. When a commander of a besieged place expels the noncombatants, in order to lessen the number of those who consume his stock of provisions, it is lawful, though an extreme measure, to drive them back, so as to hasten on the surrender.

19. Commanders, whenever admissible, inform the enemy of their intention to bombard a place, so that the non-combatants, and especially the women and children, may be removed before the bombardment commences. But it is no infraction of the common law of war to omit thus to inform the enemy. Surprise may be a necessity.

20. Public war is a state of armed hostility between sovereign nations or governments. It is law and requisite of civilized existence that men live in political, continuous societies, forming organized units, called states or nations, whose constituents bear, enjoy, and suffer, advance and retrograde together, in peace and in war.

21. The citizen...of a hostile country is thus an enemy, as one of the constituents of the hostile state or nation, and as such is subjected to the hardships of the war.

22. Nevertheless, as civilization has advanced during the last centuries, so has likewise steadily advanced, especially in war on land, the distinction between the private individual belonging to a hostile country and the hostile country itself, with its men in arms. The principle has been more and more acknowledged that the unarmed citizen is to be spared in person, property, and honor as much as the exigencies of war will admit.

23. Private citizens are no longer murdered, enslaved, or carried off to distant parts, and the inoffensive individual is as little disturbed in his private relations as the commander of the hostile troops can afford to grant in the overruling demands of a vigorous war.

* * *

Section II. *Public and private property of the enemy—Protection of persons, and especially of women; of religion, the arts and sciences—Punishment of crimes against the inhabitants of hostile countries.*

* * *

34. As a general rule, the property belonging to churches, to hospitals, or other establishments of an exclusively charitable character, to establishments of education, or foundations for the promotion of knowledge, whether public schools, universities, academies of learning or observatories, museums of the fine arts, or of a scientific character—such property is not to be considered public property in the sense of paragraph 31; [para. 31 lists such things as public money, public moveable property, and all revenues coming from real property] but it may be taxed or used when the public service may require it.

* * *

37. The United States acknowledge and protect, in hostile countries occupied by them, religion and morality; strictly private property; the persons of the inhabitants, especially those of women; and the sacredness of domestic relations. Offenses to the contrary shall be rigorously punished.

* * *

40. There exists no law or body of authoritative rules of action between hostile armies, except that branch of the law of nature and nations which is called the law and usages of war on land.

41. All municipal law of the ground on which the armies stand, or of the countries to which they belong, is silent and of no effect between armies in the field.

* * *

44. All wanton violence committed against persons in the invaded country, all destruction of property not commanded by the authorized officer, all robbery, all pillage or sacking, even after taking a place by main force, all rape, wounding, maiming, or killing of such inhabitants, are prohibited under the penalty of death, or such other severe punishment as may seem adequate for the gravity of the offense.

A soldier, officer, or private, in the act of committing such violence, and disobeying a superior ordering him to abstain from it, may be lawfully killed on the spot by such superior.

* * *

47. Crimes punishable by all penal codes, such as arson, murder, maiming, assaults, highway robbery, theft, burglary, fraud, forgery, and rape, if committed by an American soldier in a hostile country against its inhabitants, are not only punishable as at home, but in all cases in which death is not inflicted the severer punishment shall be preferred.

* * *

Section III. *Deserters—Prisoners of war—Hostages—Booty on the battlefield.*

* * *

49. A prisoner of war is a public enemy armed or attached to the hostile army for active aid, who has fallen into the hands of the captor, either fighting or wounded, on the field or in the hospital, by individual surrender or by capitulation.

* * *

56. A prisoner of war is subject to no punishment for being a public enemy, nor is any revenge wreaked upon him by the intentional infliction of any suffering, or disgrace, by cruel imprisonment, want of food, by mutilation, death, or any other barbarity.

* * *

59. A prisoner of war remains answerable for his crimes committed against the captor's army or people, committed before he was captured, and for which he has not been punished by his own authorities.

All prisoners of war are liable to the infliction of retaliatory measures.

* * *

65. The use of the enemy's national standard, flag, or other emblem of nationality, for the purpose of deceiving the enemy in battle, is an act of perfidy by which they lose all claim to the protection of the laws of war.

* * *

70. The use of poisons in any manner, be it to poison wells, or food, or arms, is wholly excluded from modern warfare. He that uses it puts himself out of the pale of the law and usages of war.

* * *

75. Prisoners of war are subject to confinement or imprisonment such as may be deemed necessary on account of safety, but they are to be subjected to no other intentional suffering or indignity. The confinement and mode of treating a prisoner may be varied during his captivity according to the demands of safety.

76. Prisoners of war shall be fed upon plain and wholesome food, whenever possible, and treated with humanity.

They may be required to work for the benefit of the captor's government, according to their rank and condition.

* * *

80. Honorable men, when captured, will abstain from giving to the enemy information concerning their own army, and the modern law of war permits no longer the use of any violence against prisoners in order to extort the desired information, or to punish them for having given false information.

* * *

Section IX. *Assassination*

148.The law of war does not allow proclaiming either an individual belonging to the hostile army, or a citizen, or a subject to the hostile government an outlaw, who may be slain without trial by any captor, any more than the modern law of peace allows such international outlawry; on the contrary, it abhors such outrage. The sternest retaliation should follow the murder committed in consequence of such proclamation, made by whatever authority. Civilized nations look with horror upon offers of rewards for the assassination of enemies as relapses into barbarism.

Appendix B

The Nuremberg Laws[*]
(*des Nürnberger Gesetzes vom 15 September 1935*)

1935 *RGBI* I 1146.

The Reich Citizenship Laws of 15 September 1935 [*Reichsbürgergesetz:* this law made a distinction between a "citizen" and a "subject" of the Third Reich].

The Reichstag has adopted by unanimous vote the following law which is herewith promulgated.

Article 1(a) A subject of the state is one who belongs to the protective union of the German Reich, and who, therefore, has specific obligations to the Reich.

---

[*] As quoted in John Bradley, *The Illustrated History of the Third Reich* 252 (1978).

(2) The status of the subject is to be acquired in accordance with the provisions of the Reich and the State Citizenship Law.

Article II(1) A citizen of the Reich may be only one who is of German or kindred blood, and who, through his behaviour, shows that he is both desirous and personally fit to serve loyally the German people and the Reich.

(2) The right of citizenship is obtained by the grant of Reich Citizenship papers.

(3) Only the citizen of the Reich may enjoy full political rights in consonance with the provisions of the laws.

Article III The Reich Minister of the Interior, in conjunction with the Deputy to the Führer, will issue the required legal and administrative decrees for the implementation and amplification of this law.

The Law for the Protection of German Blood and German Honor 15 September 1935 [*Gezetz zum Schutze des deutschen Blutes und der deutschen Ehre;* the law on mixed marriages].

Imbued with the knowledge that the purity of German blood is the necessary prerequisite for the existence of the German nation, and inspired by an inflexible will to maintain the existence of the German nation for all future times, the Reichstag has unanimously adopted the following law, which is now enacted:

Article I(1) Any marriages between Jews and citizens of German or kindred blood are herewith forbidden. Marriages entered into despite this law are invalid, even it they are arranged abroad as a means of circumventing this law.

(2) Annulment proceedings for marriages may be initiated only by the Public Prosecutor.

Article II Extramarital relations between Jews and citizens of Germany or kindred blood are herewith forbidden.

Article III Jews are forbidden to employ as servants in their households female subjects of German or kindred blood who are under the age of 45 years.

Article IV(1) Jews are prohibited from displaying the Reich and national flag and from showing the national colors.

(2) However, they may display the Jewish colors. The exercise of this right is under state protection.

Article V(I) Anyone who acts contrary to the prohibition noted in Article I renders himself liable to penal servitude.

(2) The man who acts contrary to the prohibition of Article II will be punished by sentence to either a jail or penitentiary.

(3) Anyone who acts contrary to the provisions of Articles III and IV will be punished with a jail sentence up to a year and with a fine, or with one of these penalties.

Article VI The Reich Minister of Interior, in conjunction with the Deputy to the Führer and the Reich Minister of Justice, will issue the required legal and administrative decrees for the implementation and amplification of this law.

Article VII This law shall go into effect on the day following its promulgation, with the exception of Article III, which shall go into effect on 1 January 1936.

First Supplementary Decree of 14 November 1935

On the basis of Article III of the Reich Citizenship Law of 15 September 1935 the following is hereby decreed:

Article I(1) Until further provisions concerning citizenship papers, all subjects of German or kindred blood who possessed the right to vote in the Reichstag elections when the Citizenship Law came into effect, shall, for the present, possess the rights of Reich citizens. The same shall be true of those upon whom the Reich Minister of the Interior, in conjunction with the Deputy to the Führer, shall confer citizenship.

(2) The Reich Minister of the Interior, in conjunction with the Deputy to the Führer, may revoke citizenship.

Article II(1) The provisions of Article I shall apply also to subjects who are of mixed Jewish blood.

(2) An individual of mixed Jewish blood is one who is descended from one or two grandparents who, racially, were full Jews, insofar that he is not a Jew according to Section 2 of Article V. Full-blooded Jewish grandparents are those who belonged to the Jewish religious community.

Article III Only citizens of the Reich, as bearers of full political rights, can exercise the right of voting in political matters, and have the right to hold public office. The Reich Minister of the Interior, or any agency he empowers, can make exceptions during the transition period on the matter of holding public office. These measures do not apply to matters concerning religious organizations.

Article IV(1) A Jew cannot be a citizen of the Reich. He cannot exercise the right to vote; he cannot occupy public office.

(2) Jewish officials will be retired as of 31 December 1935. In the event that such officials served at the front in the World War [World War I] either for Germany or her allies, they shall receive as pension, until they reach the age limit, the full salary last received, on the basis of which their pension would have been computed. They shall not, however, be promoted according to their seniority in rank. When they reach the age limit their pension will be computed again, according to the salary last received on which their pension was to be calculated.

(3) These provisions do not concern the affairs of religious organizations.

(4) The condition regarding service of teachers in public Jewish schools remain unchanged until the promulgation of new regulations on the Jewish school system.

Article V(1) A Jew is an individual who is descended from at least three grandparents who were, racially, full Jews....

(2) A Jew is also an individual who is descended from two full-Jewish grandparents if:

(a) he was a member of the Jewish religious community when this law was issued, or joined the community later;

(b) when the law was issued, he was married to a person who was a Jew, or was subsequently married to a Jew;

(c) he is the issue from a marriage with a Jew, in the sense of Section I, which was contracted after the coming into effect of the Law for the Protection of German Blood and Honor of 15 September 1935;

(d) he is the issue of an extramarital relationship with a Jew, according to Section I, and born out of wedlock after 31 July 1936.

Article VI(1) Insofar as there are, in the laws of the Reich or in the decrees of the National Socialist Labor Party and its affiliates, certain requirements for the purity of German blood which extend beyond Article V, the same remains untouched....

Article VII The Führer and the Chancellor of the Reich is empowered to release anyone from the provisions of these administrative decrees.

———

Appendix C

Regulation on Military Government Courts, Issued by Letter of Headquarters, U.S. Forces, European Theater
Dated July 16, 1945, AG 000.5-2CAP*

Subject: Trial of War Crimes and Related Cases....

1. General

a. As a matter of policy, cases involving offenses against the laws and usages of war or laws of occupied territory or any part thereof commonly known as war crimes, together with such other related cases within the jurisdiction of Military Government courts as may from time to time be determined by the Theater Judge Advocate, committed prior to 9 May 1945, shall be tried before the specially appointed courts provided for in this directive. Such trials in the United States Army zone of occupation will hereafter be conducted before Military Government courts, except where otherwise directed by the Theater Commander.

b. Charges against persons accused of offenses of the character described above will originate in the Office of the Theater Judge Advocate, will be processed through Army Judge Advocates to trial by specially appointed Military Government courts, and will be reviewed by Army Judge Advocates prior to approval of sentences in accordance with procedures herein provided.

1. Procedural Matters before Trial.

a. *Charges.* Charges in the cases contemplated will be prepared under the direction of the Theater Judge Advocate in the form prescribed for Military Government courts.

b. *Reference for Trial.* The Theater Judge Advocate, or the authority designated by him, will forward charges to the appropriate Army Military District Commander for reference to trial before Military Government courts. Such charges when forwarded will be addressed "Attention: Staff Judge Advocate." The charges will be referred to the court for trial by the Army Military District Commander or in his discretion by his Staff Judge Advocates.

c. At the time of forwarding such charges to the Army Military District Commander the Theater Judge Advocate will in each case designate those United Nations, if any, which in his judgment should be invited by such commander to send observers to the trial.

3. *Appointment of Courts.* Military Government courts will be appointed by Army Military District Commanders for the special purpose of the trial of cases herein con-

———

* As quoted in Maximilian Koessler, "American War Crime Trials in Europe," 39 *Georgetown Law Journal*, 18; 110–112 (1950).

templated, the personnel for the courts to be selected from the officer personnel of military organizations under the command of the appointing authority. General Military Courts and Intermediate Military Courts appointed under the authority hereof shall consist of not more than five members and not less than three members respectively. The orders appointing such courts will designate one or more prosecutors and defense counsel. The senior member present at each trial will be the president and presiding officer of the court. At least one officer with legal training will be detailed a member of such courts.

4. *Trial.* The trial will be conducted according to pertinent Military Government directives and instructions, except that no person shall be convicted or sentenced by the courts provided for herein except by the concurrence of two-thirds of all members present at the time vote is taken.

5. Post-Trial Action.

a. Irrespective of the result of the trial, the accused will be returned to custody pending final disposition.

b. The prosecuting officer will be responsible for the preparation of the record of trial which, after being properly authenticated, will be forwarded to the Staff Judge Advocate of the appointing authority who will prepare a written review of the case for submission to the approving authority. No administrative examination by any other legal officer on the staff of the appointing authority will be required.

c. In taking the action prescribed in sub-paragraph *b*, above, the Staff Judge Advocate will take into consideration and include in the discussion and recommendations made in such written review any Petition for Review filed by or on behalf of the accused. Final action on each case will be deferred for the ten-day period described under Military Government court procedure for filing of such petition.

d. No sentence of Military Government Court appointed under the authority hereof shall be carried into execution until the case record shall have been examined by the Army Military District Judge Advocate and the sentence approved by the officer appointing the court or by the officer commanding for the time being, except that such approving authority may designate an officer for such action on sentences of Intermediate Military Courts appointed hereunder. The action taken will be entered on the case record in the space provided... over the signature of the appointing authority or, in the case of intermediate military courts, of his designee.

e. No sentence of death shall be carried into execution until confirmed as prescribed for Military Government courts.

f. Approving authorities will in each case where a death sentence is adjudged advise the Theater Judge Advocate... of the approval of any such sentence, and will withhold execution after confirmation pending receipt of clearance from the Theater Judge Advocate in connection with each person so sentenced.

6. The execution of death sentences, designation of places of confinement, and the effective date of prison sentences will be as provided for other Military Government Courts.

7. All directives and instructions of this and subordinate headquarters relating to the conduct of trials by Military Government Courts are modified to the extent necessary to give effect to the provisions of this letter....

Appendix D

Regulation on Military Commissions, Issued by Letter of Headquarters, U.S. Forces, European Theater

Dated August 25, 1945, File AG 250.4 JAG-AGO

Subject: Military Commissions.

1. *General*

a. *Authority to Appoint.* You are hereby authorized to appoint military commissions for the trial of persons subject to the jurisdiction of such commissions who are charged with violations of the laws and customs of war, of the law of nations, or of the laws of occupied territory, or any part thereof. You are not authorized to redelegate such appointing powers.

b. *Cases to be Tried.* As a matter of policy no case shall be referred to trial before a military commission except when directed by this headquarters. Applications for authority to proceed with such trials will be forwarded to the Deputy Theater Judge Advocate, War Crimes Branch, this headquarters, APC 757.

c. *Composition.* Military commissions shall be composed of not less than three commissioned officers of the United States Army. There shall also be appointed a trial judge advocate and defense counsel.

d. *Conviction or Sentence.* The concurrence of at least two-thirds of the members of the commission present at the time of voting shall be necessary for the conviction and for the sentence.

e. *Approval of Sentence.* No sentence of a military commission appointed under the authority cited in sub-paragraph a, above, shall be carried into execution until the same shall have been approved by the officer appointing the commission or by the officer commanding for the time being.

f. *Confirmation of Death Sentence.* No sentence of death shall be carried into execution until it shall have been confirmed by the Theater Commander or his designee.

2. *Rules of Procedure.* Military Commissions shall have power to make, as occasion requires, such rules for the conduct of their proceedings, consistent with the powers of such commissions, and with the rules of procedure herein set forth, as are deemed necessary for a full and fair trial of the accused, having regard for, without being bound by, the rules of procedure, and evidence prescribed for general courts-martial...

3. *Evidence Admissible.* Such evidence shall be admitted before a military commission as, in the opinion of the president of the commission, has probative value to a reasonable man.

4. *Charges and Specifications.* Formal charge and investigation as contemplated in Article of War 70 are not necessary in proceedings before military commissions.... The charge should designate the offense by its legal name or describe to an Article of War. The specification should set forth the details of the act charged with sufficient definiteness to show the jurisdiction of the commission and the status of the accused. The accused shall be furnished with a copy of the charges and specifications. Although no oath is necessary, the charge should be signed by a person subject to military law. At some state prior to the trial, the charge should be investigated sufficiently to enable the ap-

pointing authority to determine that the offense merits trial by military commission. Before directing the trial of any charge, the appointing authority will refer the case to his staff judge advocate for consideration and advice.

5. *Challenges.* Members of the military commission may be challenged by the accused or the trial judge advocate for cause stated to the court. Peremptory challenges shall not be allowed.

6. *Oaths.* Making such changes as necessary, the appropriate oaths contained in Article of War 19 shall be administered to members of the commission as well as to the prosecution and to others connected with the trial. All witnesses will be sworn.

7. *Pleas.* General and special pleas of the accused should be heard and passed upon by the commission in order to insure a fair and impartial trial.

* * *

11. *Sentence.*

a. *General.* Subject to limitations imposed by this headquarters, military commissions may adjudge any type of punishment referred to in paragraph 45, War Department FM 27-5, subject: "Military Government and Civil Affairs," dated 22 December 1943. Commissions may be guided by, but are not limited to, the penalties authorized by the Manual for Courts-Martial, the laws of the United States, and of the territory in which the offense was committed or the trial is held.

b. *Places of Confinement.* Places of confinement will be designated by the appointing authority as in the case of prisoners sentenced to imprisonment by military government courts.

12. *Review.*

a. Every record of trial by military commission will be referred by the appointing authority to his staff judge advocate for review before he acts thereon.

b. Every record of trial in which a death sentence is adjudged, if such sentence is approved and not commuted by the appointing authority, will be forwarded to the Deputy Theater Judge Advocate, War Crimes Branch, APO 757, for review by the Theater Judge Advocate or his deputy and presentation with appropriate recommendations to the confirming authority for action.

* * *

15. *Mitigation, Remission, etc.* The power to order the execution of a sentence, or to confirm a death sentence, of a military commission includes the power to disapprove or vacate in whole, or in part, any finding of guilty, and to mitigate, remit, approve and commute, suspend or to remand for further proceedings or for rehearing before a new military commission.

Appendix E

Regulations Governing the Trials of Accused War Criminals, GHQ, Supreme Commander for the Allied Powers [Tokyo]

December 5, 1945, amended December 27, 1946*

1. ESTABLISHMENT OF MILITARY COMMISSIONS.

a. *General.* Persons accused as war criminals will be tried by commissions to be convened by, or under the authority of, the Supreme Commander for the Allied Powers.

b. *Number and Types.* The commissions will be established dependent upon the number, nature of the offenses involved and the offenders to be tried. Such commissions may include, among others, international military commissions consisting of representatives of several nations or of each nation concerned, appointed to try cases involving offenses against one (1) or more nations.

2. JURISDICITON.

a. *Over Persons.* The military commissions appointed hereunder shall have jurisdiction over all persons charged with war crimes who are in custody of the convening authority at the time of trial.

b. *Over Offenses.*

(1) Military commissions established hereunder shall have jurisdiction over all offenses including, but not limited to, the following:

(a) The planning, preparation, initiation or waging of a war of aggression or a war in violation of international treaties, agreements or assurances, or participation in a common plan or conspiracy for the accomplishment of any of the foregoing.

(b) Violations of the laws or customs of war. Such violations shall include, but not be limited to, murder, ill-treatment or deportation to slave labor or for any other purpose of civilian population of or in occupied territory, murder or ill-treatment of prisoners of war or internees or persons on the seas or elsewhere; improper treatment of hostages; plunder of public or private property; wanton destruction of cities, towns or villages; or devastation not justified by military necessity.

(c) Murder, extermination, enslavement, deportation and other inhuman acts committed against any civilian population before or during the war or persecutions on political, racial or religious grounds in execution of, or in connection with, any crime defined herein, whether or not in violation of the domestic laws of the country where perpetrated.

(2) The offense need not have been committed after a particular date to render the responsible party or parties subject to arrest, but in general should have been committed since or in the period immediately preceding the Mukden incident of September 18, 1931. [The beginning of the Japanese conquest of Manchuria].

---

* National Achieves, Record Group 331, File M112, Roll 1.

3. MEMBERSHIPP OF COMMISSION.

A. *Appointment.* The members of each military commission will be appointed by the Supreme Commander for the Allied Powers, or under authority delegated by him. Alternates may be appointed by the convening authority. Such alternates shall attend all sessions of the commission, and in case of illness or other incapacity of any principal member, an alternate shall take the place of that member. Any vacancy among the members or alternates, occurring after a trial has begun, may be filled by the convening authority, but the substance of all proceedings had and evidence taken in that case shall be made known to that new member or alternate before the trial proceeds. This fact will be announced by the president of the commission in open court.

b. *Number of Members.* Each commission shall consist of not less than three (3) members.

c. *Qualifications.* The convening authority shall appoint to the commission persons whom he determines to be competent to perform the duties involved and not disqualified by personal interest or prejudice, provided that no person shall be appointed to hear a case which he personally investigated, nor if he is required as a witness in that case. A commission may consist of Army, Navy or other service personnel, or of both service personnel and civilians. One specially qualified member shall be designated as the law member whose ruling is final insofar as concerns the commission on an objection to the admissibility of evidence offered during the trial.

d. *Voting.* Except as to the admissibility of evidence, all rulings and findings of the commission shall be by majority vote, except that conviction and sentence shall be by the affirmative votes of not less than two-thirds (2/3) of the members present.

e. *Presiding Member.* In the event that the convening authority does not name one of the members as the presiding member, the senior officer among the members of the commission present shall preside, or such other member as the senior member shall designate.

4. PROSECUTORS

a. *Appointment.* The convening authority shall designate one or more persons to conduct the prosecution before each commission. Where offenses involve nationals of more than one nation, each nation concerned, in the discretion of the convening authority, may be represented among the prosecutors.

b. *Duties.* The duties of the prosecution are:

(1) To prepare and present charges and specifications for reference to the commission.

(2) To prepare cases for trial and to conduct the prosecution before the commission of all cases referred for trial.

5. POWERS AND PROCEDURES OF COMMISSIONS

a. *Conduct of the Trial.* A commission shall:

(1) Confine each trial strictly to a fair, expeditious hearing on the issues raised by the charges, excluding irrelevant issues or evidence and preventing any unnecessary delay or interference.

(2) Deal summarily with any contumacy or contempt, imposing any appropriate punishment therefore,

(3) Hold public sessions except when otherwise decided by the commission.

(4) Hold each session at such time and place as it shall determine, or as may be directed by the convening authority.

b. *Rights of the accused.* The accused shall be entitled:

(1) To have in advance of trial a copy of the charges and specifications clearly worded so as to apprise the accused of each offense charged.

(2) To be represented, prior to and during trial, by counsel appointed by the convening authority or counsel of his own choice, or to conduct his own defense.

(3) To testify in his own behalf and have his counsel present relevant evidence at the trial in support of his defense, and cross-examine each adverse witness who personally appears before the commission.

(4) To have the substance of the charges and specifications, the proceedings and any documentary evidence translated when he is unable otherwise to understand them.

c. *Witnesses.* The commission shall have the power:

(1) To summon witnesses and require their attendance and testimony under penalty; to administer oaths or affirmations to witnesses and other persons and to question witnesses.

(2) To require the production of documents and other evidentiary material.

(3) To delegate to the Prosecutors appointed by the convening authority the powers and duties set forth in (1) and (2) above.

(4) To have evidence taken by a special commissioner appointed by the commission.

d. *Evidence.*

(1) The commission shall admit such evidence as in its opinion would be of assistance in proving or disproving the charge or such as in the commission's opinion would have probative value in the mind of a reasonable man. The commission shall apply the rules of evidence and pleading set forth herein with the greatest liberality to achieve expeditious procedure. In particular, and without limiting in any way the scope of the foregoing general rules, the following evidence may be admitted:

(a) Any document irrespective of its security classification which appears to the commission to have been signed or issued by any officer, department, agency, or member of the armed forces of any government without proof of the signature or of the issuance of the document.

(b) Any report which appears to the commission to have been signed or issued by the International Red Cross or a member thereof, or by any doctor of medicine or any medical service personnel, or by an investigator or intelligence officer, or by any other person whom the commission considers as possessing knowledge of the matter contained in the report.

(c) Affidavits, depositions or other signed statements.

(d) Any diary, letter or other document, including sworn or unsworn statements, appearing to the commission to contain information relating to the charge.

(e) A copy of any document or other secondary evidence of its contents, if the original is not immediately available.

(2) The commission shall take judicial notice of facts of common knowledge, official government documents of any nation, and the proceedings, records and findings of military or other agencies of the United Nations.

(3) A commission may require the prosecution and the defense to make a preliminary offer of proof, whereupon the commission may rule in advance on the admissibility of such evidence.

(4) The official position of the accused shall not absolve him from responsibility, nor be considered in mitigation of punishment. Further, action pursuant to order of the accused's superior, or of his government, shall not constitute a defense, but may be considered in mitigation of the punishment if the commission determines that justice so requires.

(5) All purported confessions or statements of the accused shall be admissible in evidence without any showing that they were voluntarily made. If it is shown that such confession or statement was procured by means which the commission believes to have been of such character that they may have caused the accused to make a false statement, the commission may strike out or disregard any such portion thereof as was so procured.

e. *Trial Procedure.* The proceedings at each trial will be conducted substantially as follows, unless modified by the commission to suit the peculiar circumstances:

(1) Each charge and specification will be read, or its substance stated, in open court.

(2) The presiding member shall ask each accused whether he pleads "Guilty" or "Not Guilty."

(3) The prosecution shall make its opening statement.

(4) The presiding member may, at this time or any other time, require the prosecutor to state what evidence he proposes to submit to the commission, and the commission may thereupon rule upon the admissibility of such evidence.

(5) The witnesses and other evidence for the prosecution shall be heard or presented. At the close of the case for the prosecution, the commission may, on motion of the defense for a finding of not guilty, consider and rule whether the evidence before the commission supports the charges against the accused. The commission may defer action on any such motion and permit or require the prosecution to reopen its case and produce any further available evidence.

(6) The defense may make an opening statement prior to presenting its case. The presiding member may, at this or any other time, require the defense to state what evidence they propose to submit to the commission, whereupon the commission may rule upon the admissibility of such evidence.

(7) The witnesses and other evidence for the defense shall be heard and presented. Thereafter, the prosecution and defense may introduce such evidence in rebuttal as the commission may rule admissible.

(8) The defense, and thereafter the prosecution, shall address the commission.

(9) The commission thereafter shall consider the case in closed session and unless otherwise directed by the convening authority, announce in open court its judgment and sentence, if any. The commission may state the reasons on which the judgment is based.

f. *Record of Proceedings.* Each commission shall make a separate record of its proceedings in the trial of each case brought before it. The record shall be prepared by the prosecutor under the direction of the commission and shall be submitted to the defense counsel. The commission shall be responsible for its accuracy. Such record, certified by the presiding member of the commission or his successor, shall be delivered to the convening authority as soon as possible after the trial.

g. *Sentence.* The commission may sentence an accused, upon conviction, to death by hanging or shooting, imprisonment for life, or for any less term, forfeiture of real or personal property, fine, or such other punishment as the commission shall determine to be proper.

h. *Approval of Sentence.* No sentence of a military commission shall be carried into effect until approved by the officer who convened the commission, or his successor. Such officer shall have the authority to approve, mitigate, remit in whole or in part, commute, suspend, reduce or otherwise alter the sentence imposed, or (without prejudice to accused) remand the case for rehearing before a new military commission; but he shall not have authority to increase the severity of the sentence. No sentence of death shall be carried into execution until confirmed by the Supreme Commander for the Allied Powers. Except as herein provided, the judgment and sentence of a commission shall be final and not subject to review.

Appendix F

Military Government—United States Zone Ordinance No. 7
October 18, 1946, as amended by Ordinance No. 11, February 17, 1947*

ORGANIZATIONS AND POWERS OF CERTAIN MILITARY TRIBUNALS

Article 1. The purpose of this Ordinance is to provide for the establishment of military tribunals which shall have power to try and punish persons charged with offenses recognized as crimes in Article II of Control Council Law No. 10, including conspiracies to commit any such crimes. Nothing herein shall prejudice the jurisdiction or the powers of other courts established or which may be established for the trial of any such offenses.

Article II. (a) Pursuant to the Military Governor for the United States Zone of Occupation and further pursuant to the powers conferred upon the Zone Commander by Control Council Law No. 10 and Articles 10 and 11 of the Charter of the International Military Tribunal annexed to the London Agreement of 8 August 1945 certain tribunals to be known as "Military Tribunals" shall be established hereunder.

(b) Each such tribunal shall consist of three or more members to be designated by the Military Governor. One alternate member may be designated to any tribunal if deemed advisable by the Military Governor. Except as provided in subsection (c) of the Article, all members and alternates shall be lawyers who have been admitted to practice, for at least five years, in the highest courts of one of the United States or its territories or the District of Columbia, or who have been admitted to practice in the United States Supreme Court.

(c) The Military Governor may in his discretion enter into an agreement with one or more other zone commanders of the member nations of the Allied Council Authority

---

* As quoted in Howard S. Levie, *Terrorism in War: The Law of War Crimes* 563–570 (1993).

providing for the joint trial of any case or cases. In such case the tribunal shall consist of three or more members as may be provided in the agreement. In such cases the tribunal may include properly qualified lawyers designated by the other member nations.

(d) The Military Governor shall designate one of the members of the tribunal to serve as presiding judge.

(e) Neither the tribunals nor the members of the tribunals or the alternates may be challenged by the prosecution or by the defendants or their counsel.

(f) In cases of illness of any member of a tribunal or his incapacity for some other reason, the alternate, if one has been designated, shall take his place as a member in the pending trial....

(g) The presence of three members of the tribunal, or of two members when authorized pursuant to subsection (f) *supra* shall be necessary to constitute a quorum. In the case of tribunals designated under (c) above, the agreement shall determine the requirements for a quorum.

(h) Decisions and judgments, including convictions and sentences, shall be by majority vote of the members. If the votes of the members are equally divided, the presiding member shall declare a mistrial.

Article III. (a) Charges against persons to be tried in the tribunals established hereunder shall originate in the Office of the Chief of Counsel for War Crimes, appointed by the Military Governor pursuant to paragraph 3 of the Executive Order Numbered 9679 of the President of the United States dated 16 January 1946. The Chief of Counsel for War Crimes shall determine the persons to be tried by the tribunals and he or his designated representative shall file the indictments with the Secretary General of the tribunals (see Article XIV, *infra*) and shall conduct the prosecution.

(b) The Chief of Counsel for War Crimes, when in his judgment it is advisable, may invite one or more United Nations to designate representatives to participate in the prosecution of any case.

Article IV. In order to ensure fair trial for the defendants, the following procedure shall be followed:

(a) A defendant shall be furnished, at a reasonable time before his trial, a copy of his indictment and of all documents lodged with the indictment, translated into a language which he understands. The indictment shall state the charges plainly, concisely and with sufficient particulars to inform defendant of the offenses charged.

(c) A defendant shall have the right to be defended by counsel of his own selection, provided such counsel shall be a person qualified under existing regulations to conduct cases before the courts of defendant's country, or any other person who may be specially authorized by the tribunal. The tribunal shall appoint qualified counsel to represent a defendant who is not represented by counsel of his own selection.

(d) Every defendant shall be entitled to be present at his trial except that a defendant may be proceeded against during temporary absences if in the opinion of the tribunal defendant's interests will not thereby be impaired, and except further as provided in Article 6(c). The tribunal may also proceed in the absence of any defendant who has applied for and has been granted permission to be absent.

(e) A defendant shall have the right through his counsel to present evidence at the trial in support of his defense, and to cross-examine any witness called by the prosecution.

(f) A defendant may apply in writing to the tribunal for the production of witnesses or documents. The application shall state where the witness or document is thought to be located and shall also state the facts to be proved by the witness or the document and the relevancy of such facts to the defense. If the tribunal grants the application, the defendant shall be given such aid in obtaining production of evidence as the tribunal may order.

Article V. The tribunals shall have the power

(a) to summon witnesses to the trial, to require their attendance and testimony and to put question to them;

(b) to interrogate any defendant who takes the stand to testify in his own behalf, or who is called to testify regarding another defendant;

(c) to require the production of documents and other evidentiary material;

(d) to administer oaths;

(e) to appoint officers for the carrying out of any task designated by the tribunals including the taking of evidence on commission;

(f) to adopt rules of procedure not inconsistent with this Ordinance. Such rules shall be adopted, and from time to time as necessary, revised by the members of the tribunal or by the committee of presiding judges as provided in Article XIII.

(g) the presiding judges, and, when established, the supervisory committee of presiding judges provided in Article XIII shall assign the cases brought by the Chief of Counsel for War Crimes to the various Military Tribunals for trial.

* * *

Article VI. The tribunals shall

(a) confine the trial strictly to an expeditious hearing on the issues raised by the charges;

(b) take strict measures to prevent any action which will cause unreasonable delay, and rule out irrelevant issues and statements of any kind whatsoever;

(c) deal summarily with any contumacy, imposing appropriate punishment, including the exclusion of any defendant or his counsel from some or all further proceedings, but without prejudice to the determination of the charges.

Article VII. The tribunals shall not be bound by technical rules of evidence. They shall adopt and apply to the greatest possible extent expeditious and nontechnical procedure, and shall admit any evidence which they deem to have probative value. Without limiting the foregoing general rules, the following shall be deemed admissible if they appear to the tribunal to contain information of probative value relating to the charges: affidavits, depositions, interrogations, and other statements, diaries, letters, the records, findings, statements and judgments of the military tribunals and the reviewing and confirming authorities of any of the United Nations, and copies of any documents or other secondary evidence of the contents of any document, if the original is not readily available or cannot be produced without delay. The tribunal shall afford the opposing party such opportunity to question the authenticity or probative value of such evidence as in the opinion of the tribunal the ends of justice require.

Article VIII. The tribunals may require that they be informed of the nature of any evidence before it is offered so that they may rule upon the relevance thereof.

Article IX. The tribunals shall not require proof of facts of common knowledge but shall take judicial notice thereof. They shall also take judicial notice of official government documents and reports of any of the United Nations, including the acts and documents of the committees set up in the various Allied countries for the investigation of war crimes, and the records and findings of military or other tribunals of any of the United Nations.

Article X. The determinations of the International Military Tribunal in the judgments in Case No. 1 [*United States et al. v. Wilhelm Göring et al.*] that invasions, aggressive acts, aggressive wars, crimes, atrocities or inhumane acts were planned or occurred, shall be binding on the tribunals established hereunder and shall not be questioned except insofar as the participation therein or knowledge thereof by any particular person may be concerned. Statements of the International Military Tribunal in the Judgment in Case No. 1 constitute proof of the facts stated, in the absence of substantial evidence to the contrary.

* * *

Article XV. The judgments of the tribunals as to the guilt or innocence of any defendant shall give reasons on which they are based and shall be final and not subject to review. The sentences imposed may be subject to review as provided in Article XVII, *infra.*

Article XVI. The tribunal shall have the right to impose upon the defendant, upon conviction, such punishment as shall be determined to be just, which may consist of one or more of the penalties provided in Article II, Section 3 of Control Council Law No. 10.

Article XVII. (a) Except as provided in (b) *infra*, the record of each case shall be forwarded to the Military Governor who shall have the power to mitigate, reduce or otherwise alter the sentence imposed by the tribunal, but may not increase the severity thereof.

(b) In cases before tribunals authorized by Article II(c), the sentence shall be reviewed jointly by the zone commanders of the nations involved, who may mitigate, reduce or otherwise alter the sentence by a majority vote, but may not increase the severity thereof. If only two nations are represented, the sentence may be altered only by the consent of both zone commanders.

Article XVIII. No sentence of death shall be carried into execution unless and until confirmed in writing by the Military Governor. In accordance with Article III, Section 5 of Law No. 10, execution of the death sentence may be deferred by not to exceed one month after such confirmation if there is reason to believe that the testimony of the convicted person may be of value in the investigation and trial of other crimes.

Article XIX. Upon the pronouncement of a death sentence by a tribunal established thereunder [*sic*] and pending confirmation thereof, the condemned will be remanded to the prison or place where he was confined and there be segregated from other inmates, or be transferred to a more appropriate place of confinement.

Article XX. Upon the confirmation of a sentence of death the Military Governor will issue the necessary orders for carrying out the execution.

Article XXI. Where sentence of confinement for the term of years has been imposed the condemned shall be confined in the manner directed by the tribunal imposing sentence. The place of confinement may be changed from time to time by the Military Governor.

Appendix G

Convention on the Prevention and Punishment of the Crime of Genocide

December 9, 1948*

Article I. The Contracting Parties confirm that genocide, whether committed in time of peace or in time of war, is a crime under international law which they undertake to prevent and punish.

Article II. In the present Convention, genocide means any of the following acts committed with intent to destroy, in whole or in part, a national, ethnical, racial or religious group, as such:

(a) Killing members of the group;

(b) Causing serious bodily or mental harm to members of the group;

(c) Deliberately inflicting on the group conditions of life calculated to bring about its physical destruction in whole or in part;

(d) Imposing measures intended to prevent births within the group;

(e) Forcibly transferring children of the group to another group;

Article III. The following acts shall be punishable:

(a) Genocide;

(b) Conspiracy to commit genocide;

(c) Direct and public incitement to commit genocide;

(d) Attempt to commit genocide;

(e) Complicity in genocide.

Article IV. Persons committing genocide or any other acts enumerated in Article III shall be punished, whether they are constitutionally responsible rulers, public officials or private individuals.

Article V. The Contracting Parties undertake to enact, in accordance with their respective Constitutions, the necessary legislation to give effect to the provisions of the present Convention and, in particular, to provide effective penalties for persons guilty of genocide or any of the other acts enumerated in Article III.

Article VI. Persons charged with genocide or any other acts enumerated in Article III shall be tried by a competent tribunal of the State in the territory of which the act was committed, or by such international penal tribunal as may have jurisdiction with respect to those Contracting Parties which shall have accepted its jurisdiction.

Article VII: Genocide and the other acts enumerated in Article III shall not be considered as political crimes for the purpose of extradition.

---

* *1948–49 Yearbook of The United Nations* 959 UN: Lake Success, New York (1950).

The Contracting Parties pledge themselves in such cases to grant extradition in accordance with their laws and treaties in force.

Article VIII. Any Contracting Party may call upon the competent organs of the United Nations to take such action under the Charter of the United Nations as they consider appropriate for the prevention and suppression of acts of genocide or any of the other acts enumerated in Article III.

Article IX. Disputes between the Contracting Parties relating to the interpretation, application or fulfillment of the present Convention, including those relating to the responsibility of a State for genocide or any of the other acts enumerated in Article III, shall be submitted to the International Court of Justice at the request of any of the parties to the dispute.

Appendix H

Convention for the Protection of Cultural Property in the Event of Armed Conflict
The Hague, May 14, 1954*

Article 4

1. The High Contracting Parties undertake to respect cultural property within their own territory as well as within the territory of other High Contracting Parties by refraining from any use of the property and its immediate surroundings or of the appliances in use for its protection for purposes which are likely to expose it to destruction or damage in the event of armed conflict; and by refraining from any act of hostility directed against such property.

2. The obligations mentioned in paragraph 1 of the present Article may be waived only in cases where military necessity imperatively requires such a waiver.

3. The High Contracting Parties further undertake to prohibit, prevent and, if necessary, put a stop to any form of theft, pillage or misappropriation of, and any act of vandalism directed against, cultural property. They shall refrain from requisitioning movable cultural property situated in the territory of another High Contracting Party.

4. They shall refrain from any act directed by way of reprisals against cultural property.

* * *

1. Apart from the provisions which shall take effect in time of peace, the present Convention shall apply in the event of a declared war or of any other armed conflict which may arise between two or more of the High Contracting Parties, even if the state of war is not recognized by one or more of them.

---

* 249 U.N.T.S. 240; S/T 745.

* * *

Article 28

The High Contracting Parties undertake to take, within the framework of their ordinary criminal jurisdiction, all necessary steps to prosecute and impose penal or disciplinary sanction upon those persons, of whatever nationality, who commit or order to be committed a breach of the present Convention.

Appendix I

Convention on the Non-Applicability of Statutory Limitations to War Crimes and Crimes against Humanity
November 26, 1968*

Article 1

No statutory limitation shall apply to the following crimes, irrespective of the date of their commission:

(a) War crimes as they are defined in the Charter of the International Military Tribunal, Nurnberg, of 8 August 1945 and confirmed by resolutions 3(1) of 13 February 1946 and 95(1) of 11 December 1946 of the General Assembly of the United Nations, particularly the 'grave breaches' enumerated in the Geneva Conventions of 12 August 1949 for the protection of war victims;

(b) Crimes against humanity whether committed in time of war or in time of peace as they are defined in the Charter of the International Military Tribunal, Nurnburg, of 8 August 1945 and confirmed by resolutions 3(1) of 13 February 1946 and 95(1) of 11 December 1946 of the General Assembly of the United Nations, eviction by armed attack or occupation and inhuman acts resulting from the policy of *apartheid*, and the crime of genocide as defined in the 1948 Convention on the Prevention and Punishment of the Crime of Genocide, even if such acts do not constitute a violation of the domestic law of the country in which they were committed.

Article II

If any of the crimes mentioned in article I is committed, the provisions of this Conventions shall apply to representative of the State authority and private individual who, as principals or accomplices, participate in or who directly incite others to the commission of any of those crimes, or who conspire to commit them, irrespective of the degree of completion, and to representatives of the State authority who tolerate their commission.

---

* UNGA Res. 2391 (XXIII), 26 November 1968, 74 U.N.T.S. 73; S/T 925 (1969).

Appendix J

International Covenant on Civil and Political Rights
March 23, 1976*

Article 14

1. All persons shall be equal before the courts and tribunals. In the determination of any criminal charge against him, or of his rights and obligations in a suit at law, everyone shall be entitled to a fair and public hearing by a competent, independent and impartial tribunal established by law. The Press and the public may be excluded from all or part of a trial for reasons of morals, public order (*ordre public*) or national security in a democratic society, or when the interest of the private lives of the parties so requires, or to the extent strictly necessary in the opinion of the court in special circumstances where publicity would prejudice the interests of justice; but any judgment rendered in a criminal case or in a suit at law shall be made public except where the interest of juvenile persons otherwise requires or the proceedings concern matrimonial disputes or the guardianship of children.

2. Everyone charged with a criminal offense shall have the right to be presumed innocent until proved guilty according to law.

3. In the determination of any criminal charge against him, everyone shall be entitled to the following minimum guarantees, in full equality:

(a) To be informed promptly and in detail in a language which he understands of the nature and cause of the charge against him;

(b) To have adequate time and facilities for the preparation of his defence and to communicate with counsel of his own choosing;

(c) To be tried without undue delay;

(d) To be tried in his presence, and to defend himself in person or through legal assistance of his own choosing; to be informed, if he does not have legal assistance, of this right; and to have legal assistance assigned to him, in any case where the interests of justice so require, and without payment by him in any such case if he does not have sufficient means to pay for it.

(e) To examine, or have examined, the witnesses against him and to obtain the attendance and examination of witnesses on his behalf under the same conditions as witnesses against him;

(f) To have the free assistance of an interpreter if he cannot understand or speak the language used in court;

(g) Not to be compelled to testify against himself or to confess guilt.

4. In the case of juvenile persons, the procedure shall be such as will take account of their age and the desirability of promoting their rehabilitation.

5. Everyone convicted of a crime shall have the right to his conviction and sentence being reviewed by a higher tribunal according to law.

---

* 999 U.N.T.S. 171, 176.

6. When a person has by a final decision been convicted of a criminal offence and when subsequently his conviction has been reversed or he has been pardoned on the ground that a new or newly discovered fact shows conclusively that there has been a miscarriage of justice, the person who has suffered punishment as a result of such conviction shall be compensated according to law, unless it is proved that the non-disclosure of the unknown fact in time is wholly or partly attributable to him.

7. No one shall be liable to be tried or punished again for an offence for which he has already been finally convicted or acquitted in accordance with the law and penal procedure of each country.

Appendix K

Protocol I Additional to the Geneva Conventions of 12 August 1949, and Relating to the Protection of Victims of International Armed Conflicts
[8 June 1977]*

Article II—Protection of Persons

1. The physical and mental health and integrity of persons who are in the power of the adverse Party or who are interned, detained or otherwise deprived of liberty as a result of a situation referred to an Article1 shall not be endangered by any unjustified act or omission. Accordingly, it is prohibited to subject the persons described in this Article to any medical procedure which is not indicated by the State of health of the person concerned and which is not consistent with generally accepted medical standards which would be applied under similar medical circumstances to persons who are nationals of the Party conducting the procedure and who are in no way deprived of liberty.

2. It is, in particular, prohibited to carry out on such persons, even with their consent:

   (a) physical mutilations;

   (b) medical or scientific experiments;

   (c) removal of tissue or organs for transplantation,

Except where these acts are justified in conformity with the conditions provided in paragraph 1.

3. Exceptions to the prohibition in paragraph 2(c) may be made only in case of donations of blood for transfusion or of skin for grafting, provided that they are given voluntarily and without any coercion or inducement, and then only for therapeutic purposes, under conditions consistent with generally accepted medical standards and controls designed for the benefit of both the donor and the recipient.

4. Any willful act or omission which seriously endangers the physical or mental health or integrity of any person who is in the power of a Party other than the one on which he

---

* UN Doc. A/32/144 Annex I.

depends and which either violates any of the prohibitions in paragraphs 1 and 2 or fails to comply with the requirements of paragraph 3 shall be a grave breach of this Protocol.

* * *

Article 20 — Prohibition of reprisals

Reprisals against the persons and objects protected by this Part are prohibited.

* * *

Article 35 — Basic Rules

1. In any armed conflict, the right of the Parties to the conflict to choose methods or means of warfare is not unlimited.

2. It is prohibited to employ weapons, projectiles and materials and methods of warfare of a nature to cause superfluous injury or unnecessary suffering.

3. It is prohibited to employ methods or means of warfare which are intended, or may be expected, to cause widespread, long-term and severe damage to the natural environment.

* * *

Article 37 — Prohibition of Perfidy

1. It is prohibited to kill, injure or capture an adversary by resort to perfidy. Acts inviting the confidence of an adversary to lead him to believe that he is entitled to, or is obliged to accord, protection under the rules of international law applicable in armed conflict, with intent to betray that confidence, shall constitute perfidy. The following acts are examples of perfidy:

   a. the feigning of an intent to negotiate under a flag of truce or of a surrender;

   b. the feigning of an incapacitation by wounds or sickness;

   c. the feigning of civilian, non-combatant status; and

   d. the feigning of protected status by the use of signs, emblems or uniforms of the United Nations or of neutral or other States not Parties to the conflict.

2. Ruses of war are not prohibited. Such ruses are acts which are intended to mislead an adversary or induce him to act recklessly but which infringe no rule of international law applicable in armed conflict and which are not perfidious because they do not invite the confidence of an adversary with respect to protection under that law. The following are examples of such ruses: the use of camouflage, decoys, mock operations and misinformation.

Article 38 — Recognized Emblems

1. It is prohibited to make improper use of the distinctive emblem of the red cross, red crescent or red lion and sun or of other emblems, sign or signals provided for by the conventions or by this Protocol. It is also prohibited to misuse deliberately in an armed conflict other internationally recognized protective emblems, signs or signals, including the flag of truce, and the protective emblem of cultural property.

2. It is prohibited to make use of the distinctive emblem of the United Nations, except as authorized by that Organization.

Article 39 — Emblems of nationality

1. It is prohibited to use in an armed conflict of the flags or military emblems, insignia or uniforms of neutral or other States not Parties to the conflict.

2. It is prohibited to make use of the flags or military emblems, insignia or uniforms of adverse Parties while engaging in attacks or in order to shield, favour, protect or impede military operations.

3. Nothing in this Article or in Article 37, paragraph 1(d), shall affect the existing generally recognized rules of international law applicable to espionage or to the use of flags in the conduct of armed conflict at sea.

Article 40 — Quarter

It is prohibited to order that there shall be no survivors, to threaten an adversary therewith or to conduct hostilities on this basis.

Article 41 — Safeguard of an enemy *hors de combat*

1. A person who is recognized or who, in the circumstances, should be recognized to be *hors de combat* shall not be made the object of attack.

2. A person is *hors de combat* if:

(a) he is in the power of an adverse Party;

(b) he clearly expresses an intention to surrender; or

(c) he has been rendered unconscious or is otherwise incapacitated by wounds or sickness, and therefore is incapable of defending himself;

Provided that in any of these cases he abstains from any hostile act and does not attempt to escape.

3. When persons entitled to protection as prisoners of war have fallen into the power of an adverse Party under unusual conditions of combat which prevent their evacuation as provided in Part III, Section 1, of the Third Convention, they shall be released and all feasible precautions shall be taken to ensure their safety.

Article 42 — Occupants of Aircraft

1. No person parachuting from an aircraft in distress shall be made the object of attack during his descent.

2. Upon reaching the ground in territory controlled by the adverse Party, a person who has parachuted from an aircraft in distress shall be given an opportunity to surrender before being made the object of attack, unless it is apparent that he is engaging in a hostile act.

3. Airborne troops are not protected by this Article.

Article 43 — Armed Forces

1. The armed forces of a Party to a conflict consist of organized army forces, groups and units which are under a command responsible to that Party for the conduct of its subordinates, even if that Party is represented by a government or an authority not recognized by an adverse Party. Such armed forces shall be subject to an internal disciplinary system which, *inter alia*, shall enforce compliance with the rules of international law applicable in armed conflict.

2. Members of the armed forces of a Party to a conflict (other than medical personnel and chaplains covered by Article 33 of the Third Convention) are combatants, that is to say, they have the right to participate directly in hostilities.

3. Whenever a Party to a conflict incorporates a paramilitary or armed law enforcement agency into its armed forces it shall so notify the other Parties to the conflict.

Article 44—Combatants as prisoners of war

1. Any combatant, as defined in Article 43, who falls into the power of an adverse Party shall be a prisoner of war.

2. While all combatants are obliged to comply with the rules of international law applicable in armed conflict, violations of these rules shall not deprive a combatant of his right to be a combatant or, if he falls into the power of an adverse Party, of his right to be a prisoner of war, except as provided in paragraph 3 and 4.

3. In order to provide protection of the civilian population from the effects of hostilities, combatants are obliged to distinguish themselves from the civilian population while they are engaged in an attack or in a military operation preparatory to an attack. Recognizing, however, that there are situations in armed conflicts where, owing to the nature of the hostilities an armed combatant cannot so distinguish himself, he shall retain his status as a combatant, provided that, in such situations, he carries his arms openly:

(a) during each military engagement, and

(b) during such time as he is visible to the adversary while he is engaged in a military deployment preceding the launching of an attack in which he is to participate.

Acts which comply with the requirements of this paragraph shall not be considered as perfidious within the meaning of Article 37, paragraph 1(c).

Article 45—Protection of persons who have taken part in hostilities

* * *

2. If a person who has fallen into the power of the adverse Party is not held as a prisoner of war and is to be tried by that Party for an offense arising out of the hostilities, he shall have the right to assert his entitlement to prisoner-of-war status before a judicial tribunal and to have that question adjudicated. Whenever possible under the applicable procedure, this adjudication shall occur before the trial for the offence. The representative of the Protecting Power shall be entitled to attend the proceedings in which that question is adjudicated, unless, exceptionally, the proceedings are held *in camera* in the interest of State security. In such a case the detaining Power shall advise the Protecting Power accordingly.

* * *

Article 51—Protection of the civilian population

* * *

2. The civilian population, as such, as well as individual civilians, shall not be the object of attack. Acts or threats of violence the primary purpose of which is to spread terror among the civilian population are prohibited.

* * *

4. Indiscriminate attacks are prohibited. Indiscriminate attacks are:

(a) those which are not directed at a specific military objective;

(b) those which employ a method or means of combat which cannot be directed at a specific military objective; or

(c) those which employ a method or means of combat the effects of which cannot be limited as required by this Protocol;

And consequently, in each such case, are of a nature to strike military objectives and civilians or civilian objects without distinction.

5. Among others, the following types of attacks are to be considered as indiscriminate:

(a) an attack by bombardment by any method or means which treats as a single military objective a number of clearly separated and distinct military objectives located in a city, town, village or other area containing a similar concentration of civilians or civilian objects; and

(b) an attack which may be expected to cause incidental loss of civilian life, injury to civilians, damage to civilian objects, or a combination thereof, which would be excessive in relation to the concrete and direct military advantage anticipated.

6. Attacks against the civilian population or civilians by way of reprisals are prohibited.

* * *

Article 53 — Protection of cultural objects and places of worship

Without prejudice to the provisions of the Hague Convention for the Protection of Cultural Property in the Event of Armed Conflict of 14 May 1954, and of other relevant international instruments, it is prohibited:

(a) to commit any acts of hostility directed against the historic monuments, works of art or places of worship which constitute the cultural or spiritual heritage of peoples;

(b) to use such objects in support of the military effort;

(c) to make such objects the object of reprisals.

Article 54 — Protection of objects indispensable to the survival of the civilian population

1. Starvation of civilians as a method of warfare is prohibited.

* * *

4. These objects shall not be made the object of reprisal.

Article 55 — Protection of the natural environment

1. Care shall be taken in warfare to protect the natural environment against widespread, long-term and severe damage. This protection includes a prohibition of the use of methods or means of warfare which are intended to or may be expected to cause such damage to the natural environment and thereby to prejudice the health or survival of the population.

2. Attacks against the natural environment by way of reprisals are prohibited.

Article 56 — Protection of works and installations containing dangerous forces

1. Works or installations containing dangerous forces, namely, dams, dykes and nuclear electric generating stations, shall not be made the object of attack, even where these objects are military objectives, if such attack may cause the release of dangerous forces and consequent severe losses among the civilian population.

* * *

4. It is prohibited to make any of the works, installations or military objectives mentioned in paragraph 1 the objects of reprisals.

* * *

Article 75 — Fundamental Guarantees

1. In so far as they are affected by a situation referred to in Article 1 of this Protocol, persons who are in the power of a Party to the conflict and who do not benefit from more favourable treatment under the Conventions or under this Protocol shall be treated humanely in all circumstances and shall enjoy, as a minimum, the protection provided by this Article without any adverse distinction based upon race, colour, sex, language, religion or belief, political or other opinion, national or social origin, wealth, birth or other status, or any other similar criteria. Each Party shall respect the person, honour, convictions and religious practices of all such persons.

(a) violence to the life, health, or physical or mental well-being of persons, in particular:

(i) murder;

(ii) torture of all kinds, whether physical or mental;

(iii) corporal punishment; and

(iv) mutilation.

(b) outrages upon personal dignity, in particular humiliating and degrading treatment, enforced prostitution and any form of indecent assault;

* * *

3. Any person arrested, detained or interned for actions relating to the armed conflict shall be informed promptly, in a language he understands, of the reasons why these measures have been taken. Except in cases of arrest or detention for penal offences, such persons shall be released with the minimum delay possible and in any event as soon as the circumstances justifying the arrest, detention or internment have ceased to exist.

4. No sentence may be passed and no penalty executed on a person found guilty of a penal offence related to the armed conflict except pursuant to a conviction pronounced by an impartial and regularly constituted court respecting the generally recognized principles of regular judicial procedure which include the following:

(a) the procedure shall provide for an accused to be informed without delay of the particulars of the offence alleged against him and shall afford the accused before and during his trail all necessary rights and means of defence;

(b) no one shall be convicted of an offence except on the basis of individual penal responsibility.

(c) no one shall be accused or convicted of a criminal offence which did not constitute a criminal offence under the national or international law to which he was subject at the time when it was committed; nor shall a heavier penalty be imposed than that which was applicable at the time when the criminal offence was committed; if, after the commission of the offence, provision is made by law for the imposition of a lighter penalty, the offender shall benefit thereby;

(d) anyone charged with an offence is presumed innocent until proved guilty according to law;

(e) anyone charged with an offence shall have the right to be tried in his presence;

(f) no one shall be compelled to testify against himself or to confess guilt;

(g) anyone charged with an offence shall have the right to examine, or have examined, the witnesses against him and to obtain the attendance and examination of witnesses on his behalf under the same conditions as witnesses against him;

(h) no one shall be prosecuted or punished by the same Party for an offence in respect of which a final judgment acquitting or convicting that person has been previously pronounced under the same law and judicial procedure;

(i) anyone prosecuted for an offence shall have the right to have the judgement pronounced publicly;

(j) a convicted person shall be advised on conviction of his judicial and other remedies and of the time-limit within which they may be exercised.

* * *

6. Persons who are arrested, detained or interned for reasons related to the armed conflict shall enjoy the protection provided by this Article until their final release, repatriation or reestablishment, even after the end of the armed conflict.

* * *

8. No provisions of this Article may be construed as limiting or infringing any other more favourable provision granting greater protection, under any applicable rules of international law, to persons covered by paragraph 1.

Article 76 — Protection of Women

1. Women shall be the object of special respect and shall be protected in particular against rape, enforced prostitution and any other form of indecent assault.

* * *

Article 82 — Legal advisors in armed forces

The High Contracting Parties at all times, and the Parties to the conflict in time of armed conflict, shall ensure that legal advisors are available, when necessary, to advise military commanders on the appropriate level on the application of the Conventions and this Protocol and on the appropriate instruction to be given to the armed forces on this subject.

* * *

Article 85 — Repression of breaches of this Protocol

2. Acts described as grave breaches in the Conventions are grave breaches of this Protocol if committed against persons in the power of an adverse Party protected by Articles 44, 45 and 73 of this Protocol, or against the wounded, sick and shipwrecked of the adverse Party who are protected by this Protocol, or against those medical or religious personnel, medical units or medical transports which are under the control of the adverse Party and are protected by this Protocol.

3. In addition to the grave breaches defined in Article 11, the following acts shall be regarded as grave breaches of this Protocol, when committed willfully, in violation of the relevant provisions of this Protocol, and causing death or serious injury to body or health:

(a) making the civilian population or individual civilians the object of attack;

(b) launching an indiscriminate attack affecting the civilian population or civilian objects in the knowledge that such attack will cause excessive loss of live, injury to civilians or damage to civilian objects, as defined in Article 57, paragraph 2(a)(iii);

(c) launching an attack against works or installations containing dangerous forces in the knowledge that such attack will cause excessive loss of life, injury to civilians, or damage to civilian objects, as defined in Article 57, paragraph 2(a)(iii).

(d) making non-defended localities and demilitarized zones the object of attack;

(e) making a person the object of attack in the knowledge that he is *hors de combat;*

(f) the perfidious use, in violation of Article 37, of the distinctive emblem of the red cross, red crescent or red lion and sun or of other protective signs recognized by the Conventions or this Protocol.

4. In addition to the grave breaches defined in the preceding paragraphs and in the Conventions, the following shall be regarded as grave beaches of this Protocol, when committed willfully and in violation of the Conventions or the Protocol:

(a) the transfer by the Occupying Power of parts of its own civilian population into the territory it occupies, or the deportation or transfer of all or parts of the population of the occupied territory within or outside the territory, in violation of Article 49 of the Fourth Convention;

(b) unjustifiable delay in the repatriation of prisoners of war or civilians;

(c) practices of *apartheid* and other inhuman and degrading practices involving outrages upon personal dignity, based on racial discrimination;

(d) making the clearly recognized historic monuments, works of art or places of worship which constitute the cultural or spiritual heritage of peoples and to which special protection has been given by special arrangement, for example, within the framework of a competent international organization, the object of attack, causing as a result extensive destruction thereof, where there is no evidence of the violation by the adverse Party of Article 53, subparagraph (b), and when such historic monuments, works of art and places of worship are not located in the immediate proximity of military objectives;

(e) depriving a person protected by the Conventions or referred to in paragraph 2 of this Article of the rights of fair and regular trial.

5. Without prejudice to the application of the Conventions and of this Protocol, grave breaches of these instruments shall be regarded as war crimes.

* * *

Article 91 — Responsibility

A Party to the conflict which violates the provisions of the Conventions or of this Protocol shall, if the case demands, be liable to pay compensation. It shall be responsible for all acts committed by persons forming part of its armed forces.

Appendix L

[United Nations] Security Council Resolution Condemning Hostage Taking

U.N. Security Council Resolution 579 (1985)*

The Security Council,

Deeply disturbed at the prevalence of incidents of hostage-taking and abduction, several of which are of protracted duration and have included loss of life,

Considering that the taking of hostages and abductions are offences of grave concern to the international community, having severe adverse consequences for the rights of the victims and for the promotion of friendly relations and co-operation among States,...

1. *Condemns unequivocally* all acts of hostage-taking and abductions;

2. *Calls for* the immediate safe release of all hostages and abducted persons wherever and by whomever they are being held;

3. *Affirms* the obligation of all States in whose territory hostages or abducted persons are held urgently to take all appropriate measures to secure their safe release and to prevent the commission of acts of hostage-taking and abduction in the future;

4. *Appeals* to all States that have not yet done so to consider the possibility of becoming parties to [various Conventions listed]...;

5. *Urges* the further development of international co-operation among States in devising and adopting effective measures which are in accordance with the rules of international law to facilitate the prevention, prosecution and punishment of all acts of hostage-taking and abduction as manifestations of international terrorism.

Appendix M

United States Code: *The War Crimes Act of 1996*

18 U.S.C. §2401

(a) Offense.—Whoever, whether inside or outside the United States commits a grave breach of the Geneva Conventions, in any of the circumstances described in subsection (b), shall be fined under this title or imprisoned for life, or any term of years, or both, and if death results of the victim, shall also be subject to the penalty of death.

(b) Circumstances.—The circumstances referred to in subsection (a) are that the person committing such breach or the victim of such breach is a member of the Armed Forces of the United States or a national of the Untied States (as defined in section 101 of the Immigration and Nationality Act).

---

* As quoted in *International Criminal Law, Cases and Materials,* 2d ed. (Jordan J. Paust et. al. eds.). 962–963 (2000).

(c) Definition. — As used in this section, the term "grave breach of the Geneva Conventions" means the conduct defined as a grave breach in any of the international conventions relating to the laws of warfare signed at Geneva 12 August 1949 or any protocol to such convention, to which the United States is a party.

Appendix N

Tables of International Legal Regimes and War Incident Values*

III. Observations and Analysis

Table 2.
Hague Conventions: War Incidence Values
[1899–1919]

Hague Conventions Wars	Battle Deaths (Est.)
Russo-Japanese War	130,000
Central American War	1,000
Central American War II	1,000
Spanish-Morrocan War	10,000
Italo-Turkish War	20,000
First Balkan War	82,000
Second Balkan War	60,000
World War I	12,000,000
Hungarian Allies War	11,000
Russian Civil War	5,000
Greco-Turkish War	50,000
Total Battle Deaths	12,370,000

Table 3.
League of Nations: War Incidence Values
[1919–1945]

League of Nations Wars	Battle Deaths (Est.)
Manchurian War	60,000
Chaco War	130,000
Italo-Ethiopian War	20,000
Sino-Japanese War	1,000,000
Russo-Japanese War	19,000
Russo-Finnish War	90,000
World War II	15,000,000
Total Battle Deaths	16,319,000

---

* As quoted in William C. Bradford, "International Legal Regimes and the Incidence of Interstate War in the Twentieth Century: A Cursory Quantitative Assessment of the Associative Relationship," 16 *American University International Law Review* 647; 688; 696; 708 (2001).

Table 4.
United Nations: War Incidence Values
[1945–2000]

United Nations Wars	Battle Deaths (Est.)
Indonesian War	1,400
Palestine War	8,000
First Kashmir War	3,000
Korean War	2,000,000
Sino-Tibetan War	10,000
Tunisian Independence	10,000
Moroccan Independence	10,000
Guatemala War	1,000
Russo-Hungarian War	32,000
Sinai War	3,230
Nicaragua-Honduras War	1,000
Algerian Independence	15,000
Sino-Tibetan War	40,000
United States-Lebanon War	1,000
Belgium-Congo	2,000
India-Portugal (Goa)	2,000
Bay of Pigs [Cuba]	5,000
Sino-Indian War	1,000
Indonesian-Malaysia	10,000
United States-Dominican Republic	1,500
Second Kashmir War	6,800
Vietnam War	2,000,000
Mozambique-Portugal	20,000
Six Day War [Israel]	20,000
U.S.S.R.-Czechoslovakia	10,000
El Salvador-Honduras	4,000
Third Kashmir War	14,000
October War	35,000
Turkey-Cyrus	40,000
Indonesian-East Timor	200,000
Muritania-Morocco	20,000
Somalia-Ethiopia	50,000
Vietnam-Kampuchea	200,000
Uganda-Tanzania	40,000
China-Vietnam	50,000
Libya-Chad	10,000
U.S.S.R.-Afghanistan	1,000,000
Israel-Lebanon-Syria	20,000
Falklands War	4,500
United States-Granada	1,500
Armenia-Azerbaijan	40,000
United States-Libya	1,000
United States-Panama	4,000
Operation Desert Storm	200,000
Yugoslavia-Croatia	100,000

Yugoslavia-Bosnia	200,000
Rwandan Genocide	100,000
Peru-Ecuador	1,000
NATO-Yugoslavia (Kosovo)	30,000
Ethiopia-Eritrea	50,000
Total Battle Deaths	7,638,930

Glossary

A contrario: Opposite; Contrary; Oppossed.

A minor ad majorem: From minor to major.

Abwehr: The espionage, counter-espionage and sabotage division of the German High Command in WW II presided over during most of the conflict by Admiral Wilhelm Canaris.

Ad hoc: special; for the particular purpose.

Allegemeine-SS: name applied to the (General) SS which was strictly civilian; many ambassadorial, legal and cultural staff of the Nazi Party were members of the *Allegemeine-SS.*

Alsace-Lorraine: a French province bordering Germany that was in constant dispute between the two countries between the Franco-Prussian War of 1871 up until the end of WW II.

Amicus curiae: "friend of the court"; Latin term applied to an individual(s), group(s) or organizations who have an intense, but indirect, interest in certain litigation, other than those of the parties to the conflict; these entities or individuals may be allowed to file briefs "amicus curiae" in support of their particular position.

Anschluss: union; term denoting the annexation of Austria into the Third Reich in February, 1938; as a result of the *Anschluss,* Austria was incorporated as a province (Ostreich) of Nazi Germany.

**Ardennes*:* heavily forested, hilly and thinly populated region of southeastern Belgium, extending into Luxembourg and northeastern France; site of the Third Reich's last offensive operation in the West during the Battle of the Bulge, 1944–45.

Arguendo: for the sake of argument; during the course of argument.

ARVN: Army of the Republic of Vietnam (South Vietnam).

Assize: the early common law name applied to a court session or to a council.

Auschwitz: the largest Nazi concentration camp in WW II situated in southern Poland, southeast of Kotowice, where millions of Jews and other "undesirable elements" were murdered between 1941 and 1945; camp consisted of Auschwitz 1, the original installation, Auschwitz 2, at Birkenau, and Auschwitz 3, the industrial camp at Monowitz.

Auschwitz Trial (1963–1965): Trial by a West German Federal Court under the *Strafgesetzbuch* (German Penal Code), in Frankfurt, a/M that began in December, 1963, and lasted approximately six months. Twenty Auschwitz so-called "perpetrators" were put on trial for alleged atrocities committed between 1940 and 1945; trial concluded on August 8, 1965, in a 900-page judgment wherein all but three defendants were convicted of either murder or complicity in murder; six defendants received a punishment of life imprisonment while the remaining fourteen were either acquitted or received prison terms of between three and ten years; unlike the IMT-Nuremberg, the Auschwitz prosecution relied heavily on witness testimony in opposition to documentary evidence.

Babi Yar: A site near the Russian city of Kiev where some 35,000 Jews who were resident in that community were rounded up, marched to a ravine, and summarily executed on orders from Field Marshal Walther von Reichenau.

Balfour Declaration (1917): British Foreign Secretary, Lord Balfour, on November 2, 1917, expressed support on behalf of Great Britain for "a national home for the Jewish people" in Palestine.

Balkans: that area of southeastern Europe which generally includes the countries of Albania, Greece, Bulgaria, European Turkey, Yugoslavia and southeastern Romania.

Barbarossa: the military code name for the German invasion of the Soviet Union in WW II on June 22, 1941.

Beria, Lavrenti Paviovich (1899–1953): head of the Soviet NKVD, executed for treason, 1953.

Berlin Protocol (October 6, 1945): amended Article 6(c) of the IMT-Nuremberg "Charter" to define crimes against humanity as: "murder, extermination, enslavement, deportation and other inhumane acts committed against any civilian population, before or during the war, or persecution on political, racial or religious grounds in execution of or in connection with any crime within the jurisdiction of the Tribunal, whether or not in violation of the domestic law of the country where perpetrated."

Black Reichswehr: a secret organization established by General Hans von Seeckt under the name of *ArbeitsKommandos* (Labor Commandos); its mission was to provide secret reinforcements for the allotted 100,000-man *Reichswehr* of the Weimar Republic; dissolved in 1923.

Blitzkrieg: "lightning war'; a swift military offensive thrust employing armor spearheads with supporting airpower and mobile infantry, especially effective in the early years of WW II in German advances into France and the Soviet Union.

Brest-Litovsk, Treaty of (1918): Russo-German Peace Treaty of March 3, 1918, that freed Imperial Germany in WW I from a two-front war; Russian Bolsheviks were compelled to cede extensive territorial assets in the bargain, including their Baltic Provinces, Poland, White Russia (Belorus), Finland, Bessorabia, the Caucasus region and the Ukraine.

Brigand: bandit; an early term applied mostly to robbers who inhabited mountainous or forested regions of a country.

Buchenwald: a village located near Weimar in central Germany which was the site of a Nazi concentration camp from 1937 to 1945.

Burgomeister: mayor or local authority figure in a German community.

Bushido, Code of: Japanese warrior code that considered death in the service of the Emperor to be a combatant's highest honor; surrender was considered ignominious; this mindset in Japanese military culture was responsible, in part, for numerous war crimes committed against Allied POWs in Japanese custody where post-war statistics reflected that in the Pacific Theater in WW II, 27% of Allied POWs died in captivity, compared to 4% of POWs in the European theater.

Cairo Conference (1943): meeting between Roosevelt, Churchill and Chiang Kai-shek of China in December, 1943; this conference marked a change in the United States military strategy and sub-ordinated China to a supporting role only in the overall offensive against Japan.

Canaris, Wilhelm (1887–1945): German Admiral and Chief of the German secret service, the *Abwehr*, in WW II; implicated in the July 20, 1944, plot to assassinate

Adolf Hitler: Canaris was imprisoned in a concentration camp and was executed shortly before the end of WW II in Europe in 1945.

Casablanca Conference (1943): meeting in French Morocco between Roosevelt and Churchill and their military advisors in January, 1943, concerning the allocation of Anglo-American military assets in the Pacific war with Japan.

Central Powers: Imperial Germany, Austria-Hungary, Ottoman Turkey and Bulgaria, all foes of the Allied and Associated Powers in WW I.

***Certiorari,* writ of:** a discretionary writ issuing from a superior (or appellate) court calling up the record of a trial from a lower (of inferior) court in order to review claimed errors or irregularities made by the lower court; *certiorari* in United States practice is the principal procedural device for bringing a criminal case up for review by a higher tribunal.

Chamber d'accusation: the criminal division of a French Court of Appeal.

Chiang Kai-shek (1877–1975): Chinese Head of State, or a first-among-equals; leader of the Kuomintang (Nationalists) after 1925; Chinese Nationalists were defeated in civil war with the Communists and the Kuomintang was expelled from the mainland to the island of Formosa in 1949.

Churchill, Sir Winston (Leonard Spencer) (1874–1965): British Statesman, Prime Minister (1940–1945: 1951–1955): Nobel Prize for Literature, 1953.

Colloborator: to cooperate; assist another; as employed in World War II, the term signified one who works with an enemy of one's own country. Term gained currency apparently from a speech by Marshal Pétain of France made in December, 1940, shortly after he had met with Adolf Hitler at Montoire, France.

Commando Order, *Kommandobefehl* (1942): Adolf Hitler's "Top Secret Commando Order" was issued on October 17, 1942. It read, in part: "From now on all enemies on so-called commando missions in Europe or Africa challenged by German troops, even if they are in uniform, whether armed or unarmed, in battle or in flight, are to be slaughtered to the last man."

Commissar Order, *Kommissarbefehl* (1941): Issued to the *Wehrmacht* on June 8, 1941, by Field Marshal Walther von Brauchitsche, on direct orders from Adolf Hitler, through General Franz Halder of the German General Staff; it read, in part: "The war against Russia…will be such that it cannot be conducted in a knightly fashion…the commissars are the bearers of ideologies directly opposed to National Socialism. Therefore, the commissars will be liquidated. German soldiers guilty of breaking international law…will be excused. Russia has not participated in the Hague Convention and therefore has no rights under it."

Commission on the Responsibility of the Authors of War and on Enforcement of Penalties (1919): inter-governmental commission established at the Preliminary Peace Conference (Paris) to investigate and report on the responsibility of those who initiated WW I so that they could subsequently be prosecuted and punished.

Concert of Europe (1799–1899): considered by many to be the first international legal regime established to regulate, in very crude form, the employment of force at the international level; not a formal or highly structured international legal regime on the same order as either the League of Nations or the United Nations.

Contumacy: stubborn; disobedient; resistant to authority.

Corpus Juris Civilis: term applied to the entire body of ancient Roman law codified by the Emperor Justinian in the 6th century A. D.

Corregidor: a fortified island at the entrance to Manila Bay in the Philippines where United States and Philippine forces were defeated by the Japanese in May, 1942.

Customary International Law: article 38 of the Statute of the International Court of Justice recognizes that "customary" international law is a "general practice accepted as law" by some majority of States in the international community; the 1907 Hague Convention No. IV preamble stated that the "law of nations… [results] from the usages established among civilized peoples, from the laws of humanity, and from the dictates of the public conscience"; it is recognized that long-term "usage" coupled with patterns of *opinio juris* can eventually ripen into customary international law.

Cour d appel: Court of Appeals (France).

Cour d' assises: Court of Assizes (French criminal court).

Cour de cassation: another term for a French court of appeal.

Dachau: site of the first Nazi concentration camp in Germany; located some 10 miles northwest of Munich and opened in March, 1933; the United States Army turned Dachau into a military prison and put some 1,672 Germans on trial there for war crimes during the post-war "subsequent proceedings" period.

DAF: abbreviation for *Deutsche Arbeitsfront* (German Labor Front) organized by the NSDAP to replace various trade unions that flourished in Germany under the Weimar Republic.

Dayton Accords (1995): peace conference held at Dayton, Ohio, in November, 1995, to end the Balkan conflict in Bosnia; provided for a new Bosnian State, divided into two entities: the Croat-Bosniac Federation and the Republika Srpska; established a NATO Implementation Force (IFOR) to be employed in the region to enforce separation of opposing armies and keep the peace; IFOR was later transformed into a so-called Stabilization Force (SFOR).

Debellatio: subjugation; a term denoting a nation's complete defeat so that the victor nation(s) may alone decide the fate of the vanquished State's territory; classic example was the state of affairs in Nazi Germany at the conclusion of WW II in May, 1945, after the surrender of the Döenitz Government.

Declaration of St. Petersburg (1868): parties to this Declaration renounced the use of projectiles below a certain weight; this Declaration was a precursor to subsequent refinements in international agreements regarding weapons and the laws of war.

De facto: from the fact; by one's own authority; in point of fact; in international relations, a *de facto* government is considered illegitimate, but is one in actual effect and in control of a country.

De jure: by right; from the law.

De jure belli: the law of war.

De lege ferenda: from law to be passed.

Dictum: a statement by a court of an opinion thought to be authoritative because of the status of the jurist making it, but not the actual ruling of "holding" of the court on the issue in question.

Dolchstosslegend: The view, after WW I, that the German Army had not been defeated in the field, but had been "stabbed in the back" (*Dolchstoss*) by cowardly politicians and other civilians on the home front. Ultimately, the "*Dolchstosslegend*" found willing adherents not only in the military, but in the wider German population during the 1920s and 1930s.

Dolus specialis: a special wrong; special aggression or, in criminal law, a special form of criminal intent, often termed "fraud."

Dresden: a German city in Saxony, often in Pre-WW II years compared to Florence, Italy, and called by many "the Florence of the Elbe," because of its magnificent baroque architecture; attacked and largely destroyed on the evening of February

13–14, 1945, by 244 bombers of the R. A. F. which dropped high-explosive and incendiary ordnance on the city which unleashed firestorm winds reaching temperatures of more than 1,000-degrees Fahrenheit; air raid killed between 50,000 and 135,000 persons, mostly civilians; death toll probably exceeded those of the atomic attacks on Hiroshima and Nagasaki later that same year in Japan.

Drumhead courts-martial: a form of courts-martial without traditional procedural protections; held for summary trial of those charged with the commission of certain offenses during periods of military operations; most defendants involved in a Drumhead Courts-Martial face almost certain execution.

Eifel Offensive: the German designation for the Battle of Bulge in Belgium, winter, 1944–45.

Einsatzgruppen: battalion-size special mobile units of the SIPO and members of the SD that conducted terroristic activities behind and alongside regular German army units; charged with rounding up Jews, "Asiatic inferiors," communists, gypsies, homosexuals and others who were considered unfit in the world-view of the Third Reich and either executed on the spot or herded into concentration camps; all four *Einsatzgruppen* were under the overall control of the RSHA.

Enabling Act (1933): legislation passed by the Nazi-dominated Reichstag on March 24, 1933, which accorded newly-elected Chancellor Adolf Hitler absolute power to change the statutory and constitutional law of Germany; in effect, the *Enabling Act* abolished the Weimar Republic.

Endlösung: "Final Solution": the Nazi euphemism for the extermination of the European Jews.

Entente cordiale: a friendly understanding, generally between two governments.

Ex parte: upon or from one side only.

Ex post facto: after the fact.

Fait accompli: something already accomplished, done or decided.

Fascist: in WW II, a person belonging to the party of Benito Mussolini, who supported Fascism in Italy between 1923 and 1943; Fascist movement was a political ideology that supported dictatorial government, right-wing social and political programs and an extreme form of nationalism.

Freikorps: free corps; consisted of volunteers who were idealistic activists from the armed forces whose main mission was to defend Germany during the years immediately following WW I from Bolshevism and other subversive elements; some historians maintain that Germany would have succumbed to communism had it not been for the presence of the *Freikorps.*

Führerprinzip: leader or leadership principle; a Nazi article of faith that held that only the highest *führer* (or leader) is responsible to the German nation; the *führer* delegates power (*führergewalt*) to subordinates who, in turn, delegate to lower subordinates.

Gauleiter: a Nazi Party district leader; during WW II, *Gauleiters* were responsible for civil defense and local Party administration, among other things; Germany was divided into some 34 districts, or *Gaue,* which were presided over by a *Gauleiter* appointed by Hitler.

Generalgouvernement: name applied to German-occupied Poland in WW II under the initial administration of the German civilian, Hans Frank.

Geneva Accords (1954): after the French defeat in Vietnam at Dien Bien Phu on July 21, 1954, an agreement was reached for a cessation of hostilities between the commanders of the French Union Forces in Indochina and the People's Army of Vietnam;

political structure of the country was to be decided by secret ballot scheduled for July, 1956, under the supervision of an international commission; the Accords established a demarcation line between North and South Vietnam at the 17th parallel.

Geneva Conventions (1949): on August 12, 1949, the Geneva delegates signed four Conventions: (i) Convention for the Amelioration of the Conditions of the Wounded and Sick in Armed Forces in the Field; (ii) Convention for the Amelioration of the Condition of the Wounded, Sick and Shipwrecked Members of the Armed Forces at Sea; (iii) Convention Relative to Treatment of Prisoners of War; and (iv) Convention Relative to the Protection of Civilian Persons in Time of War; these were major international agreements by mid-century that laid the foundation for additional treaties and protocols regulating armed conflict.

GHQ: the abbreviation for "General Headquarters" of the Supreme Allied Commander for the Far East, General Douglas MacArthur, in Tokyo, Japan.

Götterdammerung: from Richard Wagner's *Die Götterdammerung* (The Twilight of the Gods); in German mythology and in Wagner's tragic music of the death of the gods, the final days of Hitler's Third Reich are played out in the awesome grandeur of *Die Götterdammerung;* there were credible reports that in the closing days of the Battle of Berlin, as the Red Army was tightening its grip on the city, the final performance played by the Berlin Philharmonic Orchestra in the blacked-out Beethoven Hall was Wagner's *Die Götterdammerung.*

Grave breaches: the term "grave breaches" as used in the language of the 1949 Geneva Conventions include such acts as the willful killing, torture, inhumane treatment and other specified delicts committed against persons protected under the provisions of those Conventions; the list of "grave breaches" from the 1949 Conventions is reproduced in Article 2 of the **ICTY Statute.**

Grotius, Hugo (1583–1645): Dutch jurist and statesman; considered by many to be the Founding Father of international law.

Habeas Corpus, Writ of: "that you have the body"; a common law writ of ancient lineage whose purpose it is to bring an incarcerated individual before a court to have that court determine the legality or illegality of the prisoner's detention.

Hadamar: A German state sanitorium located in the town of Hadamar, Germany, specializing in the treatment of the mentally ill; between 1941 and 1944, some 10,000 German citizens who were allegedly mentally ill were admitted to Hadamar and put to death; between June 1944 and March 1945, some 400-plus Polish and Russian men, women and children were sent to Hadamar and executed by the Nazis ostensibly because they were infected with tuberculosis.

Heer: the Germany Army.

Heligoland: a German island in the North Sea.

HIL: an acronym for Hegemonic International Law.

Hitlerjügend: Hitler Youth: a NSDAP youth organization for boys in WW II under the leadership of Baldur von Schirach.

Hokaido, Honshu, Kyushu and Shikoku: the four main islands comprising the landmass of Japan.

Holocaust: from the Greek *holo* ("whole') and caustos ("burned"); refers to any widespread human catastrophe; when written with a capital "H" the term refers to the annihilation of nearly six million European Jews by Nazi Germany during WW II.

Hors de combat: out of condition to fight.

Hostis humani generis: an enemy of all mankind.

in camera: in private; a hearing held by a judge, generally in chambers outside the presence of jury and/or the public.

ICC: International Criminal Court; an international criminal tribunal created by treaty in 1998 to serve as a permanent court for the prosecution of selected international crimes.

IFOR: acronym for Implementation Force (NATO) created to keep the peace in Bosnia as a result of the Dayton Accords.

in absentia: in the absence of someone; a Continental European practice of trying an individual for a crime even though that person is not present in court.

In flagrante delicto: in the very act of committing a criminal offense.

In limine: at the threshold; at the outset; a motion presented to a judge, normally before the commencement of a trial.

In situ: on site.

Inter alia: among other things.

Inter arma silent leges: during war the law is silent.

Jackson, Robert H. (1892–1954): Associate Justice of the United States Supreme Court and Chief of Counsel for the United States, IMT-Nuremberg, 1945–1946.

Judge Advocate: an officer and lawyer in the United States military charged with the administration of military justice, either as legal counsel in trial proceedings or conducting appellate proceedings, as the situation dictates.

Judg d' instruction: in French criminal procedure, felony cases are first sent to an investigating magistrate (*juge d' instruction*) who assembles a *dossier* and reviews all of the evidence, then recommends whether or not the evidence is sufficient to support an indictment and subsequent trial.

Jus cogens: in international law, a preemptory norm which supercedes all other treaty rights and obligations, including the U. N. Charter; the international prohibition against genocide is an example of customary *jus cogens*, as well as proscriptions against slavery, torture, piracy and extra-judicial capital punishment.

Jus gentium: the law of nations.

Jus ad bellum: just war; under the U. N. Charter, *jus ad bellum* is no longer considered an acceptable international benchmark for determining when armed force is lawful; the U. N. Charter mandates, instead, that the legitimate use of force hinges on the self-defense provisions of Article 51 of the Charter.

Jus in bello: "just conduct" in warfare, or, in other words, abiding by the laws of war under such general concepts as proportionality, military necessity and the prevention of unnecessary suffering.

Jus talionis: law of retaliation; punishment should be meted out in kind, that is, be the same type as the original harm administered.

K. B.: English abbreviation for King's Bench in British legal citations.

Kameradenschinder trials: name designating a series of trials held by West German civil courts during the twelve-year period, 1948–1960, of Germans who were former POWs in Soviet prison camps who, while there, aided and abetted their Soviet captors by collaborating with the Russians against other German POWs that placed some of their fellow comrades in peril of further punitive treatment by Soviet authorities.

Kamikazi: "divine wind"; term derived from a legendary Japanese victory over the Mongols in the 13th century; a typhoon (or Kamikazi) wind destroyed the Mongol fleet that was threatening the Japanese home islands. Japanese *Kamikazi* units in WW II were established in 1944 after the Battle of the Philippine Sea; the Battle of Leyte Gulf saw the introduction of the first *Kamikazi* attacks against the U.S. Navy.

Kapp *Putsch* **(1920):** an abortive military revolt occurring in Berlin in March, 1920, led by General Walther von Lüttwitz, commander of the Berlin Military District, Captain Hermann Erhardt, commander of the Second Marine Brigade and a Prussian civil servant by the name of Wolfgang Kapp; aim of the *Putsch* was to overthrow the Weimar Government because their officials had decided to reduce the size of the German Army to 100,000 men in line with the provisions of the Treaty of Versailles.

Katyn Forest: a forest located near Smolensk, USSR, where, in February, 1943, a mass grave containing some 14,000 Polish officers, cadets and enlisted personnel were found; Nazi Minister of Propaganda, Josef Goebbels, announced on April 13, 1943, that Polish officers had been murdered by the Russians; Russians retorted on April 15, 1943, alleging that Polish POWs were executed by "German Fascist hangmen," however, it was later firmly established that the Soviet NKVD, on orders from Josef Stalin, were the actual perpetrators; Soviet culpability for the Katyn Forest Massacre was conveniently overlooked during the IMT-Nuremberg proceedings in order to maintain Allied unity.

Kellogg-Briand Pact (Pact of Paris, 1928): known officially as "The General Treaty for the Renunciation of War as an Instrument of National Policy"; signed August 27, 1928; this document condemned recourse to armed conflict for the solution of international disputes and was cited by both the IMT-Nuremberg and the IMTFE-Tokyo as the basis for certain charges leveled against Axis defendants from both nations.

Kelsen, Hans (1881–1973): Austrian international law and jurisprudence scholar; taught law at the universities of Vienna, Cologne, Prague, at the Graduate Institute of International Studies, Geneva, at the Harvard Law School and political science at the University of California.

Kesselring, Albert (1883–1960): Chief of Staff of the *Luftwaffe* (1936); Commander of 1st Air Fleet, Polish Campaign (1936); Commander of 2nd Air Fleet, invasion of the USSR (1941); Commander-in-Chief, West (1945); tried for war crimes by the British in 1947; sentenced to death, but sentence later commuted to life imprisonment; released from captivity in 1952.

Khrushchev, Nikita Sergeyevich (1894–1971): Soviet Premier, 1958–1964 and First Secretary of the Soviet Communist Party.

Kristallnacht: "Night of Broken Glass"; occurred on November 10, 1938, following the assassination of a Nazi diplomat in Paris by young Jew; as a result, German synangogues were set ablaze, thousands of Jews were arrested and Jewish-owned shops and businesses throughout Germany were destroyed, their storefront glass broken and their contents looted; *Kristallnacht* sent a clear signal to the German Jewish community that Jews were no longer welcome in the Third Reich.

Kurile Islands: a small group of islands off the northeastern coast of Japan, extending from northern Japan to the southern tip of Kamchatka Peninsula; the Kurile Islands provided the staging area for the Imperial Japanese Combined Fleet before it set sail for the attack on Pearl Harbor; Japan renounced sovereignty over the Kuriles after WW II.

Kwantung Army: name given to the Japanese Field Army during the Manchurian campaign in the 1930s.

Lausanne, Treaty of (1923): the Lausanne Treaty of July 24, 1923, replaced the Treaty of Sevres of August 10, 1920; it restored peace with Turkey, one of the members of the Central Powers in WWI; the Treaty of Lausanne made no mention of war crimes or war crime trials on the part of the Turkish Government and failed to include Turkish recognition for an independent state of Armenia.

Lauterpacht, Sir Hersh (1897–1960): former judge, International Court of Justice and British international law scholar who played a major role in preparing Justice Robert H. Jackson for his assignment as Chief of Counsel for the United States at the IMT-Nuremberg.

Lebensborn: "Life Springs"—an SS organization founded in 1935 that provided safe homes for both married and unmarried women who had children by SS personnel; in reality, the *Lebensborn* project was an SS mating organization disguised as maternity homes.

Lebensraum: Living space or living room; term employed by the Nazi regime to justify conquests of additional territory for the Third Reich, primarily in Eastern Europe and European Russia.

Lenin, Vladimir Ilyich (1870–1924): Leader of the 1917 Russian Revolution and Soviet Premier (1918–1924).

Letters Rogatory: a multi-stage legal procedure by which a foreign tribunal seeks assistance from another foreign court in obtaining evidence, witness testimony or documents; in the United States, the Department of State acts as a diplomatic intermediary and forwards Letters Rogatory to the United States Department of Justice, which then reviews the request and forwards it to the appropriate United States court; under 28 U.S.C. §1782, a United States District Court "may" order testimony or documentary production to be transmitted to a foreign tribunal, but it is not required to do so.

Lidice: a village in Western Czechoslovakia in what is now the Czech Republic; Lidice was the site of a 1943 massacre by Germans in reprisal for the assassination of SS-General Reinhard Heydrich by the Czech resistance; a reign of terror quickly descended on Bohemia and Moravia where more than 1,300 Czechs were executed; all male inhabitants of Lidice were slaughtered on a trumped-up charge that the village had harbored Heydrich's assassins; Lidice was completely obliterated and plowed under at the specific direction of Adolf Hitler.

Lieber Code (1863): a set of rules established by the United States in an attempt to codify the laws of war for Union forces during the American Civil War; written by professor Francis Lieber of Columbia College and revised by a board of Army officers and issued by the War Department under the title "Instructions for the Government of Armies of the United States in the Field 1863," and originally published as "General Orders No. 100, War Department, Adjutant General's Office, April 24, 1863."

Liebstandarte—SS Adolf Hitler **(1933):** SS-Bodyguard Regiment Adolf Hitler; established September, 1933, nine months after Hitler became Chancellor of Germany; the *Liebstandarte* was the first and arguably the most famous *Waffen-SS* unit to be established in the Third Reich and was garrisoned at Lichterfelde Barracks in Berlin.

London Agreement (1945): Great Britain, France, the Soviet Union and the United States signed the so-called "London Agreement" on August 8, 1945, establishing an international military tribunal for the trial and punishment of the major German Axis war criminals; out of this agreement came the *Charter* which was the legal foundation for the establishment of the IMT-Nuremberg.

Lytton Commission (1932): commission appointed by the League of Nations at the urgent request of China and under the direction of Lord Lytton of Great Britain, to investigate Japanese hostilities in Manchuria, which, by 1932, was spilling over into China; the Lytton Commission Report was severely critical of Japanese intervention in Manchuria in violation of the Covenant of the League of Nations; Commission Report called upon the Japanese Government to voluntarily withdraw its armed forces from all areas occupied in Manchuria; Japanese denounced the findings of the Lytton Commission, and, in 1933, Japan withdrew from the League of Nations.

M. R.: English legal abbreviation for Master of the Rolls.

MacArthur, Douglas A. (1880–1964): General of the Army; Supreme Allied Commander in the Pacific Theater in WW II; Japanese Occupation Commander after Japan's surrender in September, 1945; often mercurial and controversial; dismissed from command of U. N. Forces in the Korean War by President Harry S. Truman for his apparent insubordination and his desire to cross the Yalu River and take the war to Communist China.

Manchukuo: name of the puppet state created by the Japanese after their conquest of Manchuria; League of Nations demanded that Japan quit Manchuria and gave no international recognition to such an entity, refusing to deal with the Japanese-installed Head-of-State.

Mandamus, writ of: "we command"; a writ issued by a superior court to compel an inferior court or governmental official to perform mandatory or purely ministerial duties on pain of contempt.

Mandate System (League of Nations): a system designed by the League of Nations to remove territories from colonial domination and provide appropriate mechanisms for them to attain peaceful independence; the League Mandates, however, were quite limited and one-sided; they applied only to two of the nations defeated in WW I—Germany and Turkey; Great Britain, France and the United States, all colonial powers, were exempt.

Martens Clause (IV Hague Convention 1907): clause states that "[p]ending the preparation of a more complete code of the laws of war, the high contracting parties deem it opportune to state that, in the cases not provided for in the rules adopted by them, the inhabitants and the belligerents shall remain under the protection of and subject to the principles of the law of nations, as established by the usages prevailing among civilized nations, by the laws of humanity, and by the public conscience;" clause was drafted by Fedor Fedorovitch Martens, a Russian representative to the 1907 Hague Conference and an expert on international law; the Martens Clause in the preamble to the Convention laid the groundwork for the later concept of "crimes against humanity."

Martial law: law that is imposed by State or subordinate military forces to keep order where the civil authority has either broken down or is non-existent.

Mengele, Josef (1911–1979): SS-physician who joined the Waffen-SS in 1940; appointed later by Heinrich Himmler as chief medical officer at Auschwitz where he conducted gruesome and inhumane experiments on human subjects, earning the sobriquet "Angel of Death"; escaped to Argentina after WW II and apparently died of a heart attack in Sao Paulo, Brazil in 1979.

Mens rea: "guilty mind"; in criminal law, one of the two essential elements of every serious crime, the other being the *actus reus* or "guilty act."

Model, Walther (1891–1945): German Field Marshal, Panzer Division and corps commander (1940–1941); Commander of 9th Army, Eastern Front (1942–1944); Commander-in-Chief, West, and then Army Group B (1944–1945); committed suicide in the Ruhr Pocket in 1945.

Molotov, Vyacheslav Mikhailovich (1890–1986): Soviet Foreign Minister, Commissar of Foreign Affairs (1939–1949) and (1953–1956); co-signer (along with von Ribbentrop) on behalf of the USSR of the German-Russian Non-Aggression Pact of August, 1939, in which both powers secretly pledged to divide Poland into their own spheres of influence shortly before the outbreak of WW II on September 1, 1939.

Moscow Proclamation (1943): proclamation issued at a conference of Foreign Ministers of the United Kingdom, the Soviet Union and the Secretary of State of the United States, in Moscow, October 30, 1943; proclamation referred to the "punishment" for the major Nazi Axis war criminals whose offenses had no particular geographic location, and promised that the Allied Powers would seek "swift and sure justice."

Munich Settlement (1938): an agreement reached between German Chancellor Adolf Hitler and British Prime Minister Neville Chamberlain on September 27, 1938; Great Britain, with the apparent acquiescence of France, gave in to Hitler's demands that Czechoslovakia grant Nazi Germany, without a plebiscite, most of the German demands made on that nation, including its important defense and industrial areas, otherwise Hitler threatened to take Czechoslovakia by military force; Britain and France thus failed to uphold the territorial integrity of Czechoslovakia as they were duty-bound to do under the terms and conditions of the Covenant of the League of Nations; the Munich Settlement became a key symbol in the ongoing pre-war appeasement by Britain and France that, in part, led to the initiation of WW II in Europe in 1939.

NATO: North Atlantic Treaty Organization (1949); established at Washington, DC and headquartered in Brussels, Belgium, the original alliance consisted of twelve nations of the Atlantic Pact, together with Greece, Turkey and the Federal Republic of Germany (West Germany) as a collective defense force to resist Soviet and Soviet-bloc designs on Western and Southeastern Europe; in recent years NATO has expanded its membership by inclusion of some Eastern European nations after the collapse of the USSR.

Nero Decree (1945): issued by Adolf Hitler on both March 19 and March 30, 1945, the "Nero Decree" ordered the destruction of "all military, transportation, communications, industrial and supply facilities, as well as all resources within the Reich that the enemy might use immediately or in the foreseeable future for continuing the war"; Armaments Minister Albert Speer used his influence to prevent the decree from being executed.

NGO: an abbreviation for non-governmental organizations.

Night and Fog Decree (1941): this decree (*Nacht und Nebel Erlass*) was issued by Adolf Hitler on December 7, 1941; purpose was to authorize the seizure of all persons who posed a security threat to the Third Reich who were not immediately slated for execution and to have them simply vanish without a trace into the "night and fog"; families of the victims were never given any official information as to their whereabouts, nor even the location of their gravesites, if they had been executed.

Night of the Long Knives (the Röhm Purge, 1934): name given to the plot by the SS and Hitler to eliminate Ernst Röhm, the SA Chief of Staff; when confronted with his fate, Röhm refused to commit suicide and was shot point-blank by two SS men on July 1, 1934, in the company of *Brigadeführer* Theodor Eicke in a cell at Stadelheim Prison; many other high-ranking SA officials were also murdered in Bavaria, Berlin and elsewhere in Germany because Hitler was convinced that Röhm and the SA were plotting to overthrow the Nazi Party and the German Army.

NKVD: Peoples' Commissariat of Internal Affairs (USSR): secret State Police of the Soviet Union (1935–1943).

Non-bis-in-idem: a term found in many statutes regulating procedures in trials conducted by international criminal tribunals giving the accused protection against double jeopardy, that is, multiple prosecutions for the same offense.

NSDAP: the abbreviation for *Nationalsozialistissche deutsche Arbeiter Partei* (National Socialist German Workers' Party) or "Nazi" for short.

Nuremberg Laws (1935): a series of three statutes passed in September and October, 1935, which redefined German citizenship, outlawed "racial pollution" and required all German couples contemplating marriage to undergo a medical examination and counseling; the law of mixed marriages, entitled *Laws for the Protection of German Blood and German Honor (Gesetz zum Schutze des deutschen Blutes und der deutschen Ehre)* forbade marriage and sexual relations between Germans and Jews; the *Reich Citizenship Law (Reichsburgergesetz)* established a legal distinction between "citizens" and "subjects" with Jews being classified as "subjects"; the third racial law was captioned *Law for the Protection of the Genetic Health of the German People (Gesetz zum Schutze der Erbgesundheit)* and mandated that German couples receive a "Certificate of Fitness to Marry" from public health officials before a marriage license could be issued.

Obersalzberg: a mountain in the Bavarian Alps northeast of Berchtesgaden where Adolf Hitler had his private villa, the *Berghof.*

Obiter dicta: a comment in a legal opinion said "by the way" or "in passing."

OHKA bomb: a Japanese suicide weapon of little notoriety carried on the underside of a twin-engine aircraft; with stubby wings and a small cockpit, released near a target and delivered to its destination on a one-way mission by an on-board pilot; Americans dubbed it the "foolish bomb."

OKH: abbreviation for *Oberkommando des Heeres* (High Command of the Army).

OKL: abbreviation for *Oberkommando der Luftwaffe* (High Command of the Air Force).

OKM: abbreviation for *Oberkommando der Kriegsmarine* (High Command of the Navy).

OKW: abbreviation for *Oberkommando der Wehrmacht* (High Command of the Armed Forces) replaced the former Reich War Ministry in 1938.

ORPO: abbreviation for *Ordnungspolizei* (Order Police) who dealt with routine law enforcement in urban and rural areas, but was also involved in mass executions in Poland and the USSR, functioning alongside the *Einsatzgruppen.*

Passive Personality: in international law, a form of jurisdiction assumed by a court located in the victim's State of nationality; criticized by some international law scholars, the passive personality principle was invoked by the State of Israel to try Adolf Eichmann for crimes against humanity during the Holocaust in WW II.

Peace of Westphalia (1648): treaty ending the Thirty-Years War in Europe, signed in Westphalia, now a part of North Rhine-Westphalia in northwestern Germany; considered by some to be the nascent foundation for subsequent development of international law.

Per curiam: by the court (as a whole) instead of an opinion by one or more judges individually.

Plenipotentiary: a person vested with full state power to act with complete authority for the State that individual represents; such person or persons could be an ambassador, an envoy, or State delegate given full authorization to act on behalf of a government or a sovereign.

Potsdam Conference (1945): from this conference held in Potsdam, Germany, a declaration emerged called the "Potsdam Declaration" issued on July 26, 1945, by the governments of the United States, the United Kingdom, China (and later the Soviet

Union) announcing their collective intention to prosecute high-level Japanese for war crimes; during the Potsdam Conference, President Harry S. Truman received a coded message "Babies satisfactorily born" indicating the successful testing of the world's first atomic bomb at Alamorgordo, New Mexico, on July 16, 1945.

Presidium: An administrative committee of the Soviet Government.

Prima facie: at first view; plain, clear; self-evident.

Prohibition, writ of: an extraordinary judicial remedy issued by an appellate court to prevent a lower court from exceeding its jurisdiction or to prevent a non-judicial officer or public entity from exercising a certain power.

Putsch: the German equivalent of a *coup d'etat;* a sudden revolt or uprising in an attempt to change a government illegally, usually by force and violence.

Q. B.: an English legal abbreviation for Queen's Bench.

Qui facit per alium, facit per se: he who acts for another, acts himself.

Ratio decidendi: the reason for deciding; the actual "rule" of law upon which a court's opinion is premised.

Ratio materia: by reason of the matter involved.

Ratione personae: by reason of the person concerned.

Realpolitik: politics and political decisions based upon a pragmatic view of the situation rather than on some ethical, moral or theoretical construct.

Reichsführer: the highest rank in the SS; held during WW II by Heinrich Himmler.

Reichsleiter: the name given the highest ranking Nazi Party official or officials appointed directly by Hitler.

Reichstag: the German Parliament.

Reichswehr: name of the German armed forces during the years of the Weimar Republic (1919–1933); in 1935, the *Reichswehr* became the *Wehrmacht.*

Reprisal: a swift, but limited, military action taken by one State in direct response to a prior action taken by another State (or by partisan organizations) that does not rise to the level of an armed attack; reprisals are punitive in nature and do not have the same legal effect in international law as acts committed in self-defense.

Res adjudicata: a thing or matter adjudged on its merits by a court of competent jurisdiction; the same matter cannot be relitigated by the same parties.

RFP (Rwanda): Rwandan Patriotic Front.

Röhm, Ernst (1887–1934): SA Chief of Staff and an early and ardent supporter of Adolf Hitler and the Nazi Party; called back to Germany from Bolivia in 1930, Röhm took charge of the SA (*Sturmabteilung* or Storm Detachment) and built it into a mass army of brownshirted "Storm Troopers" who assisted the Nazi Party in security and political demonstrations during the early 1930s; executed by the SS on July 1, 1934, in a Nazi purge called "Night of the Long Knives."

Rome Conference (1998): officially termed the "United Nations Diplomatic Conference of Plenipotentaries on the Establishment of an International Criminal Court," the Rome Conference began its work on June 15, 1998, to enact a statute for a permanent International Criminal Court; as finalized, the Rome Statute, so-called, consists of thirteen parts with substantive law definitions for war crimes, crimes against humanity and genocide; the crime of aggressive war, however, remains undefined as of mid-2005; the ICC is a treaty-based tribunal, not an ad hoc court and the Statute has its own text of governing law, thereby avoiding the pitfalls of *ex post facto* and *nulla crimen sine lege* arguments that bedeviled previous international criminal tribunals.

Rommel, Erwin (1891–1944): German Field Marshal, commanded Hitler's bodyguard during Polish Campaign (1940); Commander of *Deutsches Afrika Korps* (1941):

Panzergruppe Afrika and *Panzerarmee Afrika* and Army Group Africa (1942–1943); Commander, Army Group B, Northern Italy and France (1944); wounded by air attack, 1944; implicated in the plot to assassinate Adolf Hitler at the *Wolfsshanze*, July, 1944; given choice of being tried for treason or taking his own life and having a State Funeral with full military honors, he chose the latter and committed suicide, October 14, 1944.

RSHA: Reich Main Security Office (*Reichssicherheitshauptamt*) established September 27, 1939, originally headed by SS-General Reinhard Heydrich; top security agency of the SS.

RTLM (Rwanda): Radio Television Libre des Mille Collines; a media outlet in Rwanda often employed for propaganda purposes to incite inter-tribal hatred and violence between the Hutus and the Tutsis.

Russo-Finnish War (1939–1940): Finland attacked by the Soviet Union on November 30, 1939; after heavy fighting in several sectors, an armistice between the two nations took effect on March 13, 1940; for its aggression against Finland, the USSR was expelled from the League of Nations and the Germans viewed the sometimes halting Soviet assault on Finland as evidence that the USSR was relatively weak and unable to defend itself.

Ruthenia: a province incorporated into Czechoslovakia in 1919; annexed by Hungary in 1939; annexed by the USSR in 1944 and in 1991 became the most westerly part of the independent Ukraine.

Scapa Flow: The large British Naval Base located in the Orkney Islands off the northern coast of Scotland where the WW I German High Seas Fleet was anchored as a result of armistice negotiations preceding the signing of the Treaty of Versailles: German Admiral von Reuter ordered the fleet to be scuttled in the harbor at Scapa Flow on June 21, 1919: Fifty German vessels were sunk or capsized; eighteen destroyers, three cruisers and one battleship was saved.

Schlieffen Plan (1905): a military blueprint developed by Alfred von Schlieffen for a German attack on France through Belgium and Holland into northern France, bypassing the heavily fortified French frontier facing Germany.

Schmachparagraphen: "shame paragraphs:" the name the Germans gave to several clauses in the Treaty of Versailles including the articles requiring Germany to surrender the Kaiser for trial as a war criminal: the "war guilt clause" and a list of both generals and admirals, yet unnamed whom the allies wanted for trial as war criminals.

Sevres, Treaty of (1920): original peace treaty between the Allied and Associated Powers with Turkey after WWI which recognized the war crimes committed by Turkey during that conflict and also recognized the right of the Allies to try Turkish accused before military tribunals; treaty ultimately rejected by Turkey; replaced in1923 by the Treaty of Lausanne which omitted any reference to Turkish war crimes or war crimes trials.

SFRY: Socialist Federal Republic of Yugoslavia.

SIPO: Acronym for Security Police (*Sicherheitspolizei*); this force was composed of members of the Gestapo, the Criminal Police and the Border Police.

SS: abbreviation for *Schutzstaffel* (Protective Squads); formed in 1923 as a small group of personal bodyguards for Adolf Hitler; subsequently developed into a Nazi Party police force, an institution overseeing a huge conglomerate of concentration camps and a regular army (*Waffen-SS*) within, but separate from, the regular German Army; *Waffen-SS* units were noted for their fierce loyalty to Nazi ideology and their unrelenting and unforgiving tactics of warriorhood, many of which were flagrant violations of the laws and customs of war.

Stalin, Josif Vissarionovich (1879–1953): General Secretary of the Communist Party of the U.S.S.R. (1922–1953): Premier of the U.S.S.R (1941–1953).

St. James Declaration (1942): this document emerged from a meeting of representatives of nine nations under German occupation on January 13, 1942, in St. James Palace, London; text of the Declaration read, in part, that the signatories "place among their principal war aims the punishment, through the channel of organized justice, of those guilty of and responsible for these crimes whether they have ordered them, perpetuated them or in any way participated in them"; also out of this conference came the establishment of the United Nations War Crimes Commission (UNWCC).

Stare decisis: to stand by things decided; Latin term describing the common law doctrine of precedent in which a court is to follow previous judicial decisions involving the same points of law.

STAVKA: name of the Soviet Supreme Military Command in WW II.

Subsequent Proceedings: term applied to occupation court trials in Germany between 1946 and 1949; twelve of these trials were held in the Palace of Justice at Nuremberg after the IMT-Nuremberg had concluded its work; altogether, 195 defendants were charged with various violations of international criminal law in the following cases tried by the United States: (i) the *Krupp Case*; (ii) the *Ministries Case*; (iii) the *Hostages Case*; (iv) the *Justice Case*; (v) the *High Command Case*; (vi) the *Medical Case*; (vii) the *RuSHA Case*; (viii) the *Milch Case*; (ix) the *Flick Case*; (x) the *Pohl Case*; (xi) the *Einsatzgruppen Case*; and (xii) the *I. G. Farben Case.*

Sudentenland: a mountainous region located in central Czechoslovakia comprising approximately one-quarter of the country, inhabited by some 3 million German-speaking inhabitants; as a result of the Munich Settlement of 1938 between Chamberlain and Hitler, the German Army marched into the Sudentenland unopposed on September 30, 1938, annexing the region to the Third Reich.

Sui generis: of its own kind; unique; peculiar.

Supreme Soviet: The legislature of the U.S.S.R., consisting of an upper and lower house.

Tanaka Memorial (1927): in July, 1927, a conference was held in Mukden attended by then Japanese Prime Minister Baron Tanaka and civil and military officials of Manchuria; the 11-day conference was ostensibly held to review and determine Japanese policies in the Far East; shortly after the conference, the Chinese published what they claimed to be the so-called "Tanaka Memorial" the contents of which laid out a blueprint for Japanese control of Manchuria, Mongolia and China through a combination of economic and military means.

Tojo, Hideki (1884–1948): Japanese General; Chief of Staff, Kwantung Army; War Minister and Minister of Munitions; succeeded Prince Fumimaro Konoye as Prime Minister (1941–1944); Tojo Government collapsed after the Allied invasion of the Marianas in July, 1944; replaced by a cabinet headed by General Koiso Kiniaki and Admiral Yonai Mitsumasa.

Toyoda, Soema, Fleet Admiral (1885–1957): Last commander of the Imperial Japanese Combined Fleet; under Toyoda's command, the Japanese Navy suffered terminal defeats in the Battles of the Philippine Sea and Leyte Gulf.

Tripartite Pact (1940): Germany, Italy and Japan signed the Tripartite Pact in Berlin on September 27, 1940; its object was to hasten the goal of a "New Order" in Europe and a "Greater East Asia Co-Prosperity Sphere" in the Far East; the three powers agreed among themselves to assist one another against any nation that joined the British side, but they specifically excluded the Soviet Union from their "pro-British" list.

Triple Entente: an informal alliance in WW I between Great Britain, France and Czarist Russia that was terminated in 1917 when the Bolsheviks came to power in Russia as a result of the Russian Revolution.

Tu quoque: thou also; a principle which purports to justify the conduct of a State which violates international law and the rule of armed conflict on the grounds that the State upon whom or upon whose subjects the harm has been inflicted has engaged in similar conduct; *tu quoque* is essentially a retributive argument based on the Old Testament's "an eye for an eye" argument; the concept shares a common denominator with reprisals—that of collective punishment.

UCMJ: abbreviation for the *Uniform Code of Military Justice.*

Ultra: code name for the British top-secret decrypts of coded German ciphers during WW II.

Ultra vires: beyond legal power or authority.

Universality Principle: the most expansive jurisdictional theory in international law; the universality principle allows a State to exercise jurisdiction over individuals regardless of any connection that particular State may have had with the offense in question, the offender, or the victim.

Untersuchungsrichter: German term for investigating magistrate, similar to *juge d'instruction* in French criminal procedure.

Versailles, Treaty of (1919): Peace Treaty signed between Germany and the Allied and Associated Powers on June 28, 1919, with representatives of twenty-seven victor nations signing the 200-page document in the "Great Hall of Mirrors" in the Palace of Versailles outside Paris; the treaty came into force on January 1, 1920; article 228 provided for the creation of Allied tribunals to prosecute those accused of violating the laws and customs of war, while article 229 provided for trials before military commissions; an Allied Control Commission was established to oversee German disarmament and Germany was forced to submit to the payment of astronomical reparations for war damage she allegedly wrought.

Verscharfte Vernehmung: an aggravated form of interrogation.

Volksdeutsche: German ethnic groups who lived outside the geopolitical boundaries of the Third Rich.

Volkssturm **(1944):** People's Army; a primarily civilian defense force composed mainly of the very young and the elderly (ages between sixteen and sixty-five) formed in the summer of 1944 after Josef Goebbels was appointed Reich Plenipotentiary for Total War; the *Volkssturm* was pressed into service during the final months of WW II, but was generally ineffective against the combined might of the Allied war machine.

VOMI: the acronym fro Repatriation Office for Ethnic Germans.

von Brauchitsch, Walther (1881–1948): German General and Commander-in-Chief of the Germany Army (1938); retired in 1941 and died in British captivity in 1948.

Von Brockdorff-Rantzau, Count Ulrich (1869–1928): German Foreign Minister in the Weimar Republic government during the Versailles Treaty negotiations and one of Germanies most successful diplomats: he failed, however, to persuade the Allies and Associated Powers to amend the harsh terms of the Versailles Treaty levied upon Germany, in part, because of his intemperate rhetoric, and, in part, because he perfectly fit the Western stereotype of the arrogant and monocled Prussian official; resigned as Foreign Minister of the Scheidemann government on June 20, 1919.

von Manstein, Erich (1885–1973): German Field Marshal and one of Adolf Hitler's most brilliant military strategists; Chief of Staff, Army Group South, Poland (1939); Commander, Army Group South (Russia, 1942); dismissed in 1944; tried by the British for war crimes in 1949 and sentenced to 18 years' imprisonment; sentence reduced and released from captivity in 1953.

von Rundstedt, Gerd (1875–1953): German Field Marshal; Commander, Army Group South (Poland, 1939); Commander-in-Chief, West (1939–1940); Commander, Army Group South, Eastern Front (1941); retired, 1941; Commander-in-Chief, West (1942–1945); sacked by Hitler in July, 1944 and again in March, 1945; charged by the British with war crimes but was considered medically unfit for trial and released from captivity, 1949.

Waffen-SS: the armed SS; an elitist military organization whose members took an oath of unconditional loyalty to Adolf Hitler which stated: "I Swear to thee Adolf Hitler, as Führer and Chancellor of the German Reich, Loyalty and Bravery, I vow to thee and to the superiors whom thou shall appoint Obedience unto death So help me God"; originally termed the *Verfugungstruppen,* it was renamed the *Waffen-SS* in the winter of 1939–1940; its divisions were comprised of volunteers not only from Germany but also from Belgium, France, Holland, Norway, Lithuania, Denmark, Sweden, Hungary and Romania.

Wagner, Richard (1813–1883): German composer and a favorite of Adolf Hitler and many members of the Nazi Party hierarchy; as a young man, Hitler became enamoured with Wagner's *Lohengrin, Die Meistersinger* and *Tristan und Isolde,* among others.

Wannsee Conference (1942): a secret government meeting called by Reinhard Heydrich at a villa in an up-scale Berlin suburb located on Lake Grosser Wannsee, on January 20, 1942, and attended by those Nazis involved in the "final Solution" to the Jewish question, including Adolf Eichmann; the Wannsee participants planned to sweep up all European Jews and transport them to five extermination camps located at Auschwitz, Belzec, Treblinka, Sobibor and Majdanek.

War criminal classification-IMTFE: defendants in the IMTFE-Tokyo trial were "Class A" war criminals, meaning that at least a portion of the indictment against them charged a violation of "Crimes Against Peace"; "Class B" and "Class C" offenders were tried for violating the conventional laws of war and were tried separately from "Class A" offenders; in a six-year period from 1945 to 1951, some 5,700 Japanese were charged and tried for committing "conventional" war crimes; of those 1,000 were executed and 3,000 were sentenced to various terms of imprisonment.

Wehrmacht: armed forces; term was first employed in 1935 to refer collectively to the three branches of the German military.

Weimar Republic (1919–1933): the democratic government of Germany from the end of WW I until Adolf Hitler came to power in January, 1933; named such because the first National Assembly met in Weimar, a town in central Germany, in 1919, to draft a new Constitution and establish a new republic.

Wilhelm II of Hohenzollern, Kaiser (1859–1941): German Head of State and Emperor during WW I; the grandson of Queen Victoria of Great Britain; abdicated in November, 1918, shortly before the Armistice that ended WW I and fled to Holland who granted him political asylum and where he remained until his death in 1941.

Wolfsshanze: Wolf's Lair; Adolf Hitler's military headquarters located in a dense forest near Rastenburg, East Prussia; here the Nazi leader directed the German war against the Soviet Union; Hitler vacated the *Wolfsshanze* for the final time on November 20, 1944, in advance of the Red Army and returned to Berlin and his underground bunker.

Yalta Conference (1945): site of a conference in the Crimea, USSR, on the Black Sea, between Roosevelt, Churchill and Stalin, February 4–12, 1945; among other things, the Yalta Conference determined the areas of Germany each nation was to administer; France was subsequently allotted its own zone of occupation; Yalta was the final "Big Three" conference of WW II attended by Franklin D. Roosevelt before his death on April 12, 1945.

Yamamoto, Isoroku, Fleet Admiral (1884–1943): Commander of the Japanese Combined Fleet; initiated the Japanese surprise attack on Pearl Harbor and the Battle of Midway; presided over the Japanese defeat at Guadacanal; killed by an American air attack on his personal aircraft in 1943.

Yamashita, Tomoyuki Hobun (1885–1946): Commander, Japanese 25th Army in Malaya and Singapore; later appointed Commander, Japanese Forces in the Philippines where he conducted a lengthy defense of the island of Luzon; charged with the devastation of Manila; tried, convicted and executed for war crimes in 1946.

Yokohama: Japanese city located in the southeastern portion of Honshu in central Japan on Tokyo Bay; Yokohama was the site of numerous post-WW II military trials of lesser Japanese defendants accused of war crimes.

Yokosuka: site of the first United States and British Occupation Forces landing on Japanese soil near end of WW II at Yokosuka Naval Base, Sagami Bay, Japan, August 30, 1945.

Zhukov, Georgi Konstantinovich (1896–1974): Chief of the Soviet General Staff; commanded defense of Moscow (1941); First Deputy Defense Commissar (1944–1945); Commander of Soviet Occupation Zone in Germany (1946–1947); Deputy Defense Minister of the USSR (1953–1955); Defense Minister of the USSR (1955–1957).

References

Books

A Functional Index to the Proceedings of the International Military Tribunal, Far East (Paul S. Dull & Michael T. Umemura eds.). Ann Arbor, MI: University of Michigan Press (1957).

A Treatise on International Criminal Law. (2 vols.), (M. Cherif Bassiouni & Ved O. Nanda eds.). Springfield, IL: Thomas (*1973*).

Abarinov, Vladimir, *The Murderers of Katyn.* New York: Hippocrene Books (1993).

Adams, R.J., *The Great War, 1914–1918: Essays on the Military, Political and Social History of the First World War.* College Station, TX: Texas A&M University Press (1990).

Akehurst, Michael A., *A Modern Introduction to International Law.* London: Allen & Unwin (1977).

Alexander, Bevin, *How Hitler Could Have Won World War II: The Fatal Errors That Led to Nazi Defeat.* New York: Three Rivers Press (2000).

Alexander, Edward, *A Crime of Vengeance: An Armenian Struggle for Justice.* New York: Free Press (1991).

Al-Hammadi, Abdullah & Abdulateef Al-Abdalrazaq, *Atlas of Iraqi War Crimes in the State of Kuwait.* Al Qabas Commercial Press-Kuwait (1995).

Allen, Beverly, *Rape Warfare: The Hidden Genocide in Bosnia-Herzegovina and Croatia.* Minneapolis, MN: University of Minnesota Press (1996).

Allen, Thomas & Norman Polmar, *Code-Name Downfall: The Secret Plan to Invade Japan—and Why Truman Dropped the Bomb.* New York: Simon & Schuster (1995).

Allen, William S., *The Nazi Seizure of Power: The Experience of a Single German Town 1930–1935.* Chicago: Quadrangle Books (1965).

Allison, Graham, *Nuclear Terrorism: The Ultimate Preventable Catastrophe.* New York: Times Books (2004).

Alperovits, Gar, *The Decision to Use the Atomic Bomb and the Architecture of an American Myth.* New York: Knopf (1995).

Aly, Gotz, *'Final Solution': Nazi Population Policy and the Murder of the European Jews.* London: Arnold (1999).

Aly, Gotz & Susanne Heim, *Architects of Annihilation: Auschwitz and the Logic of Destruction.* London: Orion (2002).

Ambrosius, Lloyd E., *Wilsonian Statecraft: Theory and Practice of Liberal Internationalism during World War I.* Wilmington, DE: Scholarly Resources (1991).

American Exceptionalism and Human Rights (Michael Ignatieff ed.). Princeton, NJ: Princeton University Press (2004).

Americans as Proconsuls: United States Military Government in Germany and Japan, 1944–1952 (Robert Wolfe ed.). Carbondale, IL: Southern Illinois University Press (1984).

Amtliches Material zum Massenmord von Katyn (Official material concerning the Katyn massacre). Berlin: Zentravlverlag der NSDAP, F. Eher Nachf. (1943).

Anatomy of the Auschwitz Death Camp (Yisrael Gutman & Michael Bevenbaum eds.). Bloomington, IN: Indiana University Press (1994).

Annan, Noel, *Changing Enemies: The Defeat and Regenaration of Germany.* New York: Norton (1995).

Appleman, John A., *Military Tribunals and International Crimes.* Indianapolis, IN: Bobbs-Merrill (1954).

Arad, Yitzhak, *Belzek, Sobibor, Treblinka: The Operation Reinhard Death Camps.* Bloomington, IN: Indiana University Press (1987).

Arend, Anthony C., *Legal Rules and International Society.* New York: Oxford University Press (1999).

Arendt, Hannah, *Eichmann in Jerusalem: A Report on the Banality of Evil.* New York: Penguin Books (1977).

Armstrong, David, Korna Lloyd & John Redmond, *From Versailles to Maastricht: International Organizations in the Twentieth Century.* New York: St. Martin's Press (1996).

Askin, Kelly D., *War Crimes Against Women: Prosecution in International War Crimes Tribunals.* Cambridge, MA: Martinus Nijhoff (1997).

Asprey, Robert B., *The German High Command at War: Hindenburg and Ludendorff Conduct World War I.* New York: Morrow (1991).

Aufricht, Hans, *Guide to League of Nations' Publications: A Bibliographical Survey of the Work of the League, 1920–1947.* New York: Columbia University Press (1951).

Austin, John, *The Province of Jurisprudence Determined,* 5th ed. London: John Murray (1885).

Aymar, Brandt & Edward Sagarin, *A Pictorial History of the World's Great Trials: From Socrates to Eichmann.* New York: Crown (1967).

Bailey, George, *Germans: Biography of an Obsession.* New York: Avon Books (1974).

Balakian, Peter, *The Burning Tigris: The Armenian Genocide and America's Response.* New York: Harper-Collins (2003).

Balfour, Michael & Julian Frisby, *Helmut von Moltke: A Leader Against Hitler.* London: Macmillian (1972).

Ball, Howard, *Prosecuting War Crimes and Genocide: The Twentieth Century Experience.* Lawrence, KS: University Press of Kansas (1999).

Bankier, David, *The Germans and the Final Solution: Public Opinion Under Nazism.* Cambridge, MA: Harvard University Press (1992).

Barber, Benjamin R., *Fear's Empire: War, Terrorism and Democracy in an Age of Interdependence.* New York: Norton (2003).

Bardakjian, K., *Hitler and the Armenian Genocide.* Cambridge, MA: Harvard University Press (1985).

Barenblatt, Daniel, *A Plague Upon Humanity: The Secret Genocide of Axis Japan's Germ Warfare Operation.* New York: Harper-Collins (2004).

Barnett, Michael, *Eyewitness to Genocide: The United Nations and Rwanda.* Ithaca, NY: Cornell University Press (2003).

Barton, Omer, *Mirrors of Destruction: War, Genocide and Modern Identity*. New York: Oxford University Press (2000).

Bartov, Omer, *Hitler's Army: Soldiers, Nazis and War in the Third Reich*. New York: Oxford University Press (1992).

_____, *Murder in Our Midst: The Holocaust, Industrial Killing, and Representation*. New York: Oxford University Press (1996).

_____, *The Eastern Front, 1941–1945: German Troops and the Barbarisation of Warfare*. New York: St. Martin's Press (1986).

Bartov, Omer, Atina Grossman & Mary Nolan, *Crimes of War: Guilt and Denial in the Twentieth Century*. New York: New Press (2002).

Bass, Gary T., *Stay the Hand of Vengeance: The Politics of War Crimes Trials*. Princeton, NJ: Princeton University Press (2000).

Bassiouni, M. Cherif & Peter Manikas, *The Law of the International Criminal Tribunal for the Former Yugoslavia*. New York: Transnational (1996).

Beals, Walter, *The First German War Crimes Trial*. Chapel Hill, NC: Documentary (1985).

Bederman, David J., *The Spirit of International Law*. Athens, GA: The University of Georgia Press (2002).

Beigbeder, Yves, *Judging War Criminals: The Politics of International Justice*. New York: St. Martin's Press (1999).

Belknap, Michal R., *The Vietnam War on Trial: The My Lai Massacre and the Court-Martial of Lieutenant Calley*. Lawrence, KS: University Press of Kansas (2002).

Bell-Falkoff, Andrew, *Ethnic Cleansing*. New York: St. Martin's Press (1996).

Benedict, Ruth *The Chrysanthemum and the Sword*. Boston: Houghton Mifflin (1946).

Bennett, D. Scott & Allan C. Stam, *The Behavioral Origins of War*. Ann Arbor, MI: University of Michigan Press (2004).

Benvenisti, Eyal, *The International Law of Occupation*. Princeton, NJ: Princeton University Press (1993).

Bergamini, David, *Japan's Imperial Conspiracy*. New York: Morrow (1971).

Berman, Paul, *Terror and Liberalism*. New York: Norton (2003).

Bernstein, Victor, H., *Final Judgment: The Story of Nuremberg*. New York: Boni & Gaer (1947).

Beschloss, Michael, *The Conquerors: Roosevelt, Truman and the Destruction of Hitler's Germany, 1941–1945*. New York: Simon & Schuster (2002).

Bessel, Richard, *Germany After the First World War*. New York: Oxford University Press (1993).

Best, Geoffrey, *Humanity in Warfare*. New York: Columbia University Press (1980).

_____, *War and Law Since 1945*. Oxford, UK: Clarendon Press (1994).

Bilton, Michael & Kevin Sim, *Four Hours in My Lai*. New York: Viking Press (1992).

Binion, Rudolf, *Hitler Among the Germans*. 2d corrected printing, New York: Elsevier (1979).

Blishchenko, I. & Zhdanov, N., *Terrorism and International Law*. Moscow: Progress (1984).

Blitzkrieg to Defeat: Hitler's War Directives 1939–1945 (H.R. Trevor-Roper ed.). New York: Holt, Rinehart & Winston (1964).

Bloom, Mia, *Dying to Kill: The Allure of Suicide Terror*. New York: Columbia University Press (2005).

Borkin, Joseph, *The Crime and Punishment of I.G. Farben*. New York: Free Press (1979).

Bory, Francoise, *Origin and Development of International Humanitarian Law*. Geneva: International Committee of the Red Cross (1982).

Bosch, William J., *Judgment on Nuremberg: American Attitudes Towards the Major War Crimes Trials*. Chapel Hill, NC: University of North Carolina Press (1970).

Bosworth, R.J.B., *Explaining Auschwitz and Hiroshima: History of Writing and the Second World War, 1945–1990*. New York: Routledge (1993).

Bottigliero, Ilaria, *Redress for Victims of Crimes Under International Law*. Leiden/Boston: Martinus Nijhoff (2004).

Bower, Tom, *Blind Eye to Murder: Britain, America and the Purging of Nazi Germany — A Pledge Betrayed*. London: Andre Deutsch (1981).

Boyajian, Dickran H., *Armenia: The Case for a Forgotten Genocide*. Westwood, NJ: Educational Book Crafters (1972).

Boyle, Francis A., *Foundations of World Order: The Legalist Approach to International Relations, 1918–1922*. Durham, NC: Duke University Press (1999).

Bracher, Karl D., *The German Dictatorship: The Origins, Structure, and Effects of National Socialism*. New York: Praeger (1970).

Brackman, Arnold C., *The Other Nuremberg: The Untold Story of the Tokyo War Crimes Trials*. New York: Morrow (1987).

Bradley, John, *The Illustrated History of the Third Reich*. London: Gramercy Books (1978).

Braham, Randolph L., *The Eichmann Case: A Source Book*. New York: World Federation of Hungarian Jews (1969).

Braun, Otto, *Von Weimar zu Hitler*. New York: Europa Verlag (1940).

Breitman, Richard, *The Architect of Genocide: Himmler and the Final Solution*. New York: Knopf (1991).

Brendon, Piers, *The Dark Valley: A Panorama of the 1930s*. New York: Knopf (2000).

Brooker, Paul, *Twentieth Century Dictatorships: The Ideological One-Party States*. New York: N.Y.U. Press (1995).

Brooks, Lester, *Behind Japan's Surrender*. New York: McGraw-Hill (1968).

Broomhall, Bruce, *International Justice and the International Criminal Court: Between Sovereignty and the Rule of Law*. New York: Oxford University Press (2004).

Broszat, Martin, *German National Socialism 1919–1945*. Santa Barbara, CA: Clio Press (1966).

_____, *The Hitler State*. New York: Longman (1981).

Browder, George C., *Foundations of the Nazi Police State: The Formation of the SIPO and SD*. Lexington, KY: The University Press of Kentucky (1990).

_____, *Hitler's Enforcers: The Gestapo and the SS Security Service in the Nazi Revolution*. New York: Oxford University Press (1996).

Browne, Courtney, *Tojo: The Last Banzai*. New York: Holt, Rinehart & Winston (1967).

Browning, Christopher R., *Nazi Policy, Jewish Workers, German Killers*. Cambridge, UK: Cambridge University Press (2000).

_____, *Ordinary Men: Reserve Police Battalion 101 and the Final Solution in Poland*. New York: Harper (1992).

_____, *The Path to Genocide: Essays on Launching the Final Solution*. Cambridge, UK: Cambridge University Press (1992).

_____, *The Origins of the Final Solution: The Evolution of Nazi Jewish Policy, September 1939–March 1942*. Lincoln, NE: University of Nebraska Press (2004).

Buchheim, H., *The Third Reich: Its Beginning, Its Development, Its End*. Munich: Kosel (1961).

Buhite, Russell D., *Decisions at Yalta: An Appraisal of Summit Diplomacy*. Wilmington, DE: Scholarly Resources (1986).

Bujosevic, Dragan & Ivan Radovanovic, *The Fall of Milosevic: The October 5th Revolution.* New York: Palgrave Macmillian (2003).

Bull, Hedley, *The Anarchical Society: A Study of Order in World Politics.* New York: Columbia University Press (1977).

Bullock, Alan, *Hitler and Stalin: Parallel Lives.* New York: Knopf (1992).

Bumgarner, John R., *Parade of the Dead.* Jefferson, NC: McFarland (1995).

Burleigh, Michael, *Death and Deliverance.* Cambridge, UK: Cambridge University Press (1994).

_____, *Ethics and Extermination: Reflections on Nazi Genocide.* Cambridge, UK: Cambridge University Press (1997).

_____, *The Third Reich: A New History.* New York: Hill & Wang (2000).

Buruma, Ian, *The Wages of Guilt: Memories of War in Germany and Japan.* New York: Farrar, Straus & Giroux (1994).

Buscher, Frank W., *The U.S. War Crimes Trial Program in Germany, 1946–1955.* Westport, CT: Greenwood Press (1988).

Butler, Harold, *The Lost Peace.* London: Faber & Faber (1941).

Butow, Robert J.C., *Japan's Decision to Surrender.* Stanford, CA: Stanford University Press (1954).

_____, *Tojo and the Coming of the War.* Princeton, NJ: Princeton University Press (1961).

Calic, Edouard, *Reinhard Heydrich: The Chilling Story of the Man Who Masterminded the Nazi Death Camps.* New York: Morrow (1985).

Calvocoressi, Peter, *Nuremberg: The Facts, the Law and the Consequences.* New York: Macmillan (1948).

Cannon, Michael, *Pearl Harbor Betrayed.* New York: Holt (2001).

Carr, Caleb, *The Lessons of Terror: A History of Warfare Against Civilians: Why It Has Always Failed and Why It Will Fail Again.* New York: Random House (2002).

Carr, Edward H., *The Twenty Years' Crisis, 1919–1939.* London: Macmillan (1946).

Carr, William, *Hitler: A Study of Personality and Politics.* New York: St. Martin's Press (1979).

Carroll, Berenice, A., *Design for Total War: Arms and Economics in the Third Reich.* The Hague: Mouton (1968).

Cecil, Lamar, *Wilhelm II.* (2 vols.). Chapel Hill, NC: University of North Carolina Press (1989).

Cecil, Robert, *Hitler's Decision to Invade Russia, 1941.* London: Davis-Poynter (1975).

Century of Genocide (Samual Totten, William S. Parsons & Israel W. Charney eds.). New York: Garland (1997).

Chadwick, Owen, *Britain and the Vatican during the Second World War.* New York: Cambridge University Press (1986).

Chalk, F & K. Jonassohn, *The History and Sociology of Genocide, Analyses and Case Studies.* New Haven, CT: Yale University Press (1991).

Chandler, David P., *The Tragedy of Cambodian History: Politics, War, and Revolution Since 1945.* New Haven, CT: Yale University Press (1991).

Chang, Iris, *The Rape of Nanking: The Forgotten Holocaust of World War II.* New York: Basic Books (1997).

Charney, Israel W., *Genocide: A Critical Bibliographic Review.* New York: Facts on File (1988).

Chen, John H.M., *Vietnam: A Comprehensive Bibliography.* Metuchen, NJ: Scarecrow Press (1973).

Children of Cambodia's Killing Fields: Memories of Survivors (Kim DePaul ed.). New Haven, CT: Yale University Press (1998).

Chimni, B.S., *International Law and World Order: A Critique of Contemporary Approaches*. Newbury Park, CA: Sage (1993).

Chinnery, Philip D., *Korean Atrocity: Forgotten War Crimes 1950–1953*. Annapolis, MD: Naval Institute Press (2000).

Christopher, Paul, *The Ethics of War and Peace: An Introduction to Legal and Moral Issues*. Englewood Cliffs, NJ: Prentice-Hall (1994).

Chuter, David, *War Crimes: Confronting Atrocity in the Modern World*. Boulder, CO: Reinner (2003).

Clark, Alan, *Barbarossa: The Russian-German Conflict*. New York: Quill (1965).

Clark, Ramsey, *The Fire This Time: U.S. War Crimes in the Gulf*. New York: Thunder's Mouth Press (1992).

Clarke, Richard A., *Against All Enemies: Inside America's War on Terror*. New York: Free Press (2004).

Coffey, Thomas M., *Imperial Tragedy: Japan in World War II: The First Days and the Last*. New York: World (1970).

Cohen, Marshall, Thomas Nagel & Thomas Scanlon, *War and Moral Responsibility*. Princeton, NJ: Princeton University Press (1974).

Cohn, Norman, *Warrant for Genocide: The Myth of the Jewish World Conspiracy and the Protocols of the Elders of Zion*. Hammandsworth, Middlesex, UK: Pelican (1970).

Cole, David & James X. Dempsey, *Terrorism and the Constitution: Sacrificing Civil Liberties in the Name of National Security*. New York: New Press (2002).

Coll, Steven, *Ghost Wars: The Secret History o f the CIA, Afghanistan and bin Laden, from the Soviet Invasion to September 10, 2001*. New York: Penguin Press (2004).

Combs, William L., *The Voice of the SS: A History of the SS Journal DAS SCHWARZE KORPS*. New York: Peter Lang (1986).

Compton, James V., *The Swastika and the Eagle*. Boston: Houghton Mifflin (1967).

Conot, Robert, *Justice at Nuremberg*. New York: Harper & Row (1983).

Conover, Helen F., *The Nazi State, War Crimes and War: A Bibliography*. Washington, DC: Library of Congress (1945).

Contemporary Genocides: Causes, Cases, Consequences (Albert J. Jongman ed.). Leiden: Ploom (1996)

Cook, Haruka T. & Theodore F. Cook, *Japan at War: An Oral History*. New York: New Press (1992).

Corni, Gustavo, *Hitler's Ghettos: Voices from a Beleagued Society 1939–1944* (Nicola R. Iannelli trans.). London: Arnold (2002).

Cornwell, John, *Hitler's Pope: The Secret History of Pius XII*. New York: Viking Press (1999).

_____, *Hitler's Scientists: Science, War, and the Devil's Pact*. New York: Viking Press (2003).

Craig, Gordon A., *The Politics of the Prussian Army, 1640–1945*. New York: Oxford University Press (1955).

Craig, Gordon A. & Alexander L. George, *Force and Statecraft: Diplomatic Problems of Our Time*. New York: Oxford University Press (1983).

Craig, William, *The Fall of Japan*. New York: Dial Press (1967).

Crankshaw, Edward, *Gestapo: Instrument of Tyranny*. New York: DaCapo Press (1956).

Crawford, James, *The International Law Commission's Articles on State Responsibility: Introduction, Text and Commentaries*. Cambridge, UK: Cambridge University Press (2002).

Creek, George, *War Criminals and Punishment*. New York: McBride (1944).

Crimes of War: A Legal, Political, Documentary and Psychological Inquiry into the Responsibility of Leaders for Criminal Acts in War (Richard A. Falk, Gabriel Kolko & Robert J. Lifton eds.). New York: Random House (1971).

Crnobrnja, Mihailo, *The Yugoslav Drama*. Quebec: McGill-Queens University Press (1996).

Crutwell, Charles R.M.F., *History of the Great War, 1914–1918*. Oxford, UK: Oxford University Press (1936).

Dadrian, Vahakn N., *The History of the Armenian Genocide: Ethnic Conflicts from the Balkans to Anatolia to the Caucasus*. Providence, RI: Berghahm Books (1995).

Dallin, Alexander, *German Rule in Russia, 1941–1945: A Study of Occupation Policies*. London: Macmillan (1957).

D'Amato, Anthony A., *The Concept of Custom in International Law*. Ithaca, NY: Cornell University Press (1971).

Das Diktat von Versailles. (3 vols.), Essen: Essener Verlagsanstalt (1939).

Davidson, Eugene, *The Making of Adolf Hitler*. New York: Macmillan (1977).

_____, *The Nuremberg Fallacy: Wars and War Crimes Since World War II*. New York: Macmillan (1973).

_____, *The Trial of the Germans: An Account of the Twenty-One Defendants Before the IMT at Nuremberg*. New York: Macmillan (1966).

_____, *The Unmaking of Adolf Hitler, Columbia*, MO: University of Missouri Press (1996).

Davis, Calvin DeH., *The United States and the Second Hague Convention*. Durham, NC: Duke University Press (1975).

Dawidowicz, Lucy S., *The War Against the Jews, 1933–1945*. New York: Holt, Rinehart & Winston (1975).

Deák, István, *Weimar Germany's Left-Wing Intellectuals*. Berkeley, CA: University of California Press (1968).

Dedijer, Vladimir, *The Yugoslav Auschwitz and the Vatican: The Croatian Massacre of the Serbs during World War Two*. Buffalo, NY: Prometheus Books (1992).

Deist, Wilhelm, "The Road to Ideological War, 1918–1945" in *The Making of Strategy: Rulers, States and War* (Williamson Murray. Macgregor Knox & Alvin Bernstein eds.). New York: Cambridge University Press (1994).

Delarue, Jacques, *The Gestapo: A History of Horror*. New York: Morrow (1964).

Democaratic Accountability and the Use of Force in International Law (Charlotte Ku & Harold K. Jacobson eds.). Cambridge, UK: Cambridge University Press (2002).

Derso, Alois & Emery Kelen, *Le testament de Genieve*. Paris: Georges Lang (1931).

Destexhe, Alain, *Rwanda and Genocide in the Twentieth Century*. London/East Haven, CT: Pluto Press (1995).

Deutsch-russische Zeitenwende Krieg und Frieden 1941–1995. Baden-Baden: Hans-Adolf Jacobsen (1995).

Devil's Dairy: The Record of Nazi Conspiracy and Aggression (John L. Stipp ed.). Yellow Springs, OH: Antioch Press (1955).

deVisscher, Yoram, *War, Aggression and Self-Defense*. Cambridge, UK: Grotius (1988).

De Zayas, Alfred M., *Nemesis at Potsdam: The Anglo-Americans and the Expulsion of the Germans*. London: Routledge & Kegan Paul (1977).

_____, *The Wehrmacht War Crimes Bureau, 1939–1945*. Lincoln, NE: University of Nebraska Press (1989).

Dictionary of International and Comparative Law, 3d ed. (James R. Fox ed.). Dobbs Ferry, NY: Oceana (2003).

Dietrich, Otto, *Hitler* (Richard & Clara Winston trans.). Chicago: Regnery (1955).

Dinstein, Yoram, *The Defense of 'Obedience to Superior Orders' in International Law.* Leyden: A.W. Sijthoff (1965).

Divine, Robert A., *The Reluctant Belligerent: American Entry Into World War II.* New York: Wiley (1965).

Documents of Destruction: Germany and Jewry, 1933–1945 (Raul Hilberg ed.). Chicago: Quadrangle Books (1971).

Döenitz at Nuremberg: A Reappraisal—War Crimes and the Military Professional (H.K. Thompson & Henry Strutz eds.). New York: Amber (1976).

Dollinger, Hans, *The Decline and Fall of Nazi Germany and Imperial Japan.* (Arnold Pomerans trans.). New York: Crown (1967).

Domarus, Max, *Hitler: Speeches and Proclamations 1932–1945.* (2 vols.), Wauconda, IL: Bolchazy-Carducci (1990).

Dower, John W., *Embracing Defeat: Japan in the Wake of World War II.* New York: Norton/New Press (2000).

_____, *War Without Mercy: Race and Power in the Pacific War.* New York: Pantheon Books (1986).

Drost, Peter, *The Crime of State: Penal Protection for Fundamental Freedoms of Persons and Peoples.* (2 vols), Leyden: A.W. Sijthoff (1959).

DuBois, Josiah E. & Edward Johnson, *The Devil's Chemist: 24 Conspirators of the International Farben Cartel Who Manufacture Wars.* Boston: Beacon Press (1952).

Dworkin, Ronald, *Freedom's Law: The Moral Reading of the American Constitution.* Cambridge, MA: Harvard University Press (1996).

Eichmann Interrogated: Transcripts from the Archives of the Israeli Police (Jochen von Lang, ed.). New York: Farrar, Straus & Giroux (1982).

Eisenberg, Azriel, *Witness to the Holocaust.* New York: Pilgrim Press (1981).

El-Dakkak, M. Shokry, *State's Crimes Against Humanity: Genocide, Deportation and Torture.* Kuala Lumpur: A.S. Noordeen (2000).

Ellis, John, *Eye-Deep in Hell: Trench Warfare in World War I.* Westport, CT: Praeger (1996).

Elshtain, Jean B., *Just War Against Terror: The Burden of American Power in a Violent World.* New York: Basic Books (2003).

Essays on ICTY Procedure and Evidence in Honour of Gabrielle Kirk McDonald (Richard May et al. eds.). The Hague: Kluwer Law International (2001).

Evans, Richard J., *The Coming of the Third Reich.* New York: Penguin Press (2004).

Eyck, Erich, *A History of the Weimar Republic.* (2 vols.), Cambridge, MA: Harvard University Press (1962–63).

Facing My Lai: Moving Beyond the Massacre (David L. Anderson ed.). Lawrence, KS: University Press of Kansas (1998).

Falconi, Carlo, *The Silence of Pius XII* (Bernard Wall trans.). Boston: Little, Brown (1970).

Falk, Stanley L., *Bataan: The March of Death.* New York: Jove (1983).

Feig, Konnilyn G., *Hell on Earth: A Holocaust Bibliography.* San Francisco: Multilith (1981).

_____, *Hitler's Death Camps: The Sanity of Madness.* New York: Holmes & Meier (1981).

_____, *The Voyage of the Damned: An Essayed Bibliography of the Holocaust.* Portland, ME: University of Maine (1974).

Feis, Herbert, *Between War and Peace: The Potsdam Conference.* Princeton, NJ: Princeton University Press (1960).

_____, *The Road to Pearl Harbor: The Coming of the War Between the United States and Japan.* Princeton, NJ: Princeton University Press (1950).

Feldman, Noah, *After Jihad: America and the Struggle for Islamic Democracy.* New York: Farrar, Straus & Giroux (2003).

Fenno, Richard, *The Yalta Conference.* Boston: Heath (1955).

Ferencz, Benjamin B., *An International Criminal Court: A Step for World Peace.* Dobbs Ferry, NY: Oceana (1980).

_____, *Defining International Aggression: The Search for World Peace: A Documentary History and Analysis.* Dobbs Ferry, NY: Oceana (1975).

Ferguson, Niall, *The Pity of War.* New York: Basic Books (1999).

Ferrell, Robert H., *Peace in Their Time: The Origins of the Kellogg-Briand Pact.* New York: Yale University Press (1952).

Fest, Joachim, *Speer: The Final Verdict.* New York: Harcourt (1999).

Field, Geoffrey G., *Evangelist of Race: The Germanic Vision of Houston Steward Chamberlain.* New York: Columbia University Press (1981).

Filipovic, Zlata, *Zlata's Dairy: A Child's Life in Sarajevo.* New York: Viking Press (1994).

Finkelstein, Norman G. & Ruth B. Birn, *A Nation on Trial: The Goldhagen Thesis and Historical Truth.* New York: Holt (1998).

Fischer, Fritz, *From Kaiserreich to Third Reich: Elements of Continuity in German History, 1871–1945* (Roger Fletcher trans.). Boston: Allen & Unwin (1986).

Fischer, Klaus P., *Nazi Germany: A New History.* New York: Barnes & Noble (1995).

FitzGibbon, Louis, *Katyn: A Crime Without Parallel.* New York: Scribner's (1979).

Fleming, Gerald, *Hitler and the Final Solution.* Berkeley, CA: University of California Press (1982).

Fleming, Thomas, *The Illusion of Victory: America in World War I.* New York: Basic Books (2003).

Fontette, Francois de, *de Proces de Nuremberg.* Paris: Presses Universitaires de France (1996).

Forever in the Shadow of Hitler (James Knowlton & Truett Cates trans.). Atlantic Highlands, NJ: Humanitites Press (1993).

Fraenkel, Ernst, *Military Occupation and the Rule of Law: Occupation Government in the Rhineland, 1918–1923.* London: Oxford University Press (1944).

Frank, Richard B., *Downfall: The End of the Imperial Japanese Empire.* New York: Random House (1999).

Fraser, Lindley, *Germany Between Two Wars: A Study of Propaganda and War Guilt.* London: Oxford University Press (1945).

Frei, Norbert, *National Socialist Rule in Germany: The Führer State, 1933–1945* (Simon B. Steyne trans.). Oxford, UK: Blackwell (1993).

Fried, Hans E., *The Guilt of the German Army.* New York: Macmillan (1942).

Friedlander, Henry, *Origins of Nazi Genocide: From Euthanasia to the Final Solution.* Chapel Hill, NC: University of North Carolina Press (1995).

Friedlander, Saul, *Reflections on Nazism: An Essay on Kitsch and Death* (Thomas Weyr trans.). New York: Harper & Row (1984).

Friedman, L., *The Law of War: A Documentary History.* (2 vols.). New York: Random House (1972).

Frischauer, Willi, *Himmler, the Evil Genius of the Third Reich.* Boston: Beacon Press (1953).

Fritzsche, Peter, *Germans into Nazis.* Cambridge, MA: Harvard University Press (1998).

From Nuremberg to My Lai (Jay Baird ed.). Lexington, MA: Heath (1974).

From Peace to War: Germany, Soviet Russia and the World, 1939–1941 (B. Wegner ed.). Providence, RI: Berghahn Books (1997).

Fuchser, Larry W., *Neville Chamberlain and Appeasement: A Study in the Politics of History.* New York: Norton (1982).

Fulbrook, Mary, *A Concise History of Germany.* Cambridge, UK: Cambridge University Press (1990).

Gallagher, Richard, *Nuremberg: The Third Reich on Trial.* New York: Avon (1961).

Gallo, Max, *The Night of the Long Knives.* New York: Harper & Row (1972).

Gannon, Michael, *Pearl Harbor Betrayed.* New York: Holt (2001).

Garrett, Stephen A., *Ethics and Airpower in the World War II: The British Bombing of German Cities.* New York: St. Martin's Press (1993).

Gaskin, Hilary, *Eyewitnesses to Nuremberg.* London: Arms & Armour Press (1990).

Gellately, Robert, *The Gestapo and German Society: Enforcing Racial Policy, 1933–1945.* New York: Oxford University Press (1990).

Geller, Daniel S. & J. Singer, *Nations at War: A Scientific Study of International Conflict.* New York: Cambridge University Press (1998).

Generalfeldmarshall Wilhelm Ritter von Leeb, Tagebuchaufzeichnungen und Lagebeurteillungen aus zwei Weltkrigen. Stuttgart: Georg Meyer (1976).

Genocide and Democracy in Cambodia (Ben Kiernan ed.). New Haven, CT: Yale University Southeast Asia Studies (1993).

Genocide in Cambodia and Rwanda: New Perspectives (Susan E. Cook ed.). Piscataway, NJ: Transaction (2005).

German Democracy and the Triumph of Hitler: Essays in Recent German History (Anthony Nicholls & Erich Matthias eds.). New York: St. Martin's Press (1971).

Germany Speaks: By 21 Leading Members of Party and State (with Preface by Joachim von Ribbentrop). London: Thornton Butterworth (1938).

Gershen, M., *Destroy or Die: The True Story of My Lai.* New Rochelle, NY: Arlington House (1971).

Geyer, Michael, "German Strategy in the Age of Machine Warfare, 1914–1945" in *Makers of Modern Strategy* (Peter Paret ed.). Princeton, NJ: Princeton University Press (1986).

Gilbert, Gustav M., *Nuremberg Diary.* New York: Farrar, Straus (1947).

Gilbert, Martin, *Auschwitz and the Allies.* New York: Holt (1981).

_____, *The First World War: A Complete History.* New York: Holt (1994).

_____, *The Holocaust: A History of the Jews of Europe During the Second World War.* New York: Holt (1985).

Gildea, Robert, *Marianne in Chains: Daily Life in the Heart of France During the German Occupation.* New York: Metropolitan Books (2003).

Ginn, John L., *Sugamo Prison, Tokyo.* London: McFarland (1992).

Gisevius, Hans B., *To the Bitter End: An Insider's Account of the Plot to Kill Hitler, 1933–1944.* New York: DaCapo Press (1998).

Glantz, David M. & Jonathan House, *When Titans Clashed: How the Red Army Stopped Hitler.* Lawrence, KS: University Press of Kansas (1995).

Glass, James M., *"Life Unworthy of Life:" Racial Phobia and Mass Murder in Hitler's Germany.* New York: Basic Books (1997).

Glennon, Michael J., *Limits of Law, Prerogatives of Power, Interventionism after Kosovo.* New York: PalgraveMacmillan (2003).

Glueck, Sheldon, *The Nuremberg Trial and Aggressive War.* New York: Knopf (1946).

_____, *War Criminals: Their Prosecution and Punishment.* New York: Knopf (1944).

Göebbels, Paul Josef, *The Göebbels Diaries.* New York: Eagle (1948).

Goemans, H.E., *War and Punishment: The Causes of War Termination and the First World War*. Princeton, NJ: Princeton University Press (2000).

Goerlitz, Walther, *History of the German General Staff, 1857–1945*. New York: Praeger (1953).

Gold, Hal, *Unit 731: Testimony*. Tokyo: Yen Books (1996).

Goldhagen, Daniel J., *Hitler's Willing Executioners: Ordinary Germans and the Holocaust*. New York: Knopf (1996).

Goldstein, Joseph, Burke Marshall & Jack Schwartz, *The My Lai Massacre and Its Cover-up*. New York: Free Press (1976).

Gonen, Jay Y., *The Roots of Nazi Psychology: Hitler's Utopian Barbarism*. Lexington, KY: The University Press of Kentucky (2000).

"Gott mit Uns": der Deutsche Vernichtungskrieg im Osten 1939–1945 (Ernst Klee & Willi Dressen eds.). Frankfurt/am Main: S. Fisher (1989).

Gourevitch, Philip, *We Wish to Inform You That Tommorrow We will Be Killed with Our Families: Stories from Rwanda*. New York: Farrar, Straus & Giroux (1998).

Graber, G.S., *The History of the SS*. New York: David McKay (1978).

Greene, Joshua M., *Justice at Dachau: The Trials of an American Prosecutor*. New York: Broadway Books (2003).

Greenspan, Morris, *The Modern Law of Land Warfare*. Berkeley, CA: University of California Press (1959).

Gregor, A. James, *The Ideology of Fascism: The Rationale of Totalitarianism*. New York: Free Press (1969).

Greil, Lothar, *Oberst der Waffen SS Joachim Peiper und der Malmédy Process*. Munich: Schild-Verlag (1977).

Griffin, Michael, *Reaping the Whirlwind: The Taliban Movement in Afghanistan*. London: Pluto Press (2001).

Grotius, Hugo, *De Jure Belli Ac Pacis Libri Tres: The Classics of International Law* (James B. Scott ed. and Francis W. Kelsey trans.). Oxford, UK: Clarendon Press (1925).

Grunberger, Richard, *The 12-Year Reich: A Social History of Nazi Germany 1933–1945*. New York: Ballantine Books (1972).

Grunfeld, Frederic V., *The Hitler File: A Social History of Germany and the Nazis 1918–1945*. New York: Random House (1974).

Guérin, Daniel, *The Brown Plague: Travels in Late Weimar and Early Nazi Germany*. Durham, NC: Duke University Press (1994).

Gutman, Roy, *Witness to Genocide*. New York: Macmillan (1993).

Habeck, Mary, *Storm of Steel: The Development of Armor Doctrine in Germany and the Soviet Union, 1919–1939*. Ithaca, NY: Cornell University Press (2003).

Haffner, Sebastian, *Defying Hitler: A Memoir*. New York: Farrar, Straus & Giroux (2000).

Hagan, John, *Justice in the Balkans: Prosecuting War Crimes in the Hague Tribunal*. Chicago: The University of Chicago Press (2003).

Halder, Franz, *Hitler as Warlord*. New York: Putnam (1950).

Hammer, R., *The Court-Martial of Lt. Calley*. New York: Coward, McCann & Geoghegan (1971).

Hardach, Gerd, *The First World War, 1914–18*. Berkeley, CA: University of California Press (1977).

Harries, Meirion & Susie Harries, *Soldiers of the Sun: The Rise and Fall of the Imperial Japanese Army*. New York: Random House (1991).

Harris, Marshall R., Bruce Hitschner, Michael P. Scharf & Paul R. Williams, *Making Justice Work*. New York: Century Foundation Press (1998).

Harris, Sheldon H., *Factories of Death: Japanese Biological Warfare 1932–1945 and the American Cover-Up*. London: Routledge, Kegan Paul (1994).

Harris, Whitney R., *Tyranny on Trial: The Evidence of Nuremberg*. Dallas, TX: Southern Methodist University Press (1954).

Hartigan, Richard S., *Lieber's Code and the Law of War*. Chicago: Precedent (1983).

Harwood, Richard, *Nuremberg and Other War Crime Trials: A New Look*. Ladbroke, UK: Historical Review Press (1978).

Hastings, Max, *Armageddon: The Battle for Germany, 1944–1945*. New York: Knopf (2004).

Hatheway, Jay, *In Perfect Formation: SS Ideology and the SS-Junkerschule-Tölz*. Atglen, PA: Schiffer (1999).

Hauser, Gideon, *Justice in Jerusalem*. New York: Harper & Row (1966).

Hausser, Paul, *Waffen SS im Einsatz*. Gottingen: Plesse (1953).

Hawkins, Kike, *Social Darwinism in European and American Thought, 1860–1945: Nature as Model and Nature as Threat*. New York: Cambridge University Press (1997).

Headland, Ronald, *Messages of Murder: A Study of the Reports of the Einsatzgruppen of the Security Police and the Security Service, 1941–1943*. Rutherford, NJ: Fairleigh Dickinson University Press (1992).

Heiden, Konrad, *Der Füehrer: Hitler's Rise to Power* (Ralph Manheim trans.). Boston: Houghton Mifflin (1944).

Herrmann, David G., *The Arming of Europe and the Making of the First World War*. Princeton, NJ: Princeton University Press (1996).

Hersey, John *Hiroshima*. New York: Knopf (1946).

Hersh, Seymour M., *Chain of Command: The Road from 9/11 to Abu Ghraib*. New York: Harper Collins (2004).

_____, *Cover-Up: The Army's Secret Investigation of the Massacre at My Lai*. New York: Random House (1972).

Herwig, Holger, *The First World War*. London: Arnold (1997).

Hesse, Fritz, *Hitler and the English* (F.A. Voight trans.). London: Wingate (1954).

Heydecker, Joe J. & Johannes Leeb, *The Nuremberg Trial: A History of Nazi Germany as Revealed Through the Testimony at Nuremberg* (R.A. Downey ed.). Cleveland, OH: World (1952).

Hilberg, Raul, *Perpetrators, Victims, Bystanders: The Jewish Catastrophe, 1933–1945*. New York: Harper Collins (1992).

_____, *The Destruction of the European Jews*. New York: Harper Colophon (1979).

Hildebrand, Klaus, *Das Dritte Reich*. Munich: Oldenbourg (1980).

Historical Atlas of the Holocaust. United States Holocaust Memorial Museum, New York: Macmillan (1996).

Hitler, Adolf, *Mein Kampf* (Ralph Manheim trans.). Boston: Houghton Mifflin (1971).

_____, *Mein neu Ordnung*. (Raoul de Roussyde Sales ed.). New York: Reynal & Hitchcock (1941).

Hitler and His Generals: Military Conferences 1942–1945 (Helmut Heiber & David M. Glantz eds.). New York: Enigma Books (2003). (Originally published as *Hitler's Lagebesprechungen: Die Protokollfragmente seiner militärischen Konferenzen 1942–1945*. Stuttgart: Deutsche Verlags-Anstalt (1962)).

Hitler's Letters and Notes (Werner Maser ed. and Arnold Pomerans trans.). New York: Bantam Books (1976).

Hitler's Second Book: The Unpublished Sequel to Mein Kampf (Gerhard L. Weinberg ed. and Krista Smith trans.). New York: Enigma Books (2003).

Hitler's Third Reich: A Documentary History (Louis L. Snyder ed.). Chicago: Nelson Hall (1981).

Hodedeman, Paul, *Hitler or Hippocrates: Medical Experiments and Euthanasia in the Third Reich*. Sussex, UK: Book Guild (1991).

Höess, Rudolf, *Commandant of Auschwitz*. New York: World (n.d.).

_____, *Death Dealer: The Memoirs of the SS Kommandant at Auschwitz* (Steven Paskully ed.). Buffalo, NY: Prometheus Books (1992).

Hofer, Walther, *War Premeditated, 1939* (Stanley Godman trans.) London: Thames & Hudson(1955).

Hoffman, Peter, *The History of the German Resistance, 1933–1945*. Cambridge, MA: MIT Press (1979).

Hohne, Heinz, *The Order of the Death's Head: The Story of Hitler's SS*. New York: Coward-McCann (1969).

Hoito, Edoin (Hoyt, Edwin), *The Night Tokyo Burned: The Incendiary Campaign Against Japan, March–August, 1945*. New York: St. Martin's Press (1987).

Honig, Jan W. & Norbert Both, *Srebrenica: Record of a War Crime*. New York: Penguin Books (1996).

Horne, Alistair, *To Lose a Battle: France 1940*. Boston: Little, Brown (1969).

Horne, John & Alan Kramer, *German Atrocities, 1914: A History of Denial*. New Haven, CT: Yale University Press (2001).

Horwitz, Solis, *The Tokyo Trial*. New York: Carnegie Endowment for International Peace (1950).

Höss, Rudolf, *Kommandant im Auschwitz: Autobiographische Aufzeichnungen von Rudolf Höss* 2d ed., Stuttgart: Deutsche Verlags Anstalt (1961).

Hudson, Manley O., *International Tribunals: Past and Future*. Washington, DC: Carnegie Endowment for International Peace (1944).

Human Rights: An Agenda for the Next Century (Louis Henkin & John L. Hargrove eds.). Washington, DC: American Society of International Law (1994).

Hyde, Harlow A., *Scraps of Paper: The Disarmament Treaties Between the World Wars*. Lincoln, NE: Media (1989).

Ienaga, Saburo, *The Pacific War, 1931–1945, A Critical Perspecitve on Japan's Role in World War II*. New York: Random House (1978).

Ignatieff, Michael, *The Lesser Evil: Political Ethics in an Age of Terror*. Princeton, NJ: Princeton University Press (2004).

Infield, Gleen B., *Secrets of the SS*. New York: Military Heritage Press (1981).

In Pursuit of Justice: Examining the Evidence of the Holocaust. Washington, DC: U.S. Holocaust Memorial Council (1996).

International Crimes, Peace, and Human Rights: The Role of the International Criminal Court (Dinah Shelton ed.). Ardsley, NY: Transnational (2000).

International Criminal Law (3 vols.), (M. Cherif Bassiouni ed.). Dobbs Ferry, NY: Transnational (1986).

International Criminal Law: Cases and Materials, 2d ed. (Jordan J. Paust *et al.* eds.). Durham, NC: Carolina Academic Press (2000).

International Law and the War on Terror: International Law Studies (vol. 79), (Fred L. Borch & Paul S. Wilson eds.). Newport, RI: Naval War College (2003).

Iriye, Akira, *Power and Cuture: The Japanese-American War 1941–1945*. Cambridge, MA: Harvard University Press (1981).

Irving, David *Apocalypse 1945: The Destruction of Dresden*. Cranbrook, WA: Veritas (1995).

Jackel, Ebergard, *Hitler's World View: A Blueprint for Power* (Herbert Arnold trans.). Cambridge, MA: Harvard University Press (1981).

Jackson, Julian, *The Fall of France: The Nazi Invasion of 1940.* New York: Oxford University Press (2003).

Jackson, Robert H., *The Case Against the Nazi War Criminals: Opening Statements for the United States of America and Other Documents.* New York: Knopf (1946).

James, David H., *The Rise and Fall of the Japanese Empire.* London: Allen & Unwin (1951).

Japan at War: An Oral History. New York: New Press (1992).

Japanese Prisoners of War (Philip Towle, Maragret Kosuge & Yoichi Kibata eds.). London: Hambledon & Londen (2000).

Japanese War Crimes: The Search for Justice (Peter Li ed.). New Brunswick, NJ: Transaction (2003).

Joachimsthaler, Anton, *The Last Days of Hitler: The Legends, the Evidence, the Truth* (Helmut Bogler trans.). London: Arms & Armor Press (1996).

Johnson, Eric A., *Nazi Terror: The Gestapo, Jews, and Ordinary Germans.* New York: Basic Books (2000).

Johnson, James T., *Just War Tradition and the Restraint of War.* Princeton, NJ: Princeton University Press (1981).

Jonassohn, Kurt & Karin S. Bjornson, *Genocide and Gross Human Rights Violations in Comparative Perspective.* New Brunswick, NJ: Transaction (1998).

Jones, Dorothy V., *Toward a Just World: The Critical Years in the Search for International Justice.* Chicago: The University of Chicago Press (2002).

Judis, John B., *The Folly of Empire: What George W. Bush Could Learn from Theodore Roosevelt and Woodrow Wilson.* New York: Scribner (2004).

July, 1914, The Outbreak of the First World War (Imanuel Geiss ed.). New York: Scribner's (1967).

Just War Theory (Jean B. Elschtain ed.). New York: N.Y.U. Press (1992).

Kahn Arthur D., *Experiment in Occupation: Witness to the Turnabout, Anti-Nazi War to Cold War 1944–1946.* University Park, PA: Pennsylvania State University Press (2004).

Kahn, Leo, *Nuremberg Trials.* New York: Ballantine (1972).

Kaiser, David, *Politics and War: European Conflict from Philip II to Hitler.* Cambridge, MA: Harvard University Press (1990).

Kalshoven, Frits, *The Law of Warfare: A Summary of Its Recent History and Trends in Developemnt.* Leiden: Sijthoff (1973).

Kamenetsky, Ihor, *Hitler's Occuapation of Ukraine, 1941–1944: A Study of Totalitarian Imperialism.* Milwaukee, WI: Marquette University Press (1956).

Kamm, Henry, *Cambodia: Report from a Stricken Land.* New York: Arcade (1998).

Kaplan, Morton & Nicholas deB. Katzenbach, *The Political Foundations of International Law.* New York: Wiley (1961).

Karsten, Peter, *Law, Soldiers, and Combat.* Westport, CT: Greenwood Press (1978).

Keane, Fergal, *Season of Blood: A Rwandan Journey.* New York: Viking Press (1995).

Keenan, Joseph & Brendan F. Brown, *Crimes Against International Law.* Washington, DC: Public Affairs Press (1950).

Keitel, Wilhelm, *The Memoirs of Field-Marshal Keitel* (David Irving trans.) New York: Stein & Day (1966).

Kelly, Alfred, *The Descent of Darwin: The Popularization of Darwinism in Germany, 1860–1914.* Chapel Hill, NC: University of North Carolina Press (1981).

Kelsen, Hans, *Peace Through Law*. Chapel Hill, NC: University of North Carolina Press (1944).
_____, *Principles of International Law*. New York: Rhinehart (1959).

Kershaw, Ian, *The Nazi Dictatorship: Problems and Perspectives of Interpretation*. 4th ed. New York: Oxford University Press (2000).

Kessler, Leo, *SS Peiper: The Life and Death of SS Colonel Joachim Peiper*. London: Cooper (1986).

Kiernan, Ben, *The Pol Pot Regime: Race, Power, and Genocide in Cambodia under the Khmer Rouge, 1975–1979*. New Haven, CT: Yale University Press (1996).

Kirakossian, Jon S., *The Armenian Genocide, the Young Turks Before the Judgment of History*. Madison, CT: Sphinx Press (1992).

Klemperer, Klemens V., *German Resistance Against Hitler*. Oxford, UK: Clarendon Press (1992).

Kneeshaw, Stephen J., *In Pursuit of Peace: The American Reaction to the Kellogg-Briand Pact, 1928–1929*. New York: Garland (1991).

Knell, Hermann, *To Destroy a City: Strategic Bombing and Its Human Consequences in World War II*. Cambridge, MA: DaCapo Press (2003).

Knopps, Geery-Jan G.J., *Defenses in Contemporary International Criminal Law*. Ardsley, NY: Transnational (2001).

Knox, Donald, *Death March: The Survivors of Bataan*. New York: Harcourt, Brace, Jovanovich (1981).

Koch, H.W., *In the Name of the Volk: Political Justice in Hitler's Germany*. New York: St. Martin's Press (1989).

Kochavi, Arieh J., *Prelude to Nuremberg: Allied War Crimes Policy and the Question of Punishment*. Chapel Hill, NC: University of North Carolina Press (1998).

Koenigsberg, Richard A., *Hitler's Ideology: A Study in Psychoanalytic Sociology*. New York: Library of Social Science (1975).

Krausnick, Helmut, Hans Buchheim, Martin Broszat & Hans-Adolf Jacobsen, *Anatomy of the SS State*. New York: Walker (1968).

Kuper, Leo, *Genocide: Its Political Use in the Twentieth Century*. New Haven, CT: Yale University Press (1981).

Lael, Richard, *The Yamashita Precedent: War Crimes and Criminal Responsibility*. Wilmington, DE: Scholarly Resources (1982).

Laffin, John, *Hitler Warned Us: The Nazi's Master Plan for a Master Race*. New York: Barnes & Noble (1995).

Langbein, Hermann, *Der Auschwitz-Prozess, Eine Dokumentation* (2 vols.). Frankfurt a/M: Neue Kritik (1995).

Laquer, Walter, *The Terrible Secret: Suppression of the Truth About Hitler's "Final Solution."* New York: Penguin Books (1982).

Laternser, Hans, *Der Andere Seite im Auschwitz-Prozess, 1963–1965*. Stuttgart: Seewald (1966).

Law Reports of Trials of War Criminals: Selected and Prepared by the United Nations War Crimes Commission. (15 vols.). London: H.M. Stationery Office (1947).

Lemkin, Raphael, *Axis Rule in Occupied Europe: Laws of Occupation, Analysis of Government, and Proposals for Redress*. Washington, DC: Carnegie Endowment for International Peace (1944).

Lensen, George A., *The Strange Neutrality: Soviet-Japanese Relations During the Second World War, 1941–1945*. Tallahassee, FL: Diplomatic Press (1972).

Lentin, Anthony, *Lloyd George and the Lost Peace: From Versailles to Hitler, 1919–1940*. New York: Palgrave (2001).

Les process de Nuremberg et de Tokyo (Annette Wieviorka ed.). Paris: Editions Complexe (1996).

Lescure, Karine & Florence Trintignac, *International Justice for Former Yugoslavia: The Workings of the International Criminal Tribunal of the Hague*. The Hague: Kluwer Law International (1996).

Levie, Howard S., *Terrorism in War: The Law of War Crimes*. Dobbs Ferry, NY: Oceana (1993).

Lewin, Ronald, *The America Magic: Codes, Ciphers and the Defeat of Japan*. New York: Farrar Straus & Giroux (1982).

Lewis, Anthony, *The Black Book of Bosnia: The Consequences of Appeasement*. New York: Basic Books (1996).

Lewis, John, *Uncertain Judgment: A Bibliography of War Crimes Trials*. Santa Barbara, CA: ABC-Clio (1979).

Lewy, Guenter, *The Catholic Church and Nazi Germany*. New York: McGraw-Hill (1964).

Lifton, Robert J., *The Nazi Doctors: Medical Killing and the Psychology of Genocide*. New York: Basic Books (1986).

Lindsey, Hal, *The Everlasting Hatred: The Roots of Jihad*. Marietta, GA: Oracle House (2004).

Lost Liberties: Ashcroft and the Assault on Personal Freedom. (Cynthia Brown ed.). New York: New Press (2003).

Lottman, Herbert R., *The Fall of Paris*. New York: Harper-Collins (1992).

Lukas, Richard C., *The Forgotten Holocaust: The Poles Under German Occupation*. Lexington, KY: The University Press of Kentucky (1986).

McCarthy, Mary, *Medina*. New York: Harcourt, Brace, Jovanovich (1972).

McCoubrey, Hilaire & Nigel D. White, *International Law and Armed Conflict*. Aldershot, UK: Dartmouth (1992).

McDougal, Myres S. & F.P. Feliciano, *Law and Minimum World Public Order*. New Haven, CT: Yale University Press (1961).

McKee, Alexander, *Dresden 1945: The Devil's Tinderbox*. New York: Dutton (1982).

McNamara, Robert S. & James G. Blight, *Wilson's Ghost: Reducing the Risk of Conflict, Killing, and Catastrophe in the 21st Century*. New York: Public Affairs (2001).

MacLean, French, *The Cruel Hunters: SS-Sonderkommando Dirlewanger, Hitler's Most Notorious Anti-Partisan Unit*. Atglen, PA: Schiffer (1998).

MacMillan, Ian, *Orbit of Darkness*. San Diego, CA: Harcourt, Brace Jovanovich (1991).

MacMillan, Margaret, *Paris 1919: Six Months That Changed the World*. New York: Random House (2001).

Machiavelli, Nicolo, *The Prince*, 2d ed. (Harvey C. Mansfield trans.). Chicago: The University of Chicago Press (1998).

Mackey, Chris & Greg Miller, *The Interrogators: Inside the Secret War Against al Qaeda*. Boston: Little, Brown (2004).

Maddox, Robert J., *Weapons for Victory: The Hiroshima Decision Fifty Years Later*. Columbia, MO: University of Missouri Press (1995).

Magnarella, Paul J., *Justice in Africa: Rwanda's Genocide, Its Courts, and the U.N. Criminal Tribunal*. Brookfield, VT: Ashgate (2000).

Mageheimer, Heinz, *Hitler's War: Germany's Key Strategic Decisions, 1940–1945*. New York: Barnes & Noble (1997).

Maguire, Peter, *Law and War: An American Story*. New York: Columbia University Press (2000).

Malekian, Farhad, *International Criminal Law: The Legal and Critical Analysis of International Crimes.* Uppsala: F. Malekian (1991).

_____, *The Monopolization of International Criminal Law in the United Nations: A Jurisprudential Approach.* Stockholm: Almquist & Wiksell International (1993).

Maltitz, Horst von, *The Evolution of Hitler's Germany: The Ideology, the Personality, the Moment.* New York: McGraw Hill (1973).

Manchester, William, *American Caesar: Douglas MacArthur 1880–1964.* Boston: Little Brown (1978).

_____, *The Arms of Krupp, 1587–1968.* New York: Bantam Books (1968).

Mandel, Maud S., *In the Aftermath of Genocide: Armenians and Jews in Twentieth Century France.* Durham, NC: Duke University Press (2003).

Mann, Robert, *A Grand Delusion: America's Descent Into Vietnam.* New York: Basic Books (2001).

Maogoto, Jackson N., *War Crimes and Realpolitik: International Justice From World War I to the 21st Century.* Boulder, CO: Reinner (2004).

Maraniss, David, *They Marched Into Sunlight: War and Peace Vietnam and America, October 1967.* New York: Simon & Schuster (2003).

Markusen, Eric & David Kopf, *The Holocaust and Strategic Bombing: Genocide and Total War in the Twentieth Century.* Boulder, CO: Westview Press (1995).

Marrus, Michael R., *The Holocaust in History.* New York: Penguin Books (1987).

_____, *The Nuremberg War Crime Trial 1945–46, A Documentary History.* Boston: Bedford Books (1997).

Martin, Bernd, *Deutschland und Japan im Zweiten Weltkrieg.* Göttingen: Musterschmidt (1969).

Martin, Roy A., *Inside Nuremberg: Military Justice for the Nazi War Criminals.* Shippensberg, PA: White Mane Books (2000).

Maser, Werner, *Nuremberg: A Nation on Trial.* New York: Scribner (1979).

Mayer, Arno J., *Why Did the Heavens Not Darken? The Final Solution in History.* New York: Garland (1988).

Mendelson, John, *The Use of Seized Records in the United States Proceedings at Nurnberg.* New York: Garland (1988).

Mercier, Michele, *Crimes Without Punishment: Humanitarian Action in Former Yugoslavia.* London/East Haven, CT: Pluto Press (1995).

Meron, Theodor, *War Crimes Law Comes of Age: Essays.* New York: Clarendon Press/Oxford (1998).

Merkl, Peter H., *Political Violence Under the Swastika.* Princeton, NJ: Princeton University Press (1975).

Middlemas, Keith, *The Strategy of Appeasement: The British Government and Germany, 1937–39.* Chicago: Quadrangle Books (1972).

Mihan, George, *Looted Treasurers: Germany's Raid on Art.* London: Alliance Press (1944).

Miller, Richard L., *Nazi Justiz: Law of the Holocaust.* Westport, CT: Praeger (1995).

Minear, Richard H., *Victor's Justice: The Tokyo War Crimes Trial.* Princeton, NJ: Princeton University Press (1971).

Minow, Martha, *Between Vengeance and Forgiveness: Facing History After Genocide and Mass Violence.* Boston: Beacon Press (1998).

Miskowiak, Kristina, *The International Criminal Court: Consent, Complimentarity and Cooperation.* Copenhagen: DJF (2000).

Moir, Lindsay, *The Law of Internal Armed Conflict.* New York: Cambridge University Press (2000).

Morgan, John H., *The Great Assize: An Examination of the Law of the Nuremberg Trials.* London: J. *Murrary (1948).*

Morris, Ivan, *Japan, 1931–1945—Militarism, Fascism, Japanism?* Boston: Heath (1963).

Morris, Virginia & Michael P. Scharf, *An Insider's Guide to the International Criminal Tribunal for the Former Yugoslavia: A Documentary History and Analysis.* (2 vols.). Irvington-on-Hudson, NY: Transnational (1995).

Morrison, Wilbur H., *The Elephant and the Tiger: The Full Story of the Vietnam War.* Central Point, OR: Hellgate Press (2001).

Morse, Arthur D., *While Six Million Died: A Chronicle of American Apathy.* New York: Random House (1968).

Mosier, John, *The Blitzkrieg Myth.* New York: Harper Collins (2003).

Mosley, Leonard, *On Borrowed Time: How World War II Began.* New York: Random House (1969).

Moss, Norman, *19 Weeks: America, Britain, and the Fateful Summer of 1940.* New York: Houghton Mifflin (2003).

Mosse, George L., *The Crisis of German Ideology: The Intellectual Origins of the Third Reich.* New York: Grosset & Dunlap (1964).

_____, *The Fascist Revolution: Toward a General Theory of Fascism.* New York: Howard Fertig (1999).

_____, *The Nationalization of the Masses: Political Symbolism and Mass Movements in Germany from the Napoleonic Wars through the Third Reich.* New York: New American Library (1977).

Moynihan, Daniel P., *On the Law of Nations.* Cambridge, MA: Harvard University Press (1990).

Mueller, Gerhard O.W. & Edward H. Wise, *International Criminal Law.* South Hackensack, NJ: Rothman (1965).

Mueller, John, *The Remnants of War.* Ithaca, NY: Cornell University Press (2004).

Muller, Ingo, *Hitler's Justice: The Courts of the Third Reich* (Deborah L. Schneider trans.). Cambridge, MA: Harvard University Press (1991).

Mullins, Claud, *The Leipzig Trials: An Account of the War Criminals Trials and a Study of German Mentality.* London: H.F.G. Witherby (1921).

Murphy, John F., *The United Nations and the Control of International Violence: A Legal and Political Analysis.* Totowa, NJ: Allanheld Osmun (1982).

Musmanno, Michael A., *The Eichmann Kommandos.* Philadelphia: Macrae Smith (1961).

Naumann, Bernd, *Auschwitz: A Report on the Proceedings Against Robert Karl, Ludwig Mulka and Others before the Court at Frankfurt.* New York: Praeger (1966).

Nazi Conspiracy and Aggression: Opinion and Judgment. (8 vols.), Office of the United States Chief of Counsel for Prosecution of Axis Criminality, Washington, DC: U.S. Government Printing Office (1946).

Nazi Mass Murder: A Documentary History of the Use of Poison Gas (Eugen Kogon, Kermann Langbein & Adalbert Ruckerl eds.). New Haven, CT: Yale University Press (1993).

Nazism 1919–1945: A History in Documents and Eyewitness Accounts. (2 vols.), (J. Noakes & G. Pridham eds.). New York: Schocken Books (1990).

Neave, Airey, *Nuremberg: A Personal Record of the Time of the Major Nazi Criminals in 1945–46.* London: Hodden & Stroughton (1978).

_____, *On Trial at Nuremberg.* Boston: Little, Brown (1978).

Neier, Aryeh, *War Crimes: Brutality, Genocide, Terror and the Struggle for Justice.* New York: Times Books (1998).

Nelson, Robert E. F., *Revolution and Genocide: On the Origins of the Armenian Genocide and the Holocaust.* Chicago: The University of Chicago Press (1992).

Neumann, Franz, *Behemoth; The Structure and Practice of National Socialism 1933–1944.* New York: Harper & Row (1966).

Newman, Robert P., *Truman and the Hiroshima Cult.* East Lansing, MI: Michigan State University Press (1995).

Ninkovich, Frank, *Modernity and Power.* Chicago: The University of Chicago Press (1994).

Northedge, F.S., *The League of Nations: Its Life and Times.* Leicester, UK: Leicester University Press (1986).

O'Brien, William V., "The Nuremberg Principles" in *A Conflict of Loyalties* (James Finn ed.). New York: Pegasus (1968).

_____, *The Conduct of Just and Limited War.* New York: Praeger (1981).

O'Donnell, James P., *The Bunker: The History of the Reich Chancellery Group.* New York: DaCapo Press (1978).

O'Neil, Robert J., *The German Army and the Nazi Party.* London: Cassell (1966).

Offner, Arnold A., *America and the Origins of World War II.* Boston: Houghton Mifflin (1971).

Ohnuki-Tierney, Emiko, *Kamikaze, Cherry Blossoms, and Nationalisms: The Militarization of Aesthetics in Japanese History.* Chicago: The University of Chicago Press (2002).

Olshansky, Barbara & Greg Ruggiero, *Secret Trials and Executions: Military Tribunals and the Threat to Democracy.* New York: Seven Stories Press (2002).

Osiel, Mark J., *Mass Atrocity: Collective Memory and the Law.* New Brunswick, NJ: Transaction (1997).

_____, *Obeying Orders: Atrocity, Military Discipline, and the Law of War.* New Brunswick, NJ; Transaction (1999).

Ottaway, Susan, *Hitler's Traitors: German Resistance to the Nazis.* South Yorkshire, UK: Lee Cooper (2003).

Overy, Richard, *The Penguin Historical Atlas of the Third Reich.* London: Penguin Group (U.K.) Ltd. (1996).

Padfield, Peter, *Himmler: Reichsfuhrer-SS.* New York: Holt (1990).

Palmer, Alan, *The Kaiser: Warlord of the Second Reich.* New York: Scribner's (1978).

Papadatos, Peter, *The Eichmann Trial.* New York: Praeger (1964).

Paris, Erna, *Unhealed Wounds: France and the Klaus Barbie Affair.* New York: Grove Press (1985).

Parker, Danny S., *Battle of the Bulge: Hitler's Ardennes Offensive, 1944–45.* Conshohocken, PA: Combined Books (1991).

Parssinen, Terry, *The Oster Conspiracy of 1938.* New York: Harper Collins (2003).

Paston, David G., *Superior Orders as Affecting Responsibility for War Crimes.* New York: H.G. Publications (1946).

Paul, Allen, *Katyn: The Untold Story of Stalin's Polish Massacre.* New York: Scribner's (1991).

Pearlman, Mosche, *The Capture and Trial of Adolf Eichmann.* London: Weidenfeld & Nicolson (1963).

Peers, William R., *The My Lai Inquiry.* New York: Norton (1979).

Pelz, Stephen E., *Race to Pearl Harbor: The Failure of the Second London Naval Conference and the Onset of World War II.* Cambridge, MA: Harvard University Press (1974).

Perito, Robert M., *Where is the Lone Ranger When We Need Him? America's Search for a Postconflict Stability Force.* Washington, DC: U.S. Institute of Peace Press (2004).

Perlmutter, Amos, *FDR and Stalin: A Not So Grand Alliance,* 1943–1945. Columbia, MO: University of Missouri Press (1993).

Persico, Joseph E., *Nuremberg: Infamy on Trial.* New York: Penguin Books (1994).

Petrova, Ada & Peter Watson, *The Death of Hitler: The Full Story with New Evidence From Secret Russian Archieves.* New York: Norton (1995).

Peukert, Detlev J.K., *Inside Nazi Germany: Conformity, Opposition, and Racism in Everyday Life.* New Haven, CT: Yale University Press (1987).

Phillips, Peter, *The Tragedy of Nazi Germany.* New York: Praeger (1969).

Phillipson, Colemen, *International Law and the Great War.* London: T. Fisher Unwin (1915).

Piccigallo, Philip R., *The Japanese on Trial: Allied War Crimes Operations in the East, 1945–1951.* Austin, TX: University of Texas Press (1979).

Poland Ministry of Information, *The German New Order in Poland.* New York: Putnam's (1942).

Poltorak, A., *The Nuremberg Epilogue.* Moscow: Progress (1971).

Pompe, Cornelius, A., *Aggressive War: An International Crime.* The Hague: Martinus Nijhoff (1953).

Posner, Gerlad & John Ware, *Mengele: The Complete Story.* New York: McGraw-Hill (1986).

Potter, John D., *Yamamoto.* New York: Viking Press (1965).

Power, Samantha, *A Problem From Hell: America and the Age of Genocide.* New York: Basic Books (2002).

Primakov, Yevgeny M., *A World Challenged: Fighting Terrorism in the Twenty-First Century.* Washington, DC: Brookings Institute Press (2004).

Prunier, Gerard, *The Rwanda Crisis, 1959–1994: History of a Genocide.* London: Hurst (1995).

Punishment for War Crimes: The Interallied Documents Signed at St. James Palace, London, 13 January 1942, and Related Documents. (2 vols.). British Foreign Office, London: H.M. Stationery Office (1942).

Ramsey, Paul, *The Just War: Force and Political Responsibility.* Savage, MD: Littlefield Adams (1983).

Randall, Kenneth C., *Federal Courts and the International Human Rights Paradigm.* Durham, NC: Duke University Press (1990).

Ratner, Steven & Jason S., Abrams, *Accountability for Human Rights Atrocities in International Law: Beyond the Nuremberg Legacy.* New York: Clarendon Press/Oxford (1997).

Raus, Erhard, *Panzer Operations* (Steven E. Newton trans.). Cambridge, MA: DaCapo Press (2003).

Read, Anthony, *The Devil's Disciples: Hitler's Inner Circle.* New York: Norton (2003).

Read, James M., *Atrocity Propaganda, 1914–1918.* New Haven, CT: Yale University Press (1941).

Reardon, Betty & Curtis Colby, *War Criminals, War Victims.* New York: Random House (1974).

Rector, Frank, *The Nazi Extermination of Homosexuals.* New York: Stein & Day (1980).

Redlich, Fritz, *Hitler: Diagnosis of a Destructive Prophet.* New York: Oxford University Press (1999).

Reel, Frank, *The Case of General Yamashita.* Chicago: The University of Chicago Press (1949).

Rehnquist, William H., *All the Laws But One: Civil Liberties in Wartime.* New York: Knopf (1998).

Reiners, Ludwig, *The Lamps Went Out in Europe* (Richard & Clara Winston trans.). New York: Pantheon Books (1955).

Reisman, W., Michael, *Nullity and Revision: The Review and Enforcement of International Judgments and Awards.* New Haven, CT: Yale University Press (1971).

Reitlinger, Gerald, *The Final Solution: The Attempt to Exterminate the Jewish People of Europe 1939–1945.* New York: Beechhurst Press (1953).

_____, *The SS: Alibi of a Nation 1922–1945.* New York: Viking Press (1957).

Renouvin, Pierre, *World War II and Its Origins: International Relations, 1929–1945* (Remy Inglis Hall trans.). New York: Harper & Row (1969).

Resistance Agaisnt the Third Reich, 1933–1990 (Michal Geyer & John W. Boyer eds.). Chicago: The University fo Chicago Press (1994).

Restraints on War: Studies in the Limitation of Armed Conflict (Michael Howard ed.). Oxford, UK: Oxford University Press (1979).

Reynolds, Michael, *The Devil's Adjutant: Joachim Peiper, Panzer Leader.* New York: Sarpedon (1995).

Rhodes, James M., *The Hitler Movement: A Modern Millenarian Revolution.* Stanford, CA: Hoover Institution Press (1980).

Rhodes, Richard, *Masters of Death: The SS Einsatzgruppen and the Invention of the Holocaust.* New York: Knopf (2002).

Rich, Norman, *Hitler's War Aims: Ideology, the Nazi State, and the Course of Expansion.* (2 vols.)., New York: Norton (1973).

Rieff, David *Slaughter House: Bosnia and the Failure of the West.* New York: Simon & Schuster (1996).

Ritter, Gerhard, *Der Schlieffenplan: Kritik eines Mythos.* Munich: Oldenbourg (1956).

_____, *The German Resistance: Carl Goerdeler's Struggle Against Tyranny.* New York: Praeger (1959).

Ritter, Maria, *Return to Dresden.* Jackson, MS: University Press of Mississippi (2004).

Robinson, Jacob, *And the Crooked Shall be Made Straight: The Eichmann Trial, the Jewish Catastrophe, and Hannah Arendt's Narrative.* New York: Macmillian (1965).

Rock, Steven R., *Appeasement in International Politics.* Lexington, KY: The University Press of Kentucky (2000).

Röling, B.V.A. & Antonio Cassese, *The Tokyo Trial and Beyond: Reflections of a Peacemonger.* Cambridge, UK: Polity Press (1993).

Ronayne, Peter, *Never Again: The United States and the Prevention and Punishment of Genocide since the Holocaust.* Lanham, MD: Rowman & Littlefield (2001).

Rosenbaum, Alan S., *Prosecuting Nazi War Criminals.* San Francisco: Westview Press (1993).

Rosenbaum, Ron, *Explaining Hitler.* New York: Random House (1998).

Rossino, Alexander B., *Hitler Strikes Poland: Blitzkrieg, Ideology, and Atrocity.* Lawrence, KS: University Press of Kansas (2003).

Ruckerl, Adalbert, *The Investigation of Nazi Crimes, 1945–1978.* Hamden, CT: Archon Books (1980).

Rummel, L.R.J., *Death by Government.* New Brunswick, NJ: Transaction (1994).

Rumpf, Hans, *The Bombing of Germany.* New York: Holt, Rinehart & Winston (1963).

Russell, Edward F.L., *The Knights of Bushido: A Short History of Japanese War Crimes.* London: Greenhill Books (1958).

_____, *The Scourge of the Swastika: A Short History of Nazi War Crimes*. New York: Philosophical Library (1954).

Saburo, Ienaga, *The Pacific War, 1931–1945* (Frank Baldwin trans.). New York: Pantheon Books (1978).

Sadat, Leila N., *The International Criminal Court and the Transformation of International Law: Justice for the New Millenium*. New York: Transnational (2002).

Sadler, A.L., *The Beginner's Book of Bushido* (Daidoji Yuzan trans.). Tokyo: Kokusai Bunka Shinkokai (1941).

Safferling, Christoph J.M., *Towards an International Criminal Procedure*. New York: Oxford University Press (2001).

Sakomizu, Hisatsune, *Secret History of the End of the War*. Tokyo: Jikyuku Geppo (1946).

Samelson, William, *Warning and Hope: The Nazi Murder of European Jewry*. Portland, OR: Vallentin Mitchell (2003).

Sapinsley, Barbara, *From Kaiser to Hitler: The Life and Death of a Democracy, 1919–1933*. New York: Grosset & Dunlap (1968).

Sarat, Austin, *When the State Kills*. Princeton, NJ: Princeton University Press (2001).

Sasuly, Richard, *I.G. Farben*. New York: Boni & Gaer (1947).

Schaffer, Ronald, *Wings of Judgment: American Bombing in World War II*. New York: Oxford University Press (1985).

Scharf, Michael P., *Balkan Justice: The Story Behind the First International War Crimes Trial Since Nuremberg*. Durham, NC: Carolina Academic Press (1997).

Schlabrendorff, Fabian von, *The Secret War Against Hitler*. New York: Putnam (1965).

Schleunes, Karl A., *The Twisted Road to Auschwitz: Nazi Policy Toward German Jews, 1933–1939*. Urbana, IL: University of Illinois Press (1970).

Schmidt, Matthias, *Albert Speer: The End of a Myth* (Joachim Neugroschel trans.). London: Harrap (1985).

Schramm, Percy, *Hitler: The Man and the Military Leader* (Donald S. Detwiler trans.). Chicago: Quadrangle Books (1971).

Schuman, Frederick L., *The Nazi Dictatorship: A Study in Social Psychology and the Politics of Fascism*. New York: Knopf (1935).

Schultz, William, *Tainted Legacy: 9/11 and the Ruin of Human Rights*. New York: Thunder's Mouth Press/Nation Books (2003).

Schwarzenberger, Georg, *International Law and Totalitarian Lawlessness*. London: Jonathan Cape (1943).

Scott, George, *The Rise and Fall of the League of Nations*. New York: Macmillan (1973).

Scott, James B., *The Hague Peace Conferences of 1899 and 1907*. New York: Garland Library of War and Peace (1972).

Seabury, William, *Wilhelmstrasse: A Study of German Diplomats Under the Nazi Regime*. Berkeley, CA: University of California Press (1954).

Segev, Tom, *Soldiers of Evil: The Commandants of the Nazi Concentration Camps* (Haim Watzman trans.). New York: McGraw-Hill (1987).

Sells, Michael A., *The Bridge Betrayed: Religion and Genocide in Bosnia*. Berkeley, CA: University of California Press (1998).

Sereny, Gitta, *Albert Speer: His Battle With Truth*. New York: Knopf (1995).

Shandley, Robert R., *Unwilling Germans? The Goldhagen Debate*. Minneapolis, MN: University of Minnesota Press (1998).

Shattuck, John, *Freedman on Fire: Human Rights Wars and America's Response*. Cambridge, MA:; Harvard University Press (2003).

Sherwin, Martin J., *A World Destroyed: The Atomic Bomb and the Grand Alliance*. New York: Knopf (1975).

Shirer, William L., *The Collapse of the Third Republic: An Inquiry into the Fall of France in 1940*. New York: Simon & Schuster (1969).

_____, *The Rise and Fall of the Third Reich: A History of Nazi Germany*. New York: Simon & Schuster (1960).

Shiroyama, Saburo, *War Criminal: The Life and Death of Koki Hirota* (John Bester trans.), Tokyo: Kondansha International (1974).

Shklar, Judith N., *Legalism, Laws, Morals, and Political Trials*. Cambridge, MA: Harvard University Press (1964).

Shotwell, James T., *War as an Instrument of National Policy and Its Renunciation at the Pact of Paris*. New York: Harcourt Brace (1929).

Sigal, Leon V., *Fighting to the Finish: The Politics of War Termination in the United States and Japan*. Ithaca: NY: Cornell University Press (1988).

Silber, Laura & Allan Little, *Yugoslavia: Death of a Nation*. New York: Penguin Books (1996).

Skates, John R., *The Invasion of Japan:* Columbia, SC: University of South Carolina Press (1994).

Small, Melvin, *Victors' Justice: The Tokyo War Crimes Trial*. Princeton, NJ: Princeton University Press (1971).

Smethhurst, Richard, *A Social Basis for Pre-War Japanese Militarism*. Berkeley, CA: University of California Press (1974).

Smith, Bradley F., *Reaching Judgment at Nuremberg*. New York: Basic Books (1977).

_____, *The American Road to Nuremberg*. Stanford, CA: Hoover Institution Press (1982).

Snyder, Louis L. *Encyclopedia of the Third Reich*. New York: Paragon Press (1976).

Snydor, Charles W., *Soldiers of Destruction: The SS Death Head Division, 1933–1945*. Princeton, NJ: Princeton University Press (1993).

Sofsky, Wolfgang, *The Order of Terror: The Concentration Camps* (William Templer trans.). Princeton, NJ: Princeton University Press (1993).

Spector, Ronald, *Eagle Against the Sun: The American War with Japan*. New York: Vintage Books (1985).

Speer, Albert, *Inside the Third Reich: Memoirs* (Richard & Clara Winston trans.). New York: Collier (1970).

Sprecher, Drexel, *Inside the Nuremberg Trial*. New York: University Press of America (1999).

Spetsial'naya Komissiya po Ustanovleniyu i Rassledovaniyu Obstoyatel'stv Rasstrela Nemetsko-Fashistskimi Zakhvatchikami v Katynskom Lesu Voennoplennykh Pol'skikh Ofitserov. (Special Commission for ascertaining and investigating the circumstances of the shooting of Polish Officer prisoners by the German-Fascist invaders in the Katyn Forest). Moscow: Supp. to *Novoe Vreyma*, no. 10 (1952).

Staeglich, Wilhelm, *Auschwitz: A Judge Looks at the Evidence* (Thomas Francis trans.). Tübingen: Grabert Verlag (1986).

Staff, Ilse, *Justiz im Dritten Reich: Eine Dokumentation*. Frankfurt, a/M: Fisher-Bucherei (1964).

Stein, George H., *The Waffen SS: Hitler's Elite Guard at War, 1939–1945*. Ithaca, NY: Cornell University Press (1966).

Steiner, Henry J. & Philip Alston, *International Human Rights in Context: Law, Politics, Morals*. Oxford, UK: Oxford University Press (2000).

Stephan, Robert W., *Stalin's Secret War: Soviet Counterintelligence Against the Nazis, 1941–1945.* Lawrence, KS: University Press of Kansas (2004).

Stern, J.P., *Hitler: The Führer and the People.* Berkeley, CA: University of California Press (1975).

Stern, Jessica, *Terror in the Name of God: Why Religious Militants Kill.* New York: Harper Collins (2003).

Sternhell, Zeev, with Mario Sznajder & Maia Asheri, *The Birth of Fascist Ideology: From Cultural Rebellion to Political Revolution* (David Maisel trans.). Princeton, NJ: Princeton University Press, (1947).

Stettinius, Edward R., Jr., *Roosevelt and the Russians: The Yalta Conference* (Walter Johnson ed.). Garden City, NJ: Doubleday (1949).

Stierlin, Helm, *Adolf Hitler: A Family Perspective.* New York: Psychohistory Press (1976).

Stoessinger, John G., *Why Nations Go to War.* New York: St. Martin's Press (1998).

Stolleis, Michael, *The Law Under the Swastika.* Chicago: The University of Chicago Press (1998).

Stone, Julius, *Aggression and World Order: A Critique of United Nations Theories of Aggression.* London: Stevens (1958).

_____, *Legal Controls of International Conflict: Treatise on the Dynamics of Disputes and War-Law.* New York: Rinehart (1959).

_____, *The Eichmann Trial and the Rule of Law.* Sydney: International Commission of Jurists (1961).

Storey, Robert G., *The Final Judgment?: Pearl Harbor to Nuremberg.* San Antonio, TX: Naylor (1968).

Strange, Susan, *The Retreat of the State: The Diffusion of Power in the World Community.* New York: Cambridge University Press (1996).

Sunga, Lyal S., *Individual Responsibility in International Law for Human Rights Violations.* Dordrecht: Martinus Nijhoff (1992).

Swearingen, Ben, *The Mystery of Hermann Göering's Suicide.* New York: Harcourt Brace Jovanovich (1985).

Takamae, Eiji, *Inside GHQ: The Allied Occupation of Japan and Its Legacy.* New York: Continuum (2002).

Takeyn, Ray & Nikolas K. Grosdev, *The Receding Shadow of the Prophet: The Rise and Fall of Radical Political Islam.* Westport, CT: Praeger (2004).

Takushiro, Hattori, *The Complete History of the Greater East Asia War* (4 vols.). Tokyo: Masu (1953). (English trans. on file in U.S. Army Center for Military History).

Tanaka, Uki, *Hidden Horrors: Japanese War Crimes in World War II.* Boulder, CO: Westview Press (1996).

Taylor, A.J.P., *The Origins of the Second World War.* New York: Atheneum (1961).

Taylor, Telford, *Nuremberg and Vietnam: An American Tragedy.* Chicago: Quadrangle Books (1970).

_____, *The Anatomy of the Nuremberg Trials.* New York: Knopf (1992).

Temes, Peter S., *The Just War.* Chicago: Ivan R. Dee (2003).

Terrorism and the Law (Yonah Alexander & Edgar H. Brennen eds.). Ardsley, NY: Transnational (2001).

Teson, F.R., *Humanitarian Intervention: An Inquiry into Law and Morality.* Irvington-on-Hudson, NY: Transnational (1988).

The Armenian Genocide in Perspective (Richard Hovannisan ed.). New Brunswick, NJ: Rutgers University Press (1986).

The Buchenwald Report (David A. Hackett ed.). Boulder, CO: Westview Press (1995).

The Burning of the Reichstag: Official Findings of the Legal Commission of Inquiry. London: Relief Committee for the Victims of German Fascism (1933).

The First Hague Peace Conference. Boston: World Peace Foundation (1912).

The First World War, 1914–1918 (4 vols.), (David Stevenson ed.). Frederick, MD: University Publications of America (1989).

The Great War: Perspectives on the First World War (Robert Cowley ed.). New York: American Historical Publications (2003).

The Holocaust: Introductory Essays (David Scrase & Wolfgang Mieder eds.). Burlington, VT: Center for Holocaust Studies, University of Vermont (1996).

The Holocaust: Origins, Implementations, Aftermath (Omer Bartov ed.). New York: Routledge (2000).

The Impact of Nazism: New Perspectives on the Third Reich and Its Legacy (Alan E. Steinweis & Daniel E. Rogers eds.). Lincoln, NE: University of Nebraska Press (2003).

The International Criminal Court: The Making of the Rome Statute, Issues, Negotiations, Results (Roy S. Lee ed.). The Hague: Kluwer Law International (1999).

The Kaiser and His Court: Note Books and Letters of Admiral Georg Alexander von Muller, Chief of Naval Cabinet 1914–1918. London: MacDonald (1961).

The Law of War (Richard I. Miller ed.). Lexington, MA: Lexington Book (1975).

The Law of War Crimes: National and International Approaches (Timothy L.H. McCormick & Gerry L. Simpson eds.). The Hague: Kluwer Law International (1997).

The Law of Land Warfare: Department of the Army Field Manual 27–10. Department of the Army, Washington, DC: U.S. Government Printing Office (1956).

The Laws of Armed Conflict. 3d ed. (Dietrich Schindler & Jiri Toman eds.). Dordrecht: Martinus Nijhoff (1988).

The Laws of War: A Comprehensive Collection of Primary Documents on International Laws Governing Armed Conflict (W. Michael Reisman & Chris T. Antonious eds.). New York: Vintage Books (1994).

The Laws of War: Constraints on Warfare in the Western World (Michael Howard, George J. Andreopoulos & Mark R. Shulman eds.). New Haven, CT: Yale University Press (1994).

The Life and Letters of Francis Lieber (Thomas S. Perry ed.). Boston: J.R. Osgood (1882).

The Nanking Massacre: Its History and Historiography (Joshua A. Fogel ed.). Berkeley, CA: University of California Press (2000).

The Nazi Revolution: Germany's Guilt or Germany's Fate? (John L. Snell ed.). Boston: Heath (1959).

The 9/11 Commission Report: Final Report of the National Commission on Terrorist Attacks Upon the United States. New York: Norton (2004).

The Nuremberg Trial and International Law (George Ginsburgs & V.N. Kudriavtsev eds.). Dordrecht: Martinus Nijhoff (1990).

The Path of Genocide: The Rwanda Crisis From Uganda to Zaire (Howard Adelman & Astri Suhrke eds.). New Brunswick, NJ: Transaction (1999).

The Pearl Harbor Papers: Inside the Japanese Plans (Donald M. Goldstein & Katherine V. Dillon eds.). Dulles, VA: Brassey's (1993).

The Permanent International Criminal Court: Legal and Policy Issues (Dominic McGoldrick, Peter Rowe & Eric Donnelly eds.). Portland, OR: Hart (2004).

The Problem of Chemical and Biological Weapons (6 vols.), Stockholm International Peace Research Institute. Stockholm: Almquist & Wiksell (1971–1975).

The Prosecution of International Crimes (Roger S. Clark & Madeleine Sarin eds.). New Brunswick, NJ: Transaction (1996).

The Reports of the Hague Conferences of 1899 and 1907 (James B. Scott, ed.). Oxford, UK: Oxford University Press (1917).

The Rise and Fall of Imperial Japan (S.L. Mayer ed.). Greenwich, CT: Bison Books (1984).

The Search for Justice: Japanese War Crimes (Peter Li ed.). New Brunswick, NJ: Transaction (2003).

The Specter of Genocide: Mass Murder in Historical Perspective (Robert Gellately & Ben Kiernan eds.). New York: Cambridge University Press (2003).

The Speeches of Adolf Hitler, April 1922–August 1939 (2 vols.), (Norman H. Baynes ed.). New York: Oxford University Press (1942).

The Third Reich (18 vols.), New York: Time-Life Books (1989).

The Tokyo Judgment: The International Military Tribunal for the Far East (IMTFE) (3 vols.), (B.V.A. Röling & C.F. Rüter eds.). Amsterdam: APA University Press (1977).

The Tokyo War Crimes Trial: Proceedings of the Tribunal (22 vols.), (R. John Pritchard, Sonia M. Zaide (eds.). New York: Garland (1981).

The Trial of Adolf Eichmann: Record of the Proceedings in the District Court of Jerusalem (6 vols.), Jerusalem: Ministry of Justice, State of Israel (1992–95).

The United States and the International Criminal Court (Sarah B. Sewall & Carl Kaysen eds.). Lanham, MD: Rowman and Littlefield (2000).

The UN Security Council: From the Cold War to the 21st Century (David A. Malone ed.). Boulder, CO: Reinner (2003).

The Vietnam War and International Law (4 vols.), (Richard A. Falk ed.). Princeton, NJ: Princeton University Press (1968–1976).

The War on Our Freedoms: Civil Liberties in an Age of Terrorism (Richard C. Leone & Greg Angrig eds.). New York: BBS Public Affairs (2003).

This Time We Knew: Western Responses to Genocide in Bosnia (Thomas Cushman & Stjepan G. Mestroul eds.). New York: New York University Press (1996).

Thorne, Christopher, *Allies of a Kind: The United States, Britain and the War Against Japan.* London: Hanish Hamilton (1978).

Tobias, Fritz, *The Reichstag Fire.* New York: Putnam (1964).

Toland, John, *Adolf Hitler: The Definitive Biography.* New York: Anchor/Doubleday (1976).

_____, *The Last 100 Days.* New York: Random House (1965).

_____, *The Rising Sun.* New York: Random House (1970).

Toynbee, Arnold J., *Armenian Atrocities: The Murder of a Nation.* London: Hadden & Stroughton (1915).

_____, *The German Terror in Belgium: An Historical Record.* New York: Doran (1917).

_____, *The Treatment of the Armenians in the Ottoman Empire, 1915–1916.* London: H.M. Stationery Office (1918).

Trainin, Aron N., *Hitlerite Responsibility under Criminal Law.* New York: Hutchinson (1945).

Trask, David F., *Victory Without Peace: American Foreign Relations in the Twentieth Century.* New York: Wiley (1968).

Trefousse, Hans L., *What Happened at Pearl Harbor?* New Haven, CT: College & University Press (1958).

Trial of the Major War Criminals Before the International Military Tribunal (42 vols.), Nuremberg: Secretariat of the Tribunal, Allied Control Council of Germany (1947).

Trooboff, P.D., *Law and Responsibility in Warfare: The Vietnam Experience*. Chapel Hill, NC: University of North Carolina Press (1975).

Truman, Harry S., *Memoirs, 1945: Year of Decision*. Garden City, NJ: Doubleday (1955).

Turner, Henry A., *German Big Business and the Rise of Hitler*. New York: Oxford University Press (1985).

Tusa, Ann & John Tusa, *The Nuremberg Trial*. New York: McGraw-Hill (1983).

Tutorow, Norman E., *War Crimes, War Criminals and War Crimes Trials* (ann. bibliography). New York: Greenwood Press (1986).

Twagilimana, Aimable, *The Debris of Ham: Ethnicity, Regionalism, and the 1994 Rwandan Genocide*. Lanham, MD: University Press of America (2003).

Tzu, Sun, *The Art of War* (Samuel B. Griffith ed.). Oxford, UK: Clarendon Press (1963).

Unanswered Questions: Nazi Germany and the Genocide of the Jews (Francois Furet ed.). New York: Schocken (1989).

United Nations War Crime Commission, *Law Reports of Trials of War Criminals: Four Genocide Trials*. New York: Fertig (1992).

United States Hegemony and the Foundation of International Law (Michael Byers & George Nolte eds.). Cambridge, UK: Cambridge University Press (2003).

U.S. State Department, *1994 Report on Bosnia and Herzegovina Human Rights Practices*. Washington, DC: U.S. Government Printing Office (February, 1995).

Valentino, Benjamin A., *Final Solutions: Mass Killing and Genocide in the 20th Century*. Ithaca, NY: Cornell University Press (2003).

Vanderwerff, Clorrine, *Kill Thy Neighbor*. Boise, ID: Pacific Press (1996).

Veale, Frederick J.P., *Advance to Barbarism: The Development of Total Warfare from Sarajevo to Hiroshima*. London: Mitre (1968).

_____, *War Crimes Discreetly Veiled*. New York: Devin-Adair (1959).

Vermeil, Edmund, *Germany in the Twentieth Century: A Political and Cultural History of the Weimar Republic and the Third Reich*. New York: Praeger (1956).

Victor, George, *Hitler: The Pathology of Evil*. Washington, DC: Brassey's (1998).

Viereck, Peter, *Metapolitics: The Roots of the Nazi Mind*. New York: Capricorn Books (1965).

Viscount Maugham, *U.N.O. and War Crimes*. Westport, CT: Greenwood Press (1975).

Volkogonov, Dimitri, *Stalin: Triumph and Tragedy* (Harold Shukman trans.). Rocklin, CA: Prima (1992).

von Clausewitz, Karl, *War, Politics, and Power: Selections from On War and I Believe and Profess* (Edwin M. Collins trans.). Washington, DC: Regnery Gateway (1962).

von Manstein, Erich, *Lost Victories: The War Memoirs of Hitler's Most Brilliant General*. Novato, CA: Presidio (1994).

von Weizsacker, Richard, *From Weimar to the Wall* (Ruth Hein trans.). New York: Broadway (1999).

Vulliamy, Edward, *Seasons in Hell: Understanding Bosnia's War*. London: Simon & Schuster (1994).

Waite, Robert G.L., *The Psychopathic God: Adolf Hitler*. New York: Basic Books (1997).

Walters, F.P., *A History of the League of Nations*. London: Oxford University Press (1952).

Walzer, Michael, *Arguing About War*. New Haven, CT: Yale University Press (2004).

_____, *Just and Unjust Wars: A Moral Argument with Historical Illustrations*, 2d ed. New York: Basic Books (1991).

War and Morality (Richard A. Wasserstrom ed.). Belmont, CA: Wadsworth (1970).

War Crimes in International Law (Yoram Dinstein & Malalo Tabory eds.). The Hague: Matinus Nijhoff (1996).

Warlimont, Walter, *Inside Hitler's Headquarters.* New York: Praeger (1962).

Warner, Denis & Peggy Warner, *The Sacred Warriors: Japan's Suicide Legions.* New York: Van Nostrand (1982).

Wawro, Geoffrey, *The Franco-Prussian War: The German Conquest of France in 1870–1871.* New York: Cambridge University Press (2003).

Webster, Paul, *Pétain's Crime: The Full Story of the French Collaboration in the Holocaust.* Chicago: Ivan R. Dee (1991).

Wechsler, Herbert, "The Issues of the Nuremberg Trial," in *Principles, Politics, and Fundamental Law.* Cambridge, MA: Harvard University Press (1961).

Weinburg, Gerhard L., *Guide to Captured German Documents.* New York: Columbia University Press (1952).

_____, *The Foreign Policy of Hitler's Germany: Starting World War II, 1937–1939.* Chicago: The University of Chicago Press (1980).

Weindling, Paul J., *Nazi Medicine and the Nuremberg Trials: From Medical War Crimes to Informed Consent.* New York: Palgrave Macmillan (2004).

Weingartner, James J., *A Peculiar Crusade: Willis M. Everett and the Malmédy Massacre.* New York: New York University Press (2000).

_____, *Crossroads of Death: The Story of the Malmédy Massacre and Trial.* Los Angeles: University of California Press (1979).

_____, *Hitler''s Guard: The Story of the Liebstandarte SS Adolf Hitler, 1933–1945.* Carbondale, IL: Southern Illinois University Press (1974).

Weiner, Jan,. *The Assassination of Heydrich.* New York: Grossman (1969).

Weintraub, Stanley, *The Last Great Victory: The End of World War II, July–August 1945.* New York: Dutton (1995).

Weisburd, Mark A., *Use of Force: The Practice of States Since World War II.* University Park, PA: Pennsylvania State University Press (1997).

Weiss, John, *Ideology and Death: Why the Holocaust Happened in Germany.* Chicago: Ivan R. Dee (1996).

_____, *Nazis and Fascists in Europe, 1918–1945.* New York: Harper & Row (1967).

Weitz, Eric D., *A Century of Genocide: Utopias of Race and Nation.* Princeton, NJ: Princeton University Press (2003).

Welch, J.M., *The Tokyo Trial: A Bibliographic Guide to English-Language Sources.* Westport, CT: Greenwood Press (2002).

Werrell, Kenneth P., *Blankets of Fire: U.S. Bombers Over Japan During World War II.* Washington, DC: Smithsonian Institution Press (1996).

Wheatcroft, Andrew, *Infidels: A History of the Conflict Between Christendom and Islam.* New York: Random House (2004).

Wheaton, Eliot B., *The Nazi Revolution, 1933–35: Prelude to Calamity.* New York: Doubleday (1969).

Wheeler-Bennett, John W., *Munich: Prologue to Tragedy.* New York: Duell, Sloan & Pierce (1948).

_____, *The Nemesis of Power: The German Army in Politics, 1918–1945.* London: Macmillan (1961).

Whiting Charles, *Massacre at Malmédy: The Story of Joachim Peiper's Battle Group, Ardennes, December, 1944.* New York: Stein & Day (1971).

Why Germany? National Socialist Anti-Semitism and the European Context (John Milfull ed.). Providence, RI: Bert (1993).

Wighton, Charles, *Heydrich: Hitler's Most Evil Henchman*. New York: Chilton (1962).

Williams, Emilio, *A Way of Life and Death: Three Centuries of Prussian-German Militarism*, Nashville, TN: Vanderbilt University Press (1986).

Williams, Paul R., & Michael P. Scharf, *Peace With Justice? War Aims and Accountability in the Former Yugoslavia*. Lanham, MD: Rowman & Littlefield (2002).

Williams, Paul R. & Norman Cigar, *A Prima Facie Case for the Indictment of Slobodan Milosevic*. London: Alliance to Defend Bosnia-Herzegovina (1996).

Williams, Peter & David Wallace, *Unit 731: Japan's Secret Biological Warfare in World War II*. New York: Free Press (1989).

Willis, James F., *Prologue to Nuremberg: The Politics and Diplomacy of Punishing War Criminals of the First World War*. Westport, CT: Greenwood Press (1982).

Willis, William N., *The Kaiser and the Barbarians: An Authoritative Record of the Crimes Committed by the Germans in France and Belgium in the Name of War: Together with the Official Reports of the Commission of Enquiry Appointed by King Albert of Belgium*. London: Anglo-Eastern (1914).

Wistrich, Robert S., *Weekend in Munich: Art, Propaganda and Terror in the Third Reich*. London: Pavillion Books (1995).

_____, *Who's Who in Nazi Germany*. London: Weidenfeld & Nicolson (1982).

Woetzel, Robert K., *The Nuremberg Trials in International Law with a Postlude on the Eichmann Case*. New York: Praeger (1962).

Woods, Randall B. & Howard Jones, *Dawning of the Cold War: The United States' Quest for Order*. Athens, GA: University of Georgia Press (1967).

Wormuth, F.D., *To Chain the Dog of War*. Urbana, IL: University of Illinois Press (1989).

Wright, Quincy, *A Study of War*, 2d ed. Chicago: The University of Chicago Press (1967).

Wyman, David S., *The Abandonment of the Jews: America and the Holocaust, 1941–1945*. New York: Pantheon Press (1984).

Yoshiaki, Yoshimi, *Comfort Women: Sexual Slavery in the Japanese Military During World War II* (Suzanne O'Brein trans.). New York: Columbia University Press (1995).

Yoshitsu, Michael M., *Japan and the San Francisco Peace Settlement*. New York: Columbia University Press (1983).

Young, Louise, *Japan's Total Empire: Manchuria and the Culture of Wartime Imperialism*. Berkeley, CA: University of California Press (1998).

Zawodny, J.K., *Death in the Forest: The Story of the Katyn Forest Massacre*. Notre Dame, IN: University of Notre Dame Press (1962).

Zimmerman, Warren, *Origins of Catastrophe: Yugoslavia and Its Destroyers—America's Last Ambassador Tells What Happened and Why*. New York: Times Books (1996).

Zuccotti, Susan, *Under His Very Windows: The Vatican and the Holocaust in Italy*. New Haven, CT: Yale University Press, (2000).

Zuckerman, Larry, *The Rape of Belgium: The Untold Story of World War I*. New York: New York University Press (2003).

Periodicals and Secondary Sources

Abbott, Kenneth., "International Relations Theory, International Law, and the Regime Governing Atrocities in Internal Conflicts," 93 *American Journal of International Law* 361 (1999).

Adams, William, "The American Peace Commission and the Punishment of Crimes Committed During War," 39 *Law Quarterly Review* 245 (1923).

Addicott, Jeffrey F. & William A. Hudson, Jr., "The Twenty-Fifth Anniversary of My Lai: A Time to Inculcate the Lessons," 139 *Military Law Review* 153 (1993).

Akehurst, Michael, "Custom as a Source of International Law," 47 *British Yearbook of International Law* 1 (1974).

Akhavan, Payam, "Beyond Impunity: Can International Criminal Justice Prevent Future Atrocities,?" 95 *American Journal of International Law* 7 (2001).

_____, "Justice and Reconciliation in the Great Lakes Region of Africa: The Contributions of the International Criminal Tribunal for Rwanda," 7 *Duke Journal of Comparative and International Law* 325 (1997).

_____, "Punishing War Criminals in the Former Yugoslavia: A Critical Juncture for the New World Order," 15 *Human Rights Quarterly* 262 (1993).

_____, "The International Criminal Tribunal for Rwanda: The Politics and Pragmatics of Punishment," 90 *American Journal of International Law* 501 (1996).

Alderman, Sidney, "Background and High Lights of the Nuernberg Trial," 14 *I.C.C. Practitioner's Journal* 99 (November, 1946).

Aldrich, George, "Jurisdiction of the International Criminal Tribunal for the Former Yugoslavia," 90 *American Journal of International Law* 64 (1996).

Alexander, Leo, "Destructive and Self-Destructive Trends in Criminalized Society: A Study of Totalitarianism," 39 *Journal of Criminal Law and Criminology* 553 (1949).

_____, "War Crimes and Their Motivation: The Socio-Psychological Structure of the SS and the Criminalization of Society," 39 *Journal of Criminal Law and Criminology* 298 (1948).

Alvarez, Jose E., "Crimes of States/Crimes of Hate: Lessons from Rwanda," 24 *Yale Journal of International Law* 3654 (1999).

_____, "Nuremberg Revisited: The Tadic Case," 7 *European Journal of International Law* 245 (1996).

_____, "Rush to Closure: Lessons of the Tadic Judgment," 96 *Michigan Law Review* 2031 (1998).

_____, "The Quest for Legitimacy: An Examination of 'The Power of Legitimacy Among Nations,'" 24 *New York University Journal of Law and Politics* 199 (1991).

Amann, Diane M., "Harmonic Covergence? Constitutional Criminal Procedure in an International Context," 75 *Indiana Law Journal* 809 (2000).

Anderson, John, "An International Criminal Court: An Emerging Idea," 15 *Nova Law Review* 433 (1991).

Anderson, Kenneth, "Nuremberg Sensibility: Telford Taylor's Memoir of the Nuremberg Trials," 7 *Harvard Human Rights Journal* 281 (1994).

_____, "What To Do With Bin Laden and Al Qaeda Terrorists?: A Qualified Defense of Military Commissions and United States Policy on Detainees at Guantanmo Bay Naval Base," 25 *Harvard Journal of Law and Public Policy* 591 (2002).

Andrews, Lucas W., "Sailing Around the Flat Earth: The International Criminal Tribunal for the Former Yugoslavia as a Failure of Jurisprudential Theory," 11 *Emory International Law Review* 471 (1997).

Annas, George A., "Mengele's Birthmark: The Nuremberg Code in United States Courts," 7 *Journal of Contemporary Health Law and Policy* 17 (1991).

April, Nathan, "An Inquiry into the Juridical Basis for the Nuernberg War Crimes Trial," 30 *Minnesota Law Review* 313 (1946).

Aptel, Cecile, "The Intent to Commit Genocide in the Case Law of the International Criminal Tribunal for Rwanda," 13 *Criminal Law Forum* 273 (2002).

Arbour, Louise, "The Prosecution of International Crimes: Prospects and Pitfalls," 1 *Washington University Journal of Law and Policy* 13 (1999).

Arend, Anthony C., "International Law and the Recourse to Force: A Shift in Paradigms," 27 *Stanford Journal of International Law* 1 (1990).

Armstead, J. Holmes, Jr., "The United States vs. William Calley: An Opportunity Missed," 10 *Southern University Law Review* 205 (1984).

Arnold, Roberta, "The Mens Rea of Genocide Under the Statute of the International Criminal Court," 14 *Criminal Law Forum* 127 (2003).

Askin, Kelly D., "Prosecuting Wartime Rape and Other Gender-Related Crimes Under International Law: Extraordinary Advances, Enduring Obstacles," 21 *Berkeley Journal of International Law* 288 (2003).

Arsanjani, Mahoush H., "The Rome Statute of the International Criminal Court," 93 *American Journal of International Law* 22 (1999).

Astorino, Samuel J., The Impact of Sociological Jurisprudence on International Law in the Inter-War Period: The American Experience," 34 *Duquesne Law Review* 277 (1996).

Aydelott, Danise, "Mass Rape During War: Prosecuting Bosnian Rapists Under International Law," 7 *Emory International Law Review* 585 (1993).

Baade, Hans W., "The Eichmann Trial: Some Legal Aspects," 1961 *Duke Law Journal* 400.

Bachrach, Michael, "The Protection and Rights of Victims Under International Criminal Law," 34 *International Lawyer* 7 (2000).

Baez, Jose A., "An International Criminal Court: Further Tales of the King of Corinth," 23 *Georgia Journal of International and Comparative Law* 289 (1993).

Baker, James A., III., "Law, Power and Politics After the Cold War," 34 *Columbia Journal of Transnational Law* 531 (1996).

Bakker, Jeanne L., "The Defense of Obedience to Superior Orders: The Mens Rea Requirement," 17 *American Journal of Criminal Law* 55 (1989).

Balint, Jennifer, "Conflict, Conflict Victimization, and Legal Redress, 1945–1996," 59 *Law and Contemporary Problems* 231 (1996).

_____, "The Place of Law in Addressing International Regime Conflicts," 59 *Law and Contemporary Problems* 103 (1996).

Bantekas, Ilias, "The Contemporary Law of Superior Responsibility," 93 *American Journal of International Law* 573 (1999).

Barry, John V., "The Trial and Punishment of Axis War Criminals," 17 *Australian Law Journal* 43 (1943).

Bass, Gary J., "War Crimes and the Limits of Legalism," 97 *Michigan Law Review* 2103 (1999).

Bassiouni, M. Cherif, "A Comprehensive Strategic Approach on International and Transnational Criminality, Including the Establishment of an International Criminal Court," 15 *Nova Law Review* 354 (1991).

_____, "Combating Impunity for International Crimes," 71 *University of Colorado Law Review* 409 (2000).

_____, " 'Crimes Against Humanity:' The Need for a Specialized Convention," 31 *Columbia Journal of Transnational Law* 457 (1994).

_____, "Enslavement as an International Crime," 23 *New York University Journal of International Law and Politics* 445 (1991).

_____, "Establishing an International Criminal Court: Historical Survey," 149 *Military Law Review* 49 (1995).

_____, "From Versailles to Rwanda in Seventy-Five Years: The Need to Establish a Permanent International Criminal Court," 10 *Harvard Human Rights Journal* 11 (1997).

_____, "International Crimes: Jus Cogens and Obliogatio Erga Omnes," 59 *Law and Contemporary Problems* 63 (1996).

_____, "International Law and the Holocaust," 9 *California Western International Law Journal* 201 (1979).

_____, "Islam: Concept, Law and World Habeas Corpus," 1 *Rutgers-Camden Law Journal* 160 (1969).

_____, "Negotiating the Treaty of Rome on the Establishment of an International Criminal Court," 32 *Cornell International Law Journal* 443 (1999).

_____, "Nuremberg Forty Years After: An Introduction," 18 *Case Western Reserve Journal of International Law* 261 (1986).

_____, "Nuremberg: Forty Years Later, in Panel Session: Forty Years After the Nuremberg and Tokyo Tribunals: The Impact of the War Crimes Trials on International and National Law," 80 *American Society of International Procedure* 56 (1986).

_____, "Searching for Peace and Achieving Justice: The Need for Accountability," 59 *Law and Contemporary Problems* 9 (1996).

_____, "The Penal Characteristics of Conventional International Criminal Law," 15 *Case Western Reserve Journal of International Law* 27 (1983).

_____, "The International Criminal Court in Historical Context," *1999 St. Louis-Warsaw Transatlantic Law Journal* 55.

_____, "The Proscribing Function of International Criminal Law in the Processes of International Protection of Human rights," 9 *Yale Journal of World Public Order* 193 (1982).

_____, "World War I: 'the war to end all wars' and the Birth of a Handicapped International Criminal Justice System" 30 *Denver Journal of International Law and Policy* 244 (2002).

Bassiouni, M. Cherif & Christopher L. Blakesley, "The Need for an International Criminal Court in the New International World Order," 25 *Vanderbilt Journal of Transnational Law* 151 (1992).

Battle, George, C., "The Trials Before the Leipsic [sic.] Supreme Court of Germans Accused of War Crimes," 8 *Virginia Law Review* 1 (1921).

Baxter, Richard R., "The First Modern Codification of the Law of War — Francis Lieber and general Order No. 100," 3 *International Review of the Red Cross* 171 (1963).

_____, "So-Called 'Unprivileged Belligerency': Spies, Guerrillas and Saboteurs," 28 *British Year Book of International Law* 323 (1951).

Bazyler, Michael J., "Reexamining the Doctrine of Humanitarian Intervention in Light of the Atrocities in Kampuchea and Ethiopia," 23 *Stanford Journal of International Law* 547 (1987).

Beard, Jack M., "America's New War on Terror: The Case for Self-Defense Under International Law," 25 *Harvard Journal of Law and Public Policy* 559 (2002).

Beck, Robert J., "Munich's Lessons Reconsidered," 14 *International Security* 161 (Fall, 1969).

Beiner, Theresa M., "Due Process for All? Due Process, The Eighth Amendment and Nazi War Criminals," 80 *Journal of Criminal Law and Criminology* 293 (1989).

Belknap, Michal R., "A Putrid Pedigree: The Bush Administration's Military Tribunals in Historical Perspective," 38 *California Western Law Review* 433 (2002).

_____, "The Supreme Court Goes to War: The Meaning and Implications of the Nazi Saboteur Case," 89 *Military Law Review* 59 (1980).

Bellott, Hugh H.L., "War Crimes and War Criminals," 36 *Canadian Law Times* 754 (1916).

Beres, Louis R., "After the Gulf War: Prosecuting Iraqi Crimes Under the Rule of Law," 24 *Vanderbilt Journal of Transnational Law* 487 (1991).

_____, "Iraqi Crimes and International Law: The Imperative to Punish," 21 *Denver Journal of International Law and Policy* 335 (1993).

_____, "Prosecuting Iraqi Gulf War Crimes: Allied and Israeli Rights Under International Law," 16 *Hastings International and Comparative Law Review* 41 (1992).

_____, "Toward Prosecution of Iraqi Crimes Under International Law: Jurisprudential Foundations and Jurisdictional Choices," 22 *California Western International Law Journal* 127 (1992).

Berger, Jacob, "The Legal Nature of War Crimes and the Problem of Superior Command," 38 *American Political Science Review* 1203 (1944).

Bernays, Murray, "Legal Basis of the Nuremberg Trials," 35 *Survey Graphics* 390 (January, 1946).

Bernbaum, John A., "The Captured German Records: A Bibliographic Survey," 32 *Historian* 564 (1970).

Bernstein, Barton J., "Compelling Japan's Surrender without the A-Bomb, Soviet Entry, or Invasion: Reconsidering the US Bombing Survey's Early-Surrender Conclusions," 18 *Journal of Strategic Studies* 101 (June 1995).

Bial, Louis C., Note: "The Nuremberg Judgment and International Law," 13 *Brooklyn Law Review* 34 (1947).

Bickley, Lynn S., Comment: "U.S. Resistance to the International Criminal Court: Is the Sword Mightier than the Law,?" 14 *Emory International Law Review* 213 (2000).

Biddle, Francis, "Nuremberg: The Fall of the Supermen," 13 *American Heritage* 65 (August 1962).

_____, "The Nuremberg Trial," 33 *Virginia Law Review* 679 (1947).

Binder, Guyora, "Representing Nazism: Advocacy and Identity at the Trial of Klaus Barbie," 98 *Yale Law Journal* 1321 (1989).

Birmingham, Robert L., Note, "The War Crimes Trial: A Second Look," 24 *University of Pittsburgh Law Review* 132 (1962).

Birnbaum, David, "Denaturalization and Deportation of Nazi War Criminals in the United States: Upholding Constitutional Principles in a Single Proceeding," 10 *New York Law School Journal of International and Comparative Law* 201 (1989).

Birov, Victoria A., "Prize or Plunder: The Pillage of Works of Art and the International Law of War," 30 *New York University Journal of International Law and Politics* 201 (1997/1998).

Bishop, Joseph W., Jr., "The Question of War Crimes," 54 *Commentary* 85 (1972).

Bix, Herbert P., "Japan's Delayed Surrender: A Reinterpretation," 19 *Diplomatic History* 197 (Spring 1995).

Black, Naomi, "Decision-making and the Munich Crisis," 6 *British Journal of International Studies* 278 (Octobr 1980).

Blakesley, Christopher L., "Jurisdiction as Legal Protection Against Terrorism," 19 *Connecticut Law Review* 895 (1987).

_____, "Jurisdiction, Definition of Crimes, and Triggering Mechanisms," 25 *Denver Journal of International Law and Policy* 233 (1997).

Blewett, George F., "Victor's Injustice: The Tokyo War Crimes Trial," 4 *American Perspective* 282 (1950).

Bliss, Tasker H., "The Armistices," 16 *American Journal of International Law* 509 (1922).

Bloch, David S., "Dangers of Righteousness: Unintended Consequences of Kadic v. Karadzic," 4 *Tulsa Journal of Comparative and International Law* 35 (1996).

Blodgett, Nancy, "Cambodia Case: Lawyer Wants Genocide Trial," 71 *American Bar Association Journal* 31 (November 1985).

Bohlander, Michael, "Last Exit Bosnia: Transferring War Crimes Prosecutions from The International Tribunal to Domestic Courts," 14 *Criminal Law Forum* 59 (2003).

Boling, David, "Mass Rape, Enforced Prostitution, and the Japanese Imperial Army: Japan Eschews International Legal Responsibility?," 32 *Columbia Journal of Transnational Law* 533 (1995).

Bolton, John R., "The Global Prosecutors: Hunting War Criminals in the Name of Utopia," 78 *Foreign Affairs* 1 (January–February 1999).

_____, "The Risks and Weaknesses of the International Criminal Court from America's Perspective," 41 *Virginia Journal of International Law* 186 (2000).

Boozer, Jack S., "Children of Hippocrates: Doctors in Nazi Germany," 450 *Annuals of the American Academy of Political and Social Science* 83 (July 1980).

Borchard, Edwin M., "The Multilateral Treaty for the Renunciation of War," 23 *American Journal of International Law* 116 (1929).

Bower, Graham J., "The Law of War: Prisoners and Reprisals," 1 *Transactions of the Grotius Society* 23 (1915).

Bowett, Derek, "Reprisals Involving Recourse to Armed Force," 66 *American Journal of International Law* 1 (1972).

Boyle, Francis A., "Law of Power Politics," *1980 University of Illinois Law Forum* 901.

_____, "The Irrelevance of International Law: The Schism between International Law and International Politics," 10 *California Western International Law Journal* 193 (1980).

_____, "The Relevance of International Law to the 'Paradox' of Nuclear Deterrence," 80 *Northwestern University Law Review* 1407 (1986).

Bradford, William C., "International Legal Regimes and the Incidence of Inter-State War in the 20th Century," A Cursory Quantitative Assessment of the Associative Relationship," 16 *American University International Law Review* 647 (2001).

Brand, James T., "Crimes Against Humanity and the Nürnberg Trials," 28 *Oregon Law Review* 93 (1949).

Brierly, J.L., "Do We Need an International Criminal Court?", 8 *British Year Book of International Law* 81 (1927).

_____, "Some Implications of the Pact of Paris," 10 *British Journal of International Law* 208 (1997).

Broomhall, Bruce, "Looking Forward to the Establishment of an International Criminal Court: Between State Consent and the Rule of Law," 8 *Criminal Law Forum* 317 (1997).

Brown, Bartrum S., "U.S. Objections to the Statute of the International Criminal Court: A Brief Response," 31 *New York University Journal of International Law and Politics* 855 (1999).

Bullitt, William C., "*How We Won the War and Lost the Peace,*" *Life*, August 10, 1948, at 83–97 and September 6, 1948, at 86–103.

Burley, Anne-Marie S., "International Law and International Relations Theory: A Dual Agenda," 87 *American Journal of International Law* 205 (1993).

Burns, Peter, "An International Criminal Tribunal: The Difficult Union of Principles and Politics," 5 *Criminal Law Forum* 341 (1994).

Bush, Jonathan A., "Nuremberg: The Modern Law of War and Its Limitations," 93 *Columbia Law Review* 2022 (1993).

Cadoux, C.J., "The Punishing of Germany After the War of 1914–1918," 43 *Hibbert Journal* 107 (January 1945).

Caloyanni, Megalos, A., "An International Criminal Court," 14 *Transactions of the Grotius Society* 69 (1928).

Campbell, A.H., "Fascism and Legality," 62 *Law Quarterly Review* 141 (1946).

Carcano, Andrea, "Sentencing and the Gravity of the Offense in International Law," 51 *International and Comparative Law Quarterly* 583 (2002).

Carnegie, A.R., "Jurisdiction Over Violations of the Laws and Customs of War," 39 *British Year Book of International Law* 402 (1963).

Carroll, Christina M., "An Assessment of the Role and Effectiveness of the International Criminal Tribunal for Rwanda," 18 *Boston University International Law Journal* 163 (2000).

Carter, E.F., "The Nuremberg Trails: A Turning Point in the Enforcement of International Law," 28 *Nebraska Law Review* 370 (1949).

Cassell, Douglass, "The ICC's New Legal Landscape: The Need to Expand U.S. Domestic Jurisdiction to Prosecute Genocide, War Crimes, and Crimes Against Humanity," 23 *Fordham International Law Journal* 378 (1999).

_____, "Empowering United States Courts to Hear Crimes Within the Jurisdiction of the International Criminal Court," 35 *New England Law Review* 421 (2001).

Cassese, Antonio, "Reflections on International Criminal Justice," 61 *Modern Law Review* 1 (1998).

_____, "Terrorism is Also Disputing some Crucial Categories of International Law," 12 *European Journal of International Law* 996 (2001).

Cavicchia, Joel, "The Prospects for an International Criminal Court in the 1990s," 10 *Dickinson Journal of International Law* 223 (1992).

Charney, Jonathan L., *Editorial Comment:* "Progress in International Law," 93 *American Journal of International Law* 452 (1999).

Chesterman, Simon, "An Altogether Different Order: Defining the Elements of Crimes Against Humanity," 10 *Duke Journal of Comparative and International Law* 307 (2000).

Chinkin, Christine, "Rape and Sexual Abuse of Women in International Law," 5 *European Journal of International Law* 326 (1994).

Clark, J.B., "Shall There be War After War,"? 11 *American Journal of International Law* 790 (1917).

Clark, Roger S., "Medina: An Essay on the Principles of Criminal Liability for Homicide," 5 *Rutgers-Camden Law Journal* 59 (1973).

Clarke, R. Floyd, "Germany Under International Law," 53 *American Law Review* 401 (1919).

Coan, Christin B., "Rethinking the Spoils of War: Prosecuting Rape as a War Crime in the International Criminal Tribunal for the Former Yugoslavia," 26 *North Carolina Journal of International Law and Commercial Regulation* 183 (2001).

Cohen, Laurie A., Comment, "Application of the Realist and Liberal Perspectives to the Implementation of War Crimes Trials: Case Studies of Nuremberg and Bosnia," 2 *U.C.L.A. Journal of International and Foreign Affairs* 113 (1997).

Cohn, Ernst J., "The Problem of War Crimes Today," 26 *Transactions of the Grotius Society* 125 (1940).

Colby, Elbridge, "War Crimes and Their Punishment," 8 *Minnesota Law Review* 40 (1923).

Combs, Nancy A., "Copping a Plea to Genocide: The Plea Bargaining of International Crimes," 151 *University of Pennsylvania Law Review* 1 (2002).

Commission on the Responsibility of the Authors of the War and on Enforcement of Penalties, *Report Presented to the Preliminary Peace Conference,* 14 American Journal of International Law 95 (1920).

Comyns-Carr, Arthur S., "The Judgment of the International Military Tribunal for the Far East," 34 *Transactions of the Grotius Society* 141 (1949).

Conlen, William J., Robert H. Jackson & Walter Lippman, "The Legal Basis for Trial of War Criminals," 19 *Temple Law Quarterly* 133 (1946).

Cowles, Willard B., "Trial of War Criminals by Military Tribunals," 30 *American Bar Association Journal* 330 (June 1944).

_____, "Trials of War Criminals (Non-Nuremberg)," 42 *American Journal of International Law* 299 (1948).

_____, "Universality of Jurisdiction Over War Crimes," 33 *California Law Review* 177 (1945).

Cramer, Myron C., "Military Commissions: Trial of the Eight Saboteurs," 17 *Washington Law Review* 247 (1942).

Creta, Vincent M., Comment, "The Search for Justice in the Former Yugoslavia and Beyond," 20 *Houston Journal of International Law* 381 (1998).

Cryer, Robert, "The Fine Arts of Friendship: Jus in Bello in Afghanistan," 7 *Journal of Conflict and Security Law* 37 (2002).

Current Notes: "German War Trials: Report of the Proceedings Before the Supreme Court in Leipzig," 16 *American Journal of International Law* 628 (1922).

Currie, David P., "The Constitution in the Supreme Court: The Second World War, 1941–1946," 37 *Catholic University Law Review* 1 (1987).

Curtin, Philip J., Comment, "Genocide in East Timor?," 19 *Dickinson Journal of International Law* 181 (2000).

Cushman, Robert E., "The Case of the Nazi Saboteurs," 36 *American Political Science Review* 1082 (1942).

D'Amato, Anthony A., "Peace vs. Accountability in Bosnia," 88 *American Journal of International Law* 500 (1994).

_____, "Is International Law Really 'Law'?," 79 *Northwestern University Law Review* 1293 (1984).

D'Amato, Anthony C., Harvey L. Gould & Larry D. Woods, "War Crimes and Vietnam: The 'Nuremberg Defense' and the Military Service Resistor," 57 *California Law Review* 1055 (1969).

D'Zurilla, William T., "Individual Responsibility for Torture Under International Law," 56 *Tulane Law Review* 186 (1981).

Dadrian, Vahakn N., "Genocide as a Problem of National and International Law: The World War I Armenian Case and Its Contemporary Legal Ramifications," 14 *Yale Journal of International Law* 221 (1989).

Damrosch, Lori F., "The Role of the Great Powers in United Nations Peace-Keeping," 18 *Yale Journal of International Law* 429 (1993).

Daniel, Aubrey M., III, "The Defense of Superior Orders," 7 *University of Richmond Law Review* 477 (1973).

Danner, Allison M., "Constructing an Hierarchy of Crimes in International Criminal Law Sentencing," 87 *Virginia Law Review* 415 (2001).

_____, "Enhancing the Legitimacy and Accountability of Prosecutorial Discretion at the International Criminal Court," 97 *American Journal of International Law* 510 (2003).

Darenshori, Sara, "Inching Toward Justice in Rwanda," *N.Y. Times,* Sept. 8, 1998, at A25.

Dautricourt, Joseph Y., "Crimes Against Humanity: European Views on Its Conception and Its Future," 40 *Journal of Criminal Law and Criminology* 170 (1949).

David, Marcella, "Grotius Repudiated: The American Objections to the International Criminal Court and the Commitment to International Law," 20 *Michigan Journal of International Law* 337 (1999).

Davis, George, B., "Doctor Francis Lieber's Instructions for the Government of Armies in the Field," 1 *American Journal of International Law* 13 (1907).

Dawson, Grant M., "Defining Substantive Crimes Within the Subject Matter Jurisdiction of the International Criminal Court: What is the Crime of Aggression?," 19 *New York Law School Journal of International and Comparative Law* 413 (2000).

Deák, István, "Post World War II Political Justice in a Historical Perspective," 149 *Military Law Review* 137 (1995).

DeGiulio, Anthony P., "Command Control: Lawful versus Unlawful Application," 10 *San Diego Law Review* 72 (1972).

Delbrück, Jost, "A More Effective International Law or a New 'World Law'? — Some Aspects of the Development of International Law in a Changing International System," 68 *Indiana Law Journal* 705 (1993).

Deming, Stewart H., "War Crimes and International Criminal Law," 28 *Akron Law Review* 421 (1995).

Derby, Daniel, "Duties and Powers Respecting Foreign Crimes," 30 *American Journal of Comparative Law* 523 (Supp. 1982).

De Zayas, Alfred, "The Right to One's Homeland: Ethnic Cleansing and the International Criminal Tribunal for the Former Yugoslavia," 6 *Criminal Law Forum* 257 (1995).

Diessenbacker, Hartmut, "Explaining the Genocide in Rwanda," 52 *Law and State* 59 (1995).

Dinstein, Yoram, "International Criminal Law," 20 *Israel Law Review* 206 (1985).

Dixon, Rod, "Developing International Rules of Evidence for the Yugoslav and Rwanda Tribunals," 7 *Transnational Law and Contemporary Problems* 81 (1997).

Documents on German Foreign Policy 1918–1945. Washington, DC: U.S. Government Printing Office (1957).

Doman, Nicholas R., "Aftermath of Nuremberg: The Trial of Klaus Barbie." 60 *University of Colorado Law Review* 449 (1989).

_____, "The Nuremberg Trials Revisited," 47 *American Bar Association Journal* 260 (March, 1961).

Douglas, Lawrence, "Film as Witness: Screening *Nazi Concentration Camps* Before the Nuremberg Tribunal," 105 *Yale Law Journal* 449 (1995).

Downey, William G., Jr., "The Law of War and Military Necessity," 47 *American Journal of International Law* 251 (1953).

Draper, G.I.A.D., "Human Rights and the Law of War," 12 *Virginia Journal of International Law* 326 (1972).

Drumbl, Mark A., "Looking Up, Down and Across: The ICTY's Place in the International Legal Order," 37 *New England Law Review* 1037 (2003).

_____, "Punishment, Postgenocide: From Guilt to Shame to *Civis* in Rwanda," 75 *New York University Law Review* 1221 (2000).

_____, "Rule of Law and Lawlessness: Counseling the Accused in Rwanda's Domestic Genocide Trials," 29 *Columbia Human Rights Law Review* 545 (1998).

_____, "Toward a Criminology of International Crime," 19 *Ohio State Journal on Dispute Resolution* 263 (2003).

Dunbabin, J.F., "The League of Nations' Place in the International System," 78 *History* 421 (1993).

Dunbar, N.C.H., "Act of State and the Law of War," 75 *Juridical Review* 246 (1963).

_____, "Military Necessity in War Crimes Trials," 29 *British Year Book of International Law* 442 (1952).

Dyer, Gwynne, "Turkish 'Falsifiers' and American Deceivers: Historiography and the Armenian Massacres," 12 *Middle Eastern Studies* 99 (1976).

Dzubow, Jason A., "The International Response to the Civil War in Rwanda," 8 *Georgetown Immigration Law Journal* 513 (1994).

Eckhardt, William G., "'Command Criminal Responsibility': A Plea for a Workable Standard," 97 *Military Law Review* 1 (1982).

Edwards, Charles S., "Law of War in the Thought of Hugo Grotius," 19 *Journal of Public Law* 371 (1970).

Ehard, Hans, "The Nuremberg Trial Against the Major War Criminals and International Law," 43 *American Journal of International Law* 223 (1949).

Eide, Asbjorn, Allan Rosas & Theodore Meron, "Combating Lawlessness in Gray Zone Conflicts Through Minimum Humanitarian Standards," 89 *American Journal of International Law* 215 (1995).

Eisner, Douglas, "Humanitarian Intervention in the Post-Cold War Era," 11 *Boston University International Law Journal* 195 (1993).

Ellis, Mark S., "Achieving Justice Before the International Crimes Tribunal: Challenges for the Defense Counsel," 7 *Duke Journal of Comparative and International Law* 519 (1997).

Enloe, Cortez F., Jr., "The German Medical War Crimes—Their Nature and Significance," 30 *Rhode Island Medical Journal* 801 (1947).

Erickson, Otto, "A Judicial Reckoning for William Hohenzollern," 22 *Law Notes* 184 (January 1919).

Esgain, Albert J. & Waldemar A. Solf, "The 1949 Geneva Convention Relative to the Treatment of Prisoners of War: Its Principles, Innovations, and Deficiencies," 41 *North Carolina Law Review* 537 (1963).

"Essays on the Laws of War and War Crimes Tribunals in Honor of Telford Taylor," 37 *Columbia Journal of Transnational Law* 649 (1999).

Eulau, Heinz, "The Nuremberg War Crimes Trials: Revolution in International Law," 113 *New Republic* 625 (November 12, 1945).

Evered, Timothy C., "An International Criminal Court: Recent Proposals and American Concerns," 6 *Pace International Law Review* 121 (1994).

Everett, Robinson O. & Scott L. Stilliman, "Forums for Punishing Offenses Against the Law of Nations," 29 *Wake Forest Law Review* 509 (1994).

Falk, Richard A., "International Law and the United States Role in the Vietnam War," 75 *Yale Law Journal* 1122 (1966).

_____, "The Shimoda Case: A Legal Appraisal of the Atomic Attacks on Hiroshima and Nagasaki," 59 *American Journal of International Law* 759 (1965).

Falvey, Joseph L., Jr., "United Nations Justice or Military Justice: Which is the Oxymoron? An Analysis of the Rules of Procedure and Evidence of the International Tribunal for the Former Yugoslavia," 19 *Fordham International Law Journal* 475 (1995).

Farrior, Stephanie, "Moulding the Matrix: The Historical and Theoretical Foundations of International Law Concerning Hate Speech," 14 *Berkeley Journal of International Law* 1 (1996).

Faulkner, Stanley, "War Crimes: Responsibilities of Individual Servicemen and of Superior Officers," 31 *National Lawyers Guild Practitioner* 131 (1974).

Fawcett, J.E.S., "The Eichmann Case," 38 *British Year Book of International Law* 181 (1962).

Feil, Scott R., "Preventing Genocide: How the Early Use of Force Might Have Succeeded in Rwanda," *A Report to the Carnegie Commission on Preventing Deadly Conflict.* Washington, DC: (April 1998).

Fredrick, William J., "Should Crimes Against Humanity Replace War Crimes?", 37 *Columbia Journal of Transnational Law* 767 (1999).

Fenwick, Charles G., "Germany and the Crime of the World War," 23 *American Journal of International Law* 812 (1929).

Ferencz, Benjamin B., "Nuremberg Trial Procedure and the Rights of the Accused," 39 *Journal of Criminal Law and Criminology* 144 (1948).

_____, "The Nuremberg Principles and the Gulf War," 66 *St. John's Law Review* 771 (1992).

_____, "War Crimes Law and the Vietnam War," 17 *American University Law Review* 403 (1968).

Ferstman, Carla J., " Domestic Trials for Genocide and Crimes Against Humanity: The Example of Rwanda," 9 *African Journal of International and Comparative Law* 857 (1997).

Finch, George A., "Jurisdiction of Local Courts to Try Enemy Persons for War Crimes," 14 *American Journal of International Law* 218 (1920).

_____, "Retribution for War Crimes," 37 *American Journal of International Law* 81 (1943).

_____, "The Nuremberg Trial and International Law," 41 *American Journal of International Law* 20 (1947).

Findlay, D. Cameron, "Abducting Terrorists Overseas for Trial in the United States: Issues of International and Domestic Law," 23 *Texas International Law Journal* 1 (1988).

Firmage, Edwin B., "Law and the Indo-China War: A Retrospective View," 1974 *Utah Law Review* 1.

Fisher, Barry A., "The Bosnia War: Religion, History and the Gypsies," 17 *Whittier Law Review* 467 (1996).

Fleming, Rebecca A., Comment, "Holding State Sovereigns Accountable for Human Rights Violations: Applying the Act of State Doctrine Consistently with International Law," 23 *Maryland Journal of International Law and Trade* 187 (1999).

Fletcher, George P., "On Justice and War: Contradictions in the Proposed Military Tribunals," 25 *Harvard Journal of Law & Public Policy* 635 (2002).

Fliess, Peter J., "Review of the Yamashita Precedent," 78 *American Journal of International Law* 256 (1984).

Florini, Ann, "The Evolution of International Norms," 40 *International Student Quarterly* 363 (1996).

Fogelson, Steven, Comment, "The Nuremberg Legacy: An Unfulfilled Promise," 63 *Southern California Law Review* 833 (1990).

Forbes, Allison L., "Ethics and Authority in International Law," 22 *Suffolk Transnational Law Review* 335 (1998).

Forbes, Gordon W., "Some Legal Aspects of the Nuremberg Trial," 24 *Canadian Bar Review* 584 (1946).

Forsythe, David P., "Politics and the International Tribunal for the Former Yugoslavia," 5 *Criminal Law Forum* 401 (1994).

Franck, Thomas M., *Editorial Comment:* "The 'Powers of Appreciation': Who is the Ultimate Guardian of U.N. Legality?," 86 *American Journal of International Law* 519 (1992).

Fratcher, William F., "American Organization for Prosecution of German War Criminals," 13 *Missouri Law Review* 45 (1948).

Fredman, Jonathan M., "American Courts, International Law, and the War in Vietnam," 18 *Columbia Journal of Law and Social Problems* 295 (1984).

Freeman, Alwyn V., "War Crimes by Enemy Nationals Administering Justice in Occupied Territory," 41 *American Journal of International Law* 579 (1947).

Fried, J.H.E., "Transfer of Civilian Manpower from Occupied Territory," 40 *American Journal of International Law* 303 (1946).

Friedel, Frank B., Jr., "General Orders 100 and Military Government: Rules for Occupying Armies Formulated in the United States Civil War," 32 *Mississippi Valley Historical Review* 541 (March 1946).

Friedlander, Robert, "The Enforcement of International Criminal Law: Fact or Fiction," 17 *Case Western Reserve Journal of International Law* 79 (1985).

_____, "The Foundation of International Criminal Law: A Present Day Inquiry," 15 *Case Western Reserve Journal of International Law* 13 (1983).

Friedmann, Wolfgang, Note, "Law and Politics in the Vietnamese War: A Comment," 61 *American Journal of International Law* 776 (1967).

Gallant, Kenneth S., "Jurisdiction to Adjudicate and Jurisdiction to Prescribe in International Criminal Courts," 48 *Villanova Law Review* 763 (2003).

Ganoe, John T., "The Yamashita Case and the Constitution," 25 *Oregon Law Review* 143 (1946).

Gardam, Judith G., "Proportionality and Force in International Law," 87 *American Journal of International Law* 391 (1993).

Garner, James W., "Punishment of Offenders Against the Laws and Customs of War," 14 *American Journal of International Law* 70 (1920).

Gasser, H.D., "Internationalized Non-International Armed Conflicts: Case Studies of Afghanistan, Kampuchea and Lebanon," 33 *American Universities Review* 145 (1983).

Gault, P.F., "Prosecution of War Criminals," 36 *Journal of Criminal Law and Criminology* 180 (1946).

George, Shobha V., "Head-of-State Immunity in the United States Courts: Still Confused After All These Years," 64 *Fordham Law Review* 1051 (1995).

Gerlach, Christian, "The Wannsee Conference, the Fate of German Jews, and Hitler's Decision in Principle to Exterminate All European Jews," 70 *Journal of Modern History* 759 (1998).

Ginsburgs, George, "Laws of War and War Crimes on the Russian Front During World War II: The Soviet View," 11 *Soviet Studies* 253 (1960).

Glennon, Michael J., "State-Sponsored Abduction: A Comment on *United States v. Alvarez Machain*," 86 *American Journal of International Law* 746 (1992).

_____, "The Fog of Law: Self-Defense, Inherence, and Incoherence in Article 51 of the United Nations Charter," 25 *Harvard Journal of Law and Public Policy* 539 (2002).

Glueck, Sheldon, "Trial and Punishment of the Axis War Criminals," 4 *Free World* 138 (November 1942).

_____, "War Criminals—Their Prosecution and Punishment," 5 *Law Guild Review* 1 (1945).

Goertz, Gary & Paul F. Diehl, "Toward a Theory of International Norms: Some Conceptual and Measurement Issues," 36 *Journal of Conflict Resolution* 634 (1992).

Goldsmith, Jack L. & Eric A. Posner, "A Theory of Customary International Law," 66 *University of Chicago Law Review* 1113 (1999).

Goldstone, Richard J., "Prosecuting Rape as a War Crime," 34 *Case Western Reserve Journal of International Law* 277 (2002).

Goodhart, Arthur L., "The Legality of the Nuremberg Trials," 58 *Juridical Review* 1 (1946).

Gordon, Ed, "American Courts, International Law and 'Political Questions' which Touch Foreign Relations," 14 *International Law* 297 (1980).

Gottlieb, Gidon, "Relationism: Legal Theory for a Relational Society," 50 *University of Chicago Law Review* 567 (1983).

Gray, Talitha, Notes, "To Keep You is No Gain, To Kill You is No Loss—Securing Justice Through the International Criminal Court," 20 *Arizona Journal of International and Comparative Law* 645 (2003).

Green, A. Wigfall, "The Military Commission," 42 *American Journal of International Law* 832 (1948).

Green, Leslie C., "Is There an International Criminal Law?," 21 *Alberta Law Review* 251 (1983).

_____, "New Trends in International Criminal Law," 11 *Israel Year Book of International Law* 9 (1981).

_____, "The Eichmann Case," 23 *Modern Law Review* 507 (1960).

_____, "The Rule of Law and Human Rights in the Balkans," 37 *Canadian Year Book of International Law* 223 (1999).

_____, "The Tokyo War Crimes Trial: An International Symposium," 12 *Dalhousie Law Journal* 190 (1989).

Greenwood, Christopher, "International Law and the War against Terrorism," 78 *International Affairs* 301 (2002).

Gregory, S.S., "Criminal Responsibility of Sovereigns for Wilfull Violations of the Laws of War," 6 *Virginia Law Review* 400 (1919–1920).

Grew, Wilhelm G., "History of the law of Nations: World War I to World War II," 7 *Encyclopedia of Public International Law* 252 (1984).

Griebel, Walter, "German Prosecutions of Nazi War Criminals," 11 *New York Law School Journal of International and Comparative Law* 333 (1990).

Griffin, James B., Note, "A Predictive Framework for the Effectiveness of International Criminal Tribunals," 34 *Vanderbilt Journal of Transnational Law* 405 (2001).

Gross, Leo, "Criminality of Aggressive War," 41 *American Political Science Review* 205 (1947).

Grossman, Claudio, "War Crimes Tribunals: The Records and the Prospects: International Support for International Criminal Tribunals and an International Criminal Court," 13 *American University International Law Review* 1413 (1998).

Guy, George F., "The Defense of Yamashita," 4 *Wyoming Law Journal* 153 (1949–1950).

Haag, E.Van Den, "When is a Crime a War Crime?," 23 *National Review* 1227 (November 5, 1971).

Haensel, Carl, "The Nuremberg Trial Revisited," 13 *DePaul Law Review* 248 (1964).

Halberstam, Malvina, "What Price Peace: From Nuremberg to Bosnia to the Nobel Peace Price," 3 *ILSA Journal of International and Comparative Law* 571 (1997).

Halverson, Karen, "Is a Foreign State a 'Person'? Does It Matter?," Personal Jurisdiction, Due Process and the Foreign Sovereign Immunities Act," 34 *New York University Journal of International Law and Politics* 115 (2001).

Hannum, Hurst, "International Law and the Cambodian Genocide: The Sounds of Silence," 11 *Human Rights Quarterly* 82 (1989).

Harhoff, Frederik, "Consonance or Rivalry? Calibrating the Effects to Prosecute War Crimes in National and International Tribunals," 7 *Duke Journal of Comparative and International Law* 571 (1997).

Harris, Whitney R., "A Call for an International War Crimes Court: Learning from Nuremberg and Vietnam: Command Responsibility Reappraised," 25 *Naval War College Review* 19 (1972).

Harvard Research in International Law, "Draft Convention on Jurisdiction With Respect to Crime," 29 *American Journal of International Law, Special Supplement*, 435 (1935).

Heazlett, Elizabeth, Note, "Eichmann—International Law?," 24 *University of Pittsburgh Law Review* 116 (1962).

Henkin, Louis, "Law and War After the Cold War," 5 *Maryland Journal of International Law and Trade* 147 (1991).

_____, "Viet-Nam in the Courts of the United States: 'Political Questions'," 63 *American Journal of International Law* 284 (1969).

Hermes, Ferdinand A., "The 'War Guilt' of the German People," 3 *American Journal of Economics and Sociology* 201 (1944).

Hessler, Curt A., Note: "Command Responsibility for War Crimes," 82 *Yale Law Journal* 1274 (1973).

Hill, Norman, "Was There An Ultimatum Before Pearl Harbor?," 42 *American Journal of International Law* 355 (1948).

Hirsh, Felix, "Lessons of Nuremberg," 11 *Current History* 312 (October 1946).

Hobbs, Malcolm, "Nuremberg Indecent Burial," 69 *Nation* 634 (December 3, 1949).

Hockett, Jeffrey D., "Justice Robert H. Jackson, The Supreme Court, and the Nuremberg Trial," 1990 *Supreme Court Review* 257.

Hockhammer, Karl A., Note, "The Yugoslav War Crimes Tribunal: The Compatibility of Peace, Politics, and International Law," 28 *Vanderbilt Journal of Transnational Law* 119 (1995).

Hofmannsthal, Emilio von, "War Crimes Not Tried Under Retroactive Law," 22 *New York University Law Quarterly Review* 93 (1947).

Hollis, Brenda J., "The Thomas P. Kienan Memorial Lecture: The International Criminal Tribunal for Yugoslavia," 39 *Air Force Law Review* 37 (1996).

Honda, Michael M., "Japan's War Crimes: Has Justice Been Served?," 21 *Whittier Law Review* 621 (2000).

Hoover, Glenn, "The Outlook for 'War Guilt' Trials," 59 *Political Science Quarterly* 40 (March 1944).

Horsky, Charles A., "Status of Prosecutions against German and Japanese War Criminals," 6 *Lawyers Guild Review* 485 (1946).

Horton, Regina, Comment, "The Long Road to Hypocrisy: The United States and the International Criminal Court," 24 *Whittier Law Review* 1041 (2003).

Howard, Kenneth A., "Command Responsibility for War Crimes," 21 *Journal of Public Law* 7 (1972).

Huyse, Luc, "Justice After Transition: On the Choices Successor Elites Make in Dealing with the Past," 20 *Law and Social Inquiry* 51 (1995).

Hwang, Phyllis, "Defining Crimes Against Humanity in the Rome Statute of the International Criminal Court," 22 *Fordham International Law Journal* 457 (1998).

Hyde, Charles C., Editorial Comment: "Japanese Executions of American Flyers," 37 *American Journal of International Law* 480 (1943).

IMT-Nuremberg: "Judgment and Sentences, October 1, 1946," 41 *American Journal of International Law* 172 (1947).

"Indictment Against Major Nazi War Criminals — International Military Tribunal," 19 *Temple Law Quarterly* 172–235 (1945–46).

"International Criminal Court: *Special Issue,* 10 *Criminal Law Forum* 1–45 (1999).

International Military Tribunal for the Far East (IMTFE), MF-302, 36 microfilm reels, CRL Monographs, OCLC # 27023371, Library of Congress, Washington, DC.

International Military Tribunal for the Far East, Papers, Journals, Exhibits and Judgments of the IMTFE, 1946–1948, Washington, DC: U.S. Army Signal Corps, Photo Division, 1948, Microfilm 279 (61 reels), Naval War College Library, Newport, RI. *E-mail: libre@nwc.navy.mil*

Inventory of Japanese War Crime Documents, 1946–48, The University of New Mexico, Albuquerque, NM: General Library, Center for Southwest Research, Collection No. MSS 413 BC. *E-mail: http://www.unm.edu/~cswrref/*

Ireland, Gordon A., "Ex Post Facto from Rome to Tokyo," 21 *Temple Law Quarterly* 27 (1947).

Isikoff, M., "Justice in the Shadows: Invoking Wartime Powers, Bush Can Try Suspected Terrorists in Secretive Military Tribunals," *Newsweek,* November 26, 2001, at 39.

Ivy, Andrew C., "Nazi War Crimes of a Medical Nature," 139 *Journal of the American Medical Association* 131 (1949).

Jackson, Robert H., "Closing Arguments for Conviction of Nazi War Criminals," 20 *Temple Law Quarterly* 85 (1946).

_____, "Nuremberg in Retrospect: Legal Answers to International Lawlessness," 35 *American Bar Association Journal* 813 (October 1949).

_____, "The Law Under Which Nazi Organizations Are Accused of Being Criminal," 19 *Temple Law Quarterly* 371 (1945–46).

Jaffe, Sidney, "Natural Law and the Nurnberg Trials," 26 *Nebraska Law Review* 90 (1946).

Jamison, Sandra L., "A Permanent International Criminal Court: A Proposal that Overcomes Past Objections," 23 *Denver Journal of International Law and Policy* 419 (1995).

Janis, Mark W., "The Utility of International Criminal Courts," 12 *Connecticut Journal of International Law* 161 (1997).

Janowitz, Morris, "German Reactions to Nazi Atrocities," 52 *American Journal of Sociology* 141 (1946).

Jessup, Phillip, "The Crime of Aggression and the Failure of International Law," 62 *Political Science Quarterly* 1 (March 1947).

Jinks, Derek, "September 11 and the Laws of War," 28 *Yale Journal of International Law* 1 (2003).

Jochnick, Chris af & Roger Normand, "The Legitimation of Violence: A Critical History of the Laws of War," 35 *Harvard International Law Journal* 49 (1994).

Joyner, Christopher C., "Arresting Impunity: The Case for Universal Jurisdiction in Bringing War Criminals to Accountability," 59 *Law and Contemporary Problems* 153 (1996).

_____, "Enforcing Human Rights Standards in the Former Yugoslavia: The Case for an International War Crimes Tribunal," 22 *Denver Journal of International Law and Policy* 235 (1994).

Joyner, Christopher C. & Anthony C. Arend, "Anticipatory Humanitarian Intervention: An Emerging Legal Norm?," 10 *Journal of Legal Studies* (USAFA) 27 (1999–2000).

Judicial Decisions, "International Military Tribunal (Nuremberg), Judgment and Sentences," 41 *American Journal of International Law* 172–333 (1947).

Kader, David, "Law and Genocide: A Critical Annotated Bibliography," 11 *Hastings International and Comparative Law Review* 381 (1988).

Kalshoven, Frits, "State Responsibility for Warlike Acts of the Armed Forces," 40 *International and Comparative Law Quarterly* 827 (1991).

Kaplan, Naomi, "A Failure of Perspective: Moral Assumptions and Genocide," 23 *Boston College Third World Law Journal* 359 (2003).

Karla, M.S., "Forced Marriage: Rwanda's Secret Revealed," 7 *University of California-Davis Journal of International Law and Policy* 197 (2001).

Kastenberg, Joshua E., "The Right to Assistance of Counsel in Military and War Crimes Tribunals: An International and Domestic Law Analysis," 14 *Indiana International & Comparative Law Review* 175 (2003).

Kastrup, Dieter, "From Nuremberg to Rome and Beyond: The Fight Against Genocide, War Crimes, Crimes Against Humanity," 23 *Fordham International Law Journal* 404 (1999).

Katyal, Neal K. & Laurence H. Tribe, "Waging War, Deciding Guilt: Trying the Military Tribunals," 111 *Yale Law Journal* 1259 (2002).

Katyn Forest Massacre, U.S. Congress; U.S. House of Representatives, 82nd Congress, 1st & 2nd Sessions; 1951–52, Washington, DC, U.S. Government Printing Office (1952).

Kaufman, Mary M., "Judgment at Nuremberg—An Appraisal of Its Significance," 40 *National Lawyers Guild Practitioner* 62 (Summer 1993).

Kaul, Hans-Peter, "Towards a Permanent International Criminal Court: Some Observations of a Negotiator," 18 *Human Rights Law Journal* 169 (1997).

Kelly, J. Patrick, "The Twilight of Customary International Law," 40 *Virginia Journal of International Law* 449 (2000).

Kelly, Michael J., "Can Sovereigns Be Brought to Justice? The Crime of Genocide's Evolution and the Meaning of the Milosevic Trial," 76 *St. John's Law Review* 257 (2002).

Kelsen, Hans, "Collective and Individual Responsibility in International Law with Particular Regard to the Punishment of War Criminals," 31 *California Law Review* 530 (1943).

_____, "Collective and Individual Responsibility for Acts of State in International Law," 1948 *Jewish Year Book of International Law* 226.

_____, "The Rule Against Ex Post Facto Law and the Prosecution of the Axis War Criminals," 2 *The Judge Advocate Journal* 8 (1945).

_____, "Will the Judgment in the Nuremberg Trial Constitute a Precedent in International Law?," 1 *International Law Quarterly* 153 (1947).

Keohane, Robert O., "International Relations and International Law: Two Optics," 38 *Harvard International Law Journal* 487 (1997).

King, Henry T. & Theodore C. Theofrastous, "From Nuremberg to Rome: A Step Backward for U.S. Foreign Policy," 31 *Case Western Reserve Journal of International Law* 47 (1999).

Kirsch, Philippe, *Keynote Address:* "The International Criminal Court: Concensus and Debate on the International Adjudication of Genocide, Crimes Against Humanity, War Crimes, and Aggression," 32 *Cornell International Law Journal* 437 (1999).

Kirsch, Philippe & John T. Holmes, *Developments in International Criminal Law:* "The Rome Conference on an International Criminal Court: The Negotiating Process," 93 *American Journal of International Law* 2 (1999).

Kittrie, Nicholas N., "A Post Mortem of the Eichmann Case—The Lessons for International Law," 55 *Journal of Criminal Law, Criminology & Police Science* 16 (1964).

Kleinberger, Thomas R., "The Iraqi Conflict: An Assessment of Possible War Crimes and the Call for Adoption of an International Criminal Code, and Permanent International Criminal Tribunal," 14 *New York Law School Journal of International and Comparative Law* 69 (1993).

Koch, H.W., "Hitler and the Origins of the Second World War: Second Thoughts on the Status of Some of the Documents," 11 *Historical Journal* 125 (1968).

Koessler, Maximilian, "American War Crime Trials in Europe," 39 *Georgetown Law Journal* 18 (1950).

Kolb, Robert, "The Jurisprudence of the Yugoslav and Rwandan Criminal Tribunals on Their Jurisdiction and on International Crimes," 71 *British Year Book of International Law* 259 (2000).

Komarow, Gary, "Individual Responsibility Under International Law: The Nuremberg Principles in Domestic Legal Systems," 29 *International and Comparative Law Quarterly* 21 (1980).

Kopelman, Elizabeth S., "Ideology and International Law: The Dissent of the Indian Justice at the Tokyo War Crimes Trials," 23 *New York University Journal of International Law and Politics* 373 (1991).

Koran, J.M., "An Analysis of the Jurisdiction of the International Criminal Tribunal for War Crimes in the Former Yugoslavia," 5 *Journal of International and Comparative Law* 43 (1998).

Kranzbuhler, Otto, "Nuremberg Eighteen Years Afterwards," 14 *DePaul Law Review* 333 (1965).

Krass, Caroline D., "Bringing the Perpetrators of Rape in the Balkans to Justice: Time for an International Criminal Court," 22 *Denver Journal of International Law and Policy* 317 (1994).

Kraus, Herbert, "The Nuremberg Trials of the Major War Criminals: Reflections After Seventeen Years," 13 *DePaul Law Review* 233 (1964).

Kresock, David M., "Ethnic Cleansing in the Balkans: The Legal Foundation of Foreign Intervention," 27 *Cornell International Law Journal* 203 (1994).

Krug, Peter, "The Emerging Mental Incapacity Defense in International Criminal Law: Some Initial Questions of Implementation," 94 *American Journal of International Law* 317 (2000).

Ku, Julian G., "Customary International Law in State Courts," 42 *Virginia Journal of International Law* 265 (2001).

Kunz, Josef L., "Bellum Justum and Bellum Legale," 45 *American Journal of International Law* 528 (1951).

_____, "Sanctions in International Law," 54 *American Journal of International Law* 324 (1960).

Lahav, Pnina, "The Eichmann Trial, the Jewish Question, and the American Jewish-Intelligentsia," 72 *Boston University Law Review* 555 (1992).

Lambert, Thomas F., Jr., "Recalling the War Crimes Trials of World War II," 149 *Military Law Review* 15 (1995).

Lansing, Robert, "Notes on World Sovereignty," 15 *American Journal of International Law* 13 (1921).

Laternser, Hans, "Looking Back at the Nuremberg Trial with Special Consideration of the Processes Against Military Leaders," 8 *Whittier Law Review* 557 (1986).

Lauterpacht, Hersch, "The Law of Nations and the Punishment of War Crimes," 21 *British Year Book of International Law* 58 (1944).

Lemkin, Raphael, "Genocide as a Crime Under International Law," 41 *American Journal of International Law* 145 (1947).

Leventhal, Harold, Sam Harris, John M. Woolsey, Jr. & Warren F. Farr, "The Nuremberg Verdict," 60 *Harvard Law Review* 857 (1947).

Levie, Howard S., "Prosecuting War Crimes Before an International Tribunal," 28 *Akron Law Review* 429 (1995).

Levy, Albert G.D., "Criminal Responsibility of Individuals and International Law," 12 *University of Chicago Law Review* 313 (1945).

Linton, Suzannah, "Cambodia, East Timor and Sierra Leone: Experiments in International Justice," 12 *Criminal Law Forum* 186 (2001).

Lippman, Matthew, "Genocide: The Crime of the Century. The Jurisprudence of Death at the Dawn of the New Millenium," 23 *Houston Journal of International Law* 467 (2001).

_____, "The Nazis Doctors Trial and the International Prohibition on Medical Involvement in Torture," 15 *Loyola Los Angeles International and Comparative Law Journal* 395 (1993).

_____, "The Trial of Adolf Eichmann and the Protection of Universal Human Rights Under International Law," 5 *Houston Journal of International Law* 1 (1982).

Luban, David, "A Theory of Crimes Against Humanity," 29 *Yale Journal of International Law* 85 (2004).

McClelland, Gregory A., "A Non-Adversary Approach to International Criminal Tribunals," 26 *Suffolk Transnational Law Review* 1 (2002).

McDougal, Myres S. & F.P. Feliciano, "International Coercion and World Public Order: The General Principles of the Law of War," 67 *Yale Law Journal* 771 (1958).

McKinley, James C., Jr., "Machete Returns to Rwanda, Rekindling a Genocide War," *N.Y. Times*, Dec. 15, 1997, at A1.

Magnorella, Paul J., "Expanding the Frontiers of Humanitarian Law: The International Criminal Tribunal for Rwanda," 9 *Florida Journal of International Law* 421 (1994).

Maier, Harold G., "The Authoritative Sources of Customary International Law in the United States," 10 *Michigan Journal of International Law* 450 (1989).

Manner, George, "The Legal Nature and Punishment of Criminal Acts of Violence Contrary to the Laws of War," 37 *American Journal of International Law* 407 (1943).

Matquardt, Paul D., "Law Without Borders: The Constitutionality of the International Criminal Court," 33 *Columbia Journal of Transnational Law* 73 (1995).

Martin, David A., "Reluctance to Prosecute War Crimes: Of Causes and Cures," 34 *Virginia Journal of International Law* 255 (1994).

Martins, Mark S., Comment, "National Forums for Punishing Offenders Against International Law: Might U.S. Soldiers Have Their Day in the Same Court?," 36 *Virginia Journal of International Law* 659 (1996).

——————, "War Crimes' During Operations Other Than War: Military Doctrine and Law Fifty Years After Nuremburg," 149 *Military Law Review* 145 (1995).

Massey, Stephen J., "Individual Responsibility for Assisting the Nazis in Persecuting Civilians," 71 *Minnesota Law Review* 97 (1986).

Matas, David, "Prosecuting Crimes Against Humanity: The Lessons of World War I," 13 *Fordham International Law Journal* 86 (1990).

Mellanby, Kenneth, "Nazi Experiments on Human Beings in Concentration Camps in Nazi Germany," 1 *British Medical Journal* 148 (1947).

Meltzer, Bernard D., "'War Crimes': The Nuremberg Trial and the Tribunal for the Former Yugoslavia," 30 *Valparaiso University Law Review* 895 (1996).

Mendelsohn, John, "Trial by Document: The Problem of Due Process for War Criminals at Nuremberg," 7 *Prologue* 227 (1975).

Meron, Theodor, "From Nuremberg to the Hague," 149 *Military Law Review* 107 (1995).

——————, "International Criminalization of Internal Atrocities," 89 *American Journal of International Law* 554 (1995).

——————, "Is International Law Moving towards Criminalization?," 9 *European Journal of International Law* 18 (1998).

——————, "Prisoners of War, Civilians and Diplomats in the Gulf Crisis," 85 *American Journal of International Law* 104 (1991).

——————, "Rape as a Crime Under International Humanitarian Law," 87 *American Journal of International Law* 424 (1993).

——————, "The Case for War Crimes Trials in Yugoslavia," 72 *Foreign Affairs* 122 (1993).

——————, "The Continuing Role of Custom in the Formation of International Humanitarian Law," 90 *American Journal of International Law* 238 (1996).

——————, "The Geneva Convention as Customary Law," 81 *American Journal of International Law* 348 (1987).

——————, "War Crimes in Yugoslavia and the Development of International Law," 88 *American Journal of International Law* 78 (1994).

Miller, Richard I., "Far Beyond Nuremberg: Steps Toward International Criminal Jurisdiction," 61 *Kentucky Law Journal* 925 (1973).

Miller, Robert H., "The Convention on the Non-Applicability of Statutory Limitations to War Crimes and Crimes Against Humanity," 65 *American Journal of International Law* 476 (1971).

Miller, William, "Slobodan Milosevic's Prosecution by the International Criminal Tribunal for the Former Yugoslavia: A Harbinger of Things to Come for International Criminal Justice," 22 *Loyola Los Angeles International and Comparative Law Journal* 553 (2000).

Minow, Martha, "Between Intimates and Between Nations: Can Law Stop the Violence?," 50 *Case Western Reserve Law Review* 851 (2000).

Mintz, John, "On Detainees: U.S. Faces Legal Quandary," *Washington Post*, Jan. 27, 2002, at A22.

Moore, John N., "International Law and the United States Role in Viet Nam: A Reply," 76 *Yale Law Journal* 1051 (1967).

——————, "The Lawfulness of Military Assistance to the Republic of Viet-Nam," 61 *American Journal of International Law* 1 (1967).

Morris, Fritz, "Security, Intelligence Reform and Civil Liberties in the Untied States: September 11, 2001, through a Historical Lens," (Unpublished research paper, Carr Center for Human Rights Policy, Kennedy School of Government, Harvard University, June 2002).

Morris, Madeline, "By Force of Arms: Rape, War, and Military Culture," 45 *Duke Law Journal* 651 (1996).

_____, "The Trials of Concurrent Jurisdiction: The Case of Rwanda," 7 *Duke Journal of Comparative and International Law* 349 (1997).

Mueller, Gerhard O.W., "International Criminal Law: *Civitas Maxima:* An Overview," 15 *Case Western Reserve Journal of International Law* 1 (1983).

Mullins, Claude, "War Criminals Trials," 116 *Fortnightly Review* 417 (September 1921).

Murphy, Cornelius F., Jr., "The Grotian Vision of World Order," 76 *American Journal of International Law* 477 (1982).

Murphy, John F., "The Future of Multilateralism and Efforts to Combat International Terrorism," 25 *Columbia Journal of Transnational Law* 35 (1986).

_____, "The Quivering Gulliver: U.S. Views on a Permanent International Criminal Court," 34 *International Lawyer* 45 (2000).

Murphy, Sean D., "Progress and Jurisprudence of the International Criminal Tribunal for the Former Yugoslavia," 93 *American Journal of International Law* 57 (1999).

Musmanno, Michael A., "The Objections *in limine* to the Eichmann Trial," 35 *Temple Law Quarterly* 1 (1961).

Myjer, Eric P.J. & Nigel O. White, "The Twin Towers Attack: An Unlimited Right to Self-Defence," 7 *Journal of Conflict and Security Law* 1 (2002).

Nagan, Winston P., "International Criminal Law and the *ad hoc* Tribunal for Former Yugoslavia," 6 *Duke Journal of Comparative and International Law* 127 (1995).

National Archives and Records Administration, College Park, MD: Microcopy No. T-918, Court Papers, Journals, Exhibits, and Judgments of the International Military Tribunal for the Far East, Record Group 238, Rolls 1–52 (1946–1948). *E-mail: http://www.archives.gov*

Nerone, F. Regan, Comment, "The Legality of Nuremberg," 4 *Duquesne University Law Review* 146 (1965).

Nersessian, David L., "The Razor's Edge: Defining and Protecting Human Groups Under the Genocide Convention," 36 *Cornell International Law Journal* 293 (2003).

Neumann, Franz, "The War Crimes Trials," 2 *World Politics* 137 (October 1949).

Newman, Frank C., "Redress of the Gulf War Violations of Human Rights," 20 *Denver Journal of International Law and Policy* 213 (1992).

Niebuhr, Reinhold, "Victor's Justice," 15 *Common Sense* 6 (1946).

Nishigai, Makoto, Note, "The Comfort Women Case in the United States: A Note on Questions Resolved or Unresolved in *Hwang v. Japan* for War Crimes," 20 *Wisconsin International Law Journal* 371 (2002).

Noyes, John E., Association of American Law Schools Panel on the International Criminal Court, 36 *American Criminal Law Review* 223 (1999).

Nurick, Lester, "The Distinction Between Combatant and Noncombatant in the Law of War," 39 *American Journal of International Law* 680 (1945).

Nussbaum, Arthur, "Just War—A Legal Concept?," 42 *Michigan Law Review* 453 (1943).

O'Brien, James C., "The International Tribunal for Violations of International Humanitarian Law in the Former Yugoslavia," 87 *American Journal of International Law* 639 (1993).

O'Brien, William V., "The Law of War: Command Responsibility and Vietnam," 60 *Georgetown Law Journal* 605 (1972).

_____, "The Nuremberg Precedent and the Gulf War" (Special Section on Iraqi War Crimes), 31 *Virginia Journal of International Law* 391 (1991).

O'Connell, Mary E., "Continuing Limits on U.N. Intervention in Civil Wars," 67 *Indiana Law Journal* 909 (1992).

O'Neill, Kerry C., "A New Customary Law of Head of State Immunity: Hirohito and Pinochet," 38 *Stanford Journal of International Law* 289 (2002).

Orentlicher, Diane F., "Settling Accounts: The Duty to Prosecute Human Rights Violations of a Prior Regime," 100 *Yale Law Journal* 2537 (1991).

Osiel, Mark, J., "Ever Again: Legal Remembrance of Administrative Massacre," 144 *University of Pennsylvania Law Review* 463 (1995).

_____, "Obeying Orders: Atrocity, Military Discipline, and the Law of War," 86 *California Law Review* 939 (1998).

Osofsky, Hari M., Note, "Domesticating International Criminal Law: Bringing Human Rights Violators to Justice," 107 *Yale Law Journal* 191 (1997).

Paasche, Franz W., "The Use of Force in Combating Terrorism," 25 *Columbia Journal of Transnational Law* 377 (1987).

Paetel, Karl O., "The Black Order: A Survey of the Literature on the SS," 12 *Weiner Library Bulletin* 34 (1959).

Pal, Rahadbinod, "What is Aggressive War?," 4 *Indian Law Review* 99 (1950).

Panel Discussion: Responses to World War Two War Criminals and Human Rights Violators: National and Comparative Perspectives," 8 *Boston College Third World Law Journal* 3 (1988).

Pannenbecker, Otto, "The Nuremberg War Crimes Trial," 14 *DePaul Law Review* 348 (1965).

Park, Byoungwook, "Comfort Women During World War II: Are U.S. Courts a Final Resort for Justice?," 17 *American University International Law Review* 403 (2002).

Park, Kyeyoung, "The Unspeakable Experiences of Korean Women under Japanese Rule," 21 *Whittier Law Review* 567 (2000).

Parker, John T., "The Nuremberg Trial," 30 *Journal of the American Judicature Society* 109 (December 1946).

Parks, W. Hays, "A Few Tools in the Prosecution of War Crimes," 149 *Military Law Review* 73 (1995).

Parsons, George R., Note, "International Law: Jurisdiction Over Extraterritorial Crime: Universality Principle: War Crimes: Crimes Against Humanity: Piracy, Israel's Nazi and Nazi Collaborators (Punishment) Law," 46 *Cornell Law Quarterly* 326 (1961).

Partan, Daniel G., "Legal Aspects of the Vietnam Conflict," 46 *Boston University Law Review* 281 (1966).

Patel, Krishna R., "Recognizing the Rape of Bosnian Women as Gender-Based Persecution," 60 *Brooklyn Law Review* 929 (1994).

Paton, G.W., "The War Crimes Trials and International Law," 3 *Res Judicatae* 123 (October 1947).

Paulson, Stanley L., "Classical Legal Positivism at Nuremberg," 4 *Philosophy and Public Affairs* 132 (1975).

Paust, Jordan J., "After My Lai: The Case for War Crimes Jurisdiction over Civilians in Federal District Courts," 50 *Texas Law Review* 6 (1971).

_____, "Aggression Against Authority: The Crime of Oppression, Politicide and Other Crimes Against Human Rights," 18 *Case Western Reserve Journal of International Law* 283 (1986).

_____, "Antiterrorism Military Commissions: Courting Illegality," 23 *Michigan Journal of International Law* 1 (2001).

_____, "Antiterrorism Military Commissions: The Ad Hoc DOD Rules of Procedure," 23 *Michigan Journal of International Law* 677 (2002).

_____, "Applicability of International Criminal Laws to Events in the Former Yugoslavia," 9 *American University Journal of International Law and Policy* 499 (1994).

_____, "Customary International Law: Its Nature, Sources, and Status as Law of the United States," 12 *Michigan Journal of International Law* 59 (1990).

_____, "Is the President Bound by the Supreme Law of the Land? — Foreign Affairs and National Security Reexamined," 9 *Hastings Constitutional Law Quarterly* 719 (1982).

_____, "My Lai and Vietnam: Norms, Myths, and Leader Responsibility," 57 *Military law Review* 99 (1972).

_____, "The President Is Bound by International Law," 81 *American Journal of International Law* 377 (1987).

_____, "The Reach of ICC Jurisdiction Over Non-Signatory Nationals," 33 *Vanderbilt Journal of Transnational Law* 1 (2000).

_____, Universality and Responsibility to Enforce International Criminal Law: No. U.S. Sanctuary for Alleged Nazi War Criminals," 11 *Houston Journal of International Law* 337 (1989).

Paust, Jordan J. & Albert P. Blaustein, "War Crimes Jurisdiction And Due Process: The Bangladesh Experience," 11 *Vanderbilt Journal of Transnational Law* 1 (1978).

Pearl, Elizabeth L., "Punishing Balkan War Criminals: Could the End of Yugoslavia Provide an End to Victor's Justice?," 30 *American Criminal Law Review* 1373 (1993).

Peeler, Calvin, "The Politics of Memory: Restructuring Vichy and the Past the French Chose to Forget," 19 *Whittier Law Review* 353 (1997).

Pejic, Jelena, "The International Criminal Court Statute: An Appraisal of the Rome Package," 34 *International Lawyer* 65 (2000).

Pella, Vespasien V., "Towards an International Criminal Court," 44 *American Journal of International Law* 37 (1950).

Penrose, Mary M., "It's Good to be the King: Prosecuting Heads of State and Former Heads of State Under International Law," 39 *Columbia Journal of Transnational Law* 193 (2000).

Persian Gulf: *The Question of War Crimes, 1991: Hearings before the Committee on Foreign Relations, 102d Cong., 1st Sess.* (1991).

Phillimore, Walter G.P.F., "An International Criminal Court and the Resolutions of the Committee of Jurists," 3 *British Year Book of International Law* 79 (1922–23).

Pickard, Daniel B., "Proposed Sentencing Guidelines for the International Criminal Court," 20 *Loyola Los Angeles International and Comparative Law Journal* 123 (1997).

Podgers, James, "The World Cries for Justice," 82 *American Bar Association Journal* 52 (April 1996).

Posner, Eric A., "A Theory of the Laws of War," 70 *University of Chicago Law Review* 297 (2003).

Potter, Pitman, B., "Offenses Against the Peace and Security of Mankind," 46 *American Journal of International Law* 101 (1952).

Preuss, Lawrence, "Punishment by Analogy in National Socialist Penal Law," 26 *Journal of Criminal Law and Criminology* 847 (1936).

Prevost, Ann M., "Race and War Crimes: The 1945 War Crimes Trial of General Tomoyuki Yamashita," 14 *Human Rights Quarterly* 303 (1992).

Prinz, Barrett, "The Treaty of Versailles to Rwanda: How the International Community Deals with War Crimes," 6 *Tulane Journal of International and Comparative Law* 553 (1998).

Pritchard, R. John, "Lessons from British Proceedings Against Japanese War Criminals," 3 *Human Rights Review* 104 (1978).

_____, "The Gift of Clemency Following British War Crimes Trials in the Far East, 1946–1948," 7 *Criminal Law Forum* 15 (1996).

Quigley, John, "State Responsibility for Ethnic Cleansing," 32 *University of California-Davis Law Review* 341 (1999).

Radin, Max, "International Crimes," 32 *Iowa Law Review* 33 (1946).

_____, "War Crimes and Crimes of War," 21 *Virginia Quarterly Review* 497 (1945).

Ragavan, Chitra, "Law in a New Sort of War," *U.S. News*, April 26, 2004, at 34.

Randall, Kenneth C., "Federal Questions and the Human Rights Paradigm," 73 *Minnesota Law Review* 349 (1988).

_____, "Universal Jurisdiction Under International Law," 66 *Texas Law Review* 785 (1988).

Rashba, Jeffrey D., "Finishing the Work of Nuremberg: Nazi War Criminals and American Law," 20 *Connecticut Law Review* 633 (1988).

Ratner, Steven R., "New Democracies, Old Atrocities: An Inquiry in International Law," 87 *Georgetown Law Journal* 707 (1998).

_____, "The Schizoprenia of International Criminal Law," 33 *Texas International Law Journal* 237 (1998).

Ratner, Steven R. & Anne-Marie Slaughter, "Appraising the Methods of International Law: A Prospectus for Readers," 93 *American Journal of International Law* 291 (1999).

Ray, Amy E., "The Shame of It: Gender-Based Terrorism in the Former Yugoslavia and the Failure of International Human Rights Law to Comprehend the Injuries," 46 *American University Law Review* 793 (1997).

Reik, Otto E.,"War Crimes—A Refutation of Objection," 39 *Kentucky Law Journal* 317 (1951).

Reisman, W. Michael, "Assessing Claims to Revise the Laws of War," 97 *American Journal of International Law* 82 (2003).

_____, "Coercion and Self-Determination: Construing Charter Article 2 (4)," 78 *American Journal of International Law* 642 (1984).

_____, "Criteria for the Lawful Use of Force in International Law," 10 *Yale Journal of International Law* 279 (1985).

_____, "Institutions and Practices for Restoring and Maintaining Public Order," 6 *Duke Journal of Comparative and International Law* 175 (1995).

_____, "International Legal Responses to Terrorism," 22 *Houston Journal of International Law* 3 (1999).

_____, "Legal Responses to Genocide and Other Massive Violations of Human Rights," 59 *Law and Contemporary Problems* 75 (1996).

_____, "Peacemaking," 18 *Yale Journal of International Law* 415 (1993).

_____, "Nuclear Weapons in International Law," 4 *New York Law School Journal of International and Comparative Law* 339 (1983).

_____, "Sovereignty and Human Rights in Contemporary International Law," 84 *American Journal of International Law* 866 (1990).

_____, "War Powers: The Operational Code of Competence," 83 *American Journal of International Law* 777 (1989).

Reitlinger, Gerald, "The Truth About Hitler's 'Commissar Order,'" 28 *Commentary* 7 (1959).

Renault, Louis, "War and the Law of Nations in the Twentieth Century," 9 *American Journal of International Law* 1 (1915).

Reston, James B., Jr., "Is Nuremberg Coming Back to Haunt Us?," 53 *Saturday Review* 14 (1970).

Reuter, Paul, "Nurnberg 1946—The Trial," 23 *Notre Dame Lawyer* 76 (1947).

Rheinstein, Max, "The Legal Status of Occupied Germany," 47 *Michigan Law Review* 23 (1948).

Rie, Robert, "The War Crimes Trials," 48 *American Journal of International Law* 470 (1954).

Roberts, Adam, "The Laws of War: Problems of Implementation in Contemporary Conflicts," 6 *Duke Journal of Comparative and International Law* 11 (1995).

Roberts, Guy B., "Self-help in Combating State-Sponsored Terrorism: Self Defense and Peacetime Reprisals," 19 *Case Western Reserve Journal of International Law* 243 (1987).

Robinson, Jacob, "The International Military Tribunal and the Holocaust: Some Legal Reflections," 7 *Israel Law Review* 1 (1972).

Roch, Michael P., "Forced Displacement in the Former Yugoslavia: A Crime Under International Law?," 14 *Dickinson Journal of International Law* 1 (1995).

Rogers, A.P.V., "War Crimes Trials Under the Royal Warrant: British Practice 1945–1949," 39 *International and Comparative Law Quarterly* 780 (1990).

Roht-Arriaza N., "State Responsibility to Investigate and Prosecute Grave Human Rights Violations in International Law," 78 *California Law Review* 451 (1990).

Rolph, John W., "Perfecting an International Code of Crimes," 39 *Federal Bar News and Journal* 528 (1992).

Root, Elihu, "Francis Lieber and General Orders 100," 7 *American Journal of International Law* 453 (1913).

Roth, John K., "Holocaust Business: Some Reflections on *Arbeit Mach Frei*," 450 *Annals of the American Academy of Political and Social Science* 68 (July 1980).

Roth, Kenneth, "The Court the U.S. Doesn't Want," *N.Y. Review of Books*, November 19, 1998, at 45.

Rovine, A.W., "Memorandum to Congress on the ICC from Current and Past Presidents of the ASIL," 95 *American Journal of International Law* 967 (2001).

Rubin, Alfred P., "Legal Aspects of the My Lai Incident," 49 *Oregon Law Review* 260 (1970).

_____, "The International Criminal Court: Possibilities for Prosecutorial Abuse," 64 *Law and Contemporary Problems* 153 (2001).

Russell-Brown, Sherrie L., "Rape as an Act of Genocide," 21 *Berkeley Journal of International Law* 350 (2003).

Sack, Alexander N., "War Criminals and the Defense of Superior Orders in International Law," 5 *Lawyers Guild Review* 11 (1945).

Sadat, Leila N. & S. Richard Carden, "The New International Criminal Court: An Uneasy Revolution," 88 *Georgetown Law Journal* 381 (2000).

Sammons, Anthony, "The 'Under-Theorization' of Universal Jurisdiction: Implications for Legitimacy on Trials of War Criminals by National Courts," 21 *Berkeley Journal of International Law* 111 (2003).

Sarker, Lotika, "The Proper Law of Crime in International Law," 11 *International and Comparative Law Quarterly* 446 (1962).

Schabas, William A., "Blending Criminal Procedure at the Ad Hoc Tribunals," 24 *Michigan Journal of International Law* 887 (2003).

_____, "International Law and the Abolition of the Death Penalty," 55 *Washington and Lee Law Review* 797 (1998).

_____, "Justice, Democracy, and Impunity in Post-Genocide Rwanda: Searching for Solutions to Impossible Problems," 7 *Criminal Law Forum* 523 (1996).

_____, "Sentencing by International Tribunals: A Human Rights Approach," 7 *Duke Journal of Comparative and International Law* 461 (1997).

Schachter, Oscar, "In Defense of International Rules on the Use of Force," 53 *University of Chicago Law Review* 113 (1986).

_____, "Self-Defense and the Rule of Law," 83 *American Journal of International Law* 259 (1989).

_____, "The Decline of the Nation State and Its Implications for International Law," 36 *Columbia Journal of Transnational Law* 7 (1997).

_____, "The Extraterritorial Use of Force against Terrorist Bases," 11 *Houston Journal of International Law* 309 (1989).

_____, "The Right of States to Use Armed Force," 82 *Michigan Law Review* 1620 (1984).

Scharf, Michael P., "Have We Really Learned the Lessons of Nuremberg?," 149 *Military Law Review* 65 (1995).

_____, "The Amnesty Exception to the Jurisdiction of the International Criminal Court," 32 *Cornell International Law Journal* 507 (1999).

_____, "The Case for an International Trial of the al-Qaeda and Taliban Perpetrators of the 9/11 Attacks," 36 *New England Law Review* 911 (2002).

_____, "The ICC's Jurisdiction over the Nationals of Non-Party States: A Critique of the U.S. Position," 64 *Law and Contemporary Problems* 67 (2001).

_____, "The Legacy of the Milosevic Trial," 37 *New England Law Review* 915 (2003).

_____, "The Letter of the Law: The Scope of the International Legal Obligations to Prosecute Human Rights Crimes," 59 *Law and Contemporary Problems* 14 (1996).

_____, "The Tools for Enforcing International Criminal Justice in the New Millennium: Lessons from the Yugoslavia Tribunal," 49 *DePaul Law Review* 925 (2000).

Scheffer, David J., "A Negotiator's Perspective on the International Criminal Court," 167 *Military Law Review* 1 (2001).

_____, "The International Criminal Court: The Challenge of Jurisdiction," 93 *Proceedings, American Society of International Law* 68 (1999).

_____, "The United States and the International Criminal Court," 93 *American Journal of International Law* 12 (1999).

Schick, Franz B., "Crimes Against Peace," 38 *Journal of Criminal Law and Criminology* 445 (1948).

_____, "International Criminal Law—Facts and Illusions," 11 *Modern Law Review* 290 (1948).

_____, "The Nuremberg Trial and the International Law of the Future," 41 *American Journal of International Law* 770 (1947).

Schuster, George, "Hanging at Nuremberg: The Truth Was Not Allowed to Emerge," 45 *Commonweal* 110 (November 15, 1946).

Schwartz, Stephen, "Rape as a Weapon of War in the Former Yugoslavia," 5 *Hastings Women's Law Journal* 69 (1994).

Schwartzenberger, Georg, "The Eichmann Judgment: An Essay in Censorial Jurisprudence," 15 *Current Legal Problems* 248 (1962).

_____, "The Judgment of Nuremberg," 21 *Tulane Law Review* 329 (1947).

Schwelb, Egon, "The United Nations War Crime Commission," 23 *British Year Book of International Law* 363 (1946).

Seelye, Katharine Q. & David E. Sanger, "Bush Reconsiders Stand on Treating Captives of War," *N.Y. Times,* January 29, 2002, at Al.

Shamsey, John, "80 Years Too Late: The International Criminal Court and the 20th Century's First Genocide," 11 *Journal of Transnational Law and Policy* 327 (2002).

Sharp, Walter G., Sr., "International Obligations to Search for and Arrest War Criminals: Government Failure in the Former Yugoslavia?," 7 *Duke Journal of Comparative and International Law* 411 (1996).

_____, "The International Criminal Tribunal for the Former Yugoslavia: Defining the Offenses," 23 *Maryland Journal of International Law and Trade* 15 (1999).

Shraga, Daphna & Ralph Zacklin, "The International Criminal Tribunal for Rwanda," 7 *European Journal of International Law* 501 (1996).

Sheppard, Steve, "Passion and Nation: War, Crime, and Guilt in the Individual and the Collective," 78 *Notre Dame Law Review* 751 (2003).

Sherman, Antonio, Comment, "Sympathy for the Devil: Examining a Defendant's Right to Confront Before the International War Crimes Tribunal," 10 *Emory International Law Review* 833 (1996).

Silving, Helen, "In re Eichmann: A Dilemma of Law and Morality," 55 *American Journal of International Law* 307 (1961).

Simma, Bruno & Andreas I. Paulus, "The Responsibility of Individuals for Human Rights Abuses in Internal Conflicts: A Positivist View," 93 *American Journal of International Law* 302 (1999).

Simpson, Gerry J., "Didactic and Dissident Histories in War Crime Trials," 60 *Albany Law Review* 801 (1997).

Sims, John S., Jr., Comment, "Act of State vs. International Law," 13 *Mercer Law Review* 370 (1962).

Sluiter, Göran, "The Surrender of War Criminals to the International Criminal Court," 25 *Loyola Los Angeles International and Comparative Law Journal* 605 (2003).

Smidt, Michael L., "Yamashita, Medina, and Beyond: Command Responsibility in Contemporary Military Operations," 164 *Military Law Review* 155 (2000).

Sofaer, A.D., "Terrorism as War," 96 *American Society of International Law Proceedings* 254 (2002).

Sohn, Louis B., "From Nazi Germany and Japan to Yugoslavia and Rwanda: Similarities and Differences," 12 *Connecticut Journal of International Law* 209 (1997).

_____, "The New International Law: Protection of the Rights of Individuals Rather Than States," 32 *American University Law Review* 1 (1982).

Solf, Waldemar A., "A Response to Telford Taylor's Nuremberg and Vietnam: An American Tragedy," 5 *Akron Law Review* 43 (1972).

Solf, Waldemar A. & Edward R. Cummings, "A Survey of Penal Sanctions Under Protocol I to the Geneva Conventions of August 12, 1949," 9 *Case Western Reserve Journal of International Law* 205 (1977).

Spears, Jeffrey L., "Sitting in the Dock of the Day: Applying Lessons Learned from the Prosecution of War Criminals and Other Bad Actors in Post-Conflict Iraq and Beyond," 176 *Military Law Review* 96 (2003).

Standard, William L., "United States Intervention in Vietnam Is Not Legal," 52 *American Bar Association Journal* 627 (July 1966).

Stephen, Sir Ninian, "International Criminal Law and Its Enforcement," 74 *Australian Law Journal* 439 (2000).

Steven, Lee A., Note, "Genocide and the Duty to Extradite or Prosecute: Why the United States is in Breach of Its International Obligations," 39 *Virginia Journal of International Law* 425 (1999).

Stimson, Henry, "The Nuremberg Trial: Landmark in Law," 15 *Foreign Affairs* 179 (January 1947).

Stoelting, David, "Military Commissions and Terrorism," 31 *Denver Journal of International Law & Policy* 427 (2003).

Stone, Julius, "Hopes and Loopholes in the 1974 Definition of Aggression," 71 *American Journal of International Law* 224 (1977).

Storey, Robert G., "The Nuremberg Trials," 19 *Tennessee Law Review* 517 (1946).

Supernor, Christopher M., "International Bounty Hunters for War Criminals: Privatizing the Enforcement of Justice," 50 *Air Force Law Review* 215 (2001).

Symposium: "Appraising the Methods of International Law: A Prospectus for Readers," 93 *American Journal of International Law* 291 (1999).

Symposium: "Legality of United States Participation in Viet Nam Conflict," 75 *Yale Law Journal* 1084 (1966).

Symposium: "Milosevic, Killing Fields, and Kangaroo Courts: Symposium on an Emerging International Criminal Justice System," 9 *U.C. Davis Journal of International Law and Policy* 7 (2002).

Symposium: "1945–1995: Critical Perspectives on the Nuremberg Trials and State Accountability," 12 *New York Law School Journal of Human Rights* 453 (1995).

Symposium: "Nuremberg and the Rule of Law: A Fifty Year Verdict," 149 *Military Law Review* 1 (1995).

Symposium: "The Hague Peace Conferences," 94 *American Journal of International Law* 1 (2001).

Symposium: "Terrorism and the Law," 60 *University of Colorado Law Review* 447 (1989).

Symposium: "The ICTY at Ten: A Critical Assessment of the Major Rulings of the International Criminal Tribunal Over the Past Decade Forward," 37 *New England Law Review* 865 (2003).

Symposium: "The International Criminal Court," 8 *Journal of International Law and Practice* 1 (1999).

Symposium: "Toward an International Criminal Court? A Debate," 14 *Emory International Law Review* 159 (2000).

Symposium: "War Crimes, Bosnia and Beyond," 34 *Virginia Journal of International Law* 255 (1994).

Symposium: "War Crimes Trials," 24 *University of Pittsburgh Law Review* 73 (1962).

Szasz, Paul C., "The International Conference on the Former Yugoslavia and the War Crimes Issue," 87 *Proceedings of the American Society of International Law* 29 (1993).

Taft, Donald R., "Punishment of War Criminals," 11 *American Sociological Review* 439 (1946).

Taulbee, J.L., "A Call to Arms Declined: The United States and the International Criminal Court," 14 *Emory International Law Review* 105 (2000).

Tavenner, Frank S. Collection; Inventory of Personal Papers and Official Records from the IMTFE. Special Collections, MSS 70-3, University of Virginia Law Library, University of Virginia, Charlottesville, VA. *E-mail: maw9b@virginia.edu*

Taylor, Telford, *Final Report to the Secretary of the Army on the Nuremberg War Crimes Trials Under Control Council Law No. 10* (August 15, 1949). Washington, DC: U.S. Government Printing Office (1949).

Tenet, George, "The Worldwide Threat in 2003: Evolving Dangers in a Complex World," Testimony before the U.S. Senate Select Intelligence Committee, Washington, DC: February 11, 2003.

"The Holocaust As Catalyst for International Justice," International Law Association Panel Discussion, Summary of Extemporaneous Remarks, Benjamin B. Ferencz, 9 *ILSA Journal of International and Comparative Law* 349 (2003).

Tieger, Alan, "Non-State Actors and the Case Law of the Yugoslavia War Crimes Tribunal," 92 *American Society of International Law* 48 (1998).

Travalio, Gregory M., "Terrorism, International Law, and the Use of Military Force," 8 *Wisconsin International Law Journal* 165 (2000).

Treves, Vanni E., "Jurisdictional Aspects of the Eichmann Case," 47 *Minnesota Law Review* 557 (1963).

"Trial of Sovereigns for State and War Offenses," 43 *Juridical Review* 175 (1931).

Tribe, Lawrence H., Letter to the Editor, "Military Tribunals: Too Broad a Power," *N.Y. Times,* December 7, 2001, at A28.

U.S. Legal Briefs: "The Legality of the Untied States Participation in the Defense of Vietnam, March 4, 1966," 60 *American Journal of International Law* 565 (1966).

Vagts, Detlev F., "In Defense of World Public Order," 95 *American Journal of International Law* 833 (2001).

van der Vyver, Johan D., "Prosecution and Punishment of the Crime of Genocide," 23 *Fordham International Law Journal* 286 (1999).

van Schaak, Beth, "The Crime of Political Genocide: Repairing the Genocide Convention's Blind Spot," 106 *Yale Law Journal* 2259 (1997).

Verdross, Alfred, "Jus Dispositivum and Jus Cogens in International Law," 60 *American Journal of International Law* 55 (1966).

Vincent-Daviss, Diana & Radu Popa, "The International Legal Implications of Iraq's Invasion of Kuwait: A Research Guide," 23 *New York University Journal of International Law and Politics* 231 (1990).

von Elbe, Joachim, "The Evolution of the Concept of Just War in International Law," 33 *American Journal of International Law* 665 (1939).

Walkinshaw, Robert B., "The Nuremberg and Tokyo Trials: Another Step Towards International Justice," 35 *American Bar Association Journal* 299 (April 1949).

War Crimes Studies Center, University of California—Berkeley, Berkeley, CA. *E-mail: warcrimescenter@socrates*

Warner, A.M., "The Case Against Saddam Hussein—The Case for World Order," 43 *Mercer Law Review* 563 (1991–92).

Washburn, John, "The Negotiation of the Rome Statute for the International Criminal Court and International Lawmaking in the 21st Century," 11 *Pace International Law Review* 361 (1999).

Washington, Ellis, "The Nuremberg Trials: The Death of the Rule of Law (in International Law)," 49 *Loyola Law Review* 471 (2003).

Watson, Geoffrey R., "The Humanitarian Law of the Yugoslavia War Crimes Tribunal: Jurisdiction in *Prosecutor v. Tadic,*" 36 *Virginia Journal of International Law* 687 (1996).

Webb, John, Note, "Genocide Treaty—Ethnic Cleansing—Substantive and Procedural Hurdles in the Application of the Genocide Convention to Alleged War Crimes in the Former Yugoslavia," 23 *Georgia Journal of International and Comparative Law* 377 (1993).

Wedgwood, Ruth, "Combatants or Criminals? How Washington Should Handle Terrorists," 83 *Foreign Affairs* 126 (May–June, 2004).

_____, "Responding to Terrorism: The Strikes Against bin Laden," 24 *Yale Journal of International Law* 559 (1999).

Weller, Marc, Note, "The International Response to the Dissolution of the Socialist Federal Republic of Yugoslavia," 86 *American Journal of International Law* 569 (1992).

Wenner, Scott J., "The Indochina War Cases in the United States Court of Appeals for the Second Circuit: The Constitutional Allocation of War Powers," 7 *New York University Journal of International Law and Politics* 137 (1974).

Wexler, Leila S., "Reflections on the Trial of Vichy Collaborator Paul Touvier for Crimes Against Humanity in France," 20 *Law and Social Inquiry* 191 (1995).

_____, "The Interpretation of the Nuremberg Principles by the French Court of Cassation: From Touvier to Barbie and Back Again," 32 *Columbia Journal of Transnational Law* 191 (1995).

_____, "The Proposed International Criminal Court: An Appraisal," 29 *Cornell International Law Journal* 665 (1996).

Wierda, M.L., "What Lessons Can be Learned from the ad hoc Criminal Tribunals?," 9 *U.C. Davis Journal of International Law and Policy* 13 (2002).

Williams, Kenneth A., "The Iraqi-Kuwait Crisis: An Analysis of the Unresolved Issue of War Crimes Liability," 18 *Brooklyn Journal of International Law* 385 (1992).

Williams, J.F., "The Covenant of the League of Nations and War," 5 *Cambridge Law Journal* 1 (1933).

Williams, P.R., "Trying the Butcher of Omarska," 10 *Criminal Law Forum* 147 (1999).

Williamson, J.A., "Command Responsibility in the Case Law of the International Criminal Tribunal for Rwanda," 13 *Criminal Law Forum* 365 (2002).

Wilner, Alan M., "Superior Orders as a Defense to Violation of International Criminal Law," 26 *Maryland Law Review* 127 (1966).

Wippman, David, "Change and Continuity in Legal Justifications for Military Intervention in International Conflict," 27 *Columbia Human Rights Law Review* 435 (1996).

Wise, Edward M., "General Rules of Criminal Law," 25 *Denver Journal of International Law and Policy* 313 (1997).

_____, "International Crimes and Domestic Criminal Law," 38 *DePaul Law Review* 923 (1989).

Wolfe, Robert, "Putative Threat to National Security as a Nuremberg Defense to Genocide," 450 *Annals of the American Academy of Political and Social Science* 46 (July 1980).

Wright, Lord, "The Killing of Hostages as a War Crime," 25 *British Year Book of International Law* 296 (1948).

_____, "War Crimes Under International Law," 62 *Law Quarterly Review* 40 (1946).

Wright, Quincy, "International Law and Guilt by Association," 43 *American Journal of International Law* 746 (1947).

_____, "International Law and Ideologies," 48 *American Journal of International Law* 616 (1954).

_____, "Legal Positivism and the Nuremberg Judgment," 42 *American Journal of International Law* 409 (1948).

_____, "The Escalation of International Conflicts," 9 *Journal of Conflict Resolution* 434 (1965).

_____, "The Legal Liability of the Kaiser," 13 *American Political Science Review* 120 (1919).

_____, "War Criminals," 39 *American Journal of International Law* 257 (1945).

Yarnold, Barbara M., "Doctrinal Basis for the International Criminalization Process," 8 *Temple International and Comparative Law Journal* 85 (1994).

Zacklin, Ralph, "Bosnia and Beyond," 34 *Virginia Journal of International Law* 277 (1994).

Zaid, Mark S., "Trial of the Century? Assessing the Case of Dusko Tadic [Prosecutor v. Tadic, International Criminal Tribunal, Case No. IT-94-1-T, Feb. 13, 1995] before the International Criminal Tribunal for the Former Yugoslavia," 3 *Journal of International and Comparative Law* 589 (1997).

_____, "Will or Should the United States Ever Prosecute War Criminals? A Need for greater Expansion in the Areas of Both Criminal and Civil Liability," 35 *New England Law Review* 447 (2001).

Zemach, Ariel, Comment, "Fairness and Moral Judgments in International Criminal Law: The Settlement Provision in the Rome Statute," 41 *Columbia Journal of Transnational Law* 895 (2003).

About the Editors

JOHN C. WATKINS, JR., a native of Mobile, Alabama, is professor *emeritus* of criminal justice and Founding Chair, Department of Criminal Justice, College of Arts & Sciences, at The University of Alabama, Tuscaloosa, Alabama. He is a graduate of The University of Alabama School of Law where he held several visiting appointments; Northwestern University School of Law, Chicago, Illinois; and the School of Criminology, Florida State University, Tallahassee, Florida, where he was an NIMH Fellow in criminology. Professor Watkins was a staff law clerk on both the Supreme Court of Alabama and the Fifth United States Circuit Court of Appeals. His previous books by Carolina Academic Press include *The Juvenile Justice Century: A Sociolegal Commentary on American Juvenile Courts* (1998) and *Centennial Sourcebook on Selected Juvenile Justice Literature, 1990–1999: A Transdisciplinary Index* (2001). Professor Watkins served as a company-grade officer in the Army of the United States with the U.S. Army Security Agency (Europe), 7th United States Army, Heilbronn, Germany.

JOHN PAUL WEBER, a native of New York, New York, is assistant professor and Chair, Department of Criminal Justice, Judson College, Marion, Alabama. He is a graduate of the United States Military Academy, West Point, New York; the School of Law of the College of William and Mary, Williamsburg, Virginia; and the Department of Criminal Justice, College of Arts & Sciences, at The University of Alabama, Tuscaloosa, Alabama. Professor Weber, among other assignments, was Staff Judge Advocate, United States Forces, Grenada, West Indies, Chief, Criminal Law Division, Ft. Jackson, South Carolina, Command Judge Advocate, Ft. Buchanan, Puerto Rico, saw combat in Vietnam where he was awarded the Purple Heart and was Commanding General of the New Mexico State Defense Force. He has also held other legal positions in both New Mexico and in Alabama. Professor Weber is the author of *The German War Artists,* Cerberus (1979), and, as a retired Flag Officer in the Army of the United States, served as military law consultant to the lead editor.

Name Index

Addicott, Jeffrey P., 463
Adoiphus, Gustavus, 219
Akayesu, Jean-Paul, 502, 549–550, 551–552, 556–559
Akufo-Addo, 404
Al Odah, Fawzi Khaled, 503, 649–650, 681
Alstoetter, Joseph, 192
Alvarez, Jose E., 527
Amann, Diane Marie, 558
Ambrosius, Lloyd E., 78
Anderson, Kenneth, 653
Annan, Kofi, 509, 578
Araki, Sadeo, 287, 324–325
Arbour, Louise, 575, 777
Arendt, Hannah, 371, 440–441
Aroneanu, Eugene, 389
Artukovic, Andrija, 412
Ashcroft, John, 654
Ashida, Hiroshi, 356
Aus Dem Bruch, Kurt, 259, 260

Baccus, Rick, 651
Badoglio, Marshal, 506
Ball, George, 447
Barbie, Klaus, 418–420, 422–424, 427–428, 440–441
Barker, Frank, 463, 465, 472
Barnes, Sir Thomas, 107
Barr, Bill, 610
Barr, Bob, 654
Barre, Kjell, 264, 267
Bassiouni, M. Cherif, 274, 440, 506, 509, 581, 689
Battle, George C., 6, 67
Beigbeder, Yves, 78, 352–353, 365, 503, 507, 509, 578
Belknap, Michal R., 443–445, 498,
Ben Gurion, David, 370
Berg, Franz, 259–261

Berg, Toralf, 264–266, 270
Bergold, Friedrich, 144
Berk, Malcolm A., 495
Beria, Lavrenti P., 505
Bernard, Henri, 286, 337
Bernays, Murray C., 81, 181
Berrigan, Philip, 492
Berry, Lucien S., 250
Bersin, Valentin, 250
Biddle, Francis, 82, 143
Bilien, Valentina, 254–255, 257
Bilton, Michael, 465, 498
bin Laden, Osama, 604, 639, 653
Birkett, Norman, 82, 143
Birmingham, Robert L., 117
Birn, Ruth B., 97, 755
Bizimungu, Pasteur, 544
Blaskic, Tihomir, 502, 535–536, 538, 540–541
Blaskowitz, Johannes, 229, 231–232, 234, 246
Boldt, John, 51, 53, 63, 67
Bolton, John, 609–610, 689
Boltz, Marcel, 253–254
Borg, Erling, 265, 269
Bormann, Martin, 83, 120, 155, 157–158, 160–161
Boudarel, George, 431
Bradford, William C., 3–4, 76–77
Brandegee, Frank, 76
Brandt, Karl, 192
Brooker, Paul, 96
Brooks, Steven, 465
Bruning, Heinrich, 90
Bruttel, Emil, 259–261
Burger, Ernst Peter, 617, 619
Bush, George W., 503, 638–640, 643–644, 651
Bye, Hans Fredrik, 264, 267

Calley, William L., Jr., 235, 443–444, 447, 464–467, 470, 472–475, 477–487
Canaris, Wilhelm, 227, 235, 617–618
Carpenter, Alva C., 308
Carrico, Terry, 651
Carroll, Christina M., 542
Cassesse, Antonio, 521
Chamberlain, Neville, 224
Churchill, Sir Winston, 504
Clarke, R. Floyd, 43, 68
Clark, Tom, 311
Claus, Gustav, 254–255
Clemenceau, Georges, E.B., 37
Cline, William, 651
Clinton, William J., 588, 601, 639
Coffey, Thomas M., 281, 289, 367
Coke, Edward, Lord Chief Justice, 148
Colburn, Lawrence, 464
Conder, Raymond C., 250
Cook, Haruka T., 352–372
Cook, Theodore F., 352, 752
Cooper, Norman G., 475
Covert, Clarice, 633, 635
Cox, Simon, 553,
Cramer, Myron C., 286, 326, 690
Crawford, James, 203, 578, 752
Crawford, Johnson, T., 203
Cruscius, Benno, 52–53
Czar Nicholas II, 3, 5, 30

Dadrian, Vahkn N., 14
Dalbey, Josiah T., 250
Daniel, Aubrey, III, 473, 498
Daniell, Robert, 78
Dasch, George John, 617, 619
Delarue, Jacques, 274, 429
deMenthon, M. Francois, 82, 127, 162
de Ribes, M. Champetier, 82, 143
de Vabres, Donnedieu, 82, 143
de Villers, Tremolet, 431
Demmerich, Richard, 254–255, 258
Derso, Alois, 27
Des Forges, Alison, 553–554
Dietrich, Joseph Sepp, 248–249, 251, 253
Dithmar, Ludwig, 6, 51, 53, 63, 67
Dix, Rudolf, 144
Dixon, Richard D., 196
Dobbs, Eugene H., 224
Dobbs, Michael, 617, 690
Döenitz, Karl, 83, 113, 120, 124, 144, 154, 157, 160–161
Doherty, William F., 465
Dohihara, Kenji, 287, 324

Dollfuss, Englebert, 139
Dollinger, Hans, 315–316
Dostler, Anton, 191
Douglas, William O., 346
Dowell, Cassius M., 618
Dower, John W., 313, 367
Drexler, Anton, 72
Dulles, John Foster, 444, 457, 459
Dursi, James J., 478
Dworkin, Ronald, 687

Eckart, Dietrich, 72
Eessling, Georg, 254
Ehard, Hans, 162
Eichmann, Adolf, xvii, 123, 369–374, 383, 399–400, 403, 406, 440–441
Einstein, Albert, 350
Eisenhower, Dwight David, 444, 459
Ekornes, Konrad, 264
Elliott, Robert, 466
Ellis, Burton F., 250
England, Gordon R., 644
Erdomovic, Drazen, 502, 527–528, 532
Everett, Willis M., Jr., 250
Exner, Franz, 144

Fabry, Jose, 407
Falco, Robert, 82, 143, 573
Falk, Richard A., 362
Feder, Gottfreid, 73
Fenrick, William, 575
Ferdinand, Francis, 4
Ferencz, Benjamin B., 197, 498
Fermi, Enrico, 350
Ferrell, Robert H., 77
Finkelstein, Norman G., 97
Finta, Imre, 433–434
Fischer, Klaus P., 72, 95
Fitch, B.M., 322
Flaechsner, Hans, 144
Flem, Magne, 264
Flesch, Gerhard Friedrich Ernst, 263–265
Flick, Friedrich, 193
Flint, Fritz, 254
Foch, Ferdinand, 22
Fogelson, Steven, 181
Frank, Hans, 83, 121, 144, 154, 157, 160–161, 198
Fredman, Jonathan M., 489
Frick, Wilhelm, 83, 121, 154, 157, 160–161
Fritsche, Hans, 83, 121, 155, 160–161
Fritz, Heinz, 144
Fritzsche, Peter, 73–74, 145, 157–158

Funk, Walter, 83, 121, 144, 154, 157, 160–161
Furuno, Shuzo, 356

Garner, J.W., 225
George, David Lloyd, 75–76
Gerike, Heinrich, 95, 254–258
Gibbon, Edward, 684
Goebbels, Paul Josef, 73, 81, 157–158, 229
Göering, Hermann Wilhelm, 83, 122, 127, 131, 142, 145, 153, 157–159, 160–161, 189, 190
Goldhagen, Daniel J., 97
Gonzales, Alberto, 657, 663
Graf, Mathias, 203
Green, L.C., 532
Greifelt, Ulrich, 196, 203, 207–209, 212, 216
Grey, Sir Edward, 29
Gritz, Sidney, 463
Grotius, Hugo, 182, 384, 392
Guy, George F., 307, 310, 313

Habib, Mamdouh, 652, 681
Habyarimana, Jevenal, 543, 553, 549, 553–554, 561
Haig, Alexander, 466
Halder, Franz, 231–232, 235–236
Hale, Winfield B., 217
Hamdi, Esam Fouad, 666
Hamdi, Yaser Esam, 664–665, 674, 676
Hansen, Peter Helland, 264
Hart, Liddell, 238
Hartjenstein, Fritz, 259–260
Hashimoto, Kingoro, 287, 324
Hata, Shunroku, 287, 324
Haupt, Herbert Hans, 617, 619, 623, 669, 675–676
Hausner, Guideon, 372, 382
Haussmann, Emil, 199
Heinck, Heinrich, 617, 619
Hebert, F. Edward, 485
Helms, Jesse, 588–589, 599
Henriot, Phillipe, 431
Herring, George, 445
Hertkorn, Hans, 250
Hess, Richard Rudolf, 73, 83, 122, 145, 153, 157, 160–161, 253, 409–410, 412
Hessling, Georg, 157, 201, 255–257
Heydrich, Reinhard, 157, 201, 235, 265, 369, 372–373
Heynen, Karl, 6, 51, 53–54
Hicks, David, 649, 681

Higgins, John P., 286, 326
Himmler, Heinrich, 81, 122, 141, 157–158, 205, 207–208, 211–213, 229, 266, 370, 372, 408, 435
Hiranuma, Kiichiro, 287, 323
Hirohito, Emperor, 287–288, 316, 323, 337, 352
Hirota, Koki, 287, 323, 337, 343
Hitler, Adolf, xvii, 5, 72–74, 75, 81, 83–84, 94–98, 118–119, 127, 129, 133–134, 141, 156–157, 158, 168, 198, 200, 202, 204, 207, 211, 213, 214, 218, 223–224, 227, 232, 239, 241, 245–254, 405, 408, 418, 435, 572, 617–618
Ho Chi Minh, 444, 454
Hockhammer, Karl A., 519
Hodges, Kenneth L., 465
Hoepner, Erich, 242
Höess, Rudolf Franz, 78, 370
Hollidt, Karl, 234, 241, 246
Holm, Ingeborg, 264
Holmes, Oliver Wendell, 220
Homma, Masaharu, 332–333
Horn, Martin, l44
Horne, Alistair, 418, 440
Hoshino, Naoki, 287, 324
Hoth, Hermann, 233, 240–242, 246
Hovey, Alvin P., 612
Howard, Kenneth A., 487
Hudson, William A., Jr., 463, 498
Hull, Cordell, 80, 281–282, 285
Hussein, Saddam, 502, 604
Hutson, Max, 465
Hutto, Charles E., 465, 473, 475

Ignatieff, Michael, 684
Irving, David, 510
Itagaki, Seishiro, 287, 324

Jackson, Robert H., 82, 105–106, 127, 143, 145, 151–152, 162, 166, 177, 182
Jaranilla, Delfin, 286, 326
Jodl, Alfred, 83, 122, 154, 157, 160–161
Johnson, Lyndon B., 445
Jones, Dorothy V., 7
Joseph, Francis, 29

Kagami, Paul, 544
Kaiser, David, 17
Kaltenbrunner, Ernst, 83, 123, 154, 157, 160–161, 369
Kant, Immanuel, 119
Kato, Takahisa, 356

Kauffmann, Kurt, 144
Kaya, Okinori, 287, 324, 356
Kayibanda, Gregoire, 552
Keitel, Wilhelm, 83, 123, 154, 157–158, 160–161, 230, 235, 242
Kelen, Emery, 27
Kelsen, Hans, 112
Kemal, Mustafa, 14
Kennedy, John F., 445, 573
Kerling, Edward John, 617
Kerwin, Walter T., Jr., 463
Keynes, John Maynard, 74
Khan, Tafazzal H., 569
Khoman, Thanat, 457
Khrushchev, Nikita Sergeyevich, 505
Kido, Koichi, 287, 323
Kimura, Heitaro, 287, 325
King, Edward P., 332
Kiniaki, Koiso, 287
Kipling, Rudyard, 611
Kirsch, Philippe, 591
Kittrie, Nicholas N., 399
Klarsfeld, Beate, 115
Klement, Ricardo, 370
Koch, Ilse, 187
Koessler, Maximilian, 186
Koiso, Kunaiki, 287, 325
Konoye, Fumimaro, 281
Kopelman, Elizabeth S., 346
Kotouc, Eugene M., 464
Kraemer, Fritz, 248, 253
Kranzbuehle, Otto, 144
Kraunch, Carl, 194
Krauthammer, Charles, 609
Krupp, Alfried Felix Aiwyn, 185, 194, 529
Krupp, Gustav von Bohlen und Halbach, 83, 120, 127, 160, 185
Kruska, Benno, 53
Kubuschok, Egon, 144
Kubwimana, Silas, 553
Kurusu, Saburo, 282
Kvernrod, Ole, 264, 269

Lahousen, Erwin, 617
Laird, Melvin, 484, 495
Lammers, Hans Heinrich, 211
Lansing, Robert, 18, 43
Laternser, Hans, 217, 237–238, 241, 244
Lathrop, Robert H., 473
Laule, Adolph, 53
Lauterpacht, Sir Hersch, 108, 279
Lawrence, Sir Geoffrey, 82, 143–145, 162
Leer, Eugene, 250

Lehmann, Rudolf, 227, 230, 233–236, 241–242, 246
Lehnert, Michael, 651
Leiling, Otto, 250
Lenin, Vladimir Ilyich, 501
Lentin, Anthony, 75
Levie, Howard J., 708
Ley, Robert, 83, 120, 126, 160
Lincoln, Abraham, 454, 615–616, 685
Lindh, John Philip Walker, 658
Lippmann, Matthew, 370, 440
List, Sigmund Wilhelm, 195
Lodge, Henry Cabot, Sr., 76
Ludendorff, Erich Friedrich Wilhelm, 51

McDonald, Gabrielle Kirk, 570
McDougal, E. Stuart, 286
McGrath, Howard, 311
McHaney, James M., 204
McIntire, Alison M., 595
McNamara, Robert H., 445–447
McVeigh, Timothy, 655–656
MacArthur, Douglas, 285, 288, 292, 295, 305, 317, 322, 337, 341, 343
Maguire, Peter, 17, 43, 51
Mao, Tse-tung, 502
Maples, Robert E., 478
Marr, Melanie A., 678–679
Marshall, Richard J., 322
Marx, Hans, 144
Matsui, Iwane, 287, 325
Matsui, Yasuhiro, 356
Matsuoka, Yosuke, 287
Maxwell-Fyfe, Sir David, 108, 416
Meadlo, Paul D., 478–479
Medina, Ernest L., 444, 463, 465, 467, 470–471, 473, 475, 477–479
Meier, Emil, 259–260
Mengele, Josef, 353
Mesic, Strip, 520
Milch, Erhard, 192
Milligan, Lambdin P., 503, 612–614
Milosevic, Slobodan, 572–573, 575
Minami, Jiro, 287, 325
Minami, Noboru, 356
Mitchell, David, 465
Mizuta, Kenichi, 356
Mladic, Ratko, 528
Mobbs, Michael, 666
Molotov, Vychesslav M., 95
Morgan, Ted, 419, 441
Morgenthau, Henry, Jr., 17, 80
Morikawa, Kinju, 356

Morris, James W., 618
Moyers, Bill, 447
Müller, Emil, 6, 51, 53, 56
Muller, Hermann, 254–255, 258
Musmanno, Michael A., 196, 441
Mussolini, Benito, 79, 218
Muto, Akira, 287, 325
Myers, Richard B., 644, 651

Nagano, Osami, 287
Nagumo, Chuchi, 282
Ndimubanzi, Francois, 550
Nelte, Otto, 144
Neubauer, Hermann Otto, 617
Neumann, Karl, 6, 53, 60
Neumann, Robert, 53
Niedermari, Paul, 217
Niemöeller, Pastor Martin, 139
Nikitchenko, I.T., 82, 105–106, 143, 145,
    161, 573
Nixon, Richard M., 465
Nomura, Kichisaburo, 281
Northcroft, Erima Harvey, 286
Noth, Werner, 254–255
Ntaryamira, Cyprien, 549, 561

O'Connell, Daniel T., 203, 216
Ohlendorf, Otto, 196, 203
O'Neill, Kerry C., 287
Oka, Takasumi, 287, 325
Okawa, Shumei, 287
Oliver, Covey, 383
Ono, Masao, 356
Oppenheimer, J. Robert, 350
Oshima, Hiroshi, 287
Overy, Richard, 48, 89–90

Padilla, José, 664, 677–678
Paine, Thomas, 306
Pal, Rahadbinod M., 286, 326, 337, 341, 347,
    350
Pannenbecker, Otto, 144
Papadatos, Peter, 373–374, 441
Parker, Danny S., 249
Parker, John J., 82, 143
Pasa, Talat, 14
Patrick, Lord, 286
Patzig, Helmutt, 51, 66–67
Paust, Jordan J., 307, 499, 576
Peers, William R., 463, 467–468
Peiper, Hinrich, 250
Peiper, Joachim, 81, 248–249, 252–254
Percival, Sir Arthur, 313

Perl, William R., 250
Pétain, Henri Phillipe, 419
Pevik, Johnny, 264, 268, 270
Pfister, Franz J., 250
Piedmontese De Maistre, 239
Pohl, Oswald, 196
Pol Pot, 502, 509
Pomerans, Arnold, 315–316
Pompidou, Georges, 428
Pope Paul VI, 581
Prevost, Ann M., 311
Priess, Hermann, 248, 253
Princip, Gavrilo, 4
Prophet Mohammad, 581
Pu Yi, 279

Queen Victoria, 6
Quigley, John, 533
Quirin, Richard, 617–618
Quisling, Vidkun, 83

Raeder, Erich, 83, 124, 154, 157–158,
    160–161
Ramdohr, Max, 52–53
Ranariddh, Norodom, 509
Raach, Otto, 199
Rasul, Shafiq, 649
Rathenau, Walther, 89
Rau, Max, 250
Rehnquist, William H., 616
Reinecke, Hermann, 227, 233, 235, 241,
    246–247
Reinhardt, George-Hans, 233–234, 241–242
Reismann, W. Michael, 606
Resor, Stanley R., 468, 474, 484
Reynolds, Michael, 249
Riad, Fouad, 527
Ridenhour, Ronald L., 464–465, 467
Röehm, Ernst, 72, 158
Rohde, Werner, 96, 259–260
Roling, Bernard Victor A., 286, 337, 354
Rommel, Erwin, 313
Roosevelt, Franklin D., 283, 285, 350, 610,
    617
Roosevelt, Theodore, 3, 7
Rosenberg, Alfred, 83, 124, 144–145, 154,
    157, 160–161
Rosenfeld, A.H., 250
Rostow, Walt, 445
Royall, Kenneth C., 618
Rudenko, R.A., 82, 127, 144, 167
Rumsfeld, Donald H., 644, 651, 660, 678
Rusk, Dean, 457

Russell, Lord Edward F.L., 275, 278, 286, 367
Rutaganda, Georges A.N., 502, 561, 564, 569
Ruter, C.F., 354

Sacher, Liesel, 259
Safire, William, 654
Sato, Kenryo, 287, 324
Saukel, Fritz, 83, 125, 157, 160–161, 265
Sauter, Fritz, 144
Schact, Hjalmar, 83, 125, 145, 154, 157,
    160–161
Scharf, Michael P., 572, 588
Scheffer, David J., 591
Schiel, Kenneth, 465
Schmidt, Ella, 259
Schniewind, Otto, 232, 234, 241–242,
    246–247
Schumann, Horst, 404
Schwarzenberger, Georg, 174, 441
Scott, James Brown, 18
Seidl, Alfred, 144
Sen, Hun, 509
Servatius, Robert, 144
Seyss-Inquart, Arthur, 83, 126, 134, 155,
    157, 160–161
Shawcross, Sir Hartley, 82, 127, 144
Shigemitsu, Mamoru, 287, 316, 323
Shigenori, Togo, 287, 323
Shimada, Shigetaro, 287, 324
Shimoda, Ryuichi, 356, 365
Shinagawa, Sumio, 356
Shiratori, Toshido, 287, 324
Shirer, William L., 72, 88, 94
Shiro, Ishii, 353–354
Shklar, Judith, 115
Sidwa, Rustam S., 528
Siemers, Walter, 144
Sim, Kevin, 465, 498
Simpson, Gerry L., 113, 272
Skorzeny, Otto, 218
Sledge, Charles, 478
Smith, Dorothy, 634
Smith, Gerald A., 465
Speer, Albert, 83, 126, 155, 157, 159,
    160–161, 192
Speight, John J., 196
Sperrle, Hugo, 227, 232, 234, 242, 246–247
Stalin, Josef V., 501, 504–505, 508
Stahmer, Otto, 144
Steinbauer, Gustav, 144
Stenger, Karl Franz, 51–53
Steward, Wilfred H., 250
Stimson, Henry L., 80–81, 348

Stone, Harlan Fiske, 307, 314
Storass, Kaare, 264
Strasser, Gregor, 73
Strasser, Otto, 73
Straub, Peter, 259–261
Streicher, Julius, 83, 126, 154, 157, 160–161
Stresemann, Gustav, 49, 92, 223
Styer, Wilhelm D., 289–292, 305, 310
Suharto, General, 508
Suzuki, Teeiichi, 287, 324
Suzuki, Toru, 356

Tadic, Dusko, 502, 518–519, 525, 527, 535,
    538–539
Taft, Robert, 573
Takemae, Eiji, 280
Taney, Roger, 183
Taylor, Maxwell, 445
Taylor, Telford, 182, 218–219, 314, 402, 498
Thiel, Heinrich Werner, 617
Thoma, Alfred, 144
Thompson, Hugh C., Jr., 464, 469
Tibbets, Paul W., 351, 356
Todt, Fritz, 126
Togo, Shigenori, 287, 323
Tojo, Hideki, 281–282, 287, 314, 323, 333,
    337, 348
Tommerass, Arne, 264
Torres, Escquiel, 465
Touvier, Paul, 418–419, 428–432, 441
Toyoda, Soemu, 312
Tribe, Lawrence, 656
Trooen, Ingar, 264, 269
Truman, Harry S., 307, 330, 356, 359, 459
T'Souvas, Robert W., 465
Tudjman, Franjo, 574–575
Tusa, Ann, 79, 103, 144
Tusa, John, 79, 103, 144
Tyrolt, Georg, 258

Uchida, Count, 92
Umezo, Yoshiiro, 316, 324
Usami, Hatsuo, 356

Vagts, Detlev F., 608
Vick, Penny, 466
Viermetz, Inge, 216
Volchkov, A.F., 82, 143
von Below, Herr, 31
von Brauchitsch, Walther, 233, 234,
    240–242
von Brockdorff-Rantzau, Ulrich, 481
von Clausewitz, Karl, 5, 239–240

von Hindenburg, Paul, 51, 96, 223
von Kuechler, George Friedrich-Wilhelm, 233, 241–242, 266, 247
von Leeb, Wilhelm Ritter, 195, 217, 233–234, 241–242, 244, 246–247
von Lercenfeld, Count, 31
von Lersner, Kurt, 53
von Luedinghausen, Otto, 144
von Moltke, Helmuth James, 29
von Neurath, Constantin Freiheer, 123, 155, 157, 160–161
von Papen, Franz, 83, 124, 144–145, 155, 157, 160–161
von Paulus, Friedrich, 240
von Ribbentrop, Joachim, 83, 95, 124, 145, 154, 157–158, 160–161, 207
von Roques, Karl, 233–234, 241–242, 246
von Rundstedt, Gerd, 252
von Salmuth, Hans, 233–234, 242
von Schirach, Baldur, 125, 145, 154, 157, 160–161
von Schleicher, Kurt, 223
von Schlieffen, Alfred, 5
von Schobert, Eugen Ritter, 233
von Schock, Hans, 53
von Schoen, August, 30
von Schushnigg, Kurt, 134, 139, 159
von Seeckt, Hans, 94, 222–223
von Stuelpnagel, Otto, 225
von Tirpitz, Alfred, 51

Walker, Samuel J., 351
Warlimont, Walter, 227–229, 233–234, 236, 241–242, 247

Washington, George, 616
Watkins, James C., 250
Webb, Sir William F., 286, 325–326, 347
Weiland, Paul H., 250
Weisenthal, Simon, 115
Weizsaeker, Ernst, 193
Wemyss, R.E., 22
West, Bland, 467
Westmoreland, William C., 314, 446, 468, 484
Wexler, Leila S., 428
Wieland, Heinrich H., 250
Wilhelm II of Hohenzollern, Kaiser, 5–6, 30, 37, 42–43, 46, 595
Willingham, Thomas K., 465
Wilson, Thomas Woodrow, 5, 17, 25, 27, 43, 49, 76–77
Winder, John H., 183
Winthrop, William, 482
Wirz, Henry, 183
Witze, Lothar, 617
Wochner, Magnus, 259, 260–261
Woehler, Otto, 234, 241–242, 246, 260
Wolff, Karl, 213
Wright, Quincy, 69, 93, 275
Wyatt, Lee B., 203

Yamashita, Tomoyuki, 191, 288–289, 299, 302, 306–315
Yoshio, Tamura, 353
Young, John C., 217

Zaryanov, I.M., 286
Zeuss, Wolfgang, 259–260

Subject Index

ABCD Powers, 282
Abwehr (German Intelligence Agency), 617–618
Act of State, 82, 84, 183, 359, 383, 390–392
action civile, 432
Administrative Procedure Act, 651, 681
Afghan Northern Alliance, 649, 651, 664–665, 667
Afghanistan, 92, 168, 571, 610, 639, 643, 649–651, 656, 659–662, 664–670, 674, 680
Akagi, Kaga, Soryu, Hiryu, Zuikaku, Shokaku, 282
'Aktion Reinhard', 379
al Qaeda, 639–641, 643, 650, 653, 655–656, 658, 660–662, 664–667, 669, 677, 680
Alamorgordo, NM, 350
Alderson, WV, 634
Aleutian Islands, 284
Alexandria, Egypt, 122, 408
Allied Control Commission, 48, 175
Allied Control Council Law No. 10, xvii, 78, 85, 95, 109, 112–113, 120, 185, 191, 215, 245–247, 385
Allied Kommandatura for Berlin, 409
Allied Military Prison: Spandau/Berlin, 408, 410
Alien Tort Act, 651, 681
allocution, 144
Alsace-Lorraine, 19–21, 44, 48, 214–215
Amagansett Beach, L.I., 619
Americal Division, 463, 466, 468–470
American Servicemembers' Protection Act, 588–589, 599–600
ANACR (*Association Nationale des Anciens Combattants de la Resistance*) 421
Andersonville, GA, 183
Anklageschrift (brief of accusation), 189

Anschluss (annexation), 107, 123–124, 126, 133, 158–159, 369
Anti-Fascist Action Front, 90
apartheid, 567, 584
Ardennes Offensive, 249, 251–252
Armenian Genocide, 14–17, 68–69, 531
Arusha, Tanzania, 541
ARVN (Army of the Republic of Vietnam), 469–470
'Asiatic inferiors', 201
Assembly of Bordeaux, 44
'Asymmetrical' warfare, 608
AUMF (Authorization for Use of Military Force), 669–670, 676, 678
Auschwitz, 78, 197, 370, 372–373, 375–376, 380, 404, 406–408, 419, 434, 440
Austria-Hungary, 18, 21, 31
Austro-Hungarian Empire, 519

Baguio, Luzon, 300
Baky Order, 434–436
Balfour Declaration, 394
Balkars, 504
Bangladesh, 510, 596
Barbarossa Jurisdiction Order, 195, 236
Bastille Day, 249
Bataan Death March, 285, 326, 332, 349, 367
Baugnez crossroads, 248, 253
Beit Ha'am Municipal Theatre, 371
Belzec, 372, 375
Bergen-Belsen, 78
Berchtesgaden, 134
Berlin, Treaty of, 415
Bernays Plan, 105
Biafra, 510
Birkenau, 434
Black Reichswehr, 94
blitzkrieg (lightning warfare), 135, 418
Bock's Car, 351

815

Bosnia-Herzegovina, 519–520, 523, 525,
    535–536, 606
Brandenburger Tor (Brandenburg Gate), 419
Brest-Litovsk, Treaty of, 21
British RAF Bomber Command, 510
Buchenwald, 119, 159, 187, 377
Bulge, Battle of the, 81, 95, 249, 251
Bush Administration, 588–591, 594, 600,
    653–654, 658–660, 662–663, 680

Cairo Conference, 285
Cairo Declaration, 340, 345
Camp Dachau, 248, 250
Camp O'Donnell, 332
Camp X-Ray/Camp Delta, 651
Canadian Charter of Rights and Freedoms,
    433, 440
Canadian Criminal Code, 433, 437–438,
    440
Central Powers, 4, 30, 49, 130, 175
Chambre d'accusation, 423–424, 427
Chambre du Conseil, 424
Charter of the International Military Tri-
    bunal for the Far East, 285, 287, 317,
    322, 325–326, 335, 343, 345, 347, 350,
    382, 385, 398, 422–423, 487, 595
Charter of the International Military Tri-
    bunal-Nuremberg, 98, 148–150, 152,
    160, 163–173, 176, 178–181, 184, 317,
    325–326, 345, 382, 385, 398, 422–423,
    595
Chechen-Ingush Autonomous Republic, 504
*Chef des Füehrungstabes des Oberkommando
    des Wehrmacht* (Chief of the Operations
    Staff of the High Command of the
    Armed Forces), 143
Chef des Generalstabes des Heeres (Chief of
    the General Staff of the Army), 142
Chef des Oberkommando der Wehrmacht
    (Chief of the High Command of the
    Armed Forces), 143
Chef der Seekriegsleitung (Chief of Naval War
    Staff), 142
Chelmno, 373–375
Cherry Society, 278
Ching Dynasty, 279
Chinese Exclusion Act of 1882, 312
Christ, 118
CIA, 445, 507
'Climb Mount Niitaka', 282
Columbus, GA, 465–466
Combined Fleet Operations Order No. 1,
    330–331

Commando Order, 195, 226–228, 229, 231,
    235, 243–244
Commissar Order, 195, 233–234, 240–243
Commission on the Responsibility of the Au-
    thors of the War and on Enforcement of
    Penalties, 28, 32–33, 42, 46, 50, 68, 401,
    517, 539, 548, 577, 579, 624, 642
Compiegne, 418
Concert of Europe, 15
Consolidated Naval Brig, 678
'Copperhead', 612
Cour d'assises, 423–424, 428
Cour d'assises du Rhone, 424, 428
Court of Appeals of Paris, 430
Court of Appeals of Versailles, 430
Covenant of the League of Nations, 22, 25,
    27, 75–76, 93, 278
corpus juris civilis, 384
Croatia, 412, 519–521, 532, 535–536, 574,
    589
customary international law, 3, 40, 174–179,
    181, 341, 357–358, 362–363, 365–366,
    387–388, 396–399, 413, 415, 523–524,
    526, 536, 541, 559–560, 566–567,
    592–593, 596–597, 610, 657, 660, 663
Cyprus, 510

Dachau, 78, 187–190, 218, 248–250, 377
Dachau trials, 187–190
Danzig, 21, 45–46, 48, 51, 92, 135, 182, 209
*Das Korps der Politischen Leiter der National-
    sozialistischen Deutschen Arbeiterpartei*
    (Leadership Corps of the National So-
    cialist German Workers' Party), 82, 140,
    162
Dayton Accords, 521
debellatio, 175
Declaration of Paris, 39
Department of State Bulletin, 451
de lege ferenda, 172
Democratic Republic of the Congo, 544
Der Stürmer (The Stormer), 126
Deschenes Commission, 437
Dienbienphu, 444
Dienstelle Eichmann (Eichmann Authority),
    376
Die Geheime Staatspolizei (State Secret Po-
    lice-Gestapo), 82, 142, 162, 202, 265,
    373, 377, 382
Die Reichsregierung (Reich Cabinet), 82, 140
*Die Schutzstaffeln der Nationalsozialistschen
    Deutschen Arbeitterpartei* (Protection
    Squad of the National Socialist German

Workers' Party-SS) 82, 141–142, 154, 162, 192–194, 196, 207–208, 213, 218, 259, 263

Die Sicherheitsdienst des Reichsfuehreres-SS (SD-Intelligence Service of the SS), 82, 141–142, 154, 162, 192–194, 196, 207–208, 213, 218, 259, 263, 382

Die Spinne (The Spider), 370

Die Sturmabteilungen der Nationalsozialistschen Deutschen Arbeiterpartei (Storm Detachment of the National Socialist German Workers' Party-SA), 82, 142, 162

'dignity test', 689

Dijon, 249

District Court of Jerusalem, 369, 371, 374, 383, 402, 406

Dolchstosslegend ('stab in the back' legend), 94

dolus specialis, 555

Donner Pass, 312

Dover Castle, 53, 60–62

Draft Rules of Air Warfare, 358

Dresden, 114, 510

Dunkirk, 226

East Prussia, 45, 48, 617

Ecole Technique Officielle (ETO), 562

Eichmann Trial (Indictment), 374

Eifel Offensive, 251

Einsatzgruppen (Special Action Groups), 95, 196–201, 206, 235, 244–245, 373, 375, 389, 419

Einsatzkommandos (Special Action Group Commandos), 235, 265

Elba, island of, 118

English Habeas Corpus Act, 675

English Statute of Treasons, 674

Enola Gay, 351

entente cordiale, 238, 281

Espionage Act of 1917, 622

'ethnic cleansing', 518, 520, 531–534, 541

Etorofu Island, 282

European Commission on Human Rights, 409, 412

European Court of Human Rights, 410

Exodus, 119

Falstad Concentration Camp, 264–265, 269

Far Eastern Commission, 345

Farben, I.G., 193–194

Federal Republic of Germany (West Germany), 371, 403–404, 408–411

Federal Republic of Yugoslavia, 520, 528, 570

'Final Solution', 97, 159, 370, 372

Flavy-le-Martel, 57

'flier cases', 189

'Folkdom and Soil', 209

Fort Benning, 447, 466, 473, 483–484

Fort Leavenworth, 465–466

'Fourteen Points', xvi, 5, 17

Four Year Plan, 97

franc-tireurs, 240

Franco-German Armistice, 1940, 419

Franco-Prussian War, 4, 238

Frankfort, Treaty of, 44

Freikorps (Free Corps), 89, 94, 123

Führerprinzip (leadership principle), 97, 130, 146, 201

Fürth, 82

Gauleiter (Nazi Party District Leader), 83, 125–126, 140, 190, 212, 254, 257, 264

Geheimer Kabinettsrat (Secret Cabinet Council), 140

'General Plan East', 206

Geneva Accords, 444, 451, 454–457

Geneva Convention of 1864, 10, 39

Geneva Conventions, 114, 173, 191, 224, 301, 413, 461, 512, 521–525, 527, 533, 536, 540–542, 545, 549, 551–552, 554, 558–559, 561, 563, 569–570, 585–587, 611, 654, 657–658, 660–661, 687

Geneva Protocol of 1924, 75, 169, 177

Geneva Testament, 27

Genocide Convention, 385–389, 399, 401, 505, 508, 532, 552, 555, 558–559, 564–565

German Democratic Republic (GDR-East Germany), 273

German General Staff, 79

German-Polish Pact of 1934, 135

German-Soviet Non-Aggression Pact of 1939, 95

Germany, Treaty of Peace with, 6, 43, 47, 74, 76

'Great Depression', 74, 96, 281

'Great Leap Forward', 508

Great Purge, 1936–38, 504

'Greater East Asia Co-Prosperity Sphere', 278, 280, 284

Guantanamo Bay, 644, 647–653, 662, 666, 680, 683

Guantanamo Naval Base, 644, 647–650, 653, 662, 666, 680, 683

Gulf of Tonkin, 444, 446, 460

Gulf of Tonkin Resolution, 444, 446, 458, 460, 496

Ha'am Ha'yehudi, 392
Hadamar, 190
Hadamar trial, 190
Hague, The, 1, 3–4, 7–8, 13, 29, 31, 34, 38–42, 61, 63–64, 113, 127, 139, 170, 176, 182, 201, 215, 217, 220, 224–225, 227, 239, 255, 257–258, 260–261, 266–267, 274, 291, 293–294, 301, 327, 357–359, 394, 409–410, 413, 415, 440, 502, 518–519, 523–524, 532–533, 536, 541, 571–572, 579, 582, 595, 611, 622–623
Hague Conventions, 1899/1907, xv, 7–8, 13, 40, 41, 176, 182, 255
Halifax, N.S., 64
Hall of Knights, 7
Hall of Mirrors (Versailles), 48
Hamidian Massacres, 14, 16
Hawaiian Organic Act, 624, 626–629, 675
Heligoland, 22
High Court of Calcutta, 346
High Court of Ghana, 404
HIL ('Hegemonic International Law'), 608–610
Hiroshima, 288, 348, 350–352, 356–359, 362–365, 366, 510
Hitlerjügend (Hitler Youth), 125
Hitler-Ludendorff *Putsch* 222
Hitokappu Bay, 282
Hoheitstraeger (Bearers of Sovereignty), 141
Hohenzollern Empire, 85, 94
Holocaust, the, 185, 369, 371, 393, 440–441
hostis humani generis, 185
Hotel Campo Imperatore, 218
House in the Wood, the, 7
Hutu(s), 534, 541–543, 553, 556–558, 562
HVO, 536–537

ICC Statute, 576, 578, 580, 582
ICTR, 501–502, 511, 538–542, 558–560, 566, 569, 571
ICTR Statute, 542, 544, 558–560
ICTY, 501–502, 511, 518–519, 521, 523–525, 535, 537, 539–542, 543, 569–571, 574
ICTY Statute, 511, 537
IFOR (Implementation Force), 521, 535
ILC (International Law Commission), 576, 595
Immigration Act of 1924, 313
Imperial Rescript, 12/8/41, 288

Imperial Rescript, 8/14/45, 352
Imperial Rescript, 9/2/45, 316
IMT-Nuremberg, 71, 75, 78, 81, 84–85, 112–113, 120, 127, 143, 192, 247, 285–286, 322, 355, 369, 373, 408–409, 421
IMTFE-Tokyo, 75, 192, 285–286, 288, 323, 325–326, 350, 353–354
Indonesian Communist Party (PKI), 507
Ingush peoples, 504
'Inkotanyi', 554
'Interahamwe', 561–563
Inter-Allied Control Commission, 221, 223
International Commission of Inquiry, Mediation and Arbitration, 34
International Control Commission, 451, 458
International Court of Justice, 386–387, 409–410
International Covenant on Civil and Political Rights, 421–422, 657
International Criminal Court (ICC), xvi, 502–503, 581–582, 588, 600–601
International Disarmament Conference, 133
International Law Commission (ILC), 114, 117, 577
Islamic Jihad, 604

Japanese Medical Association, 354
Japanese Ministry of Health, 354
Japanese Reservations to the Commission on Responsibilities, 37
Jencks Act, 485–486
Jewish National Home, 394
Judenrein (free of Jews), 533
Judiciary Act of 1789, 645, 681
juge d'instruction, 104, 430
jus cogens, 184–186
jus talionis, 119

Kalmyk Republic, 504
Kamerandenschinder trials (former German POW in USSR), 273
Kampfgruppe (Battlegroup) Peiper's 1st *SS-Leibstandarte Adolf Hitler* Panzer Division, 248
Kapp *Putsch*, 90, 222
Katyn Forest Massacre, 481, 573
KDS (*Kommando der SIPO und SD*), 419
Kellogg-Briand Pact, xvii, 75, 91–92, 135, 165, 167, 169, 176, 182, 401
Kemalist Regime, 16
Keraterm, 526
Khmer Rouge, 508–509

Knesset, 370, 384, 397–398
Korea, 284, 325, 340, 455, 459, 510, 639
Ku Klux Klan Act, 675
Kosovo, 509, 519–520, 532, 572, 590, 606, 639
Kreigsmarine (German Navy), 83, 94, 120, 142
Kristallnacht ('Crystal Night'), 377
Kurile Islands, 282
Kuwait, 606, 651
Kwantung Army, 278–279, 323–324, 329

Landsberg Prison, 73, 122, 249–250, 253–254, 629, 682
Language Arbitration Board, 287
Lausanne, Treaty of, 49, 531
Law for the Ordering of National Labor (1934), 98
League of Nations, 3–4, 17–18, 22–25, 27, 44–45, 48–49, 67–68, 75–77, 84, 93, 133, 169–170, 177, 223, 277–279, 335, 394, 416, 590
Lebanon, 459, 510
Lebensborn ('life springs'), 207–208, 212
Lebensraum ('living space'), 97, 129, 135, 204–205, 208, 211
'Lebenssunwerten Lebens' ('of life unworthy to live'), 408
Leibstandarte-SS Adolf Hitler (SS Bodyguard Unit 'Adolf Hitler'), 218–248
Leipzig, 6–7, 49, 51–52, 54, 56, 60, 63, 69, 80, 108, 114, 511
Leipzig trials, 7, 51–52, 69, 80, 108, 511, 531
lex imperfecta, 169
Leyte Gulf, Battle of, 299
Lidice, Czechoslovakia, 381
Limitations and Reductions of Naval Armaments, Treaty for, 278
Linz, 369
Llandovery Castle, 51, 53, 63–66
Locarno, Treaties of, 49, 75, 133, 182
London Naval Conference, 278–279
London, Treaty of (1831), 39, 81, 103, 278
London, Treaty of (1839), 31
Los Alamos Laboratory, 351
Los Baños Prison Camp, 311
lo stato, 118
Lusitania, 37
Luxemburg, 31, 214–215
Luzon Campaign, 300
Lysander, 65
Lytton Commission 278–279

MAAG (Military Assistance Advisory Group), 444–445, 458
MACV Directive Number 20–4, 461–462, 472
Madagascar, island of, 159
Majdanek, 372–373, 375
Malmédy, 81, 248, 252–253
Malmédy trial, 187, 190, 248–249
Manchukuo, 279, 314, 324
Manchuria, 278, 282, 284, 334, 337, 341
Manhattan Project, 351
Manila, Battle of, 284
Mauthausen, 78, 190
Mein Kampf (My Struggle), 73, 84, 122, 157–158, 204–205, 211, 253–254
Memorandum of Reservations (United States), 35
Milice, 428–430
Military Government Ordinance No. 7, 192, 247
Military Order, 11/13/01, 640
Military Reconstruction Act, 616
Ministerrat für die Reichvertiedigung (Council of Ministers for the Defense of the Reich), 140
Mobbs Declaration, 666–667, 671
Montenegro, 19, 415, 519–520, 527–528
Moscow Conference, 80, 251, 317
Moscow Declaration, 80, 105–106, 109, 251, 421, 506
MRND (Mouvement Republicain National pour le Developpment et le Democratic), 561
Mukden, 278–279
'Mukden Incident', 278
multilateralism, doctrine of, 76
Munich Beerhall *Putsch* 73, 130
Munich Settlement, 135
Munsungen Asylum, 406
My Lai, 444, 463–467, 470–472, 475, 477–481, 483, 485–486, 490

'Nacht und Nebel Erlass' ('Night and Fog Decree'), 226, 229–231, 258, 268
Nagasaki, 114, 288, 348, 350–352, 357–359, 362–363, 364, 510
Nanking, 277, 279–280, 324–325, 367, 629, 682
Nanking Massacre, 277, 280
Nanking, Rape of, 280, 324, 367
National Constiuent Assembly, 72
National Emergencies Act, 638
NATO (North Atlantic Treaty Organization), 459, 520–521, 574–575, 589, 606–607

Nazis and Nazi Collaborators (Punishment) Law, 374, 376, 380, 381–384, 397
Neuilly-sur-Seine, Treaty of, 49
New Bilibid Prison, 308
NKVD (Soviet Secret Police), 505
N.S.D.A.P., 72–73, 82, 129, 257, 372, 377, 382, 432
nulla poena sine lege, 116, 164–165, 168, 178, 396, 579
nullem crimen sine lege, 116, 164–165, 167, 170, 178, 396
Nuremberg Laws (1935), 97
Nuremberg Principles, 120, 172, 184–185, 219, 272–273, 347, 389, 398, 401, 428, 440, 490, 502

Oberbefelshaber des Heeres (Commander-in-Chief of the Army), 142
Oberbefelshaber der Kreigsmarine (Commander-in-Chief of the Navy), 142
Oberbefelshaber der Luftwaffe (Commander-in-Chief of the Air Force), 143
Oberreichsanwalt (Public Prosecutor), 52
Oberst Peiper Denkmal (Peiper Memorial Monument), 249
ODESSA (Organization der SS Angehoeringen—Organization of SS Members), 370
Omarska, 526
Office of Reich Commissioner for the Strengthening of Germanism, 207–211
OKH, 227–228, 232, 234–235, 241
OKW, 123, 161, 218, 226–232, 234–236, 240–241, 243
Operation Attila, 419
Operation Order No. 8, 201
Operation Pastorius, 617–618
Order of the American Knights, 612
Ordinance No. 7, American Military Government, Berlin, 192, 247
Ottoman Empire, 15, 19

Pakistan, 510
Palestine, 394, 510
Palestine Mandate, 394
Paris Peace Conference (1919), 25, 48, 52, 76
passive personality principle, 402
PAVN (People's Army of Vietnam), 452
pax americana, 346
pax Germanica, 204
Peace of Westphalia, 39
Pearl Harbor, 95
Peers Commission Report, 444, 467–468

Permanent Court of International Justice, 24, 396, 572
Politschen Leiter (Political leader), 140–141
Polizei Kommandeurs (Police Commanders), 269
Ponte Vedra Beach, FL, 619
Potsdam Conference, 350
Potsdam Declaration, 285, 292–293, 315, 317, 326–327, 340–341, 345, 350, 352, 363
Presidium, 505
Proclamation by the Supreme Allied Commander for the Allied Powers (SCAP), 1/19/46, 285, 316
Proclamation 7463, 9/14/01, 638
Profiles of Courage, 573
Protocol Supplementary to the Treaty of Peace between the Allied and Associated Powers and Germany, 47
Protocol to the Southeast Asia Collective Defense Treaty, 450
Public Law 107-39, 107th Congress, 604
Public Law 107-40, 107th Congress, 605

Quai d'Orsay, 30
Quang Ngai Province, 463, 467–468, 470, 483
Quenz Lake Camp, 617
'quisling', 83

'racial hygiene', 78
Radio Television Libre des Mille Collins (RTLM), 554, 561
Rapallo, Treaty of, 222–223
realpolitik, 27, 272, 511, 572, 581
Red Terror, 503–504
'Reflections on the Treatment of Peoples of Alien Races in the East', 211–212
Reich Chancellor, 86, 96, 126, 140, 221
Reichsgericht (Supreme Court), 51
Reichstag (Parliament), 86, 90, 96, 123, 125–126, 130, 133, 153, 198
Reichstag fire, 130
Reichswehr (State Defense Forces), 84
Reichswehrministerium (State Defense Ministry), 221
REP (Rwandan Patriotic Front), 543, 550
Report of the Commission on the Authors of the War and on the Enforcement of Penalties to the Preliminary Peace Conference (1919), 28, 33–34, 35, 37
Report to the President (IMT-Nuremberg, 1945), 182

Republic of Cuba, 92, 647, 652, 680, 682
retributive theory, 432
Rhineland, 20–21, 48, 74, 77, 132–133, 182, 221, 223, 369
Rillieux-la-Pape, 428
RKVFD, 207
Rome Conference (ICC), 578, 595–596, 599
Rome Treaty of, 578, 582, 588, 591, 593–594, 598, 601
Royal Hungarian Gendarmerie, 432, 434–435
RSHA (*Reichssicherheitshauptampt* — Reich Main Security Office), 123, 370, 373, 375
Rumania, 18, 53, 92, 168, 376, 415
Rundstedt Offensive, 252
RuSHA (Race and Settlement Main Office), 196, 207–208, 212
Russo-Japanese Neutrality Agreement (1941), 280–281
Russo-Japanese War, 312
Russo-Turkish War, 238
Rwandan Penal Code, 556

Saarland, 48, 74, 419
Saint-Germain-en-Lave, Treaty of, 49–50
San Francisco Conference, 148, 454
Sarajevo, 4
SCAP (Supreme Commander Allied Powers), 355
Schlieffen Plan, 5
'Schmachparagraphen' (shame paragraphs), 49
Schwäbisch Hall, 249
SEATO Treaty, 444, 448, 456–459, 498
Second Reich, 5, 87, 94, 119, 418
Security Council (U.N.), 371, 502, 519, 533–534, 541–542, 598, 663
Serbia, 30, 519
Serbian Republic of Bosnia-Herzegovina, 520
Sevres, Treaty of, 49, 150, 531
SFRY (Socialist Federal Republic of Yugoslavia), 519–520, 537
Simpson Commission, 249
Sixth Pan American Conference (1928), 169
Sixth Panzer *Armee*, 248
Slovenia, 519–520
Snowdrop, 65
Sobibor, 372, 375
Solingen, 369
Sonderkommandos (Special Commandos), 249
Son My, 464, 468–472, 528
Spa, Belgium, 6

SPD (Social Democratic Party), 90
Spanish-American War, 680
Statute of Treasons (1350), 674
Staunton, VA, 77
Stellvertretender Chef des Füehrungstabes des Oberkommando der Wehrmacht (Deputy Chief of the Operations Staff of the High Command of the Armed Forces), 143
St. James Declaration, 79
St. Petersburg Declaration, 357
Stuthof/Natzweiler Concentration Camp, 259
Suddeutsche Juristen-Zeitung (South German Legal Newspaper), 162
Sudentenland, 134, 224, 265
Sugamo Prison, 287
Superior Administrative Court for the *Land* (State) of North Rhineland-Westphalia, 410
'Support Group for the Release of Rudolf Hess', 410
Supreme Court of the Empire, 6, 54, 56, 60, 63, 289
Supreme Soviet, 503
Suspension Clause, 674, 677

Taba, 558
Taliban, 639, 643, 650, 658, 661, 664–667, 669–670, 673, 680, 690
Talmud, 582
Tanaka Memorial, 278
Task Force Barker, 463–464, 468–471, 477–478
Tatars, 504
Tcheka, 504
'Terror Flier' orders, 226, 241
Theresienstadt, 377
Third Geneva Convention, 657–662
Thirty Years' War, 118, 219
'Tiger of Malaya', 308
Traves, France, 249
Treblinka, 372, 375
Trianon, Treaty of, 49
Tribunal Permanent des Forces Armees de Lyon, 420, 424
Tripartite Pact (1940), 136, 277, 280
Triple Entente, 4, 14, 277
Truppenamt (Office of Troops), 94
tu quoque, 114, 119, 241, 354, 574–575
Tutsi(s), 534, 541–543, 553, 556–558, 562
Tyrrhenian Sea, 60–61

UCMJ (Uniform Code of Military Justice), 443, 471, 480, 487, 633, 636, 658

ultra vires, 392, 433
Ukranian famine, 505
UNAMIR (United Nations Assistance Mission-Rwanda), 543, 552–553
Union Generale des Israelites de France, 419
Unit 731, 337, 353–354
United Nations Charter, 172, 371, 398, 400, 410, 448–449, 451–456, 460–461, 511, 533, 583, 601, 607, 609, 663
UNWCC (United Nations War Crime Commission), 80, 506, 529
United States Strategic Bombing Survey, 351
Untermenschen (subhumans), 84
USS Cole, 640
USS C. Turner Joy, 446
USS Maddox, 446
USS Missouri, 285, 324
Ussher Fort Prison, 404
utilitarian theory, 432

V-Men, 617–618
'Versailles diktat', 72
Versailles, Treaty of, 3, 6, 48–49, 51–52, 71, 74, 84, 94, 129, 132–133, 154, 171, 182, 214, 220–221, 222–223, 225, 582, 595, 632
Vichy France, 419
Vienna Congress of 1815, 39
Vienna Convention on the Law of Treaties, 184
Vietcong, 445, 447, 464, 471–472, 480
Volksgemeinschaft ('Community of the People'), 73, 97

VOMI (*Volksdeutsche Mittelstelle* — Repatriation Office for Ethnic Germans), 207, 212

Waffen-SS (Armed SS), 218, 248–249
Wannsee Conference, 372
'war guilt clause', 49
War Powers Resolution, 606
Warsaw, 373
Washington Naval Conference, 277–278
Wehrmacht (Armed Forces), 123, 143, 223
Weimar Constitution, 71, 85, 88–89, 130, 224
Weimar Republic, 7, 46, 71–74, 78, 85, 92, 94, 124, 130, 220–224, 244–245
Weltanschaung ('world view'), 96
West German Federal Administrative Court, 412
West German Federal Constitutional Court, 409, 411
Westphalia, Treaty of, 39
Wolfschanze ('Wolf's Lair'), 617
World Trade Center, 604, 638–640

Yalta Conference (1945), 148
Yangtze River, 280
'Yellow Peril', 312–313
Yokohama, 355
Yugoslav People's Army, 520

Zentralstelle für Jüdische Auswanderung (Central Authority for the Emigration of Jews), 375, 379
Zeppelin atrocities/operations, 38, 40